THE AMERICAN INSTITUTE OF ARCHITE

MW01008700

The Architecture Student's Handbook of Professional Practice

Fifteenth Edition

WILEY

Cover design: Wiley

This book is printed on acid-free paper.

Copyright © 2016 by The American Institute of Architects. All rights reserved. "AIA" and the AIA logo are registered trademarks and service marks of The American Institute of Architects.

Published by John Wiley & Sons, Inc., Hoboken, New Jersey

Published simultaneously in Canada

For general information about our other products and services, please contact our Customer Care Department within the United States at (800) 762-2974, outside the United States at (317) 572-3993 or fax (317) 572-4002.

Wiley publishes in a variety of print and electronic formats and by print-on-demand. Some material included with standard print versions of this book may not be included in e-books or in print-on-demand. If this book refers to media such as a CD or DVD that is not included in the version you purchased, you may download this material at http://booksupport.wiley.com. For more information about Wiley products, visit www.wiley.com.

Library of Congress Cataloging-in-Publication Data:

Names: American Institute of Architects.
Title: The architecture student's handbook of professional practice.
Description: Fifteenth Edition. | Hoboken, New Jersey : Wiley, [2017] |
    Includes bibliographical references and index.
Identifiers: LCCN 2016033846| ISBN 9781118738979 (paperback) | ISBN
    9781118739006 (epub)
Subjects: LCSH: Architectural practice—United States—Handbooks, manuals,
    etc. | Architectural services marketing—United States—Handbooks,
    manuals, etc. | BISAC: ARCHITECTURE / General.
Classification: LCC NA1996 .A726 2017 | DDC 720.1—dc23 LC record available at
    https://lccn.loc.gov/2016033846

Printed in the United States of America

SKY10044894_032223

Contents

Fifteenth Edition Student Handbook Participants

Advisory Board
Phillip Bernstein, FAIA
Renee Cheng, AIA, NCARB
Joseph Fleischer, FAIA
David Heymann, FAIA
Michael Hricak, FAIA
Brian Kenet
David McHenry, FAIA, LEED AP
Bruce McMillan, AIA
Valerian Miranda, Ph.D.
Roger Schluntz, FAIA

Contributing Authors
James B. Atkins, FAIA, KIA
Catherine Berg
Phillip G. Bernstein, FAIA, RIBA,
LEED AP
Glenn W. Birx, FAIA, LEED AP
Brian Bowen, FRICS
Ann Casso, Hon. AIA
William C. Charvat, AIA
David S. Collins, FAIA, NCARB
Kenneth C. Crocco, FAIA
Philip R. Croessmann, AIA, Esq
Dana Cuff, Ph.D.
Clark S. Davis, FAIA, LEED AP
Randy Deutsch
Donald W. Doeg, Esq., PE, LEED AP
Cornelius R. Dubois, FAIA
David A. Ericksen, Esq.
Harry M. Falconer, Jr., AIA, NCARB
Kristine K. Fallon, FAIA
Joseph L. Fleischer, FAIA
Scott R. Fradin, Esq., AIA,
Phillip H. Gerou, FAIA
David Greusel, AIA
Lowell V. Getz, CPA
Sally A. Handley, FSMPS
Gregory Hancks, Esq., AIA
Douglas C. Hartman, FAIA, FCSI, CCS,
CCCA, SCIP, LEED AP

Robert G. Hershberger, FAIA, PhD
Travis L. Hicks, AIA
Mark Jussaume, PE
Calvin Kam, Ph., AIA, PE, LEED AP
David F. Kinzer III, CPA
David Koren, Assoc. AIA, FSMPS,
CPSM
Peter Gifford Longley, AIA, CSI CCS,
LEED AP
John-Paul Lujan, Esq.
Nadav Malin
Nancy Malone, AIA, LEED-AP
Peter Piven, FAIA
William C. Ronco, Ph.D.
Pat Rosenzweig
Andrea S. Rutledge, SDA, CAE
Fredric W. Schultz, CPCU
Jessica Sheridan, AIA, LEED, AP, BD+C
Henry Siegel, FAIA
Grant A. Simpson, FAIA
Debra L. Smith, AIA, AICP
Larry Strain, FAIA, LEED-AP
Frank Stasiowski
Steven G. M. Stein, Esq.,
Lee W. Waldrep, Ph.D.

Wiley Project Staff
Margaret Cummins
Lauren Olesky
Kerstin Nasdeo
Doug Salvemini
Kalli Schultea

Editor
Bradford Perkins, FAIA, MRAIC, AICP

Research Assistant
Judith Perkins Schiamberg

About The Architecture Student's Handbook of Professional Practice

The practice of architecture is complex and its complexity is increasing each year. The knowledge required to plan, design, and administer the construction phase of a new building or major renovation has always required a depth of knowledge but each year new building types, design concepts, materials, systems, digital tools, construction techniques, and many other important areas of technical knowledge have to be mastered by architects. At the same time architects have to be effective managers of both their projects and their practices. Most architectural schools focus almost all their classes on providing their students with an introduction to the design and technical challenges of the profession. The vast body of knowledge required to effectively manage architectural projects and practices is usually compressed into one course—the practice course—for one semester.

In my own practice class, I note that I will be introducing topics that often consume the vast majority of a senior architect's day. It is not possible to cover any of these important topics in any depth in one semester, but it is essential that all architects get an introduction to the most important subjects so that they can gain the skills required to be an effective professional.

This 15th edition of the *Student Handbook* is structured to be a companion textbook for architectural practice classes. It is also intended to be a reference text for young architects at the beginning of their careers while they are learning their profession with the assistance of intern development programs.

TITLE AND ORGANIZATION OF THE BOOK

As was the prior (14th) edition, this book is not simply an abridged version of *The Architect's Handbook of Professional Practice*, 15th edition. Recognizing its use as required reading in professional practice courses and sometimes as a companion in studio courses—along with the fact that the information needs of architecture students are not the same as those of professionals—this book contains knowledge specific to the needs of students and emerging professionals that has been organized to be approachable for them. To reflect this increased focus on the needs of students and interns, the publisher John Wiley & Sons and the American Institute of Architects (AIA), as author, chose to name this book *The Architecture Student's Handbook of Professional Practice*.

Like *The Architect's Handbook of Professional Practice*, 15th edition, published in 2013, *The Architecture Student's Handbook* is presented in four parts. However, the names of the parts—The Profession, Practice, The Project, and Contracts and Agreements—and the organization of the material within them are different. The progression of material makes the book suitable for use as a professional practice course outline, beginning with consideration of the concepts of professionalism through the construction and closeout of projects, as well as consideration of the legal agreements used for project delivery.

Content Structure

Content from *The Architect's Handbook* has been either included in *The Architecture Student's Handbook* in its entirety or edited or abridged as appropriate for the student reader. This volume also contains new material prepared specifically for *The Architecture Student's Handbook* that does not appear in *The Architect's Handbook*. This text was written for those beginning to learn about the architecture profession or navigating the beginning of their careers. Conceived as a true handbook, this volume is a resource to be used in the examination of all aspects of architecture practice, including research, programming, professional relationships, the design process, and the intricacies of delivering a project.

In addition, the book contains unique content on changes under way in the design and construction industry that are having a profound impact on the practice of architecture. This material invites readers to explore new possibilities in architecture practice and to redefine both what architects do and how they accomplish their goals. The variety of subject matter makes *The Architecture Student's Handbook* a useful resource for design studios, seminars, and research efforts, in addition to its use as a professional practice textbook and intern development programs.

A NEW APPROACH TO PRACTICE

A theme running through this edition is the protection of the design integrity of projects, a greater concern as architects increasingly rely on electronic tools. Behaviors and practices necessary to accomplish this goal, which both protects client interests and allows for professional satisfaction and reward, are discussed. In today's design and construction marketplace, architects are called on to consider accepting new risks and responsibilities. Students studying architecture, as well as recent graduates, can use the same creative impulse in use in the studio to design a method of practice that ultimately makes it possible to deliver the projects conceived.

In accepting the 2005 AIA/ACSA Topaz Medallion, Edward Allen, FAIA, spoke to the issue of art versus science in architecture education. He suggested that these two categories have long been inadequate for describing what architecture truly is and offered the following alternate perspective: "Architecture is neither art nor science; it belongs to a realm of intellectual endeavor called design. Its goal is to produce new products to solve human problems."

It is through practice that design becomes useful. Practice provides a framework that enables the architect to progress confidently from concept to completion. *The Architecture Student's Handbook* introduces the concept of professional practice to students so they will enter the profession with a well-rounded education that has readied them for all aspects of architecture practice.

The editor of *The Architecture Student's Handbook of Professional Practice*, 15th edition, is the founder, Chairman, and CEO of Perkins Eastman Architects, a New York–based practice that has a staff of 1000 and 15 offices around the world. He is on the faculty at Cornell's College of Architecture, Art and Planning, where he teaches the Professional Practice course.

CAREERS FOR ARCHITECTS

This *Handbook* has been developed primarily for those who choose to follow a traditional professional career path into an architectural practice or into one of the other typical architectural careers in public agencies, architectural education, or construction. Many people who have gone to architectural school, however, have found their education to be a good foundation in a wide variety of other careers. Some have moved into other related arts including animation, environmental graphics, and the traditional fine arts while others have gone on to run major corporations, star in the movies, and serve in Congress.

—Bradford Perkins, FAIA

PART 1
THE PROFESSION

CHAPTER **1**

Professional Life

1.1 Architecture as a Profession

Dana Cuff, Ph.D.

Architecture is in the family of vocations called professions, all of which share certain qualities and collectively occupy a special position in society. Architects' status as professionals provides them with an underlying structure for their everyday activities.

To be a professional means many things today. One can be a professional athlete, student, or electrician. Each of these occupations uses the term in ways distinct from what we mean by the professional who is a doctor, lawyer, or architect.

Typically, we distinguish professionals who do certain work for a living from amateurs who work without compensation. The term *amateur* connotes a dabbler, or someone having less training and expertise than a professional.

We also differentiate between professions and other occupations. Expertise, training, and skill help define those vocations that "profess" to have a specialized territory of knowledge for practice. While many occupations require expertise, training, and skill, professions are based specifically on fields of higher learning. Such learning takes place primarily in institutions of higher education rather than in vocational schools or on the job. Universities introduce prospective professionals to the body of theory or knowledge in their field. Later, this introduction is augmented by some form of internship in which practical skills and techniques are mastered.

A high level of education is expected of professionals because their judgments benefit—or, if incompetently exercised, endanger—the public good. Thus people who are attracted to the professions usually have altruistic concerns for their society.

Dana Cuff is a professor in the Architecture and Urban Design department of the School of the Arts and Architecture at the University of California, Los Angeles.

The status of professions, their internal characteristics, and their relationship to society are constantly, if not always perceptibly, changing. The professions have grown dramatically in recent years, in keeping with the rise of the postindustrial, service economy. Growth in professional employment has accompanied expansion of the service sector of the economy, estimated today to be 78 percent of the labor force. In a service economy, information and knowledge industries become dominant, creating the context in which professions can rise among occupations.

CHARACTERISTICS OF A PROFESSION

Professions are dynamic entities that reflect our society, our economy, and, generally, our times. There is no widely accepted definition or list of features that covers all professions. Nevertheless, they have some characteristics in common, which have appeared throughout history.

Lengthy and Arduous Education

Perhaps the most frequently cited characteristic of a profession is a lengthy and sometimes arduous education. A professional must learn a body of technical knowledge and also develop an ability to exercise judgment in the use of that knowledge. Thus, all established professions incorporate long periods of high-level education.

Professional education is also a form of socialization. Like a rite of passage for initiates, architecture, medical, and law schools are places where future practitioners are introduced to the knowledge, values, and skills of their profession. Students undergo tests of their commitment and ability. In architecture schools, a good example is the charrette (often involving all-nighters), during which students concentrate all their efforts to finish a project. These experiences instill tacit beliefs about the significance of architecture, the work effort required to do a good job, and the commitment needed to become an architect. Through selective admissions, carefully designed curricula, and rigorous graduation standards, schools guide the formation of their professional progeny. Professional schools play a key role in developing the shared worldview that characterizes a professional community.

Expertise and Judgment

Professions traffic in ideas and services rather than in goods or products. Rather than marketing a better widget, professionals sell their expertise. They have knowledge outside the ken of the layperson. Professions are based upon a balance of technical knowledge, reasoned judgment in applying such knowledge, and inexplicable, even mysterious talents that some call artistry. Thus, while doctors need a high degree of scientifically based knowledge, they also need diagnostic ability and a good bedside manner.

Expertise begins with theoretical knowledge taught in universities, but being a competent professional also means knowing how to apply this knowledge. Among practitioners, both expertise and experience contribute to quality performance. While initial skills are taught in school, a large share of professional training comes from the practicum or internship; it then continues in lifelong learning through the gathering of experience and the application of new concepts and technologies.

Registration

Because professional judgments affect the public good, professionals generally are required to be licensed in order to practice. This serves as a means of protecting the public health, safety, and welfare. Professions require sophisticated relationships with people and information. To become licensed, professionals are usually required to meet education and experience standards and to pass a compulsory comprehensive examination.

Relative Autonomy

Because professionals exercise considerable judgment and discretion, professional work is intended to be more autonomous and self-determined than work controlled by owner-managers as in the production of goods.

Other Traits

In addition to these primary characteristics, a number of other traits are typical of professions:

- Because they are well trained to perform complex services, professionals generally command relatively high incomes and high prestige in their communities.
- As a group, professionals attach a large part of their identity to their careers, rarely changing vocations.
- Within each profession, members usually hold a set of common values; they often speak what amounts to a dialect that is not easily understood by outsiders.
- Professionals understand the importance and value of lifetime learning.
- Professions are relatively well organized, and a significant proportion of their members belong to a national professional organization such as the American Medical Association, the American Bar Association, or the American Institute of Architects.

These characteristics are in constant evolution. For example, the prestige of a given profession may suffer under consumer dissatisfaction or be enhanced by significant developments in the field that have positive social repercussions. The professional degree that was once optional becomes a necessity. Professional organizations are periodically strengthened by programs that capture practitioners' attention. Such evolution depends in part upon the participation of professionals themselves—in their schools, professional associations, and communities.

ARCHITECTURE AMONG THE PROFESSIONS

Many of the trends influencing architectural practice have parallels in other professions. For example, the tensions created by complexity and specialization, consumer influences, and divergence of goals among practices can also be seen in the professions of law and medicine.

These common influences notwithstanding, each profession introduces its own variations and idiosyncrasies. Looking at architecture among the professions, we observe the following features.

Relationships with the Arts

The qualities that most clearly set architecture apart from other established professions are its close ties to the arts and its similarities to artistic endeavors. Creativity is crucial to all professions, but for the architect it is of the highest priority. Moreover, architects produce objects that are fixed in space, highly public, and generally long-lasting.

Importance of Design

Although all professions are based on a balance of technical and indeterminate knowledge, some stress one over the other. Architecture emphasizes an artistic, relatively inexplicable domain of expertise—design—as the core of the practitioner's identity. Design requires rational knowledge of how buildings are put together, how they will function, historical models for building types, materials, mechanical systems, structures, and so on. But being a good architect also presumes that the professional possesses something extra—aesthetic sensibility, talent, or creative ability, whatever we choose to call it.

Place in the Social Structure

According to one study that compared a number of professions on a variety of dimensions, architecture ranked high in terms of prestige but in the middle range in average years of education, average income, and proportion of members belonging to professional organizations. This suggests that architecture's respected place in the social structure has been granted by society rather than defined through numbers, dollars, or professional control.

The profession's position in the social structure has been changing. Historically, the church, the state, and powerful individuals were the primary patrons for architectural services. Now, industrial and commercial enterprises have become major clients as well. During the 1960s, when community design emerged as a subdiscipline, architects sought and secured a role in housing and neighborhood revitalization; this activity has evolved into a growing presence in community and urban design.

Architectural practice is developing in new ways that allow architects to intermingle with a broader population. One recent study argues that architecture is more closely connected to a large, relatively affluent middle class than to a small group of the very rich. In a similar vein, the composition of the profession is changing, particularly as more women and ethnic minorities become architects.

Place in the Economic Structure

The well-being of the architectural profession depends upon ties to a healthy building industry. The level of construction activity both nationally and internationally significantly determines the amount and type of services architects will render.

As the United States urbanized and industrialized, the demand for buildings was great and the architectural profession grew rapidly. In more recent times, however, construction has declined proportionately in the national economy. With the evolution from a goods-producing economy to a service economy, there are fewer major new building projects.

At the same time, the demand for architectural services has increased—especially in the predesign and postconstruction phases. This suggests a repositioning of the profession, along with other professions, as part of the service economy. New roles and markets for services have been created. In addition, new roles and specializations mean that more professionals are doing what was once one individual's job.

Internal Social Structure

Within any profession, there are social divisions that complement and compete with one another. Those who study professions call these divisions "the rank and file," "the administrators," and "the intelligentsia."

In the architectural profession, the rank and file might be considered to include drafters and junior design and production people; the administrators to include principals, senior designers, and project managers; and the intelligentsia to include academicians, critics, practitioner-theorists, and those architects who push the parameters of architecture outward and whose work often establishes precedents for others to follow.

The values and objectives of each group are likely to conflict with those of other groups at times. The first two groups have very different convictions, agendas, and knowledge of the way practice operates. These differences become important in a profession where, even though a majority of architecture firms are small, the provision of architectural services has been heavily influenced by larger firms in which many of the architects are wage-earning employees who work not for clients but for their architect-employers. Data from the 2012 AIA Firm Survey confirm this: Only 1.4 percent of offices have 100 or more employees but these offices employ over 20 percent of the profession. Firms with 50 or more employees earn more than 40 percent of all fees generated.

Initially, an increase in intraprofessional stratification brought a greater need to formalize professional control. Firms created organization charts, personnel policies, and manuals governing project procedures. Many professionals devoted themselves to managing the organization. As firms grew, they dealt with these phenomena in different ways. Compare, for example, the large law firm, which is a collection of relative coequals (the main distinction being seniority among partners), and the hospital, which has a stricter hierarchy of medical administrators, senior physicians, residents, and interns. In recent years, however, there seems to be a general trend away from stratification in architecture firms—even in large firms. The advent of the second generation of digital technology and the maturing of the architectural profession in its use, along with the increased demand for a growing number of specialized areas of expertise has encouraged firms to be more horizontally organized and much less hierarchical.

PROFESSIONS AND SOCIETY

Professionals possess knowledge and ability not accessible to the public. As a result, the public establishes a special relationship with professional groups, essentially granting each a monopoly in its area of practice. Society thus grants members of professional groups certain rights and privileges:

- A certain level of prestige and respect
- A certain amount of autonomy and authority
- A relatively high level of compensation
- A standard of reasonable care with which to judge the appropriateness of professional actions

In return for these rights and privileges, society expects a profession to assume certain obligations:

- Establishing and maintaining standards for admission and practice
- Protecting public health, safety, and welfare
- Considering the public good when working for an individual client
- Respecting public welfare over personal gain

Every profession participates in a coordinated body of tasks necessary to fulfill its obligations to the public and to manage the profession. These tasks include establishing a body of professional knowledge, regulating entry to the profession, and maintaining standards for practice. Each profession develops mechanisms for accrediting educational programs, licensing professionals to practice, encouraging continuing education, and regulating professional ethics and conduct.

By and large, these mechanisms are designed, staffed, and implemented by professionals. Architects have the major voice in where and how new architects are educated. They sit on registration boards, write and grade the licensing examination, and recommend laws and administrative guidelines for registration. Architects conduct disciplinary hearings and, through the AIA, establish and enforce codes of ethical behavior. Like all professionals, architects have substantial voices in establishing their own destiny.

1.2 Demographics of Practice: 2012 AIA Firm Survey

Bradford Perkins, FAIA

The architectural profession is not one of the larger professions. According to the Bureau of Labor Statistics, there were 107,400 architectural jobs in the United States in 2012. In contrast there were 759,800 jobs for lawyers and 691,400 for

Bradford Perkins, FAIA, is the founder, chairman, and CEO of Perkins Eastman Architects, a large New York–based international architecture, interior design, and planning firm that has won many design awards. He lectures regularly at architecture schools and other institutions and is on the faculty of Cornell University's College of Architecture, Art, and Planning. He has published seven books and numerous articles on design and architecture management issues.

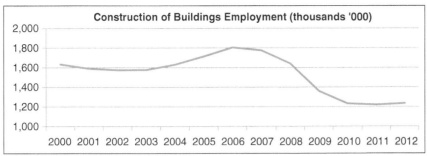

FIGURE 1.1 **U.S. Construction of Buildings Employment**

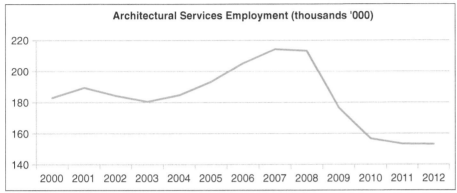

FIGURE 1.2 **U.S. Architectural Services Employment**

physicians and surgeons. Since architectural firms employ many people who are not trained as architects, total employment in architecture is higher than 107,400, but it still is a relatively small percentage of the total professional employment in the country.

The 2012 AIA Firm Survey was conducted as the traumatic recession that began at the end of 2007 was finally ending for the architectural profession. The sharp impact of the recession on construction and architectural employment is clearly illustrated in Figures 1.1 and 1.2. Since 2012 architectural employment has been rising and is projected to rise 7.3 percent by 2022 according to the U.S. Bureau of Labor Statistics.

This chapter introduces you to a statistical profile of the profession today. As this chapter and the 2012 Survey outlines, most firms (over 80 percent) have fewer than 10 employees, but approximately 65 percent of the profession work in firms with 20 or more employees. More than a quarter of the profession work in the 1 percent of firms that have 100 or more employees.

The majority of firms were formed within the last 20 years and a third within the last 10 years, but there are a few of the larger firms that were founded 80 to 100 years ago. In the past the majority of these firms only offered architectural services, but today an increasing number are adding other services, such as interior design, planning, and sustainable design consulting.

STAFF AT ARCHITECTURE FIRMS

Nearly 40 Percent of Staff at Firms Are Licensed Architects

Overall, almost two in five employees at architecture firms are licensed architects with another 16 percent of staff comprising interns on the path to licensure (Figure 1.3).

An additional 13 percent of staff is nonlicensed architecture staff that is not on the path to licensure. In general, the share of nonarchitecture staff, which might include engineers, interior designers, and landscape architects, increases with firm size.

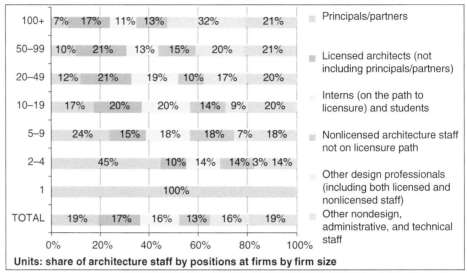

Firm size	Principals/partners	Licensed architects	Interns/students	Nonlicensed	Other design	Other nondesign
100+	7%	17%	11%	13%	32%	21%
50–99	10%	21%	13%	15%	20%	21%
20–49	12%	21%	19%	10%	17%	20%
10–19	17%	20%	20%	14%	9%	20%
5–9	24%	15%	18%	18%	7%	18%
2–4	45%		10%	14%	14% 3%	14%
1	100%					
TOTAL	19%	17%	16%	13%	16%	19%

■ Principals/partners

■ Licensed architects (not including principals/partners)

Interns (on the path to licensure) and students

■ Nonlicensed architecture staff not on licensure path

Other design professionals (including both licensed and nonlicensed staff)

■ Other nondesign, administrative, and technical staff

Units: share of architecture staff by positions at firms by firm size

The Business of Architecture: 2012 AIA Survey Report on Firm Characteristics

FIGURE 1.3 **The Share of Nonarchitect Staff Typically Increases with Firm Size**

Finally, approximately 20 percent of workers at firms are nondesign staff, which includes professionals such as accountants, marketers, information technology, and human resources managers.

Most Firms Use Engineering Consultants

Since the majority of architecture firms are small or midsize businesses, they rely heavily on consultants and part-time staff to provide flexibility.

The 2012 AIA Firm Survey found that 85 percent of firms regularly hired engineers as consultants in the past three years, by far the most hired group of professionals. This is due, in part, to the fact that most owner-architect agreements call for the architect to provide structural, mechanical, electrical, and plumbing engineering. The share of firms that regularly use interior design consultants has increased, on average, 3 percentage points since 2005 and nearly 10 percentage points since 2002.

The types of consultants that firms use also tend to vary by firm specialization. Mechanical, electrical, and plumbing (MEP) engineers are hired as consultants more frequently at firms with commercial/industrial and institutional specializations, whereas residential firms are more likely to use civil and structural (CS) engineers as consultants. Landscape architects are also used by many firms that have an institutional specialization, which may include projects like public buildings, museums, and recreational structures. In general, it is more common for firms with a commercial/industrial or institutional specialization to hire code consultants and other specialty consultants, as there are more features to incorporate into their projects, such as security and communication networks (Table 1.1).

LEED AP Certified Staff Nearly Doubles in Four Years

Two-thirds of architecture firms now have at least one Leadership in Energy and Environmental Design accredited professional (LEED AP) on staff, versus just one-third in 2008. Ninety percent of firms with 10 or more employees have at least one LEED AP on staff, and more than half of small firms have at least one LEED AP certified staff member, compared to just under one-quarter in 2008 (Figure 1.4).

TABLE 1.1 The Largest Share of Firms Use MEP and CS Engineers as Outside Consultants

	Total (%)	Residential (%)	Commercial/ Industrial (%)	Institutional (%)
MEP engineers	85	74	93	92
Structural engineers	78	81	76	78
Landscape architects	56	50	52	65
Interior designers	31	35	33	29
Sustainability consultants	20	17	17	24
Spec writers	17	13	19	20
Planners	6	4	4	9
Other specialty consultants	27	18	28	35

Units: Use of outside consultants in last three years, percent of firms by specialization
The Business of Architecture: 2012 AIA Survey Report on Firm Characteristics

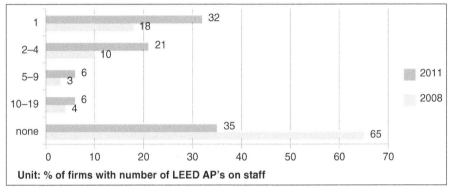

The Business of Architecture: 2012 AIA Survey Report on Firm Characteristics

FIGURE 1.4 **The Number of LEED APs on Staff Nearly Doubles in Three Years.**

FORMATION OF FIRMS

S Corporation Is Most Widely Employed Business Structure

When starting a business, one of the first decisions the owner has to make is the type of business to create. The business type that is best suited for the firm's situation and objectives may vary by firm size or specialization. Liability protection and tax concerns may also play a major role in this decision.

According to the Internal Revenue Service, 70 percent of all businesses start out as sole proprietorships, since they are relatively easy to start and give the owner discretion to make decisions. On the downside, these firms have unlimited liability for all debts against the business, including personal assets.

The share of architecture firms that use the sole proprietorship legal structure has continued to decline in recent years, with a drop of 5 percentage points from 2008 to just one in five firms in 2011 (Figure 1.5). The share of firms using the sole proprietorship legal structure has declined significantly since 1997, when nearly half of all firms were classified as such.

As of 2011, the most common legal structure among all firms, with the exception of sole practitioners, is the S corporation, with more than one-quarter (28 percent) of firms reporting having been formed under this legal business structure. The percentage of firms structured as limited liability companies (LLCs), a legal structure that is now permitted in most states, increased moderately to 22 percent, from 17 percent in 2008.

▶ See Section 2.2 in Part 2 "Firm Legal Structure," which discusses the most commonly used structures for architecture firms.

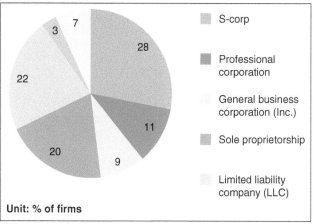

The Business of Architecture: 2012 AIA Survey Report on Firm Characteristics

FIGURE 1.5 **The S Corporation Is the Most Common Legal Structure, While Sole Proprietorship Continues to Drop.**

At firms with 50 or more employees, the General Business Corporation (Inc.), also known as a C corporation, is the second choice. Among the firms with 10 to 49 employees, the Professional Corporation (PC), LLC, and the General Business Corporation are evenly divided, averaging around 16 percent for each of the legal business formations.

Diversity and Demographics Are Changing

The architectural profession has traditionally not been as diverse as other professions.

Most Firms Are Less Than 20 Years Old and Formation of New Firms Grows

The weak economy from 2007-2011 sparked new firm formations. Six percent of existing firms were formed between 2009 and 2011, and almost one-quarter of firms were formed since 2005. More than one-half of firms were formed since 1995.

In comparison, fewer than one-tenth of firms were founded before 1970. However, more than three-quarters of firms with 50 or more employees were established before 1980. Two in five sole practitioners started their firms since 2005. Not surprisingly, firm size is indicative of its longevity, since firms generally need time to grow (Table 1.2).

TABLE 1.2 Over One-Third of All Firms Formed After 2000								
	Number of Employees							
	2011 (%)	1 (%)	2–4 (%)	5–9 (%)	10–19 (%)	20–49 (%)	50–99 (%)	100+ (%)
2010–2012	6	12	6	3	1	0	0	0
2005–2009	17	27	20	9	5	2	0	0
2000–2004	14	17	16	15	9	6	3	0
1990–1999	25	22	25	26	25	23	9	3
1980–1989	19	13	19	25	28	21	18	9
1970–1979	10	6	10	10	17	16	20	20
1960–1969	4	2	2	5	7	12	18	31
1950–1959	2	1	1	3	4	10	8	6
Before 1950	3	0	1	4	4	10	24	31

Units: Percent of firms
The Business of Architecture: 2012 AIA Survey Report on Firm Characteristics

TABLE 1.3 Multiple Offices at the Largest Firms Decrease Considerably

Number of Offices	All Firms 2011 (%)	All Firms 2008 (%)	Number of Employees			
			2011 50–99 employees (%)	2008 50–99 employees (%)	2011 100+ employee (%)	2008 100+ employees (%)
5+	2	3	20	18	43	60
4	1	1	16	9	9	7
3	2	2	13	14	20	10
2	7	7	21	26	20	5
1	88	87	30	33	9	18

Units: Percent of firms
The Business of Architecture: 2012 AIA Survey Report on Firm Characteristics

Number of Offices Decline at Largest Firms

The majority of architecture firms have one office, although just over 10 percent have multiple offices (Table 1.3). Approximately two-thirds of firms with 10 to 49 employees and one-quarter of firms with 50 or more employees have one office.

South Atlantic Regional Share of Firms Increases While Middle Atlantic Sees Largest Decrease

The 2012 AIA Firm Survey geographical breakout (based on the U.S. Census: www .census.gov/geo/www/us_regdiv.pdf) showed the Pacific Southwest and South Atlantic regions continue to have the greatest share of firms, 22 and 18 percent, respectively. The East South Central region has the smallest share of firms, with just 4 percent, followed by West North Central, with 6 percent.

Nearly Half of All Firms Have Small Business Status

According to the Small Business Administration (SBA), small businesses represent the majority of all employer firms and employ about half of all private sector employees. This is true for the architecture profession as well.

The share of firms that are federally recognized women-owned business enterprises (WBE) is 6 percent, and the share of businesses that are state/local recognized WBEs is 8 percent.

Approximately 4 percent of firms are federally recognized minority-owned businesses enterprises (MBEs), while 3 percent of firms are federally recognized as a Small Disadvantaged Businesses or Disadvantaged Business Enterprises (SDBs or DBEs).

For More Information

AIA Diversity and Inclusion Initiative: www.aia.org/about/initiatives/AIAS078656

Beverly Willis Architecture Foundation: http://bwaf.org/

National Organization of Minority Architects: www.noma.net/

The following backgrounder adds information and context to the topic of diversity and inclusion:

- *AIA Diversity History Timeline.* Since the early 1990s, the AIA has institutionalized an effort to engage its membership with issues of diversity and inclusion. This brief timeline highlights some of the significant moments in AIA diversity history.
- *Forging a Diverse Culture: The Shepley Bulfinch Experience.* This case study of a diversity-award-winning firm contains practical advice for fostering and implementing a culture of diversity and inclusion.

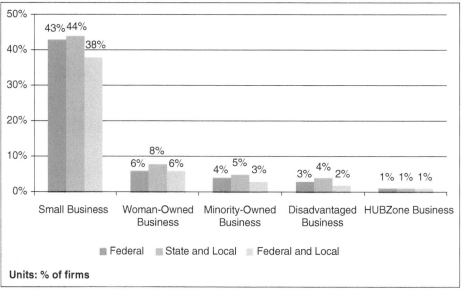

The Business of Architecture: 2012 AIA Survey Report on Firm Characteristics

FIGURE 1.6 **Nearly Half of All Firms Are Recognized as Small Business Entities**

BACKGROUNDER

AIA DIVERSITY HISTORY

Marga Rose Hancock, Hon. AIA

In 2011, AIA Diversity and Inclusion commissioned the development and online publication of an AIA Diversity History, excerpted here. What follows is a brief history of activities by the AIA directed at study and redress of the underrepresentation of women and racial/ethnic minorities in the profession, with statistical references and participant observations.

Marga Rose Hancock has taken an active role in AIA Diversity initiatives, as a founding member of the AIA Seattle Diversity Roundtable in 1986 and a 1992 appointee to the national Diversity Task Force. In 2011, AIA Diversity and Inclusion commissioned Rose Hancock to develop and publish an online AIA Diversity History.

DIVERSITY IN PROFESSIONAL PRACTICE

Women and people of color have practiced architecture and taken active roles in the profession, but at a rate substantially below their counterparts in other professions. Concern regarding the underrepresentation of these constituencies has engaged AIA leaders: The U.S. civil rights movement of the mid-1960s saw the initiation of policies and programs seeking to address this concern, as detailed in Table 1.4.

Following the Institute's 1857 establishment, in 1888 Louise Blanchard Bethune, FAIA, became the first woman to join the AIA, and in 1923 Paul Revere Williams, FAIA, became the first African American member.

According to U.S. Department of Labor/U.S. Bureau of Labor Statistics, compared with law and medicine, architecture lags in the percentage of women and minorities employed in the field (see Table 1.4).

TABLE 1.4 Comparison of Diversity in Architecture to Medicine and Law (2011)

Occupation	Percentage of total employed			
	Women %	Black/African Americans %	Asian %	Hispanic or Latina %
Architects	20.7	1.6	5.5	4.1
Lawyers	31.9	5.3	4.2	3.2
Physicians	33.8	5.3	16.1	6.6

Diversity is now improving. While 88 percent of the AIA's retired members are classified as Caucasian, the percentage among active members is now 72 percent. Among Associate members it is 58 percent and over 40 percent among students in accredited architecture programs. The same can be seen for women in the profession.

A further comparison: As of May 2012, the BLS also notes, "Fourteen percent of architects and engineers and 34 percent of physicians and surgeons were women, whereas 61 percent of accountants and auditors and 82 percent of elementary and middle school teachers were women."

TABLE 1.5 AIA Diversity Timeline 1968–2011 (excerpted)

1968	In his keynote address to the AIA Convention in Portland, Oregon, Urban League head Whitney M. Young, Jr. challenges the AIA on issues of social responsibility and diversity within the profession: "We are going to have to have people as committed to doing the right thing to inclusiveness as we have in the past to exclusiveness."
1970	AIA/AAF Minority Disadvantaged Scholarship initiated, supporting an average of 20 students per year.
1971	Establishment of National Organization of Minority Architects at AIA Convention, Detroit.
1972	AIA presents first Whitney M. Young Award, recognizing "architects and organizations that exemplify the profession's proactive social mandate," to Robert J. Nash, FAIA.
1974	AIA hires Robert T. Coles, FAIA, as Deputy VP for Minority Affairs, to develop "a master plan for minority awareness," and, working with Leon Bridges, FAIA, and Marshall Purnell, FAIA, to establish the AIA Commission on Community Services.
1980	Norma Merrick Sklarek, FAIA, the first African American woman licensed as an architect, becomes the first elevated to the AIA College of Fellows.
1982	Women constitute 3.6 percent of AIA membership.
1989	"The number of female architects, less than 1,500 in 1970, now approaches 5,000. The number of black architects has grown from about 1,000 to 2,000, remaining at about 2 percent of the total." —Robert Coles, FAIA, "Black Architects: An Endangered Species," *Progressive Architecture* (July 1989)
1992	First meeting of the AIA President's "Task Force on Equal Rights and Proactive Action" in Washington, D.C., charged by then AIA President W. Cecil Steward, FAIA, to develop a comprehensive strategic plan to implement the 1991 civil rights policy, for presentation to the AIA Board. Named the Diversity Task Force, this group developed a vision of the AIA in the year 2000 as a multicultural organization.
1992–93	Susan Maxman, FAIA, serves as the first woman president since AIA's 1857 founding. L. Jane Hastings, FAIA, serves as the first woman chancellor of the AIA College of Fellows.
1994	Diversity Conference I: "Breaking the ICE" (Washington, D.C.) Keynoter: Charlotte, NC, Mayor Harvey Gantt, FAIA. AIA membership includes 7.3 percent "all minorities," 10.45 percent women, 0.99 percent minority women.
1996–97	Raj Barr-Kumar, FAIA, serves as first AIA president of color.
1996	Diversity Conference III: "Crossing Lines" (Boston, MA). Keynoter: Patricia Carbine, co-founder of *Ms.* Magazine.
1997	Diversity Conference IV: "Beyond the Rainbow" (Seattle, WA), proceeded by "Dancing in Design" National Conference for Women in Architecture organized by Seattle Association for Women in Architecture (AWA). Keynoters: Seattle Mayor Norm Rice, Professor Sharon Sutton, FAIA, and AIA President Ronald Altoon, FAIA.
1998	Diversity Conference V: "Opening Doors," Atlanta, GA. Keynoter: Atlanta Mayor Andrew Young.
2001–02	Gordon Chong, FAIA, serves as first Asian American AIA president.
2005	AIA sponsors study of architecture demographics by Holland & Knight: "Of its members, approximately 2% are Hispanic/Latino, 3% are Asian, and 1% are Black. . . . As of December 2004, approximately 12% of all of the AIA's architect members are female. The AIA does not collect information on disability or sexual orientation."
2007–08	Marshall Purnell, FAIA, serves as the AIA's first African American president.
2008	First AIA Diversity Plenary "MultiFORMity" in St. Louis brings together individuals representing architecture, other professions, business, academia, associations, and AIA components to identify best practices for implementation by the AIA and its partners in order to move the profession toward a more diverse and inclusive future by improving the recruitment, retention, and promotion of diverse individuals in architecture. The outcome of the plenary, the "Gateway Commitment," leads to the development of a multiyear action plan to address these issues, with a mandate to create a diversity toolkit designed to engage firms on the issue of diversity and inclusion. Leers Weinzapfel Associates selected as first woman-owned firm recipient of the AIA Architecture Firm Award. AIA recognizes Norma Merrick Sklarek, FAIA, as the first woman recipient of the Whitney Young Award. "Only 1.5 percent of America's architects are African American (at a time when the U.S. Census shows that African Americans comprise approximately 12 to 13 percent of the total population)." —Robert Ivy, FAIA, "Room for All Our Talents," *Architectural Record* (May 2008)
2009	Inaugural AIA Women's Leadership Summit, Chicago, IL: "The first national gathering of women who serve as firm principals and in other professional leadership roles drew upon their talents and experiences to describe the issues women face and sought to raise their profile within the profession." Second AIA Diversity Plenary, "Value: The Difference—a Toolkit for Firms." San Francisco plenary brings together AIA Board members, collateral organizations, related organizations, firm representatives, interns, and students to identify tools, resources, and approaches to increase diversity and inclusion within architecture firms. Adoption of the "NOMA/AIA Memorandum of Understanding," and adoption of "AIA Diversity Action Plan, 2009–2013," with strategies to (1) expand the racial/ethnic, gender, and perspective diversity of the design professions to mirror the society we serve; and (2) nurture emerging professionals and influence a preferred future for the internship process and architecture education. "According to the latest figures from the National Architectural Accrediting Board, architecture schools are still dominated by men, though by a decreasing margin. Of all the enrolled and matriculating students of architecture, 59% are men and 41% are women. The gender gap is much wider among faculty, however, with a split of 74% men, 26% women." —Lance Hosey, "Women Rule," *Architect* (December 2009)

(continued)

| TABLE 1.5 *(continued)* | |

2010	AIA hosts Women's Leadership Summit, New York. Diversity Best Practice Awards recognize the contribution of individuals, firms, and AIA component programs to the aim of advancing diversity in architecture.
2011	AIA Women's Leadership Summit, Kansas City,
2016	Carole Wedge FAIA elected Chair of the AIA Large Firm Roundtable.

DIVERSITY WITHIN THE AIA

The United States' tumultuous and turbulent past with regard to racial and gender equality set the stage for consideration of diversity and inclusion in the workplace. According to the 1960 U.S. Census, virtually all doctors, attorneys, architects, engineers, executives, and managers were white men. The civil unrest of the sixties provided a catalyst for change.

In 1964, the Civil Rights Act was passed, which made it illegal for the organizations to engage in employment practices that discriminated against employees on the basis of race, color, religion, gender, national origin, age, and disability. In 1965, Executive Order 11246 was passed, requiring all government contractors to take affirmative actions to overcome past patterns of exclusion and discrimination. While these federal mandates plus several others helped to eliminate formal policies that discriminated against various classes of workers, professions and the organizations that represented them were slow to make changes toward a more diverse membership.

At the 1968 AIA National Convention in Portland, Oregon, Whitney M. Young Jr., civil rights activist and Executive Director of the National Urban League, in his keynote speech challenged the AIA membership on the issues of human/civil rights, diversity, and inclusion.

It took a great deal of skill and creativity and imagination to build the kind of situation we have, and it is going to take skill and imagination and creativity to change it. We are going to have to have people as committed to doing the right thing, to inclusiveness, as we have in the past to exclusiveness.

—*Whitney M. Young (1968)*

In 2012, 44 years later, it is instructive to understand how the situation has changed and has not changed. Unless otherwise noted, the source of demographic information shown is *The Business of Architecture: 2012 AIA Survey Report on Firm Characteristics*.

In 2012, current emeritus AIA members embody the ethnic makeup of the profession during the second half of the twentieth century (see Figure 1.7).

The ethnic demographics of AIA member architects in 2012, as shown in Figure 1.8, reflect the status quo in the early twenty-first century. It is worth noting that over the past 20 years, the percentage of African American AIA architect members has remained at only 1 percent.

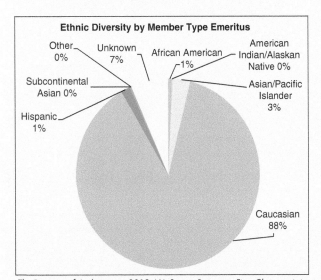

The Business of Architecture: 2012 AIA Survey Report on Firm Characteristics

FIGURE 1.7 **Ethnic Diversity: AIA Emeritus Members**

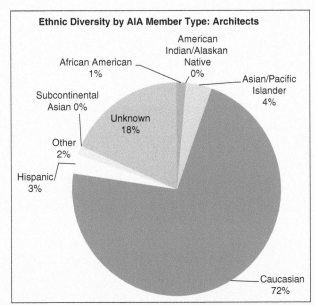

The Business of Architecture: 2012 AIA Survey Report on Firm Characteristics

FIGURE 1.8 **Ethnic Diversity: AIA Architect Members**

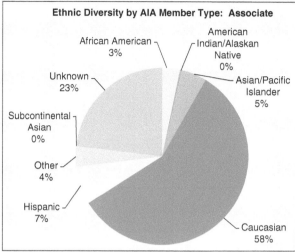

The Business of Architecture: 2012 AIA Survey Report on Firm Characteristics

FIGURE 1.9 **Ethnic Diversity: AIA Associate Members**

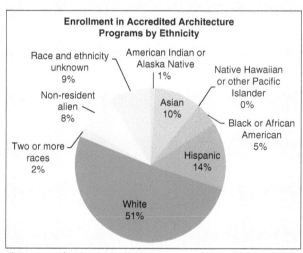

The Business of Architecture: 2012 AIA Survey Report on Firm Characteristics

FIGURE 1.10 **Enrollment in Accredited Architecture Programs by Ethnicity**

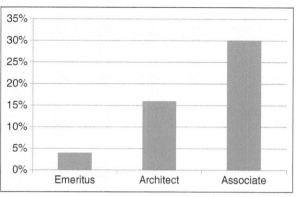

NAAB Accreditation Report, 2011

FIGURE 1.11 **Percentage of Women in AIA Member Categories**

Nevertheless, the 2012 ethnic makeup of associates (see Figure 1.9) portends a future AIA and architectural profession with more non-Caucasian participants.

For women the trend is similar, as Figure 1.11 shows. Only 4 percent of emeritus members are women, while women make up 16 percent of Architect members, and 30 percent of Associates.

At the university level there appears to be evidence of some change, as shown in Figure 1.10. In many architecture programs, women make up 50 percent or more of the students, with the average being about 40 percent. Although gender balance among architecture students has been in place since the mid-1980s, the number of women architect members of the AIA has remained flat at around 16 percent. Judging by the 2012 percentage of minority AIA associate members (30 percent), minority participation in architecture programs must also be improving. Nevertheless, it clearly still lags behind what is needed to significantly increase ethnic diversity in the profession.

CONCLUSION

A diverse and inclusive workforce is a reflection of a changing world and marketplace. Diversity among clients, especially in the global marketplace, can in itself be a challenge. Diversity and inclusion at all levels brings high value to organizations and promotes the firm's ability to adapt to any situation. In addition, diversity and inclusion will help a firm attract and retain top candidates that can add capacity and competitiveness in the global marketplace.

THE PRACTICE

Most Design Specialty Offerings Increase

Nearly all firms (97 percent) report that they offered architecture services at their firm in 2011, with a significant share also reporting that they offered the design-related disciplines of predesign services (61 percent), space planning (57 percent), interior design (57 percent), and planning (52 percent).

TABLE 1.6 Despite the Economic Downturn, Share of Firms Offering Most Design-Related Specialties Has Increased

Firm Type	2011 (%)	2008 (%)	2005 (%)
Architecture	97	97	97
Predesign services	61	n/a	n/a
Space planning	57	54	50
Interior design	57	54	49
Planning	52	50	48
Consulting	n/a	42	44
Sustainable/green design	49	50	31
Historic preservation	30	30	29
Design-build	22	21	20
Construction management	18	17	16
Urban design	17	16	15
Landscape architecture	11	11	10
Engineering	8	8	8
Practice-based research	6	n/a	n/a
Other	7	10	8

Unit: Percent of firms
The Business of Architecture: 2012 AIA Survey Report on Firm Characteristics

The share of firms offering the sustainable/green design specialty grew significantly from 2005 to 2008, but changed little from 2008 to 2011, with nearly half of firms offering this specialty in 2011. The share of firms offering the interior design, space planning, and planning design specialties grew modestly in these three years (Table 1.6).

Fewer than half of small firms reported that they offer sustainable design services, while over two-thirds of the midsize firms, and four in five large firms, do so. Of firms with an institutional specialization, 57 percent report offering sustainable design as a specialty in their practice, in contrast with an average of 45 percent of firms with a commercial/industrial or residential specialization.

Multidisciplinary Firms Continue to Grow

The economy is going through a transformation and so is the architecture industry. The share of architecture firms that describe their practice as single-discipline continued to decline in 2011, falling below 60 percent, as more than one-third of firms report that they are now multidisciplinary (with architecture as the lead discipline) versus just over one-quarter a decade ago (Figure 1.12).

The share of multidisciplinary architecture firms has doubled in the past 15 years. More than four in five firms with 50 or more employees now characterize themselves as multidisciplinary.

In 2011, nearly two-thirds of firms with fewer than 10 employees and one-third of firms with 10 to 49 employees described their practice as single-discipline.

BIM Software Used by Slightly More than One-Third of Firms

On average, just over one-third of firms were using building information modeling (BIM) software as of 2011. At the same time, 36 percent of firms do not use BIM software and do not plan to use it in the near future. About one-quarter of firms that are not using BIM software are considering the purchase of this tool in the next few years.

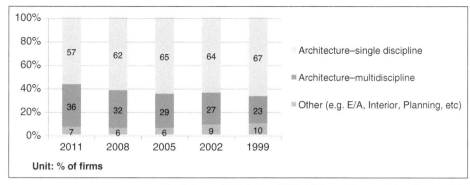

The Business of Architecture: 2012 AIA Survey Report on Firm Characteristics

FIGURE 1.12 **The Single-Discipline Architecture Firm Continues to Decline**

The majority of firms with 100 or more employees are using BIM software, while three-quarters of firms with a staff size of 20 to 99 employees are doing so.

The firms using BIM software for billable work indicate that they are most likely to use it for design visualization services (91 percent of firms), coordinated construction documents (74 percent), and sharing models with consultants (55 percent). Larger firms also indicate that resolving conflicts with other disciplines (clash detection) and sharing models with constructors/trade contractors are primary uses of BIM software in their office (Table 1.9).

					Number of Employees		
Firm Type—Architecture	All Firms (%)	1 (%)	2–4 (%)	5–9 (%)	10–19 (%)	20–49 (%)	50–99 (%)	100+ (%)
Single discipline—2011	57	74	63	49	39	20	11	1
Single discipline—2008	62	79	69	59	41	23	9	7
Multidiscipline—2011	36	17	30	46	54	68	79	86
Multidiscipline—2008	32	12	26	37	51	64	79	80
Other discipline—2011	7	9	7	5	7	12	10	13
Other discipline—2008	6	8	5	4	8	13	12	13

TABLE 1.7 Multidiscipline Firms Increase Another 10 Percent from Three Years Ago

Units: Percent of firms
The Business of Architecture: 2012 AIA Survey Report on Firm Characteristics

TABLE 1.8 Less Than One-Third of Firms Using BIM for Billable Work

					Number of Employees		
	Total (%)	1 (%)	2–4 (%)	5–9 (%)	10–19 (%)	20–49 (%)	50–99 (%)	100+ (%)
Yes, we are using it for billable work	29	16	22	28	54	71	79	100
Yes, but we are not yet using it for billable work	9	9	8	14	10	7	10	0
No, but plan to acquire within the next 12 months	7	7	8	8	8	5	0	0
No, but plan to acquire sometime (not within the next 12 months)	19	17	23	21	13	9	5	0
No, and do not plan to acquire	36	51	39	30	15	8	6	0

Units: Percent of firms
The Business of Architecture: 2012 AIA Survey Report on Firm Characteristics

TABLE 1.9 Design Visualization and Construction Documents Most Widely Used on BIM Software

	Total (%)	1 (%)	2–4 (%)	5–9 (%)	10–19 (%)	20–49 (%)	50–99 (%)	100+ (%)
					Number of Employees			
Design visualization	91	92	91	91	89	94	90	94
Coordinated construction documents	74	63	68	67	83	91	92	97
Sharing models with consultants	55	31	44	55	69	79	83	80
Resolving conflicts with other disciplines (clash detection)	46	28	30	43	55	75	87	86
Sharing models with constructors/ trade contractors	34	22	28	25	37	55	71	66
Quantity takeoffs/estimating	27	30	27	25	22	26	37	31
Energy/performance analysis	24	19	19	17	25	31	58	51
In the learning phase of the software	2	2	4	1	0	1	0	0
Other	3	4	3	1	3	3	6	0

Units: Percent of firms (those who currently use BIM—multiple selections permitted)
The Business of Architecture: 2012 AIA Survey Report on Firm Characteristics

CONSTRUCTION SECTORS SERVED

Majority of Firm Billings Derived from New Construction Projects

While new projects still constitute the overall majority of firm billings, renovations, rehabilitations, additions, and other construction projects have markedly increased their share, particularly at midsize and larger firms. At firms with fewer than 10 employees, the majority of their firm billings continue to be from renovations, rehabilitations, additions, and historic preservation, as in the past.

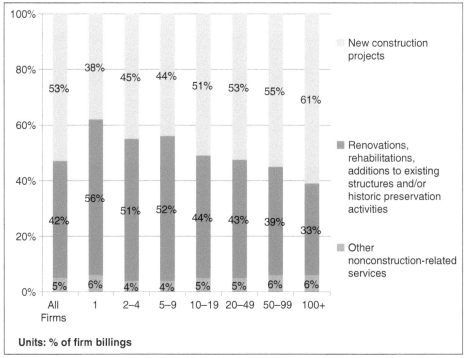

The Business of Architecture: 2012 AIA Survey Report on Firm Characteristics

FIGURE 1.13 **New Construction Projects Account for Just Over Half of Firm Billings**

Institutional Projects Make Up Biggest Share of Firm Billings

When considering the distribution of architecture firm billings by project type, institutional projects continue to account for the largest share of billings at all firms (except for the smallest-sized firms), accounting for an average of 58.2 percent of firm billings (Table 1.10).

Majority Share of Billings from Repeat Clients

Architecture firms report that nearly two-thirds of their firm billings are from basic design services (an average of 64 percent of billings for all firms). Approximately 10 percent of billings are from planning and predesign services, 9 percent from nonarchitectural design services, and 8 percent from expanded design services.

On average, more than two-thirds of 2011 architecture firm billings (68 percent) were from projects for repeat clients.

Firms with a commercial/industrial specialization reported the largest share of their firm billings from repeat clients (75 percent), while firms with a residential specialization indicated that nearly half of their billings (45 percent) were from new clients.

Nearly One-Third of Firm Billings from Government Clients

Clients from state and/or local government entities remain the most common client type for architecture firms of all sizes, accounting for one-quarter of all firm billings in 2011, while at midsize firms they accounted for nearly one-third of their billings (Table 1.13). Small firms reported that nearly half of their billings were from private individuals, but overall private individuals accounted for just 12 percent of billings at all firms.

TABLE 1.10 Nearly 60 Percent of Firm Billings Are from Institutional Projects		
	2011 (%)	2008 (%)
Single-family residential	6.2	5.5
Multifamily residential	7.5	5.8
Residential Total	**13.7**	**11.3**
Office	9.2	11.3
Retail, food services, warehouses, etc.	7.6	8.4
Hospitality	3.7	4.8
Industrial	3.3	3.6
Commercial/Industrial Total	**23.8**	**28.1**
Education (K–12)	12.4	9.0
Education (college/university)	12.4	9.0
Health care	17.2	18.2
Justice (e.g., corrections, courthouses)	1.6	2.3
Other government/civic (e.g., Post Office, federal office buildings)	6.4	5.9
Religious	2.0	2.2
Cultural (e.g., museums)	2.0	1.7
Recreational (e.g., sports centers, theme parks)	2.2	2.3
Transportation (e.g., airports, rail, bus, mass transit)	2.2	2.9
Institutional Total	**58.4**	**53.5**
Other construction projects	2.3	6.0
Nonconstruction projects	1.8	1.1

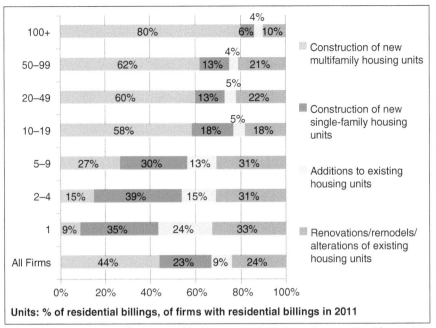

Units: % of residential billings, of firms with residential billings in 2011

The Business of Architecture: 2012 AIA Survey Report on Firm Characteristics

FIGURE 1.14 **Two-thirds of Residential Billings Involved New Construction**

TABLE 1.11 Majority of Firms Have a Residential or Institutional Specialization

| | All Firms 2011 (%) | All Firms 2008 (%) | 1 (%) | Number of Employees | | | | | |
				2–4 (%)	5–9 (%)	10–19 (%)	20–49 (%)	50–99 (%)	100+ (%)
Residential	33.5	35.0	47.2	39.0	26.2	13.6	8.8	5.0	3.0
Commercial/ industrial	21.7	21.0	20.6	23.6	20.5	19.3	20.3	23.4	26.4
Institutional	32.9	27.0	18.3	24.2	42.1	59.4	64.8	63.2	64.5
Mixed	11.9	18.0	13.9	13.2	11.2	7.6	6.1	8.3	6.1

Units: Percent of firms with 50 percent or more of 2011 firm billings in given sector
The Business of Architecture: 2012 AIA Survey Report on Firm Characteristics

TABLE 1.12 Repeat Clients Account for Larger Share of Firm Billings Than in Past

	All Firms 2011 (%)	All Firms 2005 (%)	Residential (%)	Commercial/ industrial (%)	Institutional (%)
Repeat clients, noncompetitive selection	43	48	48	55	37
Repeat clients, competitive selection (interview, proposals, etc.)	25	10	8	20	29
New clients, noncompetitive selection	10	26	21	10	7
New clients, competitive selection (interview, proposals, etc.)	23	16	24	15	26

Units: Percent of firm billings
The Business of Architecture: 2012 AIA Survey Report on Firm Characteristics

TABLE 1.13 More Than One-Quarter of Firm Billings from State/Local Government Clients

	All Firms (%)	Number of Employees						
		1 (%)	2–4 (%)	5–9 (%)	10–19 (%)	20–49 (%)	50–99 (%)	100+ (%)
State or local government (including public schools)	25.4	8.6	13.7	25.6	29.6	32.4	30.7	17.6
Other business, commercial, or industrial companies	19.9	11.7	16.7	18.6	13.7	22.1	22.8	21.8
Nonprofit institutions (e.g., private schools, museums, churches)	15.8	10.2	11.4	9.6	11.9	10.8	11.6	29.3
Developers, construction companies	14.4	14.4	14.0	15.3	12.4	16.7	14.1	13.3
Private individuals	12.1	44.2	37.1	22.7	18.5	7.3	4.9	3.6
Federal government	7.0	0.4	1.1	4.0	7.9	6.6	9.1	8.7
Other architects, engineers, design professionals	4.3	8.2	5.1	3.1	3.9	3.5	3.5	5.7
Other	1.2	2.2	0.8	1.1	2.1	0.5	3.3	0.0

Units: Percent of firm billings
The Business of Architecture: 2012 AIA Survey Report on Firm Characteristics

Business, commercial, and industrial companies are also popular clients, accounting for 20 percent of firms' billings, while nonprofit institutions accounted for 16 percent (and nearly one-third of billings at firms with 100 or more employees). Regardless of firm size, very little work was done for the federal government in 2011, although there were some firms that derived a significant part of their fees from federal projects.

Pro bono work is relatively common at many firms, with 6 in 10 having provided pro bono work in 2011. Large firms were much more likely to provide pro bono work than small firms, with 67 percent of firms with 50 or more employees providing the service in contrast to 55 percent of firms with four or fewer employees. Firms with an institutional specialization were also much more likely to report having offered pro bono work than those with residential or commercial/industrial specializations.

CONCLUSION

In an effort to document emerging trends in the practice of architecture, the American Institute of Architects periodically has conducted comprehensive surveys of its member-owned firms. These *Business of Architecture* reports present benchmarks that allow firms to assess their practices and evaluate their operations in comparison to their peers. In this way, the architecture profession can monitor its current performance while pursuing shared goals for the larger architecture community.

During the survey, conducted in early 2012, firms provided information on characteristics and operations in 2011. The analysis in part compares these results to earlier surveys to assess how the profession is changing. Generally, firm activity is compared and contrasted by the size of the firm (number of employees on payroll), the region of the country, and the construction sector concentration of the practice (residential, commercial/industrial, and institutional) for those firms that received 50 percent or more of their annual revenue from one of these three sectors.

Unless otherwise specified, all information in this report was generated by the American Institute of Architects.

1.3 Ethics and Professional Conduct

Phillip H. Gerou, FAIA

Architects are confronted daily with moral choices, competing loyalties, and ethical dilemmas. Although such situations can be ambiguous or paradoxical, basic tenets held in common by the profession can help architects determine how to respond to them.

The need to articulate and advocate ethical standards has never been more critical. Concern about professional ethics, while not a recent development, has certainly become more conspicuous in recent years. This visibility has led to extensive inquiries into the sources, development, interpretation, and enforcement of ethical codes. Principles guiding professional conduct are based on the core values held by that profession. These core values originate in legal definitions, social mores, moral codes, and common business practices.

Legal systems are based on historical precedent and commonly accepted social interactions between individuals or legal entities. The rights of individuals are protected by mutual acceptance of this legal structure. Contractual and other legal responsibilities and their consequences are generally well defined in law and in written agreements. But when these responsibilities and their consequences are specific to a profession, they may prove difficult to legally enforce.

There are many social conventions, moral beliefs, and ethical dilemmas that are not legislated or enforced by any regulatory agency. These may include widely accepted values but are not part of our legal system because they lack consensus or represent conflicting opinions. These values are often defined by religious doctrine, corporate policies, or societal rules. While morality describes behavior that is generally accepted as either correct or incorrect, ethical situations often present dilemmas in which equally relevant positions compete.

Ethics is traditionally defined as the rules or standards for moral behavior. Often the terms *morality* and *ethics* are used interchangeably, and to many there is no distinction between the two. The definition of ethics has also evolved to express a set of values held by a unique and finite group of individuals, such as a corporation, legislature, industry, or profession. Ethical codes are based on common values and moral laws such as religious doctrine, social conventions, secular beliefs, and traditional philosophies; they may even incorporate the values of courtesy, civility, mutual respect, or equality. Ethical standards for doctors or priests are different in their details from those of architects or engineers, although the core beliefs and the moral guidelines on which they are founded may be nearly identical. The distinction in ethical standards depends on the specific practices of a particular group.

Ethics also define fairness and equity and quite often relate to issues in which two parties may hold opposing but equally valid points of view or an individual may be torn between two compelling positions. For example, an individual may find that speaking the truth could breach a confidence, someone's dedication to a friendship might result in injury to others if an obligation to protect the public is ignored, or a client's goals could be at odds with protection of the environment. In certain situations, ethical standards may take precedence over other important standards. For

Phillip H. Gerou is a former director and vice president of the American Institute of Architects and served six years as a member and chairman of the AIA National Ethics Council.

example, life safety issues are usually perceived as a primary concern in comparison to, for example, obligations to employers. Although a solution that positively addresses each competing issue is preferred, occasionally a choice is necessary. Ethical codes address such situations, but it is often left to an informed and impartial observer to make the final judgment.

ETHICAL STANDARDS FOR ARCHITECTS

In the United States, there are two widely used standards of conduct for architects. In 1977 the National Council of Architectural Registration Boards (NCARB) issued a set of model rules of conduct for use by its member boards. NCARB rules are guided by certain core values as they pertain to the protection of the life, safety, and welfare of the public, issues to which architects are legally bound by individual state licensure laws. NCARB's rules of conduct have been adopted, with modifications, by various NCARB member boards as part of the licensing regulations that apply to individual architects.

The American Institute of Architects has established a Code of Ethics and Professional Conduct. This code addresses life safety and public welfare issues, and also includes rules of conduct that deal with professional interactions between architects and their colleagues and their clients. Members of the AIA are also held accountable by the code for such broad issues as seeking aesthetic excellence and respecting the environment.

The first AIA ethical code was established in 1909. By today's standards, some of the original principles seem out-of-date. Under the original code, design-build was a forbidden practice and paid advertising by architects was not allowed. The code also prohibited architects from competing on the basis of fees or entering design competitions that were not in keeping with Institute principles. These restrictions were derived more from the common business practices of the day than universal core values or widely accepted moral principles.

By the late 1970s, the AIA code of ethics had been significantly amended. Design-build became an accepted approach to project delivery, and advertising was no longer the anathema it had been. By 1972 the U.S. Justice Department had determined that the 1890 Sherman Antitrust Act demanded that architects be allowed to compete on the basis of fees and that not doing so constituted an unreasonable restraint of trade. In a 1978 case involving the National Society of Professional Engineers, the Supreme Court ruled that unfettered competition was essential to the health of a free-market economy, and the only lawful way competition could be constrained was through state or federal legislation. In its opinion, the court dismissed arguments stressing the possible negative effects of fee competition on the health, safety, and welfare of the public.

In 1977, an architect sued the Institute for civil damages when his AIA membership was suspended for violating the AIA code of ethics by supplanting another architect on a project. Although the violation was not disputed, in 1978 a federal district court ruled that enforcement of this particular rule in the code violated federal antitrust laws and the accused architect was awarded substantial monetary damages.

In response to these rulings, in 1980 the AIA suspended its code of ethics. The following year a statement of ethical principles was established as a guideline for the voluntary conduct of members. Recognizing a need for mandatory professional guidelines, the AIA Board of Directors subsequently appointed a task force to propose a substitute Code of Ethics and Professional Conduct. In 1986 the membership adopted the new code at the AIA National Convention. Since that time, minor revisions have been made to keep pace with current technologies, economic realities, and changing social demands.

AIA Code of Ethics and Professional Conduct

The current AIA Code of Ethics and Professional Conduct defines in detail the obligations of AIA members. The code is organized into five canons that describe broad

Some ethical situations are not regulated by the AIA Code of Ethics and Professional Conduct. For example, the profession of architecture as a whole may aspire to contribute to the preservation of historical and cultural resources by helping to develop appropriate building codes or formulating aesthetic guidelines. Nonetheless, some architects are more suited to such tasks than others; for instance, participation in this effort may not be a reasonable requirement for an AIA member whose expertise lies in financial management or graphic design. Similarly, it is not a requirement that all AIA members provide pro bono services, as some may choose to support causes or organizations by other means. A code of ethics cannot embrace every aspiration of a profession. Rather, it must exhibit restraint in defining actions to which all members may reasonably submit.

principles of conduct: general obligations, obligations to the public, obligations to the client, obligations to the profession, and obligations to colleagues.

Each canon is defined by a number of ethical standards. These standards provide more defined goals, which members should aspire to in their professional performance and behavior. Individual ethical standards incorporate specific rules of conduct that are mandatory and enforceable. Violation of a rule by an AIA member may be grounds for disciplinary action by the Institute. Commentary, which is offered to clarify or elaborate the intent of the rule, is provided for some of the rules of conduct.

The code applies to the professional activities of all AIA members regardless of their membership category and is enforced by the AIA National Ethics Council. Only AIA members are obligated to comply with these standards.

AIA National Ethics Council

The National Ethics Council (NEC) is made up of seven AIA members selected and appointed according to specific credentials. Each of the seven members represents a diverse constituency. They come from various regions of the country and different types of practice and professional backgrounds, and they are representative of the general membership based on diverse demographic criteria. Prospective NEC members are recommended to the AIA Board of Directors, which makes the final decision and appointment. Appointments are for a three-year term, although members of the NEC may be, and usually are, reappointed for a second three-year term. An NEC member may not serve more than two consecutive full terms.

The full ethics council meets three times per year to hear and consider complaints. The particulars of each case, along with a recommendation for resolving it, are presented to the NEC by one of its members who serves as a hearing officer. This individual is then excused while the remaining NEC members consider the report and recommendation and ultimately decide whether to accept, reject, or modify the hearing officer's recommendation or to return the case for rehearing.

The principal responsibility of the NEC as defined by the AIA Bylaws is enforcement of the AIA Code of Ethics and Professional Conduct. However, the NEC also provides guidelines to the public and within the Institute on a variety of professional topics. In addition, the NEC presents programs at the AIA National Convention, to AIA components, and to schools of architecture throughout the country.

AIA NATIONAL ETHICS COUNCIL PROCEDURES

Local AIA components manage ethical situations in a variety of ways. Some components provide advice and mediation for ethical violations through experienced members or established committees, while others simply refer local inquiries to the national organization. The general counsel's office at the national component is available to answer technical questions concerning the AIA Code of Ethics and Professional Conduct and can provide other information to members and nonmembers.

The AIA National Ethics Council has established strict rules of procedure for considering ethics cases. If it is believed that a member has violated the code of ethics, anyone—a member or nonmember of the AIA—may initiate a formal complaint. The NEC then initiates its review and hearing process.

If the architect is found to have violated the ethics code, the penalties available to the NEC are as follows:

Ethics complaints against AIA members should be addressed to:

Chair, National Ethics Council, The American Institute of Architects, 1735 New York Avenue NW, Washington, D.C., 20006

- *Admonition (private).* A letter of the ruling is sent to the parties involved and kept in the respondent's membership file.
- *Censure (public).* A letter is sent and notification of the case and ruling is published to the AIA membership.
- *Suspension of membership.* The respondent's membership is suspended for a period of time, usually one or two years, and the ruling is published.
- *Termination of membership.* The respondent's membership is terminated and the ruling is published.

The respondent may appeal the NEC's decision to the AIA Executive Committee, whose subsequent ruling is final except in cases in which termination of membership is the penalty. Those cases are automatically appealed to the AIA Board of Directors.

COMMON ETHICS VIOLATIONS

Although the AIA Code of Ethics and Professional Conduct regulates a wide range of professional activities, several issues generate the majority of complaints. These include the following:

- Attribution of credit (i.e., stating or giving proper credit for project involvement)
- Accurate representation of qualifications
- Attainment and provision of examples of work
- Basic honesty

The predominant reason these four issues continually resurface is that each has an identifiable injured party—an angry colleague or an upset client—who is intent on seeing justice served. Also, even if the alleged infraction does not have legal or contractual consequences, it may still indicate an ethical breach. More serious issues, such as misappropriation of a client's or partner's funds, tend to be presented to the NEC less frequently. If a member knowingly violates the law (Rule 2.101) or displays discrimination (Rule 1.401), for instance, other forums with more severe remedies are available to the offended party.

To offer some guidance on issues commonly presented to the NEC, the following detailed illustrations are offered.

Attribution of Credit

Architecture is a profession in which design capability and originality is prized. Intellectual property is the most common proof of worth in terms of talent and experience. However, the collaborative nature of contemporary practice sometimes obscures the individual contributions of each team participant. The more complex the project and the more prolonged the design and construction process, the more individuals may lay valid claim to credit for some part of the work.

The most frequent violation of the code of ethics is improperly taking or not giving appropriate credit and recognition. The NEC recognizes that these infractions are frequently due to an incomplete understanding of the ethical standards and rules of conduct that direct members in this area. The following ethical standards apply to this issue:

Ethical Standard 4.2, Dignity and Integrity: Members should strive, through their actions, to promote the dignity and integrity of the profession, and to ensure that their representatives and employees conform their conduct to this Code.

Ethical Standard 5.3, Professional Recognition: Members should build their professional reputation on the merits of their own service and performance and should recognize and give credit to others for the professional work they have performed.

The rules associated with these standards mandate the required professional conduct:

Rule 4.201: Members shall not make misleading, deceptive, or false statements or claims about their professional qualifications, experience, or performance and shall accurately state the scope and nature of their responsibilities in connection with work for which they are claiming credit.

Rule 5.301: Members shall recognize and respect the professional contributions of their employees, employers, professional colleagues, and business associates.

Based on these standards and rules, the NEC has adopted guidelines to help AIA members determine how to handle this concern, although individual cases may present circumstances not explicitly covered. These guidelines are recommended for application to any oral, written, or graphic representation of an architect's work, whether it was developed for use in a public or private presentation.

Following are the AIA "Guidelines for the Attribution of Credit" (also published on the AIA website) that should be considered when making representations of an architect's work:

- An architectural project, built or unbuilt, involves any of the services provided by or under the direction of an architect.
- In analyzing attribution-of-credit issues, the National Ethics Council typically views the Architect-of-Record as the legal entity that has contracted for and completed the work in question. [The entity] can be a corporation, partnership, or individual architect. If the Architect-of-Record takes credit for a project, there is no further need to define the role or state "Architect-of-Record." Unless specific attribution is noted, it is assumed the Architect-of-Record is making a representation of complete responsibility for a project, including the design, production of construction documents, and construction observation.
- A Member taking credit for a project or a specific role on a project other than as the Architect-of-Record must clearly define that role. In addition to the Member's specific role, the Architect-of-Record must be acknowledged.
- It is not necessary to present a complete or exhaustive list of all the team participants. The acknowledgment of major team participants is recommended.
- Designation of the Member's role and/or the Architect-of-Record must be obvious, plainly visible, and legible at the anticipated viewing distance. The reference text should be no less obvious than the text used to describe the project. The description must be specific enough to make clear the services the Member rendered on this project. In the instance of a mailer/postcard that shows only an image of a project on the front, it is necessary to give the appropriate credit on the other side. The Member shall not overstate, actually or implicitly, his/her involvement in a project.
- If attribution of credit is not previously defined in a written agreement, and to avoid potential conflict, it is recommended that Members open a dialogue between all concerned parties prior to making any representations.

Accurate Representation of Qualifications

It is human nature and good business practice to present professional qualifications in the best light. However, overstatement, even if well-intentioned, can lead to unrealistic expectations on the part of the client or other project participants and thus to subsequent owner dissatisfaction. The architect-of-record must ultimately be responsible for complying with laws and codes as well as with other commitments, such as the project budget, a client's goals, a building's function, or environmental standards.

Rule 1.101: In practicing architecture, Members shall demonstrate a consistent pattern of reasonable care and competence, and shall apply the technical knowledge and skill which is ordinarily applied by architects of good standing practicing in the same locality.

Rule 3.102: Members shall undertake to perform professional services only when they, together with those whom they may engage as consultants, are qualified by education, training, or experience in the specific technical areas involved.

As an architecture firm evolves, its expertise may become somewhat different from that stated in promotional materials or in a previous statement of qualifications. Members are obliged to always ensure that the expertise and resources presented match those that are currently available.

Professionals are often compelled to make commitments regarding time, cost, or results based more on the urgency of the moment than on rational evaluation. Too often, architects make changes that affect the scope or budget of a project without presenting viable options or possible ramifications of the proposed changes. Architects may also feel pressure to articulate results by describing the final product of the work in terms that naturally speak well of the process and the architect's capabilities to attain those results. Great care and restraint should be taken in clarifying expectations relating to budget, building function, quality of materials, and other anticipated results of the design process. Project and individual responsibilities should be clearly defined contractually and verbally. Revisiting the following statements of obligation periodically throughout the life of a project is beneficial:

- *Rule 3.103:* Members shall not materially alter the scope or objectives of a project without the client's consent.
- *Rule 3.301:* Members shall not intentionally or recklessly mislead existing or prospective clients about the results that can be achieved through the use of the Member's services, nor shall the Members state that they can achieve results by means that violate applicable law or this Code.

Helping the client reach realistic expectations is important. The medical profession characterizes this as informed consent, where a patient must be informed of a situation to the level of understanding that allows an informed decision. Clients in every profession deserve the same consideration.

Attainment and Provision of Samples of Work

In light of current technologies and the variety of roles that architects perform, defining an architect's work is increasingly difficult. For example, should an architect who predominantly created or adapted computer software or developed unique technical details be given copies of that work upon leaving a firm? How can the rights of the firm and of the employee be protected? Ethical Standard 5.3 pertaining to professional recognition provides a framework for guidance (see above). The specific rules that apply to this question are these:

The AIA has published a Best Practices article titled "Personal Use of Documents: A Sample Firm Policy" to help firms establish policies for the ethical use of documents during and after employment. (AIA Best Practices are available on the Internet.)

Rule 5.302: Members leaving a firm shall not, without the permission of their employer or partner, take designs, drawings, data, reports, notes, or other materials relating to the firm's work, whether or not performed by the Member.

Rule 5.303: A Member shall not unreasonably withhold permission from a departing employee or partner to take copies of designs, drawings, data, reports, notes, or other materials relating to work performed by the employee or partner that are not confidential.

It seems simple enough to be honest, but even well-meaning professionals from time to time are presented with competing obligations, such as family responsibilities or religious convictions. For example, employees may decide to work outside the office to build a client base, take advantage of opportunities to demonstrate design talent, or simply make money. In doing so, they may unwittingly expose the firm to liability and may compromise their own ability to perform adequately for the compensation they are receiving. Or, an employee may use the firm's software for personal use, believing that no harm is done by making a copy of it. Architects have certainly lied, stolen, defrauded, or taken advantage of a situation. Sometimes the individual is well-intentioned, sometimes not, but almost always he or she feels justified in his or her actions.

Architecture is a profession replete with competing values. Within every project are decisions to be made about quality of materials versus budget constraints, owner-prescribed requirements versus building codes or architectural review committees, and confidentiality versus truthfulness. Resolving these conflicts does not require decisions about right and wrong, but rather decisions to resolve situations in which competing principles are equally correct but may be mutually exclusive.

In addition, the code provides the following commentary: "A Member may impose reasonable conditions, such as the payment of copying costs, on the right of departing persons to take copies of their work."

The best advice is that the question of whether and how copies of work will be granted to an employee should be discussed before an employee decides to leave a firm or at least during the departure process. This discussion may help mitigate an awkward, emotional, or volatile termination process. A departing employee should expect to receive reasonable *examples* of work; the employer is not obligated to make the entire volume of work produced by the employee available. The intent is to allow the employee a reasonable opportunity to present qualifications to future employers or potential clients. It is equally important for the firm to retain proprietary or confidential materials and the work products it rightfully owns, such as renderings, photography, or proprietary software.

ETHICS AT ALL LEVELS

Michael Hricak, FAIA

Responsibility for ethics extends to all members of a firm, not just the principals or those in management positions. Members of the firm at all levels are in positions that require a clear understanding of ethical behavior.

Entry-level professionals and interns, as part of their daily responsibilities, make choices and perform tasks that need to be guided by a code of ethics. With the trend toward flattened, less hierarchical professional organizations, these firm members are attending meetings with clients, conducting daily tasks, and issuing project communications. The skills necessary to perform in these situations are seldom discussed, much less taught, within the architectural curriculum. As a result, the young architect is left to learn them on the job. The understanding of ethical behavior that should guide all firm members is thus often introduced in a work situation.

Questions of ethics can arise from examining seemingly routine or common behaviors:

- Discussing details of a proposal or comparing fee structures with colleagues in another firm

- Repeating information gathered within the context of a project or client meeting
- Casually sharing digital files (text, drawings, renderings, objects, and so on) with a colleague in another firm to bring each other up-to-date as to "what are you working on"
- Using the firm's Internet connection for personal instant messaging or other online activities not related to work
- Installing personal software on an office computer to assist in the production of a project, marketing material, or particular task at hand
- Working on personal projects in the workplace after hours using office resources

These examples touch on actions that are often misunderstood or not even considered as issues by those entering the profession and often by those in practice.

CONFIDENTIALITY

Everyone has a certain expectation of confidentiality. In a work situation, these expectations are formalized and there are often implications if a confidence is breached. Clients have the right to expect that their project, project information (e.g., schedule, budget, legal hurdles, and public reviews and approvals), and communications will be kept confidential. Sending project information over the Internet to a colleague—whether or not the project is in a sensitive stage of the approval process—is a clear violation of this expectation.

The firm has a certain level of expectation of discretion on the part of its employees. While exposing secrets and violating confidences appears to be a part of daily life in the media, office gossip and the sharing of situations within the workplace is seldom useful or appropriate. An architecture firm is not just any job, and firm members are not simply employees. A profession demands more of all those involved, both seasoned practitioners and aspiring professionals.

Employees likewise have certain expectations of their employers. They have a right to assume that personal information, whether health, financial, or behavioral in nature, will be held in trust by the firm.

Ethical practice is not merely a two-way street, but a network of complex relationships and behaviors.

INTELLECTUAL PROPERTY

Although there may be shades of gray in situations involving ethical behavior, many legal issues are black and white.

Software appropriately acquired while an individual is in school is provided by most software developers with the understanding and explicit agreement that it be used for academic purposes only. Many of these digital products are offered free or at substantial discounts to the student. Even the private, personal use of these products after graduation is questionable. Without question, bringing these products into a work setting, even in an attempt to support the efforts of the firm, exposes the firm to considerable legal liability, undue risk, and the possibility of fines and penalties. Such unauthorized use of software within a firm also exposes the employee to actions by the employer since, once this use is discovered, the firm is obligated to respond appropriately.

As professionals, architects have made considerable progress in protecting their intellectual property. The Architectural Works Copyright Protection Act of 1990 allows for protection of both technical drawings and building designs. Other work products (e.g., specifications, reports, etc.) may be covered under other provisions of copyright law.

If, as creative professionals, architects seek legal protection for what they produce, it is appropriate that they respect the efforts of others and equally value their intellectual property. This is not only the ethical response but also the legal one.

PERSONAL COMMITMENT

While the term "multitasking" is used to describe the ability to conduct several operations simultaneously, the work of an architect, or someone who aspires to become one, requires focus, concentration, and commitment to the task at hand. Design issues, buildings, the project delivery process, and the entire construction industry have become increasingly complex. It is essential for architects to use available technology to improve the process and better serve both their firms and their clients. At the same time, the ever-improving digital tools used by architects may make the actual act of design increasingly demanding. Building information modeling (BIM) software gives the members of the project team tremendous power in the creation of the information set necessary to construct a building.

Very unlike years past, there is no "backroom" filled with drafters performing routine and often mindless tasks. The cut-and-paste 2-D world of the last decade is rapidly giving way to operations that require a much more knowledgeable and thoughtful person at the controls, entering and monitoring the quality of the information being contributed to the building information model. For these and countless other reasons, everyone involved in the project delivery process must acknowledge and take responsibility for the quality of the work, since so many hands are involved in its creation.

PERSONAL PROJECTS/MOONLIGHTING

Taking on outside projects, whether for financial reward or professional satisfaction, is often attractive. Pro bono work, which at the outset appears to be a harmless allocation of a person's free time, also falls into this category.

Seldom do individuals involved in such outside projects realize the implications of their actions. In some cases, a person's energy and attention to the work of the firm is compromised. In others, there are conflicts with commitments made and deadlines and agreements that must be met within the firm.

No matter the size and scope of a personal project, it often requires time during the workday to manage issues and attend to problems. This activity compromises both the time available for the firm's work and the quality of service provided to the moonlight job and client.

In addition to distracting an employee from full commitment to the success of the firm, moonlighting can also expose the firm to legal liabilities. Several court cases have held the parent firm responsible for the actions of an employee, even though the firm had not authorized or even known about those actions.

If the firm's work does not provide the personal, professional, and/or financial rewards an architect seeks, the best action is to improve his or her role and responsibilities within the firm, look for new employment, or start a firm.

THE AMERICAN
INSTITUTE
OF ARCHITECTS

FROM THE OFFICE OF GENERAL COUNSEL

2012 Code of Ethics & Professional Conduct

Preamble
Members of The American Institute of Architects are dedicated to the highest standards of professionalism, integrity, and competence. This Code of Ethics and Professional Conduct states guidelines for the conduct of Members in fulfilling those obligations. The Code is arranged in three tiers of statements: Canons, Ethical Standards, and Rules of Conduct:
- Canons are broad principles of conduct.
- Ethical Standards (E.S.) are more specific goals toward which Members should aspire in professional performance and behavior.
- Rules of Conduct (**Rule**) are mandatory; violation of a Rule is grounds for disciplinary action by the Institute. Rules of Conduct, in some instances, implement more than one Canon or Ethical Standard.

The **Code** applies to the professional activities of all classes of Members, wherever they occur. It addresses responsibilities to the public, which the profession serves and enriches; to the clients and users of architecture and in the building industries, who help to shape the built environment; and to the art and science of architecture, that continuum of knowledge and creation which is the heritage and legacy of the profession.

Commentary is provided for some of the Rules of Conduct. That commentary is meant to clarify or elaborate the intent of the rule. The commentary is not part of the **Code**. Enforcement will be determined by application of the Rules of Conduct alone; the commentary will assist those seeking to conform their conduct to the **Code** and those charged with its enforcement.

Statement in Compliance With Antitrust Law
The following practices are not, in themselves, unethical, unprofessional, or contrary to any policy of The American Institute of Architects or any of its components:
(1) submitting, at any time, competitive bids or price quotations, including in circumstances where price is the sole or principal consideration in the selection of an architect;
(2) providing discounts; or
(3) providing free services.

Individual architects or architecture firms, acting alone and not on behalf of the Institute or any of its components, are free to decide for themselves whether or not to engage in any of these practices. Antitrust law permits the Institute, its components, or Members to advocate legislative or other government policies or actions relating to these practices. Finally, architects should continue to consult with state laws or regulations governing the practice of architecture.

CANON I

General Obligations

Members should maintain and advance their knowledge of the art and science of architecture, respect the body of architectural accomplishment, contribute to its growth, thoughtfully consider the social and environmental impact of their professional activities, and exercise learned and uncompromised professional judgment.

E.S. 1.1 Knowledge and Skill:
Members should strive to improve their professional knowledge and skill.

Rule 1.101 In practicing architecture, Members shall demonstrate a consistent pattern of reasonable care and competence, and shall apply the technical knowledge and skill which is ordinarily applied by architects of good standing practicing in the same locality.
Commentary: By requiring a "consistent pattern" of adherence to the common law standard of competence, this rule allows for discipline of a Member who more than infrequently does not achieve that standard. Isolated instances of minor lapses would not provide the basis for discipline.

E.S. 1.2 Standards of Excellence:
Members should continually seek to raise the standards of aesthetic excellence, archi-

tectural education, research, training, and practice.

E.S. 1.3 Natural and Cultural Heritage:
Members should respect and help conserve their natural and cultural heritage while striving to improve the environment and the quality of life within it.

E.S. 1.4 Human Rights:
Members should uphold human rights in all their professional endeavors.

Rule 1.401 Members shall not discriminate in their professional activities on the basis of race, religion, gender, national origin, age, disability, or sexual orientation.

E.S. 1.5 Allied Arts & Industries: Members should promote allied arts and contribute to the knowledge and capability of the building industries as a whole.

CANON II

Obligations to the Public

Members should embrace the spirit and letter of the law governing their professional affairs and should promote and serve the public interest in their personal and professional activities.

E.S. 2.1 Conduct: Members should uphold the law in the conduct of their professional activities.

Rule 2.101   Members shall not, in the conduct of their professional practice, knowingly violate the law.

Commentary: The violation of any law, local, state or federal, occurring in the conduct of a Member's professional practice, is made the basis for discipline by this rule. This includes the federal Copyright Act, which prohibits copying architectural works without the permission of the copyright owner. Allegations of violations of this rule must be based on an independent finding of a violation of the law by a court of competent jurisdiction or an administrative or regulatory body.

Rule 2.102   Members shall neither offer nor make any payment or gift to a public official with the intent of influencing the official's judgment in connection with an existing or prospective project in which the Members are interested.

Commentary: This rule does not prohibit campaign contributions made in conformity with applicable campaign financing laws.

Rule 2.103   Members serving in a public capacity shall not accept payments or gifts which are intended to influence their judgment.

Rule 2.104   Members shall not engage in conduct involving fraud or wanton disregard of the rights of others.

Commentary: This rule addresses serious misconduct whether or not related to a Member's professional practice. When an alleged violation of this rule is based on a violation of a law, or of fraud, then its proof must be based on an independent finding of a violation of the law or a finding of fraud by a court of competent jurisdiction or an administrative or regulatory body.

Rule 2.105   If, in the course of their work on a project, the Members become aware of a decision taken by their employer or client which violates any law or regulation and which will, in the Members' judgment, materially affect adversely the safety to the public of the finished project, the Members shall:
(a) advise their employer or client against the decision,
(b) refuse to consent to the decision, and
(c) report the decision to the local building inspector or other public official charged with the enforcement of the applicable laws and regulations, unless the Members are able to cause the matter to be satisfactorily resolved by other means.

Commentary: This rule extends only to violations of the building laws that threaten the public safety. The obligation under this rule applies only to the safety of the finished project, an obligation coextensive with the usual undertaking of an architect.

Rule 2.106   Members shall not counsel or assist a client in conduct that the architect knows, or reasonably should know, is fraudulent or illegal.

E.S. 2.2 Public Interest Services: Members should render public interest professional services, including pro bono services, and encourage their employees to render such services. Pro bono services are those rendered without expecting compensation, including those rendered for indigent persons, after disasters, or in other emergencies.

E.S. 2.3 Civic Responsibility: Members should be involved in civic activities as citizens and

professionals, and should strive to improve public appreciation and understanding of architecture and the functions and responsibilities of architects.

Rule 2.301   Members making public statements on architectural issues shall disclose when they are being compensated for making such statements or when they have an economic interest in the issue.

CANON III

Obligations to the Client

Members should serve their clients competently and in a professional manner, and should exercise unprejudiced and unbiased judgment when performing all professional services.

E.S. 3.1 Competence: Members should serve their clients in a timely and competent manner.

Rule 3.101   In performing professional services, Members shall take into account applicable laws and regulations. Members may rely on the advice of other qualified persons as to the intent and meaning of such regulations.

Rule 3.102   Members shall undertake to perform professional services only when they, together with those whom they may engage as consultants, are qualified by education, training, or experience in the specific technical areas involved.

Commentary: This rule is meant to ensure that Members not undertake projects that are beyond their professional capacity. Members venturing into areas that require expertise they do not possess may obtain that expertise by additional education, training, or through the retention of consultants with the necessary expertise.

Rule 3.103   Members shall not materially alter the scope or objectives of a project without the client's consent.

(continued)

PART 1: THE PROFESSION

E.S. 3.2 Conflict of Interest:
Members should avoid conflicts of interest in their professional practices and fully disclose all unavoidable conflicts as they arise.

Rule 3.201 A Member shall not render professional services if the Member's professional judgment could be affected by responsibilities to another project or person, or by the Member's own interests, unless all those who rely on the Member's judgment consent after full disclosure.

Commentary: This rule is intended to embrace the full range of situations that may present a Member with a conflict between his interests or responsibilities and the interest of others. Those who are entitledto disclosure may include a client, owner, employer, contractor, or others who rely on or are affected by the Member's professional decisions. A Member who cannot appropriately communicate about a conflict directly with an affected person must take steps to ensure that disclosure is made by other means.

Rule 3.202 When acting by agreement of the parties as the independent interpreter of building contract documents and the judge of contract performance, Members shall render decisions impartially.

Commentary: This rule applies when the Member, though paid by the owner and owing the owner loyalty, is nonetheless required to act with impartiality in fulfilling the architect's professional responsibilities.

E.S. 3.3 Candor and Truthfulness:
Members should be candid and truthful in their professional communications and keep their clients reasonably informed about the clients' projects.

Rule 3.301 Members shall not intentionally or recklessly mislead existing or prospective clients about the results that can be achieved through the use of the Members' services, nor shall the Members state that they can achieve results by means that violate applicable law or this Code.

Commentary: This rule is meant to preclude dishonest, reckless, or illegal representations by a Member either in the course of soliciting a client or during performance.

E.S. 3.4 Confidentiality:
Members should safeguard the trust placed in them by their clients.

Rule 3.401 Members shall not knowingly disclose information that would adversely affect their client or that they have been asked to maintain in confidence, except as otherwise allowed or required by this Code or applicable law.

Commentary: To encourage the full and open exchange of information necessary for a successful professional relationship, Members must recognize and respect the sensitive nature of confidential client communications. Because the law does not recognize an architect-client privilege, however, the rule permits a Member to reveal a confidence when a failure to do so would be unlawful or contrary to another ethical duty imposed by this Code.

CANON IV

Obligations to the Profession

Members should uphold the integrity and dignity of the profession.

E.S. 4.1 Honesty and Fairness:
Members should pursue their professional activities with honesty and fairness.

Rule 4.101 Members having substantial information which leads to a reasonable belief that another Member has committed a violation of this Code which raises a serious question as to that Member's honesty, trustworthiness, or fitness as a Member, shall file a complaint with the National Ethics Council.

Commentary: Often, only an architect can recognize that the behavior of another architect poses a serious question as to that other's professional integrity. In those circumstances, the duty to the professional's calling requires that a complaint be filed. In most jurisdictions, a complaint that invokes professional standards is protected from a libel or slander action if the complaint was made in good faith. If in doubt, a Member should seek counsel before reporting on another under this rule.

Rule 4.102 Members shall not sign or seal drawings, specifications, reports, or other professional work for which they do not have responsible control.

Commentary: Responsible control means the degree of knowledge and supervision ordinarily required by the professional standard of care. With respect to the work of licensed consultants, Members may sign or seal such work if they have reviewed it, coordinated its preparation, or intend to be responsible for its adequacy.

Rule 4.103 Members speaking in their professional capacity shall not knowingly make false statements of material fact.

Commentary: This rule applies to statements in all professional contexts, including applications for licensure and AIA membership.

E.S. 4.2 Dignity and Integrity:
Members should strive, through their actions, to promote the dignity and integrity of the profession, and to ensure that their representatives and employees conform their conduct to this Code.

Rule 4.201 Members shall not make misleading, deceptive, or false statements or claims about their professional qualifications, experience, or performance and shall accurately state the scope and nature of their responsibilities in connection with work for which they are claiming credit.

Commentary: This rule is meant to prevent Members from claiming or implying credit for work which they did not do, misleading others, and denying other participants in a project their proper share of credit.

Rule 4.202 Members shall make reasonable efforts to ensure that those over whom they have supervisory authority conform their conduct to this Code.

Commentary: What constitutes "reasonable efforts" under this rule is a common sense matter. As it makes sense to ensure that those over whom the *architect exercises supervision be made generally aware of the **Code**, it can also make sense to bring a particular provision to the attention of a particular employee when a situation is present which might give rise to violation.*

CANON V

Obligations to Colleagues

Members should respect the rights and acknowledge the professional aspirations and contributions of their colleagues.

E.S. 5.1 Professional Environment: Members should provide their associates and employees with a suitable working environment, compensate them fairly, and facilitate their professional development.

E.S. 5.2 Intern and Professional Development: Members should recognize and fulfill their obligation to nurture fellow professionals as they progress through all stages of their career, beginning with professional education in the academy, progressing through internship and continuing throughout their career.

Rule 5.201 Members who have agreed to work with individuals engaged in an architectural internship program or an experience requirement for licensure shall reasonably assist in proper and timely documentation in accordance with that program.

E.S. 5.3 Professional Recognition: Members should build their professional reputation on the merits of their own service and performance and should recognize and give credit to others for the professional work they have performed.

Rule 5.301 Members shall recognize and respect the professional contributions of their employees, employers, professional colleagues, and business associates.

Rule 5.302 Members leaving a firm shall not, without the permission of their employer or partner, take designs, drawings, data, reports, notes, or other materials relating to the firm's work, whether or not performed by the Member.

Rule 5.303 A Member shall not unreasonably withhold permission from a departing employee or partner to take copies of designs, drawings, data, reports, notes, or other materials relating to work performed by the employee or partner that are not confidential.

Commentary: A Member may impose reasonable conditions, such as the payment of copying costs, on the right of departing persons to take copies of their work.

CANON VI

Obligations to the Environment

Members should promote sustainable design and development principles in their professional activities.

E.S. 6.1 Sustainable Design: In performing design work, Members should be environmentally responsible and advocate sustainable building and site design.

E.S. 6.2 Sustainable Development: In performing professional services, Members should advocate the design, construction, and operation of sustainable buildings and communities.

E.S. 6.3 Sustainable Practices: Members should use sustainable practices within their firms and professional organizations, and they should encourage their clients to do the same.

RULES OF APPLICATION, ENFORCEMENT, AND AMENDMENT

Application

The **Code of Ethics and Professional Conduct** applies to the professional activities of all members of the AIA.

Enforcement

The Bylaws of the Institute state procedures for the enforcement of the **Code of Ethics and Professional Conduct**. Such procedures provide that:

(1) Enforcement of the **Code** is administered through a National Ethics Council, appointed by the AIA Board of Directors.

(2) Formal charges are filed directly with the National Ethics Council by Members, components, or anyone directly aggrieved by the conduct of the Members.

(3) Penalties that may be imposed by the National Ethics Council are:
    (a) Admonition
    (b) Censure
    (c) Suspension of membership for a period of time
    (d) Termination of membership.

(4) Appeal procedures are available.

(5) All proceedings are confidential, as is the imposition of an admonishment; however, all other penalties shall be made public.

Enforcement of Rules 4.101 and 4.202 refer to and support enforcement of other Rules. A violation of Rules 4.101 or 4.202 cannot be established without proof of a pertinent violation of at least one other Rule.

Amendment

The **Code of Ethics and Professional Conduct** may be amended by the convention of the Institute under the same procedures as are necessary to amend the Institute's Bylaws. The **Code** may also be amended by the AIA Board of Directors upon a two-thirds vote of the entire Board.

***2012 Edition.** This copy of the **Code of Ethics** is current as of September 2012. Contact the General Counsel's Office for further information at (202) 626-7348.*

THE FUTURE

Defining professional ethics for the architecture profession will remain the duty of the American Institute of Architects and its National Ethics Council. As they have in the past, the AIA Board of Directors and NEC will periodically reevaluate the Code of Ethics and Professional Conduct based on the profession's core values while responding to societal pressures, changing business practices, advancing technologies, and lessons learned from the results of future litigation.

For More Information

The AIA website at www.aia.org/about_ethics provides current information and resources. The process for filing a complaint is described. Also posted are the NEC's previous decisions and advisory opinions, the rules of procedure, the AIA Code of Ethics and Professional Conduct, guidelines for attribution of credit, and answers to frequently asked questions. Specific questions may be directed to the Office of the General Counsel at (202) 626–7311. Members of the AIA National Ethics Council may be available to offer programs, which include case studies, at AIA national and local events.

1.4 Regulation of Professional Practice

Cornelius R. DuBois, FAIA

Individuals are licensed to practice architecture, and in doing so, to protect the health, safety, and welfare of the public. Licensing regulations vary among the 54 U.S. jurisdictions, and each architect is responsible for understanding, observing, and abiding by the appropriate statutes, rules, and policies.

THE BASIS FOR THE REGULATION OF THE PRACTICE OF ARCHITECTURE

In order to practice architecture, individuals must hold a license in the jurisdiction in which they wish to practice. The regulation of architecture and of other professions in the United States falls under the authority of the 50 states, three territories (Guam, Puerto Rico, and the U.S. Virgin Islands), and the District of Columbia. This authority is left to the states by the Tenth Amendment of the U.S. Constitution, in the Bill of Rights.

> Amendment X ("States Rights") of the U.S. Constitution says, "The powers not delegated to the United States by the constitution, nor prohibited by it to the States, are reserved to the States respectively, or to the people." This is why there are 54 different licensing jurisdictions, each with its own statute, rules, and policies. This provides challenges to professionals seeking to practice in multiple states, and it can mystify, at first, those from other countries with a single licensing or credentialing authority. The National Council of Architectural Registration Boards (NCARB) has developed our system of reciprocal licensure in part as a response to this reality.

HISTORY OF THE LICENSURE OF ARCHITECTS

Regulation of the practice of architecture is a relatively recent development, especially when one considers for how many centuries architects and proto-architects have been designing buildings. The regulation of some professions, particularly those of medicine

Cornelius R. (Kin) DuBois has practiced architecture since 1979. He has served as 2010–2011 president of the National Architectural Accrediting Board and 2007 president of AIA Colorado, and is a former member of the NCARB Board of Directors.

(beginning with the Code of Hammurabi in 1700 BCE) and law (300 AD), had been in place and tested for many years before registration laws for architects in the United States came into being.

Regulation of architecture did not happen overnight. The first law was enacted in the State of Illinois in 1897, establishing a licensing board in 1898. Other states gradually adopted their own statutes and set up their own registration boards over the next 50-plus years, with Wyoming and Vermont as the final states to adopt licensure in 1951. The territories of Puerto Rico, the U.S. Virgin Islands, and Guam subsequently joined the licensing jurisdictions to create, with the District of Columbia, the current total of 54.

A generally accepted philosophy of regulation guides the process for both statute and rule: to establish the minimum threshold of regulation necessary to ensure the protection of the public. While the concept of minimum threshold may be subject to personal or political interpretation, this approach offers some assurance to counter the tendency of a statute to accumulate superfluous or inappropriate provisions over time. Whether this is always effective may be questioned, but this principle provides a consistent yardstick that must be held up to set any discussion of amendments or revisions to a licensing law.

ELEMENTS IN COMMON THROUGHOUT LICENSING LAWS

Interchangeable Terminology: The terms "registration" and "licensure" are used interchangeably. "Registration board" and "licensing board" are also used in this article, as are "states" and "jurisdictions." The states, territories, and the District of Columbia have "licensing statutes" and "registration boards." The one term that does not lead to interchangeability is "architect." There is no acceptable use of a term such as "unlicensed architect."

Despite the forces that would seem to pull 54 statutes in 54 separate directions, there are many key elements consistent among virtually all architectural licensing laws, which:

- Establish a board and the rules governing its composition, authority, and operation
- Define the practice of architecture
- Set the requirements for licensure and entry into the profession
- Include exemptions for certain structures not requiring an architect
- Define professional conduct and misconduct
- Establish sanctions and the parameter for the application of these when the statute is violated

Licensing laws may include a range of other elements that are specific to the jurisdiction and not in common with all others, such as requirements for continuing education, for corporate practice, or for supplemental examinations or qualifications for practice. The balance of this article will include detailed discussion of all of these.

DEFINITION OF THE PRACTICE OF ARCHITECTURE

Every licensing law (usually at the beginning of the statute and often within a section on "definitions") contains a definition of the practice of architecture. A few states take the most direct approach and adopt the *NCARB Legislative Guidelines and Model Law, Model Regulations* without modification. Others use the NCARB document as a template for their statutes, modifying to suit local conditions and politics and reviewing and adapting to revisions and updates as they may be implemented through the resolution process held at the NCARB Annual Meeting.

The practice of architecture is not typically defined by means of an exclusive list of items of practice but is, rather, a collective definition. Architects do many things in the course of programming, designing, creating documentation, and administering the construction of buildings, and elements of these are shared with other occupations. In the course of their work, architects accept a unique professional responsibility that is not shared with others. Interests from other professions, trades, or occupations may seek to limit the definition of architectural practice when a licensing statute is subject to amendment or undergoing a Sunset Review process. The outcome may be a definition of practice that is at variance with that in the *NCARB Legislative Guidelines* or it may be in the form of specific exemptions.

There is a long history of the interface of the definition of the practice of architecture and that of engineering. In some states, a clear distinction is established between the activities of the two professions, while in others engineers may engage in aspects of architectural practice—or specific building types—if it falls within their "area of expertise." Likewise, architects may be permitted to "engineer" (that is, to calculate and size) structural elements in some instances, such as for smaller residential buildings. In either case, an added consideration will be the willingness of a code official to accept such work when permitting a set of construction documents.

Statutes respecting other allied professions such as landscape architecture and interior design may also overlap or conflict with the definition of the practice of architecture. An architect practicing in a new jurisdiction would be well advised to scan the corresponding statutes and rules for these to confirm that there are no potential conflicts. Another consideration that must be weighed is that some of these professions may be regulated only via title acts instead of practice acts.

As with the overlapping practices of architecture and engineering, the ability of other professionals to stamp and submit construction documents for building permit approval will always be subject to some degree of discretion on the part of the building official. In a state where there is no statewide building code, the window of what is and what isn't acceptable may vary from one municipality or county to the next.

USE OF THE TITLE

The privilege to use the title "architect" in any form is specific to a licensing jurisdiction, and an individual licensed to practice in one jurisdiction may not use the title in another until he or she has been granted a license there.

Not only is the title "architect" regulated, but so is use of the title in combination with other terms and in the form of what is commonly called "the derivative." Not only is this a subject that can vary significantly from state to state, but individual jurisdictions, through the legislative or rule-making process, also may make changes in these provisions from time to time. This is a particularly sensitive issue affecting interns. A few states allow the use of "intern architect," while a greater number allow only "architectural intern" (use of the derivative). Still other jurisdictions allow neither, in which case an intern is an intern.

While an intern proceeding diligently through the Intern Development Program for three years or more may be flying under the radar screen, using a title on resumes, business cards, and firm marketing materials that is contrary to what is allowed, carelessness can get an intern into difficulty when actually applying for a license. This can result in fines or other sanctions, as well as delays in issuing the license. The fact that some of the offending material may have been produced by the firm for which the intern is working (possibly without the intern's knowledge) may not obscure the fact that it is the individual intern who is ultimately responsible.

Examples of Violations of Use of the Title "Architect"

Violations of the use of the title can come in many forms, some of which are referred to in the discussion above, and professionals may inadvertently find themselves paying the price, even when there has been no intent to deceive the public. An architect from another state may prematurely use the title on a proposal, or may even do preliminary work on a project before receiving a license. Interns may use the disallowed title ("intern architect" or "architectural intern") on resumes, business cards, marketing materials, listings on awards, or magazine articles. A firm may list an intern as "project architect," when "project manager" or some alternative would be more appropriately consistent within the licensing statute. Out-of-state firms and individual practitioners may find themselves referenced inappropriately in the press, or they may directly violate the statute by entering a competition in a jurisdiction where a license is required.

Although a design firm may be called to task in some of these situations, requiring an appearance before the board, it is ultimately the individual who must take responsibility for how he or she is represented to the public. If called before the registration board, an honest account is without question the best approach.

> Licensing boards do not view the use of "AIA" after someone's name as an inappropriate use of the title—unless the title has clearly been used or manipulated (such as "AIA architect") so that it may appear as an attempt to mislead the public in a state where the individual is not licensed.

Licensing boards must also contend with complaints about misuse of the title by nonprofessionals. There may be deliberate misuse of the title by disguising it in combination with other terms, such as "design architect" or "architectural renderer" (where the derivative is not allowed). In these cases, boards take seriously their responsibilities to protect the public and the consumer while not unnecessarily tying up their or the administrative department's time with frivolous or pointless complaints.

USE OF THE STAMP OR SEAL

Licensing statutes require that every architect have a stamp or seal in his or her possession. Depending on the jurisdiction, this may be in the form of a rubber stamp or an embossing seal. Some boards require verification that the licensee has indeed acquired the stamp. The particular requirements (dimensions, required text) are typically included in the rules of the registration board and not in the statute. These rules, from one jurisdiction to another, are evolving with respect to electronic documents and whether these can be "stamped" electronically, with or without an encrypted signature.

The use of the stamp on a set of documents (both drawings and specifications) submitted for a building permit signifies that the architect has been in "responsible control" of the preparation of the drawings. Responsible control is defined in the *NCARB Legislative Guidelines and Model Law, Model Regulations*, and tends to be consistently applied throughout the United States. The architect must stamp only those documents prepared under his or her control: The NCARB Model Law makes it clear that "Reviewing, or reviewing and correcting, technical submissions after they have been prepared by others does not constitute responsible control." In other words, an architect has no business stamping and signing someone else's shop drawings.

Building departments, which are ultimately responsible for the acceptance or rejection of the construction documents, may refer to the "Architect of Record." This terminology may not appear in the licensing statute, but it essentially implies the same thing. A building department may require a stamp on other documents, such as a written response to a plan correction notice. The architect must comply with these requirements. However, a stamp should never be used for extraneous purposes; for example, on a certification required by a lender on a project.

The term "plan-stamping" refers to the inappropriate use of a stamp by an individual not in responsible control of the preparation of the documents. This is a serious violation of any statute, and it is discussed below in the section on discipline.

QUALIFICATIONS FOR LICENSURE

Licensing statutes define the qualifications for licensure, dealing in different ways with the same three topics—education, experience, and examination:

- *Education.* While the majority of jurisdictions now accept only a NAAB-accredited degree as a prerequisite to licensure, a declining number of jurisdictions allow a lower threshold for education. The bar may be set at: a minimum four-year pre-professional degree, such as a Bachelor of Science in Architectural Studies; a four-year degree in an unrelated field; a two-year associate's degree from a community college or technical college; and in some cases, a high school diploma.

- *Experience.* The second area of requirements for licensure applies to experience. Typically, this means completion of the Intern Development Program (IDP). When a state allows a lower education threshold it will usually require a longer term of internship (experience) before an individual without an accredited degree can qualify for the Architect Registration Examination® (ARE®). These jurisdictions may also allow some parallel means to documenting experience that is nevertheless based on and parallel to the IDP.

- *Examination.* This is the final step. The licensing jurisdiction must determine when the individual has qualified to take the ARE, in some cases allowing early eligibility to take portions of or the entire exam before completion of the experience requirement. Whereas in the past, the "three legs of the stool" (education, experience, examination) were seen as being assembled sequentially, it is now not unusual to have candidates begin to acquire qualified experience while still enrolled in a degree program and to begin the exam before completing the experience requirement. In all cases, however, a jurisdiction will not issue a license until all steps have been successfully completed.

Upon successfully meeting their registration board's education, examination, and experience requirements, a candidate for licensure will then have to complete that board's application and fulfill any additional requirements of that jurisdiction. These will certainly require the payment of a fee, but there may also be a supplementary exam covering local conditions or a jurisprudence exam, typically a take-home open-book test of the candidate's knowledge of local licensing laws and rules. Only upon completion of all requirements will a license then be issued.

There are potential disqualifications for licensure, such as past felony convictions including specific convictions for sex-related offenses or for failure to pay child support.

Foreign-Educated and Trained Professionals

Individuals educated in other countries, and even those who have been practicing as architects in their home country, have additional hurdles to clear in order to become licensed to practice in any of the 54 U.S. jurisdictions. This may include obtaining an EESA-NCARB evaluation (performed by Education Evaluation Services for Architects) of a foreign-educated architect to determine in what areas additional education might be required. In this evaluation, the candidate's transcript (in English) is weighed against the NCARB *Education Standard.* Some states also accept individuals licensed in other countries who have demonstrated competence through the NCARB Broadly Experienced Foreign Architect Program. Other jurisdictions will not allow a foreign-educated individual to take the ARE unless he or she acquires a NAAB-accredited degree.

The difficulty of understanding the wide variation of applicable regulations is made more daunting by the fact that many foreign-educated professionals come from countries where there is a single licensing authority and a single set of rules.

RENEWAL OF A LICENSE

Licensing requirements include different renewal cycles or terms. These can be one-, two-, or three-year cycles. Although a licensing board may send out renewal notices, it is incumbent upon the individual to know when a license is due to expire. Some jurisdictions allow for a grace period for overdue renewals, and this may include an additional fee penalty. In a jurisdiction where no grace period is allowed, or where a license has lapsed beyond the period allowed, an individual is likely to have to start the licensing process all over again.

In many states, mandatory continuing education (MCE) is now a requirement for re-licensure.

The renewal form, likely to be available online, will typically include a series of questions, including those relating to whether the licensee has been the subject of disciplinary action related to a stamp held in another jurisdiction or whether another license has been voluntarily relinquished (this may be indicative of a stipulated agreement to resolve a disciplinary action). When the fee has been paid and an architect's stamp is renewed, the licensee will receive a new license to post on the wall as well as a new wallet card.

▶ The accompanying backgrounder on continuing education provides a detailed discussion of MCE requirements.

RECIPROCITY

There are two principal means of obtaining a license in a jurisdiction beyond the original one in which an architect was registered. The first, and the most common, is referred to either as "comity" or "endorsement." Even though the terms have slightly different meanings, they are essentially the same thing. The technical meaning of comity is accepting as a courtesy the qualifications for licensure from another state. Even when comity is applied, most jurisdictions will require the applicant to have a certified NCARB Council Record, which is then forwarded to the state in addition to filling out the application form and sending in a fee. In a state using the term "endorsement," the process will be the same.

The second means for reciprocal licensure is where a registration board will accept the NCARB Certificate on its own. This includes those states that will accept applicants who have qualified for NCARB certification via the Broadly Experienced Architect (BEA) program or the Broadly Experienced Foreign Architect (BEFA) program. The option applies to architects without a NAAB-accredited degree who have been licensed in another state for a minimum period of time (6 to 10 years, depending on the level of education attained). Through this process, the architect must demonstrate equivalent learning through practice in order to fulfill each of the requirements specified in the *NCARB Education Guidelines*. The BEFA option applies to architects licensed by a foreign credentialing authority. The BEFA process requires establishment of an NCARB Record, preparation of a dossier to demonstrate experience, and a personal interview.

▶ See the backgrounder on NCARB Certification at the end of this chapter for related information.

For a number of reasons, especially pertinent to applicants under the BEA program, it often proves valuable for architects to retain a license in the first state in which they were registered. In a new state, the same rules pertaining to new licensees are likely to apply with respect to supplemental or jurisprudence exams, and some jurisdictions also include an affirmation that the architect has passed a seismic exam or taken the ARE after a certain date (1965) at which seismic content was included.

EXEMPTIONS

Perhaps no subject engenders more heated discussion of licensing statutes in the legislative arena than that of exemptions to the requirements that buildings be designed by architects. The reasons for these exemptions, which exist across the spectrum of jurisdictions, are often philosophical, practical, or purely political.

There are several types of exemptions, the most common being those for buildings not intended for human habitation or occupancy (for instance, some agricultural structures). The next most common are for residential structures, defined either by size, height, the number of occupants or families, or construction cost. These vary widely among the jurisdictions and are subject to push and pull every time an architectural licensing law is opened up to legislative and public scrutiny. Anyone designing a structure that is exempt because of size or cost must be especially attentive to the definition applying to that exemption. For example, how is cost defined? The final cost of a project might exceed a preliminary estimate and thus place the structure out of the protection of the exemption.

In addition to exemptions for types of buildings, there may be exemptions for categories of practice: A statute, in deference to the Supremacy Clause of the U.S. Constitution (which says that the federal government must operate free of interference by the states) may be specific that federal employees are exempt from the requirements of the licensing statute. Also, as discussed earlier, there may be partial or full exemptions for other professions to engage in architectural practice in some form.

Likewise, the licensing statutes of these other professions may allow reciprocal exemptions for architects, for both title and practice. A simple example is when an architect is allowed to engage in site design even though this may also fall into the description of the practice of landscape architecture. Another might be when an architect is allowed to describe "interior design" services when a title act for interior designers also exists. These nuances require architects to be aware of not only their own licensing laws but also those applying to related fields.

THE ARCHITECT IN RELATION TO OTHER PROFESSIONS

Architects practice in a broader context of related and allied professions. There are corresponding exemptions in the regulation of other professions, just as architectural licensing laws have exemptions for others to engage in aspects of practice that might fall under the definition of the practice of architecture. As architects continue the trend of expanding services both horizontally and vertically, they must become particularly attentive to the full breadth of the law and not just what is found in architectural licensing statutes.

Finally, there is an important paradox relating to exemptions and exempt structures: One does not have to be an architect in order to design an exempt structure. However, if a nonarchitect is holding out as an architect while advertising for or designing an exempt structure, they will likely be found in violation of the statute.

CORPORATE PRACTICE

Some jurisdictions require firms as well as individuals to be registered in some form. In some states the firm name must be registered with (and approved by) the licensing board. This may require an annual fee.

Beyond the mechanics of corporate registration, corporate practice requirements in licensing laws may comprise several, sometimes complex, areas. One of the most common governs the composition of firms. Depending on whether a firm is a sole proprietorship, a partnership, a professional corporation, or another type of entity, there may be a requirement for a certain number of the firm's principals or directors to be—or for a minimum percentage of stock ownership to be held by—architects licensed in the jurisdiction.

Firm names may also be regulated, and an architectural practice from another state may discover that it is operating under a name that is not acceptable in a new state. Firm name requirements may govern the use of what are termed "fictitious business titles," and may require a formal approval by the regulatory agency. "Fictitious" may be a confusing term for an architecture firm that sees itself as anything but imaginary, but it applies to a firm name that does not indicate the ownership of the firm. For instance, a firm called "Architectural Partnership" doesn't include the names of the actual partners in its title and is thus a fictitious business title.

Other provisions may limit how long a firm can keep the name of a deceased or retired partner or principal. Architecture practices may find themselves removing the name of a deceased partner or resorting to initials in order to comply with regulations in their home states or in order to practice without reincorporation in multiple jurisdictions. Similarly, a firm with only a single registered architect cannot use "Architects" in its title.

NCARB.ORG

The website of the National Council of Architectural Registration Boards, NCARB.org, is an invaluable source of information on licensing requirements, including documents such as the *Rules of Conduct* and the *Legislative Guidelines and Model Law/Model Regulations*. The site also offers a Registration Requirements Comparison Chart and provides links to the sites of the individual registration boards. Please refer to the "For More Information" section at the end of this discussion for specific links to documents.

COMPLAINTS

Any member of the public (whether a client, a building user, or another architect) can file a complaint with a licensing board. Once received, the complaint is reviewed first by the staff and then by the board, which will choose among several courses of action.

The duty to file complaints does not fall solely on members of the public. Indeed, architects have a duty to report violations of the statute, whether committed by an architect or an unlicensed individual. Architects also have a responsibility to self-report life safety issues, including those that result in insurance claims. This duty to report may be either when an event occurs or in the course of filling out the license renewal form.

The responsibility to report violations of the statute is one that architects are often uncomfortable with. An architect must, however, consider the possible consequences (to the public or to the occupants of a building) should a violation of a licensing law not be reported.

DISCIPLINE

As discussed above, there are two basic types of violations considered by licensing boards:

- *Violations by untrained and unlicensed individuals.* Discipline in such cases may not fall under the purview of the licensing board and must be referred to another agency, such as the state attorney general's office.
- *Violations by trained individuals*, either those licensed and already practicing in the jurisdiction or those who are not yet licensed there.

Those not yet licensed may have an application already in process, or they may be interns "moonlighting" (performing services outside of their regular employment and without a license). In these and in similar instances, the registration board has a purview and may ultimately grant a license pending payment of a fine and acknowledgment of the violation per a stipulated agreement.

Perhaps the most common instances leading to major disciplinary actions are those involving plan-stamping or misuse of the title (holding out). Registration boards, with the advice and guidance of their administrative agencies or state attorneys, have a range of options from which to choose, ranging from a letter of admonition to suspension or revocation of the person's license.

CONCLUSION

The regulation of architects, for which the overarching purpose is to protect the public health, safety, and welfare, is a complex world, covering many aspects of individual and corporate practice. The dynamics of regulation among the 54 separate jurisdictions can seem confusing, but it is important to consider that this complexity—and indeed richness—reflects our society, our national history and the U.S. Constitution, regional particularities, and the evolving conditions in which architects practice. It is the responsibility of each professional to keep pace with this context and to understand the laws and rules of the jurisdictions in which he or she practices or wishes to practice.

THE U.S. ARCHITECT AND GLOBAL PRACTICE

More U.S. architects are practicing or seeking to practice in some form in countries around the world. As much as regulation varies in our country from one jurisdiction to the next, global regulation appears in even more forms. Some countries don't regulate at all, while others credential the title only. In some cases, the title of "architect" may be granted upon graduation from an architecture degree program. In the face of confusing—and occasionally ambiguous—regulation abroad, many architects wisely choose the option of teaming with a local firm instead of attempting to operate solo in another country. As with our own requirements, a foreign country may not accept education here as comparable to what is approved in that location, and if there is an examination requirement, that test will most likely be given in the language of that country. International practice is still in many ways an untested and rapidly evolving area, making attention to the particulars of architectural regulation especially important.

For More Information

NCARB Legislative Guidelines and Model Law: www.ncarb.org/Publications/~/media/Files/PDF/Special-Paper/Legislative_Guidelines.pdf.

NCARB Rules of Conduct: www.ncarb.org/Publications/~/media/Files/PDF/Special-Paper/Rules_of_Conduct.pdf

Broadly Experienced Architect (BEA) program: www.ncarb.org/Certification-and-Reciprocity/Alternate-Paths-to-Certification/Broadly-Experienced-Architect-Program.aspx

Broadly Experienced Foreign Architect (BEFA) program: www.ncarb.org/en/Getting-an-Initial-License/Foreign-Architects.aspx

EESA-NCARB evaluation process: www.eesa-naab.org/home.aspx

MANDATORY CONTINUING EDUCATION

Cornelius R. DuBois, FAIA

A majority of licensing jurisdictions now include requirements for mandatory continuing education (MCE) as a condition for renewal of a license to practice architecture. As with licensing laws in general, the requirements for MCE vary, and it is up to the licensee to track and comply with those in each jurisdiction.

THE RATIONALE FOR MANDATORY CONTINUING EDUCATION

Architects live and practice in a rapidly changing world. The body of knowledge required for the practice of architecture is always changing.

CATEGORIES OF MANDATORY CONTINUING EDUCATION

The U.S. licensing jurisdictions (the 50 states, the District of Columbia, Guam, Puerto Rico, and the U.S. Virgin Islands) have different requirements for the types of MCE that qualify for credit. Generally, these fall into four categories:

- Health, Safety, and Welfare (HSW)
- Sustainable Design (SD)
- Accessibility (ADA)
- Other (Non-HSW)

Many jurisdictions require only HSW subjects. The rationale for this is tied directly to the reason that architects are licensed to practice in the first place—to protect the health, safety, and welfare of the public and to provide for consumer protection.

ACCEPTABLE PROVIDERS

Generally, course content from the following provider organizations will be approved, with each jurisdiction having its own specific requirements:

- AIA Components, through AIA/CES (Continuing Education System)
- AIA/CES program registered providers
- NCARB (Monographs)
- Some state boards offer a limited number of their own courses.
- Registered providers to the state registration boards
- Institutions offering NAAB-accredited architecture degree programs
- State and local governments and agencies
- Many other organizations, such as the U.S. Green Building Council (USGBC), Urban Land Institute (ULI), and American Planning Association (APA)

NCARB CERTIFICATION

Douglas Morgan

Architects must be licensed in each jurisdiction in which they seek to practice. The NCARB Certificate, administered by the National Council of Architectural Registration Boards (NCARB), is a recognized professional credential that helps facilitate reciprocal registration for licensed architects among U.S. and Canadian registration boards.

Douglas Morgan is the Director of Records for the National Council of Architectural Registration Boards. With over 20 years of records management experience, Morgan has modernized and transformed NCARB records management to provide effective regulation and enhanced customer service to NCARB Record and NCARB Certificate holders.

After initial licensure, an architect can pursue NCARB certification, which helps facilitate reciprocal registration in other jurisdictions (see Figure 1.15). Reciprocity (also commonly referred to as "comity" or "endorsement") is achieved when applications for licensure in additional jurisdictions are approved based on jurisdictional review and acceptance of

verified documentation showing that the architect has satisfied all of the requirements for reciprocal registration.

The NCARB Certificate is the most common and widely accepted means of gaining reciprocity, with more than half of

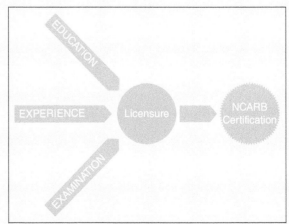

Kenji Bohlin NCARB

FIGURE 1.15 Path to NCARB Certification

U.S. registration boards requiring it for reciprocal registration. It certifies that an architect has met the national standards of eligibility for licensure established by the boards and recommends registration of the architect without further qualification.

NCARB certification helps streamline the process and reduce the amount of time needed to receive a reciprocal license in most states. The reality of architectural practice today is that many firms, whether large or small, practice in multiple jurisdictions. Because it expedites reciprocity, certification can help architects or their firms more quickly mobilize in pursuit of new business or meet expanding client needs across state lines. Some jurisdictions also allow the benefit of soliciting work or participating in a design competition prior to licensure if the architect holds an NCARB Certificate.

When applying for reciprocity, NCARB-certified architects pay a Record transmittal fee and request transmittal of their NCARB Record, which is sent by NCARB to the jurisdiction of interest. The fee includes the services provided as part of the Record storage, verification, and transmittal processes, and also helps subsidize the cost of programs that NCARB provides to the profession, such as the Architect Registration Examination.

Those who have an active NCARB Certificate may use the letters "NCARB" after their name, indicating that they have earned and maintain this recognized professional credential and are licensed architects.

STANDARD PATH TO CERTIFICATION

Earning NCARB certification is a relatively straightforward process. The architect needs to establish and hold an active NCARB Record in order to apply for certification. The NCARB Record is a detailed, verified record of architecture education, experience, and examination used to establish qualification for licensure and certification. The architect must also meet the following requirements:

- Be of good character as verified by employers and an NCARB Member Board where the architect is registered
- Document completion of a professional degree in architecture from a program accredited by the National Architectural Accrediting Board (NAAB)
- Document completion of the Intern Development Program (IDP)
- Have passed the Architect Registration Examination® (ARE®) or its then-current predecessor
- Hold an active registration in good standing in a U.S. jurisdiction

ALTERNATE PATHS TO CERTIFICATION

Architects who don't hold a professional architecture degree from a NAAB-accredited program, or those credentialed by a foreign authority, may qualify for NCARB certification through the Broadly Experienced Architect (BEA) program or the Broadly Experienced Foreign Architect (BEFA) program. While most jurisdictions accept an NCARB Certificate through

these programs for reciprocal licensure, it is important for each BEA and BEFA applicant to confirm to specific registration requirements, including those for reciprocity, with the individual jurisdiction in which they would like to be licensed.

Broadly Experienced Architect Program

The BEA program provides eligible architects registered in a U.S. jurisdiction an alternative to the education requirement for NCARB certification. Eligible architects can demonstrate their learning through experience by meeting the requirements of the *NCARB Education Standard*, which approximates the requirements of a professional degree from a NAAB-accredited program. The BEA program requires establishment of an NCARB Record and preparation of an education dossier to demonstrate learning through experience, and may also require an education evaluation.

Broadly Experienced Foreign Architect Program

Architects credentialed by a foreign authority are eligible to apply for an NCARB Certificate through the BEFA program. The multistep BEFA process requires establishment of an NCARB Record, preparation of a dossier to demonstrate experience, and a personal interview. An architect intending to pursue this alternative should complete and submit the BEFA Eligibility Verification form prior to applying for an NCARB Record.

Alternatives to the Intern Development Program

Architects who did not complete the IDP may retroactively document the IDP for purposes of NCARB certification. This is the most prudent course of action and offers the best chance of securing future reciprocity, as many jurisdictions specifically require the completion of the IDP to gain reciprocal licensure.

A second alternative is available and fully explained in the NCARB *Certification Guidelines*; however, it is worth noting that some jurisdictions may not accept this alternative and may require formal IDP documentation for reciprocal licensure. To use this alternative, applicants must be licensed by a U.S. jurisdiction for five consecutive years, must verify that their experience as an architect met the intent of the IDP, and must have that experience verified by one or more other architects. This alternative does not apply to architects licensed after January 1, 2011.

For More Information

NCARB certification and reciprocity: www.ncarb.org or by contacting NCARB Customer Service at customerservice@ncarb.org

NCARB *Certification Guidelines*: www.ncarb.org/en/Certification-and-Reciprocity/Certification-Overview/~/media/Files/PDF/Guidelines/Cert_Guidelines.ashx

NCARB Education Guidelines: www.ncarb.org/Studying-Architecture/~/media/Files/PDF/Guidelines/EDU_Guidelines.pdf

Registration requirements for each U.S. jurisdiction, including those for reciprocal registration: www.ncarb.org

1.5 Entering the Profession

Bradford Perkins, FAIA

One of the most important steps in a career in architecture is the first. Finding a first job is often the hardest and the most important for one's career. Therefore, getting the right first job should be regarded as an important task for all students. This first job will often expose a student or recent graduate to the initial experiences that clarify initial career goals. As the second section of this chapter will outline, a career should be planned, But first a career begins with a first job.

GETTING THE FIRST JOB

There are 11 basic rules for getting a first job.

Do your homework: The objective is not to just get a job. It should be to get the right first job. This requires research. Firms are different. Each one has its strengths and weaknesses. Not every firm will be a good fit for you.

Do not limit your search to "name" firms: For many people, the right firm for a first job will be one that gives you the most opportunities to learn. Sometimes that can be a well known firm, but for some it might be a firm that specializes in a field or is in a location of particular interest to you. The one constant is to always seek to work for a firm whose work you respect and is generally respected in the architectural profession. It is important to learn about quality from the best firms, but all job searches should be about what is best for you.

Know yourself: What are you good at and what do you need to learn, how hard are you willing to work, what special talents do you have, and where do you want to live today and in the future are just a few of the things you should think about before applying for a first job.

Make sure you are prepared: Your resume and portfolio should be carefully proof-read and graphically attractive. Make sure both highlight any special skills—languages, software knowledge, etc. Have these materials reviewed by someone who is knowledgeable about architectural hiring processes and ask this person or employed friends what to expect in an employment interview.

Dress appropriately, be relaxed, and focus on answering the questions you are asked: Most firms are looking for people who are personable, appear to be team players, listen, and have strong design and computer skills. Some are also looking for people with special skills such as a relevant foreign language or prior work experience in a foreign country or on a particular project type.

The first job should be about the experience and its potential to get you to the next level in your career: Working for a famous firm can be the right choice. Often, however, there are better choices where you will be given more responsibility and experience early. Spending two years detailing the core of a high-rise tower for a famous firm is not necessarily the right first job experience.

Use all of your relationships to contact your preferred employers: Merely sending a letter, digital portfolio, and resume is rarely the best way to introduce yourself to a potential employer. It should be, but at this time most good firms are too busy to focus on letters and resumes. Do not be shy about using any relationships—classmates, professors, relatives, etc.—that allow you to create a personal point of contact with a firm your research indicates might be a desirable first employer. All firms give preference to potential employees referred by friends, employees, and clients.

Know the firm: Prior to the interview research the firm and be prepared to answer such basic questions as "Why are you interested in our firm?" and "What part of our practice is of most interest to you?" Speak to others about the firm so that you are able to relate your interests and special skills to their practice.

Focus on what you want from a first job: Do not prejudge a job because the firm is "large" or "small," led by a star, or any other arbitrary screen.

Show more interest in the job, what you can learn, and what opportunities there are for growth than in the starting salary and benefits: The salary and benefits are, of course, relevant but they should not appear the primary concern.

Avoid firms that are known to treat their employees badly: Sadly, some firms routinely underpay and overwork their staff. A little research can usually identify these firms.

PLANNING AND MANAGING A CAREER

For most architects, the first job is an initial stepping stone in a career. There is nothing wrong with finding that you like your first job and deciding to stay for your entire career. Most architects, however, try out two to four firms before settling on a preferred choice. Still others use their initial jobs as a platform for starting their own firms.

The key in the early years is to learn your profession and become competent with the basic skills necessary to practice. If possible try to participate in such key tasks as business development, project management, presentations and other forms of communication, and client management. Build your leadership skills, develop a network of professional and personal relationships, and look for people who you think you might want to work with in the future. Get licensed as early as possible and plan your career.

Set goals. Again, it is important to ask yourself what you want to do, where you want to live and work, how independent you want to be, who you want to work with, how much money you need and/or want to make, how much security is important, and what is your career timeline.

All job changes should be analyzed against your goals. Only move to a new firm for a good reason such as what you will learn, the potential for growth, a better work environment, etc.

Make sure you are visible to and appreciated by the senior people in the firm who can help you learn and accelerate your growth.

After the first six to eight years, do not work for a firm where the leadership will not actively help you with your professional development and career.

Do not jump around. Try to stay at each job at least three or four years. Employers consider a series of short-term jobs a warning sign that you are not stable or are a potential problem employee.

Do not let your career stall. In the early years if you are not seeing growth, consider moving on.

Even if you are happy where you are, be open to other opportunities. Employers are not comfortable if they hear you are looking for a new position, but most are understanding when an opportunity comes to you. If an interesting opportunity does come, be flexible and evaluate it against your goals.

Be willing to take some risk when going to a new job if you can afford it. Some of the best opportunities come with some risk—especially the decision to start your own firm or to join a young promising, but not yet established, firm.

Make a commitment if and when the fit is right and you feel you could see staying with a firm. For most architects making a commitment to a preferred firm or career path happens by your mid-30s.

Do not burn bridges. It is often very important to have former employers and colleagues available to provide you with a strong reference.

And as in your first job avoid: abusive employers, dead-end positions with no potential for growth, firms that are in decline, firms where it is all about the head of the firm, and firms where you do not look forward to going to work in the morning.

Most architects who have had successful careers have consciously or subconsciously followed these basic guidelines. There are many potentially satisfying careers in architecture, but relying on luck alone rarely leads to a satisfying career. We tell our clients to plan their projects and the same advice applies to our own careers.

1.6 The Career Paths of an Architect

Lee W. Waldrep, Ph.D.

This article describes career designing—a process of developing a career that parallels the architectural design process—and the roles an architect can pursue both in the architecture profession and outside traditional practice. As well, it outlines those career paths beyond architecture, often referred to as nontraditional careers.

To study architecture is to study all things.

—John Ruskin

Architects are broadly qualified to practice in a wide variety of roles and settings within the architecture profession and building enterprise.

—David Haviland, Hon. AIA

After the rigors of an architecture education, work experience, and examination, becoming an architect may seem the simple and direct path for a career. However, other paths exist not only for the new graduate but also for the experienced architect wanting or needing to make a change.

> *The building of a career is quite as difficult a problem as the building of a house, yet few ever sit down with pencil and paper, with expert information and counsel, to plan a working career and deal with the life problem scientifically, as they would deal with the problem of building a house, taking the advice of an architect to help them.*

> —Frank Parsons, 1909

As the father of vocational guidance Parsons states, the building of a career—the process of career development—is a difficult but important task. Yet few individuals prepare for their careers in a thoughtful, careful, and deliberate manner. Instead, many often fall into a career, while others make random career choices that show little commitment to their occupation. This approach frequently leads to dissatisfaction.

Currently the assistant director at the School of Architecture at the University of Illinois at Urbana-Champaign, Lee W. Waldrep has 20 years of experience in higher education. With degrees from American University, ASU, and Michigan, he is the author of *Becoming an Architect: A Guide to Careers in Design*, 2d edition (Wiley 2010).

Career Designing

Deliberately designing one's career path maximizes career success at any point in a profession. As with architectural projects, careers can be planned. Actually, designing a career is parallel to designing a building. Programming, schematic design, design development, working drawings, and construction are replaced in the career designing process with assessing, exploring, decision making, and planning.

Assessing

Know thyself.

—Inscription over the Oracle at Delphi, Greece

When an architect designs a project, programming is the first step in the process. As William Pena points out in *Problem Seeking*, the main idea behind programming is the search for sufficient information to clarify, understand, and state the problem. In a similar manner, when designing a career, the process begins with assessing.

Assessing involves learning about yourself. Assess where you want to be; analyze what is important to you, your abilities, the work you would like to do, and your strengths and weaknesses. Just as programming assists the architect in understanding a particular design problem, assessment helps determine what a person wants from his or her career. This ongoing process must be revisited throughout a person's entire employment. The details of assessment include examining values, interests, and skills.

Values

Values are feelings, attitudes, and beliefs held close to the heart. They reflect what is important to a person; they tell you what you should or should not do. Work values are the enduring dimensions or aspects of work that are regarded as important sources of satisfaction. Values traditionally held high by architects include creativity, recognition, variety, independence, and responsibility.

As a quick inventory, circle which of the following you value most in your work:

- Social contributions
- Creativity
- Excitement
- Working alone or with others
- Monetary reward
- Competition
- Change and variety
- Independence
- Intellectual challenge
- Physical challenge
- Fast pace
- Security
- Responsibility
- Making decisions
- Power and authority
- Gaining knowledge
- Spiritual/Transpersona
- Recognition

Your responses provide insight on a career path within the profession. For example, an architect who values contributions to society most highly might look for opportunities for work in public interest design.

Interests

Interests are those ideas, events, and activities that stimulate enthusiasm; they are reflected in choices you make about how you spend your time. In simplest terms, interests are activities that an individual enjoys doing. Typically, architects have a breadth of interests because the field of architecture encompasses artistic, scientific, and technical aspects. Architects enjoy being involved in all phases of the creative process—from original conceptualization to a tangible finished product.

To determine your interests, complete the following exercise: In 10 minutes of continuous writing, never removing pen from paper or fingers from keyboard, answer the question: *What do I like to do when I am not working?*

Career development theory dictates that an individual's career path should follow his or her interests; if they do, the person will see success.

Skills

Skills or abilities can be learned. There are three types of skills—functional, self-management, and special knowledge. Having a functional skill means being able to perform some specific type of activity, action, or operation with a good deal of proficiency. According to the Bureau of Labor Statistics, an architect needs the following skills: analytical, communication, creativity, critical-thinking, organizational, technical, and visualization. Self-management skills speak to one's personal characteristics, while special knowledge skills are skills you have that may not necessarily pertain to your career.

The importance of knowing one's skills is echoed by Richard Bolles in *The Quick Job Hunting Map*: "You must know, for now and all the future, not only what skills you have, but more importantly, what skills you have and enjoy." With respect to skills, think back over the past five years. What were your five most satisfying accomplishments? Next to each, list the skills or abilities that enabled you to succeed. Similarly review your failures to determine traits or deficiencies you want to overcome. Knowing your skill set is important as it helps you direct your career path.

A variety of techniques may be used to conduct an assessment. The few listed here are simply to get started; others include writing an autobiography and undertaking empirical inventories or psychological assessment with the assistance of a career advisor. Regardless of the method you choose, only you can best determine what skills you have acquired and enjoy using; the issues, ideas, problems, and organizations that interest you; and the values that you care about for your life and career. By assessing yourself, you will better be able to make decisions related to your career path.

Exploring

Students spend four or more years learning how to dig data out of the library and other sources, but it rarely occurs to them that they should also apply some of the same new-found research skill to their own benefit—to looking up information on companies, types of professions, sections of the country that might interest them.

—Albert Shapero

Schematic design follows programming in the design process. Schematic design generates alternative solutions; its goal is to establish general characteristics of the design, including scale, form, estimated costs, and the general image of the building, the size and organization of spaces. In addition, schematic design identifies major issues and makes initial decisions that serve as the basis of subsequent stages.

In career designing, exploring is parallel to schematic design. It develops alternatives or career choices. Career exploration is the process of accumulating information about the world of work. Its goal is to obtain career information on a plethora of careers or specializations within a particular career. Even if you already have chosen architecture as a career, it is still a valuable and necessary process. Instead of exploring careers, you can explore firms, possible career paths within architecture, and other areas that affect your architectural path; understanding exploration will help you be flexible and adaptable when the economy or other factors require it.

To begin, collect career information from a variety of sources, both people and publications. Conduct an *information interview*—interviewing someone to obtain information.

People to interview might include a senior partner in a local firm, a faculty member, a classmate or colleague, or a mentor. Other ways to explore are through attending lectures sponsored by the local AIA chapter or a university, volunteering time through a local AIA committee or other organizations of interest, becoming involved with a mentor program, and observing or shadowing someone for a day.

As Shapero states, use research skills to access any and all information on a career. Visit your local library and inquire about the following publications: *The Dictionary of Occupational Titles (DOT)*, *Occupational Outlook Handbook (OOH)*, *Guide to Occupational Exploration (GOE)*, and *What Color Is Your Parachute?* Ask a reference librarian to identify other resources that might be valuable. In addition, investigate resources at your local AIA chapter or the library/resource center at an area architecture program.

Decision Making

What most people want out of life, more than anything else, is the opportunity to make choices.

—David P. Campbell

The heart of the design process is design development. Similarly, decision making is the heart of the career development process. Design development describes the specific character and intent of the entire project; it further refines the schematic design and defines the alternatives. Decision making means selecting alternatives and evaluating them against a predetermined set of criteria.

How you make decisions? Do you rely on gut-level reactions? Or do you follow a planned strategy of weighing alternatives? Whatever your method of deciding, be aware of it. While some decisions can be made at the drop of a hat, others, including career designing, require more thought.

Decision making can be difficult and time-consuming, but knowing the quality of decisions is affected by the information used to make them, you quickly realize that making informed decisions is an important skill to learn. Decision making is making the decision based on what you learned from assessing and exploring.

Both exploring and decision making are critical steps to successful career designing. Once a decision is made and a path chosen, the next step, planning, is about taking action to realize your goals.

Planning

If you do not have plans for your life, someone else does.

—Anthony Robbins

Planning is bringing the future into the present so that we can do something about it now.

—Alan Lakein

Planning is key to fulfilling your career goals. After the owner/client decides on a design for a potential building, the next step is the development of plans. These plans—construction documents, specifications, and construction schedules—all play an important role in realizing the design. As part of the career development process, planning ensures that a successful career will be realized.

In his book *The 7 Habits of Highly Effective People*, author Stephen Covey states that a mission statement focuses on what you want to be (character) and to do (contributions and achievements) and on the values or principles on which being and doing are based. To start the planning process, draft your mission statement by asking yourself: What do I want to be? What do I want to do? What are my career aspirations? Review the mission statement example below:

I desire to act in a manner that brings out the best in me and those important to me—especially when it might be most justifiable to act otherwise.

After you have crafted your mission statement, the next step is to develop goals that will lead to its fulfillment. Goals are future-oriented statements of purpose and direction to be accomplished within a specified time frame. They are stepping stones in achieving long-range aims and should be specific and measurable. Write down your goals. It has been said that the difference between a wish and a goal is that a goal is written down.

Once you establish your goals, you are ready to develop the action plan that will help you accomplish them. Action plans are steps on the path toward your goals; they are stepping stones in achieving related short-range intentions. Look at your accomplished goals. What steps must you take to accomplish them? As with career goals, write down your action plan, including specific completion dates.

The final step in planning is to review your action plans and goals regularly. Cross out the goals you have accomplished and revise, add to, or delete others. Be honest with yourself. Are you still committed to achieving your goals? You can change them, but remember that the magic road to achievement is *persistence*. Abandon goals only if they have lost meaning for you, not because they are tough or you have suffered a setback.

Now that you understand the career designing process—assessing, exploring, decision making, and planning—you can implement it. This process is never-ending and cyclical as you progress through your professional career. As soon as you have secured an ideal position in a firm, you will wish to assess your new life situation and make adjustments to your career design accordingly. Designing your career is one of the most important tasks during your lifetime.

Career Paths

Careers in Architecture

Pursuing architecture prepares an individual for a vast array of career possibilities. Many of these are within traditional architecture practice, but many are also available in related career fields.

Within the traditional architecture firm, graduates may obtain a beginning position as an intern and progress to junior designer, project architect, and, eventually, associate or principal. Getting to the top does not happen overnight; it can take a lifetime. Aspiring professionals may pursue their careers in traditional firms regardless of their size (small, medium, or large) or may choose to work in a different setting, such as a private corporation, a government agency, or a university—or, after obtaining professional licensure, may choose to start their own firms.

► Entrepreneurial Practice: Starting an Architecture Firm (see Section 2.1 in Chapter 2) discusses why and how to start one's own firm.

► "Intern Development" (see Section 1.7) discusses the IDP in detail.

Architectural Practice

How does a career in architecture begin? How does a person progress from graduation to become an architect? Following the AIA Definition of Architect Positions, the path seems linear, progressing from an intern to architect; once licensed (and depending on the firm), the path continues to architect I (3 to 5 years) and architect/designer III (8 to 10 years). From there, the path progresses to project manager, department head or senior manager, junior principal/partner, and concludes with senior principal/partner.

Of course, the path of a career in architecture is not strictly linear; however, it is helpful to understand these titles with the knowledge and responsibility associated with them, as outlined in Dana Cuff's *Architecture: The Story of Practice*. Upon entry into the profession, the intern is building upon his or her educational foundation through practical experience under the supervision of an architect; and the intern is tracking his or her experience in the Intern Development Program (IDP), an essential step in becoming an architect. Once licensed, the architect is demonstrating competence, gathering responsibility, and gaining autonomy and management tasks. When at the full-fledged stage, the architect is gaining fiscal responsibility on a widening sphere of influence.

The entering graduate does face challenges. Given the gap between education and practice, what happens in the studios of schools is much different than the studios of

- *Senior Principal/Partner*: Typically an owner or majority shareholder of the firm; may be the founder. Titles include president, chief executive officer, or managing principal/partner.
- *Mid-Level Principal/Partner*: Titles include executive or senior vice president.
- *Junior Principal/Partner*: Recently made a partner or principal of the firm. Title may include vice president.
- *Department Head/Senior Manager*: Senior management architect or nonregistered graduate; responsible for major department(s) or functions; reports to principal or partner.
- *Project Manager*: Licensed architect or nonregistered graduate with more than 10 years of experience; has overall project management responsibility for a variety of projects or project teams, including client contact, scheduling, and budgeting.
- *Architect/Designer III*: Licensed architect or nonregistered graduate with 8 to 10 years of

experience; responsible for significant aspects of projects; responsible for work on minor projects. Selects, evaluates, and implements procedures and techniques used on projects.
- *Architect/Designer II*: Licensed architect or nonregistered graduate with 6 to 8 years of experience; responsible for daily design or technical development of a project.
- *Architect/Designer I*: Recently licensed architect or nonregistered graduate with 3 to 5 years of experience; responsible for particular parts of a project within parameters set by others.
- *Intern*: Unlicensed architecture school graduate under supervision of an architect.
- *Entry-Level Intern*: Unlicensed architecture school graduate in first year of internship.
- *Student*: Current architecture student working during summer or concurrently with school.

PART 1: THE PROFESSION

the firms. For this reason, architecture students are strongly encouraged to seek intern positions in architecture firms during their academic years.

Those seeking licensure will find it essential to secure employment within an architecture firm to gain the necessary experience under the direct supervision of an architect and meet the requirements of the Intern Development Program; however, in recognition of opportunities to go beyond traditional practice—such as working under registered professionals in related professions like landscape architecture, or working under an architect outside of a firm setting—interns can gain experience in other work settings.

When seeking employment, one should consider firm size as a factor when deciding where to work; in large firms, an intern will be exposed to a broad scale of projects and full-service work, but may be limited in exposure to aspects of practice. In a small firm, the intern will see the full spectrum of projects, but the projects may be limiting in scope and size. Where one works at the start of his or her career can have an impact on the future career trajectory in architecture.

Within what is typically referred to as traditional practice, there are firms that develop specialties. While they are still architecture firms, these specialties provide opportunities to showcase talent or strong interest. Examples of such specialties include programming, design, specifications, construction contract administration, or sustainability.

Some firms focus on particular building types, such as healthcare, religious, justice facilities, housing, interiors, sports facilities, educational, and/or institutional. One firm—for instance, Animal Arts in Boulder, Colorado—focuses on facilities related to animals, including veterinary hospitals, shelters, and pet resorts. As a specialist in healthcare, an architect can become a certified healthcare architect with the American College of Healthcare Architects (ACHA). Certain Knowledge Communities of the AIA that focus their energies on building types or specialties include the Academy of Architecture for Health, the Academy of Architecture for Justice, the Committee on Architecture for Education, and the Interfaith Forum on Religion, Art and Architecture, among others.

Another means to expand a career within the profession is through supplemental architectural services. Because of the recent economic downturn, the AIA created the Supplemental Architectural Services program, a series of detailed essays and slide presentations to offer assistance to architects in expanding their consulting services.

Supplemental architectural services can:

- Help architects generate income
- Increase the value of the firm through diversification
- Help attract new clients or keep the firm involved with existing patrons
- Be used as special projects for young professionals to nurture their development

The AIA has identified 48 supplemental architectural services, listed below. More information on each of these—required knowledge and skills, why clients need the deliverables, associated tasks, and the AIA Contract Document that can be used in conjunction with the service—can be found at the AIA Architects Knowledge Resource, Supplemental Architectural Services (http://www.aia.org/practicing/akr/AIAB089194).

- Accessibility Compliance
- Architectural Acoustics
- Building Measurement
- Code Compliance
- Commissioning
- Contract Administration/Construction Contract Administration/Design and Construction Contract Administration
- Construction Defect Analysis
- Construction Documentation—Drawings
- Construction Documentation—Specifications
- Construction Management
- Construction Procurement
- Demolition Planning Services
- Detailed Cost Estimating
- Digital Architecture Survey Technologies
- Energy Analysis and Design
- Energy Monitoring
- Environmental Graphic Design
- Expert Witness Services
- Facility Evaluation Services
- Facility Management/Facility Support
- Furniture, Furnishings and Equipment Services/FFE Design
- Geotechnical Services
- Historic Preservation
- Indoor Air Quality Consulting
- Interior Design/Architectural Interior Design
- Land Surveying Services
- Lighting Design
- Model Construction
- Move Management
- On-Site Project Representation
- Parking Planning Services
- Postoccupancy Evaluation
- Program Management Services
- Programming
- Project Financing and Development Services
- Record Drawing
- Regional or Urban Planning
- Renderings
- Research Services
- Security Evaluation and Planning Services
- Seismic Analysis and Design
- Site Analysis/Site Evaluation and Planning
- Space Planning
- Strategic Facility Planning
- Sustainable Building Design
- Urban Design Services
- Value Analysis
- Zoning Process Assistance

Outside Traditional Practice

Beyond traditional practice, architects work in a number of other settings. While no exact statistics are kept, it is estimated that one in five architects work outside private practice. These are traditional architect roles in nonarchitectural settings.

- *Corporations and institutions.* Do you want to work at McDonald's? It may come as a surprise that McDonald's hires architects, as do many businesses and corporations. Corporate architects may serve as in-house architects, but in most cases they represent the interests of the corporation to the outside architects they hire. Depending on the industry, they may be involved with all phases of a project.
- *Government and public agencies.* Federal, state, and local governments commission more than one-quarter of construction annually. As such, opportunities exist for architects in public agencies. Many departments of government, including the military, employ architects. In addition to traditional tasks, architects manage facilities and projects and oversee construction. Emerging professionals may find it difficult to start a career in a public agency, but such careers can be extremely worthwhile. Employers of public architects (as represented on the 2012 Advisory Group of the AIA Public Architects Knowledge Community) include the State of Ohio, Texas

A&M University, the U.S. Army Corps of Engineers, Thomas Jefferson National Lab, the City of Dallas, and the Judicial Council of California.

- *Education and research.* For some architects, a substantial career path is teaching and research. According to the National Architectural Accrediting Board (NAAB), there were over 6,231 faculty members within the accredited programs of architecture in the academic year 2013–2014, most of whom were adjunct faculty. Additionally, with over 300 programs in architectural technology at the community college level, many more opportunities exist for architects to teach at this level. In addition to teaching, architects serving as faculty will pursue research interests to test ideas that connect education and practice. Aside from teaching future architects, many faculty members also maintain a practice.

As a profession, architecture offers a myriad of possibilities for rewarding careers.

—Irene Dumas-Tyson

I am certain that architectural graduates who are in command of the powerful problem-defining and problem-solving skills of the designer will be fully capable of designing their own imaginative careers by creating new definitions of meaningful work for architects that are embedded in the social landscape of human activity and life's events.

—Leslie Kanes Weisman

Beyond Architecture

An architecture education is excellent preparation for many career paths beyond architecture. In fact, the career possibilities with an architecture education are truly limitless. Anecdotal estimates suggest that only one-half of architecture graduates pursue licensure. By applying the ideas listed earlier in "career designing," one can launch a successful career beyond architecture.

Career paths beyond traditional practice tap into the creative thinking and problem-solving skills developed from an architecture education. The interest in these paths is growing; the results of the most recent AIA/NCARB Internship and Career Survey of interns and emerging professionals indicate that nearly one-fifth of the respondents do not plan on pursuing a traditional career in architecture, although they still plan to obtain their license.

Over the last four years, Archinect, an online forum for architecture, has featured over 25 architects who have applied their backgrounds in architecture to other career fields through its "Working Out of the Box" series. While most are still connected to design in some form, the range of career fields is quite diverse: filmmaker, organic farmer, artist, design director at a resort hotel chain, user experience designer, information designer, and design technology consulting. Also, the reasons for pursuing these are varied and typically are not tied to the recent economic downturn.

For purposes of his doctoral thesis, Robert Douglas, FAIA, studied nontraditional careers (maverick architects) and found those whom he studied credited "design thinking" as helpful in their careers beyond architecture. From his research, architecture graduates and architects pursued careers in law, investment banking, real estate development, computer software, lighting design, film production and set design, cultural policy, architectural criticism and journalism, facilities planning, land planning and management, industrial and product design, arts programming, structural engineering, highway design, public arts installation, architectural photography, painting and sculpture, and clothing design.

A June 2008 issue of *Columns*, the AIA Pittsburgh magazine, entitled, "It's a Wonderful Life," highlighted architects who built new careers after first having one as an architect. First, the article outlines the path of actor Jimmy Stewart, who graduated from Princeton University having studied architecture but instead pursued acting (hence the title of the article). Next, it highlights four individuals who, after successful careers as architects, moved to new career paths—development, needlepoint (fiber art), community design, and construction supervisor. In each case, they discuss how their education and background in architecture paved the way for their new chosen career.

- *Related design professional (landscape architecture, interior design, urban design).* Given the parallel education of design, it is clear why some architects pursue the related career fields of landscape architecture, interior design, and urban design. Many architects pursue careers in interior architecture or space designing, while others pursue the profession of landscape architecture to design outdoor spaces. Still others combine their talents in design to focus on urban design.
- *Engineering and technical.* As architecture is both an art and a science, many architects will pursue careers in engineering or more technical fields. Many with a joint degree in architecture and engineering will pursue civil or structural engineering, but there are other opportunities that exist if there is an interest in the technical side of the profession.
- *Construction.* Because of the connection between design and construction, many architects have pursued careers in construction as construction managers, general contractors, and/or related associates. Architecture firms have expanded their services to include design-build and construction management, bridging the two disciplines.
- *Art and design.* Because much of what architects do is considered an art, it is no surprise that many architects pursue careers in art and design; this extends from fine arts (painting) to applied arts (graphic design and furniture design). Some will determine a way to combine their background in architecture more directly with art, while others truly move away from architecture to pursue their art.
- *Architectural products and services.* Perhaps less obvious are careers in architectural products and services. As these manufacturers market and sell their products and services to architects, who better to serve in these positions but those trained as architects? With an interest in and talent for sales, opportunities exist for a rewarding and fulfilling career.
- *Other.* As stated in the quote from Irene Dumas-Tyson, an education in architecture offers myriad career possibilities. But what other career paths are open to architecture graduates, emerging professionals, or architects? The true answer: There are over 25,000 occupations as defined by the Bureau of Labor Statistics that potentially highlight skills and fulfill passion. Truly, the only limitation to possible career paths is one's imagination.

Real estate. More recently, more architects have become involved with real estate development, the creation of communities, and the repositioning of land or buildings into a higher or better use. For architects wishing to expand their influence on the building process, real estate may be a good fit, as it connects multiple disciplines (engineering, architecture, planning, finance, marketing, law, and environmental impact).

Katherine S. Proctor, FCSI, CDT, AIA, former director of student services at the University of Tennessee, shares her perspective:

> For an individual interested in the career of architecture, the possibilities are endless. I have seen students graduate and become registered architects, professional photographers, lawyers, bankers, business owners, interior designers, contractors, and artists. The education is so broad, with a strong liberal arts base, that it provides a firm foundation for a wide array of exploration. This comes from the content of the curriculums but also from the methodology. The design studio, which is the core of the curriculum, provides a method to take pieces of intellectual information and apply it within the design process. The movement from thinking to doing is powerful. The ability to integrate hundreds of pieces of information, issues, influences, and form and find a solution is a skill that any professional needs to solve problems, whether they are building issues or life issues.

Emerging Careers

The future is not a result of choices among alternative paths offered by the present, but a place that is created—created first in the mind and will, created next in activity. The future is not some place we are going to, but one we are creating. The paths are not found, but made, and the activity of making them changes both the maker and the destination.

—John Schaar, Futurist

Most would agree that the architecture profession is changing; as a result of this change, opportunities are being created to expand the profession beyond what it is now. For example, sustainability has already created new emerging career paths for architects.

Many within the profession have pursued becoming a Leadership in Energy Efficient Design Accredited Professional (LEED AP). As outlined by the Green Building Certification Institute, those credentialed as LEED APs are building industry professionals who have demonstrated a thorough understanding of green building and the LEED® Green Building Rating System™ developed and maintained by the U.S. Green Building Council (USGBC).

Technology such as building information modeling (BIM) will continue to play an increasing role within the architecture profession and will also create new career paths. Firms have emerged that are assisting architecture firms in creating virtual designed environments. Additional career options, such as BIM management and facilitation, are being created as a result of technology.

BEYOND ARCHITECTURE

OUTSIDE TRADITIONAL PRACTICE

Academic Dean/Administrator
Architectural Historian
Corporate Architect
Facilities Architect
Professor
Public Architect
Researcher
University Architect

RELATED PROFESSIONAL

Interior Designer
Landscape Architect
Urban Designer

ENGINEERING AND TECHNICAL

Architectural Acoustics
Building Pathologist
Cartographer
Civil Engineer
Computer Systems Analyst
Construction/Building Inspector
Illuminating Engineer
Marine Architect
Structural Engineer
Urban Planner

CONSTRUCTION

Carpenter
Construction Manager

Construction Software Designer
Contractor
Design-Builder
Estimator
Fire Protection Designer
Land Surveyor
Project Manager

REAL ESTATE

Property Assessor
Real Estate Agent/Broker
Real Estate Developer

ART AND DESIGN

Architectural Illustrator
Architectural Photographer
Art/Creative Director
Artist
Clothing Designer
Exhibit Designer
Filmmaker
Furniture Designer
Graphic Artist/Designer
Industrial/Product Designer
Lighting Designer
Museum Curator
Set Designer
Toy Designer
Web Designer

(continued)

ARCHITECTURAL PRODUCTS AND SERVICES
Product Manufacturer Representative
Sales Representative

OTHER
Architectural Critic
Author/Writer

City Manager
Environmental Planner
Golf Course Architect
Lawyer
Preservationist
Public Official

Other influences that are creating new career opportunities for architects are integrated project delivery (IPD) and other alternative project delivery methods, international practice, and public interest design.

To adequately prepare for your future in architecture or beyond, consider reading *The New Architect: A New Twist on the Future of Design* (Greenway Communications, 2007) by James P. Cramer and Scott Simpson.

CONCLUSION

As stated by David Haviland, Hon. AIA, "Architects are broadly qualified to practice in a wide variety of roles and settings within the architecture profession and building enterprise." To maximize one's path, this chapter highlighted "career designing"—the process of assessing, exploring, decision making, and planning.

Further, the chapter outlined the myriad possible career paths of an architect, both within traditional practice (extending from intern to architect to principal) as well as careers outside traditional practice and beyond architecture. Finally, emerging and potential trends for design professionals were listed.

FOR MORE INFORMATION

AIA Supplemental Services program, a series of detailed essays and slide presentations: www.aia.org/practicing/akr/AIAB089194

Archinect: http://archinect.com/

The New Architect: A New Twist on the Future of Design (Greenway Communications, 2007) by James P. Cramer and Scott Simpson

Occupational Outlook Handbook: www.bls.gov/ooh/

What Color Is Your Parachute? A Practical Manual for Job-Hunters and Career-Changers (Ten Speed Press, 2013) by Richard N. Bolles: www.jobhuntersbible.com/

The Dictionary of Occupational Titles (DOT): www.occupationalinfo.org/

SUCCEEDING IN THE BUILT ENVIRONMENT

H. Alan Brangman, AIA

H. Alan Brangman is vice president of facilities, real estate, and university architect, Howard University, Washington, D.C.

I became an architect because I have always had a fascination with building things. I initially went to school at the University of New Hampshire to study civil engineering. At the beginning of my sophomore year I met an art professor who was a former instructor at Cornell University. He suggested that I transfer to Cornell. My degree is the Bachelor of Architecture.

My greatest challenge as an architect has and continues to be convincing other professionals that architects are capable of doing much more than just architecture. As the university architect at Howard University, my job responsibilities are more in line with those of a principal in a real estate development firm. I am responsible for implementing and monitoring programs and processes to achieve short-term and long-term Howard-wide strategic and operational goals as they relate to facilities and real estate. I am also responsible for the hiring of design and planning consultants and for providing program, planning, and design oversight for all university facilities, as well as monitoring construction projects on campus.

Initially, I pursued a nontraditional career path because I had an interest in something more than just designing buildings. I spent nine years with the Oliver T. Carr Company, a real estate development company in Washington, D.C. That opportunity opened my eyes to the breadth of the built environment and provided me with a much more global perspective on place making.

When I started my career in real estate development, I had been counseled to consider obtaining an MBA. I did not want to commit the time required to return to graduate school. I decided to pursue the path of learning through experience. Since I had been schooled as an architect and architects are taught to solve problems, I was able to manage any of the issues that were part of my job responsibilities quite well. After getting a few years under my belt, I obtained the Real Estate Development Primer Certificate from Harvard Graduate School of Design and Wharton School of Business as a way of confirming what I had learned. It worked.

1.7 Developing Leadership Skills

Success in an architectural career requires the development and refinement of a variety of skills. Few students and recent graduates are born with some of the most important basic skills they will need. Among the most critical are learning to be a leader, learning to communicate effectively, and learning the basic technical skill necessary to competently participate in the profession. Only the last of these three is directly addressed in the formal Intern Development Program (IDP) that all young graduates must participate in prior to licensure in the United States. The other two basic skills should be learned in school and in the important early years of a career.

William C. Ronco, Ph.D., and Mark Jussaume, PE

Leadership is an essential component of successful architecture practice. Through professional development efforts, firms can help staff members attain the skills they need to become effective leaders.

Many architects are deeply interested in leadership and committed to becoming better leaders. Because there are different and conflicting views about the nature of effective leadership, numerous methods are available to architects who want to improve their leadership skills and performance. This article clarifies the different views on leadership and offers guidelines to help architects hone their leadership effectiveness.

Why Architects Must Care About Leadership

The profession places architects in a wide range of leadership positions. Beyond managing projects, architects also lead firms, studios, and committees within firms; mentor young professionals; teach in formal and informal settings; and serve in community and civic groups. In small firms and individual practice, architects also lead in their relationships with clients, stakeholders, government officials, and the community. To be successful in these positions, architects must guide and inspire the actions of others. Leading creates the groups, relationships, and organizations that provide the environments that nurture creative design. Leading enables architects to get their designs built and improve their designs in the process.

Serving as a leader is often challenging and difficult, however. "Leadership is not a walk in the park," observes Richard

> Leadership is the most important thing we can provide our clients. Lots of people can draw lines on paper, but it takes leadership to draw the right conclusions. . . . We are in the leadership business; design is our medium.
>
> —Scott Simpson, FAIA, president, Stubbins Associates

William C. Ronco is president of Gathering Pace Consulting in Bedford, Massachusetts. He consults on strategic planning and leadership training and is a coauthor of *The Partnering Solution*. **Mark Jussaume** is Chief Executive Officer for TRO Jung|Brannen in Newton, Massachusetts. The original version of this topic appeared in Handbook Update 2005.

Leadership is a reciprocal process between those who choose to lead and those who choose to follow. To be successful as an architect, developing leadership skills is essential. Research has identified four important leadership skills. To balance our understanding of leadership, let's take a look at the expectations people have for their leaders. In other words, what do people look for and admire in someone they would willingly follow?

Research about what constituents expect of leaders has yielded fairly consistent results over time and across the globe, transcending a variety of individual, interpersonal, and organizational differences. For people to follow someone willingly, the majority of constituents must believe the leader is competent, honest, forward looking, and inspiring.

COMPETENCE

Constituents must believe the person they follow is competent to guide them where they are headed. Leaders must be viewed as capable and effective. Competent leadership is reflected in the leader's track record and ability to get things done and guide the entire organization, whether the group is large or small.

HONESTY

Honesty is the single most important ingredient in the leader-constituent relationship. Before people will follow someone, they want to be assured that person is worthy of their trust. They are looking for consistency between word and deed. Constituents appreciate leaders who take a stand on important principles; they resolutely refuse to follow those who lack confidence in their own beliefs. Constituents simply do not trust people who cannot or will not communicate their values, ethics, and standards.

VISION

The ability to look ahead is one of the most sought-after leadership traits. Leaders are expected to have a sense of direction and a concern for the future of the group or organization. No matter what this ability is called, the message is clear: Leaders must know where they are going if they expect others to follow.

THE ABILITY TO INSPIRE

People expect their leaders to be enthusiastic, energetic, and positive about the future. It is not enough for a leader to have a dream about the future. A leader must be able to communicate that vision in ways that encourage people to sign on for the duration.

Fitzgerald, director of the Boston Society of Architects. "It's a mind-set born of commitment to ourselves. Although architects clearly are the visionaries who should be leading clients from dream to reality, too often the leadership role is ceded to or usurped by others." Shifting definitions of legal liabilities and changing contract forms have contributed to these changes. Construction managers and client representatives in particular have taken on some of the key decision-making responsibilities formerly assumed only by architects.

RELEVANT LEADERSHIP CONCEPTS

How can architects become better leaders? The first step is to understand what leadership is. Hundreds of articles and books on leadership are published annually, and many are useful for architects, but four leadership concepts have special relevance for architects: behavioral, contingency (or situational), transformational, and Level 5 leadership. An understanding of these concepts can provide the foundation for effective leadership training for architects.

Behavioral Theory

Behavioral theory provides a foundation for leadership training appropriate for architects that incorporates the following concepts:

- Articulating and following a vision and clear goals
- Communicating effectively
- Demonstrating passion and energy
- Demonstrating high standards, morals, and ethics
- Questioning the status quo
- Expecting more from others
- Demonstrating design sensibility

Contingency Theory

This approach to leadership implies that architects who want to lead must develop both a variety of leadership behaviors and an ability to read and adapt to changing situations. This focus results in leadership training that devotes a good deal of effort to understanding, appreciating, and working with a wide range of different kinds of people.

Contingency theory validates the interest architects have in the multiple leadership roles they must play. Familiar roles that permeate architects' descriptions of leadership include these:

- Theoretician
- Business development hunter
- Project management warrior
- Civic/community advocate
- Coach/counselor
- Teacher
- Marketing director
- Project manager
- Coach/counselor/mentor
- Renaissance person

Such a variety of leadership roles means there are different paths to leadership success.

Transactional/Transformational Leadership

Transactions are trades and deals that leaders make. Transformation is the learning and development that both leader and follower can experience in the process of leadership. Architects relate to this approach because defining and conducting transactions with clients, subordinates, and peers is a fundamental part of professional practice. The "performance" descriptors of leadership are easily applied to many of these transactions.

James MacGregor Burns, in his 1978 book, *Leadership*, points out, however, that leadership is more than simply conducting transactions; it has the potential to transform both the follower and the leader. This potential is especially important for architects because it speaks to the inspiration that can take place when architects educate clients, coach and mentor younger professionals, or devote their energies to civic causes. Burns' ideas remind architects of the potential they have as leaders to go beyond simply getting others to do what they want and truly transforming both themselves and others. It's possible, and quite important, for architects to learn from clients and others.

Level 5 Leadership

Level 5 leadership is an important leadership theory for architects because it adds a dimension to the meaning of leadership beyond the image of someone who fills multiple roles, initiates structure, and is "considerate." Level 5 involves a selfless dedication to the organization that, in many cases, may conflict with an architect's own ego.

Level 5 leadership is distinguished by its combination of a unique, counterintuitive quality of humility with unwavering perseverance. Level 5 leaders are selfless "servant" leaders.

I would love to be able to give you a list of steps for becoming a Level 5 [leader], but we have no solid research data that would support a credible list.

—James Collins, *Good to Great*

Leadership Basics

Consideration of the four leadership concepts described above yields five statements that summarize them and can serve as a foundation for leadership training:

Leaders fill different and sometimes conflicting roles. For example, a principal of an architecture firm demonstrates a strong ability to design as well as to bring a project in under budget, mentor younger staff, and build a lasting organization.

Architects need to lead in small firms and individual practice as well as in large firms. Leadership tasks, responsibilities, and opportunities occur in everyday practice with clients, stakeholders, government, and community, as well as in large AE firms.

Both extroverted and introverted leadership styles work. There is a recurring and noticeable tension between extroverted, authoritative styles of leadership and more introverted, reflective servant leadership. More recent leadership theories recognize the power and validity of the more introverted leadership model and question the apparent superficiality of the more traditional extroverted approach. However, for architects, the most effective leadership combines both extroverted (communicating a vision, connecting, building relationships) and introverted (developing concepts, modesty, sharpening focus, refining goals) styles.

Architects must do more than fill multiple roles—they must perform well in them. Architects recognize the need to fill multiple leadership roles, but they also want to see clear evidence of performance in those roles, not mere figureheads.

A concern for "higher" matters is part of leadership. Caring, inspiration, and the transformation of both the follower and the leader are as much a part of leadership for architects as winning design awards, landing big projects, and building strong client relationships. This transformational/inspirational aspect of leadership is especially important for architects because of its link to the learning and growth inherent in the creative process.

For More Information

Several books on leadership provide a sound background for embarking on a leadership training and development program. In *Good to Great* (Harper Collins, 2001), Jim Collins puts forth his Level 5 leadership theory. Several large A&E firms have successfully used internal reading groups of *Good to Great* to develop increased understanding of leadership and organizational concepts.

Max DePree's books, *Leadership Is an Art* (Currency, 2004) and *Leadership Jazz* (Dell, 1993), provide insight and understanding into the nature of effective leadership.

The MBA text *Organizational Behavior* (Merrill, 1984), by Jerry L. Gray and Frederick A. Starke, provides extensive information about leadership theories and their evolution over time. This approach to leadership contrasts in interesting ways with thinking on leadership by famous architects. For example, Cesar Pelli's *Observations for Young Architects* (Monacelli, 1999) provides another view.

The Reflective Practitioner (Ashgate Publishing, 1995), by Donald Schon, is especially geared to architects. Schon writes eloquently about the nature of personal development in the professions and in architecture in particular. Another book on leadership of value to architects is *The Partnering Solution* (Career Press, 2005), by William and Jean Ronco. It features a chapter on leadership that links partnering methods with leadership approaches.

Books about interpersonal relations can be a good place to learn about improving leadership skills. *People Styles at Work* (AMACOM, 1996), by Robert Bolton, provides useful insights into the nature of effective communication and other interpersonal skills that are especially important for architects. In *Leader Effectiveness Training* (Perigree, 2001), Thomas J. Gordon provides very clear instruction for essential leadership communications skills. Stephen Covey's *Seven Habits of Highly Effective People* (Free Press, 2004) looks at the need for listening: "Seek first to understand before trying to be understood." Covey's *Principle-Centered Leadership* (Free Press, 1992) is also useful.

Laurie Beth Jones provides practical, usable instruction for the complex task of writing a personal vision statement in *The Path: Creating Your Mission Statement for Work and for Life* (Hyperion, 1996).

1.8 Developing Communication Skills

David Greusel, AIA

Generally, architects are better known for their graphic skills than their verbal or writing skills. However, effective oral and written communications benefit a design practice in many ways.

Communication is at the center of architecture practice. An exceptionally gifted designer may not achieve success if he or she is unable to effectively communicate ideas to others. The construction process requires collaboration between many people, and architects must be able to communicate in a clear, concise, and unambiguous manner for a project to be successful.

Of course, architects communicate many ideas visually, but this represents only one of many forms of communication. This topic will focus on common communication problems, describing methods and techniques to help architects listen, speak, and write in a manner that is understandable and useful to clients and others involved in the approval, review, and construction process.

COMMUNICATION BASICS

The purpose of communication is to transmit ideas and facts, from simple social or emotional concepts ("I'm fine, thanks, and you?") to sets of highly complex instructions (e.g., a specification for an escalator). Whatever the idea, if information transferred from one person is not understood by another, communication has not taken place. Communication is, at best, a challenging proposition, but one that can be improved by developing certain skills and techniques.

Because message erosion occurs so easily, the method by which information is communicated is significant. Communication can be casual or formal, polite or terse, clear or muddled—and these variables apply to both spoken and written communication. Because architects communicate so often with so many people in a typical day, they tend to give little thought to the quality of their communications. However, all players in the project delivery process—officials, manufacturers, fabricators, consultants, engineers, contractors, subcontractors, and, particularly, clients—make judgments about the professionalism and effectiveness of architects based on how well they communicate. For example, potential clients may view poorly delivered communications as a sign the architect is a sloppy and inattentive practitioner—not the sort of architect most owners want to hire.

Communication Goals

Professional communication has three basic goals: to inform, to persuade, and to instruct.

Informing. At the outset, much of the communication between architect and client is intended to inform the client about the architecture firm, the services it offers, the design process, the way the firm works, or particular aspects of a design solution. As the project proceeds, the architect is called upon to keep the client and other project participants aware of the status of the activities necessary for the work to proceed, the tasks accomplished, the milestones met, and the overall schedule. When a message is necessary, include a call for action to alert the recipient to its purpose. Even the most

David Greusel is the founding principal of Convergence Design in Kansas City. He is the author of *Architect's Essentials of Presentation Skills*. The original version of this topic appeared in the 2003 Update volume of the Handbook.

mundane memorandum should identify a requested action, such as "Please file this memo for future reference" or "Kindly acknowledge receipt of this memo."

Persuading. Another goal of communication is to encourage the recipient to take action, make a decision, or agree with a particular point of view. Marketing communications come to mind, since the goal of most marketing messages is "hire our firm!" Project communications are also routinely meant to be persuasive, as when an architect asks an owner to release a payment to a contractor, approve a change order, or pay an invoice. In one respect, persuasive messages are simpler to communicate than informative ones because the reason for them is usually more obvious.

Since the purpose of a persuasive communication is more readily grasped, a good first principle of communication is this: Before undertaking any communication, oral or written, determine whether it has a persuasive purpose and identify that purpose. The initial result of consistently applying this principle should be the generation of far fewer unnecessary or competing messages. Bear in mind, however, that keeping someone informed of progress on a project or a task can be a perfectly good reason for sending a message.

Instructing. The last goal of communication is to instruct the recipient on how to proceed. Architects, in the course of a typical project, issue hundreds of sets of instructions. These can appear as drawings, sketches, specifications, product or material literature, details, clarifications, memos, and letters. In fact, it would be fair to say that the main vehicle an architect uses to do his or her work is instructions to those who perform the activities necessary for construction of the project.

The clarity and precision of this category of communication is an important ingredient in the success of any project.

Learning Other Languages

Architects at times are accused of couching their design presentations in obscure academic language or professional jargon that is incomprehensible or confusing to the audience. Clients, too, use terms and jargon particular to their field of expertise or business. These specialized and often competing "languages" can result in misunderstandings and confusion. Thus it is helpful if the architect clarifies the terms and concepts used by all those involved in a project.

If an architect's work involves many projects of a particular type (e.g., laboratories, schools, courthouses, etc.), learning the language of that specialty and learning it well is essential. Here are specific suggestions for speaking a client's language:

Read what your clients read. One of the best ways to improve your client communication skills is to subscribe to and study the trade publications clients read. It does not matter if the publication is *Banker's Week* or *Assisted Living Monthly*, as long as it pertains to a client's field. It is important to be exposed to and familiar with the professional jargon and vocabulary your clients use. As a side benefit, architects can also acquire a better understanding of issues confronting their clients' industries.

One reason trade publications are good for study is that trade journalists usually explain acronyms and jargon in their articles. A story about REITs, for example, will somewhere (usually when it first appears) explain that a REIT is a "real estate investment trust." By reading what your clients read, you can learn their vocabulary.

Attend client events. Attending events sponsored by organizations the client belongs to is also an effective way to learn a specialized language. Attendance at these events is usually not restricted and, more often than not, industry organizations are glad for the architect's interest (and registration fee). Programs, lectures, and conferences by client groups can provide a realistic idea of how clients speak among themselves. Unlike trade journals, however, program speakers do not always take care to explain the terms they are using. So although client events are useful for learning client language, some translation may still be needed. And obviously, this sort of "fieldwork" is more expensive and time-consuming than reading trade publications.

Delve into glossaries and references. It can also be helpful to purchase or download a glossary or reference work pertaining to the client's field. Just as there are dictionaries of architecture terms, there are dictionaries or glossaries for most other professions. Usually, the hardest part is tracking down the publisher, since dictionaries of, say, biochemical research are not likely to be found at a local bookstore. Client trade and professional associations are the best place to start a search for client language references. Often these glossaries can be found online at trade association websites.

Learning to speak a client's or specialist's language is an important skill by which an architect can remove potential barriers to good communication. Equally important is the architect's willingness to cultivate listening skills and to improve speaking and writing skills.

LISTENING

We tend to think of communication skills as those skills that help us transmit a message. In fact, the most important communication skill is the means by which we receive messages from others. The most effective and least-used communication tools are the ears. You can learn a lot just by listening.

A Marketing Tool

Listening to clients is perhaps the most effective marketing strategy. Although it is seldom taught in schools, listening is compelling to both current and prospective clients. Clients consistently report selecting an architect because they

> You can observe a lot by just watching.
>
> —Yogi Berra

felt the candidate or firm demonstrated a willingness to listen. Another positive result of listening is that selection committees routinely rank lower those design firms that come into a project interview acting as though they have all the answers.

Why is this? Listening connotes a cooperative and collaborative spirit, which is both effective and persuasive when dealing with clients. Listening implies a willingness to learn and to be fully committed to the client's idea of a successful project. In addition, listening shows respect for the client.

Despite its large and obvious benefits, listening is among the least valued communication skills because it is not glamorous—that is, becoming a better listener does not seem to add much to an architect's professional stature. Indeed, one precondition of good listening is the willingness to learn from clients instead of enlightening them. Humility is rarely the topic of best-sellers, although in *The Seven Habits of Highly Effective People*, author Stephen Covey advises readers to "seek first to understand, then to be understood."

Empathetic Listening

The essence of good listening is to listen with empathy, which requires you to view an interaction from the other person's point of view. Putting oneself in another's shoes will make it much easier to understand that person's message and the motivation behind it. Empathetic listening requires architects to lay aside personal agendas, professional pride, and natural defensiveness in order to enter into a discussion with clients as a person willing to learn.

Keys to empathetic listening. The strategies described below are essential to being an empathetic listener. Architects who learn to cultivate these skills in their interactions with clients should find it much easier to achieve professional and business goals.

> Listen. Listen. Listen better. Understand our culture. Get immersed in what we do, who we are.
>
> —Charles Andrews, assistant vice president for space planning and construction, Emory University

- *Check your ego at the door.* Empathetic listening requires a humble attitude. Professional pride is the biggest obstacle to being a good listener. Learn to focus more on what the client wants you to hear and less on what you have to say.

- *Acknowledge your biases.* Everyone has a frame of reference. Yours will always be different from your client's.
- *Establish a "plane of connection."* Attitude is not just a mental disposition. Empathetic listening requires a literal horizontal connection with the speaker, so that communication takes place between equals.
- *Avoid commentary.* Resist the urge to evaluate every statement a client makes for its validity or usefulness. Learn to listen without immediately judging either the speaker or the content of the message.
- *Show interest.* Although it may seem insincere, adopting an interested posture (leaning in, eyes front and not preoccupied) will help you *become* interested.
- *It's not all about you.* Resist the urge to share your own stories, however relevant they may seem. Especially resist the urge to top each point a client makes with an anecdote about how the same thing happened to you.
- *Be affirmative.* Learn to use words and actions that affirm the speaker without necessarily expressing agreement. Affirmation means letting a speaker know his or her message is being received, not that you agree with everything that is said.
- *Take notes.* Taking notes is almost always permissible, unless clients specifically say their comments are "off the record." When you do take notes, you'll be surprised at how much better you remember the conversation later.
- *Be in the moment.* Being in the moment requires full participation in the conversation taking place. This means paying attention to a client while he or she is speaking, not thinking back on something that happened earlier in the day and not anticipating something that might happen later.
- *Respond appropriately.* Reinforce the communication process by restating the speaker's main points, acknowledging expected actions, and asking clarifying questions. Inappropriate responses include reciprocal attacks, defensive posturing, and changing the subject to something of greater interest to you.
- *Frames of reference.* A major consideration when listening empathetically is to remember that architects and clients generally do not share the same frame of reference. In fact, architects are likely to encounter individuals with many different frames of reference within a client organization.

Challenge yourself to think, before a conversation takes place, about how your frame of reference may differ from that of the client. Clues to an individual's frame of reference can be found by observing the following:

- What does he or she seem passionate about?
- What are his or her measures of effective performance?
- To whom does this individual report? What are his or her accountabilities?
- What other constituencies must this person answer to?

Comparative Frames of Reference	
Role in Client Organization	**Likely Frame of Reference**
Executive	Image, theme, first cost, schedule
Department manager	Functional layout, efficiency, flow
User	Convenience, control, personal space
Facility manager	Standardization, efficiency, lifecycle cost
Maintenance staff	Durability, ease of repair, materials, standards

Architects should also be aware of how their own frame of reference filters communications they receive. Are you most passionate about design? About client satisfaction? About profitability? About larger social concerns (e.g., the environment)? The issues an architect cares about most deeply (e.g., design, client satisfaction,

Here are 10 good ideas to keep in mind when making a formal presentation to a client:

1. Show up. Be physically prepared for your presentation, recognizing that how you "dance" is part of the message.
2. Know your motivation. Have a clear purpose for your presentation and a call to action. Build your presentation around a story line, rather than just technical facts.
3. Know your lines. Over-preparation (having more to say than you actually say) is the key to confident presenting.
4. Be visible. Know the setting where the presentation will take place, and keep yourself lighted during audiovisual presentations.
5. Face out. Build energy, empathy, engagement, enthusiasm, and entertainment into your talk. Never turn your back to the audience.
6. Keep going. Recognize that things can (and will) go wrong during your presentation. Strategize ahead of time about how to handle them.
7. Project. Speak so you can be heard by the person farthest away from you in the room.
8. Stay in the moment. Concentrate on what you are saying, not on extraneous problems unrelated to your presentation.
9. Remember your props. Think about what sort of visual aids will help you achieve your objective.
10. Know when to stop. Plan generously, so you can finish your presentation before your allotted time runs out.

Adapted from Architect's Essentials of Presentation Skills, *by David Greusel, AIA*

profitability, the environment, etc.) define the edges of his or her frame of reference. As a design professional, it is your job to understand both your frame of reference and your client's.

Gender differences. The majority of architects are still male, and some have observed that men do not always model good listening skills. Author Tom Peters points out that women more often exhibit the collaborative skills, like listening, that are needed to succeed in the twenty-first century. In addition, women are generally better at entering into a conversation openly, without jockeying for status, and at responding empathetically rather than defensively to what they hear.

Should male architects therefore abandon the quest to become better listeners? Of course not. However, in many instances, men face greater challenges in becoming good listeners. Thus, when opportunities arise, they should observe how women communicate and their sensitivity to context and nuance, and they should seek to cultivate those qualities in their own listening.

Focusing on the Message

One barrier to effective listening is a natural tendency to judge the communication skills of others. The solution is to focus on the *content* of the message and not the person delivering it. Because people can listen much faster than others can talk, the "rate gap"—the difference between the two—can be used to determine what the person speaking is trying to say. Turning listening into a challenging mental game will minimize distractions caused by a client's less-than-perfect delivery.

Avoiding Distractions

Obviously, good listeners avoid distracting themselves. This means not making (or taking) phone calls when speaking with someone, not sending (or reading) e-mails on a wireless device, not doodling, and not looking out the window. For those who are easily distracted, avoiding distraction may take a concerted effort, but the dividends gained in better communication with your clients is well worth it.

VERBAL COMMUNICATION

Once you have begun to learn a client's language and to practice empathetic listening, you will be well on your way to establishing good communications. The next step is learning to speak to clients in a way that fosters mutual understanding.

Dialogue vs. Monologue

The most practical way architects can improve verbal interactions with clients is to stop making "speeches." In a society where a thirty-second television commercial is considered long, it hardly makes sense for an architect to discourse for an hour or more on a topic before asking for questions. This truth applies to design presentations, marketing efforts, and speeches to clients or public groups.

Darling, for a speech to be immortal, it need not be interminable.

—Muriel Humphrey

How can a monologue be turned into a dialogue? By deciding to do it ahead of time. The decision to interact, rather than just talk, is the key to client engagement. Once that decision is made, crafting a dialogue becomes fairly easy.

Asking Questions

A simple way to interact with a client is to ask questions—lots of questions. Begin with a question, either innocuous ("How are you this morning?") or profound ("What adjective best describes your attitude toward this project?"). Continue asking questions throughout the meeting. It is not an exaggeration to say that asking questions is the single most effective way to achieve high-quality communication with clients—assuming you listen to the answers.

Some architects may think, "I've spent a lot of time preparing for this meeting. I have a lot to say! If I'm asking all these questions, how can I make the points I need to make?" The idea is not only to ask questions at the outset, but also to punctuate your presentation with questions throughout. If you find yourself going on about some aspect of a design that particularly interests you, pull yourself up short and say, "It's obvious that I'm having fun. Is any of this making sense to you?" Questions create breathing space in a discussion and allow architects to redirect their remarks to keep the client's interest.

One concern about asking questions is that doing so will make the architect seem weak or tentative, but this is almost never the case. Although asking questions requires a certain level of humility, doing so shows respect for a client's views by inviting him or her into the discussion. Many of the best teachers ask questions of their students, even teachers with vastly superior knowledge. Through the use of questions, teachers engage their students' minds in a discussion. Like the philosopher Socrates, skilled inquisitors can steer a conversation in any direction they want by the questions they ask.

A third objection expresses a basic fear: "What if I ask questions and no one answers? I'm supposed to be making a *presentation*—the panel is there to hear me talk. They don't want to hear themselves talk. What if they simply don't respond?" This fear, as often as it is raised, rarely becomes a reality. All that is needed to get a quiet client to respond to questions is patience. Wait a moment, restate the question, then wait another moment. Eventually someone will break the ice, and more comments will follow.

Crossing Cultural Barriers

As the United States becomes increasingly multicultural, so do architects' clients. It is obvious that the makeup of building committees, architect selection panels, zoning boards, and city councils is far more diverse today than in years past. As a result, it is important for architects to recognize, respect, and be sensitive to cultural differences when communicating with clients and other groups involved in their work.

First—and this should go without saying—avoid potentially offensive jokes or comments altogether. Racial, ethnic, or religious humor has no place in professional communications, no matter how informal.

More to the point, architects should take cultural differences into account as they make presentations. Are all members of the building committee fluent in English? If not, what adjustments should be made to reach them? Are there persons with disabilities needing some type of accommodation? Did everyone in the audience attend college? Considering such questions will help you gear your presentation to the cultural atmosphere of the meeting.

The most important cultural accommodation you can make is to be aware that there will be cultural differences. Following are additional suggestions for addressing such differences.

Communicating with speakers of other languages. One advantage of foreign travel is the empathy it creates for being inexpert in the local language. When communicating with clients or others for whom English is an acquired skill, it may help to remember how you have felt in a non-English-speaking country. Without being patronizing (speaking too loudly, for instance), moderate the pace of conversation to allow listeners less comfortable with English to follow along. Avoid using lofty vocabulary words (e.g., *orientation*) when a plainer expression (such as *facing north*) will suffice. Stopping frequently to ask questions would be helpful as well.

Nonverbal communication. Sometimes nonverbal communication reveals more than is intended. Do you know when to present a business card with one hand and when to use two (as opposed to the American style of flipping it across the conference table like a winning hole card)? Do you understand cross-cultural protocols for handshakes, introductions, and seating locations? These matters are important in dealing with clients of other cultural backgrounds. Remember to be sensitive to nonverbal cues when communicating across cultural boundaries, and take time to do the research that will help prevent a *faux pas.*

Clothing issues. As American business attire veers perennially toward greater casualness, architects should be aware that many cultures (including some American subcultures) view appropriate attire as important. While polo shirts and cotton pants may suffice for many business encounters in the United States, "business attire" often has an entirely different meaning abroad, to foreign clients inside the United States, and even to some American clients whose cultural norms are not in the mainstream. Be aware of cultural expectations, and dress accordingly.

Personal space and other cultural taboos. In dealing with clients from different cultural backgrounds, it is important to avoid actions that are simply unacceptable. For example, failing to reciprocate an "air kiss" or using the left hand may seem innocent to Americans, but these are, in some cultural contexts, major gaffes that can start interactions on a negative footing. Another common cultural difference is the distance deemed appropriate for personal communication. More formal cultures tend to communicate at greater distances as an indication of rank and respect. Other cultures are more comfortable with intimate conversation, and "rubbing shoulders" with the client may be more literal than Americans expect. If you misunderstand your clients' expectations about personal space, you risk being seen as either obnoxious or aloof. To avoid running afoul of these and other cultural taboos, do your homework before dealing with clients from a different culture.

Avoiding jargon and "tech speak." One of the largest barriers in communicating with clients is "architect-ese"—the language of academic architectural criticism. Too easily picked up from lectures, critiques, or professional journals, this transgression is the inverse of "learning a client's language." It's expecting a client to learn the architect's language.

For example, if an architect discusses "the dialectical use of materiality to enhance the phenomenology of the space" during a presentation, clients may wonder if the

This [letter] would not be so long had I but the leisure to make it shorter.

—Blaise Pascal

Although it is tempting to think of e-mail as a conversational medium, it is a type of written communication and thus the basic rules of written communication apply. Because e-mail is a rapid and seemingly informal medium, a few special rules are worth pointing out:

- Spelling counts. Just because you are responding to a client from a handheld device in an airport does not mean you don't have to correctly spell—or punctuate—your messages. Every message is a reflection of your firm's commitment to quality.
- Context matters. Because e-mail "threads" can be read sequentially from the bottom up, it is tempting to write telegraphic responses like "No problem," or "I agree." While acceptable for internal communications, do your clients the favor of at least restating the question in an e-mail response.
- Don't yell. Typing in all capital letters comes across as shouting.
- Put your name on your paper. It's a good idea to include an automatic signature with basic contact information in every e-mail sent. This allows the recipient to reach you in other ways, if necessary.
- It's on the record. E-mail correspondence is always part of a project's written documentation, and it is acceptable as evidence in court. Architects should bear this in mind before firing off an ill-considered response to a client or a contractor. "Recalling" an inappropriate message does not work; it may still have been received and saved by the recipient. In addition, the firm should retain copies of all work-related e-mail messages and have a method for retrieving them.
- It represents your firm. It bears repeating that e-mail is written communication, despite its apparent informality. Any opinion you express, statements of fact you assert, or project details you clarify are a fixed expression of your professional thought. Rules for more formal, hard-copy written communications apply. The same principle applies for jokes or Internet links architects might forward to clients. A good question to ask before sending an e-mail is, "Would I put this on company letterhead and mail it to my client?"

goal is to inform them or to impress them with an obscurity (and by implication, profundity) of thought. If your goal is truly to inform rather than impress, using obtuse vocabulary is certainly not the way to do it. Avoiding jargon is even more important when a client has a different cultural background.

Using acronyms (such as HVAC for heating, ventilating, and air conditioning) is another barrier to clear communications. Although using acronyms saves time and effort when architects communicate with similarly trained professionals, they can be a constant source of frustration for clients. Most clients will not stop an architect in mid-sentence and ask him or her to explain an acronym, but the humiliation of not being in the know can have a lasting negative effect.

It is not difficult to talk about design in clear, unornamented English. Just speak plainly, using short sentences, and get to the point. Architects should also use common vocabulary and explain any technical terms necessary to present a project. When you can trust yourself (and your work) enough not to lean on obscure rhetoric to describe it, your communication with clients will improve.

WRITTEN COMMUNICATION

Architects often do not excel at written communication. Perhaps because of their graphic and spatial reasoning skills, architects can find stringing words together into a coherent sentence a daunting task.

Given the opportunity to review other firms' literature, architects will likely be surprised by the sameness in the written communications. The carefully crafted words of your own promotional materials may be echoed in the marketing materials of others. You may also be surprised by numerous grammatical and spelling errors, so visible in others' work but so hard to spot in your own.

Fortunately, good professional writing doesn't require brilliant feats of creativity. In fact, it often is the desire to insert creativity where it does not belong that is the greatest problem. Leave it to novelists to reinvent the English language.

Keep It Simple

In their classic book *The Elements of Style*, authors E. B. White and William Strunk Jr. recommend a prose style that is simple, elegant, and to the point. Architects would do well to follow their advice in most professional communications. Do not mistake convoluted prose for deep thought. If the purpose of written communication is to communicate rather than to dazzle or impress, it is best to write with economy and simplicity. A few simple rules for elegant writing follow.

Trim your train of thought. Run-on sentences are a common problem in architectural prose, even in published writing. It is much easier to write punchy, captivating prose when thoughts don't ramble on for 50 or 70 words.

Deliver just the facts. In most professional communications, it is not necessary to embellish a point beyond the facts. In fact, such embellishment can seem self-serving or patronizing.

Leash your word power. It is one thing to understand long, difficult words; it is quite another to inflict them on other people. If your goal is to communicate simple ideas effectively, use commonly understood words.

Give the reader a break. It is possible to write a coherent paragraph that spans several pages, but this doesn't mean that you should. Look at a newspaper: Rare is the paragraph that contains more than one or two sentences. Chopping text into smaller chunks makes it easier for the reader—your client—to digest.

Use vivid language. Most architects use the same dry, professional prose to cover every topic from initial contacts to a final punch list. Although it is possible to overdo it, make an effort to find more lively ways to express your thoughts. For example, *cut* may work better than *reduce*, and *show* can replace *indicate*. Use active instead of passive voice (e.g., "we designed" instead of "was designed by our firm"). Architects need not deviate from the goal of sticking to the facts to make their writing more vivid, and hence, memorable.

Avoid Jargon

As mentioned above, no one appreciates being spoken to in a foreign language. For many clients, the language that architects use to describe their work seems foreign. As with oral presentations, architects should avoid using jargon in written communications with their clients. If an architecture firm's written materials contain words such as *tectonic* and *morphology*, the firm has a jargon problem.

Jargon can fall into several categories. It's easy to identify (and make fun of) the obtuse academic jargon common in the design press. But other types of jargon can be just as bad. Consider these examples:

> We architects demand clarity and rigor in our designs. But we ignore them in our writing as we massacre syntax, chop-shop metaphor, and reach for exactly the wrong polysyllabic word.
>
> —Robert Campbell, FAIA

Technical jargon. Does your client know what "eefiss" is? Project architects and contractors frequently toss around this word, which has become a common pronunciation for the acronym EIFS (exterior insulation and finish systems). Don't use such shorthand unless you are certain your client understands it.

Process jargon. Process terminology is another source of obscure abbreviations. Rare is the architect who actually spells out "design development" instead of writing "DD." More to the point, clients may not be familiar with the term "design development" at all, let alone its abbreviation. Acquainting clients with such commonly used process terminology can enhance communications.

Academic jargon. Architects may use academic jargon in an attempt to relate their work to books and magazines about architecture. Almost comical in its obscurity, academic jargon includes such words as *Miesian* and *Corbusian*, *phenomenology*, and *deconstructivism*, as well as obscure references such as *Robie-esque* or *Piranesian*. Unless you are writing a thesis, avoid this type of jargon; it will not usefully address your client's space needs.

Avoid Puffery

Architects who use puffery in written communications can also confound their clients. Puffery refers to the liberties an advertiser takes in describing a product to make it irresistible to consumers. Puffery is easily detectable because it makes vague claims that cannot be substantiated, such as "Best in town!" "Low, low prices!" or "Nothing else like it!"

While architectural puffery may be less shrill, it is no less annoying to clients. This is especially true when, for example, clients wading through their ninth or tenth written proposal read yet another claim to be "uniquely responsive to client needs." If all the architects vying for a project are "uniquely responsive," then what is unique about that?

A better approach to marketing communications is to write about the most distinctive areas of an architecture practice in clear, concise prose. For example, if your firm has won a number of design awards, cite the actual awards instead of a vague phrase such as "commitment to design excellence expressed in our many award-winning projects." To highlight a firm's technical skills, cite its low incidence of change orders (using an actual number or percentage), rather than mentioning a "commitment to quality documentation." If you believe your firm's design process is unusual, state what makes it so, rather than claiming "clients love our collaborative approach to design." Puffery is not always untrue, but it sounds untrue to cynical clients and, as such, it wastes their time and your effort.

RULES TO REMEMBER

This article has dealt briefly with four principal skills integral to good communication with clients: learning a client's language, listening to clients, speaking with clients, and writing for clients. These same skills are applicable and useful in all professional communications. In summary, here are some important principles to keep in mind.

Challenge Your Assumptions

Every client approaches interactions with architects with a different set of assumptions. One of the most effective communication tools architects can use is to constantly challenge their assumptions about what the client knows, what the client expects from the architect or firm, and what the client desires for the project.

Consistently, client surveys show that the goals clients and architects have for construction projects are seldom in perfect alignment. Architects may view each new commission as an opportunity for peer awards or publication. Although clients may have similar aspirations, more often they do not. Rather, they are focused on the practical goals of meeting the budget, finishing on time, and getting a certain quantity and quality of useful space.

Because architects and their clients often enter into projects with different expectations and assumptions, miscommunication is common. One way to counteract this is for architects to spend time with their clients, clarifying expectations early in the relationship. Architects should keep in mind their client's frame of reference, and how it resembles (and differs from) their own, throughout project delivery. This awareness will facilitate communications that flow from a shared understanding rather than divergent goals.

Keep an Empathetic Perspective

Another essential rule for effective client communication is viewing relationships with clients from an empathetic perspective. This means learning to see the world from the perspective of the client. An architect may not agree with a client's worldview, but it is not necessary to endorse the client's view to understand it. When designing libraries, it helps if an architect thinks like a librarian, or at least understands how librarians think. The purpose of viewing projects with empathy is to build a mutual understanding that will result in successful communications and ultimately in a successful project.

It is often said that architects (and other professionals) who reach the top of their profession are not the most skilled practitioners but rather the best communicators. Aspiring to be a successful communicator may not position you to win the Pritzker Prize. However, honing your communication skills with the same intensity you bring to improving your design and technical skills can help you be more effective in all aspects of practice.

For More Information

The following books address the communication elements of writing, listening, and giving presentations. *Writing for Design Professionals*, second edition (W. W. Norton, 2006), by Stephen A. Kliment, discusses how to master the complexities of effective writing in design practice, with a focus on proposals, letters, brochures, portfolios, reports, presentations, and job applications. Madelyn Burley-Allen's *Listening: The Forgotten Skill* (Wiley, 1995) is a guide to learning the techniques for being an effective listener. In *Architect's Essentials of Presentation Skills* (Wiley, 2002), David Greusel covers all aspects of making effective oral presentations.

1.9 Intern Development

P rior to taking the registration exam required to become a licensed architect, young architects must participate in a continuing education program while they are working under the supervision of a licensed architect. While there is considerable variety in the Intern Development Program (IDP), the primary goal of these programs is to give a young architectural graduate the full range of basic skills necessary to practice architecture.

Harry M. Falconer, Jr. AIA, NCARB, and Catherine Berg

Completing a period of professional internship is essential to an architect's development—and is an important component of the licensure process. Gaining practical experience under the guidance of experienced professionals is invaluable to aspiring architects and prepares them for independent practice.

The Experience Component of Licensure

Only individuals who are licensed by one of the 54 architectural registration boards may call themselves architects.

Architects are responsible for the health, safety, and welfare of the people who live or work in the buildings and environments they design. It is because of this significant responsibility that an individual must be licensed in order to practice architecture or use the title of architect. Licensure signifies to the public that an individual has completed the education, experience, and examination necessary to practice architecture.

Harry M. Falconer Jr. is director of experience + education for the National Council of Architectural Registration Boards (NCARB). He joined the Council in 2006 and assumed his current position in 2012. He is licensed to practice in Virginia and holds the NCARB Certificate. Catherine Berg currently works in the Internal Communications department at Latham & Watkins and she is the former senior writer of the Communications Directorate for NCARB.

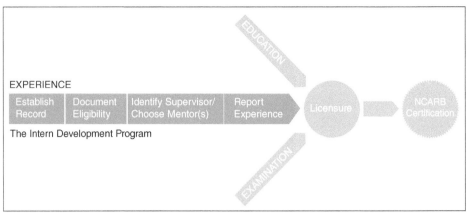

Kenji Bohlin, NCARB

FIGURE 1.16 **Path to Licensure: Experience Requirement**

Gaining experience in the profession is an essential step on the path to become an architect (see Figure 1.16). It is a key component of licensure and offers an important opportunity to develop the knowledge and practical skills necessary to practice architecture.

WHO IS AN INTERN?

The term "intern" refers to any individual in the process of satisfying a registration board's experience requirement. This includes anyone not registered to practice architecture in a U.S. jurisdiction, graduates from professional degree programs accredited by the National Architectural Accrediting Board (NAAB), architecture students who acquire acceptable experience prior to graduation, and other qualified individuals identified by a registration board.

▶ "Regulation of Professional Practice" and the backgrounders on the Architect Registration Examination and NCARB Certification further discuss the process of achieving licensure.

The Intern Development Program

Through the Intern Development Program (IDP), interns learn about the daily realities of architecture practice, acquire comprehensive experience in basic practice areas, explore specialized areas of practice, develop professional judgment, and refine their career goals.

Upon completion of the program, an intern should essentially be able to complete the design of a building from start to finish and manage the project through all phases, from programming to project closeout. This means having the ability to fulfill tasks such as performing site analysis, establishing project cost and feasibility, preparing schematic design documents, applying sustainable design principles, performing code analysis, and preparing construction documents. At the completion of the IDP process, interns should be able to demonstrate knowledge and skills in a wide range of areas, such as basic engineering principles, site design, constructability, and contract negotiation. These are just some of the many tasks and knowledge/skills that the IDP identifies as essential for the independent practice of architecture as a licensed professional.

Many Opportunities to Earn Experience

The IDP is designed with both rigor and flexibility in mind, identifying the experience interns will need and providing a range of opportunities to earn the required experience. It's the nature of the profession that no two interns' experiences will be exactly alike; however, upon completion of the IDP, all interns should possess the knowledge and skills required for the independent practice of architecture as a licensed professional.

Learning Firsthand from Architects

All interns must spend a period of their experience in an architecture firm, working under the supervision of an architect. Learning the practice of architecture directly from architects is integral to the development of emerging professionals.

The collaborative and mentoring relationship between intern and supervisor provides a structured environment for making the transition from school to the profession. Working in a firm under an experienced architect gives interns a grounding in the

PATH TO LICENSURE

Along the path to licensure, there are a number of choices available to aspiring architects—from selecting a professional degree program, to determining how and where to fulfill internship requirements, to deciding when to take the examination and where to seek initial licensure. Each of the key components of licensure—education, experience, and examination—plays a critical role in an architect's development, and proactively planning for how to satisfy requirements is an important way to take charge of one's career and make the most of each experience along the way.

The architectural registration board in each jurisdiction controls licensure and determines the requirements for initial and reciprocal registration in that jurisdiction. Reciprocity is when a registered architect in one jurisdiction applies for registration in another jurisdiction by presenting documentation that he or she meets that jurisdiction's registration requirements. Checking with an individual board is the best way to verify current requirements.

EDUCATION

In most jurisdictions, earning a professional degree from a program accredited by the National Architectural Accrediting Board (NAAB) is the most accepted way—and often the only way—to satisfy the education requirement for licensure.

EXPERIENCE

All registration boards require a minimum period of internship in order to fulfill experience requirements for licensure. The Intern Development Program is required in most jurisdictions and identifies the experience needed for the independent practice of architecture.

EXAMINATION

The Architect Registration Examination® (ARE®) is required in all 54 U.S. jurisdictions and assesses whether a candidate has the knowledge, skills, and ability required for competent practice upon initial licensure. The ARE evaluates the skills that are necessary for protecting the public health, safety, and welfare.

A jurisdiction's architectural registration board ultimately determines whether a candidate has met the requirements for licensure. In addition to the education, experience, and examination requirements, there may be other jurisdictional requirements that must be met in order to complete the licensure process.

Once architects have achieved licensure, they may earn NCARB certification, which helps facilitate reciprocal registration in other jurisdictions.

fundamentals, opportunities to exercise critical thinking, and the chance to experience firsthand how the business of architecture works.

Interns looking to gain international experience may also earn a portion of their IDP experience working abroad for an architecture firm, under the supervision of an architect who is credentialed by a foreign authority.

Beyond Traditional Practice

Architects can be found in a wide range of professional environments where their skill sets are in demand. In recognition of the opportunities to go beyond traditional practice, there are additional professional settings in which interns can earn experience:

- Working under registered professionals in related professions, such as landscape architecture or engineering
- Working under the direct supervision of a licensed architect in an organization that's not engaged in the practice of architecture, such as a facilities management company

Academic Internships

Interns also earn IDP credit through qualifying academic internships, giving them a jump-start in fulfilling program requirements while still in school. Any internship that is integrated into an academic program, whether it be as a requirement or as an elective, is considered an academic internship.

The IDP specifies a variety of ways interns can earn experience outside of a traditional setting.

Taking advantage of options to earn supplemental experience demonstrates an intern's initiative and proactive approach to augmenting his or her professional development. Some activities can be completed under the supervision of mentors, providing an invaluable opportunity to deepen relationships and to broaden professional networks. Supplemental experiences like pro bono Leadership and Service, and service to Community-based Design Centers, offer interns the opportunity to engage the greater community. In addition, the work that results from experiences such as design competitions can contribute toward the intern's professional portfolio.

Supplemental experience options include interactive, online, and self-directed activities. Unless otherwise noted, nearly all of these experiences can be completed whether or not the intern is employed, and depending on the opportunity, will earn credit for either core or elective hours.

INTERACTIVE EXPERIENCE

- *Leadership and service.* Interns need to earn a minimum number of hours through pro bono leadership and service in support of an organized activity or a specific organization. The experience may be design industry–related (e.g., Habitat for Humanity); education-related (e.g., English for Speakers of Other Languages [ESOL] teacher, critic at design review); related to strengthening of the community (e.g., soup kitchens, civic participation); or related to a regulatory or professional organization (e.g., volunteering for the AIA or the Green Building Certification Institute).
- *Site visit with mentor.* Interns can earn core hours by visiting construction sites with their mentors. Site visits allow interns to see the progress of a job over time and engage in a dialogue with their mentors. The experience is meant to be interactive, with opportunities to discuss how issues related to the specific project were resolved and why particular decisions were made.
- *Community-based design center or collaborative.* Interns can earn core hours in most IDP experience areas for volunteer service in support of a preapproved charitable organization. The work must be in support of "building" or "planning" projects. NCARB provides a list on its website of organizations it currently recognizes.
- *Design competitions.* Under the supervision of a mentor, interns can earn core hours for completion and submission of a design competition entry for a "building" or "planning" project. Entering design

competitions creates regular opportunities for the intern and mentor to interact, and offers a great way to earn core IDP hours across all related IDP experience areas.
- *Teaching or research employment.* Elective hours may be earned through teaching or research employment in a NAAB-accredited program under the direct supervision of a person experienced in the activity.
- *Design- or construction-related employment.* Under the direct supervision of a person experienced in the activity (e.g., design of interior space; engaging in building construction; working for a general contractor), interns can earn credit for employment in design- or construction-related activities.

ONLINE EXPERIENCE

- *Emerging Professional's Companion (EPC) activities.* The EPC was jointly developed by the AIA and NCARB and provides free, Web-based experience opportunities outside of the studio or work environment. EPC chapters are aligned with IDP experience areas and include activities that are identified as qualifying for either core or elective credit.
- NCARB's *Professional Conduct* monograph. Interns can earn core hours by reading NCARB monographs and passing the related quizzes. NCARB monographs are written by experts in their fields and explore topics relevant to architecture practice. Interns can download PDFs of the monographs at no charge through their NCARB Record.

SELF-DIRECTED EXPERIENCE

- *AIA Continuing Education System.* Interns can earn experience by completing AIA-approved continuing education resources and programs. One AIA learning unit equals one IDP elective hour.
- *Green Building Certification Institute (GBCI) LEED AP credential.* Interns can earn elective hours by obtaining the GBCI LEED AP credential (with or without specialization).
- *Construction Specifications Institute (CSI) Certification Programs.* Interns can earn experience for completing any of these CSI certification programs: CSI Certified Construction Documents Technologist; CSI Certified Construction Specifier (CCS); or CSI Certified Construction Contract Administrator.

IDP REQUIREMENTS

The IDP has a set of requirements that all interns must satisfy in order to document completion of the program. The *IDP Guidelines* provide a comprehensive overview of all IDP requirements, including information relevant for those serving as supervisors or mentors for interns.

NCARB Record

Establishing an NCARB Record is essential for documenting the IDP. Throughout an architect's career, the NCARB Record serves as a detailed, verified record of his or her education, experience, and examination used to establish qualification for licensure and certification. Interns interested in earning NCARB certification, which facilitates reciprocal registration, can save money simply by keeping their NCARB Record active while they complete the steps for licensure.

Eligibility

To earn IDP experience, interns must establish an eligibility date, which can be based on either education or experience. In some cases, students may be able to begin documenting IDP experience after high school graduation.

Experience Settings

Interns earn IDP experience hours in "experience settings." The experience setting is defined by the type of organization, the work performed, and who verifies the experience. Interns can earn the required experience across a range of settings, and a number of experience opportunities can be completed whether or not employed.

Supervision

Interns work under the direct supervision of an IDP supervisor who is responsible for verifying the intern's experience. "Direct supervision" can include supervising interns through a mix of personal contact and remote communication; and in certain settings, supervisors need only be licensed in any U.S. jurisdiction (not necessarily where their office is located). In most experience settings, the supervisor must be a licensed architect; however, in certain settings, a professional from another discipline, such as landscape architecture, engineering, or construction, may act as an IDP supervisor.

Experience Categories and Areas

The required experience categories and areas in which an intern must gain experience have been derived from the NCARB Practice Analysis of Architecture. Each experience area is weighted based on its importance to the independent practice of architecture. The distribution of hourly requirements across the experience areas is designed to align the IDP with current practice.

Reporting

Interns report their experience hours through an online reporting system. To help facilitate more accurate reporting, interns are required to submit their experience in reporting periods of no longer than six months, and to file the reports within two months of completing the reporting period. Reporting at regular intervals helps both the intern and the supervisor better plan, track, and discuss the intern's progress through the IDP.

1.10   The Path to Licensure

By Jessica Sheridan, AIA, LEED AP BD+C

In order to practice architecture, and for an individual to be called an architect, there are three milestones that must be met: education, internship, and examination. Although there are commonalities across the United States and the U.S. Territories, it is important to understand that each jurisdiction has different guidelines that a candidate must meet in order to qualify to become a licensed architect.

The most standard path to licensure includes obtaining a professional degree from a school accredited by the National Architectural Accrediting Board (NAAB) or by the Canadian Architectural Certification Board (CACB); then, completing the Intern Development Program (IDP), established by the National Council of Architectural Registration Boards (NCARB); and finally passing all divisions of the Architect Registration Examination (ARE).

Because there are many variables if a candidate decides to pursue a career in architecture with an alternate path—and each jurisdiction differs in their requirements—this discussion will focus mainly on the standard track.

Education

In order to qualify to begin the IDP and ARE process, one must be enrolled in a program that offers a professional degree in architecture. NAAB and CACB both establish criteria to evaluate and maintain standards for architectural education. The curriculum includes general studies, professional studies, and electives. By obtaining a degree in one of these programs, it is ensured that your education has provided you the competency in a range of intellectual, spatial, technical, and interpersonal skills; the understanding of historical, sociocultural, and environmental context of architecture; the ability to solve architectural design problems, including the integration of technical systems and health and safety requirements; and an understanding of architects' roles and responsibilities in society.[1] The three types of degrees that satisfy the education requirement are a Bachelor of Architecture (B.Arch) degree, Master of Architecture (M.Arch) degree, and a Doctor of Architecture (D.Arch) degree.

If you are not attending a NAAB- or CACB-accredited program, or if you are pursuing a nonprofessional degree, you must satisfy equivalent requirements that may be evaluated on a case-by-case basis by the jurisdiction in which you plan to be licensed. If you are attending an international school, NCARB has a service, called Education Evaluation Services for Architects (EESA), to evaluate if your degree meets the standard education requirement. NCARB also has two ways to

Jessica Sheridan, AIA, LEED AP BD+C, is an Architect and Project Manager at Gensler, where she leads accounts for several professional services firms and manages financial and tech company projects worldwide. She served as the Editor-in-Chief of e-Oculus, the American Institute of Architects (AIA) New York Chapter's e-zine, from 2005–2012, and continues to contribute to various architectural publications on a freelance basis. Currently, Sheridan is a New York State Regional Representative on the national AIA Strategic Council. She has served on the NCARB Internship Advisory Committee and ARE 5.0 Case Study Task Force Committee. Sheridan lectures regularly about the architectural licensure process, both at Cornell University and at the Center for Architecture in New York City.

---

[1] National Architectural Accrediting Board. Accessed March 20, 2015. www.naab.org/about/home.

evaluate your experience if you have been working in the field without an accredited degree. The Broadly Experienced Architect (BEA) program allows an individual to demonstrate that their experience in the architectural profession is sufficient to have met the education requirement. Depending on the highest degree level, one must work a prescribed number of years to qualify. In addition, the Broadly Experienced Foreign Architect (BEFA) program allows foreign architects to demonstrate competence in the profession that is sufficient to satisfy the education requirement.

IDP

The Intern Development Program, which is administered by NCARB, was established to provide comprehensive experience to candidates. To enroll in IDP you must maintain an active NCARB record, which involves filling out an application and paying a fee to maintain an active record. Most jurisdictions accept IDP as a means to fulfill the experience requirement, and some require IDP to become a licensed architect; therefore, most candidates maintain an active record of their experience through IDP.

IDP is a program to document experience hours. At the time this chapter is being written, candidates are required to complete a total of 5,600 hours to fully complete IDP. The required hours are spread across a wide range of categories so individuals may understand the full breadth of the profession upon completion. Currently those categories align with the way architects practice, with required hours in Schematic Design; Engineering Systems; Construction Cost; Codes and Regulations; Design Development; Construction Documents; and Material Selection and Specifications. NCARB adjusts the requirements periodically, so it is important that you regularly familiarize yourself with the categories and hourly requirements.

Although all of the hours may be obtained while working under direct supervision of a licensed architect in the United States or Canada, a percentage of IDP hours may be accumulated in other work settings as well. Other settings include working under:

- Direct supervision by a licensed architect in the United States or Canada for an organization not engaged in the practice of architecture
- Direct supervision by an architect not registered in the United States or Canada, practicing architecture outside of the United States or Canada
- Direct supervision by a landscape architect or registered engineer
- Academic internships.[2]

In addition, candidates may obtain some of their experience through alternate opportunities, called Supplemental Experience. These categories include design- or construction-related employment; leadership and service by doing pro bono design-related work; as well as a range of other activities, including design competitions, completing alternate certification programs, and working in community-based design centers. As there are limits to each category, it is important to review requirements in these categories carefully prior to submitting them for record.

To catalog hours, you must complete reports regularly to document your experience. To earn full credit for experience, reports must be submitted within eight months. Reports submitted for experience, more than eight months in the past and up to five years after the submission date, may be accepted for partial value. Any experience more than five years prior to submission will not be able to be submitted. To submit hours NCARB hosts an online reporting program to record your time and have your supervisor approve those hours.

---

[2] National Council of Architectural Registration Boards. Accessed March 20, 2015. www.ncarb.org/Experience-Through-Internships/IDP2-Experience-Settings.aspx.

ARE

The Architect Registration Examination® (ARE®) is intended to help assess candidates on their knowledge, skills, and ability to provide various services required in the practice of architecture.[3] To pass the exam means that you have demonstrated competence to successfully protect the health, safety, and welfare of the public.

Each jurisdiction sets the requirements for exam eligibility, so it is important to understand the requirements of the jurisdiction in which you are obtaining a license. Many jurisdictions allow ARE/IDP concurrency—in other words, candidates may sit for the exam while in the process of completing the IDP experience requirements. However, some jurisdictions require candidates to fully complete the experience requirement prior to sitting for the exam.

When ready to start taking the exam, you must submit an application to the jurisdiction in which you wish to become licensed and pay a fee to receive an Authorization to Test letter. If you maintain an active NCARB record (which includes a profile, IDP progress report, and degree of education) you may request to transmit it to your jurisdiction for review and approval.

The exam itself consists of several divisions that cover a range of topics. Candidates schedule to sit for each division separately. There is a fee to take each division of the exam, and different exam centers that administer each division. In order to pass the full ARE, you must pass all divisions.

NCARB develops the exam content and updates the exam every six to ten years. At the time of this publishing it is in the process of transitioning from ARE version 4.0 to 5.0.

Version 4.0 is a seven-division exam that is topic-based:

- Construction Documents & Services
- Programming, Planning & Practice
- Site Planning & Design
- Building Design & Construction Systems
- Structural Systems
- Building Systems
- Schematic Design

The exam consists of multiple choice, fill-in-the-blank, and check-all-that-apply questions, as well as graphic vignettes. Each division has a different proportion of both, so in addition to becoming familiar with the content it is important to understand the format of each division, as well. ARE 4.0 will be offered through June of 2018.

Version 5.0 is a six-division exam that aligns with the way architects practice:

- Practice Management
- Project Management
- Programming & Analysis
- Project Planning & Design
- Project Development & Documentation
- Construction & Evaluation

This exam integrates graphics throughout the exam, in addition to the more traditional testing questions. Case studies are also introduced, providing scenarios about which candidates must evaluate and answer a series of questions. ARE 5.0 is expected to launch in late 2016.

Once candidates pass their first division, all divisions must be passed within five years. If a candidate is unable to pass all divisions within the five years, the candidate must retake any of the divisions that fall outside of that timeframe. This is called the "rolling clock."

---

[3] National Council of Architectural Registration Boards. Accessed March 20, 2015. www.ncarb.org/ARE .aspx.

In addition to the ARE exam, some jurisdictions require supplemental exams. It is important to make arrangements to complete any additional requirement(s) directly with the jurisdiction in which you plan to be licensed.

Licensed Architect Status

Upon successful completion of the education, internship, examination, and any other jurisdiction-specific requirements, you qualify to be a licensed architect. Each jurisdiction is different in processing requirements, but once your information is fully processed you may call yourself a Registered Architect in that jurisdiction.

After you have established your registration, most jurisdictions have requirements for you to maintain your license. These requirements may include continuing education hours, and a set frequency to renew and keep your license active.

If you want to practice architecture outside of the jurisdiction in which you are licensed, you will need to apply for reciprocity. You will need to become familiar with the requirements in that jurisdiction and ensure that you satisfy all of those requirements, as well. Often there is a fee to apply in addition to filling out an application. If you maintain an active NCARB Record, NCARB offers a Certificate to help facilitate reciprocal registration as an option to help maneuver through the system.

Maintaining an architectural license means that you are legally empowered to practice architecture. You may call yourself an architect and contract to provide architectural services. You may seal, stamp, and sign your own drawings for submission to local jurisdictions. Also, you may own, or take ownership of, an architecture firm.

BACKGROUNDER

ARCHITECT REGISTRATION EXAMINATION® (ARE®)

Erica J. Brown, AIA, NCARB

The Architect Registration Examination® (ARE®) assesses a candidate's knowledge, skills, and abilities to perform the various services required for the independent practice of architecture.

Erica J. Brown is director of the Architect Registration Examination for the National Council of Architectural Registration Boards (NCARB). She oversees the development, administration, and management of all divisions of the exam. She is licensed to practice architecture in Indiana and holds the NCARB Certificate.

Each U.S. jurisdiction sets its own requirements for initial registration. In addition to fulfilling education and experience requirements, a candidate must meet his or her jurisdiction's examination requirement (see Figure 1.17). All 54 U.S. jurisdictions require the completion of the Architect Registration Examination to satisfy their examination requirement.

Developed and administered by the National Council of Architectural Registration Boards, the ARE concentrates on those skills necessary for protecting the public health, safety, and welfare. Figure 1.17 illustrates the ARE process on the path to licensure.

HISTORY OF ARCHITECTURE EXAMINATION

Licensure examinations weren't always standardized across states and jurisdictions. Previously, each registration board prepared its own test specifications and questions, and set its own passing standards. Because the examination process varied from jurisdiction to jurisdiction, an effective system for reciprocal licensure was not possible.

To address this need for standardization, NCARB worked with its Member Boards to create the first nationally recognized exam for architects in 1965, and in the ensuing years, continued to make significant improvements to the exam. In 1997, after extensive research and development, all exam divisions were delivered and scored by computer, making the ARE more accessible to candidates and providing the flexibility to test year-round. By establishing a single examination that all jurisdictions rely on, the process for achieving reciprocity was streamlined.

It is worth noting that in addition to the ARE, some Boards require candidates to pass jurisdiction-specific, supplemental exams in order to satisfy the examination requirement for licensure.

EXAMINATION OVERVIEW

The ARE is developed and regularly reviewed and validated by subject–matter–expert architects, and conforms to standards

(continued)

established by national testing organizations. A strong research and development culture drives the ARE, with significant annual investments being made by NCARB into its continual development and evolution. In all cases, the process is rigorous, time-consuming, and necessary to ensure the ARE remains legally defensible and psychometrically valid.

Every five to seven years, NCARB conducts a practice analysis of architecture by surveying the profession to identify the tasks and knowledge/skills necessary for independent practice. Findings from the practice analysis serve as the basis for updating the ARE test specification.

Any modifications to the exam are made after deliberate, studied, and controlled evaluation. Exam updates are made for two essential reasons: to ensure questions reflect current architectural practice and to use technology that accurately assesses the ability of candidates to practice architecture independently.

As noted in the previous section, the exam is in a continual state of development. For the most current information about the ARE, contact NCARB or visit its website.

Format and Focus of the Examination

In addition to testing for competence in specific subject areas, NCARB is aware of the responsibilities an architect may have for coordinating the activities of others involved in the design/construction process. The ARE attempts to determine a candidate's qualifications not only in performing measurable tasks, but also in exercising the skills and judgment of a generalist working with numerous specialists. In short, the objective of the exam is to reflect the practice of architecture as an integrated whole.

The examination includes seven divisions:

- Programming, Planning & Practice
- Site Planning & Design
- Building Design & Construction Systems
- Schematic Design
- Structural Systems
- Building Systems
- Construction Documents & Services

Six of the seven divisions contain a section of multiple-choice items and a separate section including one or more graphic vignettes, which are problems used to assess candidates' knowledge, skills, and abilities in the different facets of architectural practice, such as site zoning and structural layout. One division contains only graphic vignettes. It is recommended that candidates use the free practice software provided by NCARB to become familiar with the software interface used for the graphic vignettes in the examination.

Eligibility

While all jurisdictions require the ARE to satisfy their licensure examination requirement, candidates will want to understand and stay informed of the requirements specific to the jurisdiction where they plan to seek initial licensure. For example, some states allow concurrent completion of the Intern Development Program (IDP) and the ARE, so candidates should contact the individual registration board to verify when they can become eligible to begin testing.

Candidates are responsible for maintaining their eligibility status. Once made eligible to take the exam, candidates must take at least one division every five years in order to maintain their eligibility to test.

Exam Administration

Candidates may take the exam divisions in the order of their choosing and must pass all divisions to complete the ARE. The ARE is administered exclusively on computers through a network of approximately 300 test centers across the United States, its territories, and Canada.

Rolling Clock

Under the terms of NCARB's rolling clock policy, candidates must pass all divisions within five years; a passing grade for any division of the ARE will be valid for five years, after which time the division (or any equivalents) must be retaken unless all divisions have been passed. Candidates should also be aware that there is a mandatory six-month waiting period before one can retake a failed division of the exam; candidates may sit for other exam divisions during this waiting period. In addition to NCARB's rolling clock policy, jurisdictions may have their own retake limit/exam validity time frame, so candidates should contact their jurisdiction directly to determine their exam status under the jurisdiction's rules and policies.

Resources

NCARB provides a number of resources, accessible on its website, to help candidates plan and prepare to take the ARE; however, it is ultimately the candidate's responsibility to acquire the knowledge and skills necessary to demonstrate competency. The NCARB *ARE Guidelines* are essential reading for anyone preparing for the exam. They include further detail on the exam, the rolling clock policy, exam eligibility information, and the steps to take and complete the ARE. NCARB also offers free Exam Guides and Practice Programs to help candidates study and practice for each division of the exam.

Preparation Tips

Planning for the ARE is critical. There are a number of steps candidates can take to prepare for the examination:

- Take time to review and understand the requirements for the jurisdiction where seeking initial licensure. If in doubt, contact the jurisdiction directly to get clarification on its requirements.

- Review the *ARE Guidelines* to understand eligibility rules and other requirements.
- Be proactive, and create a plan for taking the exam: Determine when and where you are eligible to sit for it, in what order to take the exam divisions, and how to prepare.
- Use the exam guides and practice programs provided by NCARB. Additional references are listed in the back of the exam guides—many of these resources include professional publications that are commonly available in libraries and offices.

- Form a study group with other candidates, either through work or locally. Regional AIA chapters may be able to connect candidates with one another as well.
- Discuss plans with supervisors or mentors for preparing and taking the exam.
- Take advantage of the resources, support, and benefits firms may offer interns taking the exam.

For More Information

Architect Registration Examination: www.ncarb.org/ARE.aspx
Registration requirements for each U.S. jurisdiction: www.ncarb.org

1.11 Serving Your Community and Participation in Professional Development Organizations

As a young architect becomes engaged in a career, he or she will find many opportunities—outside their place of employment—to use their training and skills to assist their communities and/or their profession. While the primary motivation should be to serve, such service can also help build a professional's career, enhance his or her reputation, and expand a network of contacts.

SERVING YOUR COMMUNITY

Bradford Perkins, FAIA

It is common for architects to volunteer their time in a wide variety of important ways. Some of the most common include:

- Local planning, design review, zoning, landmarks and other land use boards
  - Except in larger communities, land use and other review boards are staffed by volunteers. Most seek participation by volunteers with architectural training.
- Building committees
  - Many civic, not-for-profit and religious organizations form building committees to strengthen their ability to manage their often-intermittent building programs.
- Building and land use code development and review
  - Many architects participate in committees created to draft, review, or edit new or existing codes and regulations.
- Disaster recovery efforts
  - Disaster recovery teams—helping communities recover from floods, hurricanes, earthquakes, and other natural disasters—often need volunteers with technical skills to help guide the recovery efforts.
- Citizen engagement
  - Sometimes the involvement may be in the form of participating in public hearings on projects, legislation, and public policy where architectural training and experience can help inform the debate.
- Public design education
  - A growing number of organizations ranging from AIA Chapters to design-focused educational entities, such as the Chicago Architectural Foundation and

New York's Municipal Arts Society, sponsor exhibits, lectures, tours, awards programs, and other public services to promote a greater understanding and appreciation of architecture and urban design to the general public.

- Architectural education
  - Many architects have paid teaching appointments but probably an even greater number volunteer their time to help teach architecture in elementary and secondary schools as well as in formal college-level programs.

1.12 Participating in Professional Organizations

Andrea S. Rutledge, SDA, CAE

Participating in professional organizations can help architects enrich their careers and contribute to the advancement of the profession.

It seems as though there is an association for everything. Nearly every profession, vocation, avocation, or trade has a society or association organized to meet the specific needs of its members, and the United States has the most fully developed association sector in the world. Even Garrison Keillor spoofed our national proclivity for forming associations, inventing the American Duct Tape Council as a fictitious sponsor of his radio show, *A Prairie Home Companion.*

GETTING INVOLVED

Architects may choose to belong to several organizations related to their careers, from a broadly focused organization such as the AIA to groups with a narrower focus such as the Construction Specifications Institute, International Facility Management Association, American College of Healthcare Architects, U.S. Green Building Council, or Design-Build Institute of America. The decision about which organizations to join is personal; each architect must determine which groups will provide the information most likely to advance his or her professional life. One strategy is to begin by joining just one organization and later add memberships in others as your experience broadens and your career matures.

For a list of professional and related trade organizations in the design and construction industry, Allied Professional Organizations are introduced in the following pages of this chapter.

The first step to involvement is to join the organization. Nearly all professional organizations have membership criteria, forms, and other materials available on their websites. Some groups permit individuals to join directly from the website; others require additional information and original signatures on the application form.

Members of professional societies of all sorts generally get more from their membership when they become involved in the activities of the organization, whether it is at the national, state, or local level.

For More Information

Information about opportunities to participate in the AIA at national, regional, and local levels can be found on the AIA website at www.aia.org. *AIA Public Policies and Position Statements* and the *AIA Member Benefits Guide*, updated annually, are available in PDF at www.aia.org.

Andrea Rutledge, executive director of the National Architectural Board in Washington, D.C., was formerly managing director, Alliances, at the AIA.

The AIA was formed, according to its bylaws, to "organize and unite in fellowship the members of the architectural profession of the United States of America; to promote the aesthetic, scientific, and practical efficiency of the profession; to advance the science and art of planning and building by advancing the standards of architectural education, training, and practice; to coordinate the building industry and the profession of architecture to ensure the advancement of living standards through their improved environment; and to make the profession of ever-increasing service to society." The AIA achieves a contemporary expression of its historical vision and mission through its services, products, and support of the architectural profession.

MEMBER PARTICIPATION

Today, the AIA has more than 83,000 members worldwide in several membership categories, including Architect, Associate, International Associate, Emeritus, and Allied members. The AIA supports its members in the development of their careers in a creative, constantly evolving profession and provides information that helps them sustain the growth and health of their firms. It also offers some benefits, such as insurance, that support the business of architecture.

AIA members can participate at three levels of membership: national, state, and local. In addition to traditional governance roles (e.g., board member, committee chair, or regional director), members can participate in the AIA through knowledge communities organized by type of practice or special interest (e.g., historic preservation, small practice, building science and performance, and architecture for education) and member affinity groups (e.g., the Young Architects Forum), which are organized to a certain extent by length of time in the profession. Across the AIA, there are many possibilities for participation; for example, opportunities to serve include roles such as the following:

- Chair of the state design awards program
- Regional associate director on the National Associates Committee
- Young Architects Forum regional liaison
- Local AIA component board member
- Member of the national Committee on the Environment advisory group
- State vice president
- Regional treasurer
- National regional director
- College of Fellows bursar

Among the AIA's national leaders are architects whose careers have included decades of service in local, state, and national roles.

AIA PROGRAMS

The Institute routinely researches what services, products, and other opportunities its members find valuable. In particular, the AIA carries out a member needs assessment every six months, polls members on advocacy issues each year, surveys interns every three years, collects and evaluates comprehensive information on firms every three years, and analyzes economic data and the projected impact on architecture and construction each month. From this information, the Institute develops position statements, products, services, programs, and other resources in formats that most closely meet members' expressed needs. Some items are available on the AIA website, while others are in print; still others (especially continuing education) are presented in person. Recognizing that not all products, services, and programs will meet the needs of all members all of the time, the intent is to provide a mix that will meet the needs of most members.

Continuing Education

The AIA offers many education programs at the national, state, and local levels and supports a continuing education system (CES) that serves both members and program providers. AIA/CES provides members with access to programs that enable them to meet the continuing education requirement for AIA membership (18 units per year, of which 8 must be in subjects related to protecting the health, safety, and welfare of the public), as well as state continuing education requirements for licensure. The AIA/CES registered provider program supports learning partnerships with firms, AIA components, and other continuing education providers. In addition, AIA/CES provides a third-party system for recording participation in professional learning activities.

AIA National Convention and Design Exposition

Each year the AIA national convention and expo offers members and others a major educational opportunity. This four-day event features continuing education sessions (seminars, workshops, and tours), networking and socializing events (e.g., regional receptions and alumni gatherings), presentations on significant issues or from well-known architects (e.g., a panel on integrated practice or a presentation by a recent Gold Medal winner), honors and awards presentations, and a trade show. Members can earn all required continuing education units for membership for the year (and for many, state continuing education requirements) while attending the national convention.

(continued)

Knowledge Communities and Knowledge Resources

Members have access to specialized architecture knowledge through the AIA knowledge communities. These groups comprise members who share a common interest in a given area of practice and collaborate to sponsor educational and networking opportunities with like-minded others. More than 20 knowledge communities address a variety of professional interests in different aspects of professional practice. Groups have formed around such issues as international practice, the concerns of emerging professionals, practice management, historic preservation, leadership for architects, and sustainable design and the environment, as well as specific building types (e.g., architecture for education, healthcare architecture, religious architecture, interior architecture, housing, and retail and entertainment architecture).

The AIA also provides knowledge resources to its members through its library and archives, websites, and publishing partnerships. With John Wiley & Sons, the AIA produces the *Architect's Handbook of Professional Practice* and *Architectural Graphic Standards* and supports the publication of other practice titles such as the *Architect's Essential* series. With Taunton Press, the AIA publishes specialized works on residential architecture intended to familiarize the public with the benefits of working with an architect.

Lobbying

The AIA advocates on legislative, regulatory, and related issues of importance to AIA members before federal, state, and local governments and other policy-making bodies. These efforts include lobbying for legislation that either benefits member practices (e.g., tax cuts for small businesses) or advances issues that architects believe are important (reducing the energy consumption of buildings). Advocacy activities take place in Washington before the U.S. Congress on such matters as federal tax credits for sustainable design and historic preservation, health insurance for small businesses, transportation studies, and federal grants to ensure that historic properties damaged by catastrophic storms can be restored. AIA components also lobby for members at the state and local level. This often takes the form of advocacy to prevent encroachment on the title "architect" by other design professionals whose professional qualifications do not meet the standards for architecture education, experience, and examination.

Programs for Emerging Professionals

The AIA supports its younger members as they advance in the profession, encouraging them to complete an internship and the architect registration examination (ARE) process in a timely, rigorous, and respectful manner. To that end, the AIA provides ARE preparation

courses, tools to assist in completing the Intern Development Program (IDP), mentoring information, and the *Emerging Professional's Companion*, an online study tool for earning supplemental IDP credit.

AIA Contract Documents Program

With their 120-year history, AIA Contract Documents are the "gold standard" for design and construction contract documents in the United States. More than 100 contracts and forms have been developed through a consensus process that involves owners, contractors, attorneys, engineers, and others, as well as architects. The documents establish relationships between architects and other parties that protect the interests of both. The AIA continually updates the documents to stay current with trends and practices in the construction industry.

Honors and Awards Programs

The Institute recognizes its members for outstanding work and for service to the profession through a number of different programs, including the College of Fellows, AIA Honors and Awards, and the Gold Medal and Architecture Firm awards.

The AIA College of Fellows honors architect members for outstanding service to the profession over time. Nominations can be made in five categories: design, education, service to the profession, service to the community, and technical advancement of the profession. Fellows are permitted to use the designation "FAIA" after their names on business cards and in professional settings.

In addition to its recognition of the contributions of individuals, the College of Fellows is actively engaged in supporting research in the profession through the Latrobe Prize. Awarded biannually in odd-numbered years, this award is granted to an architect or group of architects working in partnership with scientific and/or academic institutions to develop a specific body of scientific knowledge that will be applicable to architecture practice. Past Latrobe recipients have focused on manufacturing methodologies, neuroscience, and healthcare.

The AIA Honors and Awards Program seeks to recognize the best work in a given year in the categories of Architecture, Interior Architecture, and Regional and Urban Design. Other groups within the Institute recognize excellence in specific project types through juried competitions. For example, the Housing Knowledge Community recognizes excellence in housing design each year and the Committee on the Environment honors designs that meet specific criteria for sustainable design, such as use of recycled products, and other green factors.

The AIA Gold Medal is conferred on an individual architect by the national AIA Board of Directors in recognition of a significant body of work of lasting influence on the theory and practice of architecture. The Architecture Firm Award is the highest honor the AIA can bestow on an architecture firm to recognize the consistent production of distinguished architecture.

MEMBER BENEFITS

Some AIA efforts fall more into the category of general member benefits than programs related to the practice of architecture.

The AIA established the AIA Trust in 1952 as a separate entity to develop, and make available at the greatest possible value, insurance and other benefit programs for members and components of the AIA and to serve as a risk management resource for the practice of architecture. The Trust selects member programs in conjunction with independent consultants to meet high standards of quality, value, financial stability, service, and coverage.

Members can also use the services of the AIA's Affinity partners. These are companies and service providers (e.g., computer sellers, special package delivery services, car rental companies) that have agreed to offer their services to AIA members at a discount. Many sole proprietors and small firms are able to save considerably by taking advantage of these programs.

A CONSORTIUM OF LIKE-MINDED PROFESSIONALS

For AIA members, many of the issues architects face today are similar to those faced when the Institute was founded. Each year, the AIA and its members look for new solutions to "old" problems, as well as emerging ones, and work with each other and their communities to create healthy, secure, and sustainable places to live and work. More information about the AIA can be found at www.aia.org.

In addition to the AIA, there are many other organizations that are relevant to architects. Involvement in one or more may be an important aspect of an architect's career.

PARTIAL LIST OF PROFESSIONAL ORGANIZATIONS SHAPING THE PROFESSION

It would be nearly impossible to list all of the organizations that relate to the profession of architecture; it is also difficult to suggest that some are somehow more important than others. Each organization serves an important cause, advocates for an important issue, or represents a critical constituency and therefore helps shape the profession of architecture. However, there are several that are particularly important to know because they influence the practice of architecture directly.

The Five Collateral Organizations

AIA: The American Institute of Architects

Within the profession of architecture, each of the five collateral organizations plays a complementary role, addressing issues of advocacy, education, licensure, and practice. The five collaterals are: The American Institute of Architects (AIA), the American Institute of Architecture Students (AIAS), the Association of Collegiate Schools of Architecture (ACSA), the National Architectural Accrediting Board (NAAB), and the National Council of Architectural Registration Boards (NCARB).

AIAS: American Institute of Architecture Students

The student-run AIAS serves as the official voice of architecture students in North America, furthering its mission of promoting excellence in architecture education, training, and practice, fostering an appreciation of architecture and related disciplines, enriching communities in a spirit of collaboration, and organizing students and combining efforts to advance the art and science of architecture.

AIAS is divided into four geographic "quads," which serve to facilitate communication between the institution-based chapters and the Board. Current AIAS activities include the AIAS journal *Crit*, the national convention (FORUM), Quad Conferences, the Freedom by Design™ program, as well as numerous activities organized by individual chapters. In addition, representatives from AIAS participate on the National Architectural Accrediting Board's Board of Directors and on the NAAB teams, which visit institutions for accreditation, as well as on the Association of Collegiate Schools of Architecture's Board of Directors, the AIA's Board of Directors, and some NCARB committees.

ACSA: Association of Collegiate Schools of Architecture

With the primary purpose of advancing architecture education through the support of its member schools, faculty, and students, the Association of Collegiate Schools of Architecture represents over 250 schools. Founded in 1912, the ACSA engages in multiple activities, including faculty awards and student competition programs, conferences, and publications such as the *Journal of Architectural Education* and *ACSA News*, as well as developing and supporting studies on issues affecting the architecture profession and architecture education.

NAAB: National Architectural Accrediting Board

The National Architectural Accrediting Board was established in 1940 by the Association of Collegiate Schools of Architecture, the American Institute of Architects, and the National Council of Architectural Registration Boards, eight years after the ACSA abandoned the "standard minima" needed by schools in order to be granted membership.

Today, the NAAB "develops and maintains a system of accreditation in professional architecture education that is responsive to the needs of society and allows institutions with varying resources and circumstances to evolve according to their individual needs." It is the only agency in the United States authorized to accredit professional degree programs in architecture.

The Board of Directors has 14 members: 3 members each from ACSA, AIA, and NCARB, 2 members from AIAS, 2 public Board Members, and 1 Executive Director. Accreditation decisions that are made by the Board rely on school visits performed by a rotating pool of volunteers who evaluate the programs based on established criteria.

NCARB: National Council of Architectural Registration Boards

The National Council of Architectural Registration Boards is a nonprofit corporation comprising the legally constituted architectural registration boards of the 50 states, the District of Columbia, Guam, Puerto Rico, and the U.S. Virgin Islands as its members. Founded in 1919, NCARB protects the public health, safety, and welfare by leading the regulation of the practice of architecture through the development and application of standards for licensure and credentialing of architects. NCARB provides a range of important services to the profession, such as developing and administering the Intern Development Program (IDP), the Architect Registration Examination® (ARE®), and NCARB certification, which facilitates reciprocal registration.

Additional Organizations

The organizations listed in Table 1.14 are intended to be a representative sample of the many diverse organizations that exist in their respective fields. There are numerous other associations, each with their own opportunities for participation, learning, and networking. For a more exhaustive list, please see the latest edition of the *Almanac of Architecture and Design*.

AAF: American Architectural Foundation

Headquartered in Washington, D.C., the nonprofit American Architectural Foundation (AAF) seeks to educate and inspire "elected officials, educational leaders, and other public-spirited decision makers to use design to create better communities." To achieve this, the AAF assembles design teams and connects them to community and government

TABLE 1.14 Key Organizations

Name	Acronym	Founded	Focus	Website
Constituency-Based Professional Organizations				
Association of Collegiate Schools of Architecture	ACSA	1912	Education and Educators	www.acsa-arch.org
American Institute of Architects	AIA	1857	Practice	www.aia.org
American Institute of Architecture Students	AIAS	1956	Education	www.aias.org
American Society of Interior Designers	ASID	1975	Interiors	www.asid.org
Beverly Willis Architecture Foundation	BWAF	2002	Women in Architecture	http://bwaf.org/
International Interior Design Association	IIDA	1994	Interiors	www.iida.org
National Architectural Accrediting Board	NAAB	1940	Education	www.naab.org
National Council of Architectural Registration Boards	NCARB	1919	Licensure	www.ncarb.org
National Organization of Minority Architects	NOMA	1971	Profession and Practice	http://noma.net
Union of International Architects	UIA	1948	Practice and Architects	www.uia-architects.org
Cause-Based Professional Organizations				
American Architectural Foundation	AAF	1943	Architecture	www.archfoundation.org
Architecture for Humanity		1999	Public Service	www.architectureforhumanity.org
The Green Building Initiative	GBI	2004	Sustainability	www.thegbi.org
Public Architecture		2002	Public Service	http://www.publicarchitecture.org/
U.S. Green Building Council	USGBC	1993	Sustainability	www.usgbc.org
Knowledge-Based Professional Organizations				
American College of Healthcare Architects	ACHA	1986	Healthcare Architecture	www.healtharchitects.org
Association for Computer Aided Design in Architecture	ACADIA	1981	Digital Technology and Research	www.acadia.org
The Construction Specifications Institute	CSI	1948	Construction	www.csinet.org
Design-Build Institute of America	DBI	1993	Construction	www.dbia.org
Facility Guidelines Institute	FGI	1998	Construction	www.fgiguidelines.org
International Academy For Design and Health		1997	Research, Science, Health, and Culture	www.designandhealth.com
National Institute of Building Sciences	NIBS	1974	Research	www.nibs.org/

leaders, whose decisions have the ability to shape our communities. The AAF's programs include the Mayors' Institute on City Design, the Sustainable Cities Design Academy, and Great Schools by Design.

ACHA: American College of Healthcare Architects

The American College of Healthcare Architects (ACHA) offers board certification within the specialized field of healthcare architecture. The nonprofit organization recognizes four classes of certificate holders: Founding Affiliate, Affiliate, Fellowship, and Emeritus. Architects can apply to the Affiliate level if they have been licensed for at least five years, have practiced primarily in the healthcare field for at least three of those, and have passed the Board Certification examination. Affiliates are eligible to be nominated for Fellowship by a fellowship committee after five years of exemplary performance.

ASID: American Society of Interior Designers

The American Society of Interior Designers (ASID) is the largest professional organization for interior designers. Although ASID was officially founded in 1975, its history predates that, through its predecessor organizations: the American Institute of Interior Designers and the National Society of Interior Designers. It is "committed to the belief that interior design, as a service to people, is a powerful, multifaceted profession that can positively change people's lives. Through education, knowledge sharing, advocacy, community building and outreach, the Society strives to advance the interior design profession and, in the process, to demonstrate and celebrate the power of design to positively change people's lives."

ASID represents more than 18,000 practicing interior designers and 10,500 interior design students through its 48 local chapters. Professional members must possess an accredited design education or work experience, and pass the accreditation examination administered by the National Council for Interior Design Qualification (NCIDQ).

Architecture for Humanity

Founded in 1999, Architecture for Humanity is a nonprofit organization that seeks to "promote architectural and design solutions to global, social, and humanitarian crises." The original Architecture for Humanity competition sought to build transitional housing to returning Kosovo refugees. The public interest generated both inside and outside the design communities through that competition, as well as the media exposure, was translated into an organization that connects the talents and expertise of over 40,000 professionals with communities that would otherwise not have access to design services. The organization counts community-based organizations, housing developers, institutions, nongovernmental organizations (NGOs), and government entities as their clients.

BWAF: Beverly Willis Architecture Foundation

The Beverly Willis Architecture Foundation (BWAF) was founded in 2002 by Beverly Willis, FAIA, together with Heidi Gifford and architectural historians Diane Favro, Ph.D., and Lian Mann, Ph.D., with the purpose of "advancing the knowledge and recognition of women's contributions to architecture." Currently, the Foundation offers a variety of programs that include museum programs, films, tours, industry roundtables, internships, and research grants.

CSI: The Construction Specifications Institute

With the original purpose of improving the quality of construction specifications, the Construction Specifications Institute (CSI) was founded in 1948 by a group of government specification writers. Evolving with the times, today CSI's mission is to "advance building information management and education of project teams to improve facility performance."

Current programs include a series of certification levels (CDT, CCS, CCCA, CCPR), educational opportunities, the CONSTRUCT tradeshow, and the CSI Annual Convention. Local chapters also host educational sessions and networking opportunities, among other activities. In addition, CSI administers three formats for construction data organization: MasterFormat®, GreenFormat™ and UniFormat™. MasterFormat® is an organization system for building specifications; GreenFormat™ is a Web-based tool that standardizes construction products' sustainability properties; and UniFormat™ arranges information by systems, disregarding specific product selections. This allows for early construction cost estimates, among other uses.

DBIA: Design-Build Institute of America

The Design-Build Institute of America (DBIA) brings together leaders in the design and construction industry. Its membership comprises architects, engineers, owners, contractors, manufacturers, suppliers, students, and faculty. Headquartered in Washington, D.C., and established in 1993, the DBIA "promotes the value of design-build project delivery and teaches the effective integration of design and construction services to ensure success for owners and design and construction practitioners."

GBI: The Green Building Initiative

The Green Building Initiative's (GBI's) mission is to "accelerate the adoption of building practices that result in energy-efficient, healthier, and environmentally sustainable buildings by promoting credible and practical green building approaches for residential and commercial construction." Originally created as a way to help bring sustainable building practices into the mainstream, the GBI also currently administers the Green Globes® environmental assessment and rating tool in the United States, as well as their professional certifications programs: Green Globes Professional (GGP) and Green Globes Assessor (GGA).

GBI's board of directors includes representatives from construction companies, architecture firms, academic institutions, and industry representatives.

IIDA: International Interior Design Association

The International Interior Design Association (IIDA) was born in 1994 as the result of a merger between the Institute of Business Designers (IBD), the International Society of Interior Designers (ISID), and the Council of Federal Interior Designers (CFID). Currently, the IIDA supports 13,000 members in 31 chapters worldwide through its mission of creating "a strong niche for the most talented and visionary Interior Design professionals, to elevate the profession to the level it warrants, and to lead the way for the next generation of Interior Design innovators."

NIBS: National Institute of Building Sciences

Authorized in 1974 by the U.S. Congress through the Housing and Community Development Act, the National Institute of Building Sciences (NIBS) is a nonprofit organization that provides common ground where representatives of government, the professions, and industry and consumer interest groups can focus on shared problems that affect the construction industry. The Institute serves as an authoritative source of information for both the private and public sectors.

NOMA: National Organization of Minority Architects

During the 1971 AIA National Convention in Detroit, 12 African-American architects joined together to form the National Organization of Minority Architects (NOMA). Founded in recognition of the need to fight discriminatory policies that limited minority architects' opportunities, NOMA currently "champions diversity within the design professions by promoting the excellence, community engagement and professional development of its members."

Public Architecture

Public Architecture is a nonprofit entity that "puts the resources of architecture in the service of the public interest." Founded in 2002 by John Peterson of Peterson Architects, the organization launched "The 1%," a program through which firms pledge 1 percent of billable hours to pro bono work. Through The 1% website, nonprofits in need of design services and design firms participating in the program can connect with each other. The program counts over 900 participating firms, which range from some of the largest in the country to sole practitioners.

USGBC: U.S. Green Building Council

Committed to sustainability, the U.S. Green Building Council (USGBC) is a nonprofit organization based in Washington, D.C. Pulling together local affiliates, companies, organizations, and individuals, the organization seeks to "transform the way buildings and communities are designed, built, and operated, enabling an environmentally and socially responsible, healthy, and prosperous environment that improves the quality of life." Most notably, the USGBC administers the LEED® Green Building Rating System™, but other programs include the LEED AP professional credentialing program, educational sessions, the Greenbuild International Conference and Expo, and advocacy for sustainable policies and initiatives. Nationwide, the USGBC has 79 regional chapters.

PART 2
PRACTICE

Introduction

Bradford Perkins, FAIA

This second section of the Handbook covers the basic issues involved in developing and running an architectural practice. For those who have not actually practiced architecture, the business can appear simple: you just need to get projects, do the projects, and get paid enough so that you have the resources to get and do the next projects. Moreover, most architectural firms are small and have comparatively modest revenues and expenses to manage.

In reality architecture is a challenging business as well as a challenging profession. Few architects have business training and must learn the basics on the job. All businesses require basic skills in a number of disciplines to survive and prosper, and architects usually must acquire these basic skills without much formal training. This chapter introduces students and recent graduates to these required capabilities.

The factors that make architecture a challenging business have been present throughout the history of modern practice. First, architecture is a very competitive business. Very few projects are awarded without a competitive selection process, and in most cases there is more than one highly qualified firm competing for the project. Thus, getting projects is not easy. This is often illustrated with the story of the mother whose son was considering becoming an architect, approaching H. H. Richardson for advice. "Mr. Richardson, what is the most important thing in the practice of architecture?" she reportedly asked. "Getting a job," he replied. She responded, "I know getting a project is very important, but what is the next most important thing?" "Getting the next job!" Richardson replied. Getting work, however, is only one of seven issues that make even a small architectural firm a relatively complex business to run.

A second challenge is the fact that the financial management of a firm is usually complicated by unpredictable workloads and cash flow, narrow profit margins, and the complexity of completing complicated technical tasks over long project durations often within the structure of a fixed fee for services. There is little room for error, and an architectural firm's profitability and cash flow must be actively managed if a firm is going to remain healthy. Architects do not have to become accountants, but they do need to understand, monitor, and act on their firm's financial projections and results even if the financial reports are being prepared by someone (a bookkeeper, accountant, etc.) with professional training.

Third, the practice of architecture and the building of projects often involve more risk than many other businesses. Disputes are common and many of them, if not properly managed, can result in expensive litigation and related problems. Thus, knowledge of risk management techniques and related legal and insurance topics become important skills to acquire. Moreover, the business of architecture must also deal with all of the other day-to-day legal issues that impact most other businesses.

Fourth, an architectural firm's assets go home at night. Hiring, developing, managing, motivating, and retaining talented staff is complex. Even managing project teams (a subject covered in Part 3, Chapter 9.1) is complex.

Fifth, after many decades without significant advances in the technologies used in practice, architecture is now dependent on an increasingly complex digital platform. This change came on very quickly and has required most of the profession to radically change how projects are designed, documented, presented, and implemented. Cost effective management of this rapid change is still another major challenge in the business or architecture.

Sixth, architecture is highly sensitive to economic cycles. Architects are among the first to feel a slowing economy. In the deeper economic recessions, such as the very difficult period from 2008 through 2010, most architectural firms were hit hard. Revenues declined faster than expenses could be cut, and many firms suffered serious economic hardship. Only the ones who quickly took the necessary measures to get through that period emerged without significant damage.

And last but not least, planning, designing, and building architectural projects is a very complicated task. Most architects are learning new skills and information every week, and mastering even one building type in one locale can take years. This constant learning process, of course, is one of the many things that make architecture such an interesting and rewarding profession.

This combination of factors actually makes architecture a challenging business as well as a challenging profession. Part 2 is an introduction to the basic subjects that one needs to master to be able to be a leader in an existing firm or to run one's own practice. The first sections of Chapter 2 address the issues of setting up a firm and getting work. The next sections deal with financial management and other key aspects of running a practice.

CHAPTER **2**

Starting and Organizing a Practice

2.1 Developing a Practice

STARTING AN ARCHITECTURAL FIRM

Bradford Perkins, FAIA and Peter Piven, FAIA

Having their own practice is the goal of many design professionals. A new firm that is successful and achieves its founders' basic goals can be a very satisfying way to pursue a career in the field. But while the rewards (in self-expression, if not income) can be significant, so too can the risks. Most new businesses—whether architectural, engineering, and interior design firms or restaurants—never get off the ground. Some manage to launch and survive, but never really achieve much more than a modest success. A few, however, manage to surmount the inherent problems and achieve success as a business, as well as become what most professionals hope for: a respected firm that is both professionally and financially successful.

HAVE A GOOD REASON FOR STARTING YOUR OWN FIRM

Assuming you are considering "going on your own," the first question to ask yourself is: Why do you think that having your own firm is the right thing for you? We have spoken to hundreds of people who have started their own firms and no two cite exactly the same motivations. Nevertheless, we've found the answers can be placed into 10 categories, which all share a central theme: the desire for greater control over your future. These categories are:

1. Ability to realize your own goals and follow your own interests.
2. Greater ability to balance your personal and professional lives.
3. More direct relationship between effort and recognition for your professional accomplishments.

4. More direct relationship between effort and financial reward (the opportunity to make more money than is possible as an employee of someone else).
5. Greater control over your own destiny, design, and other issues of personal importance.
6. Survival during bad economic times.
7. Satisfaction of building your own practice.
8. Ability to be involved in everything.
9. Failure to "fit" into an established organization.
10. Desire to work with friends, a spouse, or others of your own choosing.

It's important to point out that in some ways the concept of greater control is illusory because the founder of a new firm soon finds out that he or she has exchanged the control by a boss for the pressures exerted by demanding clients, making payroll, and carrying out the greater range of tasks expected of the head of even a small firm. Nevertheless, when you have your own firm and face these issues, you usually feel that you are in control because they are yours to deal with.

The new pressures on the individual starting his or her own firm, however, are usually more than balanced by the benefits of one—or all—of the reasons listed for starting a firm. Few people who have started their own firm and reached the point at which its survival is no longer in question would ever go back to working for someone else.

Having a strong reason to go out on your own is a prerequisite, because the risks, effort, and initial financial investment can be significant. Without a strong reason, most design professionals decide that they are better off having a career within an existing organization. Your reason might be as simple as the prospect of having one or two interesting clients that could help launch a practice or, as for Thom Mayne of Morphosis, it can be recognizing that your personality and work habits are ill-suited to a large corporate practice. As Mayne put it, there was "no other way." The point is, not everyone is cut out to run his or her own firm, but if you feel you have compelling reasons for doing so, there are a number of steps to take before you make the final decision:

1. Be clear as to why you are doing it.
2. Define the type of firm you want to have.
3. Set goals for the first year and for the long term.
4. Look at successful models and research how they succeeded.
5. Define what special services or abilities you will offer that potential clients need.
6. Decide if you have all the basic capabilities necessary to succeed, or if you will need partners and/or colleagues.
7. Decide how you will support yourself until the firm is generating an adequate income to pay you.

KNOW THE TYPE OF FIRM YOU WANT

Part of your motivation should be that you have a specific concept of the type of firm you want to launch. David Grumman began his successful mechanical engineering firm, Grumman/Butkus Associates, in 1973, because he wanted to work directly for owners involved in the rapidly emerging energy conservation arena. He explained, "I wanted to have a different kind of consulting firm, and I did not want to work for architects."

It is not enough to just hang out a shingle that says "architect," "engineer," or "interior designer," and announce, "Hello world, here I am!" It is very important to define what your practice will offer, why it is special or unique, and why people should hire you. The answers to these questions may evolve over time as the firm matures, but it is important to have clear answers in your own mind from day one.

One way to help clarify what you want your firm to be is to define goals that will help measure progress or success. In the first year, some of the goals can be pretty basic, for example:

- To survive.
- To successfully complete three or four assignments.
- To secure enough work for the next year.

Even though it may seem impossible to set goals for 7 to 10 years out (the minimum time it takes most firms to mature from a start-up to an established firm), the exercise can help establish priorities for your efforts.

If, for example, your goal is to have a practice that is considered a leader in three or four building types, this should help focus your marketing and other efforts of the early years. Or if your goal is to run a firm of choice for a wide variety of assignments in a particular community, this will focus your efforts in a different way.

MODEL TYPES

In clarifying the type of firm you want to have, and defining a path to get there, it can be very helpful to look at how other firms became successful. Success, of course, should be measured against one's own goals, but for most professionals success includes achieving professional respect, producing interesting work, earning an adequate income, and other basic objectives.

In our experience, 10 common models can be used to launch a successful firm, and there is something to be learned from each. These models are:

1. Major client as "booster rocket"
2. House for mother
3. Academic incubator
4. Better mousetrap
5. Supersalesperson
6. Sponsor
7. Golden handshake
8. Spin-off
9. Rebuild of an existing firm (the phoenix)
10. Starting small in a good market

Some feel that achieving distinction as a successful new design firm is as much about public relations and salesmanship as it is about substance, but generally this is not true. Most design professionals accomplish their goals the old fashioned way: they achieve them by creating a firm with distinctive capabilities and consistent high-quality work. For young firms, achieving success without compromising on other goals (such as making payroll) requires both talent and commitment, especially since they typically must build their practices on a foundation of small projects with limited fees.

Let's review the model types one by one.

Major Client as First-Stage Booster Rocket

The firm is founded or taken beyond the start-up with the support of a single client willing to gamble on a young firm. The combination of the client and the work of the firm act as a booster rocket that lifts the firm above the crowd to where it can be seen. Most successful firms can trace their success back to one or two important early clients or projects. For architects, a rare variation on this is the firm that wins a major, open competition.

House for Mother

For some new firms, the booster rocket comes in the form of a project for a family member or one completed using family money. Charles Gwathmey, Robert Venturi, and Philip Johnson are only a few examples of well-known architects who became visible thanks to such projects.

Academic Incubator

Many of the best-known design firm principals have relied on their teaching positions to provide them with the basic income, time, credibility, and exposure to lay the foundations of a practice. Only when their practice becomes too demanding do they cut their academic ties. Thom Mayne of Morphosis relied on his Southern California Institute of Architecture teaching salary until his practice finally took off.

Finding a Need and Filling It (the Better Mousetrap)

Some firms see an unmet need and set out to fill it. In past years, this has included firms that first focused on specialties, such as recycling historic structures, or smaller projects in communities not served by enough strong local designers, or, currently, sustainable design.

Supersalesperson

A few firms—Kohn Pedersen Fox being one of the best known—got off the ground due in large part to the exceptional sales skills and client relationships of one or more of the founders. All successful architects have some sales skills, but only a handful can convince clients to hire a new firm for major projects over the established competition.

Sponsor

A few firms—among them some of the best known—have had other established professionals act as their booster rockets. This takes various forms. Well-known architects, Charles Moore being the most prolific, have lent their names and skills to young firms. In a few cases, elder statesmen, among them Philip Johnson, promote emerging stars. Philip Johnson's role in winning Michael Graves his first major commission, the Portlandia Building competition, is a well-known example.

Golden Handshake

Sometimes the architect's former employer provides the new firm's initial work. When Dwight Perkins (my grandfather) had to leave his position as head of the drafting room of Burnham and Root in the contraction after the 1893 Columbia Exposition, Daniel Burnham helped get him his first commission. A short time after they started, Voorsanger & Mills (later reorganized into two firms, Voorsanger & Associates and Edward I. Mills & Associates) received a major subcontract from I. M. Pei, their former employer, which sustained their start-up.

Spin-off

Among the most common models are the spin-offs—firms that break away from established ones where the new-firm members have built their reputations, skills, and potential client base. In some cases, the spin-offs are led by senior partners of major firms. Kohn Pedersen Fox, founded by the former leadership of John Carl Warnecke's New York office; Elkus/Manfredi, founded by a former partner of The Architects Collaborative; and Brennan Beer Gorman, founded by the former leadership of Welton Becket's New York office, are three major examples. More typically, the founders of a new firm spend their early years rising to senior positions below partner level in their former firms, and while there build strong personal reputations and reference lists, as well as a modest base of "moonlight" clients too small for their former employers. Then they break away.

Phoenix

The converse of the spin-off is the takeover. In a few cases, a new young leadership takes over a declining or moribund existing organization and revives and reshapes it into a new, vibrant firm. Johnson, Fain and Pereira Associates OFPA, now Johnson Fain) is a well-known example of this model. This model is very complex because, as at JFPA, it involves assuming substantial financial liabilities, an established image, and an established senior organizational structure. Scott Johnson and Bill Fain had to deal with all these while reshaping the design direction of a large practice.

Starting Small

Some firms are content to begin by doing small projects and building on that base. For Tod Williams, Billie Tsien and Associates, a small dormitory at Princeton University gave them credibility at an institutional level. After several smaller projects had been published, Princeton included them on a list of alumni architects to be interviewed for what was to be a small addition. Instead, it became a new building, which won several awards and was widely published. This, in turn, brought them increasingly important design commissions that eventually led to their internationally respected practice today.

THE LAUNCH

As Massachusetts architect Earl Flansburgh wrote, "There is no good time to start a new firm, only better times." Obviously, it is usually easier to get started in a booming economy, when there is a lot of work, but many successful practices started during recessions. Perkins+Will was founded during the Great Depression. Lawrence Perkins, FAIA, considered it, on balance, a good time to start, because as the economy recovered, clients were willing to consider new, younger firms since so many established firms had gone out of business.

Two typical triggers usually are enough to get a new firm off the drawing board and into practice:

- The belief that the firm can get work
- The assumption that the principals have the resources to survive the limited cash flow of a start-up

If both these basics are in place, most new firms then must quickly implement the following steps:

1. Decide on whom, if anyone, you want to work with.
2. Decide on a start date.
3. Draw up a business plan that includes:
   - A vision statement and a list of goals for the first year
   - A description of the services you intend to offer
   - A list of sources from which work will come
   - A budget for the start-up costs and for the first 12 months
   - An initial cash flow projection to define the initial capital requirements
   - A list of the support you will need to provide your services at the desired level of quality
4. Obtain initial clients and identify the probable source of the next clients.
5. Verify that you have met the necessary legal (licensing, corporate registration, etc.) requirements.
6. Choose a name, design business cards and stationery, and plan other actions that will help set the right image.
7. Obtain start-up capital.
8. Decide where to locate.
9. Select advisors: legal, financial, insurance, general business.
10. Promote your practice: Send out announcements; call friends and former colleagues.
11. Set up the office: equipment, a basic accounting system, telecommunications, files, stationery, and so on.
12. Identify back-up resources: administrative and technical.
13. Begin practicing.

Now let's consider these steps more closely.

PARTNERS AND ASSOCIATES

One of the most critical decisions you have to make is whom, if anyone, you want to work with. As discussed in earlier chapters, it is unusual that an individual has every skill necessary to lead and build a successful practice. There are exceptions, of course, such as firms led by sole practitioners who have chosen to focus on smaller projects that can be successfully carried out by a single design professional. But most practices with more far-reaching ambitions have to consider the question of partners.

The classic leadership mix for a new firm unites individuals who-in combination-have:

- New business development skills to get work
- Technical skills to successfully complete the work
- Basic management skills to keep the practice solvent

Ideally, each of the firm leaders will appreciate the importance of, and participate in, all three of these basic responsibilities.

LAUNCH DATE

It is important to set a date to start up the office, for, as with most deadlines, it imposes a degree of discipline into the planning and preparations.

There is little conventional wisdom regarding the best time of year to start a firm. If your plan calls for an immediate major effort to see a potential client, August and December might not be good choices because many people are away. September and January, however, are both good times to find people back at work.

In any case, often external factors—the need to sign a lease on office space, a first client who wants you to begin work immediately, or even losing one's full-time job—will override the selection of an arbitrary date.

THE FIRST BUSINESS PLAN

A firm's future should be built on the foundation of a plan, and the first-year plan is often the most important.

The first vision statement for most firms changes significantly over time. In one typical new firm, the principals wanted to be the day-to-day project architects on all jobs. As the firm grew, however, this had to change. But what did not change was their commitment to remain focused on building types where their research, experience, and other sources gave them a knowledge base and real expertise to bring to each new challenge. The initial vision remains a core belief for the firm.

DEFINITION OF SERVICES

It is important to formulate a clear statement of the services you intend to offer. Labels such as "Architecture" or "MEP Engineering" might be sufficient in a small town, where you have to be a generalist, but in most other locations, you should differentiate yourself and begin building a supportive image. If you have special skills or interests, make sure you emphasize them.

It is also imperative that you offer services that you can deliver—and well. This does not mean that you should hesitate to offer services that you have not done before, just be prepared to do whatever it takes to do them well.

LOCATION

Many new, small firms are launched from the founder's home. Often this is the only financially viable alternative, but it comes at a cost. To be efficient, most of us need a clear boundary drawn between home and work. Moreover, you are more likely to be viewed as a serious practitioner if you have a "real" office.

FIRST CLIENTS AND MARKETING PLAN

We strongly recommend that you launch only after you have the clear promise of work and a plan to get more work in the future. Avoid taking unethical advantage of your former employer, but recognize that most new firms are planned while the founders are working for someone else. Marketing and sales are ongoing processes, and few firms can afford to wait to start these processes until the day they open their firm.

FIRST BUDGETS

Two budgets are essential parts of the plan: one for the start-up costs and one for the costs for each of the first 12 months. These budgets, of course, should be tied into a realistic projection of cash flow and calculation of your capital requirements. (See Figure 2.1, "Startup Costs Checklist," and the accompanying sidebar for more on this.)

Start-Up Costs Checklist

Expense	Estimated Cost	Actual Cost	Date to Pay
Business licence/permit(s)			
Professional licence			
Business opening announcement			
Rental deposit on office (if not in home, two months' rent)			
Telephone installation/deposit			
Answering service			
Utility deposits (if not in home)			
Internet service			
Insurance			
Health			
General liability			
Professional liability			
Valuable papers			
Life			
Theft			
Hazard or tenant			
Disability			
Auto			
Legal			
Initial consultation			
Form of business papers			
Accounting			
Initial consultation			
Format resolution			
Professional association dues			
Local			
State			
National			

Source: Architect's Essentials of Starting, Assessing, and Transitioning a Design Firm, Bradford Perkins (Author), Peter Piven (Co-Author), John Wiley & Sons, Inc.: 2008

FIGURE 2.1 **Start-up Costs Checklist**

Expense	Estimated Cost	Actual Cost	Date to Pay
Initial Business Brochure			
Letterhead/business cards			
Equipment/furniture			
Computer hardware			
Computer software			
CADD software			
Typewriter			
Drafting desk(s)			
Desk(s)			
Adding machine			
Lamps			
File cabinet(s)			
Flat file(s)			
Conference table			
Chair(s)			
Telephone			
Telephone answering machine			
Facsimile machine			
Car phone/pager			
Photocopying machine			
Diazo machine			
Coffee machine			
Reference library (code books design books, this book, etc.)			
Library shelving			
Supplies			
Pens/pencils			
Markers			
Mylar			
Bumwad/tracing paper			
Vellum			
Drafting tape			
Paper clips			
Post-Its®			
Legal pads			
Telephone message pads			
Computer disks			
Light bulbs			
Measure tapes			

FIGURE 2.1 *(continued)*

Elena Marcheso Moreno writes about architecture, construction, and related business issues from McLean, Virgina.

After a business plan has been developed and refined, many tasks must be attended to before a firm formally opens its doors. The list below includes most of these, although a firm may omit or modify some or add others, depending on its circumstances.

Legal/Regulatory Issues

☐ Engage legal counsel.
☐ Register firm (as regular corporation, S-corporation, LLC, etc.).
☐ Verify that required professional registrations are current.
☐ Obtain required business licenses/permits.
☐ Obtain tax ID.

Financial

☐ Obtain start-up capital (from SBA, bank loans, equity lines, credit cards, family, personal savings, etc.).
☐ Prepare loan proposal, if required.
☐ Establish banking services/accounts.
☐ Engage accountant or accounting services.

Facilities

☐ Obtain office space (purchase, lease, lease to buy, etc.).
☐ Arrange for utility service hookups (phones, heat, power, etc.).
☐ Get keys/access devices for staff.
☐ Obtain office furniture and furnishings.
☐ Obtain office signage.
☐ Obtain or designate firm automobile.
☐ Obtain and set up computers and required software licenses.
☐ Obtain and set up copiers, fax machines, scanners, etc.
☐ Obtain miscellaneous equipment (camera, measuring devices, etc.).

☐ Obtain or arrange for coffee and vending machines, etc.
☐ Arrange for staff parking.

Staffing/Consultants

☐ Engage professional staff.
☐ Engage administrative/support staff.
☐ Line up design and technical consultants.

Insurance/Benefits

☐ Obtain workers' compensation insurance.
☐ Obtain professional liability insurance.
☐ Obtain general liability insurance.
☐ Obtain property/contents insurance.
☐ Obtain key person insurance or officer/director insurance.
☐ Obtain auto insurance.
☐ Set up employee healthcare insurance.
☐ Set up employee life and disability insurance.
☐ Set up employee savings plan [401(k), ESOP, etc.].

Administration/Support

☐ Set up office filing systems.
☐ Set up bookkeeping/accounting system.
☐ Set up tax withholding accounts (federal, state, local).
☐ Obtain and set up reference library/resource files.
☐ Purchase supplies.
☐ Obtain business stationery, forms, business cards, etc.
☐ Obtain printed contract documents (if software is not used).
☐ Obtain Internet provider.
☐ Set up LAN, Intranet, etc.
☐ Design and initiate Web page.
☐ Prepare firm policy/procedures manual.
☐ Select provider for repro services.

Marketing/Public Relations

☐ Develop initial marketing plan (based on a full business plan).
☐ Prepare announcements of firm opening.

THE OPENING

Stage the opening of your office as an event. Give a party and send announcements to all of your family, friends, past clients, professional contacts, and anyone else you can think of.

With these decisions made, and a plan and resources in place, you are as ready as most design professionals when they started. If your firm is successful, you will have a constantly rewarding and challenging career. Good luck.

2.2 Firm Legal Structure

Philip R. Croessmann, AIA, Esq., and David F. Kinzer III, CPA

Regardless of their size and structure, architecture and engineering firms are organized and behave according to certain basic principles established in state and federal law.

An architecture firm may be established as a proprietorship, partnership, corporation, or limited liability company. Although there are important legal, financial, tax, and operational factors to consider when selecting a form of practice, certain legal requirements apply to all forms.

SOLE PROPRIETORSHIPS

From a legal, compliance, and taxation standpoint, a sole proprietorship is the simplest form of practice. By definition, a *sole proprietor* is an individual conducting business in an unincorporated format. The sole proprietor makes no legal arrangements with other individuals, is not required to file state documents and federal tax forms to conduct the practice, and has full, personal control of the firm. Although a sole proprietorship may have employees, the individual and the unincorporated firm are legally one and the same.

Some of the simplicity inherent in this form of practice can be jeopardized if the proprietor fails to take special efforts to isolate the activities of the architecture practice from personal and unrelated business endeavors. In particular, keeping business and personal finances separate is part of an important management discipline that can contribute to the financial success of a practice. A sole proprietorship does not file a separate federal tax return; rather, relevant information is allocated and included with the proprietor's personal tax return. Preparation of this information for the IRS can be made much easier by keeping personal and business financial matters separate, although there is no legal requirement to do so. For example, the IRS regards business expenses differently—and more favorably—than personal expenses, permitting deductions for certain business expenses. Separate bookkeeping simplifies proper reporting of these expenses.

Two other factors should be considered when determining whether to establish a sole proprietorship: legal liability and the effect of death or retirement on the firm.

Liability. A sole proprietor's liability for professional errors and omissions and for business debts is unlimited. Both a professional liability claimant and a vendor of business services or products can reach all of the assets of the proprietor—except those that may be protected pursuant to state bankruptcy statutes. A professional liability insurance policy will protect the proprietor, to a certain extent, from losses associated with professional liability claims. Nonetheless, the proprietor remains fully liable for all adjudicated business claims.

"Risk Management" assesses professional liability insurance as part of a firm's risk management strategy.

Death or retirement. The death or retirement of the proprietor terminates the proprietorship. Unless a provision has been made for a successor to purchase the

Philip R. Croessmann, an architect and attorney, is a member in the law firm of Westberg Croessmann, P.C., based in Arlington, Virginia. He has extensive experience in construction litigation and contract law and has authored many articles on these and related subjects. **David F. Kinzer III** is a licensed CPA in Virginia performing accounting, tax, and consulting services in the Washington, D.C., metropolitan area. His work focuses primarily on the design, architecture, and construction industries.

102 Starting and Organizing a Practice

practice or assume the proprietor's projects, the only way to wrap up a sole proprietorship is through an appropriate estate and liquidation plan. Because there are advantages to placing certain assets in trust, such as avoiding probate, a proprietor could consider the use of a trust instrument in conjunction with an estate plan. To determine the best options, a proprietor should seek estate-planning counsel.

"Insurance Coverage" provides details about professional liability coverage for design errors and omissions.

PARTNERSHIPS

A *partnership* is an unincorporated association of two or more persons or entities for the purpose of operating a business with the intention of making a profit. The partnership, however, is not a separate legal entity distinct from the partners, and general partnerships are not required to file state organizational documents or federal tax identification forms.

The Partnership Agreement

Partnerships are more complex than proprietorships. A partnership agreement should be in writing and should address issues such as the following:

- Financial (capital) contributions of the partners
- Responsibility and authority of the partners
- Fiduciary duties of the partners
- Liabilities of the partners
- Operation and management of the partnership
- Distributions of profit and loss
- Transferability of interests
- Admission of new partners
- Resolution of disputes
- Dissolution of the partnership

Nearly all states have enacted some variation of a model statute called the Uniform Partnership Act. The Act establishes certain legal requirements to govern relationships between the partners (unless the partners themselves have made other specific arrangements) and between the partnership and other parties.

Establishing a partnership with a specific written agreement is preferable, for several reasons, to relying on state statutes to supply the terms of agreement between partners. For example, partnership statutes presume that all partners share income and losses equally, and do not commonly recognize a partnership's intention to treat certain parties differently with respect to income, losses, or both. Also, the laws do not take into account that certain assets or efforts contributed by the partners should be treated differently if the partnership succeeds or fails. Furthermore, most state statutes do not recognize a partner's contribution of effort in excess of other partners' efforts as the equivalent of making a cash contribution. Thus, if a partnership fails, the state law will allocate the losses according to capital contributions and will ignore the contribution of services.

Partner Liability

Each partner has potential liability for all of the business and professional liability debts of the partnership jointly and severally. Therefore, in the event that a business vendor or a professional liability claimant enforces a judgment against the partnership, each partner's personal assets may be reached to satisfy the full amount of the claim.

Architects considering becoming a partner in a firm should carefully weigh the amount of liability they will take on, particularly whether their capital contribution might soon be lost to existing creditors and claimants.

What liabilities does an incoming partner assume or an outgoing partner retain? In most states, incoming partners become responsible only for partnership debts incurred after they became partners, except that the new partner's capital is subject to claims by prior claimants or debtors. Departing partners remain liable for all partnership debts incurred by the partnership while they were partners. This is because, technically, when a partner retires or terminates the relationship with a partnership, the partnership is dissolved and a new partnership composed of the remaining partners automatically comes into being. However, a partnership agreement can be drafted to overcome this result.

Another matter to consider before joining a partnership is whether the rules concerning death and disability are addressed to the incoming partner's satisfaction. Often a retiring or deceased partner may be entitled to compensation far beyond what the partnership can or should pay for the partner's contribution. Joining such an arrangement leaves a new partner at risk should the existing partners die or retire.

Requirements for Professional Registration

Many states require that all partners be registered architects in the state where the firm is located. Some states specify that a certain percentage of the partners must be registered architects if the firm is to be classified as an architecture partnership. If a partnership consists of practitioners of multiple disciplines, the registered partners must be identified with their respective disciplines—for example, "architects and engineers."

Architects engaged in general contracting—as developers, design-builders, or construction managers—may find it necessary to obtain a contractor's license in states where they intend to engage in construction.

Income Taxes

A partnership files a separate federal tax return (called an information return), but it does not pay federal income tax on profits. A schedule showing each partner's share of the profits or losses and other reportable tax information is filed with the partnership's tax return and is given to each partner. Partners must transfer the information to their individual income tax returns and pay taxes on their share of the partnership's profits, whether or not those profits are distributed. Requirements related to partnership taxes and tax returns vary by state and locality.

CORPORATIONS

Corporations are separate legal entities that can conduct necessary business operations—including bringing suit and being sued—in their corporate name. Because corporations have "lives" of their own, they are perhaps the most complicated to establish and maintain. Articles of incorporation must be filed with the state to notify the public of the corporation's existence and some of its key characteristics. A federal tax number must also be obtained to identify the entity as a legal taxpayer. There are legal requirements for boards of directors, shareholder meetings, and a variety of other organizational issues. A corporation can be much more stable (in a legal sense) than a sole proprietorship or a partnership because its existence transcends the individuals who own and manage it.

Federal, state, and local income tax laws and regulations can be complex. They change frequently and are reinterpreted constantly, making it advisable to have a firm's accountant keep the owners apprised of changes that affect the practice. Table 2.2, at the end of this section, provides a summary of some provisions.

Many states have separate statutes for general business and professional corporations. General business corporations may be formed for any legal purpose and are subject to the requirements of the state's general corporation laws. Every state allows the establishment of general business corporations, although some do not allow stockholders or employees to practice architecture through the general corporation.

Professional corporations, on the other hand, are established specifically to provide professional services and are subject to restrictions enumerated in the professional corporation statute. Professional corporations normally must be owned or at least controlled by professionals licensed to practice in the state. Moreover, the corporate entity usually does not protect individual stockholders or employees from professional liability. Professional corporations may be required to pay income taxes as general business corporations or may be subject to special tax considerations.

Practicing architecture in a corporate form is not permitted in a few states. Some states require architects who want to incorporate to do so as a professional corporation authorized and certified by the secretary of state. Most states permit practice through either a professional corporation or a general business corporation, but some states permit architects to choose either type of entity. The number of principals in the corporation who must be registered architects varies according to the state in which the corporation conducts its practice.

"Agreements with Owners" notes legal issues that partnerships and corporations should be mindful of when entering into project agreements (or any business agreement).

A corporation seeking to practice in a state other than the one in which it is incorporated must register as a foreign corporation in the other state to avoid jeopardizing certain legal rights, including the right to enforce legal claims for fees.

Ownership and Control

A position as shareholder does not necessarily mean an individual's compensation will be proportional to his or her ownership. Compensation in a corporation is based on an oral or written agreement between the corporation and an individual and may or may not be set in relation to the number of shares owned. Such legal differences also apply to management and control of the corporation. It is possible, although uncommon, for ownership of a corporation and its control and management to be in different hands. This is uncommon because most shareholders elect the board of directors, which then appoints the officers. Under most circumstances, the individual or group who owns the majority of shares is able to elect directors who will appoint the individual or group or its designees as officers.

Employees offered shares of a corporation should consider the answers to these questions:

- Is the cost of the shares justified by an increase in compensation?
- Will the value of shares increase over time?
- Will the employee's control over management of the firm increase?

If owning shares does not increase the compensation to which an architect is entitled, there may be no value in purchasing them. This is particularly true if the number of shares to be purchased is small compared with the holdings of others, in which case the new shareholder may have little or no say about the election of directors and appointment of officers. Further, if there is no market for the shares or no buy/sell agreement that will allow the shareholder to sell the stock, the shares may have only minor investment value.

Liabilities

In a corporation, unlike in a proprietorship or a partnership, the personal assets of shareholders cannot be reached to satisfy the corporation's bona fide business debts. If the corporation purchases services or goods in its own name and fails to pay for them, the vendor can look only to the assets of the corporation for payment, not to the assets of individual shareholders.

Professional liability is a different matter. In many states, an architect remains personally liable for his or her professional errors or omissions, even if they were committed while the architect was employed by a corporation. Some states hold the owners of the corporation jointly and severally liable for professional errors and omissions in the same way they would be if they were partners. In other states, practicing architecture as a corporation shields architects from personal liability for errors and omissions.

Because the laws governing the liability of architects practicing in a corporation vary significantly from state to state, professional liability insurance is an important way to manage these risks. Those considering the purchase of shares of a corporation will want to look into how the firm handles professional liability risks. Is the corporation adequately insured against professional errors and omissions? What do the relevant state statutes say about the liability of the new shareholder for such errors and omissions?

Changes in Ownership

As in partnerships, a shareholder who retires or dies may have rights to compensation granted through his or her employment agreement. To determine whether a corporation will be viable into the future, those deciding whether to buy shares should first understand the potential liability the corporation will have to departing shareholders. Similarly, provisions for incoming shareholders' ultimate retirement or termination should be drafted in a way that fairly compensates the existing shareholders for the efforts they have made during their tenure.

Ownership transition in a corporation is, in many respects, easier than in a partnership. Shares of more than one type and variety may be bought and sold under a large number of circumstances to facilitate an orderly ownership transition and to provide severance pay to retiring shareholders.

The usual method for compensating departing shareholders is commonly known as a buy/sell agreement. These agreements require departing shareholders to sell their shares back to the corporation or its shareholders to keep the shares in the "family" of shareholders. This arrangement may be mandated by a state registration statute that requires all shareholders to be licensed architects. An effective buy/sell agreement establishes a purchase price and method of sale for the departing shareholder's shares and may also determine the price to be paid by incoming shareholders. Because such devices affect the long-term viability of a corporation, a prospective shareholder (or his or her counsel) should carefully review the buy/sell agreement to determine the corporation's prospects for viability after the other shareholders depart.

Architects who plan to establish a corporate form of practice should seek legal counsel and accounting advice to ensure they understand the tax ramifications and conditions of practice in the states where they plan to practice.

Income Taxes

Unless a "Selection" is made under federal tax law, a corporation is a separate taxable entity. Individual shareholders who are employees of the corporation are taxed on their salaries. The corporation itself reports as gross income the professional fees received and deducts salaries and other business expenses. Any amount remaining is taxable at the corporate tax rate. The corporation has several options for using the remainder in a way that will make its distribution tax deductible. For example, the earnings may be used to pay bonuses, make contributions to a qualified profit-sharing or pension plan, or, under recent federal tax provisions, be distributed to shareholders as dividends. Under certain circumstances, if earnings are not distributed to shareholders, an accumulated earnings tax may be imposed on the corporation.

Subchapter S Corporations

A corporation may elect to be treated as an S corporation for federal income tax purposes if it meets certain technical requirements. The shareholders of an S corporation are treated similarly to the partners of a partnership for tax purposes. That is, the shareholders of an S corporation are taxed on their pro rata share of the corporation's income, regardless of whether it is distributed. The S corporation itself, however, is subject to income tax only in special circumstances. Architects who establish an S corporation can avoid or mitigate the double tax that may be imposed on portions of corporate income, or they can take advantage of more favorable tax rates.

TABLE 2.1 Comparative Legal Attributes of Legal Structures

Legal Attribute	Sole Proprietorship	Partnership	S Corporation	Regular Corporation	Limited Liability Company
Liability	Individually liable for all liabilities of business	General partners individually liable (for partnership's liabilities; limited partner liable only up to amount of his/her capital contribution	Same as regular corporation	Shareholder's liability in most cases is limited to capital contribution	Shareholder's liability in most cases is limited to capital contribution
Qualified owners	Single individual owner	No limitations; however, need at least two partners (including general partner)	Only individuals, estates, and certain trusts may be shareholders (limited to 75 shareholders)	No limitation	No limitation except for professional LLCs, for which members must conform to the applicable licensing requirement
Type of ownership interests	Individual ownership	More than one class of partner permitted	Only one class of stock permitted	More than one class of stock permitted	One class of member
Transfer of ownership	Assets of business transferable rather than business itself	New partnership may be created; consent of other partners normally required if partnership interest is to be transferred	Shares can only be transferred to individuals, certain types of trusts, or estates; no consent to Subchapter S election is needed; restrictions may be imposed by shareholder agreement	Ready transfer of ownership through the use of stock certificates; restrictions may be imposed by shareholder's agreement	A new limited liability company may be created; consent of other members normally required if partnership interest is to be transferred
Raising capital	Capital raised only by loan or increased contribution by the proprietor	Loans or contributions from partners	Loans or contributions from shareholders; "straight debt" avoids second class of stock	Met by sale of stocks or bonds or other corporate debt	Loans or contributions from members
Business action and management	Sole proprietor makes decisions and can act immediately; proprietor responsible and receives all profits or losses	Action usually depends on unanimous agreement of partners or, at least, general partners. Limited partner actively participating in management may lose limited liability	Same as regular corporation except unanimous consent is required to elect S status; more than 50% of shareholders needed to revoke Subchapter S status	Unity of action based on authority of board of directors	Managed by professional managers or the members
Flexibility	No restrictions	Partnership is contractual agreement, within which members can conduct business subject to the partnership agreement and applicable state laws	Same as regular corporation	Corporation is a legal entity created by the state, functioning within powers granted explicitly or implicitly and subject to judicial construction and decision	Great flexibility is given in management and ownership

TAX CONSIDERATIONS

As suggested so far, the various forms of legal organization are subject to different federal and state income tax methods. Additional income tax considerations follow.

Tax Rates

Under current law, federal income tax rates imposed on individuals are usually lower than the 35 percent corporate income tax rate imposed on architecture and other personal service corporations. As a result, many architecture corporations choose to file for chapter S status.

Tax Year

Sole proprietorships, partnerships, and corporations are generally required to use a calendar taxable year (i.e., January 1 through December 31) unless they can establish sufficient business reasons to adopt a fiscal year (a year that begins and ends on dates other than January 1 and December 31). A corporation engaged in architecture or

TABLE 2.2 Comparative Tax Attributes of Legal Structures

Tax Attribute	Sole Proprietorship	Partnership	S Corporation	Regular Corporation	Limited Liability Company
Taxable year	Usually calendar year	Generally a calendar year is required, unless §444 or a business purpose test is met	Generally a calendar year is required, unless §444 or a business purpose test is met	Any type of year available; however, personal service corporation has restrictions	Generally a calendar year is required, unless §444 or a business purpose test is met
Ordinary/distributions to owners	Drawings from the business are not taxable; net profits are taxable and proprietor is subject to tax on self-employment income	Generally not taxable, but distribution in excess of basis is taxable as capital gain	Payment of salaries deductible by corporation and taxable to recipient; distributions generally not taxable; however, certain distributions can be taxable as dividends; distributions in excess of basis = capital gains	Payments of salaries are deductible by corporation and taxable to recipient; payments of dividends are not deductible by corporation and generally are taxable to recipient shareholders	Generally, not taxable, but distribution in excess of basis is taxable as capital gain
Limitation on losses deductible by owners	Subject to at-risk, hobby loss, and passive activity loss rules.	Subject to basis limitation; partner's investment, plus his or her share of partnership liabilities; at-risk and passive activity loss rules may apply	Subject to shareholder's basis, including loans to the corporation; at-risk and passive activity loss rules may apply	No losses allowed to individual except upon sale of stock or liquidation of corporation. Corporate carryback and carryover rules may apply. Closely held corporations limited by at-risk and modified passive activity rules	Deductible by owners subject to basis limitation; partner's investment, plus his or her share of partnership liabilities; at-risk and passive activity loss rules may apply
Dividends received	Fully taxable	Conduit—fully taxable	Same as partnership	100% dividend-received deduction	Conduit—fully taxable
Former election required to obtain tax status	No	No	Yes	No	Yes
Capital gain	Taxed at individual level	Conduit—taxed at individual level	Conduit—taxed at shareholder level; possible corporate built-in gains tax	Taxed at corporate level	Conduit—taxed at individual level
Capital losses	Carried forward indefinitely; limited to $3,000 per year	Conduit—carried forward indefinitely at partner level; limited to $3,000 per year	Same as partnership	Carry back three years and carryover five years as short-term capital loss offsetting only capital gains	Conduit carried forward indefinitely at partner level; limited to $3,000 per year
Section 1231 gains and losses	Taxed at individual level—combined with other §1 231 gains or losses of individual; net gains are capital gains for individual; net losses are ordinary losses for individual	Conduit	Conduit; possible corporate built-in gains tax	Taxable or deductible at the corporate level	Conduit
Basis for allocating income to owners	All income is reported on owner's return	Profit and loss agreement may have "special allowances" of income and deductions if they have substantial economic effect	Pro rata portion of income based on per share, per day allocation	No income allocated to shareholders	Profit and loss agreement may have "special allowances" of income and deductions if they have substantial economic effect

Tax Attribute	Sole Proprietorship	Partnership	S Corporation	Regular Corporation	Limited Liability Company
Basis for allocating a net operating boss	All losses flow through to owner's return	Profit and loss agreement may have "special allocation" of income and deductions if they have substantial economic effect	Pro rata portion of income based on per share, per day allocation	No losses allocated to stockholders	Profit and loss agreement may have "special allowances" of income and deductions if they have substantial economic effect
Group hospitalization and life insurance premiums and medical reimbursement plans	100% of self-employed person's health insurance premiums may be deducted from gross income	Cost of partners' benefits generally treated as compensation, deductible by the partnership and includable in the partner's income; 100% self-employment health insurance premiums available as a deduction	Cost of benefits to more than 2% of shareholders treated as compensation, deductible by the corporation and included in shareholders' income; 100% of self-employed health insurance premiums available as a deduction	Cost of shareholder-employee coverage generally deductible as a business expense if plan is "for the benefit of employees"; normally excluded from employee's income	Cost of partners' benefits generally treated as compensation, deductible by the company and includable in partners' income; 100% self-employment health insurance premiums available as a deduction
Retirement benefits	Limitations and restrictions basically same as regular corporations	Limitations and restrictions basically same as regular corporations	Limitations and restrictions basically same as regular corporations	Limitations on benefits from defined benefit plans and from defined contribution plans; special restrictions for top-heavy plans; 401(k) limitation began in 1992	Limitations and restrictions basically same as regular corporations
Organization costs	Not applicable	Amortizable over 60 months	Amortizable over 60 months	Amortizable over 60 months	Amortizable over 60 months
Charitable contributions	Subject to limits for individuals; gifts for use of private foundations, 20% of AGI; gifts to public charity, cash, 50% of AGI; appreciated property, 30% of AGI; other limitations for specific items contributed	Conduit	Conduit	Limited to 10% of taxable income before special deductions	Conduit
Tax preferences (Alternative Minimum Tax)	Graduated from 26% of the first $175,000 of AMTI, 28% of anything over that; applied to minimum taxable income, including tax preferences in excess of $20,000 ($40,000 for joint returns); payable to extent exceeds regular tax	Conduit	Conduit	Taxed at corporate level; 20% on preferences and adjustments in excess of $40,000 or regular tax liability, whichever is greater (does not apply to corp. with < 7,500K gross revenue averaged over 3 years)	Conduit
Character of income and deductions	Taxed at individual level; limitation on investment interest deductions	Conduit	Conduit	Taxed at corporate level	Conduit
Self-employment tax	Half of SE tax paid deductible from gross income	Same as proprietorship	Not applicable	Not applicable	Same as proprietorship

other personal services, whether organized as a professional corporation or a regular business corporation, should consult an accountant to confirm that it is entitled to use a fiscal year for tax planning purposes.

Accounting Method

An architecture firm organized as a sole proprietorship, partnership, or S corporation is entitled to compute its taxable income under the cash method of accounting. Under this method, fees are reported as income only when actually received and not when billed. Similarly, expenses are deductible only when actually paid, not in the year in which they accrue. An architecture firm organized as a corporation that has not made an S election may use the cash method only if its gross receipts do not exceed certain amounts and if certain other requirements of the Internal Revenue Code are met.

Other Taxes

Many states and some cities impose their own income taxes and professional services or gross receipts taxes. Other federal taxes that may affect individual architects and architecture firms include employer and employee Social Security taxes (and the comparable self-employment tax in the case of partnerships and sole proprietorships) and the unemployment tax on compensation paid to employees.

LIMITED LIABILITY COMPANIES

Limited liability companies (LLCs) are complex hybrids of corporations and partnerships. They are separate entities under state law that can conduct business in their own name, and they have many of the characteristics of a corporation. They are, however, classified as partnerships for federal tax purposes. This distinction makes them suitable as investment vehicles and as a business structure for individuals who wish to pass losses through to their personal income while still limiting their liability.

The use of LLCs for architecture practice varies among states. States either permit architecture firms to use general LLCs without any restrictions, prohibit the use of general LLCs for the practice of architecture, or have statutes creating professional LLCs.

Ownership and Control

Under the organizing statutes, the owners of an LLC are called *members*. LLCs do not have to be managed by the members of the company. State statutes generally provide that an LLC may be managed by professional managers, who are afforded limited liability for their acts on behalf of the company yet do not have to be members of it. On the other hand, an LLC that is managed directly by its members or any group of members can provide significant management and ownership flexibility, and can offer creative opportunities for attracting capital. A detailed operating agreement should be developed to tailor management to the needs of the company. Operating agreements, like corporate bylaws and partnership agreements, grant authority to managers and members and establish how the organization will conduct its business.

Liabilities

Like a corporation, the members of an LLC have limited personal liability. In many states, however, architects remain liable for their professional errors or omissions, even if they were committed while the architect was an employee of the company. While laws regarding architect liability vary among the states, design professionals generally cannot avoid professional liability through the use of an LLC.

Other Options

Some states permit still other options: Design Professional Corporation (DPC), Limited Liability Partnership (LLP), and others. Thus, architects should always seek professional advice before choosing an option for their firm.

2.3 Legal Issues

Architects and the Law

Donald W. Doeg, Esq., PE, LEED AP

Architects, like other professionals, render their services in a difficult and complex environment. In order to be successful, knowledge of the basic components of the legal requirements that govern their profession is essential.

Legal Overview

Architects, like many other professionals, are confronted with legal issues on a regular basis and thus must have a basic understanding of the law in order to successfully practice architecture in today's complex world. A wide spectrum of sources creates legal requirements that dictate standards under which an architect must practice. These sources include, but are not limited to: statutes passed by federal, state, or local legislative bodies under their constitutional authority; administrative rules and regulations; building codes and standards; local ordinances; obligations established by contract between two or more parties; and law established by precedent of prior interpretations by the courts and administrative agencies regarding these requirements.

In order to meet the applicable standard of care (which will be discussed in more detail later in this section) it is the architect's obligation and duty to practice in compliance with all applicable laws, codes, and regulations. While most of the existing construction-related law will apply to architectural practice in some manner, there are laws and other legal obligations that may not be applicable to particular parties, such as the architect. For instance, certain OSHA obligations are directed to the means and methods by which a contractor performs its work on a project. Unless the architect specifically assumes some specific obligation through its contract, those obligations may not extend to the architect.

In a very broad sense, issues of law impacting architects can be broken into two general categories: party disputes and administrative proceedings. Party disputes, the focus of this section, occur when problems arise on a project, such as delays, failures, or potential failures relating to the work performed, fee controversies, and a long list of other issues. Problems don't always result in disputes and disputes don't always result in legal action. However, it is important to understand that the outcome of many of those disputes will rest heavily on whether the parties have met their legal obligations.

Administrative issues and proceedings also play a very significant role in an architect's life. Administrative issues arise from regulations developed to implement civil statutes and other legal requirements, such as the area of professional licensing. Typically, this area of the law is overseen by public officials charged with ensuring compliance with certain laws, standards, and regulations. Under their statutory authority, state registration boards, code officials, and other administrative agencies are given the power to develop, implement, and enforce regulations needed to do their jobs. Individuals and entities subject to regulation typically have opportunities to seek variances or appeal decisions through administrative channels (e.g., zoning boards of appeal). When administrative avenues have been exhausted, it is possible to seek review of administrative decisions in the courts.

▶ "Managing and Avoiding Disputes" discusses the effective and strategic use of methods for resolving project disputes.

▶ "Building Codes and Standards" and "Community Planning Controls" further discuss the myriad regulations concerning building design, planning, and zoning.

PART 2: PRACTICE

Don Doeg is a principal at Updike, Kelly & Spellacy, P.C., in Hartford, Connecticut, and the chairman of the firm's Construction Law and Design Professional Law practice groups. His practice is devoted to assisting clients in all aspects and stages of construction projects, including resolution of any dispute that may arise.

COMMON CLAIMS AGAINST ARCHITECTS

If formal disputes arise relating to construction projects, attorneys will articulate their clients' claims in the lawsuits based upon various legal theories. The two legal theories most often alleged in claims against architects are "negligence" and "breach of contract."

Negligence

Overview of Negligence

The existence of negligence is often more difficult to determine than whether a breach of contract has occurred. Under the law, there are four components that must be proven in order to prevail when asserting a negligence claim. They are as follows:

- *Duty.* The architect must owe a legal duty to the person making the claim. In other words, the architect has a legal obligation to do something or refrain from doing something.
- *Breach.* The architect fails to perform the duty or does something that should not have been done.
- *Cause.* The architect's breach of duty is the proximate cause of harm to the person making the claim. That is, was the claimant injured or harmed as a consequence of the act and/or omission of the architect without any intervening cause?
- *Damage.* Actual harm or damage must have resulted from the breach.

Standard of Care

In claims against professionals, including architects, it is often difficult or impossible for a layperson to unilaterally determine the duty component of negligence as defined above. As such, the law has established that that duty is to meet a standard of reasonable care for the performance of the work. The standard of care for an architect is generally defined as what a reasonably prudent architect would do in the same general locale, in the same time frame, given the same or similar facts and circumstances. The architect's legal responsibilities to a client are examined in light of what reasonably prudent architects would have known and done at the time services were performed.

In order to prove whether the standard of care has been met in a particular instance, the courts in most states require expert witness testimony. That is, since a layperson judge or jury would not have the requisite knowledge to determine what a reasonably prudent architect would have done under similar circumstances, each of the parties must retain an expert witness to provide an opinion as to the applicable standard of care for the case (what should or should not have been done by the architect). The judge or jury is ultimately charged with applying the standard of care that they believe is most credible to the facts of the case and determining whether the architect acted appropriately.

Despite the thoughts of some owners and/or their attorneys, the law does not require perfection from an architect based upon a typical standard of care scenario. If given enough time, an experienced third-party reviewer would likely find some glitches or inconsistencies on any set of architectural drawings currently in existence. However, the mere existence of a few minor glitches or inconsistencies within project documents does not mean that the author has failed to meet the prevailing standard of care. Despite the existence of alleged "flaws," another expert may well opine that the standard of care has nonetheless been met. The outcome of these types of disputes is dependent upon the particular facts in each case.

It should also be noted that since architecture is an integration of art and building science, in virtually all situations there is more than one way to design a project or even a portion of a project. The fact that another architect would have used different details or materials does not necessarily dictate a violation of the prevailing standard of care. The successful practice of architecture is based upon reasoned judgment and skill and the law recognizes that even if there is differentiation among various designs, it does not necessarily mean any of them were performed negligently.

▶ "Owner-Generated Agreements" discusses a systematic approach to evaluating terms in agreements provided by owners.

▶ "Insurance Coverage" covers the terminology and the necessary considerations and alternatives when selecting insurance for one's firm.

The standards of care applicable to a particular project can be modified by contract or conduct. The most frequent example of this practice is an attempt by owners to elevate the standard of care. Rather than applying the typical standard of care described above, some owners' contracts seek to require a standard of "best practices," "highest prevailing standards," or some other similar language that elevates the mandated standard of care for those projects. Architects should be wary of such heightened standards for at least two reasons: (1) the new standard may not be adequately defined in the industry, which may lead to a great deal of subjectivity and debate if a conflict ever arises; and (2) such standards may not be insurable under many typical professional errors and omissions policies.

Each of the components of the aforementioned definition of the professional standard of care can be subjective in nature. Depending on the specific issue at hand, courts have given some latitude to the "in the same general locale" component. For instance, it would not be prudent for an architect in the southern states to incorporate a large factor for snow load on the roofs of their designs, and, similarly, architects in the north central states may not have the same concerns about hurricane loads as their colleagues in the southeastern states. Yet in other instances, courts have held that knowledge about basic design concepts and/or certain building products (both good and bad) should be known by architects throughout the country. This nationwide knowledge can be applied in several manners by the courts. For instance, the level of knowledge of certain questionable materials may be consistent throughout the country (e.g., use of asbestos or the risks of fire-retardant plywood) regardless of the size or nature of the specific architectural practice. In other situations, architects with certain building type specialties (e.g., large sports stadiums, large museums, and major hospitals) may have a national practice and may be compared to other architects with the same specializations, even if their respective offices are many states away.

The "in the same time frame" component has also been heavily litigated. In general, the applicable standard of care is the one in place at the time of the project, not the one in place at the time of the dispute, which can be years later. As such, experts who subsequently assert that the prevailing standard should have resulted in the use of materials or techniques that were unknown or in their formative stages at the time of the project are not persuasive with the courts. Last, but not least, the "same or similar circumstances" component must also be strongly considered. For instance, the owner's budget will significantly impact a project. The standard of care must be determined for an architect working within the same budget, and under the same constraints, as were encountered for the underlying project. Alternatively, the "same or similar circumstances" also includes the type of project and the experience of the architect. That is, a small local architectural firm designing residences in a certain locale will not be held to the same standard as a national architectural firm that routinely designs large and complex facilities such as sports stadiums or healthcare facilities. Unfortunately, meeting the relevant standard of care may not be enough to protect an architect from litigation. A lawsuit can be commenced by almost anyone, in most states even by a party with whom the architect had no contractual relationship. However, if an architect is mindful during the course of the project of the standard of care that must be met, it will go a long way toward both diminishing the chances of the commencement of litigation as well as providing good defenses to the architect if litigation does arise.

Modifying the Standard of Care by the Architect's Actions

Even though the law requires only reasonable and prudent behavior, an architect can expand or raise the standard of care. This may be done either consciously or inadvertently. The standard of care can be altered in literally countless ways by the architect's actions, such as promising a specific project result (e.g., that the roof or basement will not leak); taking on the contractor's responsibilities (e.g., dictating means and methods or designing something that the contractor was required to do as part of a performance

▶ "Risk Management Strategies" addresses how to determine whether a risk is worth taking and how to manage risks.

specification); or promising a specific supplier performance result (e.g., delivery of certain materials by a specific date).

It is important to realize that raising the standard of care increases the architect's liability exposure by making the architect responsible for more than the professional standard requires. Sometimes design professionals—under pressure from clients or contractors or propelled by their own drive for perfection—raise the standard of care that will be applied to their services without intending to do so.

Damages

Damages for negligence claims are typically measured by the standard of the plaintiff being entitled to compensation to remedy the negligence of the architect. If the case were litigated or arbitrated, the judge, jury, or arbitrator would have to decide what that compensation would entail based upon the arguments set forth by the litigants. For instance, if litigation resulted in a finding that an architect improperly designed a set of stairs that did not meet the applicable building code and those stairs were subsequently constructed in accordance with those faulty plans, an owner may be entitled to the cost of removing the stairs and installing another set of stairs that met the applicable code.

Breach of Contract Claims

Overview of Breach of Contract Claims

"Breach of contract" claims are relatively self-explanatory. Such claims are based upon an allegation that a specific duty or duties existed pursuant to a contract between two parties and one of those parties either failed to perform that duty or did not perform it properly. For instance, an owner-architect agreement may specifically require that the architect provide record drawings at the conclusion of the project. If the architect fails to do so, a breach of contract claim may ensue.

The elements of a breach of contract action are the formation of an agreement, performance by one party, breach of the agreement by the other party, and damages. To form a valid and binding contract there must be a mutual understanding of the terms that are definite and certain between the parties. Each must be found to have been based on an identical understanding by the parties and an agreement must be definite and certain as to its terms and requirements.

Contractual Protections

Logic dictates that the quality of the architect's contract will have a large impact on the potential claims and defenses against the architect. It is imperative that the architect spend time on each and every contract to understand and negotiate each of the clauses. Each and every contractual clause may prove to be either a significant defense available to the architect or a huge detriment.

Owner-architect contracts can be either written or oral. Written contracts are preferred by almost everyone in the design industry. Perhaps the largest benefit of a written contract is the fact that it preserves a written articulation of the agreement between the parties, including all critical components, which can be referenced if a subsequent dispute arises. Coming to a common understanding of the terms of the original agreement often proves very difficult if an oral agreement is in place and a dispute subsequently arises. In addition, the applicable statutes of limitation may vary depending upon whether the contract was in written or oral form.

▶ The "AIA Documents Program" details what AIA Contract Documents offer the parties involved in the design and construction of buildings.

It is important to recognize that written architectural contracts take many forms, depending upon the particular project and parties. The most common construction contracts in the industry are form contracts that are published by various construction industry groups, the industry standard being the AIA documents. The provisions included in these form contracts have been formulated over many years' use in the industry. While many parties opt to use the industry forms "as is," there are other situations in which one or both parties may seek to modify one or more of the provisions, sometimes significantly. In addition to the industry form contracts, there are many other types of contracts prepared by specific owners, design professionals, or others that also are used.

The following are some key provisions that, if properly included in an architectural contract, will go a long way toward protecting the architect.

The Absolutely Essential Terms: Whether an agreement is written on the back of a napkin or consists of a long-form agreement, it is absolutely critical that the agreement include a written summary of the project scope, the time frame in which it will be performed, and the fee agreement for the project.

- *The Project Scope*: It is critical to describe the scope of work to be accomplished. In some instances, it is equally or even more critical to describe any exclusions (e.g., in some instances the architect does not plan to be involved in the construction administration phase, but the owner may not comprehend that fact).
- *The Project Time Frame*: Many disputes have occurred because the owner and architect did not specifically discuss the time frame for the project and assumed vastly different parameters for the start and completion dates (and other critical milestones) of the work.
- *Project Fees*: It is essential that the architect and owner agree on the type of payment (e.g., lump sum, hourly, not to exceed, etc.) and the time frames for the payment (e.g., monthly, one payment at end of project, percentage of project completion).

Other Key Terms: The following are a few of the many contract terms that can have a significant impact on an architect's exposure should problems arise during the course of the project. These terms are but a few of the many critical contract provisions that may exist for a particular project:

- *Limitations of Liability Clauses*: These clauses will limit claims by the owner against the architect to a certain amount (e.g., a set dollar limit or the balance of the remaining insurance policy) should a dispute between the parties arise. These clauses have been enforced in many, but not all, states.
- *Mutual Waiver of Consequential Damages*: This is a standard clause in many AIA form contracts, but is often stricken by owner's counsel. Consequential damages are those that are not direct damages, but only arise as a consequence of some act or omission. In the prior example, if an architect failed to design a set of stairs to code and they subsequently had to be replaced prior to a certificate of occupancy being granted, the cost to do the replacement work would be direct damages. The delay in the opening of the facility would be consequential damages and, if the waiver was part of the contract, the owner would not be able to collect damages of this type from the architect.
- *Indemnification Provisions*: Many owners attempt to add indemnification clauses to the agreements with their architects, which, in essence, are a contractual requirement that the architect reimburse the owner for damages caused by the architect's acts and/or omissions. It is absolutely critical that the architect confer with his/her insurance broker and/or attorney prior to agreeing to any such clause. Many of these clauses, as proposed, are so broad and onerous that they are not insurable by the architect's professional malpractice carrier and therefore put the architect at tremendous risk if the language is not modified.

Changes in Scope of Service

It is equally important that architects properly document any changes to their agreement with the owner during the course of the project. Almost every project is a very dynamic process, with changes occurring rapidly that impact the architect's scope of work and fee as well as the project schedule. Just as it is critical to properly document the agreement between the parties in the initial contract, it is equally important to document any subsequent changes during the course of the project. If a subsequent dispute arises, written change orders documenting any changes to the original

▶ "Defining Project Services" addresses the centrality of scope definition in developing effective agreements for professional design services.

▶ "Architectural Services and Compensation" discusses the variables for architects to consider in setting compensation, as well as various methods of compensation and strategies for getting paid.

agreement will be essential to allow a court to determine the agreement between the parties. It is essential that the architect documents these changes and brings them to the attention of the owner. If possible, a formal change order should be prepared and signed by all parties. In some instances, it may be difficult to get the owner to sign off on a change order during the course of a project. In those instances, it is critical to nonetheless document the changes in writing and send it to the owner advising them that a change has been made to the contract scope/time frame/fee and outline those changes. That documentation will be very helpful in proving the changes were known and agreed upon should a subsequent dispute arise.

Damages

Damages for breach of contract claims are typically measured by the standard of the plaintiff being entitled to compensation that would put them back in the position they would have been in if the contract had not been breached. If the case were litigated or arbitrated, the judge, jury, or arbitrator would have to decide what that compensation would entail based upon the arguments set forth by the litigants. In the previous example regarding the failure to produce record drawings, a judge, jury, or arbitrator may decide that the owner is entitled to the cost of having another design professional prepare those documents.

Vicarious Liability

In General

Agency relationships are common in everyday practice. That is, one party acts on behalf of another relating to a particular project or task. However, certain obligations and liabilities arise out of these relationships. The world of construction is no different. For instance, an architect's employee acts as an agent of the architect on a project. A corporate officer acts as an agent of a corporation in signing an agreement for professional services. Partners are agents and, under the law, also principals for each other. That is, partners are agents when they act for other partners (principals) and principals when their other partners (as agents) act for them.

Under an owner-architect agreement, the architect may have an agency relationship with the owner for certain designated activities. The central question in agency relationships is the scope of authority the agent has been granted to act on behalf of the principal. Thus, architects acting as agents of the owner need to know the limits of their authority in dealing with the contractor and other third parties. Firms will want every person who can be perceived as acting as the firm's agent to understand the limits of his or her agency authority. Staying within the limits of their authority is the best protection agents can give themselves and the principals they serve.

For Consultants

In many typical projects, the architect enters into a contract with the owner for all, or virtually all, of the design services for the project. The architect, in turn, retains consultants (typically engineers in various disciplines) to perform portions of the overall scope of design work. Consultants who perform professional services on behalf of architects under the terms of an architect/consultant agreement are independent consultants. In those situations, the consultant may sometimes act as an agent of the architect.

While the law will hold these consultants to the standard of reasonable care applicable to their professional expertise, the architect may be found to have liability for the consultants should an issue arise during the course of a project. In essence, many courts have found that the architect was contracted to provide the entire scope of design services and therefore has liability if a problem arises. While the architect may likely have a claim against its consultant for indemnification in such instances, such a claim may not fully exonerate the architect for future claims by an owner if, in the intervening period, the consultant has become financially unable to take responsibility or the consultant's insurance coverage proves to be inadequate.

▶ "Project Design Team Agreements" addresses agreements between architects and consultants and those who establish joint ventures between firms.

In some instances the owner, not the architect, engages certain consultants and the architect's obligations with respect to those consultants may be limited. Typically, the architect has far more limited exposure relating to the acts and/or omissions of those consultants. In these types of situations, the terms of engagement should be clearly stated in writing. Architects usually are not responsible for project consultants hired directly by the owner unless the architect agrees to this responsibility in the owner-architect agreement or acts in a way that makes the architect responsible, such as signing a Certificate for Payment or a Certificate of Substantial Completion for the consultant's work.

For Employees

Similarly, the architectural firm is responsible for its employees during the course of a project. The courts will generally hold the architectural firm itself responsible for the acts and/or omissions of each employee. A possible exception to this responsibility is if the employee clearly acts beyond its role and tasks required of it by the architectural firm. For instance, if, unknown to the architectural firm, the employee sells illegal drugs while on the job site, the architectural firm will likely not be culpable for those acts.

Alternative Project Relationships

The types of relationships between members of the construction community seem to constantly evolve and expand. In addition to the conventional owner, design team, and construction team relationship, a number of other alternative relationships are being employed in the industry. Two examples of these alternative relationships are contractor-led design-build and joint ventures.

Contractor-Led Design-Build: In this variation of the conventional construction project delivery, the owner contracts with one entity, the contractor, to provide all design and construction services for the project. The architect typically subcontracts directly with the contractor to provide services for the project. While this type of arrangement may offer many advantages on certain types of projects, it also raises certain potential risks to the architect that do not exist with the more conventional project arrangement. For instance, the conventional construction project arrangement is set up, in part, to provide a layer of checks and balances that protect the owner. In such situations, the architect typically has certain obligations to identify problems relating to the contractor's work and the contractor has similar obligations regarding the architect's work. These obligations may not exist, or at a minimum are severely compromised, in a design-build relationship. Many architects have been placed in very difficult situations when their client, the contractor, wishes to perform work in a way the architect may not agree with. The drafting of the agreements in these types of arrangements is critical in order to protect the architect from these types of problems.

Joint Ventures: It is common for the courts to consider the parties to a joint venture to be jointly and separately responsible for the actions of the joint venture. That is, if an injury occurs because of the negligence of either party to the joint venture, the joint venture can be sued collectively or the parties to the joint venture can be sued individually. Therefore, professional responsibility and liability should be carefully allocated in contractual agreements between the parties to a joint venture. Because many states qualify how and under what circumstances professional responsibility may be shifted to another party, legal advice should be sought when preparing such agreements.

Third-Party Actions

In addition to their obligations for damages to the party with whom they contract, architects can also be held liable for negligent acts, errors, or omissions that physically injure or damage third parties with whom the architect has no contractual relationship. These third parties include construction workers, passersby, and occupants or users of projects.

▶ "Project Delivery Methods" presents an overview of available models for project delivery.

The obligations to third parties stem from a variety of sources. In many states, statutes, regulations, and prevailing case law requires architects to safeguard life, health, public safety, and property and to promote the public welfare. In fact, many of those states use this obligation for licensed architects as one of the key considerations to justify the licensing and registration statutes themselves.

Prior to 1956, the legal concept of privity barred third-party actions. Privity required the litigating parties to prove they had a direct contractual relationship with each other and that the injury occurred in the course of that relationship. Since that time, the courts in many states have, with regard to physical injury and in some cases property damage, extended the group of individuals to whom architects may owe duties to include third parties whom architects can reasonably foresee will depend on them to provide services in a non-negligent manner. However, the law differs from state to state regarding the issue of privity and it is important to get legal advice to determine the law that applies to each particular project.

The types of potential third-party actions vary widely. For instance, a worker hurt on a construction site may opt to sue a wide range of entities involved in the project, including the architect, despite the fact that they had no direct contract with any of those entities. Alternatively, a visitor to the facility after completion may opt to commence litigation against the architect, owner, or others if they are injured during their visit due to alleged design or construction defects.

DEFENSES TO CLAIMS

Overview

In the unfortunate, but not infrequent, event that a dispute does arise on a construction project, the architect may have a variety of contractual or statutory defenses to bolster the factual arguments that may be made. While the law varies from state to state, the following are some issues that may impact claims against an architect.

Statute of Limitations

With very few exceptions (such as criminal charges for murder), the states have established specific time frames in which claims must be asserted, or they are permanently barred. For instance, generally stated, a claim based upon negligence against a design professional must be asserted within 3 to 10 years (depending upon the particular state's statute) after the completion of the project. As such, an aggrieved party could know about a potential claim during the construction phase of the project, but not be obligated to commence litigation until just before the statute of limitations expires. That is, the party could wait the full 3- to 10-year period of the applicable statute and then file a claim a few days before the statutory time frame expires. A breach of contract claim may be subject to a different time frame, even within the same state. While there are a few situations that would allow an exception (e.g., the existence of fraud on the part of the architect), these statutes have proven to be very helpful in protecting architects from older claims.

Statutes of Repose

Some states have incorporated statutes of limitation, while others use statutes of repose. Statutes of repose are similar to statutes of limitation and serve to set time limitations under which claims can be made against architects and others. Differing slightly from the statutes of limitation, statutes of repose commence running at the time that the alleged digression is discovered, and the statutory period for bringing a claim after discovery of the discretion is typically much shorter than a statute of limitation period. In addition, there is also a strict cutoff date for rights of action. For instance, a statute of repose against an architect could run for two years from the date a plaintiff knew or should have known about a claim, but that same statute would limit any potential claims to those filed less than six years from the date of substantial completion of the project. Under the preceding example, if a potential plaintiff knew or should have known of a potential claim at the time that the project was substantially completed but did not initiate a lawsuit until three years later, the claim would be barred. Similarly, under the same statute, if the potential plaintiff first learned of the potential claim five years after substantial completion, they would only have one year to make a claim since all claims would be barred that are not initiated within six years under that theoretical statute.

Betterment

This concept applies to some negligence claims asserted against architects. A negligence claim can be asserted against an architect either for (a) an error in some act performed (such as not designing the stairs to code, resulting in the necessity of replacing them); or (b) an omission [the architect did not include a component of the project in its design (such as not showing carpeting that was required in a hallway) and that component needed to be part of the project for a successful completion]. While the law differs from state to state, generally the architect would be responsible for the costs arising from its errors, but may only be responsible for a fraction of the cost attributable to its omissions. In a situation such as described above, in which the architect did not specifically designate carpet for a particular hallway, resulting in a change order from the contractor, the courts have generally found that the owner would have had to pay for the carpeting anyway, had it been shown on the plans originally. Since the courts do not want to allow the owner to get something for free, and many courts recognize that a contractor may charge a premium for such a change order, the damages typically awarded by the courts against the architect are only the costs of that premium.

Collection Actions for Architectural Fees

Studies by some professional malpractice carriers have shown that one of the leading reasons for claims against an architect is the architect's initial pursuit (whether in formal litigation or not) of fees due on the project. There is a belief in the industry, although not scientifically proven, that the reason that some owners file counterclaims against architects is an attempt to get the architects to compromise, or walk away from, their outstanding fees.

The time and cost expended in defending such a claim may exceed any fees that are ultimately realized. As such, all architects must thoroughly consider the potential risks and benefits of asserting such a claim before commencing such a demand. It is critical that architects employ diligence during the course of the project to ensure that their fees do not fall into significant arrears, as well as to include contractual provisions when first forming their contract with the owner that will assist them if such a situation arises.

CLAIMS AVOIDANCE

There is a belief held by many in the construction industry that if an architect practices long enough, he or she is almost certain to be involved in a claim of some sort. In reality, many architects are never formally personally made a party to litigation, but almost everyone is ultimately involved in one or more disputes involving a project and at least threatened with litigation. Notwithstanding that fact, the architect can definitively and substantially reduce the odds of being included in a claim as well as the odds of being found liable if a claim unfortunately arises by taking proactive preventative steps. For instance, having a proper contract, as discussed above and elsewhere, is invaluable. Two other key steps that each and every architect should employ on a regular basis are proper communication with their client and using proper documentation on each project.

A staggering percentage of claims in the construction industry is based, in whole or in part, on the failure of the parties to properly communicate. On construction projects, problems often arise when the failure in communication leads to a failure to

▶ Suggestions regarding proper documentation are more fully discussed in the backgrounder, Project Documentation, which accompanies this article.

manage the expectations of the other party. On construction projects, project participants often come to the table with markedly different backgrounds, experiences, and goals, which all result in each of the participants having significantly different expectations. Those differences are typically most acute in the relationship between architects and clients. Many clients have limited or no prior construction experience and do not understand the nuances involved in the process. Such clients have high expectations for their projects, beyond anything ever contemplated by the architect. The problem is often that both sides *assume* that the other has similar thoughts and expectations as they do regarding critical components of the project. By the time those differences become evident, significant problems may exist on the project.

It is incumbent upon the architect not to assume that the owner is of the same mindset of the architect. At the risk of being too elementary or redundant, the architect must continuously endeavor at each and every step of the project to assist the owner in knowing what to expect in both the short term and long term during the design/construction of the project.

For instance, owners may also fail to realize that professional judgment, and potentially owner input, is required at each step, since the architect makes the recommendations and the owner makes the decisions. Architects need to remind these project participants that buildings, unlike automobiles, cannot be pretested. Despite the effort, care, and conscientiousness of the architect, the process of taking a project from drawing to reality has a lot of unknowns. The architect must make the owner aware of these unknowns, their potential impact on the project, and what is being done to address them.

BACKGROUNDER

PROJECT DOCUMENTATION

Donald W. Doeg, Esq., PE, LEED AP

Perhaps the most critical component to a successful construction project is effective communication. Among the many benefits of proper communication, one of the most compelling is that it will mitigate, and perhaps even eliminate in certain circumstances, any potential claims. Project documentation is perhaps the most essential element of communication in the construction industry.

It is critical that architects maintain appropriate documentation for each and every project. Not only is it beneficial to the daily activities for each project, it is invaluable if claims ultimately arise. If a construction dispute goes to litigation, the adjudication of many construction claims often takes place literally years after the event(s) in question occurred. In many of those disputes, the exact wording and timing of the critical communications plays a large role in the outcome of the case. Unfortunately, many of us cannot remember what we had for dinner a few days ago, let alone all of the nuances of a conversation that occurred several years prior. However, contemporaneous documentation during the project is generally allowed as evidence during a trial and can greatly influence the final outcome of the trial, in either a positive or negative way.

Documentation accomplishes a number of purposes:

- Provides a written record of the contractual relationships between the parties

- Provides a written record of the scope of the work to be accomplished
- Serves as an ongoing communication process that tends to raise the level of understanding between the parties and eliminate problems
- Provides a chronology of the events of the project
- Provides a consolidated record if the parties have to revisit the project at a later date

Perhaps one of the best rules of thumb to use when deciding the amount of paperwork to generate is for the architect to try to put himself in the shoes of the recipient. In generating paperwork to the owner-client, the architect wants to keep the owner informed of all of the significant events of the project. However, the architect may not want to besiege the owner with superficial details or small issues that the architect, as the professional who the owner retained to perform the project, should handle.

Another key consideration in deciding the type and volume of paperwork to generate is that, as the project architect, it is critical that an architect **manage the expectations** of the owner and others on the project. The architect should generate paperwork that enables other parties to understand his position and what may be expected in the future. Managing expectations goes a long way toward mitigating or eliminating problems on construction projects. Proper management of expectations can be accomplished in a variety of ways; it is important that the architect finds a style that works best for him or her and the firm.

In order to persuasively present or defend a claim, adequate documentation will be needed. The goal should be to be able to re-create exactly what happened on a job, when, and why. Among the documents suggested for use from the beginning of a job, before there is any reason to even think about claims, are:

- Diary/daily notebook or site observation reports (if electronic devices are not used).
  - Write in ink.
  - Use bound or spiral notebooks (they add credibility that the notes were contemporaneous if a dispute later arises since one cannot add new pages between existing notes).
  - Number and/or date pages sequentially (no gaps).
  - Keep contemporaneous records: The purpose of the project diary is to identify and discuss key events on the project at the time they occur for reference at some time in the future.
- Electronic devices: Establish an office protocol for contemporaneously accumulating in one location all notes taken in the field.
- Photographs/videos.
- Correspondence.
- Status letters: As part of efforts to manage expectations, your client should be updated on a regular basis.
- "Issue" letters. Flag significant changes or potential problems, because no one likes surprises:
  - Confirm issues that can later become subject to debate; for instance, changes to scope of work

or determining owner's desires for project (such as owner identifying on a certain date that he wanted to accomplish X).

- Letter sent to confirm owner's position can serve to lock him in said position.
- Letter sent to question owner's position if contractor or others (with whom you have no contractual ties) dictate certain changes and indicate that owner has represented that it is to be done.
- When writing letters, do not assume that the owner knows everything or is doing certain tasks. If your response to the issue or recommended actions are based on assumptions, *let the owner know each and every assumption in the letter.*

- Minutes of meetings.
- Memos of telephone conversations.
- Project scheduling information.
- Change order logs.
- Shop drawing logs.
- Progress payment logs (both from owner and to consultants).
- Payroll records.
- Equipment use records.
- Accounting records/cost reports.
- Estimates.
- Bids.
- Material invoice files.
- Claim reports.

BACKGROUNDER

COPYRIGHT LAW FOR ARCHITECTS

Joseph H. Jones Jr., Esq., AIA

Joe Jones is a risk management attorney and director of Schinnerer's risk management services. He provides risk management advice to Schinnerer and CNA clients, and is a resource on evolving areas of professional liability exposure for both design professionals and contractors.

Original creative expression is an intrinsic part of an architect's professional services. An understanding of copyright law and how it applies to an architect's professional service is an important part of any successful architectural practice.

U.S. copyright law protects the creativity captured in the architect's instruments of service, such as design and construction drawings, models, and other design representations, as well as the built structure. To protect themselves from copyright infringement, architects should be familiar with their rights under the law.

Architects need to understand the intellectual property rights intrinsic in their professional services. With some clients viewing professional services as a commodity and the plans, specifications, reports, and other documents that architects produce as products, architects should understand the business and liability issues relating to the use, ownership, and control of their designs and instruments of service.

As clients look for more ways to reduce the costs of design and construction, many view the "reuse" of designs as a way to eliminate the need to hire another architect and save money. Actions like this may put the architect at risk for professional liability from any problems that develop from subsequent uses of the same plans. In addition, the architect may lose fees if the client neglects to acquire the copyright to a design.

(continued)

Maintaining the copyright to their designs gives architects a level of control over their creative and professional endeavors. Clients will have to retain them for future projects, which may help an individual architect or firm maintain a steady stream of new business. In addition, surrendering copyright could lead to liability problems for the architect if that issue is not properly addressed in the professional services agreement.

COPYRIGHT BASICS

Intellectual property rights fall into three main areas: trademarks, including service marks; patents; and copyrights. Trademarks and patents are registered by the U.S. Patent and Trademark Office, while copyrights are registered with the U.S. Copyright Office. Architects appear to have the greatest exposure to copyright issues, which are the focus of this discussion.

According to statistics from the CNA/Schinnerer design professional liability program, 44 percent of intellectual property claims against architects and engineers from 2002 to 2011 involved allegations of copyright infringement. Of those claims, 66 percent involved architects and 55 percent involved residential projects. Interestingly, these statistics show that design professionals brought more than 57 percent of all claims for copyright violation.

It is a common misconception that copyright is a subject of interest only to the creators of copyrighted material. Both users and creators of copyrighted material must understand the limits of copyright protection as well as what constitutes fair use of copyrighted material.

WHAT CAN BE COPYRIGHTED

In brief, the U.S. Copyright Act protects "original works of authorship fixed in a tangible medium of expression." It does not extend to items such as procedures, processes, and systems, which are typically matters for patent law.

USE OF COPYRIGHTED MATERIAL

A common misconception is that *ownership* of a thing is the same as *copyright* of that thing. The difference between ownership and copyright can be illustrated by what happens when you purchase a book, burn it, or give it as a gift, but you do not own the copyright. Copyright laws give the creator of an original work the exclusive right to reproduce or display that copyrighted work.

Clients who fail to realize that the architect's designs and instruments of service are copyrighted may duplicate a set of drawings and specifications with the intention of using them for future projects. This misuse of the architect's materials opens the client to a possible copyright infringement claim and may cause liability problems for the architect because the project may not be properly designed for another site.

2.4 Insurance Coverage

Ann Casso and Fredric W. Schultz, CPCU

Architecture firms use insurance as an instrument to help them manage the inherent risks of business and the specific risks associated with projects.

As key players in the highly complex design and construction process, architects must protect their firms against a multitude of risks that can jeopardize the future of their practice, the firm, and the individual financial well-being of themselves and others. Insurance is a means to manage risks by transferring them to an insurance company.

As a firm owner and licensed professional, an architect obtains insurance coverage for professional liability, property loss, and personal loss. As a firm grows, it is useful for staff recruitment and retention to consider providing staff benefits as well, including various insurance and retirement plans.

Ann Casso is the executive director of the AIA Trust, and Ric Schultz is an advisor to the AIA Trust.

Some of the categories of insurance an architect should consider include the following:

Firm programs

- Professional liability insurance
- Business owners insurance (may include general liability, property and casualty, valuable documents, workers' compensation, business auto, umbrella, and employment practices)
- Life insurance for firms and components
- Business disability insurance
- Members retirement plan—includes 401(k)s, profit-sharing, SEPs, IRAs
- Practice-related legal information service

Individual programs

- Individual 10-year level term life insurance
- Personal disability insurance
- Short-term and student medical insurance
- Prescription and healthcare discounts
- Dental insurance
- Accident insurance
- Medicare supplement plan
- Long-term care insurance
- Automobile insurance
- Homeowner's/home office/tenant insurance
- A service to identify individual and small group healthcare plans for members and components, until an endorsed medical plan may be secured in the future.

PROFESSIONAL LIABILITY

For architects, the most devastating professional and business risks are almost certainly from litigation alleging negligence in the performance of professional services. Alleged negligent acts, errors, or omissions may cause damage to owners, contractors, or other third parties. In addition, the architect's firm may be found liable for these damages. A professional liability insurance policy (sometimes called errors-and-omissions, or E&O, insurance) absorbs a portion of such claims in exchange for the premiums paid to the insurance company.

Architects may be held liable for design errors and omissions that fall below the professional standard of reasonable care.

SELECTING INSURANCE BROKERS AND INSURANCE COMPANIES

Buying insurance is a major business decision. An architecture firm therefore will want to select a broker in much the same way it selects a lawyer and accountant—with care and scrutiny as to the broker's qualifications, independent judgment, offered services, cost, understanding of the profession, and ability to work with the firm. Independent insurance consultants are available to help architects select an insurance broker or decide between the product of an exclusive agent and those offered by an insurance broker.

An independent broker—in contrast to an agent for a specific carrier—will examine the insurance market and obtain premium quotes for specific levels of coverage and service, evaluate the quotes, and provide a professional opinion as to which policies fit the architecture firm's needs. An architect pays for this expertise and service. While some brokers work on a fee basis, most receive a commission—essentially the architect's money—paid to them by the insurance carrier out of the premium. Commission rates vary, and the architect has a right to know the commission level for each quoted premium. In some cases, a broker actually is an agent of a specific company, and while the agent may be able to offer coverage from other carriers, he or she may have a financial incentive to direct the architect

(continued)

to that company. Again, architects have a right to know whether a broker has an agency relationship with a specific company. The architect has the right to request that the broker work on a fee basis instead of for a commission.

A broker can do more than advise in the selection of insurance carriers and policies. Brokers can prepare the application, represent the architect in disputes with the insurer, and send claim notices to the insurer on behalf of the architect. A firm also may rely on a broker to help the firm:

- Communicate with insurance markets regarding all aspects of the firm's insurance needs.
- Evaluate the firm's range of liability exposures and identify various forms of insurance available to protect it from financial loss.
- Evaluate and recommend a specific insurance program based on criteria such as the company's stability and financial strength; premium cost, limit, and deductible programs; coverage terms; claims management; and risk and practice management techniques.
- Analyze the insurability implications of changes in the organizational structure or nature of the practice.
- Review proposed contractual provisions affecting insurability while the professional services contract is being drafted.
- Monitor claims administration.

Once premium quotes have been obtained, the decision about which policy to accept should not be made on price alone. A number of factors should be scrutinized when considering which carrier best meets a firm's needs.

POLICY CONSIDERATIONS

- What is the scope of coverage being offered, what endorsements are available to expand coverage, and what is being excluded from coverage?
- What is the proposed cost of the basic policy and any endorsements?
- Is the firm buying insurance to meet a coverage requirement or as a key component of its financial management program?

ATTRIBUTES OF THE INSURER

- How extensive is the insurance company's experience in underwriting professional liability for architects? In

particular, what is its track record during hard markets, when few carriers offer insurance?

- How flexible is the company in meeting the firm's needs? Does it offer project insurance and coverage for design-build, prior acts, and retirement?
- How strong is the company? A. M. Best Company rates an insurance company's relative financial strength and ability to meet its contractual obligations based on its profit, cash liquidity, reinsurance quality, adequacy of reserves, and management strength. This rating is part of the annual insurance survey conducted by the AIA and engineering societies, and the rating is also one of the AIA commendation requirements. Standard & Poor's rates a company's ability to pay claims over time. Moody's also rates aspects of an insurer's financial strength.
- Is the company a licensed or admitted carrier? Such a carrier subjects itself to all of a state's insurance rules and regulations. In many states, a state commission reviews and approves company rates and policies before they can be implemented. In all states, having a licensed (admitted) carrier means the insured is covered by guarantee funds, which may provide coverage should the company fail. Coverage for architects under guarantee funds varies by state. Generally, the protection provided by such funds has become more restrictive in terms of limits of liability and eligibility. Nonadmitted (or excess-and-surplus) carriers are not subject to the same regulation and oversight. The state neither regulates their coverage nor evaluates their rates. This translates into extra flexibility for the carrier, which historically in soft markets has produced low premiums and in hard markets has made insurance less available.
- How extensive is the company's experience in the management of professional liability claims against architects? What claims services will it provide that will benefit the firm?
- How will the legal defense of claims be handled? Against what criteria are the company's defense attorneys evaluated and appointed? How much say will the architect have in the selection of counsel and in the conduct of a legal defense, mediation, arbitration, or in settlement decisions?
- What professional liability risk management services will the insurance company offer? Does it offer reference publications, contract review services, education programs, and risk management updates?

Some firms decide not to purchase professional liability insurance, a business decision usually based on the cost of the coverage. However, not having insurance could ultimately put the firm and its architects in jeopardy. Even firms that buy professional liability insurance retain some risk, such as expenses within their deductible, costs exceeding their policy's limits of liability, or costs for claims excluded from the scope of coverage.

Professional Liability Coverage

Generally, a professional liability insurance policy covers the insured firm's liability for negligent acts, errors, or omissions resulting from the performance of professional services as an architect, provided these services are performed within the geographical territory defined in the policy. All policies cover the United States, its territories, and its possessions, and many offer worldwide coverage in the basic policy or by specific endorsement.

A basic policy provides legal defense of claims covered by the policy and pays defense costs subject to the policy limit and deductible. Most insurance companies retain attorneys who are experienced in the defense of professional liability claims. When a defense attorney is selected and approved by the policyholder, the policy-holder—not the insurance company—is the defense attorney's client. Some companies may allow firms to choose their own defense counsel.

Broad policies insure not only the firm but also any partner, executive officer, director, stockholder, or employee of the insured firm when that individual is acting within the scope of professional duties. Some lower-cost policies may not automatically provide such broad coverage.

Policy limits. How much insurance a firm buys is a function of its financial needs (including those of its principals), its tolerance for risk, its risk management abilities, and the demands of its clients. Minimum annual aggregate limits of liability for E&O

MEETING PROJECT INSURANCE NEEDS

Architects should understand that a firm's practice policy covers the firm for negligence in providing services during the life of the policy. They also should know that professional liability claims from all projects can draw on that one policy or on the firm's own resources for indemnification. As a result, owners sometimes ask firms to acquire additional insurance that would not be eroded by claims from other projects. Such insurance can be provided in several ways. For example, the CNA/Schinnerer program offers firms three choices: project insurance, additional liability limits, and split limits.

Project insurance. A separate policy can be purchased for a specific project that covers the entire design team's negligence for that project. Neither the claims nor the billings of the project policy have any effect on a firm's practice policy. The policy can last up to 10 years.

Additional liability limits. This arrangement allows firms to purchase an endorsement that can provide up to $5 million of coverage for a specific project in conjunction with their practice policy limit.

Split limits. This choice allows a firm to secure a per-claim limit of liability and a larger term aggregate limit of liability. Although the coverage is not dedicated to any single project, an owner who wants a $1 million dedicated limit might find it acceptable for the firm to have a practice policy with a $1 million limit per claim and a $2 million aggregate limit.

Of course, a firm may always increase its overall practice policy limits. Again, while not dedicated in any way to an owner's project, higher limits give a firm more assets with which to pay all claims on all projects should the need arise. The lists below highlight the various forms of coverage.

Project Insurance
- Guaranteed term
- Guaranteed rate
- Unlimited number of policies
- Costs easily identifiable to owner
- Limits up to $30 million available
- Claims do not affect practice policy.
- Project billings do not affect practice policy.
- Covers entire design team's negligence
- Dedicated limits

Additional Liability Limits
- Annual renewal option
- Annual rate (not guaranteed)
- Only two endorsements per policy
- Costs easily identifiable to owner
- Limits up to $5 million available
- Claims can affect practice policy.
- Project billings affect practice policy.
- Covers only the insured firm's negligence
- Limits may be shared.

Split Limits
- Annual or multiyear term option
- Term rate (not guaranteed)
- Per-claim limit available to all projects
- Must estimate cost for project owner
- Claims can affect practice policy.
- Project billings affect practice policy.
- Covers only the insured firm's negligence
- Aggregate limit sharing during policy term

insurance are usually set at $250,000, with maximum limits running as high as $15 million (even higher limits can be arranged for special circumstances).

Deductibles. To encourage risk management, insurance companies require a deductible amount that a firm must pay to defend each claim or after each determination of negligence. Deductibles as low as $1,000 are available, but many firms increase their deductibles to lower their premium costs. As with most insurance, the higher the level of risk retained by the insured through the deductible, the lower the premium cost.

Costs of insurance. The premium for each firm is calculated individually by an insurer's underwriter, based on such factors as the firm's practice, project mix, claims experience, coverage needs, and resulting risks to the insurer. This makes comparing premiums of different firms difficult at best. Therefore, a firm should work with a broker who can present the firm well to an insurance company. Insurers increase the cost of insurance if risks cannot be clearly delineated, so the more specific and unambiguous the information a firm can provide, the lower the premium will be.

ESTABLISHING PROFESSIONAL LIABILITY INSURANCE PREMIUMS

Insurance seems like a simple business. Companies have to collect enough premiums to cover costs, make enough money to stay in business, and keep investors happy. Insurance company costs are many, and most are not apparent to the buyer. They include funds to cover administrative costs, costs of buying reinsurance, broker commission costs, state and federal government taxes, costs associated with insurance commission funds, stockholder dividends, and the investigation, defense, and payment of claims. Insurers operate on the "law of large numbers," which allows pooled premiums to offset individual losses. Over 10 years or so, the combined premium collected should approximate these combined costs. In any given year, however, either the insurance company or the insured individuals or firms may benefit more than the other.

The simplicity of insurance, however, often is influenced by the complexity of the financial markets. When interest rates are high, insurance companies try to bring in as much premium as possible to invest. Because there is a lag time between premium payment and the cost of claims, some insurers enter the market, collect premiums for investment, and leave the market before claims mature. When stock prices are increasing, some insurers enter the market offering low premiums to show an increase in their value to stockholders because of the influx of cash. After their stock prices rise and their investments in other stocks increase, they then can abandon the market before claims are brought against their policyholders and enter another venture on a short-term basis.

How does the insurance company calculate the precise premium a firm will pay? Sound underwriting management suggests that the insurer should actually measure the risk posed by the practice. As an example, an insurance company might consider these factors:

- *Billing volume.* Basically, the more services a firm provides, the greater its exposure to claims. This exposure is

influenced by the number of projects making up the annual billings. For instance, on an equal-dollar basis, in 1999 small firms were 14 times more likely to have a claim paid by an insurer than very large firms. Part of this is simply the number of clients and size of each project. The severity (the cost of each claim paid) for small firms, however, was only one-sixth as high as each claim paid on behalf of large firms.

- *Types of services.* On a properly underwritten risk, premium levels mirror claims data. Firms should separate billings for types of services as carefully as possible. If an insurer has less information, the premium will include an "ambiguity cost" to cover the potential effects of unknown risks.

- *Project types.* Firms that do lower-risk projects may pay lower premiums. However, some types of projects, such as condominiums, generate more claims than others because of complexity or number of clients.

- *Firm claims experience.* Premium levels also mirror the firm's claims history. Firms with claims-free histories can get as much as a 25 percent credit off the standard rate charged for similar firms. (State insurance commission regulations generally permit no greater credit.) Firms with bad histories can pay 100 percent higher rates than similar firms with average claims histories; firms with very bad histories may be uninsurable. Each insurance company has its own definition of "bad" and "very bad." In soft markets, when insurers want to write business to bring in cash, the definition loosens. In hard markets, it tightens.

- *Geographic location.* Firms in low-risk states pay lower premiums than those in high-risk states. Again, claims data define high-risk states. In 1999, for example, firms practicing in California or Florida paid significantly higher rates for insurance than firms practicing in Vermont or Kansas.

- *Continuity.* The longer a firm is with a professional liability insurer, the more comfortable the insurer feels in accepting the firm's risk. These clients receive not only better consideration (that is, lower premiums) during tight markets but also the benefit of the doubt should they suffer a series of claims. The value of this "longevity credit" can be substantial.

- *Competition.* The professional liability insurance market is highly competitive. Companies enter and leave the market all the time. The architect should be wary of a quote that looks too good. The history of the industry shows that some companies price their policies lower to bring in premiums and then disappear when the claims roll in, leaving the architect with no coverage. Disappearing or underfunded insurance companies are a key problem with claims-made policies.

- *Coverage.* Based on its assessment of firm risk, an insurer calculates various coverage-deductible-endorsement-exclusion combinations and their premium costs. Firms can exercise some control over their premiums by negotiating these four factors through their broker. For example,

agreeing to a higher deductible reduces the insurer's exposure and hence the cost of the insurance premium. Small firms with low deductibles and many small projects create a higher risk of paid claims than firms with higher deductibles. Higher deductibles increase a firm's exposure to claims payments but also provide a greater incentive for careful client selection and practice management.

If you are working with an independent broker who is being paid to represent your interests, give that broker as much information as possible. Your application should accurately reflect your practice. If you have a claim that needs explaining, insist that your broker attach the explanation to your application. If you institute new quality management programs, tell the company about them. If you have continuing clients, make sure that fact is recognized. Anything you and your broker think would help the company evaluate your firm as a risk will be welcomed by insurance companies following sound underwriting procedures. And if you do not understand your premium, have your broker call the insurance company for an explanation.

Insurability issues. Insurability problems arise when owners ask architects in a contract to hold them harmless or otherwise indemnify them for the owner's negligence. Professional liability insurance companies provide coverage only for the insured firm's negligence in performing or furnishing professional services and exclude coverage for express warranties and guarantees. Certificates that have the effect of warranties, without a known fact or qualified professional opinion, are also excluded.

An extension of coverage is needed when an architect agrees by contract, in writing or orally, to indemnify and hold harmless some other person, such as the owner or contractor. However, if the architect is indemnifying the other person for the architect's own negligence, the coverage may be automatic with many policies. In most other contractual liability situations, such coverage may not be possible.

The architect should look for hold-harmless provisions before signing any contract for professional services. A clause that otherwise appears innocuous might contain such a provision. An architect who finds or suspects such a clause should submit the provision to the architect's attorney and insurance advisor. A promise to indemnify may fall within the scope of professional liability insurance coverage, but broad wording may mean that the promise is a contractual obligation that cannot be covered by insurance.

Interprofessional relationships. Architects routinely retain consultants. This relationship means that the architect also has vicarious liability for damage caused by the consultant's negligence. Insured architects will want to review their consultant's insurance status because, ultimately, they will serve as their consultant's insurer if that status is inadequate. Similarly, if an architect agrees by contract to limit the liability of a consultant, the architect may find that the risk of the consultant's negligence has been shifted to the architect and the architect's insurer. At times architects are subconsultants to other professionals or subcontractors to construction contractors. Examining the coverage of the prime design professional or the professional liability coverage of a construction contractor can alert the subconsultant architect to gaps in coverage that could result in the architect becoming the only target of a claim.

Joint ventures. From a legal standpoint, a joint venture is similar to a partnership, except that the joint venture has a more limited scope or purpose. If a professional liability claim is filed against a joint venture, one or all of the members can be held liable for any judgment rendered against it. Broad policies provide automatic joint venture coverage, while others exclude joint ventures from the basic policy and require a special endorsement that will not cover other participating firms in the joint venture.

Each member of a joint venture should obtain evidence from other joint venture partners that their policies have been properly endorsed, if necessary, to cover participation in the joint venture.

Project professional liability insurance. Project insurance covers the design team participants—even those who do not have practice insurance. The policy covers the architect and named professional consultants for the term of the project and for a predetermined discovery period after completion of construction. Depending on the insurance carriers of the firms covered by a project policy, coverage may then revert to the individual firms' professional liability policies.

Project insurance is intended to cover only one project and is usually paid for by an owner who wants coverage beyond that normally carried by architecture firms.

Expanded project delivery approaches. Insurance companies have begun to provide coverage for architects practicing in roles such as design-builder, construction manager, and land developer. While some companies offer endorsements for these services to the basic policy, potential gaps should be investigated to prevent uninsured liability. For example, a construction manager, as advisor to the owner, is covered under most professional liability policies, but the at-risk construction manager, acting as a general contractor, is not.

Claims. In the arena of professional liability insurance, there are two common triggers in a policy that require report of a claim. The first is obvious—receipt of a demand for money or services with an allegation of a wrongful act. This definition produces a clear reference point indicating when the insured and the insurance company should intervene. It also is broad enough to cover not only a lawsuit but also angry calls from clients demanding that the architect "fix it." The second trigger is more subjective—the threat of an action, or just a very troubling circumstance, that requires alerting the insurance company of a potential problem, even though it may not become a formal claim. A careful review of these policy terms is important, as failure to report a claim in a timely manner may jeopardize coverage.

Some policies permit firms to decide whether or not to report an incident and trigger claims assistance. Other policies mandate incident reporting.

Settlement issues. Most professional liability policies require the insurance company to have the consent of the insured before settling claims. In cases involving a disagreement about settlement between the insured and the insurance carrier, the insured may be liable for any judgment plus the cost of defense above the amount for which the insurance company could have settled the claim. Similarly, the insurance company may be liable for the cost of any judgment above the amount that the insured asked the company to settle for. This check-and-balance approach encourages the insurer and the insured to work together to manage claims.

OTHER LIABILITY INSURANCE

In addition to professional liability, an architecture firm may want to carry general liability and employment practices liability insurance.

Commercial General Liability

Other liability exposures, such as slips and falls, libel and slander claims, and property damage to third parties, can arise from an architect's office operations and nonprofessional activities at the job site. To cover such exposures, architects should carry a commercial general liability policy. The following are elements of protection provided by a general liability policy.

Coverage. A commercial general liability policy provides coverage for claims arising against the insured involving third-party legal liability, but it does not cover professional, automobile, and workers' compensation exposures.

Contractual liability. In addition to professional service contracts, the architect can encounter a variety of business contracts, including office leases, purchase orders, service agreements, and the like, any of which may contain a hold-harmless provision that will contractually transfer another person's legal liability to the architect. The architect must check all contracts, agreements, leases, and purchase orders for hold-harmless agreements. The commercial general liability policy automatically provides contractual liability coverage subject to policy exclusions.

Business automobile liability. Business automobile liability protection is an essential part of the architect's insurance program. The insurance should be written with adequate limits of liability to cover the business use of automobiles by the policyholder, by employees, or by others. The policy should name, as insured persons, the individual architect, all partners in a partnership, and all officers and directors of the corporation.

Coordination of liability insurance. Professional, general, automobile, and other liability policies are interrelated. The architect should seek insurance counsel to avoid gaps in protection or duplication of coverage and to correlate limits. Umbrella or excess liability policies may sometimes be needed to provide higher limits than those offered by basic liability coverage.

Excess (umbrella) liability policies. When higher limits of liability are required, certain underlying policy limits can be increased through the purchase of an excess, or umbrella, liability policy. This policy provides higher limits in conjunction with underlying general liability, automobile, and employer's liability policies.

Employment Practices Liability Insurance

No one likes to think that their employees may sue them one day, but employment practices claims are becoming an increasingly common basis of civil litigation. Recent changes in the laws related to employment have dramatically magnified both the complexity and the potential legal dangers inherent in any professional service firm's personnel management function. The number of employee harassment, discrimination, and wrongful termination charges filed has increased correspondingly.

Sound management practices will help deter claims and lawsuits—and will help provide a strong defense when allegations are made against a firm. Employment practices liability insurance is another form of protection.

OTHER BUSINESS INSURANCE

In addition to liability insurance, an architecture firm may choose to purchase insurance for other business risks.

Architect's Property Insurance

The architect's office building or the leasehold improvements where the architect is a tenant should be insured by a standard policy or by a broader all-physical-loss form. Careful attention should be given to establishing an accurate insurable value for the building or improvements. The amount of insurance always should be adequate to meet business requirements, such as purchasing insurance for the building improvements on a replacement cost basis rather than on a depreciated cash value basis. All leases and mortgages should be reviewed, as they frequently stipulate coverage requirements.

Office Contents

The architect's office contents can be insured by a standard policy covering fire, windstorm, and other extended coverage perils. Separate burglary and theft insurance also can be written to cover office contents. However, broader coverage of office contents is generally available to insure them against all risks of direct physical loss except as excluded in the policy.

Such insurance covers drawings that are damaged, but only to the extent of the cost of labor and materials to produce them. It does not cover the cost of the research that went into their preparation, although such coverage may be obtained by purchasing valuable-documents insurance.

Portable equipment that may be used outside the office can be insured under an all-risk floater policy. Money, securities, checks, travel tickets, and other negotiable instruments can be insured under a blanket crime or similar policy.

Valuable Papers and Records

Insurance coverage for valuable papers and media is critical for protection of an architect's property and generally must be specified as part of the overall coverage in a business owner's package policy. It covers the total value of documents lost or destroyed by any of the means described in the policy and is generally an all-risk coverage. Coverage also is available for client documents in the custody of the architect.

Business Interruption

Business interruption insurance reimburses the architect for continuing fixed expenses and for loss of profits in the event fire or other insured casualty interrupts normal business operations. This insurance can be written to cover fire, windstorm, computer crashes, and other hazards.

Options are available to reimburse the architect for the expenses of continuing business at another location while the damaged premises are being repaired.

Fidelity Bonds and Loss of Money and Securities Insurance

Usually all persons involved with the custody or disbursement of funds, management of firm finances (receivables and disbursements), authorization of payments to contractors or others, purchasing, and other activities requiring the use of funds or liability for the misuse of funds of others should be bonded. A blanket form of bond covering all employees is typically recommended.

Money, securities, checks, and other negotiable paper may be insured both inside and outside the firm's premises under a broad-form money and securities policy to include loss by robbery, burglary, theft, or disappearance and destruction by fire or other causes.

Comprehensive bonds or blanket crime policies are available. They combine coverage for loss of money, securities, and other property under a blanket fidelity bond. The architect's professional liability policy does not cover claims and losses stemming from the dishonest acts of associates or employees.

EMPLOYER-RELATED INSURANCE

Architects with employees must face the prospect of additional insurance coverage for their employees. Some of this coverage is mandated by statute; some is at the discretion of the firm. This insurance is designed to protect the health and income of the employee and often of the employee's family.

Workers' Compensation

By statute, an employer is required to carry workers' compensation insurance. Sold by commercial insurance companies (or, in some states, available through state-run facilities), workers' compensation policies provide protection for work-related injuries. Benefits are prescribed by statute and include medical expenses, lost wages, and death benefits. These benefits are provided regardless of employer or employee negligence. Employees are precluded from suing their employers for injuries covered by workers' compensation.

A workers' compensation policy is rated, based on the firm's payroll, to cover various classes of employees. A full-time field architect performing construction contract

The AIA Trust was established in 1952 to develop life, healthcare, disability, and other insurance programs, as well as benefit and financial planning programs of the greatest-possible value, and to make them available to all AIA members. It is governed by a board of trustees, composed of AIA members and an AIA component executive.

Today the Trust offers comprehensive benefits and services at affordable rates to AIA members. All Trust programs are listed at www.TheAIATrust.com with detailed descriptions and application forms, eligibility requirements, and contact information to obtain personalized quotes. In addition, links to related risk management and healthcare reports, as well as useful articles for reference from the quarterly newsletter *AIA Trust News*, may be found on the Trust site. The Trust sponsors numerous education seminars at AIA conventions and for AIA components on a wide variety of topics, including risk management, legal issues, and retirement planning.

The following plans are available to AIA members and, as appropriate, to their employees and families; most are also available to component executives and their staff:

- The AIA Commended Professional Liability Insurance
- Business owner's coverage for general liability coverage for firms and optional riders for valuable documents,

workers' compensation, employment practices, and umbrella
- Healthcare programs including dental, long-term care, short-term medical, and Medicare supplement insurance, as well as healthcare discounts. The AIA Trust currently offers a Medical Brokerage Desk service to find individual and small group healthcare insurance plans for members.
- Life insurance, with 10-year level premiums, for individuals. Group plans for firms are also offered.
- Accidental death and dismemberment insurance
- Disability insurance for personal and business overhead expenses
- Auto and homeowner's insurance
- Retirement plans such as 401(k) plans for small firms and component offices
- LegaLine, a legal information service

Many of the programs offered by the AIA Trust are aimed at serving the AIA's largest constituency—the small firm. The services the AIA Trust offers AIA members have evolved over the past 50 years and will continue to evolve to meet the future needs and practice requirements of members.

administration services will have a higher rate than an architect who does not perform these services. Care should be exercised in the classification of employees to ensure proper coverage and rates applicable to the hazards involved. Improper classifications can result in much higher premiums.

Health Insurance

Healthcare is a major but costly consideration for employees, the beneficiaries of the coverage, and employers, whose professional livelihood depends on a productive and healthy staff.

The cost of health insurance has been increasing at a rate far higher than that of inflation and wages for the past four decades. As a result of spiraling healthcare costs, health insurance plans and healthcare delivery systems have undergone significant changes in recent years, and employers have had to develop strategies to control the increases in their benefits costs.

Medical insurance. The types of health insurance plans available in the marketplace continue to change, and the distinction between plan types has become somewhat blurred. In general, health insurance plans fall under one of the following categories:

- Indemnity plans
- Preferred provider organizations (PPOs)
- Health maintenance organizations (HMOs)
- Point-of-service plans (POS)
- Consumer-directed plans
- Limited medical plans

It is important to keep up-to-date in the fast-moving health insurance arena. The national emphasis on healthcare reform and the Affordable Care Act have produced substantial changes and requirements for both employers and employees.

Indemnity plans, which have become rare except in rural locations or under collective-bargaining agreements, provide the same level of benefits for all providers and generally require an up-front deductible and co-insurance for covered services.

PPO plans provide enhanced benefits if services are rendered by a provider that is part of the vendor's preferred provider network but generally still require some cost sharing through co-payments or co-insurance. A PPO plan also provides benefits when care is obtained through providers that are not part of the PPO network, but requires more patient cost sharing than in-network services.

HMO plans generally limit services to those provided by a network of providers except in emergency situations. In addition, with many HMOs, a primary care physician (PCP) acts as a "gatekeeper" for services, with benefits for non-PCP services being paid only if the PCP provides a referral. Patient cost sharing in an HMO plan is usually lower than a PPO plan.

Similar to HMOs, many POS plans require coordination through a PCP. To receive in-network benefits, care must be recommended and referred by the patient's PCP. Otherwise, out-of-network benefits will apply. However, POS plans frequently have fewer restrictions on the referral process; these are often called "open access" POS plans.

In an attempt to control rising healthcare costs, new types of account-based medical plans, called consumer-directed plans, have been developed to increase patient awareness of the true cost of healthcare and provide tools to make patients better healthcare consumers. The two distinct types of consumer-directed plans available are health reimbursement accounts (HRAs) and health savings accounts (HSAs).

HRAs combine an employer-funded reimbursement account that can be used for qualified medical expenses, with a high-deductible health plan if the funds are exhausted. Unused funds in the HRAs can be rolled over from year to year but are forfeited if the employee leaves the employer plan.

HSAs are generally more uniform than HRAs. For instance, to qualify for an HSA, a participant must be enrolled in a high-deductible health plan with a minimum deductible. Enrollees in a qualified high-deductible health plan can set up a separate HSA and accrue tax-free money in this account that can be used for qualified medical expenses. While there is an annual maximum that can be contributed to the HSA, there is no limit to the total amount of money that a participant can accrue in this account. In general, HSAs are funded by the individual, but some employers have chosen to also put money into these accounts for employees who elect high-deductible plans. It is important to note that employer money in an HSA belongs to the employee and remains with the employee, even if the employee terminates employment.

Another new trend is limited medical plans, which offer basic healthcare coverage with relatively low claim limits and thus maintain reasonable premiums but do not cover catastrophic situations.

When purchasing health insurance, a firm must be aware of state and federal rules and regulations that govern health insurance. A key federal regulation that affects health insurance offerings is the Health Insurance Portability and Accountability Act (HIPAA), which became law in 1996. HIPAA was designed primarily to make health insurance more portable for employees when they change jobs, and to increase availability of health coverage for small employers.

In general, there are three distinct markets within health insurance: individual coverage, small group coverage, and large group coverage. Individual coverage is used when people buy coverage on their own, outside of their employer's coverage (if offered). With individual coverage, insurance companies can request and review medical information and potentially deny individuals who apply for individual coverage. If accepted for coverage, individuals may be required to pay different rates based on their age or health status. The only exception is when an individual switches from a group plan to an individual plan. In this circumstance, there is a special HIPPA protection that requires that the individual be offered a policy with no preexisting limitations; otherwise, HIPAA protections generally do not apply to individual plans.

Small group coverage is an employer-sponsored plan that covers 2 to 49 employees. (Depending on the state, a sole proprietor may qualify for small group coverage.) In the small group market, insurance companies may not turn down employees for coverage, but they can review medical information and adjust their rates based on medical conditions, age, industry, or other factors. Each state regulates how much adjustment insurance companies are allowed to make.

Large group coverage generally refers to groups with 50 or more covered employees. Large group coverage generally has more flexibility in plan design and uses the claims experience of the covered population to establish rates.

The health insurance marketplace has seen significant change and consolidation in the past several years. The number of insurance companies selling health insurance has shrunk to just a handful, and many regional managed care companies have merged with larger national insurance companies.

The small firm owner who lacks buying power may not have access to a great deal of choice in coverage options. Therefore, a key consideration should be selecting a stable insurance provider with a proven track record in offering similar coverage. An employer will also have to weigh the balance between offering a plan with more freedom of choice, such as a PPO, with the cost of a less-managed plan.

Dental insurance. Benefits for dental care required as a result of illness or injury may be provided under a medical insurance plan. Insurance to cover regular dental care can be obtained through either an indemnity plan or a dental HMO or PPO. Typical dental plans provide full coverage for preventive care (cleanings and exams) and require patient cost sharing (deductible and co-insurance) for nonroutine and more expensive treatments.

Vision care. Vision care plans typically provide benefits on the basis of a schedule, paying a flat dollar amount toward the cost of one routine eye examination and a set of appropriate lenses, frames, and contact lenses every 12 to 24 months.

Healthcare flexible spending accounts. These plans, authorized under federal tax laws, allow participants to make pretax contributions to a special employer-managed account and then be reimbursed from this account for eligible, uninsured, out-of-pocket healthcare costs. Contributions are exempt from FICA, federal, and most state income taxes.

Federal tax laws also authorize similar accounts for dependent care expenses. These accounts permit an employee to pay for work-related child-care expenses with pretax dollars. Regulation of such accounts is an especially fast-moving field, and advice from the firm's accountant is essential.

Income Protection and Replacement Benefits

In addition to health benefits, a firm may offer life insurance and long-term disability protection.

Life insurance. These plans provide benefits in the event of the death of the insured. They should be thought of as income protection for the spouse or other employee beneficiaries and also as a potential source of protection for the firm in the event of the death of the owner or a principal. Group term life insurance (such as the product marketed by the AIA Trust) is commonly provided to all employees as a fixed-dollar amount per employee or as a multiple of salary.

Disability benefits. State disability benefit laws provide benefits for employees who are disabled due to non-work-related injury or illness. Not all states require this coverage, but in those that do, minimum benefits are fixed and prescribed by statute. For states where disability benefits are not mandated, or in situations where the architect wishes to increase mandated coverage, voluntary disability coverage is available through a number of commercial insurance companies, as well as through the AIA Trust.

Disability benefits are provided in several forms. Short-term disability benefits protect against absence from work of short duration, typically three to six months. Both small and large employers often self-insure against the risk of short-term disabilities through a sick leave program, although it is possible to buy insurance for this purpose.

Long-term disability benefits protect against extended disabilities, often until the employee recovers or reaches age 65. The cost of this insurance is quite modest, and long-term disability insurance provides greater assurance that the financial resources to pay a claim will be available indefinitely. A third party is often needed to determine the continuance of disability; for architects, it is important that the test of disability be their ability to practice their chosen profession. This is the test used in the AIA Trust policy.

Business overhead expense (BOE). BOE disability benefits are similar to long-term disability benefits except that BOE protects business-related expenses in the event of total disability of a business owner. Benefit periods range from 12 to 24 months, and this low-cost insurance helps a business owner cover ongoing business expenses (e.g., rent, mortgage interest, utilities, and employee salaries). This valuable insurance coverage allows a disabled owner to maintain the business viability or avoid a forced sale of the business should the disability condition be long-term or permanent.

CHAPTER 3

Marketing and Strategic Planning

3.1 Firm Identity, Image, and Expertise

Bradford Perkins, FAIA

Neither of the adjacent quotes is entirely correct, but it is true that virtually all successful architectural firms depend a great deal upon their image and perceived expertise for their success. Most successful firms also work hard to establish the image they think they need for success. This chapter briefly summarizes some of the strategies that firms employ to build expertise and a positive image.

Over time all firms establish an image. For smaller firms operating within a limited geographic area this image is often closely tied to the public perception of the founding principal or principals as well as a few of the firm's best known projects. For larger firms operating nationally or internationally with multiple principals, the firm's image may be very different in different locales and to different people. Whether large or small, however, all architects need to establish an image that supports their professional aspirations.

Some well-known consultants have confused this issue by trying to divide firms into a few categories. One came up with the very unhelpful distinction of "design" and "service" firms. Virtually all architects aspire to an image that they are good at both. Another came up with six categories: Innovators, Project-type Specialists, Full-service Client Partners, Community Contributors, Project Management Experts, and Cost and Quality Leaders. Again, while most thoughtful firms choose an approach to their practice based on their interests, strengths, demands of the market, and many other factors; they also often seek to create a positive image for their firms in all of these categories. The lesson here is that few firms can be sorted into a category with a simple definition, and even fewer should aspire to be so categorized.

While the reality of most firms' desired image usually defies simple categorization, many firms work hard to build strong images as project-type specialists, innovators, effective project managers, and valued client partners. At the same time most firms seek to create a unique image that separates them from other firms in their market or markets.

"Clients in all markets seek value from their architects. A firm's distinctive expertise should match what its ideal clients value most."

—Jack Reigle, President of SPARKS: The Center for Strategic Planning

"Image is Everything."

—1990 Andre Agassi Canon Commercial

For those firms seeking to build an image as a strong designer or design firm, the first step is doing good work. This, however, is rarely enough. There is a lot of interesting work being done, and it usually takes an aggressive effort to get good work widely recognized and attributed to the design architect or firm. The typical techniques include cultivation of the press, getting work published, entering and winning design awards, and participating in design activities such as awards juries, speaking at schools or design symposia, teaching design at architectural schools and related activities. It also typically requires that the firm pay particular attention to all of the things that the public and potential clients see: the office design, stationery, brochures, websites and other marketing materials, project photography and presentation materials, and the like. It also may require careful editing of the work that the public sees and attributes to the architect or the firm. One prominent firm with a strong design reputation made much of its revenue doing prisons but almost never publicized this experience outside the justice facility market.

Given the preference by the public and press for relating project designs to personalities, many successful architects also cultivate personal personas that support their image as talented designers. This does not necessarily require Frank Lloyd Wright's flowing hair, cape, and pork pie hat (or the current fashion in some architectural circles of black clothing and designer glasses); but it does require the ability to communicate design ideas in a way that engages other design professionals, opinion leaders, and the public.

For those who want to be viewed by the public and potential clients as experts in a particular project type, doing successful work for prominent clients in the field is a necessary first step. Many well-known firms became known because of one particularly successful project that they effectively publicized. Perkins+Will's international reputation for school design was launched by the widely published and innovative Crow Island School in Winnetka, Illinois. For Kohn Pedersen Fox's distinguished practice in commercial high-rise architecture, their design of 333 Wacker Drive in Chicago gained them national attention. Both firms—as well as most other large firms—do far more than one building type but they continue to promote an image that they are leaders and innovators in the building types that form the core of their reputation.

Once a firm begins to develop a reputation for a particular project type, they will reinforce it by getting projects published or writing articles for client publications (such as *American School & University* or *School Planning & Management*, or *Health Care Design for Health Care Facilities*), enter and win design awards sponsored by client organizations (such as the AIA and Leading Age's Design for Aging Awards for Senior Living Projects, or The Council of Educational Facilities Planners, International for schools), attending and speaking at client-oriented conferences, writing a textbook or articles on the subject, creating Apps or computer-based databases relevant to the typical client's issues and concerns, as well as other activities that reinforce the firm's image as experts in the field. Gensler's development of an impressive library of benchmark data on different types of corporate interiors is just one of the tools they have used to become an international force in this specialized field. Ayers Saint Gross helped build their reputation for campus master planning with a similar database of leading college and university master planning information.

Other firms build their images around research and/or new technologies. Kieran Timberlake emerged as a leading firm in part because of their commitment to research. As they highlight on their website, "we seek ways to improve the art, quality, and craft of architecture through research into new materials, processes, assemblies and products." William McDonough + Partners rose to prominence due to Bill McDonough's early leadership in the sustainable design movement that has now become a major theme in architecture today.

For firms who want to convey their project management expertise, again it starts with actually having the expertise as well as respected clients that will provide confirming references for your expertise. Firms that have created particularly strong images for their project management prowess, however, typically reinforce their image with carefully documented systems and procedures for such basic issues as schedule and cost management, quality control, and project closeout. Again, websites that speak to this expertise, writing articles and books, speaking at conferences, and other activities reinforce the desired image.

For firms that want to be seen as the leaders in their communities for a wide range of building types, deep involvement in community activities is usually required. As Jack Reigle wrote in the 14th edition of this *Handbook*, "Many design professionals begin with a small, local practice. The difference between being a high performing community firm and an underperforming generalist is the relationship of the firm, particularly its principals, to community organizations and individuals. Community knowledge firms are so woven into the fabric of the community that they open doors that are closed to outsiders. They can expedite decision making by virtue of their professional and personal relationships in the community." (Page 100, 14th Edition)

An often-overlooked aspect of an architect's image related to the firm's and its principals' is its reputation for being ethical, responsive to client concerns, and easy as well as fun to work with. This is usually dependent upon client references and the principals' interactions with others in the community, and it can be critical. Clients usually know that they will be spending a good deal of time with their architect and that they will be relying heavily on the architect's expertise and advice for success. Thus, they want to like and trust the firm they choose. Moreover, others in the community—including other design professionals—are more likely to recommend an architect who they like and trust to clients and others who can be helpful in an architect's career.

In every instance outlined above, getting to the top ranks in the profession is dependent upon building an image for quality work and good service. You can be a project-type specialist, a strong project manager, a pillar of the community, and many other things, but without an image as an architect who does high-quality work and provides responsive service, some of the rewards of a successful practice will be beyond your reach.

Ambitious architects often strive to build an image that will appeal to their clients and support their mission as a firm. For the larger firms, as well as some smaller firms, this often requires the firm to build a multifaceted image. More than one architect has complained that his or her firm is known for just one thing when that is only one of the many things they do well. This is why trying to force high-quality firms into a short list of categories is usually unfair. Most firms and architects can do more than one thing well and their goals for their practices typically defy preconceived boundaries. Thus, no two firms or architects will have identical images, but most successful architects and firms actively try to build an image that will support their practice's goals.

3.2 Marketing and Business Development

David Koren, Assoc. AIA, FSMPS, CPSM

MARKETING ARCHITECTURAL SERVICES

To build a successful architecture practice, pay close attention to everything the firm does to attract new business and retain existing clients. A strategic approach to marketing enables a firm to allocate resources to support activities that serve the growth of the practice. This article provides an overview of how architecture firms secure work.

David Koren was Vice President of Business Development and Design at ESI Design. Prior to ESI, he held senior marketing positions at WSP, Perkins Eastman, and Gensler—all global design firms. He is a past president of the NYC Chapter of the Society for Marketing Professional Services, and author of *Architect's Essentials of Marketing* (Wiley, 2004).

Introduction

Marketing is the process of bringing new business to a firm in order to sustain and grow the practice. Marketing is much more than proposals and presentations; it involves everything that helps to spread the word about a firm, communicate with prospective and existing clients, and get the work in the door—including correspondence, the firm's website, the quality of the firm's design work, the firm's reputation, even the way the receptionist answers the phone. No matter what role an individual plays in a firm, and no matter how large or small a firm is, every employee has an important part in the marketing process by working to satisfy the needs of existing clients and attract new clients to the firm.

Many firms approach marketing in a somewhat haphazard way, but it is important to market thoughtfully and strategically in order to allocate resources efficiently to effectively attract and retain clients. This article and the four that follow discuss marketing-related topics including the basic principles of marketing an architecture firm, the strategic process, research, brand strategy, budgeting for marketing, website development, media relations, business development, networking, social media, the sales process, positioning, targeting new clients, and lead development and tracking.

The topics discussed in this chapter apply to firms of every size. Whether the firm is a sole practitioner or a very large firm, the basic process and principles of marketing are the same, and are vital to the success and growth of the practice.

Marketing Architectural Services

Marketing architectural services is different from marketing other services or marketing a product. Architecture involves a complex mix of creative and technical skills. In the marketing process, convincing prospective clients of a firm's creative and problem-solving abilities, attention-to-detail and follow-through, and passion for the project can all be vitally important. Because what the client or potential client is actually buying is the individual expertise and ability of the team members, differentiating a firm from the competition happens on an individual and personal level.

While it is easy to believe that a prospective client's decision of which firm to hire is rational (that they will hire the firm that has the best experience, capabilities, and fee), the fact is that the prospective client is a person or a group of people, and which firm they choose will also be based on emotional factors. People tend to select people whom they like and trust, people whom they believe will be good to work with and will help them achieve their desired results.

In building credibility with prospective clients and conveying that the firm is the right one for a specific project, the firm's portfolio of prior work is important, but the portfolio will not win the job on its own. The portfolio lets the prospective client know that the firm has done this kind of work before and is capable of doing it for them. From there, the prospective client will make a personal and emotional decision among similarly qualified firms. All the facts about the firm that a prospective client has gathered along the way—including project experience, the quality of work, fee, and so forth—serve to reinforce and justify the decision of whom to hire.

While the marketing efforts of many architecture firms are focused on winning work from new clients, it is important not to forget about existing clients. It is generally much easier and less expensive to win new work from an existing client than from a new one. If a firm has worked for a client and has done a good job, the client has no reason not to hire the same firm again. A firm's first priority in marketing is to keep existing clients happy. If existing clients are happy, they will not only hire the same firm again, they will also recommend that firm to other people they know who may be considering an architectural project. No recommendation is more valuable than the endorsement of a satisfied client.

In marketing an architecture firm, relationships are everything—with clients and with other third-party influencers in the marketplace such as contractors, consultants, real estate brokers, and so forth. People talk, and the relationships that individuals in the firm have will influence the way that others perceive the firm: Positive relationships can help, and negative relationships can hurt. When pursuing work with a new client, it is vital that members of the firm build a relationship with the individuals involved in making the purchase decision. Without some kind of relationship, some kind of natural affinity that helps the client to like and trust the key individuals from the firm who will be servicing the project, it is unlikely that the firm will prevail in a competitive environment. Unfortunately, if a firm enters the selection process without an existing relationship with the prospective client, it is probably already too late—one of the competitors is probably way ahead, and now has the "inside track" with the potential client.

The Purchase Decision

To many architects and other professionals, "sales" is a dirty word. The idea that they would have to "sell" something makes them break out in a rash. Many people hate to sell. "Business development" has a much better ring to it than "sales." It sounds professional; it sounds like there is an established process for bringing in work.

From the architect's perspective, the business development process is about convincing the prospective client that the firm is the best firm for the job. The conventional selection process is often conceived and explained as very straightforward and linear—moving from hearing about a project to getting more information to presenting qualifications, a proposal, and a presentation; and then, if all goes well, entering negotiations and winning the project.

Instead of a straight line, if we think of this process from the client's perspective, it looks more like a funnel: Many firms are qualified, fewer will be invited to submit a proposal, fewer still will be asked to present, and only one firm will be selected.

Of course, the competitive landscape and selection process vary based on the client's industry. In more public selection environments, such as in government facilities or schools, an opportunity will likely be publicly advertised, resulting in a large number of competitors. When the client is a private company or institution, such as a developer or a corporation, there may be fewer competitors from the outset, possibly an invited list of firms known to have expertise in the specific facility type being planned. And when the client is an individual or a closely held corporation with whom the firm has a long-standing relationship, the firm may have the privilege of being the only firm under consideration.

Before entering any selection process, it is important to understand who the client is, what their priorities are, and what the competitive landscape is. Does anyone in the firm know the client personally? Is it possible to meet with the individual or individuals who will be making the decision? Are the client's objectives and concerns for this project clear to the proposing team? How important is the architect's fee in their selection decision? At what point in the process will fee be discussed? How many firms will be considered? How relevant is the firm's previous experience to the project in question?

Once enough information has been gathered about the project, the client, their objectives and concerns, and the competitive landscape, a decision can then be made about whether to pursue the project or not. This is commonly called the "go/no-go decision."

Once a decision has been made to "go," all efforts should be geared toward addressing the client's specific questions and concerns about the project. The goal in the process of preparing qualifications, developing a proposal, and presenting to the client should be to position the firm not only as qualified and capable but also as the best firm for the project, the firm best able to deliver a project that meets the client's objectives.

The Importance of Good Decision Making

Pursuing new work can be expensive. Depending on the size of the potential project and the amount of effort put into the pursuit, it is possible to spend a great deal of time as well as significant financial resources on printing, binding, models, renderings, travel, meals, client entertainment, and the like. Resources, in terms of time and money, are always finite, even in a large firm. Pursuing one major opportunity may mean that there are fewer resources to pursue other opportunities. This is why it is absolutely critical that good decisions are made about which clients and opportunities to chase, and which to decline.

Being strategic, by definition, means saying no to some opportunities. If a firm pursues every opportunity that appears, this is not acting strategically, or even with a strategy in mind. By developing a strategic approach to marketing and by allocating resources intelligently, focusing on the key opportunities that the leaders of the firm really want and believe they can win, the key individuals in the firm can take more control over their destiny as professionals.

In order to make good decisions about where to put limited resources, it is important to understand the client and the competitive environment, and to approach decision making in an objective frame of mind. Research about the client and the project should be conducted in as dispassionate a way as possible. Then, it is important for the individuals leading the pursuit to try to assess the situation from an objective perspective, asking questions such as, "If I were this client, would I hire my firm for this project? If I were this client, and I could hire any firm at all, whom would I pick? Which firm is the absolute best choice for this project? Who has the most experience in this project type? Who has the best press in this area? Which firm feels like the right choice?" It may be helpful to have a conversation with a friend, associate, advisor, or mentor who knows the industry well to ask these questions and gain the benefit of a broader perspective.

Architects often learn about a new opportunity and respond with, "We can do that!" no matter what the project type is or whether they have designed something similar before. But unless no one has ever done a project like this before, the client is likely to hire the firm with the most experience, or at least a firm that has done enough similar projects to convince the client that they are intimately familiar with this type of project. There is usually no point for the client in taking a risk on a less experienced firm.

That said, the value of a relationship with the client cannot be overstated. If a firm's leader has a strong existing personal relationship with a decision maker, they may be able to overcome concerns about inexperience relative to the competition. Clients hire design consultants they like, trust, and want to work with. And that will be easiest to gauge if they have worked with a firm before.

Because of this, when determining how to prioritize efforts, what to pursue, what to decline, and how to spend resources, it is vitally important not to take existing clients for granted, or prioritize gaining new clients over keeping existing clients happy. A firm is far more likely to be awarded work from people who already know the firm, and like and trust its principals, than they are from people they have not met or barely know. It is vitally important to spend enough time and attention on the relationships the firm already has, and not to spend too much time courting new clients at the expense of those existing relationships.

How Passion Fits In

One often-overlooked factor that can distinguish a firm from the competition is its passion for the project. Because what is being sold is the promise of future performance and the firm's abilities to deliver on that promise, enthusiasm for a project can make a huge difference in influencing a potential client to hire the firm. It is important to find ways to demonstrate how much key individuals in the firm want to do the project, in a way that is natural and proportionate to the project. For example, on a very important project, it may be perfectly appropriate to say, "This is the most exciting project that has happened in this city in years, and we are very excited at the opportunity to work with you on it!" However, if the project is small or not very exciting, the passion of,

"We really want to work with you!" may be all that can be mustered. It is important for the firm's principals to decide why they want to do this project and then figure out how to express this passion to the client. In a close race between competitors, enthusiasm can be the factor that wins the job for one team over another.

That said, passion can also get in the way of objective decision making. It is too easy to take the attitude that, "This project is important and we really want to win it, so the facts aren't really important here. We're going after it full-on no matter what." It is critical to step back and consider the possibility that the firm may lose the project and really evaluate objectively whether the pursuit makes sense. The firm may decide to pursue it anyway. But at least then the firm's principals are entering the process with their eyes open, and making good decisions about how they are prioritizing their time, and how much energy they are devoting to this pursuit at the expense of other activities.

MARKETING STRATEGY

Marketing efforts will be most successful when they mesh with the vision and operations of a firm. To create an effective plan for improving marketing and building business, your firm's long-term goals must be clear. This includes setting goals for business growth, as well as goals based on the design aspirations of the firm's principals and staff.

The firm's business plan can provide a good starting point for developing a marketing strategy. A business plan is a high-level discussion of the basis and objectives for beginning a new business venture, and for its overall operations over time. Depending on how your firm has developed its business plan, it may contain some indication of target markets, financial goals, and hiring and staffing strategies.

To begin the marketing planning process, it is advisable to bring key firm leaders together for a strategy meeting. Below are 10 key questions that can form the agenda for a productive strategy meeting, one that results in answers that form a basis for the firm's marketing strategy. It will be helpful to do some research before the meeting to have information handy on the firm's markets, competitors, and clients to help facilitate discussion of each question.

1. *Who are we?* Key firm leaders must agree on their vision for the firm and its basic identity. What kind of practice is it? What do the leaders of the firm believe in? What is the firm known for? Is the firm a design-based practice, known for a signature design style that can be applied to many kinds of projects, or is it a specialist practice, expert in the design of a specific facility type?

   There are advantages and disadvantages in being either a generalist or a specialist. A strategy of *generalization*, of pursuing work in a number of markets, can enable a firm to grow by pursuing new kinds of work. This strategy is often more stable, as downturns in one market may be offset by opportunities in others. A strategy of *specialization*, of pursuing work in one or just a few markets, can be incredibly profitable while the targeted market is hot but does not usually enable the same long-term stability as the generalist strategy. When a firm "owns" a market—when it becomes the obvious leader in a given area—a lot less time and money are required to bring in new work, and the firm's profitability can soar. In practice, many firms follow a hybrid strategy that involves specializing in several key markets, ideally providing the firm with some of the stability of a general practice and some of the benefits of a specialist practice.

2. *What markets do we serve?* Key markets should be defined carefully. Markets can be defined by geography, service, client industry, and facility type. Members of a firm could define its market by saying, "We provide architectural and interior design services for academic institutions in the Midwest, with a special emphasis on dormitory projects." There should be a clear distinction between the markets the firm works in now and the markets the firm would like to move into. It is important to have a clear, realistic picture of the firm's position in each desired market, and to

consider the competition in each market. Who is your firm competing against? Which firms are the most successful? Make a list of all major competitors, and briefly discuss the strengths and weaknesses of each.

3. *What are our strengths?* What is your firm really good at? The answer could be design, service, or some special knowledge or expertise. In listing a firm's strengths, it is important to emphasize those that are truly unique to the firm. A generic strength such as "We're responsive to clients" is something any service provider in business today should be able to claim, and therefore would not differentiate a firm from others.

4. *What are our weaknesses?* It is vitally important in the marketing strategy process to be honest about liabilities. What are the things that your firm does not do as well as it could? List everything that might affect the firm's performance, or the perception of the firm's performance—both internally and externally. Establishing an understanding of weaknesses is the first step to overcoming them, and it can minimize the amount of time spent chasing opportunities that will be difficult to capture.

5. *What are our opportunities?* Consider each market in which the firm is active and identify opportunities in those markets for growth or for developing greater depth in existing areas. What's changing in these markets? Are there trends that could be capitalized on to achieve growth? Could the firm offer new services, explore new geographies, or become expert in designing new facility types? It may be helpful to ask, "What will we be doing in 10 years that we are not doing now? What opportunities do we need to take advantage of now to get there?"

6. *What threats do we face?* Threats are factors in the marketplace that could hurt a firm's current position. An honest appraisal of threats is invaluable in planning the firm's future direction. What are competitors doing that threatens the firm's position in its existing markets? Is the firm facing new competitors? Are there trends in existing markets that may negatively affect your firm and its business? One way to get at the heart of this subject is to ask, "What keeps us up at night?"

7. *What's our vision for the firm?* A vision statement is a written expression of the firm's highest aspirations. This is the place to use superlatives: best, leading, largest, most, finest. What is your firm all about? Design? Innovation? Efficiency? Service? How does the firm's work improve the lives of its clients? How does the firm change the world for the better with every project? A vision statement could be something like this: "AB&C is a design firm that improves the lives of hospital patients and medical professionals by taking a fresh look at healthcare design and applying best practices from around the world to our projects." A vision statement should be as concise as possible. When you are crafting one for the first time, it may help to begin by writing it as long as it needs to be and then to cut out what is not absolutely essential. Try to pare it down to one key idea, if possible. The final statement should be as active and as ambitious as possible.

8. *What's our mission?* A mission statement is much more directed than the vision statement. It describes where the firm is going. It describes how the firm would like to change its practice in the future. It is important to think big, but at the same time a firm must create a mission that is practical and achievable. A sample mission statement might be, "Our mission is to be the most respected laboratory design firm on the West Coast. We intend to accomplish this by hiring the best staff, rigorously improving the quality and accuracy of our designs, and delivering on our promises." When developing a mission statement, it helps to ask, "Where do we want to go now?" Is there an existing market the firm ought to penetrate further? Is there an area of existing practice the firm could strengthen? Be as specific and focused as possible.

9. *What are our goals?* The next step is to identify goals that will help your firm accomplish its mission. What does your firm need to do to accomplish its mission? Does the firm need to hire new kinds of staff, modify the design process, look for different

kinds of work, or make other significant changes in strategy or operations? Discuss how firm members are going to work to achieve these goals. Who will be responsible for following through with each goal? How soon will firm leaders reconvene to evaluate progress?

10. *How do we communicate our strategy?* Everyone in the firm has a role to play in marketing; therefore, it is vital for everyone to understand and participate in the marketing strategy. Consider creating a one-page marketing strategy summary that includes all 10 of these questions with brief summaries of the firm's answers and action plan, and then distributing it to all staff. It is a mistake to have the strategy shared only by the firm's leaders. The marketing strategy will be most effective if everyone is on board with where the firm is headed and if each person understands his or her role in helping the firm move forward.

"Firm Identity, Image, and Expertise" discusses how architecture firms can create strong firm identities.

Branding

Branding is a familiar concept in the world of products. Think of a few great product brands—Sony, Nike, Mercedes, Apple, Volvo: These names are closely associated with product attributes or even marketing slogans, such as safety for Volvo or "Just Do It" for Nike. Brands are an incredibly effective means of communication between companies and their customers. If a company has a clear and consistent brand, customers will know what to expect and will associate the company with certain key ideas.

Service companies have brands just like products companies do. Many service providers, however, are more comfortable using the word "reputation" than "brand," but both words have essentially the same meaning: what people have in mind when they think of a given firm. Brand is critical in differentiating one firm from another.

A firm's brand is built by every single interaction that people have with the firm. It is the consistency of experiences with the firm and its work that defines its brand. Once a firm decides on a specific brand message, the message should be conveyed to key audiences in a memorable way. If a firm declares it is all about service, for example, and if the firm's staff delivers on this promise so that everything its clients and the public see supports this, the firm will become known for service.

Once a firm has gone through the strategy development process and carefully considered its vision, mission, and identity, the firm can proceed with spreading the word to existing clients, prospective clients, and other audiences. Building a communications plan around your brand is a five-step process:

1. *Define your audiences.* What specific industries or organizations is the firm focusing on? Who are the people at these organizations the firm is trying to reach? How do these targeted clients interact with the firm now?

2. *Get a clear picture of how your firm is perceived.* This may require some research—asking people in various audiences what they think of the firm. It may be helpful to periodically take current or former clients to lunch and ask them directly to share what they think the firm's strengths and weaknesses are.

3. *Identify the firm's message.* The message should be as simple and clear as possible, and should be a direct reflection of the firm's vision statement. If possible, summarize the message in one keyword, such as "service," or a short phrase.

4. *Determine how to transmit the firm's message.* A firm's audiences can be reached in many ways. Consider your firm's work, staff, logo, office environment, business cards, advertising, proposals, and marketing materials. How can the firm make use of every contact with potential clients to get its message across?

5. *Make sure your firm "walks the talk."* No matter what, the brand must be backed up with action. A brand is empty and hollow if it is not consistent with the service the firm provides and the quality of the firm's work. If there's any fibbing, the staff will know, and before long the clients will, too.

One of the most important tools in a firm's brand communication is its name. It is important to consider the significance a name has to people who hear it, and how it supports the firm's vision and brand. The best names are distinctive and memorable.

Most architecture firms have one of the following types of names:

- *Multiple proper names.* Difficult to remember, and usually shortened to a set of letters that quickly lose their meaning. Examples: HOK, SOM, NBBJ, HLW, KPF, BBB, WATG, P+W.
- *Single name of signature architect or company founder.* Generally calls up the image of a visionary founder. Examples: Gensler, Jerde, Rockwell.
- *Anything other than a person's name.* Less ego is implied, but such a name can also seem less personal. Examples: Studios, Morphosis, Pentagram, Arquitectonica, Ennead, Populous.

When choosing a firm name, think about it carefully and objectively. Consider both how it looks on paper and how it sounds when people say it. Is it easy to spell? Is it easy to say? Consider any connotations the name has in your mind and the mind of your audience. Does it sound like anything else? Do you have an emotional response to it? Does it sound like the firm you want to be? If the firm carries a person's name or one combined from several surnames, what associations or connotations do those names have?

Positioning

Positioning is the application of a firm's brand to a specific market. While branding is the process of trying to influence the perception various audiences have of the firm, positioning is the process of packaging the company for a specific target market and determining how to define it relative to the competition in that market. The brand applies to the entire firm, in all markets, and should originate from the firm's vision statement. The position, however, applies to only one market. When figuring out how to position the firm, you need to ask, "How can we present the firm to this market, and how can we differentiate our firm from the competition?"

The value of market position becomes most apparent when a firm is in pursuit of a specific opportunity. A firm's position is its starting point and consists of what clients and potential clients think of the firm before they open a proposal or grant an interview. What do they know about the firm? What do they think of its work? How is the firm positioned in this particular market? Is it the leader or the underdog?

In their landmark book *Positioning: The Battle for Your Mind* (McGraw-Hill, 2000), Al Ries and Jack Trout describe positioning in terms of ladders in the audience's mind: Each ladder is a market, and each rung is a brand. Where a brand fits on the ladder is its positioning. For example, imagine what the positioning ladder looks like for cola drinks: rung 1: Coca-Cola, rung 2: Pepsi-Cola, rung 3: RC Cola, rung 4: everybody else.

Once the arrangement of a ladder has been set in the mind of the public, it is very tough for a brand to move up the ladder. Even though Pepsi generally wins in blind taste tests, it cannot knock Coke out of its position at the top. In another example, if an architecture firm is competing against Populous, formerly HOK Sport, in the sports arena market, it may be able to beat the firm on one project, but it will be very difficult to knock it off the top rung of the ladder. Populous is often the first firm a prospective client thinks of for sports arena design, and there is not much other firms can do about that.

The challenge is to define each market (that is, each ladder) as specifically and concisely as possible so that people can accept it as a unique market, remember it, and associate your firm with it. It is vitally important to define your markets carefully. What does your firm offer this market? Why should the firm pursue the market, and how will it become a leader in it? Much as the vision statement describes the firm's aspirations, the positioning statement sums up a specific market and the firm's position in it. For example, a positioning statement might read, "JKL is the leader in the design of intermodal transportation facilities. We are different from the competition because we have a thorough understanding of the complex circulation issues of people, trains, buses, and cars."

Developing a positioning statement is a four-step process that includes considering and answering the following questions:

1. *What is the market?* The market is defined by service, facility type, client industry, and/or geography. It can be any area that could have a marketable specialization and any permutation of those four factors. For example, a market could be the interior design (service) of retail locations (facility type) for fashion companies (industry) in the western United States (geography). Or a market could be only one or two of those factors, for example, real estate developers in Boston.

2. *What does the market need?* An assessment of the needs of the market requires input from clients and prospective clients. Find out what they would like to do differently but so far have not been able to. Find out what their hot issues are. Find out what the trends are. Identify any unsatisfied opportunities in the market. Then determine if your firm can fulfill any of these needs better than your competitors.

3. *Who is the competition?* To position a firm within a market, it is essential to know as much as possible about the competition. What other architects work in this market? How are they perceived? What is their positioning? Is another firm the clear leader in the market? (If so, you may want to redefine the market and try a new "ladder.") Are there any weaknesses in the competition against which a firm could position itself? For example, "We're just as good as RST, but we are cheaper!"

4. *What do we offer?* Most important to determining your firm's positioning is zeroing in on what the firm can bring to this market that none of the competitors can match. What experience, capabilities, or attributes does the firm offer that are truly unique? Why would a prospective client in this market be foolish to hire the competition?

Answers to these questions will help a firm put together a clear positioning statement, such as, "PQR is the leader in designing mini storage facilities in the Midwest. We can design and deliver a mini storage facility faster than anyone." Once the statement has been crafted, the next step is to spread the word in every communication the firm has with the identified market, and to back up the positioning by delivering on its promises.

The Marketing Plan

A marketing plan provides structure to marketing efforts on a continuing basis. Where there is a plan, there is a common understanding of marketing goals and objectives and what actions the firm will take to build its business. It is a measuring stick that guides decision making. When any kind of opportunity arises—whether a project or publicity or joint venture—the marketing plan provides a context for evaluating the opportunity and determining how to proceed.

Most firms create marketing plans in an attempt to expand their practice, whether in overall size, profitability, or the types of opportunities for which the firm can compete. Without a plan, a firm can probably win work and sustain client relationships, but it will be difficult to penetrate new markets or significantly increase market share in existing markets.

Developing a Marketing Plan

A firm should aim to have a marketing plan for each of its markets. If the firm does some retail work, some residential work, and some academic work, it should have a marketing plan for each. A marketing plan should be no more than a page long, if possible. A short and simple plan is most likely to be read and followed. The following is a short outline for what should go into a one-page marketing plan.

The market. Define the market as precisely as possible in terms of geography, service, industry, and facility type.

The mission. What do we want to accomplish? Describe specifically the impact the firm would like to have in this market. What is the major goal of this marketing plan? What do you want your firm's position in this market to be?

Current position and client base. Who are our current clients in this market? Describe where the firm is right now in this market. Is the firm a veteran, an underdog, or a newcomer?

As part of the planning process, consider carefully how much emphasis to place on new clients and how much to place on existing clients. The mix will vary depending on the firm's focus, current position in the market, and goals. Existing clients make great references for potential clients to talk to, and can also recommend your firm to their friends and business associates.

Market size and trends. How big is the market? What is changing? This may be the time to do some research to learn more about the market. How many projects are there each year in this market? How profitable are they? What trends in this market can your firm take advantage of?

Competitors. Which firms is your firm competing against? What are their strengths and weaknesses? Prospective clients will compare your credentials with those of other firms. What other firms will your firm be positioning itself against?

Positioning. Where do you want your firm to stand in this market? Have you defined the market in such a way that your firm can be the leader in it?

Objectives. Break down your firm's mission into smaller pieces. What can you do to achieve your mission? Do you need to do more business development, reach out to existing clients more, or work on media relations? Be as specific as possible here. If there is anywhere in the plan to add additional detail, it is here. This is the heart of the marketing plan—what firm leaders and staff members intend to do to fulfill the identified mission.

Responsibilities. It is important to assign specific responsibilities to individuals to make sure the objectives can be accomplished. Spread around responsibility. Everyone involved in this market should share in the responsibility of fulfilling the plan.

Schedule. Make it very clear in the plan when firm leaders will check on progress. By what date is each person named supposed to have accomplished his or her objective? Give them a time frame. If this is a one-year plan, it may make sense to review the plan every month or two to check progress, update the plan, and make new assignments.

Budget. The budget should quote a specific dollar amount for the firm's marketing efforts in this market. It should include hard costs (printing, networking expenses, etc.) and soft costs (staff time). Consider breaking out big-ticket items, such as a new brochure or attendance at a trade show.

Determining the Marketing Budget

Budgeting can be a difficult process. It is tough to put dollar values on expenses that have not appeared yet and expect to live by them for the lifespan of the budget. It is probably impossible to predict how many award submissions the firm will complete, or how many presentations will be made over the course of a year. This is why a budget is so important—it is a guideline for determining whether an opportunity is reasonable in terms of its cost.

To prepare a budget, start by developing broad categories for expenses. This may include marketing materials, photography, market research, public relations, business development, proposals, and presentations. Then make a rough guess at a reasonable amount for each category over the course of the next year, using any existing historical data as a benchmark. The first budget will be the most difficult to prepare; in subsequent years, as expenses are tracked, the firm will have more perspective on what is reasonable and which areas require investment of more resources.

SAMPLE ONE-PAGE MARKETING PLAN

The market: Architectural design of garages for shopping centers in Florida.

The mission: We want to be the leading designer of garages for shopping centers in Florida. We want to double our revenue in this market in the next year.

Current position and client base: We have designed three multistory garages for shopping centers in the last year for three different clients. However, we are often thought of as a designer of garages for corporate offices, not shopping centers.

Market size and trends: Ten to twenty new shopping centers are built in Florida each year. In addition, older shopping centers are being reclaimed as corporate offices (five to ten last year). There may be an opportunity to leverage our corporate office parking garage experience to expertise in shopping centers.

Competitors: VWX designs shopping centers and parking garages. RST designs parking garages and lots, mostly for sports arenas and amusement parks. CDE designs anything, anywhere.

Positioning: We are the leading firm in designing parking garages for shopping centers. Unlike our competitors, we are specialists in this project type. We have deep experience in parking garage design, not only for shopping centers, but also for corporate offices.

Objectives: We intend to

- Build our network of shopping center developers
- Redesign our marketing materials
- Conduct a Web-based marketing campaign
- Get articles placed in trade publications
- Be more aggressive in closing the deal

Responsibilities: [Put at least one name next to every item on your objectives list.]

Schedule: The time frame of this plan is one year. We will check on progress next month.

Budget: Our marketing budget for the year is $20,000. Of this, $5,000 will be for printing new marketing materials and the rest for networking and pursuing specific opportunities.

A Living Document

The best marketing plans are living documents. The marketing plan should not be filed away, but kept close at hand for reference and revisions. Over the life of the plan, unanticipated opportunities will come up. There may be serious setbacks for one reason or another, or the market may change dramatically. Whenever market conditions change, the plan should be updated accordingly. A plan that is not able to change over time runs the risk of becoming obsolete or irrelevant. When opportunities arise that had not been envisioned, the response should be carefully considered. An opportunity can be outside the parameters of the plan and still serve the mission—the spirit of the plan. The following questions will help determine how to evaluate a new opportunity:

- Does this opportunity serve the mission?
- What is the potential benefit?
- What is the total cost?
- Does it fit the budget?
- What is the risk?
- Is it worth it?

If the opportunity supports the mission, the plan can be changed to encompass the new opportunity. Otherwise, it makes sense to defer to the existing plan and decline the opportunity.

Business Development and Sales

The word "sales" can suggest an uphill battle of convincing someone to buy something he or she does not really want or need. Nobody likes to be "sold." Fortunately, the

Many firms budget 5 to 7 percent of their net fee revenues for marketing. Firms entering new markets or seeking to grow aggressively may budget more while established firms primarily serving existing clients budget and spend less.

—2012 AIA Firm Survey

BUDGETING MATRIX

This sample budget matrix has columns for different markets (in this case, academic, labs, and offices) to break down the budget by market sector. The top portion of this budget covers soft costs (principal, staff, and marketing time—probably the biggest dollar-value item on your budget). The bottom portion itemizes specific hard costs, such as project photography, brochure printing, and so on.

(continued)

SAMPLE BUDGET MATRIX

SOFT COSTS: STAFF TIME	ACADEMIC	LABS	OFFICES
PRINCIPAL TIME			
STAFF TIME			
MARKETING STAFF			

HARD COSTS: EXPENSES			
PHOTOGRAPHY			
BROCHURES			
REPRINTS			
DIRECT MAIL			
AWARD ENTRIES			
PUBLICITY			
TRADE SHOWS			
SHORT-RUN PRINTING			
RESEARCH			
TRAVEL			
NETWORKING			
MEMBERSHIPS			
TRAINING			

process of winning new business does not have to be about "selling." An architect needs to communicate that his or her firm is the right one for the project by making a personal and compelling case to the client that the firm has the best solution for the client's needs. Professionals win business by being truthful, competent, and personal. People who are hiring an architect generally seek to hire someone they like and trust—not someone who has "sold" them something.

The business development process can be approached in a number of ways. Many established firms are reactive in their approach: Clients and potential clients who know about a firm through prior experience or reputation send requests for proposals (RFPs) to the firm, which responds, hopefully winning a satisfactory portion of work to sustain its business. A proactive approach to business development is one in which a firm carefully selects the individuals and organizations it wants to work for and pursues them. A proactive approach gives a firm more control over whom it works for and the kinds of work it will take on, and can open up significant new opportunities and areas of growth. This approach can require considerable work, but it can also be highly rewarding.

Whatever approach is followed, relationships are critical to the process of winning new work. In an ideal situation, a firm will already have a strong relationship with the project decision makers when they begin the process of selecting an architect. Even if your firm has to compete to satisfy additional stakeholders (a board of directors or a public agency's purchasing policies), if you have a strong relationship, the firm will have an advocate in the decision-making group and will be able to get more accurate information from the potential client as to the real issues guiding the selection process.

If the firm's relationship with the potential client is not strong, or the firm does not have any relationship at all at the start of the process, it can be much harder to compete or even to have a sense of how the competitive process is going to unfold. All you can do is listen carefully to the potential clients and try to figure out who they are and where they are coming from, consider their objectives and priorities carefully, and respond with your qualifications and proposal, tailored to your understanding of the potential client and project.

Networking

Networking is vital to the marketing success of business-to-business services like architecture. A good network can make the difference between a flourishing practice and one that is struggling to survive.

Many people think of a network as a set of artificial relationships, a social convention that exists to fulfill a business purpose—sharing and trading information. But a professional network is essentially a circle of friends. The relationships in the network are real; they are based on authentic interpersonal connections.

Networking is an ongoing process; it should not happen just when the firm is pursuing work.

An architect builds his or her network the same way that an individual looks for new friends. Potentially beneficial contacts can be found in social situations—industry events, parties, and even on projects—or anywhere there are people with whom an individual feels a natural connection and where there is the possibility of a mutually beneficial relationship. What each side offers the other can be almost anything: industry information, connections, a good laugh, knowledge of the local community, gossip. All that is important is that the friendship is real and that each party has something to offer the other.

There are many different ways to build a network. Some people seem as if they want to know everybody, while others try to build tight bonds with a limited number of people. There is not a right or wrong way to build a network; you could build a great network with five friends (if the relationships are strong and they have information and connections) or with 600. Either way, the network needs constant attention to grow and evolve.

If an architect has built a strong network of people in related disciplines (engineers, contractors, real estate brokers, developers, and consultants), they can share information on upcoming projects. Initially, with newer contacts, the sharing may be more guarded and exploratory: "Have you heard anything about this new project?" With more established contacts, professional acquaintances will be thinking of projects for each other: "I heard about a new project that would be perfect for your firm."

Targeting Clients

Firms that are proactive in their business development efforts are much more likely to win projects that members of the firm are truly interested in, from individuals and organizations they want to work for. Being proactive means deciding which organizations you would like to work with, researching them, getting to know the decision makers, building relationships, and eventually pursuing and winning work from them. It can be a long process, but it is very important to building a business and taking it in new directions.

Start by identifying prospective clients with whom you would like to do business. Survey the markets in which your firm is currently working (defined by industry, facility type, service, or geography). Are there organizations the firm has not worked for in these markets that would make attractive clients? Make a list of 10 to 20 prospective clients to target.

Be realistic. Each potential client on the list must be an achievable target for the firm. Do not consider organizations for which there are serious roadblocks, such as those that only work with firms that are very different from yours, or organizations for whose projects your firm has no relevant experience.

Once you have assembled a list of ideal clients, begin to research them. Go online and find out everything you can. Ask people about them. Most important, try to connect with the key decision makers in these organizations. Who are they? What are their backgrounds? Whom do you know who knows them? How can you meet them? What can be your pretext for approaching them and getting to know them? Pursue the top targets aggressively, and try to make connections and build networks that get you closer to the decision makers.

Of course, you will not be able to get a meeting with every ideal client on the list right away. Simply having a list of target clients, and keeping up-to-date with their businesses and ongoing projects will prepare the firm to act on an opportunity when it appears.

Developing Leads

A lead on a potential project can come from practically anywhere—a friend, a work associate, a client, a family member, or even the newspaper. The more people who are familiar with the work an architecture firm does, the greater the likelihood someone will think of the firm when they hear about appropriate new projects. When a lead to a potential new project comes along, the following questions should be asked:

- *What is the project?* How big is it? Where is it? What is the budget?
- *What is driving the project?* Why is it happening now? What is changing in the potential client's business that necessitates this project? What objective is the potential client trying to achieve by undertaking this project?
- *Is it right for your firm?* Is this project not just something the firm *can* do, but something it is truly qualified to do, experienced in doing, and passionate about?
- *Who is the competition?* Which other firms will be considered for this project? If the answer is "none," great! If the answer is "an open field of 50 or 100 firms," not so great.
- *Does your firm have an existing relationship?* Does the firm have any connection to the people who are involved with this project? Whom can you meet? How can you connect yourself to the decision makers?
- *What is the timing?* If word about the project has hit the street (or if the project has been publicly announced), it may be too late—there are probably other firms already lined up to do the project. If the project is still being planned, there may be time to help the potential client with the process of defining the project and position the firm for the work.
- *Can you win the job?* Realistically, given the potential client and the project, and an assessment of the firm's experience, relationships, and competition, what are the chances of winning this project?
- *What should you do next?* Given everything that is known about the client and the opportunity, what is the best first step to pursuing this project?

Answering these questions puts a firm in a much better position to evaluate the lead and determine the appropriate level of investment. Many people hear about a lead and rush headlong into the pursuit, but it is much better to step back, evaluate the lead objectively, and then determine how high a priority this lead is and the proper course of action.

An important part of the process of pursuing leads is having a system for tracking them. If an architect is working alone to track a few leads, the system can be fairly simple—a notebook or a simple spreadsheet. But if the information needs to be shared with others within an organization, the firm may want to invest in a more robust lead-tracking database system. Generally, there's far more to be gained by sharing, as colleagues can help if they know someone related to the project. There is no one-size-fits-all system for tracking leads in the architecture business, however. Each firm has to find the system that works best.

The Case for Marketing Strategically

Many leading design firms have achieved success somewhat accidentally, through the personalities, connections, and panache of their founders. It is a rare firm that looks at marketing as an ongoing strategic process that is integrated into the operations of the firm. For those that do, the benefits are immense, including sustaining the firm, expanding its business, earning higher fees, and gaining access to preferred types of clients and projects.

Professionals who ignore marketing and do not develop their marketing and strategic thinking skills will have the terms of their work life—type of client, type of work, and even compensation—determined by someone else. The better an architect or architecture firm is at marketing, and the more strategically focused, the more likely the sole practitioner or firm will be able to work on truly interesting, profitable projects.

COLD CALLS

No matter how hard you try, there are times when you cannot find a connection to the decision makers on a project, or to anyone who knows them. When all other possibilities for contact have been exhausted, your alternatives are reduced to two: Pick up the phone and call "cold," or forget about the lead.

Cold calling is not a particularly effective means for bringing in work, so it should be your absolute last resort, after you have exhausted your network but still want the project and believe it is right for your firm. Relationships, more than any other factor, are what win work, and trying to build a relationship from a cold call is very difficult. In such calls, the person you are calling has no idea who you are—which is why it's called a "cold" call. Any warmth that arises from the situation will have to be your own. Even a warm call is better—when the person you are calling has heard about you or your firm before.

Despite its difficulties, if you are honestly interested in a project and believe your firm is qualified, a cold call may be worth a shot. Following are a few basic rules to follow.

Know whom you are calling. Know as many details as you can about the person you want to talk to. Know his or her name, title, role in the project, history, and anything else you can find out before you pick up the phone. The goal of the call is to get a personal meeting. Personal relationships are not built over the phone. Have a strong hook (something in your portfolio the person you are calling will want to see) that will get you the meeting.

Rehearse what you are going to say. When you get on the phone with the person, you may not have much time to break through his or her "sales filter" and convince him or her it would be valuable to meet you. Plan it, write it down, and rehearse it.

Be specific and direct. You are calling to talk about a specific project. Ask about it. Do not be shy about why you are on the phone.

Ask questions. Prepare good questions to ask about the project to show you have thought about the project—not just about the selection process. Ask questions the person you are talking to may not have considered.

Be yourself. Your goal is to build a relationship with the person on the other end of the phone line. Strike a balance between being as professional as possible while still letting your energy, enthusiasm, and personality shine through.

Send information, and always follow up. As a follow-up to your call, always send some information about your firm. Make it as specific to the project as possible. It should not be just your standard brochure; it should be specific information that will be interesting to the contact.

Marketing Systems

The technological systems that architecture firms use in the process of marketing their services have evolved rapidly in recent years. Knowledge management is vital to the success of a firm's marketing efforts and growing its business. Knowledge management includes all the systems—whether electronic, physical, or procedural—that enable staff to easily store, find, and utilize valuable information. Databases and filing systems can help, but it is unreasonable to start with a filing system or database and expect organization to be the natural result. Each firm has to begin with an organization system that feels natural, then add and build systems to formalize the organization and communicate how information is to be captured and shared.

Some firms have cultures that more effectively support knowledge management than others. Knowledge management requires people to be comfortable freely sharing information with each other. If a firm has a culture in which, for whatever reason, people with knowledge are regarded as more important than those without it, and where people are not comfortable sharing their information, it is going to be very difficult to institute an effective knowledge-sharing system. Real estate brokers are notoriously bad at institutional knowledge management, because the professional success of a broker is predicated on the broker having information that his or her colleagues do not have.

For firms that get it right, knowledge management can be a true differentiator, demonstrating a clear difference between a firm and its competition. When a client asks a question to which an architect does not personally know the answer, whether it is about one of the firm's past projects or which audiovisual consultants they work with, how long does it take to find the answer? Does the architect need to ask a person, or can the answer be found in some easy-to-use electronic or physical resource? If the architect can find the right information quickly, he or she will look much smarter to the client.

Think about all the different kinds of information a company needs to capture and maintain—on projects as well as in areas related to finance, legal issues, human resources, and marketing. Categories of information necessary for marketing and for which firms often implement knowledge management systems include research, leads, people, projects, and staff.

Research: Trends, Articles, White Papers, Thought-Leadership

Many professionals are conducting informal research all the time, through the articles they read and the formal and informal conversations they have with fellow professionals. Research is in many cases difficult to store and track because it can often be free-form information. It does not usually fit into a database, because the information generally is not easily separated into neat fields that can be searched later. Research information can also appear in lots of different formats, some of which are on paper: newspaper and magazine articles, white papers, reports, notes, and so forth. To support a firm's marketing efforts, it is important to create a system for storing research and other information that relates to the work of the firm.

Leads: Managing Information Down the Marketing Pipeline

In order to manage the business development process, it is important to find a way to track opportunities as they develop from leads to prospects, and then to projects. Some firms use customizable off-the-shelf systems to do this, while others develop their own systems. Lead-tracking software applications are commonly referred to as client (or customer) relationship management systems, or CRMs. Some providers refer to their systems as "sales automation software."

People: Clients and Contacts

Lead-tracking software is generally able to store and share information on contacts as well as information on opportunities. It is critical to have an effective system for collecting, updating, and sharing contact information on clients and other people that the members of the firm have relationships with.

Projects: Past Experience

When a firm is pursuing a new project, it is important to identify the firm's previous experience that is most relevant, and then to prepare qualifications to represent this experience. If the firm is small or is a new firm without a significant portfolio, this will be a somewhat easier task than if it is a large firm or a firm with a long history. But whatever the size of the firm, it is critical for the firm to institute some sort of system for tracking project information.

The file system is the simplest to start, and if it is set up right, it can easily be converted to a database later. Create a basic form (see Table 3.1, for example) for information on projects, fill out the form for each project (one file per project), and store all the files in the same folder. Make the form using a two-column table, with questions/categories down the left (project size, facility type, etc.) and answers on the right side. Then, when an opportunity comes up and relevant projects need to be identified, use your computer's search feature to look for any files in the folder that contain certain text (such as "laboratory" or "Rhode Island") to find the appropriate projects.

When the project is finished and documented through snapshots or professional photographs, store those with other project documents in a physical project file, as well as in an electronic project file.

There has been a lot of innovation in image database or gallery applications, like Extensis Portfolio. These systems enable the tagging or keywording of thousands of images, and, depending on the system, may enable the images to be exported in a wide variety of ways, or to be displayed in galleries on the firm's website.

Staff: Resumes and Statistics on the Firm's Staff

Like project information, readily accessible information on the firm's staff is vitally important when pursuing a project. It may be important to know which architects are registered in a certain state, or speak a certain language, or have worked on laboratory projects. Resumes, of course, are the primary place where this information exists, and it is worth putting in the effort to make sure that resume files include all the information that may be needed later on any individual staff person.

TABLE 3.1 Sample Project Information Form
Client name:
Project name:
Project location:
Project size (in sf, sm, acres, hectares, etc.):
Other key quantities (number of keys for hotels, number of beds for hospitals, number of units for apartment buildings, etc.):
Services provided (architecture, interior design, planning, etc.):
Project budget (construction cost):
Project fee (if a public project):
Firm team members who worked on the project:
Consulting team (firm name and discipline):
Project start date:
Construction start date:
Project completion date:
Project description (100–150 words):
Sustainability factors (LEED certification, etc.):
Client contact:
OK to use as reference? (Y/N):

Conclusion

This chapter is a very high-level overview of key topics in the marketing process, from strategy, to public relations, to business development and networking, to the sales process. This is ideally an integrated part of the way every architecture firm operates on an ongoing basis, as a practice grows over time.

It is important to bear in mind that the common practice in marketing changes over time with evolutions in social trends and the development of new technology. It is important to view each new marketing activity as an experiment, so that those involved can learn from it, getting better and more practiced over time, continually improving in their ability to communicate with potential clients in order to bring more work to the firm.

For More Information

Society for Marketing Professional Services: www.smps.org

Rainmaking: The Professional's Guide to Attracting New Clients, 2nd edition (Adams Media Corp., 2008) by Ford Harding

It's About THEM: Building the Market-Driven Organization (Jacques Management, 2010) by Richard G. Jacques, AIA

Architect's Essentials of Marketing (Wiley, 2005) by David Koren

Marketing Professional Services (Prentice Hall, 2002) by Philip Kotler, Paul Bloom, and Thomas Hayes

Marketing Handbook for the Design & Construction Professional, 3rd edition (BNi Publications, 2009) by the Society for Marketing Professional Services

Architect's Essentials of Starting, Assessing, and Transitioning a Design Firm (Wiley, 2008) by Peter Piven and Bradford Perkins

In *Selling the Invisible: A Field Guide to Modern Marketing* (Texere, 2001), Harry Beckwith, a leading writer and speaker on marketing for service firms, provides great perspective and insight into marketing services. Also recommended are Beckwith's later books, *The Invisible Touch: The Four Keys to Modern Marketing* (Texere, 2001) and *What Clients Love: A Field Guide to Growing Your Business* (Warner Books, 2003).

The Marketing Team

Described throughout this chapter are important activities related to marketing the architecture firm. A challenge for each firm lies in determining which of the activities described are reasonable and necessary for this firm and how much help is required to do it. There is some rough correlation between the size of a firm and the number of marketing staff. Generally, firms hire their first full-time marketer when they have 25 to 35 staff members, and their second when they have around 65 to 70. From there, the ratio of marketers to staff is about 1 to 50, or a little lower. It depends, of course, on how diverse the practice is, how effective their marketing efforts are, and how hard the firm is pushing into new markets.

3.3 How Clients Select Architects

Pat Rosenzweig

The values held by an organization are reflected in its criteria for selecting an architecture firm.

Pat Rosenzweig, who passed away in 2015, had more than 30 years of experience in marketing architecture, previously as director of marketing for OWP/P as well as Perkins+Will and owner of Rosenzweig Professional Services Marketing. Her specialty was developing strategies for sales efforts and coaching for interviews.

Prospective clients, whether organizations or individuals, select their architects in many ways, but the approaches used can be grouped into four broad categories: cost based, qualifications based, value based, and direct hire. Most often the selection criteria are a blend of these categories, but one is likely to dominate. Usually, entities or individuals that seek architectural services do not announce their primary selection criteria. Even when prospective clients share the points they will attribute to each factor, these often allow for subjective judgments.

The architect's challenge is to discern what the selection criteria actually are. How is the prospective client accustomed to working? What are its concerns about this particular project? Many times, when the process is over and a short list is released or selection made, the reason for the selection is "chemistry." Many architects interpret this pejoratively, thinking their competitor's style or salesmanship won the job. In reality, however, jobs are won through the ability of the successful team to convey that it understands the prospect's functional and process issues. Once a prospect becomes a client, the firm can maintain the relationship by recognizing it is always at risk unless the firm maintains the values on which the selection was made throughout the project.

Making a judgment about selection category is not always as easy as it appears. Looking at a request for proposal (RFP), an architect might think, "This is a government office building. This is a QBS [qualifications-based selection] project. We'll show our government office buildings." While experience designing government office buildings is one criterion the architect needs to meet, is it the only one? Are there operational concerns, such as the ability to manage the size of the project or the complex team required? Is the owner concerned about the cost of the project? Is the project going to pursue LEED™ certification at a certain level? In a qualifications-based selection approach, the question is: qualifications for what? At the same time, the architect must determine how to meet the formatting and technical requirements of the solicitation and still show the qualifications that will connect with the client.

The following discussion covers each of the common architect selection approaches and suggests ways to determine what the issues really are, along with suggestions about how to respond to a prospective client.

> Across all client types, the selection process criteria are largely the same: cost, chemistry and relationship, and relevant experience.
>
> —The Client Experience (AIA, 2002)

Cost-Based Selection

Cost is always an issue and cost-driven clients base their decisions predominantly on the basis of the architect's proposed fee.

Types of Clients That Tend Toward Cost-Based Selection

Clients that have a complete program, experience with the project type, and explicit design standards usually (but not always) favor cost-based selection. These clients are typically, though not exclusively, from the private sector. However, clients interested in architects who provide innovation and leadership in a collaborative relationship are less likely to rely on cost and more likely to consider other factors. Cost-based selection is often used for branch facilities of restaurants, retail properties, financial services organizations, data or call centers, or industrial processing facilities for which the client or an operations consultant will handle mechanization.

Owners rarely make decisions on a pure cost basis. In many cases, the prospect has researched the qualifications of several firms. The short list or final decision then boils down to cost. Similarly, if fees submitted by two firms are very close, other criteria—especially experience—will be decisive. Whether a prospective client reviews qualifications before issuing a request for proposal or in reaction to a submitted proposal, a review of the architect's prior experience is relevant to even the cost-oriented prospect. A lack of similar project experience on the part of the architect could suggest that the client will pay for the architect to learn.

Knowing if the project will require multiple layers of decision making by the client helps the architect determine if the proposed fee is realistic for the effort needed to meet the client's expectations.

Determining If Cost Is the Most Important Criterion

Clients do not always say their decision will be based on the lowest fee. Therefore, the architect must find ways to judge how strong a role fee will play in client decisions.

Are there questions in the RFP related to cost and cost control, such as enumeration of change order requests and budgeted and final construction costs? An unusual number of such questions may indicate the prospective client was burned on past projects by out-of-control budgets or schedules. On the other hand, such clients may be unsophisticated school boards or municipal clients who did not effectively evaluate earlier project proposals or did not know how to manage their architects and want to ensure they do not make the same mistake again. They ask questions in the RFP and interviews in an attempt, however inappropriate, to find a more responsive architect.

An RFP from either a public or private client may also include information on the status of the project, such as the existence of a developed floor plan, site plan, or elevation and other program details. If a project is to be part of a chain of similar facilities, the architect should ask about the existence and scope of a prototype or design standards.

Sometimes cost- and schedule-based questions that appear in an RFP seem out of place. This may happen when one organization borrows an RFP from another and does not adapt it fully to its own needs. Nothing can resolve conflicts or ambiguities in the language of an RFP better than contacting the prospect directly.

Some prospective clients are unwilling to talk to the architect about the competition and believe they have no obligation to the architect beyond supplying performance standards and specifications. Similarly, a client may not realize that knowing who the competition is can help architects understand what the client is actually seeking, which will help them provide a more meaningful response to the RFP. "After all," this client thinks, "you all do the same thing, so what does it matter?" In addition, some facility owners believe that if they talk to the architect, the playing field will not be level—that one architect may have an unfair advantage. There are subtle differences among these attitudes. The former signals a cost- and commodity-based approach to selection, and the latter suggests naiveté or perhaps respect for the architect's contribution to a successful facility.

The objective in talking to prospective clients is to learn as much as possible about their programs and their commitment to existing planning documents, how they will manage their projects, and who will be involved in decision making. For projects in the cost-based selection category, it is vitally important to learn anything that can help the architect create an appropriate fee.

Contacting allied professionals with whom a prospective client has worked, such as contractors and engineers, can provide insight into how the client works. This enables the architect to construct a fee appropriate to the client's work style and to make project cost assumptions consistent with the client's expectations.

WHAT TO ASK A PROSPECTIVE CLIENT

- Who is on the selection committee? Who are the leaders of the selection committee? What particular concerns does each have?
- Who will our firm work with on a day-to-day basis?
- Can you tell us a little about the person/group/committee that makes decisions?
- Can you describe the program? Is it room-by-room, or departmental? Do you know how many people will use the facility? What is this assessment based on?

- Have you identified the site? Where is it? If the site has not been identified, how much control over its location do you have?
- What worries you about this project? What about this project keeps you up at night?
- How do the worries of others on the selection committee differ from yours?
- Why are you doing this project *now*?

Responses to a Cost-Based Prospect

The architect must first adhere to the rules of the RFP. Answer every question thoroughly and with respect. Try to understand the client's point of view. As examples, select projects with stellar references for which budgets and schedules were met. Remember, rigorous responses signal rigorous cost control. Here are a few guidelines:

- Provide budget adherence information, even if it is not requested.
- Respond respectfully to what appear to be "dumb" questions (e.g., those about change orders).
- Provide a schedule as detailed as the information permits. Frequently fee, construction cost, and schedule are closely linked in a prospect's value system. If there is not enough information to provide a detailed schedule, provide alternative scenarios, thoroughly explaining the assumptions for each.
- Provide an absolutely clear fee for the requested scope only. If the firm strongly believes additional services or a different weighting of activities is required to meet project demands, these should be presented separately. For example, if the architect suspects the program is not as complete as the RFP represents, the primary scenario would assume the level of programming verification the RFP states; in a second scenario, the architect could suggest a reason to do more extensive programming based on other information the client has provided (e.g., appointment of a new board or an acquisition).
- For a planning study (whether a master plan, feasibility study, or other type), determine how the client intends to use the plan. Is it to establish a rough budget or to test site capacity before executing an option? In such cases, only a modest fee suitable for assessing major system requirements is appropriate. Resist the temptation to provide more information than the client needs. However, if a client needs to submit the proposal to a regulatory body, the cost analysis and imagery may need to be more extensive to allow agencies to assess the validity of the cost. These studies will command appropriately higher fees, as will traditional master plans that identify future construction requirements.
- Do not take lightly any requests for elaborate matrixes showing hours-by-phase-by-person and "related experience" of personnel. This information is not necessarily requested to put the architect through the wringer. The request allows sophisticated clients to assess whether the fee is realistic (i.e., a reasonable number of hours); whether they would be getting enough time from the right level of personnel; whether the scope and complexity is over- or underestimated, and thus whether the fee is realistic; and whether the team assigned really has the same experience as the firm.
- Carry the same awareness of cost into the interview. Bring the schedule. Whether it is formally presented or not, have it available for discussion during Q&A. If it is part of the formal presentation, highlight critical and, if possible, innovative strategies that will ensure deadlines are met and perhaps save costs. Highlight cost-saving measures taken in the design or implementation of previous firm projects and have their costs on the tip of your tongue. When an RFP requires the submission of data showing staff hours by project task or discipline, know that information inside out. For many major corporations, the discussion of this information will be the sole issue in the interview.

Qualifications-Based Selection

Experience, or qualifications, is the starting point for just about every type of selection, even cost-based selection. Conversely, cost ultimately plays a role in architect selection in nearly every project. Clients using qualifications-based selection (QBS) methods select architects primarily on the basis of the similarity of an architect's prior work with the proposed project, under the assumption the architect's fee will be fair, competitive, negotiable, and consistent with the requirements of the project.

Mandated QBS

Federal projects, many state and local government projects, and projects from owners that build many projects, such as public or private hospitals and universities, often mandate QBS. These clients usually follow a schedule that dictates fee ranges in accordance with the size and complexity of a project. Thus, once the firm has been selected, the fee negotiation focuses on project scope rather than on team qualifications.

"Defining Project Services" describes steps for effectively identifying and defining the scope of project services.

Government agencies using QBS have formal processes with which firms must comply. The selection processes used by the Government Services Administration (GSA) are all qualifications based but vary depending upon the scope of the project and its position in a community. More information about these approaches to qualifications-based selection can be found in the accompanying sidebar.

FEDERAL ARCHITECT SELECTION PROCESS

In June 2004, the federal government formally updated its standard forms 254 and 255 to the new, consolidated Standard Form 330, Architect-Engineer Qualifications. The new form is more concise than previous versions, allowing federal clients to assess the qualifications of architects and their consultant teams more easily. (In many cases, the form can be completed using fewer than 20 pages.) Countless publications and software applications are available to help architects fill out these forms, but common sense should reign. As with previous versions, Form 330 rewards firms that highlight work of appropriate size and offer strong references. Form 330 also allows architects to emphasize work that has been designed by the proposed team.

Other federal procurement methods include the highly praised Design Excellence Program, operated through GSA's Public Buildings Service. Started more than a decade ago, this program has afforded firms of all sizes the opportunity to design new federal buildings, major additions, and comprehensive renovations of existing federal architecture. In fact, most projects under $20 million in construction value are set aside for small businesses.

In this program, firms are recognized and selected based on the quality of their design and, in particular, the design skills of the proposed lead designer. Competition for these projects is heated. A five-person panel consisting of government officials and practicing architects selects the lead designer and prime A/E firm,

usually from a pool of more than 50 statements of qualifications. At the earliest stage, the exemplary projects of the lead designer do not need to be exactly the same as the project being pursued, which is a significant departure from the practices supported by Form 330 and other qualifications-based selection processes. In some cases, the short-listed firms are asked to compete in a single-day charrette or—even more rare—a month-long design competition before a winner is chosen.

The odds of winning these Design Excellence competitions are obviously slim, but successful teams can be rewarded with projects that have solid construction budgets and a broad public profile. These projects may also allow the firm to work with new building types.

The criteria for Design Excellence portfolios are standardized, and brevity is almost always preferred. Design teams should submit a limited number of images (usually no more than three pages per project) and even less text (no section permits more than three pages of description). The Design Excellence Program has been so successful that other public and nonprofit agencies have adopted its standards to structure their requests for qualifications.

For detailed requirements, visit GSA online at www.gsa.gov. Look for the Web page on "New Construction and Modernizations," which outlines design process and related submission requirements and provides information about the Design Excellence Program.

A variation of the federal QBS process is a "task order agreement," commonly used by universities, government agencies, and corporations. Firms compete to be on a list of professionals deemed qualified to perform projects of a specified nature and scope. To be considered for a particular project, prequalified architects may be required to enter a fee competition. In this case, the design firm submits a chart to identify the fee per square foot for various project functions and sizes, whether renovation or new construction. If the client requests this information, further competition may be unnecessary. If provided at the initiative of the firm, it may enable a direct hire without further competition.

Voluntary QBS

Clients using qualifications-based selection approaches generally believe their architects know the fundamental program, materials, and sources for their particular facility or industry type (e.g., hospital casework standards and suppliers or furniture systems consistent with a particular client's budget). Use of this approach to selection may also reflect a prospective client's appreciation for an established relationship with an architect or interest in gaining insight into what their peers are doing. QBS is sometimes used for projects in virtually every market segment.

Identifying the Qualifications Wanted

A client's idea of "relevant experience" and other appropriate qualifications varies from market sector to market sector, but several general types of experience are of interest to all clients.

Experience with project type. QBS generally signals the importance of a firm's past experience. Some RFPs may include precise requirements, such as a request for presentations of a certain number of public libraries, middle schools, or law firms completed by the firm in the past decade. They may also request examples of projects

DESIGN COMPETITIONS

Ordinarily a design competition connotes a selection process independent of traditional questionnaires with their lists of related qualifications. However, it is increasingly common that after creation of a short list, the finalists are expected to present a concept for the project. However the competitive aspect is framed, client goals are the same—they seek design innovation.

Whether a competition is composed of an invited list of competitors or advertised in design publications, the competition process can be fierce. While architects should be compensated for all stages of the competition or at least for a final round, it is the rare firm that stays within the budget suggested by the fee that is offered. Similarly, many competitions do not guarantee the project will go forward or that the winning firm will actually be awarded the project.

So why does a firm enter competitions? They are an excellent way for a firm to gain experience in a market or building type. Participation in competitions provides great team building and can boost staff morale, particularly among younger professionals. Some firms do no marketing except for entries in design competitions because many competition entrants are published.

Design competitions are frequently criticized, however. Complaints include that insufficient program

information is provided for the architect to do a responsible job and that the jury is led to believe it can actually have a project at its anticipated cost even when some competitors disregard the stated budget.

The more precise the design program information is, the better firms can assess the risks of participating. A solicitation with a well-developed program, a precise articulation of payment provisions and process, opportunities to meet with the sponsoring organization, a list of jury members, clear and consistent rules on the method of presentation, and a budget will provide more security than one that is vague in any of these respects.

Above all, design solutions for competitions must be inspiring and understandable. If a short list will be made without benefit of an in-person interview, presentation boards and any required models have to be self-explanatory. Make sure text on the boards is concise and large enough to read easily.

For project interviews, the architect should remember that the jury is far more likely to remember a designer's enthusiasm and clarity of thought than a lot of details. Rely on the Q&A period to communicate all but the basic concept, logic, and most significant examples of how the concept is reflected in the design.

Above all, follow the rules.

of "similar scope and complexity." Firms with deep experience usually can respond easily to these types of requests.

Firms with project type expertise may still be challenged if their experience is not with the same kind of client. For example, firms that have completed swimming pools and emergency departments may not have the experience to compete for a university natatorium or an emergency department of a certain size. Or a firm that has designed a significant number of K–12 schools may not have the experience to tackle a freestanding K–8 school with a small-school philosophy.

Experience with project size and complexity. The relative importance of scope, complexity, function, and philosophy may be perceptible if an RFP includes an explanation of the evolution of the project. If a prospect also asks for a fee amount, this does not necessarily signal the selection will be based on fee. Rather, it may be a preliminary screening to eliminate a firm whose fee is way off base. A sophisticated client may eliminate a candidate whose fee is too low because the prospect recognizes the respondent does not understand the client's objectives or the complexity of the project.

Understanding of client needs. Clients may also want to know how a firm will "approach" the work. Usually this question is asked to find out how the firm will interact with the project's stakeholders. The client can learn whether applicants have over- or underestimated the number of meetings that will be required, can meet the schedule, and understand the nature of the client organization and decision-making process. Owners are likely to be interested in who from the architecture firm will lead the various stages of a project. This is particularly true for large projects and those that include associated firms or consultants, such as healthcare and higher education clients.

Researching the Client's Values

Others with whom a prospective client has worked know the client's values. They know how much stakeholders are involved in project development and delivery; the importance of the facility to the owner's marketing, recruitment, and retention; how the prospect makes decisions and who is involved; and how the prospect approaches risk.

The client's website can also provide some insight into the character of a company, government agency, or institution, but much more in-depth and objective information can be gained from other sources, especially direct client contact.

Responses to a Qualifications-Based Prospect

Responding to an RFP in a QBS process is likely to require both a written proposal, with accompanying exhibits, and a project interview.

Written proposal elements. The project proposal should showcase the firm's qualifications and tell what the firm will provide for the project.

USE THE INTERNET CAREFULLY

The Internet can be a useful way to learn about a prospective client, but some caution is required. Here are some things to consider when researching on the Internet:

- The corporate roles of members of the architect selection committee may be available on the company or institutional website. Based on these roles, the architect can make some presumptions as to what each person's priorities may be. If HR is involved, workplace environment or growth may be a consideration, while a CFO may be worried about cost. Sometimes architects can leverage existing relationships with board members.
- The website may show pictures of various existing facilities, which can indicate the degree of design freedom a prospective client may allow the architect.

- Those sections of a client's website directed at recruitment may suggest the importance of facilities, especially of amenities and a firm's priorities with regard to sustainability and workplace comfort. These sections may also reveal locations where the client is growing or where recruitment is difficult. Facility design will need to respond to such concerns.
- The vision, mission statement, or list of programs an organization posts on its website can provide information the architect can use to initiate discussion, as well as an idea of what will be involved in programming efforts for this client.
- Be cautious when using the Internet to discern information about a corporate culture. Marketers often prepare websites, and their views may not be consistent with the way an organization actually operates.

To begin, the cover letter should never be simply a letter of transmittal. It directs attention to the firm's experience and knowledge that can serve the client's needs. It should be specific: "During the past ten years, we have designed more than fifty emergency departments for community hospitals. Of special note are the ABC and QRS projects highlighted in Section 2 which, like yours, were designed to segregate pediatric and adult trauma areas."

An executive summary allows the architect to present seemingly dissimilar qualifications and can be useful when following the rules does not allow the architect to shine. For example, when an RFP has page limits, an executive summary can give the firm more space to describe the depth of its experience. Similarly, if an RFP does not include questions that address a design or process perspective in which the architect excels, an executive summary will allow the architect to highlight that expertise.

Short narratives can be used to explain the relevance of previous projects and the talents of staff who will be assigned to the client's project. These explanations may allow the use of standard, unedited project description pages or resumes. The tone of such language might read like these examples:

- "We have selected these projects because they exemplify our experience working with banks on new branches and on other projects with highly specific design standards."
- "The team we have selected includes personnel who have managed projects of this scale."

Never leave it to the client to figure out why particular projects and people have been included in your proposal. Obviously, projects listed should include only those that can offer good references.

Explanatory exhibits. Lawyers call these demonstrative exhibits; they are documents that address gaps in the architecture firm's direct qualifications.

A matrix of qualifications (see example in sidebar) can be used to demonstrate how the firm has previously met similar project requirements. The items in the matrix can be highly specialized functional spaces, delivery methods, cost parameters, leadership roles, or geographic or regulatory agency experience—any subjects that communicate the full scope of the firm's strengths to the client. This tactic is particularly useful when a firm has experience with all of the components of a project (e.g., training rooms, open offices, food service, dry labs, and 24/7 building systems) but has not done a project that combines all of them.

A matrix is also useful when a firm wants to propose a staff that includes new hires and associated specialists because it allows the firm to highlight individual staff member experience without improperly suggesting the firm has experience with projects it has not previously delivered. Finally, a matrix is useful when research indicates a key decision maker has a short attention span, as it provides a snapshot of what the firm has to offer.

Concept diagrams or block models are increasingly being used during project interviews. The firm's interview team can employ them to facilitate discussion about the project, which is almost always desirable. In addition, at the RFP stage, a concept diagram can inspire the client and demonstrate knowledge and abilities of the architecture firm that may not be evident in the written part of the proposal.

A diagram may also be useful when the firm's portfolio is dominated by small projects and the proposed project is substantially larger. For example, a diagram of conceptual solutions to parking and access sequences might be effective. Or, if the firm is not known for its design, an inspiring elevation or sketch could be helpful. If the prospect has identified a provocative approach to an operational issue, a drawing of a well-annotated floor plan may be effective.

Qualifications-based interviews. Jobs are won and often lost at the interview stage. Winning at this stage is about connecting with the values and priorities of the client better than the competition does. Thus it is incumbent on the architecture firm to find out from the client or from an architecture network who the competition is. Once the competition is known, the firm can shape its proposal content and interview methods to highlight its winning strengths.

This qualifications matrix for a proposed regional electronics assembly facility matches the needs of the project with the abilities of the architecture firm. The project is to be located in a suburb of a major city. It will be approximately 100,000 square feet in size and needs to be completed within one year. The company's personnel will be a blend of its own relocated employees and employees of a recently acquired competitor. The architecture firm submitting a proposal specializes in hospital design. The firm is associating with a world-class M/E/P firm for the project and has assigned a new hire with corporate experience to the project.

Prior Projects of Team Members	Experience Needed for Electronics Assembly Facility Project					
	Zoning in Suburb A	Projects of 100,000 s.f.	Dry Labs or Designer-Led Design-Build	Fast-Tracked Merged Organizations	Programming	Clean Rooms
University of Q Physics Addition						
ABC Company						
Suburb A Community Hospital Surgicenter						
University of Z Electrical and Mechanical Engineering School						
Suburb A Community Hospital Parking Structure						
QRS, Inc. Headquarters						

PART 2: PRACTICE

It is equally important to know who will represent the client at the interview, what the role and voting power of those people will be, and how much they have been involved in the selection process to date. In most groups, there is a person who has ultimate decision-making power, knowledge, or persuasiveness. It is critical to know who that person is so the interview can be shaped with that person's interests in mind.

Those determining the short list may not be the same as those making the final selection. This is particularly true in public education, where the superintendent or other senior staff manages the short-list process but the board often chooses the winning firm. If the architecture firm does not already know the opinions of the members of the board of education, researching the local newspapers for their positions on certain issues, as well as their professions, can be helpful. Most firms seeking work with local public bodies make it their business to attend board meetings, not just to be seen, but to learn the issues and positions of the members.

More than a few architects with great strategies have lost in the details. Common mistakes during interviews include the following:

- *The organization chart is not clear.* The client must know and see who is in charge. There should be only one leader.
- *Weak presenters are in key positions.* This error has its roots at the RFP stage. The firm must anticipate the interview when selecting the project team members. If management is a key issue, the project manager or director needs to be assertive and methodical. A designer needs to inspire. Manage the message and the time allotted to each person according to his or her ability to command attention.
- *The interview is not focused.* The interview replicates the RFP response; it is not a catalog. It should address the issues the client deems important, not what the architect believes are the key issues and challenges that should drive the project. To the degree the interview is about design, architects should discuss only those projects that parallel an issue of specific interest to this client, rather than highlighting a laundry list of projects. A rule of thumb is that each visual should deal with no more than two thoughts.
- *The team, especially the project manager, goes into unnecessary detail.* An interview is about making connections with an audience on issues relevant to meeting their objectives. Highlight, don't bore. Show that you respect the time of the client's interviewers and know what is important.
- *During Q&A, the senior manager on the team either does not control the responses or dominates them.* Unless a question is asked directly of a team member, the team leader should grab each question and direct it to the appropriate member of the team. If other team members jump in to respond, it will appear they do not trust the leader, but if the leader answers all the questions, the client may wonder about the strength of the team.
- *Answers to questions wander.* Q&A responses should be treated like a deposition. Answer directly and briefly. Your answer can be followed with, "Did I answer your question?"

Value-Based Selection

Qualifications-based selection and value-based selection can look very similar. However, there are two significant differences between clients using QBS and those using value-based selection. The latter group is looking for an architect who is not only qualified to do the job but can take a leadership role in helping the client achieve its goals. The two bulleted paragraphs below illustrate this concept.

- The client has a project that fills a significant strategic role, but the client is inexperienced with the project type. Therefore, the client looks to the architect for ideas gained from working with other innovative clients. Often, a real estate decision has not been made and programming is not complete, giving the architect an opportunity to provide knowledge and recommendations beyond those required when the client is familiar with the project type.

- The client's predominant interest is in design. Government clients using the GSA Design Excellence Program and design competitions in qualifications-based selection of architects are looking for architects who can provide superior innovation, superior aesthetics, and superior sensitivity to context and history—in other words, value.

Client contact is almost mandatory to distinguish value-based criteria from pure qualifications-based criteria. In fact, clients may not be aware that architects could lead a team to meet their strategic needs. For example, a discussion may reveal the prospect does not know whether to lease, buy, develop, or engage in a sale/leaseback to acquire property for a project. An architecture firm knowledgeable about these client challenges can distinguish itself from the competition by submitting a response that includes relevant information from an associated real estate professional.

Responses to a Value-Based Prospect

The value-based RFP response should demonstrate leadership. It is still a qualifications-based response, but project descriptions should be tailored to the primary concern of the client. For example, if the client's priority is to compete with its peers (e.g., to be the best music school or the best trading company work environment), the firm can present past projects that highlight the client's best-in-class competition. The prospect is interested in learning what its competition does and that the proposing architect can provide such information.

If the client is looking for process leadership, on the other hand, the RFP response can include a broad mix of projects. For example, if a proposed project requires programming a science facility that will bring together formerly competing departments, the client may fear it will be difficult to reach an agreement between the departments, resulting in program creep. To address this concern, the RFP response can include project examples highlighting the firm's ability to lead a process with competing interests and accommodate needs in a reasonable time frame, such as design of a project for the merger of two companies with dissimilar cultures.

To communicate the architect's role in a useful way to the prospective client looking for value, standard project pages will have to be tailored for use in the proposal. A cover letter or executive summary is essential to quickly give the selection committee an understanding of why, for example, the architect is using a corporate facility to demonstrate experience relevant to the design of their biology/physics building.

To illustrate process leadership, the proposing firm also needs to identify and describe the steps in its project delivery process, whether or not the client has requested this. Identify which members of the proposing team will lead the process at each stage and their relationships with the client and stakeholders along the way. This can be done with a diagram supported by simple, clearly understandable text.

Direct Hire

An organization often rehires an architect they have worked with before without requiring the architect to compete for the project. However, it is rare for an owner to establish a new relationship with an architect without a traditional selection process.

New Clients

When a firm finds itself in a noncompete situation with a new client, it is likely the client's colleagues have provided laudatory references for the architect. Nonetheless, it is crucial for the architect to understand the requirements, priorities, status, budget, schedule, decision-making process, and relationship the prospective client anticipates having with the architect before entering into even the most superficial agreement. Be prepared to walk away if the client's temperament and expectations suggest a poor relationship will ensue. Remember, the great advantage of the traditional selection process is that much of this information is revealed during the architect's pursuit of the project.

Existing Clients

Keeping existing clients is a primary way many architects get work. To maintain a good relationship, never take the client for granted. Architects who understand that their relationships with clients are always at risk are likely to keep those clients. Relationships will not survive on client loyalty alone. Thus, it is important for architects to relate to their existing clients with the same enthusiasm, creativity, and attentiveness they bring to establishing new client relationships. The following techniques can help architects maintain these relationships:

- Initiate process or design innovations. Don't wait to be asked.
- Initiate fee reviews. Don't wait to be challenged.
- Keep a stable team and notify the client if the team must change.
- Have senior staff develop personal relationships with clients.

Despite the architect's efforts, an existing client may still ask a familiar firm to interview for a new project. This can happen for a number of reasons, including new leadership in the client organization, a problem on a past project, the client's desire to "keep you honest," or the organization's policy to periodically review relationships. Whatever the client's reason for bidding a project, the architecture firm should use the advantage of inside knowledge to discover why the client is looking for something new and to try to address those issues. For example:

- If the client has had a change in administration, the new leaders may have an existing relationship with another architect. Get to know the new administrators, and let them know your firm's experience and qualifications. Learn the new priorities, especially with regard to process, cost, and management, and find out what internal operational changes the administration wants to make. Shape the proposal or interview to focus on the new people—looking forward and not backward.
- If the administration is not new and nothing else appears to be different, the firm could try to identify something new in the client's situation and use that to suggest change or improvement. This should be handled delicately, however, so as not to criticize the client's actions.
- If the client has already progressed to the interview stage with another architect because of a known problem with your firm, it may be too late to save the relationship, but an effort should still be made. Find out if your firm has advocates on the selection committee. Acknowledge problems, and ask for a trial period to implement solutions. The firm can also consider appointing different staff members to communicate with the client. These latter two suggestions challenge the architect's ability to introduce change without raising the question, "Why haven't you done this already?"

Summing Up

When organizations or individuals seek architecture services, they have certain expectations for their relationships with the architecture firm. These expectations, or values, are reflected in the criteria they use to choose an architect. To connect with the client and stay within the confines of the RFP rules and interview constraints, the firm must accurately assess the client's values by carefully analyzing information obtained during the selection process.

For More Information

In *The Tipping Point* (Little, Brown, 2000), Malcolm Gladwell provides insight into the importance of message clarity and obtaining information directly from clients.

Sally A. Handley, FSMPS

Responding to RFPs and preparing for short-list interviews are two of the most important marketing functions. A thoughtful approach along with advance planning and organization can help minimize the effort and maximize a firm's hit rate.

Spotting a publicly advertised request for proposal (RFP) for a project that firm leaders or marketers have been tracking, or receiving an RFP from a long-pursued prospective client, can be cause for celebration. At long last, there is a feeling that the firm's long-range marketing efforts are paying off. But euphoria can quickly turn to panic as the RFP is reviewed and the magnitude of the task ahead is understood. In firms both large and small, the proposal process can often be chaotic and overwhelming.

There are three basic steps every firm can take to reduce the anxiety surrounding the proposal process: The first is to take a good, hard look at the RFP and determine the likelihood of winning the project. The second is to approach the proposal with the same degree of organization with which a design project is approached. Finally, and most important, procedures and processes must be developed to organize the information most commonly asked for in client RFPs.

THE GO/NO-GO POLICY

Frequently firms respond to too many proposals without really considering how realistic their chances are for winning. The more proposals prepared, the more diluted the proposal effort becomes, because time is finite, and even if people work 24/7, the more proposals put out, the less time there is to spend on each one. The secret to a successful proposal effort starts with a good go/no-go policy. Pursuing work that the firm is not qualified for and is unlikely to win is self-defeating and diverts time and money that can be better spent on marketing activities that are more likely to result in jobs won.

There are many ways to approach a go/no-go policy. One size does not fit all. Some firms focus on whether or not a project has the potential to yield a profit. Others focus on a project's potential for publicity that can increase name recognition and identity. Whatever approach is used, policy guidelines should be summarized in writing and a scoring system should be used to give the policy teeth. Here are some sample questions that cover the issues firms should be considering before beginning the proposal effort:

- Does the project fall under our mission?
- Is the project in a target market sector?
- Is the project in our geographic range?
- Is the project the appropriate size?
- Is the budget realistic? Funded?
- What is the potential for profit?
- What is the client's reputation and payment schedule?
- Who is our competition?
- How were we selected to receive the RFP?
- Can we demonstrate relevant experience?
- Can we provide a truly responsive proposal in the time frame?

Sally A. Handley is a writing and marketing consultant with over 30 years' experience in the AEC industry. She is the author of *Marketing Metrics De-Mystified: Methods for Measuring ROI and Evaluating Your Marketing Effort* (2007) and *When Can You Start? The AEC Guide to Recruiting, Managing and Retaining a Marketing Coordinator* (2009).

Firms can develop their own scoring scheme. Three or more noes to the first six questions is a likely no-go. The last five questions require more analysis.

There may be overriding reasons why the firm might say yes to a project that doesn't pass the go/no-go test. For example, the client may have lots of profitable work and a reputation as a great client. Often firms may be asked to propose on a project smaller than their no-go minimum. Clearly, this is a test opportunity that most firms may not want to pass up.

This detailed approach to judging whether or not an RFP is a go or no-go reduces long-shot proposal efforts that actually diminish the effectiveness of an overall marketing effort. If a go/no-go sheet is developed and completed each time a proposal is prepared, a chart can be created that demonstrates over time where marketing hours and dollars are being spent with no return, and where dollars spent are winning work.

THE PROPOSAL PROCESS

Reading the RFP

In order to complete the go/no-go assessment, be sure to read the entire RFP. This may sound obvious, but all too often in a hectic-paced environment, it is tempting to cut to the chase and just read what needs to be done, skipping the full scope of services and going right to project description, the proposal requirements section, and the due date. A thorough reading of the RFP is a must. It's possible to discover that the firm doesn't qualify to respond because of certain requirements.

Taking time to read the project description and scope of services, as well as the extraneous requirements that don't always appear on the requirements page, will actually save time and result in a much better proposal. There is nothing worse than finding at the end of the proposal process that a lengthy form mentioned elsewhere in the RFP was overlooked. Also, there may be specialty subconsultant requirements that have to be met. These are issues no one wants to deal with after they are nearly done with the RFP response, a day or two before it is due.

THE RELEVANCE FORMULA

This is a formula for determining the relevance of past project experience to a current proposal. The project might match each one of these criteria:

- *Client*: It's the same client.
- *Service*: The same service was performed.
- *Market sector*: The client was in the same market sector—for example, transportation or pharmaceutical.
- *Facility (if applicable)*: The project type is the same—for example, a bridge or laboratory.
- *Attributes*: Special attributes, requirements, or situations are the same. For example, the project must be LEED Silver or BSL-3.
- *Location*: The assignment or client is in the same location (city, county, state, or region).

An appropriate order can then be built based on the projects that have the best mix of criteria matches.

Here it is: This is the formula, in order from best to worst projects to use:

- Client, service, market sector, facility, attributes, location
- Client, service, market sector, facility, attributes
- Client, service, market sector, attributes
- Service, market sector, facility, attributes, location
- Service, market sector, facility, attributes
- Service, market sector, attributes
- Client, service, market sector, facility, location
- Client, service, market sector, facility
- Service, market sector, facility, location
- Service, market sector, facility
- Service, market sector
- Service, location
- Service

By applying this formula, the right projects will be in the right order every time.

From *Proposal Development Secrets: Win More, Work Smarter, and Get Home on Time* (Amazon Kindle edition, Feb. 9, 2012) by Matt Handal, reprinted with permission.

Both small-firm practitioners and principals in large firms need to conduct a brief strategy session to get the proposal off to a good start. The purpose of the strategy session is to determine answers to the following questions:

1. What is known about the client?
2. What is known about the project?
3. Who is the competition?
4. Why should the client choose us for this project?

No matter the firm or staff size, these questions need to be answered in order to develop a proposal that demonstrates understanding of the project and the client. Knowing who else received the client RFP, or which firms are most likely to respond to a publicly advertised RFP, is important in order to understand the context in which the firm is competing. Finally, a compelling argument for why the client should select the firm must be articulated clearly and concisely.

Relevant project experience is a key element of any argument for why a firm should be selected. Projects that illustrate a firm's capabilities, but that are not similar in size or scope to the project being proposed on, may not be relevant. Clients want to know that the design firms they select have experience with similar projects and understand the issues and nuances of a particular project type. Clients renovating a vehicle maintenance facility may not be impressed by a design portfolio consisting of renovations to office buildings or schools, even if those projects won awards. The Relevance Formula in the accompanying sidebar provides guidelines for determining what is most relevant to a client and how to order relevant projects in a proposal.

If a team is working together to produce a proposal, all of the key individuals involved need to participate in the strategy session. Depending on the firm size, these might include the principal-in-charge, the project architect, the project manager, the proposal manager, and/or marketing coordinator. The proposal manager or the marketing coordinator should be assigned the task of taking notes that will be distributed to anyone involved in preparing the proposal. Additional tasks to be completed during the strategy session include the following:

1. If it hasn't already been done, designate the principal-in-charge and the project manager.
2. Create a checklist, schedule, and budget.
3. Select subconsultants who will constitute the project team. (Be sure to review any requirements, such as MWBE (Minority/Women-owned Business Enterprise) goals or specialty consultants, needed for the project team to be compliant.)
4. For large projects, define responsibilities and how the team will interact, and create an organization chart.

During the strategy session, the note taker also wants to compile a list of questions that come up. Note any RFP requirements that are vague or about which there is uncertainty and clarification is needed. Every RFP has a point of contact or a specific procedure for asking questions. When the questions are compiled into a single list, one member of the proposal team should call the point-of-contact to get answers.

Often clients hold pre-proposer conferences and/or walk-throughs of the project site in order to make clear their project goals and answer questions. A member of the proposal team should always attend. Ideally, the project manager is the right person to attend. When that is not possible, the proposal manager or marketing coordinator may attend. Although not always technically oriented, marketers often are adept at discerning client concerns underlying the technical challenges.

Following the strategy session, the designated note taker needs to compile a checklist. The checklist should include deliverables, responsible individuals, deadlines, and

TABLE 3.2 Sample Proposal Checklist		
Deliverables	Who's Responsible	Due Date
Cover letter		
Executive summary		
Scope of work		
Project approach		
Schedule		
Team resumes		
Experience		
References		
Fee proposal		
Packaging		
Delivery method		

packaging and delivery method. Table 3.2 is a standard checklist that is a start and can be altered for each proposal. Circulate the checklist immediately, and post it to a central spot for team access. The checklist is a dynamic document and may change based on information obtained throughout the proposal process. Everyone needs to be notified when changes are made.

Whether or not there is an individual on staff with the title of Proposal Manager, one individual needs to be designated the proposal manager, champion, or advocate for any given proposal. This individual is the keeper of the checklist and the individual who monitors daily the status of all deliverables. It is best if this individual is not a principal, who is most likely to have client- and project-related responsibilities that will take priority over the proposal process.

For sole practitioners, the checklist is a must. Any amount of time set aside to work on the proposal should begin with a review of the checklist. This valuable tool keeps the process organized, ensuring that long lead items don't get lost in the process.

Subconsultants

The value of long-standing relationships notwithstanding, subconsultant selection should not be something done on autopilot. Subconsultants should be selected based on their ability to enhance the chances of winning a project. Sometimes that means reaching out to new firms that have specialized experience with the project type or client being pursued. In addition, there must always be a good-faith effort to comply with client MWBE requirements.

Optimally, meeting subconsultants is something done on an ongoing basis, so as not to have to scramble to locate the appropriate MWBE or specialty subconsultant for the first time during the proposal process. Pre-proposer conferences, which generally make attendee lists available, are an excellent way to meet potential team members already pursuing the project. Keeping a database of firms cross-referenced by their disciplines, client connections, and certifications will make subconsultant selection much easier at proposal time.

As soon as possible after subconsultants have been selected, notify them of the intention to include them on the project team. Determine exactly what subconsultants need to provide, the format in which their qualifications are to be prepared, and the deadline for receipt. The proposal manager or coordinator should be in charge of this effort, and be the point of contact for any questions the subconsultant might have.

When the firm I worked for decided to pursue an on-call contract with the Veteran's Administration, we realized that we needed to be strategic in selecting subconsultants for our team. We had plenty of experience with on-call work for government agencies, but no experience with the VA.

First, we contacted the subconsultants we worked with most frequently to see if they had VA experience. We invited those who did to join our team. Next, we reviewed the qualifications of other firms we had in our database to see if they had VA experience. We assembled a subconsultant team composed entirely of firms who had successfully worked for the VA.

Next, we interviewed each subconsultant to determine the VA's hot-button issues. Every subconsultant was happy to share with us the things that were most important on VA jobs on which they had previously worked. For example, noise abatement during construction was understandably a major concern at VA hospitals. We made sure to emphasize our understanding of and sensitivity to the issues that would be of concern to the VA on any project awarded under the on-call contract. We were short-listed, and subsequently won the contract.

The Mock-Up or Dummy Copy

A good practice throughout the proposal production process is to create a physical mock-up of the proposal. As the various elements are completed, insert them into the mock-up copy. Use colored paper to indicate outstanding items still to be inserted. This simple practice gives everyone a good idea of the status of the proposal. In addition, proofreading the printed page yields better results than proofreading on a computer screen.

While some clients request digital copies, multiple hard-copy submissions remain the norm. The mock-up copy can facilitate the actual, physical production of the proposal. As sections of the proposal inserted into the mock-up are judged final, copies can be printed and collated. For obvious reasons, it is preferable to print completed sections as they are finalized, rather than leave all printing to the end.

Crafting a Responsive Proposal

Of utmost importance is making sure that the proposal is responsive to all of the requirements. The RFP process is highly competitive, particularly in the institutional and public sectors. Clients who receive many responses to proposals start by looking for nonresponsive proposals in order to narrow down the field for serious consideration.

If the proposal is being prepared by one person working alone, the proposal must be read cover to cover, highlighting every item required by the client, even those that fall outside the "proposal format" section of the RFP. If there is a marketing staff, it is the responsibility of the proposal manager or marketing coordinator to make sure all required elements are on the checklist.

Additional Solicitation Requirements

Government forms, schedules, licensing, and insurance requirements should be completed early. Lead time for obtaining certain certificates can be lengthy, so, as tempting as it is to let these go until the end, it is not advisable.

Writing Persuasive Proposal Content

In the case of proposals and requests for qualifications, there is a great deal of information provided by the client in the form of the RFP requirements. If the process begins by jumping to the proposal requirements section, the most important step in persuasive writing will be skipped—understanding the client that the proposal is trying persuade! Start looking at the RFP as the best source of information about the client.

Search the RFP for clues about the issues most important to the client. Do they want an iconic building that makes a statement about them and their business? Are they committed to sustainability and desirous of a building that will not adversely impact their environment? Are they concerned about neighborhood resistance to their facility? Do they want a new addition to blend seamlessly with adjacent buildings? Are they a government agency committed to design excellence for public buildings?

Next, verify how the firm will be evaluated. The criteria that will be used to judge proposals are almost always provided in client documents, and can be a key to client hot buttons. Consider changing the focus from the proposal requirements to the evaluation criteria. Make a thorough review of the criteria a significant part of the preparation process. Print it out, maybe even blow it up and pin it somewhere in view. While completing all of the required proposal elements is very important, paying equal attention to the evaluation criteria is just as critical.

Suppose the evaluation criteria look like what are shown in Table 3.3

Now let's jump ahead and suppose the RFP has been read thoroughly, questions have been answered by the point of contact, and the walk-through has been completed. Additionally, at the walk-through a subconsultant confides that the last project done for this client had huge cost overruns because the project manager was inexperienced. This warrants a look at the evaluation criteria one more time. Eighty points are devoted to the firm's experience, the experience of the project manager, and the management plan. This further confirms that effective management is a hot-button issue for the client.

The next step is to write a statement of purpose, indicating what must be communicated in this proposal. Don't overthink this and get into analysis paralysis. Just quickly either jot it down or type it. For the example above, the purpose statement may be as simple as: "In addition to our firm's experience with all the elements of the proposed project, we also need to show that our project manager has experience with all or most of the elements of this project and demonstrate that s/he has a track record for controlling costs and completing projects on or near original estimates."

Once a statement of purpose is written, everything that goes into the proposal is there because it will help accomplish that purpose. Every project example, every staff resume, and every question answered must fulfill the purpose; otherwise it is at best filler and at worst a distraction. Remember, every word written must add to the argument.

TABLE 3.3 Proposal Element Evaluation Criteria	
Evaluation Criteria	**Points**
Required experience	35
Quality of key personnel	35
Quality of management plan	10
Overall firm capability	20
TOTAL POSSIBLE SCORE	100

HOW LONG SHOULD X BE?

Once someone asked me how long the cover letter should be. When I said one page, the individual proceeded to tell me there was no executive summary in the RFP to which they were responding, and they felt they needed to put more of their persuasive argument in the letter. My response: "Then by all means, make your cover letter longer."

(continued)

Remember, while there are general guidelines for writing proposals, there is no *one* right way to do this. I recall being asked to work on a proposal for a new branch office my firm had acquired. Our main office had significant experience in designing parking garages, and the branch office had tried two or three times to win parking projects at a local university hospital. A firm they were teaming with had spoken to the client contact at the university hospital and reported to us that the client said they just didn't know who we are. I asked to look at the previous proposals that had been sent and saw that our branch office had not really done a good job of explaining the "new identity."

Hence, my mission was to make it clear who this new firm was. If we didn't reach the short list, at least the client would know who we were going forward. I wrote a three-page letter describing our firm, the services we provided, the relationship of the branch office to the main office, and who from the main office would be working on the project. We got short-listed. The point is that I understood my client's hot button: They didn't know us, and nothing we had previously sent clearly explained how the experience from the main office was going to be tapped for their local work. Now they understood. I violated the one-page guideline, but I knew my audience and what was needed to persuade them to consider us.

Next, create a working outline or table of contents (TOC). The TOC may change throughout the proposal writing process, but it's best to start with a solid outline. In some instances, the client may have very specific guidelines for the TOC, and that makes the job easier. If not, consider organizing the proposal according to the evaluation criteria.

Proposal Content: Less Is More

In a letter to a friend, seventeenth-century French philosopher and mathematician Blaise Pascal wrote, "I have made this letter longer than usual, only because I have not had time to make it shorter." Proposal writers frequently make the mistake of thinking that, in order to be effective, proposals need to be lengthy. The fact is that reviewers of submissions spend approximately 18 minutes reviewing a proposal! That is the reason proposal advertisements often limit the number of pages, sometimes even cautioning that elaborate submissions will be rejected.

Clients want an RFP that tells them what they need to know in order to make a decision. They ask specific questions and they want succinct answers, not every piece of boilerplate ever written at a firm. In order to write a persuasive proposal, tailor the boilerplate to the client. Clearly and succinctly demonstrate that the audience is known and their special needs and requirements are understood—that there is sensitivity to their hot-button issues.

Avoiding Jargon

STEPHEN KLIMENT'S PRINCIPLES FOR WRITING IMPACT

1. Write as you would talk.
2. Keep sentences short.
3. Shun jargon or "designer babble."
4. Be specific.
5. Keep it simple.
6. Use the active form or voice.
7. Don't forget people.
8. Know what you want to say.

PART 2: PRACTICE

In his classic *Writing for Design Professionals*, Stephen Kliment, former editor in chief of *Architectural Record*, cautions writers to avoid technical jargon and "designer babble" that can actually make it more difficult for the reader or reviewer of the proposal. Technical professionals sometimes forget that even the most knowledgeable clients are not necessarily technical. If technical details are going to be included, make clear to the reader the *benefit* of the technical information. Here's a description that does this very well:

> Established to promote greater public understanding of the United States Constitution, the National Constitution Center is a structure of complex geometries articulated in limestone, granite, and glass. The architect's sophisticated design relies on an elaborate frame of interconnected steel systems designed to achieve the building's bold structural form. Long-span, column-free solutions and special connection details accommodate the building's vast, open spaces.

The last sentence does an especially good job of explaining the benefit of the technical design without jargon that loses the reader.

Quality Control: Assessing the Proposal

The schedule set in the strategy session should always include enough time for a thorough proofread and final edit. When all the checklist items are complete, and the proposal is assembled, ask the following questions:

- Does this proposal demonstrate an understanding of the project?
- Have we identified potential problems?
- Are our project examples truly relevant?
- Do resumes show relevant projects?
- Have we clearly established our technical expertise?
- Have we demonstrated that we have the capacity to handle the project and meet the schedule?
- Have we provided all of the information and documentation required?
- Is the proposal easy to read and easy for the client to locate the most important information?

Part of quality control is allowing enough time for proofing, printing, binding, production, and delivery of the final package. It doesn't matter how good the content is if there isn't enough time to create a high-quality deliverable. Just like a schedule for a project deadline needs to allow adequate time for drawing coordination and printing, so does a marketing proposal schedule. Be sure to factor this in to the original proposal schedule at the beginning of the process.

QUALIFICATIONS: ORGANIZING STANDARD PROPOSAL ELEMENTS AND THE BOILERPLATE

Ironically, this step really should precede the previous two, because an organized database of the firm's qualifications—that is, of the types of information and standard write-ups (boilerplate) asked for in a proposal—is the key to an efficient proposal effort.

The sample proposal checklist shown in Table 3.2 contains the most commonly required elements in any RFP. While each client, project, and proposal is unique, most RFPs request some form of the same basic information. Many firms start each new proposal by using the last proposal submitted as a template. The limitations of that approach to proposal writing become clear when hours are wasted searching for a proposal that predates the most recent one because it contains a perfectly crafted response to the same question asked in a current RFP.

One of the keys to an efficient proposal process is the organization of the firm's qualifications—information that is asked for repeatedly. Designate a folder "Boilerplate Library." This folder will contain a basic list of the standard documents and responses to typical RFP questions that could be included. Create subfolders for items such as Project Approaches. While each project approach must be tailored to the project currently being pursued, previously written project approaches may contain introductions or paragraphs that can be incorporated into current proposals. For example, the approach to historic restoration will probably always start with a site visit and review of existing documents.

The time invested in developing a well-organized boilerplate library of the firm's qualifications will yield tremendous time savings in the future. The added benefit is that the time can be used to better research the client's needs and tailor the boilerplate to prepare a truly responsive proposal.

THE SHORT-LIST INTERVIEW

Every planning session, every market research question, every networking event, every cold call, every letter written, every trade show attended, every piece of communication sent, especially the proposal, is intended to get the firm in front of the client for a real opportunity to win a project. The joy of being short-listed is frequently short-lived, however, because the time frame is often less than a week, and the interviews never seem to be scheduled at a "good" time—that is, a time that is convenient for everyone who must participate. Particularly when there are project deadlines in-house, key staff members may be tempted to say, "I don't have time to participate in a strategy session or to practice or rehearse." All of the marketing hours and dollars expended thus far are wasted if the key players don't make preparation for the short-list interview a high priority. For small-firm practitioners working without a marketing department, this is no different. Remember, getting new work is as important as executing the work already acquired.

Begin by taking the same exact approach as the proposal. Let everyone who will participate, including consultants and those who will assist in preparation, know the time and date of the interview. Circulate copies of pertinent material, and hold a strategy session. Who needs to attend? The partner-in-charge, the project architect/manager, key consultants, the marketing coordinator, and/or manager.

Start by reviewing the proposal submitted—after all, it is what got the firm short-listed. Ask again: What does everyone know about the client? The project? What is not yet known? Why do the same questions need to be asked? Because much could have changed since the RFP response was submitted, both with the client and with the firm. Everything needs to be seen with fresh eyes. Possibly someone in the firm or one of the consultants on the team may have new information that may be valuable. Perhaps the client, or the project, has been in the news, and this information provides additional insight into the client that can be used to prepare for the interview.

At a minimum, learn who is on the selection committee, who the competition is, and the physical conditions of the interview room. If this information is not provided by the client, a call should be made to the point-of-contact to ask questions. Not all clients are willing to provide the names of the selection committee or the other short-listed firms, but it is always worthwhile to ask. Subconsultants are often on more than one team and often are willing to share the names of the teams they are on, even if the client won't.

Why Us?

Review the key reasons in the proposal submission for why the client should select the firm's team. Have these changed? Has the intelligence and reconnaissance revealed information that requires an amendment to the original "why us" statement? Whether or not the statement changes, make sure that the key points being used to advance the firm's argument are crystal clear to everyone going to the interview—everyone in-house and every subconsultant. Every individual's presentation should support the overall strategy.

At this point, in larger firms there should be a reassessment of principal-in-charge and project architect/manager designations. Sometimes there is a significant lag between submitting a proposal and making the short list. The workload of the individuals submitted in the proposal may have changed drastically, and they may no longer be available to work on the project. The number-one complaint of clients is that the individuals who attend the interview are not the ones assigned to work on the project. The short-list interview is the last opportunity to make a change to proposed project staffing.

The same holds true for subconsultants. Perhaps there have been performance problems with a subconsultant on a project since the proposal was submitted, and this has caused second thoughts about working with him or her again. In addition, there may be a need for a specialty consultant that was not originally on the team. This is the time to let the client know of any project team changes.

Once the team is finalized, especially for large projects, create an organization chart that clearly defines responsibilities. Clients want to know how team members will interact with them and with each other. Most important, they want to know who their day-to-day contact will be, whom they will contact when they have a question or problem—in other words, who's in charge?

Whoever is in charge of the project must also be in charge of the interview, and this needs to be completely clear to everyone attending the interview. Usually the partner-in-charge (PIC) from the architecture firm leads the interview, but it could also be handled by the project manager (PM). There may be good reasons why the PM is the right one to lead, particularly if project management is a client hot-button issue. Also, the PM may be the right person to lead the interview because of a previous working relationship with the client.

The interview is a good opportunity for the PIC or the PM to demonstrate leadership of the project team. The interview leader opens and closes the presentation. Questions not directed at individuals by the selection committee should be fielded by the PIC or PM, who will answer the question or direct the question to the appropriate individual on the team.

The Agenda

Be sure to check whether or not the client already has an agenda for the interview, and share that agenda with all participants. Does the one-hour interview consist of a 45-minute presentation and a 15-minute Q&A, or are there 30 minutes for presenting and 30 for Q&A? The ability to present within the time frame provided is the client's first opportunity to observe how well directions are followed, as well as the leader's time management skills.

Prepare an outline with the name of each presenter that will be given to the client at the start of the interview. Prepare a second version with the number of minutes each participant has for his or her presentation. Distribute the second version to each participant. The principal-in-charge or the project manager should discuss with each participant his or her vision for the content of the individual's portion of the presentation. Everyone should be advised to prepare a bullet-point list that can be referred to at the actual presentation, not a document to be read. The goal is that the presentation be as conversational as possible.

The Checklist

Similar to the proposal preparation process, create a checklist and schedule for the short-list interview at the strategy session (see Table 3.4). For interviews for large projects, this may require air travel, models, video presentations, and so forth. There may also be a need to develop a budget. In addition to expenses, the hours spent by key staff can quickly add up, something often not considered at the proposal stage.

Deadlines are crucial because of the very tight turnaround time for short-list interview preparation. There is no margin for error. Similar to the proposal process, this

TABLE 3.4 Sample Interview Checklist

Deliverables	Who's Responsible	Due Date
Agenda		
Visuals		
Key points for PPT or boards		
Leave-behind		
Schedule		
Fee proposal		
Travel arrangements/reservations		
Rehearsal scheduling		

interview process needs a manager or champion. This is the keeper of the checklist and the individual who monitors daily the status of all deliverables. Again, it is best if this individual is not a principal, but rather someone for whom the short-list interview becomes his or her short-term highest priority. Principals of smaller firms may want to assign an administrator or even a staff member to manage this process.

The Leave-Behind

There is no one answer to what should go into the leave-behind. Every presentation is unique, and the decision on what to include should be based on this particular project. Was the site visited and photos taken? Should they be included in a leave-behind? Is there a team member whose material was not in the original submission? Is the team especially complex? Perhaps the organization chart should be included.

There are two things, however, that most presentation coaches seem to agree on. First, creating a leave-behind that consists of what was already in the proposal is redundant and serves little purpose. Second, the leave-behind should be exactly that—something *left behind*. It should not be distributed to the selection committee during the presentation, because all eyes and attention should be on the presenters.

Planning the Presentation

Crafting an opener that grabs the selection committee's interest is key to getting the interview off to a good, memorable start. Most speakers begin the interview saying something like this: "Good afternoon. I'm John Doe, principal of Doe Enterprises. We want to thank you for this opportunity to present to you this morning. Blah, blah, blah." Imagine if, instead of sounding just like everyone else, the interview started with an attention-getting opening such as: "Educating young people is your most important mission. Designing the buildings that make that possible is ours." That opener is far more likely to get the selection committee's attention than the generic opener.

Management consultant to the AEC industry and president of the Clayton Consulting Group, Dr. Janet A. Sanders, says: "Telling got you to the presentation; *selling* is what will win it. You're not giving the client a reason to select you if you're saying the same thing as everyone else."

Simply recounting credentials is not a good proposal strategy. Stress that what the team will design will serve the client's best interest. At the end of the interview, the client needs to feel that all their problems will be over if they select your firm. "Emphasize what you're going to do *for them*, rather than what you do in general," Sanders further advises.

Throughout the interview, focus on the strategic selling points—the "why us." Use a problem-solving approach, not a past performance review. The project examples shown at the interview should very specifically relate to the client's projects. They should be examples of how the team solved problems that were similar to the client's problem. The ultimate criterion for what is said in the presentation is: What does the client want and what will best advance the overall proposal strategy?

Rehearsal

Once the presentation outline is in place, and participants know their assignments, a rehearsal should be scheduled. For anyone who thinks this is an unnecessary use of otherwise billable time, consider the following words of former New York Knick and New Jersey senator Bill Bradley: "Just remember, when you're not practicing, someone, somewhere is. And when you meet them, they will win."

Rehearsals are an essential part of interview preparation, *and* the entire presentation team must rehearse together. The "I'll rehearse in the car" ploy is simply not an option. Every member of the team needs to hear what the others are saying. Otherwise, there is a risk of redundancies or contradictions during the interview that can make the team appear uncoordinated and unprepared.

The rehearsal session also allows everyone to get familiar with the "props." Have the subconsultants seen what will appear on the screen when they are speaking? If boards are being used, who is handling them? Who is handling the LCD projector? Are participants advancing their own slides? These are just a few of the questions the team does not want to face in the presentation venue minutes before the start. The natural nervousness that anyone about to make a presentation feels can be minimized if all of the physical logistics are worked out in advance through a rehearsal.

Finally, another key reason why the presentation team should rehearse together is to brainstorm possible questions in advance of the Q&A session. To a fault, most professionals know their weaknesses, and know the questions that would be difficult to answer. Don't go into the interview hoping the client will not ask the difficult questions. Go to the interview with prepared answers.

Coaching the Presenters

The rehearsal should be observed by at least one individual not involved in the presentation. This individual should watch the clock to make sure everyone completes his or her assignment within the allotted time. The observer also should take notes of nervous habits and general observations.

As previously mentioned, presenters should refer to bullet-point outlines at the interview, and should have been already told that reading their portion of the presentation would not be permitted. Carol Doscher, presentation trainer and president of Graceworks, says, "It's the human connection that will put your presentation on top." Selection committee members are making a decision about whom they will be working with for the next few months, or even years. They do not want to be read to. The interview team needs to connect with the selection committee on both a professional and a personal level.

Not all professionals are good presenters. Preparation and rehearsal go a long way toward increasing the comfort level of all presenters, but, for some, that is not enough. Professional training may be the answer for individuals who are not good presenters, but who are key staff members whose participation in interviews is essential for success. Principals of small firms should also rehearse and seek feedback, perhaps from a staff member or someone from an office down the hall. When needed, coaching for a sole-proprietor principal is even more critical, since it will be the same person presenting the same capabilities at every interview.

After the Interview

A thank-you letter to the selection committee should be sent after the interview. The follow-up letter can serve several purposes: First, it is the last opportunity to restate interest in the project. Second, it allows a restatement of the team's strengths. Third, it affords a chance to address a point that may have inadvertently been omitted during the presentation, or that came up during the Q&A.

In the best of all possible worlds, the firm will be notified soon after the interview that the team has won the project. If, however, the firm did not get selected, call the point-of-contact to get a debrief. It is preferable for a person who did not attend the interview to make the call because he or she is more likely to get an honest response. The caller should ask for genuine candor and honesty from the client. This is especially important for sole proprietors, who, of course, will need to conduct the debrief themselves.

Some clients are experienced with debriefs and may already have a format they follow, which usually includes a review of the score sheet or selection committee comments. For the clients who do not, have a clear agenda for the call that includes four key areas: (1) technical competence, (2) communication, (3) the team organization and approach, and (4) future projects.

Be prepared with specific questions, such as the following:

- Did the selection committee feel that we clearly conveyed our technical ability to accomplish the project?
- Did we clearly communicate our project approach and our interest in the project?
- Was the selection committee satisfied with our team? With our proposed approach?

The caller should take notes and make no comments in response to the debriefer's answers. This is not the time to debate or refute the client's take on the interview. Doing so could cause the debriefer to stop being candid, or even terminate the call. Questions to clarify an unclear answer are acceptable. End the call by thanking the debriefer and by expressing interest in future opportunities.

3.5 Strategic Planning for a Design Firm

Bradford Perkins, FAIA, and Peter Piven, FAIA

A central theme of this *Handbook* is the observation that most successful firms are built within the framework of a plan. Though this plan may be as simple as making a list of goals, itemizing a budget, and conducting research on potential clients, almost always it is worth the extra effort to take a more comprehensive planning approach, one that establishes an integrated plan for all aspects of the practice.

There is no standard format to follow for devising a comprehensive plan, but many experienced firms find it advantageous to develop both strategic and business plans. Most also institute a process for updating their plans (usually annually), and then commit the plan to writing. Both the process and the written plan are important.

The process is important because it provides a way to think about, refine, and document the various elements of the future practice. The plan derived from the process documents the results of the planning and serves as a checklist for measuring the progress toward achieving the stated goals. In this discussion, we'll delve into the benefits of both strategic and business planning. First, however, familiarize yourself with the 10 guiding principles given in "The Practice Plan."

STRATEGIC PLANNING

A strategic plan in this context is defined as a clear and coherent *vision* for the future as seen by the firm's stakeholder(s), and an *action plan* for implementing the vision, with clearly identified tasks, responsibilities, priorities, and milestones.

When you begin to consider your vision for the future—a vital step in the planning process—recognize that some front-end "blue-sky" thinking is acceptable, and may even be energizing; but it is important to keep in mind that your vision should identify a future that is reasonable, achievable, and, to the greatest degree possible, measurable, so that the stakeholders can ensure that they are making progress toward realizing their goals.

Strategic Planning Process

Here we look at two strategic planning models—one longer and more complex than the other—both of which provide a useful framework for incorporating frequently used planning terms and issues. First we'll look at the long-form model, which is a nine-step process.

Values. Establish the underlying philosophical concepts on which you intend to build your future, that lead to a . . .

Mission. Make this an inspiring, but general, description of what you want to be, leading to definition of a . . .

Vision. Articulate your overall goals, the description of which should include major areas of emphasis to move you toward your mission, leading to identification of . . .

Obstacles. Identify anything or anyone that stands in the way of you fulfilling your mission, leading to identification of . . .

Areas of focus. Know where you have to focus to overcome the obstacles, leading to definition of . . .

Goals. Do this for each focal area listed in Step 5, leading to the shaping of . . .

Strategies. Decide on the approaches you will take to achieve your goals, leading to the development of . . .

Action plans. Specify how you intend to implement the strategies, leading to the . . .

Business plan. Annualize, budget, follow up, and keep implementation on track.

For a start-up firm, however, this long process is probably more layered than is really necessary to develop a strategic plan. When the founders have an intuitive understanding of their own values, which they undoubtedly do, then they can use the relatively simple three-step process:

1. Perform a SWOT analysis
2. Formulate a vision
3. Do action planning

We'll explore each of these steps more fully, using case studies of our fictional firm, Able & Baker Architects.

SWOT Analysis

SWOT is an acronym for strengths, weaknesses, opportunities, and threats. In a SWOT analysis, founders start by identifying what they understand to be their strengths, weaknesses, opportunities (in the marketplace), and threats against potential success. This will provide information, in a general way, to help complete the more specific visioning process in Step 2.

The Practice Plan

Follow the leaders. Most successful firms plan their future. At a minimum, your plan should include: a vision statement and summary of goals, a marketing plan, a financial plan, an operations (including technology) plan, and a human resources plan.

Set realistic goals. Have an intermediate and a long-term vision of where you want to go.

Know yourself. This means know your strengths and weaknesses. Perform a strengths, weaknesses, opportunities, and threats (SWOT) analysis (defined later in the discussion).

Build a firm with the required skills. Plan to build or acquire the capabilities to accomplish your goals.

Focus on ways to get work, build momentum, and establish the desired image. A realistic marketing plan is a central feature of any plan.

Create a financial foundation. This will enable you to support the practice and build reserves.

Accept change. Change occurs whether we like it or not, so be prepared for inevitable changes that will take place in personnel, organizational structure, the marketing and financial climates, and other areas.

Plan for excellence. Excellence is not achieved by talent alone. Plan for it. *Never be satisfied.* No successful firm rests on its laurels.

Be flexible. This means be ready and willing to take advantage when opportunity knocks. As Yogi Berra once said, "When you reach a fork in the road, take it."

ABLE & BAKER ARCHITECTS' SWOT ANALYSIS

As the partners in Able & Baker Architects approached the end of their third year of practice, they decided to develop a strategic plan for the next three years. At an evening meeting, they performed an informal SWOT analysis and identified the following:

- *Strengths*: design ability, client service, growing reputation as experts in healthcare facilities
- *Weaknesses*: staff quality and quantity, inefficient principal-to-staff ratio, inconsistent quality assurance procedure (although no serious liability problems)
- *Opportunities*: large and diverse healthcare marketplace, large and diverse employee pool
- *Threats*: other capable healthcare firms in the market

Visioning

In this step, founders reflect on, and then document, their vision of what they intend the firm to be at a fixed future time, usually between three and five years out. (Less than three years rarely provides sufficient time for substantive change and achievement, and more than five is usually too far out, considering the substantive change, either internally or externally, that could occur in that time frame.) For the point in time chosen, at a minimum, the firm's founders should consider the firm's:

- Location
- Capabilities
- Services offered to the marketplace
- Design philosophy
- Size, in numbers of people
- Volume of fees (to be) sold, in net revenues
- Profit to be earned
- Markets, expressed geographically and by client type
- Human resources (the nature and quality of staff)
- Technology (nature and quality)
- Reputation in the marketplace, in the eyes of both clients and prospective employees
- Culture (what it "looks and feels like" inside the firm)
- Ownership (who will own the firm)

In addition, the founder(s) should document how they define:

- Their roles
- Their base salaries
- The time they expect to expend in the interest of the firm

By thinking about and documenting these key elements, founders will have identified virtually every important aspect of the firm they're planning.

ABLE & BAKER ARCHITECTS' VISIONING PROCESS

During the week following their SWOT analysis, the partners thought about and documented their personal visions for the firm at the end of the next three-year period. The following Saturday they met to discuss their respective visions. At that meeting, both partners presented their personal vision, which revealed both a great deal of congruence, but also incongruence regarding the firm's size and markets. Able expressed a desire to grow at an aggressive rate of 20 percent per year, compounded, while Baker wanted to grow at a more modest rate.

Moreover, Able also articulated a desire to expand the firm's markets into medical office buildings and nursing homes, which he saw as connected to the firm's essential expertise while creating some diversity; Baker wanted to continue to focus on the firm's core strengths. After discussing the issues, Able agreed to modify his vision to reflect a more modest growth rate of 15 percent, and to treat medical office buildings and nursing homes as "targets of opportunity," rather than seek that work proactively.

- *Location:* New space in the same city
- *Size:* Staff of six
- *Volume:* Net revenue, $500,000
- *Profit:* 15 percent of net revenue
- *Capabilities:* Comprehensive architectural services
- *Markets:* Healthcare institutions within a one-and-a-half-hour radius
- *Human resources:* Well-educated, well-trained, client-centered staff
- *Technology:* Fully integrated at an appropriate level for the practice
- *Reputation:* Expert in our field; firm of choice in our market; professional and caring place to work
- *Culture:* Professional, ethical, hard-working, focused on project success
- *Ownership:* Same as current

They will have, in a manner of speaking, painted a picture of their firm in a way that enables them to begin to identify specific steps to take to realize that vision.

Action Planning

With a vision for the future clearly drawn, the founders are ready to begin action planning. Appropriately, the visioning process is the responsibility of the stakeholders, as only those who are, or will be, at risk have the right to determine the firm's future. Metaphorically, they decide where their train is going. In contrast, the action planning process is more successful when a broader group of people participate. Employees, advisors, colleagues, and others who "are on the train" but who do not set its direction, can, nevertheless, make a significant contribution to the quality of the action planning.

A proven successful technique for participants to use in the action planning process is to time travel; that is, to imagine themselves in the future, celebrating the successful achievement of their vision at the end of the defined planning period. After visualizing a successful outcome, it is easier to identify the things they *would have done*, individually and collectively, to be successful. This visualization process frees the action planning participants from the constraints and limitations of the present, and allows them to think more freely and expansively about the future.

To that end, each of the participants in the action planning process (guided by a facilitator, if possible) makes a list of actions that they imagine would have been done to realize the vision established by the stakeholders. They then share their lists with each other and discuss them. The participants then set relative priorities on each of the items on their list—to identify which items they see as more or less important to achieving the overall vision.

Next, the participants identify the individual or group of individuals they believe to be best equipped to ensure that each identified action is accomplished, along with a reasonable milestone for each.

In the end, the strategic plan should include every important element necessary for success, as determined by the stakeholders, plus an action plan for accomplishing them.

Strategic Planning Summary

When firms are very small, most of the work involved in carrying out the action plan will fall on the principals. As the firm grows, however, it will be possible for many of the actions to be accomplished by others.

Like all planning activities, strategic planning is dynamic, not static. Regardless of the thoroughness and specificity with which you prepare a strategic plan, a number of factors may cause the plan to change over time—perhaps the people and their goals, the clients and their needs, technology, the macro-economy, or something else. Therefore, you should review your strategic plans periodically, ideally annually or semiannually.

And because strategic plans typically are made to cover several years, keep in mind that the goals explicit in the vision are not intended to be accomplished in a few weeks. Rather, the goals are meant to express longer-range aspirations that require time, energy, and money over the long term. In the meantime, business must continue as usual, meaning that the time, energy, and money required to meet future goals must be expended *in addition* to the resources being used currently. By conducting a semiannual or annual review, you'll be able to easily identify which short-term objectives have been realized, or have failed to be realized. The review will also help guide you as you change the plan to reflect or respond appropriately to any external changes that have occurred during the established time frame.

Once they had articulated a clear and coherent vision for the next three years, the partners and the new staff member they had hired met to develop an action plan to implement the vision. Working individually, they identified the specific actions that they believed would have to be taken to realize the vision; they then shared their thoughts, documenting suggested actions as they were mentioned. The actions they suggested included:

(continued)

Recruit and hire an experienced healthcare architect.

Initiate a firm-wide 401(k) plan.

Prepare project sheets to use as promotional pieces.

Develop a manual of drawing standards and guidelines.

Upgrade the CAD software.

Write articles on new developments in healthcare design.

Start every new project with a formal kickoff meeting.

Become active in the Academy of Healthcare Architects.

Schedule "client satisfaction" meetings with all clients.

Institute regular staff reviews.

Delegate budget and schedule monitoring responsibilities to key project staff members.

Develop a specific marketing plan.

Write programs for new offices for the firm when it grows.

Create a specific description for every position.

Plan firm-wide social events.

During the discussion, the participants also determined that for the firm to realize its vision, the most important actions they had to focus on were numbers 1, 7, 11, and 12:

1. Recruit and hire an experienced healthcare architect.

7. Start every new project with a formal kickoff meeting.

11. Delegate budget and schedule monitoring responsibilities to key project staff members.

12. Develop a specific marketing plan.

Therefore, they immediately assigned responsibilities and initial milestones for each of those items and agreed to meet quarterly to review progress.

Business Planning

In contrast to the strategic plan, which identifies goals that can be achieved over relatively long periods of time—generally three to five years—the purpose of a business plan is to integrate the firm's marketing, finance, operations, and human resources in a shorter time frame, usually on an annual basis. The business plan is the instrument that helps principals to plan, in both a general and detailed way, exactly how they expect to use the firm's resources in the coming year.

Each element in the plan relates to the others. Revenue targets generate marketing goals and the need for appropriate professional/technical staff and overhead support. Staff growth (in numbers of people or expense) creates the need to produce revenues to pay for them, and technical and other indirect expenses, to support them. The desire to step up the marketing effort or to increase any other component of indirect expense adds to the total overhead expense, thereby increasing the overhead rate, thus creating the need for additional revenue.

Clearly, then, business planning is an iterative process. There are only three parts to the financial equation: revenue, expense, and profit or loss, and it is possible to start the planning process with any one of those three factors. That said, the conventional approach for firms that have been in business for several years is to begin the planning process with revenues—the fees and other monies it expects to earn the following year. Firms that have a more sophisticated management structure and that have sufficient knowledge of their marketplace usually can reasonably and accurately project the next year's revenue. Less sophisticated firms will simply extrapolate from what they have earned in fees during the current year. In either case, the business planning process starts by identifying next year's revenues. The initiating assumption might be something like this: "We'll do $x in net revenues this year; next year we can do $x times $y."

With a defined revenue amount as the starting point, planners can next specify the expenses likely to be related to those revenues. To do this they must answer a series of questions:

- What will we have to do to earn those revenues?
- How many people will we need? With what level of experience and ability? At what salaries?

- How much consulting help will we need?
- How much will we have to spend in other direct expenses? How much in nonsalary indirect (overhead) expense?
- What will those revenues and those expenses leave in profit?
- Is that profit sufficient?

If the answer to the last question is no, the planning process is reiterated with different assumptions that will yield the desired profit.

Smaller or newer firms with insufficient historical data on which they can rely may choose to start the planning process from the point of costs, from which they generate income. Their initiating assumption might be: "We have a current payroll of a to which we expect we will have to add raises of b, yielding a new payroll cost of c. Based on current payroll utilization and our traditional salary multiplier, those labor dollars will generate d in net revenues. We also expect that overhead expense will increase by e percent, so our total cost will be f." Subtracting the total operating cost (f) from revenues (d) yields profit. Again, if profit is sufficient, and an examination of the various line items does not turn up other significant problems, the planning process is over. If, however, profit is insufficient, the planning process is reiterated using different assumptions.

A very few firms begin the planning process by identifying the amount of profit they wish to earn in the coming year. Then, starting with profit, they identify the overall revenues and expenses that will be required to produce that profit; next, they analyze those amounts to ascertain that they are reasonable, achievable, and consistent with the firm's vision for the future. Again, the process becomes iterative if any element is deemed to be unreasonable or unachievable.

Take a look now at two business plans for Able & Baker Architects, first using the revenue generation method and then the cost projection method.

Business Planning Summary

Regardless of the starting point, whether revenue, labor cost, or profit, the result is a business plan that identifies the relationship between productive (utilized) staff salaries and revenue, the revenues that must be produced by those responsible for marketing the firm, the staff required to produce those revenues, and the related overhead expenses (including marketing, of course) that will be required to operate the firm.

The numerical relationship between direct and indirect salary expense is called the *utilization rate*: direct hours or direct salary expense divided by total hours or total salary expense. The range within which most profitable firms operate is .60 to .65.

The numerical relationship that describes the amount of indirect (overhead) expense that must be covered by each dollar of direct salary expense is called the *indirect expense* (or *overhead*) ratio: total indirect expense divided by direct salary expense.

ABLE & BAKER ARCHITECTS' BUSINESS PLAN USING THE REVENUE GENERATION METHOD

Using as a template the firm's Income and Expense Statement at the end of the first year of practice, Able and Baker set about developing a business plan for the following year. Confident they will be successful in securing new commissions, they intend to add a professional/ technical staff person to enable them to allocate more time for marketing. They start by creating a revenue target based on their goal to

increase the firm's net revenues by 25 percent, or $200,000 × 1.25 = $250,000 for the first year.

Assuming that consultants and other direct expenses will grow proportionally, they project $50,000 for consultants and $15,000 for other direct expenses.

They calculate direct salary expenses as a function of their first year's history of achieving a net multiple of 2.8

(continued)

times salary (though they had hoped to do better). Although they expect their own utilization to drop, they also anticipate that the new employee will be highly utilized.

They expect payroll and benefits expenses to increase in proportion to salaries, to $30,000, while occupancy and general and administrative expenses are expected to increase to $11,000 and $24,000, respectively, bringing indirect expenses to $125,000, a combined 25 percent increase.

The resulting profit planned for the year is $35,000, 14 percent of planned net revenues and 11.1 percent of planned total revenues. Able & Baker Architects' planned income statement using the revenue generation method for the end of the next year is shown in Table 3.5

Although the current norm for established firms approximates 1.50, it will probably be lower for start-up firms and each firm should establish the level at which it can operate comfortably and be profitable. Most new firms will operate at an overhead ratio of 1.0 or less in their early years.

TABLE 3.5 Able & Baker Architects' Planned Income Statement Using the Revenue Generation Method		
Revenues		
Gross Revenues	$315,000	
Reimbursable revenue—Consultants	(50,000)	
Reimbursable revenue—Repro, travel, etc.	(15,000)	
Net revenue—Architectural fees	$250,000	100.0%
Direct and Reimbursable Expenses		
Direct salary expense	$ 90,000	36.0%
Consultants' expense	50,000	20.0%
Repro, travel, etc.	15,000	6.0%
Total direct expenses	$155,000	62.0%
Indirect Expenses		
Indirect salary expense	$ 60,000	24.0%
Payroll and benefits expense	30,000	12.0%
Occupancy expense	11,000	4.4%
General and administrative expense	24,000	9.6%
Total indirect expenses	$125,000	50.0%
Profit (Loss)	$ 35,000	14.0%

The numerical relationship between the revenues produced by the firm's staff and the cost of the labor to produce that revenue is called the net multiple, or net earned multiple: net revenues divided by direct salary expense. Although the current norm is very close to 3.0, each firm should establish the net multiple it is able to charge clients in order to produce good work and make an acceptable profit.

The financial or business plan is covered in more detail in the next chapter.

CHAPTER **4**

Running a Practice

4.1 Financial Planning

Lowell V. Getz, CPA

Financial planning is the process whereby performance goals are established and reports are prepared to measure whether these goals are being achieved.

The principal task of financial management systems is to help firms achieve their financial goals. Effective financial management requires guideposts that show where a firm is versus where it wants to be next month, next year, and beyond. The guideposts come from firm objectives: profit targets, staffing needs, and the costs of providing the level of service that management deems appropriate.

Business Planning

As noted in the previous chapter, strategic planning enables the principals in an architecture firm to chart its course instead of reacting to situations and opportunities as they arise. Planning begins with "big-picture" strategic thinking and positioning. Goals and strategies are then translated into a business plan—a set of financial projections and operational plans that guide the principals in managing the firm.

Business plans may be prepared with different degrees of formality, from a few ideas and numbers on a single sheet of paper to a carefully prepared document that can be presented to a bank when seeking a loan. Frequency of preparation varies, although the usual approach is to prepare or update the plan before the start of each year.

Annual financial plans typically include four components:

- A *revenue projection* that outlines anticipated revenues from projects under contract, those in the negotiation stages, and estimated revenues from projects not yet obtained

---

Lowell Getz is a financial consultant to architecture, engineering, planning, and environmental service firms. He has written, taught, and lectured widely on financial management.

- A *staffing plan* that defines the size and cost of the staff required to provide the services outlined in the revenue projection
- An *overhead expense budget* that identifies the indirect costs of supporting the staff as it provides the services outlined in the revenue projection
- A *profit plan* that establishes and budgets the profit required to sustain the firm and allow it to meet its goals

These components are closely interrelated, and decisions made about any one will affect the others, so it is necessary to develop them concurrently. As shown in Figure 4.1, the planning process can proceed along one of two paths:

- *Path A.* Start with the workload that is expected, and determine what staff and other resources will be needed.
- *Path B.* Start with the staff available, and determine the workload it can support.

It is also possible to begin with an achievable profit margin and determine the relationship of revenue and expenses needed to produce it. All of the approaches set profit goals, help in deciding billing rates, and provide yardsticks for monitoring progress and making course adjustments to keep the firm on track.

Revenue Projection

The planning process starts with a projection of what revenue management can expect to achieve in the plan year. The projection should be neither too optimistic nor too pessimistic, but should reflect the best estimate based on market conditions over the next 12 months. Beginning with projects in hand and projecting the possibility of acquiring projects from outstanding proposals, this plan establishes marketing goals for the firm over the planning period. The revenue projection covers these categories of projected income:

- Existing projects to be completed
- Proposals that are outstanding
- Unidentified future work

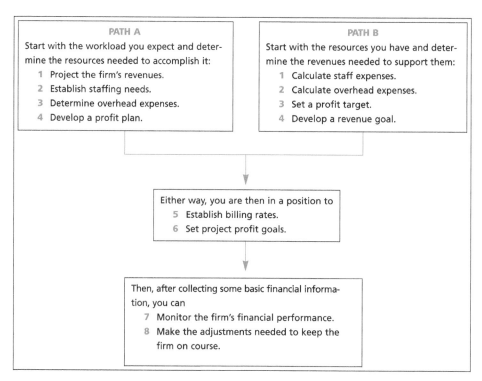

FIGURE 4.1 **Paths to Profit Planning The discussion in the text follows Path A. The discussion in the sidebar titled "A Streamlined Financial Planning Process," at the end of this topic, follows Path B.**

Work to be accomplished on existing projects is budgeted by month for the balance of the year. Work that extends beyond the plan year is budgeted in total for the following year. The sum of these projects is the firm backlog. The backlog figure is an important planning tool and needs to be continually monitored. An early warning sign of impending problems is a shrinking backlog. If the backlog is not replenished at the rate revenue is realized from it, the firm will face a shortfall of work in the months ahead. Likewise, if the backlog is increasing, it is a sign that management may need to hire more staff. The hiring process often takes months to accomplish.

Preparing a monthly projection may seem unnecessary, but this effort will help a firm plan its cash flow. It is as important to know when cash is likely to arrive as how much is expected.

The revenue projection list includes a section on proposals that are outstanding, with an estimate of the probability of this work being awarded. An estimate is also made regarding when this work is likely to begin. The revenue estimate is then made by month and entered into the plan.

Management knows that some portion of the revenues for the next year will come from projects that have not yet been identified. Using experience to project what is likely to happen, the planner estimates how much new work can be expected. Follow-on work from existing projects is also included in this estimate.

Staffing Expenses

The next step is to develop a staffing plan, starting with a list of firm staff and anticipating salary increases over the next year. In larger firms, staff members are grouped into categories such as junior or senior architects. The plan may be modified through new hires and attrition to coordinate it with the revenue projection.

Certain assumptions need to be made when developing a staffing plan. For example, the percentage of billable time (utilization ratio) for each individual or category of personnel should be estimated. Vacations and holidays need to be considered, as do allowances for training new personnel and continuing professional education for the staff.

Staffing plans require development of billing rates, either for individuals or for categories of staff. This process begins with direct labor costs (hourly salary) and adds payroll burden (payroll taxes and fringe benefits), general and administrative expenses, and a target profit that the firm hopes to achieve.

For example, assume the firm has an architect whose salary is equivalent to $115.00 per hour. The billing rate can be calculated as follows:

TABLE 4.1 Billing Rate Calculation	
Architect's hourly rate	$115.00
Indirect expense*	172.50
Subtotal	$287.50
Profit @ 25%	71.75
Hourly billing rate	$359.25

*Includes payroll burden @ 150%

The overhead and profit rates used in this calculation come from other portions of the business plan. Using the figures shown in the example produces a billing rate that is 3.124 times the cost of direct salary. In other words, a multiplier of 3.124 covers the cost of direct labor and overhead and also yields the desired profit in the example. It is important for a firm to calculate the multiplier it requires to meet its goals so it can price its services correctly.

OVERHEAD EXPENSES

The next step is to develop an estimate of overhead or indirect expenses for the coming year. Each element of indirect expense should be listed with the actual expenses for the previous year. Then assumptions are made about what is likely to happen in the plan year.

This sidebar and the sidebars titled "Staffing Plan," "Overhead Expense Budget," and "Profit Plan" provide views of the business plan of a hypothetical firm as it appears at the beginning of the year just ended.

An analysis of the revenue projection shows the firm undertakes many projects of short duration. On the date this version of the plan was prepared (January 1), the firm had a backlog of $650,000 in expected revenues over the next nine months. Three outstanding proposals total $300,000 in fees. After applying probability factors for actually receiving these projects, the principal preparing the plan assumed the firm would realize $105,000 in revenues from these proposals beginning in March. (The firm includes outstanding proposals by applying a probability factor to each one. For example, Project Z has an expected fee of $120,000, and the firm estimates it has a 25 percent chance of acquiring the project. Thus only $30,000 is included in the projection.) The firm estimates that $60,000 to $70,000 in revenue is required each month to sustain its staff and meet its overall goals; this figure is derived from the staffing, overhead expense, and profit plans shown in the next three sidebars, as well as an assessment of how much of the projected revenue will be passed through to consultants. The "unidentified future work" figures, taken from the firm's marketing plan, establish the revenue that must be raised to meet the firm's revenue goals.

Given the nature of the firm's projects, its revenue projection is updated monthly. Both backlog and outstanding proposals are carefully tracked, giving the firm a clear idea of the marketing effort required if it is to meet its goals.

TABLE 4.2 Revenue Projection

Existing Projects		Total	Jan	Feb	Mar	Apr	May	June	July	Aug	Sept	Oct	Nov	Dec
Project A		$360*	$40	$40	$40	$40	$40	$40	$40	$40	$40			
Project B		120	20	20	20	20	20	20						
Project C		170	45	45	40	40								
Total backlog		$650	105	105	100	100	60	60	40	40	40			
Proposals Outstanding														
Project X	60 @ 25%	15			5	5	5							
Project Y	120 @ 50%	60					20	20	20					
Project Z	120 @ 25%	30					15	15						
Total proposals		$105			5	5	40	35	20					
Unidentified Future Work														
Institutional clients		5										2		3
Planning studies		5										3		2
Total future work		$10										5		5
Grand Totals		$765	105	105	105	105	100	95	60	40	40	5		5

*All figures are in thousands of dollars.

Known cost increases, such as an increase in rent or insurance, should be factored in at actual amounts. Other expenses should be examined and, where necessary, adjusted to account for inflation and historical trends. It is better to make realistic assumptions based on what is likely to occur rather than to increase all expenses by a flat percentage to account for inflation.

It is now possible to set the projected overhead rate for the coming year. Most architecture firms use the direct salary expense (DSE) approach, in which the total overhead (indirect expense) budget is divided by the total budgeted direct salary expense to arrive at an overhead rate.

Other firms use a direct personnel expense (DPE) approach. Under this method, payroll burden on direct salaries is removed from overhead and added to direct salaries before the overhead rate is calculated.

The hypothetical firm has a staff of five. For each staff member, the planner first calculates an hourly rate for direct labor (by dividing the individual's annual base salary by the number of hours available to be worked over the year, assumed at 2,080—52 weeks at 40 hours per week—for a full-time person employed for a full year). Since all staff hours cannot be billed directly to projects, a utilization ratio (percent chargeable) is projected for each staff member. The resulting chargeable hours are translated into direct salary expense (chargeable hours times hourly rate) and then into total billable revenue (direct salary expense times the firm's multiplier). The last column shows the portion of each staff member's salary that is not expected to be charged to projects and that will become part of the overhead (indirect) expense budget.

This firm must bill approximately $700,000 during the year in net revenues (i.e., exclusive of consultants and reimbursable expenses) to sustain the level of staffing shown, cover its overhead, and meet its profit goal.

TABLE 4.3 Staffing Plan

	Base Salary	Hours per Year	Hourly Rate	Percent Chargeable[1]	Chargeable Hours	Direct Salary[2]	Billable Revenue[3]	Indirect Salary[4]
Principal	$110,000	2,080	$52.88	60%	1,248	$66,000	$211,000	$44,000
Registered architect	75,000	2,080	36.06	70%	1,456	53,000	170,000	22,000
Technical employee	55,000	2,080	26.44	85%	1,768	47,000	150,000	8,000
Technical employee	55,000	2,080	26.44	85%	1,768	47,000	150,000	8,000
Secretary	40,000	2,080	19.23	12.5%	260	5,000	16,000	35,000
Totals	$335,000				6,500	$218,000	$697,000	$117,000

[1] It is important to recognize the distinction between the terms billable and chargeable and their implications. Time spent on projects is chargeable and may or may not be billable. If the project fee is anything other than an hourly fee (with or without a maximum), then none of the hours charged to the project are billed. Billing is a percentage of the fee for work completed. Therefore, billable hours are possible only on hourly fee projects.

[2] Direct salary is calculated by multiplying the chargeable hours by the staff member's hourly rate.

[3] Billable revenue is calculated by multiplying direct salary expense by the firm's DSE multiplier (3.20—see "Profit Plan" sidebar).

[4] Indirect salary is calculated by multiplying non-chargeable hours (available hours minus chargeable hours) by each staff member's hourly rate.

OVERHEAD EXPENSE BUDGET

The hypothetical firm anticipates that its overhead expenses will total $341,000 for the planning year. Dividing this figure by the total projected direct salary expense ($218,000, from the staffing plan) yields an overhead rate of 1.56 or 156 percent of direct salary expense (DSE); this rate is used to determine multipliers (for hourly billing rates).

TABLE 4.4 Overhead Expense Budget

Overhead Expenses	Prior Year	Budget Year	Change
Indirect labor	$115,000	$117,000	$2,000
Payroll burden (on total salary)	96,000	101,000	5,000
Rent	20,000	20,000	0
Utilities	9,000	10,000	1,000
Telephone	3,200	4,000	800
Equipment purchase/maintenance	12,000	10,000	(2,000)
Postage and shipping	3,000	3,000	0
Publications	2,000	2,000	0
Insurance	27,000	25,000	(2,000)

(continued)

PART 2: PRACTICE

TABLE 4.4 *(continued)*

Office supplies	10,600	10,000	(600)
Travel	7,000	8,000	1,000
Printing	7,000	5,000	(2,000)
Marketing tools	9,200	10,000	800
Professional development	6,000	8,000	2,000
Legal and accounting expenses	6,000	6,000	0
Other general/administrative expenses	2,000	2,000	0
Totals	$335,000	$341,000	$6,000

Calculation of Overhead Rate Based on Direct Salary Expense (DSE)

Total overhead	$341,000
Divided by total salary expense (staffing plan)	218,000
Yields overhead rate	1.56 (156%)

Calculation of DSE Break-Even Multiplier*

Total direct salary expense + total overhead	$559,000
Divided by total direct salary expense	218,000
Yields DSE "break-even" multiplier	2.56

Calculation of DPE Break-Even Multiplier*

Total direct personnel expense	
Total direct salary expense	$218,000
Direct payroll burden @ 30%	65,000
Total personnel expense	$283,000
Total overhead (without direct payroll burden)	276,000
Total direct personnel expense + total overhead	$559,000
Divided by total direct personnel expense	$283,000
Yields DPE break-even multiplier	1.97

*These are called break-even multipliers because a profit target has yet to be considered.

THE PROFIT PLAN

Profit is budgeted in the same manner as any other item in the plan. That is, the firm should have an expected level of profit and should budget for it in the same way that it budgets for staffing and overhead expenses.

PROFIT PLAN

The profit plan presented here includes the information developed above. To provide a complete picture, it adds the amount the firm expects to pay for outside consultants ($189,000) and for reimbursable expenses ($55,000). The plan shows a profit target of $140,000, or 20 percent of net revenues (gross revenues minus pass-throughs to consultants and reimbursable expenses).

This, and the previous three commentaries, all provide insights into the hypothetical firm's business plan and performance. The information shows how the firm's budget, revenue, staffing, overhead expense, and profit plans relate to and interact with each other.

There is, however, a great deal that we don't know about the hypothetical firm: What are its overall goals, and how is it positioning itself? Are its utilization rates going up or down? Are accounts receivable aging and collection periods lengthening? Is the firm financially healthy over the long run? Is the firm producing quality architecture? Business plans and financial reports can't answer the first and last questions. As they are produced, updated, and compared with past performance, however, these financial plans and reports—and the judgments drawn from them—produce a picture of the firm and its ability to realize its financial goals.

TABLE 4.5 Profit Plan	
Profit Target	
Projected gross revenues	$943,000
Minus reimbursable expenses	(55,000)
Minus outside consultant expenses	(189,000)
Projected net fees	$699,000
Minus projected expenses:	
Direct salary expense	$218,000
Indirect expenses	341,000
Total projected expenses	$559,000
Profit target (20% of projected net fees)	$140,000
Net DSE Multiplier Required to Attain Profit Target	
Total projected net fees	$699,000
Divided by direct salary expense	$218,000
Yields net DSE multiplier (rounded)	3.2

Profits are required to provide bonuses to employees, to fund capital expenditures, and to reward the owners for their risk. Some profits are reinvested in the firm. It may not be possible to earn the targeted profit on all projects, but the important point is to establish an overall expectation for the firm that will balance profits and losses on all projects.

The most common method of estimating profit in an architecture firm is to establish it as a percentage of net revenue. Another approach to establishing a profit target is to consider owner investment in the firm, establish a reasonable return on that investment, and then calculate how much must be earned at the expected level of activity both to achieve that return and to provide bonuses or profit-sharing contributions as well.

Once the profit target has been set, each new project should be reviewed in light of this target. Projects that do not achieve the target reduce the overall profit margin of the firm.

Individual Project Planning

An architecture firm accomplishes its profit plan one project at a time. Each project is a building block that helps achieve, or detracts from, the firm's practice goals. Following are keys to meeting firm profit targets:

- Acquire clients and projects that are right for the firm.
- Price projects appropriately to the firm and its clients.
- Negotiate contracts that implement the firm's goals.
- Hire staff and consultants with the talent and experience to provide the services offered by the firm.
- Manage projects, relationships, and risks well.

The remaining implementation details involve other aspects of the firm's financial management, such as acquiring and maintaining the proper levels of cash, billing and collecting funds, and keeping a steady hand on the financial tiller.

The following is a simplified approach to financial planning and management.

STEP 1: ESTABLISH A PROFIT PLAN

Financial guideposts come from a profit plan—which is also an estimated operating budget. Here is a bare-bones method for profit planning for the small firm:

- Estimate your expenses. Include salaries of principals and staff (include any planned adjustments), payroll taxes and benefits, and office expenses (use past history as a starting

point and estimate anticipated changes over the next year). Do not include passthroughs such as reimbursables and fees for project-related outside consultants.

- Set a profit goal. Each firm sets its own profit goal. In the case illustrated here, the firm has established a goal of 20 percent of net revenues before any federal income taxes are paid.

- Calculate the net revenue goal by adding estimated expenses and the profit goal. This is called net because you have omitted reimbursables and outside consultant fees.

Sample Profit Plan (Excludes Consultants and Reimbursable Expenses)

Expenses

Salaries		
Principal	(1 @ $110,000)	$110,000
Registered architect	(1 @ $75,000)	75,000
Technical employees	(2 @ $55,000)	110,000
Secretary	(1 @ $40,000)	40,000
Total salaries		$335,000
Payroll taxes and benefits (@ 30%)		$101,000
Office expenses		
Rent		$20,000
Utilities		10,000
Telephone		4,000
Equipment purchase, lease, maintenance		10,000
Postage, shipping		3,000
Publications		2,000
Insurance (auto, office, liability)		25,000
Office supplies		10,000
Travel		8,000
Printing		5,000
Marketing tools		10,000
Professional development costs		8,000
Legal and accounting fees		6,000
Other expenses		2,000
Total office expenses		$123,000
Total expenses		$559,000
Profit goal @ 20% of net revenues		140,000
Net *revenue goal*		$699,000

STEP 2: RESTATE THE PROFIT PLAN TO REFLECT EFFICIENCY

In architecture firms, revenue (and profit) are generated by direct services labor—people working on projects. The most easily used common denominator for planning and measuring financial performance is direct salary expense:

Direct salary expense (DSE) = Salary cost of hours charged to projects (billable time)

PART 2: PRACTICE

Financial guideposts in the form of DSE multipliers can easily be calculated from a profit plan that has been restated to isolate expected DSE. This can be done by applying an expected utilization ratio to total salaries:

$$\text{Utilization ratio} = \text{Direct salary expense} \div \text{Total salary expense}$$

Stated another way:

$$\text{Direct salary expense} = \text{Total salary expense} \times \text{Utilization ratio}$$

Utilization ratios are different for different firms, but statistical surveys indicate that most achieve about 65 percent overall efficiency (averaging all principals and employees) to maintain reasonable profitability. The other 35 percent is spent on nonbillable (indirect) time such as that spent for marketing, staff development, general office administration, vacations, holidays, sick leave, and so on.

The utilization ratio should be monitored because it reflects the firm's ability to generate revenue. A low percentage means low revenue potential, and a high percentage means high revenue potential.

Using the utilization ratio just described, the firm's profit plan can be restated:

Restated Profit Plan (using a 65% utilization ratio)

Direct salaries	($335,000 x 0.65)	$218,000
Indirect expenses		
Indirect salaries	($335,000 x 0.35)	$117,000
Payroll taxes and benefits		101,000
Office expenses		123,000
Total indirect expenses		341,000
Total direct salaries + indirect expenses		$559,000
Profit goal @ 20% of revenues		140,000
Net *revenue goal*		$699,000

STEP 3: CALCULATE NET MULTIPLIERS

The next step is to calculate the planned DSE multipliers for each major item in the restated profit plan. Divide each major item by the direct salary expense amount as shown. The results for the illustrated firm are shown on the following page:

A low utilization ratio increases the necessary breakeven multiplier because there are more indirect hours and fewer direct hours, which results in a lower profit margin.

To pay for direct salary expenses	$218,000 ÷ $218,000	1.00
To pay for indirect expenses	341,000 ÷ $218,000	1.56
Equals the firm's break-even multiplier		2.56
To add profit	140,000 ÷ $218,000	0.64
Equals the planned net multiplier		3.20

STEP 4: USE THE NET MULTIPLIER TO SET MINIMUM HOURLY BILLING RATES

Using the sample firm's 3.20 net multiplier yields the hourly billing rates show (at 2,080 hours in a year, rounded to the nearest dollar). These are the minimum rates needed to meet the profit plan. Actual rates charged may also reflect the value of the services and market considerations.

Principal (@ $110,000)	$52.88 × 3.2 = $169/hour
Registered architect (@ $75,000)	$36.06 × 3.2 = $115/hour
Technical staff (@ $55,000)	$26.44 × 3.2 = $85/hour
Clerical/administrative staff (@ $40,000)	$19.23 × 3.2 = $62/hour

(continued)

STEP 5: SET PROJECT PROFIT GOALS

To meet its profit plan, this firm needs to set aside 20 percent of its net revenues. When a project comes in, 20 percent off the top of the net fee must be set aside as untouchable. The project must be done for the money left if the profit plan is to be met.

STEP 6: USE ACTUAL NET MULTIPLIER EARNED TO MONITOR FINANCIAL PERFORMANCE

This can be done quickly, easily, with reasonable accuracy, and without accountants. The only information needed is

- Net revenue earned (derived from fees invoiced)
- Direct salary expense (project hours at hourly salary rate as recorded on time sheets)

Following is a sample current project analysis using the break-even multiplier established as this firm's goal in Step 3. All figures except multipliers are rounded to the nearest $1,000.

The break-even multiplier is the only variable factor in this analysis. It should be recalculated periodically using accrual-based financial information (you will probably need your accountant for this). In the meantime, check your utilization ratio. If it is holding about as planned, your break-even probably hasn't changed much—unless, of course, some large indirect expense has come up unexpectedly.

Although it is not 100 percent accurate (due to possible variations in the break-even multiplier), this method of monitoring provides a simple and timely means of staying abreast of financial performance—and determining if and on which projects corrective action is needed.

Sample Current Project Analysis

	Step 1		Step 2		Step 3		Step 4		Step 5	Step 6
	Net Revenue Earned	÷	Direct Salary Expense (DSE)	=	Net Multiplier Earned	−	Break-Even Multiplier	=	Profit Multiplier	Approximate Profit or (LOSS)
Project A	$220,000		$75,000		2.93		2.56		0.37	$28,000
Project B	135,000		42,000		3.21		2.56		0.65	27,000
Project C	112,000		53,000		2.11		2.56		(0.45)	(24,000)
Project D	242,000		101,000		2.40		2.56		(0.16)	(17,000)

Adapted from "The Minimalist Financial Manager" by William H. Haire, AIA, Oklahoma State University, in previous Handbook editions.

4.2 Financial Management Systems

Lowell V. Getz, CPA

Managing the finances of a firm and monitoring financial performance on a regular basis are essential for a successful practice.

Architects who understand how to manage the financial operations of a firm can achieve better performance and a higher level of success. People can be hired to perform the accounting function, but the responsibilities of management cannot be delegated.

To manage firm finances, it is necessary to have a financial control system in place. Principals require a clear, timely, and accurate method of monitoring financial performance of individual projects and the firm as a whole in order to:

- Know if the firm is meeting its financial goals and making a profit. To remain in practice, an architecture firm must earn a profit—an excess of revenue over expenses that sustains the firm and allows it to provide the level of service it aspires to offer.

Lowell V. Getz is a financial consultant to architecture, engineering, planning, and environmental service firms. He has written, taught, and lectured widely on financial management.

- Know if there will be cash to cover payroll and other current expenses. Even a profitable firm will have difficulty meeting its obligations if it does not maintain a positive cash flow.
- Plan for capital expenditures. As new and improved technology becomes available, it is necessary to set aside funds for acquiring capital equipment.
- Provide quality professional services priced at competitive levels.

Sources and Uses of Funds

To understand the financial aspects of an architecture firm, it is necessary to become familiar with certain terms.

Revenues

Revenues to operate the firm come from projects, that is, from fees received for providing professional services. Additional sources of funds include the following:

- Infusions of capital from the founders when the firm is started and from new principals as ownership is expanded
- Revenue from associated business ventures, such as real estate development
- Income from interest, rents, sale of assets, or other miscellaneous sources

Direct (Project) Expenses

Like revenues, a significant portion of a firm's expenses are incurred in providing project services. These *direct expenses* are identified with specific projects and categorized as:

- Direct salary expenses, representing time charged by professional and technical staff in providing project services, as well as time spent administering and coordinating consultant services.
- Expenses for outside consultants working on projects.
- Other direct expenses for providing project services, such as travel, telephone, and printing expenses. Such expenses may be non-reimbursable (included in the architect's fee) or reimbursable (paid for separately by the client).

Reimbursable Expenses

Reimbursable expense categories are specified in the owner-architect agreement and may include travel, lodging and meals, telephone, reproduction expenses, and similar project-related costs. Charges are billed to the client and any requested documentation is provided, such as copies of telephone charges. Reimbursable expenses invoiced to the client usually include a markup of approximately 10 percent. A "not-to-exceed" limit on reimbursable expenses is sometimes included in the owner-architect agreement. The architect, therefore, needs to develop a reasonable estimate that includes a contingency amount.

> Government agencies may have their own definitions of what are considered to be direct and indirect expenses, and what indirect expenses are allowed within a firm's overhead rate or multiplier.

Indirect Expenses

Indirect expenses are those expenses that do not directly support project activities. Indirect expenses are classified as payroll burden or general and administrative expenses.

Payroll burden is the cost of benefits provided to staff members and includes health insurance, workers' compensation insurance, federal and state unemployment insurance, and payroll taxes.

General and administrative expenses consist of salaries and benefits for management and staff members when they are not working on projects. These nonproject activities may include management, marketing, professional development, civic functions, and other activities that are important to the firm but cannot be charged to a billable project. The cost of renting space, office operations, business taxes, liability insurance, and depreciation are also indirect expenses.

Indirect expenses, often called overhead, represent a significant portion of a firm's expenses. In making a proposal for services, the usual practice is to include overhead either as a percentage of direct salary expense (for example, 150 percent of DSE, Direct Salary Expenses) or as a breakeven multiplier applied to direct salary expense (in the same example, 2.5 times DSE). Adding a 20 percent profit arrives at a multiplier for billing purposes of 3.0 times DSE. Some firms apply overhead rates and multipliers to direct personnel expense (DPE). DPE includes direct salary expense plus associated payroll burden. Payroll burden on direct salaries is therefore removed from overhead.

In the above example, if payroll burden represents 30 percent of direct salaries, a breakeven multiplier of 1.9 times DPE equals a breakeven multiplier of 2.5 times DSE ($1.3 \times 1.9 = 2.5$). Adding a 20 percent profit results in a multiplier for billing purposes of 2.3 times DPE ($1.3 \times 2.3 = 3.0$).

Profit

Defined as the difference between revenues and expenses, *profit* # represents the funds required to sustain the practice in lean times, buy capital equipment, reward staff members for outstanding performance, and allow firm owners to achieve a return on their investment.

Accounting Systems

An accounting system consists of a chart of accounts and a coding system.

Chart of Accounts

A *chart of accounts* is a list of the various accounts used by the firm. In a sense, it is a directory that evolves to meet firm needs. The chart of accounts classifies accounts under the following six headings:

- *Assets* (everything owned by the firm or owed to the firm by others)
- *Liabilities* (claims of creditors against these assets; what the firm owes to others)
- *Net worth* (claims of the firm owners against its assets; what the firm owes to its owners)
- *Revenues* (amounts earned by a firm during an accounting period)
- *Expenses* (what it costs the firm to produce its revenue)
- *Profit or loss* (the difference between revenue and expenses)

EXPENSES

DIRECT EXPENSES

In addition to the expenses of salaries and outside services, architecture firms incur other expenses that can be charged directly to a specific project. These expenses, which may be non-reimbursable or reimbursable, often include costs for

- Printing, duplication, and plotting, including reproduction of drawings and specifications
- Photography
- Diskettes, tapes, and other electronic media requested by the client
- CAD and other computer services associated with the project

- Items purchased on the client's behalf (e.g., fees, permits, bid advertising, models, renderings)
- Project meeting expenses
- Transportation, including expenses to and from the job site
- Lodging and meals
- Long-distance telephone, fax, telex, etc.
- Postage, courier, and overnight delivery
- Project professional liability insurance premiums
- Additional premiums for project professional liability insurance in excess of basic firm coverage
- Other project-related insurance premiums
- Legal and accounting services related to the project
- Financing and carrying costs of professional services at the client's request

GENERAL AND ADMINISTRATIVE EXPENSES

Indirect or overhead expenses—expenses that cannot easily be attributed to a specific project in the office—include salaries not charged to a project, payroll burden (fringe benefits), and a wide variety of general and administrative expenses. These G&A expenses may include costs for the following items:

CURRENT OPERATING EXPENSES

- Rent (or equivalent), utilities, operation and maintenance, and repair of buildings, equipment, and automobiles
- Printing, duplication, photographs, and similar items for marketing and other nonproject uses
- Printing of in-house check sets and consultant base sheets
- Computer hardware, software, and operating expenses
- Postage and messenger services
- Travel and entertainment for marketing and firm or staff development
- Office supplies
- Library materials, books, periodicals
- Telephone, facsimile, electronic mail, information services
- Taxes (e.g., real estate, personal property)
- Professional dues and licensing fees
- Seminars, conventions, in-house training, and professional development

- Marketing and proposal preparation
- Public relations
- Charitable and civic contributions
- Insurance (e.g., automobile, contents, building, principals' life, valuable papers, comprehensive general liability, equipment, professional liability)
- Interest on loans and credit lines
- Bond premiums

CAPITAL EXPENDITURES

- Depreciation (e.g., furniture, equipment, automobiles, buildings)
- Amortization on leasehold improvements

LOSSES

- Theft or casualty loss not covered by insurance
- Expenses to correct design errors and omissions, including deductibles on insurance payouts
- Uncollectible compensation and bad debts

PREPAID EXPENSES

Expenses that affect operations beyond the current fiscal year and that the Internal Revenue Service requires to be spread over more than one year (e.g., long-term insurance premiums, certain taxes, equipment leases, licenses/fees, organization expenses)

Accounting Codes

A *coding system* is the shorthand used to record various entries in the proper accounts. Each project is assigned a number. In more complex systems, subcodes may be used for departments, phases, or tasks. Accounting codes are listed in the chart of accounts and identify various types of expenses. Accounting codes allow a firm to track expenses by project, by phase or task, or by type of expenditure to better control costs and to improve budgeting.

The financial management system uses the chart of accounts and coding system to provide reports on individual projects (project accounting), as well as for the firm as a whole (general accounting).

Project Accounting

Reports from the project accounting system contain information on the time and expenses directly assigned to projects. Time sheets are used to record hours spent working on projects and nonproject activities. Other direct expenses are coded to projects either when they are incurred or when they are paid. Overhead expenses are assigned to projects as a percentage of direct labor expense. Project accounting compares project labor spent with revenue earned to determine whether a profit or loss was incurred on the project. Project control systems produce reports that compare actual project expenses with budget to determine whether the project is proceeding in accordance with the work plan.

Accounting systems vary in complexity. A wide range of software is available so that even the smallest firms can obtain timely and accurate information for project control.

General Accounting

General accounting software produces reports needed to prepare financial statements and tax returns. The general accounting system consists of payroll records, receipts and disbursements journals, accounts receivable, accounts payable, and the general ledger. These various records are used to summarize transactions and prepare financial statements and management reports.

Accounting Methods

There are two primary methods of accounting: the cash and accrual methods. A firm accounting system may use one, or more likely, both methods.

Cash Method

Cash accounting records entries at the time they impact cash. For example, revenue is recorded when checks are received from clients, and expenses are recorded when cash is paid out. Transactions that do not involve cash are not recorded until they do. When an invoice is sent to a client, it is not recorded as revenue until the check arrives.

Cash accounting is very straightforward. However, revenue is not matched with expenses. Certain cash expenses, such as salaries and vendor invoices, are paid shortly after the obligation is incurred. However, revenue for services provided may not be received until later. Cash accounting statements therefore record only the excess or deficit of cash that occurred.

For income tax purposes, most professional services firms pay tax on a cash basis, since few want to pay taxes on money that has not been collected. These firms keep accrual records for management purposes, which are then converted to a cash basis for tax purposes at the year's end.

Accrual Method

The accrual system of accounting records revenue when it is earned and expenses when they are incurred. For example, if labor and expenses are charged to a project in January, the revenue earned is reported in January as well, even though the cash has not yet been received. The drawback, of course, is that the firm may not collect the cash for the reported revenue. The revenue is then written off when the bad debt is discovered, which may be several months later. However, this should be a rare occurrence.

Similarly, expenses are recorded in the accounting period when they are incurred rather than when paid. For example, a vendor invoice for supplies provided to the firm in January is recorded as an expense in January even though it may not be paid until February. The invoice is recorded as an account payable to match it against the corresponding revenue. Likewise, certain expenses such as insurance premiums that are paid in advance (prepaid) are spread over the entire period to which they apply.

Many firms prefer accrual accounting because it addresses the question of profitability by matching revenue with expenses. Additionally, the revenue earned but not yet billed (work in progress) and its billed revenue (accounts receivable) are recorded as assets on the balance sheet. By reporting these amounts each month, the firm principals can see how much they are owed and can take steps to collect it. Similarly, unpaid expenses are recorded as liabilities, indicating how much the firm owes to others.

The emphasis on accrual accounting does not minimize the importance of cash and the need to monitor the firm's cash position on a regular basis. The reporting system needs to supply both cash and accrual information, but for management purposes, accrual statements give the most pertinent information. Firms that are organized as regular corporations generally are allowed to pay taxes on the cash basis. The outside accountant converts the accrual income statements to a cash basis at year-end for purposes of calculating corporate taxes owed.

Financial Reports

Financial control systems produce reports that can be used to keep the firm and its projects on track.

Income Statements and Balance Sheets

The most common statements used to describe the financial status of a firm are the income statement and balance sheet. Taken together, these statements present a complete picture of the firm's current financial position. In essence, an income statement is a moving picture, whereas a balance sheet is a snapshot. The income statement presents the results of operations or a summary of revenue, expenses, and profit for a period of time, such as a month, quarter, or year. The balance sheet, on the other hand, is a report of the current condition of the firm showing the status of assets, liabilities, and net worth as of a particular date.

The income statement can be used to monitor various key ratios, such as profit margin, multipliers, utilization, revenue per employee, and overhead factors. The balance sheet can be used to monitor working capital and average collection period. These statements provide indicators of the firm's ability to manage debt (leverage), pay current debt (solvency), and convert assets to cash (liquidity).

Management Reports

The financial management system produces invoices, summaries of amounts owed to and owed by the firm (accounts receivable and accounts payable), reports for tax and regulatory agencies, and other information for management. Project reports track actual expenses against budget. These reports provide detail to help project architects manage the financial aspects of their projects. The reports also provide summary information on project performance for management.

CASH AND ACCRUAL ACCOUNTING

Accrual accounting provides an accurate picture of the firm's revenues and expenses within a given time frame—in the case of our example, the month of January. This picture is not skewed by cash coming in or going out that does not relate to the month's activities.

Look at this simple example: On a cash basis, this firm recorded a surplus of $16,000 in January. In reality, though, much of the revenue producing this surplus resulted from old invoices not paid by the firm's clients until this month—perhaps as the result of a year-end effort to clean up accounts receivable. In January the firm actually committed to spend $10,000 more than it earned.

TABLE 4.6 Cash and Accrual Accounting

January–Cash Basis	
Revenues received by the firm:	
October invoices	10,000
November invoices	27,000
December invoices	30,000
Total January revenues	$67,000
Expenses dispersed for salaries, vendors, etc.	$51,000
Net cash revenue for January	$16,000
January–Accrual Basis	
Revenues earned from clients	$80,000
Expenses incurred in January	
Billable to clients (project services)	65,000
Not billable (marketing)	15,000
Other expenses	10,000
Total January expenses	$90,000
Net income (or loss) for January	($10,000)

How often should financial statements be prepared? The answer is a function of the size and complexity of the firm and how often management needs to review financial performance. Many firms operate with weekly summaries of project hours spent and monthly financial statements. Others input timesheets daily online and access information whenever it is needed—sometimes in the form of "flash reports" or summaries of critical information, such as project status or cash on hand. Firms also need to prepare reports for banks, insurance companies, and various government agencies. These requirements may influence the frequency of reporting.

INCOME STATEMENT AND BALANCE SHEET

Shown here are the income statement and balance sheet for a hypothetical nine-person firm for the year just ended.

As shown in the income statement, the firm took in $1,057,000 in revenues and incurred $969,000 in expenses, ending the year with a profit of $88,000. (This is labeled net profit before taxes because no federal income taxes have been deducted.)

While the principals may have considered this profit level to be adequate, the firm missed its budgeted profit of $154,000. An analysis of the income statement shows that revenues from fees were below estimates, the firm was able to keep direct labor and other direct expenses within budget, and it was less successful at controlling indirect (overhead) expenses.

In budgeting for the coming year, this firm will need to boost fees, control overhead expenses, or establish a more realistic profit target.

On the balance sheet, the firm ended the year with $510,000 in assets, $300,000 of which represents work billed but not yet paid by clients (accounts receivable) and another $100,000 of which is work in progress.

The firm's liabilities, including a few bills payable and a note to the bank, totaled $45,000. Subtracting this amount from assets produces a net worth (owners' equity) of $465,000.

Note that the balance sheet is only a snapshot. It produces some valuable information (for example, the firm has only $10,000 in cash on hand—not enough to cover its accounts payable of $20,000) and flags significant problems (for example, the need to track and collect accounts receivable). To be most useful, however, this balance sheet would need to be compared with one from the end of the previous period to determine if assets, liabilities, and owner's net worth are increasing or decreasing.

TABLE 4.7 Income Statement and Balance Sheet

Income Statement (for the period beginning January 1 and ending December 31)

Revenues	Budget	Actual	Variance
Fees	$1,200,000	$1,000,000	$200,000
Reimbursable expenses	61,000	57,000	4,000
Total revenues	$1,261,000	$1,057,000	$204,000
Expenses			
Direct expenses			
Direct personnel cost	$321,000	$273,000	$48,000
Outside consultants	212,000	189,000	23,000
Other direct expenses	31,600	24,000	7,000
Total direct expenses	564,000	486,000	78,000
Indirect expenses			
Indirect personnel	222,000	211,000	11,000
Other indirect expenses	1 88,000	217,000	(29,000)
Total indirect expenses	410,000	428,000	(18,000)
Reimbursable expenses	133,000	55,000	78,000
Total expenses	$1,107,000	$969,000	$138,000
Net profit before taxes	$154,000	$88,000	66,000

TABLE 4.7 *(continued)*

Balance Sheet (as of December 31)

Assets

Cash	$15,000	$10,000	($5,000)
Accounts receivable	280,000	300,000	20,000
Work in progress	80,000	100,000	20,000
Fixed assets (less depreciation)	75,000	100,000	25,000
Total assets	$450,000	$510,000	60,000

Liabilities and owner's equity

Accounts payable	$40,000	$20,000	($20,000)
Notes payable	45,000	25,000	(20,000)
Total liabilities	85,000	45,000	(40,000)
Owner's equity	365,000	465,000	100,000
Total liabilities and equity	$450,000	$510,000	$60,000

Using Financial Reports

Architects do not have to be accountants to manage the financial aspects of their firms. Architects need to understand the significance of financial information rather than the details of how reports are prepared. They are then in a position to ask questions, seek clarification, and have enough information to make the decisions necessary to maintain a successful practice.

4.3 Maintaining Financial Health and Navigating Economic Cycles

Peter Piven, FAIA

Well-managed firms continually assess their financial health and take appropriate measures to stay on track.

Architects aspire to financial health. The reason is simple—they cannot attain their practice goals unless they do. They must practice at whatever level of profitability is required to stay in business, fulfill promises made to clients, and fulfill their own practice goals, including providing appropriate rewards for performance and risk and a reasonable return on the investment of firm owners.

MAJOR FINANCIAL PLANNING FACTORS

Financial health requires understanding, planning, monitoring, and controlling three interrelated aspects of the firm's financial picture:

- *Profitability* (the ability to create an excess of revenue over expenses)
- *Liquidity* (the ability to convert an asset to cash with relative speed and ease and without significant loss in value)
- *Solvency* (the ability to meet financial obligations as they come due)

Architects serve an extremely cyclical sector of our economy. To thrive, therefore, they need to be able to adjust to the regular ups and downs of the construction industry.

—Kermit Baker, Ph.D., Hon. AIA

"Financial Management Systems" describes the revenue and expenses, as well as cash and accrual accounting methods, of architecture firms.

Profitability

Profitability is required at three levels:

* For the firm, generally in the form of retained or reinvested earnings, so it can provide for capital investment, endure downward economic cycles, and sustain growth
* For those who produce the profit, as a reward for having done so
* For the risk taken by firm owners and as a return on their investment in the firm

By attending to profitability, architects ensure that they will not incur more expense than revenue on a project or on a firm-wide basis. The normal project cash cycle includes three steps: performing services, invoicing, and collecting cash to cover the costs—both direct and indirect—of performing the services. If the architect manages successfully, this cycle not only yields sufficient cash to cover costs but also returns profit to the firm. Practicing at a loss means two things: There is no profit and, even worse, essential costs are not being covered. Regardless of whether the firm uses the cash method or the accrual method for its accounting, losses eventually result in a cash drain—more is expended than is taken in.

Liquidity

In operating their practices, architects acquire both fixed (long-term) and current (short-term) assets. *Fixed assets* are assets such as real estate, leasehold improvements, furniture, fixtures, equipment, and automobiles that they do not intend to convert to cash in the foreseeable future. *Current assets* include both cash and other assets that must be converted to cash, especially *accounts receivable* (the value of services billed but not yet collected) and *work in progress* (the value of services performed but not yet billed).

THE IMPORTANCE OF UNDERSTANDING ECONOMIC CYCLES

Whether architects like it or not, they are extremely exposed to economic cycles. Since architects receive most of their revenue from services provided to the construction sector of the economy, and since the construction industry is one of the most cyclical industries in the economy, architects are vulnerable to the regular ebb and flow of activity in the economy.

The impact of the economy on architecture practice has been particularly apparent with recent cycles. The past national economic expansion that began in late 2001 reached a peak at the end of 2007. The tail end of that expansion saw healthy growth in the economy, and with it even stronger growth in most nonresidential construction sectors. However, at this phase of the upturn, the overall construction sector was seeing more modest growth. The housing market peaked much earlier in the cycle—the beginning of 2006 was the high-water mark of the cycle for home building—and declines after that offset gains in the nonresidential construction sector over the 2006–2008 period. The deep recession which followed was painful for most architects.

To keep a practice financially viable, the architect must maintain the liquidity of the firm; this is accomplished by invoicing regularly with the goal of continually converting work in progress to accounts receivable. Then, to convert accounts receivable to cash, the architect must follow up by assiduously maintaining collections (see Figure 4.2).

Solvency

Solvency is the firm's ability to pay its bills. Solvency and profitability are closely related; a firm that is unprofitable will, in the long run, not have enough money to pay its debts. In the extreme, the inability to pay debts when they come due leads to insolvency and bankruptcy.

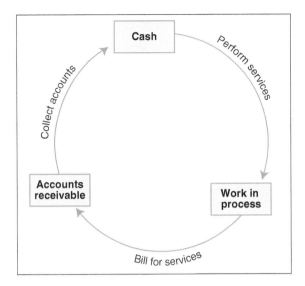

FIGURE 4.2 **Cash Cycle**

Managing Cash

Keeping solvent requires sound cash management. Solvency is a cash issue: How much cash is needed? For what purposes? When? From what sources?

Cash management is a systematic procedure for forecasting and controlling the cash that flows through the firm. The objective of cash management is to ensure that adequate cash is always on hand and that cash surpluses, when they exist, are invested wisely.

Cash Flow Projections

The best tool for addressing these questions and evaluating firm solvency is *cash budgeting*. This involves forecasting anticipated flows of cash into and out of the firm over time by gathering and reporting information about the amounts, timing, and certainty of future cash receipts and payments. The cash budget predicts cash flow. Its purpose is to provide a plan to indicate when cash receipts and disbursements can be expected. The forecast should indicate needs for short-term borrowing as well as surpluses available for short-term investing.

The steps in developing a cash budget are listed here:

- Forecast billings
- Forecast amounts and timing of cash receipts (collections) from those billings
- Forecast cash receipts from sources other than project revenues, such as investments, rents, and sale of assets
- Forecast cash disbursements, including payroll, consultants, other direct (project) expenses, indirect (overhead) expenses, reimbursable expenses, and capital expenditures
- Combine receipt and disbursement schedules and calculate net monthly cash increases or decreases

Monthly increase or decrease, when combined with the beginning cash balance, indicates the cash position of the firm at the end of each month. The ending cash balance of one month is the beginning balance for the next month.

Cash Flow Controls

Cash budgeting is planning in advance for cash that will be required in the future. Controlling cash flow requires measuring actual performance against the budget and taking corrective action as needed. Techniques for managing cash include the following:

- Sustaining backlog by developing a continuing flow of new projects and services
- Billing promptly and correctly, ensuring that clients are aware of the services provided

This cash projection, made as of March 1, looks at anticipated revenues in terms of when the firm expects to collect them. For example, a total of $72,000 was billed in January; of this, $18,000 was paid in January, an additional $43,200 in February, and the remaining $10,800 is projected for collection in March. Similarly, 25 percent of the anticipated billing for March ($16,500 of $66,000) is expected to be earned in March, another 60 percent ($39,600) in April, and the final 15 percent ($9,900) in May.

Adding receipts from sources other than billings (e.g., interest) provides the total cash figure for each month. Subtracting disbursements leaves the firm with an expected monthly cash gain or loss. Adding the cash balance at the end of each previous month produces the projected cash balance for each month. Adding the actual $3,000 cash balance from February to the projected $7,900 net cash gain from March brings the month-ending cash balance for March to the $10,900 shown.

TABLE 4.8 Cash Flow Projection Process

Cash Flow Projection: March 1	January	February	March	April	May
Total billings					
Actual					
Projected	$72,000	$68,000	$66,000	$76,000	$80,000
Collections on accounts receivable					
First month (25%)	18,000	17,000	16,500	19,000	20,000
Second month (60%)		43,200	40,800	39,600	45,600
Third month (15%)			10,800	10,200	9,900
Other (nonoperating) receipts			2,000	2,000	2,000
Total cash receipts (cash in)			$70,100	$70,800	$77,500
Cash disbursements					
Direct expenses			$29,800	$31,000	$34,000
Indirect expenses			32,000	35,000	30,400
Other (nonoperating disbursements)			400	0	12,000
Total cash disbursements (cash out)			$62,200	$66,000	$76,400
Net cash gain (loss) during month			$7,900	$4,800	$1,100
Cash balance at beginning of month			3,000	10,900	15,700
Cash balance at end of month		$3,000	$10,900	$15,700	$16,800

Robert F. Mattox, FAIA

- Monitoring cash receipts and pursuing collections
- Controlling disbursements
- Preparing cash budgets on a regular basis and using them to monitor actual cash flow

Billing and collection are especially important in managing cash flow. From an overall practice perspective, clients who are slow to pay may be in the process of becoming less satisfied or even dissatisfied with the firm's professional service—or perhaps experiencing other problems that do not bode well for the project.

In managing cash flow, timely billing and collections are only half the problem; the other half involves controlling disbursements. Careful timing of disbursements can be an effective way to control cash outflow. The firm has more ability to control when it makes a disbursement than when it receives a cash payment. It can defer payment to vendors and other payees, reduce the draws or salaries of principals and, if necessary, borrow funds on a short-term basis.

If cash projections indicate a continuing deficit, financing from other, longer-term sources may be needed. Following are some possibilities:

- Refinancing a major asset with a long-term note or mortgage
- Adding capital from existing partners, new partners, or shareholders
- Retaining additional corporate earnings rather than distributing all profits
- Deferring capital or other expenditures

Financial Strength

There are many indicators of financial performance and financial health. Often these indicators are expressed as simple ratios of numbers created in everyday operations and reflected in the firm's income statement or balance sheet. These ratios can be useful in establishing the need for working capital, assessing productivity, managing overhead and project expenses, establishing fees, and seeking credit.

Working Capital

The architect needs to know not only how much cash will be required to meet expenses in the near term but also the firm's general requirements for working capital. Working capital is the minimum amount of liquid capital needed to sustain the firm in business. More specifically, it is the minimum amount needed to maintain the flow from cash to work in progress to accounts receivable and again to cash. Practically, it is calculated in this way:

$$\text{Working capital} = \text{Current assets} - \text{Current liabilities}$$

Current assets include cash or other assets that are readily convertible into cash (such as work in progress and accounts or notes receivable). Current liabilities are liabilities that come due within the next 12 months.

Receivables

The largest single current asset of an architecture firm is usually its accounts receivable. The liquidity of this asset is extremely important to the firm's financial well-being. It is critical to convert accounts receivable (receivables) to cash in a consistent and timely manner.

If the firm invoices for services at the end of the month in which services are performed and collects two months later, it will need funds to cover three months of operations. This amount represents one-quarter of the firm's annual revenues. Therefore, working capital requirements are closely related to the cycle on which the firm collects its receivables—its average collection period.

Although it is advisable to keep track of individual invoices rendered for collection purposes, it is also valuable to know the rate at which *all* invoices are being collected. The calculation is as follows:

$$\text{Average collection period (in days)} = \text{Accounts receivable} \div \text{Average revenue per day}$$

To calculate the average revenue per day, divide gross revenues by the number of days in the period being considered. As a convention, most analysts use 30 days per month and 360 days per year.

Architects are well advised to keep the average collection period as close to 30 days as possible, although this time period will clearly be difficult to meet with certain kinds of clients.

Revenues per Employee

Another measure of financial health is earned revenue per employee. This ratio can be based on gross revenues (total revenues, including consultants and other project expenses) or a net figure (after subtracting all project consultants and other nonsalary expenses). It can also be calculated per *technical* employee or for *all* employees. Gross revenue per total employees is probably a more useful figure in analyzing the firm's overall volume of activity (such as dollars expended for marketing and business development), while net revenue per total employees is most useful in analyzing matters of operational productivity (such as the effectiveness of computer-aided design systems).

Firm-wide Profit

As a percentage of net revenue, profit is an important indicator. Average profitability in the profession was low for many years, with some surveys reporting average profits, before taxes and discretionary distributions, in the range of 7 to 8 percent. More recently, profitability as a percentage of net revenue has increased to 11 to 12 percent, with some firms having profitability as high as 25 to 30 percent. A reasonably attainable profit for many firms might be in the 10 to 15 percent range. (Although it is possible to calculate profit as a percentage of gross revenue, profit divided by net revenue is a more useful and appropriate indicator because of the differences in the way firms use consultants and other nonsalary direct expenses, both firm-by-firm and project-by-project.)

Managing Overhead

To continue in practice, an architecture firm incurs indirect (overhead) expenses that are necessary to keep the firm in operation and that are not chargeable to any specific project. Indirect expenses can amount to 30 to 40 percent of revenues and 100 to 200 percent of direct salary expense.

Indirect expense must be managed. If it is too high, the firm will probably not be able to produce a profit, regardless of how efficiently projects are being produced. If it is too low, the firm may be spending too little on marketing, management, benefits, administrative services, or other important areas that ultimately affect the quality and quantity of its services.

Indirect Expense Factor

It is important to understand the relationship between indirect expenses and projects. Although there are many ways to view this relationship, the most useful is the indirect expense (or overhead) factor, which is the ratio of all indirect expenses (including payroll burden and general and administrative expenses) to DSE:

$$\text{Indirect expense factor} = \text{Total indirect expense} \div \text{DSE}$$

An indirect expense factor of 1.75, or 175 percent, indicates that the firm requires $1.75 in indirect expense to support each $1.00 of DSE; conversely, each $1.00 of DSE requires $1.75 in overhead. Although this ratio will fluctuate on a month-to-month basis, it is possible to plan for, monitor, and control overhead to keep the indirect expense factor appropriate for the firm.

If the firm finds its indirect expense factor acceptable (i.e., the firm is operating within its overhead budget), there may be no specific need to examine individual overhead items. If, on the other hand, the factor is higher than planned or desired, the architect should examine individual overhead items to identify areas of excess.

Indirect Salary Expenses

The most important category of indirect expense is likely to be indirect salaries—salaries paid for clerical services, firm management, marketing, education and training, civic activities, downtime between project tasks, and paid time off, including vacation, holiday, sick, and personal time.

Low payroll utilization frequently contributes to excessive overhead. Utilization is the ratio between DSE and total salary expense:

$$\text{Time utilization ratio} = \text{Direct hours (charged to projects)} \div \text{Total hours}$$
$$\text{Payroll utilization ratio} = \text{DSE} \div \text{Total salary expense}$$

The most important thing to understand about utilization ratios is this: As the amount of personnel time and expense charged to projects *decreases*, overhead time and expense *increases* (given a stable staff). Under normal circumstances, shifting staff from project assignments to overhead activities will result in reduced project effort and revenues and, at the same time, increased indirect salary expense and increased total overhead.

Two instruments can be used to monitor utilization:

- A time analysis that records individual and cumulative expenditures of staff time
- An income statement that records direct and indirect salary expenses

Note, too, that utilization is a valid measure only to the extent that the firm is *actually paid* for the direct labor. Charged time is not always billable time. Charging time to projects without expecting to bill the client (as in the case of a fixed fee that is already spent) will result in a flawed view of utilization; the utilization ratio will be high, suggesting low overhead and efficient operations, but the profit will be reduced. On the other hand, it is important for staff to report their chargeable time so that the firm has an accurate idea for estimating the fee required for future projects. Some firms report using a utilization ratio (UR) chart in combination with a project progress report, which compares actual to budgeted time, as an effective way of managing office efficiency.

Other Indirect Expenses

If overhead is excessive and indirect salary is not the cause, a review of the other items on the firm's indirect expense budget is in order.

These items can be budgeted by projecting prior-year expenses forward, by considering specific new needs, or by using a zero-based budgeting technique that requires thoughtful consideration and justification of any item to be included. Individual items (accounts), subtotals, and totals can be planned and monitored either absolutely (i.e., with the specific dollar amounts) or relative to other items, such as total payroll, total expenses, or total revenues. Exceptions or variances from budget should be noted and examined and corrective action taken as appropriate. If it is not possible to modify overhead expenses to bring them within the budget, it is usually necessary to revise the firm's overall financial plan.

Managing Project Expenses

Project expenses include DSE, consultants, and other direct expenses, such as project-related travel, reproductions, models and renderings, long-distance telephone calls, and similar expenses. Of these, the largest expense—and the one over which the architect has the most control—is DSE, the salaries of the staff engaged on projects. The two most important principles in managing DSE are as follows:

- *Utilization* (keeping the staff engaged on projects)
- *Productivity* (the degree to which the direct efforts of the firm can generate revenue; this is measured by the net multiplier)

The most common instrument for measuring productivity is the net multiplier, which measures the dollars of revenue generated by the firm overall or on a project basis (net revenue excludes the cost of consultants and other nonsalary direct expenses, such as travel, reproductions, postage, long-distance telephone, and so on, whether reimbursable or not) as a ratio of each dollar of DSE:

$$\text{Net multiplier} = \text{Net revenues} \div \text{DSE}$$

The net multiplier is the best basis for measuring productivity because it eliminates all pass-through expenses, leaving as net revenue only those revenues produced by the

PART 2: PRACTICE

This report, an excerpt from a standard report produced from Deltek Vision™ software, looks at the time reported by firm members over the past month, breaks it into direct and indirect hours, indicates the use of indirect hours (vacation, sick time, etc.), and calculates three ratios: (A) direct hours divided by total hours charged, (B) direct hours divided by hours actually worked, and (C) the target ratio negotiated with each employee and entered into the system.

TABLE 4.9 Sample Time Analysis Report

Time Analysis Report: Apple & Bartlett, PC　　　　**As of March 31, 2008**　1:17:38 PM

Period	Total Hours	Direct Hours	Indirect Hours	Ratio A	Ratio B	Ratio C	Vacation	Sick	Holiday	Bus dev	Mgmt	Acctg	Prof	Mktg
Employee Number: 00001 Apple, William														
Employee Name: Apple, William														
00001			**Apple, William**											
MTD	578	504	74	87	91	50	18	4	16	21	7			
YTD	2,440	2,187	253	90	91	50	26	4	32	38	81			
Total for Apple, William														
MTD	578	504	74	87	91	50	18	4	16	21	7			
YTD	2,440	2,187	253	90	91	50	26	4	32	38	81			
Total For 00001														
MTD	578	504	74	87	91	50	18	4	16	21	7			
YTD	2,440	2,187	253	90	91	50	26	4	32	38	81			
Employee Number: 00002 Bartlett, James														
Employee Name: Bartlett, James														
00002			**Bartlett, James**											
MTD	503	441	62	88	94	40	32		8	12				10
YTD	2,438	2,168	270	89	93	40	88	8	24	71	4			75
Total for			**Bartlett, James**											
MTD	503	441	62	88	94	40	32		8	12				10
YTD	2,438	2,168	270	89	93	40	88	8	24	71	4			75
Total for 00002														
MTD	503	441	62	88	94	40	32		8	12				10
YTD	2,438	2,168	270	89	93	40	88	8	24	71	4			75
Employee Number: 00003 Cohen, Grace														
Employee Name: Cohen, Grace														
00003			**Cohen, Grace**											
MTD	319	307	12	96	99	65	8			4				
YTD	2,000	1,916	84	96	98	65	40			44				
Total for Cohen, Grace														
MTD	319	307	12	96	99	65	8			4				
YTD	2,000	1,916	84	96	98	65	40			44				
Total for 00003														
MTD	319	307	12	96	99	65	8			4				
YTD	2,000	1,916	84	96	98	65	40			44				

Note: Ratios: A = Direct/Total, B = Direct/(Total - Benefit), C = Target.

PART 2: PRACTICE

firm's own forces. A net multiplier of 3.0, for example, indicates that each $1.00 of DSE is generating $3.00 of revenue for the firm.

As suggested in the "Financial Planning" topic in this chapter, it is possible to look at an architecture firm as a series of DSE multipliers. For example:

To pay for DSE:	$1.00
To pay for indirect expenses:	$1.50 ($1.50 = 1.5)
Breakeven:	$2.50 (DSE multiplier = 2.5)
Profit:	$0.50 ($.50 × $1.00 = 0.50)
Revenue:	$3.00 (Net DSE multiplier = 3.0)

Multipliers are useful in project pricing and in overall firm planning—especially in comparing current multipliers with past performance and with those reported by other architecture firms. Architects commonly establish anticipated project expenses by determining the hours (and thus the DSE) needed to perform services and by using the firm's multipliers to be sure indirect expenses and profit are appropriately considered.

Generally speaking, clients do not need to know about a firm's use of multipliers, unless the firm chooses to inform them. Some approaches to compensating architects, for example, involve multiples of DSE or DPE. (The latter approach includes the payroll burden associated with DSEs as part of the base rather than as an indirect expense.)

For architecture firms that do not provide engineering services in-house, consultant expenses may equal or exceed DSE, especially on large, complex projects. Other direct expenses, such as travel, reproductions, models, and renderings, are generally in the range of 20 to 25 percent of DSE.

Sound management of project expenses requires planning these expenses before they are incurred (creating a project budget and work plan), monitoring revenues and expenses as the project proceeds, and taking corrective action when actual performance varies from the plan.

For More Information

In Chapter 4 of *An Architect's Guide to Financial Management* (AIA Press, 1997), Lowell V. Getz describes financial ratios and analytical methods used to measure the financial health of a firm.

The AIA undertakes periodic firm surveys, which include a number of statistics related to firm billings. *The Business of Architecture: 2012 AIA Firm Survey* contains data on billings by firm size and per employee. Other surveys are listed below. Check the AIA website (www.aia.org) for availability, coverage, and prices.

The *Deltek Operating Statistics Survey*, published by Deltek Systems, Inc., can be downloaded from www.deltek.com.

PSMJ Financial Statistics Survey, published by PSMJ, is available from Practice Management Associates, 10 Midland Avenue, Newton, MA 02158, (617) 965–0055. PSMJ also publishes surveys on design fees, executive compensation, and human resources practices. Its Web address is www.psmj.com.

ZweigWhite publishes several surveys on financial performance, finance, and accounting for architects, engineers, and environmental consultants. For a complete list, contact ZweigWhite Research at One Apple Hill Drive, Suite 2, Natick, MA 01760, (800) 466–6275 or www.zweigwhite.com/research.

The Institute of Management and Administration (IOMA) publishes monthly newsletters and an extensive series of guides about cost management and control. Contact IOMA at (212) 244–0360 or www.ioma.com.

PART 2: PRACTICE

4.4   Setting Fees and Alternative Fee Types

Bradford Perkins, FAIA, and Peter Piven, FAIA

Sales and finance come together when it is time to negotiate the fee for the services being offered. Obviously, it is essential to a firm's financial health that the design professionals learn to do this task well. All design professionals find setting fees a challenging task, especially because most clients want to know in advance what the fee will be for their project, even when the scope is unclear and the service will be provided over several years.

One approach is to do what one young engineering consultant did with his first client. He sent a letter of proposal for an energy audit of the client's building and left a blank for the client to fill in the fee. The client filled in $300. Most experienced professionals do not recommend this approach.

In the past this task was far simpler because most of the professions published recommended fee curves to help guide their members' efforts in setting fees. These curves have been declared anticompetitive and illegal, and the only people who still use established fee schedules are some of the large public and institutional clients. Needless to say, these client-generated fee curves are lower than those created by the professions.

The demise of the standard fee curves was a positive step not only from a legal standpoint, but in other ways as well. These curves were built on the fallacious concept that any two projects that were of the same construction budget, building type, and mix of new and renovation would require the same effort and cost to carry out. In fact, the research done on the costs to complete various types of projects, which formed the underlying basis for the fee curves, showed widely varying results for projects that were supposed to be similar. In national surveys, for example, almost 25 percent of the projects lost money.

Projects, clients, schedules, required services, and many other factors have continued to grow in complexity since the cessation of fee schedules. This has forced the design professionals to face the fact that calculating and negotiating appropriate fees is a major task requiring considerable skill and effort.

ANALYZING THE COST OF PROVIDING A SERVICE

There are five basic steps to setting a fee:

1. Calculate costs.
2. Do a competitive analysis.
3. Do a risk analysis.
4. Choose a fee method.
5. Negotiate the fee.

Calculate Costs

One method, often referred to as *top-down* budgeting, starts with the assumed or desired fee and calculates how much can be allocated to the various services and phases. A second approach is to estimate the time and cost to do each task and phase. This is often called *bottom-up* budgeting. Probably, the first pass at the bottom-up method will yield a higher number than the expected fee, and further analysis will be necessary to reconcile it with the top-down calculation. If and when both methods yield the same results, this can be a good starting point. Nevertheless, it is not necessarily the right fee to quote if you are still competing for the project.

Do a Competitive Analysis

The next step in establishing a fee is to research the "going rate" for the service and the fees your competitors are likely to quote. A common range for comparable jobs exists in most cases and can often be checked with other experienced firms that are not competing for the same project. This "comparing of rates" is done all the time, and a principal in either a new or established firm should not be shy about asking for advice.

Determining what your competition will charge is much more difficult. Sometimes, other firms can help you, but in most cases you have to guess at this. Established firms are likely to quote within a certain range if it is consistent with their own bottom-up and top-down analyses. Smaller, younger firms are far harder to evaluate.

Do a Risk Analysis

The next step in determining a fee is to analyze the risks. This subject, too, requires judgment, which will improve with experience. Among the most common areas of potential risk encountered on many projects are:

- *An indecisive client.* These can be hard to spot in advance, but benchmarks include: reputation from previous jobs, a vaguely worded description of their proposed project, and the impression they give during preproposal contacts. A client with poor decision-making capabilities always adds to the cost of providing services.
- *An unreasonable client.* Good clients expect their design team to make a profit, and will work to help ensure that happens. An unreasonable client does not care, and argues against even reasonable requests for additional compensation when the scope changes. Other clients—such as the large committees set up for some projects—are inherently indecisive even if they are well meaning. These clients often cannot be avoided, but some contingency should be built into the fee or contract to account for the extra time it takes to deal with them.
- *An extremely tight budget.* A tight budget can significantly increase the effort necessary to reach a final design. If the budget is so tight that it is unreasonable, it may be indicative of an unreasonable client. Moreover, it may make it difficult to make the proposed fee seem reasonable in proportion to the total project cost.
- *A very tight or an unpredictable schedule.* Many clients talk about unreasonably short schedules. As with budgets, if it is too tight, it may be indicative of a naive or unreasonable client. Conversely, tight, reasonable schedules are advantageous to the design firm since many of the design team's costs increase over time. Thus, of equal concern is an indefinite schedule that stops and starts or extends beyond the time required, because many of the design team's costs are a direct function of time.
- *An interrupted work process.* Some projects are done in phases with indefinite breaks between stages to secure financing, obtain land use approvals, and the like. Each interruption can add to cost as a firm shuts down or remobilizes its efforts.
- *A difficult approval process.* Clients often like to shift risk. For example, if they foresee risk in obtaining financing or land use approvals, they often will try to shift fee payments until after these hurdles have been overcome. Moreover, if these steps are risky, they are likely to require added effort by the design team.
- *Slow payment.* Some clients are notoriously slow payers. This can place a real burden on a young design firm, hence should be a factor in both the fee and the contract negotiation. To reward prompt payment, therefore, it is often worth giving something extra to a client that does so. One early client paid within 24 hours of receiving the invoice. This sensitivity to the firm's cash flow needs resulted in the client being given first priority throughout the life of the project.
- *A difficult construction phase.* With a good contractor or construction manager, one site visit a week is more than required; with a bad one, five days a week is not enough. As for an indecisive client, a difficult construction phase is almost impossible to predict at the beginning of a project. Therefore, it is important to clearly tie the basic fees to an assumed level of service (number of site visits, length of construction, etc.), with any overages compensated as extra services.
- *An insecure client or a client in trouble.* Many in the profession believe that the most dangerous client is one that is insecure or already in trouble. If a client gets into

financial or other difficulty, expect it to impact the design team. The only protection is to be sensitive to early signs of trouble.

Choose a Fee Method

The next step is to select the most appropriate fee method. There are many, each with its advantages and disadvantages, and no one works for all situations. The final choice often depends upon client preference. The most common are defined in the following subsections.

Percentage of Construction Cost

For decades, this was the most common method for setting fees. Its great advantage is that the fee increases automatically as the scope (as reflected in the budget) increases. Its major disadvantages are: it is arbitrary (if not based upon a project cost analysis); it penalizes the effort to contain or reduce budget, and clients view this conflict with suspicion; and the fee goes down if the cost goes down. Because of these disadvantages, this method should be used with caution, though it can be the right choice if the client has set an unrealistically low budget.

Percentage of Approved Budget

This method resolves any perceived conflict of interest. It is best used when the scope is unclear at the start of the design process.

Lump Sum

This is becoming the most commonly used method for some firms and experienced clients. If based on a careful cost and risk analysis, it can be the appropriate choice. Its major disadvantage is its underlying assumption that the scope is fixed. Lump sums are inflexible and clients usually resist requests for extra services.

Hourly

Hourly billing is the ideal method when the scope is unclear. Most clients will, however, accept this method only for small projects or for the phases for which the scope clearly cannot be defined.

Hourly with a Cap (or Limit or Maximum)

The cap is the most common way to respond to clients' concerns about the open-ended nature of hourly billing. Some agreements permit hourly billing without an *upset amount* or fixed cap until the scope is defined and a maximum upset can be set. If a maximum, or cap, is set, it should be higher than the lump sum that could have been negotiated. In a lump sum, the design team keeps any amount under the maximum. In hourly up to a cap, the client keeps the difference. Of course, any amount over the cap is a loss to the design professionals under either arrangement.

Dollars per Square Foot or per Unit

Some fees are quoted on a unit basis (square foot, residential unit, etc.). This is common for corporate interiors, multifamily housing, and a few other building types. This is the equivalent of a lump sum if the unit total is known in advance.

Prototypes and Reuse Fees

In certain circumstances, a builder may ask the architect to design several prototypes (such as houses or chain stores) that will then be used repeatedly. In this case, part or all of the basic cost of designing the prototype is recovered in the original prototype fee, with a smaller additional amount paid for each reuse to cover site adaptation and the rest of the prototype fee. In some cases this does not have to cover continuing services and is thus a royalty for reuse of the original design.

Performance Bonus or Success Fees

Some clients will offer bonus or success fees if certain targets (budget, schedule, etc.) are met. Since so many of these targets are under the client's control, the agreement must be clear.

Composite

Among the many other approaches to setting fees, one of the most common is to combine two or more of the preceding methods. For example, when there is a variable scope, a variable form such as hourly charges can be used for design, public approvals, and construction administration, and a fixed fee is used for the scope (usually design development and contract documents) under the design team's control.

Negotiate the Fee

Fee negotiation is more an art form than a skill, but to some extent it can be learned. The most effective teacher is experience. Absent experience, keep these basics in mind when negotiating fees:

- *Avoid setting fees while still selling.* When your priority is to be selected by the client, you may lose your focus on maintaining the fee you need. If a client asks you to set a fee during the marketing sales process, try to build in the flexibility to negotiate a more accurate fee later. Also, quote fee ranges rather than a single number; provide separate fee estimates for any consultants so that their fees do not distort your own proposal; and try to get the client to accept a fee quote for a limited initial phase of work where the scope and risks can he clearly defined. If all else fails, be as vague as possible, in the hope that it will gain you some negotiating room later.

- *Avoid setting fees before the scope has been clarified.* If a client asks for a fixed fee before the scope has been clarified, be very clear about the assumptions that form the basis of the fee. Make it plain that any material changes in the assumptions are likely to require an adjustment to the fee quotation. Refer to the risk areas discussed earlier in the chapter for the issues (such as schedule, number of meetings, scope of construction phase services, etc.) to be covered by assumptions.

- *Avoid the volitional fallacy.* The "volitional fallacy" is the assumption that because you want something to be true it will be true. Analyze your probable cost, keep and refer to records of actual costs on past jobs, and don't talk yourself into believing an unrealistically low fee will somehow work out because "this job is different."

- *Ask the client to commit to a limited first phase.* This is called "setting the hook." Once most clients have agreed to retain you for an initial scope of service, such as a site selection study or a master plan, you can usually avoid negotiating the overall fee while still competing with others. It is worth offering a very competitive fee for a limited first phase to avoid setting fees while still selling or while the scope is largely unknown.

- *Play on the client's sense of fairness.* If you think the client is fair, it's a good idea to try to make fairness a part of the negotiation. Consider sharing the underlying cost analysis that you prepared for your fee estimate. If the client asks you to cut your fee, counter by asking which part of the labor estimate they think you should cut. Most reasonable clients will not push back too hard when confronted with this choice. Some clients, even large, corporate clients, will respond favorably when faced with the fact that their unfairness is inconsistent with the company's corporate ethic.

- *Get it upfront.* When setting the overall fee, try to negotiate a fee that covers the full list of known services. Some firms like to leave open the potential to negotiate extra services later, but experience proves that most clients resent this. No two clients are the same, but it is often easier to get a fair fee at the beginning rather than by detailing a long list of extra services.

- *Be prepared to walk away.* One of the easiest ways to get a fair fee is to not need the job. If you can walk away, it strengthens your negotiating stance. Unfortunately, it is rare for a new firm to be in this position. There are, however, times when even a new firm should walk away.

- *Remember, some low-fee jobs are worth taking.* There are times when it is worth taking a project for which the fee is too low; for example, if the project is relatively small, if it will lead to future work, and/or if it uses time that is uncommitted. Remember, having some income is better than none, especially for a struggling young firm.

These important points are reiterated in the box titled "Guidelines for Setting Fees."

GUIDELINES FOR SETTING FEES

- Don't set fixed fees while still selling or when the scope is unknown.
- Know the competition and understand the norms.
- Always estimate the cost to provide the service and define the net direct labor that will be available for the likely fee.
- Understand the areas of risk.
- Keep records and know your costs.
- Pick the most appropriate fee method:
  - Percent of construction cost (actual final cost or approved budget)
  - Lump sum
  - Hourly (open-ended or an agreed-to limit)
  - Square footage

- Prototype and reuse fee
- Bonuses, success fees, shared savings, and so on
- Mixed methods
- Present the fee in the most attractive manner possible.
- Negotiate with consultants the following:
  - Terms consistent with yours
  - Fees that work within the overall budget
  - No open-ended terms within a fixed fee contract
- Build in clear limits on open-ended scope items.
- Negotiate a fair deal up front rather than through extra services.

Source: *Architect's Essentials of Starting, Assessing, and Transitioning a Design Firm*, Bradford Perkins (Author), Peter Piven (Co-Author), John Wiley & Sons, Inc.: 2008

4.5 Building a Quality Design Practice

Bradford Perkins, FAIA, and Peter Piven, FAIA

The purpose of the firm's strategic and business plans is twofold: to address financial, marketing, and other business issues, and to facilitate the achievement of excellence, the latter of which should be the greatest concern of any successful firm.

While it is true that most significant works of architecture are usually developed under the guidance of a single strong design leader, credit for such works must always be given to the role played by the many other participants in the design process. Typically, more than 10 people (architects, engineers, interior designers, specialist-consultants, construction managers and, of course, clients) are involved in the design decision-making process for most significant projects, and many have 50 or more.

As any experienced architect with his or her ego in check will admit, design excellence is, in part, a result of successful management of a complex team, all of whose members contribute to the quality of the final result. Thus, the ability to select, manage, and train this team of individuals is always critical to a design firm's success. David H. Maister, in his book *Practice What You Preach* (New York: The Free Press, 2001) listed nine statements he regards as best predictors of financial performance (see the accompanying box).

Don't misunderstand: We are not saying that design excellence can be achieved by management alone, or even that it is the most important factor. Management skill cannot substitute for high-quality design, but it can make those with design ability more effective. Thus, design quality, and helping to achieve it, must be a central management issue in any firm concerned with design excellence. And, as a central issue, it should be addressed in the firm's plans for the future.

At first, it may seem that saying design quality should be a central management issue blurs the traditional boundary between design and management in architectural practice. Certainly, most design professionals make a careful distinction between management and design; one has to do with finance, administration, and other related matters, while the other is the core of a design practice. We argue that management and design cannot be separated in practices that aspire to achieve consistent quality. Consider these situations that illustrate this point:

- The new firm that is spending so much effort surviving that it cannot focus enough on design. How does it reduce the effort required just to survive?
- The established firm with a solid—but dull—reputation that, more often than not, is losing out on the best jobs and whose staff members are moving to other firms with "hotter" design reputations. How does the firm meet this challenge?
- A firm that is growing rapidly, thanks to the design skills and reputations of the founding principals, who no longer can find the time to design, and so are assigning the work to a constantly changing group of employees, thereby relinquishing consistent quality of design. How do the principals regain control over quality?
- The firm that more frequently is asked to compete on a design basis for jobs, none of which it manages to win. The losses are expensive and demoralizing. Can the firm be restructured to compete more effectively? Should it make the effort to compete at all?
- The firm that has done good work on small projects but that cannot break into larger, more professionally challenging projects. How does the firm obtain the design opportunities it wants and needs to grow?
- The firm that is organized such that design, production, and construction are run by different people, resulting in designs that are often unrecognizable by the time they are built. How can design control be combined with management efficiency?
- The firm that always seems to encounter project problems—whether in budget, schedule, or client dictates—that prevent it from achieving the quality of design it seeks. How can this firm effectively control the process of designing and constructing a building?

As you can see, wherever design is carried out by a team (as is the case in most major projects today), wherever design depends on having and guiding receptive clients (as most good design does), or wherever the process of doing a project has an impact on the result (as most processes do), management is a factor in producing quality design. If effectively planned and controlled, the interaction between management and design can be a significant help in achieving the highest possible design quality within the inherent constraints of each project.

ACHIEVING CONSISTENT QUALITY IN DESIGN

As stated at the beginning of this section, consistent design quality depends primarily on the skill and force of the firm's design leadership (keeping in mind that leadership is a human characteristic and cannot be conferred). But it is also dependent on these other factors as well:

- How the firm defines its goals for design in conjunction with other aspects of its practice.
- The types of project the firm secures.

BEST PREDICTORS OF FINANCIAL PERFORMANCE

- Client satisfaction is a top priority at the firm.
- The firm has no room for those who put their personal agenda ahead of the interests of the clients or the office.
- Those who contribute the most to the overall success of the office are the most highly rewarded.
- Management gets the best work out of everybody in the office.
- You are required, not encouraged, to learn new skills.
- Invest a significant amount of time in things that will pay off in the future.
- People within the office always treat others with respect.
- Quality supervision on client projects is uniformly high.
- Quality of the professionals in the office is as high as can be expected.

- How the firm defines the design process, allocates resources to each phase of this process, and monitors this process as the project is executed.
- How the firm is organized.
- How the firm relates to its clients.
- How, in this media-influenced era, the firm builds its design reputation so that it attracts the clients and staff it requires to perpetuate both its image and the substance of design excellence.
- How the firm uses and manages the talent, experience, energy, and will of the entire project team.

Each of these factors affects design quality differently in every firm, so we cannot offer a definitive answer to any of the questions raised, but what is clear is that the search for the right framework is an essential step toward achieving consistent design quality.

Setting Goals

The values and objectives of a firm's principals—no matter how loosely expressed—set that framework. To state that the overriding goal is to provide the client top-quality services that result in building solutions that are esthetically, technically, and functionally advanced, and are of consistently high quality, is not enough. Every goal set by the principals has an impact on how the firm responds to the design quality factors just listed. Firm targets for size, profitability, growth, type of projects, ownership, control, and other areas all have a direct or indirect impact on design quality.

For example, a firm that plans to grow into a 100-person office with a practice targeting the market for hospitals and laboratories will have to pursue design excellence using a different set of constraints than a firm that pursues housing and office projects and that does not want to expand beyond the number of projects that can be personally directed by the firm's founding principals. The former will have to be able to support more than one principal designer, plus a core staff comprised of senior technical specialists who share project leadership; the latter firm, in contrast, will be able to maintain centralized control in the hands of a single design principal.

But what may have the most direct impact on design quality is how the principals define design quality and set goals to achieve it. It is particularly important to avoid the tendency to use only *quantitative values* as the basis for measuring the firm's achievement. When this happens, those primarily involved in design will find the going rough if the firm measures success solely in terms of optimized revenues and minimized expenses. Creativity, taste, and problem-solving skill factors that defy quantitative measure must be given significant weight in the final structure of a firm's objectives.

In recent years, ideas about how to measure design quality have proliferated. For example, whether explicitly stated or not, some firms' objectives include one or more of the following:

- *To do something innovative or newsworthy on each project.* This is a common goal of firms focusing on establishing a reputation.
- *To redefine the traditional design response to a particular building type.* This is a goal for many firms with specialized institutional practice (schools, hospitals, etc.).
- *To design buildings that emphasize the functional, maintenance, cost, and other performance objectives of the owner, rather than aesthetic criteria.* This is perhaps the objective of some office, hospital, and housing specialists.
- *To consistently impose on each project a single design theory or vocabulary.* This goal is common among firms dominated by a single strong personality.

No doubt you see the point: Regardless of what your design goals are, once they are defined, they will influence how your firm approaches its work, allocates its resources to a project, guides and judges its own design efforts as the projects develop, selects and develops staff, and deals with many other issues that affect design quality.

Recognizing the Impact of Practice Mix on Design Goals

Design goals, are, as stated, directly affected by a firm's projects. Therefore, the type of projects a firm gets is usually a function of what the firm seeks. If a firm wants to establish a strong design reputation, it must find a way to obtain work from clients with the desire, budget, and program to generate public interest and make design excellence possible.

Obviously, it is far more difficult to build an image from completing, say, small additions to proprietary nursing homes, small industrial buildings, or low-income housing than it is by designing a corporate headquarters building or a college performing arts center. The point here is that the realism, and even the definition, of the firm's design goals are in large part dependent on the direction and success of the firm's marketing efforts.

Moreover, a firm's design goals must address the needs of the building type and client. Different building types generate very different design constraints. These differences must be reflected in the firm's design philosophy and process. High-technology, code-constrained programmatic buildings, such as hospitals and laboratories, often present more difficult esthetic challenges than those of an office building or a luxury condominium, where a different combination of a client's decision-making process, program, budget, and technical priorities govern.

More than one solid, old-line firm has seen its reputation damaged by breaking away from its roots to embrace design philosophies and processes that are incompatible with its traditional projects' needs. This is usually done in a misguided attempt to rapidly upgrade design quality and image. A typical sequence is:

1. The firm loses several projects in part because of a reputation for dull design.
2. The principals decide they must upgrade their image and skills.
3. The firm hires a designer from a "design firm," and tries to import new process as well.
4. The firm turns its back on the skills that brought in clients.
5. Its image fails to change and clients and old-time staff become alienated.
6. The design "savior" is fired and the firm reverts to its former ways, often in a weakened condition.

An alternative scenario is the following:

1. The firm hires a star designer.
2. The firm fails to alter its project delivery process or budgets to reflect the new, design-driven needs of the new "star."
3. The star designer resigns in frustration.

It is important to remember that design excellence is not imported, but instead requires a long-term effort directed from the top down and integrated with every aspect of the firm's activities. It is a firm's real goals, in conjunction with the projects it works on, that help establish the context for the development of a design process.

Designing the Design Process

The term *design process* is used here to refer to the way a firm allocates and controls its design resources (people, consultants, time, etc.) and manages them to execute a project. To improve design quality and efficiency of the project team, as well as to promote meaningful interaction between the client and the project team, time must be spent on designing the design process.

For each of the participants [owner(s), architect(s), consultant(s)], a clear, well-documented and agreed-upon definition of this process will include:

- Scope of the work
- Schedule
- Work plan

The work plan serves to organize the efforts of the team and is a vehicle for communicating the sequence of these efforts to the client. Note, however, there are major differences even among "design-oriented" firms in this area. Some of the typical ones are:

- *Length of time devoted to each phase.* Some firms spend far more time in program and site analysis; other firms allocate as much time as possible to schematic design and design development; still others are careful to allocate adequate resources to the late design-development, contract-document, shop-drawing, and field phases, in the belief that "God is in the details."

- *Who does what.* In any design-oriented firm, the proper matching of staff with projects is the critical first step in the successful execution of the project. Some individuals are better at small projects; others are best in design development; still others are good at working through complex problems. The natural tendency is to make do with the staff available. This, however, can result in the most important projects being assigned to staff no one knew what to do with, since they are available because the best design talent is busy on other projects.

> *Asked what his most important job was, legendary ice hockey coach Scotty Bowman, replied: "To get the right players on the ice."*
>
> —Quoted in *The Game*, by Ken Dryden

- *How each phase is carried out.* This refers to decisions about when to involve engineers, which tools (models, renderings, etc.) to use during the design phase, how to study the key design issues, and how to resolve these issues.

- *When to involve consultants.* Most architects will, when asked, say they like to involve engineers at the beginning of design, but in practice, many do not. Moreover, many engineers discourage such early involvement because they want to do the job only once. Still, failure to seek creative engineering input early can significantly affect the development of a building design.

- *How progress is monitored.* At specific times during the development of a project, there is a need to pause for a review. The firm must decide when these reviews are needed, how they should be structured, and who should participate. Sporadic reviews by poorly briefed principals that result in a lot of rework are all too common and often give reviews a bad name. Well-run design firms find some way to provide regular review and participation by the firm's design leadership. In sum, these reviews should evaluate progress based on the management, design, and technical goals established for the project. They should suggest areas for further study and establish guidelines for further development. In an environment where clients want projects "yesterday," it is tempting to cut out the so-called soft parts of the design process, and the design development phase is the most typical victim today. Ironically, it is during this phase that some important details require extra time to work out. What a shame it would be, for example, to see a separate accounting for a chair rail detail that was a central theme in an interior project because it took several weeks to resolve. These soft periods are often gestation periods, when the design concept matures. Or firms are faced with the need to rethink a design decision that cuts into fee budget, project schedule, and client patience. The firms with design ambitions are careful to preserve their flexibility in all aspects of the process in order to bring additional skills, time, and effort to a project when necessary. These factors can all play a role in effectively focusing the resources of a firm so that the design concepts established by the principal designer can result in an excellent completed work of architecture.

- *How the firm deals with other members of the project team.* Over the last several decades, the size of teams has grown and the roles and responsibilities have changed. Now, many specialist consultants, owners' reps, construction managers, and others have direct access to the client. Almost every firm today has lost some important aspect of the project design decision because of the advice of one of these other team members. Conversely, in an era of skeptical clients, a united front of architect and construction manager or other consultant can often serve to resolve an important design issue. Therefore, how a firm controls the entire project team—in particular its relationship with the source of such key owner concerns as cost and time—will have a great impact on the success (or failure) of a given project.

Organizing the Firm

Communication and interaction are central to the effectiveness of every aspect of the design process. In simpler times, when the problems, the project, and the practice were all on a smaller scale, the practice of architecture could be based on individual intuition. Today, with larger projects, complex functional, technical, and environmental problems, and larger groups of client/architect/consultant teams working to solve these problems, organized and effective communication and interaction are imperative to success.

Some firms—even some large national ones—try to centralize design in the hands of a single person. And though management theory says that most individuals can control only the details of four to six complex issues (such as design projects) at one time, this has not deterred some architects from trying to handle more. Centralization of design decision making is normally most effective only in small firms; it is difficult to achieve in large ones.

Medium and large firms usually take one of three more decentralized options: *departmental*, *project team*, and *studio*. The first breaks the project into specialties, often with different specialists or departments doing the planning, programming, design, production, and construction administration. Under this option, a project manager weaves the common thread throughout each project. The second option has a single team take the project from planning through construction, with specialists and draftspeople added to the core team as required. The studio is an expanded team, with most or all of the skills and personnel to handle several projects organized under a single design/management leadership.

All of these options (and variants) have their advantages and disadvantages. The central organizational issue, with respect to design quality within each option, is the role of the principal designers. More specifically, do designers or managers control decision making for the project? On this point much blood has been shed. If it is not the designer, how do important design decisions get made? Is the principal designer involved throughout the process?

Firms that confine the principal designer to schematic design and design development have been compared to multistage rockets with each stage controlled by a different guidance system. The satellite may get launched, but not necessarily into the orbit intended by the first-stage rocket. Peter Samton, of the Gruzen Samton Partnership, now IBI Group Inc., did a study of how a few of their more respected competitors organized themselves to achieve design quality. While his sample was limited to relatively large firms (with more than 100 staff), his conclusions are relevant for most firms:

- Design excellence is achieved only when there is effective design leadership at the principal level throughout the process.
- All firms studied were very concerned about process, organization, and most of the other issues covered in this section, and were working to find the right approach for their firm.
- No two firms were identical in the way they achieved excellence, but all had found some way to address each issue.

Managing Clients

A key figure in any project organization is the person who manages the client relationship, whether that person is the principal designer or someone else. The design quality of many projects is often won or lost depending on who fills this role. On some projects, it is easier to go along with a client's wishes than to defend a design solution the client does not support. But while it is easier to "ride a horse in the direction it is going," this decision can often lead to a compromised design concept.

Few owners today accept their architect's design decisions unchallenged. Often, owner opinions directly cause key budget and esthetic trade-offs. If there is no one on the architect's side who understands what is important in the design, and who can sell it to the client, many of the firm's design ideas will fall prey unnecessarily to unsupported arguments based solely on "taste" or budget. This does not need to happen. An understanding client is essential to a good result, and it is part of the architect's job to gain this understanding. To quote Eero Saarinen, "Let's see if we can make this guy into a great client."

One popular architectural argument says that good design does not necessarily cost more. This is often true, but unfortunately it is also true that the heart of many designs has been cut out in last-minute budget reductions because of poor client and construction cost management. Many budget reductions also alienate clients, who end up feeling misled by their architects and lose the essential quality they, too, had counted on. Thus, the careful management of client expectations and project budget are critical to design.

Another essential part of the client management process is the effective communication of the design team's ideas and recommendations. Whoever presents the design must be supplied with adequate visual and technical support to make his or her arguments. It is no coincidence that the best-known design firms typically produce the most compelling design presentations.

Building a Public Image

Obtaining client support for a design proposal is easier, of course, if the firm has a strong reputation for design excellence. When dealing with a recognized design talent, clients generally defer to their acknowledged architectural judgment. Design image also has the more tangible reward of attracting more notable clients and talented staff. This has always been true, but it appears to have become even more important in recent years. The success of developers, such as Gerald Hines, together with a growing public interest in architecture, has made being a design celebrity an important competitive asset.

Image-building methods employed vary considerably, but those used most often today include:

- Cultivation of the press
- Aggressive publication of the firm's work. (In more than one case this has involved subsidizing a publisher to produce a book on the firm.)
- Active participation in the design establishment's activities: teaching, speaking, preservation efforts, art openings, panel discussions, juries, and the like.
- Organizing architectural exhibits or writing about architecture, featuring one's own work
- Working to make the firm's office, graphics, and the other visual elements consistent with the desired image

Of course, the time-honored methods of entering—and winning—competitions or design award programs are still among the most effective approaches. Being active and respected in the design community tends to increase success in competitions and awards programs. Merely creating an attractive submission is not always enough.

Promoting Design Talent

This brings us full circle. As stated at the beginning of the chapter, the most important figures in achieving design excellence are the lead designer and the design team that work on each project. No matter how good the goals, the projects, the process, or the salesmanship, great (or even good) design is possible only when you have a good design team led by a superior design talent.

Firms that have strong reputations have little trouble attracting such talent, but building a new organization, or rebuilding an older tarnished one, is a far more difficult task. In the latter case, the firms that have done so have had to aggressively seek out, train, and integrate talent into established organizations that may have had powerful antibodies to resist change. At the very least, this takes several years to accomplish.

It is very rare to see a firm such as C. F. Murphy (now Murphy/Jahn) emerge quickly as a design leader. The large staff layoff at SOM following completion of the Air Force Academy, however, combined with the Richard J. Daley–directed load of public work gave that firm an opportunity for staff and projects with real design potential. They took this opportunity and ran with it. Some firms have tried the quick fix by importing outside talent to lead the design effort. More often than not this has failed because the effort stopped with the hiring of one or two stars. As many expensive free agents in baseball have proven, a few stars are not enough to make a winning team.

CONCLUSION

As with any other aspect of successful architectural practice, consistent design excellence cannot be achieved by accident. It is the product of an intense multifaceted effort. At the core of a successful effort is an individual (or individuals) with design talent in a leadership role. But though essential, a strong leader is not enough to achieve consistently high design quality. Consistent high-quality design is also a central management issue, and as such it should be built into the firm's plan for the future.

Source: *Architect's Essentials of Starting, Assessing, and Transitioning a Design Firm*, Bradford Perkins (Author), Peter Piven (Co-Author), John Wiley & Sons, Inc.: 2008

4.6   Risk Management Strategies

Peter Gifford Longley, AIA, CSI CCS, LEED AP

Being in the business of architecture means taking risks. But any good endeavor, like the privilege of practicing architecture, is worthy of some risk. The best approach is to know the risks, and then know how to manage them.

How Does the Architect Manage Risk?

The word "risk" derives from the archaic Italian word *riscare*, which means "run into danger," or to imperil, endanger, or jeopardize. All choices in life entail some risk; for example, play and risk injury, or pass and risk boredom. When a decision is made to risk one thing or another, security lies only in *managing* the risk.

There are four classic strategies, all used by prudent firms to manage risk. These are manifested in the practice of architecture as shown in Table 4.10.

Peter Longley is an architect with more than 35 years of experience. He has developed and authored firm standards for documentation and quality control. As director of operations for Tsoi/Kobus & Associates, he is responsible for the firm's risk management and quality assurance/quality control practices.

TABLE 4.10 Strategies to Manage Risk			
Avoid Risk	**Transfer Risk**	**Assume Risk**	**Control Risk**
Marketing selects project types that fit with prior experience, working for clients with excellent reputations.	Contracts transfer risk appropriately to the client, or downward to a consultant. Insurance transfers risk to a business financial partner.	Accept appropriate work, but maintain enough cash to responsibly satisfy insurance deductibles.	Adopt best practices, and educate staff. Seek good counsel to prevent or reduce losses when claims emerge.

Identifying Sources of Risk

Some aspects of the practice of architecture are, by nature, more likely to create unmanageable risk—risk of claims that place a firm's reputation, even its existence, in jeopardy. Professional liability insurance companies track actual claims by category, frequency, and cost. These data are used to determine premiums—costly for customers servicing areas of greater risk, and less so for those where risks are low.

Measured liability losses, organized by category, form a quantifiable basis for decoding areas of greatest risk. Professional liability insurance provider XL Group identifies nine such categories in its Risk Drivers research:

1. Communication
2. Project team capabilities
3. Client selection
4. Negotiation and contracts
5. Budget control
6. Schedule control
7. Loss prevention issues
8. Construction phase services
9. Billing procedures

XL Group's Risk Drivers research reveals that one or more of areas 1 through 4, shown in Figure 4.3, were present in 93 percent of all claims. Therefore, a focus on these four areas will address most causes of risk to architects—to determine best practices to avoid, to transfer, or to control risk . . . reasoning, alternatively, which risk is reasonable to assume.

The four greatest areas of risk that architects face are examined below, with potentially effective means to manage each of them also discussed.

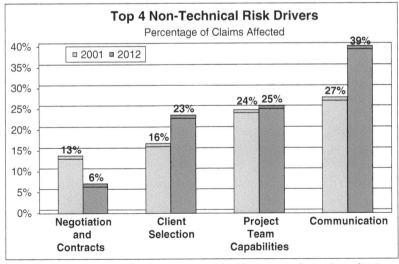

Risk Drivers data provided by The Design Professional unit of XL Group

FIGURE 4.3 **Chart Depicting the Four Greatest Areas of Claims**

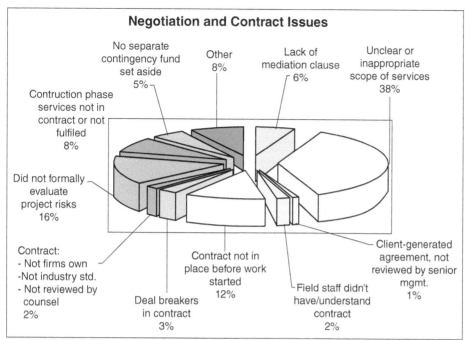

Negotiation and Contract Issues

- No separate contingency fund set aside 5%
- Contruction phase services not in contract or not fulfiled 8%
- Did not formally evaluate project risks 16%
- Contract: - Not firms own - Not industry std. - Not reviewed by counsel 2%
- Deal breakers in contract 3%
- Contract not in place before work started 12%
- Other 8%
- Lack of mediation clause 6%
- Unclear or inappropriate scope of services 38%
- Client-generated agreement, not reviewed by senior mgmt. 1%
- Field staff didn't have/understand contract 2%

Risk Drivers data provided by The Design Professional unit of XL Group

FIGURE 4.4 **Chart Depicting Negotiation and Contracts Claims by Type**

No. 4: Negotiation and Contracts

Claims almost always appear in a legal form, targeted directly at the failure of the architect to comply with some term of their design services agreement—the document that set forth the responsibilities now in dispute. (See Figure 4.4.) Not surprisingly, the contract is the first piece of paper consulted when a claim comes to light. Designers frantically examine it to learn if the claim has any basis in reality. Copies are requested by attorneys and insurance companies. Everyone scours it for the magic words that prove their perspective, supporting or refuting the claim.

Long before the claim emerged, times were happier. At the beginning of the project everyone is excited about getting started. Still, the project is, after all, a business deal—a contract—a fee paid for services rendered. Central to both the client's and architect's mind are the large matters: the project description, the site, the program, the schedule, the budget. Next comes the means to get there: the team, the consultants, the services needed, what's included, what's not, and the fees. Finally come the terms and conditions: all the legal fine print governing everything mentioned, and then some. The main characters typically lose interest at this point—the prime reason projects often begin without a contract in place. They turn over the business of sorting out the details to other people.

These main characters are the same ones who frantically reach for the contract (if it was ever executed) once the claim notice arrives. They need to see what was previously agreed. That day's conclusion will likely be determined by how well the agreement was negotiated.

Deal Makers and Deal Breakers

From the architect's perspective, the key issues in agreements are profitability and insurability. Simply put, if a profit can't be made with the deal as stated, the commission shouldn't be accepted. Likewise, agreeing to take on responsibilities excluded by a firm's professional liability insurance policy could leave the firm uninsured when a claim emerges. Either issue can put a firm out of business. Both present unmanageable risk. Both are deal breakers.

Negotiation is the time to identify and remove deal breakers. If they can't be removed, some way must be found to offset the risk—something that would instead be a deal maker. Finding the deal makers are theoretically possible (e.g., a large enough fee can compensate for increased risk), but require willpower and skill to negotiate.

Below are noteworthy deal makers and deal breakers.

Working Without an Agreement

Working without an agreement is an unmanageable risk. If a claim emerges before the contract is executed, there are no clear rules for settlement. The party due something may have to walk away without anything, perhaps even having to pay. In the case of the architect, that means real trouble. The effects of working without an agreement are many. Foremost concerns include:

- Difficulty in getting paid, or getting paid all that the architect believes it is entitled to be paid
- Claims of architect responsibility for any and all things not the firm's fault—such as the client's consultants' negligent services, the presence of hazardous waste on-site, inaccuracy of client's budget, changes in the code, bad construction safety, poor performance of the builder
- Claims of architect responsibility for broader scope than may have been intended or understood by the architect
- Claims of the architect causing delay due to a lack of written schedule, or definition of the schedule approval or amendment process

Most architects would probably never work with just a handshake, wink, or nod. But exchanging draft agreements that never get signed has the same net effect—no written agreement. There are too many skilled attorneys and different-minded judges who would dismiss those unsigned pieces of paper, regardless of arguments about payments made ("course of conduct"). Architects need to get the agreement negotiated and signed before issuing documents for use by the client or the builder. Once the work product is delivered, the architect loses the leverage necessary to get the client to the signing table.

Heightened Standard of Care

The standard of care is the basis against which architects are measured to determine whether they are performing to a level of legal competence. The standard of care does not require performing services perfectly. Rather, when errors and omissions occur, they are judged against a standard consistent with the work of other architects doing similar projects. Errors and omissions that fall short of this "norm" constitute a failure to meet the standard of care, amounting to legal negligence. The key to the concept is that there is a norm—and the norm is not perfection.

Textbook definition of *standard of care*: Rendering services with the ordinary degree of skill and care that would be used by other reasonably competent practitioners of the same discipline under similar circumstances, taking into consideration the contemporary state of the art and geographic idiosyncrasies.

The standard of care flows from a concept in English law that recognizes that professional services—from doctors, lawyers, architects, and engineers—are rendered based upon learned opinion. Such professional opinions are provided by gifted human beings who have plied their trade over time, developing varied pathways to success. There isn't always a single solution.

To determine whether an architect has been negligent, performance will be measured against what architects would typically have done in the same situation.

The problem with nearly all client-developed agreements is that they seek to prescribe a standard of care that is higher than the norm. Problematic words abound that define the architect's enhanced performance level, including "best," "better," "high," and "higher." These words are red flags and should be stricken not only from agreements but also from marketing materials and proposals.

What is the problem with being contractually required to perform at a higher standard of care? Professional liability insurance does not cover such a higher performance level. Architects are insured against acting negligently in performing their services. Beyond that, they are on their own.

How does establishing a higher standard lead to claims? When architects are required to be near-perfect, the client will expect them to pay for every problem on the plans, everything missed, every mistake that the typical architect would be forgiven. *Everything*.

Thankfully, most clients will accept pushback on this negotiation issue and will agree to take out the words "best" and "highest." As businesspeople, they understand the limits of insurance. They also recognize that if the policy does not cover their claim, the only other assets the architect has are used desks and computers—which don't amount to much.

Indemnities

Almost every client-furnished agreement comes with a professional services indemnity provision—most are horribly written. The AIA has addressed client demands for such contractual indemnities in the major 2007 versions of the AIA's standard architectural services agreement forms. The AIA's language was reviewed by professional liability insurance carriers and determined to be insurable under typical professional liability insurance policies.

The principle of the professional services indemnity is that the architect ought to reimburse the client for claims brought against it by a third party—claims arising from the architect's negligence.

Indemnities of other types actually benefit the architect:

- Client indemnity to the architect for claims arising from the presence of hazardous materials on the job site
- Client indemnity to the architect for claims from the client's misuse of the architect's drawings
- Mutual indemnities between the architect and consultants, making each party legally responsible for their own mistakes and *not* for the mistakes of the other

Problems with professional services indemnities occur when they become too broad, holding the architect responsible for performance beyond professional liability insurance policy coverage. Common examples include:

- Indemnifying persons or entities not a party to the agreement
- Indemnifying the client from their own mistakes
- Indemnifying for errors and omissions not rising to the level of legal negligence
- Defending the client against third-party claims—providing legal defense—prior to legally establishing negligence

Overbroad indemnities provide unmanageable risk. Therefore, read every proposed indemnity carefully. Use the AIA version (e.g., AIA Document B103TM–2007, section 8.1.3 and B503TM, which provides model language) as a good model. Always seek legal advice before agreeing to the client's version of an indemnity clause.

MARKETING MATERIALS: SINGING OUR PRAISES

A professional carefully negotiates an agreement and then, unwittingly, attaches the proposal to it—too lazy to retype the scope. There, lurking in the proposal, are the promises of performing among the best in the nation or region at one thing or another. Plaintiffs' attorneys can take those promises to the bank.

▶ The "AIA Documents Program" details the range of AIA contract documents that capture and convey the expectations, relationships, responsibilities, and rules that bring parties together for the design and construction of buildings.

THE LIABILITY BUCKET

Sophisticated clients may try to come up with ways to quantify or measure the standard of care. One such attempt is to express the barrier in terms of construction change orders. For example, any amount of error and omission (E&O) change orders in excess of, say, 1.5 percent means that the standard of care has been breached. So each time an E&O change order is classified, it is dumped into a "liability bucket." When the amount in the bucket rises to the established rim, in this case 1.5 percent, the architect pays for the rest that spills over.

The liability bucket is a noble idea. It has its basis in facts, as expert witnesses often quote normal change order

(continued)

percentages, such amounts varying by project size, complexity, new or renovated construction types, and the like. This seems like a fair and reasonable way to establish expectations of performance. Doesn't it?

The problem is that there is no statutory or judicial percentage threshold for an across-the-board definition for the standard of care. None.

The standard of care must be argued before the finder of fact (arbitrator, judge, or jury) and legally established for each element in every claim. Plaintiff's experts opine as to how bad the services in question were, how the mistakes were so egregious that, regardless of change order amount, "no other competent architect would have made *that* mistake." Then after hearing the charges, defendant's experts explain why everything that happened on the job was no different from any other project. In the end, the decision by the finder of fact will boil down to how convincing the arguments were, considering the credentials of the opposing experts—it's the proverbial "battle of the experts." The fact remains: There is no clear legal definition of a breach of the standard of care.

Therefore, there is a problem in trying to establish a contractual measuring stick for the standard of care. Doing so removes the insurance company's ability to argue against claims that breach the contractual standard, but might arguably *not* have breached the standard of care. That is why underwriters specifically exclude "contractual breaches" from coverage. Check the firm's policy. The liability bucket may be uninsurable.

Construction Means and Methods

The architect designs the finished project. How it gets built, the "means and methods" to get there, are determined by the builder. Construction means and methods ought not, and generally are not, the responsibility of the architect.

▶ See "Agreements with Owners" in Part 4, Chapter 11.1 for more information related to the contract with the client.

Means and methods claims examples include excavation cave-ins, scaffolding failures, and crane collapses. Fortunately such claims are rare, but the result is almost always tragic, with property damage, personal injuries and death involving workers and members of the general public. These accidents turn into media events, with plaintiff awards that amount to tens of millions.

AIA standard agreements have effectively managed this issue for decades, with carefully considered language in the architectural services agreements and the general conditions for the contract for construction. Take advantage of this language in AIA agreements—language tested in the courts.

Guarantees and Certifications

Architects are often asked to guarantee or certify the quality or completeness of their design. There is real danger here. The only guarantee that the law typically requires, and that professional liability insurance policies cover, is a guarantee to perform to the standard of care. Beyond this, guarantees and certifications are excluded from coverage.

The words *guarantee* and *warranty* should either be stricken from the agreement, or at least used properly—for example, "Architect makes no guarantee of performance." Other terms take on the same meaning—"ensure," "assure," "insure," "confirm," "verify," "thorough," "any," "all," and even "100% complete." Each may be placed in a context requiring that the architect perform at a level of perfection—to provide any and everything needed at the architect's expense.

Certifications are far more common than guarantees, and cannot realistically be avoided. Building officials and jurisdictions require certifications stating that drawings have been prepared per code, or, after construction, that the project was completed per plans and specs. Other common certifications are requested by project financiers, banks, and lending institutions—all requesting the same thing: that architects promise that they didn't make any mistakes.

There is a simple solution to any certification. Remember the standard of care—that the architect is a professional who exercises judgment. An architect should only certify "in my professional opinion" or "to the best of my knowledge, information, and belief." The contract should give the architect the ability to review and reasonably limit certifications before signing them. Do not certify perfect performance.

Proper Scope

Badly written scopes of services lead to claims and lost revenue. Unclear scopes can make architects responsible for the performance of someone not under their direct control. Overbroad scopes rob architects of the ability to invoice for extra services. Bad scopes can ruin a firm, damaging its relationship with the client.

Good scopes of services set forth with precision the services the architect will provide, and exclude those he or she won't. Spend time getting it right. Review it with the client and other members of the team; include the junior staff who will work on the project. Getting the words right will clarify everyone's expectations and may eliminate later disputes.

▶ "Defining Project Services" further discusses the centrality of scope definition to effective agreements for professional design services.

Administration of the Contract for Construction

During the construction phase, the task for the architect is to "administer the contract for construction" between the owner and builder—various services that collectively are commonly referred to as "CA." These CA tasks include field observations, reviewing contractor's payment applications, answering contractors' questions about the drawings and specifications, reviewing contractors' submittals, reviewing and approving change orders, issuing revised documents for changes, and inspecting for substantial completion.

Clients sometimes want to save on professional design fees by eliminating CA services. They reason that after the construction documents have been prepared, the architect is done with design.

▶ "Construction Contract Administration" (Part 3, Chapter 7.4) covers the architect's evaluation and reporting of the progress and quality of the work and its conformance to the design intent expressed in the contract documents.

But "design" is not done until the project is built. Changes occur during construction, brought about by contractor substitutions, products and systems purchased off of performance specifications, unanticipated field conditions, modifications to accommodate construction means and methods, owner changes, and errors and omissions. Plans are never perfect, nor are they "complete."

With these change forces at work, the architect must continue to protect the client's core interest—the design. In protecting the design, architects also protect their own reputation and liability. Costs from fixing systems not properly integrated, not meeting code, or not functioning could become a basis for claims.

Professional liability insurance providers recognize a rise in claims among firms that do not provide CA services—because the architect is not around to correct their documents or to defend them, to interpret and explain them, to preempt or minimize costly construction mistakes. Some underwriters will not insure firms that take on commissions for construction that do not include CA services.

Limitation of Liability

Without a limitation of liability (LOL), there is "no limit" to an architect's liability. If a professional liability insurance policy has a per-claim limit of $10 million, a firm is not protected for any claim in excess of that limit. A $20 million claim, if enforced, could put a firm out of business. Uninsured loss is an unmanageable risk.

A limitation of liability is an agreement not to seek damages in excess of a pre-established and agreed-upon amount. To be legal, the limit must provide fair payout in relation to the value of the services; unreasonably low LOLs have been struck down by courts. An enforceable LOL can be an effective way to manage risk. Most underwriters offer a break in premiums if all the insured's projects, or at least a significant percentage of them, have an LOL.

LIMITING THE LIABILITY OF A CONSULTANT

Jay S. Gregory, Esq., founding partner of the Boston office of LeClairRyan, PC, tells the story of an architect he represented who had unwittingly agreed to certain fine print in the contract of a structural engineering consultant. When the structural design of the project turned out to be defective, resulting in repairs totaling several million dollars, his client turned to the engineer to make good. The engineer immediately produced the contract and turned to the fine print, which stated a limitation of liability in the amount of $100,000. The engineer freely admitted guilt—"Here, I'll get my checkbook and write you a check for one hundred thousand."

The architect, holder of the prime agreement with the client, was responsible for the rest of the damages—damages arguably not his fault.

What is a reasonable value for an LOL? Some advise that it should equal the compensation received on the project. But that can amount to a big number, exceeding policy limits. A reasonable target is to set the LOL at the "proceeds of available insurance." Doing so will ensure that the firm never has to pay out of pocket, even if the annual policy limit (aggregate) has been eroded by claims on other projects. [Note: Savvy clients may require that eroded limits be replaced with the purchase of add-on coverage. Even so, that is a better deal than no LOL.]

Significantly, LOLs should apply to the full sum of any and all claims on the project. Otherwise, the LOL may not do what it is supposed to do—set a limit on liability.

Making Better Agreements
Establish Standard In-House Practices

There are firms with no standard approach to developing, executing, and maintaining design services agreements. Almost anyone can authorize work and sign contracts, committing the firm to situations of unmanageable risk.

Consider these tips to address this risk:

- Appoint a single person or, for larger firms, a team of individuals, to review and negotiate all contract terms and conditions. People who review contracts all the time know what to look for, acquiring the skills to effectively negotiate with difficult clients and attorneys. It takes years of training and experience to develop these skills. Consider hiring someone with a legal background or a licensed attorney to perform this role. Contracts legally obligate a firm and should be reviewed and approved by select firm members only.
- As part of the review process, the project manager (PM) should review his or her own contracts. He or she will manage the project and ought to play a role in shaping what the contract says. However, the PM should not be the *only* person reviewing the contract.
- Provide access to signed agreements for review by the entire project team.
- Save electronic copies of every agreement with the electronic project records. Also save a copy in a general office directory of the firm's contracts. When a problem emerges on a project, perhaps several years after the records have been archived, there will be a dash to find the contract. Make it readily available on that day.

Get Professional Support

If there is a claim, a firm will need support from an attorney, but attorneys can also help avoid a claim before it happens. Attorneys specialize in areas of legal expertise; contract law is one such specialty, and construction contracts a subset within it. There are attorneys who work with owners, builders, or design firms. Finally, there are attorneys who specialize in developing agreement text, and others who are called in to resolve disputes. At times, help may be needed from both of these subspecialties.

To find the right attorney, ask other architects in the area or a professional liability insurer for recommendations, or attend seminars in risk management conducted by attorneys to get a glimpse of what they know. Take time to make the right choice. Architects should select an attorney with relevant experience, clients, and references.

A qualified attorney can help with the review of contracts, or perhaps just with difficult agreement clauses. Some architects use outside counsel to negotiate contract terms—speaking attorney to attorney to the one representing the other party. While this is an extra expense, it could avoid a far more costly contract claim later that stems from improper review.

In addition to paid attorney consultation, many insurance providers offer contract reviews. These reviews best address matters of insurance and insurability. Using both outside insurance and legal counsels will combine to make the contracts best suited to preserve the interests of the firm.

Use Standard Agreement Forms

Most professional liability insurance carriers offer discounts to their clients that use standard agreement forms, such as AIA documents. AIA forms have been tested by the courts. In addition, clients recognize and respect these forms, making the negotiation process with these as a starting point much easier.

Standardized forms can be used "as is," but it is more typical that they be modified beyond project particulars and changes to common services, to include technical edits to the legal terms and conditions in response to the advice of legal and insurance advisors.

One way to use outside legal and insurance counsel is in the development of a suite of standard agreement forms customized for use by the firm. These documents may seldom be adopted as is by the client, but they will be very useful as a reference to a firm's preferred language. There will be many times when client's counsel is pushing for certain text in the client's standard form. In that situation, an architect can transmit the firm's preferred paragraph for consideration—a good negotiation strategy.

There are several key customized agreement forms to have on hand:

- *Full services agreements* of the types most frequently used.
- *Small or limited-scope agreements*: Short-form terms and conditions for projects where there is no construction involved, such as feasibility studies, programming, and planning services.
- *Notice to proceed*: Brief letter agreement used to get a project going until the final agreement is executed. Such notices include limited items to agree on quickly: definition of limited scope and payment, intent to execute the final agreement, and rules to terminate or extend.
- *Consultant agreements*: These should always be tied to the terms and conditions of the prime agreement between the architecture firm and the client. Never sign the consultant's proposal—and avoid attaching it to a consultant's agreement form—where its terms and conditions might conflict.
- *Common exhibits*: Rate schedules, reimbursable expenses schedules, sample invoices, standard scopes of services for each type of consultant regularly hired, consultant standards.

No. 3: Selecting the Client

The third most frequent source of claims comes from client selection. (See Figure 4.5.) It is the client who most frequently sues the architect for failing to fulfill his or her duty. A client who is unsophisticated, or short on the cash needed to fund the project, or has a record of litigation, or is completely unknown to the architect, is one to avoid.

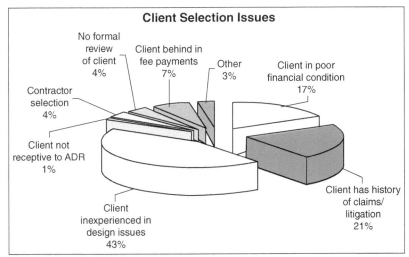

Client Selection Issues

No formal review of client 4%
Client behind in fee payments 7%
Other 3%
Client in poor financial condition 17%
Contractor selection 4%
Client not receptive to ADR 1%
Client inexperienced in design issues 43%
Client has history of claims/litigation 21%

Risk Drivers data provided by The Design Professional unit of XL Group

FIGURE 4.5 **Chart Depicting Client Selection Claims by Type**

Know the Firm's Expertise—Know the Market

An architect who keeps designing the same thing, over and over again, necessarily develops an expertise in that one thing. The purest example of this is the prototype building. Examples include box stores and fast-food outlets. Each successful franchise solves a series of problems very effectively—established brand recognition, optimal layout for both customer service and product preparation, predictable construction cost and schedule, and significant reduction in errors and omissions. These prove a simple principle—if architects were given the opportunity to design a project just like their last one, they would likely expect to do a better job. We see that specialization helps mitigate risk, while establishing a record of accomplishment.

Sophisticated clients want to select firms that have successfully designed and completed projects similar to theirs. Such is their means of managing risk.

Know the Client

Before beginning to work with a client, an architect should know them. Are they an experienced developer, having previously done projects like the one proposed? Can they afford the project? Do they have a reputation for negotiating fairly? Do they have a long list of architects they have hired—and if so, who? What is their track record for paying? Do they have a history of litigation?

The more that is known about a potential new client, the better equipped a firm will be to make a proper decision. Seeing the potential pitfalls and negotiating with these in mind helps avoid a bad client relationship. This information is often available in the community of architects or from the firm's insurance agent.

Condominium Projects

Residential projects are among the riskiest and condominium projects are particularly risky. Condominium projects begin with a client, the developer. But the moment that the developer sells the first unit, there is a new client—an owner of the design product. With each unit sold, the architect acquires another new client—one whom they didn't select and have no relationship with, and who might have unreasonable expectations.

ONE GOOD LAWSUIT DESERVES ANOTHER

A design firm completed a commission for a major institution and received popular recognition for a job well done. The client was happy. There was good publicity. Awards were given. But not everyone on the team was satisfied.

Several years after the project was completed, three of the major trades filed suit over change orders that were long denied and never paid—three separate suits in three different jurisdictions. Whom did they sue? The architect.

The subs each lost money on their contracts, primarily because there were unanticipated changes to the schedule that led to labor overruns. Despite these facts, the basis of the suits alleged that the plans were incomplete and uncoordinated, leading to their losses. This basis quickly faced an important legal obstacle: the architect, a third party to the construction contract, does not have a legal duty to save the builder's subcontractors from economic loss due to defective plans. Only the owner, through the general contractor, has this legal duty. But the builder did not want to sue his client to aid his subcontractors—the same client he wanted to work for again in the future. The subs didn't want to sue the builder

for the same reason. At this point in the claim, summary judgment, with dismissal of the claims against the architect, seemed possible.

Ensuing legal discovery exposed the faults of all team members—not surprisingly, no one had been perfect. Meanwhile, both the general contractor and owner, neither a defendant in the suits, watched with interest from the sidelines. Both suspected that at any time, they could get pulled into the fray.

In the end, the owner and builder, the ones with legal agreements relevant to the claims, succumbed to pressure to do right by the subcontractors. Both volunteered to participate in mediation and settlement with the parties. The architect settled for six figures, about one-tenth of the stated claim value. The owner also kicked in seven figures. The parties agreed to settle, ending what could have been a much costlier trip to court, where anything could have happened. There is no justice in settlement—only conclusion.

The lesson that the architect learned was this: People to whom you owe no legal "duty" can sue—and they may obtain something for their effort, even in claims lacking merit.

As a result, condo projects are notorious for claims. Professional liability insurance companies will charge substantial premiums for covering this project type.

Repeat Clients Are Like Gold

Surveys of architectural firms across America indicate that most current clients are repeat clients. The repeat client rate can vary between 60 and 85 percent, and for a few firms, be even higher. There are two messages in these data: (1) It's very hard to break in with a new client who has previously worked with another architect, and (2) clients and their designers, after they've worked together, generally like and trust each other. Respect is key to these relationships. Where there is respect and clear expectations, there is a reduction in claims.

Get the Right Builder

A good builder can make a project a big success. Likewise, a bad builder—one who causes delays, can't follow the plans, or charges extra for everything—can make a project into a financial disaster, and not just for the owner. When a builder fails to perform well, everyone pays in one way or another. To the extent that architects have a voice in the decision, they should help their client choose a builder who is well organized, understands and respects the architect's role, and appreciates the value of all of the relationships involved.

Impact of the Project Delivery Method

How the project is contracted for construction is known as the delivery method. Some of the most common alternatives are explained below, with an eye toward identifying risk.

▶ "Project Delivery Methods" (Part 3, Chapter 8.1) provides an overview of the available models for project delivery.

Hard Bid

Hard bid is the so-called traditional method, or design-bid-build method (DBB). Under this option, the architect (design team) completes the plans and specifications (construction documents) and puts them out to bid. Regardless of the many options for selecting bidders, the bottom-line goal of the bidder is to get low and win.

On the surface, the hard-bid scenario sounds like it should be the best approach for reducing claims. The design process is linear, flowing uninterrupted from schematics, through design development, and then finishing with construction documents—suggesting no impediment to completing and coordinating the documents before they are put out to bid. The true difficulty is that no set of documents is ever fully complete or perfectly coordinated. This fact plays right into the hand of a skilled estimator—one who is looking for any advantage he or she can find over the competition. In the bid situation, the goal is to get low—quality in construction is *not* a priority for those who plan to win. Missing information in the bid documents affords opportunity to achieve the low bid. The real payday comes later, *after* award, when the seed of missing information yields a harvest in change orders. Mounting change orders—uncontrolled project costs—puts undue strain on the owner-architect relationship.

Claims histories show that there are more claims by percentage of type of project delivery method on DBB projects than any of the other project delivery types.

▶ "Bidding and Negotiation Phase" (Part 3, Chapter 7.3) discusses the processes involved in selecting a contractor.

Negotiated Contracts

Negotiated contracts are said to produce the best quality for the lowest price. In this option, the owner interviews and selects the builder independent of a bid process. Qualifications may include the cost of the builder's services, but more important drivers will be reputation for quality, on-time delivery, and effective cost management.

Negotiated contracts come in a variety of forms. The builder might take on a purely advisory role (construction manager, advisor) with all of the "subs" under separate contracts direct with the owner; or the builder may build the project with his or her own forces and subcontractors. The cost model may be in the form of reimbursement for all costs plus a fee, a fixed fee, or a guaranteed maximum price (GMP).

Regardless of the many combined options, negotiating a contract with a good, qualified builder is most apt to bring the best results, and produce the lowest risk to all involved.

Fast Track

Fast-track construction involves phasing of design activities to overlap the construction process—construction commences in one phase before design is complete for the next. Under this option, a series of "bid packages" are organized and scheduled.

Throughout the fast-track process, the biggest (highest-cost) decisions are made first, the smallest (lowest-cost) decisions last. The risk in the process is that decisions are always made and implemented without complete information, and may later need to be changed at some expense. This risk is an outfall of the owner's decision to speed the construction process. The need for speed, over quality and first cost, is the owner's choice—and the owner ought to weigh the decision carefully. Architects should attempt to highlight this point in the contract. At minimum there should be a record of discussion with the client regarding the increased risk of change orders. Managing this risk is mostly about clarifying expectations in advance. AIA Document B103™– 2007 contains good cautionary language for the fast-track method.

Other Project Delivery Methods

A number of other delivery methods are available, including contractor-led design-build (CLDB), architect-led design-build (ALDB), construction management (CM), and integrated project delivery (IPD). In each of these, the traditional roles of the architect, builder, and owner are modified to some degree, creating the potential for increased risk. In each case, understanding and clearly limiting the responsibilities of the architect, while maintaining insurability, is one way to keep the risk model from crumbling into disarray.

Public vs. Private Clients

There are many opportunities to compete for public design contracts. However, public contracts offer significant problems over private client relationships:

- Terms and conditions are often one-sided against the architect, with little or no room for negotiation.
- Profit margins are tight. The parties that fund the project have to answer to their taxpaying constituents.
- The press often has a field day with public projects, magnifying and misstating problems that leak out—sometimes without fact checking, and without understanding the construction or design trades.
- Public officials owe more to their constituents than they owe to the design team. This can make it hard to establish a normal designer-client relationship.
- Public officials come and go. After an election, an architect could be working for a person who previously opposed the project.

Any of these issues can increase risk on public projects. Understand the risks and figure out how best to manage them.

Establish a Reasonable Fee

Examine a client's expectations and degree of sophistication and take into account the real level of risk inherent in the project. Then formulate the processes needed to prevent anticipated problems. After quantifying these processes, determine the real cost of taking the commission. Add profit to that figure to establish a fee. If the client consents to that sum, then, and only then, will it be known that the project constitutes a manageable risk.

▶ "Architectural Services and Compensation" (Part 3, Chapter 5.3) covers the variables when determining what to charge for services, methods of compensation, and strategies for getting paid.

No. 2: Project Team Capabilities

The second most frequent source of claims comes from the risk category known as project team capabilities. (See Figure 4.6.) Dominating this category are claims arising from the use of inexperienced staff. Coming in a close second and third are similar issues—inexperienced staff on site, and an inexperienced PM. To proactively help avoid these kinds of claims, hire or train qualified staff and, as much as possible, have

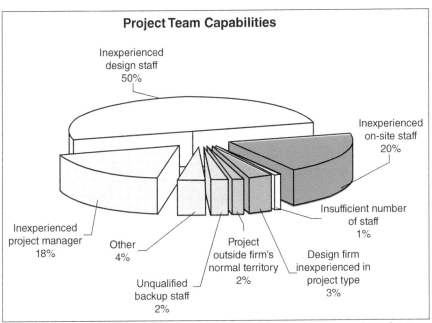

Project Team Capabilities

Inexperienced design staff 50%

Inexperienced on-site staff 20%

Insufficient number of staff 1%

Inexperienced project manager 18%

Other 4%

Unqualified backup staff 2%

Project outside firm's normal territory 2%

Design firm inexperienced in project type 3%

Risk Drivers data provided by The Design Professional unit of XL Group

FIGURE 4.6 **Chart Depicting Project Team Capability Claims by Type**

the most qualified people working on each project and each phase of the project. This includes a thoughtful division of labor, taking advantage of the lower billing rates of less-experienced staff for tasks that are appropriate to their skill level. A successful work plan requires enough senior level experience to balance the inexperience of youth. Managing this risk, while turning a profit, requires finding the right mixture of less-experienced interns and experienced architects.

Use of Technology

In the "old days," when drawings were prepared by hand, the plans were almost always drawn by the most senior staff. The plans required more depth of experience; more things had to be known to draw them properly—the program, the structural grid, the clearances for a toilet, what the walls are made of (how thick), the code, what's going on overhead, how to label, how to dimension. The details, on the other hand, were far more one-dimensional. With a small amount of coaching, and reference to prior projects' working drawings as examples, an intern could in short order be equipped to become productive at drawing the details. Thus interns began their drawing careers with exciting tasks like door schedules and toilet room details.

In the current day, drawings are prepared entirely on the computer—increasingly in 3D. The older experts are often less computer-savvy, becoming hands-off. The new generation, however, uses the computer with great familiarity, but lacks expertise in design and construction—they don't know what to draw. Neither can operate effectively entirely on their own. This can create a significant risk. Both generations need the skill that the other possesses.

Below is a series of ways to manage the multigenerational approach:

- Train senior-level staff to draw again—on the computer, to become hands-on in the building information model being created in the computer. There are things in the model that cannot be seen on a print. Senior staff need to be able to see them.
- Train junior-level staff to know what they should draw, and why.
- Manage the generational differences. Break down barriers between old and young so they can communicate effectively, respecting the different but needed value each brings to the team.

- Foster mentoring. Senior staff possesses a wealth of experience to share with the next generation. Some will share, but only if asked. Effective mentoring happens when mentor and mentee both see the value. Both must be motivated to make it happen.
- Hire and maintain a good mixture of staff at the various levels.

Firms should invest in training staff of all ages in the proper use of technology.

Staff Continuity on Projects

People come and go for a variety of reasons. Whatever the cause, their departure creates a void in the knowledge base of the project team—the perfect opportunity for unresolved issues to fall through the cracks. Take these steps whenever someone leaves:

- Obtain a written "to do" list from the person leaving, documenting unfinished items and design decisions yet to be made.
- Get commitments from remaining team members to pick up and close out the loose ends that result with the departure.
- When appropriate, bring in the right replacement. If the position vacated was senior, the client may want to interview or review qualifications of the replacement; obtaining client approval might even be a contractual obligation. Regardless, make the client aware in a timely fashion of the change. Demonstrate intent to fulfill contractual commitments.

Office Standards

Standards exist for good reasons. They portray the signature of a firm, its image, its attitude. They establish a quick solution to a problem, avoid reinventing the wheel, and save money in the process. They also exist as a repository of firm knowledge, a reference in how to avoid failures in quality. Standards are indeed great, but only when they are used.

Firms can now host their quality plans online—available for reference by every employee as their home page. These online documents set forth the firm's policies and procedures for how to do almost everything—providing instant access to checklists, templates, and forms. They can provide handy links to resources, such as online building codes, industry standards, an electronic library of past project drawings and specifications, image databases used for marketing, case studies, white papers, and lessons learned. Company intranets and online quality plans have become essential tools for today's architecture firms. These require significant investment of time and money, both to develop and then to maintain. But this investment is returned many times over by improving quality and reducing risk.

No. 1: Communication

The most frequently cited cause of claims is poor communication. (See Figure 4.7.) More than half of communication complaints arise out of a lack of procedures to identify conflicts, errors, and omissions. Secondarily prevalent are the problems that happen when people don't follow procedures that are in place. For the project to proceed without problems, people must communicate effectively.

Peer Reviews: Quality Assurance/Quality Control (QA/QC)

One sure way to prevent mistakes is to check the work—the benefit best characterized in the carpenters' saying, "Measure twice, cut once."

On any given project there are hundreds, even thousands of decisions that have to be communicated. Any decisions not made by the design team will be made by someone else, and the architect may not like that decision or its impact on the project. This situation is less likely when a system is employed for managing or controlling quality.

Here are several practical ways to manage quality:

- Self-checking: All team members must be responsible for the quality of their own work. They know their piece of the project better than anyone else. They can use

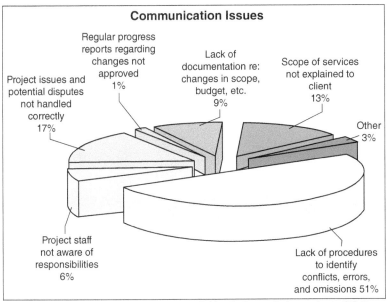

Communication Issues

- Regular progress reports regarding changes not approved 1%
- Lack of documentation re: changes in scope, budget, etc. 9%
- Scope of services not explained to client 13%
- Project issues and potential disputes not handled correctly 17%
- Other 3%
- Project staff not aware of responsibilities 6%
- Lack of procedures to identify conflicts, errors, and omissions 51%

Risk Drivers Data provided by The Design Professional unit of XL Group

FIGURE 4.7 **Chart Depicting Communication Claims by Type**

checklists from the company standards, or a list developed by their immediate supervisor. Either way, expectations and communications need to be clear.

- In-house third-party review: A "fresh set of eyes"—experienced eyes—can be a big help. Third-party reviews ought to occur at the conclusion of every major project phase, *before* deliverables are issued. Project leaders should see written proof that the reviews have occurred before they issue the documents.
- Peer reviews: Some jurisdictions require independent, outside consultant "peer" reviews before they will issue a building permit—at least for some critical portions of the work. For projects with which a firm does not possess significant prior experience, or when working with a new consultant, it might be prudent to have a peer review. Some institutional clients may even require it. Small firms can greatly benefit from a peer review.
- Building information models: BIM can take advantage of electronic checking, employing clash-detection software. These software add-ons produce reports that still have to be reviewed by humans to determine which clashes are real and which are incidental. Nonetheless, the thoroughness of the reports is a remarkable benefit.

Remember the simple goal of checking: to identify and correct a mistake before it becomes too expensive to fix. Checking, regardless of which tool or method is employed, helps members of a project team learn to communicate better—to provide better design.

Know the Contract

Nothing is as disappointing as a failure to meet expectations. Clients readily become dissatisfied because the architect didn't do things the way they had expected. Likewise, many project leaders become dissatisfied because the members of the team didn't complete tasks as they expected. Why does this happen? Bad communication.

One simple way to address this concern is to review the services agreement—the written expectations—with everyone. Sit down with the client and go over the scope of work. Show examples of the deliverables that will be produced. Listen to the client. Their preferences might alter the standard approach.

Likewise, review the agreement with the team at the beginning of the project. At appropriate times, pull out a copy of the agreement to confirm the written rules—expectations—for key deliverables.

It is always better to discuss matters and review a change of strategy or approach in advance. The alternative, which is to make assumptions, often results in disappointment.

Conduct Proper Meetings

Meetings should never happen just because they're on the calendar. Meetings should be organized to complete a set of distinct decisions along the road to finishing the project. Each meeting deserves attention to the advanced development of an agenda, planning who should be there, and the topic of necessary decisions.

The written outcome of meetings is the minutes. Minutes need not be lengthy. They just need to record date and location, attendees, a summary of each item discussed, decisions made, and identification of action items, assigning who is responsible for each. The key in this record is decisions.

The architect is often the one responsible for preparing and issuing minutes during the design phase. Once construction commences, this responsibility often shifts to the builder. Regardless of formal responsibility, it is essential that the architect take written notes of some form at *every* meeting. Minutes issued by other parties should be reviewed promptly. If there is any disagreement, write and send a record of comments or corrections right away.

In the ebb and flow of the project, often spanning several years, the minutes represent a key record of who said what, what they knew, and when they knew it—documenting the involvement of people no longer around or available for comment. These become the means to affirm prior decisions, dissolve disagreements, or to resolve claims.

Document Control

Every paper document issued by the architect needs several points of identifying information: the author, who it is being issued to, the date issued, and, in the case of contract documents, a reference number. Documents that are revised and reissued, such as drawings, need a revision date. Last, copies of each document issued must be saved in the project record.

In resolving disputes, the resolution hinges on who knew what and when they knew it. For example, change orders arise over information added or subtracted from the contract documents. Reference to copies of the documents of the two dates in question, before and after the change, will support or disprove the claim.

Practice throughout the entire construction industry is moving toward a paperless exchange of information. E-mail is used to transmit documents of modest size. The courts now accept electronic records as a means of storing data for use in litigation. The benefit of this decision saves significant money on printing and delivery. In addition, re-access to the data is improved, since many document storage systems are databases that can be electronically searched.

Regardless of the system in place, access to important project records must be preserved long after the project has been completed—until the statute of limitations or repose (if any) precludes litigation. If project records are saved remotely during the life of the project, obtain a copy for safekeeping. If appropriate, convert the files into an electronic format that will still be recoverable by computer systems toward the end of the potential litigation period—some 6, 10, or 15 years from now.

▶ "Managing and Avoiding Disputes" (Part 2, Chapter 4.7) covers strategic and effective use of mediation, arbitration, and litigation.

Warning Signs of a Claim

When someone has made a mistake, the human tendency is to hide. This is true in all relationships, including that between architect and client. Sooner or later mistakes will come out. Though difficult, it's always better to face one's own mistakes head-on—to tell the client about a problem before they hear about it from someone else. That, at least, gives the architect some measure of control.

See It First

Many claims begin with the architect being among the first to know of a problem. If they aren't among the first, it's likely because they're not listening or paying attention to what is going on.

The discovery of an error often begins with denial. After this comes the realization that the problem needs to be fixed.

Start with fact checking. Speak to the people involved with the situation; find out everything about it. Check out the timing on the issue; who knew or did what, and when. At the same time, formulate what has to change to resolve the matter. Is a change really needed? A partial change? What are the options? What is the cost? How would the schedule be impacted?

Any serious mistake can damage the relationship with the client. If a claim could erupt, call in outside legal and insurance counsels for advice. Don't wait for the claim letter from the client's attorney. After the problem and its implications are understood, and good advice received from insurance providers or legal counsel, the next step is to tell the client.

How to Preserve the Client Relationship

It is important to be open with clients. At the same time, this is a business relationship, based on a contract. If the architect *believes* they are at fault, they should resist the first tendency to admit fault. First seek the advice of outside counsel, before taking responsibility for a repair.

On examination, the facts could well prove the architect caused the problem. But that doesn't necessarily mean the architect has a legal obligation to fix it. Remember the standard of care. There may also be contractual or legal bases for excusing compliance with the standard of care (e.g., a force majeure clause). The law does not require the architect to be perfect, and hopefully the contract does not require perfection either. Do not offer to remedy the situation without approval from the insurer. Professional liability insurance policies exclude from coverage situations in which they are not involved in authorizing a settlement.

Conclusion

The practice of architecture involves risk—risk that has the potential to strike directly at the ability of the professional to remain in business. Much risk can be avoided or transferred by simply being savvy, making good contracts, and getting good advice, then following through on it. The balance of the risk stems from being human, being fallible—architects do make mistakes. Architects need to manage this risk.

Errors and omissions are never planned, and many could have been avoided. Reducing human error requires nothing less than hard work, a commitment to excellence, and getting serious about improving the process by which services are rendered. A firm that is disinterested in risk management "processes" may feel invincible, but it is wise to beware. When risk isn't being carefully watched, claims will rear their ugly heads.

4.7 Managing and Avoiding Disputes

David A. Ericksen, Esq.

Project disputes are an unfortunate reality. They are also time-consuming, expensive, and stressful. The first goal should be to avoid or contain the potential for disputes. However, when they do arise, they are best resolved by the strategic and effective use of mediation, arbitration, litigation, and even compulsory direct negotiations.

David Ericksen is president of Severson & Werson in San Francisco and leads the Construction Practice. He specializes in the representation of architects, engineers, construction managers, and other construction professionals. He graduated from the University of California School of Law in Berkeley and clerked for the Washington State Supreme Court.

▶ "Risk Management Strategies" (Part 2, Chapter 4.6) further discusses how to know one's risks and how to manage them.

Simply stated, the best way to resolve a dispute is to prevent the dispute from ever beginning, or at least to prevent it from gaining any serious momentum. Although they are discussed elsewhere, it bears repeating that the three most powerful tools in doing so are the successive steps of client selection, client education, and contract documentation. Client selection is obvious. Investigate and then choose those clients most in tune with the architect's vision and with the least likely impulse toward claims and litigation. Most architects pay at least some heed to these issues. Where most fail is in client education and the even more important step of documenting the verbal understandings in the contract and other documents. The too-frequent inevitable results are missed expectations, misunderstandings, and litigated disputes.

Client education should be centered on the design and construction process and the practical realities and limitations of that process. These realities will be both generic and project-specific. The real key is that this education should and must take place *prior* to entering the agreement, and then become a part of the agreement. Any valid contract provision is supposed to reflect a "meeting of the minds" between the parties. Too often, it is the first, last, and only time architects and their clients actually have a reliable meeting of the minds. When the parties have signed an agreement, courts and arbitrators will generally assume that the provision accurately reflects their mutual understanding and expectation. In AIA Document B101™–2007, the exchange of initial information is included as an exhibit and was included in the document itself in AIA Document B103™–2007. These documents are an excellent *starting point* for this process. Ideally, it will go far beyond those introductory steps and then be reflected in the agreement through project recitals and assumptions, potential additional services, excluded services, and contingencies, as well as the clarification of the roles and responsibility of various project participants.

Beyond the broad value of client education culminating in a contractual meeting of the minds, the two contractual issues, which can lead to more avoidable disputes, claims, and losses than any other issues, are "absolutes" and "ambiguities." Absolutes, because few (if any) design and construction projects proceed perfectly, and they are not expected by the law or covered by professional liability insurance. Nevertheless, expectations of perfection are often asserted and claimed by unhappy or opportunistic clients. Ambiguities, because open-ended obligations create potentially limitless responsibilities. Fortunately, each of these concerns can be managed and contained by some relatively simple contract provisions establishing a touchstone for a meeting of the minds and precluding later revisionist views.

The first is set forth in the 2007 and later versions of the AIA owner-architect agreements, which now include a standard of care clause that is consistent with the prevailing legal standards for professional skill and care. The clause recognizes that perfection is rare and is not to the legal standard. AIA Document B101TM–2007 provides:

§ 2.2 The Architect shall perform its services consistent with the professional skill and care ordinarily provided by architects practicing in the same or similar locality under the same or similar circumstances. The Architect shall perform its services as expeditiously as is consistent with such professional skill and care and the orderly progress of the Project.

In itself, the standard of care is a great start to overcome the burden of alleged obligations of professional perfection. However, even this clear statement of the law is, by itself, often not enough.

INTEGRATE POINTS OF AGREEMENT OR THEY VANISH

Including any important points of agreement and understanding into the actual contract or by express reference is critical. If not, it may be as if they never existed. The integration clause from all the AIA documents provides, essentially, "This Agreement represents the entire and integrated agreement between the Owner and the Architect and supersedes all prior negotiations, representations or agreements, either written or oral." (AIA Document B101™–2007, Art. 13.1.) Even absent this provision, the law provides the same result through the "parole evidence rule," which may lead to a similar and potentially devastating result. In one situation, at the outset of the project, the architect and client spent three days negotiating a memorandum of understanding with over 100 points specifically agreed to and initialed. However, when the agreed-upon points were not reflected in the AIA-based written agreement that followed, the memorandum was excluded in its entirety from consideration in the $7.5M claim.

First, just as compliance with the building code is often rightly seen as the floor, and not the ceiling, of the design professional's obligation, clients may wrongly assume that the standard of care is the floor for responsibility and not the fulfillment of responsibility. For that reason, adding language to clarify that the standard of care is also the limit of the architect's responsibility can be very helpful. Whatever words are used, the goal is to make clear that the standard of care represents the limit of the architect's design duties for the project and under the agreement.

Second, even with a clear statement of the standard of care, it often remains difficult for clients, lay jurors, and even nonspecialist judges to understand that even this "ordinary" standard for licensed professionals could contemplate imperfections. To make this even clearer and to avoid any potential implied obligation of absolute perfection, it is often useful to expressly disclaim perfection and to advise the client to prepare for the corresponding contingencies that would thereby be their financial responsibility. Such a clause might provide: "Architect's professional standard of care is not a warranty or guarantee of perfection and Architect shall have no such obligation. Accordingly, Owner shall provide appropriate contingencies for cost and schedule impacts resulting from reasonable design clarifications, additions, and corrections."

For client satisfaction and project success (and thereby dispute avoidance), the most important section of any architectural agreement remains a qualitatively and quantitatively detailed scope of work. Nevertheless, some provisions will inevitably carry some potentially open-ended or result-oriented clauses that can also be open-ended. In addition, the inherently fluid nature of the design and construction process, as well as the ingrained service mind-set of architects and their design teams, means that new issues can arise and the original scope of work may be stretched or expanded by ambiguities, events, or conduct. This is broadly referred to as "scope creep," and it presents multiple grounds for disputes and the prolonging of those disputes. First and foremost, once a well-defined scope of work is exceeded, absent a written confirmation and agreement, there is no longer any obvious limit to the expanded services. As a result, there is no easy way to either define the duty or say that it has been satisfied. In addition, such services are by definition "extra-contractual" and outside of the procedures and important controls established by the agreement. For these reasons, architects should consider two additions to the scope of work to contain these potential ambiguities.

The first is to simply avoid the ambiguous expansion of duties. The agreement would provide: "Architect shall have no obligations or responsibilities for the Project except as expressly set forth in this Agreement."

While this may be close to other provisions in many agreements, most such clauses refer to modification of the agreement. This is expressly focused on "the Project" and thereby can be used to avoid or mitigate alleged scope creep.

The second addition turns on the quality of the agreement. Assuming it is a quality agreement, such as an AIA agreement or even an agreement including a limitation of liability clause, it can be important to make clear that all project-related activities, whether expressly referenced in the agreement or not, get the benefit of the contractual protections. For those reasons, a leading introduction or closing provision to any scope of work might include: "All of Architect's services, actions, communications, and documentation relative to the Project shall be covered by this Agreement."

PLAYING OUTSIDE THE CONTRACT

Tremendous effort often goes into the drafting and negotiation of agreements. If so, it should be valued and honored by following and remaining within the scope of work. In one situation, a design professional had a very limited role and, accordingly, had a limitation of liability clause limiting exposure to the nominal fee received. The project had a significant failure. When the claim came, the obvious course seemed to be to honor the limitation of liability and quickly exit the dispute. However, the claimant disagreed and argued that the claim was for those services provided outside the agreement as uncompensated extra-contractual services, and therefore the contract and limitation of liability did not control. The claim ultimately cost over 100 times the limitation of liability to resolve.

DOCUMENTATION CHECKLIST

The need to document mid-project issues will vary, but a starting list for issues to be documented and conveyed would be:

1. Agreements
2. Notifications
3. Information relied on
4. Requests for significant action or information
5. Allocated roles and responsibilities

With these provisions in place, any dispute relative to the project will be subject to the certainty of the agreement and the corresponding dispute resolution provisions.

The final two steps in the critical process of dispute and claim avoidance are really performance issues. The first is consistent, timely, and proactive documentation. The reality is that memories can and do differ, and progressively so as time passes. Small misunderstandings or false assumptions and expectations can grow into full-blown failures and disputes. Prompt communication, followed by corresponding documentation, is the key to avoiding this. In a claims context, a written document properly conveyed will almost always triumph over varying recollections and oral testimony.

Finally, the most important key to avoiding disputes is to adopt proactive and responsive behavior that promptly addresses issues rather than allowing them to fester. Simple misunderstandings grow into frustration and anger, intensified disputes, and, ultimately, claims if attention is not paid to them. Similar to the dispute procedures discussed below, this is best done with an escalating or phased sequence of actions and communications. For instance, it is seldom effective to start with written position statements. While sometimes uncomfortable and even intimidating, it is almost always best to start with a conversation or meeting to identify and talk through the issues before reducing positions to writing. As the issues are identified, it is likewise important to attach a schedule and plan of action to each issue with corresponding follow-up actions. Simply identifying the issues and then ignoring them may actually be the worst of all possible paths and the one most likely to lead to a difficult-to-defend claim.

Dispute Resolution Methods: Mediation, Arbitration, and Litigation

Where a third-party neutral becomes a part of the dispute resolution process, there are three primary paths to resolution: mediation, arbitration, and litigation. There are also countless variations to each path, and even some that blend them in some ways. However, understanding the basic process, advantages, and disadvantages of each is really the first stepping stone in the successful and strategic use of the options. As an introductory point, it is important to distinguish first between mediation on the one hand and arbitration and litigation on the other. Mediation is really a facilitated negotiation of a dispute. Disputes cannot be settled in mediation absent the agreement of the parties. In arbitration and litigation, on the other hand, the decision making passes to a third party who will ultimately make the decision based on the applicable facts and law presented.

Mediation

Mediation is "a process in which a neutral person or persons facilitate communications between the disputants to assist them in reaching a mutually acceptable agreement" (*Jeld-Wen, Inc. v. Superior Court* (2007) 146 Cal.App.4th 536,540). As stated above, mediation is so favored by the AIA that it is the default first step in the dispute resolution process. Mediation has proved to be so useful in efficiently and cost-effectively resolving design professional claims that many professional liability carriers provide significant financial incentives to architects and engineers who can resolve their claims by this means.

Absent an advance agreement, there are typically few rules or procedures applicable to mediations. The one rule that does generally apply to all mediations is that it is a confidential and privileged process such that any statements made in mediation cannot be cited, quoted, or otherwise used against a party in any subsequent proceeding or elsewhere (Federal Rules of Evidence, Rule 501). Nevertheless, most mediations will typically follow a similar format and process. Depending on the extent of material and positions exchanged in advance, most mediations begin with a group session facilitated by the mediator during which there is a presentation of positions by each side through counsel, experts, and the parties. From there, most mediations shift to "shuttle diplomacy," with the mediator moving between separate rooms of parties. This involves an effort to provide feedback, develop arguments and positions, and move the parties toward resolution by the exchanges of various settlement offers and demands. In many mediation contexts, it is not at all unusual for the parties to remain completely separated following the group session until there is either a settlement to be consummated or there is an impasse such that the parties cannot reach agreement.

There are five factors that can be most influential toward the potential for success in mediation. They are:

1. Party Participation and Authority

The goal of mediation is to bring the parties together to agree among themselves to a resolution of a dispute. In the process, a collateral benefit may even be the preservation or resurrection of an important relationship. The chances of achieving either objective decrease dramatically if the necessary parties are not personally present. "Telephone standby" is simply not an adequate substitute.

Party representation must include those with adequate factual knowledge to address and evaluate the factual issues in contention. Mediations can stall over the lack of factual research, or input from the "technical people," or the presence of those with the authority to make the decision to reach a resolution. Authority involves the express legal credentials needed to settle as well as the financial backing to support the process. Those necessary persons should be identified well in advance of the mediation with the verified commitment that they will be personally present as participants.

2. Selection of Mediator

One of the key advantages of the mediation process is the opportunity to independently evaluate and voluntarily select a mediator. In contrast to publicly appointed judges and commissioners who regularly hear a wide variety of unrelated matters, few of which actually relate to construction or architects, mediators can be selected for their particular expertise in the subject matter, experience with design and construction disputes, reputation, and approach. The most important considerations for the selection of a mediator include the following:

Expertise

Expertise in the subject matter and the mediation process is important for two reasons: It creates credibility and it empowers the mediator as the guide in the process. Each is critical to the success of the mediation. Subject matter expertise makes the process far more efficient and creates credibility in the feedback and evaluation. Process expertise facilitates the efficient and productive exchange of information, which then flows into an efficient process of feedback and negotiation, tempered by a mediator with the skill to avoid or work around impasses. Because these combined talents are rare in combination, most mediators tend to be retired judges or attorneys who have practiced in the subject matter. Each has its merits. Under both the AIA and the Association of General Contractors (AGC) model agreements, both mediation and arbitration are referred to the American Arbitration Association (AAA), which has rules expressly tailored to the construction industry and which tends to be dominated by attorney mediators with some construction professionals as well. The other major competitor nationally is the Judicial Arbitration and Mediation Service (JAMS), which tends to have a far higher percentage of retired judges in its panel. There are also countless other local and regional providers for both mediation and arbitration services.

Energy

Good mediation is hard work. It takes focus and energy to take in and quickly analyze information, which the parties may have been dealing with for years, listen to their positions, provide relevant feedback, and then facilitate a negotiation to resolution. Passive mediators generally add nothing to the process other than a conference room and the forced experience of having to explain positions to a third party. The other reality is that not all mediations are immediately successful on the initial effort. Good mediators will take the time and have the drive to follow up and continue to pursue resolution for the parties rather than simply providing a one-time forum.

Empathy

Generally speaking, mediators do not make decisions. As a result, mediation resolves a dispute only if the parties themselves agree. To move parties to that position, one of the most important traits and tools of any mediator is the capacity to truly listen and convey an understanding of that party's position. They must connect. With that as a backdrop, the mediator can also then juxtapose that position as to the other positions to help lead the party into making their own decision for resolution.

Perspective and Persuasion

Finally, good mediators frequently put themselves on the line. As one of the leading construction mediators in the country will frequently say, the mediator's only tool is the "power of persuasion." Their capacity to do so is ultimately the greatest key to selection and the greatest differentiator. Persuasion is driven by the mediator's capacity to convey two perspectives with credibility: that is, the perspective of a third party who might ultimately decide such a matter if not resolved by agreement, and the perspective of a party who has confronted similar disputes many times. Good mediators are willing to share these perspectives. Not surprisingly, the quality of this perspective and its persuasive power builds largely on the first three components of expertise, energy, and empathy.

3. Adequate Advance Exchange of Information and Positions

"Mediation by surprise" does not work. If parties receive information and positions for the first time on the day of mediation, they really are unprepared. In this situation, the parties have little chance of adequately considering the information and adjusting their own positions accordingly, in order to be prepared for resolution. Nevertheless, it is amazing how often parties come to mediation without an advance exchange of information provided with adequate time to evaluate. Although each situation is unique, as a general rule, it is important that the parties share their positions with each other and the mediator at least a week to 10 days in advance. Depending on the circumstances, it may be appropriate to lengthen this time and even provide a time for responses to the position statements.

In addition to the open statements, parties may have information they do not want to share with the other side or publish, but which may be useful to the mediator. Most mediators will operate under two levels of confidentiality. One level is that confidentiality and privilege attach to the mediation process under the rules of evidence and civil procedure. The other is an internal level of confidentiality whereby a party can share information only with the mediator with the understanding that it will not be shared with the other side. With respect to position statements, this internal level of confidentiality is sometimes best accomplished by providing a second confidential statement to the mediator alone.

4. Timing

The final issue is timing. Mediation can occur at any time in a dispute and even after a "final" judgment is handed down by a judge, jury, or arbitrator. However, by that time, countless dollars have been spent and hours lost to the process. Moreover, the underlying relationships may have been irreparably damaged. For that reason, the AIA, AGC, and other model agreements call for mediation as an initial step. However, absent a specific provision to the contrary, mediation can often be slow to start and can drag on for an indeterminate period of time. Ideally, the mediation would be contractually mandated to proceed within a short period of time (e.g., 30 or 60 days) and to be declared completed within some short period of time thereafter which allows for follow-up, but not an endless process (e.g., 2 weeks or 15 days). The AIA B101, Art. 8.2.2 defers to the AAA Construction Industry Rules for deadlines, but effectively establishes a minimum 60-day deadline by suspending other litigation for that time period. The AGC ConsensusDoc 240 is more specific and provides that the mediation shall commence within 30 days of the demand and shall be completed within 45 days.

5. Settlement

Although mediation is not required to achieve it, the goal of mediation is a "settlement" resolving the dispute. Whether as a result of mediation or direct negotiation, just as with the contract, it is critically important that this settlement agreement be reduced to a written agreement as soon as possible, to avoid differing recollections and "buyer's remorse." In addition to any monetary terms, it is important that the settlement agreement be specific as to the parties included and the scope of the release. The goal should be a final resolution of all issues as to all parties and even the project as a whole. Generally, this is referred to as a "project release." If it is less than a complete release, the agreement should be very specific as to what is included and what is not.

Arbitration

Arbitration is the process whereby the parties voluntarily submit their disputes for resolution by one or more impartial third persons instead of by a judicial court process. Absent an agreement to arbitrate in the services agreement or a subsequent agreement at the time of the claim, there can be no arbitration. Although arbitration may take many procedural forms, a dispute resolution mechanism is not really arbitration unless it has all four of the following characteristics:

1. A private/third-party decision maker chosen by the parties or by a service provider chosen by the parties
2. A mechanism for ensuring neutrality in the rendering of the decision
3. An opportunity for both parties to be heard
4. A binding decision or result (*Cheng-Canindin v. Renaissance Hotel Assocs.* (1996) 50 Cal.App.4th 684)

A TALE OF THREE BATTLES

In one recent condominium claim, an architect learned the importance of coordinated dispute resolution provisions the hard way. As a result of differing arbitration provisions with the owner and consultants, which preselected two different arbitration providers, and an owner-contractor agreement, which made no provision for arbitration, the architect was forced to simultaneously participate in two separate arbitrations and a separate lawsuit.

Parties can be included in and bound by arbitration only if they have agreed to do so. Most design and construction disputes are not isolated to a single party, but may also include multiple other parties such as other design professionals, contractors, subcontractors, and supplier/manufacturers. Although there may be very isolated strategic exceptions, it is generally critical for efficiency and fairness that all such parties and disputes be resolved in a single arbitration. Accordingly, the agreements should and must be coordinated for those purposes.

If a consistent contractual template such as the AIA standard form agreements is used for all parties, generally the arbitration or dispute resolution provisions will be coordinated. The AIA provisions then provide for permissive joinder of all related claims and actions into a single proceeding (See AIA B101, § 8.3.4 CONSOLIDATION OR JOINDER), and require that disputes with consultants that involve the owner be resolved according to the dispute resolution method selected in the owner-architect agreement. However, the 2007 AIA agreements and the AGC Consensus-Docs each present a potential failure point for arbitrations that may involve the contractor, because arbitration is no longer the automatic or default option and the parties may elect either arbitration or litigation. If different options are selected for different parties, there may not be a single proceeding and venue for resolution.

The AGC ConsensusDocs seeks to overcome this by affirmatively requiring that all parties be committed to the same dispute resolution process. It provides:

> 9.6 MULTIPARTY PROCEEDINGS The Owner and Architect/Engineer agree that all Parties necessary to resolve a claim shall be Parties to the same dispute resolution procedure. Appropriate provisions shall be included in all other contracts relating to the Project to provide for joinder or consolidation of such dispute resolution procedures.

Arbitration has many fans. It has been a preferred option for both the AIA and AGC. It is included in many public works agreements and private developer agreements.

Each proponent likely has its own reasons for arbitration, but the most common perceived advantages to arbitration are as follows:

- Private—the dispute is not confidential, but arbitration awards are not published. Limitations on this privacy may exist on public projects.
- Greater control over selection of decision maker, and better-qualified and experienced decision makers.
- Faster due to avoidance of court congestion and timing and more limited prehearing procedures and discovery.
- Less costly, due to little or no discovery and shorter path to hearing. However, the arbitrator(s) themselves must be compensated.
- Avoidance of lay juries.

However, there are also downsides. Among those most often mentioned as a reason to avoid arbitration are the following:

- Scant discovery. Generally, absent an agreement by the parties there is no right to "discovery" by deposition, interrogatories, or requests for documents. As a result, much of the information is revealed at the arbitration itself and can be a surprise.
- Less opportunity for dispositive motions such as demurrers, motions for summary judgment, and motions to strike, although arbitration rules may accommodate them.
- Can be costlier than civil litigation. The fees for even a short arbitration can run well into five figures.
- Limited judicial review. Decisions from trial courts may generally be appealed to a higher court, but arbitration decisions may only be reviewed for abuse of arbitrator discretion.
- Perception that arbitrators practice "justice by halves" and are more likely to issue compromise awards.
- Limited rights to join third parties.

As a result, the decision whether to elect arbitration is not one to be taken lightly. The decision-making process should consider the following:

- Are all necessary parties included in the same arbitration process?
- Are there issues or tools such as lien rights, stop notices, foreclosures, or bonds that are not available in arbitration?
- Is it likely the dispute is better decided by an arbitrator than a judge/jury? If not, is there a part of the dispute or a limited dollar value that would be?
- If there is a dispute, will the parties likely have all of the necessary information or will they need recourse and access to it?
- Is publicity a likely concern for a dispute on this project? Can privacy realistically be maintained by arbitration (i.e., not a public entity claim)?
- Will the expense of arbitration be a problem?

Once arbitration is selected as the dispute resolution forum, there are then multiple considerations for the arbitration itself and the success of that process. Among those issues to be prioritized for consideration are the following:

- *The arbitration provider.* While arbitrators need not be affiliated with an organization or provider, most arbitration will utilize a provider. As stated above, the AIA and AGC contracts both designate the AAA as the provider. One great advantage to that selection is that the AAA has developed arbitration rules specifically applicable to the construction industry. Other providers have some rules of their own. The key advantage to such rules is that they create a predictable structure and process that might otherwise be lacking. The fee structures and policies of various providers can also vary widely. Accordingly, a good provider is a critical first choice and there are many local, national, and international options.
- *The number of arbitrators.* Most arbitration will proceed with a single arbitrator or a panel of three. The advantage of the panel is that it provides a sense of balance with

the expectation that each side will have some perspective on the panel. It also triples the cost and can greatly slow the process.

- *The selection of the arbitrator.* The preferred option would always be for the parties to mutually agree as to the selection of the arbitrator. Most providers will give the parties an opportunity to do so from a panel, and the parties would generally have that option in any event. Where they cannot agree, providers such as the AAA will generally give the parties the opportunity to strike and rank potential arbitrators from a panel and then appoint the arbitrator with the highest combined ranking.

The attributes of a good arbitrator are similar to those of a good mediator—in particular, the first two qualities of expertise and energy. From there the key attributes of an arbitrator would likely be intelligent, open-minded, and fair. Each will have these to some extent; and each party inevitably will seek to secure an arbitrator whom they perceive as more sympathetic to their perspective. Most often this comes out of some perceived industry bias, but this can also be a danger because an arbitrator with that historical alliance may go to some considerable lengths to avoid any such perceived bias.

Finally, and sometimes most elusively, a good arbitrator must have the genuine capacity to make decisions. Arbitration is about a dispute. Generally, someone will or should win and someone will or should lose. Too often arbitrators are stereotyped as being inclined toward compromise awards so as to avoid hard feelings. Arbitration providers deny the stereotype, but it is still pervasive. It is important to find arbitrators who can and will make the difficult decisions and, if required, make them early in the dispute to eliminate or truncate claims and save costs.

The arbitration procedures and discovery. As stated above, the default for most arbitration is a very limited exchange of information, which may be as little as an exchange of documents and proposed exhibits. While very efficient, most participants agree that it is too little and does not really allow for adequate preparation or for an arbitration that is efficient and reliable. Accordingly, most arbitration participants will seek to and do negotiate some limited terms of exchange and discovery. A good starting point for such a plan would include the following:

- Statement of claims and response
- Exchange of relevant project records
- Third-party discovery through document subpoenas or depositions
- Limited party depositions
- Expert identification and exchange of reports
- Limited expert depositions
- Pre-arbitration briefing and identifications of exhibits
- Pre-arbitration motions and rulings to limit arbitration hearing

The key to the foregoing is to make it limited and tailored. To do otherwise would convert the arbitration into the equivalent of private litigation, with all of the costs and waste of unfettered discovery. (See Table 4.11.)

TABLE 4.11 Comparing Arbitration and Litigation	
Arbitration	**Litigation**
Parties have input as to decision maker	Court-appointed decision maker
Expertise of decision maker	General judge or lay jury
Private	Public
Faster	Delayed
Limited parties	All parties
Limited discovery	Unlimited (and expensive) discovery
Limited procedures	Extensive procedures
Less attorney's fees/more hard costs	More attorney's fees/less hard costs

Litigation

Litigation is the default resolution venue. Absent an agreement to the contrary, this is where nearly all disputes involving architects end up. It is simply the public court system provided by local, state, and federal governments and it is subject to the rules and procedures adopted by those governments. It is "the American way." It can be slow (years), expensive, distracting, time-consuming, and public. The good news is that generally the out-of-pocket costs to access the courts can sometimes be less than arbitration, and the procedures are time tested and well known.

The "Special Master" Hybrid

In response to the competing issues with mediation, arbitration, and litigation as well as the congestion of the courts, many states and jurisdictions now frequently make use of "Special Masters" who effectively act as a hybrid of arbitrator, discovery referee, and mediator. A construction dispute is filed in the courts and the judge appoints a private Special Master to oversee the exchange of information and facilitate settlement discussions. Rather than allowing the wide-open, inefficient, and wasteful discovery of general litigation, such Special Masters will often tailor processes and orders for the exchange of information, which is similar to the efficient exchanges of most arbitrations. Armed with that insight as well as the Special Master's own expertise, settlement discussions essentially equivalent to mediation are then incorporated into the process.

Early Non-Facilitated Resolutions

All of the foregoing discussion regarding mediation, arbitration, and litigation contemplates the involvement of third parties to assist in or resolve the dispute. This is often critical to getting the parties to come together or to achieving a resolution. However, others may rightly suggest that what may be needed is merely for the participants to just talk to each other and to listen. Human nature being what it is, this does not always happen on its own. To compel such a process, many agreements incorporate such required communications into their dispute resolution process and even as a required precursor to formal processes. The AGC ConsensusDocs is such an example (see AGC ConsensusDoc 240, Section 9.2).

Ideally such a process is a rapid, phased, and escalating process with limited rounds. In the most streamlined of processes, it would start with a mandatory meeting between the project managers within five business days. If they cannot resolve the issues, it would then "escalate" to the principal level for a second discussion within five business days based on written summaries provided by the project managers to both principals. It is amazing how often such processes will resolve issues before they escalate into a genuine dispute. If that is the happy result of such a process, it is important that the resolution be memorialized in writing and signed by both "sides." If not properly motivated, however, parties may abuse required discussions to further delay the path to a formal process.

Conclusion

As a final word, there are three admonitions that will serve architects well in resolving disputes. They are:

- *Engage.* Dispute avoidance and resolution is not a passive process. It takes a proactive, pragmatic, and strategic energy from the participants and an open mind. Bring all of this energy to the issue.
- *Use your support network.* While architects can and often do seek to resolve issues alone, they need not do so, and do themselves a disservice in the process. Professional liability insurance brokers and carriers provide a ready network of support. As appropriate, architects should also engage experienced attorneys and consultants to guide and support them. Choose professionals that have seen these issues before and bring with them both experience and third-party detachment.

- *Secure closure.* Too often, issues are ignored or postponed. Even when architects think the issue has resolved or gone away, it may reappear unless there is a definitive written and communicated resolution of the issue. Documentation and distribution of agreements is critical to dispel uncertainty and recurrence.

For More Information

American Arbitration Association: www.adr.org.

Judicial Arbitration and Mediation Service: www.jamsadr.com.

"Mediation 101 for Architects," *Architectural Record* (September 2008) by B. J. Novitski.

4.8 Technology in Practice Overview

Calvin Kam, Ph.D., AIA, PE, LEED AP

When navigating technology, architects encounter an array of applications that make it difficult to objectively analyze the potential value and impact of adoption decisions. This article reviews common tools in practice, and categorizes them to support an objective evaluation of their capabilities and value to a project or a firm.

INTRODUCTION

Technology plays an integral part in our daily lives. Computers, mobile Internet access, smartphones, and a host of applications and software are familiar tools in our daily experience, and are transforming the efficiency and quality of our communication and entertainment. Mirroring the rise and proliferation of technology in daily life, technology has brought sweeping changes to architectural practice. These include not only software and hardware innovations but also the way owners define requirements and deliverables; the methods through which designers, engineers, and builders collaborate; the processes through which governments validate and approve permit submissions; and, gradually, the expectations from building occupants and the public at large.

With the rapid evolution of technology and the concurrent improvements in design and delivery processes, designers are increasingly finding themselves at a crossroads of technology adoption. Many are choosing to invest in incremental improvements to traditional processes by simply pairing conventional practice with new technology and tools; visionary innovators, however, are challenging the status quo by investing in an entirely new integration of organization, process, and technology to realize transformative benefits and revolutionize their existing business practices. This is illustrated in the integrated enterprise example presented in Figures 4.8a and b, where sustainable design was empowered by multidisciplinary building information modeling and analyses, through collaboration among owner, architect, and construction manager as an integrated enterprise. Whether or not a firm or professional is a

Dr. Calvin Kam is the founder of bimSCORE.com, the director of industry programs and a consulting faculty member at Stanford University's Center for Integrated Facility Engineering, a co-founder of GSA's National BIM Program, an active AIA volunteer, and an expert advisor to a number of international public and private owners. The author would like to acknowledge the contributions of colleagues and coworkers in developing this article, particularly Justin Oldfield, Claire Matthews, Tony Rinella, and Martin Fischer.

FIGURE 4.8 (a) Sustainable design supported by building information modeling

FIGURE 4.8 (b) An array of models and model-based analyses employed in practice today: multidisciplinary models, energy simulations, daylighting and solar analyses, cost estimation, automated model checking, and 4D simulations

technology visionary or a mainstream adopter, informed decisions must be made about the degree and maturity of technology adoption, balancing potential values and the risks of change.

This article explores an array of value propositions and technological applications for architects to consider, using seven categories of technology's contribution to enterprise and project performance:

1. Communication
2. Design Exploration & Facility Performance
3. Cost
4. Schedule
5. Safety
6. Project Delivery
7. Knowledge Management

These categories were formulated at Stanford University's Center for Integrated Facility Engineering (CIFE) as part of the BIM and Virtual Design and Construction (VDC) Scorecard Research led by the author. The Scorecard will be introduced later in this article (see sidebar), but its genesis lies in the fostering of objective decision making in technology management in the AEC industry. These seven categories are part of a larger evaluation framework and vocabulary for assessing BIM and VDC maturity in practice, established to inform and improve business decision making, and help identify specific areas for potential improvement within a firm or project. Outside of BIM and VDC, this same framework can also be applied more generally to technology management.

Definitions

Throughout this article, the discussion of technology applications and tools will focus on their value to practice. Short definitions are provided below to supplement this value-oriented discussion by describing the basic functions and characteristics of common tools and processes.

3D Modeling

3D modeling refers to the creation of a three-dimensional, virtual representation of an object's surfaces or forms. 3D surfaces are composed of a collection of 3D points that are usually connected by triangles or lines to create a polygonal mesh, or otherwise connected via curved surfaces such as non-uniform rational Bézier splines (NURBS). NURBS are defined by weighted control points, which can be modified by changing their location or weight in order to alter a surface's shape. 3D objects can be solid, representing the volume of the object, or a surface or shell, representing the outer surface or boundary of an object.

4D Modeling

By incorporating the fourth physical dimension of "time" into 3D building information models, 4D simulations of facility phasing and construction sequencing can be generated. These animations or simulations can be used to identify spatial and temporal conflicts in the construction process and analyze different sequencing scenarios.

Technology vendors may have used analogous terms such as "5D" and "6D" to describe adding cost and facility management information to a model, respectively. But unlike 4D, these misnomers are not grounded in actual physical dimensions, and are instead creating labels which are merely "information" that is embodied in the "i" of "building information modeling." Thus, readers are recommended to use terms like "BIM for cost estimating" or "BIM for facility management," rather than ungrounded terms such as 5D, 6D, or nD.

Building Information Modeling

Building information modeling (BIM) has been defined by several industry and academic organizations, but generally each of these definitions incorporates several key ideas and components. BIM is the generation of a digital representation of design intent and construction specification, including a facility's physical and functional characteristics. The resulting building information model can be used by designers, builders, and facility operators as a shared knowledge resource, condensing the information needs of many users into one central and integrated source for easy extraction and analysis throughout a facility's lifecycle.

By linking attributes to model objects, BIM can incorporate a vast array of geometric and nongeometric information into a 3D model. This provides access to a wealth of information for model-based analyses and design and construction support. Model attributes include parametric information that allows object form and behavior to be controlled through modifying object parameters, both of the object itself and the parameters of adjoining or related objects. Parametric behavior effectively embeds design intent into objects and the relationships between objects, facilitating efficient design exploration and revisions by propagating changes to all related objects. This is further enabled by parametric modeling tools, which will be described in a later section.

Computer-Aided Design

Computer-aided design (CAD) refers to the many computer systems and software applications that assist the design and drawing process. Traditionally, CAD refers to 2D drawing systems used for design and construction documentation, as well as for assisting with facilities management operations. Yet as technology has developed, CAD has come to refer to 3D drawing tools as well, described in the 3D definition above.

Clash Detection

Frequently led by BIM managers or coordinators, clash detection is the use of BIM applications to integrate discipline-specific models into an aggregated model (also known as a federated model) in order to detect undesirable geometric or spatial conflicts among various building systems and assemblies. This includes not only direct spatial conflicts but also objects that violate acceptable clearances required for construction or proper installation.

Computer Numerical Controlled

The term CNC (computer numerical controlled) machine refers to fabrication equipment that accepts and reads precise geometric information, and aids in or automates the creation of fabrication and sequencing instructions to cut, drill, mill, grind, or otherwise alter a block of material to produce an object. CNC machining involves a carefully planned fabrication process, since the CNC machine may need to perform cutting, routing, or other procedures in a certain sequence, possibly with manual work in-between. Geometric information defining an object's shape can be in many formats, including CAD files and, more recently, 3D fabrication models generated from BIMs.

Integrated Concurrent Engineering

"Integrated Concurrent Engineering (ICE) uses: a singularly rapid combination of expert designers; advanced modeling, visualization, and analysis tools; social processes; and a specialized design facility; to create preliminary designs for a complex system" (J. Chachere, J. Kunz, and R. Levitt. "Observation, Theory, and Simulation of Integrated Concurrent Engineering: Grounded Theoretical Factors That Enable Radical Project Acceleration", 2004). As the name implies, ICE relies on concurrent design tasks to reduce design duration, and integrates many project stakeholders to reduce decision and response latency and properly account for the needs and performance of a product during all phases of its lifecycle.

Virtual Design and Construction

Virtual design and construction (VDC) is the use of integrated multidisciplinary performance models of design-construction projects, including the product, organization, and processes of the design-construction-operation team, in order to support business objectives (cife.stanford.edu).

BIM and VDC Maturity

Generally speaking, most practitioners have a subjective basis upon which to rest their claim to knowledge, accomplishment, or experiences with BIM. In reality, technology and BIM come in many forms, maturity levels, and purposes; and it is necessary to be more precise in defining, differentiating, and relating the levels of technology maturity. Without a systematic method of evaluation it can be difficult to effectively navigate technology adoption decisions, making practitioners susceptible to short-sighted technology investments and advancements. Lacking explicit definitions, the stages of BIM maturity have become vague as users have different expectations and assessments of BIM adoption. The architecture industry could greatly benefit from a holistic and objective BIM evaluation framework that outlines the many purposes and business needs of BIM, their gaps, their interrelationships, and their levels of maturity.

As part of the BIM and VDC Scorecard research, technology and BIM applications have been categorized into five groups, separating their key functions and maturity. As listed, they generally progress from least mature—(1) Visualization—to most mature, (5) Automation and Optimization. These classifications are only part of the larger framework of the BIM and VDC Scorecard, which aims to provide a common vocabulary and structure for assessing BIM and VDC maturity within a firm or project. Subsequent sections will focus more on the contributions of specific tools, but the categories defined below provide a broad overview of the varying levels of technology's value to practice. Using these categories, professionals are more likely to see BIM adoption as including clash-detection or model-based simulation, and less likely to assess their level of BIM adoption as solely based on the creation or existence of 3D models.

Visualization

Tools for visualization enhance our ability to quickly view and understand a design, component, or process. These include 3D models and BIMs, which in their basest forms are mediums for design visualization, and other technologies such as Cave Automatic Virtual Environments (CAVE) that provide 3D, immersive environments for design review. Visualization tools are considered less mature applications of technology because although they may expedite and enhance design and review, they don't have a direct or significant impact on optimizing design performance or increasing design productivity.

Documentation

Documentation tools aid in generating, organizing, and presenting many forms of project documentation. This includes creating design, construction, and as-built documents from models or drawings, incorporating product or system specifications into models for facility management, and using 3D laser scanning to verify as-built or existing facility conditions. This level of technology maturity extends beyond visualization, as the model assists directly with typical documentation tasks while maintaining tolerances and precision adequate for design and construction requirements.

Model-Based Analyses

Model-based analyses refer to a wide range of simulations and studies that leverage building information models to predict facility behaviors and simulate design and construction impacts on building performance, structural integrity, project cost, energy consumption, and other facility lifecycle issues. While the term "BIM" may equally refer to virtual artifact (building information modeling), this article uses the acronym to refer to the latter. For the former, "virtual model" or "building information model" is used. Such analyses include spatial validations for program compliance, structural analyses, daylighting and energy analyses, and model-based estimation. The primary shared characteristic of these and other similar tools is the use of model geometry and attributes to drive a performance analysis.

Integrated Analyses

Integrated analyses combine multiple analyses and discipline-specific interests into a single analysis process, thereby increasing efficiency, consolidating data, and reducing redundant information exchanges. Such integration is achieved in clash detection, which resolves conflicts between different systems and trades, and integrated scope-cost-schedule applications, which combine multiple construction management tasks into one platform. These integrated platforms use 3D model geometry to drive model-based estimation and scheduling, facilitating nearly automated revisions to estimates and schedules as model quantities change throughout design and construction.

Collaborative, integrated forms of project delivery provide environments conducive to optimizing the value of these tools, as designers and builders can more effectively interact and integrate shared information during early project stages. Builders can analyze cost and schedule impacts to aid in design decisions, and designers can assist in resolving many questions and issues before construction begins. This results in fewer changes and delays, and ultimately more value and quality for the project owner.

Automation and Optimization

Software and hardware tools in this category automate typical design and construction tasks, increasing the productivity of designers, builders, and regulatory agencies.

4.9   Practicing in a Global Market

Bradford Perkins, FAIA

Introduction and Historical Overview

Virtually every aspect of the North American economy has been affected by globalization. Design professionals—architects, engineers, planners, interior designers, and more than a dozen other design disciplines—are currently engaged in countries around the world. For a few, international projects are an essential part of their practice; but for most, such work is an interesting—but secondary—part of their workload. For many, professionally challenging and profitable, but for others it has been a serious drain on their firm's human and financial resources.

All trends, however, point to international clients and projects becoming increasingly important in the future. All young architects—in particular ones who choose to work in larger firms—should expect international practice to be part of their career experience.

While the majority of the fee volume earned on projects overseas is earned by the larger firms, many smaller firms are actively engaged in international projects. Few firms are actively working in more than two or three countries at a time, and most of us who work internationally have experienced how quickly conditions can change.

An Historical Overview

When my grandfather's firm designed the original campuses of two universities in China—Shandong and Nanjing—the required travel was a commitment of months. Years later, when I was growing up in the 1950s, I remember going with my father to the airport because it was a special event; he was flying to Germany to start Perkins+Will's first international project—a school for the children of U.S. Army personnel in Frankfurt, Germany. Except for the architectural divisions of large engineering and design-build organizations, international practice was not a major part of most firms' practice at that time. Today, my children and the children of hundreds of my contemporaries find nothing extraordinary about their parents taking another flight to another foreign project.

In the 1960s, the rapid expansion of international air travel, as well as many other factors, began to change design professionals' view of international practice. A growing number of firms—such as The Architects Collaborative, which was retained to plan and design a new technical university in Baghdad—began seeking and receiving major commissions from clients other than the U.S. government and North American corporations with operations overseas.

It was the great U.S. recession, as well as the Organization of Petroleum Exporting Countries (OPEC)–related shift of wealth, in the mid-1970s that permanently changed things for the architectural profession in North America. During those years many sought international work due to a sharp drop-off in domestic commissions (particularly in such major centers as New York City) and the availability of huge new commissions in countries with limited domestic architectural resources. In that period, many firms made major commitments to international practice, and large numbers of my contemporaries got a taste for both the rewards and the strains of working overseas.

The OPEC countries became a less important part of international practice when Europe, Hong Kong, Japan, and other countries opened up to North American architects in the 1980s. In addition, North American clients, such as Olympia & York, Disney, and IBM, as well as international clients imported many firms for their expertise in those most American of building types: high-rise office buildings, shopping centers, mixed-use and corporate interiors. The draw of major projects in such glamorous places as London, Paris, and Madrid was irresistible, and many firms even committed to permanent offices overseas.

When the real estate boom of the 1980s hit the wall at the end of the decade, a large number of firms had developed the skills, organization, and need to continue to seek work overseas. Just as the European and Japanese firms finally caught up with us in our traditional areas of expertise, a new real estate boom took off in Asia.

The Asian boom—and the steep North American recession that lasted into the early 1990s—drew more firms overseas, this time to the overheated economies of Indonesia, Thailand, Korea, Taiwan, Malaysia, Singapore, and the emerging giant, China. North American firms continued to work in the Middle East and, if a firm had a local office or marketable design reputation or expertise, in Europe. A reduction in barriers to foreign design firms also opened markets in South America, Eastern Europe, and Russia.

Many of these markets crashed in the mid-1990s, just as the U.S. economy was recovering. Some firms reduced their commitments to work overseas; but the majority of the large firms, as well as many smaller firms, now regarded international practice as a basic part of their strategies for their firms' futures.

Today, North American firms are engaged in projects in dozens of countries around the world. China is the hottest market, until their own domestic design capabilities grow to meet the demand; but the stable, oil-rich countries of the Middle East and several other regions have also become big markets. Hundreds of firms now work in these as well as dozens of other countries around the world.

The *Engineering News Record* (*ENR*) annual "Top 500 Design Firms Source-book" records the steady increase in international practice. The 1965 version does not refer to international work even though many firms had started to work outside the United States and Canada. The 1975 issue, on the other hand, noted the rising importance of international work, particularly the emerging market in the Middle East. Reported projects there tripled from 1972 to 1974. Central and South America, in the 1970s, still accounted for the largest number of projects, followed by Africa and a growing number in Indonesia. By 1985 the top 500 had over $1 billion in foreign billings and almost half of that came from the Middle East. Overall, 210 of the 500 firms were working abroad—89 of which had projects in Saudi Arabia. By 1995 Europe, which had been a busy market, was now according to some "a very mature market," and Asia had become "the top attraction for international design firms."

Why Consider an International Practice

International practice sounds glamorous and fun, but is it something that your firm should consider? The cyclical nature of the North American economy was one of the factors that stimulated international practice at many firms. A growing number have used overseas work to balance periodic declines in domestic workload. This, however, is a rationale that is typically used after a firm has already committed to pursuing international work. Few firms have been able to anticipate the periodic North American recessions, and even fewer have been able to shift their practice from domestic to international on short notice.

Eight Reasons to Consider International Practice

While a balance of domestic and international work can be a valid long-term rationale for pursuing an international practice, most firms begin their involvement overseas for other reasons. Eight of the most common reasons are listed in the sidebar.

1. *A strong personal interest:* Most firms are a direct reflection of the personal interests and capabilities of the senior principals. If one of those interests is international work, it can be a valid basis for pursuing work overseas. Because of this interest, one or all of the principals may have developed a network of relationships overseas that eventually leads to project opportunities. In my own case, an undergraduate degree in Latin American studies led to a lifelong interest in the region and several of my first international projects.

2. *An influential foreign friend or business associate:* Many of us have been drawn overseas by an individual who claimed to have access to international projects, and most of us have found that this is not always true. Unfortunately, most of us have stories about con "artists" who convinced us to fund unproductive business development efforts overseas. This approach is valid often enough to be one of the major starting points for many firms' international practice. Nevertheless, learning to judge who can, and who cannot, really help you get work in a country is an essential and hard-to-learn international practice skill.

COMMON REASONS TO START WORKING INTERNATIONALLY

1. Strong personal interest
2. Influential foreign friend or business associate
3. Introductions from friends and family
4. Clients who take you overseas
5. International clients seeking expertise
6. Foreign design firms seeking expertise
7. Targets of opportunity
8. A planned effort

3. *Introductions from friends and family:* Many North American architects or their firms' employees are foreign-born and educated, or they have friends and family overseas. Many of the first projects may start with requests for assistance on or introductions to overseas opportunities from these relationships.

4. A *client who takes you international:* All firms owe a good part of their success to a few clients who give them the projects that become the foundation of the practice. This is true for international practice as well. Many firms have been taken overseas by clients (including the U.S. government) whom they met and worked for in North America.

5. *International clients seeking specific expertise:* Some firms establish a reputation that attracts international interest. In some cases it is a reputation for design innovation and creativity; but in most cases it is a demonstrated track record in a building type or service that is perceived as relevant and needed by international clients.

6. *Foreign design firms seeking expertise:* In this increasingly global world, overseas design firms also seek out U.S. and Canadian firms that have the experience needed for their projects.

7. *Targets of opportunity:* Many firms' first overseas opportunities happen by chance. A principal meets someone at a conference, a college classmate makes an introduction, and so forth, and it eventually leads to a first project.

8. A *planned effort:* Possibly the least-followed start to an international practice—but the one strongly recommended here—is a plan. Some firms plan the effort that leads to their first project.

International practice, however, should not be justified by the cliché used by some mountain climbers to justify their dangerous sport—"because it is there." Overseas work can be expensive, disruptive, and a serious distraction. Some firms have even destroyed their domestic practice by diverting too much energy and too many resources to foreign work. The Architects Collaborative (TAC) of Cambridge, Massachusetts (and my first architectural employer), is just one of the more prominent examples. TAC, once one of the country's leading firms, had many problems in its later years, but its heavy commitment in the Middle East left it overextended when Saddam Hussein's invasion of Kuwait brought a sudden halt to several large projects.

Since international practice is inherently riskier, why do it? Interest in foreign culture, a desire to travel, and other personal motivations can be valid justifications; but there are some typical business justifications as well. Among the most often cited are the following:

1. *Growth:* Some firms are committed to growth; they see it as a way to keep the firm challenging and profitable for the principals and staff. At some point in the development of these firms, a number of the better growth opportunities were outside of North America.

2. *A hedge against North American economic cycles:* An interest in international work has often been stimulated by an economic downturn in the United States. Few firms can shift from domestic to international work on short notice; but with planning, overseas work can be a

"Basically we followed Wal-Mart into Canada, Puerto Rico, and Mexico. With Mexico the work was extensive enough to warrant an office. Wal-Mart was moving into those regions, and we were doing work for them."

—Thomas F. Keeter, Vice President, Operations, BSW International, Inc. Tulsa, Oklahoma

"[The firm] had completed several first-rate, widely recognized equestrian training and boarding centers in the eastern and western United States, mainly for race and show animals. The firm loved doing the work, and I think we had become the best in the country in this niche market. But the domestic market for that kind of work had become pretty saturated, so I started researching where else in the world there were racehorses. Then I wrote lots of letters, enclosing examples of our work. We got new work very quickly in Europe and the Middle East. It was very lucrative, and [the firm] is still internationally recognized as a leader in the field."

Architect who asked to not be named.

REASONS TO HAVE AN INTERNATIONAL PRACTICE

1. Growth
2. Hedge against domestic downturns
3. New markets for specialized expertise
4. Creation of an interesting practice
5. Building credibility for future domestic opportunities
6. Scope and challenge
7. Profit
8. Mission
9. Globalization

healthy way to balance changes in domestic workload. In addition, if one takes a long view, some projections suggest that the majority of the world's design and construction activities will shift from the developed to the developing countries over the next two decades.

3. *A new market for a specialized capability:* Some of us have specialized practices, and we are always on the lookout for clients who need that expertise. SOM and KPF are just two of the firms whose commitment to high-rise office design makes it logical that they pursue opportunities overseas where many of the most challenging high-rise projects are being planned.

4. *Creation of an interesting practice:* I used to refer to our initial international projects as "yeast"—they helped make the dough (our practice) rise. This might be a clumsy analogy, but creating a challenging and interesting practice is a valid objective. Interesting practices attract better staff, media attention, and clients. As Burt Hill's (now part of STANTEC) former CEO, Peter Moriarty, noted, "The prospect of overseas travel and international work could and should be a recruiting and retention assist—especially since so many of our staff in the future will be immigrants or their children—many of whom will retain ties to their country of origin."

5. *Building credibility for future domestic opportunities:* Some firms find that they can get projects overseas that enhance their ability to get similar work back home. Because international clients are often not as focused on demonstrated expertise in a particular project type, it is often possible to get projects that can be used to convince a more focused North American client that you are qualified to design their project.

6. *The scope and challenge:* The scope and challenge of some overseas projects is unmatched domestically. For those who find the opportunity to design multimillion-square-foot, mixed-use developments, entire new university campuses, and new cities exciting, most of these opportunities are overseas.

7. *Profit:* Some international work can be extremely profitable. The 2012 AIA Survey on "The Business of Architecture" found that the surveyed firms reported that, while the cost of doing business internationally is higher, "profitability is comparable" (AIA 2006, p.57, Figure 7.6).

8. *Mission:* Some of us believe in the old-time religion—that our design expertise can change people's lives for the better. In our case, our professional commitment to the belief that the physical environment plays a part in the health and healthcare as well as the housing of the frail elderly has helped support our involvement overseas. We—and many other firms—believe we can make a meaningful difference in people's lives, and that alone justifies the effort to work overseas.

9. *Globalization:* National boundaries are becoming less relevant each year. Firms are not only working internationally but using international resources to carry out the work. Each year more firms are outsourcing drafting, rendering, and other tasks to the highly talented, low-cost resources developing in countries like India and China.

Reasons to Be Cautious

All of the above are valid reasons to pursue work outside of the United States, but these rationales should be balanced by a clear understanding of the risks. International practice is far more difficult and risky than working near home. Differences in language, privacy, trust, and accessibility all make the foreign design project quite different from the U.S. project, and all can have negative impacts that at times appear insurmountable. There can be good reasons to pursue work overseas, but one should do so with eyes

REASONS TO BE CAUTIOUS IN PURSUING WORK OVERSEAS

1. Drain on senior resources
2. Financial risk
3. Impact on domestic clients
4. Lack of legal recourse
5. Physical risk
6. Professional compromises
7. Lack of recognition
8. Challenges to integrity
9. Limited control
10. Currency and tax surprises

open to these risks. In addition, the economic, political, and social volatility of many countries means that conditions can change rapidly. Among the most frequently cited concerns, however, are the following:

1. *Drain on senior resources:* Most international practices are built on the efforts of the firms' most senior personnel. The 13th Edition of the AIA *Handbook's* chapter on practicing in a global market correctly states that "working with clients abroad will demand more time than most architects expect, so be prepared . . . People [in many foreign countries] spend more time with each other and can be quite offended by the American 'gotta go' working methods" (Williams and Meyer, AIA Handbook of Professional Practice, 13th Edition, 2001, p.106). During the peak years when I was building our practice in China, I spent as many as 100 days per year there. Not only did that leave me slightly vague about what time zone I was in, but it also meant I was often unavailable for important presentations, meetings, and decisions back home.

    One should be realistic about these issues and not commit to more than is good for both your own health and the health of your firm. As one of my friends noted, he knew he was traveling too much when on his return from a trip, he went to the movies with his family and tried to find the seatbelt after he sat down.

2. *Financial risk:* Many of the first international efforts are very expensive. It is not uncommon for firms to find they have invested hundreds of thousands of dollars before they get their first project. Even after the work begins to flow, the risk of substantial loss often equals the potential for profit and probably the greatest risk is not getting paid.

3. *Impact on domestic clients:* At first, some domestic clients are impressed and supportive. Over time, however, their tolerance erodes when you are not available for key meetings. The rapid improvement in international communications has reduced this problem, but I have had many overseas trips cut short by the need to be back in the United States to deal face to face with an important client. This is in addition to the phone calls I am expected to take at two in the morning when I am in China.

4. *Lack of legal recourse:* In most foreign countries, if a client does not pay, the only recourse is to stop work. Therefore, if your payments do not cover the work to date, the normal options—liens, legal action, etc.—are not available. Almost every firm working internationally has stories that reinforce the basic advice: "Do not let them get ahead of you!" As almost every firm will acknowledge, however, that it is easier said than done.

5. *Physical risk:* Many countries are as safe as the United States and Canada, but many are not. I stopped going to Lebanon in the 1970s, where I was working on a plan for the American University of Beirut, when the dean of the architectural school was shot and killed 12 hours after I had dinner with him in his home in East Beirut. In some countries the risks are more likely to be the food and water, but physical risk should be a consideration—particularly for people with young children.

6. *Professional compromises:* Getting a project built that is consistent with the original design intent is even harder in most overseas locations than it is in the United States. Very few countries have the commitment to quality seen in Japan and some European countries. In too many cases, the design drawings done in North America are just a general guideline.

7. *Lack of recognition:* If a tree falls in a forest and no one is there to hear it, does it make a sound? Many firms active in the Middle East during the 1970s complained that their years of effort resulted in projects no one ever saw or acknowledged.

8. *Challenges to integrity:* It is rare for any firm working overseas not to come up against some moral—and sometimes legal—choices. The Arab states' enforcement of a boycott of Israel was one such issue in the past, but the more common problem both then and now are situations where payments are expected that look too much like bribes or kickbacks. Some of these are governed by the Foreign Corrupt Practices Act, but many fall into a gray zone. For example, is a payment to an agent a payment for professional advice, or is it a payment to influence a potential client

to hire you? For those who do not want to be faced with frequent moral and ethical judgments, avoid international practice in many developing countries.

9. *Limited control:* Many international practices require the commitment of staff to overseas offices. Managing domestic branch offices is a difficult task, but managing offices in a foreign country is even harder. Firms really have to trust the managers of their foreign offices and projects because detailed oversight is usually impossible.

10. *Currency and tax surprises:* Most firms with international practices have experienced sudden currency devaluations, inability to convert local currency, and/ or unexpected taxes. All can be very unpleasant and expensive surprises.

If, on balance, these risks do not outweigh the positives, the effort to build an international practice can be a worthwhile investment in a firm's future.

PLANNING AN INTERNATIONAL PRACTICE

Many firms—mine included—stumble into their first international project. It is not uncommon to react like a dog that chases a bus and, to its surprise, catches it. Then what?

Most experienced firms agree that any international practice should be governed by a plan—even if it is developed after securing the first one or two projects. The costs and risks of international practice are too great to just play it by ear.

There is no standard format for a plan, but there are at least six basic issues that should be addressed: market analysis, goal setting, analysis of strengths and weaknesses, development of a marketing plan, management and operations, and a financial plan.

> "If you are buying, you can get away with operating in your own tongue. If you're selling, it certainly helps to speak the customer's language."
>
> —George Bain, Principal of the London Business School, *Fortune,* January 24, 1994

Market Analysis

The first questions should be:

- What makes working in this country of interest?
- Is there a need for our services? For how long?
- Are good design and quality building valued?
- Who else is there?
- What does it take to be competitive?
- Are the prevailing fee levels adequate?
- Can the fees be paid in American dollars? Are there tax issues?
- What special skills, resources, and advisors are needed?
- What have the major risks and rewards been for the firms already working in the country?
- Are there local resources that can help us get and do the work efficiently?

Often the best sources for answers to these questions are other firms with experience in the country. Some of this is shared in conferences, some comes from friends in other firms, and some advice comes from other firms in related disciplines—engineers, builders, and consultants. Useful information can also be obtained from the commercial section of the country's U.S. Embassy; a variety of book, magazine, and online sources; and the firsthand impressions gained in an exploratory trip.

Some combination of these sources is usually enough to develop preliminary answers to the questions listed above. Only firsthand experience and a constant effort to learn about working in a country will result in the answers needed to be really successful.

Setting Goals

Setting realistic goals is an important part of any plan. Some of the goals should be set in a firm's discussions of the issues raised in this chapter. Others should be more specific:

- What country or countries will be the primary focus?
- What projects or project types will be targeted?
- How much time and expense will be budgeted?
- What results (new projects, types of projects, sales revenues, profits, etc.) make the effort worthwhile?
- What results will trigger abandonment of the effort?
- Does the long-term strategy involve a commitment to a permanent presence in the country? Will it be a marketing or representative office, a local technical liaison and support office, or an office able to offer services on its own?

An Evaluation of Strengths and Weaknesses

The first step toward achieving international goals is often a realistic evaluation of the firm's strengths and weaknesses. A recognized specialty, size, strong contacts overseas, an able local partner, management depth, and spare financial resources are all important strengths. Even with some or all of these, a firm must ask itself:

- Are my services needed in the target country?
- Are we competitive with the international and local firms we will be competing with?
- Do we have the contacts, knowledge, and local relationships to operate effectively in the country?
- Can we communicate effectively?
- Can we spare the senior management time required?
- Do we have the financial resources to ante up for the initial effort?

If the answer to any of these questions is no or maybe, the plan should include proactive measures to compensate for the perceived weakness(es). The right local advisor, a specialty consultant, and/or a joint venture partner or team with complimentary skills and resources are just some of the ways to deal with a gap in the firm's capabilities.

A Marketing Plan

This part of the plan should cover all of the major issues in any marketing plan:

RANGE OF CLIENT TYPES

"An existing American client expanding its business to overseas markets. The client in this case is a known entity. With a relationship of trust between client and architect, the American architect should have an advantage in pursuing international design work for this client. Examples of client categories and international building types include:

- **Corporations**—regional or foreign headquarters, manufacturing facilities, and staff housing
- **Special Uses**—American lifestyle/expertise, retail, other services and products
- **Hospitality**—resorts, hotels, and spas
- **Entertainment**—amusement and theme parks, sports venues
- **Technology and science**—laboratories, research, health care, and environmental facilities

American and foreign joint venture developers with American specialties. These building types are quite similar to those mentioned in the American client category. This client type differs only because it is partly foreign and will require marketing efforts to be expended in more than one country. Typical building types include:

- Retail
- Entertainment and sports facilities
- Technology
- Transportation
- Hospitality
- Convention facilities

Institutional and governmental organizations. Various institutions and the U.S. government are good sources for international projects. Among those building projects are:

- Embassies and military installations, including military housing
- Trade and commodities associations
- Educational institutions, from international schools to universities

The foreign individual or company. Citizens of many foreign countries have a special interest in American design. Reasons foreign clients have for hiring American architects vary and frequently depend on the level of development in the client's own country. Many clients are searching for a "signature designer" and are less demanding of specialized knowledge for a particular building type. Others are searching for the design expertise, perhaps for program, function, or feasibility that they cannot get at home.

Highly industrialized nations, such as Canada, Australia, Japan, and those in the European Union, are likely to be interested in hiring firms with expertise in the following:

- Communications technology
- Retail shops or centers
- Corporate interiors
- Senior and special needs housing

- Sustainable design and resource management
- Universal design

Private and government clients in developing nations are typically searching for designers who can help them build a solid foundation for their country. Some projects they would commission, in addition to those listed for industrialized countries, are:

- Infrastructure—roads, utilities, commercial districts, and the companion buildings for each
- Transportation facilities
- Housing for both urban and rural settings, with special attention to energy conservation
- Medical and health care, including hospitals, clinics, and medical buildings
- Industrial facilities for the manufacture of products from raw materials and from capital resources

Foreign corporations in the United States. International work includes buildings on American soil for clients from other countries. While U.S. law, standards, and contracts will prevail, the architect will encounter foreign cultures."

—Williams Meyer 2001, 101–102.

Who are our target clients? In the 2001 edition of the AIA *Handbook* essay on Practicing in a Global Market provides an overview of the range of client types to consider (see the accompanying sidebar).

Other questions that should be covered in the marketing plan include:

1. How do we generate leads?
2. How do we qualify leads and determine whether they are worth pursuing?
3. Who is going to follow up and how?
4. What is the normal process? Is it qualifications based, is it fee based, is it a design competition, or is it some other process unique to the country? While U.S. and Canadian clients tend to follow North American practices for their projects overseas, most foreign clients do not. Many foreign clients like to see some work up front before selecting an architect. In some cases, this is in the form of legitimate competitions and (see sidebar "Guidelines for Foreign Competitions"). And, in many other cases, it is just clients looking for free work to help them make a choice. Therefore, it is essential to research how the process works in each country of interest and to determine whether the selection process is acceptable.
5. What are the prevailing fee levels? How are contracts structured to keep them adequate?
6. Who is going to make the sales presentations, and what are the important issues? Many firms work hard to establish a local network of advisors, associate firms, and friends if they intend to make a major commitment to a particular country. Other firms focus on U.S. clients and the federal government.
7. Are there government resources that can help us with introductions and marketing assistance?
8. What special skills are required to be successful? The marketing skills a firm has acquired in North America are usually relevant to international work, but there are new skills required in almost every foreign country.

"I would say most smaller or midsize firms that don't have offices overseas don't really have the luxury to have someone go out and start knocking on doors. It's better if the people who have the need identify who you are and then, once you're out there, you can make the most out of those opportunities and start to do business in that region. What has allowed us to do a fair amount of international work is that we have developed a specialty practice. And, through that, we have been able to develop a reputation, to be published, to win awards. This gives us visibility within a specialty. . . . I think there are more complex and interesting projects being done overseas, particularly in the retail industry, because many of these countries are now coming of age. Here we have a well-built-out retail infrastructure."

—James Fitzgerald, FAIA, FRCH Worldwide (Courtesy of Thomas Vonier)

GUIDELINES FOR FOREIGN COMPETITIONS

"We have some criteria for entering competitions. Our firm tries to follow three basic rules regarding competitions: The first is not to participate in any competition without an honorarium. We have experienced ranges of compensation from US $50,000 to US $100,000 and above. Although these sums do not come close to the cost of entering the competition, it is our opinion that awarding any sum of money as an honorarium shows a measure of good faith on the part of the client. Our second rule is not to join in open competitions because the risk is already high and we do not wish to enter competitions in which there is no limit to the number of entrants. The third rule is related to number two in that we do not enter invited competitions when the number of firms exceeds five; in rare instances we will enter one with a maximum of six. Anything beyond that results in confusion for the client in making a selection."

—Fred W. Clarke (Principal, Pelli Clarke Pelli Architects), "Case Study 2: Malaysia" in Southeast Asia: ArchitecturalMarkets and Practice Conference, Hong Kong and Shenzhen, China, November 5–11, 1994 (Washington, D.C.: American Institute of Architects, 1995), p. 19.

Management and Operations

This part of the plan is even more important than the plans for a domestic practice initiative. Working internationally presents new and more complex challenges. Among the most common issues to be addressed include the following:

- Who is going to manage the marketing effort, and who is going to follow through if projects are obtained?
- What will be done in the home office and what will be done in the project country?
- How will projects be done so that travel and other direct costs are minimized?
- What local resources are available to facilitate projects?
- What technology is necessary to facilitate the work?
- What steps (registrations, etc.) have to be taken to operate legally with minimum tax exposure?

It is important to remember that international work requires the commitment of senior people. What is more, when they are 6 to 12 time zones away, the senior people must be able to operate independently. Critical, also, to successful overseas projects is appropriate and skilled local support as well as a reliable technology umbilical cord to the main office.

Many international projects cannot afford large teams traveling to the site. What is more, few firms can afford to have large numbers of senior people away from the office at the same time. Both of these facts make it vital for firms managing the people who do go overseas to have the right people working within a well-thought-out operations plan.

Financial Plan

The final element of a basic plan is a developed financial structure and budget. The financial plan should include answers to such basic questions as:

- What should the budget be for exploratory trips, marketing, and (if part of the process) competitions?
- How much is the maximum that can be invested before project income starts coming in?
- What is the projected cash flow for the first 12 to 24 months of operations?
- What are the accrual-basis projections for revenues and expenses for the first 12 to 24 months? While accurate projections are always difficult to calculate, the effort will clearly bring out serious issues. Most experienced firms will reflect that their initial forays into international practice cost far more than they had expected. Moreover, if they had been working within a carefully constructed budget, they might not have invested so much.

Together, these six basic parts of a plan can set an initial framework for either a first international effort or for the first steps in a new country. Whichever it is, it is worth remembering the advice of Harold Adams, FAIA, former chairman and president of RTKL, who made the following comments at a conference on international practice:

- "Set aside enough seed money to conduct your marketing—you must have a sound financial base.
- Learn the civilities [of the country or countries you are interested in working in] and culture.
- Know what you're getting into—learn about this region before plunging in.
- Have something special to offer.
- Stay legal. [Use experienced attorneys and tax advisors and be conscious of the U.S. Foreign Corrupt Practices Act.]
- Run your own business. [Beware of agents and "free" design competitions.]
- Use partnerships and joint ventures as a way to get into the market and understand it.
- Watch the political situation closely and always have a strategy for unrest."

FIRST STEPS

So, you have decided you want to have an international practice, and you have the beginnings of the plan. Now what?

Usually, the first step is getting a strong lead or even a project. To paraphrase H. H. Richardson: "Get the job and then get the next job!" As noted earlier, most of us stumbled into our first assignments. A planned approach, however, is a more effective way to build a successful international practice.

What Country Is the Right Place to Start?

The reality is that for most firms the first foreign opportunities are unplanned; but once there is the determination to pursue work overseas, there are factors that make a country a better or worse choice. Some of the factors should be uncovered by the market analysis discussed earlier in this chapter. Other factors can be judged with less

THE U.S. GOVERNMENT'S ROLE

The founder of the American Institute of Architects' Continental Europe chapter, Thomas Vonier, FAIA, RIBA, noted that the United States provides far less support than many European and Asian governments. "The U.S. government itself is a major client for overseas work, with ample opportunities for firms of all sizes and backgrounds. The U.S. Department of State, for example, maintains that its overseas building projects are open to all qualified firms. Its Bureau of Overseas Building Operations is responsible for more than 15,000 facilities worldwide. The Bureau adheres to a qualifications-based selection process for hiring design professionals, but many State Department projects require U.S. citizenship for all personnel who work on them, as well as eligibility for security clearances.

Military construction programs of the U.S. Army Corps of Engineers and the Naval Facilities Engineering Command often entail procuring architectural services, usually in accordance with qualifications-based selection processes. Most military projects require that potential awardees register in the Department of Defense Central Contractor Registration database."

—(Courtesy of Thomas Vonier)

formal analysis. Some of the other factors to consider include whether you want to spend time in the particular country, whether there is a realistic chance of getting work in the country, and whether you have a guide.

- *Do you want to spend time in the country?* I usually rationalized my initial trips to a new country as quasi vacations if the long-term prospects for work did not pan out. Recognizing that I only had the time to focus on one country, I chose China as our initial target market after preliminary trips and small assignments in a dozen other countries. My enjoyment of China and the fact that the prospect of several dozen trips in the future was something to look forward to were major motivators for my decision to work there.

- *Do you have a realistic chance of getting work?* Many of us would like to focus on England, France, or Italy; but for a firm to break into these markets, they probably should have started in the 1980s, when Europe was looking for North American experience. When reviewing his own firm's international opportunities, one CEO of a large architecture and engineering firm noted that "the economy of Western Europe is stagnant, population growth is negative, and the area is already overserved by existing well-established firms." Other regions and countries were more open to North American firms, including the more stable oil-rich countries in the Middle East, and the rapidly developing countries in Asia.

In the 1970s, the key question was "Does the country have oil?" Today, one only has to listen to the experience of other firms with international practices. If a country is open to firms with your profile of capabilities, other design professionals are often willing to advise you.

As I noted in a conference early in the profession's expansion into international practice: "A country's dollar volume of construction, taken by itself, is not the only major criterion for deciding whether or not there are opportunities there. One of the major criteria is strong need for American services, even though there may be a relatively smaller dollar volume." Moreover, the fact that there are many projects does not always mean that the market is open to North American design firms. Thomas Vonier explains:

It is not difficult to determine that a given country has launched a massive hospital or school building program, but it may not be quite as easy to determine whether foreign firms are welcome, merely tolerated, or plainly banned. If a U.S. firm's strength lies in designing advanced pharmaceutical laboratories, it may be natural and a matter of relative ease to assess where else in the world such facilities are planned. What is not always clear is how well qualified local firms are to handle such work and how inclined they may be to partner with U.S. firms. Major national investments in infrastructure projects—for tourism and leisure facilities or public transportation systems—often carry with them major opportunities for foreign participation, particularly if they involve international financial support and funding.

- *Do you have a guide?* Few firms enter a country without a guide. In some cases, the guide is a native of the country who is a principal or staff member of the firm and who has family or friends available there to help. In other cases, an agent is hired for this specific purpose; in still others, the guide is a professional advisor, joint-venture partner, or other experienced professional.

In booming markets there is no shortage of people claiming to have the ability to get you work. Most of us who have been working overseas for some time have been conned by one or more of these advisors. In my case, I remember one who had used up his retainer and travel advance before he ever left New York. When he came for a second installment, we cut our losses. Learning to distinguish the frauds from those who can really help is an acquired skill. In my experience, to glean useful information about a guide's potential, the following evaluative questions are helpful:

- Is the prospective guide from the city, region, or country that is the primary target? In China, for example, you do not usually retain an advisor from Taiwan or Singapore to help seek work in Shanghai or Beijing.
- Is the prospective guide from a well-connected family, and did he or she attend the right schools?
- Does the guide speak and write the language fluently?
- Is he or she willing to make some or most of his or her compensation contingent on success?
- Do you like and trust this person? Remember, you are likely to be spending a lot of time together sharing the stresses of building an international practice.

How to Start

Most of us start with one or more exploratory trips. These trips may or may not be paid for by some small introductory assignments. The primary objective, however, is to flesh out a plan and to obtain an understanding of the basics of finding and doing work in the country. Among the issues worth studying are the following:

1. Is there a market for our services, and how long will it last?
2. Are there enough good reasons to make the effort?
3. What are the likely pitfalls, and how can they be avoided?
4. What skills and capabilities are essential for success?
5. What peer firms are operating there now?
6. Who are the clients and what services and building-type expertise are most in demand?
7. What is the process for getting work?
8. How does one deal with the language and communication issues?
9. What are the licensing and other legal requirements?
10. Are the prevailing fee levels, payment terms, and tax structures such that it is possible to make a profit?
11. What are the major contract-negotiation issues?
12. Are there local resources—associate firms, engineers, etc.—that can help?
13. What are the design traditions and client design preferences?

"[We] had several clients domestically interested in expanding their building programs to other countries. Initially, we partnered with various professionals in the countries our clients wanted to expand into. We learned as much about the building process in each country as possible through visiting construction sites and meetings in respective offices. Our initial approach was to partner with the professionals to provide our client with the best possible mix of our expertise with their building program, combined with the host country's professional expertise with that country's building process."

—Michael D. Gallagher, BSW International, Inc., Tulsa, Oklahoma

"I was the lead architect who was interested in Japanese culture and convinced my partners to get involved after I was convinced we could be successful. My experience has been very rewarding. Not only have I developed wonderful relationships in Japan, but I have also diversified company investments without compromising our core services. Through personal interest in Japan, hosting exchange students, and volunteering with Sister Cities International, we heard about a technology-based housing system in Japan and invited the company to visit us in Minnesota. They made the visit and in turn invited us to Japan. After many months of dialogue, we were each convinced we could work together toward the mutual goal of transferring their technology to the U.S. and adapting this building system to U.S. codes and standards in exchange for cash and equity. Understanding cultural differences and communication are key factors. If I had not spent several years reading about Japanese culture and business, as well as studying the language, I might have given up after the first couple of trips without a contract."

—James Brew, President, LHB Corporation, Duluth, Minnesota

14. What code and regulatory issues are important, and how do you navigate through them?
15. What is the typical scope of services, and how do projects get done?
16. What are the typical project schedules?
17. What are the construction capabilities, normal construction practices, and sources of construction materials?
18. Is the country safe to work in?
19. What are the most common problems facing design professionals working in the country?
20. What are the most important pieces of advice you need to get during this exploratory phase?

Getting Those First Projects

For some firms the first projects come quickly, but for many others they only come after extensive groundwork. In either case, the following normal steps in the marketing process apply.

- *Lay the groundwork:* Many firms will prepare marketing materials in the appropriate language, seek lecture or teaching assignments in the country, get their work published in magazines that will make good third-party references for the firm, and take other preparatory steps.
- *Generate leads:* The first trips—as well as home-office contacts—should begin creating a network that will help identify leads for potential projects. Over time—as this network of friends, clients, consultants, and others expands—it will become relatively easy to have more leads than one can reasonably follow. In some countries, a network can be helped with the aid of an agent, representative, or broker who—for a fee or a percentage—will help find work.
- *Qualify leads:* Culling the leads worth pursuing is important due to the cost of pursuing a project overseas, particularly in those countries where competitions are a common method for architect selection. This is where a good agent can find out if the firm "is being invited to compete or invited to win."
- *Courting:* As will be noted again later, the courting stage, where leads are converted into solid opportunities, is particularly important in many foreign countries. As Williams and Meyer note in the 13th edition of the AIA *Handbook:* "The biggest challenge designers face . . . is understanding their clients . . . [and] getting close to the client—the real decision maker—is far more complicated than with domestic projects." Many international clients are looking for a personal connection before they hire a firm. My first major project in China materialized after several dinners and meetings with leaders from the Chinese Academy of Sciences. These had been arranged by a Chinese friend and were helped by the presence of my brother, who was then head of the Asia Center at Harvard. Once they were comfortable with me, we were invited to a paid competition for a new information technology campus, which we subsequently won. That project led to a close personal and professional relationship with the leadership that has resulted in a steady stream of projects.
- *Presentation:* As in North America, many projects are won before the final presentation. But the quality of the presentation is critical in many foreign settings. Particularly in less sophisticated areas, a superior presentation can beat superior substance.
- *Closing:* This is again a time when good agents should earn their keep. This is also where personal relationships matter as well. In many countries, architect selection procedures are often very informal and easily influenced by outside forces. A good agent and/or a strong personal connection can insulate the firm from these forces and reinforce the strength of your firm's proposal.

No two firms get their first jobs in the same way. While each firm usually has to deal in some way with the steps discussed here, there is a lot to be learned from the stories of other firms. Talking with peer firms with relevant experience is usually very helpful.

"The most effective method we have found to identify leads for foreign projects is through our strategic partners—local firms with whom we have established relationships. Currently, we have associations throughout the Middle East and in Korea, Vietnam, Cambodia, Italy, and the United Kingdom. In any given month I receive at least a couple of notices of design competitions from local firms looking for an American design partner. We are extremely selective with design competitions—we rarely participate in open, unpaid competitions, and we look very hard before agreeing to proceed with limited, invited ones. Competitions can be a viable way to break into international work, however, provided one is willing to risk making the investment. I have helped teams win several international design competitions in the past; but overall I feel they are a very inefficient and costly way of developing business."

—James M. Wright, AIA, PageSoutherlandPage, Washington, D.C. (Courtesy of Thomas Vonier)

Contract Issues

Once a first project is secured, the next challenge is to negotiate a contract that minimizes the major risks inherent in many overseas projects. The AIA Documents Committee is developing a set of agreements; but helpful as these will be, they are just the starting point for a full contractual agreement. Among the issues to consider are the following:

- *Does the client have the financing and is the project viable?* This is far harder to determine in most foreign countries than it is in North America.
- *What is the client's reputation?* This, too, can be hard to check. But research through the credit agencies, other firms who have worked with the client, the U.S. Department of Commerce Foreign Commercial Service, and other sources can be helpful.
- *Does the client have assets or operations in the United States or Canada?* If so, it strengthens the firm's legal options if things go wrong. Trying to use legal remedies against a foreign entity in the entity's own country is often fruitless.
- *How will you be sure to get paid?* Four potential contract provisions can help:
  - An irrevocable letter of credit can be conditioned upon the shipment of documents or an agreement with the client that your statement of project completion is acceptable evidence to the bank.
  - An escrow account can be set up that will be drawn from upon evidence of completion of a phase or task.
  - A retainer can be credited to the final invoice that is sufficient to cover all the work being done between regular payments.
  - A fixed schedule of monthly payments for a specified amount can be established, not necessarily related to the work performed.
- *How will you avoid scope creep?* The rest of the world is not as litigation-prone as the United States. Of course, international clients are aware of how hard it is for U.S. firms to enforce payment provisions offshore and will often take advantage of the situation by requesting more and more work as a basis for payment. The greatest risk in overseas work is in not getting paid. Therefore, clear contracts, payment schedules that do not let the client get too far ahead, and strong firm project management are the best way to avoid this problem.
- *How do you manage client expectations?* Foreign clients—even more than domestic ones—rarely understand what we do and don't do; what is the proper sequence and scope appropriate for each phase (design development, for example, is often considered unnecessary by foreign clients); how much work the project requires; and many other issues that can be the difference between a successful, profitable project and an unhappy experience for all parties.
- *How do you get the client to accept younger staff when they think they are retaining the firm's senior leaders?* Many foreign clients are seeking gray hair and experience, which can make acceptance of a typical project team an issue.

- *How do you convince the client that it is important to retain experienced international consulting engineers and/or specialty consultants to create the team needed?* Many overseas clients, in particular in countries with lots of engineers, are reluctant to pay a premium for these services. As in North America, however, inexperienced or inadequate consultant support can be the cause of major problems. Thus, it is usually important to insist on the right team.

- *How do you divide the work with the local design team required on most overseas projects?* It is often appropriate to create an elaborate responsibility matrix and then assign lead and support roles for the international and local teams to the list of tasks to be completed. Three-party contracts with detailed descriptions of each party's responsibilities are often appropriate.

- *How do you make sure you are compensated for extra services?* Many foreign clients do not (or choose not to) understand the concept of additional services. Thus, it is often necessary to define in greater detail when something is outside the scope of responsibilities or is an additional expense—more so than in a typical U.S. contract. This means contracts may need to detail the number of trips covered in the basic fee (and the cost of additional trips beyond that) as well as detail the hourly cost for rework due to inadequate performance of the local consultant team, and so forth.

- *How do you make sure that out-of-pocket expenses are fully reimbursed?* Many overseas clients—particularly in China and some other Asian markets—expect travel and other out-of-pocket costs (renderings, models, printing, etc.) to be built into the fee. This can be a major issue, since these costs are hard to estimate at the beginning of a project and often require a great deal of effort to manage. Learning to use local resources in the country can help control some of these costs.

- *How do you make sure that key areas of risk and professional liability are insured?* There is a need to be careful to make sure contracts do not have provisions that are uninsurable or that void coverage. Review of draft contracts with the firm's insurance advisor is often appropriate.

CONTRACT PROVISIONS

Use your contract to minimize the risk of not being paid. Then, be prepared to stand by the provisions it contains to enforce your rights.

- Confirm that all payments are net of taxes. Pass on the taxes to the client through "net of taxes" contract provisions.
- State explicitly the currency to be paid. Payment in U.S. dollars is always the best. If payment is in a foreign currency, address the issue of currency fluctuations. Architects should not be in the business of currency speculation. Consider purchasing a currency insurance policy if payment in dollars is not an option.
- Include "pay when paid" provisions in subcontractor and joint venture agreements.
- Assert the right to stop work in case of nonpayment. Contract for the right to withhold deliverables.
- Include ownership of documents and copyright provisions (which is often a sticking point).
- Address dispute resolution. International arbitration is increasingly popular and is institutionalized through the American Arbitration Association.

- Specify the right to bill electronically, which can eliminate one to two weeks on accounts receivable.
- Send two invoices, one for services and one for reimbursable expenses, so that questions about expenses will not delay payment of your fees.
- Specify what materials and services are expected from the client before architectural services can commence.
- Identify the client representative who is authorized to approve your work and payment.
- Provide suspension and termination procedures. Overseas projects have a tendency to be delayed or end abruptly. When they cease, the right to stop work and be paid is critical.
- Define reimbursable expenses explicitly. Many overseas clients are not familiar with the concept and many expect these expenses to be included in the "fee."
- Request a retainer to determine a client's intent and protect you from delayed payment.
- Be aware that foreign capital can be frozen or prohibited from leaving the country.

—Williams and Meyer, 2001, *Handbook of Professional Practice*, p. 104

- The level of completeness of each service and product should be specifically described and mutually agreed upon to avoid undefined or misunderstood deliverables.
- The true purpose of a project can be different from how it appears to the U.S. architect.
- Compensation amounts and methods are different. Foreign clients are often unfamiliar with the value of the architectural service being provided. Consequently, they are unwilling or unable to afford the level of service required for the project's success.
- The expectation of "winning" is high in many cultures, and for some foreign clients the ends justify the means.

- Negotiation tactics vary widely.
- Clients often expect "loss leaders." Thorough, uncompensated design solutions are frequently required before the architect or development/construction teams are selected.
- Clients sometimes expect the American architect to bring the money or the tenant to the project.
- Many foreign clients expect the architect to be a true generalist and provide services that in America are specialized or unrelated.

—Williams and Meyer 2001, *Handbook of Professional Practice*, p. 105.

- *How do you resolve disputes?* As noted earlier, most foreign clients are less likely to resort to lawyers. There are international arbitration panels available in some countries as well as other established approaches. In any event, it is an important subject to research and define at the outset.
- *How do you get out of a bad project?* Sometimes it is best to just walk away, but most contracts make that difficult. Therefore, termination provisions are as important for the design team as they are for the client.

Once all of these—and the many other technical and administrative issues unique to the contract for each project—are resolved, it is time to start the project.

Source: *International Practice for Architects*, 1st Edition, Brad Perkins, Author, John Wiley & Sons, Inc.: 2007

4.10 Potential Cause of Failure

Bradford Perkins, FAIA, and Peter Piven, FAIA

Most books and articles on architectural design focus on how design firms have risen from obscurity to prominence. Few address the equally instructive, if less popular, subject of why some firms fail. There are, of course, many types of failure: failure to achieve the principals' major objectives; failure to achieve a firm's full potential; failure in the form of complete organizational collapse; or just going broke. Fortunately, it is possible to trace the origins of most failures to one or more flaws in the leadership of a firm, and such an investigation can teach founders of new firms a lot about what to avoid and how.

Some flaws are noble, worthy of a Greek tragedy, but most are petty or avoidable. Both the noble and the petty are discussed in the following sections with examples of the common pitfalls presented as brief case studies.

We have distilled the most common causes of firm failure to a list of 10, introduced in the following list, then explored one by one in the following sections.

NOTE

All the case studies presented in this chapter are composites of real situations, but sufficiently disguised to be unrecognizable.

1. *Halley's Comet:* Believing a brief run of luck means you can coast.
2. *The Buggy Whip:* Ignoring the cycles inherent in most specialties.

3. *The Grass Is Always Greener:* Ignoring core clients and markets to pursue other practice areas.
4. *Cannon Fodder:* Treating key people as expendable.
5. *The Captainless Ship:* Failing to replace a strong leader when he or she retires.
6. *Peter Principle by Primogeniture:* Bringing unqualified relations into the firm's leadership.
7. *Swollen Heads and Feet of Clay:* Relying too much on strengths while ignoring weaknesses.
8. *Financial Management According to the Russian Politburo:* Managing finances incompetently.
9. *Losing Sight of the Big Picture:* Failing to market when busy.
10. *Sometimes the Batteries Run Low:* Running out of energy.

Case 1: Halley's Comet

Probably the most commonly seen form of failure is the firm that has a brief run of luck and then disappears.

Firm A spent 10 years building a reputation for consistent quality on a series of small commissions. The three principals all worked directly on each project and developed a growing list of happy former clients. Then they obtained a "dream" commission, a major project for a client willing to support an innovative design solution. The architects made the most of the job, and following favorable publicity, rapidly became a "hot" firm. As more big projects came their way, the office grew from 10 to 60 people in two years. That's when the problems began.

Too soon, the principals began believing their own publicity and playing the role of "stars." At the same time, they spread themselves too thin—a problem aggravated by their loss of interest in the details of new projects. They spent more and more time enjoying the fruits of their prosperity. Quality became inconsistent and client loyalty weakened. No organized business development program was created. As a result, when a recession hit, their work dried up, they shrank quickly back to a 10-person firm, and eventually faded into obscurity.

Case 2: The Buggy Whip

The design professions are competitive, cyclical businesses. This means a firm can never rest on its laurels, and must be in a position to respond to changes in the market.

Firm B built a strong practice in educational and other public building types in the 1960s and 1970s. The principals were confident their prosperity would continue and so regularly spent the firm's profits. Unfortunately, school populations began to decline, the economy slumped, and local tax revolts applied the coup de grace to their traditional markets by the 1980s. The firm found itself without work and without the financial strength to rebuild in another area of practice.

Case 3: The Grass Is Always Greener

Unlike Firm B, many firms are never satisfied with their current areas of practice. This, too, can lead to problems.

Firm C acquired a strong reputation for planning studies, which occasionally led to architectural commissions. Even though the firm's finished buildings never matched the quality of their predesign studies, the principals wanted to be architects, not planners, so they ignored their study work and put their efforts into getting design commissions. The basis of their reputation soon shifted from excellent planning to mediocre architecture. With this shift came the beginning of their decline.

Case 4: Cannon Fodder

It is good advice to anyone, who thinks him- or herself irreplaceable, to observe what happens when he or she withdraws his or her finger from a bucket of water. Unfortunately, this lesson has often been translated into the belief that everyone is replaceable, which, in the short term, is not necessarily true.

Firm D prospered for years under the leadership of a man who made it clear that he believed the "everyone is replaceable" axiom. Over time, the firm's reputation became more dependent on the principals who were carrying out the projects (as is generally the case today), but the founder never recognized their growing contributions or shared the fruits of the firm's success. Then a crisis came, and the key principals, who felt no loyalty to the top man, left the firm, taking their clients with them.

Case 5: The Captainless Ship

A variant on the loss of key personnel is the forcing out or failure to replace the person or persons who built the firm.

Firm E's younger partners breathed a sigh of relief when their concerted efforts finally compelled the domineering founding principal to retire. In reaction to his autocratic approach, they decided to manage by committee. All of the committee members were "inside" men who frowned on the founder's egomaniacal and wasteful interest in speeches, parties, travel, and other "nonproductive" efforts. Eventually, though, the committee found that, in the name of prudent management, they had, essentially, "lobotomized" the firm. Devoid of its personality, and constipated in its decision making, the office muddled its way into mediocrity.

Case 6: Peter Principle by Primogeniture

Like many parents, design professionals often want to pass on what they build to their children. The desire to hand down the leadership of a firm is understandable, but often ends up being a disservice to both the child and the parent-architect's colleagues who helped create the legacy.

Firm F—compelled by the insistence of its founder—promoted the founder's son to fill his father's place upon retirement. The merit of this promotion was not convincing to either clients or key staff, who soon departed.

Case 7: Swollen Heads and Feet of Clay

It is far truer to say that, "no one person is a complete design professional" than "no one is irreplaceable."

Firm G, for example, was built upon the sales skills of its principals. Unfortunately, its other skills—in design, production, and the many other capabilities necessary to serve a client properly—were not comparable. Ultimately, the principals ran out of new clientele.

Firm H, in contrast, built its reputation on design expertise, but like Firm G, never balanced its forte with other requisite skills. Tough competition and bad references cut short their moment of success.

Achieving balance is a challenge for most design firms, often because of big egos and a lack of respect for the full range of skills required to achieve excellence. Too many firms have been led by individuals who could not tolerate equals, or, when they could, had too little respect for skills other than their own to tolerate full partners with balancing capabilities.

Case 8: Financial Management According to the Russian Politburo

The financial rewards of the design professions are rarely comparable to those of other major professions and businesses. Regrettably, many design professionals do not recognize this fact.

Firm J grew and prospered, and its principals' tendency to spend grew with it. Personnel were hired in advance of need, offices were outfitted in a manner consistent with the firm's design tastes, and personal spending by the principals centered on slow whiskey and fast cars. This expensive lifestyle was financed with borrowed money and a failure to pay consultants money they were owed. In time, Firm J's credit ran out, it was nearly forced into bankruptcy, and it suffered a general dissolution of its reputation and practice.

Case 9: Losing Sight of the Big Picture

It is very easy to lose sight of long-term issues when working hard to meet current client deadlines. It should be remembered, however, that successful firms are always hungry, and they never forget that continuous marketing is a constant priority.

Firm K built a busy practice, whose principals focused all their energies on their current workload, even to the point of ignoring or turning down potential new commissions. When the projects all moved into construction and the fee volume dropped precipitously, a financial crisis ensued. The firm could not cut costs fast enough to respond to the drop in revenue and no new work had been lined up to fill the gap. It took the principals 18 months to rebuild, but the firm was so financially and psychologically weakened that it never recovered its earlier success.

Case 10: Sometimes the Batteries Run Low

Building and maintaining a successful practice requires consistent effort. It never gets easier, and the more ambitious you are, the harder it is. But even successful design professionals can burn out. After a period of success, they begin to focus on other priorities or just run out of energy.

Firm L was dominant in its county of practice. A large percentage of the major corporate, institutional, and private clients automatically considered them when they had a project. The firm was led by one principal, who was a talented designer and an effective leader; the other principals all had strong complementary capabilities but none the same as those of the senior partner. When the senior partner began to phase down and take more time off away from the office, no one could fill the void. Soon, the firm earned the reputation of being in decline, with a leader soon to retire. The firm survived only by being absorbed into another firm that could provide the absent leadership.

Lessons from Case Studies of Failure

A full list of lessons implicit in the case studies just described would require its own book, but the more important ones and their management implications can be summarized as follows:

- **Make a consistent effort to achieve excellence in all areas.** For a firm to achieve and maintain success, it must recognize that it has to be skilled at both the professional and the business aspects of architecture. In the simplest terms, a firm has to sell well, provide consistently good service on the projects it sells, and manage both its projects and its office in a way that generates a profit. There is no significant margin for error in today's competitive, demanding-client, low-profit-margin world.

- **Conduct a realistic self-appraisal.** To manage the basics well, the firm should have a plan that establishes goals, realistically assesses its own strengths and weaknesses, and then outlines logical steps to build on these strengths and overcome the weaknesses in the pursuit of the goals. This requires an *honest* self-appraisal—which is not easy, because too many design professionals begin to believe their own press releases.

- **Steadily follow a well-planned business development program.** Successful business development is usually directly related to a realistic plan, a strong reputation in a good market or markets, and ongoing efforts to develop new leads and sales. It is important to remember that once a strong reputation or momentum has been achieved, it must be maintained. Few firms are ever given a second chance. In addition, as illustrated in Case 3, a firm should not abandon an area of strength or even dilute its impact. As already noted, any expansion into new areas must be carefully governed and monitored by a realistic plan to eliminate weaknesses while building on existing strengths.

- **Be sensitive to changes in the marketplace.** A realistic plan and effective business development program must also recognize that the market is dynamic, not static. No firm can depend on one building type or a long-standing reputation to carry it into the future. Today, the pace of change in all things is accelerating, and firms must change, too, if they are to stay viable.

- **Structure an organization that can carry out the work.** The firm's organization must be structured to respond to the new work produced by business development. This means not only having the full range of technical skills required to provide excellent service, but also focusing these skills on the right problems. In Case 1, for example, the firm did not build a structure—one with new partners or a strong middle management—capable of accommodating the additional load created by growth. The one- or two-leader firm is particularly vulnerable today as clients become increasingly demanding of personal commitment and error-free service.

- **Attract and hold key staff.** Any firm seeking to grow must create a structure that attracts and holds the best available person in every key position. The principals of the typical architectural firm should take a lesson from leading attorneys, accountants, advertising agencies, investment bankers, and other firms, where there is room for more than one "star"; and in the best of them, each major position is held by a specialist whose reward and status are based more on his or her contributions to the firm's success than on an arbitrary professional caste system.

Principals should not be afraid to take on additional partners, officers, or principals. As service firms in other professions have repeatedly shown, the proper choice of additional partners to fill leadership openings can expand both the financial "pie" and the quality of the service. A partner in any category who pulls his or her weight costs nothing.

Partnerships and other principal ties are primarily business relationships—ideally, but not necessarily—strengthened by personal ties of friendship and respect. Because they are business relationships, they can be severed with far more ease than most people assume. But these relationships should be made—or severed—primarily for business, not personal, reasons. When personal jealousies, family loyalty, or other emotional issues interfere in such decisions, the results rarely benefit anyone. One of the primary roles of a firm's leaders must be to minimize the inevitable petty personal differences that can sow the seeds of the firm's destruction.

- **Plan carefully for changes in senior leadership.** Probably the most dangerous period for any firm occurs during the transition of leadership from the founder(s) to the next generation, or, as is more common in a young firm, the departure of a partner. It is at this point, more than at any other, that a realistic plan and assessment of strengths and weaknesses must be made. The holes left by the departing leaders, as well as the actions necessary to fill them, should be identified.

- **Apply the "why not the best" principle**. The "why not the best" principle should be applied when hiring to fill all positions. Failure to clear out dead wood is almost as serious as neglecting to keep staff levels closely related to the volume of work available. Given the limited fees received by most design professionals, it is imperative that funds be spent on productive personnel. This does not mean, however, to follow a hire-and-fire philosophy, as then it will be impossible to form the bonds of loyalty and respect among principals and staff that are essential to the building and maintenance of a productive, stable staff of quality personnel. Always remember that the best staff have the most options and, without good reasons to stay in their present position, will be the first to exercise those options.

- **Manage personnel costs carefully.** Because salaries constitute almost two-thirds of most design firms' expenses, and are the most easily adjustable segment, they must be the focus of financial control. Most firms—with or without such controls—make money during periods of rapid growth because personnel and other expenses usually do not catch up with volume. With controls applied to personnel, however, the other easy time to make money is when month-to-month volume remains steady and relatively little effort is required to keep all technical personnel billable. Unfortunately, few firms ever enjoy such conditions. Most experience wild swings in volume and need to expend a growing percentage of their resources on securing new work. These conditions, combined with narrow profit margins, leave no room for error or waste.

- **Recognize the importance of effective, conservative financial management.** Above all, a firm must make money to grow and prosper. To make a profit, the primary effort must always be directed at balancing volume and expenses. This requires coordination of business development, project scheduling, and staffing. The closer a firm comes to achieving a consistent balance, the more likely it is to make a profit. Financial management must, of necessity, be conservative. Owing to the cyclical nature of the building industry, it is essential that a firm accumulate cash reserves to weather the inevitable crises. There is no room for any personal behavior that wastes the firm's (and its creditors') resources on personal expenses. Too many people are hurt by such actions. Effective financial management is impossible without formal controls on volume, expenses, and cash flow.

Final Points

Of course, even the strictest adherence to all of the precepts given here cannot guarantee that a firm will achieve success or avoid failure. After all, management is not the raison d'être of a design firm. Unfortunately, as the case studies illustrate, a weakness in any management area can cause failure, and only superior professional capability can ensure success.

Source: *Architect's Essentials of Starting, Assessing, and Transitioning a Design Firm*, Bradford Perkins (Author), Peter Piven (Co-Author), John Wiley & Sons, Inc.: 2008

PART 3
THE PROJECT

Introduction

Bradford Perkins, FAIA

Two of an architect's primary roles are to act as the client's advisor and to manage a complex multiyear process. This process often begins with studies that assess project scope, define project feasibility, analyze potential sites, establish an overall schedule for the tasks that must be accomplished in order to complete the project, and provide the information that the client needs to decide to proceed. Once a project proceeds, the architect is often responsible for managing a large team that must define the project, develop an appropriate design that is within the client's budget, navigate an increasingly complex public approval process, and administer an ever more complex construction phase. For many projects, this entire process takes more than five years and many larger projects can take a decade or more to complete.

This part of the *Handbook* discusses some of the most common tasks and more important issues encountered by an architect during the course of this multiyear process. Virtually all projects face unique challenges, but there is an overall process that most projects follow. Understanding this overall process, the key players, the major decision points, and how to deal with some of the most common challenges is a basic part of an architect's services to his or her client.

This part of the Handbook divides the project process into six sections: Project Definition, Common Project Issues, Project Development, Project Delivery, Project Management, and Building Codes, Standards, and Regulations. These six sections are not a comprehensive introduction to all of the issues involved in completing an architectural assignment, but each part provides an introduction to some of the most common and important issues.

PROJECT DEFINITION

Chapters 5 covers some of the important tasks involved in starting a project: defining the services to be provided and negotiating an appropriate fee for the required services.

COMMON PROJECT ISSUES

Chapter 6 covers four issues that are increasingly important in many architectural projects: programming, evidence-based design, sustainable design, and environmentally preferable product selection.

PROJECT DEVELOPMENT

Chapter 7 discusses the traditional phases of an architect's basic services: the two design phases (schematic design and design development), construction documentation and specifications, assistance in bidding and negotiation, construction administration, and project closeouts and postconstruction services.

PROJECT DELIVERY

Chapter 8 covers the major alternative methods for translating an architect's design into a completed project.

PROJECT MANAGEMENT

Chapter 9 discusses the central role of the architect in the management of a project's development and delivery. This part also includes introductions to project scheduling, project construction cost management, and project control systems and methods.

BUILDING CODES, STANDARDS, AND REGULATIONS

Finally, Chapter 10 discusses the major role that building codes and other public regulations play in the development and delivery of almost all projects.

The understanding and mastery of all these topics are essential skill sets for most architects. Architects are expected to know the entire process from project definition and development through the increasingly complex public approval and construction phases. Larger firms may have specialists who only focus on one part of the entire process, but the project manager and principal architect typically need to have a command of the entire process. In a smaller firm, the lead project architect needs to be able to oversee the entire process.

CHAPTER 5

Project Definition

5.1 Life of a Project

Bradford Perkins, FAIA

THE TYPICAL PLANNING, DESIGN, AND IMPLEMENTATION PROCESS

Almost no two projects are identical and each has unique issues that impact the type of team required, the challenges, the schedule, and other major variables. Therefore, this discussion can only describe a representative process that touches on the 12 major steps in the typical life of a project:

1. The idea
2. Strategic planning
3. Feasibility analysis and scoping of market need and project feasibility
4. Selection and organization of the project team
5. Programming and predesign work (defining the scope of the proposed facility)
6. Schematic design
7. Obtaining client and public approvals and/or financing/premarketing and sales
8. Design development
9. Construction documentation
10. Selection of the construction and furniture, furnishings, and equipment (FF&E) teams
11. Construction and FF&E installation
12. Occupancy and project closeout

We discuss here the design team's task for each of these steps. A typical schedule for a new public school illustrates the process in Figure 5.1.

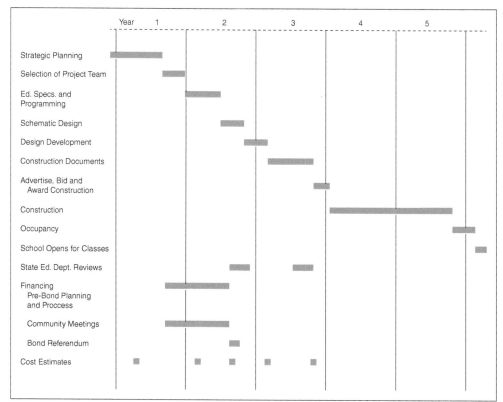

FIGURE 5.1 **Typical schedule for the planning, design, and implementation of a large, new school building. From** *Building Type Basics for Elementary and Secondary Schools,* **Second Edition.**

The Idea

The owner or client has an idea that a new building or a renovation/expansion of an existing building is needed. This could be as small as adding a new kitchen and family room to an existing house or as large as building a high-rise, mixed-use development on a vacant property.

Strategic Planning
(Typical time required: Two or four months)

Many projects are done within existing facilities or on existing campuses and even new buildings and vacant sites need to be analyzed before the decision to proceed. Therefore, most projects should be defined within the framework of a long-range plan. Even in new facilities, the initial design has to assume future growth and change.

An effective strategic plan will respond to more than site and facility issues; it will account for the way changes in technology, demography, and funding will impact the future need for and use of the facility.

Typically, design professionals evaluate existing conditions. If the project is a renovation of or addition to an existing building, this review might include studies of the condition of the existing mechanical/electrical/plumbing and fire protection systems, interior finishes, operational issues, code compliance, site conditions and constraints, and the ability of facilities to support their owner's mission. If it is a new building the initial studies might include the existing zoning and land use controls; any difficult site conditions such as steep slopes, sensitive environmental issues, potential flooding and/ or challenging geotechnical issues; solar orientation; vehicular access; adequacy of utilities, and so forth. Once these issues and any problems are defined, the design team can develop possible solutions as well as the cost and schedule for each potential development strategy. In most strategic plans, the options for the facility's expansion or modernization are then evaluated according to how well they achieve the client's goals. Then the options are reduced to a preferred strategic direction.

Feasibility Analysis
(Typical time required: Two to four months)

Once the strategic planning framework is set, the scope of the specific project can be defined. The client may do this, but it is often more efficient to include specialists in market or needs analysis as well as design professionals in this process.

The primary tasks of this step are establishing an outline program and statement of project objectives, setting a realistic schedule, outlining a preliminary project budget, and defining the professional services that must be retained. In certain cases, this step also includes some preliminary feasibility testing of a specific site or building. Because many projects face market and financial constraints, clients need confirmation early on that their project is financially viable.

For some projects the owner may now retain a market and/or financial consultant to provide an independent professional opinion of the market and financial feasibility—a basic requirement for the financing of some projects. All the project parameters—program, budget, schedule, and feasibility—must be reconfirmed and refined after the full team is selected, but it is important to have a realistic definition of the project before selecting the full team.

Selection and Organization of Project Team
(Typical time required: One to three months)

The design of any facility is a team sport; it is not uncommon for 10 or more professional disciplines to be involved. Typically, the architect retains most of these professionals and forms a single cohesive team, thereby providing the owner with a single source of responsibility. The team may include the following specialists:

- Architects
- Interior designers
- Civil engineers
- Mechanical engineers
- Structural engineers
- Electrical engineers
- Plumbing and fire-protection engineers
- Cost consultants and/or construction managers
- Telecommunications and low voltage technology consultants
- Lighting designers
- Landscape architects
- Acoustic consultants
- Food-service and laundry consultants
- Equipment specialists

There is also a second group of consultants (usually retained by the client) that could include the following:

- Surveyor
- Geotechnical engineers
- Accountants
- Financial consultants
- Market analysts
- Sales and marketing professionals
- An advertising agency
- Public approval specialists and/or land use attorneys
- Development management consultants

- Investment bankers
- Attorneys for real estate, financing, etc.
- Bond counsel
- Fundraising consultants
- Hazardous materials consultants
- Traffic analysts
- Environmental impact consultants
- Parking consultants
- Zoning consultants

The client typically selects the lead professionals (usually the architect), who, in turn, choose the remainder of the design team. Members of that team must possess all of the required professional skills. The complexity of many projects demands that the team find the expertise listed above, even if the budget curtails the degree to which some of those specialists are involved.

The selection process for the lead professionals can vary, but a typical process includes the following:

1. Research is done on firms with relevant experience.
2. A written request is sent to a "long list" of firms asking them to submit letters of interest, references, and information about similar projects they have worked on. This request, sometimes known as a request for qualifications (RFQ), includes a statement of the project's objectives, an outline of the program, a schedule, and a budget.
3. After a review of these submittals, four to six firms are placed on a short list and asked to make a formal presentation.
4. The short-listed firms are sent a request for a written proposal, known as a request for proposal (RFP), summarizing
   - The firm's understanding of the project
   - A proposed work program
   - A proposed schedule
   - Key personnel and subconsultant firms to be involved and their relevant experience
   - Proposed fees and expenses

Following formal presentations and interviews, a contract is negotiated with the selected firm. A fee is finalized once the team is retained and there is comprehensive discussion of scope, schedule, proposed specialist consultants, and other variables. No two projects are the same, so the appropriate fees should be carefully calculated on a case-by-case basis to reflect the full scope of the services to be provided. The form of contract is typically based upon one of the standard American Institute of Architects (AIA) contract forms, discussed in Part 4, but the client may edit these or have their own form of contract.

Once the lead firm is selected, the entire team must be organized. This organization must begin with the client because only the client can

- Select the team or the lead professionals who will assemble the full team
- Set the overall project goals and monitor whether they are being met
- Select the program and design solutions that best meet the objectives from among the options prepared by the design team
- Resolve differences and problems between team members (e.g., design team and builder)
- Administer the contracts with the team members
- Lead the relationship between the project team and the public

Clients who create a clear decision-making structure and build a strong team relationship with all the firms involved in the process are much more likely to be successful. Some clients have even used one- to three-day "partnering sessions" at the beginning of a project to build such team relationships. Recognizing the importance of the client's role in this relationship, the renowned Finnish-born architect Eero Saarinen would begin a project by saying to the design team, "Let's see if we can make this guy into a great client."

In some large projects, a development manager provides overall project management expertise to the owner. While such firms can provide essential expertise and manpower for some projects, they should never become a filter between the owner and the rest of the team. Most owners benefit from direct communication with the experienced leaders of the other key team members.

Programming and Predesign
(Typical time required: One to four months)

One of the most challenging steps for the design team is translating market data, owner objectives, state and local codes, and other input into an architectural program and initial concept. In the past, the client would often prepare a detailed statement of the project requirements or program during the scoping phase (see Chapter 6.1). Today, the increased complexity of the average project means that its full detailed scope must be analyzed and defined with the assistance of the design team.

Program analysis has become a standard service provided by the architects, planners, and interior designers on some—but not all—projects. Among the additional issues the design team and specialists must define include:

- The number of each type of space
- Mechanical, electrical, plumbing, and other system choices; service needs and space required
- Detailed equipment requirements
- Dimensions of each space
- The relationship between spaces

The project team also has several other tasks before design can begin, including

- A detailed assessment of existing conditions in the project area
- Preparation of base plans showing the conditions of the existing structures, a site survey, utility analyses, and subsoil analyses (if new construction is involved)
- An analysis of the zoning, building code, and public-approval issues that will influence the design
- A review of the latest evidence-based design experience and research on the particular project type
- Special analyses of any other issues (asbestos, structural capacity, etc.) that could affect the project's design, cost, schedule, or feasibility
- An outline of the sustainability goals for the project

The results of the programming and related analyses are then combined into one or more preliminary concepts, an expanded statement of project goals, and an updated project schedule and budget.

Once these materials are available, two important parallel series of tasks often start: land use approvals (zoning, site plan approvals, wetland permits, etc.) and financing. When required, the local land use approvals typically start with informal meetings with the municipal officials or planning department staff. The meetings help outline the steps in the process, identify whether any special approvals (such as zoning variances) are necessary, and define the information required at each step in the process. Most local approval processes for projects involving more than interior renovation require detailed site design and schematic building design for land use approval. On larger projects, this may also require detailed analyses of the environmental impact of increased traffic, noise, storm drainage, and similar issues before local officials grant their approval. It is not unusual for the land use approval process to take one year or more. In many cases, the architect must take the lead in this effort.

DEFINITION OF SCHEMATIC DESIGN

Schematic design documents shall establish the conceptual design of the project, illustrating the scale relationship of the project components. The schematic design documents shall include a conceptual site plan, if appropriate, and preliminary building plans, sections, and elevations.

—(American Institute of Architects, 2007)

The second task that typically begins during predesign is securing preconstruction and construction financing for the project. Few major projects are paid for with the client's own cash reserves or endowment. Most involve borrowing and/or fundraising. Financing a project can also take more than a year. During this process, the design team is often asked to assist in the required documentation, public presentations, and other steps. Once these predesign tasks near completion, it is usually time to start the traditional design process.

Schematic Design
(Typical time required: Two to five months)

Schematic design is the first phase of the traditional design process (see also Chapter 7.1).

On many projects, this phase does not begin until additional feasibility studies confirm the project's viability. During the first design phase, the basic design concept is developed for all major components of the project. The standard forms of agreement for design services provide brief definitions of schematic design as well as subsequent phases.

The standard contractual definitions of design services are based on a process that would theoretically permit the design team to move in an orderly way through the most common steps in the design, documentation, and construction of a building. This theoretical process assumes that a clear definition of the client's program exists and that the design process can progress in a linear fashion from that definition through a series of steps—each of which results in a more complete definition of the design—until the project is sufficiently detailed to go into documentation for bidding (or negotiation) and construction.

The reality is not so orderly. Evolving program requirements, budget realities, increased knowledge of site considerations (such as subsoil problems), and many other factors make it necessary to go back and modify previous steps. Design moves forward, but rarely in the straightforward fashion implied by the standard two-phase description of design. In fact, most design professionals agree that the design choices occur at every step of the process. In other words, building design neither starts with schematic design nor ends with the completion of the second phase, design development.

The process by which an architect, design team, and consultants convert all of the design influences into a specific design solution varies from project to project. In schematic design, most firms begin with a period of analysis of the key issues (function, cost, codes, aesthetics, etc.) followed by a period of synthesis into a single concept.

It is common for the design team to consider several conceptual solutions to a design problem. For this reason, most have developed a process for narrowing down to a single concept. Selection may be based on the formal grading of a concept against the original project objectives, on an intuitive judgment based on experience, or, as is often the case, on a combination of both.

In the past formulaic design solutions were used for some projects. Today most of these standard solutions are considered obsolete or do not work on the available sites. Most projects require design solutions that respond to each project's unique mix of site, program, budget, owner goals, and other key variables.

Underlying this diversity of approaches are some common themes and design tasks. The first is an expansion of the original client's goals statement to include clear design goals. These will help in making the inevitable decisions on trade-offs between budget and quality, appearance and energy efficiency, as well as the thousands of other major decisions for which competing priorities must be reconciled.

The next basic task is the development of a parti, or basic conceptual diagram for the project concept. Sometimes this concept evolves from the site and program; other times, it starts with a strong formal concept. As architect Edward Larrabee Barnes, FAIA, put it, "It is not just a case of form following function. Sometimes function follows form."

Designers also choose a design vocabulary. The vocabulary includes the formal or aesthetic ideas that will govern the development of the design concept. Some architects develop a personal vocabulary of ideas, details, and preferred materials, and soon refine it on each subsequent project. Others approach each project as a unique problem and select a vocabulary appropriate to that problem.

Beyond the first conceptual steps, the process becomes more complex. In all but the smallest and simplest projects, the steps that follow the original planning concepts involve a team of people. While it is true that significant projects are usually developed under the guidance of a single strong design leader, in most projects more than 10 people are involved in the decision-making process. Thus, design excellence is dependent upon the effective management of a complex team, all of whose members contribute to the quality of the final result.

The result of all these steps is a completed schematic design. While different projects, clients, and design teams have different definitions of the completion of this phase, there are certain commonly agreed upon objectives and delivered documents.

Objectives

The primary objective is to arrive at a clearly designed, feasible concept and to present it in a form that the client understands and accepts. The secondary objectives are to clarify the project program, explore the most promising alternative design solutions, and provide a reliable basis for analyzing the cost of the project.

Products

Communicating design ideas and decisions usually involves a variety of media. Typical documentation at the end of this phase can include the following:

- A site plan
- Plans for each level, including conceptual reflected ceiling plans
- All exterior elevations and conceptual interior elevations
- Two or more cross sections
- An outline specification—a general description of the work indicating major systems and materials choices
- A statistical summary of the floor areas in the design as well as other characteristics in comparison to the program
- A preliminary construction cost estimate
- Other illustrative materials—renderings, models or drawings—needed to adequately present the concept

Other Services

As part of the schematic design work, the design team may agree to provide the client with energy studies, lifecycle cost analyses, or other economic studies, or special renderings, models, brochures, or promotional materials.

Approvals

The final step in schematic design is to obtain formal client approval. The schematic design presentation must be clear enough for the client to understand and approve. To confirm this approval, each item in the presentation should be signed and dated by the client so that the design development phase can begin.

Obtaining Approvals and/or Financing
(Typical time required: 90 days to over 24 months)

At this stage, the design may also be subject to review by state, local, and sometimes federal agencies. For example, healthcare facilities may require approval from the state department of health. A residential condominium project may require approval of the state attorney general and projects in areas controlled by federal or state regulations may require approval from the Army Corps of Engineers or other such agency.

At the same time they are undergoing state and/or federal review, most projects also proceed with local land use approvals. For reasons that are often hard to understand, there has been widespread resistance to new development in many regions. As a result, the most complex task in many projects has become obtaining local land use approvals and permits (site plan approval, wetlands permits, approval for curb cuts, etc.).

Local land use approvals typically require detailed site engineering (public utility demand, sanitary waste disposal, etc.) and special impact studies (traffic, visual, etc.) that are far more detailed than the architectural design is at this stage. The local land use process must be carefully planned and executed. Failure to manage any of the public approvals is one of the most common reasons for projects to come to a halt.

Design Development
(Typical time required: Two to four months)

The primary purpose of the design development phase is to define and describe important aspects of the project so that all that remains is the formal step of producing construction contract documents (see Chapter 7.1).

As schedule pressures and the amount of fast-track construction have increased, some clients and design firms have attempted to cut down or even eliminate this phase. However, there are strong arguments against doing this. Design development is the period during which all the issues left unresolved at the end of schematic design can be worked out. Eliminating this phase increases the possibility that major modifications will be required during the construction contract document phase. Such changes are costly and more likely to lead to coordination problems during construction.

Effective design development results in a clear, coordinated description of all aspects of the design. This typically includes fully developed floor plans, interior and exterior elevations, reflected ceiling plans, wall and building sections, and key details. This also includes the evaluation of alternative interior finishes and furnishings. In addition, the basic mechanical, electrical, plumbing, and fire-protection systems are accurately sized and defined, if not fully drawn. No major issues should be left unresolved that could require significant restudy during the construction documents phase.

The products of the design development phase are similar to those of schematic design drawings and specifications that fix and describe the size and character of the project, as well as any recommended adjustments to the preliminary estimate of construction cost. The design development phase should be brought to a close with a formal presentation to, and approval by, the client.

Construction Documentation
(Typical time required: Three to eight months)

The design process does not really end with the completion of the design development phase, but the emphasis shifts to producing a complete coordinated set of documents to guide the purchasing, construction, installation, and initial operations steps that follow.

The construction documents typically include drawings, specifications, contract forms, and, if the project is being bid, bidding requirements (see Chapter 7.2). These four documents play an important role:

- Drawings provide the graphic description of the work to be done.
- Specifications outline the levels of quality and standards to be met.
- Contract forms include the actual contract, bond and insurance requirements, and general conditions outlining the roles, rights, and responsibilities of all parties.
- Bidding requirements set the procedures for this process.

The professional design organizations (such as the AIA and others) have model documents for the specifications, contract forms, and bidding requirements that can be adapted to incorporate each project's unique requirements (see Part 4).

The most complex part of this step is the production of a comprehensive set of drawings and technical specifications. This often takes at least four to six months and can involve over 100 sheets of architectural drawings and several hundred pages of technical specifications. Each sheet of the drawings may take 80 to 200 hours to complete because the drawings must provide a clear, accurately dimensioned graphic description of the work to be done. Moreover, each drawing must be coordinated with the many drawings of the other design professionals working on the same project.

Today most projects of any size and complexity are done using computer-based drafting systems.

Selection of the Construction and FF&E Installation Teams and Purchasing (Typical time required: Two to four months)

Once part or all of the construction documents are available, the next critical step is the selection of the builders, FF&E manufacturers, equipment suppliers, and others who will provide the construction and other installed elements of the facility. Typically, the architect either manages the selection process or is an active participant with the client.

A number of selection strategies are available (see Chapter 7.3). For selection of the builder and project delivery method there are five major alternatives:

The most common is for the construction documents to be completed and put out for a bid to companies attracted by public advertisement, solicited by the owner and design team, or selected from a list of prequalified general contractors.

For many projects, it is a good idea to hire a construction manager (CM) to work side by side with the design team. During design, the CM provides advice on cost, schedule, and constructability issues. When the construction documentation nears completion, there are two ways in which the CM may continue to be involved in the project.

In the first scheme, the CM bids all of the various subtrades and then provides a guaranteed maximum price (GMP) and becomes the general contractor.

In the second scheme, the CM is a consultant to the client during construction as well. The CM may replace the general contractor on a fee basis. The construction subcontractors may be bid, but the CM—in its professional service form—does not guarantee the price. If the price is guaranteed, too much power is placed in the hands of the CM, and he or she can no longer be expected to work solely in the client's interest—the risks are too great.

For projects whose scope is unclear or the construction must start long before the completion of design, some clients will retain a builder to work on a cost-plus basis. Most clients do not like the open-ended nature of this method, but there are times when it is necessary.

A variation sometimes occurs on projects for which common components such as sheetrock walls, electrical outlets, light fixtures, and doors can be identified. The client may negotiate unit prices for each component and can then choose to buy as many units as it needs or can afford. This works for projects such as window replacement programs, repaving of parking lots, and repetitive interior renovations.

Another common option is design-build or integrated project delivery (IPD) (see Chapter 8.2). In this alternative the client typically retains a team that includes both a builder and a design team, or a design team that includes a "builder" component. Some clients like the simplicity and the assumed higher degree of cost control and unified project objectives. The success of this approach, however, depends upon the selection of a design-build team committed to the client's interests, since the normal quality-control check provided by an independent design team is compromised. Because the design team works for or with the builder, it often cannot communicate quality and value concerns directly to the client. The IPD process has been refined to help address this concern.

For furnishings, the equivalent is the furniture procurement specialist, who bids furniture packages within the framework of a performance specification.

The selection of an approach, as well as the appropriate companies, should be carried out in a systematic fashion. Advertising for bidders and hoping the right people show up to bid is rarely enough. Most experienced design teams will research the options, identify the most qualified firms, solicit their interest, confirm their qualifications, and then limit the final proposals to the four to six best candidate firms. As is the case for many of the other steps in the process, the AIA and other professional organizations have standard forms to facilitate this. (See Chapters 11 and 12 of this *Handbook*)

The purchasing of interior finishes, furnishings and equipment involves some of the same options. Dealers, who may represent one or several manufacturers, will provide fixed-price bids for furniture and/or finishes. There are also many firms prepared to provide cost-plus services with or without a guaranteed maximum price, and there are a growing number of services offering the equivalent of a design-build approach. Finishes and furnishings are not typically purchased by the same team. Finishes and built-in elements are typically handled by the GC or CM through their subcontractors, but furniture and moveable equipment are usually not included in their scope of work.

Construction and Installation
(Typical time required: One to three years)

With the start of construction and the production and delivery of furnishings and equipment, many additional companies and individuals take on major roles. Architects and the design team are expected to provide both quality control and management throughout this process. The management role typically includes administration of the various construction and supplier contracts; review of payment requests, change orders, claims, and related contract issues; and assistance in resolving problems in the field. It is not uncommon for 20 to 30 percent of the design team's total project effort to be spent during this phase (see Chapter 8).

Occupancy and Project Closeout
(Typical time required: One to six months)

Most clients need their buildings to be effectively complete one to four months prior to occupancy, during which time the client obtains final inspections and public approvals, learns to operate the new facility, makes sure all the key systems and equipment are operating properly, and prepares for full occupancy.

The architect's work is not complete when the facility is ready for occupancy. Virtually all clients moving into new facilities require assistance during the first few months. The design team's tasks during the occupancy or "commissioning" phase fall into two categories: following-up on incomplete or malfunctioning construction, furnishing, and equipment issues; and organizing and transferring the information necessary to occupy and maintain the facility.

Occupancy frequently reveals construction, furnishing, and/or equipment that do not perform as intended. Design teams should prepare their clients for the probability of some lingering issues and assure the clients that they will be there to help resolve them (see Chapter 9.4).

This begins with the collection and transfer of operation and maintenance manuals, training information, and related materials to the client. This information should include a set of record drawings (in both electronic and hard-copy forms) describing what was actually built based on the contractors' marked-up construction documents. In addition, some design teams prepare a reference manual containing samples, supplier data, and other information on all furnishings and finishes.

CONCLUSION

The completion of most architectural projects is a challenging endeavor. The time to accomplish the 12 steps outlined above can take years to complete. The client, the architect, and their project team must understand the process and be able to deal with the inevitable issues and problems they will encounter. All projects—even the most successful—face some complications. A well-run project will surmount these challenges. The difference between a successful project and one damaged by the dilemmas it faces is usually due not to the financial strength of the owner or the natural qualities of the site but to the quality of the planning and the effectiveness of the management of a complex team and process.

5.2 Defining Project Services

Glenn W. Birx, FAIA, LEED AP

Defining project services carefully is central to developing an agreement that clearly expresses the client's expectations.

To set up a project for success, it is important for the client and the architect to establish a mutual understanding of the project's intent and to define the performance expectations for all project participants. The intent and these expectations are then incorporated into a professional services agreement. Whenever a problem arises on a project concerning architectural and engineering services that is serious enough to include attorneys and a dispute resolution process, the contract for services is the initial document referenced by both sides. All discovery and argument in the resolution process will strive to understand the services performed in the context of those defined in the project agreement. Resolution of the problem will evolve from a determination of the contracted obligations of the parties and whether those obligations were adequately performed.

Building projects are complicated, and architects would all prefer to resolve differences amicably to maintain healthy continuing relationships with clients. Accordingly, a good first step is to establish open communications with a client and to be crystal clear as to the obligations of the parties before beginning work on a project. Because architects and engineers provide many types of services, the client and the architect may have a different understanding of what those services entail. Providing your client with a clear description of services up front will help clarify the client's expectations.

A clear description of services can also serve as an appropriate basis for the architect's response to the owner's programmatic requirements, facilitate the development of an effective work plan, enable negotiation of fair contract terms, and ensure that adequate compensation is agreed to. In addition, it can provide a benchmark for determining when requested services are beyond those specified in the contract and thus require an additional fee.

STEPS FOR DEFINING SERVICES

Proposing and defining services to be provided is a critical part of practice and should not be taken lightly. Thus, the architect should not rely solely on AIA standard forms of agreement or other contracts to perform this task. Each project is unique, with varying code and local requirements and specific client expectations, site conditions, and programmatic requirements.

Glenn W. Birx is a principal with the Baltimore-based firm Ayers Saint Gross, Inc. He is responsible for technical services, including proposal generation and design contract development. Ayers Saint Gross provides design services for colleges and universities around the world.

The unique nature of most projects requires an understanding of factors that can affect the type, quality, and depth of professional services. Possible factors that can influence the level of professional services include the following:

- Programmatic requirements
- Project budget
- Project schedule
- Inclusion of engineering consultants in basic services
- Requirement for inclusion of specialty consultants under the architect's agreement (those outside your core expertise or different from those usually used with basic services)
- Provision of services by others (consultants or contractors)
- Your firm's own internal capabilities
- Regulatory requirements and public approval processes
- The client's goals, expectations, and values (if you don't know, find out)
- The client's level of knowledge and experience regarding facility development and building construction
- Required use of building information models
- The method of construction procurement (e.g., services for a design-build project will be vastly different from services for a traditional design-bid-build project)
- The form and terms and conditions of the professional services agreement
- The level of risk associated with the project services

Communication with the client is a key element in determining what services are required for a particular project. Keep in mind that clients who have worked with more than one architect may have realized they receive different services from each firm even on similar projects. Remember, too, that previous clients can change their expectations or standards.

The following steps can serve as a guide for defining services for a project.

Step 1: Verify the Project Requirements

Many factors can affect the type and quality of an architect's project services and deliverables. Among them are the program, the client's expectations, the client's level of knowledge and experience, the architect's need to retain engineering or specialty consultants, the types of other consultants to be retained by the client, the project budget and schedule, your firm's internal capabilities, and the method of project delivery and construction procurement.

The list in the accompanying sidebar provides a starting point for identifying design factors relevant to a project. Contacting others who may have worked for your client can help uncover potential services that may be expected. Be sure to ask the client in what ways other consultants have not met their expectations. Contact local code and other officials (especially in an unfamiliar locale) to find out about their processes and the extent of required project approvals. Do not skip this last step or assume that you already know these procedures. Intensive research on the factors that could affect the services required for the project will ease project delivery.

Step 2: Prepare a Proposal for the Services to Be Provided

The AIA series of owner-architect agreements (B101–2007 and its related family of documents) is a good starting point for defining services. Propose the use of these agreements whenever possible. However, be sure the client fully comprehends the scope of proposed services and has reasonable expectations of the project outcome. Many clients do not understand language in professional service agreements with respect to deliverables, requirements for the client to provide information and make timely decisions, and services provided by consultants and contractors. While AIA owner-architect agreements attempt to clarify these items in a thorough manner, direct conversation with the client regarding their extent is always prudent.

A proposal for services, in a letter or other appropriate format, should be prepared in advance of the professional services agreement. The proposal should expand on and clarify the proposed services consistent with the architect's understanding of the project. It can elaborate on specifics such as the schedule (duration of the project), number of design meetings and public presentations, type and quality of renderings, number of site visits and progress meetings during construction, and so on. In some cases, it may be advisable to define the expected number and type of drawings for each phase of the project. If selection of the architect is fee-based, the proposal should include the fee for basic services and for those that are considered additional services.

It may also be useful to provide a list of "services not included" (often termed "exclusions") in the basic services proposal to further clarify what is not included in the basic fee. The proposal should be the starting point for negotiating the professional services agreement, which will more fully describe the scope of services and fees.

Step 3: Negotiate the Final Services and the Fee

It is always better to reach agreement on the scope of services before discussing and negotiating fees. Since fees are tied directly to the services provided, it is especially important to have a clear description of services in the proposal. Therefore, if the client should ask you to reduce your fees, it is best to ask which of the proposed services are not needed, since many clients do not fully understand the relationship between fees and services. For hourly-based compensation, be prepared to provide an estimate of the required labor hours and other costs associated with each service. Remember that fees can also be based on value provided to the client rather than the hours required to perform them.

Step 4: Prepare the Professional Services Agreement

At the conclusion of negotiations, the proposal should be revised to reflect the final agreed-upon services, schedule, and compensation. Some clients will want the proposal to be included as an exhibit with the professional services agreement. In this case, the final proposal should contain a more complete and detailed description of services whether you are using AIA documents or other contract forms. Keep in mind that AIA documents and other standard contract forms include only general descriptions of services, and that the final proposal will likely incorporate a more detailed description tailored to the unique requirements of the project.

If the client does not accept the detailed description in the final proposal, as with many state or government projects, modify or provide a reference to the proposal so it is represented somewhere in the final agreement or elsewhere in the project records, such as in the client-architect correspondence file. Contracts should be written with the understanding that the signatories to them may not be around, for various reasons, at the time when disputes may arise. Absolutely do not rely on oral agreements. A written record is essential.

Step 5: Monitor and Manage Changes in Scope

A well-written agreement will make clear what services are included and which ones are not. There should be no question as to the legitimacy of a request for additional compensation in the event additional services are requested. There may be times, however, when unanticipated services arise regardless of efforts to include clarifying requirements in the proposal. Thus, members of the project team should be knowledgeable of the scope and the contract language so they can readily identify additional services when they are requested. It is best to raise the issue of additional services prior to beginning work on them. Most professional services agreements require prior client approval for the architect to be paid for additional services.

TYPES AND CATEGORIES OF SERVICES

To make it easier to understand services, it can be helpful to organize them into three groups: predesign services, design through construction phase services, and postconstruction services. Typically, most predesign and postconstruction services are considered "additional" and those associated with the design through construction phases are considered "basic," although many additional services can be provided during design and construction as well.

Predesign Services

Almost all clients need design consultation prior to the start of schematic design, and through training and experience, architects possess the knowledge to address predesign issues such as site selection and programming. Defining the problem is the first step toward solving it, and architects can assist in the predesign phase in numerous ways, which may include such tasks as scenario planning, strategic planning, facilitation of goal and visioning sessions, campus or master planning, project definition, program management, and related activities. A common predesign task for architects is facilities programming, in which the required spaces proposed for the facility are outlined, along with specific needs for these spaces, such as sizes and number of people they must accommodate, lighting and audiovisual needs, finishes, relationship to other spaces, and other issues. The program becomes an important tool for the design phases and helps the architect design more effectively.

See "Programming" for information about the processes and methods of architectural programming.

Some clients may require services prior to design to help them with fundraising activities. These might involve feasibility studies and cost estimating, renderings and models for brochures and fundraising events, graphic design, return on investment analysis, and other services. The predesign phase offers excellent opportunities for architects to provide "value-added" services for the benefit of the project and to extend relationships with clients.

Design-Through-Construction Phase Services

Most architects and clients are familiar with services traditionally provided during the five phases of basic services—schematic design, design development, construction documentation, bidding or negotiation, and construction.

It is always advisable, however, to review design-through-construction services for each project, because the client's building standards may have changed or the client may be providing some of the services or, conversely, asking for more services than usual. Services can also vary when delivery methods other than design-bid-build are used, such as construction management and design-build. The use of technologies, such as building information modeling and advanced rendering software, may also affect the level of project services and how they are carried out.

Most basic architectural services include services for structural engineering and mechanical/electrical/plumbing engineering, and sometimes for civil engineering. However, most other design-through-construction phase services are usually considered "additional." For example, some projects may require the use of specialty consultants in connection with food service (kitchen) planning, audiovisual systems, laboratories, libraries, theaters, data/communication systems, security systems, green or sustainable design, and lighting and acoustic design.

Fees for these specialty consultants can be included with the architect's fee proposal, but when this is done, it should be pointed out that such fees are not normally part of basic services. Other additional services can include renderings and animations, topographic or furniture and equipment surveys, lifecycle cost analysis and energy modeling, additional bid packages and multiple construction phasing, fast-track scheduling, building commissioning, graphic design, assistance with permits and other municipal fees, and many others. Although building owners have traditionally obtained and contracted separately for geotechnical engineering services and utility and boundary surveys, owners are increasingly requesting that these services be packaged with services of the architect. The architect should be aware that providing these site-related services carries considerable risk.

Postconstruction Services

Traditionally, the only postconstruction phase services provided by architects have been building commissioning and postoccupancy evaluation. However, architects are increasingly offering more services after construction completion. Such services include maintenance scheduling, space planning, renovations, energy analysis and monitoring, disaster planning, tenant improvements, forensic analysis, code analysis, and space scheduling.

"BASIC" VS. "ADDITIONAL" SERVICES

The importance of distinguishing "basic services" from "additional services" relates to their associated fees. Another way to differentiate services would be to describe them as "services included" versus "services excluded" from the owner-architect agreement. However, over the years, the terms "basic" and "additional" used in AIA documents have become the industry standard for describing architectural services, and the term "basic services" has become the benchmark for comparison of fees by clients. This baseline comes from the AIA description of basic services as something to which the unique requirements of a project are added or subtracted.

A detailed description of the architect's services should be provided with the fee proposal. In addition, a description of services that are not included should accompany the proposal. The accompanying sidebar further delineates the distinction between basic and additional services, according to AIA Document B101–2007, Standard Form of Agreement Between Owner and Architect.

BASIC AND ADDITIONAL SERVICES

AIA Document B101–2007, Standard Form of Agreement Between Owner and Architect, identifies and describes both basic and additional services:

BASIC SERVICES

B101–2007 categorizes and defines basic services provided by the architect in five discrete phases. The following summarizes what each of these phases includes:

Schematic design phase. The architect makes a preliminary evaluation of the owner's program, schedule, budget, project site, and the proposed method of project delivery. Based on these evaluations, the architect prepares a site plan and preliminary building plans, elevations, and sections; makes preliminary selections of materials and systems; and prepares a preliminary estimate of the cost of the work. (Schematic design documents may also include some combination of study models, perspective sketches, and digital modeling.)

Design development phase. Based on approved schematic design documents, the architect prepares design

development documents that fix and describe the character of the project in plans, elevations, sections, typical construction details, diagrammatic layouts of building systems, outline specifications for materials and systems, and an updated estimate for the cost of the work.

Construction documents phase. Based on approved design development documents and any other approved changes, the architect prepares drawings and specifications that establish in detail the requirements for the construction of the project and the quality level of materials and systems required for the project. An updated estimate of the cost of the work is also completed.

Bidding or negotiation phase. In this phase, the architect helps the owner establish a list of prospective contractors. For competitively bid projects, the architect helps organize and conduct a prebid conference, prepares addenda to respond to questions from bidders, and assists the owner in analyzing the bid results. For negotiated construction work, the architect helps procure and distribute proposal documents, organize

(continued)

and participate in selection interviews, and prepare a report of negotiation results.

Construction phase. In this phase, the architect administers the contract between the owner and the contractor. Services include responding to requests for information that are consistent with the requirements of the contract documents; interpreting the contract documents; preparing supplemental drawings as appropriate; visiting the site at "intervals appropriate to the stage of construction"; reporting on known deviations from the construction documents and observed defects and deficiencies in the work; rejecting work that does not conform to the construction documents; reviewing and certifying certificates for payment; reviewing and taking appropriate action on the contractor's submittals; preparing orders for minor changes in the work; preparing and issuing change orders and construction change directives, but not for those that require evaluation of the contractor's proposals and supporting data or revisions to the instruments of service; and making inspections for substantial and final completion.

ADDITIONAL SERVICES

Additional services are addressed in Article 4 of the B101–2007, Standard Form of Agreement Between Owner and Architect. These services are defined and described in two groups.

The first group includes additional services identified in the agreement at its signing. A matrix in the B101 allows these services to be designated along with the party responsible for them. Descriptions of additional services can be inserted into the body of the agreement or attached as exhibits to any AIA owner-architect agreement. Some of the AIA scope documents for additional services that are available include:

- B201, Design and Construction Contract Administration
- B203, Site Evaluation and Planning
- B204, Value Analysis (for use when the owner employs a value analysis consultant)
- B205, Historic Preservation
- B206, Security Evaluation and Planning
- B209, Construction Contract Administration (for use when the owner retains another architect for design services)
- B210, Facility Support
- B211, Commissioning
- B214, LEED Certification
- B252, Architectural Interior Design
- B253, Furniture, Furnishings, and Equipment Design

The second group of additional services includes services that may become necessary during the course of the project. Following are some examples:

- Revisions to architectural documents caused by changes in the initial information, previous instructions, or prior approvals from the owner
- Document revisions due to the enactment of new codes, laws, or regulations after design submissions
- Revisions due to non-timely decisions by the owner
- Material changes to the project size, quality, complexity, schedule, or budget
- Extra work caused by performance failure by owner, contractor, or owner consultants
- Preparation for and attendance at public hearings or dispute resolution proceedings
- Reviews of out-of-sequence submittals from the contractor
- Responses to RFIs when the information requested is in the contract documents or when the RFI is not submitted in conformance with the requirements of the contract documents
- Change orders requiring evaluation of the contractor's proposals and supporting data or requiring revisions to instruments of service
- Services related to fire or other damage to the project
- Reviews for an extensive number of claims
- Evaluation of substitutions and making required revisions to the contract documents for them
- Preparation of design and documentation for alternate bid or proposal requests
- Construction administration services occurring more than 60 days after the date of substantial completion, or the date anticipated in the agreement, whichever is earlier
- Assisting the initial decision maker (IDM) in evaluating claims, when the architect is not serving as the IDM
- Assisting the owner in determining the qualifications of specific bidders or persons providing proposals
- Providing services beyond the negotiated number of months from the date of the agreement
- Reviewing shop drawings, product data item, sample and similar submittals that exceed the negotiated number
- Making visits to the site that exceed the negotiated number
- Making inspections that exceed a negotiated number of inspections to determine if the work is substantially complete
- Making inspections that exceed a negotiated number of inspections to determine if final completion is reached

THE PROFESSIONAL SERVICES AGREEMENT

Once the scope of services has been defined and agreed to, it is critical to formalize that agreement in a contract. Regardless of the type of contract form used, the document must include a section outlining and defining the services, and neither party should execute the agreement without thoroughly understanding those services. Three basic types of agreements are used for architectural services: AIA owner-architect agreements, other standard forms of agreement, or owner-generated agreements.

AIA 2007 Owner-Architect Agreements

The AIA publishes a large number of coordinated standard contract forms and other documents. These are listed and discussed in Part 4 of this book.

The AIA Owner-Architect Agreement forms are widely used and an provide an excellent starting point and structure for an owner-architect. As is noted in this chapter, however, these standard forms must be amplified to reflect all of the services and other issues that constitute a full agreement between the owner and the architect.

Other Standard Agreements

Architects are often presented with other standard types of agreements, such as those produced by the Engineers Joint Contract Documents Committee (EJCDC) and the Construction Management Association of America (CMAA). All of these agreements have sections relating to the scope of services. Be sure to review this language carefully, and do not hesitate to make modifications to accommodate your specific services.

Owner-Generated Agreements

These agreements come in many forms and variations. They could be federal, state, or municipal government contracts and may not have been updated for many years. Unfortunately, some government agencies and other large clients take the position "Take this contract or leave it," and they will not entertain modifications in spite of out-of-date content.

Some owners have their attorneys prepare professional services agreements. Although some attorneys may not admit it, many have limited experience with the construction process, and the resulting contracts can be dangerous. Therefore, architects are encouraged to read these contracts carefully and have their own attorney and professional liability insurance company provide reviews and advice. These contracts may employ very broad terms (e.g., "as required" or "as necessary"), and they can raise the standard of care of an architect's contracted services to an extent that is not protected by the firm's professional liability insurance policy. As mentioned previously, it is important to be specific in terms of the actual scope of a project and to have definitive scope language placed in the contract.

When dealing with government agencies, request to speak to someone in authority (e.g., the state attorney general) who has the ability to make modifications to the contract. If this is not possible, send a letter to your client carefully outlining the scope of services and deliverables on which you have based your fee proposal. Good documentation will always come in handy should a dispute arise.

CHANGES IN SERVICES

As a general rule, never proceed with services that are considered "additional" without first requesting and receiving written owner approval for further compensation. Although time may be short, a quick e-mail can inform the owner and document your request. Architects who consistently adhere to this rule may encounter fewer disputes about services and payments. Doing the work first and then asking for payment is never received well by clients—and for good reason. Clients want to know ahead of time if additional fees are involved.

Identifying additional services requires careful management. Members of the design team, and especially the project manager, should be intimately aware of services under the project contract. Any proposed changes should be communicated to and discussed with the owner in a timely and professional manner.

Architects could take a lesson from contractors, who typically do not hesitate to submit change orders for work they consider not in their contracts. While professional services are harder to define and quantify than a set of bidding documents, architects should take the same approach to being compensated for additional effort.

Once identified, additional services should be addressed with the same care as any other professional service. Contractual language showing that the work is, in fact, additional should be cited. A reasonable proposal should be submitted in a timely manner, and work should not begin until owner approval has been received. Time spent on additional services should be invoiced separately and a clear distinction made between original contract services and the additional service.

In the event a dispute arises with the owner regarding whether a service was included in the original contract, make every attempt to immediately work out an amicable solution. Set up a meeting or meetings to discuss the issues with parties authorized to make a decision. State your case clearly and professionally, and listen to the owner's position. Architects may find that many disputes about services are caused by misunderstandings that can be cleared up quickly by discussion. Should this approach fail, follow the "dispute resolution" clause that should be contained in your contract. Act quickly, and do not let these issues linger until they become more contentious.

STEPS TOWARD SUCCESSFUL PROJECTS

The delivery of successful architectural services begins with determining what work is required, proposing the services to be provided, and negotiating the scope of services and fee. The intent is to achieve a clear description of the project's services that matches the client's expectations with the architect's capabilities. The fee proposal must be clearly linked to the services proposal. Clear definitions and lists of "basic" and "additional" services are essential. The agreement that is ultimately signed between owner and architect must adequately document the understandings reached by the architect and the client. Once the project is under way, remember to monitor and manage the scope of services as carefully as possible. Doing so can substantially reduce potential disputes, go a long way toward establishing a professional and productive client relationship, and help bring the project to a successful conclusion.

5.3   Architectural Services and Compensation

Clark S. Davis, FAIA, LEED AP

Clients are willing to compensate an architect in direct relation to the value they place on that architect's services. Therefore, architects must communicate the full range of their services to their clients as well as the benefits those services provide.

Clark S. Davis is a principal consultant at Cameron MacAllister group and was formerly vice chairman of Hellmuth, Obata + Kassabaum (HOK) and managing principal of the firm's regional offices in St. Louis and Chicago. He is past president of the St. Louis and Missouri chapters of the AIA.

Architects in all types of practice have a common challenge: identifying and receiving appropriate compensation for the services they provide. For most of the twentieth century, project-based fee structures were often calculated as a percentage of construction cost, and the AIA and other industry groups once promoted standard fee percentages. As the practice of architecture has become more complex, however, the challenge of determining appropriate compensation for an architect's work has increased.

By the end of the twentieth century, the complexity, scale, and uniqueness of many building projects had led to the use of cost-based fees for design services. This approach emphasizes the recovery of costs for labor and expenses incurred by architects in performing the work, and invites detailed negotiation of the projected services, staff salaries, overhead rates, fee multipliers, and profit margin the architect will be allowed. While it seems flexible, this cost-based approach to determining fees has some serious limitations. In particular, it evaluates the architect's services solely in terms of hours of effort and does not consider the value of an architect's ideas and results.

Several other trends have emerged in calculating compensation for architectural services as firms work to meet changing client expectations and improve their own economic performance.

- Many architects recognize that maintaining long-term client relationships (rather than focusing on individual projects) is a strong foundation for a successful architecture practice. With this approach, architects can devise flexible compensation terms to cover a wide range of services, project types, and locations.
- More projects today involve delivery methods other than traditional design-bid-build approaches. These may include third-party project management—usually by a developer, construction manager, or program manager—or design-build responsibility. Such approaches require new combinations of architectural services and thus new fee considerations.
- Architects are increasingly sensitive to the business risks imposed by different approaches to delivering their services, and they are seeking appropriate rewards in contract and compensation terms. For example, an architect who shares direct risk for construction cost may negotiate an incentive fee derived if the project comes in under the client's budget.
- Technology has changed the way architects, clients, and consultants around the world work. Significant projects have been completed by "virtual teams" collaborating electronically, and some U.S. firms have explored off-shoring of technical services or documents production to low-cost service providers in other countries. Integrated project delivery supported by building information modeling (BIM) software may change many of the basic rules and practices of the A/E/C industry.
- Architects and clients are developing a clearer sense of value based on the contribution architectural services make to the success of a client's project. More clients realize that an architect's ideas can speed business processes, draw and delight customers, attract and retain key employees, and save money through wise choices among facility options.

DEFINING SPECIFIC PROJECT SERVICES

The first step in structuring architectural services and the compensation appropriate for them is determining the scope and specificity of a client's project requirements. The services may be defined precisely or loosely, depending on the clarity of the client's goals. Understanding and communicating the scope of services can be handled in three basic ways.

Client-generated work scope. Some clients may provide detailed service requirements as part of an RFP soliciting architectural services. This approach is often employed for repetitive or standard assignments and is managed by the client's personnel, who compare competing proposals on an equal basis. Detailed RFPs may specify program requirements, site conditions, service expectations, required deliverables, and schedules.

Owner-architect agreements. Standard service agreements are useful in defining architectural services, primarily for traditional design and construction projects. This is particularly true of the 2007 series of AIA standard forms of owner-architect agreement.

Customized work plans and scope descriptions. For a set of special services, the architect creates a customized definition—after extensive consultation with the client—as the basis for a service and compensation agreement. While customized scope documents vary in level of detail, they typically include the following elements:

For more information about defining the scope of project services see "Defining Project Services." Many different types of project agreements, including AIA Contract Documents, are discussed in Chapters 11 and 12.

- Client goals and objectives for the architect's services
- Service tasks and expected work products
- Key review and decision milestones
- Schedules of tasks, phases, and milestone dates
- Requirements for information or services provided by others
- Allowances for changes or events outside the architect's control
- Exclusions and additional services available if needed

Before determining specific compensation options and pricing for the architectural services defined, architects should consider issues of value and risk related to their firm's goals, the particular client, and the project assignment.

RECOGNIZING THE VALUE OF ARCHITECTURE SERVICES

The traditional emphasis on cost-based project compensation has resulted in limited profitability for many architecture firms. Architects have been conditioned to accept marginal rates of return for their businesses, and the cyclical nature of design and construction investment has exacerbated this problem. During slow times in the industry, architects and other design professionals often compete vigorously for work performed on a breakeven or loss basis just to retain staff and cover overhead costs. However, accepting such low levels of return is not sustainable over the long term, as it hurts a firm's market position and financial performance.

Fortunately, many architects are gaining a new awareness of the value of their services and the distinct benefits they can provide to clients. Although value is ultimately defined by client perceptions, some successful firms have adopted overall business strategies and market positions based on the benefits their services can provide to clients. The principles are simple: Firms perceived to be the best in a particular arena or to offer unique services will be in demand, and clients will pay a premium for their expertise. Conversely, firms perceived to be "just like everyone else" often will be evaluated on price alone.

In *A Whole New Mind: Moving from the Information Age to the Conceptual Age*, author Daniel Pink identifies design as one of six "senses" required for personal success in the twenty-first century. "It's no longer sufficient," he says, "to create a product, a service, an experience, or a lifestyle that's merely functional. Today it's economically crucial and personally rewarding to create something that is also beautiful, whimsical, or emotionally engaging."

Value in architecture services may be perceived and delivered in a number of ways:

Design preeminence. Firms honored for the signature quality of their design work will be valued and well compensated.

Building type expertise and experience. Most clients seek architects with successful experience in similar projects.

Project leadership capability. As clients seek simpler and more efficient ways to manage facility projects, firms that can lead the delivery process through program management, construction management, or design-build services are in demand.

Unique service methods and tools. Many firms offer value through special services that improve quality, speed, and accountability in the planning, construction, and management of client facilities.

Loyal, long-term client relationships. Many successful architecture firms have built their practices on long-standing partnerships with key clients. These relationships create mutual value, often resulting in better compensation and lower risk for architecture firms.

Every firm should know its own market strategy and value proposition and how they apply to the firm's individual clients and service assignments.

RISK ASSESSMENT AND PRICING

In addition to creating positive value opportunities, architects must be sensitive to the business risks they assume in providing their services. Technical quality and completeness are considered a given in the provision of architecture services. However, many clients today are demanding unprecedented and sometimes unrealistic levels of perfection in the execution of architecture work. These rising client expectations present architects with new challenges and opportunities.

> [M]any leading professional firms . . . are rated very highly by their clients in terms of . . . expertise, but rather poorly in terms of their capabilities at relationships, including understanding their client's business, communicating effectively, being a pleasure to deal with, and creating broad business outcomes. These same clients indicate that the importance of these relationship factors is increasing. . . . In short, doing great work is not enough.
>
> —Ross Dawson, Developing Knowledge-Based Client Relationships

When anticipating risks associated with a particular client or project, the goal is either to find ways to eliminate sources of risk or to receive fair compensation for conditions that are outside the architect's control. Each project must be evaluated in terms of the risks associated with it as compensation and contract terms are developed.

Architects also face the risk that clients may misunderstand what is included in architectural services, particularly with fixed-fee contracts. For example, if two different clients hire an architect for two identical projects, the clients may have very different expectations about the level of services to be provided, causing one project to require twice the compensation of the other to be consistently profitable. To avoid such misunderstandings, AIA standard owner-architect agreements have become increasingly explicit about the architect's basic and optional responsibilities. The AIA recommends consideration of the following risks when drafting architectural services proposals:

Client decision making and approvals. The architect should know the structure and pace of the client's decision-making process. Will one or two representatives make decisions, or will the architect be required to review options with large groups of people? Will key decisions be reached in days or weeks?

Scope changes. If an assignment is expanded or substantially altered during the design and construction process, the change creates more work and cost for the entire project team. This is a particular issue when clients are experiencing rapid growth or organizational change.

Third-party project management. When a client engages a third-party program or construction manager to lead design and construction of a project, the architect is challenged with responding to direction from two or more parties, which can require more time.

Fast-track and construction-driven delivery schedules. Accelerated construction schedules often drive the demand for design decisions and bidding and construction documents. An architect who plans to produce one or two document packages could be expected to deliver numerous other documents to support a new construction schedule. Producing multiple document packages is inherently more costly and difficult to coordinate than traditional deliverables.

Construction cost responsibility and contingency structure. Architects are usually held accountable for designing to a client's budget based on a budget review and estimation of services. The risk involved is compounded, however, when the architect is asked to rely on estimates by third parties or when construction begins early, based only on partial design and pricing information. At a minimum, the architect should retain parallel estimating capability and ensure that appropriate budget contingencies exist for program uncertainties, design completion, pricing variations, and unforeseen conditions during construction.

Design-build projects also present risks related to construction cost. An architect may be required to make design changes to meet a strict design and construction budget, but may benefit—with the owner's agreement—in savings achieved if the project comes in under the budget or contract amount.

Standard of care for design and technical coordination. As instruments of service, architects' technical documents are never perfect or immune to differences in interpretation. A small percentage of the total cost of any construction project will be related to coordination issues or omissions in technical documents. Some clients and contracts overlook this reality and expect architects to share in additional construction costs attributable to normal coordination issues. This is a subject for serious contract negotiation, as higher fees may need to be charged to offset the architect's risk.

Financial resources and payment terms. Architects should confirm their clients' financial resources and intended payment practices for any project assignment. The carrying costs of unpaid invoices and any at-risk design work can substantively reduce the profitability of a project.

COMPENSATION OPTIONS

Architects can consider several compensation options when structuring a new client relationship or project assignment. The options offer different levels of flexibility, profit potential, and risk protection for the architecture firm.

Fixed (Stipulated Sum) Fees

A fixed fee is a firm compensation amount related to a particular scope of service. Fixed fees are convenient and appropriate when services can be precisely defined, a client understands what is included, and the architect is confident the services can be managed within a fixed budget.

Hourly Billing Rates and Fee Multipliers

Hourly billing is the most flexible fee option for architects and clients, and it is generally preferred when no exact service scope can be defined. For this reason, hourly billing is often used for the preliminary phases of project assignments and later converted to fixed fees.

Cost Plus Fixed Fee

Cost plus fixed fee is an hourly fee option in which a client is billed for the actual cost of an architect's effort—base salaries, fringe benefits, and firm overhead—on a rate or multiplier basis, and a fixed fee is negotiated as the firm's profit on the assignment. This arrangement can be useful when a client does not want a completely open-ended fee arrangement but there are many unknowns and establishing a stipulated sum at the outset proves difficult. Clients often see the advantage of cost-plus approaches when the uncertainties would force a prudent architect to include substantial contingencies in a fixed-fee proposal. From the architect's perspective, cost-plus approaches limit profit potential but greatly reduce the risk of losses.

Unit Cost Methods

In some cases, clients prefer to compensate professionals based on cost per square foot, room, store, building, or other unit. For example, office planning and interior design are often priced per square foot, which is the same unit used in lease rates and tenant allowances in commercial buildings. Hotel projects are often structured based on cost per room. However, unit cost estimating requires accurate and timely data on the cost of providing the services for each unit and recognition of the fact that earlier units usually require more effort than those that follow.

Percentage of Construction Cost

This method ties the architect's compensation to the budgeted or actual construction cost of a project. This once was the most common method for setting architectural fees, but is no longer used by most owners.

Reducing the construction costs can reduce the architect's fee and growth in the construction cost can raise questions in an owner's mind if it increases the architect's fee.

Disadvantages of a percentage-based contract include the assumption that construction cost is directly proportional to the architect's effort. A percentage-based fee agreement can be structured to convert to a fixed fee when the project's scope has been confirmed, often at the end of the schematic design or design development phase.

Outcome-Based Value Pricing

Business consultants sometimes tie their compensation to revenue, cost, and profitability results achieved with their assistance. Advertising firms routinely propose "idea fees" and licensing arrangements for ongoing use of their work products. Architects can propose such "value pricing" based on measurable outcomes specific to individual clients and project engagements. Examples of such metrics include sales in retail facilities, leasing successes in housing or commercial office developments, and employee satisfaction or retention in corporate workplaces.

Reimbursable and Non-Reimbursable Direct Costs

While staff effort usually represents most of an architect's cost of service, it is also important to anticipate and budget other direct costs that are related to the work but not covered in the firm's overhead structure. These typically include travel, long-distance communications, mail and courier services, printing, photography, computer services and output, professional models and renderings, and materials or equipment. These direct costs may be reimbursable (billed directly to the client at actual cost or with a markup) or non-reimbursable (covered by an architect's other fees for the assignment). Direct costs are almost always reimbursable under the hourly and cost-plus compensation options.

PUTTING IT ALL TOGETHER: SERVICE AND PRICING STRATEGY

Before proposing services for a new client or project assignment, architects should consider the potential risks and compensation options. There is no single best strategy or approach to determining the compensation for a project; architects must apply professional judgment and experience when considering what terms are appropriate to each new opportunity.

The following process works well for many firms.

Step 1: Consult with the Client About Needs and Priorities

The most important step in forming any new business relationship is knowing the client—understanding the client's needs, expectations, style, and concerns.

Step 2: Identify Service Strategy, Team, and Work Scope

Once the client's needs are understood, the architect should develop an overall service strategy to address them successfully. This should include a clear work plan, the proposed team of architectural staff and consultants, schedule, and big decision points.

Step 3: Estimate the Cost of Providing the Services

Unless the architect is proposing an open-ended hourly billing arrangement, it is important to estimate the actual cost of providing the services (including the firm's staff, the proposed fees from outside consultants, and direct costs) as the starting point for the compensation proposal. The sample compensation worksheet shown in Table 5.1 can be used as a template for this calculation on a fixed-fee assignment.

Step 4: Evaluate Risk Factors and Apply an Appropriate Contingency

The architect should evaluate the potential risks involved in providing proposed services and decide what additional compensation is appropriate to offset them. This may be a specific dollar amount added to the estimated actual cost for a fixed fee, a markup of hourly cost rates, or an increase in the base fee multiplier.

TABLE 5.1 Sample Compensation Worksheet

Apple and Bartlett
616 Highland Avenue
Maintown
USA

Phase: **Design Development**
Proj. No: 1207
Project: Clayton Elementary School
Owner: Maintown School District
Date: 10/23/2007

Project Management/Admin	Hrs	× Rate	= Cost
Principal	10	$55	$550
Project Manager	80	$38	$3,000
Architect/Designer III	0	$30	$0
Architect II	0	$25	$0
Architect I	0	$20	$0
Subtotals	90		$3,550

Cost Estimating			
Principal	0	$55	$0
Project Manager	20	$38	$750
Architect/Designer III	40	$30	$1,200
Architect II	20	$25	$500
Architect 1	0	$20	$0
Subtotals	80		$2,450

Architectural Design			
Principal	20	$55	$1,100
Project Manager	0	$38	$0
Architect/Designer III	80	$30	$2,400
Architect II	0	$25	$0
Architect I	0	$20	$0
Subtotals	100		$3,500

Documentation			
Principal	0	$55	$0
Project Manager	0	$38	$0
Architect/Designer III	20	$30	$600
Architect II	120	$25	$3,000
Architect I	240	$20	$4,800
Subtotals	380		$8,400

Consultants	
Civil	$7,200
Landscape Design	$3,200
Mechanical	$16,500
Electrical	$13,500
Lighting Design	$5,400
Subtotals	$45,800

	Summary	Total Hrs	Total Cost
1	Principal	30	$1,650
2	Project Manager	100	$3,750
3	Architect III/Designer	140	$4,200
4	Architect II	140	$3,500
5	Architect I	240	$4,800
6	Total in-house salary expense		$17,900
7	Direct personnel expense[1]		0
8	Indirect expense[2] @ 150% of line (6)		$26,850
9	Nonreimbursable direct expense[3]		$2,500
10	Total In-house expenses		$47,250
11	Consultants		$45,800
12	Estimated Total		$93,050
13	Contingency		$9,000
14	Proposed compensation		$102,050
15	Estimated reimbursables		$2,400
	Alternative Computation		
6	Direct in-house salary expense		$17,900
7	Direct personnel expense @ 1 25% of line (6)		$22,375
8	Indirect expenses @ 20% of line (7)		$4,475

Note: The figures in the above chart are not intended to reflect actual practice, but simply to illustrate the calculation procedure.

[1] Direct personnel expense is defined as the direct salaries of the architect's personnel engaged in the project and the related portion of the cost of their mandatory and customary contributions and benefits (e.g., employment taxes and other statutory employee benefits, insurance, sick leave, holidays, employee retirement plans, and similar contributions).

[2] Indirect expense is defined as all expenses not directly allocated to specific projects and is synonymous with overhead.

[3] Nonreimbursable direct expenses cover expenses not otherwise included in personnel and outside expenses (e.g., Reproduction of documents for in-house use, unreimbursed travel, and items paid on behalf of the client without specific reimbursement).

Step 5: Assess the Firm's Value Position and Add the Appropriate Profit Terms

Architects should assess the special value of their firm's services to a client and determine the most favorable fee and profit structure, based on the following considerations:

- The firm's minimum profit targets
- The value of the firm's services in the marketplace
- The value of the project to the firm even if the probable profit is low
- The fee level likely to be quoted by other firms competing for the project

At a minimum, the target profit levels will determine the architect's fixed fee, fully loaded hourly rates, or fee multiplier. It is also possible to increase compensation and profit by proposing incentive fees or bonuses to reflect high-value results from the architect's work. For example, an incentive amount might be related to a particularly aggressive schedule, tenant attraction and lease rates, or postoccupancy evaluation of building performance.

Step 6: Compare the Proposal with the Firm's Past Experience

Throughout the pricing process, most firms use previous experience with similar projects to estimate basic design service fees as a percentage of a new project's estimated construction cost. A firm should track its history of fee earnings and profitability to support this process. Given the number of variables, however—even among related projects for the same client—it is wise for several firm principals or project leaders to review proposed compensation terms before the service proposal is completed.

Step 7: Understand a Client's Administrative and Accounting Practices

An architect should discuss preferred billing and payment terms in early consultations with clients when goals, needs, and service scope are also discussed. Many clients will appreciate this as a sign of good business practice. While the details are prescribed in any owner-architect agreement, a few basic questions should be asked and answered:

- We prefer to bill for services every [state number] weeks. Is that acceptable?
- Is there a particular schedule on which invoices should be submitted?
- What documentation is required with our invoices?
- Who will review our invoices and approve them for payment?
- How quickly will payments be processed once invoices have been approved?

Step 8: Appropriate Invoicing and Payment Terms

Most architects invoice their clients for services monthly or every four weeks, depending on their internal accounting practices. Collections can be expedited if clients accept more frequent billing, particularly on hourly fee arrangements.

Although 30 days is a general standard for invoice payment, many architecture firms experience average collection periods of 60 days or more. Long collection cycles require the architect to finance the staffing and direct costs of providing services at an increased carrying cost to the firm. Efforts should be made to negotiate a contract provision requiring interest to be paid on payments overdue by more than 45 days.

Client payment patterns often reflect perceptions about the quality and value of work an architecture firm is providing. Regular invoices provide a natural opportunity for the architect to ask—on paper or in person—for a client's assessment of the firm's performance. If client payment patterns change, it is usually a sign that the perceived value of the service has changed; this is an important time for firm principals to address the client's concerns.

Step 9: Assess Special Risks and Responses

When the following are concerns, they should be addressed before a service agreement is finalized:

Uncertain credit. Like any provider of goods or services, an architect has a right to ask about a client's financial resources to support a specific project assignment. If a client's financial capacity is in doubt, the architect should consider declining the project or requiring an up-front fee and aggressive billing schedule to keep collections ahead of actual project costs.

Fee retainage. Contracts that allow retainage (amounts withheld from professional service fees until the completion of a project or work phase) dilute an architecture firm's financial performance and increase its risk. Retainage provisions should be eliminated from owner-architect agreements whenever possible.

Slow payment. Clients who describe a slow and complex payment process, or decline to commit to any specific process, present serious business risks for architects. This problem is best addressed by principals of the firm with their most senior client counterparts. Charging interest for late payments or requiring prepayment are additional responses.

Step 10: Sign the Agreement

The important final step is to actually sign the agreement and to obtain and date the owner's signature. Too many architects fail to complete the process and find that this leads to misunderstandings later in the project.

CHAPTER **6**

Common Project Issues

6.1 Programming

Robert G. Hershberger, FAIA, PhD

Architectural programming is the thorough and systematic evaluation of the interrelated values, goals, facts, and needs of a client's organization, facility users, and the surrounding community. A well-conceived program leads to high-quality design.

Architectural programming has developed as an activity related to, but distinct from, architectural design. It is considered an optional predesign service under AIA Document B101-2007, Standard Form of Agreement Between Owner and Architect. Document B101-2007 states that under "basic services," the architect is required only "to provide a preliminary evaluation of the Owner's program." Presumably after this preliminary evaluation the architect is expected to proceed with normal design services.

An increasing number of architects have found the above approach unsatisfactory and have elected to offer architectural programming as an integral part of their services. In this context, programming has evolved into a far more thorough and systematic endeavor than when it was offered as an incidental part of the architectural design process or when it was conducted by the owner.

Because of the increasing complexity of buildings and building systems, the need for programming services is likely to expand. Moreover, many clients are becoming much more sophisticated and thus more interested in understanding and managing their physical resources.

Programming led by architects can provide clients with a systematic process for decision making about organizational and project values, goals, and requirements.

Robert G. Hershberger is professor and dean emeritus of the College of Architecture at the University of Arizona. He is also a partner in Hershberger and Nickels Architects/Planners of Tucson and Tempe, Arizona. He is the author of Architectural Programming and Predesign Manager.

VALUES IN ARCHITECTURAL PROGRAMMING

Human: functional, social, physical, physiological, psychological

Environmental: site, climate, context, resources, waste

Cultural: historical, institutional, political, legal

Technological: materials, systems, processes

Temporal: growth, change, permanence

Economic: finance, construction, operations, maintenance, energy

Aesthetic: form, space, color, meaning

Safety: structural, fire, chemical, personal, criminal

—Robert Hershberger, Architectural Programming and Predesign Manager (1999)

Many clients have a limited view of the range of physical possibilities for accommodating their operations; architects have the ideal professional background to help them visualize options during programming. The programming process as led by architecture firms can expose clients to a wide range of alternative approaches and help them choose appropriate directions.

CLIENT NEEDS

All types of clients need programming services. Institutional, government, and corporate clients are most likely to recognize this need and be willing to pay for programming services, although in some cases these clients may produce programs in-house or by using other programming consultants before engaging the services of an architect.

Government agencies use programming services extensively because they often base procurement of design services on fully developed programs. Owners of complex institutional facilities such as hospitals and hotels easily recognize the need for careful up-front analysis of design issues and will often employ architecture firms to develop their programs. Owners of owner-occupied office facilities usually want quality programming in order to achieve facilities management objectives. Clients with little experience with the building industry generally appreciate the guidance an architect can provide through the programming process. Developers are the least likely to recognize the need for architectural programming services because many believe they know precisely what is needed in the market and thus see no reason to explore alternatives and weigh potential trade-offs. While some residential clients may not want to pay extra for programming, they need the service, even when they are just remodeling a few rooms.

Discussing the benefits of programming during initial interviews sometimes broadens the vision of resistant clients and helps them understand why they need to contract for these services.

Preliminary Studies

Some clients will need financial feasibility, site suitability, and/or master planning services prior to architectural programming. Financial feasibility studies explore market conditions in relation to specific sites and development plans in order to show whether a particular project will be viable. These studies can be led by architects but often require the expertise of other professionals. Site suitability studies may also be required prior to the purchase of a particular property to make certain that the site is properly zoned, has needed services, and is appropriately sized and configured for a proposed project.

Architects are ideally trained to conduct site suitability studies because of their design skills and knowledge of applicable land use and building codes and regulations. Where geotechnical issues are involved, civil engineering consultants may be brought in. Landscape architects should be consulted on projects where there are significant site planning issues.

Clients with a large site and an extensive program that will develop over time should develop a master plan before programming for any particular building or facility. Architects who provide master planning services followed by complete architectural programming services are in an excellent position to prove their value to the client and thus to be assured of obtaining the commission for design services for each phase of master plan implementation.

Architectural Programming

Architectural programming can include all of the above studies but generally commences after they are complete. It tends to focus on specific facilities identified in the master plan and includes all of the areas mentioned in the previous sections: value identification, goal setting, discovery of related facts, and development of specific project requirements. These are all developed in collaboration with the client, user, and community, but depending on the nature of the project, specialists may be required to develop some of the information. Specialists may include kitchen consultants, laboratory consultants, security consultants, data and communications specialists, and transportation and parking specialists.

Some architects specialize in offering programming services, and other professionals, including social and behavioral scientists, systems analysts, interior designers, and building management and operations specialists, have entered the field. Some programming consultants, including architects, specialize in particular building types or functions, such as hospitals, sports complexes, hotels, justice facilities, laboratories, security systems, clean rooms, and kitchens.

Costs of Services

Architects who offer programming services have had increasing success in negotiating fees to cover the cost of these services because owners recognize that the resulting buildings better serve their needs. Indeed, architecture firms that offer programming as a primary service are often recognized by their peers as producing quality architecture. Fees for programming vary. Highly technical buildings such as hospitals or laboratories can command higher figures than commercial and moderate-size institutional buildings. Fees for master planning also vary depending on the expected deliverables and project types.

SKILLS

On smaller projects, one person from the programming firm can usually handle all of the programming tasks. On larger projects, the programming team will generally include a senior architect, who handles sensitive client interviews and work session presentations (or at least introductions); a project programmer, who conducts interviews with key personnel, develops questionnaires (if needed), analyzes data, and oversees development of the programming document; and junior programmers, who do literature searches, conduct user interviews, conduct observational studies including site analysis, and assist the project programmer in developing the program document.

Specialized consultants are used to develop the criteria and parameters for particular spaces or facility types, such as laboratories, airports, prisons, kitchens, and hospitality/entertainment complexes. The involvement of specific personnel should be carefully developed in a programming work plan.

Programmers must be familiar with the fundamentals of the architectural design and building processes and be alert to the design and construction implications of program statements. But they must also have specific knowledge and skill to be effective at programming.

Expertise in information gathering is the heart of the programmer's domain and requires the ability to

- Conduct efficient literature searches
- Employ active listening skills to conduct diagnostic interviews
- Record meaningful data during a walk-through study
- Develop comprehensive space inventories
- Obtain trace evidence
- Conduct systematic observations
- Know when and how to develop and administer questionnaires

Strong verbal and management skills are necessary for group interviewing and work session leadership. Here again, active listening skills are vital, but the ability to direct the course of the session and to lead people of diverse opinions to consensus is even more important.

Data analysis skills are equally important. Knowing what to collect and then how to convert the raw data to useful information is essential to effective programming. Skilled programmers learn how to avoid "data clog," a favorite term of programming pioneer Willie Pea. The programmer must learn to collect only the needed data and then know how to convert them into meaningful (reliable and valid) information that can influence the design of the project.

Knowledge of space size standards for various building types is a fundamental requirement for programmers. Before going into the work session, they must know what the standards are for a building type as well as what space the client actually has, so they can guide the client to agreement on appropriate net space needs for a particular facility. They must also be aware of appropriate efficiencies for various building types and quality levels to be able to apply them to net totals to arrive at gross square footage requirements. Efficiency factors are often less than 70 percent for many building types. But clients rarely understand how much of a building area is consumed by such space as halls, walls, utility chases, and closets. The programmer must have the knowledge and skill to guide the client through this part of program development.

The programmer must be familiar with current construction cost information and with general project delivery timelines. In some cases it may be necessary to consult general contractors or cost estimators in order to develop realistic preliminary costing and project schedules. Where clients require full financial feasibility studies, consultants with backgrounds in real estate development and banking often are used. At this early stage, it is common to provide a contingency budget of 20 or 30 percent of the expected building cost because so many factors (land cost, soils, easements, etc.) are unknown. This percentage will be reduced as the project progresses and more is known, so that a common contingency in the master planning would be 15 percent, dropping to 10 or 12 percent in programming and 5 to 7 percent for construction.

Finally, writing skills are needed to capture and delineate the qualitative and quantitative aspects of the client requirements. An architectural programmer must be able to communicate programming information verbally and visually to the client, the users, the community, and the architect who will design the project.

Equipment

Given that virtually all architects will have a computer that can produce finished drawings and a word-processed report, the only special equipment needed for architectural programming would be a digital or other camera.

No other special equipment is necessary.

PROCESS

Architectural programming is inherently a team process. At a minimum, the programmer and client determine the program, but more often several persons from the programming firm, an array of users, and sometimes community participants are involved. The scale of the project (e.g., a building interior, one building, a building complex) will have a strong effect on team size and composition. Other factors include the type of facilities and level of specialized functions that will be required and possibly constraints on interaction with the client and users.

Client and User Values

Programming is the time to identify, consider, debate, reject, accept, and prioritize values such as institutional purposes, functional efficiency, user comfort, building economics, safety, environmental sustainability, and visual quality. These identified values and concerns can have a profound effect on the ultimate form of a building. If the program is driven primarily by concerns for functional efficiency, as is the case in many owner-produced programs, organizational decisions made during programming will significantly affect the form of the building.

If the program evolves more from the social and psychological needs of the users, prescriptions for form will also be inherent in the identified spaces and their sizes, characteristics, and relationships. If the program responds primarily to economic concerns, it is possible that numerous material and system opportunities as well as potentially unique spaces and places will be eliminated from design consideration during programming. A carefully conceived and comprehensive architectural programming process will help to ensure that all of the appropriate values have been identified and prioritized.

The values identification portion of architectural programming offers the client an opportunity to resolve important questions or make critical decisions about how the client's organization relates to the built environment. In addition, consideration should be given to how the client's values relate to the values of the community, of the users of the facility, and those of the design professionals with whom the client is working. Considering these value relationships can help the programmer manage potential conflicts of values and identify opportunities for a fuller expression of common values.

Project Goals

Once the primary values have been identified and prioritized, it is possible to develop specific project goals. What organizational objectives should be accomplished by providing a new, expanded, or renovated facility? Should the resulting building be a statement of the organization's desired image? Should it be a model of efficiency? Or should it be more loosely organized, allowing for serendipitous events or even changes in how operations are conducted? Should it be environmentally sensitive, a showpiece of "green" architecture? What is the target for overall project cost? When should the facility be ready for operation? Goals in these and many other areas need to be set during programming.

Constraints and Opportunities

Achievement of the goals will be made easy or difficult by the characteristics of the organization's operations as well as those of the site. Information must be gathered that identifies the specific nature of the constraints and opportunities. Is there enough land on which to locate the proposed facility? Is it in the right location in terms of visibility, access, service, and the like? Can the existing facilities be easily converted to new uses? Are the organization's cash flow and/or reserves sufficient to ensure that the construction and start-up costs can be managed? Questions of fact must be considered before realistic projections for new and renovated spaces can be made.

Facility Requirements

When the important values and goals of the client, user group, and community and any related facts have been identified, then and only then should the identification of specific space needs begin. Unfortunately, many client-provided programs are developed without adequate consideration of important institutional values and goals. Personnel assigned to prepare the program tend to proceed directly to identification of user needs and space requirements. Those preparing the program may be unaware that their personal value systems are influencing the decisions they are making and that a more conscious identification of institutional values and the setting of specific project goals would have a profound effect on how the specific needs of the project are developed. Often a few known and pressing facts tend to dominate the decision process, while other facts remain uncovered, even though they may be more important relative to the organization's mission.

Steps for identifying the space needs of a specific facility include the following:

- Identify required spaces.
- Establish the size and relationships of these spaces.
- Develop appropriate factors for estimating efficiency.
- Determine project budget and schedule requirements.

When determining factors for estimating efficiency, allow for nonprogrammed areas such as halls, walls, restrooms, service areas, two-story spaces, and the like. Base budget and schedule requirements on previously identified values, goals, and facts in order to get the most accurate guide for the design of proposed new facilities.

Information Gathering

Five types of information gathering are used in architectural programming: literature and code search/review, interviewing, observation, questionnaire/survey, and group sessions.

Literature and code search/review. This task comes first in the programming process, beginning even before the commission is awarded, to give the programmer background knowledge of similar facilities and a general familiarity with the client's mission and language. The literature search includes gathering reports on existing facilities, along with site surveys, construction documents, and other relevant documents that the client may possess. It also involves obtaining relevant government documents, including applicable codes and ordinances, as well as recognized building and planning standards, historical documents and archival materials, trade publications, research literature, professional publications, manufacturers' publications, and even sources in popular literature and on the Internet.

Some types of facilities—for example, healthcare, senior living, elementary and secondary schools—are governed by codes that often dictate sizes of some rooms, adjacencies, and other key program considerations. Thus, the literature search must also include a review of any relevant codes.

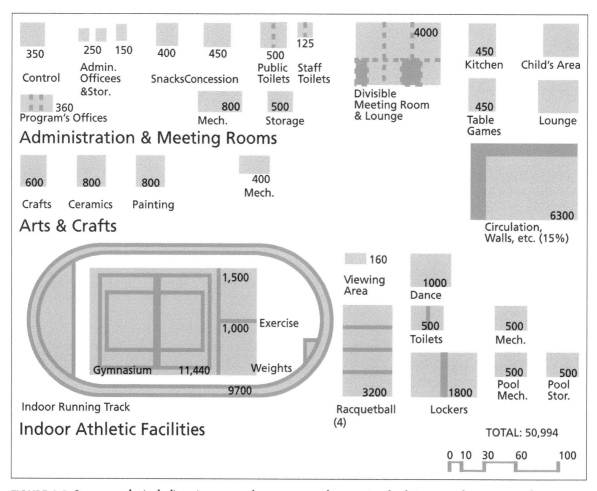

FIGURE 6.1 **Space needs, including site uses such as sports and recreation facilities, are often presented graphically to facilitate the start of the design process.**

TABLE 6.1   DATABASES

Source	Description	Location
Databases		
Associations Unlimited	Information about 444,000 international and U.S. nonprofit membership organizations in all fields	Online library database (available to library card holders)
Business & Company Resource Center (Gale)	Broker research reports, trade publications, newspapers, journals, and company directory lists	Online library database (available to library card holders)
Business Source Premier (EBSCO Host)	Full text for nearly 7,400 scholarly business journals across all subject areas. Includes detailed company profiles and country economic reports	Online library database (available to library card holders)
Expanded Academic ASAP (Gale)	Scholarly journals, magazines, and newspapers	Online library database (available to library card holders)
ProQuest	Access to more than 8,000 magazines and newspapers, including the *New York Times* and the *Washington Post*	Online library database (available to library card holders)

TABLE 6.2   WEB RESOURCES

Source	Description	Location
Web Resources		
Arts and entertainment	American Association of Museums International Society for Performing Arts National Endowment for the Arts	www.aam-us.org www.ispa.org http://arts.endow.gov
Census data	GlobalEDGE International Business North American Industry Classification System U.S. Census Bureau	http://globaledge.msu.edu www.census.gov/epcd/naics02/ www.census.gov
Corporate	American Productivity & Quality Center Annual reports via the *Wall Street Journal* Business Wire National Association of Manufacturers U.S. Securities & Exchange Commission	www.apqc.org http://wsjie.ar.wilink.com home.businesswire.com www.nam.org www.sec.gov/edgar.shtml
Education	American Association of School Administrators American Association of State Colleges and Universities Association of Higher Education Facilities Officers Design Share National Clearinghouse for Educational Facilities School Building Association School Construction News School Designs U.S. Department of Education	www.aasa.org www.aascu.org www.appa.org www.designshare.com www.edfacilities.org www.cefpi.org www.schoolconstructionnews.com www.schooldesigns.com www.edu.gov
Health care	American Association of Retired Persons American Hospital Association American Medical Association American Nursing Association Assisted Living Federation of America Center for Health Design *Health Facilities Management Journal* Modern Healthcare National Council on Aging	www.aarp.org www.aha.org www.ama-assn.org http://nursingworld.org www.alfa.org www.healthdesign.org www.hospitalconnect.com www.modernhealthcare.com www.ncoa.org
Housing and urban development	Americans with Disabilities Act Fannie Mae Freddie Mac National Apartment Association National Association of Home Builders National Association of Housing and Redevelopment National Multi Housing Council U.S. Department of Housing and Urban Development	www.usdoj.gov/crt/ada/adahom1.htm www.fanniemae.com www.freddiemac.com www.naahq.org www.nahb.org www.nahro.org www.nmhc.org www.hud.gov
Newspapers and magazines	Local business journals Local business journals Internet Public Library (Univ. of Mich.)	www.bizjournals.com http://bibliomaven.com/businessjournals.html www.ipl.org

PART 3: THE PROJECT

(continued)

Source	Description	Location
Web Resources		
Nonprofit organizations	American Society of Association Executives	www.asaenet.org
	Nonprofit Board	www.boardsource.org
	The NonProfit Times	www.nptimes.com
Real estate management and development	Building and Office Management Association	www.boma.org
	Community Associations Institute	www.caionline.org
	CoreNet Global	www.corenetglobal.org
	Facilities Net	www.facilitiesnet.com
	FM Link	www.fmlink.com
	International Facility Management Association	www.ifma.org
	National Association of Industrial and Office Properties	www.naiop.org
	National Real Estate Investor	http://nreionline.com
	National Urban League	www.nul.org
Retail	Institute of Store Planners	http://ww3.ispo.org/
	International Council of Shopping Centers	www.icsc.org
	National Retail Federation	www.nrf.com
	Retail Industry Leaders Association	www.imra.org
	Retail Source	www.retailsource.com

Research and analysis by Peggy Lawless and Wendy Pound

Interviewing. In most cases this is the core activity in programming. It begins with the client interview. At this interview, the programmer can learn more about the client's values and goals, refine a work plan and schedule, and ascertain whom to contact within the client organization. Interviews with key personnel, other users (clients, patrons, customers, etc.), and interested community members follow. Successful interviews are carefully planned. The programmer first tries to identify the basic values that will affect the design of the facility—human, cultural, environmental, technological, temporal, economic, aesthetic, and safety-related. In planning interviews, the programmer should consider what data could make a design difference, who could provide the most useful information, who has the authority to make decisions and establish priorities, the amount of time and the size of the budget that are available, and how interviewing will relate to other information-gathering techniques that may be used, such as observations or surveys.

For larger organizations, the programmer usually reviews the organizational chart with the client to identify the key officers, department heads, and other persons likely to be knowledgeable about facility needs or in decision-making positions. Others within the organization who might be interviewed include department managers, members of special committees, maintenance people, a sampling of typical employees, and employees with special needs. Those who use or visit the building but do not work for the client organization, such as suppliers, service people, fire officials, or customers, also may have important input. Interviews may take place in an individual or group setting.

Whoever is interviewed and however the interviews take place, the objective is to obtain complete and reliable information. It helps to conduct the interviews in or near the client's or user's existing environment. This setting tends to make interviewees more comfortable in answering questions, and also makes it easier for them to focus on their own architectural environment. Interviewing techniques vary widely and should match the data-gathering objectives.

Following are questions of the sort that could be used in an interview guide.

I. Your Job
    1. What type of work do you do?
    2. What activities do you perform most often?
    3. How often do you need to work alone? In small groups?
    4. Which activities or tasks are most important to your job?
    5. What barriers do you encounter in doing those tasks?
    6. What helps or hinders you when you need to be creative?
    7. Describe your most recent day at work. What did you do? Where did you go? With whom did you interact?
    8. How often do you meet with customers here? Where do you meet with them? How well does that work?
    9. How often do you travel for your job?
    10. What technology do you use on the job? How well does it meet your needs?
    11. What changes would help you do your job better?

II. Your Work Style
    1. What's your style of working?
    2. Overall, do you prefer working alone or in groups?
    3. What distracts you when you're working?
    4. How easy is it for you to ignore distractions?
    5. How much privacy do you need? How well is that need met?
    6. Under what conditions are you most productive?
    7. What do you do when you need to recharge yourself?

III. Your Office or Workspace
    1. What is your workspace like?
    2. How satisfied are you with the space you have?
    3. What do you particularly like about your workspace?
    4. What's missing that would help you do your job?
    5. Where do you work when you need to concentrate? What makes that space good for concentrating?
    6. How comfortable is your office furniture?
    7. In what ways have you personalized your office?
    8. How convenient is the location of your support services, both administrative assistants and equipment such as photocopiers and printers?
    9. What would you change in your current workspace to help you be more productive?
    10. Doing the work you do today, what would your ideal work environment be (features, atmosphere, people, interactions, equipment, feel, stimulation)?

IV. Interactions and Communication
    1. What people or departments do you work with on a regular basis?
    2. How convenient is it for you to reach those people or departments?
    3. How do you most often communicate with people? One on one? In groups of two to four people? In meetings? On the phone? Via e-mail? Which method works best for you?
    4. How common is it for you to encounter people from other departments? Where does that usually happen?

V. Meeting Space
    1. How much of your day do you typically spend in meetings? How productive is that for you?
    2. Describe the rooms that work well for meetings.
    3. How easy is it for you to schedule a meeting room?

VI. Physical Factors
    Do any of these physical factors interfere with your work? If yes, in what way(s)?
    - Too much noise
    - Too quiet
    - Lighting quality
    - Too hot or too cold
    - Air quality
    - Vibration
    - Smells

VII. Workplace or Building
    1. What is your impression of the building entrance? Lobby?
    2. How do you think guests and customers feel when they enter the building?
    3. If you were a new employee here, how easy would it be for you to get your bearings?
    4. What do you think of how the space is laid out here? What changes, if any, would you make?
    5. What do you think of the security measures for this building?
    6. Are there places for you to get food or refreshments? If so, where? What do you think of those spaces?

Research and analysis by Peggy Lawless and Wendy Pound

Observation. This task is another information-gathering technique that programmers should use. A walk-through observation of the existing facility with the property or facility manager is an excellent way to orient yourself to obvious programming requirements. A space inventory, including plans and annotated photographs of existing spaces, equipment, and furnishings, can provide important baseline information. The programmer photographs and measures existing spaces and documents existing furniture and equipment to better understand the space requirements. Trace observation documents wear and tear on existing facilities (surfaces, furniture, fixtures, and equipment) and may tell an important story about traffic and circulation patterns, use levels, and other factors that should be accounted for in the program. Behavioral observation (time-and-motion studies) can document the functions that the building occupants perform and the adequacy of the space accommodating them. For example, the programmer may observe that a hospital room has an inadequate turning radius for a wheelchair when a visitor chair is placed in the room. Quite often the programmer will be told during client or user interviews that a particular space is a problem, prompting subsequent observational study of the space to determine the cause of the problem.

Questionnaires and surveys. These are yet another information-gathering tool used in programming. Surveys are an efficient way to gather facts and quantitative details in a large organization. Furniture and equipment needs of individual users, for example, can be ascertained through a written survey form. The questions must be carefully developed using a systematic process that includes pretesting, or there is a good chance that the resulting data will be meaningless or at least difficult to analyze.

Group sessions. These are the final way to obtain needed information in architectural programming. It is important to conduct at least one group work session (usually several) as a feedback mechanism to allow the client and users to consider, debate, and eventually resolve and agree upon the true nature of the architecture problem—to reach a consensus as to which values, goals, facts, needs, and ideas should influence the design of the facility. This is a type of group interviewing process that typically involves feedback of information obtained from the other information-gathering methods. Techniques include brainstorming new ideas and rejecting as inappropriate some of the information collected earlier, concluding with prioritizing the goals and needs for the project. It is not only a way of gathering information but also a method of obtaining agreement.

Data Analysis

Throughout the data-gathering process it is important to organize data so that they can be retrieved and analyzed quickly and easily. A key technique is to seek and record only information that will be vital in making design decisions. Based on analysis of all information gathered, the programmer will develop performance and design criteria for the facility. Space requirements, space relationships, circulation, ambient environment, safety and security, needed surfaces, furnishings, flexibility, and site information are among the issues usually addressed. Graphics such as matrices showing space allocations and relationships and bubble diagrams showing adjacency relationships are also developed.

During analysis, the programmer will identify major unresolved programming issues and begin to develop some preliminary ideas about options for their resolution in the final building program. Some writers have referred to these ideas as "precepts" (a term implying a combination of "preliminary" and "concepts," yet still clearly preliminary to conceptual design). Here the programmer's task is to develop options (precepts) for solutions, to help with their evaluation, and to recommend the most effective alternatives. For example, in a residential facility such as a nursing home or a juvenile justice institution, there might be a trade-off between privacy and isolation in residents' bedrooms. Options might be single, double, or multiple-occupancy bedrooms. A recommendation might be to have a mixture of rooms to allow for occupant or staff choice. The programming team presents the various options or precepts to the client and guides the client through evaluation of the alternatives. As with interviewing, there are many different ways to structure these presentations, and the approach should be tailored to the needs of the client organization and the particular project.

Deliverables

The usual deliverable is a written architectural program, which is a comprehensive report that includes documentation of the methodology used, an executive summary, value and goal statements, the relevant facts, data analysis conclusions, and the program requirements, including space listings by function and size, relationship diagrams, space program sheets, stacking plans, precept drawings, and flow diagrams. Photographs or even videos may be used to illustrate space-planning requirements. A comprehensive program will also include project cost estimates and a project schedule.

For More Information

The following titles represent a bookshelf of publications about architectural programming that architects will find useful: Edith Cherry, *Programming for Design: From Theory to Practice* (1998); Donna P. Duerk, *Architectural Programming: Information Management for Design* (1993); Robert Hershberger, *Architectural Programming and Predesign Manager* (1999); Robert R. Kumlin, *Architectural Programming: Creative Techniques for Design Professionals* (1995); Mickey Palmer, ed., *The Architect's Guide to Facility Programming* (1981); William Pen and Steven Parshall, *Problem Seeking: An Architectural Programming Primer*, 4th ed. (2001); Wolfgang F. E. Preiser, ed., *Facility Programming* (1978); Preiser, ed., *Programming the Built Environment* (1985); Preiser, ed., *Professional Practice in Facility Programming* (1993).

6.2   Evidence-Based Design

Travis L. Hicks, AIA

Evidence-based design (EBD) is a trend in the practice of architecture that has grown out of evidence-based medicine and other evidence-based discourses. Grounded in research, EBD takes advantage of current knowledge, data, and well-informed clients to arrive at better design solutions.

Evidence-based design is ". . .a process for the conscientious, explicit, and judicious use of current best evidence from research and practice in making critical decisions, together with an informed client, about the design of each individual and unique project."

—D. Kirk Hamilton, FAIA

BACKGROUND

Since the early 1970s, evidence-based design (EBD) is one of a number of different "evidence-based" discourses among a wide range of disciplines. For example, there are similar evidence-based paradigms in medicine, education, nursing, dentistry, and policy, to name a few. Evidence-based design is a term that has come to mean many different things to different audiences at different times.

Travis L. Hicks is an NCARB-certified licensed architect and assistant professor at the University of North Carolina at Greensboro. With combined professional practice and academic experience dating back to 1997, he is a graduate of Princeton University who began his career with thesis advisor Michael Graves.

At its best, EBD is a design process that leverages best practices and current knowledge as well as primary, secondary, or tertiary evidence in order to solve a particular problem or answer a specific question through a rigorous process that resolves design issues with evidence. When misrepresented, EBD can be a convenient rhetoric used to justify what one would have done intuitively or through a more conventional design process. This discussion seeks to provide some guidelines for telling evidence-based design apart from conventional architectural practices and from research for research's sake; additionally, this section offers some suggestions for integrating an EBD program into one's practice.

Qualities of Responsible Evidence-Based Design
- The design process relies on knowledge and information gleaned through research and the gathering of evidence.
- Completed projects go through a rigorous postoccupancy evaluation, or similar analysis, in order to make subsequent projects more successful.
- Research and evidence are woven into the design process; conversely, the design process responds to research reciprocally.
- Results of research are open-ended, not predetermined, so that the design is open-ended.

Signs of Dubious Evidence-Based Design
- Architect relies solely on intuition, past projects, or standard practices to arrive at a design solution, while claiming to be practicing EBD.
- Product manufacturer points to its product data and claims it as "evidence"; however, closer inspection reveals that the data is not changing the way the product has been conceived and/or produced.

EVIDENCE-BASED DESIGN METHODS

Question

The first step in a research project is often stating a question, or questions, that will be answered through a methodical process. Understanding that the very practice of architecture is a complex problem-solving exercise that ultimately answers a plethora of questions, there is not an expectation that every problem one encounters in a project will be pursued with the same level of research and/or evidence-gathering strategies. The architecture team should determine some hierarchy of questions in much the same way one would design for formal hierarchy in a building design. Working with an informed client, the design team with evidence-based experience will organize research questions around project goals and priorities.

Sample Research Questions
- What arrangement of patient room furniture promotes the shortest hospital stay? *Project goal*: Reduce hospital stays by a certain amount of time.
- What relationship between open labs and closed labs promotes the greatest efficiency? *Project goal*: Decrease the time before a particular drug goes to market.
- How do lighting strategies and reflectivity of ceiling finishes influence student test scores? *Client's priorities*: Increase test scores above state or national averages.
- What is the relationship between work surface heights and collaboration in research and development facilities? *Client's priorities*: Promote product innovation through collaboration.
- How will a change in the materiality and geometry of the facade affect the R-value of the building enclosure? *Project goal*: Design a building envelope that reduces the building's energy consumption by a certain percentage.

Not all questions will make great research questions. The experienced design and research team will be able to establish a short list of questions that are central to the project and the client's goals. Shortly after establishing this hierarchy of questions and project goals, the architect or design team should generate a literature review to offer a background knowledge base for the research project and to hone the questions. The term "literature review" is primarily associated with academic settings; however, many of the academic literature review techniques will sound familiar to practitioners who have done background research to set project goals for a client.

Collect Data

While every step in the EBD process is important, the collection of data is a critical component to establishing the pretest attributes of the work. If, at the other end of the process, one is to assume that there's something to be studied after the project is built, then the quantitative or qualitative data that is to be compared begins with the data collected during this step in the process.

STEPS IN THE EVIDENCE-BASED DESIGN PROCESS

While there are a number of different versions of the EBD process, the following steps are common to many of these versions:

Question: Through a literature review or by virtue of previously completed projects, arrive at a question to be addressed through the design project.

Collect data: Collecting data will take on different forms, depending upon the kind of data to be collected. This collected data will inform and influence the design process.

Hypothesize: A critical step in the EBD process, stating a hypothesis the architect is beholden to prove/disprove, will make the process more rigorous.

Design: Like other architectural projects, designs that follow an EBD process will have a design process. An EBD-oriented project team will have methods and tools to evaluate a project's trajectory toward its EBD goals periodically throughout the design process.

Construct: The construction of the design based on solid evidence or knowledge is a critical component of EBD, so that a posttest or postoccupancy evaluation of the project is possible.

Analyze: The analysis of the design and construction project is commonly done through a postoccupancy evaluation, and this analysis offers insights into the project's success.

Refine question: A key to evidence-based design is that the process results in a refinement of the question or project goals, and the EBD cycle begins all over again.

Share results: Publication of the results from the EBD process will advance the collective body of knowledge in the profession.

SUGGESTIONS FOR CONDUCTING A LITERATURE REVIEW

- Seek current knowledge while still framing literature within a historical context.
- Target academic journals in addition to books or mainstream periodicals. University libraries will have access to academic journal articles.
- Seek peer-reviewed work to elevate the objectivity and accountability of source materials.
- Draw a diagram to describe relationships between different sources.
- Keep notes in an organized fashion so that they can be called upon in future phases of the project.
- Generate a spreadsheet summarizing each article, with the following headings: citation, setting, subjects, methods, and results.
- Use a citation program such as Endnote or Refworks for recording citations and inserting them in papers while you write.

Hypothesis

While in a typical design process the architect relies on previous experience, proto-types, or rules of thumb to assume the answers to all the questions, an evidence-based design process demands a suspension of belief. Stating a hypothesis or a series of hypotheses will allow for discovery and for the hypotheses to be supported or unsupported. Stating a hypothesis is one of the key differences between evidence-based design and a standard design process.

Design

How, then, does the design process change when there are evidence-based aspirations of the architect or design team? For illustration purposes, consider another component of the typical design process. For example, cost estimating is an activity that is done periodically throughout a project, generally at the ends of project phases. A project team that fails to generate periodic cost estimates will most likely find that the design is off track vis-à-vis the budget by the end of the construction drawing phase of the project. Is it possible to complete a project without a cost estimate? Yes; however, the results may be less than desirable. Is it possible to complete a project without any thought given to evidence-based design? Yes, but that project would not be able to claim EBD as an influence nor an outcome; moreover, the project would not benefit from the value that data and evidence could bring to the table. If project cost is something that needs to be evaluated periodically, then evidence is also an aspect of the project that could be evaluated periodically.

Construct

For an EBD process the construction phase will have similarities to any other construction phase. Those aspects of a construction phase that might be unique to EBD include more rigorous mock-ups for testing, higher levels of building commissioning, and rigorous testing, measuring, and balancing. Depending upon the research questions that the design team and client are trying to address, mock-ups will be important in the EBD process.

Mock-ups should be used to measure more than just aesthetics or whether the mock-up quality meets the specifications for the element constructed. Depending on its scale, the mock-up can be used to gain additional cycles from the cyclical EBD process. The mock-up can be analyzed, and the research questions can be reformulated and the design modified before the final construction is completed.

Analyze

The analysis of data will rely on different tools and techniques, depending on the data that has been collected after construction and/or occupancy. In the case of postconstruction, the design team will be able to analyze the more technical aspects of the design. Engineering systems can be tested and balanced against the design criteria; however, the aspects of the design that rely on human interaction will require a postoccupancy evaluation (POE). Architects will be familiar with postoccupancy evaluations and the techniques generally used in POEs. Surveying end users, for example, will offer insights into the project's overall success, usability, and comfort.

Refine Questions

Following through with an evidence-based design process means the research questions need to be refined so that subsequent projects take advantage of the previous project. Upon analyzing the results of the built project, the researcher, architect, or design team must determine if the hypothesis was supported, or not, through the project's outcomes. If the hypothesis was supported, then the architect can continue with similar attitudes or solutions when faced with a similar problem. If the hypothesis was not supported in the course of analyzing the project's outcomes, then the architect will alter the design or refine the question when faced with a similar problem or project.

Share Results

Disseminating one's work is critical to establishing the legitimacy and objectivity of the work. Most architects are familiar with the process of disseminating their work through monographs or journal articles; however, architects are not used to releasing the data or numbers about their work. Reasons for this reluctance to share information might result from a fear of exposing less-than-desirable conclusions or from a desire to keep information private or proprietary, thereby maintaining a competitive edge or client confidentiality.

APPLICATIONS FOR EVIDENCE-BASED DESIGN

The evidence-based design process transcends typology or context; however, there are a number of building types that lend themselves more readily to the EBD process. These building types either rely more heavily on data or numbers to be successful, or they are allied with end users or clients who themselves have evidence-based discourses.

Healthcare Environments

Evidence-based design has a well-established history in healthcare environments where the collection of quantitative patient data has been readily available. Given the interest of hospitals and insurance companies in maintaining or improving the level of patient care and employee productivity, healthcare environments have over the years focused time and energy on architecture and interior design. Patient data such as blood pressure, heart rate, other vital signs, and length of stay are monitored and tracked in the standard operation of a hospital, nursing home, or other healthcare facility; therefore, the collection of data for architects in healthcare environments is more accessible. The Center for Health Design (CHD) is an organization that advocates for better healthcare design through research and education, supporting an EBD approach to healthcare design.

The pursuit of evidence-based medicine provides a natural synergy with EBD. Healthcare professionals seek to improve patient care and, in the process, collect data that supports the work of architects and interior designers. Information about staff efficiency and effectiveness, data related to accuracy and proficiency, and numbers of patient illness or death related to staff performance are of interest to those studying evidence-based medicine. This data, when shared with architects and designers, offers some insights into the relationships between welfare and design.

Learning Environments

Learning environments such as K–12 schools or higher education spaces also offer architects access to quantitative data, such as test scores, grades, student absences, and sick days. Design goals supported by research into these project types range from improving test scores to improving indoor environmental quality. Over the years architects and researchers have concluded that daylight has a direct and positive impact on student performance, and indoor environmental quality has a similar impact on health. More recently there has been research into the relationships between teaching styles, furniture layout, and learning in academic environments. A product of this research is Steelcase's "LearnLab: Classroom of the Future," a prototype for a flexible learning environment that challenges the conventional classroom layout and structure.

Another source of data tied to learning environments is the National Clearinghouse for Educational Facilities (NCEF). Funded through the National Institute of Building Sciences, NCEF collects and disseminates information about learning environments and links to a number of allied organizations and information sources.

Learning environments are not limited to schools; libraries also fall under this category. Libraries range from academic libraries to public libraries to school libraries. As EBD expands beyond healthcare design, there are opportunities for architects to find synergies with evidence-based librarianship (EBL) or evidence-based library and information practice (EBLIP). Recent research by the author suggests that EBD principles applied to library design will affect the ways that libraries are laid out in the future.

Workplace Environments

Workplace environments are being studied relative to employee attraction and retention, reduction of sick days, productivity, and efficiency. For corporate office environments, the research is being led by furniture manufacturers such as Knoll, whose Workplace Research group is showing the way to advancements in corporate office design. Research in workplace environments has led to improved ergonomics for workers, more transparency in office partitions, and changes in standard planning modules. Ergonomic research has resulted in office accessories such as keyboard trays, monitor arms, high-end task chairs, and foot machines.

In addition to research being done by furniture manufacturers, there are leading architecture firms that are studying the relationships between design and productivity and efficiency. Gensler is one of the global leaders in this effort; through its Workplace Performance Index® it has established a tool to measure the relationships between business and design.

Retail Environments

Retail environments are another project type where research influences architectural design. Project goals for these retail environments tend to be different from the types of goals for healthcare. Retail data is generated through information technology systems linked to sales. Through studying sales figures, market research, and their relationships to retail space planning and layout, retailers are better equipped to generate retail designs that increase profitability.

An advantage that retail environment's EBD processes have over other building types is the rate at which retail spaces are designed and built and the sheer number of retail environments that exist. Compared to hospitals or laboratory buildings that take 5 to 10 years from start to finish, retail environments are generated at lightning speed. The EBD cycle is able to lead to conclusions at a similar pace, such that retail spaces are perhaps the most finely tuned environments based on research and evidence.

Science and Technology Environments

As their name implies, research laboratories are those facilities where hard science and bench research is undertaken. The people who run these laboratories are the same people who are funded by federal grants from agencies such as the National Institutes of Health or the National Science Foundation or through private investors. The kind of rigor that these agencies demand and that the researchers carry out means that the architecture of these spaces needs the same rigor.

Evidence-based design techniques will assist with a number of current issues in wet lab and dry lab architecture. For new construction projects, EBD has the potential to address questions related to daylighting, ventilation, efficiency, safety, and security. For existing laboratories in need of renovations or additions, an analysis of the existing building will generate the data needed to produce the architectural design. Airflow tests, light levels, and indoor environmental quality measurements are examples of a few metrics that can be collected and documented in existing laboratory buildings.

Importance of Evidence in Sustainable Design

One might argue that sustainable design is inextricably linked to evidence; otherwise, who would know what is actually being targeted for sustaining? In order to sustain something at a certain level, or to improve upon that level, the metrics or data of that level must be a known number to begin with. This area of metrics is where sustainable design and EBD overlap.

LEED for Existing Buildings: Operations and Maintenance, or LEED-EBOM, is a rating system that incorporates the pursuit of evidence in sustainable design. Within this system there are several categories that ask the architect or other design team member to utilize evidence gathered through energy analyses, existing building energy consumption, and other data before establishing the existing building's baseline. From this baseline of the building model or energy model, then, the design team establishes goals for improving the numbers. While the LEED rating system does not emphasize evidence-based design principles, there is a great potential for exploiting the LEED certification program in order to generate postoccupancy analyses of LEED-certified buildings with the express purpose of making design changes and then starting the cycle of research again. The mandatory five-year recertification cycle of LEED-EBOM-certified buildings will ensure that architects and owners are collecting data that can inform future design projects.

The Environmental Protection Agency's Energy Star® program encourages the collection of building energy data that gets tracked and recorded as energy use intensity per unit of floor area. Energy Star offers an interactive online Portfolio Manager® tool for building owners to monitor this resource consumption. The data collected and reported by owners is generating benchmark data for future building projects; in turn, these data provide a wealth of information for evidence-based sustainable design. The kinds of data tracked by this program have already resulted in collective building data that can be referenced as architects design buildings of similar scale and type.

EVIDENCE-BASED DESIGN ACCREDITATION AND CERTIFICATION

The Center for Health Design, founded in 1993 by a group of healthcare design professionals, has established criteria for accreditation and certification, codified through an examination. Much like the USGBC's LEED rating system and LEED examination have redefined professional practice, the CHD's Evidence-based Design Accreditation and Certification (EDAC) examination has the potential to redefine practice around evidence-based design.

According to the Center for Health Design, the "internationally recognized EDAC program awards credentials to individuals who demonstrate a thorough understanding of how to apply an evidence-based process to the design and development of health care settings, including measuring and reporting results."

The EDAC examination consists of 110 multiple-choice questions. One hundred of the questions are scored; 10 questions are pretest questions that are not scored. The test covers five different content areas: Evidence-Based Design for Health Care, Research, Pre-Design, Design, and Construction and Occupancy.

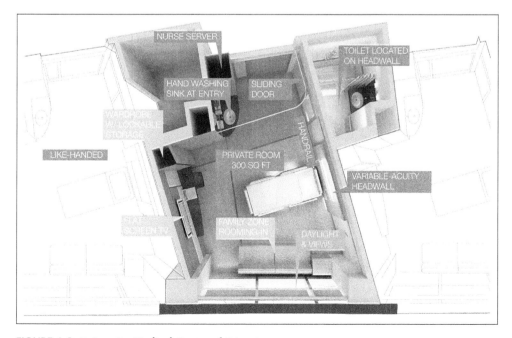

FIGURE 6.2 **University Medical Center of Princeton**

6.3   Sustainable Design

Henry Siegel, FAIA; Larry Strain, FAIA, LEED-AP; and
Nancy Malone, AIA, LEED-AP

Green building combines the best of age-old design traditions with updated construction technology. When current events point to potential environmental and energy crises, the need to understand sustainability becomes increasingly urgent.

Although ecological problems are not a recent development, in the past their results were more immediate and more visible. Today, we live in surroundings that are increasingly removed from nature, making many environmental effects less apparent. Before the Industrial Revolution, environmental problems were caused mostly by concentrated amounts of compounds that occurred naturally and over time. Today, the environment isn't always able to adapt to or assimilate the growing quantity of synthetic materials and compounds or the increased number of waste products.

The World Watch Institute estimates that population growth and increased consumption are the two leading factors contributing to environmental degradation. This is due in part to a constantly expanding economy, the creation of new markets, and planned obsolescence. Today, we use more resources and produce more waste on a per capita basis than our ancestors did.

The construction and operation of buildings contributes significantly to consumption of resources and generation of waste, and if the rate and manner in which buildings are currently constructed continues, resource consumption will accelerate. In the United States alone, an estimated 300 billion square feet of building area will be either constructed or remodeled by 2035. Unless the rate of construction is managed or changes are made in the way buildings are constructed, this development will place an increased burden on the environment.

A measure of how much land area is required to provide resources for and absorb the wastes of a person, city, or country is the ecological footprint of that individual or community. The City of London, the first major city to map its footprint, was determined to have an ecological footprint the size of Spain.

According to the U.S. Energy Information Administration, "the architecture and building community is responsible for almost half of all U.S. greenhouse gas emissions annually." That statistic is one reason architect Ed Mazria, AIA, launched the 2030 Challenge initiative in early 2006. This campaign calls upon the building community to drastically reduce fossil fuel energy consumption by designing efficient new buildings or retrofitting existing ones. Most buildings, according to the 2030 Challenge website, "can be designed to use only a small amount of energy at little or no additional cost through proper site design, building form, glass properties and location, material selection and by incorporating natural heating, cooling, ventilation and daylighting strategies."

Henry Siegel is founding principal of Siegel & Strain Architects in Emeryville, California, a firm that has received a number of awards for sustainable design. He has taught sustainable design in the School of Architecture at University of California, Berkeley, and spoken widely on ecological design. Larry Strain, a principal of Siegel & Strain, has a 30-year background in sustainable design. He cofounded the Solar Center, a solar design and installation company and developed reSourceful Specifications for environmentally considered building materials and construction methods, now part of BuildingGreen's GreenSpec Directory. Nancy Malone, a principal of Siegel & Strain, has managed many sustainable projects, and she serves on the U.S. Green Building Council's Materials and Resources Technical Advisory Group for the development of the LEED rating system.

PART 3: THE PROJECT

Once, buildings used mostly local sources of materials, water, and energy. However, the twentieth century brought inexpensive fossil fuels; widely distributed electricity and water; widely available mass-produced building components; mechanically operated elevators; heating, cooling, and ventilating systems; and large-scale construction equipment. Combined, these developments made it far easier to quickly construct ever-larger buildings and to operate them comfortably without regard to regional variations in materials or climate. Because the construction and operation of such buildings depend on fossil fuels, a rise in concern about this source of energy consequently increased interest in energy-efficient design. The energy crisis of the 1970s stirred widespread interest in energy efficiency and conservation measures, and experimentation in passive design. Progress slowed in the early 1980s as the oil crisis abated, but interest in ecological issues continued to grow.

DEFINING SUSTAINABILITY FOR THE BUILT ENVIRONMENT

Reducing environmental impacts is the first step toward sustainable design. True sustainability is more far-reaching, requiring, at a minimum, reduction of environmental impacts to a level the Earth can sustain indefinitely. The World Commission on the Environment and Development defined sustainability as "meeting the needs of the present without compromising the ability of future generations to meet their own needs."

What's missing from this definition is how we view our relationship to the natural world. Architect and environmental leader William McDonough, FAIA, argues for the need to "recognize interdependence" with the natural world, not merely to use it as a resource, and for the need to "accept responsibility for the consequences of design decisions" so safe buildings of long-term value can be created. Architects need to consider stewardship, restorative acts, and regeneration of natural capital, just as nature does.

The definition of sustainability and sustainable design continues to evolve and broaden as more is learned about what it takes to maintain natural systems. Therefore, it is important for architects to recognize that their daily practice is part of a wider web of influence that affects all living systems, and it is important for them to recognize that sustainability is not just a designer's issue but is of concern to many disciplines. Architects will need to find ways to collaborate with new kinds of team members to achieve a sustainable built environment. As author and educator David Orr has stated, "Sustainable design is the careful meshing of human purposes with the larger patterns and flows of the natural world."

MEASURES FOR ACHIEVING SUSTAINABLE DESIGN

The AIA Committee on the Environment (COTE) developed a list of criteria, known as the Top Ten Measures of Sustainable Design, that address both the quantifiable and the intangible aspects of sustainable design. (These measures are also used to choose the winners of COTE's annual Top Ten Green Projects award program.) The following section of this topic uses the Top Ten Measures—quotes from them appear in italics— as a framework for presenting sustainable design strategies available to architects.

Recognize Design Opportunities

Sustainable design embraces the ecological, economic, and social circumstances of a project.

Sustainable building design applies ecological principles and works *with* natural energy flows rather than ignoring them. It creates connections to the natural world and minimizes, or ideally reverses, adverse environmental impacts.

Architect James Wines believes that an ecological approach to design presents an opportunity to change the paradigm for design excellence, to move from "ego-centric to eco-centric." What he proposes is an analysis that reevaluates humanity's evolving relationship with nature and our place in it as the basis for design.

Sustainable design is not a style and is more than a trend. When building orientation or protection of drainage paths or the integration of energy-saving technologies is given equal weight with the classical virtues of symmetry, scale, and proportion, the definition of what constitutes good design will change. Buildings will demonstrate stronger connections to place, and new design solutions may evolve. But it is not enough to design buildings that perform well. The more traditional architectural values apply as well. Buildings that are valued by their communities are the ones that will be maintained and preserved. Ultimately, as David Orr has said, if a building is not beautiful, it is not sustainable.

Strategies for recognizing design opportunities include these:

- Consider ecological models—how nature does it—as models for design.
- Design to strengthen human connections to natural systems.
- Make sustainable design strategies drivers of design aesthetics.

Promote Regional/Community Identity

Sustainable design recognizes the unique cultural and natural character of a given region . . . promotes regional and community identity and an appropriate sense of place . . . reduces automobile travel from home, work, shopping, or other frequent destinations . . . and encourages alternative transportation strategies.

Regional and urban issues lie at the heart of a sustainable future. Buildings and other development fit within the context of local and regional habitat, resources, water, food, transportation, and community. Creating a sense of place grows from analysis and understanding of local circumstances, including cultural and historical patterns as well as local differences in landscape and topography, climate, resources, and habitat. The way architects design affects the health and well-being of natural systems as well as the effectiveness of constructed systems. Designing with an understanding of local factors not only reduces environmental impacts but contributes to the creation of meaningful, memorable places.

American cities are often fragmented by zoning or other use patterns, separating people from jobs, services, and green spaces. Suburban settlements tend to be even more specialized, with housing typically isolated from other uses. The automobile influences development everywhere, but that influence is more dominant in the suburbs. Although suburbs tend to have more open space per capita, the open space often is largely private lawns that require frequent mowing and heavy use of water, fertilizer, and weed killers.

The widespread use of cars has led to sprawl and the infrastructure that goes with it. Development eats up 1 to 1.5 million acres of land every year in the United States. The population of New York City has grown by only 8 percent since the 1960s, but the amount of urbanized land in the New York area has grown by 60 percent in the same period. Sprawl in turn contributes to how much people drive: Studies show that each year U.S. suburban dwellers drive 110 hours—the equivalent of nearly three workweeks—more than city dwellers do.

Resources are increasingly removed from the cities they support. Food is grown far away and shipped great distances. According to the Leopold Center for Sustainable Agriculture at Iowa State University, most food in the United States travels between 1,500 and 2,000 miles before it is eaten. Water is collected and piped from distant watersheds or pumped from diminishing aquifers. Other resources are supplied by global markets to ensure the lowest cost to the consumer, often ignoring proximity to resources, support for the local economy, and other undervalued ecological and social "externalities."

Externalities are costs (sometimes benefits) that are borne by parties "external" to a transaction. For example, air pollution from a power plant can negatively affect people hundreds of miles away and they, rather than the utility company, bear the social and economic costs created by this pollution without necessarily reaping any of the benefits. Traditionally, economists do not account for these external costs, often assuming that negative environmental impacts have little cost. New economic models use a "triple bottom line" method of accounting that considers profit, social equity, and environmental protection.

Similarly, waste is collected and removed from cities, taking problems somewhere else. Garbage goes to landfills or is dumped in the ocean, polluted runoff from roofs and streets is diverted to the nearest body of water, and emissions drift and pollute someone else's air.

Cities and suburbs need to be re-imagined and redesigned to provide economically and socially viable neighborhoods and communities, taking local resources and natural systems into careful consideration. Communities should be pedestrian friendly, have adequate public transportation, and provide connections to nature. Communities should, to the greatest extent possible, draw only from their local resource base, support the local economy, and handle their waste locally. Local control of food, water, and material resources makes people more aware of, and accountable to, the world around them.

Strategies for promoting local identity include these:

- Design from a sense of place.
- Encourage infill development.
- Encourage mixed-use transit development.
- Include nature by providing habitat in yards, on planted roofs and parks, and in wildlife corridors.
- Design buildings and communities in ways that support local food cultivation and suppliers.
- Collect water and protect watersheds.
- Support the local economy and use local materials that do not require transportation over long distances.
- Reuse or recycle urban waste.

Design for the Ecological Context

A project site design should respond to its ecological context. Site selection and design can relate to ecosystems at different scales, from local to regional. Even urban sites relate to ecological issues such as climate, topography, and watershed, as well as transportation and land use.

Sustainable design acknowledges that each site—whether rural, suburban, or urban—is different in resources and context, which can enhance or limit design decisions. Sustainable design requires a level of research and analysis that considers impacts on watersheds, habitats, and other natural systems that intersect a given site. It also includes identification of opportunities for transportation linkages, ways to restore habitat, and use of infill and brownfield sites, the latter defined by the Environmental Protection Agency as a property that may have pollutants or hazardous substances present.

Pulitzer Prize–winning biologist E. O. Wilson developed the theory of "biophilia"—the innate need of humans to be in close touch with the natural world. He defines biophilia as "the connections that human beings subconsciously seek with the rest of life" and proposes that the deep affiliations we have with nature are rooted in our biology. Designs inspired by biological models that are more strongly connected to nature would be plausible outcomes of applying this theory to architecture.

One way to define the extent of the area to be analyzed for a particular project is to identify the site's watershed and determine its water source and its destination for treatment and disposal. It is also essential to consider and analyze wildlife habitat, plant life, topography, and soil conditions, and respond to them in ways that minimize the effects of development and reestablish or strengthen connections to regional ecological systems. What are the important species in the watershed? How can their habitat be protected or restored? Consideration of these factors can make it possible to design landscaping that supports wildlife, while saving water and even helping to store and treat stormwater.

Opportunities exist even on most urban sites. Nearly two-thirds of the site footprint of the Solaire, a high-rise apartment building in New York City designed by Cesar Pelli & Associates (now Pelli Clarke Pelli Architects), is green. A roof garden is irrigated with captured rainwater, and some of the captured water is used to help irrigate an adjacent park. The building design has the synergistic effect of providing open space, reducing stormwater runoff and reducing the heat island affect—a condition in urban areas where tall buildings retain heat more than the same space would if it were located in an open area.

Strategies for designing in context include these:

- Utilize infill and brownfield sites to reduce development on more pristine habitat areas or productive farmland.
- Retain or restore waterways on or near the site.
- Use native plants or plants that have evolved in similar bioregions to provide and restore biological diversity.
- Use landscape to offset the impacts of the built environment. Plant trees to reduce heat islands created by paving and roofs and to offset carbon dioxide emissions from building operation.
- Use swales, check dams, and storage basins to slow and collect water and keep it on-site to reduce stormwater runoff.
- Protect air, water, and soil quality by practicing natural pest control, minimizing use of petroleum-based fertilizers, and conserving and rebuilding topsoil.
- Restore habitat and protect local species.

Engage in Bioclimatic Design

Sustainable design conserves natural resources and maximizes human comfort through an intimate connection with the natural flows and cycles of the surrounding bioclimatic region.

At the turn of the twentieth century the heating, cooling, and lighting of buildings was the domain of the architect. Since then, systems have evolved for lighting, heating, and cooling that ignore nature and function without regard to whether it is cold or hot, light or dark outdoors. By the 1950s, cheap and abundant energy allowed technology to provide comfort in any climate. One result has been the homogenization of architecture—buildings that look the same regardless of climate or culture. Another result is that architects now work with teams of highly specialized engineers for the design of building systems. In 1973 the first energy shortage revealed our heavy reliance on mechanical conditioning of buildings.

Designing *with* the climate (known as *bioclimatic*, *climate-based*, or *passive design*) is an effective way to reduce a building's dependence on nonrenewable sources of energy. By starting with bioclimatic design principles and considering how buildings will perform when "unplugged," architects can reduce the size of building systems and in some cases even eliminate them. Buildings climatically attuned to their surroundings will also have a stronger sense of place.

Buildings that rely only on locally available resources illustrate sound approaches to climate-based design because they evolved over time as best responses to local conditions. Traditional buildings in similar climate zones around the world illustrate a variety of approaches to comparable climatic conditions. Different cultures demonstrate different approaches to similar climates, and these various approaches are an important resource for design strategies and solutions.

Some understanding of human comfort and strategies for different climate zones is a prerequisite for designing with the climate. This information can be summarized in bioclimatic or psychometric charts that depict local conditions and strategies to accommodate them. These strategies are most effective when addressed at the earliest stages of the design process, when the architect is considering orientation, shape, and building massing.

While the ideal building shape varies from climate to climate, building orientation generally favors maximizing the length of the south side of a building (the north side below the equator) to take advantage of easier sun control, and minimizing eastern and western exposures for the same reason. Buildings can be shaped to aid natural ventilation and daylighting as well as to provide views and connection to the outdoors.

Window shading can help maximize heat gain in winter and minimize it in summer. Windows can be placed to optimize daylight and take advantage of prevailing winds for ventilation. High-mass materials such as concrete or masonry can be optimized to shift absorption of heating and cooling to times of the day or night when it is most needed. These long-standing principles should once again become primary criteria of good design.

Strategies vary by climate zone. Generally, climate zones can be reduced to four: hot and dry, hot and humid, temperate, and cold. A few strategies for each climate zone follow.

Design strategies for hot and dry climates
- Minimize sun exposure; minimize effects of wind.
- Use small windows.
- Optimize thermal mass to take advantage of the large diurnal temperature swing.
- Closely cluster buildings for the shade they offer one another.

Design strategies for hot and humid climates
- Minimize sun exposure; maximize natural ventilation.
- Use lightweight construction to minimize radiation of heat.
- Space buildings far apart to maximize breezes.

Design strategies for temperate climates
- Maximize solar gain in winter; minimize it in summer.
- Maximize breezes in summer; minimize them in winter.
- Take advantage of daylighting opportunities.

Design strategies for cold climates
- Orient buildings and openings for maximum protection from cold winds.
- Use south-facing windows (in the northern hemisphere) to maximize solar gain.
- Use compact shapes and small windows to minimize heat loss.

Create Healthy Indoor Environments

Sustainable design creates and maintains a comfortable interior environment while providing abundant daylight and fresh air.

North Americans spend as much as 90 percent of their time indoors, making buildings the primary locus for health, comfort, well-being, and productivity. Air quality, daylight and views, temperature and humidity, and personal control over the environment contribute to how people experience the indoor environment. While it is difficult to demonstrate which factors are most important, studies have shown that ample daylight and proper ventilation lead to greater satisfaction, an increased sense of comfort, fewer sick days, and increased productivity.

Indoor air can be many times more polluted than outdoor air, especially in poorly ventilated buildings. Illnesses identified with indoor pollutants range from mild allergic symptoms to serious and life-threatening illnesses such as heart disease and cancer. Many chemical and biological pollutants present in indoor air, such as the following, can affect human health:

- Mold, mildew, and other moisture-related contaminants
- Off-gassing from building materials and furnishings
- Maintenance products, including pesticides

- Combustion gases from appliances, automobiles, and tobacco
- Naturally occurring gases such as radon
- Outdoor pollutants that enter the building

An effective supply of fresh outdoor air can dilute the amount of airborne contaminants in a building. Natural and/or mechanical means can provide appropriate ventilation. Passive ventilation has the benefit of being more energy-efficient and less noisy, but it is more difficult to design for larger buildings. "Mixed-mode" systems that use both natural and mechanical ventilation offer a healthier alternative to sealed buildings, which are still the norm for some building types.

Natural light and views to the outdoors can help enhance physical and mental health. Ample daylight increases productivity in the workplace and test scores in schools. Daylight and views can be maximized by coupling a narrow building section with careful window placement, a legal requirement for office buildings in many European countries. Desired amounts of daylight can be achieved with the use of skylights and light shelves, the shape of windows and ceilings, and use of light-colored surfaces. However, care must be taken to avoid excessive heat gain and glare.

Temperature and humidity affect occupant comfort and can be controlled with both passive and mechanical means, depending on the climate and the building type. Postoccupancy studies indicate that building occupants are happier if they have localized or individual control over temperature and air, especially if it includes access to operable windows.

Strategies for creating healthy indoor environments include these:

- Identify potential pollutant sources and eliminate them from the building.
- Separate occupants and any pollutant sources that remain with a barrier.
- Prevent moisture intrusion and buildup.
- Set minimum ventilation rates based on ASHRAE 62–2003.
- For suspected pollutants or health risks that have no verified cause-and-effect relationship, exercise the Precautionary Principle (see following sidebar).
- Optimize daylight and reduce glare.
- Prevent excessive heat gain.
- Provide localized or individual controls for ventilation and light.

THE PRECAUTIONARY PRINCIPLE

Many practitioners make decisions about building materials or systems based on limited evidence that a selection is better for human health or the ecosystem. Sometimes the only available research about new materials is still in development or short of scientific confirmation, yet some evidence indicates a particular material may cause harm. In this situation, the decision-making process should be preventive: Avoid potential harm.

Scientists, environmentalists, and others at a January 1998 Wingspread conference developed the "Precautionary Principle" as a framework for making such decisions. Its main point is this: "When an activity raises threats of harm to human health or the environment, precautionary measures should be taken even if some cause-and-effect relationships are not fully established scientifically."

Conserve Water

Utilize building and site design strategies to conserve water supplies, manage site water and drainage, and capitalize on renewable sources.

In most parts of the United States—especially the arid West—cities, agriculture, and industry rely on large-scale water distribution systems. In California, water that falls in the Sierras as snow is diverted from rivers and streams and transported over long distances to irrigate Central Valley agribusiness and quench thirsts along the coast. As it travels downslope, this water is used to create electricity, but the system uses more electricity than it creates to pump water and is one of the state's largest consumers of electricity. Other parts of the country tap vast but shrinking aquifers, pumping water from the Earth at rates that cause the ground to subside and require deeper wells. According to the *LEED Reference Guide*, Americans extract 3,700 billion gallons more per year than they return to natural systems.

Water is becoming a major challenge in the twenty-first century, as issues from overuse to drought to pollution to privatization of sources proliferate. Continued global population growth and industrialization will make water an even more precious commodity.

Within the built environment, water is used for drinking, cooking, cleaning, bathing, transporting waste, heating and cooling buildings, and irrigating lawns and gardens. There are established methods of conservation for all of these uses, but such efforts can be further improved. For example, the concept of wastewater must be reconsidered. Graywater—the water collected from sinks and showers—and rainwater can be used to irrigate plants or flush toilets. Even blackwater—which comes from toilet flushing—can be treated to a level suitable for irrigation. All water and wastewater eventually returns to the natural hydrologic system; it should be returned as clean as possible and treated with the least amount of chemical and energy input possible.

Strategies for conserving water include these:

- Reduce potable water by employing drip irrigation and low-flow water fixtures and appliances.
- Design landscapes that minimize or eliminate the need for irrigation.
- Promote kitchen composting rather than disposal use.
- Catch rainwater for potable water and irrigation.
- Retrieve graywater for uses that do not require potable water, such as flushing toilets.
- Treat blackwater with biological treatment systems for use in irrigation.
- Return water to the site rather than disposing of it off-site.
- Promote infiltration by minimizing impermeable surfaces.

Minimize Use of Nonrenewable Energy Sources and Maximize Use of Renewable Energy

Good design of building mechanical and electrical systems and integration of those systems with passive design strategies is essential for conserving natural resources and improving building performance. . . Sustainable design carefully considers the long-term impact of current decisions in order to protect quality of life in the future.

Total operating energy used during the life of a building far surpasses the embodied energy of the materials and the energy use from construction. For green buildings, energy system design starts at the beginning of the design process, when the integrated design team meets to brainstorm best choices for passive and active approaches to energy systems.

Building systems in green buildings can be smaller and more efficient. But they can also be more complex, since they may incorporate more sophisticated control systems and use natural ventilation and daylighting. Whole systems strive to work more like an organism, to maximize opportunities for the building to breathe on its own—to heat and cool itself through good passive design—rather than letting the mechanical or electrical system do all the work. Often, green design requires a change in attitude about how to interact with a building. For example, in accepting wider temperature swings, clients can benefit from more personal control of their environment and have a closer connection to the natural world.

Renewable energy is often an exciting concept to clients—many want to start the discussion of green building with photovoltaic power, wind power, or hydrogen fuels. However, the first and most productive measures for consuming less energy from the grid involve eliminating or reducing the size of systems through good passive design; then the size of renewable energy systems, which often have high first costs, can be reduced. Green technology follows green design.

Renewable energy promises less reliance on the grid, making it possible for buildings to operate better in blackouts and when energy sources change or disappear. Eventually, buildings and communities will need to be energy-independent, producing at a minimum enough energy for their own operation and ideally enough energy for the larger community.

Strategies for reducing energy use from the grid include these:

- At the beginning of the design process, work collaboratively with engineering consultants to optimize systems.
- Design minimal, efficient systems with high-tech and sophisticated controls to improve performance rather than compensate for inefficient design.
- Use energy sources appropriately. Use high-grade energy such as electricity where it is critical, and use lower-grade thermal energy for heating, cooling, and ventilating.
- Once building systems have been optimized, use renewable energy for building operation.

Use Environmentally Preferable Building Materials

The careful selection of materials and products can conserve resources; reduce impacts of harvesting, production, and transportation; improve building performance; and enhance occupant health and comfort.

Buildings are major consumers of materials. Materials affect building performance and user comfort. There are environmental impacts at every stage of a material's life, from extraction, transport, and manufacture to use and final recycling or disposal. Typically, these consequences, generally borne elsewhere, are easily ignored.

Environmental effects must be considered over the complete life cycle of the material. How are materials made, and what are they made from? Selecting durable, regionally appropriate building materials and using them efficiently to enhance the performance of a building are essential elements of sustainable design. For example, engineered lumber can use up to 75 percent more of the wood fiber in a tree than sawn lumber; resource-efficient framing can reduce lumber use by 25 percent or more; and structural slabs can serve as finish floors, eliminating the need for additional finishes.

Individual building materials are typically part of wall, floor, or roof assemblies. It is important to understand how these assemblies work as systems, and how changes in one material can affect other materials in the assembly, the performance of the assembly as a whole, and the building.

Strategies for using environmentally friendly materials include these:

- Do not design buildings larger than needed.
- Select materials and building systems engineered for maximum efficiency, and eliminate unnecessary materials.
- Use durable materials and construction systems. Buildings that last longer use fewer resources over time.
- Avoid irreplaceable and endangered resources. This goes beyond avoiding old-growth redwood; consider irreplaceable habitats as well as individual resources. Consider the forest, not just the trees.
- Use renewable, well-managed resources.
- Use recycled, recyclable resources. Avoid recycled materials that are toxic or cannot themselves be recycled.
- Avoid materials that generate high levels of pollution during manufacturing, extraction, use, or disposal.
- Select materials with low embodied energy. Intensive use of fossil fuels contributes to global warming and other forms of pollution.
- Use materials that help conserve energy. For example, use thermal mass for energy storage, light reflective surfaces for daylighting, and radiant barriers and insulation to conserve heating and cooling energy.

Plan for the Long Term

Sustainable design seeks to maximize ecological, social, and economic value over time.

Buildings represent a huge investment of capital, resources, and energy, and if they are to be sustainable,

See "Environmentally Preferable Product Selection" for guidance on selecting and specifying building construction products with higher levels of environmental performance.

they need to last. Buildings last when their inhabitants and communities value them. Aesthetics, suitability of purpose and use, and adaptability to new uses all contribute to long life. Several strategies can help ensure this outcome.

Design new buildings so they can be more easily adapted to accommodate inevitable changes of use. Buildings that are designed too tightly to their programs are often more difficult to adapt. Buildings with longer structural spans and a separation between the structure and the skin and interior walls are generally easier to remodel. Higher ceilings provide more daylight and can make the space more adaptable to new uses.

Designing adaptable buildings does not mean they have to be infinitely flexible or programmatically neutral. Given the rapid rate of change, it may be that buildings, more than most things, can provide some needed sense of permanence and stability. Good design is the key; people will adapt to well-designed, well-built, contextually sound buildings.

Reducing the amount necessary to build is a significant contribution to sustainability. Projects may be "right sized" by, for example, multiplying uses for a space or putting circulation outside when climate and circumstances allow. A good strategy is to design buildings that can be easily expanded.

As well as accommodating changes of program or use, buildings need to be able to adapt to changes in energy, water, and material resources. Buildings that can use future fuels and technologies will last longer than those that rely on limited resources or technologies that will be obsolete long before the building itself. Buildings that perform well "unplugged" will be more likely to stay in use when energy sources change.

When designing for durability, structure is critical. Buildings located where there is a chance of extreme events such as earthquakes or hurricanes need to be designed to withstand such events. Separation of building structure and skin helps make this possible by easing access to finishes so repairs can be made without destroying the structure. The building envelope is also important. Durable materials that age gracefully and are carefully detailed to protect against water or vapor intrusion will extend the life of a building.

Strategies for taking the long view include these:

- Design for adaptability to accommodate future changes in program and use.
- Design for versatility to accommodate future changes in technology.
- Design for durability by using materials, construction methods, and structural systems that will withstand weather, long-term use, and catastrophic events.

Take Advantage of Collective Wisdom and Feedback

Sustainable design recognizes that the most intelligent design strategies evolve over time through shared knowledge within a large community.

Feedback about design and construction processes serves many purposes, from improving building operation to improving construction practice. How well sustainable measures work, or how they could be modified to make them more effective, will be useful information for all practitioners.

It is now widely viewed that commissioning of building systems should be required before building occupancy and use. *Building commissioning* is the process of ensuring that systems are designed, installed, and functionally tested for effective operation and maintenance for an owner's operational needs. *Retrocommissioning* is the systematic investigation process applied to existing buildings to improve and optimize operating and maintenance procedures.

Performance can also be monitored over the life of a building. With baseline data created at commissioning, building performance can continue to be improved as users and uses change. Recent studies by the Pacific Energy Center have shown that performance improves dramatically after commissioning, levels out after two years, and then begins to decline again. It is evident that buildings, especially those with more complicated control systems, need to be recommissioned every two to three years to provide feedback and maintain optimum performance.

Postoccupancy evaluations compare actual building performance to energy models of designs and demonstrate the success or failure of adopted strategies. They can be used to improve building performance and ultimately to improve the analysis tools themselves. Learning how well buildings work for their occupants is a key feedback component rarely utilized by designers. Postoccupancy surveys can gauge satisfaction with many factors, including comfort, lighting, acoustics, and indoor air quality.

Materials and building assemblies can take longer to evaluate, as they are tested against time and climate for durability and longevity. It is worthwhile to visit constructed projects periodically or to contact maintenance staff to see how materials are performing. Architects must also look to studies outside the construction industry for information on whether the extraction and manufacture of materials are harmful to habitats or to human health.

Lessons learned can be disseminated in case studies to establish a body of precedent that future designers can learn from. Professional lectures, conferences, and seminars are also good places to gather and disseminate information and to discuss topics with colleagues.

Strategies for obtaining feedback on the success of design efforts include these:

- Undertake postoccupancy surveys.
- Install equipment to monitor the ongoing performance of building systems.
- Create short feedback loops by designing smaller, simpler buildings and more accessible building systems.
- Develop a common language of building metrics readily understood by designers and laypeople—the equivalent of miles-per-gallon for buildings.
- Disseminate lessons learned. Share with colleagues what does and does not work.
- Create a shared set of precedents by developing a body of case studies.
- Share test results for new materials and methods of construction.

INTEGRATED DESIGN

Traditionally, architects worked closely with builders to design and construct a building and all its systems. Today, architects often develop a concept, then rely on engineers to design the systems and "make it work," and further rely on builders to interpret the design once it is complete. Sustainable design revisits the earlier model, creating a multidisciplinary team of consultants, including builders, to evaluate and identify the best choices for building systems throughout the project delivery process. This team approach is employed from very early in the project, even before programming.

Sustainable design relies on this collaborative approach, now referred to as "integrated design." The process brings the entire design team together at key points in the design process to discuss ways that site design, building form, and mechanical, electrical, and other systems can complement each other to create an effective solution. While not always possible, it is also beneficial to include the construction team in the design process. Synergies and trade-offs occur throughout design and construction, and including the entire team in these discussions allows for educated decisions that benefit the whole project.

Integrated design may require that architects and consultants take on tasks outside their typical roles. Civil engineers design biologically based stormwater treatment systems, electrical engineers design daylighting and photovoltaic systems, mechanical engineers consider how thermal mass and glazing affect their system design and model air and heat flows in increasingly sophisticated ways, and architects expand their understanding of all of these systems and how they relate to the building design. Integrated design may also require consultants outside the normal design team. Biologists or ecologists, for example, might participate in planning for a highly sensitive site. Integrated design may also require an unconventional communication process and method. How the design team members share information and ideas among themselves and with other stakeholders can significantly affect the eventual performance of the building and the satisfaction of its users.

Outlined below are the typical phases of design and a sampling of strategies related to a sustainable, integrated design process.

PREDESIGN

- Form a multidisciplinary design team.
- Complete a site analysis, including watershed, climate, solar access, views, soils.
- Set and prioritize sustainable design goals.

SCHEMATIC DESIGN

- Incorporate considerations for light, air, views, water collection, reduced site disturbance, and so on.
- Reduce demand on M/E/P systems through passive design strategies.
- Create an initial energy model, then respond to the results by adjusting the building design.
- Use a physical or virtual model to analyze daylighting effects.
- Estimate water use based on potential building systems, potential water catchment, and landscape design.
- If proposing unusual systems of any kind (structural, mechanical, water treatment, etc.), visit the local jurisdiction to discuss code requirements.
- Evaluate the schematic design against sustainable design goals.

DESIGN DEVELOPMENT

- Refine the design based on information gathered in schematic design.
- Reevaluate the design using computer and physical models.

CONSTRUCTION DOCUMENTATION

- Thoroughly document all materials, systems, and details that may not be familiar to the plan checker or builder.
- If appropriate, create a narrative of the high-performance systems to enhance understanding by the construction team.

CONSTRUCTION

- Conduct a construction kick-off meeting that includes discussion of the sustainable design goals, strategies, and construction methods.
- Require written plans for erosion control, waste management, indoor air quality, and commissioning.
- Require that the general contractor have an on-site supervisor who is responsible for the sustainable design requirements, including construction waste management and indoor air quality measures.

OCCUPANCY

- Commission all building systems prior to occupancy.
- Provide a building flush-out period prior to occupancy if necessary.
- Incorporate information in the operating manual about environmental aspects of the design and hold a training session for building owners, operators, and if appropriate, occupants.

POSTOCCUPANCY

- Evaluate building performance at one-year intervals.
- Recommission systems periodically (e.g., two to three years) to address operational problems and adjust building support systems.
- Learn from the successes and failures of the project, and share this knowledge with others.

Several tools and rating systems have been established to evaluate the performance of green buildings or their particular attributes. Some tools provide qualitative evaluation, some provide quantitative evaluation, and others provide both.

Several computer programs can be used to evaluate energy efficiency, such as DOE-2, Energy–10(tm), and eQUEST®, which have been widely used to help design buildings and meet energy codes. Programs used to predict daylighting effectiveness include Radiance, Lumen Micro, and the Lightscape visualization system. These tools provide valuable feedback during design and can help designers make decisions about components as diverse as wall assemblies, thermal mass, window size and glazing, and mechanical system size and type. They are particularly helpful in maximizing the use of passive design strategies when used early in design. Physical models can also be used to predict daylighting effectiveness and to help determine building fenestration that will provide effective winter solar gain, summer heat avoidance, and glare control (see Figure 6.3).

Green building rating systems are intended to measure the environmental performance of proposed designs and finished buildings and to help building owners and designers set performance objectives. One of the oldest and most successful rating systems is the Austin Energy Green Building Program®, first used to rate homes and now suitable for commercial projects as well. This program created a rating that measured the environmental performance of a house and created an identifiable brand that became desirable in the Austin, Texas area.

A number of local, regional, and national rating programs now exist. Nationally, the best-known is the U.S. Green Building Council's LEED Green Building Rating System™. LEED (Leadership in Energy and Environmental Design) rates projects by awarding points in five areas: site design, energy use, water use, materials and resources, and indoor environmental quality. The point total indicates the overall environmental performance of a project. LEED has been a major force for promoting green building and has gained acceptance from a wide range of stakeholders, from designers and clients to manufacturers and construction teams. This acceptance is due in part to the rigor of the certification process and the use of objective national standards and third-party certification to verify that points are given only for what is properly documented once a project is complete.

In the future, rating systems will likely include some form of environmental lifecycle assessment (LCA). LCA has been used most widely to evaluate the environmental performance of individual materials and products, but it can also be used to evaluate building assemblies and the entirety of materials in a building. LCA measures all the "inputs" to a finished product, such as raw resources, water, and energy, and all the "outputs" that are the result of manufacturing the product, such as air and water emissions, solid waste, and other by-products. Evaluating the inputs and outputs of like products—different countertop materials, for example—makes educated material selection possible. LCA is, for the most part, still the province of highly specialized consultants, but programs like BEES® (Building for Environmental and Economic Sustainability) and the Athena Institute's software tools—Athena® Impact Estimator for Buildings and Athena® EcoCalculator for Assemblies—are beginning to make such analysis more accessible to architects. BEES software, available free from the National Institute of Standards and Technology, evaluates individual building materials using LCA. The Athena software can provide LCA feedback for whole buildings and for many types of construction assemblies.

Other rating systems and design tools are also available. The widely known Energy Star program of the Environmental Protection Agency rates buildings on energy use. Many utility-sponsored programs across the country, such as the Savings by Design program funded by Pacific Gas & Electric and other California energy companies, also focus on energy use. Another EPA program, Target Finder, helps rate building performance early in the design process for specific building types. State and local agencies across the country have also developed green building guidelines. These programs range from "rule of thumb" suggestions to more sophisticated whole building analyses.

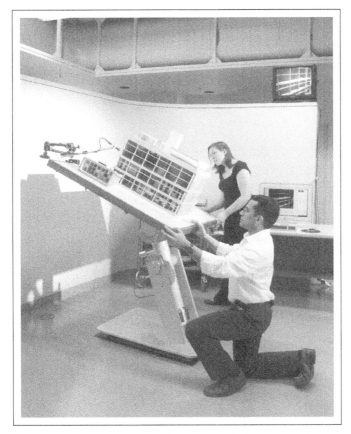

FIGURE 6.3 **The Heliodon. This device uses a light source and a physical model to simulate the effects of sunlight on a building. This process allows architects to determine during the design phases how a building will function with respect to daylighting, shading, and shadows and to identify opportunities for energy savings.**

However, none of these rating systems addresses such aspects of building design as aesthetics, comfort, and connection to nature. The Top Ten Measures developed by the AIA Committee on the Environment, outlined earlier, begin to address these intangibles.

AN URGENT CALL

In the last century, the argument that natural resources are "free" capital for human use and the related notion that the natural world has little value until developed were used to justify massive and often thoughtless development and expansion. As the driver of our economic system, growth discounts the value of natural capital and focuses on first cost without consideration of long-term costs or ecological effects. Consequences of this worldview include clear-cut forests, dammed rivers, developed prime agricultural land, and hillsides shaved away in pursuit of stone and ore. In addition, cheap and abundant fossil fuels have encouraged wasteful construction and transportation practices. The results of these actions—global warming and a host of other detrimental changes—may damage global environmental systems long before fossil fuels run out.

As society has begun to recognize the urgency of responding to these issues, sustainable design has rapidly grown in importance. The AIA has established ambitious goals to encourage significant reduction of fossil fuel use and emissions in buildings—from 50 percent reduction for all new buildings by 2010 to fully carbon neutral by 2030. Based on 2016 data, this goal may not be reached by 2030, but steady progress is being achieved. Architects have already begun broadening existing planning models

Lifecycle cost analysis provides a tool for determining long-term costs for the total building, as well as for building systems and components.

and design paradigms, and taking advantage of age-old design strategies and improved building technologies and systems. To reach the goal of sustainability, though, architects can do much to reduce, and eventually reverse, the damages that shortsighted community planning and building design have caused. We urgently need to become stewards of our limited resources and to transform our practices to create a long-term balance between the built environment and nature.

For More Information

The AIA Committee on the Environment publishes information about sustainable design and its Top Ten Green Projects program on the AIA website at www.aia.org/cote. A full version of the Top Ten measures is also available at this address.

In *Sustainable Design: Ecology, Architecture, and Planning* (Wiley, 2007), Dan Williams, FAIA, provides a primer on green building design in which sustainable design concepts are presented along with case study examples.

The 2030 Challenge program links building construction and operation to global warming and proposes a way to reverse the current impact of human development on global warming. For information about how the built environment is specifically related to global warming and the 2030 Challenge, visit www.architecture2030.org.

Natural Capitalism: Creating the Next Industrial Revolution (Back Bay Books, 2000), by Paul Hawken, Amory Lovins, and L. Hunter Lovins, is a good resource for details on the "triple bottom line" and new economic models that consider environmental protection and social equity in addition to profit.

BEES (Building for Environmental and Economic Sustainability) software can be used to evaluate individual building materials using lifecycle assessment. The software is free from the National Institute of Standards and Technology (www.bfrl.nist.gov/oae/software/bees.html).

The Impact Estimator for Buildings and the EcoCalculator for Assemblies, other lifecycle assessment tools, are available from the Athena Institute at www.athenasmi.ca.

The website of the American Society of Heating, Refrigerating and Air-Conditioning Engineers gives access to the text of the many consensus standards for the design and maintenance of indoor air environments, as well as interpretations of the standards. For example, ASHRAE 62–2003 covers minimum ventilation rates for indoor air quality. ASHRAE created a technical research group focused on sustainable building guidance and measurements. (www.ashrae.org).

6.4   Environmentally Preferable Product Selection

Nadav Malin

A universal standard is not yet available for selecting building materials and products with high levels of environmental performance. Meanwhile, building professionals can make more informed choices by becoming familiar with the

Nadav Malin is President and CEO of BuildingGreen, Inc. and a LEED Fellow. He is an experienced trainer and facilitator, convening the network of architecture firm Sustainable Design Leaders and teaching diverse groups about LEED and green building. He is a sought-after workshop facilitator and consultant to USGBC, AIA, large corporations, government agencies, and architecture firms. As President and CEO of BuildingGreen, he oversees the company's industry-leading information and community-building websites BuildingGreen.com and LEEDuser. He also served as executive editor of *GreenSource* magazine throughout its highly decorated seven-year run and as founding chair of the LEED Materials and Resources Technical Advisory Group. (The original version of this topic first appeared in the 14th edition of this *Handbook*.)

information that is available and studying the complexities and challenges associated with this task.

Whether it's simply to "do the right thing" or to comply with an agency mandate or company policy, designers often find themselves trying to assess which products are good for the environment. Adding this criterion to the standard list of cost, performance, and aesthetics introduces a whole range of additional issues and considerations for architects.

A range of programs, initiatives, and tools are available to help architects respond to client requests to use green products. This article aims to provide a general context and some background on many of those tools and initiatives, to help architects use them most effectively.

WHAT ARE ENVIRONMENTALLY PREFERABLE PRODUCTS?

As the name implies, environmentally preferable products, or EPPs, are products and materials that—for a given application—represent a better choice than most others from an ecological perspective. The U.S. Environmental Protection Agency (EPA), per Executive Order (EO) 13693 (2015), defines environmentally preferable products as "products or services that have a lesser or reduced effect on human health and the environment when compared with competing products or services that serve the same purpose."

In theory, use of these products in a building will result in the lowest ecological burden and/or the highest ecological benefit. In practice, however, the web of relationships between the built and natural environments is so complex it is not possible to determine with certainty what all those burdens and benefits will be. Despite this uncertainty, there are indications, based on what we do know, as to which products and materials are better from an environmental perspective.

GREEN PRODUCTS IN THE CONTEXT OF GREEN BUILDING

When considering EPPs, or green products, it is important to remember that the products only exist as independent entities until they are used in a building. Once it has been erected, applied, or installed, the environmental performance of an individual product in isolation is less important than the performance of the constellation of products that form a building.

The collection of products that makes up a building inherits the environmental burdens associated with each product. At the same time, how a building is designed, constructed, and used contributes significantly to its environmental impact.

The construction process itself can produce environmental impacts such as habitat disruption, erosion, noise, and pollution emissions from construction equipment. Once a building is occupied, its ongoing operation requires a constant flow of resources (e.g., energy, water, and maintenance supplies) and generates corresponding pollution emissions and waste. Some of these flows are related directly to the facility itself, while others are associated more with the activities of the occupants. However, even occupant-related resource demands and waste streams are affected by the characteristics of the building in which those activities take place. Whether or not facilities are available to help occupants recycle waste materials, for example, can determine how much material is separated for recycling.

Finally, when a building no longer serves its intended function and is renovated, altered, or demolished, yet another series of environmental impacts takes place, primarily in the form of disposal or dispersal of the materials. Older buildings often contain hazardous materials, such as asbestos, lead dust, or mercury, posing the risk that those materials will contaminate the local environment when removed. Products going into buildings today may constitute similar challenges for future generations, unless we choose those products wisely.

Many environmental impacts associated with the construction, operation, and decommissioning of a building are at least partially determined by the products and materials initially chosen for the building. In this sense, the environmental impact of a building as a whole is the sum of the environmental burdens each product carries and the impacts associated with assembling, using, and discarding those products and materials.

VARYING DEFINITIONS OF EPP

The initials "EPP" are used differently in different contexts, although these uses are generally closely related. The EPA, many other federal agencies, and state and local governments have programs to promote environmentally preferable purchasing. These EPP programs are intended to promote the use of environmentally preferable products and services, as long as they are available within the agencies' cost and performance constraints. Unfortunately, most of these programs provide relatively little guidance on what exactly constitutes a preferable product, although that situation is improving.

Some of the limited EPP guidance available comes from the Federal Trade Commission (FTC) in its effort to manage the claims manufacturers and suppliers make about their products. The FTC has indicated that when manufacturers claim a product is preferable on an environmental basis, they should be able to back up that claim with evidence that the product has a comprehensively lower environmental impact than competing products. Having a lower impact in just one area, such as recycled content, is not sufficient. Therefore, manufacturers should clearly qualify the scope of any claim of environmental preferability.

GREEN ATTRIBUTES OF PRODUCTS AND MATERIALS

For a range of social and cultural reasons, certain characteristics of building materials have been widely adopted as indicators of environmental preferability. These "green attributes" include recycled content, low indoor chemical emissions, and the ability of a product to be used in its natural state, in other words, with minimal manufacturing. Products with any one of these attributes are often selected for use in a building over other products that have a lower overall environmental impact.

INDIVIDUAL GREEN ATTRIBUTES AS PROXIES FOR ENVIRONMENTAL PREFERABILITY

Most existing EPP programs, including purchasing mandates from government agencies and state or local government, are based on specific green characteristics of products. In such cases, the term EPP is applied as a way of broadening the appeal of what is fundamentally a narrowly focused initiative. In other instances, an agency or organization may actually intend to promote the use of products that are environmentally preferable in a broader sense, but for practical purposes uses a single green attribute as a preferable environmental indicator.

A significant driver of the use of these green attributes has been the U.S. Green Building Council's and its LEED Rating Systems, which based some of its materials-related credits on such single attributes until the release of the "Version 4" rating systems in 2013. This newer version deemphasized those criteria in favor of more holistic, lifecycle and health-based indicators which are described later in this chapter.

Recycled content. Promoting recycled content, as an *overall* preferable environmental indicator, is an example of using a specific societal agenda to make particular products attractive. The recycled content prerogative is a response to the problem that emerged when recycling first became popular—an accumulation of collected material

PART 3: THE PROJECT

without a viable end use. The federal EPA, many state agencies, and other organizations all have programs that promote or mandate the use of materials with recycled content under the mantra of "closing the loop."

Nearly all recycled-content programs distinguish between post-consumer recycled materials, which have been discarded after fulfilling their intended use, and pre-consumer (or "postindustrial") recycled materials. Pre-consumer materials are those that have entered a waste stream before reaching their intended end use, such as paper trimmings at a printing plant. Most definitions of pre-consumer recycled materials specifically exclude those that are reused within a single manufacturing facility or operation, as those materials have never really become "waste" at all. For example, glass manufacturers routinely break off spec glass at the end of a processing line and melt it again to make new glass.

Further confusing matters, the EPA uses the term "recovered material" to include both post-consumer and pre-consumer recycled material, but other organizations use that term more broadly to include materials that would not qualify as recycled under most definitions. For example, the Composite Panel Association's EPP Specification includes logging slash—tree tops and limbs not usable as lumber—and logs from forest thinning operations in its definition of "recovered fiber" used in making particleboard and medium-density fiberboard.

Bio-based. In theory, building materials derived directly from plants are renewable indefinitely and, as such, represent a solution to the problem of products whose manufacture adds to the depletion of finite mineral resources. Plant-based materials tend to be less manufacturing-intensive than materials synthesized from petrochemicals, as well. Their structural qualities are typically provided by the cellular structures of the plants from which they are made. Some agricultural products, however, are grown with extensive use of pesticides and herbicides, and in a manner that contributes to the loss of topsoil.

The U.S. government has long promoted the use of agricultural materials as a way of supporting farms, including the 2002 Farm Bill, which mandates that federal agencies establish preferential purchasing programs for certain types of bio-based materials. The Department of Agriculture initiative for implementing this mandate includes a program to label and promote new markets for bio-based materials. Wood, though obviously bio-based, was excluded from the original regulation because it is deemed to have a mature market and therefore didn't require federal support, but the 2014 Farm Bill included modified language to ensure that wood is now included. To address concerns about ecological problems with bio-based materials, the Farm Bill includes a screening process based on environmental lifecycle assessment (see below).

Low in chemical emissions. In response to concerns about indoor air quality in buildings, the off-gassing of chemicals from building materials and furnishings is increasingly being scrutinized. Many of the substances under investigation fall into the category of volatile organic compounds (VOCs), a term that describes carbon-based compounds that occur as gases under ambient temperature and pressure conditions. Some VOCs are known to cause adverse health effects and discomfort, and many contribute to smog. Not all VOCs are harmful, however, and some (both harmful and benign) occur naturally in the environment.

The off-gassing of VOCs and other substances is measured by placing a sample of the product or material in a stainless steel testing chamber and collecting and then analyzing the gases emitted into that chamber. The Carpet and Rug Institute began using this process in the early 1990s as the basis of its "Green Label" program, which certifies that emissions of total VOCs and certain specific compounds from carpets do not exceed specified thresholds. Beginning in 2004, the Green Label program was replaced with a more robust and stringent program, entitled "Green Label Plus."

The carpet industry's Green Label Plus protocol was expanded to other product categories under the brand "Greenguard," which is now owned by Underwriters'

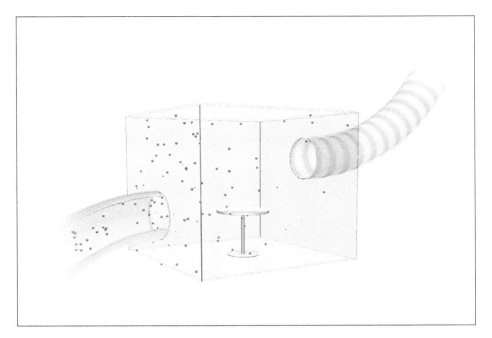

FIGURE 6.4 Technicians test for emissions from a product, by analyzing air samples from a sterile, stainless steel chamber containing the product.

Laboratories. Greenguard establishes allowable chemical emission thresholds for a wide range of materials used indoors, and certifies products that do not exceed those thresholds. Subsequently, the furniture manufacturers' trade association BIFMA International introduced its own, similar standards for testing furniture's indoor emissions. Figure 6.4 illustrates a typical chamber for testing emissions.

Meanwhile, in California, a specification was developed for state office buildings which uses a very similar type of chamber testing for products, but uses a different list of chemicals and allowable concentrations to determine compliance. This spec is now codified in the "California Department of Public Health (CDPH) Standard Method v1.1–2010." This California protocol has now become the basis of the FloorScore certification program for resilient and hard surface flooring, and the Indoor Advantage Gold product certification program from Scientific Certification Systems (SCS).

Natural and minimally processed. Although there are few formal ways to reference or certify natural materials, designers and their clients generally consider natural or minimally processed products environmentally preferable. Included in this category are natural fiber carpets and fabrics, natural stone floors, cork, linoleum, and bamboo. An exception to this mind-set, at least in North America, is the use of wood. While in Europe wood is generally considered an ecologically sound material choice, in the United States concerns about the destruction of domestic old-growth forests and deforestation in the Amazon and other tropical rainforests have discouraged some designers from embracing wood as a green material.

To assuage concerns about the sustainability of wood, several certification and labeling systems have been developed to provide some assurance that wood from certain sources is a good ecological choice. The most widely accepted of these is from the Forest Stewardship Council (FSC). This international organization establishes regional forest management plans based on its "Principles and Criteria for Forest Stewardship" and then accredits third-party organizations to certify forestry operations for conformance with these plans. The FSC also requires certification of every organization in the chain of custody for the wood to ensure that wood from certified well-managed forests is not inadvertently mixed with uncertified wood.

A number of countries, including Malaysia and Indonesia, developed their own forest certification programs, but these failed to develop credibility among wood buyers, primarily in Europe. In response to this difficulty, these programs are choosing to merge with the FSC system and meet its requirements. In North America, however, the Canadian Standards Association (CSA) and the American Forest & Paper Association (AF&PA) have created other certification programs, which are preferred by most of the forest products industry. Over time, both the CSA Sustainable Forest Management Standard and the AF&PA Sustainable Forestry Initiative have become more rigorous in an attempt to win over loyalists of the FSC system. Proponents of the industry-supported systems argue that their programs are now equivalent to the FSC's, but many environmentalists are unconvinced. Where the FSC program tends to prescribe specific forest management practices, the industry-supported programs often allow more leeway for foresters to determine the preferred approach. Given the complexity of the systems themselves, and the ecological and business environments in which they are used, comparing them is not easy.

Low embodied energy and low carbon. Another indicator used to measure environmental impact is the amount of energy used to create a product, which is often correlated with the amount of climate-change inducing greenhouses emitted in the manufacturing process. This metric is variously called "carbon footprint," "embodied energy," "embedded energy," or simply the "energy intensity" of a product. Measures of embodied energy include the quantity of fuels and electricity used to mine or harvest raw materials, transport them, and process them into a product ready for delivery to a construction site. The embodied energy of a product and its carbon footprint is not something that can readily be found on a label or manufacturer's website, but some researchers internationally have estimated embodied energy figures for certain product groups.

Embodied energy is often reported in units of Btus per pound, or Gigajoules per tonne. For these figures to be useful in product comparisons, it is necessary to also consider the weight of the material in question, and how much of it is needed to perform a given function. For example, concrete may have lower embodied energy than kiln-dried lumber on a per-pound basis, but if it takes many more pounds of concrete to perform the same job, the lumber needed to support a structure will likely have lower embodied energy. The comparison is complicated even further, however, by the question of durability or longevity. If the concrete structure will last significantly longer than the wood structure, that additional longevity should also be factored into the comparison.

LIFECYCLE ASSESSMENT: A COMPREHENSIVE APPROACH

The environmental product characteristics or attributes described above are widely referenced as preferable indicators, in part because they are often based on relatively accessible information. It is widely acknowledged, however, that they are merely indicators and do not accurately reflect the full environmental performance of a product.

Ideally, EPP claims would be based on comparisons of overall environmental performance. The most common approach to determining the environmental performance of a product is through lifecycle assessment (LCA).

Environmental lifecycle assessment is a science that attempts to quantify the resource and material input, and product and pollution output, over the entire lifecycle of a product. Based on this inventory of energy and material flows, LCA characterizes the environmental burdens associated with each type of input and output, thereby quantifying the overall environmental burdens of a product. The practice of LCA is guided internationally by ISO Standards 14040 and 14044.

Lifecycle Costing vs. Lifecycle Assessment

Lifecycle assessment is not related to lifecycle costing, which is a methodology commonly used by engineers and financial managers to determine the dollar cost of ownership of a particular item. Lifecycle costing accounts for the initial cost of an item, the cost of operating and maintaining the item, the time it will serve, and any costs associated with its eventual disposal. The result of this calculation is what the item will cost the owner throughout its service life. Lifecycle assessment, on the other hand, quantifies environmental performance rather than financial cost (although they are often related). LCA also extends the definition of "lifecycle" to include where a product comes from (raw materials extraction and manufacturing) and where it ends up after its service life is over.

The resource flows that are quantified in an environmental lifecycle assessment are typically broken down according to lifecycle stage: raw material extraction, manufacturing, transportation, construction, use, and disposal or reuse. In each stage, environmental performance is measured in terms of input (energy, water, resource materials) and output (emissions, effluents, and solid waste and co-products).

Extraction or harvesting of raw materials. The energy used to operate heavy equipment (primarily in the form of diesel or other fossil fuels) is the major input for the extraction and harvesting of raw materials. Output includes pollution associated with burning these fuels, any runoff or erosion into surface waters, and other negative effects on the immediate environment of the operation. The raw material—whether logs, ore, petroleum, or some other material—is also an output.

Manufacturing. Input into a manufacturing process includes all the raw materials and the fuels that provide energy to drive the process. In the case of electricity, the input includes the fuels used to generate the electricity at the power plant. Water is also often used in the manufacturing process.

Output from manufacturing typically includes pollutant emissions to air and effluents to water, as well as any solid waste generated. The desired output is the product itself, along with any usable by-products.

Transportation. Transportation of raw materials and finished products consumes energy and releases pollutants from the use of that energy. Some modes of transportation are more energy efficient and less polluting than others.

Construction. Construction also consumes energy, and it requires the input of products or materials. The desired output is the completed building. Unwanted output includes air emissions from construction equipment, erosion from the construction site, and job-site waste.

Use. When a product or material is in place in a building, it has become part of a larger whole. It may contribute to reduced (or increased) energy use by the building. Its ongoing maintenance and operation (for example, floor finishes and cleaning supplies, or toner and paper for copiers) will require input. In place, a product or material may release pollutants to the indoor or outdoor environment.

The resource input and pollution output vary significantly depending on the type of product, how it is applied or installed in a building, and how building occupants interact with it. For many materials, these flows continue over the life of the product and can easily dwarf impacts from upstream stages in the product lifecycle. The energy used to counteract unwanted solar gain through a window, for example, can over a few years, exceed the energy used to manufacture, transport, and install the window.

Disposal/recycling/reuse. At the end of its useful life, a product or material may become solid waste that must be disposed of, or it may become the raw material for some other product. In some cases, a product may be salvaged and reused intact. If a product has hazardous components, such as the mercury in thermostats or fluorescent lamps, those materials become a potential environmental burden that must be managed appropriately.

Practical Problems and Limitations of LCA

Quantifying all the types of input and output over the entire lifecycle of a product is no simple matter, and many assumptions and variables come into play. How broadly to set the boundaries of the study is not always obvious. For example, vehicle fuel is always considered as transportation input, but what about other fluids, such as lubricants and hydraulic fluids? And should the energy and materials used to manufacture and maintain the vehicle or the roads on which it travels be included? If researchers do not address these questions consistently by doing different studies, the results may not be comparable.

Despite the intention that LCA studies address all relevant impacts, in practice they focus on those impacts that can most readily be quantified, leaving out other concerns which may be no less important. For example, the habitat and ecosystem impacts of forestry are quite complicated, and many LCA studies make no attempt to differentiate between wood from well-managed forests and that from irresponsible, even illegal, deforestation. In addition, the human health impacts included in most LCA studies only consider the effect of a limited set of air pollutants; ignoring the effects of many hazardous substances. In this sense, LCA is susceptible to the looking-under-lamppost problem, scrutinizing impacts that are accessible to its methods while ignoring others.

Finally, LCA studies have not been performed for many products and materials because so much work is required to produce comprehensive studies. As a result, even with good LCA data for a certain product, it can be hard to interpret the results for lack of information on other products for comparison. To further complicate matters, the more comprehensive a study is, the more environmental burdens it is likely to report. As a result, product manufacturers have an unfortunate incentive to limit the boundaries of their studies as much as possible.

Translating Flows into Environmental Impacts

When the inventory for a lifecycle assessment is available, the next step is to estimate the environmental impacts associated with the resource flows. For example, the lifecycle of any given product is likely to include emissions of carbon dioxide, nitrous oxides, and methane, all of which are greenhouse gases that contribute to climate change. To estimate their collective impact on climate change, however, it is not enough to simply add up the quantities of each emitted because each gas affects the environment to a different degree. For example, according to EPA figures, methane is 21 times more powerful than CO_2 as a greenhouse gas and nitrous oxide is 310 times more powerful. Thus, the overall climate change impact associated with a product is calculated in units of "CO_2 equivalents." CO_2 equivalents are arrived at by multiplying each greenhouse gas by its appropriate factor, and then adding the resulting figures together.

A similar process is used to estimate environmental impacts in other categories. In the case of human health and eco-toxicity, however, the list of compounds that can contribute to impacts in each category can be very large, and estimating how much each one contributes is quite complicated. The categories used by the EPA's environmental impact assessment protocol—Tool for the Reduction and Assessment of Chemical Impacts, or TRACI—include ozone depletion, global warming, acidification, eutrophication, photochemical smog, human carcinogenic effects, human noncarcinogenic effects, human health criteria, eco-toxicity, fossil fuel use, land use, and water use.

Interpreting the Results

Aggregating the input and output of the various flows into impact categories is not easy, but even that doesn't give designers the simple answers they want. If two products or materials are being compared, typically one will score lower (better) in some impact categories and the other will score lower in others. In other words, it still isn't clear which is preferable. It is tempting to choose the one that is lower in more categories or that appears to be lower overall. However, that solution assumes that all the categories are equally important, which they are not likely to be.

TRANSPARENCY DECLARATIONS—AN INTERIM SOLUTION

For a comprehensive view into which products are environmentally preferable, designers are looking to LCA in combination with other information that fills in some of the gaps in LCA as it practiced today. The results of an LCA study are summarized in a report called an environmental product declaration (EPD). In addition to summarizing the results, the EPD specifies the protocols under which the LCA was performed, which are supposed to be consistent for all the products in a given category. Those protocols are known as product category rules (PCRs).

To address information about hazardous ingredients that might be missing from the LCA, there is a new "health product declaration" (HPD) format that offers a consistent, structured way for suppliers to report on the ingredients in their product and any potential health hazards associated with those ingredients. The HPD format provides a way for companies to disclose all the ingredients in a product but allows them to refrain from identifying some as long as any health hazards are revealed.

The habitat and ecosystem impacts of raw material extraction are covered by certification programs, such as those based on the Forest Stewardship Council's Principles and Criteria. Similar programs are now emerging to reward responsible practices in agricultural products and mining.

Together these three frameworks—EPDs, HPDs, and raw material sourcing certifications—address most relevant environmental and health impacts of products. Interpreting the data in EPDs and HPDs is a challenge, however, and will remain so until there is a critical mass of products providing this data in consistent and comparable ways. To help achieve that critical mass, some programs provide incentives for suppliers to provide these declarations, even when the information they reveal is not flattering to the product.

Pulling It All Together: Comprehensive Certifications

To save designers the challenge of gathering and interpreting all this data, there are third-party certifications that do the interpretation and provide Silver/Gold/Platinum-style tiered results. These include Cradle to Cradle, which covers all product categories (including many outside the building industry), and sector-specific programs such as "level" certification from BIFMA, and a series of standards from NSF International, such as the NSF–140 Standard for carpets.

Each of these programs factors in LCA results, health hazards, and raw material extraction impacts in its own way, so it's important to review a standard and understand its scoring system before specifying products based on its outcomes.

Setting an even higher bar, with aspirational goals for ideal products is the Living Product Challenge, a new program from the Living Future Institute, which brings us the Living Building Challenge. This program seeks to offset the adverse environmental footprint of a product with corresponding "handprints" that recognize beneficial impacts associated with the product's manufacture and use.

MATERIALS IN LEED®

Since it was first released in 1999, the U.S. Green Building Council's LEED Rating System has had a significant effect on the U.S. building industry. To a large degree, it has driven the demand for green buildings. As a result, designers and product manufacturers are particularly interested in the LEED approach to material selection. There are now several different rating systems under the LEED umbrella—with many variations on the original LEED for New Construction (LEED-NC).

Each of the LEED Rating Systems certifies the environmental performance of a building based on the building's conformance with a series of criteria in the LEED checklist. Each item on the list offers one or more points, depending on the level of achievement required to conform to that item. A number of the LEED criteria relate directly to the selection of products and materials. These are handled slightly differently in the different LEED rating systems, and have changed significantly with the release of the Version 4 collection of systems.

The original LEED rating systems include incentives to use materials with the following attributes:

- Salvaged materials
- Recycled content materials
- Locally harvested and manufactured materials
- Rapidly renewable materials
- Wood from well-managed forests
- Low-emitting adhesives and sealants
- Low-emitting paints and coatings
- Low-emitting carpet
- Composite wood products without urea formaldehyde binders

Each of these criteria offers points based on the use of materials with a specific green attribute. As described earlier, these attributes serve as proxies for a preference based on overall environmental performance. This approach could lead to the use of materials that have certain green attributes, but are not at all desirable from a comprehensive lifecycle perspective. LEED offsets this limitation, to some extent, by virtue of the fact that designers using LEED are not working with each criterion in isolation, but looking to achieve points over the whole system. Thus, if a carpet has high recycled content but does not meet the low-emissions requirement, it may be avoided in favor of one that meets both criteria.

LEED Version 4 takes a fundamentally different approach, seeking more comprehensive metrics of environmental preferability. For lack of a single universal standard, however, those more comprehensive metrics are divided into three core credits, on environmental product declarations, raw material extraction, and material ingredients. These credits each include both incentives for transparent reporting of product impacts and ingredients, and incentives for optimization. Future versions are likely to add a credit on social equity to that trio.

A great many points in LEED do not address material choices explicitly, but their performance requirements indirectly lead to the use of green products. This is especially true in relation to plumbing fixtures, appliances that use water, and energy-related equipment such as chillers, light fixtures, fans, pumps, and the like.

SOME GUIDING PRINCIPLES

A comprehensive, reliable, and accessible system for choosing environmentally preferable products is not yet a reality. Until LCA-based approaches become more robust and available, architects must base their decisions on less ideal methods. In light of this situation, what options do designers have? Here are some principles to keep in mind:

1. Think big-picture. Apply "lifecycle thinking" to product choices, even when reliable lifecycle data is not available. To do this effectively, learn a bit about where products come from and how they are made. When specifying a product based on certain green characteristics, ask questions about aspects of the product's environmental performance in other areas. A carpet may be low in indoor emissions, for example, but is it also efficient in its use of raw materials? Was it manufactured using renewable energy sources?
2. Focus on big-ticket items. Most of a building's materials-related impact on the environment is associated with the materials used in biggest quantities. Therefore, it makes sense to spend time evaluating the structural materials and materials used extensively for cladding or interior finishes. It does not pay to spend a lot of time seeking to optimize the environmental performance of products and materials that are only used in a small area of a project. However, if you are pursuing a LEED point for low-emitting materials, you may have to track down products that conform to the requirements even if they are used in a very limited way.

3. Remember to look at the usage phase. With all the information available on recycled content and renewable materials, it is easy to forget that a product's environmental impact once it has been installed in a building can easily overwhelm upstream considerations. Any exterior cladding, insulation, or equipment that can help reduce a building's energy use should be given careful consideration. Interior finish materials that do not require strong cleaning agents and frequent refinishing are also helpful.

4. Seek lifecycle and ingredient toxicity data when comparing dissimilar products. The environmental impact of two very different materials being considered for the same application may vary in different areas, so it is hard to know which is better overall without good lifecycle data. With or without such data, though, the final decision often comes down to a value judgment. For example, an architect may have to choose between agricultural materials with relatively high manufacturing energy requirements and petrochemical-based materials that require less energy to manufacture.

5. Differentiate products based on specific green attributes. This technique is useful when products are otherwise quite similar. In the case of ceiling tiles, for example, reflectivity is important because it can lower lighting energy demand. However, if two products are similar in terms of performance characteristics choosing one with higher recycled content and/or lower indoor emissions makes sense.

6. Look for outside sources you can trust. Because your time is precious and you can never study all the materials you might consider using, it helps to have reliable resources on which to base decisions. When reviewing these resources, consider factors such as the stated values of the organization, the methods it uses, the expertise of its personnel, and who pays its bills.

For More Information

Several organizations are working to create and implement standards for environmentally preferable products.

The Cradle-to-Cradle Products Innovation Institute provides certification of products that conform to its Cradle-to-Cradle protocol, developed and popularized by architect William McDonough and chemist Michael Braungart. (www.c2ccertified .org/)

The Living Product Challenge from the International Living Future Institute seeks to define the ultimate goal of products that not only minimize their adverse impacts but more than offset those with positive ecological and social impacts. (www .living-future.org)

Green Seal is an independent, nonprofit organization that develops standards, certifies products to those standards, and publishes reports with product recommendations. Green Seal employs an open, consensus-based process in the development of its standards. It relies on outside funding to support this process, which limits the number of standards it can develop. (www.greenseal.org)

Scientific Certification Systems, Inc. offers third-party certification services based on systems that range widely in scope, from single-issue claims to comprehensive claims of environmental preferability. (www.scscertified.com)

Other organizations are active in related areas:

The Health Product Declaration Collaborative manages the HPD reporting standard: www.hpdcollaborative.org

Carbon Leadership Forum promotes EPDs and the development of low-embodied carbon products.

UL Environment's Greenguard program certifies products that meet its published standards for low indoor air emissions. Interior furnishings, fixtures, and finishes are especially well represented in its database of certified products. (www.greenguard.org)

Forest Stewardship Council (FSC) produces guidelines for certifying forest products that originate from forestry operations that are managed in an environmentally and socially responsible manner. FSC also accredits organizations, such as SCS and Smartwood, that can certify compliance with the FSC's guidelines and bestow permission to use the FSC label. (www.fscus.org)

U.S. Life Cycle Inventory Database Project, coordinated by the National Renewable Energy Laboratory and the Athena Sustainable Materials Institute, publishes publicly available and transparent lifecycle inventory information on basic industrial processes and materials. This information can be used to improve consistency across lifecycle assessments of competing products and reduce the time and effort needed to produce those assessments. (www.nrel.gov/lci)

Green Building Materials, 2nd edition, by Ross Speigel and Dru Meadows (Wiley, 2006), provides guidance on selecting and specifying green products and materials.

BuildingGreen.com is an online resource that applies lifecycle thinking to compare material options for specific applications, and include detailed product reviews that address both the functional and environmental performance of green products. This subscription-based tool also provides lists of preferable products curated by the editors (manufacturers do not pay for listings) and a robust product information management platform for firms. (www.buildinggreen.com)

CHAPTER 7

Project Development

7.1 Design Phases

Bradford Perkins, FAIA

Design is the keystone of architecture practice. Translating needs and aspirations into appropriate and exciting places and buildings requires great skill, as well as attention to broader public concerns.

Architecture is the art of inquiry.

—Arthur Erickson

Building design begins with the architect's analysis, understanding, and response to the base of data, intentions, and impressions collected in the process of discovering what there is to know about the project.

There are many ways of looking at the design process and the design practices in which architects engage. Design decision making can be seen as private and intuitive—for, in many respects, it is—and yet many of the decisions designers make are broadly discussed and rationally analyzed. Design can be seen as complex and inaccessible, and yet it is taught to and practiced by thousands of capable architects—and hundreds of thousands more in a wide array of other disciplines. Design has moments of great inspiration and deep insight—but most of all it requires hours, months, and years of hard work.

Design is a continuous activity. It "begins" somewhere deep in the recesses of the project definition process; somewhere someone has an idea that ultimately takes form. Design never really ends; important design decisions are made at every stage of the process. Even once opened for use, buildings are constantly modified and adapted—redesigned, if you will.

Bradford Perkins, FAIA, is the founder, Chairman, and CEO of Perkins Eastman Architects, a large New York–based international architecture, interior design, and planning firm that has won many design awards. He lectures regularly at architecture schools and other institutions and is on the faculty of Cornell University's College of Architecture, Art, and Planning. He has published seven books and numerous articles on design and architecture management issues.

Most projects *do* have beginnings and ends. These points are defined by the contracts written to provide planning, design, construction, and facility management services. Design, however, is the central issue at every step. The design process has been compared to a learning curve on which each step exposes the design team to new opportunities, new problems, and new knowledge about the situation at hand.

DESIGN FACTORS

Every project situation is different. Each presents different requirements, limitations, challenges, and opportunities, as well as a unique set of cultural, environmental, technological, and aesthetic contexts. Design brings to the surface the major considerations inherent in a situation. It is both a problem-seeking and a problem-solving process. Although the particular combination is specific to each project, some of the most important design factors follow.

Program

All building projects have a series of aspirations, requirements, and limitations to be met in design. This information is included in the "program" for the project. The program may be short or long, general or specific, descriptive of needs, or suggestive of solutions. The program may be provided by the client or may be developed as an additional service by the architect.

The combination of all data collected and analyzed during programming sets up the decision-making process that leads to the synthesis that is the core of concept design. See "Programming" for a discussion of the programming process.

Community Desires

A growing number of public agency approvals influence design. Many owners and their architects must adjust their designs to satisfy community groups, neighbors, and public officials. These design adjustments are often ad hoc efforts to meet objections or to gain support rather than direct responses to codified requirements.

Codes and Regulations

Regulatory constraints on design have increased steadily. Beginning with simple safety requirements and minimal land use and light-and-air zoning, building codes and regulations have grown into a major force that regulates every aspect of design and construction.

Site and Climate

The site is, of course, a major influence. Physical characteristics (e.g., size, configuration, topography, and geotechnical issues), climate (wind, solar orientation, temperatures, humidity, and precipitation), environmental factors (views, existing vegetation, drainage), access, adjacent land uses, and many other site factors are considered in reaching the final design.

Building Context and Existing Fabric

The surrounding environment has been a site feature of major influence on many buildings. In addition to obvious effects on building configuration, neighboring structures or landscape can influence the materials, fenestration, color, and detailing chosen for the final building design. Of even more importance are any existing structures that may be incorporated into the building being designed. A growing percentage of building design problems call for working within the constraints of an existing structure.

A building should respond to the order of the city and the order of the land.

—Romaldo Giurgola, FAIA

Building Technology

Building configuration, materials, and systems are rarely arbitrarily chosen and are only partially based on aesthetic criteria. For example, the floor-to-floor height

It is becoming increasingly important for us to identify those unique aspects of each project, and explore through design, that will not only result in significant contributions to modern architecture but will also help solve the myriad environmental issues that we now face.

—Craig Curtis, FAIA of the Miller/Hull Partnership

required to accommodate structural, mechanical, lighting, and ceiling systems in a cost-effective manner varies significantly from an apartment house to an office building or research facility. Similarly, horizontal divisions are often set to achieve maximum efficiency of layout; thus, office fenestration may be based on one module and housing on another. In still other cases, these dimensions may be dictated largely by mechanical systems or even by the knowledge and preferences of the local construction industry.

Sustainability

In its broadest scope, sustainability refers to the ability of a society, ecosystem, or any ongoing system to continue functioning into the indefinite future without being forced into decline through exhaustion or overloading of the key resources on which that system depends. For architecture, this means design that delivers buildings and communities with lower environmental impacts that also enhance health, productivity, community, and quality of life. Projects today often begin with specific sustainable design goals that often strongly influence the final design.

Evidence-Based Design

Many clients want their architects to learn from successful precedents and the growing body of evidence-based design.

Special Issues

External factors, such as rapidly rising energy costs or increased security concerns, can also be major design influences. Desire for energy conservation, for example, can be a major determinant in the choice of most major building systems. Security concerns can influence everything from the site plan and entry sequence to the space program and building materials.

The best things happen when you have to deal with reality.

—Robert Venturi, FAIA

Cost

Since most projects have limited budgets, cost considerations significantly influence almost all issues from building size and configuration to material selection and detailing. Cost is rarely a simple issue. Budgets may be fixed by the amount of financing available, or they may be flexible and come into focus in the design process. Often a construction budget emerges from an analysis involving the owner and the entire project team. Some owners are willing to increase initial budgets to achieve overall life-cycle cost savings, but in most cases, there is a limit to the funds available for construction. Once defined, this limit has a major influence on subsequent design decisions.

Schedule

Because there are so many outside influences on design, it is common for the architect to make design decisions out of sequence or in time frames so compressed that some alternatives cannot be explored. For example, an alternative requiring a time-consuming zoning variance may be discarded in favor of one that can keep the project on schedule. In another project, it may be necessary to commit to a final site plan early in the process—before the building "footprint" drawn on the site plan has been fully designed.

Designs of purely arbitrary nature cannot be expected to last long.

—Kenzo Tange

The Client

A central ingredient in most successful design projects is a good client. Some clients have a clear idea of program, budget, and other project objectives, including the final appearance of the building. Others look to their architect to help them define the project objectives, as well as to design a building that meets these goals. In both cases, the effectiveness of the marriage between client and architect is a major factor throughout the design process.

DESIGN PROCESS

Almost every project has a unique set of factors that combine to make each process different. For their part, individual architects approach design in different ways and with different values and attitudes. While design has a certain linear quality (it involves analysis, synthesis, and evaluation), it is widely acknowledged the process has nonlinear qualities as well. The latter are sometimes described as "flashes of insight" and "creative leaps."

Increasingly, we recognize that the design process works with information and ideas simultaneously on many levels. Thus, the architect can be thinking simultaneously about the overall geometry of the building, the ways in which a wheelchair-bound person might experience the spaces in the building, and the materials of which the building will be constructed.

At the same time, we view designing as a reciprocal action and reflection. Architects process requirements, issues, and variables, and produce tentative design proposals. Examination and criticism of these proposals lead to new proposals. Each proposal reveals more about the problem and suggests an appropriate solution.

> The challenge is to determine, depending on the circumstances, whether to design the project from the inside out or outside in. Often the constraints of the site, program, or budget will lead to an optimum resolution of these seemingly independent criteria.
>
> —Mustafa Abadan, FAIA, of Skidmore Owings & Merrill

Analysis

However nonlinear it may be, design involves analysis. An initial step is to identify, analyze, confirm, and organize the factors that will influence the development of a design concept. Architects typically take available data from the economic feasibility, programming, and site analysis steps and organize them into a form that allows the information to be used in building design. The data may be provided by the owner or developed by the architect in the course of programming or site analysis services. The analyses—often pursued in parallel—are described in the paragraphs that follow.

Program analysis. Many architects translate the words and numbers in the program statement into graphic terms, developing charts, bubble diagrams, and sketches of design concepts. Most architects stress the need to be actively involved in the program as a critical starting point for design. As Herbert McLaughlin of Kaplan McLaughlin Diaz notes, "It is vital to understand that programming is inevitably and necessarily a part of the design process. The ideas of design should be able to influence and often change the size and, inevitably, the shape of spaces as well as their interrelationships and, frequently, their relationships with nature." Even when the owner has prepared a program, it is useful to spend time confirming the program and converting it into understandable and usable design information.

Site analysis. Important site data are typically organized into a graphic record of relevant physical, cultural, and regulatory factors. When organized in a common scale and format, these data often begin to point the way to design solutions. Ideas also present themselves in time spent walking the site, understanding both it and the surrounding community.

> The design process can be summarized in four words: ingenuity, hard work, and talent.
>
> —Hugh Stubbins, FAIA

Zoning and code analysis. Concurrent with the site analysis, many firms convert zoning and other code issues into graphic form. In the case of complex urban zoning codes, this may include graphic representations of the zoning envelope—height, bulk, setbacks, and other limits imposed by the code. When combined with parking and loading requirements, exiting considerations, building area and height limitations, and other code requirements, this analysis can help the architect begin to shape the program into a building mass that fits the site well.

Documentation of existing conditions. Many building design problems must work with or include existing structures in the solution. It is essential, therefore, to establish clear and accurate documentation of existing conditions, either by converting existing drawings into base sheets for use in design or by creating new measured base drawings. In addition to providing basic dimensional data for design, this step typically identifies existing physical and code problems.

Scheduling. The project schedule is a project management tool, but at times, it can also become an important factor in design. Such major scheduling issues as project phasing, the time it takes to seek variances, and the sequencing of design decisions to accommodate fast-track scheduling can all influence the development of a design concept.

Cost. It is important to analyze a project budget to understand its implications for the building design. Virtually all project budgets are limited. The architect must make careful use of funds, directing them to those decisions that appear to be most important to the success of the design solution. An experienced architect can usually identify the size of this discretionary portion of the budget, as well as establish clear guidelines for the basic system selections to take place during the design.

Construction industry practice. Concurrent with schedule and cost analysis, most architects consider the aspects of local construction industry practice relevant to the design assignment. This can range from availability of materials and labor to commonly used materials, systems, and detailing.

Design precedents. In many firms, an important aspect of the initial analysis is the critical assessment of relevant precedents from projects facing similar or related program, site, context, cost, or other design issues. It is common for architects to familiarize themselves with the design of buildings that deal with similar issues to stimulate solutions for their own design problems.

Synthesis

Building design begins with the architect's analysis, understanding, and response to the base data collected and analyzed. The combination of all this into a unified solution is the synthesis that is the core of concept design.

Most architects start with an analysis of the base data and then work through sketches, talking, and thinking—reciprocal action and reflection—until they reach the level of understanding necessary to form a concept. While the particular design stimuli, organizing principles, areas of emphasis, and aesthetic vocabularies may be unique to a particular architect or firm, and while firms may synthesize these in different ways, there are some common tasks in design. These are discussed in the paragraphs that follow.

Establishing design goals. The client and design team have goals for the project, expressed formally or informally. These goals create functional and aesthetic guidelines for judging design decisions, and the project objectives help establish priorities when trade-offs must be accommodated in the design solution. Compromises between budget and quality, appearance and energy efficiency, and hundreds of other decisions have to be made within the context of an understanding of project goals and priorities.

Evolving a design concept. With the design goals in hand, the architect develops a design concept—or perhaps several. This may be a plan concept, the selection of a geometric form, a decision to mass the building vertically or horizontally, or the use of an organizing element (e.g., a central mall for the interior spaces). The concept might be based on a particular image or a historic precedent. It may employ a "design vocabulary" of formal and aesthetic ideas that will govern the development of the design. Whatever the underlying principles, it is common for architects to develop several representations and variations to help them understand and articulate the evolving design concepts.

Evaluating concept alternatives. Working with these possibilities and variations, most architects have developed a process for narrowing them down to a set of workable concepts. In some cases, the selection of alternatives is based on a point-by-point evaluation of the concept against the original project objectives. In other cases, it is an intuitive judgment based on experience. In most instances, it is a combination of both.

Beyond the first conceptual steps, the process becomes more complex. In all but the smallest and simplest projects, the steps that follow development of a concept involve a team of people. As the design team is expanded, most firms begin to involve the engineers, specialist consultants, and cost consultants necessary to help test and develop the selected concepts. Architects generally agree that early participation of other project team participants leads to a more efficient and coordinated design effort. For example, engineers not only guide the selection of many building systems but also define the size, area requirements, and preferred location of these systems. In more complex design problems, engineers often help analyze the feasibility, relative cost, and other critical factors of major design options.

> In their work and writings, leading design principals express the importance of the nonrational, the indescribable, and the poetic in the creation of successful building design. At key points, judgment, taste, intuition, and creative talent take over.

CONTRACTUAL FRAMEWORK

Design is undertaken within a contractual framework that

- Outlines design tasks and requirements
- Identifies specific responsibilities for design, including those of the architect and the owner, and possibly of third parties
- Establishes a schedule, including starting and completion dates
- Often defines design phases with interim milestone dates and owner approvals to proceed

This contractual framework is established in the agreement between owner and architect. Design activities may be described in detail or, in the case of small or limited-scope projects, in a few sentences. The AIA owner-architect agreements have established five project phases:

- Schematic design
- Design development
- Construction documents
- Bidding or negotiation
- Construction

AIA Document B101–2007, Standard Form of Agreement Between Owner and Architect, assumes that a clear definition of the client's program exists. Either the owner brings the program to the start of design or the architect provides the service as part of professional services. It also assumes the process can move ahead in a linear fashion through a series of phases—each of which results in a more complete definition of the design—until the project is sufficiently detailed to go into documentation for bidding (or negotiation) and construction.

Reality is rarely so orderly. Evolving program requirements, budget realities, increased knowledge of site considerations (such as subsoil problems), public agency reviews, and many other factors make it necessary to go back and modify previous steps. Fast-track scheduling—breaking design into "packages" and awarding some before others are completed—further complicates matters. Design moves forward, but rarely in the clear, linear fashion implied by the contractual phases. Building information modeling blurs the distinctions between phases even more. As this tool has more architects designing and documenting projects in three dimensions, many of today's later-phase decisions will inevitably become part of the early design process.

Nonetheless, a contractual framework is important. It imposes an order on the process. When there are phases, the architect brings the design to an interim level of development, the owner reviews and approves it, and the project moves forward based on a mutual understanding.

Schematic Design

AIA Document B101–2007 identifies the first phase of services as schematic design. Although the completion of this phase may be defined slightly differently for each project or by different clients and design teams, certain objectives and products are commonly agreed upon.

Schematic design establishes the general scope, conceptual design, and scale and relationships among the components of a project. The primary objective is to arrive at a clearly defined, feasible concept and to present it in a form that achieves client understanding and acceptance. The secondary objectives are to clarify the project program, explore the most promising alternative design solutions, and provide a reasonable basis for analyzing the cost of the project.

Typical documentation at the end of this phase includes the following items:

- A site plan
- Plans for each level
- All elevations
- Key sections
- An outline specification
- A statistical summary of the design area and other characteristics in comparison to the program
- A preliminary construction cost estimate
- Other illustrative materials—renderings, models, computer simulations, or additional drawings—needed to adequately present the concept

Drawings. These are typically presented at the smallest scale that can clearly illustrate the concept, perhaps 1/16″ = 1′-0″ (1:200 in SI units) for larger buildings and 1/8″ = 1′-0″ (1:100) or 1/4″ = 1′-0″ (1:50) for smaller buildings and interiors.

Outline specifications. This is a general description of the work that indicates the major system and material choices for the project and provides the information necessary to communicate the appearance and function of the building.

Preliminary estimate of construction cost. The schematic design estimate usually includes a preliminary area analysis and a preliminary construction cost estimate. The level of detail is necessarily limited; the estimate may be broken down by major trades or by systems (e.g., foundations, structure, exterior closure, interior partitions and finishes, plumbing, mechanical, electrical, site work, and equipment). This may also include a preliminary analysis of the owner's budget, with recommendations for changes based on site, marketplace, or other unusual conditions encountered in schematic design. It is common for preliminary cost estimates made at this stage to include contingencies for further design development, market contingencies, and changes during construction.

AIA Document B101–2007 calls for a preliminary estimate of construction cost based on current area, volume, or other unit costs.

Additional services. As part of schematic design, the architect may agree to provide services such as lifecycle cost analyses, energy studies, tenant-related design studies, economic feasibility studies, special renderings, models, brochures, or promotional materials for the owner. These are included as "additional services" in the AIA B201 form of owner-architect agreement (Standard Form of Architect's Services).

Approvals. The final step in schematic design (and, for that matter, in each design phase) is to obtain formal client approval—in writing, if at all possible. If approval is given verbally, it is a good idea to send the client a letter confirming the architect's understanding of the approval. (You may ask the client to initial the letter and return a copy.) The importance of this step cannot be emphasized enough. The schematic design presentation has to be clear enough to gain both the understanding and the approval of the client.

Design Development

Design development is the period in which the approved schematic design receives the refinement and coordination necessary for a really polished work of architecture. The decisions made in schematic design are worked out at a scale that minimizes the possibility of major modifications during the construction documentation phase. Working

TABLE 7.1 Design Documentation by Phase

	Schematic Design	Design Development
Purpose	Drawings and other documents to indicate the scale and relationship of project components.	Drawings, specifications, and other documents fix and describe the project's size and character as to architectural, structural, and M/E/P systems and materials and other elements as appropriate. DD documents can be used to prepare preliminary construction cost estimates.
Drawings		
Title and project data sheet	Not generally required. If provided on larger projects, the project name, owner and team names, location map, possible rendering or other graphic may be included. Rarely includes sheet index, code, standards, etc.	Project name, owner and team names, possible location map, rendering or other graphic. Sheet index all disciplines. Occasionally includes code, standards, etc.
Site plan	Conceptual site plan showing land use, general building location, general parking arrangement, major site features.	Scaled site plan with building locations tied down dimensionally. Street lines, property lines, setbacks and easements shown (survey required). Preliminary grades reviewed with civil engineer. Parking lots with overall dimensions.
Floor plans	Conceptual building plans. Major plan components or departments defined. Departmental blocking and stacking indicated. General structural grid and major M/E/P components indicated. Rarely includes detailed dimensions.	Scaled building plans with building perimeter, structural grid and selected critical areas or elements dimensionally fixed. Major M/E/P systems determined (rooms, shafts, etc.) and indicated. Interior partitions shown at approximate scale. Doors and window systems indicated. Rooms or doors rarely numbered.
Enlarged floor plans	Generally not required except for highly detailed special areas.	Provided only for major typical elements if required (e.g., healthcare patient room, hotel room, correctional jail cell).
Reflected ceiling plans	Generally not required except for highly detailed special areas.	Occasionally included for major critical elements if required to define major design elements (e.g., healthcare patient room, major public lobby space). Otherwise, ceiling features indicated by vignette on floor plan.
Exterior elevations	For each major building facade, generally indicating fenestration, entrances, and design vocabulary.	For each major building facade, indicating material, fenestration, entrances, special features, floor levels, and vertical dimensions.
Enlarged elevations	Generally not required except for highly detailed special areas.	Generally not required. Include if needed to define for major critical elements.
Building sections	Conceptual building section to illustrate building shape or spatial features.	Occasionally provided where required to illustrate building shape or spatial features.
Wall sections @ 1/8″ or 1/4″	Not applicable.	Not applicable.
Wall sections @ 3/8″	Not applicable.	Full-height sections conveying basic building configuration provided for predominant or typical locations. Indicate materials, structure, foundations, flashings, etc.
Enlarged details @ 1 1/2″	Generally not required.	Generally not required.
Door schedules, door types, frame types	Generally not required.	Not generally required. Specific door types may be shown for some facility types (e.g., correctional facilities, hospitals, etc.). May be generally defined by generic door schedule using matrix or covered by outline spec.
Common door details	Generally not required.	Generally not required.
Room finish schedules	Generally not required. If necessary, generally defined in outline specifications.	Not included as a room-by-room schedule. May be generally defined by generic room type using matrix or covered by outline spec.
Partition types	Generally not required.	Generally not required although some types may be indicated for some facility types. May include standard guide sheet to establish quality, but not referenced on plans.

(continued)

TABLE 7.1 *(continued)*

	Schematic Design	Design Development
Elevator sections and details	Generally not required.	Generally not required.
Stair sections and details	Sections generally not required except for highly detailed decorative stairs. Details generally not required.	Not required for exit stairs. Occasionally may be needed to define ceremonial or monumental public area stair.
Interior elevations	Rarely included except as a background for other documents (e.g., background in atrium section).	Provided in presentation format for major public spaces. Occasionally provided in sketch format, possibly freehand, for casework, millwork, toilets, elevators, etc.
Interior details	Generally not required. When needed, provide conceptual sketches.	Generally not required. When needed, provide conceptual profile sketches.
Specifications	General outline, or bullet point list, briefly describing each primary building system.	Short-form specification briefly describing primary materials and building systems. Abbreviated, does not include execution sections.
Optional Documentation		
Renderings and presentation models	Requirements determined by design team. Generally reimbursable.	Requirements determined by design team. Generally reimbursable.

Adapted from a chart created by Grant A. Simpson, FAIA, copyright © HKS, Inc.

drawings and specifications are complex and intricately interrelated; changes in those documents are costly and likely to lead to coordination problems during construction. Thus, the primary purpose of design development is to further define and describe all important aspects of the project so that what remains is the final step of creating construction documents.

During design development, the design team works out a clear, coordinated description of all aspects of the design. This typically includes fully developed floor plans, sections, exterior elevations, and, for important areas or aspects of the building, interior elevations, reflected ceiling plans, wall sections, and key details. Often these become the basis for the construction documents. The basic mechanical, electrical, plumbing, and fire protection systems are accurately defined if not fully drawn. No major issues that could cause significant restudy during the construction documentation phase should be left unresolved.

The deliverables of the design development phase are similar to those of schematic design: drawings and specifications that fix and describe the size and character of the project, as well as any recommended adjustments to the preliminary estimate of construction cost. The design development phase usually ends with a formal presentation to, and approval by, the owner.

Design development may be a substantial undertaking, or it may be a much briefer transition from schematic design to construction documentation. Some owners require extensive schematic design services, with much of the project "developed" by the time this phase ends. For some straightforward or repetitive projects, the schematic design may be sufficiently clear for both owner and architect to proceed directly to construction documents with confidence. In these instances, design development may be brief (or in the most extreme cases, nonexistent).

In some project delivery approaches, the owner may wish to secure construction cost commitments before the design is fully developed—thus reducing or even eliminating the design development phase. This reduces one uncertainty but introduces another, for there is likely to be debate about what was included and not included in a cost estimate made on the basis of preliminary, partial, or "scope" documents.

While most design issues should be resolved by the end of design development, some will continue to be refined, resolved, or modified during the construction documentation, bidding and negotiation, and construction phases of the project.

During construction documentation, additional design issues may emerge as the design team works out the final material and system selections, details, and dimensions. Examples of such issues may clarify this point:

- The final detailing and specification of an exterior wall, including the selection of specific products and manufacturers, inevitably leads to modification of the dimensions, color, transparency, and other aspects of the wall.
- The detailing and specification of interior partitions, openings, and finishes involve a large number of minute design decisions, from the location of joints to the selection of the final materials or acceptable alternates.

Once a contractor or construction manager is selected, the need to make design decisions continues. The bidding and negotiation process inevitably leads to proposed substitutions or modifications in details to achieve cost savings or to simplify the construction process. Usually some of these are accepted and must be successfully integrated with the remainder of the design.

Design continues even through the construction phase. The construction documents require interpretation and elaboration. Field conditions and other problems may force design changes. Confronted with the reality of the project, the owner may request changes—reinforcing the elemental idea that design "never really stops" but continues through construction and everyday use of buildings and facilities.

Design is a continuous process, often broken into phases to gain commitment to more general decisions before they are developed in detail. Here is one view of the level of decision making regarding each of a building's functional subsystems as the project moves through design.

TABLE 7.2 Design Decisions

Predesign	Early Schematics	Later Schematics or Early Design Development	Design Development or Early Construction Documents
General			
Project objectives	Program interpretation	Design concept elaboration	Floor plans
Project scope	Basic design concepts	Schematic floor plan	Sections
Program codes and regulations	Siting	Schematic sections	Typical details
Project budget	Building massing		
Project schedule	Blocking and stacking		
Delivery approach	Access and circulation		
	Design vocabulary		
	Style issues and constraints		
	Sustainability		
Site			
Site selection	Siting concepts	Design concept elaboration	Site plan
Site development criteria	Site forms and massing	Initial site plan	Planting plan
Requirements for access, circulation, parking, utilities, landscaping, lighting	Access and circulation	Schematic grading, planting, paving plans	Typical site sections
	Views to/from buildings		Typical site details
	Concepts for grading, planting, paving, etc.		Outline specifications
	Acoustics and other site issues		
Foundation and Substructure			
Performance requirements for foundations, excavations, etc.	Subsurface conditions and requirements	Schematic basement plan	Foundation plan
	Exploration of special problems	Refinement of special foundation requirements	Basement floor plan
	Impacts of program, energy on underground building	Selection of foundation system	Sizing of key foundation elements
			Outline specifications

(continued)

TABLE 7.2 *(continued)*

Predesign	Early Schematics	Later Schematics or Early Design Development	Design Development or Early Construction Documents
Superstructure			
Performance requirements for floor, roof, stair, other structural elements	Relation of structure to spatial organization, elevations, etc. Selection of use modules Basic structural module Initial system selection	Structural system selection Outline framing plan Sizes of key elements	Floor framing plans Roof framing plan Sizing of elements Important details Outline specifications
Exterior Closure			
Restrictions on exterior design materials, etc. Performance requirements for walls, doors, windows, etc.	Approach to elevations, fenestration Views to/from building Initial envelope elements sizing and selection	Design concept elaboration Selection of wall systems, materials Schematic elevations fenestration	Elevations Key exterior details Outline specifications
Roofing			
Performance requirements for roofing elements	Roof type and pitch Initial system selection	Selection of roof system, materials	Outline specifications
Interior Construction			
Performance requirements for partitions, finishes, specialties Flexibility requirements	Approach to partitioning built-in furnishings Interior design vocabulary Layout of key spaces	Room designs Layout of key areas Selection of partition systems, finishes Important fixtures or theme elements	Input to plans and elevations Key interior elevations Initial finish schedules Outline specifications
Vertical Circulation and Conveying Systems			
Performance requirements for conveying systems	Basic organization and circulation scheme Need for and types of vertical circulation Need for special conveying systems	Input to plans, sections and elevations Sizing of exits, other circulation areas Basic elevator and escalator concepts Other conveying systems concepts	Input to floor plans, framing plans, sections, elevations Outline specifications Detailed systems selection
Mechanical Systems			
Performance requirements for conveying systems Performance requirements for plumbing, HVAC, fire protection Need for special mechanical systems	Impact of mechanical concepts on building planning Initial systems selection Initial distribution ideas Space allocation for mechanical areas	Mechanical systems selection Refinement of service, distribution concepts Input to plans, sections, and elevations	Initial system drawings and key details Distribution and riser diagrams Input to floor plans, framing plans, sections, elevations Outline specifications Initial equipment list
Electrical and Lighting Systems			
Performance requirements for lighting systems Performance requirements for electrical systems Need for special systems	Approaches to natural, artificial lighting Lighting quality and character Impact of site design on electrical systems Space allocation for electrical systems	Window, skylight, and glazing design Selection of lighting, electrical systems Service, power, and distribution concepts Input to plans, sections, and elevations	Detailed systems selection Distribution diagrams Key room lighting layouts, ceiling plans Input to plans, sections, and elevations Outline specifications
Equipment			
Delineation of equipment needs and performance	Impact of key equipment items on siting and design	Impact of key items on room design, framing plans, etc.	Input to plans, sections, and elevations Outline specifications Initial equipment list

David Haviland, Hon. AIA (adapted from *The Architect's Handbook of Professional Practice,* 12th edition)

For More Information

The AIA Design Knowledge Community maintains a Web page on the AIA website at www.aia.org. The site contains information about the mission, policies, initiatives, and special reports of the Committee on Design.

Numerous books and other resources on the general subject of design, designers, design theory, history, and criticism are available. The following sources include a few selected publications that address the design process, including several about presentation techniques.

In *How Designers Think: The Design Process Demystified*, 4th edition (Architectural Press, 2005), architect and psychologist Bryan Lawson delivers a readable discourse on what design thinking entails and how to understand and apply it. Many architectural examples are used. As noted by the publisher, this book is intended not as an authoritative description of how designers should think but to provide helpful advice on how to develop an understanding of design.

Architect Kenneth Allison meshes design and project management subjects into a single discussion in *Getting There by Design: An Architect's Guide to Design and Project Management* (Architectural Press, 1997). Allison addresses fundamental principles for these dimensions of practice in four major parts: project context, decisions and techniques, managing costs and fees, and cultures as action systems.

C. Thomas Mitchell's *Redefining Designing: From Form to Experience* (Wiley, 1993) contains a provocative discussion about why architects and designers need to elevate the importance of client and user needs in building design. In his *New Thinking in Design* (Wiley, 1996), Mitchell presents a series of interviews with 13 leading international designers committed to client- and user-centered design approaches.

James Marston Fitch's classic *American Building: The Environmental Forces That Shape It* (originally published in 1947 and updated and expanded in 1999) examines how buildings respond to and control environmental forces through building and system design. Stewart Brand's *How Buildings Learn: What Happens After They're Built* (Penguin, 1995) calls for rethinking the way buildings are designed so they may be more readily adapted to ever-changing user needs. Brand's theses are that buildings adapt best when their occupants constantly refine and reshape them and that architects can mature from being artists of space to becoming artists of time.

Christopher Alexander's two classic titles, *The Timeless Way of Building* (Oxford University Press, 1979) and *A Pattern Language* (Oxford University Press, 1977), deal with design approaches intended to let users participate in the design process. In each of 253 patterns, Alexander explicitly links what takes place in various kinds of spaces to the physical layout of the spaces themselves. Collectively, these patterns represent a "pattern language" that allows designers and nondesigners to communicate with each other.

Design Drawing (Wiley, 1997) by Frank Ching and colleagues describes delineation from several perspectives: drawing from observation, drawing systems, and drawing from imagination. A supplemental CD-ROM contains information and instruction elucidating a broad range of drawing concepts through animation, video, and three-dimensional models. Paul Laseau's *Architectural Representation Handbook: Traditional and Digital Techniques for Graphic Communication* (McGraw-Hill, 2000) provides a guide to traditional, new, hybrid, and emerging representational techniques, along with discussion of the roles of each in the design process. The illustrations are organized in relation to an architectural drawing "vocabulary" that includes the design activities of seeing, thinking, and communicating.

Color Drawing: Design Drawing Skills and Techniques for Architects, Landscape Architects, and Interior Designers, 3rd edition (Wiley, 2006), by Michael E. Doyle, covers drawing techniques, color theory, and presentation drawings and includes step-by-step instructions and in-depth guidance. Discussed are innovative ways to create design drawings with color copiers and the latest computer techniques.

7.2 Construction Documentation

Kristine K. Fallon, FAIA, and Kenneth C. Crocco, FAIA

Construction documents describe what is to be built, how contractors are to be selected, and how the contracts for construction will be written and administered. The process of producing construction documentation strives for efficiency, comprehensiveness, and quality.

One of the nobler professional goals of every architect should be that every project is completed, closed-out, and delivered with the same verve, intensity, anticipation, interest, effort, attention to detail, dedication, enthusiasm, skill, poise, and concern for the project, as were present and employed when the project first came into the office, all to the client's complete satisfaction and pleasure.

—Ralph W. Liebing, *Architectural Working Drawings* (1999)

Once a design has been developed and approved, the architect prepares the drawings and specifications that set forth the requirements for construction. The development of the construction documentation is an extension of the design process. Decisions on details, materials, products, and finishes all serve to reinforce the design concept—and begin the process of translating the concept into reality. Of all project phases, the preparation of the construction documentation typically takes the most time and resources.

ORGANIZATION AND CONTENT

Construction documentation serves multiple purposes that include the following:

- Communicating to the owner, in detail, what a project involves
- Establishing the contractual obligations the owner and contractor owe each other during a project
- Laying out the responsibilities of the architect or any other party administering or managing construction contracts for the owner
- Communicating to the contractor the quantities, qualities, and configuration of the elements to construct a project

In turn, the contractor uses the documentation to solicit bids or quotations from subcontractors and suppliers, and the construction documents provide the basis for obtaining regulatory and financial approvals needed to proceed with construction.

The project documents typically consist of the project manual and the project drawings. The drawings include architectural, structural, mechanical, electrical, civil, landscape, interior design, and other specialty drawings. The project manual typically includes the following:

- Bidding requirements (advertisement and invitations, instructions, available project information) and procurement forms
- Contract forms and supplements (the form of agreement to be used between owner and contractor, project forms, and certifications)
- Contract conditions (the general conditions of the contract for construction, which outline the rights, responsibilities, and duties of owner and contractor as well as others involved in the construction process, including the architect; supplementary conditions particular to the project)

Kristine K. Fallon, FAIA, is a Chicago-based consultant for computer applications in the design and construction industry. Kenneth C. Crocco, FAIA, was vice president of Chicago-based ArchiTech Consulting, Inc., a firm specializing in building specifications and information management.

- Specifications (general requirements, facility construction and facility service specifications, and site work specifications), which describe the level of quality and the standards to be met in the construction of the project

The bidding documents include the project manual and drawings, as well as revisions, clarifications, and modifications to them, including addenda (additions to any of these documents issued by the architect during the bidding or negotiation process).

"Bidding or Negotiation Phase" reviews bidding requirements and addenda.

The contract documents include all of the documents just listed except the bidding requirements. In addition, any contract modifications (orders for minor changes in the work, construction change directives, and change orders) become part of the contract documents.

The construction documents are not intended to be a complete set of instructions on how to construct a building. Construction means, methods, techniques, sequences, procedures, and site safety precautions are customarily assigned as responsibilities of the contractor to give the contractor latitude in preparing bids and carrying out the construction phase. The contractor determines the assignment of work to specific trades and subcontractors. The contractor also manages logistical matters such as the sequence of operations, scheduling, design of temporary supports and facilities, selection of appropriate equipment, and project safety.

Construction documentation contains legal and contractual information, procedural and administrative information (referred to as Division 01 General Requirements of the Project specifications and further expanded in Part 1 of each specification section), architectural and construction information (found in Divisions 02 through 48 of the specifications and in the drawings), and site and infrastructure information, such as topographical surveys and geotechnical investigation data.

PROJECT DOCUMENTS

A variety of document types must be produced to accomplish building design and construction.

The *project manual* includes the bidding requirements, contract forms and conditions, and specifications.

Bidding documents are the documents required to bid or negotiate the construction contract.

Construction documents are the drawings and the specifications the architect prepares to set forth the requirements for construction of the project.

Contract documents form the legal agreement between the owner and contractor.

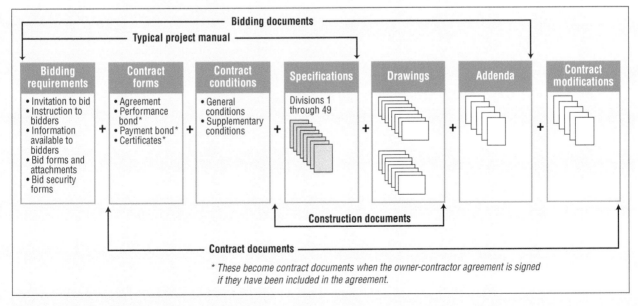

FIGURE 7.1 **Project Documents**

PART 3: THE PROJECT

"Construction Contracts" discusses contract forms and conditions.

Legal and Contractual Information

The contract forms and conditions establish the legal framework of a project by setting forth the rights, duties, and responsibilities of the owner and contractor.

On larger projects, it has been customary to physically separate the contract form from the contract conditions. The *form* is the agreement between owner and contractor enumerating the contract documents, specifying the time of performance, and stating the contractor's compensation. The *conditions* set forth the rights, duties, and responsibilities of owner and contractor and other parties to the construction process (the architect, subcontractors, and possibly the construction manager, the owner's project representative, etc.). Separating the form from the conditions allows the contractor to disclose the contract conditions to subcontractors and suppliers without revealing the contract sum or other items in the agreement that may be privately held between the owner, architect, and contractor.

The architect's responsibility. Several of the AIA owner-architect agreements require the architect to "assist the Owner in the development and preparation of (1) bidding and procurement information that describes the time, place, and conditions of bidding, including bidding or proposal forms; (2) the form of agreement between the Owner and the Contractor; and (3) the Conditions of the Contract for Construction (General, Supplementary, and other Conditions)." The architect is not required to prepare legal and contractual information but only to assist in its preparation. The architect is not in the practice of law and is not professionally qualified to give the owner legal or insurance counsel. It is common, however, for architects to assemble the bidding and contractual documents, providing them for review and approval by the owner.

The owner's responsibility. The owner is responsible for furnishing the necessary legal, accounting, and insurance services to accomplish a project. Therefore, the owner, with the advice of the owner's legal counsel, approves the bidding requirements, contract forms, and conditions.

If the owner has little experience with construction projects and contracts, it may help to provide the owner with the following information:

- AIA Document G612–2001, Owner's Instructions to the Architect Regarding the Construction Contract, Insurance and Bonds, and Bidding Procedures
- "You and Your Architect." This brochure, available from the AIA website, offers advice to clients on how the owner and architect can work together to keep a project on track throughout the design and construction process.

If used, these documents should be submitted to the owner at or prior to the beginning of construction document development because basic decisions about the handling of the construction contract affect all aspects of the project.

Some owners propose or mandate their own bidding requirements, contract forms, and conditions. Since the contractual agreements for construction are so closely related to the owner-architect contract (and any other contracts the owner may have written with a construction manager or other consultants), and since these agreements are usually already in place, it is essential that all of these agreements be carefully coordinated. It is often worthwhile for the architect's legal counsel to review owner-prepared documents with specific regard to the architect's rights, duties, and responsibilities, as well as to review clauses covering indemnification of the architect, role of the architect during construction, ownership of documents, dispute resolution, and similar provisions.

Procedural and Administrative Information

This information is typically found in three places in the construction documentation: in the conditions of the contract, in Division 01 of the specifications, and in the opening articles (Part 1) of the specifications in Divisions 02 through 48.

The general conditions of the contract for construction contain provisions common to most projects. In addition to legal and contractual information, the general conditions include requirements for a variety of contract administration activities, such as reviewing shop drawings and samples, reviewing contractor's payment requests, approving minor changes in the work, monitoring the progress of the work, issuing site observation reports, and reviewing closeout documents. AIA Document A201, General Conditions of the Contract for Construction, is widely recognized for establishing common general conditions practices.

Division 01 of the specifications expands on information in the general conditions and often includes the following:

- Standard office procedures, such as required format for shop drawing submittals, numbers of sets of submittals required, and procedures for certification of substantial completion
- Procedures required by owners, such as forms for payment requests and waivers of lien
- Procedures that govern the specific project, such as applicable codes, requirements for record documents, temporary facilities, and testing laboratory methods

Division 01 section titles include the following:

011000 Summary

011200 Multiple Contract Summary

012100 Allowances

012200 Unit Prices

012300 Alternates

012600 Contract Modification Procedures

012900 Payment Procedures

013100 Project Management and Coordination

013200 Construction Progress Documentation

013233 Photographic Documentation

013300 Submittal Procedures

013513.16 Special Project Procedures for Detention Facilities

013591 Historic Treatment Procedures

014000 Quality Requirements

014200 References

015000 Temporary Facilities and Controls

015639 Temporary Tree and Plant Protection

016000 Product Requirements

017300 Execution

017329 Cutting and Patching

017419 Construction Waste Management and Disposal

017700 Closeout Procedures

017823 Operation and Maintenance Data

017839 Project Record Documents

017900 Demonstration and Training

018113 Sustainable Design Requirements

019113 General Commissioning Requirements

Part 1 of each of the sections in Divisions 02 through 48 presents administrative and procedural information relating to the elements covered in that section including, for example:

- Definitions
- Delivery, storage, and handling requirements
- Allowance and unit price items
- Alternates
- Site condition requirements
- Submittal requirements
- Warranty requirements
- Quality assurance requirements
- Maintenance requirements

It is worthwhile to develop a consistent approach to placement of procedural and administrative requirements in the documents.

Architectural and Construction Information

Architectural and construction information encompasses the quantities, qualities, and configuration of the elements required for the project. Quantities and relationships are usually best indicated on the drawings; qualities and standards of workmanship are best placed in the specifications. The level of detail provided in the drawings and specifications responds to the needs of the project and of those who will own, regulate, and—most important—build it.

There are a steadily growing number of new software products, including those for building information modeling developed to assist construction documentation. The use of BIM software does not preclude the delivery of traditional documentation but does make other methods of communication possible. If there is no specific contractual requirement for the use of BIM software, it is prudent to verify with the contractor in advance the acceptability of using BIM technology to transmit architectural and construction information.

THE POWER OF INFORMATION MODELS

According to the National Institute of Building Sciences, a building information model is a "digital representation of the physical and functional characteristics of a facility." As such, it serves as "a shared knowledge resource for information about a facility, forming a reliable basis for decisions during its life-cycle, from inception onward." For purposes of discussion, building information modeling is a tool that enables the process of virtual design and construction.

BIM technology is different from first-generation 3D computer modeling used for animation and rendering. In the project depictions created with the first-generation software, data are stored as lines, planes, and surfaces with no other information about the objects represented. Going beyond this basic 3D geometry, a model created using BIM software includes information about material designations, product and equipment specifications, and even performance data. Another important BIM characteristic is that representations are not redundant; in

other words, information recorded once then appears in multiple views, ensuring that measurements or properties found in one view are the same in other views of the same design. This is a great improvement over the errors that can be introduced when data must be copied from one drawing to another.

A building information model can be used to check interferences and to extract bills of materials for estimating or procurement purposes. Pioneering project teams have already demonstrated that construction drawings can be bypassed altogether and a building can be constructed directly from a BIM, with any required 2D drawings—plans, sections, elevations, details—extracted from the model as needed. If as-built conditions are documented in the model, the model can then be used for operations and maintenance activities as well.

BIM technology has broad implications for work processes and sequencing, team composition, contractual relationships, and professional liability. It is unlikely the building design and construction industry will transition completely to this way of working in the near term. Nevertheless, the technological tools now exist to reorder the entire building design and delivery process. BIM tools from multiple vendors have delivered benefits to projects of all types and scales, from K–12 schools to the Beijing National Swimming Center for the 2008 Olympics.

Using an information model as the central design tool, rather than creating and coordinating information in multiple drawings, yields significant production efficiencies, including enhanced productivity, reduced design cycle time, and a better-coordinated work product. The benefit is not that architects draw faster using building information modeling, but that less drawing is required. The traditional documentation approach requires the inclusion of redundant information on multiple drawings, while the building information model is the single authoritative source for building information, and most drawings are extracted directly from it. Changes made to the model can be automatically propagated to all extracted drawings. This has the additional advantage of improving coordination among the drawings, as well as reducing time spent in coordination activities.

Using a BIM approach requires comprehensive rethinking of production techniques, including:

- *Who does what.* Development of a building information model requires more knowledge of architectural technology than production of 2D drawings.
- *CAD and data organization standards.* If a firm wants drawings produced with BIM software to conform to office graphic standards, setup and customization efforts will be required. The firm will also need to rethink how project data is organized and named (i.e., file naming and folder structure).

- *Standard CAD libraries and details.* A firm must determine how much of this information will be needed in the BIM environment and how to get it there.
- *Type and sequence of design activities.* For example, many firms find they need to model the individual components to be used in the building before they develop the building model itself.
- *Effort required in each design phase.* With a building information model, more design decisions must be made early in the design process, while time savings of 50 percent have been reported in construction drawings.
- *Value earned in each project phase.* Design firms should seek a payment schedule that parallels the new level of effort expended and value produced in each design phase.
- *Coordination procedures.* Project coordinators must understand where coordination is automated and where it is not.
- *Checking and other quality assurance procedures.* Because building components are reusable within the same project or across projects, care must be taken to ensure the accuracy and appropriateness of nongraphic attributes that may be used in downstream functions, such as schedules and bills of material.
- *How information is communicated and shared.* A major question is whether to share a particular model with outside team members or simply to provide 2D CAD files. This decision, which depends on the capabilities of the other team members, can raise serious business issues. Although BIM tools inherently produce 2D drawings, many project teams have found that a requirement to produce updated drawing sets on a regular basis becomes a bottleneck. Finally, sharing a building information model requires careful data management techniques.

DRAWINGS

The construction drawings show, in graphic and quantitative form, the extent, configuration, location, relationships, and dimensions of the work to be done. They generally contain site and building plans, elevations, sections, details, diagrams, and schedules. In addition to drawn information, they may include photographs, other imported graphics, and printed schedules.

The U.S. National CAD Standard (NCS) provides comprehensive guidance to users of two-dimensional computer-aided design (CAD) systems on the format, sequencing, and internal organization of CAD drawings. The NCS incorporates the Construction Specifications Institute (CSI) Uniform Drawing System (UDS) and the AIA CAD Layer Guidelines. It covers layer names, plotting guidelines, drawing set organization, drawing sheet layout and organization, schedule formats, drafting conventions, terms and abbreviations, symbols, notations, and code conventions.

NCS is not entirely prescriptive. Firms will find that they need to customize this standard to meet their needs, but NCS does provide guidelines for doing this. It is an excellent starting point for any firm's CAD standard. NCS can be purchased from the National Institute of Building Sciences. An order form is available at www.nibs.org.

Sequence and Sheet Formats

A set of drawings is an organized presentation of the project. To the extent possible, the drawings are organized in the sequence of construction.

Most firms develop office standards for sheet size, layout, and title blocks. Some clients, however, might dictate their own format requirements. In addition to the name, address, and phone number of the architecture firm, the title block may include the following:

- Project title and address, frequently including owner's name and address
- Drawing title and sheet number
- Names and addresses of consultants
- Notation of who worked on the drawing, including checking
- Dates drawings were issued (such as for bid, permit, and construction)
- Dates of revisions
- Architect's seal and, if required, signature
- Engineer's seal and, if required, signature
- Copyright information

The CSI Uniform Drawing System organizes this information according to the following categories:

- Designer identification block
- Project identification block
- Issue block
- Management block
- Sheet title block
- Sheet identification block

Each drawing should include the basic information required to orient the user, such as key plans showing location of partial plans, north arrows, and scales for drawings. Graphic scales are included in the event drawings are reduced. Most firms lay out the drawings early in the project. A cartooning or storyboard process may be used to determine how many and what kinds of plans, sections, elevations, details, schedules, and other graphic elements will be prepared; their scale (and thus size on the sheets); their sequence; and any interrelationships. This helps the architect conceptualize the project and understand what will be involved in developing and communicating it to the owner, regulators, and contractors.

Many architects will have "cartooned" the drawings as part of the project pricing and proposal process.

Drawing Scale, Dimensions, and Targets

Appropriate scale, dimensions, and targets (or "keys") are essential communication elements of the drawings. It is common for a firm to establish standard procedures and symbols for dimensions and targets, as well as for lettering size and style. The project manager usually determines the drawing scales to be used, as well as any variations from office standards.

Scale. The smallest scale that clearly presents the required information is chosen for a drawing. The selection of scales and lettering sizes must also take into account whether the drawings will be reduced for distribution.

Dimensions. Necessary dimensions should be numerically indicated on the drawings. Because the contractor is not permitted to scale the drawings for dimensions, drawings should contain sufficient numerical dimensions to construct the building elements shown. The system of dimensioning used in the drawings relates to horizontal and vertical reference planes (such as the structural grid) that, in turn, can be tied to one or more benchmarks established as permanent data points for the project. It is logical to establish a hierarchy of dimensions in the order of construction, using building elements that will be constructed early as dimensional benchmarks for elements constructed later. For example, it is common to first denote the dimensions of structural elements such as a column grid and then measure distances from the columns to nonstructural elements, such as interior partitions.

Dimensions are laid out in lines called *strings*. It is necessary to develop several strings to properly locate a sequence of related building elements. These sets of strings are drawn in a hierarchy of detail, with overall dimensions shown in the outermost string and detailed dimensions shown in the innermost string. To ensure that numbers indicated on the dimension strings correspond to the intended built reality, contractors and others using the drawings will add up strings of dimensions and cross-check them against one another. In some cases, the level of detail of the drawing or the construction method employed makes comprehensive strings, in which every dimension is determined, undesirable. In such cases, the critical dimensions are noted and a non-critical dimension is noted with a plus-or-minus value. This gives the contractor an idea of the desired dimension and further indicates that discrepancies during construction are to be resolved by adjusting this dimension.

Automatic dimensioning in CAD systems produces accurate dimension annotation. This reduces the need for manual cross-checking of dimensions and has the added benefit of highlighting dimensional discrepancies as the drawings are being completed. When establishing CAD standards and procedures for dimensioning, it is important for firms to thoughtfully select the display precision for their dimensioning—1/32″, 1/16″, or 1/8″—and to include that parameter in their CAD template or seed file. In the interest of accuracy and coordination, CAD users should not manually override automatically generated dimensions even though CAD systems do permit it.

The drawings should call attention to critical areas where standard construction tolerances are not sufficient or dimensions are tied to specific dimensions of manufactured assemblies. At the same time, the experienced architect recognizes that materials and construction tolerances in the field rarely approach those that can be achieved in manufacturing. For example, some architects regard field-created tolerances of less than 1/8″ (1:100 in SI units) or even 1/4″ (1:50) as unrealistic.

Targets. Sometimes referred to as "keys," targets are one of the primary methods of establishing the relationships among the drawings. Floor plans use standard symbols to locate (or target) building sections, column grids, door designations, wall types and sections, details, interior elevations, enlarged plans, and similar information. Elevations target building sections, windows, and details. It is also helpful to target details on wall sections and building sections.

Other Drawing Elements

The drawings often include the following:

- *Symbols and abbreviations.* The need to communicate a large amount of information in a limited space commonly dictates the use of symbols and abbreviations. Good practice suggests that these be defined early and used consistently.
- *Drawing/specification coordination.* Designations on the drawings should be coordinated with those used in the specifications. If, for example, only one type of elastomeric sealant is used in the project, the term "elastomeric sealant" is sufficient on the drawings. If more than one sealant type is involved, however, it is necessary to develop and use terminology that clearly differentiates among the various sealants.
- *Notes.* When drawings and specifications are separate, statements on quality and workmanship are made in the specifications. Notes on the drawings should be limited to the minimum needed to convey design intent clearly.
- *Schedules.* Information best presented in tabular form is most commonly shown in a schedule. There may be schedules for doors, windows, hardware, room finishes, paint selections, fixtures and equipment, repetitive structural elements (such as

columns, footings, or lintels), and similar items. Schedule formats vary according to office or project requirements. Many schedules can be developed and revised using spreadsheet or word-processing software programs. The Uniform Drawing System (UDS) and the U.S. National CAD Standard include a module on schedules. UDS establishes guidelines for creating schedules and complete illustrations of commonly used schedules. The UDS companion CD-ROM includes these schedules in a word-processing format.

Architectural Graphic Standards presents conventions for symbols and abbreviations.

Drawing Production Methods

For hundreds of years architectural drawings were produced manually, making their production one of the most labor-intensive and time-consuming phases of professional service. Technological advances—especially in CAD—have improved productivity in drawing production. This change has also blurred the distinction between design development and construction documentation.

Manual drafting. Some firms continue with manual drafting as the production method of choice. A number of approaches and specific techniques can be used to reduce time and increase the accuracy and utility of manual drafting:

- Standard items such as sheet borders, title blocks, symbols, and common details may be produced ahead of time and incorporated into the drawings as needed. Some firms bind reference information and standard details into the project manual.
- Schedules and other highly organized data sets may be produced using computers and spreadsheet or database programs and incorporated into the drawings or bound into the project manual.
- Photographs of existing conditions may be reproduced directly onto drawing media. Planned renovations can then be drawn directly onto the photographs.
- Individual drawing sheets may be overlays or photographic composites of individual drawings, details, schedules, and notes, allowing flexibility in formatting.

Computer-aided drafting. CAD systems offer the advantages of clarity, easy representation of elements (especially repetitive elements), fast changes, accurate dimensioning, and improved coordination among drawings as well as between drawings and specifications. Computer-produced drawings can be easy to read, with lettering and dimensioning consistent throughout. CAD software packages increasingly incorporate useful ancillary functions such as automatic area and material quantity takeoffs and concurrent development of door, window, and other schedules.

Managing drawing revisions is entirely different in the CAD environment. Telltale erasures, changes in lettering, and other marks that signal changes and revisions to manually drafted drawings are absent. The exchange of computer data files among collaborating design professionals via the Internet has underscored the need for controlling and verifying the integrity of electronically transmitted drawings. Electronic data management (EDM) systems prevent multiple persons from accessing the same drawing simultaneously, track drawing modifications, ensure that changes are not incorporated into the record copy of the drawing until properly approved, and automatically route the pending changes to the party responsible for approvals. However, EDM technology can be too costly and time-consuming to implement in multi-firm environments except on large, long-duration projects.

Another CAD approach is for each firm on the project team to manage its own drawing controls internally and post new and revised documents on secure computer bulletin boards or project websites called "project extranets."

Drawing Standards

There are different approaches to establishing standards or conventions for the uniform production of construction documents. Because the industry lacks comprehensive drawing standards, nearly all firms have developed their own standards as a way of ensuring quality, consistency, and thoroughness in this critical phase of service.

The advent of CAD technology introduces a new level of complexity for construction drawing standards. The manner in which data are created and stored is not readily apparent to the viewer without a detailed examination of the data file. The laborious task of deciphering the organizational system of another person can easily negate any gain in productivity achieved by the use of CAD technology. This underscores the necessity for establishing and adhering to CAD standards, and NCS, discussed above, is a good starting point. It also establishes a common point of reference when exchanging CAD data with consultants or the owner.

The ability to reuse design elements from previous projects is one of the principal benefits of CAD. However, if projects are developed with different layer names, line weights and colors, text fonts, and dimension styles, the reuse of design elements may require extensive editing. This prevents reaping the anticipated productivity benefits of CAD. In a CAD environment, graphic standards for drawing organization must be supplemented by CAD standards for data organization. At a minimum, these standards should address the following subjects:

- Drawing sheet sizes, layout, scales, sequence, and numbering
- Targeting and other references within the documents
- Notes, abbreviations, and graphic conventions
- Dimensioning
- Internal organization of CAD files and the relationships with reference files and drawing sheet layouts
- Where project CAD files and any reusable components should be stored on the firm's file server and how they should be named and organized (i.e., folder structure)
- Procedures for versioning, archiving, and exchanging CAD data with outside organizations

CHRONOLOGY OF STANDARDS DEVELOPMENT FOR CONSTRUCTION DRAWINGS

The development of office standards is a time-consuming overhead task, and the quality of office drawing standards varies greatly from one firm to another. Consequently, even the best of efforts can prove futile if clients and consultants do not share and use the same standards. This situation has prompted a number of independent efforts aimed at bringing industry-wide order to the production of construction documents. The following profiles present several of these efforts.

CONDOC DRAWING SYSTEM

ConDoc, developed by Onkal "Duke" Guzey, AIA, and James Freehof, AIA, in the late 1980s, was the first system for organizing construction documents. Based on a simple, uniform arrangement of drawings, a standard sheet format, a sheet identification system, and a keynote system that links drawings and specifications, ConDoc improved quality control, information management, productivity, and bidding results.

Organization of drawings. A uniform arrangement is established for locating project data within a set of drawings and for identifying individual sheets. Drawing sets are divided by disciplines, with each discipline assigned a discipline letter prefix. Discipline drawings are subdivided into groups of like information, with each group assigned a group number. Finally, each sheet within a group is assigned a sequential number. For example, A101 represents the architecture discipline (A), group plan (1), and sheet number (01).

Standard sheet format. Sheets are composed using a standard, modular format that may be subdivided into module blocks. The standard sheet has three zones. The first zone, on the right side of the sheet, contains the sheet title block and drawing keynote legend. Zone 2 is the graphics zone and contains a nonprinting modular grid. Zone 3 is the perimeter or border, with alphanumeric grid coordinates.

Keynote system. This process establishes a connecting link between graphic information shown on the drawings and the related text in the specifications. Keynotes minimize the amount of text needed on drawings without restricting the notation process. Drawing notations are identified by keynote symbols. In general, notations with their respective keynote symbols are located on each sheet in a keynote legend, while only the keynote symbols are placed in the drawing.

(continued)

Each note may be repeated in the drawing as often as needed by simply repeating the symbol.

THE UNIFORM DRAWING SYSTEM

The creators of ConDoc shared their system widely through seminars and other events, and produced a detailed workshop handbook. In 1994, recognizing the need for a more detailed system fully described in a self-contained publication, the Construction Specifications Institute embarked on a project to create the Uniform Drawing System (UDS).

The first three UDS modules, published in 1997, build upon ConDoc's organizational concepts. The Drawing Set Organization Module (Module 1) establishes consistency between disciplines through the use of standard discipline designators, sheet types, and file names. The Sheet Organization Module (Module 2) establishes graphic layout standards delineating drawing area, title block area, and production data area, as well as a grid system of blocks or modules for organizing drawings and related information on a sheet. The Schedules Module (Module 3) defines a standard format for numerous schedules used in construction documents. In 1999 the UDS was expanded to include Drafting Conventions (Module 4), Terms and Abbreviations (Module 5), and Symbols (Module 6). In 2000 the UDS was completed with the publication of Notations (Module 7) and Code Conventions (Module 8).

CAD LAYER GUIDELINES

Developed and first published by the AIA in 1990, the layer list in *CAD Layer Guidelines* is the only comprehensive system for the standard naming of CAD data file layers. The second edition, published in 1997, contains enhancements and refinements of the original edition. *CAD Layer Guidelines* offers a consistent, comprehensive yet flexible layer-naming system that can be adapted to particular needs while maintaining the integrity of the system.

In 2001 the publication was completely revised and updated and given a new name, *AIA CAD Layer Guidelines: U.S. National CAD Standard, Version 2.* The original layer-naming system has been amended to enable U.S. design firms to conform to ISO Standard 13567, Organization and Naming of Layers for CAD, while largely preserving the integrity of data located according to earlier editions. The layer list has also been expanded for disciplines such as civil, civil works,

structural, mechanical, plumbing, telecommunications, survey/mapping, geotechnical, process, and operations.

THE U.S. NATIONAL CAD STANDARD

The National Institute of Building Sciences recognized a need for a single, comprehensive national standard for electronically produced construction documents. A single standard supports the seamless transfer of building design and construction information among a broad array of users throughout the building lifecycle, including architects, planners, engineers, contractors, product manufacturers, building owners, and facility managers.

The NIBS Facility Information Council (formerly the CADD Council) provides an industry-wide forum for the standardization of computer-aided design and drafting. Membership in the council is open to all individuals and organizations with an interest in the subject matter. Components of the CAD standard include the following:

- CAD layering
- Drawing set organization
- Sheet organization
- Schedules
- Drafting conventions
- Terms and abbreviations
- Symbols
- Notations
- Code conventions
- Plotting guidelines

THE U.S. NATIONAL BIM STANDARD (NBIMS)

NIBS organized the National BIM Standard Project Committee in 2005. The mission of this committee, as defined in its charter, is to improve the performance of facilities over their full lifecycle by fostering a common, standard, and integrated lifecycle information model for the architecture, engineering, construction, and facility management industries. The basic premise underlying the development of this standard is that the true value of a building information model lies in its accessibility to different stakeholders at different phases of the facility lifecycle. The ability of each stakeholder to insert, extract, update, or modify information in the model requires a shared digital representation that can be manipulated by a variety of software applications. This interoperability must be achieved through open standards that allow for the unfettered electronic exchange of graphic and nongraphic information.

SPECIFICATIONS

The specifications present written requirements for materials, equipment, and construction systems, as well as standards for products, workmanship, and the construction services required to produce the work. The specifications are often presented in the project manual, along with the bidding requirements, contract forms, and conditions of the contract.

Organization

In its *Project Resource Manual: CSI Manual of Practice*, CSI publishes a series of widely used conventions for specifications organization, format, and development. Especially important is MasterFormat™, which establishes a master list of section titles and numbers as well as a format for the organization of individual specification sections. This widely used format is incorporated into many industry standards and products, including AIA MASTERSPEC, which includes 50 divisions. Divisions 00 through 49—the missing division numbers are reserved for future use—are labeled as follows:

Division 00 Procurement and Contracting Requirements

Division 01 General Requirements

Division 02 Existing Conditions

Division 03 Concrete

Division 04 Masonry

Division 05 Metals

Division 06 Wood, Plastics, and Composites

Division 07 Thermal and Moisture Protection

Division 08 Openings

Division 09 Finishes

Division 10 Specialties

Division 11 Equipment

Division 12 Furnishings

Division 13 Special Construction

Division 14 Conveying Equipment

Division 21 Fire Suppression

Division 22 Plumbing

Division 23 Heating, Ventilating, and Air Conditioning

Division 25 Integrated Automation

Division 26 Electrical

Division 27 Communications

Division 28 Electronic Safety and Security

Division 31 Earthwork

Division 32 Exterior Improvements

Division 33 Utilities

Division 34 Transportation

Division 35 Waterway and Marine Construction

Division 40 Process Integration

Division 41 Material Processing and Handling Equipment

Division 42 Process Heating, Cooling, and Drying Equipment

Division 43 Process Gas and Liquid Handling, Purification, and Storage Equipment

Division 44 Pollution Control Equipment

Division 45 Industry-Specific Manufacturing Equipment

Division 48 Electrical Power Generation

Division 01 of MasterFormat presents a series of general procedural and administrative requirements applicable to all portions of the work. Each MasterFormat division

The backgrounder at the end of this topic describes AIA MASTERSPEC programs for specification preparation.

contains sections designated by six-digit numbers. Each section, in turn, is organized according to the three-part format with the following article titles: General, Products, and Execution.

Methods of Specifying

For each specifications section, the architect selects the method of specifying. These methods include descriptive specifying, performance specifying (listing required performance qualities of products and assemblies), specifying by reference standards, and proprietary specifying (listing products and assemblies by one or more manufacturers and trade names). In addition, the architect may use allowances and unit prices for parts of the work that cannot be accurately quantified or qualified at the time of bidding.

Descriptive specifying. Many architects use descriptive specifications, describing exact characteristics of materials and products without listing proprietary names.

Performance specifying. Some architects believe that performance specifications are best in principle because they specify the end result required and allow contractors, manufacturers, and fabricators the flexibility and creativity to meet the requirements. In practice, however, creating performance specifications can be complicated due to the vast number of factors that can affect the finished result.

MASTERSPEC® DIVISIONS AND SECTIONS

ARCOM uses the CSI Master Format outline for its MASTERSPEC specification system. The outline below is an abridged version of divisions 01 through 14, which include the section titles most frequently used by architects.

Division 00—Procurement and Contracting Requirements

Division 01—General Requirements
  010000 General Requirements
  011000 Summary

Division 02—Existing Conditions
  024116 Structure Demolition
  024119 Selective Structure Demolition

Division 03—Concrete
  033000 Cast-in-Place Concrete
  033300 Architectural Concrete
  033816 Unbonded Post-Tensioned Concrete
  034100 Precast Structural Concrete
  034500 Precast Architectural Concrete
  034713 Tilt-Up Concrete
  034900 Glass Fiber-Reinforced Concrete
  035113 Cementitious Wood Fiber Decks
  035216 Lightweight Insulating Concrete
  035300 Concrete Topping
  035416 Hydraulic Cement Underlayment

Division 04—Masonry
  040100 Maintenance of Masonry
  040120 Maintenance of Unit Masonry
  040140 Maintenance of Stone Assemblies
  042000 Unit Masonry
  042300 Glass Unit Masonry
  044200 Exterior Stone Cladding
  044300 Stone Masonry
  047200 Cast Stone Masonry

Division 05—Metals
  050170 Maintenance of Decorative Metal
  051200 Structural Steel Framing
  052100 Steel Joist Framing
  053100 Steel Decking
  054000 Cold-Formed Metal Framing
  055000 Metal Fabrications
  055100 Metal Stairs
  055213 Pipe and Tube Railings
  055300 Metal Gratings
  057000 Decorative Metal
  057113 Fabricated Metal Spiral Stairs

Division 06—Wood, Plastics, and Composites
  061000 Rough Carpentry
  061323 Heavy Timber Construction

061500 Wood Decking

061600 Sheathing

061753 Shop-Fabricated Wood Trusses

061800 Glued-Laminated Construction

062000 Finish Carpentry

064013 Exterior Architectural Woodwork

064023 Interior Architectural Woodwork

064200 Wood Paneling

066400 Plastic Paneling

Division 07—Thermal and Moisture Protection

071113 Bituminous Dampproofing

071326 Self-Adhering Sheet Waterproofing

071353 Elastomeric Sheet Waterproofing

071354 Thermoplastic Sheet Waterproofing

071413 Hot Fluid-Applied Rubberized Asphalt Waterproofing

071416 Cold Fluid-Applied Waterproofing

071600 Cementitious and Reactive Waterproofing

071613 Polymer Modified Cement Waterproofing

071616 Crystalline Waterproofing

071619 Metal Oxide Waterproofing

071700 Bentonite Waterproofing

071800 Traffic Coatings

071900 Water Repellents

072100 Thermal Insulation

072400 Exterior Insulation and Finish Systems

072413 Polymer-Based Exterior Insulation and Finish System

072419 Water-Drainage Exterior Insulation and Finish System

072700 Air Barriers

073113 Asphalt Shingles

073116 Metal Shingles

073126 Slate Shingles

073129 Wood Shingles and Shakes

073200 Roof Tiles

073213 Clay Roof Tiles

073216 Concrete Roof Tiles

074113 Metal Roof Panels

074213 Metal Wall Panels

074216 Insulated-Core Metal Wall Panels

074243 Composite Wall Panels

074600 Siding

075100 Built-Up Bituminous Roofing

075113 Built-Up Asphalt Roofing

075116 Built-Up Coal Tar Roofing

075200 Modified Bituminous Membrane Roofing

075300 Elastomeric Membrane Roofing

075400 Thermoplastic Membrane Roofing

075556 Fluid-Applied Protected Membrane Roofing

075700 Coated Foamed Roofing

076100 Sheet Metal Roofing

076200 Sheet Metal Flashing and Trim

077100 Roof Specialties

077129 Manufactured Roof Expansion Joints

077200 Roof Accessories

078100 Applied Fireproofing

078200 Board Fireproofing

078413 Penetration Firestopping

078446 Fire-Resistive Joint Systems

079200 Joint Sealants

079500 Expansion Control

Division 08—Openings

081113 Hollow Metal Doors and Frames

081119 Stainless-Steel Doors and Frames

081173 Sliding Metal Fire Doors

081216 Aluminum Frames

081416 Flush Wood Doors

081433 Stile and Rail Wood Doors

083113 Access Doors and Frames

083213 Sliding Aluminum-Framed Glass Doors

083219 Sliding Wood-Framed Glass Doors

083323 Overhead Coiling Doors

083326 Overhead Coiling Grilles

083459 Vault Doors and Day Gates

083463 Detention Doors and Frames

083473 Sound Control Door Assemblies

083513 Folding Doors

083613 Sectional Doors

084113 Aluminum-Framed Entrances and Storefronts

084126 All-Glass Entrances and Storefronts

084229 Automatic Entrances

084233 Revolving Door Entrances

084243 Intensive Care Unit/Critical Care Unit Entrances

084413 Glazed Aluminum Curtain Walls

084423 Structural-Sealant-Glazed Curtain Walls

(continued)

084433 Sloped Glazing Assemblies

084500 Translucent Wall and Roof Assemblies

084513 Structured-Polycarbonate-Panel
Assemblies

084523 Fiberglass-Sandwich-Panel Assemblies

085000 Windows

085113 Aluminum Windows

085123 Steel Windows

085200 Wood Windows

085313 Vinyl Windows

085653 Security Windows

085663 Detention Windows

086100 Roof Windows

086200 Unit Skylights

086300 Metal-Framed Skylights

087100 Door Hardware

087113 Automatic Door Operators

087163 Detention Door Hardware

088000 Glazing

088113 Decorative Glass Glazing

088300 Mirrors

088400 Plastic Glazing

088853 Security Glazing

089000 Louvers and Vents

Division 09—Finishes

090190 Maintenance of Painting and Coating

092216 Non-Structural Metal Framing

092300 Gypsum Plastering

092400 Portland Cement Plastering

092613 Gypsum Veneer Plastering

092713 Glass-Fiber-Reinforced Plaster
Fabrications

092900 Gypsum Board

093000 Tiling

093033 Stone Tiling

095113 Acoustical Panel Ceilings

095123 Acoustical Tile Ceilings

095133 Acoustical Metal Pan Ceilings

095753 Security Ceiling Assemblies

096229 Cork Flooring

096313 Brick Flooring

096340 Stone Flooring

096400 Wood Flooring

096466 Wood Athletic Flooring

096500 Resilient Flooring

096513 Resilient Base and Accessories

096516 Resilient Sheet Flooring

096519 Resilient Tile Flooring

096536 Static-Control Resilient Flooring

096566 Resilient Athletic Flooring

096600 Terrazzo Flooring

096723 Resinous Flooring

096813 Tile Carpeting

096816 Sheet Carpeting

096900 Access Flooring

097200 Wall Coverings

097500 Stone Facing

097713 Stretched-Fabric Wall Systems

097723 Fabric-Wrapped Panels

098413 Fixed Sound-Absorptive Panels

099100 Painting

099113 Exterior Painting

099123 Interior Painting

099300 Staining and Transparent Finishing

099419 Multicolor Interior Finishing

099600 High-Performance Coatings

099633 High-Temperature-Resistant Coatings

099646 Intumescent Painting

099653 Elastomeric Coatings

099726 Cementitious Coatings

Division 10—Specialties

101100 Visual Display Surfaces

101200 Display Cases

101300 Directories

101400 Signage

101426 Post and Panel/Pylon Signage

101700 Telephone Specialties

102113 Toilet Compartments

102123 Cubicles

102213 Wire Mesh Partitions

102219 Demountable Partitions

102226 Operable Partitions

102600 Wall and Door Protection

102800 Toilet, Bath, and Laundry Accessories

104400 Fire Protection Specialties

104413 Fire Extinguisher Cabinets

104416 Fire Extinguishers

105113 Metal Lockers

105116 Wood Lockers

SECTIONFORMAT™ OUTLINE CSI AND CSC

SectionFormat is used to organize information when specifications are being written. The information is presented in three parts: General, Products, and Execution. A new version of this outline is under consideration.

Part 1 General

SUMMARY

Products supplied but not installed under this section

Products installed but not supplied under this section

Related sections

Allowances

Unit prices

Measurement procedures

Payment procedures

Alternates

REFERENCES

Definitions

System Description

Design requirements

Performance requirements

(continued)

Submittals

Product data

Shop drawings

Samples

Quality assurance/control submittals

   Design data

   Test reports

   Certificates

   Manufacturers' instructions

   Manufacturers' field reports

Closeout submittals

Quality assurance

Qualifications

Regulatory requirements

Certifications

Field samples

Mock-ups

Preinstallation meetings

Delivery, storage, and handling

Packing, shipping, handling, and unloading

Acceptance at site

Storage and protection

Project/site conditions

Environmental requirements

Existing conditions

SEQUENCING

Scheduling

   Warranty

   Special warranty

SYSTEM START-UP

OWNER'S INSTRUCTIONS

COMMISSIONING

   Maintenance

   Extra materials

   Maintenance service

Part 2 Products

MANUFACTURERS

EXISTING PRODUCTS

MATERIALS

MANUFACTURED UNITS

EQUIPMENT

COMPONENTS

ACCESSORIES

MIXES

FABRICATION

   Shop assembly

   Fabrication tolerances

   Finishes

   Shop priming

   Shop finishing

   Source quality control

   Tests, inspection

   Verification of performance

Part 3 Execution

INSTALLERS

EXAMINATION

   Site verification of conditions

   Preparation

   Protection

   Surface preparation

ERECTION

INSTALLATION

APPLICATION

   Construction

   Special techniques

   Interface with other work

   Sequences of operation

   Site tolerances

REPAIR/RESTORATION

REINSTALLATION

   Field quality control

   Site tests

   Inspection

   Manufacturers' field services

ADJUSTING

CLEANING

DEMONSTRATION

PROTECTION

SCHEDULES

Specifying with reference standards. Specifications may also incorporate references to standards published by industry associations and testing organizations. This allows designers, contractors, and suppliers to use industry-accepted standards of practice and performance. The most widely known standards associations are the American National Standards Institute (ANSI), American Society for Testing and Materials (ASTM), and Underwriters' Laboratories (UL). These groups either develop and organize performance standards or test material products and assemblies for compliance with published standards.

Proprietary specifying. Many architects use proprietary specifications for their brevity and simplicity and because they are familiar with the qualities of the specific products being specified. These specifications are frequently augmented with reference to standards, narrative descriptions of materials' qualities, and performance requirements.

Some standards, such as those published by the American Society of Heating, Refrigerating, and Air-Conditioning Engineers (ASHRAE), the National Fire Protection Association (NFPA), and the Illuminating Engineering Society (IES), focus on specific aspects of building performance. Industry associations, such as the American Iron and Steel Institute (AISI) and the American Architectural Manufacturers Association (AAMA), write standards for the products and systems produced by their members. For example, AAMA publishes test methods, standards, and guide specifications for aluminum fabrications such as storefronts, curtain walls, and windows.

Restrictive specifying. The architect also determines how restrictive the specifications are to be—whether they will permit only one manufacturer's product, several products, or any product that meets specified criteria. Publicly funded projects require full and open competition. Therefore, several brands of products are specified under the theory that qualified manufacturers should be able to compete equitably for the work. In private work, the architect will typically specify restrictively, unless the owner prefers competition. When there is a choice, the architect should determine which approach best serves the client's interests.

Master Specifications

Most firms employ some form of master specification that is modified for each project. A master specification covers an entire topic, including a range of options. The specifications editor then fills in blanks, deletes options that don't apply, and incorporates special requirements not included in the master.

The most commonly used commercially available master specification is MASTERSPEC, developed by the AIA and available through ARCOM Master Systems. It is distributed on electronic media and is regularly updated by professional staff and an AIA-sponsored review committee of architects and engineers. MASTERSPEC is well suited for use in a variety of architecture offices. It covers most types of projects and is closely coordinated with AIA standard documents and procedures. MASTERSPEC also acts as a specifications-writing tutorial, including overview and reference materials, editorial notes, and specifications and drawing coordination notes.

Other commercially available master specifications include SpecText, maintained by Construction Sciences Research Foundation Inc., and e-SPECS, created by InterSpec, Inc., which is also available integrated with MASTERSPEC. Master specifications are also available from some government agencies, such as the Veterans Administration and NASA, which developed its own automated system, NASA SpecsIntact. Government agencies that produce master specifications usually require that these be used on their projects.

Specification Production Methods

Specifications are produced using electronic word processing and software developed solely for editing specifications. As a firm finds products and procedures that work well for its markets, it will repeat much of the same information from project to project.

Moreover, specifications typically evolve through multiple drafts, and, as in CAD drawings, tracking revisions is increasingly important.

Well-coordinated drawings and specifications are essential in any set of construction documents. In particular, the architect is challenged to ensure that materials and products shown on the drawings are described in the specifications and that the language used is consistent and unambiguous. For small projects, the architect often develops the specifications concurrently with the drawings. These specifications may be included directly on the drawings, perhaps by attaching photocopies to the drawings or importing a word-processing file into CAD. For larger projects, however, it is common to include the specifications in a separate project manual. CAD and other automation tools can help architects achieve coordination, and in some cases, they provide new techniques to create more tightly integrated drawings and specifications. One important goal is maintaining consistency between the language used in drawing notations and the language used in the specifications. Inconsistency can be a major source of requests for interpretation and change orders during construction.

In addition to careful review of drawings and specifications, several production techniques are available to help architects achieve this consistency. Numerical keynoting offers one example. Instead of attaching a descriptive note, such as "batt insulation," to a component of a drawing or detail, the architect attaches a keynote number. This number is cross-referenced to a standardized keynote list, which is included on each drawing. It remains the responsibility of the architect to coordinate the keynote list and the specifications, but this technique generally makes it easier to revise drawing notations, and the notations are better coordinated. If a standard material notation changes, for example, only the keynote list needs to be updated—not every plan, section, elevation, or detail in which the material appears.

Keynote-based drawings lend themselves to automation. CAD systems allow the same information to be shared between multiple drawings using reference files. The keynote list, when attached as a reference file to many drawings, can be updated for all drawings simply by changing the master list. This can be especially helpful for international practices. By maintaining the keynote list in multiple languages, the firm's architects can select notes in their own language and output those notes in the language spoken where the building is being constructed.

The ConDoc drawing system that appeared in the late 1980s took the concept of keynotes further by using MasterFormat as the keynote numbering convention. Each material or product notation on a drawing essentially becomes a direct reference to the appropriate specifications section. At any point in the drawing process, the program can scan the drawing and print a keynote legend listing all of the materials on the drawing. Similarly, the user can locate all occurrences of a specific material within the drawings. The keynote list can be used to link drawings and specifications, helping to ensure that each building component drawn is described in the specifications.

CAD provides another mechanism to integrate drawings and specifications by allowing architects to add specifications data directly to the drawing in the form of database attributes. Predrawn standard components in the drawings (metal studs, furring channels, insulation, plumbing fixtures, etc.) can include specifications attributes. Some CAD systems can generate reports based on this information, so the architect can double-check that each component in the drawings is described in the specifications and vice versa. In addition, some systems quantify this information, producing bills of materials. Such systems require that the user know enough about specifications to enter the correct attributes or select the appropriate components.

BIM technology is particularly powerful in this regard. These systems more tightly integrate specifications attributes and permit them to be assigned to assemblies of objects—an insulated masonry wall, for example—as well as to the components of that wall. This allows complete and highly accurate extraction of bills of materials. In addition, these systems may incorporate design rules. In other words, knowledge about how buildings are designed and constructed is programmed into the software. An example might be a rule that a door inserted into a fire-rated wall must be a fire-rated door. The BIM system would prevent the insertion of a nonrated door object into a fire-rated wall.

OTHER CONSTRUCTION DOCUMENTS

Increasingly, contract documents include a code compliance summary—sometimes on the first sheet of documents—for use by the code enforcement official in reviewing the project and issuing the building permit. This and other construction information is usually presented as a combination of documents generated in the architect's office and standard forms supplied by the AIA, the owner, or other sources. AIA documents, with or without modifications, are included in the project manual in their original form; others are commonly developed as word-processed forms that can be used, with appropriate modifications, on future projects.

CONSTRUCTION DOCUMENTATION MANAGEMENT

Planning for this phase includes thinking through the documentation required (usually very early in a project, frequently as part of the proposal to acquire the project in the first place), selecting appropriate production methods, planning the production process, and managing this process to achieve the desired results.

Effective production management of construction documentation is important to meeting both a firm's project goals and its practice goals. Good production management includes these features:

- Careful production planning, scheduling, and oversight
- Documentation standards
- A library of construction information and technical references
- Effective coordination with consultants and others on the project team. (As integrated practice becomes more widespread, this project team will increasingly include contractors and subcontractors during design phases.)
- Thorough review and checking procedures
- The resources and the desire to produce high-quality construction documentation
- Approval of the construction documentation by the owner (sometimes at various stages of production).

Firms seeking continuous quality improvement usually consider construction documentation a prime candidate for attention. Creation of the documentation translates design intent into the information needed for approvals and construction. Errors and omissions in the construction documentation inevitably require reworking later and may, in fact, degrade the quality of the service provided and reduce customer satisfaction with that service.

Construction documentation is what its name implies—documentation of decisions made and agreed to in the design development phase. While changes during the construction documentation phase are inevitable, comprehensive design development documentation, carefully coordinated by the design team and approved by the owner, provides a sound foundation for preparing the construction documentation.

It may be necessary to impress upon owners that most design decisions are interrelated. Adding a new door, for example, may require changes in several drawings (floor plans, interior elevations, sections, details, and door and hollow metal schedules). It may also require a new specification section as well as changes in the electrical, mechanical, or structural work. Computers are helpful in coordinating design changes, but professional judgment is involved in even the smallest design decision.

Production Planning

Considering the many interrelationships among the construction documents, most offices identify a single production coordinator. For many projects, this person is the project architect or project manager. For larger projects, production coordination may be delegated to a technical architect, a job captain, or another specially designated individual.

With CAD systems offering the possibility of simultaneous design and production as well as integrated specifications, firms are finding that their project architects and key project staff are doing production as well as design. The traditional distinction between designers and drafters is blurring and, in some offices, disappearing entirely.

As the construction documentation phase approaches, the project manager determines, in detail, the time, staffing, and other resources required to produce the documents. Usually this involves cartooning the drawings, blocking out the specifications (which by now are in outline form), and outlining the remaining content of the project manual. Some, perhaps all, of these decisions may have been made earlier; some firms prepare design development documents in the formats planned for the construction documents.

Production scheduling and budgeting. Many architects have found that the amount of time required to produce working drawings varies greatly, depending on project complexity and the level of detail required. It is good practice to allocate time (based on the previously prepared budget) for each sheet so that each person working on the drawings knows what is expected. Data from past projects will help sharpen these estimates. One of the major challenges in introducing a building modeling approach has been the difficulty in estimating the time and staffing levels required in each design phase.

The time required to produce specifications varies widely, due to a number of factors, including:

- The project delivery approach
- Size and complexity of the project
- Competitive bidding requirements
- Specification scope (broad to narrow)
- Staff knowledge of the specified products and systems
- The level of detail already achieved in the design development phase

Construction documentation is prepared most efficiently if the decision-making process is well structured. With modern production techniques, more time can be spent researching systems and coordinating decisions than producing documents. As might be expected, the time required increases substantially if unfamiliar construction systems are used.

Selection of production methods. As suggested above, each approach to production exerts a discipline on the process. The firm may use the same production approach for all of its projects or mix and match them according to the needs of the project at hand.

"Project Delivery Methods" describes the possible options for the delivery of project services.

In a similar vein, the firm must decide how specifications are to be produced, whether separate systems will be used for outline and final specifications, and to what extent specifications are to be integrated with the drawings.

If CAD systems are used, it is especially important that the project manager or production coordinator think through the organization of the CAD data as well as the number of drawings, scales, and sheet layouts. CAD issues include whether a single CAD file or multiple files will be created, the CAD layers to be used, how drawings will be created from the CAD data, and how the data will be presented in drawings of different scales in terms of line weights, text heights, and so forth.

Typically the firm's CAD standards provide guidance on these topics, but almost every project will present some unique requirements. Sharing CAD data with outside consultants or with the client requires additional planning to ensure that all parties can use the data without extensive editing. This highlights the usefulness of industry-wide standards, such as the National CAD Standard discussed above.

If CAD data will be exchanged between different organizations, the team must address the following questions:

- Which organizations are exchanging data?
- What information does each organization need from the others?
- What format data are required?
- What are the project drafting and CAD standards?
- What is the frequency of data exchange?
- How will the data be exchanged (project website, bulletin board, e-mail, CD)?
- How much data preparation is required for each exchange and how long does the transfer take?
- Who is the person in each organization responsible for sending and receiving data?
- Who is authorized to request and release electronic data?
- How will data transfers be logged?

Archiving procedures are also important and frequently overlooked. Archiving is distinguished from data backup in that it is a complete copy of the project data at a defined point in time, typically at a project milestone. Also, deciding what and when to archive is a project

ELEMENTS OF PRODUCTION PLANNING

Sound production planning for construction documentation reflects the following:

- **The firm's experience.** Most firms accumulate historical information on which to plan projects and base compensation proposals. Past and present time records are readily adaptable to computerization using spreadsheet programs.
- **The production budget.** A large fraction of the architect's cost is budgeted for the construction documents; it is particularly important that scope, services, and compensation be in balance during this phase of services.
- **Project consultants.** On projects of any size or complexity, the consultants will prepare much of the documentation. It is essential that the architect and consultants agree on both production schedules and documentation standards.
- **Project technology.** CAD and BIM systems require careful planning and management if their potential benefits are to be realized.

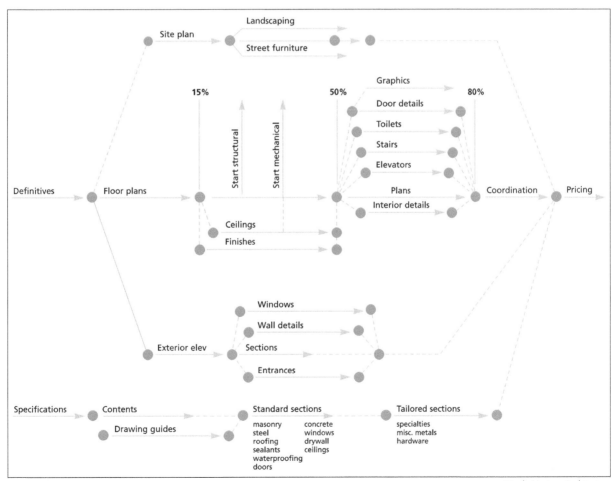

Nagle Hartray Architecture

FIGURE 7.2 **Sample Documents Production Sequence. Here is one firm's production sequence.**

management responsibility, whereas data backup is typically a system management responsibility.

When a BIM is used as the primary communication and coordination vehicle for the project team, all of the issues above must be considered. The American Institute of Steel Construction (AISC) has championed virtual design and construction for several years, including an appendix in the 2005 *Code of Standard Practice for Steel Buildings and Bridges* on what the AISC calls "product models." AISC recommends that a single entity be assigned responsibility for managing the official version of the shared model:

> When a project is designed and constructed using EDI [electronic data interchange], it is imperative that an individual entity on the team be responsible for maintaining the LPM [logical product model, or building product model]. This is to assure protection of data through proper backup, storage and security and to provide coordination of the flow of information to all team members when information is added to the model. Team members exchange information to revise the model with this Administrator. The Administrator will validate all changes to the LPM. This is to assure proper tracking and control of revisions. This Administrator can be one of the design team members such as an Architect, Structural Engineer or a separate entity on the design team serving this purpose. The Administrator can also be the Fabricator's detailer or a separate entity on the construction team serving this purpose.

A key aspect of production planning is the search for bottlenecks that may slow down the project and endanger its schedule. Coordination points, where all drawings and specifications need to be brought to a common level of development for checking, are common candidates. Plotting CAD drawings and preparing, translating, and transferring CAD files to outside consultants are other likely bottlenecks. With a BIM, the periodic need to extract and plot full sets of 2D drawings from the model can also be a choke point.

Identifying technical references. Architects increasingly recognize that before new details and construction techniques are formulated, standard approaches should be investigated and understood as part of the design process. To facilitate this research, many valuable references are available to the practitioner. These include the following:

- Building codes and regulations applicable to the project
- Technical references and standards, such as those published by ASTM, ANSI, and professional and industry associations
- Standard references, such as Architectural Graphic Standards
- Journals and other publications of professional societies and industry associations
- Manufacturers' catalogs and trade literature

The above material is available in books, journals, pamphlets, Internet websites, or compact disc format. Some of the computerized sources are integrated with product selection, analysis, and detailing routines. Increasingly, product suppliers will be providing technical information in intelligent, 3D digital objects that can be inserted in a BIM.

In addition to working with printed references, most firms find that technical representatives of industry associations, product representatives, consultants, and senior members of architecture firms are valuable resources. Most firms develop a library of technical and reference information. Information on materials and products is often filed by MasterFormat division or section number, making the library easily accessible to all members of the project team.

Documents Coordination

A goal of the construction documentation phase is a fully coordinated building description. When conventional documents are the deliverable, these documents must be internally consistent. Plans, sections, elevations, details, and schedules must agree with each other. Materials shown on the drawings must be specified, the mechanical and electrical systems must fit within the chases and plenums designed for them, and so on.

BIM software automates a great deal of this coordination, by extracting drawings as "views" of the single building model. When using a BIM tool, the firm must understand its capabilities and limitations and develop appropriate coordination procedures.

The coordination task is complicated by the reality that more than one person or firm, and usually several, will work on the construction documentation of all but the smallest projects. Staff may be in different groups within the firm or in consultant organizations. For CAD systems, it is necessary to develop protocols for who has access to what layers or drawings, exchange of updated files, and backups for all of the work. When a BIM is to be shared by multiple project team members, it is necessary to establish techniques for partitioning and sharing the model and to establish the responsibility for managing changes to the shared model.

Progress prints or plots of drawings and drafts of project manuals are commonly shared within the project team. Coordination meetings and milestone reviews may be used to achieve ongoing coordination. Projects using a shared BIM have achieved excellent results by scheduling 3D model walk-throughs on a regular basis. Although some projects have used virtual reality environments for these walk-throughs, they can also be conducted on-screen and even include remote sites through Web conferencing techniques. During these walk-throughs, the entire team can see each conflict as it is encountered and discuss possible solutions. For this technique to be most effective, the team should use software that automatically detects and highlights conflicts.

Design changes. Design changes are particularly critical. One of the responsibilities of the project manager or production coordinator is to make sure that when changes occur they are reflected in all appropriate locations in the documents. This includes notification of all disciplines. When overlay drafting or CAD systems are being used, the project manager decides when a new or revised base sheet, layer, or file is created and distributed to each discipline. BIM systems can automatically update all affected drawings when there is a change to the model. When using a building information model as the basis for coordination, the team must develop a procedure for approving design changes and incorporating them into the shared model. However, even with an agreed-upon procedure in place, it is necessary to inform other team members when model updates occur.

As updates are issued, it is good practice to note the date and purpose of the revision on drawing title blocks or on the cover of the project manual. Thus, a record of issue dates and purposes appears on the documents. Some firms note the issue date on each page in the project manual or use a different-colored paper or different binding for subsequent issues. These measures provide effective means of determining whether documents are current. In true virtual design and construction, there may be a main and multiple related submodels produced by the various team members. In those instances, data management systems are needed to track model relationships as well as changes, and apply access controls to ensure that any changes are approved. Similar systems have been used in industries such as aerospace.

Once drawings are issued for contract, it is good practice to number each set of changes, circle and label each change on the documents, and record a new issue date (e.g., "3.24.16, Revision #1").

A number of firms have found that thoughtful organization of CAD data and automation of CAD background updates has yielded significant advantages, both in productivity and in drawing quality and coordination. The key to reaping these benefits is moving beyond the idea that a CAD file is a drawing. It is not—whether the graphics are 2D or 3D, a CAD file should be seen as a model from which many drawings, or "views," can be generated. When setting up a project CAD model, users should follow these guidelines in order to avoid any major operational issues:

- Never draw anything twice.
- Create a primary CAD model and make sure as many drawings as possible reference that model. This is consistent with the sheet file/model file distinction made in the *AIA CAD Layer Guidelines* and incorporated in the NCS.

- Establish CAD standards that permit each drawing to view the appropriate subset of the model information and to plot that information in the correct graphic representation, line weights, and text heights. Consider the needs of all users and all disciplines when setting CAD standards.
- Consider how any irregular geometry or rotated plans will be handled. This may require additional software or customization.
- Consider how data will be transferred to and received from outside consultants. How can the architect ensure that all consultants are referencing the most current version of the model?

A CHECKLIST FROM REDICHECK

1. Preliminary review
   a. Quickly make an overview of all sheets, spending no more than one minute per sheet to become familiar with the project.
2. Specifications check
   a. Check specs for bid items. Are they coordinated with the drawings?
   b. Check specs for phasing of construction. Are the phases clear?
   c. Compare architectural finish schedule to specification index. Ensure all finish materials are specified.
   d. Check major items of equipment and verify that they are coordinated with contract drawings. Pay particular attention to horsepower ratings and voltage requirements.
   e. Verify that items specified "as indicated" or "where indicated" are in fact indicated on contract drawings.
   f. Verify that cross-referenced specification sections exist.
   g. Try not to indicate thickness of materials or quantities of materials in specifications.
3. Plan check—civil
   a. Verify that site plans with new underground utilities (power, telephone, water, sewer, gas, storm drainage, fuel lines, grease traps, fuel tanks) have been checked for interferences.
   b. Verify that existing telephone poles, pole guys, street signs, drainage inlets, valve boxes, manhole castings, and so on do not interfere with new driveways, sidewalks, or other site improvements on architectural site plans.
   c. Verify that limits of clearing, grading, sodding, grass, or mulch are shown and are consistent with architectural or landscaping plans.
   d. Verify fire hydrant and street light pole locations against electrical and architectural plans.
   e. Verify that profile sheets show other underground utilities and avoid conflicts.

f. Verify that horizontal distances between drainage structures and manholes match with respect to scaled dimensions and stated dimensions on both plan and profile sheets.
   g. Verify that provisions have been included for adjusting valve box and manhole castings (sewer, power, telephone, drainage) to match final or finish grade of pavement, swales, or sidewalks.
   h. Verify that all existing and proposed grades are shown.
4. Plan check—structural
   a. Verify column lines on structural and architectural plans.
   b. Verify that all column locations are the same on structural and architectural plans.
   c. Verify that perimeter slab on structural matches architectural plans.
   d. Verify that all depressed or raised slabs are indicated.
   e. Verify slab elevations against architectural plans.
   f. Verify that all foundation piers are identified.
   g. Verify that all foundation beams are identified.
   h. Verify roof framing plan column lines and columns against foundation plan column lines and columns.
   i. Verify perimeter roof line against architectural roof plan.
   j. Verify that all columns and beams are listed in column and beam schedules.
   k. Verify length of all columns in column schedule.
   l. Verify that all sections are properly labeled.
   m. Verify all expansion joint locations against architectural plans.
   n. Verify dimensions.
   o. Verify that drawing notes do not conflict with specifications.
5. Plan check—architectural
   a. Verify property line dimensions on site survey plan against architecture.
   b. Verify that building is located behind setback lines.

c. Verify all concrete columns and walls against structural.
d. Verify on site plans that all existing and new work is clearly identified.
e. Verify building elevations against floor plans. Check in particular roof lines, window and door openings, and expansion joints.
f. Verify building sections against elevations and plans. Check roof lines, windows, and door locations.
g. Verify wall sections against architectural building sections and structural.
h. Verify masonry openings for windows and doors.
i. Verify expansion joints through building.
j. Verify partial floor plans against small-scale floor plans.
k. Verify reflected ceiling plan against architectural floor plan to ensure no variance with rooms. Check ceiling materials against finish schedule, check light fixture layout against electrical, check ceiling diffusers/registers against mechanical, check soffits and locations of vents.
l. Verify all room finish schedule information including room numbers, names of rooms, finishes, and ceiling heights. Look for omissions, duplications, and inconsistencies.
m. Verify all door schedule information including sizes, types, and labels. Look for omissions, duplications, and inconsistencies.
n. Verify all rated walls.
o. Verify all cabinets will fit.
p. Verify dimensions.

6. Plan check—mechanical and plumbing
a. Verify that all new electrical, gas, water, and sewer lines connect to existing.
b. Verify all plumbing fixture locations against architectural plans. Verify all plumbing fixtures against fixture schedule and/or specs.
c. Verify storm drain system against architectural roof plan. Verify that pipes are sized and all drains are connected and do not interfere with foundations. Verify that wall chases are provided on architectural plans to conceal vertical piping.
d. Verify that sanitary drain system pipes are sized and all fixtures are connected.

e. Verify HVAC floor plans against architectural plans.
f. Verify sprinkler heads in all rooms.
g. Verify that all sections are identical to architectural/structural drawings.
h. Verify that adequate ceiling height exists at worst-case duct intersection.
i. Verify that all structural supports required for mechanical equipment are indicated on structural drawings.
j. Verify that dampers are indicated at smoke and fire walls.
k. Verify diffusers against architectural reflected ceiling plan.
l. Verify that all roof penetrations (ducts, fans, etc.) are indicated on roof plans.
m. Verify all ductwork is sized.
n. Verify all notes.
o. Verify all air conditioning units, heaters, and exhaust fans against architectural roof plans and mechanical schedules.
p. Verify that all mechanical equipment will fit in spaces allocated.

7. Plan check—electrical
a. Verify that all plans are identical to architectural plans.
b. Verify all light fixtures against architectural reflected ceiling plan.
c. Verify that all major pieces of equipment have electrical connections.
d. Verify location of all panel boards and that they are indicated on the electrical riser diagram.
e. Verify all notes.
f. Verify that there is sufficient space for all electrical panels to fit.
g. Verify that electrical panels are not recessed in fire walls.
h. Verify that electrical equipment locations are coordinated with site paving and grading.

8. Plan check—kitchen/dietary
a. Verify equipment layout against architectural plans.

—Redicheck (www.redicheck-review.com)

Review and checking. The importance of review and checking cannot be overemphasized, given the extreme time constraints under which construction documentation is often produced. Documents may be produced by individuals who do not fully understand how details fit within the larger context. Therefore, checking goes hand in hand with the ongoing education process that characterizes any professional office.

Lists to help architects check documents are available from many sources. Many offices develop their own guides for document checking—checklists that may be used by the individual in developing the drawing and by the project manager in checking it.

Checking plays a central role in any firm's quality assurance effort. Most firms establish protocols for document checking. Some examples:

- Documents are comprehensively checked at one or more milestones before they are completed.
- A senior person not associated with the project checks all documents before they are issued.
- One person checks all important dimensions.
- The person responsible for the drawings reviews the specifications, and the specifier reviews the drawings.
- Consultants review the documents produced by other contributors for coordination.
- The owner reviews and approves the documents before they are issued for bid or negotiation.

> Be sure to document the owner's approval of legal and contractual information, or you may assume liability for it.

The last point is particularly important. The owner issues the construction documentation for bidding or negotiation, and the owner signs the construction agreements with contractors, the construction manager, or the design-build entity. It is the owner's project, and it is critical—and mandated in AIA forms of agreement—for the owner to approve the construction documentation.

Of all project phases, the preparation of the construction documentation typically takes the most time and resources. New technologies, especially computing and computer graphics, are changing the nature of this work, shifting the emphasis from rote production to decision making, coordination, and communication. A sound grasp of design and construction documentation is increasingly central to successful architectural practice.

For More Information

Osamu A. Wakita and Richard M. Linde cover the skills, concepts, and fundamentals for working drawings in *The Professional Practice of Architectural Working Drawings* (Wiley, 2002). *The Working Drawing Manual* (McGraw-Hill, 1998), by Fred A. Stitt, provides systematic checklists for organizing, managing, and coordinating the data needed to prepare accurate construction documents for any building.

With updated and reorganized content, the eleventh edition of *Architectural Graphic Standards* (Wiley, 2007) continues to offer a rich collection of information that provides a basis for designing, developing, and delineating an array of building elements and components.

Several publications address standards for construction drawings. The CSI *Uniform Drawing System* establishes standards for sheet types, sheet organization, and schedules. The AIA's *CAD Layer Guidelines* establishes standard naming of data file layers. Both of these documents have been incorporated, along with plotting standards, into the *U.S. National CAD Standard* (2005). The NCS is available from the AIA Bookstore at (800) 242–3837, the Construction Specifications Institute at www.csinet.org, and the National Institute of Building Sciences at www.nationalcadstandard.org.

In-depth treatment on preparing specifications can be found in *Construction Specifications Writing: Principles and Procedures* (Wiley, 2004) by Harold J. Rosen and John Regener. Specification software is available from ARCOM, including MASTERSPEC master specification system and SPECWARE specification production software. See the AIA MASTERSPEC backgrounder at the end of this section for further descriptions of these practice tools, or contact ARCOM at www.masterspec.com.

RediCheck Associates publishes an overlay checking and interdisciplinary coordination manual as a means for making construction documents more accurate and thorough. For information, call (877) 733–4243 or visit www.redicheck-review.com.

Guidance on the use of BIM tools and the management of BIM data is rapidly emerging. The U.S. National Institute of Standards and Technology published the *Capital Facilities Information Handover Guide* in 2006. This publication assists companies in planning for the lifecycle capture and use of facility information, starting with a corporate information strategy, defining detailed information handover requirements, and then delivering the required information during design and construction. This publication can be downloaded from the NIST website: http://cic.nist.gov/staff/publications.html. Scroll down to Mark Palmer's name to find it.

The National Institute of Building Sciences website, www.nibs.org, contains information about the U.S. National CAD Standard and the U.S. National BIM Standard. Search under Facility Information Council or buildingSMART.

Leading-edge research on BIM technology and applications has been undertaken at Stanford University's Center for Facility Engineering (CIFE): http://cife.stanford.edu/Research/index.html, and in the doctoral program at the Georgia Tech College of Architecture: http://bim.arch.gatech.edu.

BACKGROUNDER

THE U.S. NATIONAL CAD STANDARD

Business software applications, including computer-aided design (CAD) applications, allow a high degree of control over the organization and classification of data and the graphic composition of printed output. These user-defined variables allow individual authors to organize and classify CAD data according to their own needs and sense of logic, and to establish their own graphic standards for printed documents. While this freedom to customize is among the benefits of computer technology, the proliferation of customized user-defined settings in the production of CAD documents has eroded the common language for data organization, classification, and communication that evolved over hundreds of years of hand drafting. Even the simplest of CAD software applications can have as many as a hundred user-definable settings. The lack of standards in this arena inhibits the sharing of data even among small design teams. The overhead costs of translating settings between organizations, or developing and enforcing office standards, cut deeply into any productivity gains from adopting CAD software.

Over the years, a number of industry organizations have addressed various aspects of this issue. The AIA published the first edition of *CAD Layer Guidelines* in 1990 to establish a common system of nomenclature for CAD data files and layer names. The second edition, revised and updated, was published in 1997. That same year, the Construction Specifications Institute (CSI) published the first three modules of the *Uniform Drawing System*. This document was intended to serve as an industry standard for the organization of construction documents, whether they are prepared electronically or by hand.

Recognizing the potential for these publications to serve as the foundation of a consensus industry standard, the National Institute of Building Sciences (NIBS) convened a coalition of building design and construction industry organizations in 1997 to explore the development of a national CAD standard.

Under the auspices of the NIBS Facility Information Council (NIBS-FIC), the AIA joined with CSI, the U.S. Coast Guard, the U.S. Department of Defense Tri-Service CADD/GIS Technology Center, the Sheet Metal and Air Conditioning Contractors National Association (SMACNA), and other construction and software industry organizations to prepare the joint publication of the standard. In addition, these groups committed to support the evolution and development of a national CAD standard to keep pace with evolving technology.

The product of a historic and unprecedented cooperative effort, the *U.S. National CAD Standard*™ (NCS) is an important step in streamlining the free flow of building construction and design data throughout the lifecycle of buildings, from initial conceptual design through eventual retirement or reuse. The NCS comprises the following items:

- "Uniform Drawing System," published by CSI (a system for the organization of building construction drawings).
- "AIA CAD Layer Guidelines," a system of nomenclature for CAD drawing file names and CAD layer names, published by the AIA. The updated version includes new layer definitions for such disciplines as telecommunications and electronic building systems. It has been revised to improve compatibility with ISO layer standards.
- The Tri-Service "Plotting Guidelines," developed by the U.S. Coast Guard and promulgated by the U.S. Tri-Service CADD/GIS Technology Center of the U.S. Department of Defense (defines colors and line weight assignments for CAD drawings).
- The "U.S. National CAD Standard Foreword, Administration and Amendments," published by NIBS (resolves minor discrepancies between the constituent documents).

Several versions of NCS have now been published. Version 1.0 came out in 1999, and version 3.1 was released in January 2005. Version 4 was released in January 2008. To date, the complete NCS has not yet been incorporated into all CAD software products.

(continued)

A uniform electronic data classification format establishes a common language for preparing building design and construction documents. It eliminates the need for developing and maintaining office standards. Newly hired employees do not have to be trained or retrained to learn file and layer naming conventions, pen assignments, line weights, drawing set organization, or sheet layout conventions. Project designers and project managers will be able to access design data without having to learn varying arcane organizational systems.

The benefits are better project management, higher-quality construction documents, reduced errors and omissions, and ultimately a better building project. Most important, design firms can provide a higher quality of service to clients by delivering data in an industry-standard format. Savvy design firms will seize the opportunity to let clients know they use the NCS format.

The NIBS-FIC National CAD Standard Project Committee (NCSPC), with representation from across the 12 NIBS public- and private-interest categories encompassing the entire building construction community, was formed to perform a broad peer review and update of the constituent NCS documents. The NCSPC follows consensus rules approved by the NIBS Board of Direction. Membership is open to industry members. Anyone with an interest in the work of the committee may participate. Most of the committee's work is conducted via the Internet.

All committee members have an equal voice and ballot vote. Details are available at the NCS website, www.nationalcadstandard.org. The U.S. National CAD Standard can be ordered by phone from the AIA Bookstore: (202) 626–7541 or (800) 242–3837 (press 4). It can also be purchased from NIBS at www.nationalcadstandard.org and the CSI online bookstore at www.csinet.org. A substantial discount is available to AIA, CSI, and NIBS members.

BACKGROUNDER

AIA MASTERSPEC

MASTERSPEC® is a master guide specification system that offers architects and engineers powerful tools for preparing construction project specifications. MASTERSPEC is a product of the AIA and is exclusively published and supported by ARCOM. Its thirteen libraries are organized by design discipline as follows:

TABLE 7.3 MASTERSPEC

Library	Abbreviation
Architectural/Structural/Civil	A/S/C
Interiors	INT
Roofing	RF
Security & Detention	SD
Structural/Civil/Landscape Architecture	S/C/L
Structural	S
Site Civil	SC
Landscape Architecture	L
Mechanical/Electrical	M/E
Mechanical	M
Fire Protection	FP
Electrical	E
General Requirements	GR

MASTERSPEC libraries are available in four formats—full length, short form, small project, and outline—and in two packages—basic and expanded.

- *Full-length* specifications are comprehensive master specifications that cover a wide range of materials, products, and applications. They include multiple methods of specifying and are the most comprehensive master specifications available in the industry.
- *Short form* specifications are condensed from, and compatible with, full-length sections. They include a limited range of products, streamlined material and quality control requirements, and concise methods of specifying.
- *Small project* specifications are the most abbreviated form of master specifications and are only available in the A/S/C and M/E libraries. These specifications are intended for projects that are limited in scope and complexity.
- *Outline* specifications provide a method for recording product and material decisions early in the documentation process. They can be used as a checklist to help the project team select products and methods during development of the project manual, to communicate design intent, and to coordinate terminology for use both on the drawings and in the project manual.
- *Basic package* sections, such as concrete and gypsum board, are the most frequently used specifications because they cover the construction products and materials most commonly used for all project sizes and types.

- The *expanded package* includes basic package sections plus more specialized sections, such as laboratory fume hoods.

Section Naming Convention

MASTERSPEC uses assigned numbers and titles according to the 2004 edition of CSI/CSC's MasterFormat™. Each section is organized into one of the CSI/CSC divisions. For example:

MasterFormat 2004

Division 06—Wood, Plastics, and Composites

Section 064023, Interior Architectural Woodwork

The MASTERSPEC table of contents lists all sections by division and section number and includes issue dates and descriptions of section contents.

Supporting Documents

MASTERSPEC full-length, short form, and small project sections include the following documents:

- *Cover.* This document describes the content of the section text, related products, and work, including products that could be inserted into the section if required. It also describes similar work normally specified elsewhere and closely related work specified in other sections. It includes a summary of changes since the last update.
- *Evaluations.* This document describes characteristics and criteria for specifying the products and materials in the section. Also included are editing instructions, which are referenced in editor's notes in the section text; the scope of the section; a description of product characteristics; special design and detailing considerations, if applicable; environmental considerations; referenced standards; suggested reference materials; and a list of manufacturers. The list of manufacturers provides telephone numbers and Web addresses. Tables of comparative information on products and manufacturers are included in some sections.
- *Section text.* This document is presented in CSI/CSC's three-part *SectionFormat* with editor's notes, alternative text, in-line optional text, and insert notes.
- *Drawing coordination checklist.* This document consists of drawing requirements related to the section content. It indicates items that should be shown on the drawings because they are not in the section text.
- *Specification coordination checklist.* This document includes a list of specification sections and requirements that relate to the section content. Small project sections do not currently include this document.

Editing Assistance

MASTERSPEC is a comprehensive master specification system. The evaluations provide editing instructions for each specification section, as well as product comparisons, a list of national manufacturers, reference standards, references, a discussion of the section topic, and graphics, when appropriate. Each section text includes editor's notes with instructions for editing and selecting alternative text, in-line optional text, and insert notes. All section text is displayed for review and editing. Editor's notes and units of measure appear on screen in color. Editor's notes are formatted as hidden text, which allows them to be toggled on or off. Instructions for editing MASTERSPEC are included in the MASTERSPEC user's guide.

Continuing Education

MASTERSPEC A/S/C Library subscribers receive updates that include specification sections to review for AIA/CES learning unit (LU) credits. MASTERSPEC licensed users complete a test covering each reviewed section to receive one LU credit for each section on which the test score is at least 80 percent. Study materials include the section text, evaluations, and other supporting documents. These LU credits fulfill health, safety, and welfare (HSW) requirements.

SPECWARE

SPECWARE® is a family of ARCOM's specification enhancement software, available to MASTERSPEC licensed users to make editing, formatting, and generating reports more efficient and consistent. SPECWARE includes the following:

- *MASTERWORKS*™. This software, which is provided with each MASTERSPEC license, enhances the capabilities of word-processing programs to simplify the editing of alternative text, to select options, to insert required text, and to add project notes. The multifile capabilities automate spell checking, searching and replacing, reporting, creating headers and footers, generating a table of contents, formatting, and other text appearance functions. Specification output formats include project manual, sheet specification, drawing notes, and outline.
- *e-SPECS Linx*™. This automated editor, developed in an ARCOM/InterSpec partnership, is available as add-on software and operates on standard full-length, short form, small project, and outline MASTERSPEC sections that are in a database format. Text elements in each section are linked together hierarchically and semantically. Using a checklist, the user selects applicable product and material requirements. All appropriate text elements are marked for deletion when a parent text element is marked for deletion. If a project has no wood decking, for example, deletion of wood decking in Section 061500/06150 would automatically delete all text related to wood decking in all parts of the section text. This software provides an efficient tool for the easy removal of large quantities of text. e-SPECS Linx also allows a user to manually edit the remaining section text, automate spell checking, search and replace text, create headers and footers, generate a table of contents, and create reports. Project collaboration is enhanced through the use of project notes and a shared

(continued)

PART 3: THE PROJECT

7.2 Construction Documentation **385**

database in which multiple users can edit the specifications at the same time.

- *e-SPECS for AutoCAD* and *e-SPECS for Revit* software, developed by InterSpec, provide the additional capability to extract product and material requirements from CAD drawings and building information models. ARCOM has integrated MASTERSPEC into this software, which allows automatic editing plus better coordination of the drawings and the specifications. Other e-SPECS functions are used to perform final editing and formatting to complete the specifications without exporting or leaving the e-SPECS environment. e-SPECS integrates the entire project team into the specification development process, streamlining the document management process.

Information about MASTERSPEC and ARCOM SPEC-WARE software is available through ARCOM by phone at (800) 424–5080, on its website at www.arcomnet.com, or by e-mail to arcom@arcomnet.com.

7.3 Bidding or Negotiation Phase

William C. Charvat, AIA

The procurement of construction services brings together the team and resources needed to translate building plans into physical reality.

In the bidding/negotiation phase, the architect assists the client in obtaining competent construction bids or negotiating the construction contract. The architect's services in this phase are most often packaged with other services such as design, construction documentation, or construction administration. However, owners will sometimes choose to treat construction procurement as a discrete service. Traditionally, this choice depended on the project, but today the demand for assistance in procuring construction contracts is increasing with the trend toward alternative delivery methods such as construction management and design-build.

Owners are motivated to seek input from the architect in decisions related to construction procurement when they do not have the experience or resources to perform the task in-house or do not wish to devote in-house resources to the task. Large, complex projects may require the owner to contract with a number of different prime contractors, which requires much coordination of the bid packages. Often such projects are on tight time schedules with phased, fast-track work plans, necessitating even greater coordination of the procurement process and a higher level of effort for the construction procurement team.

Construction procurement services require a range of knowledge and skills. Some are developed through practical experience in managing building design and construction and others through previous experience in managing procurement processes. Senior architects with project management experience are most likely to have developed the negotiation skills and the knowledge of construction procedures required to provide advice to the owner with regard to the appropriate procurement and contracting methodology for the project. Most architects possess other, more fundamental skills, including the ability to understand the design intent expressed in construction drawings and specifications and the ability to communicate with vendors and construction contractors.

William C. Charvat, AIA, is executive vice president/chief operating officer of Helman Hurley Charvat Peacock/Architects, Inc., an international architecture, planning, and interior design firm in Maitland, Florida. His practice focuses on project management, construction, and problem solving for large and complex projects.

The increase in construction claims litigation and related trends toward increased control of cost and quality have placed more emphasis on the construction procurement process. Owners want to be reasonably sure that construction contractors are well qualified, their services are obtained for a reasonable cost, and the construction contract minimizes the potential for costly changes and delays. The experienced architect can provide valuable construction procurement advice to the client, but must be mindful of the risk involved.

PREPARATORY STEPS

A decision about the delivery method for a project should be considered no later than the design phase, and ideally prior to signing an agreement with the owner, since the delivery method will affect the professional fees involved. The project delivery approach the owner chooses affects the architect's decision about how project documents will be organized and how construction documents will be developed and packaged. Also, the project team should have staff experienced in the use of the chosen project delivery method. AIA Document B101–2007, Standard Form of Agreement Between Owner and Architect, provides for identification of the construction procurement approach as part of the contract. This allows the architect and the architect's consultants to understand and accept their roles in producing the project deliverables. Each can assist in the timely completion of appropriate, well-coordinated (inter- and intradisciplinary) construction and bidding documents and construction administration communications.

Negotiating vs. Bidding

Time can be saved by eliminating the bid period when a contract is negotiated directly with a preselected contractor. Only a fee and reimbursable expenses are negotiated using AIA Document A102–2007, Agreement Between Owner and Contractor, Cost Plus a Fee with a Guaranteed Maximum Price. This can be done concurrently with completion of the construction documents. The trade contract work for this approach can be set up in a similar fashion. Under this approach, construction work usually does not start until the construction documents are complete.

Another form of negotiated contract for construction involves construction management (CM) services. Here, the construction manager negotiates to establish a fee for preconstruction services as well as CM overhead during construction. AIA Document A131/CMc–2003, Cost Plus a Fee, No Guarantee of Cost, would be used for this approach. Sometimes when using cost-of-work-plus-a-fee, the construction manager's reimbursable expenses are negotiated as a fixed, or not to exceed, amount. Using such a CM approach is different from a cost-of-work approach in the following ways:

- Inclusion of preconstruction services (cost estimating, constructability review, value analysis)
- Trade contracts bid either as lump sum or with guaranteed maximum limits
- Fast-track or phased construction
- Establishment of a guaranteed maximum cost, with final costs falling under this limit being shared with the owner on an agreed-to percentage basis

With a form of negotiated contract or the lump-sum bidding approach, basic services include documenting the construction procurement process, completing the construction documents, and obtaining responsive, reasonable bids or negotiated prices.

Impact of the Delivery Method on Design Fees

Architects are accustomed to quoting fees based on a traditional design-bid-build delivery method in which the architect and consultants produce a single set of construction documents. Design decisions, including those regarding material, systems, and acceptable manufacturers, are incorporated in the documents. The roles of the architect and consultants during construction, established by AIA Documents B101–2007, Standard Form of Agreement Between Owner and Architect, and A201–2007, General Conditions of the Contract for Construction, include making scheduled site visits to report to the owner known deviations from the contract documents and any defects and deficiencies observed in the work.

Using nontraditional procurement approaches with multiple prime contractors, fast-track phased construction, and/or construction managers can save the owner time and money. However, increased architect's fees are often necessary. The architect needs to do a detailed estimate of the required scope of work, identifying deliverables and related fees, so that proper compensation is paid to the architect and the architect's consultants. Additional fees are required for meetings with the contractor/CM; value analysis (VA, including revisions and updates to the drawings to incorporate VA changes); preparation of multiple document packages; multiple bid periods; administration of multiple construction contracts; and the ability to respond to daily questions from the contractors and/or the construction manager in a timely fashion. Additional fees of 2 to 3 percent above traditional design-bid-build fees may be justified. Architects should not underestimate the additional services required for alternative construction delivery methods.

A detailed discussion of construction contract types is found in "Construction Contracts."

Prequalification of Bidders

Prequalification of the bidders is commonly conducted when bidding will be restricted to a selected list of bidders. Investigation of the general reputation, demonstrated ability and quality of performance, financial integrity, and prior project experience of the bidders can help to determine if each bidder is appropriately qualified for a project. However, before undertaking the process, be sure to review applicable laws to ensure it is permitted. For instance, prequalification is usually prohibited for publicly funded projects. Also, to avoid contractor claims of business interference, it is important for the owner, rather than the architect, to make the final decisions relative to contractor prequalification and selection.

Prequalification of contractors is suggested when a closed bid list is being developed and/or to ensure bidders are qualified in open bidding. AIA Document A305–1986, Contractor's Qualification Statement, is used for this purpose.

Preparation of Bidding Documents

Preparation for bidding and negotiation starts with selection of the project delivery approach and structure of the construction contracts that will be awarded. Ideally, each member of the team should have experience with the method of project delivery being used.

Decisions about the structure of the construction contract must be made prior to procurement. These decisions should address such issues as whether to have

- Combined or separate design and construction services. If they are combined (design-build), the construction contract is usually awarded early in project development. Similarly, when the owner wishes to have a contractor or construction manager involved in preconstruction services, those contracts should be in place early in project development.
- Single or multiple contracts. Who will manage multiple contracts?
- Single or multiple bid packages. Multiple packages require more staffing.

- Traditional or fast-track scheduling. This decision affects the timing of numerous owner and contractor activities, as well as material, equipment, and system procurement issues.
- Open competitive bidding or direct solicitation, such as negotiation.

In addition, these issues should be considered:

- What documents will establish the initial contract sum for construction—scope documents, 50 percent construction documents, or some documents at another percentage of completion?
- What role will the design architect have in bidding and construction? Will the owner also hire a construction manager?
- What will the basis of compensation be for the contractor (e.g., lump sum, cost plus fee, guaranteed maximum price, separate fee for preconstruction services)?

Having advised the owner on decisions such as these concerning contracts and bidding, the architect frequently is requested to assemble bidding documents for the owner. A helpful document is AIA Document D200–1995, Project Checklist. The bidding documents describe the project in detail and indicate the conditions under which it will be bid and built. An experienced architect, in coordination with the owner's attorney, will be able to properly assist in the preparation of these documents.

Advertisement for Bids

For public work, the law usually requires placement of an invitation to bid in the classified advertising section of one or more newspapers in the region where the project is located. Additional announcements can be placed in contractor newsletters, magazines, plan rooms, or other media. The ad or announcement should contain, at minimum, the project description, name of the architect, bid date, and information about where bid documents may be reviewed or purchased.

Instructions to Bidders

Use of AIA Document A701–1997, Instructions to Bidders, will establish a consistent understanding of the procedures that bidders should follow in preparing and tendering their bids. The instructions in this document include provisions covering the following:

- Definitions
- Bidder's representations
- Bidding procedures
- Review of bidding documents
- Consideration of bids
- Postbid information
- Performance bond and payment bond
- Form of agreement between owner and contractor

The bidding document package includes these items:

- Instruction to bidders
- Notice to bid
- Form of owner-contractor agreement
- Performance bond
- Labor and material bond
- General and supplementary conditions of the contract
- Special contract conditions
- Drawings and specifications
- Addenda issued prior to the receipt of bids

Bid Form

For most projects, but particularly for open, publicly funded ones, a bid form should be prepared by either the owner or the architect. Use of a project-specific bid form makes it easier for contractors to submit a complete, responsive, and responsible bid.

The form should indicate the project name, bid date, and location where bids are to be received and include space for entering the name of the bidder. Space beside the bidder's name should be provided to record the amount of the bid and any further breakdown of alternates and unit prices. Space for acknowledgment of certificates of insurance, bonds, or other documents (such as certificates regarding prevailing wage standards and other worker employment statute compliance representations required of the contractor) that are required to accompany each sealed bid should also be included. More space may be needed to record additional information required by the instructions to bidders or by the specifications in the project manual. For a contractor's proposal to be considered a qualified bid, it must include all required information, as well as a completed AIA Document A305–1986, Contractor's Qualification Statement.

The bid form ensures that all bids will be submitted in an identical format, which will make the evaluation process easier and help prevent errors in recording multiple base and alternate bid amounts.

Owner-Contractor Agreement Form

The owner-contractor agreement sets forth the respective rights, duties, and obligations of the two parties for the purpose of constructing the project. It may also establish similar conditions for the architect (and possibly a construction manager), who can be retained to administer the construction contract. In addition, it is common for the architect and/or the owner to write supplementary conditions, which cover specific details related to such items as project administrative procedures, bonds, contract time, construction phasing, insurance requirements, site operations, payment procedures, change order markups, and project closeout. It is important for the architect to understand the content, terms, and conditions of the owner-contractor agreement and the general and supplementary conditions. In addition, the owner's legal and insurance counsel should be properly consulted in the development of these contract documents.

Performance Bond

This bond provides a guarantee that if the contractor defaults or fails to perform, the surety will either complete the contract in accordance with its terms or provide sufficient funds up to the penal amount for such completion. A performance bond also protects against default by subcontractors responsible to the general contractor.

Labor and Material Bond

Sometimes referred to as a payment bond, a labor and material bond constitutes a guarantee that subcontractors, material suppliers, and others providing labor, material goods, and services to the project will be paid. It protects the owner from claims against contract balances by unpaid suppliers and subcontractors in the event of the default of the contractor.

Addenda

Review of the bidding documents during the bidding period by prime bidders, sub-bidders, and material suppliers often reveals items that must be clarified, corrected, or explained. Sometimes the owner or architect will initiate revisions to the bidding documents in response to changes of circumstances or requirements. In these circumstances, written addenda, including drawings or other graphic documents, are issued to modify or interpret the bidding documents before bids are received or the contract is executed.

MANAGEMENT AND CONTROL OF THE BIDDING PROCESS

Management, documentation, and equal treatment of all bidders are important during the bid process to avoid any bid protests. A verbal response should not be given to a single bidder. All responses to bidders need to be in writing and sent to all bidders.

Distribution of the Bidding Documents

Web-based communication offers an expanded level of access to bid documents. Before the digital age, local plan rooms and the architect's office were usually the only places contractors could go to see construction drawings. Today, electronic CAD files of the drawings and the project manual can be sent via e-mail to single or multiple reprographic shops where bidders can order copies anywhere in the world. Password-protected project collaboration websites can also receive electronic documents and make them available for bidders to view. With access privileges, a reprographics company can download construction drawings from such websites and publish hard copies for use by local bidders.

In any case, a bidder should have access to at least one complete set of drawings and specifications to properly prepare a fully responsive bid. Traditionally, the cost of that set of documents would be paid for either by the owner, the architect (as a reimbursable expense), or the bidder, depending upon the terms of the owner-architect agreement and bidding documents.

To ensure the return of sets of documents sent to unsuccessful bidders, each bidder can be required to provide a security deposit that would be refunded (in whole or in part) upon the return of the documents in good condition within an established period of time.

Distribution of Addenda and Notices

A master list (AIA Document G804–2001, Register of Bid Documents) should be maintained showing the name, address (e-mail and physical), and telephone and fax numbers of each contractor who has received complete sets of bidding documents. This list may be maintained by the architect or reprographic shop that is distributing the bidding documents, whichever is more practical. The list is used to issue addenda, track returned sets, and refund deposits during and after the bidding phase. Failure to issue addenda to a bidder can result in a bid protest, causing a potentially costly delay in awarding the contract for construction.

Pre-Bid Conference

The goal of the pre-bid conference is to provide bidders with a clear and consistent understanding of the project requirements and scope. Attendance at this meeting is often required to submit a bid proposal.

Receipt of Bids

In the traditional design-bid-build delivery model, bid proposals are only received from general contractors. The instructions to bidders explain how to submit a proposal and may include a requirement or representation that each bidder identify the major subcontractors (e.g., concrete, steel, mechanical, electrical, plumbing) that will be used to do the work.

Bidding Results

Final selection of the contractor is the owner's decision, made with the architect's assistance. When the qualifications and financial background of the bidders have been determined in the prequalification process, the expectation is that the contract will be awarded to the lowest bidder. However, when bidders have not been prequalified, the expectation is that the contract will be awarded to the lowest responsible and responsive bidder. (Public owners may be required by law to accept the lowest responsible bid.)

Errors, Withdrawals, and Revocations

The bidding documents generally establish a date after which bidders cannot withdraw their bid proposal. This date should allow sufficient time after submission of bids for accurate bid evaluation and authorization of an award.

Bid Bond

Some owners require bidders to provide bid security as part of their bid. The bid security can be in the form of cash, a cashier's check, or a bond. Submittal of bid security guarantees that if a bid is accepted within the specified time, usually 30 to 90 days from the opening of the bids, the bidder will enter into a formal agreement with the owner and will furnish the required construction performance and construction payment bonds.

Evaluation of Bids

The architect usually assists the owner in the selection decision by evaluating the bid proposals received. This assistance commonly includes review and recommendations regarding any alternatives and substitutions the owner has solicited. This evaluation takes on special significance if all bids exceed the owner's budget or if acceptance of alternatives changes the order of the low bidders. The owner's options in such cases include increasing the budget, rebidding, renegotiating, revising the scope, or abandoning the project.

Negotiation of Bids

Even in competitive bidding situations, it is not uncommon for some negotiation to take place after bids have been received. Minor changes required before the contract is signed should be negotiated only with the selected bidder, and then only when permitted by the owner or the awarding authority's regulations. In public work, post-bid negotiations must be consistent with state statutes governing such activity.

Rejection of Bids

The owner customarily includes in the bidding documents the right to reject any or all bids.

Notification of Bidders

After the owner has selected the contractor(s), all bidders should be informed of the results as a matter of courtesy.

Contract Award

The architect (in cooperation with the owner, the owner's attorney, and possibly the owner's insurance consultant) prepares a contract reflecting modifications resulting from negotiations and changes. The owner and contractor(s) sign the agreement(s).

Letter of Intent

When the owner wants to move forward immediately before preparing and executing a formal agreement with the contractor, a written letter of intent may be used to give the successful bidder interim authorization to begin work. Such orders to proceed have legal implications and should be drafted by the owner's attorney for the owner's signature.

A letter of intent is also known as a memorandum of understanding or memorandum of agreement. From a business perspective, a letter of intent is a device to indicate that each party has agreed, through serious negotiations, that a formal agreement can be achieved. The letter or memorandum will set forth a timeline for negotiations, including a deadline for closing the deal and what will occur if the parties fail to meet the deadline.

Preconstruction Conference

Following the contract award and prior to the start of construction, a preconstruction conference should be held that is attended by the owner, contractor, major subcontractors, architect, and engineering consultants. The architect's project manager will work closely with the contractor's project manager to develop the conference agenda. The conference will provide everyone involved with an understanding of project procedures, requirements, due dates, and special characteristics. This meeting will encourage a smooth start to the project.

See "Construction Contract Administration" for suggested agenda items for a preconstruction conference.

AVOIDING BIDDING PROBLEMS

The goal of a bid is to establish a price for the project construction. Deficiencies in the bid documents can result in change orders, which can bring financial risk to the architect as well as the owner. Change order pricing is usually higher than bid pricing due to the small quantity of materials involved and the out-of-sequence nature of the work. An excessive number of change orders may result in the owner bringing a claim against the architect for errors and omissions.

Understanding the Bid

Bidding problems directly expand into cost problems for the owner. Incomplete or inaccurate drawings will result in many bidder questions or inclusion of contingencies in the bids to protect the bidders.

It is accepted in the construction industry that the contractor's bid proposal is only for what is shown on the drawings and written in the specifications. Contractors do not provide a cross-checking and coordination service during the bidding period. This is the design team's responsibility.

When contractors prepare a bid, they only take off quantities from one area of the drawings. Since short bid periods do not allow detailed takeoffs of specific quantities for all items, pricing is commonly established by applying trade contractor square-footage guidelines to the design intent indicated in the drawings. As a practical matter, it is not possible for bidders to detect conflicts between disciplines, incomplete details, dimensional problems, or code violations during a bidding period that is typically only four to six weeks long. Individual drawings that appear complete may have problems that can only be detected when they are compared with other drawings to confirm proper coordination.

Bids Based on Insufficient Construction Documents

If project construction drawings are not complete and have not been given interdisciplinary and intradisciplinary reviews, it is advisable to delay the bid submittal date until this has been done. Failure to take this step is likely to increase the need for addenda during the bidding process and result in cost increases and schedule delays once construction is under way.

If a situation arises in which drawings are not complete and coordinated and the bid date cannot be changed, the following suggestions may be helpful:

- Bid the project as a cost-of-work-plus-a-fee contract. Keep the design team working during the bid period so the documents can be completed early in the construction phase.
- Convert the project to a CM, guaranteed maximum price (GMP) contract, where bidding site work and foundation work can be done to start construction. Concurrently complete the documents for trade bidding by the CM for the balance of the work.
- Bid the site work and possibly the foundation work as early bid packages with the right to assign these contracts to a general contractor. Concurrently with this bidding and construction, complete the drawings for the balance of the project. Bid this work with the assignment of the earlier bid contracts for a total project lump-sum price.

When architects use the bidding period as a time to check and coordinate drawings and issue addenda, this disrupts the bidding process and can cause contractors to increase their bids. In these instances, bidders may be forced to include contingencies in their price, since receiving an addendum within one to two weeks of the bid date does not usually allow enough time for contractors to coordinate the affected work with all previously issued bid documents.

Use of Alternates/Substitutions

When an alternate building feature, material, or system is specified in the construction documents, providing only a simple description of the alternate can cause problems. Drawings, details, and complete specifications illustrating use of the alternate should be prepared to properly coordinate it with adjacent work and to make it possible for the bid to cover the complete scope of work. The number and size of alternates can be disruptive to a short bid period. Therefore, their use should be limited here.

Because voluntary alternates can be disruptive, contractors should avoid using them or substitutions during the bidding phase in most instances. However, many owners find them desirable and may allow their use. In such cases, the contractor should predicate the base bid only on what is on the bid documents, with the alternate or substitution priced separately. A complete description of the contractor's alternate or substitution must accompany the separate bid amount. An alternate should not be accepted until a complete and thorough analysis has been done, which may require the architect to clarify details and/or specification to avoid conflicts with the client's program or adjacent work. This work by the architect should be considered an additional service, which the owner may require the contractor to pay for as part of the alternate bid amount.

Managing Addenda

Addenda need to be dated and sequentially numbered. All drawings, details, and specification sections being changed must be carefully referenced to each other. If large changes result in numerous or significant revisions to the drawings, the affected drawings should be reissued. Large, complicated addenda or numerous addenda may require an extension of the bid period. The last addendum should not be issued fewer than seven calendar days before the bid date.

Keeping the Design Team Involved

Once a project is in the bid phase, it is common for staff of the architect and consultant to be assigned to other projects. However, it is essential for the architect's project manager to provide team leadership during this phase. The architecture staff and consultants who prepared the drawings and specifications must be the same people who respond to questions, especially those that result in addenda. Turning the bidding over to the firm's construction administrator, who had no involvement in preparing the bidding documents, leads to inadequate or incomplete answers.

Responding to Bidder Questions

During bidding, all bidder questions should be submitted to the architect in writing. All answers should be issued to all bidders by written addendum. These requirements must be cited in the instructions to bidders. Despite these requirements, however, suppliers, subcontractors, and contractors often call the architect or engineering consultants associated with work they are questioning. Manufacturers and suppliers also routinely call to ask the architect to list a product as an equal or alternate to what is specified. The architect's best response would be "Thank you for the question; please submit it to me in writing and the answer will be covered by an addendum." The architect must also make it clear that if no answer is issued in an addendum, bidders must apply their best judgment in preparing their bid.

Use of Legal and Insurance Consultants

Terms and conditions in the owner-contractor agreement should be developed in conjunction with the owner's attorney and an insurance agent or consultant to make sure all legal and insurance requirements in the agreement are properly addressed. These advisors also need to review the bonds and insurance certificates issued by the contractor as part of the bid and subsequent contract.

THE CONSTRUCTION TEAM

In the construction procurement process, the architect helps the owner identify, select, and engage a qualified contractor and choose an appropriate project delivery method. The selected contractor joins the architect and the owner on the construction team.

For More Information

Section 5.2 of "Module 5: Construction Documents" in *The Project Resource Manual: CSI Manual of Practice* (McGraw-Hill, 2005) addresses requirements for construction procurement and includes samples of bid invitation and bid forms.

"Module 6: Bidding/Negotiating/Purchasing" of *The Project Resource Manual: CSI Manual of Practice* (McGraw-Hill, 2005) addresses practical aspects of construction procurement including pricing considerations, project information, bidding, negotiating, and award of contract.

Chapter 6 in *A Guide to Successful Construction*, 3rd edition (BNI Publications, 1999), by Arthur F. O'Leary, discusses construction procurement including preparation of bid documents, bid openings, and award of contract.

Chapter 11, "Bidding and Contract Negotiation," of the *Emerging Professional's Companion* addresses all aspects of the construction procurement process including document preparation, pre-bid conferences, and conducting bid openings. The chapter also covers practical and legal safeguards and alternative delivery methods.

7.4 Construction Contract Administration

James B. Atkins, FAIA, KIA

The architect's construction phase services are an important part of the construction process, during which time the building design becomes a physical reality. The architect's successful administration of the construction contract can bring benefits to the owner, contractor, and architect.

The architect's duty to administer the contract for construction (CCA services) begins with the award of the construction contract and ends on the date the architect issues the final certificate for payment to the owner. If requested by the owner, CCA services can extend through the expiration of the contractor's one-year warranty period.

AIA Contract Documents delineate the architect's CCA duties, and the architect has authority to act on the owner's behalf only to the extent stated in the owner-architect agreement. Throughout the construction phase, the architect serves as a representative of, as well as an advisor and consultant to, the owner. During the architect's visits to the job site, CCA duties include the following:

- Becoming generally familiar with the work through site visits
- Keeping the owner informed about the progress and quality of the portions of the completed work

Jim Atkins, FAIA, is the founder of Consulting Solutions, a Dallas-based firm providing comprehensive litigation support, owner's representative, and lender and acquisition services throughout the United States. Formerly a principal with HKS Architects, he was responsible for construction services, education, people management, and loss prevention activities. Atkins serves on the AIA Documents and Risk Management committees and chaired the steering group for the 14th edition of the *Architect's Handbook of Professional Practice*. He has authored numerous articles, including project management topics, for *AIArchitect*.

Many states have legislated that projects requiring an architect's or engineer's seal must have CCA services provided by a licensed professional.

For information on project closeouts, see "Project Closeouts."

PROACTIVE VS. REACTIVE CONTRACT ADMINISTRATION

AIA documents require the architect to visit the job site at intervals appropriate to the stage of construction. This leaves it to the discretion of the architect to decide when and how often site visits should be made during the construction phase.

Some architects elect to make visits less frequently, relying on the owner or the contractor to call if a problem or issue arises. This "reactive" approach to contract administration denies the architect opportunities to resolve problems *before* the work is constructed and makes it more difficult for the architect to be fully aware of the overall status of the work as it progresses. For example, when the architect does not attend scheduled site meetings and does not visit the site regularly, change resolution and problem solving may be accomplished without input from the architect.

A "proactive" CCA approach involves initiating steps and measures that can produce greater value for the owner and contractor, as well as for the architect. Such steps and measures include the following:

- Spending adequate time with the owner to build a "trusted advisor" relationship
- Consulting with the contractor and participating in problem resolution and conflicts to influence the final work product
- Making input on scope changes proposed by the owner or the contractor
- Finding opportunities to correct discrepancies or errors or omissions in the contract documents before the work is constructed

The construction phase involves time- and money-induced pressures. To keep your composure while administering the construction contract, keep a professional attitude, look at problems from both sides, and remain calm when dealing with tense situations.

- Reporting observed defects and deficiencies in the work, and deviations from the construction schedule
- Determining in general if the work, when fully completed, will be in accordance with the contract documents

Of course, CCA goes beyond submittal reviews, payment certifications, and field observation reports. Effective project closeouts not only assist owners in obtaining necessary closeout documents and information, they can also leave the owner with positive memories of the architect's services. Following-up with the owner prior to the end of the contractor's one-year warranty is also prudent. Owners appreciate being contacted about the performance of their buildings and to see if corrective actions are needed for warranty issues. Caring about the owner's experiences with the finished project supports professionalism and greatly reinforces the owner-architect relationship, which, among other benefits, could result in positive recommendations to other potential clients.

ACHIEVING PROACTIVE CCA

A proactive approach to CCA can better capture its potential benefits and can help the architect avoid the pitfalls of a reactive, wait-and-see approach. Proactive CCA can be more easily achieved by pursuing the following objectives prior to and during the construction phase.

Including CCA Services in the Agreement with the Owner

CCA services cannot benefit the owner if they are reduced in scope or omitted from the owner-architect agreement by the owner. Therefore, discussions with some owners may be required to help them understand the importance of CCA services.

For example, the quality of building products and systems established in the specifications cannot be effectively monitored without submittal review. On the other hand, if submittal review is included in the architect's scope of work and site visits are not, installation of specified products and systems cannot be monitored through on-site observations. The determination in general if the work is in conformance with the contract documents is an important part of project delivery.

Staying in the Communication Loop and Being a Team Player

The construction process is not solely an owner-contractor event. Frequent discussions between the owner and the architect on scope and aesthetic matters can benefit the project. In addition, the architect participates in and conducts the preconstruction conference and owner-architect-contractor project meetings, which makes it easier for the architect to stay involved in all relevant construction activities. When the contractor comes to view the architect as a resource for resolving issues—which includes providing quick responses— a synergistic and beneficial dynamic is formed.

Maintaining Good Relationships

The construction phase can be challenging, and the pressures of the job can test everyone's self-control. However, much more can be gained through calm and friendly interaction than through hostility. When members of the project team pursue the priority of helping each other, project success can be more easily achieved.

ROLES OF CCA TEAM PARTICIPANTS

Most building design and construction projects include services of the architect and the architect's consultants, the general contractor and the general contractor's subcontractors, the owner's representative and its separate contractors, and special consultants hired by the owner, the architect, or the contractor.

FACTORS AFFECTING THE SCOPE OF CONSTRUCTION PHASE SERVICES

In determining the scope of services for administering the contract on a new project, the architect usually applies historic labor and cost data. However, certain conditions may cause those services to vary from the norm. When estimating fees and labor demands, consider the following factors.

CLIMATE AND WEATHER

Areas with weather conditions such as extreme cold or heat may prevent continuous ongoing construction, and possibly extend total construction time and cause intermittent reassignment of personnel. Areas with heavy seasonal rains can cause acceleration in the dry months to achieve early completion, or they may cause delays in the start of construction to avoid the adverse weather.

REMOTE AND FOREIGN LOCATIONS

Remote locations such as islands may require importing all construction materials in containers. Submittal review must be done before materials are shipped, and time must be allowed to clear customs upon arrival. In most foreign countries, U.S. architects usually cannot legally provide architect-of-record services. Services such as document publication, payment certification, and substantial completion may be deleted from the architect's services and provided by a local architect.

ECONOMIC FACTORS

An inflating economy can cause an increase in work activity, resulting in staffing shortages and limited product availability. The cost of labor and materials increases can cause budget challenges that drive value analysis and substitution efforts in a quest for cheaper materials and systems. As a result, schedules may be protracted, and submittal review and change process activities may increase. A recessive economy increases competition for work, often resulting in unreasonably low bids with low

contingency and general conditions amounts and minimum profit margins. The substitution process is frequently used as a vehicle for recovering costs through cheaper materials. As a result, submittal review and RFI activity may increase.

PROJECT DELIVERY APPROACH

In contractor-led design-build projects, many of the architect's duties to the owner shift to the contractor. Payment certification services may not be required, and substantial completion may involve additional participants. Submittal review may become more interactive with the contractor, and the RFI process may be more active. When construction manager-advisors, program managers, and contracted owner's representatives are involved, this can add an extra step in many construction phase procedures. Integrated project delivery approaches with the project team using real-time file-sharing could increase or decrease CCA time requirements, depending on the specific interaction of the owner and the contractor. Management of meetings may be more difficult, but submittal reviews, the RFI process, and the change order process may become less demanding due to interactive participation. Multiple prime contracts tend to require additional CCA time due to the lack of a general contractor who controls all of the work.

MULTIPLE DESIGN CONTRACTS

Projects with multiple design contracts can affect payment certification, especially if there is a single contractor who submits one application for payment. The change order process could become more complicated as well, especially if a change affects the work of more than one designer.

SCHEDULING APPROACHES

The overlapping phases of fast-track scheduling could require additional time for submittal reviews, change

(continued)

PART 3: THE PROJECT

order and RFI processing, site observation, and the determination of substantial completion due to revisions made later in the project.

RENOVATION PROJECTS

Renovation work or building additions can affect CCA services, especially if the existing facility is occupied or there is limited access to the site. These situations may require additional site observations, additional payment application reviews, and multiple inspections for substantial completion. Buildings that must be occupied during renovation may also require the work to be done at designated times such as at night, on weekends, or during specific hours of the day.

- *Architect.* Unless all services are provided in-house, the architect typically engages consultants for the structural, mechanical, electrical and plumbing, and other specialized portions of the work.
- *Contractor.* The general contractor contracts with subcontractors for portions of the work that it cannot provide with its own workforce.
- *Owner.* The owner sometimes retains an "owner's representative" to assist in administering the owner's contracted obligations. A construction manager, program manager, or another architect or engineer may provide this service. The owner may also have contracts with separate contractors to do interior finishing work or specialty construction not typically provided by a general contractor.

TABLE 7.4 The Architect's Construction Phase Activities		
Activities	**Representative Tasks**	**Documentation**
For preconstruction conference	Establish administrative procedures. Review contractor schedules. Review general contactor requirements. Review schedule of values. Review quality control procedures. Review allowances/contingencies. Review bond requirements.	Administrative procedures manual
During construction	Conduct scheduled visits. Participate in project meetings. Issue site observation reports. Send/answer RFIs. Review contractor submittals. Review value analysis/substitutions. Prepare change orders. Review applications for payment. Issue work changes proposals. Monitor allowances. Monitor contingencies. Monitor progress and quality of work. Approve minor changes. Review testing and inspection reports. Cooperate with owner consultants. Review change orders.	Site observation reports Change orders Change directives Supplemental instructions Certificates for payment Action item lists Logs
At substantial completion	Inspect project for substantial completion. Review contractor punch lists. Prepare certificate of substantial completion. Qualify owner-accepted nonconforming work. Monitor equipment start-up and commissioning.	Punch lists Certificate of substantial completion
For closeout conference	Review closeout documents. Review record documents.	Closeout lists
At final completion	Receive contractor notice of final completion. Inspect project for final completion. Review final closeout documents. Review final application for payment. Write final change order.	Record drawings for owner Closeout documents Final closeout and final application for payment to owner
For contractor warranty	Review compliance completion items (if requested by owner).	Letter to general contractor citing warranty corrections required
During follow-up review	Review warranty items to be completed or corrected prior to end of warranty (if requested by owner).	List of outstanding warranty items to owner

- *Special consultants.* These can include services for quality control testing of materials and the inspection of structural systems. Some states require special inspectors such as the "inspector of record" (California) and the "threshold inspector" (Florida). States require these services in an effort to maintain a higher level of project quality control. Special consultants are sometimes retained to design and engineer special design elements and other critical building components such as roofing and curtain wall systems.

The roles of the owner, architect, and contractor during construction are complementary and interactive. While the architect is contractually obligated to the owner and not to the contractor, AIA Document A201–2007, General Conditions of the Contract for Construction, requires the architect to maintain a neutral position when rendering interpretations concerning the owner's decisions or the contractor's performance.

> Architects in smaller firms frequently have multiple responsibilities and roles, and keeping up with construction phase activities while tending to other duties can be challenging. However, pursuing suggestions covered in this topic can be helpful to architects in firms of all sizes.

Although the architect approves submittals illustrating the contractor's work plan and final installation details, the architect cannot stop the work or independently order changes in the work that change the contract sum or contract time. However, the architect can reject work that does not conform to the contract documents.

The contractor's primary role is to supervise and direct the work. The contractor is solely responsible for and has control over means, methods, techniques, sequences, and procedures, and for coordinating all work under the contract, unless designated otherwise in the construction contract. The contractor is also solely responsible for job site safety.

The AIA general conditions require that the contractor provide an express warranty to the owner and the architect that materials and equipment furnished under the contract will be of good quality and new, that the work will be free from defects not inherent in the quality required, and that the work will conform to the requirements of the contract documents.

> The architect is required to endeavor to secure faithful performance by both owner and contractor and not to show partiality to either.

This warranty of performance and conformance supersedes the actions of the architect, including any observations, inspections, submittal reviews, or certifications; those actions are all expressly qualified in the construction contract so as not to relieve the contractor of its obligation to perform the work in accordance with the contract documents. Moreover, the AIA documents clearly state the architect will not be responsible for the contractor's failure to perform the work in accordance with the requirements of the contract documents. This includes defective work not observed or discovered during the architect's scheduled site observations.

The contractor provides two other warranties in the contractor's application for payment. The first states that title to all work covered by an application for payment will pass to the owner no later than the time of payment. The second states that all work for which certificates for payment have previously been issued and payments received shall be free and clear of liens, claims, security interests, or encumbrances. The bottom line is that the contractor is contractually responsible for the completed work regardless of whether the owner or the architect has approved or failed to observe any nonconforming work.

The owner's role during the construction phase is to furnish descriptive information such as surveys, utility locations, and a legal description of the property. The owner can also stop the work, and should the contractor fail to perform under the contract, the owner can take over and carry out the work. The owner must make payment upon receipt of the architect's certificate for payment within the time stipulated in the contract documents.

Table 7.5 illustrates the decision-making responsibilities of the owner, architect, and contractor.

Owner	Architect	Contractor	Items to Be Approved
•	•		Construction change directives
•	•	•	Change orders
•	•	•	Work conformance
•	•		Nonconforming work
	•	•	Submittals
	•	•	Application and certificate for payment
•			Special testing
	•		Minor no-cost changes
•	•		Substitutions
	•		Substantial completion
	•		Final completion

TABLE 7.5 Project Authority Matrix

• Denotes approval

COMMUNICATIONS IN THE CONSTRUCTION PHASE

Communication is vital for the successful completion of construction phase services. Project team members who communicate well with each other can detect and resolve problems much earlier and much faster. The communications protocol specified in AIA documents requires the owner and contractor to endeavor to communicate with each other through the architect.

Communications by and with consultants and subcontractors should occur as follows:

- Architect's consultants: through the architect
- Subcontractors and material suppliers: through the contractor
- Owner's contractors: through the owner

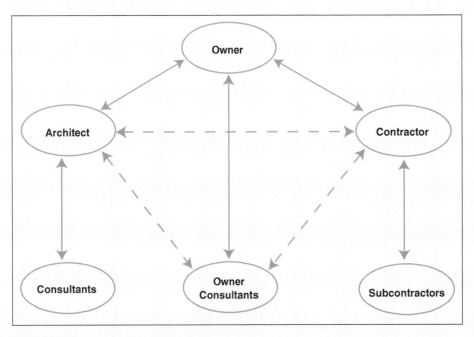

FIGURE 7.3 Communications Flow During Construction

Aggressive schedules and high levels of work coordination associated with construction work can make the architect's CCA activities challenging. By accomplishing the tasks described below, the architect can be better prepared to meet the demands of this challenge.

Review Project Agreements and Documents

The construction contract administrator should assemble sets of drawings and specifications (one for the office and one for use on the project site) and a copy of the owner-architect agreement. After obtaining a copy of the owner-contractor agreement from the owner, the construction administrator reviews this document to identify any conditions that vary from standard AIA language, and to note any atypical conditions. The owner should be advised of conditions or requirements that are or appear to be in conflict with the owner-architect agreement, especially if they prevent the execution of the architect's duties.

See "Owner-Generated Agreements" for advice and guidance on dealing with owner-architect agreements developed by the client.

Set Up the Project Database

A project database is useful for managing the processes and documents associated with the construction phase, and numerous software products on the market are suitable for this purpose. It is important to set up the database in a manner that is not biased against any team member. When the contractor purchases the software, it is often set up to track only the architect's response time on activities such as submittal reviews. Take the initiative and have the software programmed to also track the contractor's response time on activities such as work change proposal requests. As a project tool, the database should benefit all team members equally.

Update the Project Directory

The project directory should be periodically updated to include new team members, such as the contractor's personnel or the owner's consultants. If the project management software is capable, it can be programmed with the project directory to facilitate document distributions to specific team members.

Verify Team Assignments

When construction begins, some members of the team may be assigned to other projects, while others may remain. This is a good time to get everyone together and discuss CCA roles and responsibilities. A project under construction will likely need team members to review designated submittals that are unique to the project. Team members may also need to support the construction contract administrator in scheduled project meetings and to review the work in progress. When construction begins and the pace quickens, team responsibilities should be assigned and understood.

Meet with Consultants

Meet with your consultants *prior* to the start of construction to discuss their roles and to prepare for the preconstruction conference. Issues such as scheduled site visits, site observation report format, project communication protocols, and submittal procedures are among the topics to discuss. Details that can be worked out prior to the start of construction lessen the load when the dirt starts to fly and paper begins to move.

AIA Document G612, Owner's Instructions to the Architect Regarding the Construction Contract, Insurance and Bonds, and Bidding Procedures, is useful to the architect during the construction phase. It includes information about insurance and bonds, conditions for releasing retainage funds, and other relevant information.

Issue the Notice to Proceed

Construction work typically begins with the notice to proceed. The notice can be given in a variety of ways, but typically it is a letter directing the contractor to begin the

SAMPLE NOTICE TO PROCEED LETTER

ACE ARCHITECTS

Mr. John Franklin
Millennium Builders
4221 Main Street
Lincoln, Nebraska 24319
Project name: Catenville Place
Project number: 97006RE: NOTICE TO PROCEED
Dear Mr. Franklin:

The owners, Frontier Developers, have directed me to send this NOTICE TO PROCEED on the referenced project. You are hereby authorized by the owner to proceed with the work of your contract for the construction of Catenville Place. In accordance with your contract with Frontier Developers dated April 15, 2007, you have agreed to complete the contract as stated below.

Contract amount:	$22,860,562
Construction time:	401 calendar days
Start date:	May 15, 2007
Contract completion date:	July 20, 2008

Best Regards,
John H. Williams, AIA
Principal
cc: Bill Easy, Frontier Developers

SAMPLE PRECONSTRUCTION CONFERENCE AGENDA

I. Introductions
II. Project start-up requirements
   A. List of subcontractors and material suppliers
   B. Schedule of values
   C. Construction schedules
   D. Submittal schedule
   E. Site usage
   F. Quality control
III. Bonds and insurance
   A. Bonding
   B. Insurance
IV. Project procedures
   A. Correspondence
   B. Shop drawings, product data, and samples
   C. Pay applications
   D. Changes in the work
   E. Requests for information
   F. Time extensions
   G. Closeout
V. Site observations
   A. Scheduled visits
   B. Reporting
VI. Miscellaneous items
   A. Separate contracts by owners
   B. Partial occupancy
   C. Field office
   D. Project sign or banner
   E. Owner requirement for certifications

work. If initiated by the architect, the notice to proceed should be sent on behalf of the owner and at the owner's direction. The architect does not have the authority to direct the work to proceed.

Conduct Preconstruction Conference

The preconstruction conference is one of the most—if not the most—important meetings during the construction phase. This is the time when construction phase project participants meet and get to know each other, and when project procedures for the construction phase are agreed upon. Effective planning prior to the construction work start-up allows for less confusion and lack of coordination after construction begins.

CCA ACTIVITIES DURING CONSTRUCTION

CCA duties during the actual construction of the project include administering change order documents, reviewing submittals, providing supplemental instructions and information, solving problems, reviewing payment applications and stored materials, and appropriately conducting and reporting site visits and on-site observations.

Managing Changes in the Work

It is rare for a project to be constructed without a change in the work. Whether driven by design or by necessity, changes are typically a major part of the construction phase. The design team may cause changes when incorporating what it considers to be "minor touch-ups" to the issued construction drawings. Owners may institute changes as they reexamine their program requirements or when they do not like some aspect of the finished work. Other changes arise due to actual site conditions that are different from those the contractor could have expected from reviewing the contract documents.

After the execution of the owner-contractor agreement, changes in the work can be initiated by change orders, construction change directives, or by minor change instructions. A change order requires the signatures of the owner, the architect, and the contractor. A construction change directive requires the agreement of the owner and architect and may or may not be agreed to by the contractor. The architect may issue an order for a minor change without other signatures; however, it cannot change the contract sum or the construction schedule. If it is subsequently determined that the architect's instructions changed the contract sum or time, a change order will be required to properly document the scope of the revision.

Changes initiated by the contractor. The contractor can change the work by proposing substitutions during the process of "value analysis," or "value engineering." While some owners request value analysis proposals along with the construction bid, many contractors propose substitutions in an effort to convince the owner they can build the project for less money.

Changes due to nonconforming work. Other changes may occur when the contractor does not build in accordance with the contract documents. This is a common occurrence because construction is not an exact science, and the marriage of building materials and systems during the construction process often yields variations. The architect must determine if the finished work conforms closely enough to the design concept expressed in the documents.

If they wish, owners may choose to accept nonconforming work. Usually, when work is in place and can function, owners tend to want to accept it. However, the owner should not accept nonconforming work without receiving a credit to the contract sum. Because the acceptance of nonconforming work usually represents a change to the contract, any credit must be formalized in an appropriately negotiated change order. The credit may then be processed in the next payment application.

Changes due to errors/omissions. When discovered, errors or omissions in the architect's documents can prompt changes in the work. If the corrective revision changes the project scope, the contractor may be entitled to more money. If the discrepancy is discovered after the work is in place, remediation costs are typically many times greater. Architects strive to produce complete documents before the contract sum is established, but perfection is not always possible and is not required under the legal negligence standard governing the architect's performance. Including CCA services in your contract provides an additional opportunity to find discrepancies before the work is constructed.

Value analysis–induced changes. Value analysis (or value engineering) can be another source for project changes. By definition, value analysis proposals are intended to increase the value of the project. Ideally, this can be accomplished by finding a product or system of higher quality without a cost increase or by finding a product or system of equal quality for less cost. The reality is that you usually get what you pay for, and a product or system of lesser cost may be of lesser quality.

In the value analysis process, owners often expect that the product or system proposed will have the same value as the product or system originally specified. The architect should make efforts to help the owner understand the impact of the substituted item and develop a reasonable expectation of what compromises may be involved. For example, a chiller of lesser cost may have a shorter lifecycle or require a higher level of maintenance. Cheaper exterior building materials may have to be repainted or recaulked sooner.

See the AIA Contract Documents synopses in Chapter 12.2 for information on the various types of AIA documents available and their intended use.

Value analysis proposals that are accepted should be administered as substitutions. However, proposing, reviewing, accepting, and incorporating substitutions into the project take time and effort. Typically, therefore, substitutions are only proposed if they benefit the project in some way—either by lowering the cost or shortening construction time. The specifications set forth the quality of the products to be used in the construction of the work, and acceptable manufacturers are listed under the condition that their product meets the requirements of the specifications. The contractor may propose substituting a product not listed in the specifications, but only the owner can approve substitutions, after the architect evaluates them and gives a recommendation. The Construction Specifications Institute provides two forms for this process: CSI Form 13.1A, Substitution Request Form, and CSI Form 20.3, Substitution Request Checklist.

Product substitutions. Specifications prepared by an architect often reflect years of experience and the observance of product performance. When the architect is unfamiliar with a proposed substitute, caution is advised in accepting it. Because they represent a change to the contract documents, substitutions should be added to the contract by a contract modification, as required by the general conditions.

If a product is added to the contract by a contract modification, the architect could, under certain circumstances, be held responsible for its performance as if it had been

See Chapter 12.2 for AIA documents available for administering changes in the work.

specified originally. However, the architect is obligated by its contract to issue change orders and other modifications, and should not try to avoid that duty. For that reason, if the owner accepts a substitution the architect does not recommend, the architect should clarify its position in a letter to the owner and indicate on the face of the modification that the architect does not support or accept responsibility for the performance of the substitution. Such notations will not affect the enforceability of the modification, and—if the modification includes any change in the contract sum or contract time—will formalize those changes to the contract.

Managing Submittals

Submittals include detailed drawings (referred to as "shop drawings") prepared by the contractor, detailed information or data from the product manufacturer, and physical product samples. These submittals serve to illustrate in detail how the contractor plans to construct the work. Until the architect reviews and approves a submittal, the contractor is prohibited by contract from performing portions of the work associated with the submittal.

In submittal reviews, the architect does not verify or determine detailed information such as dimensions, fastening methods, or material gauges. Rather, reviews are made only for the purpose of checking for conformance with the information included in the contract documents. The submittal approval process should be a topic on the preconstruction conference agenda, and the process should be thoroughly discussed, including the required contractual obligations of the team members.

In the event project services are questioned, the architect must be able to easily reference and cite how owner-contractor agreements and owner-architect agreements are applied and used. Chapter 12 addresses AIA agreements and explains their use.

A201–2007 requires that the contractor provide a submittal schedule that is coordinated with the project construction schedule. The architect should review the submittal schedule to determine if it includes the sequence of submitted items and the allotted review times. For example, doors, hollow metal door frames, and door hardware should be submitted together to allow for proper coordination. It is also important to verify that all required submittals have been included in the schedule.

MASTERSPEC Section 013300, Submittal Procedures, identifies "action submittals" and "informational submittals" as two submittal types. Action submittals require the approval of the architect, and informational submittals do not. The purpose of receiving them is for the architect to determine if the contractor has met the contracted submittal requirements. Informational submittals, also referenced in A201, can include coordination drawings and contractor-provided engineering calculations.

The architect's contract requires it to take action in reviewing submittals in accordance with the approved submittal schedule, or if there isn't an approved schedule, with reasonable promptness. The contractor is also required to take action on submittals in accordance with the approved schedule.

Allotting review times. Owners sometimes attempt to negotiate short review times in the owner-architect agreement with the notion that it will somehow accelerate project completion. Thus, it is important that architects exercise professional judgment regarding review time. An acceptable minimum review time could be as brief as 10 business days after receipt. Some submittal reviews take longer, and if the owner attempts to fix the review time in the contract to a maximum number of days, it is wise to designate the contracted number as an average. This way, the contractor and architect can establish the submittal schedule to allow for less time on less complicated submittals and more time for more complicated ones, while maintaining the "average" review time.

Tracking of submittals. Each submittal should be stamped with the date received, and a letter of transmittal should accompany each submittal sent to another party. Letters of transmittal are important because they document a description of the items sent, the quantity, identifying control numbers, titles, and dates.

Submittals should be recorded in a submittal log. This can be done using AIA Document G712–1972, Shop Drawing and Sample Record, or in a data management system (a variety of software programs are available for this purpose). If the contractor purchases data management software as a job cost item, the contractor can dictate how the data is tracked. In such situations, it is important to communicate to the contractor how you wish the information to be reported. For example, it should indicate the amount of time that all parties, including the contractor, have to process data.

Each submittal should have its own unique control number. A popular system includes the specification number for cross-reference. For example, the first submittal of a shop drawing for metal stairs, which is specified in specifications section 055100, Metal Pan Stairs, would be numbered 055100–01A. This represents the first review of the first submittal in section 055100. The second review would be numbered 055100–01B, and a second submittal from that section would be numbered 055100–02A. Since the submittal number is referenced with the specification section, this system enables quick access to relevant project information if a problem is encountered during building operation.

Review of submittals. AIA documents require the general contractor to review each submittal *prior to submission* to the architect. This is necessary for the contractor to coordinate the work of the construction trades and to fulfill their work plan. Should the contractor choose to accept a submittal that varies from the contract documents, the contractor is required to provide notations in the submittal advising the architect of the deviations. Upon receipt of the submittal, the architect should stamp it received and check to determine that

- The submittal is required by the contract documents.
- A control number is correctly affixed.
- The required routing to a consultant for primary review is indicated.

The architect then proceeds to review submittals in a timely manner, in accordance with the approved submittal schedule. Shop drawings found to be unacceptable must be marked "revise and resubmit" and returned to the contractor. Keep in mind that time can be saved if a subsequent review can be avoided. Adding notations to the submittal with the stamp "approved as noted" can allow the contractor to proceed without resubmitting before construction is begun.

Architects should avoid reviewing submittals that are the responsibility of other design professionals. If the submittal is not in the architect's contract, return it without review. Should the submittal include the work of another contractor, highlight the area and note "not reviewed."

Related issues. In addition to tracking submittal timing and actions taken, it is important to determine if all required submittals have been provided. Equally important is determining if any submitted shop drawings are *not* required. These submittals should be returned without review. There is no need to take time to review submittals that are not part of the contract, and the architect should not review certain types of submittals, such as crane support details, earth retention designs, and temporary handrail safety cables, as those involve construction means and methods and safety procedures for which the contractor is solely responsible under the construction contract.

The fast pace of the workplace today often demands that documents be transmitted as quickly as possible. For this reason, you may choose to allow the contractor to simultaneously submit shop drawings to you, the appropriate consultant, and special consultants or owner's representatives. It is important, however, that such submittals be routed through the architect on their return to the contractor. This is to allow you to review notations from the contractor and consultant, and to check for architectural items included in the submittal that are your responsibility.

While submittals have traditionally been in paper format, electronic submittals are becoming more common. However, sufficient paper documentation of review actions should be maintained. If reviewing digital copies, you should return them in files that cannot be manipulated, such as PDFs or TIFFs.

Responding to Information Needs

Construction documents are typically not an exhaustive set of instructions on how to construct the building. It is therefore important to remember that in the construction phase, the architect can provide supplemental information by responding to requests for information (RFIs) or by issuing Architect's Supplemental Instructions.

The RFI form first appeared in the 1970s as a means for contractors to document questions for design professionals. RFIs were logged, tracked, and used to document time taken for the design professionals to answer questions or to produce drawing clarifications. Today, the RFI is a popular vehicle used by some contractors to allege that the architect's construction documentation is deficient.

> The architect's construction documentation sets forth in detail the requirements for the construction work. To carry out the construction, the contractor provides additional information, including shop drawings, product data, samples, and other similar submittals.

The reality is that all parties involved in the construction phase need information. The contractor needs interpretations from the architect, who needs submittal schedules, construction schedules, bond information, and shop drawing submittals from the contractor. The owner needs information from both the contractor and the architect. To meet these needs, the AIA published AIA Document G716–2004, Request for Information. Any team member can send this generic document to another team member. For example, the architect may wish to send an RFI to the contractor requesting the submittal schedule. The architect would log and track its own RFIs in the same way it does the contractor's RFIs.

AIA Document G710–1992, Architect's Supplemental Instructions, is used by the architect to order and record a change in the contract scope that does not affect the contract sum or contract time. It is another form of clarification of the scope that is executed in the process of communicating the design to the contractor.

Problem Solving

Identifying and resolving problematic issues are a valuable part of the construction phase. An important objective here is to identify and resolve a problem before the work is put in place. In the role of construction administrator, the architect uses problem-solving skills to resolve such issues. The following steps are suggested to resolve a problem.

- *Identify the problem.* Resolution cannot begin until the full scope of the problem has been identified. Take time to document your findings.
- *Analyze the problem.* Research and evaluate what has caused the problem. Gather information from all parties involved. Examine the documents and the construction process to determine how the problem can be avoided in the future.
- *Seek consultation.* Discuss the problem with qualified resources if necessary.
- *Identify solution options.* Review the ways to remedy the problem. Make use of available resources in-house, from the contractor, and from manufacturers.
- *Evaluate solution options.* Prioritize the options for resolution. Determine which option presents the best solution to the problems and offers the best benefit to the project.
- *Make a decision.* Decide which option is most beneficial and go with it!
- *Inform the team.* Communicate the chosen solution to the project team.
- *Implement the solution.* Move quickly to implement the solution to the problem. Complete necessary documentation to allow the contractor to proceed.

Site Visits

The architect visits the project site during the construction phase to determine in general if the completed work is installed in accordance with the construction documentation, to report observed defects and deficiencies to the owner, and to monitor and record the general progress of the work. The architect cannot physically be, and is not required to be, in all places at all times. Hundreds, and perhaps thousands, of work activities are occurring on the project simultaneously. Thus the architect may not be able to observe and report all defects and deficiencies in the work. A full-time project representative can do more observations, but likewise cannot physically see all work activities, observe all completed work, or discover all defects and discrepancies.

The design professional determines the number and frequency of site visits as well as when they are appropriate. Obviously, smaller, less complicated projects may require fewer site visits than larger, more complicated projects. For very large projects, a team of design professionals may sometimes reside on the site full-time.

A visit to the site typically presents opportunities to do more than observe the work in progress. Visits can encompass a walk with the contractor to discuss the progress and quality of the work, the scheduled project meeting, payment application reviews, observation of stored materials, and most importantly, time spent with the owner discussing the work and advising on owner decisions.

Adequate preparation helps the architect capture the most benefits from site visits. For example, it can be helpful to discuss unique design conditions with the project team prior to the site visit and to bring a digital camera to record job progress. Having an updated set of drawings during site visits is useful. However, on larger projects with larger quantities of drawings, you may wish to carry just the construction drawings or shop drawings for a specific area that you plan to visit. If the contractor has prepared coordination drawings or clarification sketches, they may come in handy as well.

The best means for documenting a site visit is in a site observation report, which the architect and design consultants issue for each visit. AIA Document G711–1992, Architect's Field Observation Report, is available for this purpose. Digital photo images of completed work may be embedded in the form using the AIA Contract Documents software. Be careful, however, to determine that any nonconforming work discernible in the image is appropriately noted.

Site observation reports should accurately reflect the status of the work, and care should be taken in word usage. For example, the architect may observe a masonry wall that appears to be complete. If the architect reports "the masonry is complete" and there is uncompleted masonry elsewhere on the project, the statement could lead to an erroneous conclusion by the reader. It is more prudent to use words like "the masonry in location X appears to be complete" to avoid a misrepresentation.

Site observation reports should be dated, sequentially numbered, and distributed to the appropriate parties. This typically includes the owner, the contractor, and the architect's consultants, but may also include a separate contractor or a special consultant, as requested by the owner.

Project Meetings

When a project meeting is scheduled, the agenda should be distributed in advance when possible. A popular agenda format is the "action item" report format, which lists numbered topics that are carried over from meeting to meeting until they are resolved. The meeting report not only serves as an agenda for the next meeting, but it also provides the attendees with an action item list for their assigned responsibilities.

Either the architect or the contractor can conduct project meetings. Those in attendance should review minutes carefully to verify content accuracy and to respond to assigned action items.

Payment Applications and Certifications

To get paid for their work, contractors submit applications for payment to the architect. AIA Document G702–1992, Application and Certificate for Payment, is a dual form that also includes the architect's certification for payment. AIA Document G703–1992, Continuation Sheet, can be used to list the scheduled values for the work. After comparing the contractor's representations in the application for payment with the completed work and stored materials observed, the architect certifies the amount that

ACE ARCHITECTS

MEETING REPORT
DATE OF MEETING: October 23, 2007
DATE OF ISSUE: October 25, 2007
PROJECT: **Catenville Place**

Project No.   97006

PRESENT: Representing **Frontier Developers (FD)**

Mr. Bill Easy

Representing **Ace Architects (AA)**

Mr. John H. Williams

Representing **Millennium Builders (MB)**

Mr. John Franklin

Representing **Default Mechanical (DM)**

Artie Millsap

LOCATION: Ace Architects

PURPOSE: Project Meeting No. 48

DISCUSSION:

Item No.	Discussion	Action Required By
I.	MAIN BUILDING	
	A. Chiller Sequence	
	The owner has requested a sequence change to allow continuous operation of the system during maintenance operations where the main chillers are offline and the system is run by chiller #4. Default Mechanical will submit recommended sequence changes for review.	DM AA
	B. Handicap Toilet Vanities	
	MM will replaced the toilet room vanities in the North Building with stone countertops as directed by the owner. AA and FD are to select the stone color.	AA FD
	C. Kitchen Makeup Air Diffusers	
	At the owner's request (CW), the general contractor has replaced the egg crate diffusers in the kitchen areas with a perforated type diffuser.	Closed

END OF MEETING

This report is assumed to be a true and accurate account of this meeting, unless written notification to the contrary is received within ten (10) working days of the date of issue of this report.

Respectfully Submitted,
John H. Williams

John H. Williams, AIA
Principal

cc: All present

FIGURE 7.4 **Sample Action Item Meeting Report**

he or she believes to be appropriate. The architect then sends the application and certificate for payment to the owner, who makes payment to the contractor.

Application processing. The contractor's application for payment, which includes work by its subcontractors and suppliers, can take substantial time to process. When the contractor receives payment, it distributes funds to subcontractors, who may distribute to sub-subcontractors, who may send payment to suppliers, who may then pay manufacturers. Payment processing, therefore, should be a priority, and contractual time requirements for payment processing should be discussed in the preconstruction conference.

The architect can make processing of the application for payment more efficient by timing site visits to allow for observation of the work in place just before the contractor submits the application for payment. This usually can be accomplished with monthly site visits. While walking the site with the contractor and reviewing a "pencil" copy of the payment application, the architect and contractor can agree on the amount, and the pencil copy can be revised accordingly. The final application copy is prepared from the pencil copy, and when it is sent to the architect, it can be approved quickly and sent on to the owner for payment.

Stored materials. Materials required for the work must be stored either on- or off-site until they can be incorporated into the work. Applications for payment typically include a list of stored materials. Off-site storage must be approved by the owner, and the location should be in a bonded warehouse or secured by other acceptable means. The application allows for payment for the stored materials. Therefore, it may sometimes be necessary for the construction contract administrator to visit off-site locations to observe the materials and confirm delivery. The architect should allow sufficient time for this, and the contractor should make adequate preparations for reviewing stored materials listed in the contractor's application for payment and confirming that bonding or other contract requirements have been met.

Representations of the work. The AIA Application and Certificate for Payment contains a representation by the contractor that the work addressed in the application has been completed in accordance with the contract documents, that all previous amounts paid have been appropriately distributed to the subcontractors, and that the current payment is due. This representation is signed and notarized, if required, by the contractor. The application for payment is further supported by the contractor's warranty to the owner and architect that the materials and equipment furnished under the contract are new, that the work is free from defects, and that it conforms to the requirements of the contract documents. This express warranty that the application is correct and the work is actually in place gives assurance to the owner that it can make payment in good faith.

As stated previously, AIA G702, Application and Certificate for Payment, also contains the architect's certificate for payment. This certification is a representation by the architect that the work has progressed as indicated, that the quality of the work is in accordance with the contract documents, and that the contractor is entitled to the amount certified. This certification is based on site observations and the data included in the application, and is made to the best of the architect's knowledge, information, and belief. The AIA general conditions provide that payment cannot be made without the architect's signed certification, and that the owner must pay the amount the architect certifies.

Related payment information. In addition to the amount applied for payment, AIA Document G702–1992 includes a change order summary, the amount of retainage for both the work in place and stored materials, and the "balance-to-finish" amount, including retainage. The balance-to-finish figure helps the architect evaluate whether there are sufficient funds to complete the work. For example, if the project is delayed or the contractor has underbid the work, the funds remaining in the contract sum may be insufficient to complete the construction, and thus the architect cannot certify the application for payment. In fact, if the amount required to complete the work exceeds the contract balance including the current application amount, the architect may have to nullify a previous certification for payment.

Whenever it is determined that funds are insufficient to complete a project, a meeting should be called with the owner and contractor to discuss the actions required for the contractor to complete the work. Certification of the contractor's application for payment is a serious matter, and care should be taken to be fair and reasonable.

When the general contractor is providing work under more than one contract with the owner, multiple contractor applications for payment could be reflected in a single application for payment. If this should occur, care should be taken not to certify work not covered by the architect's contract. The architect should only certify payment for work that is included in the architect's scope of work.

When multiple contracts are included in the payment application, discuss this matter with the owner and contractor, and have the contractor submit a separate application for payment for each design contract. If not desired by the owner, an alternative approach is to have the contractor break out the scheduled values and applied amounts on the form and to add multiple certification signature lines on additional pages. The architect's certification should include a specific cost amount that applies only to the contracted scope.

> The architect makes "observations" during scheduled site visits but makes only two "inspections"—to determine substantial and final completion toward the end of the project. The word "inspection" connotes a more thorough review and evaluation of the observed work.

Substantial Completion

When the work, or a designated portion, is sufficiently complete for the owner to occupy or use for its intended purpose, the project is considered substantially complete. This may not involve final occupancy, as in the case of shell construction with a separate contract for tenant finish-out. Building utilization requirements should be considered when determining substantial completion.

Advance preparation makes the process of substantial completion run more efficiently and smoothly. A list of items still to be completed or corrected, also known as the "punch list," is required from the contractor before the architect determines substantial completion and issues the certificate. Due to the contractor's conflict of interest, the architect sometimes assists in preparing the punch list. However, if the architect prepares the list, it does not relieve the contractor of responsibility for any items not included.

Before preparing the punch list, it can be helpful to walk the project with the owner and contractor to discuss the expected level of finish and quality. This can save time and avoid discord when the list is published. On larger projects, it may be necessary for the construction administrator to assemble additional staff members to assist in reviewing the construction status. In this event, advanced planning and budgeting is recommended. When project completion reviews involve the architect, they should be included in the contractor's construction schedule for planning purposes.

When the contractor considers that the work, or some portion of it, is substantially complete, the contractor submits the punch list to the architect. If the architect has agreed to assist in preparing the contractor's punch list, the contractor should be asked to give notice in writing to the architect when the work is substantially complete. Some architects require a formal certification from the contractor.

Upon receipt of the punch list or such written notification, the architect will conduct an inspection of the work to determine the date or dates of substantial completion. If the architect finds conditions that prevent the owner's occupancy or use of the project, the contractor must complete or correct those conditions before a certificate of substantial completion can be issued. This will require a follow-up inspection to determine if the designated work has been corrected.

The architect can use AIA Document G704–2000, Certificate of Substantial Completion, for certification. This document contains a date of issuance, which is also the date of substantial completion. If the date of issuance is different from the date of substantial completion, it will be necessary to add the date of substantial completion to the form.

Attachments to the certificate include the punch lists. Since few projects are completed without nonconforming work, care should be taken to list known nonconforming items. If the punch lists are voluminous, they can be referenced by project name and date on an attachment in lieu of attaching them to the certificate.

The contractor signs the certificate to agree on the amount of time it will take to complete or correct the punch list items and to agree with the owner regarding responsibilities for security, maintenance, heat, utilities, damage to the work, and insurance coverage. The owner signs the certificate, agreeing with the contractor on the above as well as on the date of substantial completion and the date and time the owner will assume full possession of the project.

Final Completion and Closeout

The contractor provides written notice to the architect indicating the punch list items have been completed. An additional review of the work may be necessary if the architect determines that some punch list items have not been resolved. When the architect is satisfied the items have been completed and all closeout document requirements have been met, the architect certifies payment and submits the final application for payment to the owner for processing.

Final payments. The final application for payment should include a resolution of all change orders and change issues. These can include construction change directives, reconciliation of contingencies and allowances, and resolution of any costs for additional services that resulted from additional substantial or final completion reviews by the architect. If there are varying conditions, such as a cost of

> Preparations for project closeout should begin prior to substantial completion. It is helpful to conduct a project closeout conference with the contractor and owner to review and discuss closeout activities.

the work contract with a shared savings or a completion penalty or bonus, the final contract sum must be resolved to determine the final cost of the work. This can be accomplished with the final change order. The final change order should be prepared by the architect and signed by the contractor and owner prior to submission of the final application for payment to the architect.

Closeout checklist. Closeout documents and activities can be more easily managed with a checklist, as referenced in "Project Closeouts." This checklist serves both as a list of required closeout documents and a means to record receipt and distribution of those documents. The topic also identifies various AIA documents frequently used in the closeout process. Other documents can include the contractor's marked-up drawings, record copies of submittals, warranties, extra materials stored for future use or maintenance, and any other documents required by the project specifications.

Adequate closeout planning and thorough closeout administration can help prevent miscommunications, unreasonable expectations, and disputes over requirements for completing the project. They can also leave the owner with pleasant memories and better satisfaction with how the project was delivered.

Project record keeping. Good record keeping is essential to successful construction administration. Decisions, task assignments, responses, approvals, and the like can be disputed or forgotten if not written down. Remember that if you do not keep good records, your actions will be judged by records kept by others who may not have your best interests in mind.

Primary CCA records include the owner-architect agreement and general conditions, architect-consultant agreements, owner-contractor agreement and general conditions, and an up-to-date set of contract drawings and specifications. The contracts are necessary to determine the responsibilities of the parties, and the reference documents are required to determine if the work, when constructed, is in substantial conformance.

- *Transmittal forms* are valuable for transmitting submittals, drawings, and other items that do not contain dates and subject lines as do letters, memoranda, and meeting reports.
- *Memoranda* are useful for documenting events, discussions, and decisions. They can be formal documents distributed to the various team members, or they can be a brief e-mail sent to the project file.

- *Personal journals* are a convenient way to document conversations or to record notes for future reference. Many architects use a journal to document their actions and experiences chronologically throughout the project. A journal can be kept for each project or for multiple projects. A journal with grid pages is useful for sketches or narrative. Some architects prefer using PDAs or other electronic devices to record such notes and activities.

CCA documents should be transportable and easily accessed. Although the laptop computer is today's vehicle of choice for maintaining documents, paper documents still come in handy when walking the site.

A filing system should be simple but comprehensive. If used for all projects, document retrieval can be a brief, routine endeavor.

An effective filing protocol goes hand in hand with good documentation. For this reason, it is wise to develop a filing system that is consistent for all of your projects. Without a standard system, considerable efficiency can be lost, especially when project personnel change or if a liability claim is made years after project completion. All staff members should understand the project filing system and file documents accordingly. While electronic media is becoming more practical for storage, paper documents will likely remain for the foreseeable future.

Three-Way Win

Although each project is unique, processes and procedures for construction administration are generally consistent. And with thorough planning—along with good communication—CCA services can run smoothly and efficiently. This is especially true when a "proactive" approach is taken in which members of the project team define and agree on activities and procedures in advance. When the team works to the benefit of one another, problems are discovered earlier and claims are less frequent.

In providing construction administration services, the architect makes clarifications and interpretations about the construction documentation and helps solve construction problems both before and after they arise—all of which can be valuable to the owner and contractor, as well as to the architect.

Effective construction administration by the architect can result in a three-way win. The owner benefits from the presence of a trusted advisor when construction money is being spent at a high rate. Facing expenses that are time-driven, the contractor benefits from the architect's responses to information requests and assistance in problem solving. Lastly, the architect has the opportunity to resolve problems when they arise, address discrepancies before work is put into place, and be with the owner when the keys are turned over for the completed project.

When the owner, architect, and contractor cross the finish line together, it helps forge stronger, lasting relationships that can lead to future work. A proactive approach to CCA services during the construction phase also increases your chances of pleasing your client, achieving the intended design, and minimizing construction phase problems.

For More Information

In *Why Buildings Fail* (National Council of Architectural Registration Boards, 2001), Kenneth L. Carper investigates "failure" through an enlightening mix of case studies, including failure during the design phase and errors during the construction phase.

Contractor's Guide to Change Orders, 3rd edition (Prentice Hall, 2002), by Andrew M. Civitello Jr. and William D. Locher, includes step-by-step procedures for making change order claims based on the architect's documents and actions during the construction phase. It provides insight into the contractor's strategy for claiming the architect and the high-risk areas of the architect's construction administration services.

The Construction Specifications Institute's *Project Resource Manual: CSI Manual of Practice,* 5th edition (McGraw-Hill, 2005) addresses the requirements of all participants involved in a construction project in a stage-by-stage progression, including owners, A/Es, design-builders, contractors, construction managers, product representatives, financial institutions, regulatory authorities, attorneys, and facility managers. It promotes a team model for successful implementation.

Construction Project Administration, 8th edition (Prentice Hall, 2013), by Edward R. Fisk and Wayne D. Reynolds, provides information needed by design professionals, project managers, contract administrators, and resident engineers or inspectors, and lays out steps for conducting on-site project administration, including the use of digital media.

A Guide to Successful Construction, Effective Contract Administration, 3rd edition (BNI Building News, 1999), by Arthur F. O'Leary, is designed to help construction professionals successfully manage projects through effective contract administration and minimize disputes and litigation. It defines the roles and responsibilities of the contractor, architect, owner/developer, and even the construction attorney, and includes step-by-step procedures for resolving conflicts and handling the threat of legal action.

7.5 Project Closeouts

Douglas C. Hartman, FAIA, FCSI, CCS, CCCA, SCIP, LEED AP

Clients value the closeout increment of a construction project. Effective project closeout enables completion of unfinished work, results in a completed building delivered in acceptable condition, and facilitates provision of essential postconstruction documentation to the client.

Ask most building owners who have recently completed a construction project and they will say that one of the most important aspects of the architect's services (aside from the obvious need for a functional design) is effective project closeout. Although architects tend to view the construction documents they prepare as their primary work product, most clients also consider other services essential to satisfactory project delivery. These include successful construction administration, determination of substantial and final completion of construction, orderly transfer of ownership, and guidance on operations and maintenance issues.

Project documentation that remains incomplete or work that does not meet contract requirements can lurk beneath the surface of what otherwise appears to be a successful project. Should incomplete requirements or documentation cause or contribute to problems in building function or maintenance, the situation can vary from unpleasant and disappointing to disastrous and litigious. It would be unfortunate for an architect to deliver a successful design in a timely fashion within budget only to find the owner is dissatisfied with project closeout and will not recommend the architect for future work.

Defining and clearly documenting project closeout tasks in Division 01—General Requirements of the specifications can help foster an efficient and successful closeout process. Keeping project closeout in mind during the construction phase is very important as well, and it should be a regular agenda item in scheduled project meetings.

Douglas C. Hartman, FAIA, is a Senior Virtualization Engineer at Intelligent Decisions, Inc. He was formerly the president of INSPEC, a Dallas-based specialty firm providing specifications, sustainable design, and accessibility consulting services. He regularly teaches courses in contract administration and contributed to the Construction Administration module of a previous edition of The Project Resource Manual—CSI Manual of Practice.

Tools and processes have been developed to guide the project closeout process and, if effectively utilized and implemented, these can result in project completion that meets the expectations of everyone involved. Diligence and focus on achieving a successful project and facilitating initial owner occupancy are necessary to coordinate the activities and responsibilities of all project participants.

Successful project closeout means different things to each participant. To the contractor, it means resolving the punch list, reconciling the job cost, and collecting the final payment. To the architect, it is the satisfaction of seeing the design result in a completed project that substantially conforms to the construction documents and functions as intended to meet the client's needs. To owners, however, closeout can bring nervous anticipation and anxiety as the operation and ownership of the facility are transferred into their hands. A process for an orderly project closeout, the roles of each participant in the process, and a means of measuring the relative success of project closeout accomplishments are identified in this section.

RESULTS OF POOR CLOSEOUT

Adverse effects of incomplete project closeout can range from the inconsequential to the disastrous. The following examples illustrate pitfalls that could be experienced by failing to comply with closeout requirements.

Owner Occupancy Date Omitted

AIA G704–2000, Certificate of Substantial Completion, specifies a date and time when the owner may take beneficial occupancy of a project. When the author of the document (the architect) fails to obtain and fill in this important information, and the other signers of the document do not notice this omission. Consequently, the date on which all project warranties commence is not identified, a potentially serious problem when the owner attempts to obtain subsequent warranty work. Potentially more serious is the lack of a specific date on which the owner's obligations for operation, maintenance, security, insurance, and utilities begin. If damage should occur, this omission increases the chance of a period without insurance coverage or of disputes over coverage between the property insurance companies of the owner and contractor. Attention to this detail is extremely important.

Final Change Order Omitted

The general conditions of a contract for construction require that when the cost of the work is more or less than a specified allowance, the architect will prepare and execute a change order to adjust the contract sum accordingly. One example of how this can result in a problem is the where the architect failed to prepare and execute a final change order at the end of the project to reconcile project allowances and cost contingencies. The contractor's final application for payment included the total allowance and contingency costs, although the actual cost of the work in each category was less. The owner was not aware of the cost difference, and the contractor apparently overlooked it when preparing the final payment application. Months after the project was closed out, the owner discovered the error during an audit. The owner was not successful at recovering the money from the contractor, and subsequently legal action was initiated against the contractor alleging fraud and against the architect alleging improper certification of the final application for payment.

Maintenance Training Omitted

Requirements for demonstration of the HVAC, electrical, fire protection, communication, and other systems and training of the owner's staff are clearly defined in the contract documents. While the architect's role is simply to confirm that the training was provided, the content of the training may not be clearly defined or executed by the contractor. Because the owner's staff often has limited knowledge of high-tech controls and instrumentation, operation of critical building systems may begin without adequate preparation. Operation and maintenance manuals may not be submitted during close-out. In one case the owner's staff failed to de-energize critical electrical systems before HVAC systems were shut down. The resulting damage to the HVAC system required fabrication of new equipment, which took more than a month. The owner was forced to obtain expensive temporary cooling equipment until the problem was resolved, which prompted the owner to take legal action against the architect.

INTEGRATING CLOSEOUT INTO THE PROJECT DELIVERY PROCESS

Thought should be given to project closeout before the owner-architect agreement is signed. Convincing the owner to retain an architect during the construction administration phase not only makes good sense but is mandated by law in many states (in those states, construction administration is deemed an integral part of architectural services and must be provided by a registered architect on projects that require an architect's seal). Nonetheless, the inclusion of construction administration in design services can sometimes be a hard sell, especially with owner-builder and design-builder arrangements and on projects that generally do not enlist full architect services during construction, such as residential and interior tenant improvements. Due to the serious legal implications associated with certifying substantial completion, it is not advisable for architects to agree to issue a certificate unless they periodically review the construction, review submittals and substitutions, and have the authority to reject nonconforming work.

Decisions about project closeout procedures need to be confirmed and documented during the design phase. Closeout procedures include clearly defined requirements written into Division 01–General Requirements of the specifications, including the owner's desires for items such as record documents, demonstration and training, and operations and maintenance information. Determining the owner's need for closeout documentation is no less important than determining the owner's requirements for items such as bonding, insurance, and method of contracting, as solicited in AIA Document G612–2001, Owner's Instructions to the Architect Regarding the Construction Contract, Insurance and Bonds, and Bidding Procedures. Addressing questions such as the following will help the architect learn what project closeout services the client expects:

- Is there a need for multiple substantial completion certificates?
- Does the owner wish to be involved in reviewing or administering punch lists?
- What amount of retainage is preferred, and what formula will be used to determine how it will be released?
- Is there a surety involved that may require notification when retainage is released?
- What are the owner's preferences for submission of record documents: electronic files (i.e., changes are input electronically), reproducible copies of hard-copy mark-ups, or hard-copy markups only?
- What is the preferred extent of record documents? Are only drawings required, or should record specifications (including a list of materials incorporated into the work), record submittals, or color boards and material samples also be included?
- How should warranties and certifications be organized?
- What are the owner's preferences for demonstration and training? What level of demonstration and training is needed for each specific system? Is video documentation of the demonstration and training required? What follow-up mechanical services are required at the first seasonal change?
- Does the owner want the architect to include building commissioning services?
- What are the owner's preferences for operation and maintenance manuals? How many copies are required? How should the manuals be organized?
- What are the owner's preferences for maintenance materials? What products should be included? What percentage of extra products or "attic stock" should be provided?

AIA Document D200–1995, Project Checklist, provides an opportunity to identify and plan for closeout early in the project delivery process. It contains references to closeout in Section 7, Construction Contract Administration, and Section 8, Post-Construction Services. The document can serve not only as a checklist of tasks to be decided with the owner but also as a permanent record of the decisions and actions of the owner, contractor, and architect.

Project closeout tasks continue during the construction documentation phase, as the specific requirements agreed to by the owner and the architect begin to be incorporated into a project manual. AIA Document A201–2007, General Conditions of the Contract for Construction, is a good starting point for identifying contract closeout requirements. Similar provisions are included in the engineer's version (EJCDC C-700), which is commonly used by consulting engineers on projects that consist primarily of engineering services. The provisions in these standard general conditions identify the responsibilities for action of each party, as shown in the accompanying sidebar.

These required actions should be clearly described in the general requirements sections of the specifications. In addition, the list of responsibilities should be expanded to include requirements for the following:

- Punch list procedures
- Insurance changeover requirements
- Start-up of systems
- Testing, adjusting, and balancing of systems, including commissioning reports
- Systems demonstration
- Operation and maintenance manuals
- Project record documents
- Spare parts and maintenance materials
- Warranties, workmanship bonds, maintenance service agreements, and final certifications
- Final pest control inspection and warranty
- Final construction completion photographs
- Certified survey, final property survey, and survey record log
- Delivery of tools and extra stock materials to the owner
- Changeover of permanent locks and delivery of keys to the owner

Implementation and Enforcement

It may become necessary to encourage the contractor to sustain focus on closeout procedures by enforcing any specified remedies for failure to comply with contract requirements. Such remedies can take several forms:

- Withholding a portion of periodic payments for failure to keep record documents current
- Withholding a portion of periodic payments for non-conforming work
- Refusing to release retainage until closeout documents, testing and adjusting, demonstration and training, operation and maintenance manuals, spare parts and maintenance materials, and warranties and bonds are submitted

PROJECT CLOSEOUT RESPONSIBILITIES

CONTRACTOR

- Inspects the project and prepares the punch list (outstanding items to be completed or corrected)
- Submits notice of substantial completion to architect
- Obtains agreement for the owner's acceptance of responsibility for security, maintenance, heat, utilities, damage to the work, and insurance
- Signs certificate of substantial completion
- Completes punch list items as stipulated in the certificate of substantial completion
- Submits required closeout documents and materials
- Submits notice of final completion
- Submits final application for payment and signs final change order
- Warrants to the owner and architect that the work is new, free from defects, and in accordance with the contract documents

ARCHITECT

- Reviews the contractor's punch list and supplements it as needed
- Inspects the project to determine substantial completion
- Confirms owner-accepted nonconforming work
- Prepares and issues a certificate of substantial completion with specified date, with attached punch list, if appropriate, and notes any owner-accepted nonconforming work
- Reviews closeout materials to determine contract compliance for submittals
- Prepares final change order
- Inspects project to determine final completion
- Advises contractor to submit final application for payment
- Processes final application for payment

OWNER

- Agrees to accept responsibility for security, maintenance, heat, utilities, damage to the work, and insurance
- Signs certificate of substantial completion
- Signs final change order and makes final payment

- Assessing the contractor for time and expenses of the architect (by way of additional services billing to the owner who then assesses the contractor by means of a deduct change order) when substantial completion inspections are requested before the work is ready or when the architect must repeatedly return to the site only to find that punch list work continues to be incomplete

One way to maintain everyone's focus on the importance of the closeout process is to conduct a project closeout conference before substantial completion. Such a conference can be appended to a regularly scheduled progress meeting and should include a review of all contract closeout requirements, timing requirements for each, and an identification of the party responsible for preparing, conducting, or submitting the specific requirement. A project closeout checklist that identifies the required closeout documents and activities can be distributed to the attendees.

Substantial Completion

Substantial completion is the stage in the progress of the work when the work, or a designated portion thereof, is sufficiently complete, according to the contract documents, for the owner to occupy or use the work for the intended purpose. Before requesting an inspection for substantial completion, the contractor should be required, through amendment of the appropriate portions of Division 01 of the specifications, to perform the following tasks:

1. Prepare a list of items to be completed and corrected (commonly known as a punch list), as required in AIA Document A201–2007, General Conditions of the Contract for Construction. (It is not uncommon for the architect to make major amendments to the punch list.)
2. Coordinate with the owner regarding pending insurance, maintenance, security, and utility changeover requirements, and inform the architect.
3. Submit evidence of final, continuing insurance coverage that complies with insurance requirements.
4. Instruct the owner's personnel in operation, adjustment, and maintenance of products, equipment, and systems.
5. Inform the architect of the time required to resolve punch list items.
6. Obtain and submit occupancy permits from authorities having jurisdiction (AHJs), if applicable. These can include permits from the local building official and from local and state health departments (in the case of restaurants and healthcare facilities), as well as reviews for accessibility compliance, among others.
7. Deliver spare parts and extra stock materials to a location designated by the owner.
8. Change to permanent lock cylinders and deliver the keys to the owner.
9. Complete start-up testing of systems for operating equipment.
10. Submit test/adjust/balance records for HVAC air and hydronic systems.
11. Terminate and remove temporary facilities, mock-ups, and construction tools from the project site.
12. Complete final cleaning requirements.

Once the above tasks are complete, the architect conducts an inspection of the work to determine the date or dates of substantial completion. The date of substantial completion is the date when the work (or a portion thereof) is in a condition to be occupied or utilized. This date is not determined by the owner or contractor, and it is not necessarily the date on which the owner actually occupies the project. This distinction is very important, and it is critical that it be determined independently by the architect and appropriate consultants, without the influence of any other party, particularly if the contractor is being assessed for liquidated damages for late completion.

The Construction Specifications Institute has developed a form for the punch list to be attached to the certificate of substantial completion. Form 14.1a, available electronically from CSI, can be used to organize punch list items for subcontractor

While AIA Document A201 requires the architect to observe the work during scheduled site visits, the architect must perform inspections for substantial and final completion. Inspections require a greater degree of in-depth review and verification of the work.

assignment and status determination. When the architect's inspection to determine substantial completion has been completed, items found to be incomplete or uncorrected should be attached to the certificate. This amended punch list should reference the certificate to which it is attached.

It is also important to append a list of all owner-accepted nonconforming work to the certificate of substantial completion. Very few projects conform to contract requirements in total. If latent nonconforming work is discovered that is not noted on the certificate, the architect could be at risk for misrepresenting the completed condition. As another precaution, it is also recommended that the architect obtain written confirmation from all consultants that their portions of the work are substantially complete. These written confirmations can be attached to the architect's certificate.

Final Change Order

The final application for payment cannot be processed until the final cost of the work has been determined. To accomplish this, all variables in the value of the work must be reconciled through a final change order. Examples of such variables include the following:

- Allowances, including contingency allowances
- Alternates
- Construction change directives
- Owner-accepted nonconforming work
- Extension of the one-year correction period for work not performed until after substantial completion
- Extension of the one-year correction period for work not corrected until after substantial completion

The final change order must be executed by the architect, owner, and contractor before submission of the final application for payment, which will include cost adjustments that result from the final change order.

Final Completion

Before final completion, the contractor should be required to perform the following tasks:

- Submit a final application for payment.
- Submit a copy of the architect's substantial completion punch list, with confirmation that each item has been completed or otherwise resolved for acceptance.
- Obtain consent of sureties to final payment if required.

Upon confirmation of the above and receipt of a written request from the contractor for final inspection, the architect proceeds with a final inspection or notifies the contractor of existing unfulfilled requirements. If the architect finds the work acceptable under the terms of the contract documents and the contract is fully performed, the architect may issue a final certificate for payment.

PROJECT RECORD DOCUMENTS

Typically, the contractor is required to maintain a separate set of contract documents and shop drawings at the project site. These are to be marked to show actual installations that vary from what is shown on the original contract documents. Project record documentation requirements should be reviewed in detail during the preconstruction conference. The contractor should record the data as soon as possible after obtaining it. Either the contract drawings or shop drawings may be marked, whichever most completely and accurately show actual physical conditions. If shop drawings are marked, they should be cross-referenced on the record drawings.

Preferably, the contractor will mark record sets with erasable colored pencils, using different colors to distinguish between changes for different categories of the work at the same location. When applicable, these notations should include construction change directive numbers, change order numbers, alternate numbers, and similar identification.

In addition, it is important for the contractor to submit record specifications, including addenda and contract modifications. In particular, the actual products installed should be indicated to update the list of several acceptable options included in most specifications. As well, the appropriate proprietary name and model number should be marked in the specifications for the products, materials, and equipment furnished.

Record product data submittals should be marked to indicate the actual product installed when it varies substantially from that indicated in the original product data submittal. Particular attention should be given to information about concealed products and installations that cannot be readily identified. Significant changes in the product delivered to the project site and changes in the manufacturer's written instructions for installation should also be included.

Remember that the architect checks the contractor's marked-up record drawings not for accuracy but to determine if the contractor has complied with the record-keeping and submittal requirements of the contract. The architect should discuss this activity with the owner to be sure the owner understands this distinction. In addition, the architect should affix a stamp on the record drawings that explains the source of the marked-up information.

In addition to printed copies of these documents, electronic copies should be specified and required to be provided by the contractor. Also, providing record drawings in editable digital files is invaluable to an owner when the need arises for renovation, remodeling, and additions to the facility.

OPERATION AND MAINTENANCE MANUALS

All operation and maintenance data should be assembled in manuals, bound and indexed, and placed in heavy-duty binders. This material should include a complete set of specific data for each system and piece of equipment installed in the project. Electronic format (PDF is almost universally preferred) should also be required for these manuals to serve as a permanent record in the event the printed copies are lost.

Maintenance data should include information not only for operating systems but also for building products and applied materials and finishes. Product data should include catalog number and designations as to size, composition, and color and texture of the product. Particularly important for interior finishes are instructions for care and maintenance, including the manufacturer's recommendations for cleaning agents and methods, precautions against detrimental agents and methods, and the recommended schedule for cleaning and maintenance. Moisture-control and weather-exposed products should include recommendations for inspection, maintenance, and repair.

Warranties

Copies of required warranties and bonds for each system, component, and finish specified to comply with a particular warranty period in excess of the correction period should be assembled for easy access by the owner. If the owner takes partial occupancy, warranties should be submitted within 15 days of completion of the portions of the work occupied by the owner. Warranties should be organized into an orderly sequence based on the table of contents in the project manual and bound in heavy-duty three-ring binders.

Each warranty should be marked to identify the product or installation, complete with a typed description, including the name of the product and the name, address, and telephone number of the installer.

Demonstration and Training

The owner's personnel need to be properly trained to adjust, operate, and maintain systems and equipment. The contractor must provide instructors experienced in operation and maintenance procedures, especially for HVAC and control systems. Instruction should occur at mutually agreed-upon times, and similar instruction at the start of each season should be required for equipment that requires seasonal operation. Scheduling for training, including notification of dates, times, length of instruction, and course content, should be coordinated by the architect.

The contractor should develop an instruction program that includes individual training modules for each system and for equipment that is not part of a system, provided this requirement is clearly specified in Division 01 of the specifications. For each training module, the contractor should be required to develop a learning objective and teaching outline. Instruction may occur in the following areas:

- Review of documentation
- Operations
- Adjustments
- Troubleshooting
- Maintenance
- Repair

FINAL CLEANING

Prior to final completion, the contractor is required to conduct cleaning and waste removal operations. Final cleaning should be performed by experienced workers who know and understand the substrates to be cleaned and the methods that will not damage them. Unless indicated otherwise, cleaning should result in a condition one would expect in a commercial building cleaning and maintenance program, complying with the product manufacturer's written instructions.

Cleaning that occurs prior to substantial completion should include the following:

- Removal of rubbish, waste material, litter, and other foreign substances from project site and grounds in areas disturbed by construction activities, including landscape development areas
- Broom-clean sweeping of paved and unoccupied spaces and removal of spills, stains, and other foreign deposits
- Raking of grounds that are neither planted nor paved to a smooth, even-textured surface
- Removal from project site of tools, construction equipment, machinery, and surplus material
- Cleaning of exposed exterior and interior hard-surfaced finishes to a dirt-free condition, free of stains, films, and similar foreign substances
- Removal of debris from roofs, plenums, shafts, trenches, vaults, manholes, attics, and similar spaces
- Vacuuming of carpet, removal of debris and stains
- Cleaning of mirrors and glass in doors and windows; removal of glazing compounds and other noticeable, vision-obscuring materials; replacement of chipped or broken glass and other damaged transparent materials; polishing of mirrors and glass, taking care not to scratch surfaces
- Removal of labels that are not permanent
- Touch-up and other repair and restoration of marred, exposed finishes and surfaces, including replacement of finishes and surfaces that cannot be satisfactorily repaired or restored or that already show evidence of unsuccessful repair or restoration
- Replacement of parts subject to unusual operating conditions
- Cleaning of plumbing fixtures to a sanitary condition

- Replacement of disposable filters and cleaning of permanent air filters
- Cleaning of exposed surfaces of diffusers, registers, and grills
- Cleaning of ducts, blowers, and coils if units were operated without filters during construction
- Cleaning of light fixtures, lamps, globes, and reflectors to function with full efficiency, including replacement of burned-out lamps and defective or noisy starters in fluorescent and mercury vapor fixtures to comply with requirements for new fixtures

Final cleaning requirements should include a prohibition against discharge of volatile, harmful, or dangerous materials into the drainage systems.

SUSTAINABLE DESIGN DOCUMENTATION

As the movement toward designing and constructing our built environment with an emphasis on minimizing the impact on the natural environment continues to build momentum, an important component of project closeout documentation may include assembly of documentation in support of LEED (Leadership in Energy and Environmental Design) certification. The LEED program was developed by the U.S. Green Building Council (USGBC) to help determine how "green" a project is by assigning credits for achievement of various sustainable features in the design, construction, and operation of a facility. Documentation in support of these credits can include items such as:

- MSDS (material safety data sheets) in support of VOC levels for paints, sealants, and adhesives
- Certifications from manufacturers demonstrating recycled content, VOC content, chain of custody, and other features
- Certification letters from the owner, architect, and consultants
- Calculations in support of reduced energy and water consumption
- Certification letters in support of construction waste recycling, resource reuse, and building reuse

Since documentation must come from a variety of project team members (owner, contractor, and design consultants), it is important to request this as early as possible in the submittal process to ensure credits are not lost. Although documentation may initially be assembled in print and electronic formats, the USGBC requires all formal submissions to be made in electronic files.

PROJECT FEEDBACK

The objective behind project feedback is to help design and construction teams duplicate successes and minimize future mistakes, failures, and design deficiencies. Feedback is as important to the architect as it is to the contractor, especially when an architect works with clients with prototypical needs who want to improve on the design and construction process with each project.

Mistakes do not always manifest themselves in the form of problems in need of repair or replacement. A "mistake" can simply be a poor detail or something that turns out to be difficult to construct. If recognized in a completed project, such an item can be modified in the future. The architect can focus on the outcomes from using specific materials or details in an effort to improve "corporate memory" and reinforce successful detailing and material applications.

The benefits of constructive feedback are numerous. The perspective will help architects delineate design intent more clearly on future projects, as well as reduce the need for extensive interpretation of documents and costly change orders.

CSI 16.0A, Project Feedback Form, can be used to facilitate provision of project feedback. In addition to written comments, periodic in-house seminars and field visits by design firm staff are an invaluable way to transfer knowledge to those who do not normally have a chance to be involved with construction administration duties.

POSTOCCUPANCY SERVICES

Although not part of the architect's basic services as defined in the AIA series of owner-architect agreements, services provided by the architect during the one-year correction period can greatly benefit the owner and cement a continuing relationship between the architect and the client that may lead to future work.

Systems, finishes, and other components that fail to perform during the first year of building occupancy are always a source of frustration to owners. This is usually the period when the contractor fine-tunes systems and when products and finishes that were installed incorrectly or failed prematurely are repaired or replaced. Timely response on the part of the contractor (and assistance from the architect in prompting this timely response), coupled with postoccupancy reviews at 6- and 12-month intervals, is a valuable service to the owner. Through this interaction, the architect gains a sense of ownership in the project along with the owner and may learn firsthand of valuable feedback that will improve future designs. Such postoccupancy work is beyond the scope of traditional basic services, however, and the architect must decide if a service agreement should be pursued or if the assistance will be provided through goodwill.

For More Information

Various aspects of project closeout activities, procedures, and requirements are addressed in AIA Document A201–2007, General Conditions of the Contract for Construction; Sections 017700, 017823, 017839, 017900, and 019113 of the AIA MASTERSPEC (ARCOM) master specification; and Module 7.12–Project Closeout of *The Project Resource Manual: CSI Manual of Practice*.

The following forms can also be useful for project closeout:

- AIA Document D200–1995, Project Checklist
- AIA Document G701–2001, Change Order
- AIA Document G707A–1994, Consent of Surety to Reduction in or Partial Release of Retainage
- AIA Document G707–1994, Consent of Surety to Final Payment
- AIA Document G706A–1994, Contractor's Affidavit of Release of Liens
- AIA Document G706–1994, Contractor's Affidavit of Payment of Debts and Claims
- AIA Document G704–2000, Certificate of Substantial Completion
- CSI Form 14.1A, Punch List
- CSI Form 16.0A, Feedback

CHAPTER 8

Design Project Delivery

8.1 Project Delivery Methods

Phillip G. Bernstein, FAIA, RIBA, LEED AP

The organization, strategy, and responsibilities of the key players in the building process—including the owner, architect, and contractor—comprise the project delivery method for the project. Multiple models are available, and can be chosen based on which project variables—cost, schedule, building quality, risks, and capabilities—are driving the project.

INTRODUCTION

A completed building results from a complex sequence of decisions made by the many participants in the design and construction process. For a project to run smoothly, someone must define responsibilities, organize and integrate the work of the participants, and manage the process by which the project is developed and delivered to the owner. The architect, who is deeply involved in most projects from inception to completion, may assume this role as the first construction professional hired by the owner, although this position is increasingly being assumed by construction managers and advisors. Nonetheless, the owner relies on the architect's expertise about delivery decisions, and the architect should help to determine which delivery method best suits the owner's needs. Since the project delivery model can dramatically

Phillip G. Bernstein, FAIA, is vice president for strategic industry relations of Autodesk Inc. and a former principal with Pelli Clarke Pelli Architects. Bernstein teaches at the Yale School of Architecture and lectures and writes extensively on project delivery and technology issues. He is former chair of the AIA Contract Documents Committee.

affect the results of a building project, an understanding of delivery approach options is central to the successful practice of architecture.

Conflict Resolution

The traditional design-bid-build delivery is a process fraught with conflict. The stage is set when contractors vie against one another to win the bid. Aggressive bids may allow for only the slimmest profit margins, leaving the contractor to fight any decisions that could turn profit into loss. Further, competitive bidding encourages a contractor to take the most economical approach that can be interpreted from the documents. When that interpretation does not align with the design intent, conflict can ensue.

Some owners, as well as architects, think that this conflict is good. Their view is that the documents are tested against precedent and reasonable expectation in a trial of constructability. When things don't go smoothly, both parties—builder on one side, designer on the other—argue their case. The conflict keeps both parties honest. At least, it does so in theory. In practice, owners have seen project teams dissolve into a sea of excuses and recrimination, leaving no one to deliver the owner's project. With a CM as constructor (CMc), the old divisions established in a traditional project delivery are unbound. When successful, the owner-architect-CMc relationship will create a team that works toward consensus rather than as adversaries, allowing them to concentrate their full attention on delivering the project.

Construction Experience

Construction managers are expected to have experience building buildings, but buildings are not widgets. Every project is unique, built without benefit of a prototype. Still, there are ways of executing specific project types that are best learned through experience. For example, a basic office building requires the CMc to coordinate essential trades such as electrical, mechanical, concrete, steel, etc. The most critical skill may be the ability to accelerate the schedule. CMc involvement in the design phases can help the team organize bid documents for multiple packages.

More complex projects, like performing arts buildings, have different requirements. Not only are there more demands on the essential trades to meet acoustic criteria, there are also added designers and trades that need to be coordinated. The complexity rises geometrically. Therefore, prior experience with projects similar in size and function to the one proposed can be of great benefit in both design and construction phases. A CMc who is actively building similar projects can offer advice to the AE team during the design phase, and will be able to anticipate critical activities during construction.

While "prior experience" could be applied as criteria for a design-bid-build (DBB) project as well as a CMc project, the effect would not be the same. Early involvement in the project helps the CMc to understand design intent to ensure that the scope is fully realized. The exchange of insight between architect and CM during design is one of the primary benefits of a CMc arrangement.

Cost Analysis

Most projects must adhere to a budget, and the budget is best established no later than the schematic design phase. Cost estimates performed at design milestones track the construction cost; the subcontractor bids test whether the estimates were accurate. An independent cost estimator can provide this service to the team, and can do so without bias. Another approach is to employ the constructor as the estimator. The CMc can advise on current market conditions and labor costs to help the AE team design cost-effective building options.

Schedule and Coordination

Under DBB, a single package of documents is delivered to bidders, with the package coordinated by the AE team. This is the simplest method of delivery, but not the fastest. To deliver a project quickly, document "bid packages" are released depending on their place in the overall schedule. Unfortunately, multiple bid packages released over time add uncertainty and may require changes as the documents progress. A CMc is charged with the responsibility for seeing bidders receive the appropriate information at any given time, and that the work is coordinated as it proceeds.

Matters of construction experience, cost estimation expertise, scheduling, and construction coordination expertise are discussed further below, and are essential considerations when selecting the CMc.

SELECTING THE CMC

Selecting the right CMc for a project is an important task, and the owner may ask the architect for advice and guidelines. The architect's experience on previous projects can inform the owner not only about qualifications of specific firms but also about the scope of work that should be requested when soliciting qualifications. Most importantly, the CMc will be part of a team, and the involvement of the AE team in the selection process may help promote team harmony.

Why CMc Delivery?

Before launching into the selection of a construction manager, it is important to understand what is motivating the client to do a CMc project. Is the schedule for completion aggressive? Is the cost critical? Is the scope unknown? Any of these factors could lead to the decision to choose CMc delivery.

With the driving factors known, the owner should include in the Request for Proposal (RFP) a detailed description of the CM's expected scope of services.

Define the Scope of Work

The scope of work expected of the CMc should be clearly defined in the request for qualifications/proposal. A detailed description of the project, including size, program, and materials, to the extent that they can be defined, should be included. In addition to the description of the project, AIA Document A133™–2009 can be used to set out contractual requirements for the scope of work that can be expected. The owner should make any adjustments necessary to align that agreement with their specific project, and, if necessary, any general conditions of the owner's contract for construction. In the best case, the architect will meet with the owner and discuss the scope before it is released. That way, the owner can avoid contradictions between architect and CMc agreements. Also, the architect can suggest language that may clarify what, in their experience, may have been sticking points in the past.

The AIA Contract Document A133™–2009 can be seen as the base agreement between Owner and CMc. Although this may not be the agreement those parties use, the architect should study that document to understand not only the responsibilities of each party but also matters of payment, dispute resolution, and how the cost of work is to be established.

▶ See "The AIA Documents Program" in Part 4 for more detail on the CM family of AIA Contract Documents.

Basic services for the CMc might include the following:

- Preconstruction phase:
  - Perform a preliminary evaluation of program, schedule, and budget.
  - Maintain ongoing consultation on matters pertaining to construction, constructability, and materials and labor availability.
  - Prepare and periodically update the project schedule.
  - Provide recommendations for phased construction.
  - Provide preliminary cost estimates. As the design develops, the estimates will be updated with increasing detail until a guaranteed maximum price can be established.
  - Develop subcontractors' and suppliers' interest in the project. Where demanded by schedule and market conditions, pre-purchase materials for the project.
- Guaranteed maximum price: When mutually agreed by owner, architect, and CMc, the CMc will prepare a guaranteed maximum price (GMP) proposal. The GMP will

be the sum of the CMc's estimate of the cost of the work, including contingencies and the CM's fee.

- Construction phase:
  - Solicit and obtain bids from subcontractors for the work. Review with the owner and architect to determine which bids should be accepted.
  - Administer the work of subcontractors in accordance with the contract documents.
  - Schedule and conduct meetings to discuss procedures, progress, coordination, scheduling, and status of the work. The CMc will prepare and distribute minutes to the owner and architect.
    - The owner's representative and the architect should also attend these meetings on a regular basis. The CM's ability to direct the subcontractors often relies on the involvement of the design team to clarify the documents and their intent.
- Maintain a schedule of the work, including submittals to the architect.
- Track the cost of work measured against the GMP.

This list paraphrases the scope found in AIA Document A133™–2009. It is only the starting point. Discuss with the owner how best to serve their project. Once a CMc is selected, they too may have suggestions for their scope.

Interviews

A successful team is not determined by technical qualifications alone. Team chemistry greatly affects the ability of professionals to work together toward a common goal. The CMc selection process should include an interview where the CM presents their qualifications and their team. The architect should request to be a part of those interviews. Though it should not be the primary measure, good team relationships will influence a project's success.

SAMPLE: CONSTRUCTION MANAGEMENT SERVICES

- **Team meeting leadership.** Lead regularly scheduled project meetings with members of the project delivery team for the purpose of continually assessing project status, and coordinating design and budget issues. Prepare and distribute minutes of all such meetings.
- **Action log.** Maintain the project team action log to drive and track outstanding issues and ensure timely completion.
- **Decision-making process.** Coordinate interaction and decision making among USD 443 architects, engineers, user groups, and others necessary to project decision making. Meet regularly with USD 443 to continually address key decisions required and other project issues. Includes coordination and assistance with contract negotiations for construction services.
- **Code official review.** Participate in review meetings by AE team with building official to develop a permit procedure for project.
- **Owner purchasing.** Work with USD 443 to incorporate, where possible and appropriate, to aggregate cost with other USD 443 projects and assist and advise the owner regarding owner-purchased items.
- **Cost control.** Provide an overall cost control system for the project, including monthly reconciliation with USD 443. Maintain a parallel record of project costs for review by USD 443 to serve as a permanent record. Develop and update a cash flow forecast for the duration of the project.

- **Department interface.** Coordinate interface with key USD 443 departments, including engineering, telecommunications, security, etc., to encourage participation with the project design team.
- **Documents review.** Review all design phase documents and comment on constructability, coordination, and value engineering (VE) issues. Coordinate all value engineering efforts on USD 443's behalf including facilitation of work sessions with the project design team, evaluation of proposed constructability/VE items, etc. Monitor completion of design documents to ensure constructability/VE items are incorporated as the project progresses.
- **Presentations.** Participate in other presentations, as necessary, to provide updates as to the project status. Such other presentations may include the USD 443 board or presentations to local government agencies.
- **Design process documents.** Monitor design documents relative to compliance with the approved functional program and USD 443 project objectives. Perform periodic drawing reviews to track status of the design progress and inclusion of VE objectives.
- **Conflicts and disputes.** Assist in the resolution of all project-related conflicts and disputes including coordination with USD 443 legal counsel, as required.

DEFINING TEAM ROLES

In the traditional design-bid-build project delivery method, there is a clear line marking the roles of designer and builder. While the project design is under way and documents are being prepared, management of the project is the responsibility of the architect. After the documents have been bid and a general contractor selected, management of the project passes to the contractor, although the architect remains the manager of the design team.

When both architect and construction manager are on the job, there can be some conflict as to who's running the show. Both are experienced in leadership roles, and both have significant liability for their team's performance. Taking the time early in the project to clearly establish the team members' roles can improve communication and help avoid frustration. As the architect and CM have no contractual relationship, the owner must be a party to establishing team roles. Therefore, the owner/architect agreement must be aligned with the owner/CMc agreement.

The architect should consider amending their contract to align with the owner's contract with the CM and their expectations. Included in both contracts should be a matrix or narrative description that clearly and concisely defines team roles. As always with contracts, obtain appropriate legal advice and consult with the firm's professional liability insurance provider.

Once team roles are established and documented, this documentation can be referenced throughout the project. For the CMc, two responsibilities will overshadow all others: construction schedule and construction cost. When construction begins, the architect too will be driven by schedule and cost. How those factors are defined and monitored are of crucial interest to the design team. Still, before construction starts, the CMc will make their presence known in the design phase, sometimes to the architect's chagrin.

DEVELOPING THE DESIGN

The AE team has primary responsibility for the design phase. The owner looks to them to set the schedule and to coordinate the work. At the same time, CMc input into matters of construction can help the team make informed decisions as the design develops.

Constructability Expertise

The design team should draw on the CMc's expertise in understanding the realities of actually building the design as it evolves; in other words, the design's *constructability*, which might include the following:

- *Local building conventions.* An architect may be aware of local building conventions and design standards, but not know the details of current market conditions and how they affect the local labor force. For example, while stucco might be a cost-saving alternative for exterior finish in California, the scarcity of qualified installers in Connecticut could raise the price dramatically.
- *Building systems.* While the project engineers are experts in designing building systems, current market conditions will impact the cost of the components specified. The CMc can advise the team as to which system will be most cost-effective at the time of construction. For example, the structural frame is often subject to this analysis; concrete is weighed against steel to determine which system is preferred when measured in terms of cost and schedule.
- *Site selection.* Drawing on their experience of coordinating the workforce, the CMc can offer their analysis of potential building sites. Constrained sites can be evaluated for the cost of material delivery, staging, laydown, and workforce deployment.
- *Scope limitations.* The CMc can provide oversight on the overall project scope as it develops, warning the team if it seems to be growing beyond budget or schedule limitations. The architect will need to assert their design authority if they feel that scope is being restricted without fair consideration of the owner's program.

Specifications

Final construction documents are comprised of drawings and specifications. During the early phases of design, Schematic Design and Design Development, the architect depends heavily on drawings to convey design intent to the owner. Unfortunately, as clear as the drawings may seem to the architect, they do not define the scope of construction in enough granular detail to ensure accurate pricing from the CMc. Product data, material properties, testing requirements, and quality assurance are some of the details that are too cumbersome to include in drawings. The design team must use additional tools to describe the building, pointing to the importance of specifications to establish design intent for the CMc early in the process.

The project team must agree on when the method of specification is adequate to meet the level of estimate required of the CMc for each phase of the project. Similarly, the CMc should commit to incorporating the information delivered by the preliminary specifications. Just as with the final documents, *all* design documents—drawings and specifications—make up the design intent, and should be priced accordingly.

▶ See "Construction Specifications" for more detail on specifications in traditional project delivery.

LEED Certification

It is critical to have CMc involvement in early design phases to meet LEED goals. LEED scoring requires certain construction practices if a particular point is to be gained. Equally important to the project is the cost benefit of obtaining a particular LEED point. The CMc will incorporate the cost of the LEED measures proposed by the team so that the project budget reflects the design intent.

Checking the Documents

As noted above, construction documents are by definition not prescriptive construction instructions, and at early design phases the project scope is only vaguely defined. Therefore, it's important that the architect establish the level of scope information that CM can expect for each milestone so that the CMc's advice can be calibrated accordingly. Once set, the architect can tailor their deliveries to that level, and the CMc will have the information they need to provide cost estimation and scheduling services appropriate to the phase. In addition, the scope definition by phase can act as a checklist for the design team.

The CMc can also provide, as part of their work, periodic document check to augment the architect's quality management procedures. With their knowledge of construction services and their understanding of contractors' expectations, the CMc provides insight into how the design documents will be read in the field. Any perceived gaps in scope can be filled before final documents are released for bid.

CMc involvement in quality control should not be a substitute for the design team's own quality management plan. Rather, it is a value-added service.

Conflicting or uncoordinated scope can be as damaging to cost and schedule as missing scope. The CMc can also be asked to verify that drawings are coordinated internally and with other consultants' drawings. Well-coordinated documents with adequate scope definition will go far toward meeting the design team's best contribution to meeting the project schedule.

PROJECT SCHEDULE

In the traditional design-bid-build project delivery method, responsibilities for schedule are clear. The design team is tasked with delivering a set of documents by a certain date, after which the documents are printed and issued to general contractors. The burden of schedule then shifts to the selected contractor. The design team still has schedule performance obligations, as the designers are required to turn around shop drawings and clarifications in a specific time allotted by the general conditions. But beyond that, the design team has little or no ability to affect the schedule. Similarly, prior to bid, the general contractor has no input on the design project schedule, since it is not chosen nor involved in the project until after the completion of the documents. Such is not the case when the CMc is involved.

Under CMc project delivery, the CMc has the responsibility for developing and coordinating the overall project schedule, including design phases, owner decision milestones, and work periods that include design and drawing time. The consolidated schedule is assembled, tracked, and maintained by the CMc for the duration of the project. Since many owners choose the CMc delivery method specifically to drive the project to a schedule, what unique skill does the CMc bring to a project to achieve that goal? In short, they bring the ability to accelerate the project delivery schedule.

Fast-Track Schedule

Fast track is a method of delivery that allows AE documents to be issued in multiple stages, or bid packages. While this strategy can be complex and therefore challenging, it can be of great benefit to the owner who wants to compress the project schedule. Rather than wait for a completed set of construction documents, work can begin with partial documents for the trades along the critical path. Fast-track delivery has become very common in commercial and institutional projects with accelerated schedules. Unfortunately, the risks involved in that method are not always well understood by the parties involved.

The team must have a clear understanding of how the scope definition should proceed to best allow for accurate cost estimation and, if anticipated, phased bid packages. This approach may be antithetical to the creation of a cohesive design whole, but the need cannot be ignored. The architect must maintain a coherent approach to the design even as pieces of the project are developed asynchronously in fast-tracked packages. For example, if the estimator needs details of a copper roof early in design development, the architect will need to provide them, even if they normally would not have resolved that portion of the design until much later in their process. Or if curtain wall details must be delivered months before floor plans are finalized, the team must work toward that goal. It is critical that the structure, schedule, and milestones for individual bid packaging requirements be established at the outset and properly reflected in the architect's scope of service and fees. An unclear packaging strategy will subject the design team to starts and stops that will compromise the quality of the documents, and project schedule and cost will suffer.

The architect must have a clear rationale for the design components of the schedule and be prepared to explain their schedule requirements. While there is no benefit to the CMc in a lengthy design period, the architect must be given sufficient time to complete his or her work. The CMc may pressure the architect to accept a shorter design or documentation period. Be wary of such pressures.

The CM will include the design team's schedule in their project schedule. It is important that the team not accept an unrealistic time frame that conflicts with their professional duties.

Bid Packaging

Traditional DBB allows for the straightforward production of documents, giving the design team the opportunity to coordinate documents fully before releasing them to bid. CMc with fast-track delivery introduces complexities that go far beyond producing the documents. Rather than a single set of documents, a number of sets, or bid packages, must be assembled and issued over a period of time.

Obviously, the work to customize the drawing set and release it a number of different times and ways exceeds the normal basic services that an architect provides. If it is known from the outset that the construction delivery will involve the production of multiple bid packages, make sure that the owner/architect agreement reflects that work. If multiple bid-package delivery is introduced later in the design process, the architect must negotiate with the owner to modify the contract.

Even if the design team expects and produces unique packages for each bid, there will be areas where two or more bid packages overlap. The danger of redundancy or conflict increases when the same (but revised) drawings are issued at two different times to two different contractors. It is critical that the management team know which drawings on the job are current and who is involved with the work. Both the architect and the CMc should establish document-tracking procedures that will ensure that only current drawings are on site, and that all contractors have received them.

As part of bid packaging, the CMc will include a written scope of work to accompany the design team's documents. This document in effect modifies the construction documents. While it is tempting to the designer to stand with the documents alone, that will do the project no good when the work is in progress and a piece of scope is missing. Therefore, the design team should include in their agreement time to review the CMc's scope descriptions prior to their release for bid. The architect should provide a written report on the bid package scope, noting in particular areas where the scope description doesn't appear to align with the design documents.

Release of early bid packages comes with the risk of subsequent changes that will be required when the design is further developed. As there is no fixed document set until all packages are bid, the architect may be responsible for ongoing document coordination with "as bid" conditions. Furthermore, the bid must align with the documents' intent, or a change order with accompanying additional services is in order. It should be clearly defined in the owner/CMc agreement that any deviation between the winning bid scope and the design documents be communicated—in writing—to the design team.

▶ See "Bidding and Negotiation" for more detail on construction procurement in traditional project delivery.

CONSTRUCTION COST

An architect's ability to accurately estimate construction cost is limited. At best, a firm may have in-house expertise in quantifying materials, which the architect can then extrapolate into material cost for a building. Determining labor cost is a different matter. Special expertise is needed to analyze local market conditions, not only for payroll but also for production capabilities. For this expertise, owners turn to an independent cost estimator or, very often, the CMc.

CMc as Chief Estimator

Over the last few decades, owners have increasingly turned to construction managers for cost estimation services. The reasoning is as follows:

- The CM is experienced in the valuation of construction processes and materials.
- The CM is already providing other preconstruction services.
- The CM has business relations with subcontractors that can assist in fine-tuning an estimate.
- Where the CM is constructor, they will have an incentive to provide an accurate estimate.

While these arguments are valid, they don't take into account the specific cost management challenges with the CM as constructor. Such challenges include the conceptual mind-set of the design team as opposed to a more linear ideation of the builder; more important, there is an underlying conflict of interest inherent in this system of cost estimator as constructor.

A project cost estimate in a CMc project becomes, rightly or wrongly, a key measure of the CM's competence. Thus the temptation can arise, even unconsciously, to inflate line item values to ensure that the estimate "looks good" when measured against the bid values. Conversely, the CMc may artificially lower the estimate in response to owner pressure, confident that they will find cost savings during the course of bidding and negotiation that will bring cost of construction down. As a result of these manipulations, the project can suffer in one or more ways:

- Scope that should have been included in the project is cut due to cost, albeit artificially inflated.

- The inflated estimate is leaked to bidders, who then raise their bid in response, thinking that perhaps they are missing some scope.
- The suppressed estimate goes to bid, and when the numbers come in the extent of the budget shortfall is revealed, leading to a delayed start while the team scrambles to reduce cost.

A conflict also arises for the CMc after the bids come in. If the bids exceed their estimate, a misguided CM may make behind-the-scenes side agreements with subcontractors in an attempt to bring the bid down. Loss of project quality and divergence from the design intent are the usual consequences of these deals.

Internal conflict need not result from CMc estimation. Contingencies can guard the budget against indeterminate costs. Still, the system suffers from lack of precision, with the worst culprit central to the estimate: the guaranteed maximum price.

Guaranteed Maximum Price

The guaranteed maximum price (GMP) is the amount that the CMc sets for the cost of construction based on in-progress documents provided by the architects and engineers. It is designed to allow the CMc to commit to a price while the design—often during a fast-tracked process—is still under way, giving the owner price certainty. The CMc brings the estimate to a level that aligns with the design, anticipating all materials and labor needed to complete the building, even if those pieces are not yet shown in the documents. The closer the documents are to completion, the less anticipation will be required, and the more closely the GMP will align with the final bid. Once set, the CMc "guarantees" that this cost will not be exceeded. The moment when the GMP is "set" is thus critical.

Two competing interests are in play. The first is the desire to establish the GMP as early as possible. This locks down the construction cost so that the owner is sure his or her budget is met. However, when the GMP is set early, it must be based on assumptions for scope not yet defined in the documents, as well as projections of future costs of material and labor when the project finally does bid. Therefore, the CMc may push GMP close to, if not into, the bid period so that the owner's budget is set to actual construction costs. At that point, the at-risk component of the CMc's work is minimized.

No matter when the GMP is established, the CMc runs the risk of the estimate not meeting the as-bid amount. If the owner's budget is exceeded, there must be strategies in place to reduce the construction cost while allowing the project to proceed.

Value engineering (VE) is a critical service that the CMc provides. When correctly done, the VE process introduces materials and products that will achieve the design intent at a lower cost.

Cost-cutting suggestions should not be confused with value engineering. The CMc may combine the two, but where VE achieves the same intent at a lower cost, cost-cutting will change the original design to something the CMc hopes is similar but costs less.

The CMc is charged with the task of holding the GMP as construction proceeds. With an accelerated construction start combined with multiple bid packages, the bid documents can become dangerously unraveled, with later releases diverging from early ones. Ensuring that the GMP represents the documents, and vice versa, is a crucial part of the CMc delivery.

CMC DURING CONSTRUCTION

Releasing design documents in multiple bid packages often leads to changes in work "as bid" when the design is further developed. Another force is cost; as-bid packages come in and are compared to the estimate, the CMc will get a better idea as to whether the budget will be met. If bids come in high on early packages, the design team may need to scramble in an attempt to cut costs. It is very difficult to cut costs so late in the bid process, but the team must be prepared to try. Again, meticulous tracking of documents will help ensure that only the most current design is in the field.

Construction Phase Services

An architect's responsibilities in a CMc project parallel those in a traditionally delivered project, with specific changes that anticipate the unique role of the CMc, particularly with regard to fast-tracked projects and the GMP. The architect's contract and scope must anticipate the additional complexity and risk of both approaches and fees should anticipate additional effort by the architect during a CMc project. Owners often find this idea counterintuitive, assuming that the CMc is providing services during construction that might have otherwise been performed by the architect, but quite the opposite is the case. CMc projects are often more complicated, and that means more work for the architect.

A typical example is cost management during a CMc project. Should the cost of the job begin to drift above the budget, the CMc may use various maneuvers to meet budget. "Value engineering," cost-cutting, and bid scope descriptions are ways that the CMc may stray well into the design team's territory during construction. If the team collaborates, changes can often be made and the design intent maintained. However, unilateral changes by the CMc often compromise that intent, and the architect needs to continue to act on behalf of the owner to see that the project is constructed in accordance with the contract documents.

CHOOSING CMC PROJECT DELIVERY

An experienced and reliable CMc can provide real value to a properly configured and staffed project. Such benefits might include the following:

- Up-to-date cost estimates with real-world numbers that reflect the CMc's insight about market conditions
- Constructability advice that can reduce requests for information during construction
- Document review to help reduce change orders during construction
- Advice on packaging documents for multiple bids to make the AE team's work more efficient
- With multiple bid packages, the ability to deliver a project much more quickly than would otherwise be possible. This is one of the CMc's greatest contributions to the owner.

Some interesting variants are emerging worldwide that exhibit "integrated" characteristics but don't follow the exact strictures of Integrated Project Delivery (IPD) as commonly defined. Among them are privately financed initiatives and project alliances.

Privately Financed Initiatives

In Great Britain and a growing number of other countries, consolidated design, construction, development, and building operation teams compete to deliver and operate completed buildings for extended periods as long as 50 years. The architect is one member of such teams. Owners pay a yearly fee in exchange for the use of these buildings. Many healthcare projects in the United Kingdom are using this model, notably when the government's Health Services does not wish to spend capital on building construction and operation. The *build-operate-transfer* model in Canada is a similar model. In the United States, developers are creating "lease-leaseback" arrangements, where projects are delivered for a client by a third party and then leased back to the client for a set period, with ownership reverting to the original client after an extended period, often 99 years. There are other variations on private-finance schemes, where private funds for construction of private projects have evolved as alternative financing strategies for projects; such schemes are sometimes, but not always, accompanied by consolidated design-deliver-operate project teams.

Design Assist

The increasing technical complexity of many projects, particularly those with high-performance enclosure or mechanical systems, demands the early involvement of key subcontractors and fabricators during the design phase. A new model called "design assist" has evolved accordingly, in which shop drawings generated by these subcontractors are incorporated directly in the architect's construction documents, and the architect is not required to document those systems as traditional "design intent" deliverables. This model purportedly creates more accurate and efficient working drawings, as well as improved cost control and construction operations.

Project Alliance Models

In Australia, the industry is experimenting with a radical delivery model called Project Alliance in which the entire project team—designers, contractors, and subcontractors—are bound together in a single contract that holds each jointly responsible for the project and rewards all for its success. Of interest in the Alliance model is the requirement that each project member fully support the efforts of the other, since their financial success is tied to mutual cooperation. The owner in these projects establishes measurements of this success—budget, cost, or quality, for example—and rewards the entire team based on how well these aims are achieved. Principles of Project Alliance have strongly influenced the development of IPD here in the United States.

CONCLUSION

Like many professionals anticipating the challenges of practice today, architects face increasingly complex decisions that drive the very basis of how projects will be designed and built. Advising owners intelligently about delivery options requires an understanding of the players in the building process and their roles, the key variables that affect the choice of delivery method, and, finally, the range of choices available in the current design and construction marketplace.

A new generation of delivery models based on principles of integration is coming into view. To maintain a central role in the building enterprise, architects must strive to understand, master, participate in fully, and, when necessary, invent such methods.

▶ "Emerging Issues in Project Delivery" covers particular project-delivery issues that have arisen in relation to building information modeling (BIM), IPD, and sustainable design.

8.2 Integrated Project Delivery Overview

Randy Deutsch

Integrated project delivery (IPD) methods enable project stakeholders to work together in a unified effort that shares, to varying degrees, the risks and rewards involved in design and construction. This article describes IPD as it is understood and practiced at the time this *Handbook* was published.

The building industry is inefficient, with almost a third of projects missing either budget or schedule targets. Designers and builders are separated by traditional delivery structures and contracts, creating distrust and preventing construction insight from making design more effective.

According to the AIA's research for the AIA Council of Architectural Component Executives (CACE), almost 40 percent of projects end up behind schedule and more

Randy Deutsch is a building information modeling (BIM) strategist, IPD facilitator, educator, and architect. He is the author of *BIM and Integrated Design: Strategies for Architectural Practice* (Wiley, 2011), tracking the social and organizational impacts and collaborative work process of the new technologies on individuals, teams, organizations, the profession, and industry.

than 60 percent over budget using traditional delivery models, but that percentage reduces by half for collaborative delivery models.

Owners expect significant improvements. One alternative to traditional design-bid-build or CM delivery models is an integrated approach that encourages the early involvement of project stakeholders, information sharing, and collaboration. One such response is the emergence of integrated project delivery.

In IPD methods, the project team works together to define issues, identify potential conflicts, establish performance criteria, and increase efficiency. The ultimate goal is to create a collaborative environment that produces a positive outcome for all stakeholders, improves the quality of our built environment, reduces waste, and delivers more value to the owner.

IPD DEFINED

Integrated project delivery bridges the divide between design and construction to improve communication, better coordinate documents, and increase collaboration.

The American Institute of Architects defines integrated project delivery as "a project delivery approach that integrates people, systems, business structures and practices into a process that collaboratively harnesses the talents and insights of all participants to optimize project results, increase value to the owner, reduce waste, and maximize efficiency through all phases of design, fabrication, and construction" (AIA/California Council, 2007).

As shown in Figures 8.1 and 8.2, construction productivity has not kept pace with labor productivity in other industries. IPD methods are seen as one way to address these negative trends.

If IPD were only a project delivery method, we would measure its success based on the criteria of cost, time, quality, and how the project ultimately meets its intended purpose.

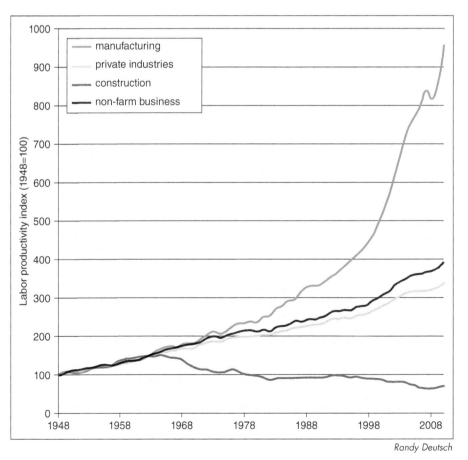

Randy Deutsch

FIGURE 8.1 **Labor Productivity Index**

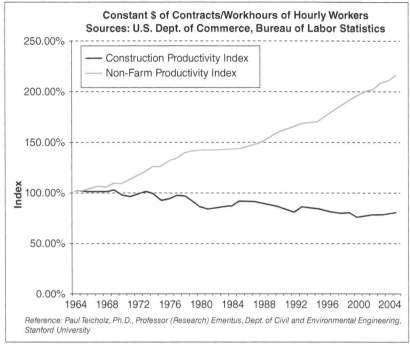

Constant $ of Contracts/Workhours of Hourly Workers
Sources: U.S. Dept. of Commerce, Bureau of Labor Statistics

Reference: Paul Teicholz, Ph.D., Professor (Research) Emeritus, Dept. of Civil and Environmental Engineering, Stanford University

Randy Deutsch

FIGURE 8.2 **Construction Productivity Index**

But IPD is also a contract strategy and a set of recommended behaviors—integration strategies sometimes informally referred to as IPD-lite or IPD-ish to distinguish them from "pure" IPD—and so the definition of IPD continues to evolve, depending on a project team's goals and tolerance for risk.

Defining Characteristics of IPD

Integrated projects are uniquely characterized by these elements:

- A formal, binding multiparty contract structure that includes, at minimum, the architect, owner, and builder
- Shared risk and reward by these stakeholders
- Support of key IPD principles
- Participation of all project stakeholders early in the design/decision-making process
- Design and construction processes focused on optimal outcomes
- Collaboration among the owner, architect, and contractor
- Indemnification from litigation for those on the project delivery team

In fact, by agreeing to not sue each other, primary stakeholders help create a safe working environment for the project. Traditional delivery methods often encourage self-protective behavior designed to shift or avoid risk; such behavior discourages collaboration.

Fundamental Principles of the IPD Approach

There are 10 fundamental characteristics of IPD.

Mutual Respect and Trust

In an integrated project, the owner, architect, contractor, subcontractors, suppliers, and consultants contractually pledge to respect each other and commit to working in the best interests of the project.

Participation in IPD requires trust in its systems and processes and a belief that information sharing during the design process leads to improved results. IPD also depends on trusting relationships that are open and transparent throughout the project.

Because it takes time and face-to-face interactions to build trusting relationships, teams that have worked together before often have the best chance of success for IPD. Collaborative organizations and teams rely openly on trust, on the belief that project team members are fundamentally capable of drawing the best from people and providing them with the means to succeed (David H. Hart, "Developing Trusting Collaborative Relationships," Oct. 25, 2007, blog.aia.org/aiaarchitect/2007). In integrated delivery, the owner sets the stage for a trusting project team environment by transparently sharing project-related information, valuing input from all project stakeholders, and trusting their own project team members to successfully get their work done.

Mutual Benefit and Reward

IPD is designed to align the interests of the project team so that everyone mutually benefits from project success. According to AIA/CC, IPD compensation structures recognize and reward early involvement based on the value added by each team member. In multiparty agreements, incentives are sometimes tied to achieving project goals and to rewarding behavior that promotes project success. IPD team members share project losses and gains from the same profit pool, providing an incentive for team members to work collaboratively. Profit in such arrangements may be paid collectively—paid to all or none—further aligning mutual interests.

Risks Identified and Accepted Early

All parties benefit equally when the most important decisions are made mutually for the best interest of the project. Similarly, when one party makes a mistake, the whole team is responsible and works to reconcile the error, challenging traditional notions of liability. This is the basis of shared risk and reward. With IPD the lines of responsibility are blurred when compared to traditional design-bid-build project delivery. Contractors contribute to the design and architects address construction issues, with risk distributed across the team. Because of the early involvement of all stakeholders and the expansion of traditional roles, risks can be identified and addressed early, making it more likely that they be mitigated well before construction begins. Thus, IPD is often characterized by the counterintuitive notion that embracing additional risk (through risk sharing) results in lowering the exposure to the project team.

Collaborative Innovation and Decision Making

The promise of IPD is that freely sharing information among all project participants leads to more innovative, informed, and balanced decision making. Ideally, in IPD ideas are judged on their strengths, regardless of the status or role of the contributor. While the expertise and judgment of each individual team member is valued, arriving at innovative ideas and creative decisions can be enhanced when accomplished collaboratively. Critical decisions are reviewed by the project team and, where possible, decided by consensus.

Early Involvement of Key Participants

The involvement of core team members from the earliest practical moment is key to an integrated approach. IPD requires the architect and all major stakeholders to be at the table with the owner early in the project development process. The timing of each team member's input is critical to the success of the project from early involvement of the project team, including consideration of the optimal time to engage manufacturers, subcontractors, and suppliers. Early involvement of key participants improves decision making and encourages the generation of informed alternatives for solving project problems as they arise.

Early Goal Definition

In IPD, project goals are jointly identified, established, and agreed upon by all participants before execution of a full contract for design and construction services. Agreement about the basic characteristics of the project, including program, cost, and schedule, is the foundation from which the team agrees to accomplish the project.

Intensified Planning

The IPD process recognizes that increased and concentrated effort in a project's earliest stages will result in improved outcomes, including increased efficiency and cost savings during construction.

Open Communication

IPD's promise of better team performance and results is based on the principle of completely open communication channels throughout the design and construction of a project, achieved by the elimination of traditional barriers to open communication. Disputes, when they do occur, can be promptly resolved in an open and transparent manner. Instead of dwelling on which party may be liable, collaboration and mutual indemnification leads to increased and open communication. Open communication begins with the owner, who must voluntarily share information, thoughts, preferences, and requirements with the rest of the team.

Appropriate Collaboration Technology

Early in the planning process, the IPD project team must identify and select the various technologies to be used throughout the design and construction of a project. No particular technology is right for use on all integrated projects. Each team has to decide—based on each participant's comfort level, familiarity, confidence, and experience—which technologies are appropriate to achieve the desired project outcomes. Regardless, the technology chosen must enhance collaboration and enable communication among all project participants through open and interoperable data exchange.

Organization and Leadership

Multiple leadership roles are played throughout an integrated delivery project. These leadership roles are determined on a stage-by-stage basis by the team. In general, the team member most appropriate for the role, skillful and experienced with the work at each portion of the project will rise to lead the team through that phase.

▶ The backgrounder on "The Need for Integrated Project Leaders" at the end of this article discusses the skills, talents, and traits of successful integrated project leaders.

IPD PROJECT CRITERIA AND CONDITIONS

While IPD is an innovative approach to project delivery, it may not be appropriate for all projects. Several considerations may combine to determine if a project should be executed under IPD.

Owner Involvement

While IPD is primarily an owner's decision, not every owner has the interest, time, or authority to participate fully in an IPD process. Some owners want the results of IPD without requiring that IPD be used in their project. Other owners may be reluctant to expend the energy and effort necessary to collaborate effectively. Owners may have no interest in addressing the unfamiliar terms of the IPD agreement, or may be skeptical of the reported cost and time savings from the IPD process. While design and construction professionals may present a convincing scenario, the fact remains: IPD cannot work without a committed owner.

If the owner does not participate fully as a team member, the team's ability to make timely, fully informed, and integrated decisions will be negatively impacted. An owner's inflexibility when it comes to process and procedures can constrain the team's ability to make decisions on a timely basis. Public owners might be further constrained by public procurement laws that favor other delivery methods. Despite these hesitations, the first condition is that the owner drives IPD.

Project Size, Type, and Complexity

All sizes of projects can benefit from an IPD approach. IPD will be effective for smaller projects when it is defined and structured. This must be done in a way that minimizes upfront expense and time commitments that may be hard to justify on a smaller project.

Smaller firms may have the ability to address issues nimbly and flexibly even though they lack the resources available to larger firms.

Due to complexity and scope, IPD may seem more appropriate for some building types than others. One building type commonly associated with IPD is the hospital, primarily due to the owner's familiarity with construction, complex building systems, and need for current technologies. However, many other building types also lend themselves to the IPD process, including commercial and institutional projects, so type of building should not constrain those considering IPD for their project.

Complex projects seem to benefit the most from an IPD approach due to the early involvement of the collaborative team. Ideally, IPD might be suitable and beneficial for any project—small or large, simple or complex. The criteria, constraints, and conditions mentioned in this section will help team members consider whether integrated delivery processes are appropriate for their project. As IPD project protocols become more widespread, the methodology will become more accessible to a broader constituency of participants.

IPD CONTRACTUAL PRINCIPLES

- Key participants bound together as equals
- Shared financial risk and reward
- Decisions based on project outcome
- Liability waivers between key participants
- Fiscal transparency between key participants
- Early involvement of key participants
- Jointly developed project goals and targets
- Collaborative decision making

IPD CONTRACTS

IPD is a delivery method that engages teams and changes the roles and behavior of team members when compared to traditional project delivery. The contractual principles below apply to "pure" IPD but can be selectively applied to integrated or "IPD-ish" contracts. To take part in pure IPD, an IPD agreement must be executed.

The IPD agreement:

- Is a contractual arrangement among multiple parties uniting the owner, architect, and contractor together in one agreement
- Is a contract based on a relationship of trust and mutual respect between the parties
- Establishes procedures that encourage specific behavioral norms
- Specifies the obligations team members have to one another

Multiparty Agreements for IPD

A standard IPD agreement is a single contract executed by the owner, architect, and contractor, representing a change from the way construction project participants have traditionally allocated risk. Standard multiparty agreements are template contracts made specifically for IPD. They are "multiparty" agreements because core team members sign one contract instead of each party signing separate contracts with the owner, engineers, and consultants. Standard multiparty contracts for IPD expand traditional responsibilities for scope of work by key participant and shift the distribution of risk.

Perhaps the greatest challenge in working with multiparty agreements is the change to work that is collaborative. Drafted with everyone's participation, the contract encourages communication among the team members prior to commencing work and reminds all parties that this is not business as usual. These conversations can create resistance, but they can also result in much stronger teams with greater alignment on key issues and project goals. People are the most complex variable in the IPD process: To overcome resistance to change, and avoid litigation, it is best to communicate early and often.

IPD Behavioral Norms

Determine the outcomes you desire, then assess the behaviors and processes you believe are necessary to achieve those outcomes. Only then do you decide what structures best support the behaviors and outcomes. It is at this last stage, not at the first, that the choice of project delivery method becomes evident.

—Howard W. Ashcraft Jr., LinkedIn discussion comment, 2011

IPD is not just about contracts; it is also a set of behaviors. IPD conforms the contract terms to the desired behaviors while protecting the project's team members. IPD creates an environment where behaviors can change in order to facilitate the process. Behaviors supported by the contract—especially optimizing collaboration and transparency—are meant to heighten team members' resourcefulness and their ability to innovate.

- Mutual respect and trust
- Willingness to collaborate
- Open communication

The IPD Team

The team is the most important element in integrated project delivery.

Team Structure

The core IPD team, in simplest form, requires an owner, an architect, and a contractor. IPD teams usually include members other than this basic triad of key players but certain players (like a specialty consultant or "sub") can be procured outside the IPD contract. Because large teams can sometimes be less productive, large projects with large teams often require teams-within-teams or cluster groups. Similarly, smaller teams might be less diverse and, as a result, could be less innovative. Irrespective of team size, select people for the core team who are critical to the project's success.

Team Experience

Teams will range from those with significant IPD experience to those who treat their pilot IPD project as a learning experience. First-time IPD teams often encounter a steep learning curve, which can be made less steep by involving those who have experience working together and by taking on less-complex projects.

Team Selection

The goal in team member selection is competency, access to a wide knowledge base, diverse points of view, and demonstrated ability to work together. IPD team members must value interdisciplinary collaboration, and have the ability to be nimble, flexible, and responsive. In IPD, where team member roles are expanded, all involved have the opportunity to contribute to the design intent, and architects can safely contribute to the means and methods. IPD removes barriers that, in traditional project delivery, kept design and construction professionals from collaborating.

BENEFITS OF PURSUING IPD

While it might be argued that a successful project is of most benefit to the owner, IPD is designed to share the rewards of that success across the members of the project team.

Benefits to the Owner

IPD provides the owner with the following benefits:

- *Predictability*. IPD can provide owners more predictable outcomes because of collaborative processes, alignment of goals, and early involvement of all stakeholders.
- *Reduced risks*. Along with predictability comes risk mitigation. People resist change because of real or perceived risk. According to Symphony LLC Partners, "remove the risk, remove the resistance."
- *Improved overall experience*. When issues do occur, IPD provides a process for dealing with inevitable unknowns. Energy is not diverted to blame and self-protection.
- *Greater flexibility*. IPD allows owners the ability to make decisions later in the design and construction process.

- *Better overall project experience.* IPD promises the elimination of adversarial relationships (typical of traditional delivery methods) and more communication, innovation, and efficiency.
- *Increased owner value.* The inherent efficiency of the IPD process reduces productivity loss in construction, thus the owner receives better value at less risk.

Benefits to the Architect

IPD affords the architect the opportunity to:

- Design and facilitate the process.
- Lead collaborative teams.
- Communicate with others in myriad ways, including architects instructing subcontractors on how to proceed.
- Develop, analyze, and evaluate a model more quickly.
- Analyze and develop options until a decision is made at the last responsible moment.
- Share knowledge and data to address the full lifecycle of the project.
- Participate in projects beyond a purely design role.
- Reduce risk while potentially increasing profit.
- Improve chances of achieving high-performance building outcomes and other goals.

Because documentation is optimized by collaboration of the architect and contractor, IPD frees architects to do what they do best, allowing them to spend less time in documentation and more time focused on their core competency: design.

Benefits to the Contractor

The contractor benefits from IPD by:

- Having an influence on construction input early in the design process
- Being made aware of and contributing to design direction and decisions by the entire project team
- Having potential to influence construction efficiency, resulting in lower overall construction cost and reduced project schedule
- Eliminating change orders by clearly defining the design documentation necessary for construction
- Working collaboratively, lessening the possibility of creating adversarial relationships

CHALLENGES OF IMPLEMENTING IPD

There are significant challenges in pursuing IPD. While design and construction professionals may struggle to adopt a collaborative approach, the greater challenge to integrated delivery processes is the skepticism of project owners. Owners who expect to award projects to the lowest bidder, for example, require that design be completed prior to bidding, which, in effect, excludes the possibility of an integrated process.

There are a number of factors working against IPD catching on and being fully adopted. First and foremost, the recent recession meant fewer projects and opportunities to implement IPD. People tend to act more conservatively in troubled economic times. The construction industry tends to be risk-averse and resistant to change. Public procurement restrictions have been mentioned, but other owner types—even entire industries—have held back from pursuing IPD due to questionable fit or suitability.

Perhaps the biggest challenge to widespread adoption of IPD is the amount of work that is involved in planning and organizing the team, the agreements, and the process.

A Committed Owner

IPD cannot work without a committed owner, who must:

- Trust the process
- Have knowledge of the industry

- Understand the impact of design decisions being made
- Agree that the best decisions are informed by key participants early on

The move to early involvement shifts increased financial outlays to earlier in the project. This change may prove detrimental for cost-sensitive and speculative projects, such as those for developer clients. Many owners are not convinced that IPD will result in cost savings. At the time of this writing, there have not been enough "pure" IPD projects completed, or accompanying cost data available, for a true comparison of delivery methods.

Owners sometimes believe that they are purchasing a product when what they are actually acquiring is a complex combination of services, knowledge, and commitment to their project. In other words, with IPD owners are investing as much in a collaborative process as a product.

Expanded Roles and Disciplinary Boundaries

In IPD, key participants are encouraged to contribute to the design intent, just as designers are free to comment on and contribute to means and methods of construction. While intended to remove obstacles and encourage collaboration, architects are sometimes threatened by the blurring of roles brought about by working in IPD. Participating in integrated delivery requires architects to redefine their position relative to the design and construction process. The blurring of roles can be seen as an expansion of services, depending on how broadly design is defined, and can result in a positive outcome for the architect.

Collaboration vs. Do-It-Yourself

In IPD, collaboration is nonoptional, foundational, and fundamental to its realization—and yet another challenge to its pursuit. Collaboration thrives in the safe environment created by IPD, empowering participants to engage in ways that result in more predictable outcomes. However, collaboration cannot guarantee consistently better results compared to working independently.

Collaborating is sometimes hard. Design professionals often have individualistic ways of working. This may be antithetical to the way many architects design projects and may be more interactive than their usual approach.

If owners could obtain diverse knowledge, breadth of expertise, and increased innovation with all key participants working independently, pursuit of IPD would seem unnecessary. Yet, trends in the construction industry productivity indicate an inability to achieve acceptable results using traditional, noncollaborative delivery methods. Despite challenges, increasing numbers of owners and design professionals are seeking out opportunities to work in integrated teams.

Legal Issues

Until IPD becomes easier to implement, architects will continue to find creative ways to work around the legal obstacles to using IPD, such as the hybrid approaches described below. Legal barriers to IPD include:

- Fluid information sharing
- Unsupportive insurance policies
- Collaborative rather than distinct responsibilities and liabilities
- Inconsistent state licensing laws

IPD principles stipulate that information produced by one party is to be made freely available to all the other team members. In terms of file sharing, some firms are concerned that the time and effort they have invested into modeling proprietary information or intellectual property becomes freely available for others to use when the model is shared among parties. This also raises the question of confidentiality, as well as liability, should the information that is borrowed without permission turn out to be faulty or misapplied. IPD exists to take advantage of information and knowledge sharing. Until barriers to sharing are satisfactorily removed, project participants will find ways to work around these and other legal challenges.

Insurance Issues

Insurers have had difficulty in confidently underwriting integrated project delivery. Insurance remains a sticking point for many teams trying to undertake an IPD approach. Some project teams continue to use traditional insurance and other standard professional liability products with the belief that special insurance isn't required in order to participate in IPD. Contractors might add professional liability to their insurance package, enabling them to participate earlier, as encouraged by IPD, in the form of preconstruction services.

There are new IPD insurance products offered by insurers, including IPD wrap-type and other project-specific insurance products. AIA Contract Documents recommend working with an insurance consultant to assist in obtaining integrated team insurance.

HYBRID APPROACHES: IPD-ISH, IPD-LITE, AND CONTRACT-FREE IPD

When a pure IPD approach through a multiparty contract is not possible for the reasons explained above, project teams may attempt to apply integrated principles to standard project delivery paradigms. They can be applied to a variety of contractual arrangements—some think of IPD as a set of philosophies that can be applied to various delivery methods. But only IPD requires that all participants place the success of the project ahead of personal gain—something that is very difficult to achieve voluntarily. Too often, such ideals are abandoned in the face of challenges without a structure in place for their amicable resolution. While design professionals are capable of working selflessly, voluntary collaboration is often fragile and should therefore be supported by integrative contract provisions.

IPD Without a Multiparty Agreement as an Intermediate Step

Architects have developed many ingenious ways to apply integrated strategies to typical delivery approaches (see case study). Hybrid IPD (IPD-ish or IPD-lite) projects follow or adapt IPD contractual and behavioral principles without strictly adhering to the constraints of the "pure" delivery method, including the use of multiparty agreements. There are certainly advantages of the IPD-ish approach. There is no checklist defining what a hybrid approach is, with agreements ranging from that required by a multiparty contract to no contractual obligation to collaborate.

Challenges of the Hybrid IPD Approaches

While IPD requires people to behave and engage differently, hybrid approaches—as sets of principles and philosophies applied to any project delivery method—don't have these same constraints. Hybrid approaches address the "what" and "why" of IPD, without addressing the critical "how" it is going to work for all involved:

- How will it happen?
- How will a safe, risk-free collaborative environment be created?
- How will aligning people and processes come about?

The transformational requirements of full contractual IPD answers these "how" questions. When it is possible to commit to a complete IPD approach, outcomes are maximized.

Project: Consolidated Forensic Lab

- Type: Government building
- Completed: 2011
- Location: 4th and School Streets, SW, Washington, D.C., USA
- Architect: HOK WDC
- Contractor: Whiting-Turner
- Area: 351,000 GSF (287,000 NSF) six-story building with two additional underground levels

As a highly complex and multidimensional organization, Consolidated Forensic Lab (CFL) needed to combine and collocate multiple independent groups into a single, state-of-the-art facility. CFL intended to realize significant operational and space efficiencies and sought to improve the Washington, D.C., crime-fighting and public health capabilities.

The project involved a complex program and a challenging site located in a dense urban area. The design team consisted of the architect and more than 30 subconsultants. With so much to coordinate, the owner insisted that the contractor complete a full 3D building information model.

The project did not use full IPD because it was awarded prior to IPD being completely defined. As a government owner, it was also constrained by public procurement laws that favor other delivery methods. The project team used a design-bid-build (DBB) delivery method but worked throughout in a spirit of cooperation.

In the DBB delivery method, the design team makes assumptions on how the work will be sequenced. These assumptions do not always work out as planned. An IPD-ish approach allows the team to coordinate and vet these assumptions early in the process.

The team took a low-tech approach of talking, openly and often, to make a high-tech approach function effectively. High-level representatives from each firm sat together in weekly meetings to go through the BIM and participate in a dialogue about the project.

THE IPD-ISH PROCESS

- Was leveraged to manage a great deal of complexity
- Allowed the owner, contractor, and design team to work together to craft the design, coordinate delivery, and control costs throughout the process
- Allowed the design team to quickly perform several different studies of the integrated facade design, and to organize about a dozen schemes for building design

RESULTS OF USING IPD-ISH MEASURES

- The actual contract value was $30 million less than the original design estimate of $165 million.
- The construction schedule was shortened by six months.
- Energy modeling achieved an expected 26 percent energy reduction over the ASHRAE 90.1 standard.
- The project achieved LEED® Platinum certification.

Documented benefits include cost, time, and energy savings from the use of BIM and the cooperative design and construction process.

Quotes from the project designer:

- "You have to be collaborative to achieve coordination like this."
- "The designer can't keep the contractor on schedule, but the designer can keep them off schedule."
- "We worked with everybody's interests in mind to facilitate the best outcome for the owner."
- "An IPD approach dramatically reduces the owner's risk, while the architect and contractor often take on more risk."
- "If your focus is on the owner's satisfaction, you will find a way to make IPD work."
- "In an IPD-ish approach, the team is under no obligation to coordinate—it is in the project's and owner's best interest to do so—especially to keep the contractor on schedule."

—Timothy O'Connell, Sr. Project Architect/Project Manager, HOK WDC

PART 3: THE PROJECT

CONCLUSION

Architects are becoming more familiar with collaborative processes and practices. The adoption of integrated project delivery methods encourages university architecture programs to foster student skills in leadership and teamwork. Architects will also be continually challenged to educate clients about IPD participation.

Despite the many challenges, owners will increasingly seek higher quality, lower cost, and faster schedules. Firms that are agile in collaboration and information sharing will be advantaged. While public sector procurement restrictions limit the use of IPD, public agencies such as the U.S. General Services Administration have shown flexibility by accommodating IPD-like principles.

To work collaboratively in IPD is to question the mind-set of the traditional practitioner. It is not necessary to be an expert in IPD or collaborative work processes to be open-minded, willing, and committed.

For IPD to catch on, contracts need to be tested in courts, the legal and insurance challenges need to be addressed, and greater education on the principles is required. In other words, these challenges need to be reframed as problems to be solved. To transform the profession and industry, there needs to be clear direction about where it is going, even if it is not going there today. IPD is one way to get there—and may be the best and highest hope for achieving shared professional goals and objectives.

For More Information

Integrated Project Delivery: A Guide (AIA, 2007): www.aia.org/contractdocs/AIAS077630

Primer on Project Delivery, 2nd edition (AIA and AGC, 2011): www.aia.org/aiaucmp/groups/aia/documents/pdf/aiab093116.pdf

BIM and Integrated Design: Strategies for Architectural Practice (Wiley, 2011) by Randy Deutsch, AIA, LEED AP: www.wiley.com/WileyCDA/WileyTitle/productCd-470572515,subjectCd-AR30.html

Integrated Project Delivery: Case Studies (AIA/AIA California Council, 2010): www.aia.org/about/initiatives/AIAB082049

Integrated Project Delivery: Updated Case Studies (AIA/AIA-Minnesota/University of Minnesota, 2011): www.aia.org/about/initiatives/AIAB087494

8.3 Emerging Issues in Project Delivery

Phillip G. Bernstein, FAIA, RIBA, LEED AP

For decades, project delivery models were stable, predictable, and repeatable, supported by standard contracts and case law. The advent of advanced digital technologies and new project objectives is stretching traditional approaches toward new models with both continual and disruptive innovations that change the roles, responsibilities, and risks of the project players.

OVERVIEW

At the turn of the twentieth century, as the modern practice of architecture was being professionalized with licensure and more formal education, projects had simple organizations and contractual models to match. Roles and responsibilities were well understood, and delivery structures were simple and streamlined. The original AIA Contract "B1" (the great-grandfather of today's AIA Document B101™–2007, Standard Form of Agreement Between Owner and Architect) explained the architect's role briefly, allocating the job of design and construction to each participant with relative clarity. Ideas like "means and methods" were created to distribute responsibilities and keep a smoothly running job site. By the 1920s, the architects of the Empire State Building had more than 200 site superintendents and managers under their direct employ, all of whom worked to complete the world's largest and tallest building in a mere 14 months, an approach almost unthinkable by modern standards. (See Neal Bascomb's *Higher: The Historic Race to the Sky and the Making of a City* [Broadway Books, 2004].)

The future of project delivery context is considerably murkier. Building construction has become both more complex and more litigious, and the means of project

Phillip G. Bernstein, FAIA, is vice president for strategic industry relations of Autodesk Inc. and a former principal with Pelli Clarke Pelli Architects. Bernstein teaches at the Yale School of Architecture and lectures and writes extensively on project delivery and technology issues. He is former chair of the AIA Contract Documents Committee.

delivery has followed suit. Multiple methods of organizing a project have evolved in the U.S. construction market, each of which is designed (putatively) to make the structure, risk, and outcomes of construction more repeatable, streamlined, and predictable. Alas, if only this were completely so.

Well-understood arguments about low industry productivity, excessive risk assumed by architects who lack the means to manage it, and ambiguous relationships to the building lifecycle are just a few of the arguments for reexamining the structures of building delivery. While models like design-bid-build and construction manager (constructor) continue to be widely adopted, new modalities are starting to emerge, catalyzed by the opportunities of new technologies, innovative owners, and industry organizations, and a growing sense that new options are necessary.

Examined here are some of the emerging innovations in project delivery processes, with a particular eye toward different approaches to changes in business structure and project structure. Designing and constructing buildings is a deliberate and careful process that is dependent on a complex, conservative supply chain of clients, designers, and builders. Systemic change therefore moves slowly, and industry participants vary widely in their appetite for radical adjustments in long-held processes—even when traditional processes yield less than satisfactory results. Therefore, some of the new ideas below can be seen as incremental (adjusting current methods toward new ends), and others disruptive (changing the underlying structure of project delivery itself).

A survey of U.S. construction owners in 2005 by the Construction Management Association of America (CMAA) concluded that almost a third of all building projects miss either their budget targets, completion dates, or both (2005 CMAA Owner's Survey). While the motivation to improve project delivery is based on this growing dissatisfaction with the results of building by everyone involved, emerging solutions depend heavily on three factors: closer collaboration of project participants, transparent exchanges of information, and reliance on advanced digital technologies like building information modeling (BIM). Innovations in methodology and technology will combine to change project delivery as a result.

INNOVATIONS IN METHODOLOGY

The separation of design and construction responsibilities and roles was an arrangement of convenience at the turn of the twentieth century, but by its end that separation became more of a gulf. The distinction between the architect's responsibility to define "design intent" through construction documents, and the contractor's obligation to follow that intent, has been and continues to be a source of tension on the job site, or, worse, lawsuits alleging negligent drawings. A more reasoned explanation of these tensions might include the acknowledgment that the separate roles of designer and builder had been exaggerated by delivery methods that optimize self-interest (in the form of risk reduction and fee protection) over communication. Thus, at the heart of most current innovations in delivery is an attempt to bridge the gulf and bring the designer and builder into closer collaboration. Such an idea implies the restructuring of the design-to-build relationship, and in many cases the revision of obligations accordingly.

Design Plus Construction Integration

Thus, two characteristics of today's traditional approaches to delivery are being questioned. First, highly sequential project delivery models like design-bid-build bring one of the most important players in the process into the project after 80 percent of the architect's efforts and the development of the job are complete, without benefit of the builder's insight. So a first principle of innovation is to bring construction expertise in early during design. This idea might involve the use of a general contractor (GC) for constructability analysis in a hard-bid project, the simultaneous selection of architect and construction manager (CM) in CM jobs, or even the use of the builder to help organize and integrate the construction documents on a project. In disruptive models like integrated project

See "Integrated Project Delivery Overview" for more detail on design plus construction integration.

delivery (IPD), the client selects an architect and builder together and holds them jointly accountable for project outcomes, sharing the risks and rewards as a result.

Second, the oft-repeated assertion that information created by the architect is for "design intent" creates controversy about the accuracy and completeness of that information for purposes of construction. In order to manage risk, architects assert that such information provided to the contractor be reviewed, coordinated, and checked vigorously before being used in the field. Such assertions create opportunities for misinterpretation, transcription errors, and argument. The digital exchange of design intent data—geometry and other information that is part and parcel of design delineation—can be transmitted, under proper arrangement, directly to the builder for accurate use. This "direct data exchange" is a basic underlying principle of almost every emerging trend in delivery today.

Integrative Strategies in Nonintegrated Delivery Models

As the industry begins to adopt "disruptive" project delivery approaches such as canonical IPD, more organic innovations for integration strategies are emerging that can be applied in more traditional delivery models, to wit:

- *Under design-bid-build*, the architect may agree to share or integrate models or other digital deliverables with subconsultants to reduce rework and increase coordination; that information could be provided to the selected general contractor for its use during construction, assuming the proper risk and compensation adjustments have been made to standard contracts.
- *Under construction management (particularly CM constructor)*, AIA contracts offer the option for the architect and builder to share common general conditions that specify particular opportunities for shared outcomes and collaborative outcomes.
- *Under design-build*, the lower contractual barriers between designer and builder offer chances to create deliverables specifically customized to the construction approach and builder's techniques.

Lean Methodology

The industry is also examining so-called Lean methodologies, developed by Toyota to streamline manufacturing of automobiles. A Lean approach involves the careful delineation of the design and construction processes by mutual agreement such that information (or materials) are created and received at the optimum moment to benefit the project. While Lean methods are making inroads with contractors, in combination with integrated strategies described above, they are likely to permeate design planning as well. And since this approach makes little distinction between design and construction activities, treating the entire process as a seamless whole, Lean approaches to project organization are by definition integrated.

Public/Private Delivery

As public entities are under increasing pressure to reduce costs, many are looking to "turnkey" services by integrated design-build-operate teams for project delivery. So-called PPP (public-private partnerships) or BOT (build-operate-transfer) projects are the answer for governments that lack both the capital funding and expertise to create complex projects like hospitals, prisons, university housing, or even infrastructure. Usually involving the participation of a developer, who provides financing and management expertise, as well as architects and builders, clients provide a specification and entertain competitive bids for the best deal based on schedule, quality, and cost.

For example, a public university in need of new student housing might offer the rights to build new dormitories on a BOT basis. The winning integrated team would finance, design, build, and operate the project, and take a large portion of the resulting revenues from housing fees, returning some of those funds to the university and relieving the institution of the obligation of running it. After a contractually agreed-upon time period (spanning 25 to 99 years in some cases) the entire project is turned back over to the originating institution.

Many architects participate in such projects in traditional roles, working for the developers who drive the projects. More recently, contractors are stepping into the lead role, using design-build contracts to create the projects. Architects who lead such projects could take advantage of this untapped market.

Outcome-Based Scopes and Services

The design and construction markets have typically been characterized by fierce competition between participants who have difficulty differentiating from each other. Lacking distinct value propositions, designers and builders compete based on only price, and the result is low profit margins. Fixed design fees for architects, lowest hard bids or fee-based compensation for builders, and behavior designed to protect those fees during the project are the result. Emerging integrated approaches are experimenting with correlating compensation with project outcomes defined at the outset of a project.

If the client, architect, and builder agree to a strongly cooperative approach (using, for example, an IPD model) at the project's outset, then outcome-based scopes and compensation can be defined by the owner to pay the architect and the contractor based on how the project is actually accomplished. Incentive payments could be based on achieving the project schedule, meeting the project budget, getting a certain LEED rating, or even meeting certain quality measures. In some IPD models, these payments are made jointly to both the architect and contractor, who decide between them how to distribute the funds among their teams. Such shared incentives are designed to align interests among project participants in the hope that decisions made to benefit the project also benefit its designer and builder.

Sustainable design objectives offer another opportunity for outcome-based scopes of service and/or compensation. They are often tied directly not just to the characteristics of the project—such as the percentage of recycled materials in construction—but also to its operational performance. Assuming proper measurements and parameters can be established at the project outset, the architect (and contractor) could establish an obligation for the building to meet certain performance requirements—such as energy or water usages against a baseline—in exchange for compensation. (Such an approach would depend, of course, on establishing operating parameters that the design and construction team could control.) The resulting project would provide not just an annuity-style revenue stream but also a more permanent relationship between the completed building and the team that created it.

Lifecycle and Facilities Management Services

As buildings increase in both technical and operational complexity (consider highly sustainable building systems, for example) owners need new strategies for running them. The design/construction team, particularly if it has created sophisticated digital and analytical models of the project during its development, brings tremendous insight to this challenge. Sophisticated owners are asking their teams to deliver digital assets (typically facilities management–based BIM) for use in operating their facilities. Forward-thinking contractors, attempting to differentiate themselves in the cutthroat construction market, are offering to not just provide that data but also to support the ongoing management of the constructed project as a service in addition to construction management. Architects who can understand and define the information and procedures that support postconstruction operation of the project can design project delivery models that connect them to that portion of the building lifecycle accordingly, as they are arguably the most knowledgeable about how projects are designed to perform when in operation.

Digital information technologies are infiltrating the entire spectrum of design and construction methodologies, with BIM at the center of the change. The creation of digital prototypes through BIM is a key characteristic in changing models of project delivery. The resulting digital information can be the basis of new methods of transparent collaboration and the generation of new kinds of information that architects can deliver for projects in various ways. As new technologies like cloud computing come into the mainstream, such methods are likely to become deeply integrated into project delivery methodologies of the future.

Performative Analysis

As the means of documenting the design shifts from paper drawings to digital models, the design process can be increasingly supported by analytical methods and procedures. Digital models, as virtual prototypes of the building, can be evaluated for performance characteristics such as energy use, occupant capacity, and even lighting or acoustic levels prior to construction, and these measured outcomes can be tied to performance aspects of the project delivery contract itself. Design ideas may be examined by scripts or computer routines to more systematically define the "solution space" within which a problem can be solved. Analytic methodologies increase the capabilities and value of the resulting buildings. The ability to deliver projects of greater value as predicted by these digital tools can be incorporated into the arrangements—contractual and financial—by which the building is delivered.

Construction Analysis, Planning, and Monitoring

A direct result of the combination of collaborative methods between architect and builder and BIM is the use of design deliverables as the basis for construction analysis and planning. Current project delivery models and contracts insist that the architects separate themselves from the so-called means and methods of construction. The resulting construction documents are intentionally agnostic to construction procedures, planning, or sequence, even if such insight is critical to achieving the final design result. Combined with the rules-based parametric analysis methods (where design logic is defined by scripts that are part of the deliverables), digital models created under integrated project delivery can instantiate sequence and logic from the builder. The BIM models become not just artifacts describing the finished state but tools to strategize and plan construction. Since many contractors operating under traditional models like CM-constructor are "rebuilding" construction phase BIM models for these ends, there is increased value to the project in combining these processes and using the combined insights of designer and builder to create information that best solves the building problem. "Disruptive" project delivery models like IPD, where the risk of construction is reallocated and refined to reflect the advantages of collaboration, are the best places to exploit this opportunity. Selected designers and builders may decide to make arrangements for the exchange of specific construction-useful information in exchange for proper financial consideration.

Once construction begins, the BIM models can be the basis for monitoring progress. Simple methods like quantity analysis support evaluation of installation and bills of materials are now possible. Advanced techniques like laser-scanning are being used by contractors, creating three-dimensional digital scans of installed work that can be compared for progress against originating BIM data. The design BIM, as the basis of such work, brings real value to the construction process while changing the relationship of the architect to the overall method of project delivery.

Digital Fabrication

Beyond mere construction planning, fabricators of building components can use geometry and other digital information created by the architect. Inasmuch as the best understanding of the geometry necessary to fabricate complex systems such as curtain walls or enclosure systems originates with the architect, it is logical to assume the architect could best guide the resulting fabrication process. Better yet, collaboration between the selected fabricator and the architect to create the geometry and supporting data necessary to create the system is most efficient, and is in fact used on many complex curtain wall designs today. Some such projects are based on integrated project delivery principles where the value of the digital information exchange is defined in the contract. In other circumstances the architect embraces the counterintuitive notion that while providing the fabricator with source geometry actually increases risk, the ability to supervise and control its use actually makes lawsuit-inducing mistakes less likely.

As building subsystems are more frequently created using manufacturing processes under tight schedules, demand for the architect's digital model to drive the fabrication process will increase. This is an opportunity for design professionals to both increase their knowledge of construction methods and add value to the construction supply chain.

Cloud, Mobile, and Social—or "The Crowd and the Cloud"

No discussion about the technological impacts on project delivery is complete without a brief examination of the implications of three critical and interrelated technologies that are changing culture, business, and, by implication, architecture: cloud computing, mobile devices, and social networking, the explanations of which may seem quaint to future readers of the *Handbook*:

- *Cloud computing*: The use of large collections of Internet-based processors and storage devices that dramatically increase the computation capabilities of any user connected to the service
- *Mobile devices*: The increasing effectiveness of battery-operated, Internet-connected devices that allow information and processes to occur away from the desktop and "at the point of work." In combination with cloud computing, mobile devices suggest that software of the future, operating anywhere from the cloud, will be increasingly independent of hardware platforms (think BIM on a smartphone).
- *Social networking*: The interconnection of large groups of like-minded individuals who rely not on formal communication mechanisms but on point-to-point electronic association, making it possible to build large, geographically disparate teams and tap the collective knowledge of a broad swath of professionals quickly.

If emerging project delivery methodologies are empowering collaboration empowered by digital technology, these trends will further accelerate new techniques and interactions. Digital information about a project will coalesce in BIM, be universally accessible on the cloud, and unconstrained by the limits of a desktop computer processor. It will be available on any Internet-connected device. As a result, the design process is untethered from the design studio, and new collaborative approaches, structures, and project delivery methods are already emerging.

For example, many of today's IPD projects are based on the concept of the "big room," a place where the design and construction team co-locate during part of each week to work collectively on the project. Some work may occur back in home offices, but the team has joint access to the project information by "moving" the place of work to a Web-based spot where they can solve it together. Once construction begins, information collectively created is delivered wirelessly to lightweight wireless devices at the new point-of-work on the job site. And even as the team may be back in their respective offices during construction, social networking methods provide easy ways for updates, decision making, and knowledge collection and insight.

SPECULATIONS ON THE FUTURE

If the history of project delivery, from the Empire State Building to the end of the millennium, was characterized by the separation of design and construction and the increasing alienation of architects and contractors (followed causally by increasing dissatisfaction of clients), the twenty-first century has begun a re-examination and bridging of that gulf. Technology has made some early techniques for reintegration possible, but it is just a means to an end. Our inefficient, environmentally challenged, risky, and low-margin industry is crying out for new approaches, and integrated project delivery models are the best vectors for reform. Today's architects and builders are beginning to realize that the answers to these questions lie in refining the ways that they work together, and realigning the project delivery models accordingly. Integrated project delivery and many of the ideas described above are the early indicators of a future that will likely include completely different definitions of the architect's role and scope, connection to the building process, and relationship to the building lifecycle.

The changes that are necessary, anticipated today by early IPD projects, are not merely procedural. Future architects and builders will likely not be able to simply "play the positions" of their predecessors and just deploy innovative contract models. New protocols, relationships, and business models—the very processes of delivery—must be redesigned, and architects can lead this process.

Practice has changed rapidly in the first 15 years of the twenty-first century as digital tools, new construction methodologies, and new responsibilities have emerged for architects. The bridging of design and construction sensibilities that integrated delivery will demand could be seen as a threat to practice, but is better seen as an opportunity for architects to define a new role for themselves and to improve building in the process. That is the best value proposition possible.

BACKGROUNDER

THE NEED FOR INTEGRATED PROJECT LEADERS

Barbara J. Jackson, PhD, DBIA

Leading integrated projects and teams requires a unique set of skills and talents. Being an architect, contractor, or engineer does not qualify or prepare a person for leading integrated projects. In addition to discipline expertise, Integrated Project Leaders (IPLs) must possess a disposition for collaboration across disciplines, demonstrating appreciation, enthusiasm, and empathy for what others contribute.

Barbara Jackson is a professor of Construction Management in the College of Architecture and Environmental Design at Cal Poly State University. She also serves as director of the Center for Integrated Project Leadership for the Built Environment and is author of *Design-Build Essentials* (Delmar Cengage Learning, 2010).

The Leadership Imperative

The one common denominator among all integrated project delivery approaches is the expectation for the team—owner, architect, and contractor, and others as assigned—to act "as one," thus capturing the collective knowledge and expertise of the multidiscipline perspective to deliver comprehensive, integrated solutions. Given our industry's historical segregated services mentality and isolated operational model, achieving such a collaborative, interdisciplinary teaming

arrangement is a tall order, and certainly one that is not going to happen by accident. It takes a unique leader with unique leadership skills to elicit such results. Unfortunately, these required leadership skills are not readily taught in architecture, engineering, or construction management schools, and yet architects, engineers, and contractors are typically the individuals who are charged with leading these integrated project approaches.

Being well trained in the disciplines of architecture, engineering, or construction project management does not usually properly prepare a design or construction professional for the task of leading a multidiscipline team of individuals with different skills and motivations. The challenge is, when bringing this diverse group together to work on an integrated project solution, if each team member only contributes their single-discipline perspectives, it's very difficult for them to view solutions from an interdisciplinary viewpoint.

What tends to happen on many projects is that each individual discipline presses for its own point of view. Architects press for enhanced design, contractors press for budgets and schedules, and each party may feel threatened by the other's point of view. While the discipline that is "leading" the team is most likely to succeed in forwarding its approach, the fact remains that the owner wants it all—an integrated solution that enhances design as well as the budget and schedule. An integrated project leader must rise above any single discipline perspective and develop a disposition for collaboration across disciplines.

The Integrated Project Leader

Most would agree that the true leader of the project is always the owner, who sets the goals, objectives, and purpose for the projects. But from a practical perspective, the owner doesn't lead, coordinate, monitor, and manage the design and construction efforts that deliver the intended and expected goals, objectives, and purpose for the project. As more projects are executed as integrated efforts between designers and builders, the question of who is best suited to lead the integrated project must be considered. Should it be the architect? Should it be the contractor? The most accurate answer is probably neither, if their discipline expertise is all that they can bring to the leadership challenge.

It is common wisdom within the construction industry, that there exists generally significant skepticism and distrust between the design and construction disciples. Both are skeptical that the other has adequate understanding, knowledge, or appreciation of elements and issues associated with their contributions, and each therefore lacks trust that a project leader of the other discipline will give them proper consideration. Anecdotally, both parties, when working together on teams, have voiced these very concerns regardless of the contract model, and whether in separate firms or integrated firms.

Successful leadership of any integrated approach to project delivery requires a new mental model for working together collectively and collaboratively. Integrated projects require individuals who can rise above their discipline bias and become the integrated project leaders that owners will need to fully leverage the collective ability of their multidisciplinary team. The integrated project leader must create an environment in which every participating party succeeds, and a comprehensive, integrated solution is achieved. In addition to managing the distinct design and construction functions as an integrated process, which poses a substantial challenge in itself, the IPL must also create and manage a teaming culture that produces the results the owner is looking for.

CHAPTER 9

Design Project Management

9.1 Managing Architectural Projects

Grant A. Simpson, FAIA

When the delivery of services for architectural projects is well managed, those projects are more likely to meet their goals and objectives and fulfill the expectations of their owners.

The design and construction industry is a project-based world. As such, project management is a key component for any architect or architecture firm. Effective project management requires an understanding of project management basics, which are equally applicable to any project, from the development of a large hospital to the design of a one-room addition to a house. Knowing how and when to apply appropriate tools and techniques will make management activities easier, more efficient, and more professional.

Except on the smallest of assignments and in smaller offices, the project manager does not personally produce the major project deliverables. Rather, the project manager must know *who* can produce the required services, *when* those services must be carried out, and *how* those services fit into the overall project delivery scheme. In short, while project managers will do some of the work, their primary role is to direct the work being done by others. In fulfilling

This topic covers the process of project management for architectural projects. The backgrounder accompanying this article, "The Effective Project Manager," addresses the desirable personal attributes and qualities of project managers.

Grant A. Simpson has served as a project delivery leader for several firms, including RTKL Associates and HKS, where his responsibilities included construction documentation, project management, and loss prevention activities. Simpson has served on the AIA Practice Management Knowledge Community advisory group and the AIA Risk Management Committee.

this role, the project manager delegates responsibilities to those with the design and technical expertise needed to complete the required work.

Project management activities for architectural projects can be clustered in the following groups:

- Organizing the project
- Facilitating the work
- Effect of client expectations on the project

These groups of activities essentially embody the full range of tasks and responsibilities that project managers will encounter in their assignments. The remainder of this topic—organized according to these groups—provides specific guidance and identifies practical methods, tools, and techniques that can be used to carry them out.

Project managers should be actively involved in the development of proposals and agreements. Both small and large offices require a certain discipline when developing these documents, since they establish the foundation for project success or failure. Ideally, the project manager will be included in the initial preparation of proposals and agreements as well as in the negotiation of final agreements. Participating in this process will give the project manager an intimate knowledge of both the firm's and the client's goals, and his or her familiarity with the issues will help the firm maintain continuity throughout the delivery process. Encouraging involvement of the project manager during this crucial stage of relationship-building with the client also demonstrates the firm's confidence in the leadership and authority of the project manager.

TWO SIDES OF PROJECT MANAGEMENT

Project management has two basic sides, which must operate in unison for success to be achieved in any project management assignment.

THE OBJECTIVE SIDE

Some project management responsibilities spring from what is objectively defined by the architect's contract for services. These include issuing notices; providing certifications; and reporting findings, decisions, and observations. Other objective responsibilities may be viewed as industry standards, including such things as attending project meetings, preparing meeting agendas, writing meeting reports, and generally attending to correspondence and documentation.

THE SUBJECTIVE SIDE

Subjective and more intangible responsibilities often require a broader application of judgment than objectively identified responsibilities. This side of project management relies on attitude, personality, behavior, and even personal habits. It involves people skills, such as being a good listener, motivating team members, and leading conflict resolution. For example, project managers are called on to remain calm and function as leaders in times of stress or duress. Project managers must frequently act as teachers to help others understand the decisions required to move the project forward.

PROJECT MANAGEMENT IN SMALL FIRMS: PYRAMID TO MATRIX

In many small architecture firms, the principals, who are usually also the firm owners, are the primary project managers. Principals do all the client contact and project tracking; all information flows through them; and they are the main decision makers. Not surprisingly, partners in these firms frequently work long hours and complain about not having time for design or for firm development.

THE PYRAMID PROBLEM

The project management model used by these firms is known as a pyramid structure. Principals, at the top of their pyramid, often become a bottleneck in the production process, causing delay and wasted effort. Because principals are frequently gone from the office, critical information can be missed and last-minute design changes may be common. If a principal were to disappear completely for some reason, much critical knowledge would also disappear, debilitating the projects and the firm.

As the day-to-day deadlines loom, firm leaders who use a pyramidal project management model may find it hard to turn their attention to firm management tasks. Even though they know they should turn their focus to outreach; to tracking backlog, cash flow, and other financial metrics; and to assessing staff effectiveness, the demands of current projects make this very difficult. Strategic thinking is put on the back burner, and short-sighted decisions are sometimes made as attention moves from one firefight to the next.

THE MATRIX SOLUTION

In the matrix model of project management, professional staff members other than the principals are the primary project managers. In addition to giving the principals more time for marketing and firm development, it gives selected employees more of the billable work. If workload declines, this can make a real difference in being able to retain highly valued staff.

(continued)

When a talented staff member assumes a project manager role, he or she is given responsibility and challenge, inevitably resulting in increased commitment and enthusiasm. The principal in charge of a project can then support the project manager with mentoring and quality review. Some principals will also serve on the project team as the lead designer or technical expert.

By letting go of project management, firm leaders are able to focus on work that enables the firm to sustain, even through troubled times. In addition, it introduces a systemic change that can result in higher productivity and employee retention. Even in a firm of two people, one owner and one professional employee, a matrix model can be applied, freeing a sole proprietor to focus on business development.

By transferring project management from principals to project architects, firm leaders will position their firm for growth, if that is their goal. In a pyramid model, growth is only possible by adding more pyramids (principals), but growth through adding pyramids is limited. While the firm may get bigger, it is unlikely it will be more profitable, more productive, or more innovative. By moving to a matrix model, growth is enabled because firm leaders are freed to do what only they can do—network, acquire projects, and set new directions for the firm.

—Rena M. Klein, FAIA (adapted from *The Architect's Guide to Small Firm Management*, Wiley, 2010)

ORGANIZING THE PROJECT

The project manager usually takes charge of planning and organizing a project. This simply means the project manager develops a primary understanding of how and when the project will be worked on and what leadership and staff will be needed to perform the work. The project manager usually interacts with firm leaders, and perhaps with other project managers, as this understanding becomes documented in a work plan.

Development of a work plan for the project begins with consideration of schedules, ways to organize relationships between the parties, the firm's available resources, and perhaps fees. In addition, how the leadership for the project will be organized and what experience and specialty levels will be required are identified.

The Manager's Organizational Tools

Organizational tools comprise some of the elements of an effective work plan as briefly described in the following. The work plan is a key part of effective project management. To be useful, a work plan need not be complicated or lengthy. For most projects, it need only include the elements listed below. Even on large projects, this information may take up no more than a few pages.

1. Project description and client requirements
2. Statement of deliverables
3. Team organization
4. Responsibility matrix
5. Preliminary project schedule
6. Preliminary staffing needs
7. Project directory
8. Internal project budget and profit plan
9. Code information (optional)

Maintaining a work plan is an ongoing process. Projections for staffing, schedules, and budgets must be revisited and adjusted as new information becomes available. When carefully prepared, items 1 through 7 can be presented to clients to illustrate how you plan to approach their projects.

Project Description and Client Requirements

The work plan includes a description of the project, including its scope and the client's budget, as well as a record of what work the client has authorized. The client's primary goals for the scope and quality of the project should also be incorporated into the project description. A project description would read something like this example:

A 300-room four-star luxury hotel, located on the waterfront at 212 Boardwalk Street in Any City, including two restaurants, conference facilities for 500 guests, a full-service spa, a resort-quality swimming pool, and landscaped grounds.

This example demonstrates how the project description can be communicated in a short statement, which can later be expanded in greater detail as the program for the project is developed.

Depending on the project phase, client authorizations may be represented in the work plan by a simple checklist of authorized work keyed to copies of signed owner-architect agreements. Client authorizations can include various kinds of documentation, ranging from letters of agreement to formal contracts to phase-completion sign-offs. The project manager tracks and monitors all of these authorizations.

Summary of Deliverables

Projects normally include a work product or deliverable produced by the architect. Such deliverables may include reports, sketches and drawings, specifications, virtual or physical models, and other items. The work plan should include estimates for the types and quantities of deliverables required to complete the work. The format of this estimate can be a simple list or a storyboard or cartoon depiction of the deliverables for each phase of the architect's services. This description and estimate provide a basis for developing the project schedule, staffing needs, and budget for the architect's work.

Team Organization

More and more, owners want information on how the architect will organize project staff, and how that staff will relate to other parties involved in the project. A chart is helpful for communicating the relationships between the project team participants.

A team chart typically reflects who the primary project leaders will be, such as the principal-in-charge, the project manager, designers, project architects, and job captains. While there can be many position titles in an architect's office, the basic intent of the team chart is to define the hierarchy of the architect's team, reflect who will be responsible for what assignments, and show primary relationships between members of the project team.

Usually, there will be one or more project leaders, regardless of project size. For a large project, several project leaders may appear on the project management team. For a small firm and a small project, the architect's project team chart may include only the firm principal.

Project Coordination Matrix

A companion task to defining deliverables is determining who will do what on the project. When a project requires consultants, it is important to have an explicit understanding of what each consultant will do. For example, it is not enough to have a seat-of-the-pants understanding that the MEP engineer will "do the MEP engineering." A more detailed understanding would distinguish responsibilities such as these: "The electrical engineer will wire and circuit the landscape architect's lighting design," or "The MEP engineer will coordinate HVAC equipment selections with the acoustical engineer." Table 9.1 illustrates a project responsibility matrix, which is a convenient way to communicate project assignments.

Preliminary Schedule

Most requests for proposals (RFPs) received or tendered by the architect relate in some manner to the project schedule. This means the work plan should delineate the preliminary project schedule as clearly and as accurately as possible. Whether the objective is to complete a retail project in time for the fall shopping season or to open a sports facility for the opening home game, the owner's goals for the project often dictate its

TABLE 9.1 Project Coordination Matrix							
Office Building		**A**	**TA**	**S**	**MEP**	**C**	**L**
1	Site Landscape & Grading					X	X
2	Site Grading & Drainage					X	X
	Site Lighting				X		X
8	Structural Engineering: Base Building			X			
9	Structural Engineering: Tenant Specialties			X			
11	Stairs: Lobby Monumental Stair	X					
13	Exterior Envelope, Roofing, and Details	X		X			
14	Doors & Hardware	X	X				
16	Interior: Main Lobby, Core Areas, and Toilets	X	X		X		
17	Interior: Tenant Areas		X		X		
23	HVAC: Base Building	X			X		
25	HVAC: Tenant Distribution		X		X		
26	Plumbing: Base Building	X			X		
28	Plumbing: Tenant		X		X		
30	Electrical: Base Building	X			X		
31	Electrical: Tenant		X		X		

Legend

A   Architect

TA   Tenant architect

S   Structural engineer

MEP   MEP engineer

C   Civil engineer

L   Landscape architect

major milestones. Into this mix, the architect must project the team's ability to perform the work within the owner's set of key dates. The preliminary schedule is one of the primary drivers of the architect's assessment of staffing needs.

Preliminary Staffing Needs

Preliminary staffing requirements can be estimated once the project scope has been delineated, the deliverables understood, the consultant's responsibilities defined, and a preliminary schedule developed. The project manager may work with upper management (in a larger firm) to determine what key personnel will be available and what support staff will be required. If available staffing becomes a greater constraint on the firm's ability to deliver the project than the client's scheduling goals, the firm may need to revisit the preliminary schedule with the client and perhaps revise it.

Project Directory

A project directory with current listings for all project entities and their key personnel should be included in the work plan. This can be prepared in a format the firm normally uses, or the entries can be printed from an e-mail management program such as Microsoft Outlook. More simply, organized copies of business cards can be used to develop a directory.

Project Budget and Profit Plan

The project manager may sometimes be assigned the duty of apportioning the project fee to the various tasks required to produce the work to help estimate and plan for the firm's profit. Often referred to as a job cost budget or a project budget, a current copy of this should be included in the work plan.

Regulatory Requirements

Information about the primary building code(s) and local amendments that will apply to the project can be a very useful part of the work plan. This information could range from a simple list of the applicable codes and ordinances to a full building code report prepared by the architect. Including this information gives the project team a close-at-hand opportunity to get an answer to the frequent question, "What code are we using?"

▶ See "Building Codes and Standards" for a detailed discussion of codes and regulations.

FACILITATING THE PROJECT

As the role of the project manager has evolved, what was once thought of as "controlling" the project has come to be more a role of "facilitating" the project. The delivery of design services is facilitated through communicating effectively; developing good working relationships with the client, contractor, and consultants; providing assistance to parties whose decisions are necessary to keep the design services moving forward; and developing and using effective documentation.

Project Staffing

When project leaders and staff positions have been identified, the project manager reviews the project organization chart and the required tasks to verify that assigned staff has the needed skills and experience for the work they will be doing. In fact, staff experience is rarely evenly matched to the project assignments, so the project manager will always need to make adjustments to effectively use the talents of everyone assigned to a project.

Project managers often face the conundrum of balancing the staff needed to do the work against the project staff the fee can sustain. In this situation, the vulnerability faced by both the firm and the project manager is the temptation to sacrifice quality for profit. The firm principals should debate this philosophical question and reach a stance that can be incorporated into the firm's culture so that this burden is taken away from the project manager. The project manager must be allowed to focus on the quality of services provided to the client.

Managing the Project Team

Managing the project team? This sounds like an overwhelming responsibility. However, the basic requirement boils down to a few key ideals. The first calls for understanding what the team is to accomplish. The second requires an understanding of who on the team has the skills to do what tasks, and where additional resources may be needed. The third is fostering a communications environment in which all parties are kept informed of what is expected of them and when their assignments are due. The key tools and techniques for accomplishing this are the work plan, effective management of project meetings, and reasonably thorough documentation of key project decisions and actions.

Client Relationships

The project manager's relationship with the client is key both to understanding the client's goals and to communicating with the client. This relationship must be close enough that the project manager can gain a comfortable understanding of the client's expectations. If the client's expectations do not align with the architect's intended services, then either the architect's services must change or the client's expectations must change. Having confidence in each other's abilities and integrity will facilitate resolution when conflicts occur. Candor and honesty are always beneficial for developing a relationship in which news and events can be presented with a neutral, unemotional attitude.

Decision Making

It is commonly understood that there are few occasions when the architect makes a decision. Instead, the architect typically gives a *recommendation* upon which the client may base a decision. For example, the architect makes decisions about substantial completion and final completion, but commonly these decisions are heavily infused with input from the owner and the contractor. In a dispute, the architect—seeking faithful performance by the owner and the contractor—renders a decision about conditions that can reasonably be inferred from the construction documents. The full range of the authority and decision-making responsibilities of the architect are generally delineated in the owner-architect agreements and in the general conditions of the contract for construction.

The architect does not decide on changes in scope, quality, or time except in specifically contracted circumstances. However, although project managers cannot make decisions for the client, they can facilitate needed decisions by providing support and explanations to the client. For example, the project manager may prepare an executive summary of the pros and cons that the client might consider in making a decision. Or the project manager might research alternative materials and costs that reflect the options the client can choose from. Such support from the architect makes the client's work easier, and will inevitably also make the architect's work easier. (The importance of carefully documenting the client's decisions is covered later in this topic.)

Managing Project Meetings

Successful project managers must learn to orchestrate and administrate project meetings. All project managers have faced the frustration of disruptions, lack of preparation on someone's part, or disruptive—even angry—people while trying to run a meeting. It is possible to take an analytical view of managing meetings and look at some ways a project manager can be more effective. A first step is to understand the obstacles to a successful meeting, which include the following:

- Too many people in attendance
- A disruptive participant
- People who don't pay attention
- Unprepared attendees
- Sidebar conversations
- Cell phone or PDA interruptions

You will have to find a way around such obstacles, even if it means bringing a gavel to the meeting. You don't want the meeting so out of control that you have to raise your voice to get attendees to pay attention.

Meetings Schedule

Arguably, for any project—but particularly for projects with more than three or four participants—it is important to hold regular meetings. Setting a routine by conducting the meetings on the same day of the week at the same time is advisable. Personal schedules tend to fall into a groove, and the participants will adapt more effectively to regularly set meetings. On smaller projects, it will save time and expense to organize the meeting via conference call if the agenda is short. Remember, it is important not to skip meetings. Missed meetings erode communication, and lack of communication is at the root of most problems on architecture projects.

Meeting Management Plan

The primary purpose of a meeting management plan is to ensure people attend the meeting when their input is required and stay away when it is not. Decisions cannot be made or obtained without the necessary participants. Conversely, you cannot facilitate decision making as effectively when non–decision makers are debating the issues.

Most projects involve a hierarchy within the client organization, design team, and contractor and subcontractor team. Not every project participant needs to attend every project

TABLE 9.2 Meeting Management Plan

Type	Purpose	Attendees from Firm	Recorded by
Executive Session			
Participants:			
Principals	Executive-level representation	Principal-in-charge	Project manager
Owner		Project manager	
Contractor/CM	Decision making		
AE team			
Design Review Session			
Participants:			
Owner	Design direction	Principal-in-charge	Project manager
Contractor/CM	Design review and approvals	Project manager	
AE team		Project architect	
Project Meeting			
Participants:			
Owner	Project planning and general decision making	Principal-in-charge	Project manager and project architect
Contractor/CM		Project manager	
AE team		Project architect	
Special consultants			
Coordination Meeting			
Participants:			
Project architects	Coordination	Project architect	Project architect
Project engineers	Work session	Job captain	
Optional			
Contractor/CM			
Owner			
Redline Work Sessions			
Participants:			
Project architect	Coordination	Project architect	Job captain
Job captains	Work sessions	Job captain	
Consultants' staff			

discussion. Whether the project is large or small, discussions run more smoothly and time is used more efficiently when meetings are divided into executive sessions, project design meetings, general project meetings, coordination sessions, and redline work sessions. Table 9.2 illustrates a meeting management plan type that can be shared with all parties.

Executive Sessions

Critical and formative decisions are made at the highest levels in an owner's organization. Whether the client is a large corporation or a couple desiring a new home, there will be key meetings during which important decisions are made. These meetings are most effective when as few attendees as possible are in the room. Meet with the owner and other key project leaders early on, and develop an understanding of who will make critical decisions about aesthetics, scope, cost, and schedule. Schedule executive sessions separately from other meetings, and invite only key decision makers.

Project Design Meetings

When design aesthetics are presented and discussed, it may not be necessary to have all the technical leaders present. For example, when lobby floor paving patterns are discussed, input from the mechanical or electrical engineer may not be needed. A generally successful approach is to make design presentations and solicit owner concurrence with the design direction early in a meeting—before most other participants arrive for a general project meeting, or even on a separate day. Owners tend to become more engaged in design issues without the distraction of unnecessary attendees. On smaller projects, owners are more engaged when design issues are kept separate from technical issues.

General Project Meetings

These are meetings when approved design direction, scope, cost, and schedule are presented and discussed with most or all of the project team members. The agenda should be carefully prepared to keep the meeting as short as possible while accomplishing the purpose of keeping everyone informed. Because general project meetings tend to involve larger groups, it can be difficult to solve detailed or worrisome issues during the meeting. The best use of everyone's time is to designate attendees who will be responsible for resolving and presenting the details of such issues. The discussions required to resolve these details can take place in coordination sessions.

Coordination Sessions

Also commonly called consultant work sessions, these meetings are the time to discuss and resolve issues related to building systems and other detailed aspects of the project. For example, the architect and MEP engineers could discuss clearances required for lights, sprinklers, and ductwork located in the plenum above the ceiling in an office building. The architect and structural engineers would discuss establishing dimension control for the structural column grid. Depending on their tolerance for long, detailed discussions, owners may or may not choose to attend such meetings. If the client does decide to attend, the project manager must take care that discussion of details is not postponed due to the client's lack of interest or patience.

Meetings with authorities having jurisdiction (AHJs), such as zoning or code officials, may be considered to be coordination sessions.

Redline Work Sessions

These are the most detailed of all project meetings. In them, basic details for arranging and coordinating the building elements are discussed. For example, the architect and structural engineer might coordinate slab edge and brick ledges, or the architect and lighting consultant might coordinate fixture types and locations. These meetings are most successful when the topic is narrowly focused and the number of attendees is minimized. Often the only agenda items are the drawings and specifications.

The meetings described above encompass most activities that must be managed during the design and documentation phases of most building projects. On larger projects, some of these meetings may actually involve separate groups, and some meetings may be held at separate times. On smaller projects, all of the meeting categories may simply be divisions of the meeting agenda for one meeting. Persons attending and documenting these meetings are assigned and requested to attend based on what the project manager expects to accomplish.

Effective Agendas

Project managers commonly arrive at a meeting with a single sheet of paper titled an agenda. This approach reflects a misunderstanding of what is to be accomplished by using an agenda. The actual purpose of an agenda is to facilitate discussion rather than to remind attendees of what is to be discussed. Therefore, in addition to the typical list of discussion topics, the agenda should be attached to other pertinent information, such as e-mails, memoranda, schedules, budgets, reports, and the like. While this consumes more paper, attaching pertinent backup information to the agenda removes the risk that an important discussion item will be tabled because a particular attendee cannot recall the details to be discussed.

It is also important to gauge the amount of time to be allocated to each agenda item. To effectively moderate the meeting, the project manager should encourage making a decision and moving on to the next topic after an appropriate amount of discussion. Just as important, however, is the ability to recognize when additional discussion is healthy and to allow the dialogue between attendees to continue without interruption.

The list of agenda topics should be distributed a day or two in advance of the meeting, along with a request for comments. Although some recipients won't bother to read them, at least everyone will have an opportunity to influence the structure of the meeting.

An effective project management tactic is to include an item that may be a sticky issue on the advance copy of the agenda to get attention, even though the item may not appear on the final agenda.

Reporting on Project Meetings

Meeting reports, sometimes called minutes, are a record of the general discussion, decisions made, directions given, and assignments accepted during the course of a project meeting. With time-driven assignments, it is advisable to publish meeting reports as soon as possible after the meeting. A copy of the agenda and any meaningful handouts presented during the meeting, along with copies of drawings or sketches, should be attached to the meeting report. The entire information package can be distributed quickly and inexpensively via e-mail. Meeting reports may be prepared by the project manager or a team leader appointed by the manager. The primary reporter for each type of meeting should be designated in the meeting management plan.

Although some managers believe meeting reports are primarily prepared for risk management purposes, the effective project manager understands the primary purpose of minutes is to facilitate communication among project participants. Meeting reports should be distributed to all pertinent persons—whether in attendance or not—so they can stay up-to-date on the project status, recent decisions, and what is expected from members of the project team.

Reports should record discussions in enough detail so that decisions and directions given—even if not expressed verbatim—can be reconstructed. The two most popular styles of meeting reports are the narrative report and the action-item report.

Narrative Meeting Report

During the design and construction documentation phases, issues tend to be a little fuzzier than during the construction phase. While the need for prompt and accurate decision making is not diminished during these phases, the narrative style tends to be less intimidating to clients and thus can actually encourage them to make more timely decisions. Functioning as more of a "history," the narrative meeting report accommodates detailed explanations of issues that may not require follow-up action.

Action-Item Meeting Report

This format consists of a list of items or issues designated with a unique, nonrepetitive number. It is helpful to key each action item to the particular meeting where the issue was raised. For example: Item 21.01 represents the first new report item for meeting 21. The item is assigned to a firm or individual and is not removed from the report until it has been fully addressed or resolved. Each item should be given a due date. This provides a constant reminder to encourage resolution of the action item in a timely fashion.

Effective managers develop personal documentation habits that become part of their daily work. Documenting key aspects of a project is not drudgery to them because it is essential to the way they manage. Writing a meeting report, making handwritten notes, or sending a client a contract proposal becomes second nature.

It does not matter if meeting reports are handwritten or typed, although many architects prefer the formality of the latter. It also does not matter what style of report is used. For example, some managers may use a simple list of bullet points to record the meeting discussions. What does matter is that the project manager communicates the discussions to everyone involved as he or she understood them, and that the directions and decisions are recorded as he or she heard them. Sharing this information gives all participants the opportunity to clarify any objections to how any item was perceived and recorded. Sharing the report also gives everyone the information they need to coordinate their efforts.

THE IMPORTANCE OF GENERAL PROJECT DOCUMENTATION

From concise contracts that define the obligations of the parties involved in a project to meeting agendas and meeting notes that facilitate effective project meetings, good documentation is the essential fabric of effective project management.

Careful documentation of milestone events and decisions—in some orderly form—is necessary for successful project management. Managers who do not retain at least a brief history of "who told what to whom" and "who decided what when" assume the risk of being unable to prove that such events occurred, a validation that could be critical for resolving any disputes that arise.

Good documentation is more than a defensive procedure to protect the architect in a dispute, however. It provides the basis for effective communication between team members and keeps all parties informed about what has taken place in the past, what is currently taking place, and expectations for what will take place in the future.

Basic Correspondence Rules

There is no industry manual for architects to follow in developing procedures for correspondence and other basic documentation. However, there are some basic principles to follow. For example, all correspondence—e-mails, letters, memos, and transmittals, as well as drawings and sketches—should bear a date and identify the project. Correspondence that cannot be connected to a specific project or cannot be placed in time in all likelihood will be virtually useless.

Memoranda

A memorandum is best used to provide an understanding of the detail of an assignment that has been accepted by a team member. Used in conjunction with a more abbreviated description that might appear in a meeting report, the memorandum provides the necessary level of detail about assignments that team members need to proceed toward delivering the project in the same orderly direction. In today's workplace, e-mail can often serve the purpose of a memorandum. If an e-mail is the preferred platform for sending a memorandum, care must be taken to include the project identifier (name or number); the date will come as a by-product of the medium.

Action-Item Lists

The action-item list is used to track the issues recorded in the meeting minutes and memoranda. If an action-item-style meeting report is being used, creation of a separate list may be unnecessary, although some clients like the "issues at a glance" convenience afforded by an action-items list, which consists of items or issues with brief descriptions given a unique, nonrepetitive number. The list itself might be numbered, or it might be sufficiently tracked by date. It is helpful to key each item to the meeting, memorandum, or other event where the issue was raised. Items may be assigned to a firm or an individual, and they are not removed from the list until they have been resolved.

Documenting Conversations

Conversations occur during meetings when others are present. Conversations also occur over the telephone or during chance encounters or in personal meetings. It is probably not necessary for a project manager to keep a record of every conversation that occurs during a project; however, it is necessary to document conversations that can meaningfully affect the project. It is important to keep a record of who generated decisions and direction, as well as when and where these actions were taken.

Important conversations that occur outside of regularly scheduled project meetings can be recorded in several ways. Some firms use a communication record or a telephone memorandum to document them. Whether typed or handwritten, a copy of these documents can be given to the person with whom the conversation took place, as well as to the entire project team, when appropriate. A decision to approve the schematic design submittal or to extend the construction documents schedule might be copied to the entire team, while the record of negotiating the client's approval of an additional service request might be copied only to the client.

E-mail

E-mail is a useful business tool, but it is double-edged. The positive side of e-mail is that it is fast. It does not require direct interaction with a person and can be prepared at any time, without regard to a set schedule. But e-mail also has a negative side. The effective project manager must be aware that the more e-mail he or she sends, the less face-to-face personal communication is undertaken. Everyone has received a seemingly rude e-mail, only to discover after further messages or phone calls that the rudeness was unintentional. Moreover, e-mail can more easily be misunderstood than a phone call or a personal conversation. For this reason, when potentially tense or complex topics requiring in-depth discussion arise, project managers should step away from the keyboard and reach for the telephone.

Personal Journal

A valuable tool for the project manager is a personal journal, as illustrated in Figure 9.1. Kept with the manager at all times, a personal journal provides an excellent opportunity to integrate contemporaneous documentation into the daily routine. Meetings, conversations, and casual notes; sketches and business artifacts, such as business cards, can all be recorded or placed in the journal. As project participants become accustomed to seeing the manager with the journal, they will begin to reference it as the project record. The manager will also become dependent on the journal as the key reference source for decisions made and direction given and other project experiences. In undertaking to keep a journal of this sort, the project manager must decide whether to keep only one journal for all ongoing projects or to keep a separate journal for each project.

Managing Information

Managing and directing the flow of project information and saving that information in an orderly manner is perhaps the most important responsibility of the project manager.

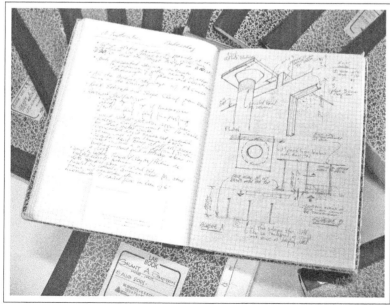

Grant A. Simpson, from 14th edition, TASHPP, 9.2: Managing Architectural Projects, p.471

FIGURE 9.1 **Sample Personal Journal**

SAMPLE PROJECT FILING SYSTEM

01 Accounting
    01 Agreements
        01 Owner-architect
        02 Owner-contractor, general conditions
        03 Consultants
        XX Other
    02 Invoices
    03 Expenses
    04 Insurance
02 Marketing
03 Correspondence
    01 Owner
    02 Contractor
    03 Consultants
    XX Other
04 Meeting Agendas and Reports
05 Memos and Lists
06 Project Data
    01 Project summary
    02 Project directory
    03 Codes
    04 Estimates
    05 Bids and addenda
    06 Schedules
    07 Site data
    08 Reference
    09 Photographs
    XX Other
07 Drawings
    01 Architectural
    02 MEP
    03 Structural
    04 Consultants
    XX Other
08 Specifications
09 Construction Phase
    01 ASIs, RFIs, CCDs
    02 Observation reports
    03 Submittals
    04 Logs
    05 Certifications and payments
    06 Change orders
    07 Closeout
    XX Other
XX Other

Of course, not all project information is created internally. As information is received from outside sources, such as the owner, consultants, or contractors, it must be processed. Processing includes noting the date the material is received, determining who requires copies, and deciding how the information will be preserved and filed.

Distribution of Information

Good project management includes making day-to-day decisions about who on the project team needs to see what. Some decisions, like sending a plumbing shop drawing to the MEP engineer, are predetermined, but others require reasoned judgment. While it is not always possible for the project manager to look at every project document or file that is received, he or she must know who is responsible to look at what documents and when they must be looked at. The project manager must either decide who will receive what or set up the protocol for others to make that decision. If the firm does not have a central receiving station where mail is received and stamped, the project manager should decide who on the team will receive mail and how it will be dated and distributed.

Project Filing System

A project filing system must be flexible and comprehensive enough to accommodate many types of project information. This includes letters, memoranda, e-mail, sketches, drawings and specifications, submittals and shop drawings, test reports, and surveys. Some of these items will be physically filed and some will probably exist only electronically, while others will be drawings, oversized materials, and physical samples. Information, regardless of its type, must be preserved in an orderly manner so it can be easily searched and retrieved. Some firms and managers, not realizing the critical importance of a project filing system, essentially use the "read and stack" method, resulting in waist-high piles of unsorted, though possibly chronologically stacked, information.

When trying to locate information that has been filed, predictability is essential. This is important for the project team as well as others who may need to access and use the project files. To make it easier to find material, most firms—large and small—develop a standard filing structure. As electronic files increasingly replace paper files, the electronic file directory structure should closely track the paper file directory structure. This means whether searching in your metal filing cabinet or on your desktop computer, you will be in familiar territory. A sample directory structure that is effective for both paper and electronic files is shown in the sidebar, "Sample Project Filing System." Additional files can be created as project-specific needs arise. For example, if the project is a theater, there will probably be an acoustic consultant file. A firm designing small projects may require fewer file categories. Firms with larger or more complicated projects may develop a more extensive system than the one illustrated.

EFFECT OF CLIENT EXPECTATIONS ON THE PROJECT

A significant ingredient for project success involves understanding and meeting client expectations. The foundation of the client's experience is the client's expectation of how the architect is to perform. The project manager who understands the client's expectations has a better chance of successfully guiding the project team's effort to meet them. If client expectations are unreasonably high, the architect may not be able to meet them even if they are fully understood. In such cases, the architect may need to help the client understand the capabilities of the firm and set more relevant and reasonable expectations.

The first step toward meeting client expectations is to discuss with the client the services to be provided. The work plan can be an effective tool for doing this. Differences between the services the client expects and the services the architect intends to provide must be resolved as early as possible. Ignoring such differences in hope that conflicts will not occur is shortsighted.

Tracking Required Services

The project manager's best efforts will not be sufficient if he or she does not monitor the progress of the project against project goals and objectives, the responsibilities established in the owner-architect agreement, and what is required by the standard of care. Project services are established by the architect's contract with the owner as well as what is expected by the standard of care for such services.

The Agreement

Project managers should keep a copy of the owner-architect agreement in a notebook at their desks at all times. As questions about services arise, the manager can refer to the contract to see if the issue is addressed. The manager should make a checklist of any contract-mandated reports or notices, schedule them, and monitor whether they are being implemented. For example, the contract may require written notice of the architect's awareness of a schedule delay. Effective project managers understand that compliance with contract requirements is *not* optional. Monitoring whether contract provisions are being met is a serious responsibility. For this reason, the project manager should have a copy of the agreement at the ready, and read it often enough that it is dog-eared and annotated to excess when the project is concluded.

Standard of Care

Not all activities the architect carries out on a project are described in a contract. Things not described might include, for example, making a subjective judgment as to how complete a set of drawings must be or how often the architect should visit the job site during construction. Such matters relate to the "standard of care" concept, which can be stated in many different ways but essentially boils down to the notion that the architect is required to do what a reasonably prudent architect would do in the same community, in the same time frame, given the same or similar facts and circumstances.

> *If one of the project parameters of scope, cost, or quality is changed, it will affect one or both of the other parameters; thus, a change in one component should not be considered without evaluating the impact on the others. The project manager should keep all issues on the table during change discussions and determine that the owner fully understands these dynamics and the potential result of any change.*
>
> —James B. Atkins, FAIA

There should be no confusion about the standard of care, which is used in the courts for adjudicating cases involving the work of design professionals. From time to time, the project manager must step back and take an introspective look at the project and the services he or she is managing. If this observation reveals something is missing, or services are not running smoothly, the manager should take corrective action.

Monitoring Client Objectives

The architect designs a building to accomplish as many of the client's stated goals and objectives as possible. Those objectives are generally focused on the scope of the project, its cost, and its desired quality. Careful attention must therefore be given to how closely the design accommodates these objectives. The project manager should make frequent comparisons of the current design to the client's objectives. If gaps or differences between the design and the client's objectives are found, the manager must take corrective action. This could mean reviewing the differences with the client to determine if the design, the construction budget, or the level of quality should be revised. Small corrective measures could simply require minor revisions to designs or candid discussions with the client.

Project Program

Clients establish programs for their project to define project uses, the project size or scope, and the desired quality. The project manager must monitor how well an evolving design addresses each of these programmatic elements. This may include periodically preparing floor-area tabulations to check the project size or obtaining samples of proposed materials and finishes to verify compliance with quality goals. It could also involve checking the detailed program to verify that the design accommodates the intended uses.

Construction Budget Targets

Although most architects are not construction cost estimators, the project manager should understand the relationship between scope, quality, and cost. The manager should have a good enough grasp of all aspects of the project to be able to make appropriate recommendations for scope or quality adjustments in the event cost estimates or bids exceed target construction budgets.

By far the best approach to meeting client expectations for construction budgets is to carefully monitor the relationship between scope, quality, and cost as a design is being developed. Architects and clients alike are frequently tempted to look past a potential conflict between budget and estimated construction costs, hoping the conflict will be resolved in competitive bidding or subsequent events.

The best practical way to resolve such conflicts—although it may be a painful experience—is to sit with the client and review and adjust one or more of the project parameters of quality, time, and cost before proceeding to the next step in the design process. To help stay on top of this issue, budget compliance or adjustment problems should find their way into meeting agendas and be discussed regularly with the client and the project team. Any statements of probable cost provided by the architect, or required by the contract, should be discussed frequently and provided at required project milestones.

Managing Consultants

The way to "do better work" for many projects involves finding a better solution to coordinating with the work of consultants. Architects and consultants face similar problems in project delivery, such as:

- Reaching the finish line at about the same time to avoid disruption when documents are issued for bidding or construction
- Making sure all parties are using the same versions of the plan backgrounds
- Uncovering and coordinating conflicts between the work of different disciplines

Project managers must allot time and resources to attend to challenges such as these.

Quality Management

Some project managers believe that quality management and quality control are relegated to the technical guys in the back room. Nothing could be further from the truth. In managing and controlling quality at the project level, quality must be a daily concern of the project manager. As with other management responsibilities, this does not necessarily mean holding a red pencil and constantly marking up the efforts of the people producing the work, any more than the project manager is required to actually prepare the drawings and specifications—although some project managers may choose to do so. It does mean the project manager must know the status of the work at all times and must oversee and direct quality management controls as they are performed.

Responsibility for Document Reviews

The project manager should consider document reviews as an opportunity to uncover mistakes and other conditions before they create problems during construction. However, many managers are reluctant to invite the criticism that results when documents are reviewed, possibly fearing being perceived as poor managers when scrutiny reveals deficiencies in the work they are directing. The irony of this thinking is that the contractor and subcontractors—through requests for information and change orders—will surely discover deficiencies that make their way into the construction drawings and specifications.

The project manager should schedule both time and resources for internal reviews of the project construction documents, if possible before the project is issued for bidding or negotiation. In small firms, the review might be made directly by the project manager. In large firms, the manager may select a reviewer, often a leader from another project. Specification writers can provide valuable internal peer reviews as their familiarity with the project helps them coordinate terminology between drawings and specifications and identify areas in the drawings where materials or systems have not been correctly represented.

The manager should always be present when review results are presented. Project managers sometimes are tempted to skip these sessions because they are tedious and technical. However, the identification and correction of errors and omissions in the architect's work is an important enough occasion to merit the attention of the primary project leader or leaders. Despite its advantages, peer review checking should not be viewed as a substitute for thorough coordination or creation of a reference set prepared by the project team.

> AIA Document D200™–1995, Project Checklist, lists tasks (organized by phase) that architects may perform on projects.

External review of the project documents can also be useful. The project manager should welcome such reviews, whether they are provided by owners, contractors or subcontractors, agencies to which applications have been made for building permits, or architects or engineers specializing in plan checking. Most external reviews provide an excellent opportunity for the project manager to improve the quality of drawings and specifications.

Setting Expectations

An effective way to meet client expectations is to help set them. This is most often accomplished through frank discussion of potentially tough issues, before they become problems.

Tackling Difficult Issues Head-On

Architects do not always talk with clients about the services they provide. Often they try to sugarcoat tough issues in an effort to be viewed as nonconfrontational. For example, although errors and omissions are a normal part of professional life, many architects avoid bringing up the subject. However, it is best to discuss difficult issues associated with project expectations directly with the client and other project participants. Determine what each participant believes is true and what is reality. With an understanding of any different perceptions, the issues can be debated in the best interest of both the client and the project. If this communication does not take place, conflicts are definitely on the horizon.

CREATIVE CONFLICT

A communication technique that can be useful for the project manager is what is called creative conflict, a process in which people engage in debate or even argument, making them more likely to recall the issues later on. Without being overtly adversarial, an effective project manager can lead a debate over an issue in an effort to gain consensus.

For example, if a client is pressing for a very aggressive schedule, the project manager can turn the focus away from

(continued)

the architect's ability to do the work faster by describing to the client realistic consequences of speeding up the work. These could be phrased something like this: "There are two alternatives for how we can proceed: (1) attempt to accomplish the more aggressive schedule, with an understanding that we all may make more mistakes as we try to work faster and acknowledgment of the relationship between the cost of mistakes and your request for speed, or (2) maintain the present schedule."

The client will likely express dissatisfaction with the concept of taking responsibility for the cost of mistakes that result

from rushing the process. The alternatives the project manager outlines must represent reasonably perceived truths that place the manager on solid ground. The client will probably not forget the conversation after such an issue has been debated.

In all cases, however, the architect's belief should be discussed with the client *when a change is requested* and not after the change has been completed. Even if the architect is overruled, the owner is likely to remember that such concerns were expressed.

A WORD ABOUT "ABSOLUTE" EXPECTATIONS

Architects frequently do not realize that they may be setting unrealistic expectations for their performance by using jargon that many clients do not understand. The use of "unqualified" language can put the architect in the position of being held to an undefined or unrealistic standard.

Architects tend to state things in absolutes because they want to explain things clearly and without ambiguity. This use of absolute terms may stem from the fact that most owner-architect agreements delineate payment of professional fees in accordance with the percentage of work completed. Thus, the architect may label a set of construction drawings "100% complete" in order to qualify for payment. However, in fact, a single set of construction drawings is unlikely to be 100 percent complete, and labeling them as such can create an expectation of performance that is unintended and even unachievable.

Table 9.3 illustrates some common absolute language encountered in project management, along with language that more accurately portrays what may realistically be expected.

If a project manager becomes an overt advocate only for the architect, he or she risks abandoning and alienating the client. The best approach is to adopt the objective attitude that a good project is a successful project, with ordinary problems and a satisfied client. Clients are likely to be more satisfied when the project runs smoothly, schedule and cost surprises are few, errors and omissions are relatively few, the client is kept informed about the construction process, and the project complies with the client's program. Avoiding unnecessary or unacceptable risks for all parties can go a long way toward achieving success.

Explaining Consequences

Discussing the potential consequences of a decision or a change is important. Clients may not always want to believe what the project manager has to say and, in fact, may disagree. Nonetheless, they usually want to hear the project manager's opinion because it is part of the service they expect. For example, if a client decides to eliminate waterproofing on the basement walls, it is not enough for the architect to simply disagree with the decision. The project manager should go a step further and explain that the decision could result in water leaking into the basement, causing damaged finishes and expensive repair costs. While such consequences may seem obvious to the experienced project manager, they might not be so obvious to the owner. Other client decisions may have

TABLE 9.3 Common Absolute Language		
Document	Unqualified Language	Suitable Alternative
Proposal letter	"We look forward to designing a first-class new school for you."	"We look forward to designing your new school project."
Drawing set cover sheet	"100% Complete Construction Documents" "50% Schematic Design Set"	"Issued for Construction" "Interim Schematic Review Set"
Field observation report	"The masonry walls have been completed."	"The masonry walls appear complete."

less obvious consequences. For instance, a decision to save money on a building system may be likely to increase maintenance expenses. The project manager should tell this to the client in plain language. As long as the potential consequences described represent the project manager's understanding of the truth, the manager is on solid ground.

MORE THAN A SERIES OF TASKS

Project management is critical to any architect or architecture firm committed to providing excellent services. While the expansive nature of project management can be challenging to describe, its basic tasks include determining by whom, when, and how the work will be done; directing and leading those who will do the work; tracking how progress compares to what was planned; taking action to make course adjustments when deviation from the plan is required; and evaluating and communicating how well the work was performed.

Yet project management is more than just a series of tasks. The project manager embodies professionalism, accountability, and integrity. In line with these more subtle and less apparent qualities, project management can also be viewed as an attitude and a way of going about one's work. For these reasons, a wise architect or other design professional will remain a student of project management throughout his or her career.

BACKGROUNDER

THE EFFECTIVE PROJECT MANAGER

Grant A. Simpson, FAIA

The project manager plays a pivotal role in orchestrating and leading the project delivery effort. The effective project manager must possess and apply a variety of skills, which together contribute to achieving desired project goals and objectives.

What Clients Appreciate in Project Managers

Recognizing that some behavior can lead to uncomfortable conflicts between the client, the project manager, and even the project design team itself, it is prudent for the project manager to understand what behaviors clients appreciate. Some of these are:

- Careful and objective use of authority
- Reliable performance
- A friendly and approachable demeanor
- Not being defensive
- Promptness in returning phone calls or e-mail
- Prompt arrival at meetings
- Being well-prepared for meetings
- Issuing timely reports and other documentation

In addition, some aspects of a project manager's behavior can make the job run more smoothly. These include:

- Being candid and honest
- Being accessible and available
- Being a good listener
- Being responsive to questions
- Using lay terms rather than industry jargon

What Makes an Effective Project Manager?

Achieving success as a project manager requires more than just performing perfunctory duties associated with the management process. It also calls for a certain frame of mind, the ability to get along with others, and an understanding of what clients expect and appreciate. Perhaps as important as any attribute is the ability to see the big picture and keep problems and issues objectively in context.

Attitude

Project managers must have not only the skills to accomplish activities and responsibilities but also the willingness to bring an appropriate attitude to their role. Most important is dedication to being a strong leader. Project management is not a passive activity. The effective project manager must be willing to make decisions and take action. The project manager cannot do all of the work on a project and must rely on others to do much of it. A willingness to believe in others is necessary. However, the project manager must also frequently look beyond this belief in others in an effort to be prepared for what could go wrong. The project manager must also have the patience to teach others how to view and participate in the project.

It is the rare project manager who perceives others as doing the work as well as he or she could do it. Yet successful

(continued)

delegation of tasks involves understanding when the work being done is good enough.

Project managers must be willing to see project circumstances from multiple points of view and to maintain a neutral attitude when conflicts inevitably arise. Nearly every aspect of project management requires give-and-take. This give-and-take must be anticipated and embraced. The project manager who finds conflict threatening or frustrating will find successful outcomes difficult when disagreements arise.

Personality and Behavior

The most effective project managers are those who can both deal effectively with conflict and get along well with other people. To a great extent, project management is infused with the need to manage continuing conflict. Problems arise and must be resolved many times throughout the day. The level of conflict may range from simple difficulty in coordinating meeting times to intense, open disagreement among members of the team. Through all of this, the project manager must recognize that his or her behavior sets the tone of leadership for the project team.

What Do Project Managers Do?

In carrying out day-to-day duties and responsibilities, project managers marshal and apply their knowledge and skills to lead, solve problems, motivate, advocate, and communicate.

Project Managers Lead

Project managers are vested with the responsibility and the authority to get the project designed and delivered. They interact with clients to determine the program and verify program compliance. They interact with their firm to determine whether staffing and resources are appropriate. They interact with the project team to help facilitate communication. They interact with contractors to help facilitate construction.

Project Managers Solve Problems

Unexpected issues arise as a part of every project. This makes problem-solving a critical part of the management process. Coupled with this is the need for project managers to successfully negotiate solutions to problems, with either the client or the contractor. Problems can be viewed as meat and potatoes for the project manager, served in great helpings on a daily basis. Problems cannot be avoided, nor are they the de facto evidence that someone has done something wrong. For the most part, design, schedule, cost, and quality problems are opportunities to improve the project

along the way. Intuition and the ability to research, understand, and resolve problems are important attributes for a project manager.

Project Managers Motivate Others

In overseeing the work of others as the project evolves, it is often necessary for the project manager to be a coach or motivator. This calls for laying the work out in a clear way and setting reasonable goals for what is to be accomplished. If the tasks or time frame are not reasonable, the manager must either revise the work plan until the tasks are more achievable or motivate the team to rise to the occasion. A project manager must realize that most teams can stretch to meet the demands of difficult assignments, but that such assignments should be an exception and not the rule.

Project Managers Serve as Advocates

The project manager must always be an advocate for the project design team. This may include standing by firm employees or the consultants working on the project. However, at times, the project manager is called upon to advocate for the client or for the contractor. Loyalty of clients usually grows from their perception that the architect is doing a good job. The project manager can build this loyalty by understanding that the client, not the project, is the firm's valuable asset. Delivering the project through dedicated service, and taking care to understand and advocate for the client's goals throughout, can help win the client's loyalty. When clients consistently feel the project manager is on their side and has their best interests at heart, success is closer at hand. The project manager also may need to advocate for the contractor, however. For example, contractors frequently make suggestions for improving a project or reducing costs but may require the project manager's assistance to explain these suggestions to the owner.

A Pivotal Role

The role of the project manager is a pivotal one. The project manager directs the efforts of others to reach desired project goals and objectives. Successfully fulfilling this role calls for the project manager to effectively plan, facilitate, and monitor the work. Whether this role is assigned to a single person or to two or more, the effective project manager must be able to understand and anticipate challenges, work through obstacles and problems as they occur, and negotiate agreement for them—all a routine part of the project management terrain.

9.2 Project Scheduling

Frank Stasiowski

Over the years, numerous systems have been devised to schedule projects. Each system has advantages and disadvantages, and each project should be scheduled using a method that best suits its scope and complexity. Also, a system must relate to the level of schedule control needed for the project. Using an overly complex scheduling method requires unnecessary effort and may, in fact, distract the project manager from the task of planning and of keeping things on track once the project begins. Table 9.4 presents some sample scheduling methods.

MILESTONE CHARTS

Perhaps the simplest scheduling method is the milestone chart (see Table 9.5). In its most basic form, this method consists of identifying the target completion date for each activity in the task outline. The chart may also include the name of the person responsible for performing each task and, later, the actual completion date for each task. The two major advantages of milestone charts are their ease of preparation and emphasis on target completion dates.

TABLE 9.4 Selecting a Scheduling Method

Evaluation Criteria	Milestone Chart	Bar Chart	Interactive Bar Chart	CPM Schedule
Ease of communication	Good	Good	Excellent	Poor
Cost to prepare	Minimal	Minimal	Moderate	High
Cost to update	Minimal	Minimal	Moderate	High
Degree of control	Fair	Good	Good	Excellent
Applicability to small projects	Excellent	Good	Good	Poor
Applicability to large projects	Poor	Fair	Good	Excellent
Commitment from project team	Fair	Fair	Excellent	Fair
Client appeal	Fair	Good	Excellent	Excellent

TABLE 9.5 Sample Milestone Chart

No.	Task	Responsibility	Target	Completed
1	Proposal cover	DB	1/15/16	x
2	Letter of transmittal	AWL	1/22/16	x
3	Introduction	AWL	1/22/16	x
4	Scope of services	MRH	2/19/16	x
5	Project schedule	MRH	2/24/16	
6	Project budget	MRH	2/24/16	x
7	Project organization	DB	2/24/16	
8	Appendix A: Qualifications	DB	2/25/16	
9	Appendix B: Biographical data	DB	3/1/16	
10	Typing and graphics	DB	3/4/16	
11	Final editing	AWL	3/8/16	
12	Printing, binding, mailing	DB	3/10/16	

Frank Stasiowski is founder and president of PSM J Resources. He is a consultant to the building and design industry and the author of numerous books and publications about management.

The best applications for milestone charts are these:

- Short design projects with few participants and little interrelationship between activities
- Preparation of presentations or proposals
- Summarizing complex schedules containing many tasks

When using milestone charts, list only key activities to avoid the excessive detail that can defeat the purpose of the chart.

A drawback of the milestone chart is that it only shows completion dates. For complex projects and key interim milestones, this may result in uncertainty about when each activity should begin. Although the tasks are listed in the order in which they are to be undertaken, the completion dates may overlap. Furthermore, comparing actual completion dates with the target dates provides only a general indication of overall schedule status. Many projects are too complex to be adequately controlled using only a milestone chart.

BAR CHARTS

Some of the drawbacks of milestone charts can be overcome by using a slightly more complex method—the bar chart, also known as the Gantt chart. Probably the most widely used planning tool among architects, the bar chart consists of a list of tasks along the left side of a page. Horizontal bars along the right side indicate the scheduled start and finish dates for each task. (See Figure 9.2.) Today there are dozens of computer programs that make this scheduling method both accessible and easy to use.

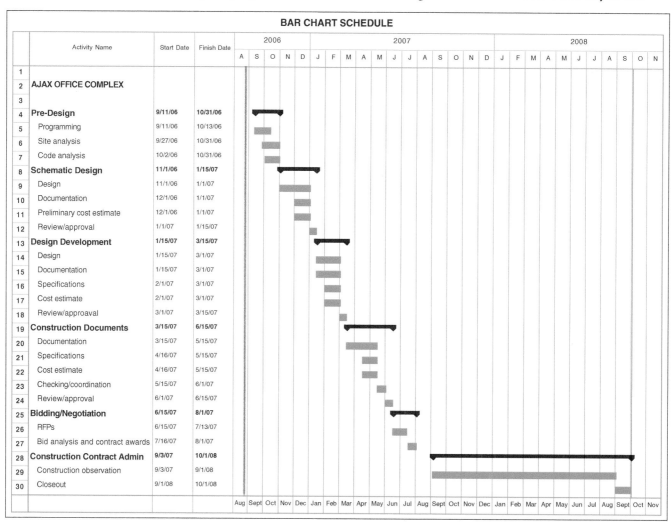

FIGURE 9.2 **Bar Chart Schedule**

Some firms create bar chart schedules in an interactive way. They will rough out a bar chart with spreadsheet or project management software before pinning it on the wall for critiques by other team members. During the scheduling meeting, the project manager can obtain commitments from all parties to accomplish their tasks on the schedule established by the group. Conflicts can be discussed and situations resolved while everyone is still in the room.

The principal drawbacks of bar charts are that they do not show interrelationships among various tasks, nor do they indicate which activities are most crucial for completing the entire project on schedule. Assigning equal importance to each activity (implicit in the bar chart method) may leave the project manager in a quandary when forced to decide which task should be delayed in the event of a labor shortage. This dilemma may result in assigning priorities to the wrong tasks. Despite these drawbacks, bar charts remain an effective method of controlling straightforward projects.

CRITICAL PATH METHOD

A highly mathematical system in which task interrelationships are defined and task schedules analyzed, critical path method (CPM) scheduling is designed for use in very complex projects with many tasks and complicated logic. CPM is not often used to schedule design projects but is frequently used by contractors to schedule construction sequences and projects.

CPM diagrams graphically show the interrelationships among project tasks: which must be started first, which cannot be started until others are completed, and which can be accomplished in parallel. Through calculation, it is possible to develop an early and late starting date (and finish date) for each activity. It is also possible to plot one or more critical paths through the project—sequence(s) of tasks that, if **delayed, would delay final completion of the project**.

A number of CPM variations have been developed. They include project evaluation and review technique (PERT) and precedence diagramming. While the physical expression and some details vary, the concepts behind these systems are comparable to CPM. Developing a critical path schedule involves these steps:

Step 1: Identify tasks and relationships. The first step is to systematically identify all tasks and the relationships among them. There are three possible relationships between two tasks: Task 1 must be completed before task 2 can begin, task 1 must be partially completed before task 2 can begin, or task 1 must be completed before task 2 can be completed.

Step 2: Construct a precedence (task interface) diagram. The precedence diagram illustrated in Figure 9.3 shows the relationships described in the first step. Study this diagram to see which of the three types of interrelationships exists between each pair of tasks. Note that in this example there is more than one type of relationship between tasks. Look at tasks C2 and C3; task C3 (cost estimates) cannot begin until task C2 (preliminary design) is partially completed, and task C3 cannot be completed until task C2 has been completed. This double relationship is quite common.

Step 3: Establish optimal task durations. The next step is to establish the length of time required to complete this activity in the most efficient manner possible—assuming that all prerequisite tasks have been completed. A tabulation for the tasks in the sample project is shown in Figure 9.4.

Step 4: Prepare the project schedule. Using the precedence diagram and duration list, prepare the project schedule. This requires calculating the earliest each task can start (and finish). When the total duration of the project as depicted in the diagram is known, then work backward to establish the latest possible finish (and start) for each task.

Step 5. Determine the critical path. The last step is to determine which tasks are critical—that is, which tasks will affect the project completion date if any delay occurs. For these tasks, the early start and late start dates are identical (as are the early finish and late finish dates). There is no float time. These tasks are darkened in the CPM schedule shown.

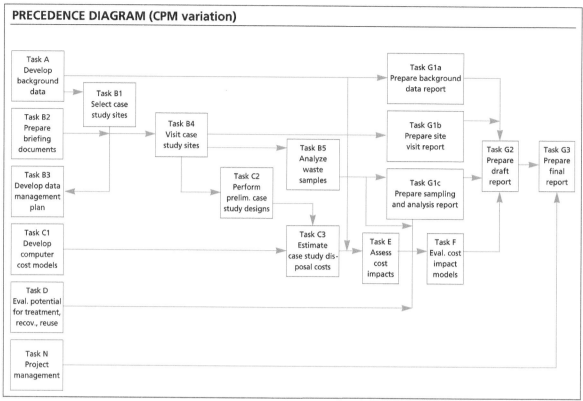

PRECEDENCE DIAGRAM (CPM variation)

FIGURE 9.3 **Precedence Diagram (CPM variation)**

Computer-based project management systems perform all these calculations quickly. They allow the scheduler to easily build, test, and modify various network schedules, and they can provide a series of analyses and reports for the project. Some software also allows the scheduler to allocate resources to each task (to help build budgets) or among multiple projects simultaneously. But use caution. Some software programs are easier to use than others, and some are designed for specific-size projects. These programs are continually evolving, with new ones being developed. It would be wise to carefully review what is currently available and consider these programs in light of your firm's needs before making a selection.

CPM TASK DURATION LIST

	Activity description	Calendar days
A	Develop background data	180
B1	Select case study sites	30
B2	Prepare briefing documents	30
B3	Develop data management plan	90
B4	Visit case study sites	180
B5	Analyze waste samples	105
C1	Develop computer cost models	90
C2	Perform preliminary case study site designs	135
D	Evaluate treatment, recovery, reuse	90
E	Assess cost impacts	60
F	Evaluate cost impact models	30
G1a	Prepare background data report	60
G1b	Prepare site data report	60
G2	Prepare draft report	60
G3	Prepare final report	60
H	Project management	(completed 60 days after the completion of all other tasks)

FIGURE 9.4 **CPM Task Duration List**

The principal advantage of a critical path method is that it shows task interrelationships clearly and highlights those activities that could create problems in meeting deadlines. It gives the project manager the most detailed control of a complex project. The major disadvantages are that CPM diagrams can be time-consuming to prepare, difficult to read, and tedious to update. Even with computers, the time and effort required to maintain a CPM chart can pose a problem for project managers with numerous project responsibilities. Moreover, most design tasks do not require such a precise level of control.

PROJECT MANAGEMENT SOFTWARE

Microsoft Corporation
One Microsoft Way
Redmond, WA 98052
Phone: 425–882–8080
www.microsoft.com
Microsoft Project is a planning, scheduling, and tracking program suitable for medium and large projects. It is compatible with Microsoft Office desktop applications and with ODBC-compliant databases. Output in PERT or Gantt formats. (Available for Windows and Macintosh.)

Primavera Systems, Inc.
3 Bala Plaza West, Suite 700
Bala Cynwyd, PA 19004
Phone: 610–667–8600
www.primavera.com
Primavera Project Planner is a program that provides planning, scheduling, and tracking capabilities for sophisticated and multifaceted projects. It allows access by multiple users. Outputs are in PERT or Gantt formats. (Available for Windows.)

Primavera also has a version intended for planning, controlling, and communicating on an enterprise-wide basis with multiuser, multiproject capabilities providing project portfolio management. Outputs are in PERT or Gantt formats. (Available for Windows.)

9.3 Construction Cost Management

Brian Bowen, FRICS

Construction cost management is too important to be left to chance. Managing costs requires skill, effort, and continuing discipline throughout design and construction.

Engaging in construction represents a substantial commitment for an owner. The costs of a project, coupled with the effort required to obtain financing, can be daunting. A project whose cost is estimated to exceed the amount borrowed or raised may have to be reevaluated or even abandoned. As a result, clients are very concerned that their projects remain within budget. Given the spotlight on construction cost in most projects, this is an area in which the architect can gain or lose credibility.

THE ARCHITECT'S RESPONSIBILITIES

The architect's responsibilities for estimating and meeting construction costs are detailed in the owner-architect agreement.

Brian Bowen is a recognized expert in cost management who has written and spoken on the subject to numerous professional societies and technical organizations around the world. Formerly a principal at Hanscomb, Inc., he has now retired.

Architecture depends on order, arrangement, eurhythmy, symmetry, propriety, and economy . . . economy denotes the proper management of materials and of site, as well as a thrifty balancing of cost and common sense in the construction of works.

—Vitruvius, On Architecture, Book 1 (25 BC)

Professional Services

If AIA standard forms of agreement are used, the architect's professional services include the following:

- *Budget evaluation.* Project scope, quality, schedule, and construction budget are interrelated, and design generally begins with an evaluation of each in terms of the other.
- *Cost estimates.* AIA Document B101–2007 specifies that the architect provide a preliminary estimate of the cost of the work when the project requirements have been sufficiently identified. The owner must be advised of any adjustments to the previous estimates that result from updates and refinements of the preliminary design.
- *Construction contract administration.* As part of construction contract administration, the architect reviews and certifies amounts due the construction contractor when the contractor requests payment. Change orders are also evaluated and agreed upon.

Depending on the owner's needs and the architect's capabilities, the owner-architect agreement may include other professional services related to construction cost. The architect may agree to provide the following:

- Market research studies
- Economic feasibility studies
- Project financing studies
- Analysis of construction alternatives or substitutions
- Construction contract cost accounting
- Lifecycle cost analysis
- Value analysis, engineering, or management
- Bills of materials
- Quantity surveys
- Detailed cost estimating

Detailed construction cost estimates are a separate service that few architects undertake unless they also have specially developed estimating capabilities.

None of these services is included in the basic services package in AIA Document B101–2007. However, the owner and architect may negotiate budgeting, budget evaluation, design analysis, or cost estimating services associated with site selection and development, planning and program options, energy or other special studies, tenant fit-up, and ongoing facility management services.

Not all architects are interested in or able to provide these additional services. Market research, financing, and economic feasibility studies require expertise in specific sales or leasing markets. Detailed construction cost estimating requires the firm to be in touch with the construction marketplace in which the project will be built. Some firms include construction cost consultants, contractors, or construction managers (CMs) on their design teams; others do not.

There is nothing absolute about construction prices—as sometimes evidenced by the wide spread among bids on a given project. Pre-contract estimating, therefore, is a hazardous business. An estimator who can bring 60 percent of the projects estimated within 5 percent of the low bid is probably doing better than expected, and it is statistically probable, on average, that one project in five will fall outside a 10 percent range, especially in volatile markets. The architect can avoid some of this hazard by including adequate contingencies and by cooperating with the client in designing contingent features into plans to allow for additions or deletions depending on bid results.

Budget for the Cost of the Work

In addition to outlining cost-related services, the owner-architect agreement establishes a budget for the cost of the work as a condition of the architect's performance. That is, the agreement may include a statement (usually as part of the project description on the cover page) that reads something like this: "New village town hall of 10,000 gross square feet floor area with a construction cost not to exceed $1,100,000."

Including such a budget in the owner-architect agreement establishes meeting the cost figure as a goal of the architect's performance. This immediately raises a number of questions that, in the interest of both owner and architect, should be addressed in the agreement:

- How is cost of the work defined? What is included and excluded? How will design and marketplace uncertainties be addressed?
- How will the architect achieve the flexibility needed to develop a design within budget?
- What options are available to the owner and architect if bids exceed the fixed limit?
- What happens if there are delays in awarding construction contracts?

These questions are addressed in AIA Document B101–2007 in this way:

- The cost of the work includes the elements of the project designed or specified by the architect and the architect's consultants, excluding their compensation.
- The architect is permitted to include contingencies for design, bidding, and price escalation in statements of construction cost.
- The architect can determine the materials, equipment, components, and types of construction to be included in the project and is permitted to make reasonable adjustments in scope.
- The architect can include alternates that, if necessary, can be used to adjust the construction cost at the time of contract award.
- Several courses of action, including revising scope and quality at no additional cost to the owner but with the owner's cooperation, are listed if the lowest bid or proposal exceeds the budget.
- The budget is to be adjusted if bidding or negotiations have not commenced within 90 days after the architect submits the construction documents.

> . . . neither the Architect nor the Owner has control over the cost of labor, materials or equipment, over the Contractor's methods of determining bid prices, or over competitive bidding, market or negotiating conditions. Accordingly, the Architect cannot and does not warrant or represent that bids or negotiated prices will not vary from the Owner's budget for the Cost of the Work or from any estimate of the Cost of the Work or evaluation prepared or agreed to by the Architect.
>
> —AIA Document B101–2007

The Architect's Performance Standard

Unless they agree to a higher standard by contract, architects are expected to use reasonable care in performing all of their professional services, including meeting the owner's construction cost objectives.

It is worth discussing reasonable care here because neither the owner nor the architect can control actual construction cost—the price that one or more contractors will ultimately charge for building the project. That price is a product of competitive market influences associated not just with the bidding contractors but also with their suppliers of materials, products, labor, and construction equipment. Under the standard of reasonable care, professionals do not have to guarantee results; rather, they are obliged to use reasonable care in performing their services.

Many owners, of course, seek guarantees. Construction represents a substantial outlay of funds, and unplanned increases in cost may create very real problems for owners. Because they have no control over the contractor, architects guaranteeing construction cost should understand that this is their choice and that they are offering to perform at a level beyond the standard of reasonable care.

Cost Services and Responsibilities of Others

Some consultants and construction organizations specialize in cost estimating and management, and these specialists may be added to the project team by the owner or the architect. Specialists may include these:

- Cost consultants who provide estimates and advice on constructability, scheduling, and the construction cost implications of functional and design alternatives

- Contractors and CMs who offer cost and constructability expertise during design. These firms may remain as advisors to the owner or architect without competing for the actual construction work, or at a predetermined time they may assume responsibility for construction, including construction cost. Some architects also offer construction management services.
- Design-build entities that assume construction cost responsibility

Some contractors may "force" higher construction costs by deluging architects with requests for information, substitutions, and proposed design changes. Architects' responses that go beyond the construction documents may be treated as "new" requirements and thus as candidates for renegotiating construction cost.

When construction cost is critical, both the owner and the architect may engage cost consultants, thus building in additional perspectives and problem-solving abilities. For small projects, the nominated contractor (or possibly a contractor engaged on an hourly basis) may provide advice on cost, constructability, and related issues. When responsibilities for providing construction cost services are divided, it is very important that responsibilities and risks be carefully spelled out, allocated among the parties, and incorporated into a series of coordinated project agreements.

Construction involves too many variables to establish generic cost objectives. These should be decided for each project.

COST MANAGEMENT PRINCIPLES

Successful management of construction costs revolves around a set of basic cost management principles.

Set Cost Objectives

It is difficult to manage well without clear intentions and objectives. Depending on the circumstances, cost objectives may include some or all of the following:

- To complete the project within the capital expenditure limitations established by the owner. These limitations may be included in the owner-architect agreement, or they may be developed by the architect and owner together.
- To provide, within budget limitations, an appropriate use of resources and value for the money
- To optimize longer-term lifecycle costs by examining alternatives that provide the best balance between initial capital expenditure and ongoing operating costs
- To provide the owner, during the course of the project, with relevant cost information related to major owner decisions and the status of the construction budget.

Pay Attention Early

The most effective benefits of cost management are gained at the beginning of a project, in establishing scope and levels of quality, making schedule decisions, selecting delivery options, and translating requirements into design concepts. The project's big decisions are made up front, and they lay the groundwork for all the decisions that follow.

PROJECT BUDGETS

There is no easy method for establishing realistic and achievable budgets, because they are usually prepared before there is a definitive project design and before good information regarding construction costs is available. A realistic budget reflects the following:

Project scope. The gross built area and volume, together with occupancy type and numbers of occupants in the building, set the stage for construction cost. Establishing the scope requires accurate identification of the owner's functional space requirements and a reasonable translation of these into gross floor area, including allowances for circulation, mechanical and electrical equipment, custodial space, and other nonusable areas. The statement of project scope should also indicate what is included in the budget for such items as equipment, furnishings, or sitework and also such "soft" costs as fees, financing, and other development costs.

Quality and performance levels. This is perhaps the most challenging set of factors because of the difficulty of adequately defining and describing quality and performance levels expected by the owner or achievable within a given budget limit. Diagrams, comparative projects, and published cost models may be helpful.

Site. The costs of developing the site and accommodating the building to it may be straightforward or complicated.

Schedule. To fix the project in time, it is necessary to establish or assume construction bid and completion dates.

Broad conceptual statement. A statement of key design and budget assumptions (e.g., the number of stories, simple or articulated building form, single or multiple buildings, quantity of above- and below-grade construction, expected levels of renovation of existing structures) is usually helpful.

Contingencies. These may be built into the various budget items, or they may be separately identified. It is common to reduce contingencies as the project moves forward in design.

Realistic figuring. Avoid the temptation to highball the budget figure (protecting yourself but jeopardizing the project) or lowball it (creating what may be unreasonable expectations).

Key assumptions. Note these in the budget statement to reduce the possibility that they will be lost as the budget is communicated, used, and revised.

Remember that the construction budget sets the stage for the project's preliminary design. It provides a framework within which all design decisions will be made. Budgeting, incidentally, provides a good opportunity to help educate the client about scope, quality, time, and cost trade-offs. Recall, too, that the budget is an estimate. Avoid language that would appear to guarantee or warrant the number. If the owner supplies the first number, do not accept it uncritically but evaluate it against program, site, schedule, and market conditions.

Draft a Realistic Budget

The most important estimate given during the course of a project's life is the first one, for this is the number everyone remembers. The budget may be prepared by the owner and evaluated by the architect or developed jointly based on an analysis of the owner's statement of requirements.

The construction budget can be developed in two fundamentally different ways. It may be a number built up from costing out the project's program and schedule requirements, or it may be a number derived from a project financing study or some other source (e.g., a public referendum). However the number is established, the design usually does not exist, so the budget is typically based on projected function, area, or other general characteristics of the project. Alternatively, it may be based on the actual cost of another, similar project.

Assign Cost Targets

Once a realistic and achievable budget has been drafted, the architect is in a position to assign cost targets to the major categories within the cost framework. The resulting cost plan provides guidance, as design begins, on the funds available for each part of the project. It may also include a cash flow projection to help the owner establish the financing schedule. A cost plan can help avoid the erosive designing/costing/redesigning that characterizes some projects.

A consistent framework for organizing cost data is an important part of the cost plan. This framework allows the architect to correlate data obtained at different stages of the project (reconciliation with original budgets and estimates is always required) and to compare data from different projects.

The MasterFormat® classification system is described in "Construction Documentation."

The most common classification in use within the industry is MasterFormat®, which is used for most specifications and construction documentation. The wide currency of this format makes it useful for cost control, but because it is oriented to construction materials and trade divisions, it is less suitable for cost management at conceptual and early design stages.

Recognizing this shortcoming, the AIA, in conjunction with the General Services Administration, developed the UniFormat™ for design cost management. This format uses functional subsystems (e.g., superstructure, exterior closure, interior construction) that parallel the way designers think about and ultimately select building components and assemblies. Design cost data are increasingly being published in the UniFormat™ categories. During the 1990s, an ASTM subcommittee undertook an extensive industry review of UniFormat™, which resulted in several changes to the original; this was published as UniFormat II, and it is now ASTM Standard E-1557–05.

TABLE 9.6 UniFormat™ Classification of Building Elements and Sitework

The UniFormat™ classification system, based on building components, provides a useful framework for developing and organizing cost information and estimates.

Level 1 Major Group Elements		Level 2 Group Elements		Level 3 Individual Elements	
A	SUBSTRUCTURE	A10	Foundations	A1010	Standard foundations
				A1020	Special foundations
				A1030	Slab on grade
		A20	Basement Construction	A2010	Basement excavation
				A2020	Basement walls
B	SHELL	B10	Superstructure	B1010	Floor construction
				B1020	Roof construction
		B20	Exterior Enclosure	B2010	Exterior walls
				B2020	Exterior windows
				B2030	Exterior doors
		B30	Roofing	B3010	Roof coverings
				B3020	Roof openings
C	INTERIORS	C10	Interior Construction	C1010	Partitions
				C1020	Interior doors
				C1030	Fittings
		C20	Stairs	C2010	Stair construction
				C2020	Stair finishes
		C30	Interior Finishes	C3010	Wall finishes
				C3020	Floor finishes
				C3030	Ceiling finishes
D	SERVICES	D10	Conveying	D1010	Elevators and lifts
				D1020	Escalators and moving walks
				D1090	Other conveying systems
		D20	Plumbing	D2010	Plumbing fixtures
				D2020	Domestic water distribution
				D2030	Sanitary waste
				D2040	Rain water drainage
				D2090	Other plumbing systems
		D30	HVAC	D3010	Energy supply
				D3020	Heat generating systems
				D3030	Cooling generating systems
				D3040	Distribution systems
				D3050	Terminal & package units
				D3060	Controls and instrumentation

TABLE 9.6 *(continued)*

					D3070	Systems testing & balancing
					D3090	Other HVAC systems and equipment
		D40	Fire Protection		D4010	Sprinklers
					D4020	Standpipes
					D4030	Fire protection specialties
					D4090	Other fire protection systems
		D50	Electrical		D5010	Electrical service & distribution
					D5020	Lighting and branch wiring
					D5030	Communications & security
					D5090	Other electrical systems
E	EQUIPMENT & FURNISHINGS	E10	Equipment		E1010	Commercial equipment
					E1020	Institutional equipment
		E20	Furnishings		E1030	Vehicular equipment
					E1090	Other equipment
					E2010	Fixed furnishings
					E2020	Movable furnishings
F	SPECIAL CONSTRUCTION & DEMOLITION	F10	Special Construction		F1010	Special structures
					F1020	Integrated construction
					F1030	Special construction systems
					F1040	Special facilities
					F1050	Special controls and instrumentation
		F20	Selective Building Demolition		F2010	Building elements demolition
					F2020	Hazardous components abatement
G	BUILDING SITEWORK	G10	Site Preparation		G1010	Site clearing
					G1020	Site demolition and relocations
					G1030	Site earthwork
					G1040	Hazardous waste remediation
		G20	Site Improvements		G2010	Roadways
					G2020	Parking lots
					G2030	Pedestrian paving
					G2040	Site development
					G2050	Landscaping
		G30	Site Mechanical Utilities		G3010	Water supply
					G3020	Sanitary sewer
					G3030	Storm sewer
					G3040	Heating distribution
					G3050	Cooling distribution
					G3060	Fuel distribution
					G3090	Other site mechanical utilities
		G40	Site Electrical Utilities		G4010	Electrical distribution
					G4020	Site lighting
					G4030	Site communications and security
					G4090	Other site electrical utilities
		G90	Other Site Construction		G9010	Service and pedestrian tunnels
					G9090	Other site systems and equipment

From UniFormat II (ASTM E-1557–05)

Cost as a Design Objective

Controlling cost as a design objective requires an understanding of the factors that affect building costs. A list of geographic, design, and marketplace factors is included in the sidebar "Factors Affecting Building Costs" later in this topic.

It is important to recognize that much of a project's cost is built into the project once its location, size, use type, and occupancy load are established; these decisions drive zoning, planning, and building code requirements. Geographic location and site set additional parameters for construction cost. The laws of supply and demand in the construction marketplace can exert great influence. Within these boundaries, the design team influences construction cost through its decisions about form, layout, systems, materials, and finishes.

Scope Control

Clearly, a major cost driver is the scope of the project: how much is to be constructed, and the levels of quality desired in the project. Increasing scope increases construction cost and may add design, financing, and operating costs, as well. Thus, scope control is an essential cost management discipline.

Many projects are subject to "scope creep," an enlargement of scope based on the many good ideas and solutions that arise during design. As the project becomes "real," owners may request changes in program requirements or levels of quality. Often these requests are small but numerous.

Most owners do not see their requests for changes as requiring changes in the budgets they have set. When budgets are fixed, scope creep forces reductions elsewhere: The chiller becomes several rooftop units. The granite facing becomes brick, then split-face block. The atrium becomes a corridor with a skylight (which ends up as an additive alternate).

An important challenge facing architects is to sit down with the owner and talk through changes, especially the small ones. The objective is to secure the client's commitment to the change and its cost implications, or to determine what other owner requirements can be changed to keep the project within budget.

Cost Monitoring and Reporting

AIA Document B101–2007 states that the architect's estimate of the cost of the work shall be based on current area, volume, or similar conceptual estimating techniques.

Construction cost should be carefully reviewed and, depending on the architect's contractual requirements, reported to the owner at each design submission or at agreed-upon intervals. Cost reports should be reconciled to the cost plan and differences explained. This is a good time to review the status of project cost with the owner and obtain commitments to any budget updates that may be mutually agreed upon.

DESIGN COST ESTIMATING

Successful cost management depends on sound estimating skills. Estimating involves two basic steps: quantifying the amount of work to be estimated and applying reasonable unit prices to these quantities.

There is a maxim among estimating professionals that the easier the measurement, the more difficult the pricing, and vice versa. Thus, it is more difficult to prepare accurate estimates at early project stages than later, when complete working drawings are available.

While there are many estimating approaches and systems, they generally fall into one of these basic categories:

- Area, volume, and other single-unit rate methods
- Elemental (assemblies and subsystems) methods
- Quantity survey methods

During predesign and even in preliminary design stages, it is usually necessary to develop construction cost estimates on the basis of one or more single units. Whether they are based on units of accommodation or on building area or volume, these estimating methods suffer from oversimplification and can produce widely varying estimates unless buildings of similar character, function, and location are being considered.

Accommodation units. This approach involves counting the units of accommodation to be provided in the proposed building—the number of apartments or dormitory rooms, beds in a hospital or nursing home, parking spaces in a parking garage—and pricing these units at an overall inclusive rate. Selecting the appropriate unit price is usually difficult, even when a reasonable body of historical evidence exists. This is true because there is wide variation in building forms and designs that contain the same units of accommodation.

Area and volume methods. For preliminary estimates, architects often use computations based on the floor area (in square feet) or, less frequently, volume (in cubic feet) of construction. These methods require care in defining and counting area and volume. Basements, balconies, covered walkways, enclosed entries, interstitial spaces, and mechanical spaces may or may not require the same level of construction cost per square or cubic foot as more conventional enclosed and inhabited space. Also, care must be used in selecting the square or cubic foot unit cost factors to be applied. Finally, these methods require skill and experience in adjusting the unit costs to the special conditions of the project.

When using historical cost data for area or volume costs of construction, the architect should ensure that the project or group of projects selected for comparison is similar to the project being estimated. The projects should be compared for similarity of use, size, site, type of construction, finishes, mechanical equipment, and economic climate during construction. The estimator can then compare characteristics and determine the modifications necessary to adjust the unit costs.

It should be noted that published single-rate unit cost figures customarily do not include the following:

- Site improvements and landscaping
- Utilities more than five feet from the building
- Unusual foundation conditions
- Furnishings and movable equipment not normally included in construction contracts
- Other items not normally included in a building of the type reported

Functional area method. This refinement of the simple area method involves separately pricing each functional space type included in the project. Thus, an estimate for a small school might include different square foot cost factors for its classroom, assembly, kitchen, and circulation spaces. This method assumes that the functions performed in the building will have a considerable bearing on its cost—a concept that holds true for interior construction but has less effect on the cost of the basic building shell. Using this method can be difficult because completed projects are rarely analyzed by the cost of individual areas, making it hard to find suitable cost data on which to base estimates.

Elemental (Assemblies and Subsystems) Methods

An approach that falls between single-unit rate methods and the extremely detailed quantity survey method involves measuring basic building systems or elements. This approach subdivides the building into a series of functional subsystems, perhaps using the UniFormat™ framework, and establishes a cost target for each subsystem.

The stage of design determines the degree of detail. In early stages, when no layouts have been designed, interior partitions can be priced on the basis of an allowance per square foot of finished area. Once layouts are done, these assemblies can be priced on a cost per linear foot of partition and, further along, on the basis of measured square foot area of the partitions, with doors, frames, and finishes priced separately.

Architectural Area and Volume of Buildings. AIA Document D101–1995, Methods of Calculating the Area and Volume of Buildings, provides a generally accepted set of definitions for establishing building area and volume. For example, an exterior balcony contributes half its floor space to the total net assignable area, while an enclosed entrance is counted at its full floor area.

The objective of using elemental methods is to produce an estimate by approaching a building as a sum of its systems and components. Construction cost is related to the configuration and construction of the building rather than just to its area, volume, or quantity of function. These methods require a sophisticated database of information.

Quantity Survey Method

This method involves detailed calculation of all the components necessary to construct the building, followed by the pricing of each component. For example, the elemental method may base plumbing costs on the number of fixtures, including roughing-in and water and waste connections. The quantity survey method measures each fixture separately, as well as the length of each piece of pipe and the quantities of fittings and trim. It applies prices to the materials involved in each construction operation, including allowances for waste, labor (crew sizes and makeup), installation time, equipment used,

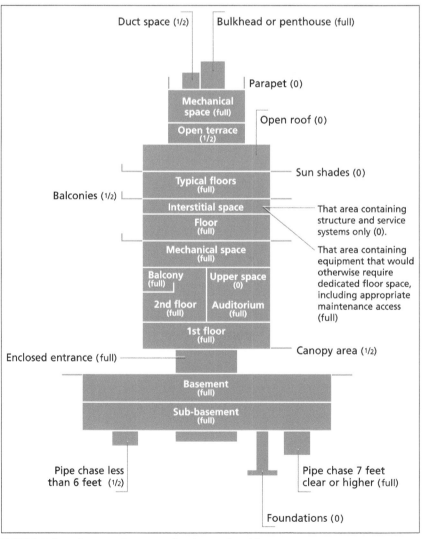

FIGURE 9.5 **Architectural Area and Volume of Buildings**

Fundamental to the development of sound cost management in design is an understanding of the basic factors that influence building costs. Some of these factors can be controlled in design, and others cannot.

LOCATION FACTORS

Location factors cover a variety of issues from characteristics of the site to local building regulations.

Geographic location. Costs will be influenced by such factors as climate and comfort requirements, building codes and regulations, ease of access, distances from sources of labor and materials, degree of union influence, and productivity of workers in the area.

Condition of the site. The bearing capacity of the soil, presence of rock, location of groundwater, slope, and existing conditions (such as old foundations or buried hazardous wastes) influence substructure costs and basic building design. Urban sites may require underpinning, extraordinary security, and limitations on access and maneuverability.

Regulations. Building design and construction are affected by a wide range of building codes and standards, as well as planning, zoning, environmental protection, construction labor, and site safety laws and regulations. These requirements, and the regulatory fees the owner must pay, may vary considerably from locality to locality.

Marketplace. Construction prices are subject to change according to the laws of supply and demand. Overstressed and under-stressed construction markets will affect the level and quality of competition, as well as the prices charged.

DESIGN FACTORS

These are design factors with a direct correlation to the cost of the building.

Plan shape. The plan dictates the amount and complexity of the perimeter required to enclose a given space. Generally, the higher the perimeter-to-floor area ratio, the greater the unit cost. Exterior closure is a high-cost item (often 10 to 20 percent of total cost) and has a secondary effect on lighting and HVAC system capacities and operating costs.

Size. As buildings increase in size, unit costs tend to decrease. This is due to more efficient perimeter ratios, better utilization of high-cost service elements (e.g., elevators, toilets, HVAC plant), and the effect of greater quantities on the contractor's purchasing power. As a rule of thumb (and, like all rules of thumb, unworkable in extreme cases), an increase or decrease in size by a given percentage is likely to lead to an increase or decrease in cost of roughly half that percentage.

Building height. Above six or eight stories, unit costs per square foot tend to increase due to the costs of increased loads, wind bracing, elevators, and fire code requirements. Taller buildings also become less efficient in their use of space, requiring more built area to house the same functions.

Story height. The greater the floor-to-floor height, the greater is the cost. The vertical elements in a building may account for 25 to 35 percent of the total cost; thus, a 10 percent reduction in story height might save 2.5 to 3.5 percent overall.

Space utilization and efficiency. To arrive at the gross building area, the architect must add circulation, toilets, mechanical and electrical space, custodial, and other nonusable spaces to the owner's stated net usable square feet requirements. The design task, which may be made more complicated by site or program adjacency requirements, is to minimize these nonusable areas and keep the net-to-gross floor area ratio as high as possible.

QUALITATIVE FACTORS

There is a direct correlation between qualitative factors, as stated in performance terms, and cost. The more demanding the performance requirements, the higher are the costs. Some owners may have specific performance concerns or aesthetic preferences. Better quality and performance may be needed to justify higher costs on a lifecycle basis over a longer term.

CONSTRUCTION FACTORS

In a marketplace with many available qualified constructors, competitively bid lump-sum contracts are generally expected to produce the best prices. Negotiated lump sums, all things considered, are often most appropriate for smaller projects, and cost-plus contracts may be useful when time or complexity of construction is a factor. Clear and complete documents reduce uncertainties (and possible contingencies) in competitive bidding.

TIME FACTORS

Accelerated schedules often increase construction costs because they require overtime, extra shifts, or other requirements. Construction during winter may have higher costs because of extra heating and protection requirements and the influences of bad weather. Time must be considered on a case-by-case basis. As an example, a winter start may ultimately make significant sums for a retail client if the project can be completed before the next major holiday shopping season.

Construction cost indexes attempt to measure changes in price during a period of time and from place to place. Like the Dow Jones or S&P 500 stock indexes, each construction cost index measures the cost of something specific. The *Engineering News Record Building Cost Index*, for example, is based on a hypothetical unit of construction requiring 1,088 board feet of 2-by-4 lumber, 2,500 pounds of standard structural steel shapes, 1.128 tons of Portland cement, and 68.38 hours of skilled labor.

Every index has a base, usually expressed as 100. This may be the value of the index in a given year (e.g., 1990 = 100) or at a given place (e.g., the 30-city index is 100). Some indexes are segmented to provide additional information. For example, the RSMeans city cost indexes are broken down by trade, revealing that while the overall city construction cost index for, say, Albany, New York, was 97.2 one year, the index for mechanical systems was 96.8 and the index for sitework was 97.4. Indexes are valuable because they facilitate comparisons. The year that Albany's index was 97.2, the index in New York City (150 miles away) was 131.9, while the index in Charleston, South Carolina, was 75.3. Looking at the change in indexes from year to year provides information on inflation and other changes in the construction marketplace.

Most published construction indexes measure change in the price of inputs to construction, such as labor, materials, and equipment. Very few attempt to modify indexes for changes in productivity, technology, design, or market conditions, so be cautious when using an index.

and for each trade, appropriate allowances for the contractor's overhead and profit.

Although such approaches to estimating are necessary for contractors, they are of limited value to architects. The designer might elect to do a careful quantity survey of alternative approaches for a given design decision or detail but is unlikely to undertake a quantity survey for an entire project.

Contingencies and Reserves

All estimates should also include reasonable provisions for the following:

Price escalation. This generally is considered from the date of the estimate to the scheduled bidding or negotiation date (if the base estimate includes escalation during the construction period) or to the midpoint of construction (if the base estimate does not include any construction period escalation).

Design contingencies. These may go as high as 20 percent for estimates based on area or volume. The completeness of the documents on which the estimate is based, the complexity of the project, the probable bidding climate, and the accuracy of the information furnished by the owner all must be considered. As design progresses and estimating becomes more detailed, this contingency will be reduced.

Construction contingencies. These generally allow up to 5 percent to provide for unforeseen changes during construction. This figure may be higher for renovation projects.

Sources of Cost Information

Architects providing construction estimates generally rely on published cost information and their own historical information.

A number of commercial sources publish cost information at three levels: area and units of accommodation; subsystems and assemblies; and individual components, products, and construction materials. The price levels in these guides represent the general market. Geographic and historical cost indexes may be used to help make the information time- and location-specific. Some guides present variations by building type, size, and general quality level. Some offer models with parameters that can be varied—within limits—to reflect the conditions the architect is facing; it may be possible, for example, to replace a masonry facade with precast concrete and calculate the resulting difference.

Construction cost guides are increasingly available in electronic form, allowing architects to enter cost information (and appropriate modifiers) into their own spreadsheets for what-if analyses and preparation of estimates.

Cost guides, of course, cannot reflect all the variations in the design or the marketplace. Intelligently used, they can help establish ballpark estimates and can assist in the choice of design features and building elements.

To supplement published cost information, many architects maintain cost data files in which their experience accumulated on completed projects is set up in a format that allows for reuse on future projects. Project cost files generally include the following:

- Basic information (e.g., location, owner, names of consultants and contractors)
- Outline project description

- Project statistics (e.g., net and gross floor areas, number of stories above and below grade, story heights, perimeter lengths at each level, exterior closure area, foundation and roof footprint areas)
- Outline specifications and performance criteria
- Cost breakdown (e.g., in UniFormat™ categories)
- Type and magnitude of change orders

Computer Programs

A number of computer-based estimating programs are available. They range from simple spreadsheet versions to powerful programs linked to databases with plenty of flexibility. They may also have capabilities for interfacing with scheduling and CAD and BIM programs. At this writing, few programs are tailored to the architecture market, so it is wise to treat vendors' claims with caution.

Presentation of Estimates

The method and information used in preparing estimates should be presented to the owner in a clear and concise manner. Depending on the circumstances and the architect's contractual requirements, the following information may be appropriate:

- Project title, location, and date of estimate
- Current project status (e.g., schematics, 50 percent construction documents)
- Estimate summary, with backup as appropriate
- Reconciliation of estimates with budget, previous estimates, or both
- Explanation of any variations and recommendations for action
- Estimating method used
- Assumed bidding and construction schedule
- Assumed delivery approach and procurement method
- Outline of items included and excluded from the estimate
- Assumptions about escalation and any escalation contingency included
- Design and construction contingencies included
- Outline specifications, and assumed performance and quality levels
- List of possible alternates or other considerations
- Comments on special conditions that might affect the accuracy of the estimate

COST ISSUES DURING PROCUREMENT

Even the most assiduous design cost management cannot ensure the marketplace will respond with quotations or bids that exactly match the construction budget. Thus, effective cost management builds in some flexibility at construction contract award time by incorporating an appropriate combination of allowances, alternates, and unit prices into the bidding or negotiation process.

Allowances

Allowances are fixed sums determined by the owner and architect before bidding takes place, and bidders are instructed to include these sums in their bids. Allowances aim to cover the costs of items whose exact character or level of quality cannot be specified at the time of bidding and therefore cannot be accurately bid. Artwork for later selection, special hardware, ornamental lighting, kitchen cabinets, custom carpeting, and similar items may be carried as allowances if the owner or bidding authority permits. If the actual cost exceeds the allowance, the contractor is entitled to additional payment; if the cost is less, the owner receives credit.

Allowances should be priced, identified, and defined in the construction documents. It also should be clear whether allowance figures include overhead, profit, delivery, and sales taxes.

Alternates

The construction documents may require the contractor to provide alternate bids. Alternates may delete work shown, require additional work, or change the level of quality specified. Alternates provide the owner with an opportunity to modify the project to ensure that construction costs fall within a fixed budget. In some cases, alternates are intended to give the owner the opportunity to select specific materials or design features after the actual cost is known. Like changes in construction cost, alternates may increase or decrease the time required for construction.

While deductive alternates are occasionally appropriate, better prices will generally be obtained for additive alternates. It is good practice not to mix the two types of alternates on bid forms. Alternates require extra work by the architect, and especially by bidders, and should be used judiciously.

Decisions about which alternates to accept are usually made by the owner on the architect's recommendation. The base bid plus selected alternates is used to determine the low bid, but the selection of alternates should not be manipulated to favor one bidder over another.

Unit Prices

Unit prices are used to provide a cost basis for changes to the contract, usually to cover unknown conditions and variables that cannot be quantified exactly at the time of bidding. Rock removal, additional excavation, additional concrete for foundations or paving, and additional piping or wiring may be identified as units to be priced by bidders. Unit prices should be specified only when reasonably necessary and when they can be accurately described and estimated. Prices for additional quantities usually exceed credits for reduced quantities, and provision should be made for this fact in the bid form. It is good advice to review unit prices carefully before recommending contract awards.

Bidding Strategies

It is wise to use the bidding process as an opportunity rather than a threat. Do everything you can to "sell" the project to the bidding contractors—provide advanced advice of the forthcoming bid, explain the importance of the work and how it will advance the successful contractor's reputation. It is also advisable to make the process itself as simple as possible:

- Make sure the bidding documents are well coordinated and complete.
- Provide enough time for bid preparation.
- Minimize (or eliminate) addenda.
- Simplify the bid form; avoid requests for cost breakdowns, lists of subcontractors, and so on; and ask for this information to be supplied within 48 hours after bid closing time.

In other words, take charge of the bidding process and make it work to the benefit of your client.

COST CONTROL DURING CONSTRUCTION

There are many opportunities to lose control of construction costs once a project is under way. Assuming the architect is engaged to administer the construction contract under the terms of AIA Document A201, following are some key areas to watch.

Schedule of Values

At the beginning of construction, the contractor submits a schedule of values that lists the various parts of the work and the quantities involved. This information helps the architect assess contractor payment requests and provides feedback for cost data files. It is recommended that a standard schedule of values be specified in the bidding documents that will enable translation between MasterFormat® and UniFormat™.

Construction Progress Payments

Under AIA standard forms of general conditions, the architect reviews the contractor's requests for payment and certifies them to the owner. To ensure fair value to the owner and fair payment to the contractor, the amounts requested are checked against the schedule of values and actual progress in the field.

Change Orders

As changes take place, the contract sum may be increased (or, rarely, decreased). Each change order is, in effect, an opportunity to renegotiate the contract sum; thus, cost control of changes is essential to effective cost management.

> "Construction Contract Administration" discusses changes in the work, contractor payment applications, and project closeout issues.

The use of unit prices (noted above) can help in the negotiation of fair cost adjustments, but more often than not, the basis of agreement is reached by negotiation based on estimated cost or actual time and material expended. One contentious item in change order negotiation is the markup for contractor overhead and profit. It is advisable to require bidding contractors to state on the bid form the percentages that will apply, or else to incorporate allowable markups into the specifications.

Claims and Disputes

Claims, too, can lead to higher construction costs. Careful administration of the construction contract, including management of conditions that might lead to disputes, is a key risk management strategy for the architect—on behalf of the project as well as the architect's practice.

> *It ain't over 'til it's over.*
>
> Yogi Berra

Construction Closeout

The closeout process provides an opportunity to wrap up the project in an expeditious way. Cost control here revolves around making inspections and punch lists, handling releases of retainage, and accomplishing the final payments with attendant approvals and releases of liens.

Postproject Review

Astute design professionals learn from their projects, gaining information and insight that helps them better plan and manage the next project. A postproject review can help the architect understand what it cost to construct a project, where the money went, and how the architect's design and project management decisions may have influenced these expenditures.

SPECIAL ESTIMATING CHALLENGES

Some project types offer more estimating challenges than others, particularly renovation or alteration of an existing structure and international projects.

Estimating Renovations and Alterations

This is a particularly challenging aspect of estimating, especially when project definition is just beginning. Renovations entail more unknowns than new construction does. Special issues will arise during renovations and will need to be accounted for with estimates. Some of these issues are as follows:

- Availability of as-built drawings
- Condition assessment

- Impact of building codes and regulations (often upgrades not included in the program are necessary to meet code requirements in older buildings)
- Continued occupancy during alterations (complicating scheduling and staging)
- Need for unforeseen structural changes
- Extent of exterior envelope renovations and alterations
- Contractor access to space and staging areas

Estimating International Projects

Estimating overseas construction costs for international projects adds to the challenge of accurate estimation.

Just as in the United States, construction prices vary from country to country according to competitive and economic factors. Sometimes exchange rates are distorted, and taxes and inflation may vary markedly from those prevailing in the United States. Availability of construction products and systems is different, as well. For example, air-conditioning might be uncommon and expensive at many locations in Europe. Drywall was not available until recently in Brazil, and at most locations, the available choices are extremely limited. Despite these circumstances, it rarely pays to import materials. Design styles and preferences are not uniform—European factory managers prefer open areas and do not like interior columns. Building codes and regulations can be bewildering to navigate—in Germany no office can be placed farther than 6.5 meters from a window, and the windows must be operable even in the presence of air-conditioning.

A common method of early estimating is to calculate the probable cost in the United States and then factor it to the overseas location. However, this is not the best method. Rather, the owner should be asked to fund a proper market survey at the overseas location to ascertain costs and pricing levels and determine other factors likely to influence the cost of the work. Retention of a local cost consultant or contractor is advised.

ORGANIZING FOR COST MANAGEMENT

In small practices, responsibility for cost estimating and management typically falls on the principals and senior staff. Less experienced staff members often do not have knowledge of factors that influence construction prices or an appreciation of current and expected market conditions.

Some practices may develop sufficient volume or depth in a specialty to justify a cost estimator on staff. In recruiting for this position, preference is usually given to candidates with conceptual estimating abilities and all-around construction pricing experience, rather than candidates with work experience in a contractor's office who may be capable of estimating for only a few trades. Cost management personnel are most effective when they are fully integrated into the design team.

The alternative to an in-house cost estimator is an independent cost consultant. It is usually best to bring cost consultants in at an early stage so that their services can be established at the outset and included in the architect's compensation. The cost consultant can provide useful services at all stages, not simply to provide a single estimate. As with all specialist firms, it is best to develop a working relationship with a cost consultant over a period of years.

It is not unusual on construction management projects for the CM to have responsibility for estimating and control, although the architect is rarely entirely relieved of this duty. The architect must be satisfied that the CM's estimates are reasonable and that cost advice is received as expected.

In whatever way the architect arranges to manage construction costs, the challenge is to establish cost as a design discipline and to sustain that discipline from the beginning to the end of the project.

9.4 Project Controls

Lowell V. Getz, CPA, and Frank A. Stasiowski, FAIA

As the project unfolds, progress is assessed against the owner's project goals—scope, quality, schedule, and budget—as well as the firm's services and compensation requirements.

Project control—tracking progress and comparing it with plans and objectives—is integral to effective project management. Without these activities, it's often not clear whether the project is on track, meeting the expectations—and requirements—established by the client and by the architect.

Project controls do not have to be elaborate, but there are some essentials:

- *Yardsticks.* A series of measuring sticks is necessary. These project objectives (services, scope, schedule, budget, and compensation) are expressed in the project agreements and work plan.
- *Measurements.* The firm periodically takes the pulse of the project, collecting vital signs—information in the form of time spent, costs incurred, and progress made.
- *Comparisons.* Comparing measured progress against the various yardsticks reveals whether expectations are being met.
- *Corrective action.* The will to address variances in progress compared to the plan is essential to keeping projects on track.

SCOPE AND SERVICES CONTROL

The project manager will need to monitor project scope—potential changes at the request of the client or introduced as part of the design process—and the services being performed to evaluate what the architect is doing against the requirements of the owner-architect agreement. Often schedule, budget, and compensation problems are the results of unplanned variations or expansions in scope or services.

A SIMPLE MONITORING TECHNIQUE

The Integrated Budget and Schedule Method (PlanTrax) is a simple project-monitoring technique developed by David Burstein, PE, and Frank Stasiowski, FAIA. The system provides the project manager with an early warning system to identify schedule and budget problems while there is still time to address them. Here are the system's key points:

- There must be a single task outline describing the scope, schedule, and budget.

- The first step involves preparing an expenditure forecast that should be thought of as forecasting the rate of progress to be made, then expressing it in terms of expenditures. Progress of a task can be reported as earned value—that is, the task budget multiplied by the actual percent completion of that task. Determining this actual percent completion is the most difficult and important part of using the system.

(continued)

Lowell V. Getz is a financial consultant to architecture, engineering, planning, and environmental service firms. He has written, taught, and lectured widely on financial management.
Frank Stasiowski is founder and president of PSMJ Resources. He is a consultant to the building and design industry and the author of numerous books and publications about management.

- The overall project progress is computed by adding all earned values for various tasks, then dividing this sum by the project budget. This is essentially the value of the work completed.
- To ascertain the actual costs expended, do not rely solely on the information provided by the accounting department. Be sure to add costs that have been committed but not yet processed (such as consultant invoices, travel costs, etc.). Don't track actual versus planned expenditures in an attempt to monitor budget or schedule status. Actual progress must also be tracked.

- Schedule status can be determined by comparing the forecast progress (or expenditures) with the actual progress (or earned value). If the actual progress is less than what was forecast, the schedule is in trouble.
- Budget status can be determined by comparing the actual expenditures with the earned value. If the earned value is less than the actual expenditures, the budget is in trouble.
- For large projects, each task should be monitored, the results graphed, and trends followed. On small projects, a simple spreadsheet format is adequate.

"Construction Cost Management" addresses "scope creep," which can be a major problem when the construction budget is fixed.

Project Scope

Project scope is made up of the owner's design requirements: program, site, area and volume, and levels of quality. During the course of design, scope can shift—and often grows—as possibilities unfold. Sometimes these shifts are clear and recognized by both owner and architect. More often, the scope of the project creeps under the pressure of owner interests or demands and the architect's enthusiasm for the evolving design.

Scope control involves asking—and answering—these questions:

- Is the scope of the project clear to you and the team?
- Do you and the client have the same view of the project?
- If the scope is changing, are you and the client formalizing those changes—including any that affect the agreement?
- If the scope is changing, are the project budget and schedule also changing as needed? If the schedule and, especially, the budget are not changing, what steps can be taken to keep the project on track?

Project Services

In the same vein, it is important to compare the services the project team is actually providing with those in the owner-architect agreement. There is a natural tendency to say yes to additional services in an effort to do the best job. It is also possible that increased scope or an extended schedule is forcing the team to provide more services than contemplated in the agreement. The best advice is to review your agreement and follow its requirements for initiating and seeking owner approval for additional services. This is not something to be left until after the fact.

Milestone Checks

While scope and services review should be ongoing, project submittals provide a handy point for a careful look at both. Frequently the owner-architect agreement sets up design phases or milestones. If this is not the case, the architect may want to establish interim points to check scope and services. Approaches may include reviews and critiques by people not on the project team.

SCHEDULE AND BUDGET CONTROL

Project schedules are developed to define target completion dates and major milestones. Schedules must be tracked and monitored to ensure that all activities and tasks

SAMPLE CONSULTANT TEAM REPORT

Week ending: 6 May 2006

DEVELOPMENT AA PROJECT
Activities completed last week

- Submitted draft layout of Parcel 13 to Client X with canal lots option
- Forwarded summary level cost information on canal lot options for Parcel 8
- Internal review of proposal for preparation of 2-B certification documents to reopen airfield
- Reviewed Contractor Y proposal for early clearing/ burning and debris removal; scheduled meeting to finalize
- Facilitated videoconference update meeting
- Facilitated Engineering Leads meeting
- Conducted Consultant Z contract status call
- Muck probes received from geotechnical engineer
- Engineering package to support platting sent out for internal QC
- Continued to facilitate progress on early work (burning, debris removal, clearing) permits
- Letters submitted to city summarizing our understanding of the path forward for servicing water and wastewater; also, submitted copy of the "Master Engineering Plan for Water, Wastewater, and Irrigation" for their information

Activities planned this week

- Submit 2-B Certification proposal to Client X for approval.
- Meet with Contractor Y to finalize debris removal proposal.
- Review and approve Consultant Z proposal for additional flushing analysis and surge analysis.
- Coordinate plan for berm with client staff.
- Submit summary level cost information on canal lot options for Parcel 13.
- Submit proposal to prepare next set of required permits, i.e., excavation for inlets, licenses to mine sand, seabed lease, beach restoration.
- Schedule meeting with Client X and Contractor Z on worker housing requirements.

    Near-term critical decisions made or to make

- Mike Smith of the city submitted his recommendation for approval of the burn permit.

    Information needed from Client X

- Finalize P-8 and P-13 layout.

    Issues

- Need to finalize decision on canal lot layout so platting efforts can resume.

proceed in an appropriate manner to reach target dates. Various scheduling techniques are used depending on the nature and complexity of the work.

Budget monitoring is usually periodic, with time and expenses charged against the project reviewed and compared to goals on a regular basis. Some firms establish a regular cycle for every project—say, every Monday. Many of these firms report separating these management meetings from design reviews—which may be scheduled on Fridays.

Sophisticated systems are not required to monitor schedules and budgets effectively. What is important is that it be done on a predictable basis so the project manager knows how the project is progressing against expectations.

Account Codes

A coding system is the shorthand used to record various entries into the proper accounts. The project is assigned a number; in more complex systems, various subcodes are used for departments, disciplines, phases, tasks, and staff levels. In addition, account codes (from the chart of accounts) permit identification of specific expenses, categorized by type. Codes are also assigned to the various indirect expense (overhead) categories in the firm's budget.

Accounting codes fine-tune project control. They allow a firm to track its expenses by project, phase or task, or object of expenditure to control costs better and to improve budgeting for future projects. As with many management techniques, there is a trade-off: Detail improves accuracy but can become cumbersome and ineffective. Keep in mind that captured data for multiple account codes will only be as successful as the accuracy reflected on time sheets and expense reports.

PART 3: THE PROJECT

Project Charges

Project control begins with recording time and expense charges against the various projects and other accounting codes in the office. Time accounting is the basis of a good reporting system. Most firms require weekly time sheets; to ensure greater accuracy and detail, some firms require them daily. Increasingly, time is entered directly into the firm's financial management software on a computer network.

The level of detail on time sheets should to some degree match the level used in project planning. It makes little sense to plan by project task if time is collected by project only. Remember, too, your firm's time and expense records become part of the database used to price upcoming projects.

Employees need to have a clear explanation of how time sheets are used and why accuracy is important. If the staff believes the firm's management values lots of overtime, they may stretch their hours to accommodate. Another employee may believe that being under budget is most important and report fewer hours than worked—essentially putting in extra time for free. Even though such actions may be performed in good faith, both examples distort the project statistics and make them less useful for planning future projects.

Depending on the firm's policy, project managers may review time charges for their projects, either before the time sheets are submitted or after they are recorded. This provides the project manager with an opportunity to make sure the proper accounting codes are charged and the results are commensurate with the work effort.

Nonchargeable or indirect time should also be monitored carefully. Indirect time can be charged to, for example, marketing, administration, new employee orientation, professional development, and civic and professional activities. In addition, time charges for vacation, holidays, and sick leave are generally recorded and monitored. In larger firms, the responsibility for monitoring indirect time generally rests with studio heads or the managing principal.

It is especially important for direct expenses the client will reimburse under the owner-architect agreement to be charged to the project (typically project related travel, printing, professional models and renderings, etc.). These expenses are not in the firm's budget; failing to charge them to projects and not billing them to clients means the firm must absorb the charges, which directly affects the bottom line.

Project Reports

Project accounting systems are intended to help project managers exercise proper control over their projects and to take corrective action to prevent unnecessary overruns. The project budget includes hours and dollars for various elements, including labor, consultants, other project expenses, and profits. The accounting system should enable the project manager to compare actual time and expenses charged to a project with the budget to determine any variances.

Managers at various levels in the organization need different kinds of reports. Project managers are likely to want frequent reports on the number of hours worked by individuals on their projects. The firm's management, however, is likely to be more interested in reports that summarize project and non-project activities and flag variances from budgets. The purpose of these reports is to give brief but easy-to-obtain information on a frequent basis so that costs can be controlled accurately.

Increasingly, offices are using financial management software to facilitate timely collection and reporting of results. Sometimes the collecting and reporting cycle is reduced to hours or even real time, providing managers with an instantaneous look at progress and potential problems.

Two examples of such reports are illustrated in Figure 9.6 and Table 9.7. Figure 9.6 tracks hours expended and billing compared to budget. Table 9.7 graphically illustrates expenditures against earned value and project plan.

TABLE 9.7 Sample Project Progress Report

APPLE & BARTLETT, PC

Project Number: 2004013.00 Waterfront Mall of Hull
Phase Number: 03A Feasibility Study

FOR THE PERIOD 5/1/05–5/31/05

Description	Current Hours	JTD Hours	Budget Hours	Balance Hours	Current Billing	JTD Billing	Budget Billing	Balance Billing	% Exp	% Rpt
Labor										
AA General										
1 Principal	18.00	42.00	48.00	6.00	1,998.00	4,662.00	5,328.00	666.00	87.50	42.00
2 Senior Architect	30.00	61.00	315.00	254.00	2,040.00	4,148.00	21,420.00	17,272.00	19.37	42.00
A Architect	81.00	196.00	700.00	504.00	4,752.00	12,172.00	35,650.00	23,478.00	34.14	42.00
M Project Manager	12.00	31.00	150.00	119.00	1,044.00	2,697.00	13,050.00	10,353.00	20.67	42.00
Total for AA	141.00	330.00	1,213.00	883.00	9,834.00	23,679.00	75,448.00	51,769.00	31.38	42.00
AB Project Admin.										
1 Principal	23.00	41.00	38.00	−3.00	2,505.00	4,503.00	4,218.00	−285.00	106.76	42.00
2 Senior Architect	17.00	34.00	270.00	236.00	1,496.00	2,992.00	18,360.00	15,368.00	16.30	42.00
A Architect	41.00	95.00	465.00	370.00	2,506.00	5,852.00	23,025.00	17,173.00	25.42	42.00
M Project Manager	13.00	22.00	117.00	95.00	1,131.00	1,914.00	10,179.00	8,265.00	18.80	42.00
Total for AB	94.00	192.00	890.00	698.00	7,638.00	15,261.00	55,782.00	40,521.00	27.36	42.00
AF Site Analysis										
1 Principal	14.00	34.00	34.00		1,554.00	3,774.00	3,774.00		100.00	42.00
2 Senior Architect	50.00	118.00	210.00	92.00	4,350.00	10,266.00	14,070.00	3,804.00	72.96	42.00
A Architect	62.00	123.00	480.00	357.00	4,152.00	8,139.00	24,395.00	16,256.00	33.36	42.00
E Engineer		7.00				504.00				
M Project Manager	9.00	15.00	105.00	90.00	783.00	1,305.00	9,135.00	7,830.00	14.29	42.00
Total for AF	135.00	297.00	829.00	532.00	10,839.00	23,988.00	51,374.00	27,386.00	46.69	42.00
AG Site Develop. Pl										
1 Principal	18.00	18.00	40.00	22.00	1,998.00	1,998.00	4,440.00	2,442.00	45.00	42.00
2 Senior Architect	18.00	33.00	265.00	232.00	1,224.00	2,244.00	18,020.00	15,776.00	12.45	42.00
A Architect	71.00	117.00	580.00	463.00	4,236.00	7,036.00	29,275.00	22,239.00	24.03	42.00
M Project Manager	9.00	15.00	125.00	110.00	783.00	1,305.00	10,875.00	9,570.00	12.00	42.00
Total for AG	116.00	183.00	1,010.00	827.00	8,241.00	12,583.00	62,610.00	50,027.00	20.10	42.00
Total for Labor	**486.00**	**1,002.00**	**3,942.00**	**2,940.00**	**36,552.00**	**75,511.00**	**245,214.00**	**169,703.00**	**30.79**	**42.00**
Expenses										
Reimbursable Expenses										
521.00 Travel, Meals, and Lodging					6,957.50	12,880.00	14,200.00	1,320.00	90.70	42.00
522.00 Reproductions					2,294.25	3,168.25	7,000.00	3,831.75	45.26	42.00
523.00 Models/Renderings/Photos					2,334.50	4,600.00	9,300.00	4,700.00	49.46	42.00
524.00 Long Distance Telephone					1,035.00	1,957.30	3,800.00	1,842.70	51.51	42.00
529.00 Miscellaneous Reimbursable Expenses					6,900.00	12,391.25	4,600.00	−7,791.25	269.38	42.00
Total for Reimbursable Expenses					**19,521.25**	**34,996.80**	**38,900.00**	**3,903.20**	**89.97**	**42.00**
Total for Expenses					**19,521.25**	**34,996.80**	**38,900.00**	**3,903.20**	**89.97**	**42.00**
Total for 03A	**486.00**	**1,002.00**	**3,942.00**	**2,940.00**	**56,073.25**	**110,507.80**	**284,114.00**	**173,606.20**	**38.90**	**42.00**
Total for 2004013.00	**486.00**	**1,002.00**	**3,942.00**	**2,940.00**	**56,073.25**	**110,507.80**	**284,114.00**	**173,606.20**	**38.90**	**42.00**

PART 3: THE PROJECT

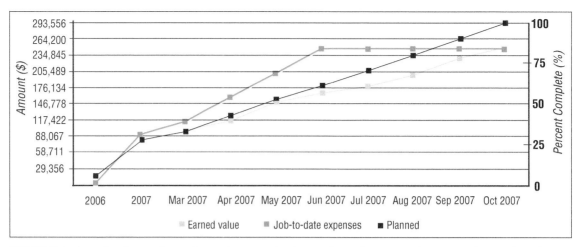

FIGURE 9.6 **Earned Value Tracking Chart. The earned value tracking chart (EVT) chart is used to track and compare budgeted costs over time with earned costs and actual job-to-date (JTD) expenses.**

Decisions about reducing overruns must be checked against the terms and conditions of the owner-architect agreement.

Overruns

Project overruns occur when project expenses exceed their budgets and, ultimately, the amount that the client has agreed to pay. The project thus incurs a loss that must be recovered out of profits on other projects.

Project overruns occur for several reasons, including poor estimating, an unrealistic fee, scope creep, and inadequate project management. Sometimes the client delays providing approvals or requests changes that were not specified in the agreement as requiring additional compensation. When overruns are projected, it is prudent to examine the options:

Additional revenue. Examine the project to determine whether, based on added services or changes in scope, there is justification to ask for additional revenue. If there is, the changes must be documented and a case made for the additional amount. Justifying the case for additional revenue will be easier if the request is made in advance (before the change is accomplished) and the client can see how much it will cost.

Overtime. Staff members may work overtime to complete the project. It is important to account for overtime hours because the firm needs to know the true costs (in both hours and dollars) of all projects in order to price similar new projects correctly.

Review alternatives for completion. Another way to overcome project budgeting problems is to reschedule and reassign the remaining portion of the work. People who can speed up the work might be assigned to the project; part-time people might help. Sometimes it is necessary to renegotiate contracts with clients or consultants.

Take the loss. Occasionally it is necessary to absorb the loss and move on.

BILLING AND COMPENSATION CONTROL

Final project control steps involve billing clients and collecting accounts.

Billing Requirements and Invoices

Requirements for billing—how often invoices are prepared, what they include, the amount of time the owner has to pay them, interest rates on overdue invoices, and related matters—are included in the owner-architect agreement. As indicated earlier, they are usually captured in some form of project authorization so the project manager (or whoever prepares invoices) has the necessary information on billing cycles, formats, allowable expenses, and other billing requirements.

TABLE 9.8 Sample Unbilled Detail Report

Apple & Bartlett, PC   9:07:38 am

Billing Status	Labor Code/ Date	Employee/ Account	Reference	Description	Hours/ Units	Billing Rate	Billing Amount
Project Number: 2004005.00 Cambridge YMCA							
Labor							
B	4/18/2005	000	00001	Apple, William	9.00	125.00	1,125.00
B	8/10/2005	000	00001	Apple, William	1.50	125.00	187.50
B	6/13/2005	001	00001	Apple, William	2.00	125.00	250.00
B	4/17/2005	030	00001	Apple, William	7.00	125.00	875.00
B	4/18/2005	030	00001	Apple, William	6.00	125.00	750.00
B	4/17/2005	030	00002	Bartlett, James	6.00	127.00	762.00
B	4/18/2005	060	00002	Bartlett, James	7.00	127.00	889.00
B	6/5/2005	00D	00302	Davidson, Emily	8.00	90.00	720.00
B	6/6/2005	00D	00301	Gonzalez, Luis	4.00	75.00	300.00
					50.50		5,858.50
Consultants							
B	4/16/2005	511.00	0000707	Haley Hart Consulting			2,760.00
B	4/16/2005	511.00	0000709	Haley Hart Consulting			5,175.00
B	4/16/2005	511.00	0000709	Haley Hart Consulting			6,095.00
B	6/5/2005	511.00	0009870	Site analysis			862.50
							14,892.50
Expenses							
B	6/10/2005	521.00	0047384	Meeting w/Board of Directors			615.25
B	4/16/2005	522.00	0000708	Blueprints, e+L95tc.			66.70
B	6/3/2005	523.00	0003456	Film			57.50
B	1/9/2006	523.00	0000263	GPI MODELS model #8855			126.50
B	5/27/2005	524.00	0005467	Conference call			40.25
B	4/15/2005	525.00	0000231	FedEx shipping			16.39
							922.59
						Total	21,673.59

Based on an example generated using DelTek software

Table 9.8 is a typical report that gives the project manager the information he or she needs to prepare a bill.

The firm will not be paid until the client receives an invoice. Therefore, full attention should be given to preparing and mailing invoices as soon as possible after the close of the accounting period. It is good practice for the project manager to review and approve invoices before they are sent to the client. However, a system should be established for approving invoices in the absence of the project manager. If the invoice requires explanation, it may make sense to call the client before it is sent.

Some firms customize their invoices to meet the needs of the client. Some send three invoices: one for regular services, one for any additional services, and one for reimbursable expenses. Some clients require that supporting documentation, such as copies of time records and expense reports, be included with all invoices. Some clients require that billing be submitted on forms prepared by and provided by the client.

PART 3: THE PROJECT

Collection

Once an invoice has been sent, the next step is to pursue collection in a timely manner. Many clients establish a payment cycle for invoices. For example, invoices received by the tenth of the month are paid in that month; otherwise, invoices are held for 30 days. If your firm knows the client's payment cycle, it is important to comply with the dates established to avoid waiting an extra month for payment.

An aging schedule for accounts receivable helps a firm keep track of how long these accounts have been outstanding. (See Table 9.11) If the firm does not regularly

---

TABLE 9.9 Invoice Format—Time and Materials

Apple & Bartlett, PC Architects and Engineers
100 Cambridge Park Drive, 5th Floor
Cambridge, MA 02140

INVOICE

May 30, 2007	
Project No:	1999007.00
Invoice No:	0000210

Mr. Charles A. Schwartz
3223 Pali Highway
Honolulu, HI 96817

Project   1999007.00   CAS Residence Design and Planning Services for Luxury Residence

Professional Services from May 1, 2007 to May 31, 2007

Professional Personnel		Hours	Rate ($)	Amount ($)
Principal				
Apple, William	5/1/07	4.00	150.00	600.00
Apple, William	5/2/07	4.00	150.00	600.00
Architect				
Gray, Barbara	5/1/07	4.00	90.00	360.00
Titony, Roberta	5/22/07	4.00	90.00	360.00
Draftsperson				
Gonzalez, Luis	5/20/07	8.00	60.00	480.00
Administrative				
Washington, Thelma	5/23/07	2.00	35.00	70.00
Totals		26.00		2,470.00
Total Labor				**2,470.00**
Reimbursable Expenses				
Structural Consultant		1.35 times	450.00	607.50
Civil & Landscape Consult		1.10 times	150.00	165.00
Travel and Lodging		1.10 times	200.00	220.00
Postage/Shipping/Deliver		1.10 times	73.25	80.58
Total Reimbursables				**1,073.08**
Unit Billing				
Interior Design				1,050.00
5/7/05 3 Bedrooms	700.0 square ft. @ 1.50			
Total Units	1,050.00			**1,050.00**
Taxes				
Sales and Use Tax	4.19% of 4,593.08			192.45
Total Taxes				**192.45**
Total This Invoice				**$4,785.53**

Invoices are due when rendered; late payments are subject to late charges.

send out invoices at the end of the month for all work accomplished during the month, then the schedule should also include columns for work in progress. It is customary for the firm's principals to review the report periodically and take action on overdue accounts.

If invoices are not paid within 30 days, the project manager may want to call the client to find out the reason for the delay. Sometimes a delayed payment is an indication of dissatisfaction with the architect's services or an indication of growing owner difficulties that may affect the health of the project, and these need to be addressed. This phone call can be followed by a reminder letter. If the project manager is not a principal in the firm, additional follow-up may best be handled by one of the firm's principals. A tickler file will help bring discipline to this process.

> If interest charges for late payments have been negotiated into the contract, they should be invoiced whenever appropriate.

Legal Recourse

Sometimes it becomes necessary to engage the services of an attorney or collection agency when a client does not pay. This decision is usually reached when the firm no longer feels it has a relationship with the client and the firm's only interest is in getting paid for its completed services. The sooner this decision is reached, the more likely the overdue bill will be collected. Statistics show that a claim against the architect often follows a demand for payment for professional services.

TABLE 9.10 Invoice Format—Percent Complete

Apple & Bartlett, PC Architects and Engineers
100 Cambridge Park Drive, 5th Floor
Cambridge, MA 02140

INVOICE

February 28, 2007
Project No: 1998005.00
Invoice No: 970

Department of Public Works
Hampshire Street
Cambridge, MA 02139

Project   1998007.00   Cambridge YMCA

Professional Services from February 1, 2007 to February 28, 2007

Fee

Total Fee				750,000.00
Billing Phase	**Percent of Fee**	**Fee**	**Percent Complete**	**Earned**
Design	25.00	187,500.00	100.00	187,500.00
Development	25.00	187,500.00	100.00	187,500.00
Construction Documents	50.00	375,000.00	0.00	0.00
Total Earned				375,000.00
Previous Fee Billing				0.00
Current Fee Billing				375,000.00
Total Fee				**375,000.00**
Total this Invoice				**$375,000.00**

Billings to Date

	Current	Prior	Total
Fee	375,000.00	0.00	375,000.00
Totals	**375,000.00**	**0.00**	**375,000.00**

Invoices are due when rendered; late payments are subject to late charge.

TABLE 9.11 Sample Accounts Receivable Aging Report

Aged as of 6/30/05

Apple & Bartlett, PC — 8:55:13 AM

Invoice	Date	Balance	Current	31–60	61–90	91–120	Over 120
Billing Client Name: Atlantic Research Corporation							
Project Number: 2004628.92 Faulkner Clinic / Principal-in-Charge: Apple / Project Manager: Anderson							
967	1/31/2005	24,000.00					24,000.00
Project Number: 2004009.00 ABC Plaza Study / Principal-in-Charge: Apple / Project Manager: Johnson							
196	4/30/2005	3,686.22			3,686.22		
554	3/30/2005	1,007.00				1,007.00	
625	6/30/2005	11,900.00	11,900.00				
955	5/31/2005	3,596.00	3,596.00				
Total for 2004009.00			15,496.00		3,686.22	1,007.00	
Project Number: 2004010.00 Johnson & Johnson Research Center / Principal-in-Charge: Bartlett / Project Manager: Anderson							
212	5/30/2005	14,990.43		14,990.43			
1035	6/15/2005	24,137.31	24,137.31				
Total for 2004010.00			24,137.31	14,990.43			
Project Number: 2000250.00 Fox Run Expansion / Principal-in-Charge: Apple / Project Manager: Anderson							
979	6/30/2005	410,540.00	410,540.00				
Project Number: 2004002.01 Novvis Headquarters Telecom / Principal-in-Charge: Bartlett / Project Manager: Anderson							
953	6/4/2005	381,250.00	381,250.00				
978	5/31/2005	131,250.00	131,250.00				
Total for 2004002.01			512,500.00				
Total for Atlantic Research Corporation			962,673.31	14,990.43	3,686.22	1,007.00	24,000.00
Billing Client Name: City of Cambridge							
Project Number: 2004005.00 City Hall Façade Replacement / Project Manager: Johnson							
166	5/15/2004	18,079.21					18,079.21
194	4/30/2005	89,093.73				89,093.73	
209	5/30/2005	21,336.05			21,336.05		
972	2/28/2005	610,293.02					610,293.02
976	4/29/2005	361.58				361.58	
Total for 2004005.00					21,336.05	89,455.31	628,372.23
Total for City of Cambridge					21,336.05	89,455.31	628,372.23

VARIANCES AND COURSE CORRECTIONS

Periodic monitoring and progress reporting is meant to uncover variances from project plans. Scope and services may shift or expand. Tasks may take too long or cost too much. The client may not render approvals in a timely fashion or pay the bills. Consultants or contractors may not meet their obligations. Given the nature of design and construction and the temporary alliances required to advance projects, variances can occur in many ways.

Each variance represents a decision item for the firm and sometimes for the client. The decision may be to do nothing. Circumstances or actions already made are expected to correct the variance, but the firm may elect to accept the variance, even though it may reduce project profit. For example, a decision to sacrifice quality documents because the design budget is overspent is not taken lightly, and the firm may decide to bite the bullet and move forward.

In other instances, the project manager will need to take corrective action, directing a change in project activity or, in some cases, coordinating the revision of project plans. Actions involving changes in architect, consultant, or client responsibilities may result in amendments to the project agreements among these parties.

Avoiding fee disputes is important in view of the facts that professional service fees do not always provide high profit margins and that firms are often strapped for working capital. As well, the architect's demand for fee payment often results in an allegation that services were not authorized by the client or were negligently performed, causing the client not to pay fees. How can the architect minimize the possibility of a fee dispute? Rely on the basics of good business practices such as the following:

Use a client-evaluation checklist. Before you sign a contract, use due diligence in evaluating the client and the project. Businesses routinely check the financial strength and payment record of their business partners. Architects should ask similar questions, such as these:

- Who are the principals involved in the project?
- What are their business reputations?
- Are they financially secure?
- Is the prospective client a limited liability company with few entity assets, or another entity that could disappear along with an unpaid fee?
- What is the client's track record with other professionals on other projects?
- Is the project financially feasible?
- Are the project scope, quality, schedule, and budget sound?

Answering these questions will inform your decision about whether to work with the client on the project. If you decide to go ahead with the project, these responses will provide insight into special provisions that should be built into the contract to protect your fee.

Make sure your contract is specific as to scope and clear as to compensation. AIA standard documents can help you do just that. Make sure the contract you negotiate addresses the following issues:

- The manner, method, and form in which fees will be paid. This should include a schedule of payment dates and an up-front "mobilization" payment, if appropriate.
- The right to suspend services until delayed payments are received and the right to terminate the contract and pursue legal remedies if the suspension is not effective. Failure by the client to make payments in accordance with the agreement should clearly be identified as "substantial nonperformance" and cause for termination or, at the architect's option, suspension of services.
- The ability of the parties to enforce the contract without the expenditure of extensive time or money. Some architects have been advised to use a prevailing-party provision that requires payment of the victorious party's

legal fees by the party found to be at fault. While this may sound good when pursuing payment of a fee, the stronger economic party (the owner) may use the provision as a threat to coerce the weaker economic party (the architect) into a settlement that might not otherwise be justified. Devices such as interest charges on unpaid amounts often are more effective. In addition, some firms attempt to solve fee disputes through the use of arbitration that is specifically authorized only for that purpose. Mediation of fee disputes is a good first-step, good-faith effort.

- The services to be provided, the manner and method in which they are to be delivered, and the time frame for their execution. A clear "meeting of the minds" on scope, timing, and deliverables is vital to preventing the misunderstandings and disappointments that lead to fee disputes.
- The specific responsibilities of the architect and client. In particular, how the parties will handle any questions or problems that might arise during design and construction should be addressed.

Finally, it is recommended that a lawyer review the firm's agreement before it is signed.

Remember the rules of communication and documentation. Clients risk the most on any project. They need to understand what is happening on their project and the value you add to the endeavor. Regular and prompt statements detailing the services provided (with appropriate references to contract clauses) should summarize the progress made since the last billing. By involving your clients in the design process, you make it easier to resolve problems and prevent an argument over fees.

Most disputes arise, in part, when clients become angry over misunderstandings that could have been avoided through good communication. Disputes over fees often become the unsatisfied client's final expression of discontent. However, the refusal to pay a fee—especially a final payment—may reflect an intentional strategy of fee avoidance or an evolution of a cost recovery scheme.

Ongoing communication also serves to keep you aware of your clients' situations. Is a client still enthused about the project, or have you been treated differently? Is something about your services making the client unhappy? Has a client's economic position changed? Delays in payment can also result from a client's internal problems. If your client is encountering financial difficulties, open architect-client communications may help detect these problems early.

Think carefully before escalating a fee dispute into adjudication. Any form of adjudication signals the end of the cooperative working relationship with a client. It probably

(continued)

PART 3: THE PROJECT

also signals the end of your opportunity to provide future services to that client. Always consider mediation. While fee disputes are often easily resolved through arbitration, nonbinding mediation affords you and your client a nonthreatening opportunity to find a third party to help you resolve your dispute as soon as you both want it resolved.

Always consider the reasons you want to pursue payment. Are you no longer pleased with the client? Is the amount owed to you substantial? Are you confident that there is no potential liability on your part? Will any judgment you obtain be collectible? Remember, the collection of fees depends on the nature of the architect-client relationship, the soundness of the initial contractual arrangements, and the ability of the architect to reinforce the client's perception of the value of the services being provided.

—Frank Musica, Esq., Assoc. AIA

Contract Changes

Every project involves changes. The approach to be taken for proposing and approving changes in scope, services, schedule, and compensation should be established (and incorporated into the project agreement) at the outset. Usually the owner's specific authorization is required. Verbal authorizations are best confirmed in writing by the architect.

Some firms issue "zero sum change orders"—that is, proposals for scope changes without added compensation to the architect—for the first one or two small changes. These firms report that this procedure establishes a discipline and reduces surprises when the client authorizes changes that do require compensation adjustments.

Documentation of Changes

The accounting department—or, depending on the firm, the bookkeeper or one of the principals acting in this capacity—maintains project files that contain copies of the project authorization, signed agreements, invoices, and other papers related to the financial aspects of the project. These files are separate from the technical files maintained by the project manager. Whenever any changes are made to the contract, such as increases in project scope or authorizations for additional services, it is important that the accounting department receive a copy of the contract amendments. This can prevent accounting and billing errors.

Suspending Services

If a client is not paying invoices or meeting other contract requirements (such as supplying required information or approvals to the architect), it may be appropriate to suspend services. This act can give the architect leverage and at the same time provide both owner and architect with an opportunity to resolve the problem before additional services (and expenses) pile up.

The possibility of suspending services should be part of the discussion with clients during negotiation of the owner-architect agreement. At that time the circumstances under which services could be stopped should be described and procedures incorporated into the owner-architect agreement. When negotiating a contract, no one enjoys

QUALITY MANAGEMENT AND THE PROJECT NOTEBOOK

The word *quality* doesn't just mean how easily a design can be built, how functional the resulting facility will be, or how attractive it will look. The discussion of quality also includes such issues as how close the project came to its intended schedule and budget, how happy the client is, and how satisfied the firm's employees are. In short, quality embraces every aspect of how a professional service firm conducts its business.

If you are like most design professionals, your first thought in setting up a quality management program is marketing and beyond that is client satisfaction. Because the term *marketing* implies internal processes and actions, a better way to consider the process is as client-focused service. Quality management then becomes an integral part of your firm; the better the job you do at aiming for and providing client service, the better the firm will do for its current clients and in attracting additional projects and clients.

A quality management program requires a systemic response in every aspect of the firm's effort. More than anything, quality management depends on better-than-average project planning and monitoring. A useful tool to help you with both is the client notebook. For each project, set up and keep a three-ring binder with the tabs listed below. This simple binder will provide an at-a-glance view of project progress—for anyone on the project team.

- *Tab 1: Client Expectations.* This is a written list of the client's expectations, reviewed and agreed to by the client. Clients seldom agree to these, but only because they are rarely asked. Make them concentrate, encourage them to let down their guard, and get them to tell you what they really want. Only then will you be prepared to deliver.
- *Tab 2: Schedule.* Place the schedule—and any updates—in this section.
- *Tab 3: Budget.* Break this section into three parts: up-front planning, ongoing project management, and post-project activity. Whenever a new report comes out on the budget, place it here.
- *Tab 4: Contract.* Describe the scope of services and other contract requirements.
- *Tab 5: Team.* Put in a complete list of people working on the project. For each staff member, consultant, contract worker, or other team member, include name, address, telephone, home telephone, fax, cell phone, and any other access number. The goal is to be able to reach everyone at any time of the day. Disasters inevitably happen at eight o'clock on Saturday morning or at nine o'clock at night.
- *Tab 6: Changes.* In this section describe precisely how you will handle design and/or construction changes throughout the project. The client should review and sign off on this section.
- *Tab 7: Communications.* This final section talks about how and when you will communicate with the client. Specify the purpose and frequency of telephone calls and meetings, your mail system, invoice system, and other communications. Get the client to sign off on this section as well.

—Frank A. Stasiowski, AIA

considering how it might be stopped; yet it may be damaging to both client and architect to allow a project to continue beyond a certain point.

AN EYE ON QUALITY

The overriding purpose of project controls is to help keep the project on track so the client's expectations and the firm's goals can be met. From an attitudinal perspective, architects can view the glass as half empty (projects sometimes veer out of control, and control helps reduce the possibility) or as half full (everyone wants a successful project, and controls provide another set of mechanisms for achieving that).

CHAPTER **10**

Building Codes
and Regulations

10.1 Community Planning Controls

Debra L. Smith, AIA, AICP

Zoning regulations have traditionally shaped the form and function of communities. Now form, function, and design reviews—along with sustainable design concepts—are beginning to shape community regulations.

Zoning, subdivision regulations, and building codes play major roles in shaping towns and cities of all sizes. Zoning is perhaps the most influential of the three because it is created at a large scale to show the big-picture interrelationships of land uses and activities throughout a community. It is the general framework used to guide decision making and interpretation of proposed new community development and redevelopment.

Zoning typically addresses issues of land use; density; floor area ratios (FAR); building envelope and massing; parking; building setbacks; signage; lighting; buffers between adjacent uses of different classifications, such as residential and commercial; and similar factors that guide community development.

Growth is inevitable and desirable, but destruction of community character is not. The question is not whether your part of the world is going to change. The question is how.

—Edward T. McMahon, quoted in *Aesthetics, Community Character and the Law* by Christopher J. Duerksen and R. Matthew Goebel

Debra L. Smith has worked for Kansas City, Missouri's Water Services Department (WSD) since 2008, using her background as an architect and urban designer and long-term planner to propose building retrofits, repairs, and improvements that are more environmentally friendly. Prior to her work with the WSD, she was Kansas City's principal urban designer. She entered the public sector after 10 years in private architecture practice. She chaired the 2006 and 2007 AIA Center for Communities by Design Committee and the 2003 Regional and Urban Design Committee Advisory Group.

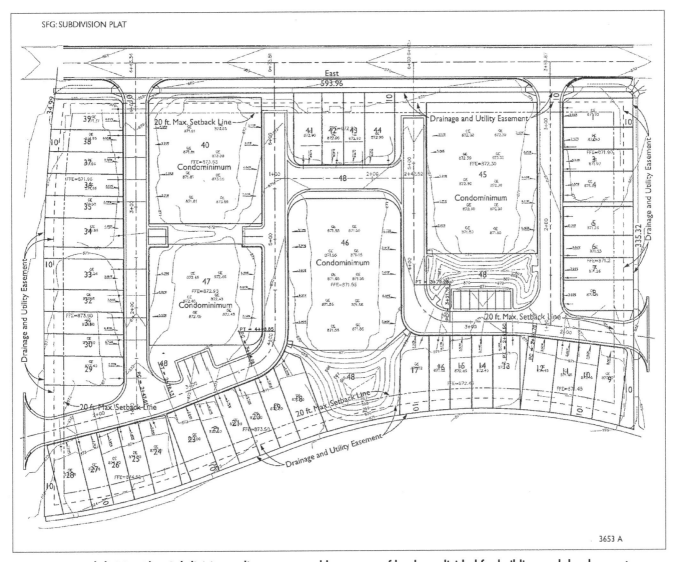

3653 A

FIGURE 10.1 Subdivision Plat. Subdivision ordinances control how tracts of land are divided for building and development purposes. Subdivision plats reflect standards for lot design and layout, streets, utilities, and other elements to ensure that these improvements are available when construction on the lots begins.

Subdivision regulations generally apply to a parcel of land within the area addressed by the zoning ordinance and the division of that parcel into lots, tracts, or other divisions of land for sale or development. (See Figure 10.1.) Many such regulations include design controls for improvements to the property.

Building codes establish minimum requirements for the construction of buildings to ensure public health, safety, and welfare (e.g., appropriate fire separations and exiting requirements).

Demographic changes across the country are causing many communities to reevaluate existing zoning ordinances and to explore new strategies to support the quality of life, character, and types of development desired by their populations. The discussion below describes these strategies along with basic zoning concepts. However, it is advisable to obtain specific information from state or local jurisdictions with respect to their zoning requirements. Regulations and their interpretation differ significantly from community to community.

See "Building Codes and Standards" for a detailed discussion of building codes and their use.

LONG-RANGE PLANNING

A zoning ordinance, or zoning code, typically is a companion document to a long-range or comprehensive plan. Such plans generally articulate a 20-year vision for a community and are intended to target locations for land use, development density, services, infrastructure, and amenities. Since planners and others involved in creating long-range plans cannot accurately predict the future, the plan provides a basic framework for development and guides public investment to support that development. Such plans may address scheduling for the installation of streets, sewers, water, and other utilities in areas where development that supports community goals and policies has been approved. Coordination of such infrastructure improvements is important to minimize demolition of recent work for new installations.

ZONING AS A REGULATORY TOOL

Zoning has existed in the United States since colonial times, when colonies regulated the location of uses such as slaughterhouses and gunpowder mills. Although the rationale to separate different and potentially incompatible land uses still serves as the basic premise for zoning today, the forces that brought about assigning the responsibility for zoning by local government occurred in 1916 when New York City adopted citywide regulations to address the quality of life issues—to reduce overcrowding and provide access to natural daylight and ventilation to building tenants and residents. These regulations became the essential "blueprint" for cities across the country for establishing their own zoning ordinances, which were tailored to meet location-specific needs and issues.

Zoning Commissions or Boards

Communities typically have a planning and zoning commission or board composed of citizens appointed by the mayor and/or the local governing body. The commissioners or board members review any comprehensive revisions to plans and zoning maps, as well as any proposed development that varies from the zoning ordinance. They make recommendations to the city council about whether proposed variations from the zoning ordinance are in the best interest of the community. Unfortunately, over time, many planning commissions have become more focused on reviewing specific project proposals rather than long-range planning initiatives.

The role and authority of planning and zoning commissions varies greatly from jurisdiction to jurisdiction. However, a common problem on these boards is lack of participation from the architecture community. As unglamorous as this type of service may appear, it can be one of the most influential arenas in which architects can help guide the shape, image, identity, and quality of life in a community.

Long-Range Plans

Most cities have adopted long-range plans to manage the preferred physical development of the municipality. These plans, in some states referred to as general plans, typically address land use, community goals, housing, transportation and infrastructure, economic development, environmentally critical and sensitive areas, agricultural land, general quality of life, implementation strategies, and related planning issues. Such documents are expected to address the effect the plan will have on neighboring communities as well.

Many communities adjust their long-range plans periodically to accommodate changing markets, needs, opportunities, and economic and social climates. For example, sustainable design is now becoming an important planning consideration for many communities.

Most states require each municipality to adopt a comprehensive plan on which to base decisions on development proposals and public investments. A long-range plan offers a general road map and goals for maintaining quality of life, supporting economic development, improving shortcomings, preserving community character, improving public amenities, and directing investment of public monies in a community.

Ideally, a long-range plan also offers consistency, despite changing political administrations and stakeholders, for pursuit of the goals stated in the plan and for strategic investment of public dollars in public infrastructure and services over time. In addition, the plan provides defensible grounds for public figures making decisions and protects property owners by providing them with advance knowledge about what may occur on their property, on adjacent property, and in the larger community.

As a final point, the planning process is iterative and the publication of a plan is rarely the end of the process. This is illustrated in figure 10.2. Most successful plans are living documents that adapt continuously to new information and conditions.

In addition to long-range plans, many communities also prepare plans for specific geographic areas within the community or to address topics of concern. Such documents include plans for neighborhoods, corridors, special districts, urban and regional design, redevelopment areas, housing, transportation, economic development, parks and open space, and environmentally sensitive areas. It is important for these plans, which usually cover at least a five-year period, to be compatible with the goals and implementation techniques identified in long-range plans.

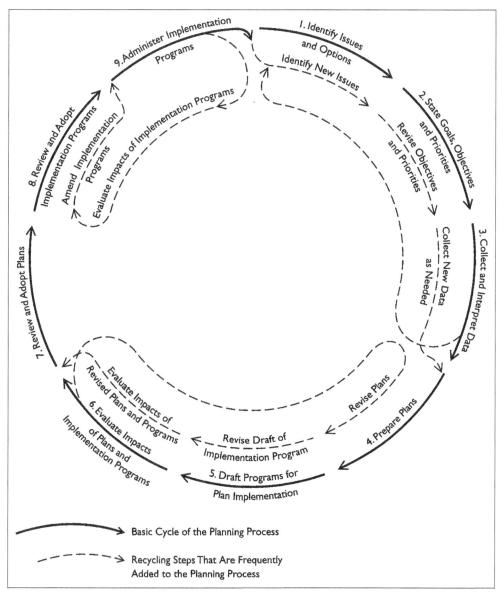

FIGURE 10.2 **The Planning Process.** The process of plan making should be viewed as a continuous cycle, with interrelationships among its phases. Information gained at a later phase can inform the outcome of an earlier phase. It is important to recognize the iterative nature of planning and to allow for continuous cycling to occur.

When designing a project and preparing for the public review process, architects and their clients should search for relevant information in comprehensive plans, plans for specific geographic areas, and any plans that address specific issues of concern in the locale.

A major advantage of preparing plans for specific geographic areas or topics is that issues and goals particular to a given stakeholder group can be addressed at a more detailed level. When decisions are being made about development, the criteria and directions in a more specific plan are usually followed, especially when they are consistent with the comprehensive plan.

Traditionally, city planners often created long-range plans with little input from the general public. However, citizens across the country have become increasingly involved in the planning process, which typically includes town-hall-style meetings, citizen advisory committees, and other ways for the general public to participate.

Long-range plans and zoning ordinances are intended to complement each other. The plan provides the community vision and goals, and the zoning ordinance provides the tools for the local government to implement the plan.

City planning departments now often use consultants to prepare long-range plans, and those consultants typically assemble multidisciplinary teams of planners, urban designers, architects, landscape architects, traffic engineers, environmental engineers, financial specialists, public relations advisors, and attorneys. The consultant team offers expertise in various areas affected by a large-scale community plan. The staff of the city planning department brings valuable knowledge about the following:

Local governments and civic leaders have realized that planning with public participation is more likely to establish buy-in and generate the civic will necessary to commit to the measures—such as approving bonds or raising taxes—required to make the plan a reality.

- Technical information about city projects
- The history, status, and priorities of various policies
- The public review process
- The political climate
- Who's who among citizen and business leaders
- Similar insights that may influence the outcome of the plan

While plans differ significantly from community to community, Figure 10.3 lists the most common elements of a comprehensive plan.

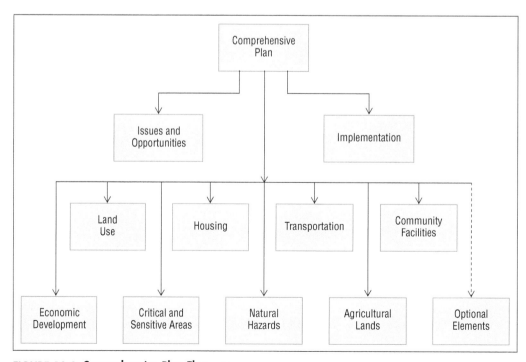

FIGURE 10.3 **Comprehensive Plan Elements**

Environmental Plans

In recent years, increasing attention has been paid to the protection of environmentally sensitive areas, such as land or bodies of water. Plans to address these areas may be independent documents that identify wetlands, mature woodlands, prairies, steep slopes, streams or rivers with water quality to be maintained or improved, or similar susceptible environmental features. Incorporation of these features as key elements in long-range plans is becoming more common, and many communities see this step as an effective approach to ensure that long-range plans strike a balance with environmental quality and stewardship.

Also, communities are starting to see the cost benefits of planning, designing, and building in ways that use more sustainable methods, such as the reduction of stormwater runoff and improved land conservation. To truly be effective, however, environmental plans should include a statement of the local government's goals, policies, and guidelines for the protection of critically sensitive areas and other environmental issues the community chooses to address.

Zoning Concepts

Zoning has evolved over decades to address changing needs, issues, and community expectations. As communities have grown and evolved, so have the types of zoning regulations. This section discusses both traditional zoning concepts and several that are emerging and gaining wider acceptance.

Euclidean Zoning

Euclidean zoning is the most prevalent form of zoning in the United States, and thus is most familiar to planners and design professionals. It has a prescriptive nature; offers objective, easy, and consistent interpretation; and has the benefit of long-established legal precedence. The U.S. Supreme Court upheld this form of zoning in 1926 in the case of *Village of Euclid (Ohio) v. the Ambler Realty Co.* for the purpose of protecting public health, safety, and welfare.

Euclidean zoning is typically characterized by a clear separation of land uses according to specific geographic districts. Typical uses include single-family residential, multifamily residential, commercial, and industrial. Limitations are often imposed on development that affects lots within each district. See Figure 10.4 for a typical land use map.

In recent years, however, Euclidean zoning has received increasing criticism. Its detractors consider it inflexible and institutionalized. Much of its theory has not kept up with current trends and preferred development patterns. For instance, mixed-use development, which promotes walkability and transit-oriented development, has grown in popularity, but the basic premise of mixed-use zoning contradicts the Euclidean approach. Hence, the exploration of alternative zoning strategies has blossomed.

There is also increasing concern that highly prescriptive zoning approaches, such as Euclidean zoning, lead to lowest common denominator results for aesthetics and development amenities. Limitations on creative solutions may simply institutionalize poor design and continue the status quo.

Flexible Zoning

As early as the 1950s, planners and communities started seeking zoning that allowed relief from the rigid methodology created by Euclidean zoning. The result was the establishment of "flexible zoning." In this approach, planners modified traditional zoning regulations to allow communities to use techniques that tie approval of unconventional uses to the review of special development plans.

Performance Zoning

The basic concept of performance zoning is regulation of land use based on consideration of the actual physical characteristics and functions of a proposed development

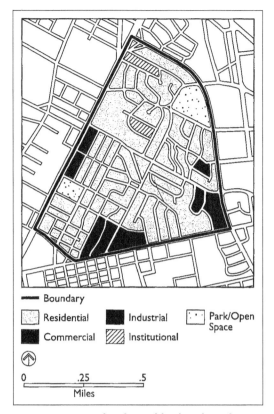

FIGURE 10.4 **Generalized Neighborhood Land Use Map**

INNOVATIONS IN ZONING

In the past several decades, a variety of new concepts and tools have emerged to improve flexibility in interpreting zoning codes and make it possible to achieve better zoning results. These concepts have included planned unit development (PUD), cluster zoning, overlay zoning, incentive zoning, flexible zoning, inclusionary zoning, and transferable (or transfer of) development rights (TOD).

More recently, smart growth, design review, and sustainability concepts have begun influencing how planning controls are created and used. As defined by the American Planning Association, smart growth uses comprehensive planning to develop communities that

- Have a sense of community and place
- Preserve and enhance valuable natural and cultural resources
- Equitably distribute the costs and benefits of development
- Expand the range of transportation, employment, and housing choices in a fiscally responsible manner
- Value long-range, regional considerations of sustainability over short-term, incremental, geographically isolated actions
- Promote public health and healthy communities

Some communities prefer to use the term "growth management" or a similar phrase to expand the goals in the smart-growth description. However, these communities typically have a similar goal in mind—to look at the needs and opportunities of the community through a larger lens and make decisions that benefit the greater good rather than a single project.

Design review has become a common tool to control the community planning process. Communities increasingly receive support from the courts for aesthetic-based regulations, provided the regulations are grounded in enabling authority and based on clear objective standards. Design review and aesthetic-based regulations in planning controls have been established largely in response to the insistence of local governments and the general public, who want a greater say in how their communities develop and what they look like.

Initially applied in historic preservation cases, design reviews are being employed in a much broader context, including new construction. Some communities are creating conservation districts, typically with design guidelines, to maintain the basic fabric and character of many existing areas. These guidelines apply to remodeling of structures, building additions, and new construction.

Design guidelines and design reviews can be applied to all-new construction if community goals, the review process, and design standards are clearly identified from the beginning. For example, New Urbanism projects typically include a pattern book to guide building forms, massing, orientation, materials, and the relationship to public spaces and adjacent buildings.

Aesthetics-based regulations are particularly effective when incorporated into and consistent with broader community goals, such as economic development and community revitalization. The extensive use of graphics, tables, and similar visual aids are valuable tools for facilitating consistent, defensible, and fair interpretations of the regulations.

Sustainability is an issue on the verge of becoming a major factor in community planning. While some communities are advocating more walkable communities along with denser, more transit-oriented development, these efforts only touch on the much larger issues of sustainable design. If governments, the general public, and the building industry decide to take on this issue aggressively, the following changes can be expected:

- Community development patterns will change to promote effective stewardship of more natural resources.
- Building designs will use environmentally preferable products and will incorporate daylighting, cross-ventilation, and energy-efficient heating and cooling systems.
- Manufacturing processes for fabricating building materials will become better balanced with maintenance and stewardship of the natural environment.

While smart growth, design review, aesthetic regulations, and sustainable design measures are becoming more common, the greatest change in zoning processes is likely to come from local governments and citizens who expect to have a stronger voice in shaping the character of their communities and a greater opportunity to create a sense of place.

when measured against predetermined criteria and standards. This is a significant shift from the Euclidean approach of assigning a land use and limiting development to only the types of uses identified as appropriate for that specific zoning district.

Performance zoning evaluates criteria such as traffic generation, noise, lighting levels, loss of wildlife or natural habitat, stormwater runoff, and flood control measures. In theory, if the criteria and standards are met, any type of land use could be located adjacent to any other type of land use. However, many elements of a development—such as site planning, building design, and facility operation—must be strictly controlled to ensure there is no damage to adjacent properties.

Performance zoning typically involves a point-based system. This allows the developer to be awarded points for meeting listed standards and criteria. Examples include the incorporation of affordable housing into a project, providing public amenities such as a new park, or mitigating environmental impacts the development may cause. If a prescribed score is reached, the project may be approved. If the score is not reached, the developer can make modifications or add special features to obtain more points.

Performance zoning offers a high level of flexibility but is often very subjective and difficult to interpret. Consequently, a high level of expertise is required to guide its review and implementation process. For this reason, performance zoning is not widely adopted as a citywide tool but is more commonly used for specifically designated areas.

Incentive Zoning

Some suburban and most urban zoning codes prescribe height limits, maximum lot coverage, maximum floor area ratios (see Figure 10.5), and other limits on a proposed development. Incentive zoning offers relaxation on some of these limits in return for specified contributions to the community.

Incentive zoning was first implemented in Chicago and New York 40 years ago. Since then, it has become more common across the country. Incentive zoning uses a reward-based system to encourage development that meets certain community goals.

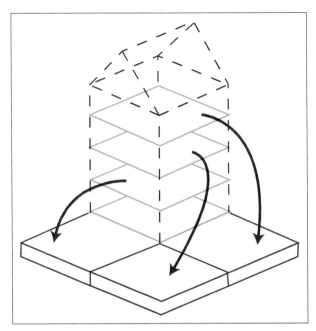

FIGURE 10.5 **Floor Area Ratio. The floor area ratio (FAR) is defined as the gross floor area of a building compared to the total area of the site. The diagram illustrates a four-story building in which each floor contains 25,000 square feet that is built on a site of 100,000 square feet. The building covers a quarter of the site, which is an FAR of 1.0.**

In return for the inclusion of provisions such as public art, public parks or plazas, or affordable housing, the developer may be awarded development incentives such as increased density, building height bonuses, a faster review process, or other bonuses. The improvements required of the developer vary from one community to another, but the above-mentioned ones tend to be the most common.

In incentive zoning, the developer must meet baseline prescriptive limitations for such things as land use, setbacks, floor area ratios, and building heights. The developer may then elect to meet any of the incentive criteria for pre-established bonuses. This form of zoning offers a significant degree of flexibility but can be complex to administer, since the level of discretionary review is proportional to the level of incentives offered. It is also important to ensure that a justifiable balance is maintained between the magnitude of the incentive given and the benefit the community receives for the developer's contribution. Following are examples of incentives used in this form of zoning:

Conditional use or special-use permits provide a way to allow a land use that normally would not be permitted in a particular zoning district, but might be allowed if additional standards and discretionary review are incorporated into the process.

Overlay zoning districts are superimposed on top of portions of one or more underlying general use zoning districts. For example, additional standards may be applied within the overlay district. These standards typically might address environmental issues, mandate a specific type of design character, or focus on a special purpose, such as historic preservation.

Floating zones are quite subjective as these areas are unmapped and the standards are described only in the zoning ordinance text. However, these zones may be applied through a rezoning process for a development that meets the district's stated standards and policies.

Planned unit developments (PUD) are typically used for large tracts of land that are planned and developed as a whole through a single development operation, or through a coordinated series of development phases consistent with a pre-established and approved master plan.

Cluster development or conservation design provides considerable flexibility in locating building sites, associated roads, utilities, and similar infrastructure so as to encourage the concentration of buildings on parts of a site. This allows a greater amount of land to be used for agriculture, recreation, preservation of environmentally sensitive areas, and other similar open-space uses. (See Figure 10.6)

Performance standards were originally used to control industrial uses. They are used to regulate the external effects of development through measurable standards directly related to the operation of the development or facility, such as noise, odor,

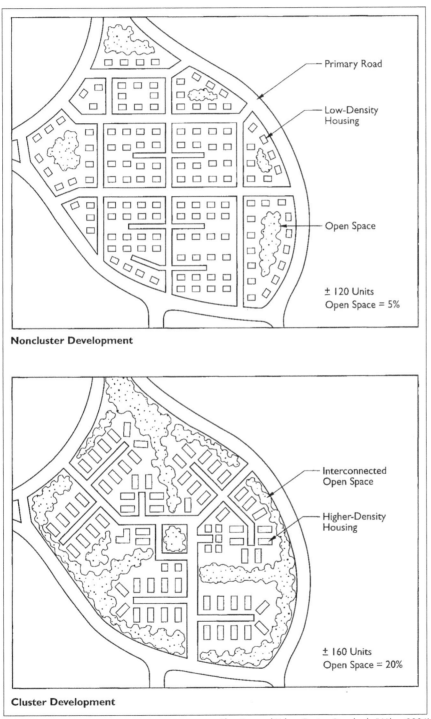

Planning and Urban Design Standards (Wiley, 2006)

FIGURE 10.6 **Noncluster Development and Cluster Development**

smoke, noxious gases, vibration, heat, and glare. This strategy may be used for all types of development to address a variety of measurable standards, such as physical appearance, fiscal impacts, traffic level, and hours of operation.

Point rating systems evaluate and rate proposed development according to preset criteria. Each characteristic has a specific number of points assigned to it. A development is required to meet minimum point thresholds, which may vary according to density. The intention is that by achieving adequate points (which are typically performance-based in nature) development will support compatibility with surrounding land uses and development.

The Uniform Development Code (UDC) consolidates the traditionally separated sections of the zoning ordinance and the subdivision regulations into a single, unified development code that provides a more consistent and efficient means of controlling development. The UDC also offers greater predictability for all involved in the development process because all stakeholders are involved throughout the process. UDC development standards often include standards for circulation, utilities, and stormwater management.

Form-Based Zoning

Form-based zoning, primarily a product of the New Urbanism movement of the late 1980s and early 1990s, is gaining momentum nationwide—largely in response to growing dissatisfaction with the perceived effects of conventional (Euclidean) zoning. Form-based zoning promotes compact, pedestrian-friendly, mixed-use communities, typically similar to pre-World War II-era development patterns. It is a regulatory approach designed to shape the physical *form* of development while setting only broad parameters for land use.

Many communities have well-maintained older neighborhoods that cannot be replicated by the current zoning ordinance for that community. Nonconforming elements typically include smaller lot sizes, insufficient setbacks, mixed-use development, a higher density of development, and other attributes characteristic of older, walkable neighborhoods. Also, neighborhoods may be considered obsolete and require variances for renovation projects because the current zoning ordinance may not offer the flexibility to approve projects that maintain the original character and integrity of the neighborhood.

In large part, the purpose of form-based zoning is to counteract two things in particular:

1. The excessive consumption of land caused by what has become the status quo—separation of land uses and limits on density
2. The erosion of the original character and sense of place in traditional neighborhoods and districts caused by the intrusion of incompatible development types allowed when a one-size-fits-all zoning ordinance is used

The sense of place in communities is decreased as formulaic, iconic stores (also known as "big boxes" and commercial strip malls) move in, cookie-cutter subdivisions spread across the landscape, and cars increasingly dominate our communities.

The general concept of form-based zoning is to focus on what is desirable, not what is forbidden. The belief is that if a development is physically compatible with its neighbors, the uses that can occur within its structure will also be compatible. One of the tools sometimes used in this form-based zoning is pattern books illustrated in Figure 10.7. The goal is to integrate private development with the public realm to optimize the mutual benefit to both public and private interests.

Form-based zoning is intended to be a community-wide approach to achieving more attractive physical development throughout a region. Form-based zoning ordinances typically include pattern books, which clearly illustrate the variety of styles and design features considered appropriate to the community.

In practice, form-based zoning does not address many secondary impacts generated by uses on neighboring properties. These include traffic, noise, hours of operation, and possible negative effects on property values. Moreover, the use of form-based zoning

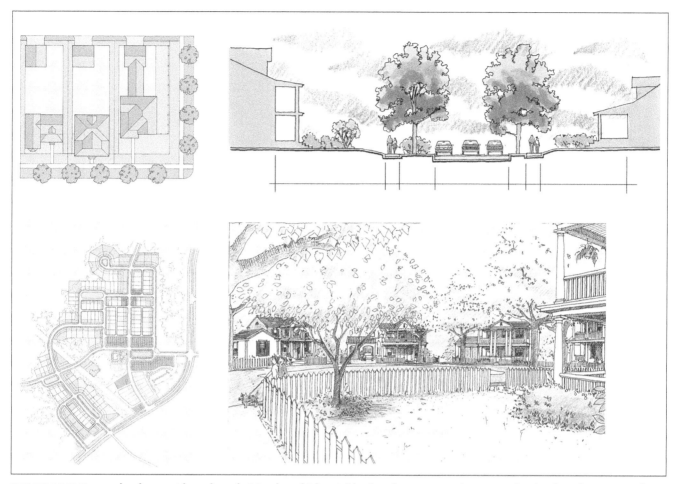

FIGURE 10.7 **Pattern books provide a shared vision by which neighborhoods, towns, and cities can be developed or renewed. They typically describe the overall character and image of the intended development; the essential qualities of public spaces, including building types; the way buildings are placed on their lots; and the architectural styles and elements for the project.**

tends to be limited to specified geographic areas for several reasons. First, the newness of the concept needs further testing to determine how to effectively apply it in a wider variety of cases (e.g., proximity to transit, topography, market needs and trends in a given area, and population patterns, including whether an area is growing, shrinking, or "graying"). Second, considerable effort is required to develop a form-based code. For instance, steps must be taken to develop a regulating plan to define which building envelope standards are to be applied where and to create a pattern book to set basic design parameters. Third, the public and policy makers are slow to accept change and invest in the time and training required to shift to form-based zoning.

To address these difficulties, more communities are exploring ways to create a hybrid zoning approach that combines form-based zoning with conventional zoning. The goals for such an approach are to balance control, enhance design quality and community character, and improve flexibility of interpretation so the ordinance can accommodate projects that meet the spirit of the zoning requirements, if not the letter of the ordinance.

Variations of Form-Based Zoning

Several variations of form-based zoning have been developed around the country. They include the following:

Smart Code zoning. The Smart Code is a zoning ordinance for an area from the center of the city to the rural edge that is based on the assumption that a mix of uses is the norm. The Smart Code allows for special-use districts where needed. This type of zoning has had limited adoption to date but is gaining momentum.

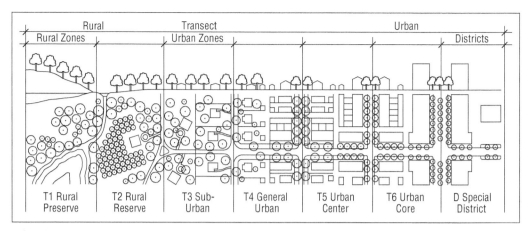

| Rural Zones | Urban Zones | | | | | Districts |

| T1 Rural Preserve | T2 Rural Reserve | T3 Sub-Urban | T4 General Urban | T5 Urban Center | T6 Urban Core | D Special District |

FIGURE 10.8 **Diagram of the Transect System**

A key component of the Smart Code is the use of a transect, or transect-based zoning, which is based on a continuum of habitats, or eco-zone, from the rural to urban core (See Figure 10.8). There are seven levels on this continuum, although not all may apply to every project. Each eco-level is distinguished by varying density and character for the built environment. Similar to form-based zoning, regulations are applied to building design standards, street design, parking requirements, and creation of a high-quality public realm; however, in this type of code the regulations on land use are limited to promote mixed-use development.

Traditional neighborhood development. Also known as neo-traditional neighborhood development, this approach to zoning refers to models of urban neighborhoods from the early to mid-twentieth century in which many of the following characteristics were common:

- Smaller lot sizes that supported a walkable scale for the neighborhood
- Access to garages from an alley
- Neighborhood parks and commercial nodes within walking distance of many houses
- Houses of varying size and price, promoting a greater diversity of age groups and income levels
- Commercial and civic functions as integral elements of the neighborhood

Transit-oriented development (TOD). This type of development focuses on planning and implementing compact development around transit, especially rail transit, stops. The goal is to offer convenience to riders by promoting the location of medium-to high-density, multifamily residential development close to retail services and offices. Such interrelationships make the choice of transit efficient and attractive. TOD designs follow many of the same principles as traditional neighborhood development, incorporating walkable scale, mixed uses, and higher density. They often use overlay zoning districts to ensure the regulations are flexible enough to create a level of density and mix of uses appropriate for supporting transit.

THE IMPORTANCE OF THE REGULATORY ENVIRONMENT

While our system of law establishes the basic framework within which an architect lives and practices, the reality is that the regulatory environment governs many of our everyday actions.

Regulations are developed and promulgated as part of what is called administrative law. The idea is that individual statutes, however well conceived by the legislative bodies that pass them, cannot possibly include all the technical and procedural provisions necessary to implement and enforce them. Thus, under the concept of administrative law, the executive branches of federal, state, and local governments draft and promulgate regulations that apply laws to everyday situations.

Consider building codes, for example. A state legislature may decide it is time to adopt a uniform statewide building code. It passes a law mandating such a code and requires that the executive branch write it. In drafting the code, a department of the executive branch (which, in this case, may be a state building code commission) follows the specific directives included in the law, as well as any legislative intent expressed in the law or in the hearings and proceedings leading to its passage. The resulting building code is very specific and detailed in its technical provisions. It also includes all of the details necessary to enforce it. Once promulgated as a regulation, it has the force of law.

Because they address complex subjects, most regulations include ways for users to seek variances, exceptions, or other forms of dispensation from the provisions. In the case of building codes, architects may find that a code does not cover their specific situation or, alternatively, that they have a better way to fulfill the intent of the code. Most codes anticipate this by setting up a variance procedure, with decisions on variances made by individuals or panels of people who represent the community and who often have some technical expertise in design and building. This administrative relief from the provisions of regulations is generally easy to access and decisions can be made in a matter of days or weeks rather than months or years.

Once a user has exhausted all administrative avenues, judicial relief (going into the courts) is still possible but rarely successful. Courts generally give great deference to administrative agencies, which have developed significant expertise in their realm of regulation.

—Ava J. Abramowitz, Esq., from *The Architect's Handbook of Professional Practice*, 13th edition

ZONING TOOLS

Zoning codes are often in place for years, even decades. This means that numerous people are involved over time in developing projects, interpreting the codes, and deciding how the codes apply to changing community needs and market forces. The tools described below offer some flexible strategies for using zoning codes to serve the interests of a community.

Long-Range Plans

Long-range plans are typically 20-year documents intended to provide broad goals, principles, and policies that create a vision for the future of a community. These plans provide a framework for evaluating proposed development projects. Zoning ordinances are the regulatory documents used to enforce long-range plans. When a proposed development differs from the zoning ordinance, it is considered a variance. A plan requesting a variance follows a different track in the review process, and different actions are required to bring it into conformity, either granting the variance or rezoning the property.

Variances

Variances typically involve only minor deviations from the specific requirements of a zoning district. It may be as simple as allowing a setback of 15 feet instead of the required 20 feet for a specific case, or allowing an extra 2 feet in building height to accommodate an auxiliary unit above a garage in an area where auxiliary units are considered appropriate to the neighborhood character, form, and density.

In order for a request for a variance to be valid, there must be an unnecessary hardship inherent in the physical characteristics of the property. Financial hardship does not constitute a valid unnecessary hardship.

Rezoning

Rezoning is the most important and most common zoning action of a local government. It involves changing the land use map to reclassify land to allow an alternate use. Because plans can only anticipate future changes in demographics and lifestyle patterns, they sometimes do not accurately predict future market trends. Sometimes unforeseen but desirable opportunities arise, and the zoning commission is asked to accommodate them.

In 1922 the U.S. Department of Commerce published the Standard State Zoning Enabling Act, and this model has been adopted by most of the states. This legislation was followed in 1928 by the Standard City Planning Enabling Act, a similar model act also published by the Department of Commerce. These model acts did not provide any effective administrative methods for amending an adopted long-range plan. Therefore, any amendment to a plan must go through the same adoption process as the original plan. This is typically a 10-step process:

1. Submission of application
2. Staff review
3. Public notice of planning commission hearing
4. Preparation of staff report to the planning commission
5. Public planning commission hearing
6. Planning commission action
7. Initial governing body action; includes setting for hearing
8. Public notice of governing body hearing
9. Public hearing of governing body
10. Governing body action

Because a rezoning or map amendment changes the law, it is a serious action. However, the governing body—typically a planning and zoning commission that offers recommendations to the county or city council for final action—has much more latitude in the degree of change it makes, as long as it stays within the broad constitutional and state legislative limitations.

ZONING BOARDS AND COMMISSIONS

City and county planners are key players in reviewing and interpreting how zoning codes are applied. However, in our democratic society, it is important to ensure that the voices of citizens are heard as well. For this reason, communities establish boards and/or commissions composed of volunteer citizens to oversee city zoning and planning goals and policies and to listen to the concerns of citizens.

City or County Planning Commissions

Most communities throughout the United States have planning and zoning commissions. These bodies typically comprise five to nine volunteer members appointed by the local governing body, such as the city council or mayor, or county council or county executive. The structure of the commission is generally governed by the state planning act or, in some cases, by the local government charter.

The role of the commission is to review and act on all planning-related matters, including master plans for a city- or county-wide comprehensive plan, neighborhood plans, and corridor plans. In these cases, the commission often has direct authority to adopt a plan or approve a subdivision. The commission may also be responsible for reviewing zoning-related matters, but typically it advises the local governing body.

Board of Zoning Appeals

The board of zoning appeals (or board of adjustment) may be a separate entity, or its responsibilities may be assigned to the planning commission. A board of zoning appeals is often the final authority in cases regarding appeals. The board hears primarily two types of cases: those requesting a variance, and those requesting a reconsideration of an earlier decision.

To approve a variance, the board must agree that a departure from the standard rules is justified because of a hardship tied to the physical characteristics of the land. To grant an appeal, the board must agree that an applicant was wrongly deprived of the opportunity to develop land due to an error in the zoning process involving a requirement, decision, or interpretation by an administrative official involved in reviewing and acting on the project application. The board may also address and rule on ambiguous provisions in the zoning ordinance.

Other Citizen Review Boards and Commissions

Communities sometimes create other types of entities to address important local issues as well. The roles of such entities may include review of projects for issues dealing with historic preservation, architectural design, urban design, landscape design, and public art. The reviews are often design-related because design matters are generally more flexible, allowing communities a greater role. Community boards may also review projects requesting tax increment financing (TIF) funds, tax abatements, or similar financing assistance using public dollars.

Governing Body

The governing body, such as the city or county council, has most of the power and responsibility for zoning decisions. The Standard State Zoning Enabling Act, which serves as the model code for most states, anticipates the local governing body will pass zoning as a local law, with the majority of the work administered by staff and interpreted by the board of appeals or adjustments. However, over time, rezoning has become necessary to accommodate development. Since rezoning is a change in the local law, involvement of the governing body is required to hear cases and make decisions.

Other government agencies also may need to be involved, such as a department of transportation, but this will become apparent during the process of working with local government and staff.

The governing body typically has three options for making a decision—to refuse a project, to approve a project as it is presented, or to approve a project subject to specific conditions or revisions. The latter decision may require a follow-up presentation to verify that revisions have been made according to the direction given.

FACTORS INTEGRAL TO ZONING REVIEW

Zoning should reflect the goals and policies of the community, and allow flexible interpretation for projects that meet the intent, if not the actual regulations, of the code. Specific factors are used to determine whether a project is in compliance with zoning regulations. The factors may vary by community, but they must be clearly stated and followed for a community to subsidize development and invest public dollars consistently and fairly.

Land Use Classifications

Land use classification is a legal term that defines permitted uses for a parcel of land. However, most communities have taken the broad categories of land use type and broken them down into very specific uses, which may result in hundreds of identified land uses in the zoning ordinance. For instance, numerous identified and acceptable uses may appear under the heading "retail sales and service," including antique shops, clothing or ready-to-wear stores, confectionery shops, and stationery stores. Even at this level of distinction, new and changing uses will arise that are not identified and therefore hard to classify, such as a live-work art studio. In addition, obsolete uses, such as "ice delivery stations" and "livery stables," are still listed in the land use classifications of many states.

Many communities are revising their zoning ordinances to condense hundreds of use types into a single table that identifies broader and more inclusive categories, avoids listing obsolete uses, and ensures flexibility to accommodate new uses that evolve over time.

Contextual Infill

Many older neighborhoods experience a resurgence of interest in new development. Often these neighborhoods offer charm and convenience (including proximity to downtown and cultural hubs) and a sense of place. Over the years, however, the needs and interests of residents have changed and the original housing stock no longer meets their expectations. This usually results in demolition of older housing stock to make way for new homes.

From a regulatory perspective, it is important for planners to know that the economic conditions leading to a teardown result from social issues unrelated to design. Teardowns often occur in desirable neighborhoods where the housing stock is sound, but dated.

—From APA's Zoning Practice Series (June 2005), "Practice Contextual Infill" by Lane Kendig

Communities facing teardowns express concern about the effect on community character and affordable housing for working-class people. One strategy for addressing such trends is to promote contextual infill through regulatory measures such as requirements for setback, building coverage, floor area ratio, building height, and building volume ratio. Such strategies can help maintain neighborhood character, while enabling property owners to make changes that accommodate modern amenities, such as upgraded kitchens and baths, and larger bedrooms and closets.

Creating design guidelines for development—whether for renovation or new construction—can also be effective in helping preserve community character. Such design guidelines should address neighborhood context, including building materials, site orientation, building height and setbacks, roof form, and windows, as well as particular neighborhood features, such as front porches or garage placement behind the house.

While keeping older building stock in communities viable for housing, local retail and business operations, and civic uses is important, the structures must also comply with local building code and related regulations. To address this issue, some states have created adjustments (or overlays) to their building codes that allow renovation of older and/or historic buildings without full compliance with requirements of the Americans with Disabilities Act (ADA) or the latest seismic codes. This allowance makes renovation of these structures more practical and financially feasible for developers and property owners, and helps maintain the original community character and building stock.

Sustainable Design and Development Patterns

Planning with regard to sustainable design and development issues promotes clustering of new development to ensure the conservation of natural resources such as wetlands, woodlands, stream and riverbanks, and steep slopes, as well as the preservation of historic resources, such as landmarks, architecturally significant buildings and districts, and the character associated with these areas. Sustainable development also includes reinvesting in existing, walkable neighborhoods, where an initial investment has already been made in streets, sewers, and other utilities. These neighborhoods often provide a density that supports public transit, thereby reducing dependence on automobiles.

Another facet of sustainable design and development is the establishment of guidelines to promote better water quality and use. Among the goals of such guidelines are a reduction in stormwater runoff to reduce pollution to bodies of water and an increase in water conservation by reducing the use of potable water for lawns and landscapes.

Sustainability is meeting the needs of the present without compromising the ability of future generations to meet their own needs.

—United Nations Commission on Environment and Development, 1987

Communities interested in using a more formal approach to incorporating sustainable standards into local zoning ordinances should start with a review of existing ordinances to determine areas for improvement and create strategies to achieve desired results.

When establishing an ordinance that considers issues of sustainable design, the following should be addressed:

- Landscaping needs, such as watering and fertilizer requirements
- Stormwater runoff and related pollution and its impact on water treatment facility capacity
- Wastewater treatment demands and costs
- Stream and wetland preservation

- Floodplain protection
- Soil erosion and sediment control
- Weed control
- Tree preservation
- Building code requirements
- Pedestrian amenities to support walkability
- Street design
- Parking requirements and opportunities for more flexible standards
- Access to multiple modes of transportation, including walking, biking, and public transit

Parking

Parking is a complex zoning issue. According to Donald Shoup, FAICP, author of the 2006 American Planning Association report *Practice Smart Parking*, there are three steps in establishing parking requirements for a specific land use:

1. Identify the land use.
2. Define the factors expected to predict peak parking demand.
3. Use the information from steps 1 and 2 to specify the number of parking spaces required to meet the anticipated need of the development.

In a 2002 survey of parking requirements, the Planning Advisory Service of the APA discovered nearly 700 land uses, each with distinct parking requirements. In addition, more than 200 factors were used to determine parking needs in various conditions and for different uses. The need for parking in different communities varied as well, often due to availability of public transit.

In the past, it was common practice to err on the side of caution to ensure an abundance of parking, rather than risk a shortage. However, as cities become more concerned about urban sprawl, stormwater management, dependence on cars, and rising gas prices, many of them are exploring strategies to reduce the amount of parking required. Following are descriptions of some of their approaches:

Implementing an effective public transit system. For example, Dallas, St. Louis, Los Angeles, and Denver are automobile-oriented cities achieving success with the relatively recent addition of transit systems.

Using shared parking opportunities. Known in some areas as a "park once" strategy, this approach facilitates the sharing of parking spaces for daytime and evening businesses and residences in mixed-use areas. Where developments provide a sufficient density of uses and a comfortable pedestrian environment, this approach encourages people to park vehicles once and walk to more than one destination without having to move their cars.

Creating strategic parking plans at a district scale. This is similar to the shared-parking plan, but on a larger scale. The general concept is to look at the land use of an area, typically no more than a half mile in diameter, estimate the parking required for that, and target preferred locations for parking to accommodate the anticipated needs of the buildings. This allows more land to be developed and creates a walkable character to the area because each land use is not required to fully provide its own parking on-site. More density, mixed uses, and opportunities to create more inviting pedestrian zones can be achieved.

Transportation Patterns, Modes, and Design

Today the United States faces rising fuel prices and related transportation costs, increasing public health concerns like obesity and type 2 diabetes, and a growing underemployed population. In light of this situation, transportation investment must be expanded from its emphasis on roads and systems that primarily support privately owned vehicles. Increasing the means of travel available to citizens in communities across the country—including walking, biking, and public transit—can serve young and elderly populations, disabled citizens unable to drive, low-income residents without cars, and those who desire alternative means of transportation. These modes of transportation also promote improved air and water quality and help maintain community character.

Community planning and design can support transportation options that encourage walkable destinations for residents, workers, and visitors by strategically increasing densities around intermodal transportation hubs; increasing desirable amenities such as parks and plazas, libraries, and shops; and encouraging mixed-use development.

Water Conservation

Water use is becoming a pressing issue around the country and is not limited to times of drought. Older cities face an aging infrastructure that needs significant repairs or complete replacement. Newer communities are struggling with finding sources of water to meet growing demand.

Several strategies commonly employed to address these issues are the use of impact fees, creation of community development districts responsible for providing infrastructure, and institution of pricing policies to cover the cost of providing water and create incentives for reducing water consumption. However, the role zoning and development patterns play in community water use is rarely addressed.

Three general categories of zoning pertain to water use: lot size, landscaping material, and leakage. Lot size relates to the amount of lawn to maintain, car washing, and similar outdoor uses. A variety of studies consistently show that these outdoor water uses can constitute up to 50 to 70 percent of overall household water use. (The statistics are similar for office uses, with the water requirements for maintaining associated landscaping.)

The plants chosen for landscaping can have a dramatic effect on the amount of water required. Plants native to an area typically require less water, and several water utilities are offering tips to homeowners who plant native vegetation. Some cities are also offering incentives to developers and property owners who landscape with plants that need minimal irrigation.

Leakage through pipes and joints occurs with all water systems. The amount of water lost to leaks is difficult to estimate because of variations in such factors as infrastructure age and condition, length of distribution systems, and water pressure. According to the May 2005 issue of the APA publication *Zoning Practice* (a special report on water conservation titled "How Thirsty Is Your Community?"), a range of typical leakage is considered to be 6 to 25 percent or more. As water becomes scarce, lost water

APPROACHING A COMMUNITY BOARD

Probably the best advice is to do your homework. Here are some guidelines to flesh out this simple maxim:

Understand what it takes to get on the agenda of a planning board meeting, zoning hearing, or other hearing. What applications need to be made? What information is required? Does the owner's request need to be denied before the owner or the owner's representative can appear in person? How much time is required to file an appeal from a negative decision? How long does it take to get on the agenda?

Sit down with the public official enforcing the regulations or the secretary of the board and learn the process. Get technical questions about the process answered, as well as an indication of how the board likes to be approached.

Find out who is on the board, what they do when they are not providing this public service, and whether *there are specific personal agendas on the table.* Most regulatory boards are appointed citizen boards, intended to represent community interests, as well as the law. Find out what those interests are.

Attend a meeting before the one at which you are scheduled to appear. Observe how the board works, how formal or informal the proceedings are, and what the important issues are. While boards operate within a carefully defined regulatory framework, they have considerable latitude in how they approach their responsibilities.

Review the law as it is applicable to your case. In constructing the case to be made, work with the owner, and perhaps the owner's attorney, to review the applicable law (for example, the conditions under which a zoning board can vote a special-use permit). Address these points.

Consider who, besides the board, will be in the room. By law, hearings and commission meetings are usually open. Public notice is given in the local newspaper, and frequently the law requires that adjacent landowners be notified. Who will come and what will be on their minds? Will the media be interested? It is one thing to present to a five-person zoning board and another to speak to a roomful of angry neighbors.

For controversial projects, suggest that the owner hold informational meetings in the community before the hearing is held. In addition to providing information, these meetings can bring concerns to the surface—concerns the owner may want to address before taking the project to the hearing where a decision will be made.

Be organized. Arrive at the hearing on time, bring the necessary materials, and make sure that everyone involved in the presentation understands their roles.

Keep your presentation short and professional. Make sure visuals are legible. When discussion begins, listen carefully to what is being said, and address concerns as directly as possible.

Be sure the owner knows what to fight for and what to give up in negotiation. Do not state a contrary position during the discussion without first huddling with the owner. Remember, this is the owner's project, not yours.

—David Haviland, Hon. AIA, from *The Architect's Handbook of Professional Practice,* 13th edition

is treated as lost money. It is predicted that curbing large water losses from leaks may save some towns or districts the cost of finding additional water sources.

THE ZONING REVIEW PROCESS

Each community has its own zoning review process. For example, some communities offer incentives, such as streamlining the process, if the applicant complies with such community goals as design character, public amenities, or the mitigation of environmental impacts. The following describes a basic review process, based on one used by Blaine County, Idaho. While it serves as an example for discussion, architects should contact the local government where a project is located to confirm the process in that particular community.

Purpose of the Review

All building permits receive zoning review as part of the building permit process. The purpose of the zoning review is to determine if the development proposal complies with the zoning requirements. If a property is located within a subdivision, compliance with the subdivision plat and plat notes will also be determined.

Review by Planning Staff

During the zoning review process, the zoning administrator or other designated planning staff member will make the following determinations:

- Whether the property is a valid "lot of record" as defined in the zoning regulations—either a lot that is part of a recorded subdivision or a lot or parcel described by metes and bounds. If the development involves an unplatted parcel, the developer should contact the planning department and request a parcel determination early in the planning process.
- Whether the proposed use is allowed as a permitted, accessory, or conditional use in the designated zoning district, such as a single-family residence in a residential zone.
- Whether the project meets the minimum building setback requirements or is located within a platted building envelope on a subdivision lot. Building setbacks are measured from the property line to the foundation wall.
- Whether the building height is within the maximum allowed, typically 35 feet as measured from existing natural grade to the highest portion of the structure for residential structures.
- Whether the subject property is located in an environmentally sensitive area such as a floodplain, wetlands, avalanche-prone area, or hillside. If so, further information

will likely be necessary and a special use permit issued by the planning and zoning commission may be required before a building permit can be issued. Special use permits and variance applications typically take a minimum of six weeks to process. It may take longer depending on the time of year, proposed use, and backlog of other applications awaiting public hearing.

- Whether the project complies with the subdivision plat and plat notes. If there is an active homeowners' association, it will be necessary to acquire its written approval before a building permit can be issued.
- Whether the conditions of approval attached to special zoning permits, such as conditional use and variances, have been satisfied.

Structural Review and Building Permit

Once it has been determined a development proposal complies with applicable zoning regulations, the plans will be referred to the county building department for structural review and issuance of the building permit as appropriate. If the development proposal does not comply with one or more of the zoning requirements, the applicant will be informed of what steps can be taken to bring the project into compliance.

Locally Specific Review Processes

Most communities include all of the steps and order of activities in the description above. However, in larger cities or municipalities with many departments, the process can be more complicated. For example, the New York City Uniform Land Use Review Procedure requires an 11-by-17-inch sheet of paper to accommodate the numerous diagrams and small type needed to outline the wide variety of issues and participants in what can be a lengthy review process that lasts 18 months or more.

SATISFYING DEVELOPMENT SOLUTIONS

In the last few decades, housing development has followed a trend where houses are geographically separated by price category. This has the effect of segregating people by socioeconomic groups and by age. It also contrasts with historic patterns in which smaller, affordable housing and larger, more expensive housing were found in the same neighborhood. Recent trends indicate that healthy, sustainable neighborhoods offer a range of housing options, allowing residents to move from apartments or small houses to larger houses and back to smaller housing as income and lifecycle needs require. When people stay in their neighborhoods by choice, they can maintain their social networks, shopping patterns, civic involvement, and other important relationships. These connections are often lost when people must move to different neighborhoods to accommodate changing housing needs.

Architects are well positioned to help communities achieve satisfying development solutions. As visual thinkers, architects can help members of the community see the possibilities in creating more livable environments with the potential to support larger community goals for health, safety, and sustainability, as well as the wants and needs of its citizens.

For More Information

Part Six of *Planning and Urban Design Standards* (Wiley, 2006), authored by the American Planning Association (APA), addresses a variety of zoning issues, including its legal foundations. The APA website at www.planning.org also provides information about community planning controls.

The Planning Advisory Service regularly publishes booklets addressing a broad range of planning issues. Its website is www.pas.gov.uk. Another website of interest is Campaign for Sensible Growth at www.growingsensibly.org, which includes an article titled "Zoning for Environmental Sustainability."

The Centers for Disease Control website, www.cdc.gov, has a wealth of valuable information addressing urban sprawl, density, and overall community development patterns and their relationship to public health.

The Institute for Transportation Engineers recently published a report titled "Context Sensitive Solutions in Designing Major Thoroughfares for Walkable Communities." It is available as a PDF file on their website at www.ite.org.

The American City: What Works, What Doesn't (McGraw-Hill, 1996), by Alexander Garvin, analyzes 250 projects in 100 cities with respect to public/private partnerships, neighborhood revitalization, zoning, and historic preservation.

Additional useful material on zoning and planning can be found in the following publications:

- *The Practice of Local Government Planning*, 3rd edition (International City/County Management Association, 2000)
- *Planning and Control of Land Development: Cases and Materials*, 6th edition, by Daniel Mandelker et al. (Matthew Bender, 2005)
- *Aesthetics, Community Character, and the Law*, by Christopher J. Duerksen and R. Matthew Goebel, cosponsored by Scenic America and APA (2000); available from the APA as Planning Advisory Service Report 489/490
- *Planning and Environmental Law*, a monthly journal of abstracts published by the APA

10.2 Building Codes and Standards

David S. Collins, FAIA, NCARB

To provide for the public welfare, government at all levels establishes and enforces building codes and regulations. The design of buildings must comply with applicable codes and regulations unless variances or alternative solutions are allowed.

As part of the police powers granted to the states by the U.S. Constitution, each jurisdiction has the legal option to establish minimum standards for safety and health in that community. States either take the authority or permit local communities to take responsibility for the adoption and enforcement of codes, and for years a variety of codes was used around the country. Today, the United States is close to having a single set of adopted codes.

As with many laws, communities have the opportunity to create their own codes or to choose a model code. Generally, a package of model codes provides guidance for communities seeking to comprehensively address how the design and construction of buildings and other facilities affect the health and safety of occupants. Model codes and standards are based on the broadest thinking about how an acceptable level of safety can be achieved and how regulations should be applied. However, in adopting model codes, a community must understand what is expected in administering the codes.

Architects, engineers, designers, and even contractors in many communities are part of the effort to regulate construction by establishing minimum levels of

David S. Collins is president and founding member of The Preview Group, Inc., a building regulatory consulting firm with offices in Cincinnati and Berkeley, California. He has served as secretary of the AIA and has managed the AIA Codes Advocacy Program. Collins serves on the NIST Construction Safety Advisory Committee investigating the World Trade Center collapse, the Underwriters' Laboratories (UL) Fire Council, and numerous ICC and NFPA committees.

performance and practice. The National Council of Architectural Registration Boards (NCARB) includes several items associated with building code compliance in the Architect Registration Examination. State licensure laws often include criteria for licensure such as preparing construction documents that conform to local law.

Many states use these types of requirements to reinforce the need for architects to be aware that local laws and regulations are an integral part of building design. In the first decade of the twenty-first century, the process of maintaining a library of regulations and standards has become increasingly difficult as the number of regulations—not to mention their complexity—increases each year. This volume is magnified by the continuous evolution of model codes and standards, many of which are modified on a three-year cycle.

To ensure that registered architects remain up-to-date on building codes, a system of mandatory continuing education is now the policy of many states and is also a membership requirement of the AIA. In general, training and education requirements call for at least 18 hours of continuing education activities, 8 hours of which are related to the protection of the health, safety, and welfare of the public.

HISTORY OF U.S. CODE DOCUMENTS

Development of modern building codes began around the turn of the twentieth century, and model codes began to appear soon thereafter. The rise of industrial cities in the United States brought many people to urban areas, resulting in the construction of housing in close proximity to industries. Responding to the hazards that could result from this juxtaposition, communities and insurance companies began writing building codes. Later, communities began sharing their knowledge and understanding of construction regulations and created regional codes.

Standards for building systems began to undergo significant changes in tandem with the development of building codes. The National Fire Protection Association traces the beginnings of NFPA 13, Standard for Installation of Sprinkler Systems, to 1895 when a group of insurers and sprinkler system installers began the process of systematizing the installation of these systems.

Committees for the development of standards typically include industry interests that are close to, and have financial interests in, the materials or systems controlled by the standard. As part of their participation, these industry representatives vote for criteria to encourage appropriate use of those materials or systems. Most model codes, on the other hand, are developed with input from industry interests, although those representing such interests are not allowed to vote on provisions included in the codes. Limiting industry involvement is intended to prevent undue influence on the codes from those with a financial interest in them.

Prior to 1994, model building codes were published in the United States by the Building Officials and Code Administrators International (BOCA), Southern Building Code Congress International (SBCCI), and the International Conference of Building Officials (ICBO). These organizations generated parallel documents and each endorsed a "common code format" that allowed users of the codes who worked in multiple jurisdictions to easily find criteria on the same subject in the same part of the three codes. It also facilitated comparisons and identification of commonalities and differences in the text of the three documents.

In 1975 the AIA Codes and Standards Committee published a white paper titled "One Code: A Program of Regulatory Reform for the United States." This document was the impetus for the consolidation of the three model codes. In 1994, BOCA, SBCCI, and ICBO officially joined together to create the International Code Council (ICC), which began producing the international family of building codes. In 1995 the new code family began with the first edition of the mechanical and plumbing codes. The 2000 edition of the International Building Code was the first publication to include all the major ICC codes.

Policy Statement	Regulation of the construction industry shapes the built environment. As stakeholders, architects must participate in the development and application of appropriate regulations and standards.
Supporting Position Statements	**22. Building Codes and Standards**

The AIA supports regulation by a single set of comprehensive, coordinated, and contemporary codes and standards, which establish sound threshold values of health, safety, and the protection of the public welfare throughout the United States.

To that end, the AIA espouses the development and adoption of model building codes that:

- Include participation by architects and the public in a consensus process;
- Are the product of informed education and research;
- Are without favoritism or bias to any special interest;
- Include provision for a prompt appeals procedure for all that might be aggrieved;
- Are cost-effective in relation to public benefit; and
- Promote building code provisions that set performance rather than prescriptive criteria.

23. Building Permits

The AIA supports governmental policies, regulatory procedures, and administration that eliminate unnecessary time delays in the construction permitting process.

Today, the ICC publishes the only family of model building codes used in the United States. The complete package of codes currently published by the ICC includes the following:

- International Building Code (IBC)
- International Residential Code for One- and Two-Family Dwellings (IRC)
- International Mechanical Code (IMC)
- International Plumbing Code (IPC)
- International Fire Code (IFC)
- International Fuel Gas Code (IFGC)
- International Energy Conservation Code (IECC)
- International Existing Building Code (IEBC)
- International Private Sewage Disposal Code (IPSC)
- International Wildland-Urban Interface Code (IWUIC)
- ICC Performance Code for Buildings and Facilities (ICCPC)
- International Property Maintenance Code (IPMC)
- International Zoning Code (IZC)
- ICC Electrical Code Administrative Provisions (IEC)

These ICC codes, along with the NFPA National Electrical Code, provide a complete bookshelf of codes appropriate for adoption and enforcement in communities throughout the United States.

In 1999 the National Fire Protection Association (NFPA) announced its intent to develop a model building code despite objections from many groups in the construction industry. Although NFPA has long published several documents, including codes and standards, none included limitations on structural loads and materials specifications. The NFPA product closest to a building code was NFPA 101, Life Safety Code, and NFPA chose that document as a model for its development of NFPA 5000, Building Construction and Safety Code™. NFPA 5000 was published in 2003 and has since undergone some revisions.

In marketing its building code, the NFPA partnered with several other organizations to provide expertise that NFPA did not have. They included the International Association of Plumbing and Mechanical Officials (IAPMO) to provide plumbing and

It is incumbent upon architects to know and understand the breadth of regulations that apply to their projects.

mechanical codes, as well as the American Society of Heating, Refrigerating and Air-Conditioning Engineers (ASHRAE) and the Western Fire Chiefs Association (WFCA) for the consolidation of its fire code with NFPA 1.

Fifty states, the District of Columbia, Puerto Rico, U.S. Virgin Islands, and Guam are using the International Building Code. Almost all are using the International Residential Code, and the International Fire Code as well. No state, however, has adopted the NFPA building code. However, virtually all of the ICC codes reference NFPA standards, such as NFPA 13 for sprinkler systems, as well as the National Electrical Code, which is used internationally as the standard for design and installation of electrical equipment.

While the IBC is now the accepted standard, there is some variation because many states and municipalities have adopted different editions of the code. As this *Handbook* goes to press, the 2015 revision was the latest, only three states have adopted it. Others use the 2012 and 2006 versions. The next major revision is planned for 2018.

Some government projects or projects that use government funding require adherence to codes and standards other than the model codes just described. A prime example is the Americans with Disabilities Act. Federal legislation established that rules were to be created to afford access to buildings by the disabled, and granted the U.S. Access Board the authority to write guidelines and the Department of Justice the authority to adopt and enforce them.

In the past, difficulty arose for architects who wanted to know which accessibility rules to follow because the Department of Justice did not adopt the 2004 guidelines issued by the Access Board until 2010 and they did not become effective until 2012.

The model code organizations have taken different approaches to building accessibility. The ICC has tried to mainstream accessible features into the general requirements of the IBC. NFPA, on the other hand, has simply incorporated the "ADA and ABA Accessibility Guidelines for Buildings and Facilities," as recommended by the U.S. Access Board in its 2004 rules, into the 2006 edition of NFPA 5000, referencing ICC/ANSI A117.1, Standard on Accessible and Usable Buildings and Facilities.

The Access Board guidelines and A117.1 are prime examples of specification requirements. The family of ICC codes and NFPA 5000 and NFPA 101 includes both specification-oriented (minimum requirements and maximum limitations) and performance options. Generally, the specification-oriented codes provide a direct response to the majority of design issues and safety concerns. However, both code groups are aware that despite efforts to be comprehensive in their documents, issues may arise that are not currently addressed or that are so far from the scope of a typical building that they require a different approach to determine what is appropriate for life safety. The performance options within the codes are intended to provide guidelines for designers and their clients looking for a means to resolve a particular problem.

While sections of NFPA 5000 are titled "performance," they actually provide very specific limits for what is to be done in the process. For example, Section 5.3 is titled "retained prescriptive requirements" and covers means of egress and all prescriptive requirements for fire protection systems and features. The ICC Performance Code provides a format for how to take a project through the performance code and indicates what considerations must be followed, but it does not establish any specific prescriptive limits. The ICC's prescriptive codes serve as the measuring stick for the performance of a design, but they do not establish absolute limits for performance.

Performance code provisions were developed to allow innovative solutions that do not fall within the typical design. The fact that the performance approach has been formalized is recognition that the codes are not able to anticipate every circumstance and every possible solution.

Choosing whether to use a prescriptive code or a performance code is a decision that must be made carefully and with the input of the client. In particular, the code choice must be supported by the authorities having jurisdiction (AHJs) that will approve the project. This may mean officials representing virtually every enforcement agency within a community who will regulate the project. According to the ICC documents, this group at least includes building and fire enforcement officials.

IBC AND IFC CODE FUNDAMENTALS

A common thread in both ICC and NFPA documents is the true integration of the building and fire codes and the standards they reference. In previous codes, the approach to code enforcement was often insulated by the document in which the requirements were located. In current codes, the fire and building requirements are totally integrated so the full understanding of what is required can only be ascertained by going to multiple documents. Reference to at least the building and fire codes is necessary to find minimum design requirements, and most often several additional referenced documents (e.g., mechanical and plumbing codes) must be checked to grasp the full impact of the codes on a given building design.

The architect, in conjunction with the client, typically makes the initial decision on occupancy or construction type appropriate for a project, while code officials (AHJs) analyze documents presented for their review. Thus, the following overview of code fundamentals, based on the International Building Code, approaches code analysis from the designer's perspective.

To determine the minimum type of construction needed to meet the code, several pieces of information are required. These include the use for the space (occupancy), the combined need for space (height and area) and, because of its occupancy classification, whether the building requires a sprinkler system (fire protection). The code also contains requirements for means of egress with respect to travel distances, paths of travel, and the design of stairs, corridors, and exits.

Occupancy

Every structure must be classified in a specific occupancy, and most buildings will require more than one occupancy classification. For example, a conference room or cafeteria within a business facility would probably be designated as an "assembly" occupancy. In the same type of structure, some supply and storage areas may be appropriately classified as "storage" use occupancies. The IBC requires identification of all the different occupancies in a space or building as part of the design process.

Because the IBC is structured to address the characteristics of the activities in a building, it is critical to understand the various occupancy categories in the code and how to distinguish among them. The categories are as follows:

- Assembly: Groups A-1, A-2, A-3, A-4, and A-5
- Business: Group B
- Educational: Group E
- Factory and Industrial: Groups F-1 and F-2
- High Hazard: Groups H-1, H-2, H-3, H-4, and H-5
- Institutional: Groups I-1, I-2, I-3, and I-4
- Mercantile: Group M
- Residential: Groups R-1, R-2, R-3, and R-4
- Storage: Groups S-1 and S-2
- Utility and Miscellaneous: Group U

Note that several of the categories are divided into subgroups to more clearly differentiate among them. For example, the "assembly" occupancy is subdivided into five different subgroups. Traditional stage theaters and motion picture theaters are classified as A-1, while an outdoor athletic stadium is classified as A-5. Although these facilities share the purpose of accommodating large groups of people watching a common demonstration, they are divided into subgroups because their needs are sufficiently different to require different approaches in a code.

NFPA 5000 has similar occupancy classifications, which are described in Chapter 6 of that code. The differences between the occupancy classifications in the IBC and NFPA 5000 are significant in some details associated with how specific conditions are to be addressed, but the major categories remain the same.

Fire Protection

Chapter 9 of both the IBC and the IFC includes limits, or thresholds, for the size and type of building that must have a sprinkler system. These limits are based on the building size or the area of an occupancy (fire area) that is enclosed by exterior walls, firewalls, or fire barriers. If the threshold for fire suppression for an occupancy classification is based on the building area, a fire area would not be part of the consideration for fire suppression. If the threshold is limited to the area of the occupancy, then the building can be subdivided into fire areas that are less than the specified threshold and not be required to have a sprinkler system.

A fire area is defined by the encompassing walls, roof, and floor that are either exterior walls, fire walls, or fire barriers. Any floor area within such enclosure is part of the fire area. For example, if a building is of Type IIB construction, the floors have zero fire resistance. If the building was three floors, all three floors would be added into the calculation of the fire area.

The ICC codes do not currently require one- and two-family dwellings and utility occupancy buildings to have sprinkler systems. However, all hospitals, nursing homes, and other institutional occupancies, as well as hotels, motels, apartments, and townhouses, are required to be protected with an automatic sprinkler system under all circumstances. Each of the other occupancies included in the IBC has a threshold after which sprinklers are mandatory; these figures are based on the size of the building, the area of the occupancy, or the number of persons the space accommodates.

Two additional conditions, which do not depend on the building occupancy classification, determine whether a structure must have a sprinkler system. Floors with no openings (the IBC sets up minimum size and spacing for openings), as well as any building with an occupied floor more than 55 feet above the lowest level that fire apparatus responding to the building can reach, must have a sprinkler system, no matter what the occupancy classification.

In NFPA 5000, thresholds for fire suppression are established in the occupancy chapter criteria. For example, an "assembly" occupancy classification in the IBC is required to have fire suppression when the occupant load exceeds 300 or the threshold of a specific occupancy area. The same 300-occupant threshold is found in NFPA 5000.

Additional fire protection thresholds for installation of automatic detection and alarm notification devices are also part of the IBC and NFPA 5000. Requirements for smoke detectors in dwelling units and the installation of pull boxes and the sound level of fire alarms are also repeated in each code.

Height and Area

The means for determining limits on height and area for a building are tied to several factors. Particularly critical are building occupancies and whether the building will be fully protected with sprinklers. Once the building height has been estimated and a concept for the layout of the floors and the location of the building on the site has been determined, the architect can easily determine the minimum type of construction for the project.

Table 503 of the IBC prescribes the base area for calculating the maximum area of a building. The base areas were derived from the area sizes permitted in the three model building codes that preceded the ICC codes. The IBC drafting committee agreed to accept the largest height and largest area of any building that would have been permitted by any of those codes. To accomplish this, the staff of each code organization was asked to determine what the largest area and height of a building would be for any given occupancy and type of construction.

Because the three previous model codes used a different method for calculating the maximum height and area, the committee chose to use the process for determining area included in the report on height and area from the Board for the Coordination of the Model Codes (BCMC). Applying that method in reverse, the values in Table 503 were developed. The formula for determining the maximum area of a building per the IBC is prescribed as follows:

$$A_a = A_t + \left[\frac{A_t I_f}{100} + \frac{A_t I_s}{100} \right]$$

where:
A_a is the allowable area for any single floor in the building,
A_t is the base area in Table 503,
I is the increase permitted for frontage, and
I_s is the increase for fire suppression.

In addition, the IBC limits the total area of the building to three times the allowable area calculated from this formula.

Although architects may begin designing a building without knowing what construction type is required, they will have a good idea of what the building configuration will be based on the program, the site and its limits, and site factors such as development and zoning requirements, drainage retention, utility easements, and so on. Given that information, a designer would be able to use the formula to solve the problem in reverse, with the actual area being known and the minimum type of construction being calculated. For example, if the program for an office building calls for 300,000 square feet of office space and supporting areas, the formula can be modified to solve for the area required for the construction type:

$$A_t = \left[\frac{A_a}{1 + I_f + I_s} \right]$$

As long as the type of construction in Table 503 has a larger area than that required for A_t, the building would be permitted for that occupancy. For example, assume a three-story office building without a sprinkler system and frontage around the building providing the minimum separation allowed to consider the building 100 percent open. The area permitted by Table 503 (A_t) would be determined by dividing the actual area (100,000 square feet) by the number of stories, and the frontage increase would be 75 percent. Thus, the formula would be

$$A_t = \left[\frac{100,000}{1 + 0.75 + 0} \right] = 57,143$$

It is then a simple matter to go to Table 503 and determine that the type of construction would have to be either Type IA or IB. However, if it was determined that installation of a sprinkler system was appropriate, the calculation would change to include the 200 percent factor and the formula would be

$$A_t = \left[\frac{100,000}{1 + 0.75 + 2} \right] = 26,600$$

The difference between the results of the two calculations indicates the effect the presence of a sprinkler system has on the construction type. The 57,143 square feet of the original required tabular area would limit the building to Type IA or IB, which is a rather unusual construction type for a low-rise building with sprinklers, however, Type IIA or IIIA would be permitted.

Note that this example uses a building with a single occupancy (business) with accessory areas of other occupancies (assembly or storage) typically found in office buildings. A mixed-use building (one with more than one principal occupancy) would require further analysis.

Additional considerations that affect the determination of construction type are requirements for fire alarms, standpipes, and means of egress. Thresholds for the installation of fire alarms are based on the use of sprinklers in the building and on the occupancy. For example, the office building just discussed would require a fire alarm if there were 100 occupants above the lowest level of exit discharge. With a total area per floor of 100,000 square feet, the occupant load would exceed 100 (100,000 square feet divided by 100 square feet per occupant equals 1,000 occupants). However, if the building has a sprinkler system and the alarm is activated by sprinkler flow, the manual pull boxes that would otherwise be a part of an alarm system are not required.

Means of Egress

Exiting, or means of egress, is one of the major code criteria that directly affect building design. Limitations are established in the code for how far a person must travel to reach an exit within a given space in a particular occupancy. These limitations include the distance when only a single path to an exit is available (common path of travel), dead-end corridor distances, and the total distance from any occupied location within the building to the exit or stairway or exit enclosure (exit access travel distance; see Figure 10.9).

The allowed distance for each of these limitations is based on the specific occupancy the means of egress is serving. The common path of travel is the initial concern for any space or layout of spaces within a building. This distance is based on the risk of not being able to access an area. The typical distance limit is 75 feet before occupants must be able to access a second route. In a suite of rooms that all discharge through a common lobby or corridor, this would apply to every space within the suite.

For example, a dead-end corridor in the area of a hospital where patients are sleeping is limited to 20 feet of travel in a direction where there is no exit. In the same building, but in areas where administrative offices are located, the dead-end corridor is limited to 50 feet of travel, assuming the entire building is protected by a sprinkler system. This difference in the dead-end limits reflects the difference in hazard to the occupants. The difference is calculated by comparing the potential response times of patients who are asleep or somehow incapacitated and people in an office area who presumably are awake and alert to an emergency.

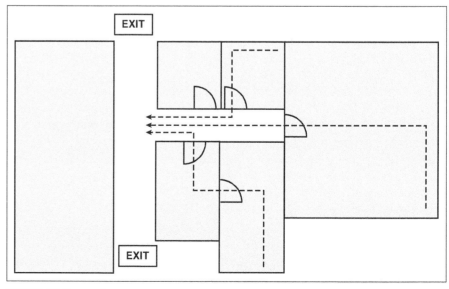

FIGURE 10.9 **Travel Distance to Exits**

The required overall travel distance will prescribe the location of the exits from a floor or the building. The typical distance to an exit for most occupancy classifications is 250 feet, which means that from any given point the distance to any exit cannot exceed that distance. Discounting any distance that would be required to travel to a central exit corridor, the exits would have to be located no more than 500 feet apart. However, the reality is that occupants would have to travel an additional distance from within a space to any such central corridor. Thus, the actual distance between the exits would have to be shorter than the optimum distance.

THE RELATIONSHIP BETWEEN STANDARDS AND CODES

Model building codes have always incorporated standards, and within the construction industry, different types of standards serve various purposes in relation to how a building is designed. Some standards regulate specific types of systems or processes. Some provide methods for testing a product in a particular application. Standards for a particular product or material include criteria as a minimum level of quality. Typically, standards are expected to parallel the building or fire code that references them and to be written in language that can easily be incorporated as an enforceable part of a code. Standards that are simply advisory, which are not written in mandatory language, are not included in model building codes.

Most NFPA standards are regulatory, the classic example being NFPA 13 for sprinklers. This standard explains the means and methods necessary to design and install a sprinkler system in a building. Its requirements are based on an industry-wide understanding of the level of hazard in various occupancies and the means needed to actively prevent the spread of a fire. NFPA 13 is considered a consensus standard because the representation of interests on the committee that reviews it and votes on revisions to its content is so broad. The group reaches consensus by balancing conflicting interests.

Standards for testing such as those promulgated by ASTM International or Underwriters' Laboratories are used to describe ways in which a material or an assembly of materials can be tested to determine a relative level of performance. ASTM E119, for example, is the fire test for floors and walls that is used to determine their ability to limit the spread of fire. The test prescribes the methods for construction of the test sample, the process of exposing it to the "standard time-temperature curve," and the levels of performance and how they are to be measured and reported. The classic measurement for a wall or floor assembly being tested using ASTM E119 is the length of time an assembly will remain in place before smoke or hot gases on the unexposed side will ignite cotton waste when exposed to these gases. The time duration is reported in hours, although the performance of an assembly in an actual fire is likely to be different from the text in the listing.

The curves for various "standard fires" rise in temperature very quickly. The ASTM E119 test goes up to almost 800°C in less than 30 minutes. At that point, a fire no longer increases at the same rate, although it does continue to increase in intensity until the test has been completed. A real fire may grow as rapidly as shown on these curves and may become even higher in intensity if the materials support rapid rates of combustion. However, a real fire typically dies down after the initial growth. This decrease is either caused by exhaustion of fuel or insufficient oxygen to feed the fire.

The purpose of standards like ASTM E119 is to establish a constant level of performance against which all tested materials can be measured. The use of the "hourly" rating is unfortunate because, as people become familiar with these ratings, the measurements become part of the lexicon of construction and an expected measure of the performance in a real fire.

There are industry standards for the production of various materials that are similar to NFPA standards and are developed using ASTM procedures. Wood, steel, concrete, and similar building products are brought to the marketplace under

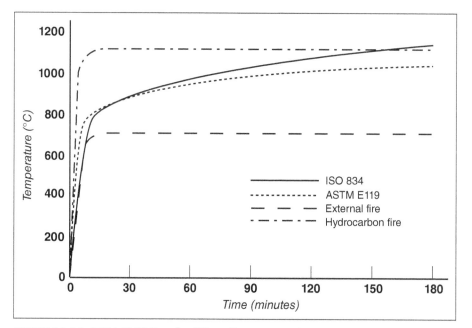

FIGURE 10.10 **ASTM E119 Standard Time–Temperature Curve**

conventions developed using these types of standards. The American Lumber Standard for wood, ACI 318 for concrete, and AISC 360 for steel, are the standards for these major building materials; they are used in combination with building codes and various engineering standards such as ASCE 7, Minimum Design Loads for Buildings and Other Structures, for the design of structures using these particular materials.

When a standard is not developed so it can be used to regulate or enforce a minimum or dictate a means and method for construction, it is considered to be advisory. Such standards may be useful to a designer dealing with a special application, but they are not required and often are not written in a way that allows their use as law.

PERFORMANCE CODES

Recently, the ICC added a performance code option to the standard specification codes that have been used for years. This code is designed to address special needs for a limited number of projects that do not fit within the norm of a typical construction and may require a level of design, investigation, and controls beyond the scope of current model codes. The concept behind a performance code is to support development of unique solutions with the acceptance of the entire project team, which could include as many players as the owner, designer, developer, and contractor, as well as building, fire, and local regulators and development officials, bankers, and so on.

This team sets the goals and objectives for the project within the parameters established in accordance with the performance code. The parameters for a particular project are determined based on the potential risk associated with the activities and an assessment of the needs of the owner and the community in which the facility will be constructed. By encouraging evaluation of risk and the effect the facility will have on identified risks, the performance code permits alternative methods for compliance.

Often, special testing or modeling tools to analyze specific risks are needed to more accurately define project parameters. For example, computer models can be used to determine egress times based on occupancy conditions. Similarly, there are models for determining how smoke would develop within a space given a specific type of fire. The

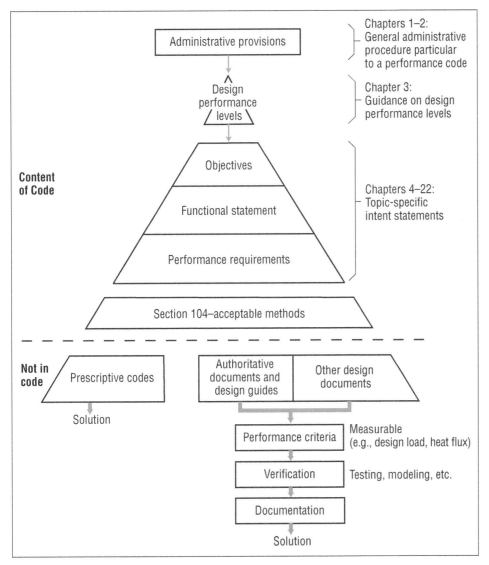

FIGURE 10.11 **ICC Performance Code**

type of fire is based on detailed analysis of the fire loading likely to be found in the space and includes consideration of factors such as the natural and mechanical ventilation available. By combining these two models, the time associated with evacuation of a given occupancy and the time associated with loss of a tenable environment can be compared and the risks evaluated.

The ICC codes include the risk of tenability for a typical environment, but often have been caught short of addressing special conditions. For instance, at one time, the IBC did not have specific criteria for a covered mall building; the use of a performance code would have been appropriate in that circumstance.

In addition, the performance codes are designed to facilitate solutions beyond those prescribed by the model codes. Typically, the codes are written as specifications and use performance options to achieve specified goals. Performance codes do not specify goals, but allow stakeholders to establish the methods and means to achieve the desired level of safety.

Evaluating risk and probable effect is key to developing appropriate performance solutions, as is being able to identify an appropriate means of testing and justifying the solutions. Often, technical specialists will be added to the design team to bring needed resources to bear on the subject.

Maximum Level of Damage to Be Tolerated

	PERFORMANCE GROUP 1	PERFORMANCE GROUP II	PERFORMANCE GROUP III	PERFORMANCE GROUP IV
VERY LARGE (very rare)	SEVERE	SEVERE	HIGH	MODERATE
LARGE (rare)	SEVERE	HIGH	MODERATE	MILD
MEDIUM (less frequent)	HIGH	MODERATE	MILD	MILD
SMALL (frequent)	MODERATE	MILD	MILD	MILD

INCREASING LEVEL OF PERFORMANCE →

MAGNITUDE OF DESIGN EVENT ↑

FIGURE 10.12 **International Building Code**

Testing and Verification

The National Institute for Standards and Technology has developed many computer software programs for evaluating building performance. Such programs are useful for determining design methods that may fall out of the standard specification for compliance. Following is a list of such programs:

- ALOFT-FT(tm)—A Large Outdoor Fire-Plume Trajectory Model—Flat Terrain
- ASCOS—Analysis of Smoke Control Systems
- ASET-B—Available Safe Egress Time-Basic
- ASMET—Atria Smoke Management Engineering Tools
- BREAK1—Berkeley Algorithm for Breaking Window Glass in a Compartment Fire
- CCFM—Consolidated Compartment Fire Model version VENTS
- CFAST—Consolidated Fire and Smoke Transport Model
- DETACT-QS—Detector Actuation—Quasi Steady
- DETACT-T2—Detector Actuation—Time Squared
- ELVAC—Elevator Evacuation
- FASTLite—A collection of procedures that builds on the core routines of FIRE-FORM and the computer model CFAST to provide engineering calculations of various fire phenomena

- FIRDEMND—Handheld Hosestream Suppression Model
- FIRST—FIRe Simulation Technique
- FPETool—Fire Protection Engineering Tools (equations and fire simulation scenarios)
- Jet—A model for the prediction of detector activation and gas temperature in the presence of a smoke layer
- LAVENT—Response of sprinkler links in compartment fires with curtains and ceiling vents
- NIST Fire Dynamics Simulator and Smokeview: The Fire Dynamics Simulator predicts smoke and/or air flow movement caused by fire, wind, ventilation systems, etc. Smokeview visualizes the predictions generated by NIST FDS.

These programs are free and are available at the NIST website at www.bfrl.nist.gov/info/software.html. Used alone, they cannot ensure that the designed level of performance will be acceptable, but the information will provide additional guidance for designs that do not fall within the specifications in the codes. Additional sources of information for performance designs are included in the reference sections of the performance codes.

PRACTICE ISSUES

As a fundamental part of any design, building codes form an important framework for developing a program to achieve the owner's objectives. Consideration of the code criteria for a particular occupancy is critical to preliminary design decisions that will affect safety and health.

Checklists

For many years, model code groups produced code checklists intended to aid in the determination of code compliance. Although these were relatively useful tools for reviewing plans from an AHJ plan examiner's point of view, they did not provide enough information for those making design decisions.

Local Adoption of Current Codes

Building codes adopted by the vast majority of jurisdictions in the United States are now or soon will be based on the ICC family of codes. While many communities make changes to portions of the building code they have adopted for local political or geographic reasons, the use of a single national code appears to be the way of the future. A list of jurisdictions and the codes they have adopted can be obtained from either the National Conference of States on Building Codes and Standards (NCSBCS) or the ICC. Both organizations publish lists of communities and the codes they have adopted. NCSBCS information is available only to members, but the ICC lists are available to anyone on the ICC Web page.

Each of the ICC model codes includes basic directions on how to use them in the form of a sample ordinance for adoption. The ICC identifies sections that must be modified because of local conditions in the sample ordinance. However, most states that adopt the model codes delete the requirements in Chapter 1 and replace them with their own legislatively mandated administrative criteria. This can work well if careful consideration is given to the requirements in Chapter 1 of each code during the adoption process. If care is not taken, however, some unfortunate conflicts can be created either between different codes or between various code enforcing agencies within a jurisdiction.

One of the most important features of the new ICC codes is the level of coordination among them. These codes are meant to be used together to comprehensively address the various elements of construction that affect life safety and health. Without appropriate integration of the code enforcement package these codes provide, a community may miss some important safety features.

For example, as parallel documents, the IBC, IMC, IPC, IECC, and IFC codes are intended to be used in a coordinated fashion. Nonetheless, the IBC and IFC include duplicate criteria for such requirements as sprinklers, means of egress, and occupancies. This duplication is meant to reduce confusion among community enforcement officials. However, the IFC establishes minimum standards for existing buildings whether or not work is being performed or occupancies are being changed. These minimum standards are only enforceable through the IFC. If a community expects to apply such standards to all buildings, adoption of the fire code and a mechanism for enforcement is critical. Similarly, requirements for alterations to an existing structure are found in two documents—the IBC and the IEBC. Although these codes are parallel in many ways, the IBC lacks several specification requirements included in the IEBC. Both codes, however, include an alternative compliance method for evaluating the safety of an existing building.

Property maintenance issues involving handrails and guardrails, addressed in the International Property Maintenance Code, are intended to be applied through adoption of the IPMC. Mechanical and plumbing requirements are referenced in the IBC, and the code includes specific designs for ventilation of an atrium or an open mall. IBC references and the IMC both include general requirements for HVAC systems, including required amounts of fresh air. The IMC and IPC provide specific criteria for plumbing and mechanical systems, which the IBC includes many of the minimum design requirements. For example, the minimum number of plumbing fixtures for an occupancy classification is described in Chapter 29 of the IBC, while the details on materials and installation of the plumbing systems are in the IPC.

The lack of coordination between code documents in the past resulted in disjointed enforcement. To address this confusion, the ICC codes were designed to be applied uniformly by any part of an enforcement team. The building and fire codes are both applicable to the design of new structures, and projects should be designed and reviewed using both documents, thus preventing subsequent conflicts. This arrangement can fall apart, however, when communities fail to recognize this structure within the model codes and adopt different codes for different aspects of code enforcement. This saddles the owner with conflicts that the designer will be forced to resolve.

CODE ENFORCEMENT

Building code enforcement typically includes review of construction plans for proposed projects followed by inspection of the built work to ensure it conforms to the approved plans. State or local building departments operate within legislated authority to determine the acceptable means of designing and constructing the buildings submitted to them. Most often it is illegal to begin construction of a building without approvals or permits from the responsible AHJs. Completion of the construction process is typically marked by the issuance of a certificate of occupancy, which means the project can be used for the purpose indicated.

Some communities have a mandatory certification process that requires the design professional to take responsibility for substantial completion in accordance with the codes. This additional level of responsibility for the designer is unusual and may lead to unnecessary liability if not handled properly.

Planning and Zoning

Planning and zoning regulations are generally found in more developed areas of the country where the land available to be developed is limited. These types of regulations are also part of a model code process, but they are not generally adopted very widely. The ICC has a model zoning code that outlines the major subjects commonly included in zoning codes, such as use districts, limitations on activities and density, location on a lot, and so on. Generally, zoning is strictly local, although planning often can be regional. It is critical during the early stages of any design project to examine the zoning limitations for the site to determine if the use is allowed and what additional requirements, such as height and setback, might affect the design.

"Community Planning Controls" addresses regulations used to shape the form and function of communities.

Water/Plumbing Codes

Criteria for water supply to a building and the plumbing fixtures required for it are established in local plumbing codes. The International Plumbing Code is designed to work closely with the IBC and IMC to specify the proper type of water supply and appropriate number of fixtures for a particular type of facility compatible with those described in the ICC codes. Some local jurisdictions maintain a local plumbing and mechanical code, and the International Association of Plumbers and Mechanical Officials (IAPMO) continues to produce the Uniform Plumbing and Mechanical Code, still in wide use in the western United States.

Controls for the design of storm and sanitary drainage systems are tied to the methods used to design and locate a structure and its site features (e.g., parking lots, sidewalks, etc.). Sites where storm drainage systems are overtaxed commonly retain stormwater.

Code Appeals

When the inevitable disagreement occurs about how a code applies, or should apply, to a particular design, the dispute can be resolved through an appeal process. Although most legal disputes are resolved in the courts, the planning and zoning and construction processes require additional opportunities for administrative review in which specific expertise can be employed to resolve a dispute. Most communities establish boards of appeal to facilitate these reviews or hearings.

Variances or equivalent means of achieving compliance to zoning codes are usually allowed under local zoning regulations. However, the ICC has limits on its appeal board as their rules state they have no authority to "waive requirements of this code." Various state laws may or may not permit adjustments to codes. For example, under the Ohio Revised Code, local appeal boards are certified and given the following specific authority:

> 112.4 Powers, local boards of building appeals. Certified municipal and county boards of building appeals shall hear and decide the adjudication hearings referred to in section 113.1 within the jurisdiction of and arising from orders of the local building official in the enforcement of Chapters 3781 and 3791 of the Revised Code and rules adopted thereunder. The orders may be reversed or modified by the board if it finds:
>
> 1. The order contrary to such laws or rules;
> 2. The order contrary to a fair interpretation or application thereof; or,
> 3. That a variance from the provisions of such laws or rules, in a specific case, will not be contrary to the public interest where literal enforcement of such provisions will result in unnecessary hardship.

Specific laws that allow variances may exist in other jurisdictions as well.

PARTICIPATION IN CODE DEVELOPMENT

Code development is a process that depends on people who take the time and make the effort to participate. Participation does not necessarily mean serving on a committee or even attending hearings on a subject. It means simply being aware of the codes and being able and willing to suggest ways in which they can better address technical issues. Web sites include forms for proposing changes to the codes, but often no more than a phone call to a staff person at the model code agency responsible for the code will begin the process of change. Many local building officials are part of a local ICC chapter that develops changes to the code, and architects can approach them about ways to fix problems or discrepancies in the model code.

Associations such as the National Association of Home Builders (NAHB), Building Owners and Managers Association (BOMA), and the AIA have resources available to help forward changes to the codes as well, and interested architects should approach them about promoting development of needed changes. In addition, staff members of the code organizations can be an invaluable resource in preparing material to enact a code change. Architects are typically the first to realize a problem with a particular provision, or to develop a unique solution to a problem not recognized in the code. By bringing forward changes that reflect a heightened awareness of what is in the code and what can work within the framework of the codes, an architect can have a profound effect on design and construction throughout the country.

For More Information

The International Code Council website provides a lot of information about the development and adoption of codes and standards. In particular, a list of jurisdictions and the ICC building codes they have adopted can be found at www.iccsafe.org/government/adoption.html.

Two heavily illustrated publications offer interpretive guidance on the 2006 International Building Code: *2006 Building Code Handbook* (McGraw-Hill, 2007), by Terry L. Patterson, and *Building Codes Illustrated: A Guide to Understanding the 2006 International Building Code*, 2nd edition (Wiley, 2007), by Francis D. K. Ching and Steven R. Winkel.

PART 4
CONTRACTS AND AGREEMENTS

CHAPTER **11**

Contracts and Agreements

11.1 Agreements with Owners

Joseph L. Fleischer, FAIA

The architect's agreement with the client should reflect the goals and expectations of both parties and establish the conditions under which services will be rendered.

The architect's *agreement* or *contract* (these terms are used interchangeably in this chapter) with the owner should be written to reflect the goals and expectations of each and to establish the conditions for working together in a professional relationship. Normally, architects think of the contract as the primary legal document recording the promises parties make about their responsibilities for the creation of a project. The contract delineates services and compensation, typically allocates risk, helps each party cope with change, and provides a method for resolving disputes. Contracts are also an excellent way to communicate and educate. They can make explicit what might otherwise be unsaid and make clear what might be misunderstood. Unstated expectations can be time bombs that explode in misunderstandings and hard feelings, potentially damaging an otherwise good working relationship. On the other hand, clearly stated goals and intentions are more likely to be mutually understood and confirmed as a basis for a good working and professional relationship. Think of a

Joseph L. Fleischer, FAIA is Partner Emeritus and past Managing Partner of Ennead Architects (formerly Polshek Partnership), where he was responsible for overseeing contracts and finances, in addition to his role as Management Partner on many of the Partnership's high-profile, award-winning projects. He has been a member of the AIA's Contract Documents Committee since 2004 and previously served as Chair of the Institute's Risk Management Committee.

contract as a means of communicating explicitly and as a way to achieve a meeting of minds between parties. The agreement with the owner also establishes the baseline for all the other relationships needed to bring a project to fruition. Contracts allocate balance to rights and rewards, and responsibilities and risks, thus aiding architects in managing their exposure to legal liability and business risks. Projects tend to run smoothly and parties tend to perform properly when they know what is expected at the outset of the work. Architects must understand that every owner represents a unique entity with specific project goals and constraints. The unique characteristics of the owner and/or of the project should be taken into consideration when negotiating and drafting the owner-architect agreement.

Experience teaches us that circumstances change over time; through contracts, architects can anticipate and prepare for future possibilities. For example, architects are commonly asked to perform services outside what are considered normal and customary basic services for construction-related projects. When writing an agreement, parties to the contract can anticipate other services and include them in the contract to create a comprehensive package of architectural services that meet the owner's needs. In general, an owner would prefer a relationship with the architect that includes under the architect's purview all of the necessary engineering and special consultant services (collectively the "architect's consultants") required to design and complete a project. It is particularly important to include as much information as is known about the project (Initial Information) at the time the agreement is executed. Because not all services can be anticipated, contracts may also need to be amended after the agreement is signed.

Finally, contracts can provide a means of resolving disputes. All contracts begin by assuming each party is operating in good faith and creating a mutually advantageous agreement. However, misunderstandings or differences of opinion are sometimes unavoidable. No contract can prescribe the resolution of every possible problem, but a good contract can specify a mechanism for resolving disputes and for maintaining a good working relationship between architect and owner while problems are resolved.

RESPONDING TO REQUESTS FOR PROPOSALS

Architects often get work by responding to a request for proposals. The AIA recommends that this type of solicitation process be based on qualifications and free from price comparison. In other words, owners should examine the talent and experience of the architect and make a selection on the basis of merit before discussing compensation. In some cases, however, and sometimes after making a short list of candidates, the owner may ask for a proposed fee to help distinguish one candidate from another. Architects may be asked first to propose the services they believe necessary along with the services requested by the owner, and then to propose compensation for performing those services. Architects should give careful consideration to the content and wording of the fee proposal. Whenever possible, it is worthwhile to include a copy of the proposed agreement form, such as AIA Document B101™–2007, Standard Form of Agreement Between Owner and Architect or AIA Document B103™–2007, Standard Form of Agreement Between Owner and Architect for a Large or Complex Project, with your proposal, particularly when a proposed fee is requested, so that it is clear to both parties, what services you expect to provide, and the terms and conditions that you expect to do business under, for the proposed fee. Depending on the nature of the request for proposal, the architect will need to include the services and fees associated with the architect's consultants that will be needed to provide all of the services described in the RFP. The AIA has also recently published a teaming agreement, AIA Document C102™–2015, that can be used as the basis for establishing the relationship between you and your other team members with regard to your pursuit of the project. The value and use of such standard form documents and agreements will be discussed later in this section.

Every fee proposal for services and compensation should cover what the owner and architect will and will not do, the timing of services, and the compensation for the services. Before preparing a response to a request for a proposal, the architect should be satisfied that these three issues can be adequately addressed in the proposal. In addition, the architect should consider the following questions:

- Is what is expected of the parties clear? Are the scope, program, site, and owner's budget (is it a construction budget or a project budget, for example) complete enough to serve as a basis for agreement? Should the architect propose, or is the owner seeking, a two-phase process, in which the first step is a simple contract of short duration to establish the program for the project? Will other professionals work on the project? Are there special legal, approval, or permitting issues the owner or architect should be aware of?
- Is the schedule clearly understood? Would a different project method provide a timelier project? Might the project be fast-tracked? Will multiple contract document packages be required?
- Is the architect being paid appropriately? What if the owner plans to pay only if the construction loan is closed?
- Will a construction manager be involved?
- Who will engage special consultants, the architect or the owner?
- What if the budget is impossible to meet or the owner proposes terms and conditions that require the architect to provide an unattainable (and uninsurable) level of performance? Is the amount of reward commensurate with the amount of risk the architect is accepting?

PROPOSALS AS OFFERS

A proposal that includes a scope of services and proposed compensation may be considered an offer to provide services. If the owner accepts the offer, a binding agreement is established.

Proposals that become agreements may be problematic, both for what is contained in the agreement and for what is omitted. For example, statements included for marketing purposes can create problems if they use superlative descriptions that induce the owner to expect a level of service that exceeds the architect's standard of care. Other problems may arise if the proposal fails to include the terms and conditions under which the architect will perform services. To avoid the latter problem, the architect, as noted above, should include and incorporate a completed standard form agreement into the proposal. A statement should be included specifying that the proposal is based on provision of services in accordance with the terms and conditions set forth in the attached agreement, which should be edited to address the specific details of the proposal. If the request for proposals already includes a proposed agreement form, the architect should review it carefully, perhaps with counsel, and clearly indicate in the proposal, what if anything in the agreement is objectionable to the architect.

ORAL AGREEMENTS AND LETTERS OF INTENT

Many times, architects feel compelled to begin work before a contract is finalized. Performing services without a written agreement can be quite risky. If things do not proceed as planned, a court or arbiter may find that the parties did not intend to be bound until the formal agreement was signed. In that case, the architect may be considered a "volunteer" to whom no compensation is owed. Clearly, without a signed agreement, the architect is at risk and will remain so until the agreement is finalized and signed.

What about oral agreements? Are they valid? They may be, but it is not the validity of these agreements that is a problem; rather, it is the proof of their terms. What was the intent of the parties? What was agreed upon? Was there really an agreement at all? These questions are usually asked when each party has a vested interest in the answer. Later, architects and owners can each be accused of remembering only what is in their best interests—and that is likely different from what the other party remembers. So, what can be done?

Always performing work pursuant to an executed written agreement will help architects avoid these issues. If an architect is unable, in certain circumstances, to withhold services until a formal written agreement is signed, the architect may consider using a letter of intent. Such a letter would state that the architect has begun to perform services on the basis outlined in the proposal pending execution of the formal written agreement, and should include the basis for being paid for services prior to execution of the agreement. The letter of intent should reference the proposed contract terms and preferred contract form, such as the AIA Document B101™–2007, Standard Form of Agreement Between Owners and Architect, if it has not already been incorporated into the written proposal.

Once the architect is performing services, the owner is likely to feel no urgency to sign a formal agreement, especially if the owner is making payments to the architect. The architect may also feel that given the choice between having a contract and being paid, being paid is the better choice. This may be true to a point, but being without a contract that protects the architect's legal rights puts the architect at considerable risk. The architect should always strive to obtain a comprehensive and fully executed written agreement as promptly as possible. Often, the lack of an agreement is used as an excuse to not pay anything to the architect. Under those circumstances, the architect may be forced to respond in kind, that he or she is unable to provide services without an agreement. That often breaks the log-jam.

WHAT TYPE OF AGREEMENT MAKES SENSE?

Architects are generally faced with three types of owner-architect agreements. The first is an owner-generated contract. Often public agencies, large institutions, or major commercial owners who have repeated and ongoing building programs and many years of experience will create a highly specific owner-architect agreement that suits their particular needs. The second source of owner-architect agreement is professional organizations other than the AIA. The third, and most often used form of agreement, is one of the AIA standard form agreements.

The AIA has published standard agreements for more than 125 years, providing the building industry with unbiased, fair, and balanced documents that represent contractual links between owners, architects, contractors, subcontractors, and consultants. AIA standard documents are periodically updated to reflect the broad changes that affect the building industry as a whole, as well as specific changes in the practice of architecture. Current AIA standard documents include revisions based on legal precedents and recommendations from national organizations representing legal, construction, engineering, and owner interests.

CHARACTERISTICS OF THE OWNER

For an architect, owners are often considered the hardest-to-understand participant in the contract equation. Unlike the legal and engineering professions, the construction industry and other design professions, owners do not subscribe to one set of tenets. Even owners that focus on building specialties, such as public schools, hospitals, or housing, usually want to see language in their contracts tailored to reflect their special interests and requirements.

Less experienced owners. These owners may not actually understand the role of an architect and thus have unrealistic expectations about the services architects can provide. The architect may need to educate such owners during contract negotiations as well as throughout the project. In a relationship with an inexperienced owner, the architect can use the contract to help keep owners' expectations and goals in line with reality.

Underfunded owners. These owners also require special attention during contract negotiations. Owners may want more building than they can afford, or they may not have the financial resources to do the project at all. Some owners may be dependent on arrangements that are conditional upon a financial closing to fund the construction and to pay for the development costs, including the architect's compensation. In such situations, architects may be at risk of not receiving all or a portion of their compensation until the closing occurs. The architect may wish to negotiate interim, nonrefundable payments, such as for direct costs and expenses, in order to cover exposure if the project is not funded or does not go forward. Keep in mind that many potential owners create single project entities to develop projects, which simply disappear if the project does not go forward. Another option may be to seek personal guarantees to cover such up-front payments. In any case, a project budget should be established at the beginning of a relationship, especially if the contract requires the architect to design within the budget. Seeing a budget at the outset will also allow the architect to understand how the compensation will be paid. Architects should make every effort to communicate to owners the importance of having a budget, including how the budget affects the project scope. Do not assume an owner has the funds for the project or fully understands the true cost of seeing the project to completion.

Owners represented by boards or committees. School boards, religious institution building committees, and condominium boards—as well as all groups using public monies or funds from members or foundations—operate under the assumption that they function as custodians of their organizations and thus their actions should be available for all to see. Legally, some owners work under "sunshine laws," legal requirements that require public disclosure. Reporting requirements sometimes make it difficult for these groups to develop and maintain consensus on goals, schedules, and budgets. As with project decisions, it may take some time to develop an owner-architect agreement, as it will have to undergo close scrutiny by many people.

This brings us to an important point in all contracts: It is helpful to both parties if the owner designates a representative authorized to deal directly with the architect in the initial information of the agreement form. The contract should specify a person on the owner's team on whom the architect can rely for decisions in a timely manner. In this particular case, this person may be the board or committee chair, whose job it will be to synthesize input from various sources and give the architect instructions on which the architect can depend.

Litigious owners. Some people and organizations are simply more litigious than others. Researching suspected litigious owners before accepting a commission is always a good idea. Architects should check with the local design community if they have any suspicion about an owner in this regard. In addition, architects may want to consult with their lawyers or check into their court records. The mere fact of past litigation should not prejudice an architect against a given owner, but architects will be better able to address potential problems and provide for their solution in their agreement if they are well informed.

How owners select their architect reveals something about their fundamental values and priorities. Some owners investigate and compare the scope and quality of services of different architects to determine what will be in their best interests. Some owners proceed with the idea that price is a consideration when professionals compete for owners and projects. Architects should ask themselves some basic questions: Does the owner understand all the services required to accomplish the project? Does a bidding requirement indicate that the prospective owner is inadequately funded and is trying to make up some of the shortfall by skimping on professional compensation? Does it indicate that the owner does not understand the nature of professional services? Is there a clear chain of command? Some owners believe that all architecture services are identical. For them, price is the only difference. When that is the case, there may be problems ahead. Owners who see the architect as the provider of a product and not as a provider of professional services will likely be disappointed and dissatisfied if the "product" isn't perfect.

The core of an architectural contract is the "fee for services" concept. As with lawyers and accountants, the documents the architect produces (drawings and specifications) are a mere representation of the services that are contracted for. The term used for these representations is "Instruments of Service," and it is an important part of the agreement, and distinguishes what architects do as opposed to what contractors do. The relationship between owner and architect is better if they are able to negotiate a level of compensation that they both believe reflects the owner's aspirations, the architect's qualifications, the nature of the project, and the type and extent of services required.

Owners who do not have the experience or staff to manage a building project may hire a project manager. In such situations, owners may outsource to a consultant, either a single individual or a company, to act as an owner's representative and manage the project on behalf of the owner. Project managers, who may also be architects, help owners make decisions about projects and help to make communications among the parties timely and adequate.

CHARACTERISTICS OF THE PROJECT

Just as types of owners influence contractual matters, types of projects do as well. Relevant project characteristics include the litigation history of the project type, jurisdictional factors, design and construction characteristics, adequacy of the construction and project budgets, and design and construction schedules.

Litigation history. Claims data from insurance companies show condominium, school, and hospital projects are involved in a relatively large number of claims. This may stem from the fact that owners and users of buildings often are not the same, and it may be difficult for architects to meet the expectations of both parties. When an owner will not be the end user of a project, the architect should take steps to add language to the agreement that protects the architecture firm from third-party claims. This language should be based on consultations with a professional liability insurance carrier and an attorney familiar with this type of agreement. It will be difficult in many jurisdictions however, to isolate oneself from such third-party claims.

Jurisdictional factors. Each state has different requirements for professional services agreements. Generally, the architect of record for the project must be legally registered in the state where the project is located. For an architecture firm to practice in a state, it must meet the requirements both for running a business in that state and for practicing professionally in the state. Architects are advised to seek legal counsel when they consider practicing in an unfamiliar jurisdiction.

One way to approach a new business opportunity in another jurisdiction is to collaborate with a local architect. Anticipating this arrangement, the AIA has created standard form documents for two types of relationships between architects. The first is a joint venture agreement, AIA Document C101™–1993, Joint Venture Agreement for Professional Services, which creates a third, new entity to undertake the project. The second is AIA Document C401™–2007, Standard Form of Agreement Between Architect and Consultant. This agreement provides for a prime-consultant relationship, with one of the architectural firms acting as the prime architect (architect) and the other firm working in an associated architect role (consultant), under the prime architect who holds the agreement with the project owner. Whatever arrangement is chosen, the relationship between the parties and the distribution of responsibilities between the two architects should be clearly spelled out in some level of detail.

Design and construction characteristics. When new, cutting-edge design or construction techniques or unusual site conditions will be part of the project, contracts should be flexible enough to reflect the possibility of design changes and a longer-than-usual design period. On the construction side, such conditions may increase construction problems, change order requests, delays, and construction costs. These occurrences are natural outgrowths of this type of project. It is important to use the contract to inform the owner about what to expect and to record the allocation of risks between owner and architect.

Budgets and schedules. Budgets and schedules can be a major source of confusion and misunderstanding. For this reason, AIA documents such as the B101™–2007, Standard Form of Agreement Between Owners and Architect, requires inclusion of budget information in the initial information recorded in a project agreement. For example, owners often confuse the construction budget with the project budget. In fact, there are many costs associated with delivering a project, and construction cost is only one of them. The architect should be prepared to discuss the entire project budget with the owner when providing the initial information. The architect should also discuss cost contingencies with an owner, as actual costs can be affected by market conditions and refinements in design.

Architects should also be realistic when discussing schedule requirements with owners and not allow unrealistic expectations to go unchallenged. Schedules included in contracts should recognize those factors that architects can control. For example, if the architect expects municipal approval of a zoning variance for the project on June 1 and it will take 60 days from that date to complete a phase of services, the contract should not state the work will be completed by August 1. Since the timeliness of municipal approval is a factor beyond the architect's control, the contract should state that services on the phase will be completed 60 days after municipal approval is granted. Owners whose projects are late are usually disappointed and unhappy. Therefore, architects should use the contract to communicate realistic expectations.

SELECTING THE DELIVERY SYSTEM

Architects are often among the first members of the design and construction team selected by owners. This position allows architects to have some influence over selection of the project delivery method, the other types of professionals to be involved, the scope of services provided by others, and how these factors will mesh with the architect's services.

In today's building industry, an increasing number of delivery systems are available to owners, including design-bid-build, design-negotiate-build, design-build, integrated project delivery, turnkey, or one of several other hybrid methods of projects delivery. Contract documents can be significantly influenced by the delivery system chosen, and it is important for the owner, with the architect's assistance, to decide early on, which delivery method to use.

Many owners may rely on a tried-and-true delivery system without being aware of the advantages of using an alternative. Thus, the architect can play a valuable role in discussing the pros and cons of alternative delivery systems. Depending on whether a project has a well-defined scope, fixed and unchangeable budget, or fixed timetable, a customized delivery system may be more economical or efficient than a standard delivery method. Likewise, when architects are involved in the planning stages of a project, they can suggest alternative methods for procurement of construction services.

Early involvement in a project gives the architect an opportunity to provide comprehensive counsel to owners regarding both design and construction. This is a strategic service that architects should contract for separately or in addition to basic architectural services. In recent years, however, many owners have turned to other third parties, such as program managers, to provide guidance to them in these preliminary stages of a project, and in many cases to assist the owner in organizing the project and overseeing the project as it moves forward. It is critically important for the architect to understand the owner's intended process and approach to managing the project, since it will significantly impact the architect's services.

UNDERSTANDING RISK

Two potential causes of increased risk and liability for architects are poor communication with the owner and negligence in the performance of the architect's and architect's consultants professional services provided to the owner. Effective communication with owners is vital. From the proposal to provide services, to the draft contract stage, to discussions and negotiations that culminate in a formal agreement, and then throughout the life of the contract, architects must strive to stay in close communication with the owner. When owners participate in essential decision making, have realistic expectations, and are kept informed of what is happening, the possibility that problems will result in claims or disagreements is reduced.

The second cause of increased risk is real or perceived shortcomings in the provision of professional services. Common examples include problems with coordination of the architect's and engineer's construction documents, design details that must be modified when prices exceed the owner's construction budget, delays in professional services according to an agreed-upon schedule, and features of a design that may conflict with the most current code or other relevant regulations.

While it is generally not possible to obtain absolution from negligent performance through the owner-architect agreement, when properly drafted, such agreements can go a long way toward minimizing areas of misunderstanding about the owner's or architect's responsibilities. Agreements that include clear descriptions of the architect's services and the owner's responsibilities can minimize risk and liability. Absent a contract provision establishing a different standard of care or level of performance, an architect is normally held to a common-law standard. The common-law standard of care typically requires the architect to exercise the degree of skill and care ordinarily exercised by other architects providing the same or similar types of services, under the same or similar circumstances, at the same time and in the same location. Sometimes clauses in the owner-architect agreement seek to reallocate or redefine the risks or standards associated with professional liability. The following examples illustrate how this might be viewed from the owner's and the architect's perspectives:

- Some owners—or their lenders—take an extreme position, asking architects to provide "warranties" or to "guarantee" their work. Architects have neither a legal nor a professional obligation to do perfect work, so accepting such language is unwise at best and generally considered uninsurable.
- Some architects take a position at the other extreme, asking owners to hold them harmless from any liability claim that may arise. An owner may reject this position, arguing that while an architect may not be expected to be perfect, the owner is entitled to some measure of protection from shoddy work and lack of professionalism.

Extreme risk-shifting clauses are usually met with resistance from the party to whom risk is shifted or from whom the burden of performance is increased. The contracting parties are more likely to agree to contract provisions that allocate risk fairly to the party in the best position either to manage and control the risk or to obtain insurance to cover it. AIA Contract Documents implement this balanced approach.

Under the common-law standard of care, the level of documentation required for a particular project relates to what would be expected of other architects under similar circumstances. The complexity of the project, the delivery method the owner selects, the timetable the owner provides, and the compensation the owner and architect agree upon will all influence the level of documentation needed for the project. For example, an owner using a single contractor to build repetitive retail facilities in many locations may request a less detailed set of construction documents from the architect than an owner constructing a one-of-a-kind museum that requires extensive and detailed documentation for unique components. Before executing the agreement, the owner and architect should discuss the issue of performance levels and the level of documentation required for the building type.

Indemnification (hold-harmless) provisions. Construction disputes are usually multiparty disputes. In the early stages of problem analysis, it is often not clear to disinterested parties whether, or to what extent, design defects, construction defects, or operation and maintenance defects have caused the problem. Therefore, all parties involved in the construction process—owner, architect, and contractor—are typically brought into any resulting claim or lawsuit. Even when it may be clear there is no fault or judgment against the architect, significant expense and effort may be incurred. In response, many architects and owners have asked the other party to indemnify and hold them harmless in cases where a third party has filed a claim in which the allegations are based on something other than the negligence of the party seeking indemnity. Some states have special requirements to make hold-harmless clauses enforceable, while others prohibit them. If asked to sign an indemnity provision, architects should seek the advice of insurance counsel.

Limitation of liability. Many AIA owner-architect agreements include mutual waivers of consequential damages, because these damages place an unbalanced risk on the architect. Consequential damages, such as the owner's lost rent, could substantially exceed the architect's insurance limits, as well as business and personal assets. When the architect is performing services in an agreement that does not contain a consequential damages waiver, architects often seek to limit to a specific sum the amount of their exposure for all claims that might arise on a project. Limitation of liability clauses used to set these monetary caps usually seek to limit the architect's monetary exposure to the amount of the architect's fees of the project, a stipulated dollar amount, or the limits of the architect's insurance coverage. The architect's ability to enforce these limitations on liability varies from jurisdiction to jurisdiction. Such limits, however, virtually never apply to third-party claimants.

Intellectual property. Some owners will view drawings and specifications as complete products and may try to reuse them for other projects in other locations and circumstances—without the architect's knowledge or consent. Drawings and specifications are instruments of the architect's services, however, and are normally intended for use only on a specific project in specific circumstances. In AIA agreements, standard contract language protects an architect from misappropriation of their drawings and specifications or other instruments of service.

OTHER CONTRACT ISSUES

As previously discussed, AIA Document B101™–2007, Standard Form of Agreement Between Owners and Architect, provides for incorporation of initial information for a proposed project into the owner-architect agreement. This information allows the owner and architect to define the use, size, location, program, budget, and delivery method proposed for a specific project. It also identifies the key individuals who will represent the owner, the architect, and architect's consultants. This information can be provided in an attachment to the agreement or written into Article 1. In comparison, AIA Document B103™–2007, Standard Form of Agreement Between Owners and Architect for a Large or Complex Project, requires the insertion of the initial information directly into the body of the agreement. It is strongly advised that the owner and architect discuss the initial information requested and come to an understanding of the requirements for the project and that those understandings become part of the agreement.

Additional services. In its simplest definition, an "additional service" is any service not included in the basic services enumerated in the AIA Document B101™–2007 agreement. Further, additional services can be identified in the owner-architect agreement or added both before and after the contract is signed. AIA Document B101™–2007 covers additional services in Article 4.

Section 4.1 of AIA Document B101™–2007 provides a simple table listing additional services that an owner might choose to incorporate into the agreement depending on their applicability to a specific project. The architect identifies those services and indicates whether the architect or the owner is responsible for them. If the architect is responsible for a particular additional service, an expanded description of that service may be placed in the space below the table or in an exhibit attached to the agreement.

Construction administration services that exceed limits stated in the owner-architect agreement are also additional services. AIA Document B101™–2007 provides places for quantifying shop drawings, product data, samples, and similar submittal reviews; visits to the site; punch-list preparation; and final inspections.

Designing to the owner's budget. AIA Document B101™–2007 contains language in Article 6 that describes the architect's obligation to design within the owner's budget for the cost of the work. If the cost of constructing the architect's design does not fall within the agreed-upon budget, the architect must redesign at his or her own cost—but with flexibility to revise the project scope and/or quality as required. It is important to note that the architect is obligated to meet the owner's budget for the cost of the work as identified in the initial information. Once a budget has been accepted and identified as adequate for the program and quality as understood, the architect accepts responsibility for designing within it. AIA Document B103™–2007, deals with this issue in a very different way, requiring the owner to provide independent cost estimating and limiting the architect's responsibility to budget compliance with the owner's adjusted budget only through to the completion of the design development phase. In either case, an architect should not agree to design to the owner's budget if the budget seems unrealistic for achieving the owner's objectives.

Dealing with changes. It is likely that both the architect and the owner will modify the standard form of agreement, deleting clauses that are inapplicable or otherwise unnecessary. Removing or adding clauses to reflect the concerns of either party that are not addressed by the standard agreement is always an acceptable way of negotiating. However, architects should be mindful that language in both AIA Document B101™–2007 and AIA Document B103™–2007 is time-tested, coordinated with the text in AIA Document A201™–2007, and crafted to balance the risks between owner and architect. For these reasons, even minor changes can have large implications. It is always best to get legal advice before making changes to these documents.

COPING WITH NONSTANDARD AGREEMENT FORMS

By choice or by regulatory requirement, some owners draft their own agreement forms. Whether they are custom documents or extensive modifications of AIA standard forms, architects presented with nonstandard agreements should approach them with care:

- Be sure you understand the services to be performed, the duties being created, and the compensation being offered.
- If a proposed agreement includes provisions that appear to redefine the architect's liability, suggest exclusions from coverage under the firm's liability insurance, or require indemnification of the owner. Have the agreement reviewed by an insurance advisor.
- Do not be afraid to modify a nonstandard agreement based on terms and conditions in AIA standard documents, and be sure to have an attorney review the proposed agreement. This review can be facilitated by carefully comparing the proposed agreement to AIA Document B101™–2007 or to a checklist developed by the architecture firm or an attorney.
- Be sure nonstandard documents are coordinated with the requirements of other project agreements, such as architect-consultant and owner-contractor agreements.

MODIFYING AN AGREEMENT AFTER SIGNING

Initial definitions of the project scope, program, site, schedule, and budget may change as the design gives shape and substance to a project. Regulatory and financing review may require design changes, and the process of bidding or negotiation may suggest or even require substitutions. In addition, detailed information from the contractor during construction—in the form of shop drawings and material and product submittals—will refine the project. Conditions encountered in the field may also require changes. For these reasons, it is important to think of owner-architect agreements as being flexible. They will be interpreted and, if necessary, modified as projects move forward.

11.2 Owner-Generated Agreements

Steven G. M. Stein, Esq.; Scott R. Fradin, Esq., AIA; and John-Paul Lujan, Esq.

Owner-generated agreements often create unreasonable legal and business risk exposures that the architect must appropriately identify and address during the contract negotiation phase.

The legitimate purpose of any agreement for the provision of design services is to allocate risk commensurate with the services and rewards promised. The standard forms of agreement published by the American Institute of Architects are generally thought to achieve this balance in a fair and equitable manner. However, agreements generated by owners do not always meet that ideal. Taking advantage of their substantial bargaining power, owners sometimes suggest contracts that allocate unacceptable risks to architects and blur the lines between the architect's responsibility, the contractor's responsibility, and the responsibilities of other participants in the project. In addition, owner-generated agreements frequently create liability exposures for architects in relation to other parties, most notably lenders. The guiding principle of this topic is to identify provisions often included in owner agreements that require architects to take responsibility for risks they cannot control or that create risk exposures for the architect that are not commensurate with the professional standard of care or ordinary fees.

"Agreements with Owners" addresses the types of agreements entered into by owners and architects and issues for architects to consider in their development.

KEY CONCERNS IN OWNER-GENERATED AGREEMENTS

The first section of this topic focuses on the key provisions and concepts typical of owner-generated agreements that potentially present the architect with the most far-reaching implications. Recognizing these provisions when they appear in an agreement and negotiating deletion, revision, or the addition of supplements to them should be the main focus of architects seeking to minimize and manage risks and potential liability exposure.

Steven Stein is a leading authority in construction law and specializes in the trial and arbitration of complex design and construction matters. He also works extensively in the drafting and negotiation of design and construction-related agreements.

Scott R. Fradin is a Principal at Much Shelist and serves as Co-chair of the firm's Construction Group. In his practice, Scott draws on his significant experience as both an attorney and a licensed architect (having practiced for several years) to draft and negotiate complex design and construction agreements on behalf of owners, architects, engineers, contractors, and specialty subcontractors.

John-Paul Lujan is a Partner at Harris Winick Harris LLP. John-Paul, trained as an architect, practices law with a focus on counseling businesses, organizations, and institutions in connection with their construction and building needs, including drafting and negotiating design, construction, and related industry contracts, as well as providing valuable advice during the construction process and through closeout to minimize and manage risk and liability.

Indemnities

Indemnities or "hold harmless" provisions are consistently the most controversial and heavily negotiated provisions in an owner-generated agreement. An indemnity is simply an agreement for one party to assume the liability of another in the event of a loss. Most, if not all, owner-generated agreements will allocate or transfer risks associated with the architect's services through the use of indemnities. In many cases, an owner-generated indemnification provision will transfer more risk and liability exposure to the architect than the law or industry standards require. Further, such provisions transfer more exposure for risks beyond either the architect's control or the scope of the architect's professional liability insurance. Consider this typical owner-generated indemnification provision:

> To the fullest extent permitted by law, Architect shall *defend*, indemnify and hold *Owner and its officers, directors, members, shareholders, employees, lender, agents, nominees, successors and assigns, and anyone acting for or on behalf of any of them* (collectively, the "Indemnified Parties") harmless from any liabilities, damages, costs, expenses, suits, losses, claims, demands, actions, fines and penalties or other liability, including, without limitation, all costs and reasonable attorneys' fees (hereinafter collectively, the "Claims") *arising out of, or in connection with the Architect's performance of the Services of this Agreement or the breach of any term or condition of this Agreement*; provided, however, the Architect shall not be required to indemnify the Owner from Claims caused *by the sole negligence of the Owner.*

The architect's main objective in responding to an owner's indemnity provision like the one present here should be to negotiate a reasonable indemnity that transfers risks the design professional can control in a manner that maximizes available insurance coverage. Because the wording of indemnities is often complex and confusing, it is recommended that the architect break down the indemnity into its most critical components. The architect should consider, at least, the following four basic questions:

All clauses herein are intended as samples only and, therefore, may require further review and/or modification by legal counsel depending on the circumstances of each project, local law, and the contract itself.

- What event will trigger the indemnification obligation?
- Who is the owner asking the architect to indemnify?
- Does the indemnity include a "duty to defend"?
- Is the owner asking the architect to indemnify the owner from claims that arise from the owner's own negligence?

What event will trigger the indemnification obligation? Perhaps the most important component of an indemnification agreement relates to the circumstances that will trigger liability and the architect's obligation to indemnify in the event of a loss on the part of the owner. Generally, to establish liability against an architect for damages, the law requires reasonable proof that the architect failed to provide the usual and customary professional care. Because this is generally the limit of the architect's obligations under the law, an architect's professional liability insurance will only cover the architect for the consequences of the architect's "negligent" acts or omissions. Accordingly, the architect should endeavor to limit exposure under an indemnity to only those claims that arise from the architect's negligent professional performance, thereby maximizing the availability of professional liability insurance. It should be noted, however, that some risks may be appropriate to allocate to an architect even though they may not be insurable, such as violation of copyright or violation of contract provisions that do not relate to adequacy.

An owner-generated agreement will seek to broaden the circumstances under which the architect's obligation to indemnify the owner will be triggered. These agreements generally attempt to provide the owner with the greatest amount of protection, often creating scenarios that are outside the control of the architect or outside the scope of losses covered under the architect's liability policy.

As in the sample indemnification provision, an owner will most commonly seek to be indemnified by the architect from claims in connection with "the performance of the Services of the Agreement." Such a request may be unreasonably broad in that it arguably includes losses arising out of anything that might be related to the services performed by the architect, without any requirement of fault or negligence on the part of the architect. Such losses, as set forth in the sample presented, may not be within the control of the architect or may not be insurable. The architect can address this issue simply by inserting the word "negligent" in front of the word "performance" in the sample owner-generated indemnity provision.

The sample provision also requires an indemnification from claims arising from the "breach of any term or condition of the Agreement." Owners have successfully used such language as a fee-shifting provision entitling the owner to attorney fees and costs under a breach of contract suit brought directly by the owner against the architect, as opposed to by a third party. Essentially, this means the architect will be funding the client's lawsuit against the architect for breach of the agreement. The owner already has a separate remedy for breach of contract, so it would be unfair, unnecessary, and excessive to award attorneys' fees to the owner, especially if there is no mutual corresponding obligation on the part of the owner. Accordingly, the architect should delete this language and/or, at minimum, add language that will expressly prevent the use of the indemnification as a way to shift responsibility for the attorneys' fee. For example, the foregoing problem may be addressed by adding the following after the words "attorneys' fees" in the sample provision: "excluding any attorneys' fees or costs associated with claims brought directly by Owner."

Who is the owner asking the architect to indemnify? The entity being indemnified by the architect is not always limited to the owner. In the sample indemnification provision presented here, the parties the architect will be indemnifying include the owner "and its officers, directors, shareholders, employees, lender, agents, nominees, and anyone acting for or on behalf of any of them." Generally, it is appropriate for the architect to indemnify the owner and any party directly part of, or related to, the owner entity, including the owner's officers, directors, shareholders, and employees. By the same token, it is generally not appropriate for the architect to indemnify parties not directly a part of the owner entity or that are otherwise not clearly defined, such as the owner's lender, agents, nominees, or anyone acting for or on behalf of the owner. The architect has no contract with these "other" parties. By including such other parties in the indemnification, a contractual right is granted to such parties at the architect's expense, often without a reciprocal obligation, or any consideration, on the part of such other parties. Their inclusion may significantly broaden the architect's risks, may not be covered by insurance and, therefore, should be deleted from the provision.

Does the indemnity include a "duty to defend"? In addition to an indemnification, an owner-generated agreement will commonly request that the architect "defend" the owner from claims arising from the acts of the architect. This will usually be achieved by adding the word "defend" to the existing indemnity provision of the agreement (as seen in the sample), or the duty to defend may be set forth in a separate provision.

The architect should understand that the duty to indemnify and the duty to defend are separate obligations. When an architect agrees to defend the owner, the architect has an obligation to essentially mount and/or fund the owner's defense against any claims under the scope of the indemnification. Without such a defense obligation, the architect may still be required to reimburse the owner for any attorneys' fees and costs incurred by the owner to defend against such claims. The difference is that this will only occur after a determination of liability against the architect (and, potentially, after several years of litigation). Professional liability insurance carriers, absent certain endorsements, will typically refuse to accommodate the architect's agreement to defend the owner.

Because the defense obligation is not something the architect's professional liability insurance ordinarily covers, the costs and expense of the defense obligation will, at least initially, be paid by the architect. Such an uninsured risk, therefore, should be avoided by deleting the word "defend" from the owner's indemnity provision or by the deletion of any separate provision requiring a defense obligation in the owner-generated agreement.

Is the owner asking the architect for indemnity against the owner's own negligence? Owner-generated agreements often contain language requiring the architect to take responsibility for claims that result not only from the negligence of the architect, but also from the negligence of the owner. The sample provision provides a typical example of an owner's request to be indemnified for all claims, *except* those claims ". . . caused by the *sole* negligence of the Owner." In other words, under circumstances in which the owner and architect jointly cause the loss or claim for which the owner seeks an indemnification, the owner will be entitled to payment from the architect for the entire loss, even if the architect is found to have been only 1 percent negligent and the owner 99 percent negligent.

Most states place strict limitations on contractual indemnity agreements, particularly those that indemnify a party against the consequences of its own negligence, and place statutory prohibitions against such agreements in certain circumstances. The indemnity language set forth in the sample provision, therefore, may or may not be enforceable, depending on the state laws that govern the provision. However, regardless of the laws that govern the indemnity in question, it is not reasonable—nor insurable, for that matter—for an architect to take on all liability for losses for which the architect may only be partially responsible. Accordingly, the architect should modify the indemnity language so that the owner takes on a requisite share of responsibility. In the sample provision, this can be accomplished by deleting the word "sole" from the last sentence.

The following illustrates the deletions and additions that an architect could propose for the sample owner-generated indemnification provision provided at the beginning of this section:

> To the fullest extent permitted by law, Architect shall indemnify and hold Owner and its officers, directors, members, shareholders, employees, successors and assigns (collectively, the "Indemnified Parties") harmless from any liabilities, damages, costs, expenses, suits, losses, claims, demands, actions, fines and penalties or other liability, including, without limitation, all costs and reasonable attorneys' fees (hereinafter collectively, the "Claims") arising out of, or in connection with the Architect's <u>negligent</u> performance of the Services of this Agreement; provided, however, the Architect shall not be required to indemnify the Owner from Claims caused by the negligence of the Owner.

Unreasonable Risk Exposure

In addition to indemnities, other concepts in owner-generated agreements are controversial and serve as a direct source of increased risk and liability exposure for the architect. These concepts include "consequential damages" and the architect's "standard of care."

Consequential damages. Consequential damages are such damages, loss, or injury that do not flow directly and immediately from the act of the party but only from the consequences or results of such an act. In the context of construction projects, this refers to an owner's economic losses, such as lost profits, loss of use of a facility, or lost opportunity resulting from delays to the project that were the result of an act, error, or omission of the architect. These losses can be significant, especially when the project being constructed is a profit-generating center. For example, delays in the completion of a production plant could result in an inability to meet orders, which, in turn, could translate into lost profits and loss of valuable customers. In the case of a condominium project, delays could result in huge financial carrying costs and the inability to sell units. Such damages may be difficult to define or calculate. Accordingly, consequential damages present the architect with the greatest exposure to potential damages on construction projects.

Owner-generated contracts usually do not address the applicability of consequential damages. Under the law, unless a contract expressly waives the right to seek consequential damages, a party who breaches a contract will be responsible for the consequential damages resulting from its breach. Therefore, when presented with an owner-generated contract, an architect should diligently search for language in the contract that expressly waives the owner's right to seek consequential damages against the architect. If no such language is present, then a provision (similar to the following example) should be added that clearly states that the architect is not responsible for any consequential damages as a result of any alleged breach:

> The Owner and Architect waive and release all claims for, or right to, any consequential, incidental, exemplary, punitive or special damages, including, but not limited to, any damages related to loss of use, lost profits, lost rent, diminution in value, or lost opportunity.

Of all concepts that must be addressed when negotiating an owner-generated agreement, the issue of consequential damages has the greatest potential to be a deal breaker for either party. Though an owner traditionally has more bargaining power, an architect should stand firm and insist on an express mutual waiver of consequential damages. When confronted and advised properly, a knowledgeable and reasonable owner will often agree that it is not fair to expose an architect to such potentially limitless liability, especially if the architect's fee is not commensurate with the potential risk. If the owner will not agree to waive rights to consequential damages, an architect may request a compromise from the owner in the form of a limitation of liability provision, either to a negotiated amount or to the extent of the architect's then-available insurance proceeds.

Standard of care. Needless to say, architects are not perfect. Unfortunately, owners often believe they are paying for perfection and they expect the drawings and specifications prepared by the architect to be free of errors. These unrealistic expectations manifest themselves in the owner's form agreements and need to be appropriately addressed by the architect.

Liability for an architect alleged to have been professionally negligent will depend on whether the architect met the agreed-upon standard of care. Under the common law and absent language in the architect's agreement to the contrary, a professional providing service is expected to do so in a reasonable and prudent manner. Therefore, a design professional should avoid agreeing to a higher standard than required by common law.

An owner-generated agreement will typically include language that attempts to raise the architect's standard of care, which can be accomplished by the owner in various ways. The most common method is to include language that requires the architect to perform services in accordance with "a high" or "the highest" standard of care. Although it is difficult to define what "high" or "highest" means in relation to the architect's services, clearly this language requires more than ordinary or typical care, and progressively moves the architect's services toward a requirement of perfection.

In other instances (sometimes in the same agreement), an owner will ask that the architect "warrant" services, or certain aspects of services. A "warranty" has an established meaning under the law and connotes an assurance or guarantee that the architect's services will be absolutely free of defects. Moreover, an architect should be wary of other, less obvious, or indirect language scattered throughout the owner's agreement that also may raise the architect's standard of care. For example, such language as "the architect represents that its employees have the expertise and experience in the design of first class facilities similar to the Project necessary to properly perform the services of this Agreement" may be argued to be an acknowledgment on the part of the architect that agreed-upon services will be better than those provided by the typical design professional.

Agreeing to any such language will expose the architect to increased risk, as its services will have to meet a standard greater than for the ordinary or reasonably prudent design professional. Moreover, the architect's professional liability insurance carrier may argue that such increase in exposure is not covered. All such language should be deleted or modified appropriately, or, alternatively, the architect should add a "catch-all" provision that will address this matter without having to find every instance of language in the agreement that arguably raises the architect's standard of care. The provision could state the following:

> The Architect, its employees and consultants agree to perform the services of this Agreement in a manner consistent with that degree of skill and care ordinarily exercised by similar professionals, currently practicing in the same geographic location and under similar circumstances. The Architect's services will be rendered without any warranty, express or implied. In no event shall any other term, language or provision contained in this Agreement be deemed to, in any way, alter, modify or otherwise increase the Standard of Care set forth in this Paragraph.

Ownership of Documents

Fundamentally, an architect is hired to prepare plans and specifications for the construction of a building. This is clearly the most valuable aspect of the owner-architect relationship. As such, the drawings and specifications become part of a tug-of-war. Architects—for both risk and artistic reasons—do not want to see their designs replicated, and owners believe that since they paid for the designs, they own them.

Most owner-generated agreements contain an ownership of documents provision that vests the owner with ownership of the architect's drawings and specifications. Generally, the decision to transfer ownership of the drawings and specifications to the owner is a business decision. However, if the architect agrees to transfer ownership of the plans and specifications to the owner, the following concepts must be addressed in order to protect the architect from future liability:

- Ownership of the drawings and specifications transfers upon payment.
- The architect retains the right to use standard design elements and architectural details.
- The owner is entitled to transfer ownership of the drawings and specifications to another entity provided that the transferee agrees to be bound by the terms of the ownership of documents provision.
- The owner must indemnify the architect for reuse of the drawings and specifications when the architect is not involved.
- Ownership does not transfer if there is a payment dispute.
- The owner must indemnify the architect if the drawings and specifications are completed by others.

In some instances, an owner-generated agreement may not contain any provisions addressing the ownership of the architect's drawings and specifications. This omission can have serious consequences if the architect is terminated before the project is completed. Although ownership of the documents remains with the architect by virtue of both common-law copyright and federal statutory copyright, the architect may lose the right to prevent the owner from using the documents after termination. This situation is exemplified by the federal court case of *I.A.E., Inc. v. Shaver*. In this case, the owner was an entity that had a design-build contract for the construction of an airport cargo hangar and subcontracted with Shaver, an architecture firm, for preparation of schematic drawings pursuant to a letter agreement. Critically, nothing more was said to Shaver about providing services for the remainder of the project. Shaver delivered the drawings to the owner under the belief that, once the drawings were approved, the firm would perform the architecture work for the remaining phases of the project. The owner, however, employed another architect to complete the remaining services. Shaver objected to the owner's use of the drawings and the owner brought an action in court to determine whether it had a right to use the drawings and whether it had infringed on Shaver's copyright.

To determine whether Shaver granted I.A.E. an implied nonexclusive license, the court considered various factors, including the language of the copyright registration certificate, the letter of agreement, the deposition testimony, and the delivery of the copyrighted material without warning that its further use would constitute copyright infringement. Applying these factors, the court held that the evidence supported the existence of a license running in favor of the owner to use Shaver's drawings to construct the air cargo building. According to the court, Shaver clearly did not have a contract for any portion of the overall project beyond the initial design phase drawings. Rather, the firm had a mere expectation that it would get further contracts for additional phases once the initial drawings were approved.

Pitfalls Within Basic Services Provisions

When it comes to a legal analysis of the design agreement, architects often gloss over the business terms of a contract, including those provisions affecting scope, fee, and schedule. However, unlike industry form agreements, such as the AIA Contract Documents, owner-generated agreements couch potentially harmful language in such provisions that increase the architect's liability exposure and affect profits. The following are examples of business terms the architect should carefully scrutinize.

Time and scheduling provisions. As set forth earlier in this discussion, an owner's profits are generally tied to how fast a new plant is up and running, or how quickly an owner can remove carrying costs and begin to sell individual residential units of a condominium project. Therefore, to an owner, time is a critical factor that often results in owner-agreements that contain very stringent and unreasonable schedule requirements and limitations that are imposed on the architect. If the architect does not address these provisions, then failure to meet these schedule requirements, no matter what the cause, may result in exposure to significant damages, including consequential damages and damages associated with delays that may have been caused by others. Consider the following owner-drafted provision:

> Time limits on the Architect's services agreed upon by Owner and Architect are of the essence. If, in performing the services, the Architect: (i) fails to complete the services in compliance with the design schedule; or (ii) impedes or prevents achievement of the Contractor's schedule, then the Architect shall be liable for and reimburse the Owner for all damages and sums the Owner incurs resulting therefrom.

Delays not only affect the owner's bottom line, they can also have an adverse effect on the architect's compensation and profits. This is the case when language in the owner-generated agreement protects the owner's profits by limiting the architect's ability to recover damages incurred as a result of any delays to the project, even if not the fault of the architect. Typical examples of such provisions are as follows:

- If the Architect fails to meet the design schedule for any reason, then Architect shall provide such services, including any additional services, to the extent necessary to cure or recover the delay with no additional compensation or reimbursement hereunder.
- The Architect's only recourse for delay, hindrance or obstruction of or to performance hereunder shall be a modification of the design schedule.

As discussed earlier, the most effective way that an architect can limit exposure to the excessive damages incurred by an owner that can arise from project delays is to include a mutual waiver of consequential damages provision. In addition to such a waiver, the architect should ensure further protection by including a provision that clearly excuses the architect from delays caused by acts of God, the owner, contractor, or causes outside the architect's control. The provision should also entitle the architect to additional compensation in the event of increased costs resulting from delays not the fault of the architect. Such a clause might read like this:

> If the Architect is delayed at any time in the progress of the Architect's services due to: the acts or omissions of Owner, Owner's consultants, Owner's cost consultant, Contractor or anyone for whom any of them are legally responsible; strikes; war; fire; abnormal weather conditions; unavoidable casualties; acts of terror; unanticipated delays by applicable governmental authorities having jurisdiction over the Project in the issuance of approvals, permits and the conducting of inspections of the Work; or other causes beyond the Architect's control, then the design schedule shall, as agreed to by the Owner and Architect, be extended by the additional time caused by such delay and the Architect's compensation shall be equitably increased.

Cost-estimating provisions. Due to the complexity of today's construction environment, the wide variety of materials available, employment of various construction techniques, and instability of prices, estimating the total costs of construction is difficult. Few architects have any training in the area of cost estimating, yet many owners look to the architect to evaluate project budgets and provide cost-estimating services as part of the architect's overall scope of basic services. Other owners prefer to separately retain the services of a professional cost consultant (or even a general contractor) during the preconstruction phase. Under either scenario, the architect should ensure that the owner's agreement incorporates the necessary protective language for the benefit of the architect.

If the owner requires cost-estimating services from the architect, the architect should consider the possibility of avoiding such responsibility in the first place, as agreeing to perform such services may result in significant risk to the architect. For example, failure to design the project within the owner's budget may result in the provision of free design services to bring the costs of construction back into conformance with the owner's budget. In addition, when actual costs of construction have greatly exceeded the architect's estimate, certain courts have held the architect responsible for the difference in construction costs. It should also be noted that not all professional liability insurance carriers cover risks associated with mistakes in cost estimation.

If the architect agrees to provide such services, the architect at least should supplement the owner-generated agreement with the following language (similar to that found in the AIA documents):

> An opinion of probable construction cost, if included in Architect's services, represents Architect's best judgment as a design professional familiar with the construction industry. It is recognized, however, that the Architect does not have control over the cost of labor, materials, or equipment, over the Contractor's methods of determining bid prices, or over competitive bidding, market, or negotiating conditions. Accordingly, Architect cannot and does not warrant or represent that bids or negotiated prices will not vary from any opinion of probable construction cost prepared by the Architect.

Such language effectively limits the owner's ability to rely on the architect's estimate or evaluation as a guarantee by qualifying the architect's services as a professional opinion, based only on the architect's experience and on uncertain market conditions. Use of the term "opinion of probable construction cost" rather than "estimate" is also preferable in conveying the intended limits on such services.

Despite such protective language, however, there is no guarantee that an architect will be completely insulated from liability when performing such services. Therefore, the architect also should consider including language that will limit the extent of liability for errors when providing an opinion of probable costs. Furthermore, as no estimate or opinion on cost can ever be perfect, the architect should also negotiate a permissible variation in actual versus estimated costs prior to the incurrence of any liability, such as the following:

> In the event the Contractor's bids or negotiated proposal exceeds the Architect's opinion of probable construction cost by _____ percent (___%) (the "Permitted Variation"), the

Owner's sole and exclusive remedy shall be the no cost performance by the Architect of those design services necessary to conform the Architect's design (or applicable portions of the design) to a cost within the Permitted Variation of the Owner-approved opinion of probable construction cost.

Finally, in the event the owner separately retains a cost consultant, the architect should request the insertion of protective language that appropriately defines and separates the obligations of the owner's cost consultant from that of the architect. The architect should also negotiate an adjustment in the architect's compensation for any redesign services required by the owner to lower the owner's estimates or to bring the design into conformance with the owner-provided estimates. To accomplish this, the following sample language can be added to the owner's provisions regarding cost-estimating services:

> Owner agrees to retain the services of a professional cost consultant to provide all necessary cost estimating services for the Project. The Architect shall be entitled to rely on such cost estimating services in the performance of the Architect's obligations hereunder. To the extent the Architect is required to redesign the Project for the purpose of reducing the Owner's approved estimate of construction cost for any reason, or for the purpose of conforming the Architect's existing design to the Owner's approved estimate of construction cost in the event exceeded by the contractors' bids or negotiated proposals, the Architect shall be entitled to an equitable increase in compensation therefor.

Submittal review. Submittals, particularly shop drawings, represent an aspect of construction where the duties of all parties involved (e.g., owner, contractor, and architect) often overlap with no clear boundaries as to where responsibilities of the parties begin and end. The result is that submittal review is a significant source of litigation against architects, as even construction-related errors committed by the contractor can readily be imputed to the architect simply based on the fact that a particular submittal was reviewed and approved by the architect. The typical owner submittal review provision may look like this:

> The Architect shall review and approve upon the Contractor's submittals such as Shop Drawings, Product Data and Samples. The Architect's action shall be taken with such promptness as to cause no delay in the Work or in the activities of the owner, Contractor or separate contractors, while allowing sufficient time to permit adequate review.

Some of the issues affecting the architect's liability exposure with respect to submittal review relate to (1) delays in the handling of a submittal by the architect, thereby exposing the architect to a claim for contractor delays in the construction; (2) the failure of the provision to limit the purpose of the architect's review to matters relating to the design as opposed to other matters that are the responsibility of the contractor, exposing the architect to the acts, errors, or omissions of the contractor or other party; and (3) the architect's approval of a submittal containing an error, which provides the potential for an argument that the design professional has personally adopted the contractor's submittal and, therefore, is liable for the error.

Consequently, precise contractual terms are necessary to ensure that the architect does not assume responsibility beyond that which is reasonable or that which is rightfully the obligation of others. Therefore, if one of the architect's services on a project is the review of submittals, the owner-generated agreement should be modified or supplemented with a provision that (1) permits the architect to handle the submittal within a reasonable time; (2) limits and defines the purpose of the architect's review; and (3) only allows for a review of the submittal, not an approval. The following provision is appropriate:

> Upon Contractor's approval of Shop Drawings, Product Data and Samples, the Architect shall review such submittals for the limited purpose of checking conformance with information given and the design concept expressed in the Contract Documents. The Architect shall have no less than _ days upon receipt of the submittal to complete the review. Review of such submittals is not conducted for the purpose of

determining the accuracy and/or completeness of details such as dimensions and quantities, or for substantiating instructions for installation or performance of equipment or systems, all of which remain the responsibility of the Contractor as required by the Contract Documents. Architect's review of a Submittal shall not constitute approval of safety precautions or of construction means, methods, techniques, sequences, or procedures. The review does not constitute an approval of a specific item or the assembly of which the item is a component.

Payment provisions/disputed amounts. From the owner's perspective, controlling payments to the architect is the owner's most convenient form of protection from damages associated with design errors. Accordingly, owner-generated agreements often contain provisions permitting an owner to withhold from the architect's invoices any amounts the owner deems appropriate or necessary. The following is a typical provision that permits the owner to withhold amounts due the architect:

> The Owner reserves the right to reject all or any portion of the Architect's invoice. If the Owner disputes the Architect's entitlement to payment for the Architect's services for any reason (the "Disputed Amount"), Owner may withhold the Disputed Amount until the dispute is resolved by the dispute resolution procedures provided in this Agreement.

From the architect's perspective, however, prompt and full payment is essential. Contractually permitting the owner to withhold sums puts the owner, at least initially, in the potentially abusive position of determining the quality of the performance of the architect's services. Ideally, this provision should be deleted. However, the architect will not always be in a position to obtain such a concession from the owner. Nevertheless, the architect can request certain changes to such a provision that an owner will have a difficult time contesting with any reasonable basis and that will afford some protection to the architect.

For example, the architect can add language to the owner's provision that requires any, all, or a combination of the following concepts: (1) written notice from the owner providing the reason(s) the owner is withholding any amounts claimed due by the architect; (2) a requirement that only an amount be withheld from the architect's invoice that is reasonably necessary to protect the owner's interest; (3) that any amounts not in dispute be released and paid in accordance with the existing requirements of the agreement; and (4) for projects with relatively significant fees, an agreement that any amounts withheld by the owner be placed in an interest-bearing escrow account mutually funded by the parties.

Other concepts that may be considered by architects when addressing such a payment provision include (1) an interest penalty placed on any amounts withheld from the architect to the extent any court, arbitrator, or other entity determines that the owner wrongfully withheld such funds and (2) the insertion of language requiring the owner to waive any right to withhold any amount from the architect's invoices in the event the owner fails to provide written notice of such disputed amount within a negotiated time period. It should be recognized that these concessions may be more difficult to obtain from an owner.

Finally, the architect should also include a statement that, despite any permission to withhold amounts from the architect's invoices, the architect's continued performance under the agreement shall not act as a waiver of any claims to any such amounts wrongfully withheld by the owner.

Owner's "Boiler-Plate" Provisions

Most owner-generated agreements contain provisions that appear to be harmless but, in reality, can result in the architect undertaking greater liability, losing valuable rights, or both. It is critical for the architect to first identify the provision, recognize the risk, and then address the risk with appropriate modifications that protect the architect.

Lender's requirements. Generally speaking, if the architect is presented with an owner-generated agreement, it is likely that the owner is a business entity rather than an individual. If the owner is a business entity, it is also likely that a commercial lender will be involved in the project. It is understandable that in such cases the lender wants as much protection from a default by the owner under the loan agreement as possible. Accordingly, the owner may attempt to insert provisions into the owner-architect agreement that are designed to protect the interest of the lender. The problem is these provisions are designed to change the rights and liabilities that the architect has under the owner-architect agreement when the owner defaults under the loan agreement.

A typical provision that an architect will encounter states that "the Architect shall comply with all Lender requirements." While this provision may seem innocuous, the fact is there is no way for the architect to know what the lender will require. For example, will the lender require the architect to subordinate a lien right to that of the lender? Will the lender require the architect to complete the project even though the architect has not been paid? Will the lender require the architect to guarantee that the designs are complete and in full compliance with all laws? Will the lender require the architect to relinquish rights to drawings and specifications? Since the architect is usually retained before the owner obtains the loan, the answers to these questions are unknown. Therefore, the following concepts should be incorporated into the Lender's Requirements provision:

- The architect shall only be required to comply with the lender's "reasonable" requirements.
- The architect shall not be required to subordinate lien rights to those of the lender.
- The architect's rights under the owner-architect agreement shall not be diminished.
- The architect's obligations under the owner-architect agreement shall not be increased.
- The architect's liabilities under the owner-architect agreement shall not be increased.

Consent to assignment. It is not unusual for the parties to a business transaction to reserve their right to assign the agreement. The standard form AIA documents address this issue as follows:

> Neither the Owner nor the Architect shall assign this Agreement without the written consent of the other, except that the Owner may assign this Agreement to an institutional lender providing financing for the Project. In such event, the lender shall assume the Owner's rights and obligations under this Agreement. The Architect shall execute all consents reasonably required to facilitate such assignment.

On the whole, this provision properly balances the interests of the owner and architect. However, most assignment provisions contained in owner-generated agreements are not as fair. Instead, they usually state the following:

> The Architect shall not assign this Agreement without the express written consent of the Owner, which consent may be withheld in the Owner's sole and absolute discretion. The Owner, in its sole and absolute discretion, shall have the right to assign this Agreement. The Architect shall execute all consents required to facilitate such assignment.

Such a provision is problematic for the architect for the following reasons:

- The owner has the absolute right to act unreasonably in precluding the architect from assigning the owner-architect agreement in the event there is a change in the architect's business form (e.g., a merger, a purchase by another firm, or a change in corporate structure).
- The owner has the unfettered right to assign the agreement to whomever it wants—even if it is to someone the architect objects to.
- The architect is contractually required to execute whatever consents the owner requires regardless of what the consents require.
- There is no requirement that the assignee assume any of the owner obligations under the owner/architect agreement (e.g., payment of past due amounts, indemnifications, and liability for owner-supplied information).

When confronted with such a provision, the architect has three options: (1) do nothing, (2) recommend using the standard AIA formulation, or (3) modify the owner's language to create a more balanced provision that does not expose the architect to additional risk. For the third option, the above provision could be appropriately modified as follows to address the most critical concerns:

> The Architect shall not assign this Agreement without the express written consent of the Owner, which consent shall not be unreasonably withheld. The Owner shall have the right to assign this Agreement upon the written consent of the Architect, which consent shall not be unreasonably withheld, provided that the assignee agrees to undertake all Owner obligations under this Agreement and cure all prior Owner defaults. The Architect shall execute all consents required to facilitate such assignment provided that such consents do not adversely affect the Architect's rights or increase the Architect's obligations under this Agreement. Notwithstanding Owner's assignment of this Agreement, the Owner shall remain fully liable under the Agreement.

Certifications. The standard form AIA documents assume that the architect will certify various matters that arise during the construction process. Typically, the architect will issue certifications concerning contractor payment applications, substantial completion, and final completion. These standard form agreements also assume that the owner may require the architect to certify matters not specifically addressed in the agreement. To limit the architect's potential exposure for providing such certifications, the standard form documents state the following:

> If the Owner requests the Architect to execute certificates, the proposed language of such certificates shall be submitted to the Architect for review at least 14 days prior to the requested dates of execution. The Architect shall not be required to execute certificates that would require knowledge, services or responsibilities beyond the scope of this Agreement.

Most owner-generated agreements, however, provide only that "the Architect shall execute such certifications as the Owner requests." This type of language, while seemingly harmless, has the potential to expose the architect to greater liability than would otherwise exist under the owner-architect agreement. More often than not, the liability concern arises when the owner is financing the project through a lender or the owner is leasing the project site. Regardless of whether a lender or a landlord is involved, the issue is generally the same—the architect is asked to make certain representations to entities that are not parties to the owner-architect agreement.

A classic example is where the owner requests that the architect certify to the lender or landlord that the plans are in accordance with all laws, codes, and ordinances. If it turns out that the plans were not in accordance with all laws, codes, and ordinances, the architect will not only be liable to the owner, but also to the lender or landlord who was the intended beneficiary of the architect's certification.

As with consents to assignments discussed above, the architect, when confronted with an overly broad certification provision, has three options: (1) do nothing, (2) recommend using the standard AIA formulation, or (3) modify the owner's language to create a more balanced provision that does not expose the architect to additional risk. With regard to the third option, the following provision can be used:

> Any certification by the Architect shall be issued only for those Contract Documents prepared by the Architect or Architect's Consultants. Such certifications shall be to Architect's best knowledge and belief and only to such matters for which Architect would have knowledge by reason of its performance of this Agreement.

Confidentiality provisions. A common provision found in most owner-generated agreements deals with confidentiality of owner-provided information. Typically, these types of provisions are designed to protect an owner's confidential and/or proprietary information from being disseminated to the owner's competition. While the owner's intention is reasonable, often such provisions fail to take into account that the architect will necessarily disclose confidential owner information when issuing the drawings and specifications to regulatory authorities during the permitting process. Similarly, the architect may be required to disclose confidential owner information when meeting with manufacturer representatives or potential contractors. In essence, a provision that does not address these issues will subject the architect to liability for breach of the contract terms.

Additionally, the scope of the typical owner-generated confidentiality provision is usually overly broad; in other words, the provision defines any information supplied by the owner to the architect as confidential. Similarly, the typical confidentiality provision either does not contain a time period or contains a time period that is so long (5 or 10 years) that it is per se unreasonable, particularly given the transient nature of the architecture profession. Lastly, this type of provision fails to address what happens in the event of litigation between the parties.

The following is a reasonable approach to dealing with a confidentiality provision:

> The Architect acknowledges and agrees that confidential information relating to the Owner including, but not limited to, the operation, management, or business thereof (collectively, "Owner Confidential Information") may be disclosed to the Architect in connection with its provision of services under this Agreement. All such Owner Confidential Information shall be clearly marked as being confidential. The Architect agrees that all Owner Confidential Information disclosed to the Architect shall not be disclosed to third parties without the Owner's prior written consent, whether during or for a period of one (1) year after the expiration or termination of this Agreement. The Architect shall require anyone directly employed by it or anyone for whose acts it may be liable to comply with this Section. Notwithstanding the foregoing, the Architect may disclose Owner Confidential Information if such disclosure is required by applicable law or by legal, judicial, administrative, or regulatory process, provided that the Architect promptly notifies the Owner so that the Owner may, if it so elects, seek appropriate remedies, or to the Architect's financial and legal advisers in the ordinary course of the Architect's business. Notwithstanding anything contained herein to the contrary, the Drawings and Specifications shall not be considered Owner Confidential Information.

Non-recourse provisions. It is common in today's marketplace for commercial owners—most commonly developers—to set up a single-purpose entity to have a project constructed. The reason is clear: The owner wants to limit its exposure to any potential losses. Typically, the only asset of this single-purpose entity is the property on which the project will be constructed. Thus, consistent with the owner's goal of limiting its exposure, the owner will likely include a "non-recourse" provision in the owner-architect agreement. As the title of such a provision makes clear, a non-recourse provision expressly provides that in the event of a claim by the architect against the owner, the architect will not go after the assets of the owner's officers, directors, shareholders, or members (which is done through a legal action referred to as "piercing the corporate veil"). Instead, the architect's only recourse will be against the assets of the entity. The following is a typical example of a non-recourse provision:

> If Owner defaults in the performance of any of Owner's obligations under the Agreement and if, as a consequence of such default, Architect recovers a money judgment against Owner, that judgment shall be satisfied only out of the right, title and interest of Owner in the Project, including the Site, as such right, title and interest may from time to time be encumbered. Architect expressly agrees that under no circumstances will any partner, member, shareholder, officer, director, or employee of Owner be personally liable for the performance of any of Owner's obligations hereunder. Additionally, none of Owner, any of its agents, or employees shall have any liability for performance of Owner's obligations under the Agreement.

Unfortunately, it is almost impossible to have a non-recourse provision stricken from the owner-generated agreement. However, there are two things that the architect should try to do when confronted with this type of provision. First, the architect should attempt to modify the provision so that it is symmetrical—that is, if the architect must agree not to seek recourse against the owner's officers, directors, shareholders, or members, the owner must agree not to seek recourse against the architect's officers, directors, shareholders, or members. Second, the architect should attempt to carve out an exception for the intentional misconduct of an officer, director, shareholder, or member of the owner. For example, if the president of the owner engages in fraudulent conduct, the architect should be entitled to seek recourse directly against the officer.

While the architect may not be able to avoid a non-recourse provision, the architect should carefully review the agreement for a no lien provision or a provision requiring the architect to subordinate lien rights to the lender, as discussed earlier. If the architect unwittingly executes an agreement with these types of contractual provisions, the architect is not likely to recover much, if any, outstanding fee in the event of owner default.

Insurance. Generally, owner-generated agreements contain detailed insurance sections specifying not only the types of insurance the architect is required to maintain but also the limits of such insurance. Commentary on the various types of insurance that owners typically require is beyond the scope of this chapter. Architects are advised to submit any owner-drafted insurance section to their insurance advisor to confirm that the owner's insurance requirements are compatible with the architect's insurance program.

There are, however, three provisions typically contained in the owner-drafted insurance section that the architect should be aware of and avoid. The first provision requires the architect to name the owner as an additional insured on the architect's professional liability policy. It is impossible for the architect to comply with this requirement. The reason lies in the nature of professional liability insurance. Professional liability insurance covers design errors and omissions. Since the owner is usually not an architect, and therefore incapable of making design mistakes, there can be no coverage for the owner. Simply put, professional liability practice policies are not written to provide for additional insured status.

The second provision the architect should avoid requires the architect's consultants to carry insurance with the same limits as those required for the architect. This requirement fails to recognize that many of the architect's consultants, including code, acoustic, audiovisual, signage, and landscape consultants, generally do not carry high limits of insurance. To avoid the risk of being exposed due to a consultant's failure to carry the same limits, the architect should modify the provision to provide that (1) the architect's consultants carry insurance at limits customarily maintained by similarly situated consultants practicing in the same locale and (2) if the owner requires higher limits, the owner will pay the cost for the increase in the cost of insurance as a reimbursable expense. The architect should bear in mind that the architect and consultants should have the minimum insurance coverage appropriate for the type of work in which they are involved. The architect should consult an insurance advisor to determine that amount.

The third provision requires that the architect maintain professional liability insurance at the same limits for a specified number of years after completion of the project. With such a provision, the owner is seeking to protect losses arising from design defects that may not manifest until many years after the completion of the project. The problem for the architect is that due to economic conditions, the architect may not be able to bear the cost of maintaining the same limit for professional liability insurance. The most effective way to deal with this requirement is to include language that states that the architect's best efforts will be used to maintain professional liability insurance with the same limits for a reasonable duration (such as three years) provided such insurance is available at reasonable commercial rates.

ADDITIONAL CONSIDERATIONS—MISSING PROVISIONS

The last section of this discussion focuses on key provisions and concepts that are typically omitted from owner-generated agreements. As the reader is undoubtedly aware, the standard form AIA documents have been developed over many years with input from both design and construction professionals. Thus, these standard forms contain provisions that design and construction professionals recognize are unique to the way architecture services are delivered and the role of the architect in the construction process. Unfortunately, most owner-generated agreements are not developed through such a considered approach. Instead, it is likely that the owner-generated agreement was cobbled together from various service agreements used previously by the owner. Thus, most owner-generated agreements are missing provisions that are essential to any owner-architect agreement.

No Responsibility for Construction Means, Methods, Techniques, and Safety

Because the architect does not construct the project, it is reasonable for the architect to disclaim responsibility for the contractor's job site activities. This disclaimer is stated in standard-form AIA owner-architect agreements and AIA owner-contractor agreements. Having a provision that clearly provides that the architect is not responsible for the contractor's construction means, methods, techniques, and safety procedures is crucial, particularly if a lawsuit results from worker injury. Often the architect is able to use this provision to be protected from a lawsuit brought by an injured worker because the provision states that the architect did not have "active control" of the job site.

Most owners fail to incorporate this type of provision in the owner-architect agreement due to lack of familiarity with the construction process. It is, therefore, reasonable for the architect to request inclusion of a disclaimer similar to that found in the standard-form AIA owner-architect agreements in an owner-generated owner-architect agreement.

No Responsibility for Hazardous Materials

One of the downsides of the Industrial Revolution is the introduction and dispersal of toxic substances into our surroundings. As owners develop projects on sites that once housed manufacturing facilities or renovate existing buildings constructed before 1972, architects are encountering these pollutants on a more regular basis.

Without question, the definition of what constitutes a hazardous substance is extremely broad. Most architects recognize that PCBs and asbestos are hazardous materials, but hazardous material means any substance, pollutant, or contaminant listed as hazardous under the Comprehensive Environmental Response, Compensation, and Liability Act (CERCLA) of 1980 and its regulations. Regardless of what a hazardous material is, however, it is not the architect's job to identify it and clean it up.

Thus, no matter how unlikely it seems that a project will involve the presence and handling of hazardous materials, it is critical that the owner-architect agreement address this possibility. The standard-form AIA owner-architect agreements make a reasonable attempt to deal with the architect's responsibility for hazardous materials. However, there are other provisions that the architect should consider negotiating into the agreement. First, there should be a clear definition of what constitutes a hazardous material. Second, in the event that a hazardous material is encountered, there should be a provision that allows the architect to suspend services while the owner abates the material. Third, there should be a clause providing that the owner agrees to indemnify and hold the architect harmless from any loss, cost, or damage resulting from the presence of a hazardous material at the job site. Lastly, the architect should attempt to include a provision providing that the owner agrees not to bring any claim against the architect because of the presence of hazardous material at the project site.

Termination and Suspension of Services

Invariably, the owner-generated agreement will contain a provision allowing the owner to terminate the agreement with or without cause. Just as often, the same agreement will make no reference to the architect's right to terminate the agreement in the event of the owner's breach. Although an unjustified failure by the owner to pay is considered to be a material breach of the contract that entitles the architect to terminate the agreement, it is strongly recommended that the agreement contain a termination provision defining the circumstances under which the architect is entitled to terminate the contract and the architect's remedies for such a termination. For example, an appropriate termination provision would allow for termination in the event of: (1) a substantial failure on the part of the owner to perform in accordance with the terms of the agreement, (2) assignment of the agreement without the architect's written consent, (3) suspension of the project or the architect's services for a specified length of time, (4) material changes in the scope of the architect's services or the scope of the project, and (5) failure of the parties to reach agreement on adjustments to the architect's compensation as the result of delays or requested additional services.

Additionally, the owner's right to terminate without cause, also referred to as a termination for convenience, should be carefully reviewed. Architects should pay particular attention to their rights to drawings and specifications and their ability to recover costs due to early termination. If the termination provision does not address these concerns, the architect should endeavor to negotiate modifications to the termination provision covering these issues.

As noted above, the unjustified failure by the owner to pay entitles the architect to terminate the agreement. In many instances, however, the architect may not want to terminate the agreement; the architect instead may want to suspend providing services until the owner cures the breach. There is a critical difference between suspending and terminating a contract. Suspension keeps the agreement in full force and effect while the duty to perform is held in abeyance. By allowing for suspension rather than termination, the architect's performance can be resumed once the reason for suspension has been abated. However, unless the agreement specifically provides the architect with this right, the only option that the architect has is to terminate the agreement. Thus, if the architect wants the right to suspend, this right has to be provided for expressly in the agreement. Further, the right to suspend should be coupled with an express waiver of any liability resulting from the suspension, a right to recover the reasonable costs the architect incurs as a result of the disruption in services, and a right to an equitable adjustment in the architect's fee and schedule of performance.

Owner-Provided Information

A fundamental concept that most owner-generated agreements fail to address is the fact that the owner is providing the architect with certain information that the architect is to use in developing plans and specifications. Such information can consist of the owner's program, budget, schedule, technical information and plans, reports, and surveys prepared by the owner's consultants. These agreements also fail to recognize that the architect is relying on that information because the architect does not have the time, the fee, or the resources to verify the accuracy or completeness of such owner-provided information. Thus, it is unfair for the owner to hold the architect liable for errors or omissions in the architect's services that result from errors or omissions in such owner-provided information.

The solution to this problem, which is the approach taken by the AIA in the standard form owner-architect agreements, is to insert a provision expressly into the agreement that states (1) what information the owner is to provide and (2) that the architect has the right to rely on the accuracy and completeness of the owner-supplied information.

The AIA Document A201 Indemnity Clause

It is a virtual certainty that if the owner has generated the owner-architect agreement, the owner is also going to generate the owner-contractor agreement. As a result, there is a high likelihood that these two agreements may not be coordinated with one another. This may cause the architect to lose certain protections afforded through the reference to AIA Document A201–2007, General Conditions of the Contract for Construction, found in the standard form owner-architect agreements.

Of particular note are two provisions found in A201–2007. The first provision is an express promise from the contractor to the architect to indemnify the architect for losses, including attorneys' fees, resulting from the performance of the construction work, provided that such loss is attributable to bodily injury, sickness, disease, or death, or to injury to or destruction of tangible property (other than the construction work itself), but only to the extent caused by the negligent acts or omissions of the general contractor, their subcontractor(s), anyone directly or indirectly employed by them, or anyone for whose acts they may be liable. The second provision is an express waiver by the contractor of any protection afforded contractors under workers' compensation acts, disability benefit acts, or other employee benefit acts. Generally speaking, these types of acts provide that a contractor's liability to an injured employee is limited to the amount that the employee receives by virtue of the act. In other words, if an employee brings a workers' compensation claim against the employer/contractor and the employee receives a payment from the workers' compensation insurer, the contractor's liability to its employee for any damages suffered by the employee is limited to the amount paid by the insurer. However, most courts have held that the protection afforded to the contractor by virtue of these acts can be waived. This is the purpose of the second provision.

From the architect's perspective, these two provisions are critical. This is particularly true in the context of a personal injury lawsuit brought by an employee of the contractor that was injured on the project site. In all likelihood, the employee will bring a lawsuit naming the architect as a defendant. In response, the architect, by virtue of the indemnity provision, will be able to seek indemnification from the contractor for any damages, including attorneys' fees that the architect incurs as the result of the lawsuit (provided, of course, that the architect was not legally responsible for the employee's injuries). Further, these provisions prevent the contractor from avoiding indemnification obligation, notwithstanding the limitations contained in workers' compensation acts, disability benefit acts, or other employee benefit acts.

To alleviate the risk that the architect will lose the protections afforded by the indemnity provisions to AIA Document A201–2007, the architect has two options. The first option is to make sure the owner incorporates the A201–2007 document into the owner-contractor agreement. This option, however, assumes the architect will be involved in the drafting of the owner-contractor agreement. However, some owners may have their own form for general conditions. In this situation, the architect should negotiate a provision into the owner-architect agreement stating that the owner agrees to include provisions substantially similar to those discussed above in any agreement it enters into with a contractor.

11.3 Project Design Team Agreements

Joseph L. Fleischer, FAIA

When architects form teams to pursue projects, and engage consultants or establish joint ventures with other firms, additional agreements result.

FORMING RELATIONSHIPS TO ACCOMPLISH PROJECT GOALS

The project design team may be a single architect who has the necessary expertise and performs all of the professional services required. More often, however, project design includes other design firms and consultants with special expertise in building engineering systems, special design issues, a particular building type or component of the building, or other aspects of the project. In these circumstances, the architect will need to enter into agreements with these other design professionals to deliver the required services. There are a variety of agreements for different purposes.

Increasingly, owners are structuring their own project teams. The owner may directly contract other design professionals, including those normally contracted through the architect, assign certain coordination responsibilities to an outside project or program manager (the AIA has recently issued program management agreement forms in response to this alternative design team structuring), or develop the project as a design-build delivery program, where the architect is itself a "consultant" to the design builder. The focus of this discussion will be to address the design team relationships within the context of a traditional design-bid-build project delivery structure. The AIA Contract Documents Program does have up-to-date families of standard form agreement documents for all project delivery strategies, including design-build and program management approaches.

Whether a project is traditionally structured, or organized in one of the alternative structures noted above, the architect's coordination responsibilities should be limited to coordinating services with those of consultants or other design professionals retained by the owner or the owner's project or program manager. In turn, all such design professionals should be contractually obligated by the owner to coordinate their services with the other consultants on the team, regardless of their contractual relationships. The architect should never assume the responsibility for the internal coordination of any other design professional's documents. In point of fact, the architect, even in its relationship with the architects' own consultants, should require each consultant to fully coordinate their own professional documents, and assist the architect in the architect's efforts with regard to overall project coordination. For example, if the architect contracts with both a lighting consultant and an electrical engineer, the architect should require each of those disciplines to coordinate among themselves, in addition to their responsibility to coordinate with the architect and the other project consultants.

Design Team Agreements

Design team agreements are the documents that describe and order the relationships among the parties within the design team. These agreements establish the duties and responsibilities the team members owe to each other, and set forth the benefits each team member can expect to receive for fulfilling its respective responsibilities. It is important that design team agreements be coordinated with each other to avoid gaps or overlaps in the parties' respective duties and responsibilities.

There are different types of design team agreements for different purposes. The more common include the following:

Agreements that include the architect and its other design professionals and consultants:

- *Teaming agreements* are employed to structure the relationships among the architect and other key design professionals and consultants in connection with pursuing a particular project or client. The AIA Contract Documents Program has just issued its first teaming document addressing the relationship and understandings between a team leader (often, but not always the architect) and other team members. The document is AIA Document C102™–2015, Standard Form of Teaming Agreement Between Team Manager and Team Member for the Purpose of Responding to a Solicitation and Pursuing a Project. A cumbersome name, but an important relationship document.
- *Consultant agreements* are typically used by an architect to retain the services of design professionals and other consultants for a project in which the architect

cannot provide all of the required services itself. This relationship is generally handled under AIA Document C401™–2007, Standard Form of Agreement Between Architect and Consultant.

- *Joint venture agreements* create and structure the relationships between an architect and another design professional or other party who wish to combine forces to provide services to their client. The basic agreement for this relationship is described in AIA Document C101™–1993.

Architect-Consultant Agreements

When other design professionals are required on a project, it is common for architects to select them and add them to the design team. These design professionals act as consultants to the architect, and the architect is responsible to the client for their professional services. The architect-consultant relationship may be established just for the project at hand; it may be a strategic alliance developed between the participants to pursue specific objectives, such as a particular client type or market segment; or the two firms may have a long-standing working relationship on a variety of projects.

The architect may seek consulting arrangements with a wide variety of design professionals and specialists—even with other architects. The most common interprofessional relationship is that between the architect and the professional engineer responsible for the detailed design and engineering of one or more of the building's systems. Most large, complex projects need special expertise in civil, structural, mechanical, and electrical design. Some architecture firms include one or more of these engineering disciplines in-house; many, however, do not.

Consultant services to the architect are outlined in the architect-consultant agreement. These services, and other contract terms and conditions, should be carefully coordinated with those in the owner-architect agreement, often referred to as the "prime agreement."

SPECIAL EXPERTISE AND CONSULTANTS

Depending on the project, a wide range of special expertise may be needed to provide professional services. Some examples of such expertise are listed here:

Building Types	Design/Practice Issues
Airports	Accessibility
Athletics/sports facilities	Acoustics
Computer facilities	Audiovisual technology
Convention centers/public assembly facilities	Building envelope
Criminal justice/corrections facilities	Building information modeling
Educational facilities	Civil engineering
Healthcare facilities	Cladding/curtain wall
Hotels	Clean room
Laboratories	Code interpretation
Libraries	Communications
Recreational facilities	Computer technology
Residential facilities	Concrete
Theater/performing arts facilities	Construction

Construction management	Materials handling
Cost estimating	Mechanical engineering
Demography	Model builder
Digital imaging	Power support systems
Display	Process engineering
Drawing review/quality assurance	Programming
Ecology	Project marketing
Economics	Psychology
Editorial issues	Public relations
Electrical engineering	Radiation shielding
Elevators/escalators	Real estate
Energy systems	Record retention
Environmental analysis	Reprographics
Equipment	Safety
Facilities management	Sanitary engineering
Financial issues	Scheduling
Fire protection	Security
Food service/kitchen	Sociology
Graphic design	Soils/foundations/earth retention
Historic preservation	Space planning
Insurance	Specifications
Interior design	Structural engineering
Landscape architecture	Telecommunications
Legal issues	Traffic/parking
Life safety	Transportation
Lighting	Urban planning
Lightning	Value engineering
Management	Window washing/exterior envelope maintenance
Market analysis	

Services

As the architect and owner establish the services to be included in the architect's agreement, both parties may consider the need for the services of other design professionals. It is advisable to review with the owner the list of services required to accomplish the project and establish who will be responsible for each. Each professional service identified may be provided by any of the following:

- *The architecture firm*, through its own staff.
- *A design professional subcontracted to the architecture firm*. The design professional may be another architect, an alliance partner, or another firm acting as a consultant to the architect.
- *A consultant to the owner*. This arrangement may include a construction manager, a project or program manager, an independent design professional for another portion of the project, or another architecture firm performing a portion of the architecture services—with or without coordination by the architect.
- *The owner*. The owner's staff may provide services themselves or by some other arrangement—with or without coordination by the architect.

- *The contractor.* The architect, or the architect's consultants, may prepare performance specifications for building components such as curtain walls, mechanical systems, or fire sprinklers. To comply with these performance specifications the contractor will retain licensed design professionals through its subcontractors and suppliers.

Clarifying responsibilities between the owner and the architect accomplishes at least two things: It helps the architect identify the services for which other design consultants will be sought, and it begins to allocate project risks among the owner, architect, and others on the project team.

Two major issues are covered in architect-consultant agreements: passing to the consultant the architect's rights and responsibilities to the owner with respect to the services to be provided by the consultant, and sharing risks and rewards. Once these key points have been worked out, it is not difficult to prepare an architect-consultant agreement that incorporates the decisions of and parallels the owner-architect agreement.

Legal Rights and Responsibilities

Usually architects want to give their consultants the same legal rights the architect has from the owner. At the same time, with respect to the consultant's professional discipline, a consultant should owe the same responsibilities to the architect that the architect owes to the owner, for the consultant's portion of the project.

Rather than restate all of these rights and responsibilities from the owner-architect agreement—and run the risk of omitting some—it is common to incorporate the owner-architect agreement (often without specifics of the architect's compensation) into the architect-consultant agreement. This binds the consultant to provide all of the services in its discipline and to be subject to the same terms and conditions the architect owes to the owner.

The architect will need to clarify with its consultants and the owner which design services each consultant will provide and what design services, if any, the contractor will provide under performance specifications. These specifics should be defined in and coordinated with the provisions of the architect's agreement with the owner, such as AIA Document B101™–2007, paragraph 2.2, and with the provisions of the owner's agreement with the contractor, such as AIA Document A201™–2007, paragraph 3.12.10; reviewed and determined to be in accordance with applicable state law; and discussed by the architect with the owner.

Risks and Rewards

In assessing the risks associated with a project, the architect should assess how risks will be shared with consultants. The best advice is for the architect and the consultant to make each other aware of the risks associated with their aspects of the project. Providing to the consultant a copy of the owner-architect agreement, generally referred to as the prime agreement, facilitates this process. With this information, the negotiation can proceed openly.

Compensation Issues

Consultant compensation is a matter for negotiation between the parties. Consultants who understand the risks and responsibilities they are assuming will be in a position to negotiate compensation with the architect. In considering compensation, architects will want to address two additional issues:

- *What level of coordination is required for the consultant services?* Because consultant services must be fully integrated with those of the architect, coordination should not be casual. The architect will commit time and money to coordination, and these factors should be considered in establishing the architect's compensation. Some firms budget coordination services directly; others budget a multiple or markup of consultant costs to reflect the need for coordination as well as the costs of administration and liability. It is recommended that you include in your consultant agreement an obligation for this consultant to coordinate with both you, the architect, as well as with other of the architect's consultants, particularly where this consultant's services directly relate to those of another consultant. Examples might be lighting to electrical engineering, or civil to landscaping. While the architect may have a contractual responsibility to coordinate the services of all the various consultants, the increasing complexities in many building typologies requires that some key consultants take on some parallel coordination responsibilities.

- *What will happen if the architect is not paid by the owner or if the project is delayed beyond reason?* Typically, the architect will not want to be obligated to pay the consultant until the architect has first been paid by the owner for the consultant's services. Architects seldom have adequate financial resources to fund such payments, which can average between 20 and 60 percent or more of the architect's total fees on a particular project. Architect-consultant agreements often include a "pay-when-paid" or a "paid-if-paid" clause, or both, for this purpose, sometimes including an agreement and release on the part of the consultant not to pursue the architect until the architect receives such funds. Consultants typically understand and accept the architect's dilemma, but in return would expect the architect to seek prompt payment from the owner. Care has to be taken in drafting such clauses, however, since state laws vary on the enforceability of such provisions, particularly with regard to "pay if paid" clauses.

Forms of Agreement

Architect-consultant agreement forms with major consultants such as engineers should parallel the owner-architect agreement. (This is normally less critical for consultants for limited purposes such as specifications, kitchens, elevators, security systems, etc.) Statements of service as well as terms and conditions should be carried consistently throughout the owner-architect agreement and the architect-consultant agreements. Using AIA Document C401™–2007, Agreement Between Architect and Consultant, achieves this goal. However, since the various standard agreement forms are often subject to modification, or where a custom agreement is used, it is important to verify that the modification is properly reflected in all the documents. This is particularly important if the scope of services portion of the owner-architect agreement is changed; in this case, the consultant agreement should be modified as well. If there is a conflict between the various documents, the direct two-party agreement will most often prevail.

Digital Practice Protocols and BIM Management Issues

Architect-consultant agreements should address protocols for e-mail, Internet, Web-based, FTP site communications, digital information sharing, and digital document storage and transfer. Protocols should also be established for building information modeling (BIM) requirements with respect to design integration among the project team members, and possibly with respect to vertical integration issues with owners, contractors, subcontractors, fabricators, suppliers, erectors, and others involved in the construction process. Along with the significant potential benefits and opportunities such digital practices can introduce to a project, they also bring new risks, possible liabilities, and some uncertainties. Such concerns can include responsibility for the integrity of the model or its constituent parts, ownership of and use rights with respect to the model and its outputs (drawings, specifications, schedules, energy analyses, cost estimates, etc.), protocols for modifications to the model, and responsibility for errors or omissions in the data included in the model. The architect-consultant agreement offers an excellent opportunity for the parties to determine and agree upon how to handle these issues. AIA Documents E201™–2007, Digital Data Protocol Exhibit, and E202™–2008, Building Information Modeling Protocol Exhibit, and the newly introduced AIA Document E203™–2013, Building Information Modeling and Digital Data

Exhibit are useful tools for organizing team members' thoughts and reflecting their agreements on these issues.

Role in Project Planning

When the architect-consultant relationship is formed early in the project, or before the project begins, the consultant can be involved in project planning. The consultant then is in a position to commit to services, scope, schedule, and fee before the architect makes these commitments to the owner.

Often it is effective to assemble the design team as part of your efforts to pursue a project. Owners whose programs require sophisticated engineering or special discipline consultants are particularly aware of the need for competent consultants, and for consultants with whom you have completed a successful project. For these owners, consultants become an important factor in the selection process. It is recommended that you utilize a teaming agreement, such as AIA Document C102™–2015, Standard Form of Teaming Agreement Between Team Manager and Team Member for the Purpose of Responding to a Solicitation and Pursuing a Project, to establish the relationship with other members of the proposed design team, particularly in the case where your team is selected, but wishes to see one or more of the consultants removed from the team.

The Responsibilities of the Architect

As the prime design professional, the architect assumes primary contractual responsibility to the owner for the accuracy and completeness of the work of the architect's consultants. If something goes wrong, at least in the first instance, the architect can be held contractually liable to the owner for services improperly performed by the architect's consultant. Obviously, you do have legal recourse against the consultant, and most forms of dispute resolution, be it litigation or arbitration allow for joinder of multiple parties. As design professionals, these consultants are required to perform their services in accordance with applicable standards of professional practice, and failure to do so may result in their direct liability to injured parties. However, their failure to meet the standard of care may also make the architect contractually liable to the owner.

This discussion underscores the importance of careful consultant selection and the need for clear agreement between architect and consultant. It is also important for the architect to understand the impact of a consultant's recommendations and to be prepared to accept initial responsibility and liability for these recommendations. This, in turn, explains why insured architects increasingly seek to retain insured consultants and request a certificate of insurance from them.

Owner-Retained Consultants

An owner may directly retain project consultants. The architect may or may not have any contractual responsibility for these consultants. If the architect is to have any contractual responsibility, then the architect must be able to review and negotiate those responsibilities.

An owner may decide to enter into an agreement directly with another consultant for a number of reasons:

- Services may be substantially different from and not overlapping with those of the architect. For example, the owner may retain a land surveyor to develop the information necessary to prepare for design services.
- The owner may have a long-standing relationship with the consultant.
- The owner may seek the benefit of direct and independent advice.
- The owner may prefer to structure the project team and then assume the responsibilities for its coordination, either through the owner's in-house staff or through a program manager.

On occasion, an owner may have motives that benefit the owner but not necessarily the project. For instance, the owner may want to save money by (usually unwisely) eliminating coordination services during design or construction, or the owner may want to keep total control of the project by retaining overall coordination responsibilities.

In some cases, it is to the architect's advantage to have the owner directly retain a consultant. This is especially true when the architect must rely on a consultant's work but is not—and does not want to be—in a position to review that work independently and take responsibility for it (e.g., in connection with land surveying and geotechnical engineering). For this reason, AIA Document B101™–2007 specifies that it is the owner's responsibility to provide any necessary land surveying and geotechnical engineering data to the architect. These consultants are engaged by the owner, and the architect is entitled to rely on the survey and geotechnical information supplied by the owner.

Whatever motivations an owner has for directly retaining consultants, someone must coordinate the services of these professionals. The owner must either assume this responsibility and the risks associated with it, or assign it to a program manager or to one of the prime professionals on the project.

Coordination is especially important from the point of view of the architect. Because architects are the generalist design professionals on building projects, others on the project team may expect the architect to coordinate professional services even though the architect may not have contractual responsibility or authority to do so. An architect who acts on that expectation and coordinates activities for other consultants may be held responsible for the results of that coordination, even when the owner has engaged project consultants directly and the architect is not responsible for them.

This situation poses unique dilemmas for the architect. As a generalist, the architect is usually in the best position to coordinate the activities of other design professionals on the project. If the architect is not assigned these responsibilities and the owner is unable or unwilling to provide them, the architect should educate the owner about potential increased costs and schedule impacts that may result from uncoordinated design services. The architect may also want to negotiate to assume these responsibilities and to be compensated for them.

The architect's coordination responsibilities with respect to consultants retained by the owner or the owner's project or program manager should be limited to coordinating its services with those of the architect's consultants. The architect should never assume the responsibility for the internal coordination of any other consultants' documents.

When the architect is assigned coordination responsibilities, owner-retained consultants should be required in their contracts with the owner to coordinate their efforts with the architect, to submit to the architect's authority to coordinate, and to look only to the owner if they have claims with respect to the architect's coordination responsibilities. And, as mentioned in the previous paragraph, whether or not the architect is to coordinate the *activities* of owner-retained consultants (such as attendance at meetings or adherence to schedules), the architect should never assume responsibility to coordinate the *documents* of such consultants (lest the architect assume responsibility for the content of the consultants' documents). Consultants should be obligated to coordinate their own documents with those of the architect; the architect's responsibility should be limited to coordinating the architect's documents with those of such consultants.

JOINT VENTURES

A joint venture is a contractual union between two or more firms for one or more specific projects. The joint venture arrangement enables firms to combine key resources, expertise, and experience to perform professional services on a specific project while allowing each participating firm to pursue other projects independent of the joint venture.

A joint venture functions essentially like a partnership. There is an agreement detailing who brings what to the venture, who will do what, and how the compensation or profit will be shared. The agreement also details how responsibilities and risks are to be allocated internally. Typically a joint venture retains no profits and pays no income taxes; it passes profits (or losses) and tax liabilities along to its participating members. Participating firms are individually and jointly liable to the client and others for the services offered by the joint venture. In other words, each joint venture partner is responsible not only for its own actions, but also for the actions of the other joint venture partners.

Generally speaking, a joint venture is formed only for the purpose of seeking and executing a specific project. After a successful project, some firms feel there is enough value in the collaboration to seek further projects that require the unique talents represented in the venture. Some joint ventures have been so successful that they have resulted in permanent mergers of the participating firms.

It is imperative that the joint venture parties have and exhibit a high degree of trust and confidence in one another. It is also imperative that before the project moves forward, the joint venture parties clearly agree on a division of responsibilities for both the professional services the joint venture will provide to the client and the business responsibilities of managing the joint venture itself. This includes decisions about who will handle the finances and banking arrangements, how key decisions will be made and by whom, and how risk for profit and loss will be allocated. Leaving any of these key decisions to be resolved in real time, when emotions may be running high and the consequences significant, creates an enormous risk that the parties' respective judgments will be unduly influenced by these factors and their ability to come to agreement severely compromised.

It may also be advisable for the design professional to confirm that forming a joint venture with another party is permitted by the relevant state's licensing or practice laws and regulations. Forming joint ventures with parties who may themselves not be licensed design professionals may be prohibited.

Reasons for Forming a Venture

A successful joint venture begins with a clear understanding of why the venture has been formed in the first place. The initiative to form a joint venture is usually taken by the architect, although it may also come from the owner. The reasons for it may be technical or political. For example, a national firm from outside the owner's geographic area may enter a joint venture with a respected local firm.

Each primary participant in a venture must make an independent decision that the venture makes sense, but the participants must make a similar decision collectively. A firm that discovers it is being used in some unexpected and undesired way—by the owner or by another firm, say, for its higher professional liability insurance limits—may have trouble remaining content and performing at its best. Finally, it is important to understand that some owners are cautious about contracting with joint ventures formed for the specific purpose of performing services on the owner's project. They may see the advantages for the firms but may not want *their* project to be the testing ground for the relationship.

Process

A joint venture is a business proposition, and it is important that a good business relationship be developed among the joint venture partners. The process of forming a joint venture begins with asking these questions: What does the project require? What are your firm's strengths and weaknesses relative to these requirements? Stated another way, what does your firm bring to the project, and what does your firm need to obtain through a joint venture? One approach is to examine these key issues:

- *Required skills.* What skills does the project require, and what does your firm have in-house (or through capable consultants)? Are other disciplines required? Is the owner expecting construction management, financing, or other specific services?

- *Background and knowledge.* What special requirements does the project have? How much expertise or experience does your firm have in accomplishing projects like the one under consideration?
- *Staffing.* Does your firm have the people with the right expertise and experience available to work on the project? If these people are committed to the project, can your firm meet its other commitments?
- *Geography.* Does the location of one or both of the venture partners bring an advantage to the project?
- *Financing.* If the joint venture needs resources your firm does not have (e.g., expanded computer-aided design or BIM capability), is your firm in a position to make the investment?
- *Insurance.* Is the scope of each firm's professional liability insurance acceptable to the others—and to the client?
- *Licensing and registration.* While each joint venture member is likely to be properly licensed and registered as a corporation, partnership, or other appropriate legal entity in its home state, will each member and/or the joint venture itself be required to be licensed or registered under the local laws of the state where the project is located?
- *Management.* Does your firm have the leadership and management capabilities to take on the project, service the client, and manage the people, processes, and risks involved?
- *Contacts.* Does your firm have the necessary contacts to secure award of the contract?

A careful and honest appraisal of what you bring to the project does two things: It helps you decide whether to pursue the opportunity, and it creates a profile of characteristics to seek in your joint venture partner(s). As the parties come to agreement on the various aspects of a joint venture, these should be written down, perhaps first as a statement of principles and then later as an outline for the joint venture agreement. In this process, trust can be developed and expectations clarified and mutually agreed to, making the drafting of a joint venture agreement less difficult. Following these steps to reaching agreement will make it clear when discussions should break off—the point at which one or more of the parties do not see the reward as justifying its risk. It is sometimes easy to coast into agreement, or at least apparent agreement. Writing it down provides the first real test. The time to discover that a joint venture is not going to work is before contractual commitments have been made to the owner. An even better time is before you pitch the owner on the merits of your team.

Joint Venture Agreements

There are many business issues, some related to the project and others related to the ways the two firms will work together, that must be addressed in forming a joint venture. The best advice is to be aware of the full range of issues and to negotiate them before the joint venture offers to provide professional services. A review of the AIA standard form of joint venture agreement, AIA Document C101™–1993, Joint Venture Agreement for Professional Services reveals the points to be considered in negotiating a formal agreement. Key issues include the following.

Overall Management

A mechanism and a budget must be created to manage the joint venture. Under AIA Document C101™–1993, a policy board includes a representative and an alternate from each participating firm. The board's responsibilities include, but are not limited to:

- *Joint venture management* to manage joint venture business operations, such as its capital needs and contributions of the parties.
- *Project management* to plan, organize, staff, direct, and control the project, and to establish project financial management and risk management/quality control systems.

PART 4: CONTRACTS AND AGREEMENTS

- *Responsibility for professional services* to understand that all of the participants are jointly and severally liable to the client for the quality of the joint venture's efforts. Internally, however, responsibilities for tasks can be allocated to individual participants. *Each firm assumes full responsibility fo*r a portion of the work. The policy board allocates specific services to each of the participants. For example, responsibility for all services is shared by the joint venture participants. The work is apportioned to individual participants based on (1) skills and experience and (2) cost and availability of resources. One participant takes the lead in providing services, and the others provide support as needed.

Financial Arrangements

Of particular importance to any joint venture are the financial arrangements and especially the allocation of risks and rewards to the participants. AIA Document C101™–1993 outlines two possible approaches to dividing rewards: *The division of compensation method* assumes that the services provided and compensation received will be divided among the parties as they have agreed at the outset of the project. *The division of profit/loss method* is based on each party performing work and billing the joint venture at cost plus a stated amount for overhead. The ultimate profit or loss of the joint venture is divided among the parties at the completion of the project. Whichever approach is selected, it is essential to budget for managing the joint venture. Sometimes joint venture participants overlook the additional time and expense involved in this management.

Insurance

The agreement should address insurance coverage for the participants, especially professional liability insurance. Participants may agree to coordinate insurance so that coverage, limits, deductibles, and other key provisions are negotiated and included in the joint venture agreement.

Digital Practice Protocols and BIM Management Issues

The parties will certainly want to agree on electronic protocols for e-mail, Internet, Web-based, and FTP site communications; information sharing; and document storage and transfer. The parties will need to address building information modeling requirements to enable design integration between the joint venture parties and among members of the entire design team. Vertical integration issues with owners, contractors, subcontractors, fabricators, suppliers, and others involved in the construction process may also be a concern.

The Resulting Agreement

Agreement on the essential business issues places all participants in a joint venture in a position to finalize the written agreement. At this point, each participant may want to involve its attorney. While it is possible to draft an agreement from scratch, it often makes sense to use, or at least to start with, AIA Document C101™–1993. This document is intended to provide for the mutual rights and obligations of two or more parties who, once they have established a joint venture, will enter into a project agreement with the owner to provide professional services. It also addresses all issues most commonly encountered in structuring a joint venture, such as those described above.

Associated Professional Firms

Sometimes two professional firms choose to represent themselves as "associated" with each other to undertake a project. From a legal standpoint, these firms have two choices: They may either form a joint venture or establish a prime-consultant relationship, with one of the firms acting as a prime consultant to the other.

Whatever arrangement is chosen, the issues discussed above should be addressed. Roles, responsibilities, risks, and rewards should be defined and delineated in a written agreement between the parties. Once an agreement has been signed, the associating firms should act with that agreement in mind. For example, two architects with a prime-consultant arrangement may hold themselves out and act so that a third party sees them as participants in a joint venture, jointly and severally liable for any resulting problems. This could result in unintended liability for one or both of the parties that would not otherwise exist if it were clear from the parties' actions that a prime-consultant arrangement existed.

Architects should approach architect-consultant and joint venture agreements—indeed, all design team agreements—with the same careful attention they pay to arrangements with owners. Both have similar purposes: to put in place an outstanding design team and a framework of arrangements that serve the client and the project well.

11.4 Construction Contracts

Gregory Hancks, Esq., AIA

The construction agreement, general conditions, and other parts of the construction contract set out what the owner, contractor, and architect are expected to do during the construction phase.

A construction contract is the formal agreement for the purchase of labor, materials, equipment, and services for building work. The construction contract

- Sets forth the rights and obligations of the owner and contractor with respect to each other and to the work
- Details the contractor's scope of work by incorporating the construction documents prepared by the architect
- Determines the total amount that the owner will pay the contractor and when payments are to be made
- Describes procedures that are to be followed in carrying out the work, including information the owner and contractor are to provide
- May set out how each party can assert a claim against the other and how disputes are to be resolved

Many owners request the architect's assistance in selecting and preparing the construction agreement, general conditions, and other parts of the contract—in addition to preparing the construction drawings and specifications. The architect is well positioned to provide the owner with practical and technical information on these matters and to identify standard form documents that are generally consistent with the owner's goals. It is always appropriate, however, to recommend that the owner also obtain the advice of legal and insurance professionals to meet the requirements of the particular project. It also should be remembered that the owner (not the architect) is entering into the contract. Decisions on contract terms are ultimately the owner's responsibility.

At the same time, the construction contract affects the services that the architect will provide during the construction phase of a project. In many projects, the architect provides administration of the construction contract. In the

The party who purchases the construction work is commonly referred to as the "owner." In some instances, this party may be the tenant or lessee of the property where the work is to be performed even though the contract documents use the word "owner." When the tenant enters into the construction contract, the landlord's interests should also be taken into account.

See "Construction Contract Administration" for a discussion of those services provided by the architect.

Gregory Hancks practices law in Kansas City, Missouri. He is the former Associate General Counsel for the AIA General Counsel Office.

role of construction contract administrator, the architect acts as the owner's representative to the extent agreed upon by the owner and architect. When a construction contract is selected or drafted, the architect should ensure that its provisions for contract administration are coordinated with the provisions of the owner-architect agreement.

For all of these reasons, the architect needs to be familiar with each part of a construction contract and understand alternative approaches that are available in drafting and administering such contracts. This knowledge will enable the architect to contribute to a successful project as well as manage the architect's own services more effectively.

THE EFFECT OF THE PROJECT DELIVERY METHOD ON A CONSTRUCTION CONTRACT

The term "project delivery method" refers to the way that relationships are structured among the primary participants in the design and construction process. A successful construction contract provides an accurate description of those relationships, including their legal, administrative, procedural, and technical aspects.

Fast-track is a project scheduling technique. Project delivery methods such as construction manager-advisor, construction manager-constructor, and design-build are commonly associated with fast-track scheduling, as are design-award-build projects, especially where multiple prime contracts are awarded.

As a result, the initial selection of a standard form agreement and general conditions for a particular project primarily depends on the project delivery method to be used. This selection also depends on the method for determining the amount the contractor will be paid, a subject discussed in detail later in this section. The project delivery method is critical because the agreement and general conditions contain more than just abstract legal provisions—these documents also describe the basic administrative procedures by which the project will be built. In other words, these documents provide the framework for what the owner, contractor, and architect will do during the construction process.

This discussion focuses on construction contracts for projects that follow the traditional design-award-build project delivery method. This method encompasses projects in which the construction contract is negotiated following completion of the design (design-negotiate-build), as well as projects that are competitively bid (design-bid-build). It is common for an owner to enter into a single contract for the general construction work on a project. For some projects, however, the owner may find it advantageous to divide the work into more than one prime contract. When the owner enters into multiple prime construction contracts, each of those contracts will likely follow the design-award-build project delivery method.

This will typically be the case, for example, when the owner enters into multiple prime construction contracts after retaining a construction manager–advisor (i.e., a construction manager who does not perform any of the construction work but serves solely as the owner's consultant). The AIA Construction Manager–Advisor (CMa) family of contract documents, including the CMa construction agreement and general conditions, fits this model and follows the design-award-build project delivery method.

When construction management services are to be provided by a construction company that will also serve as the construction contractor, the owner will normally retain those services during the predesign or design phase of the project. The AIA Construction Manager–Constructor (CMc) family of contract documents describes this project delivery method. A CMc project is not design-award-build because the owner awards the prime construction contract to the construction manager–constructor *before* the design and construction documents are completed. Once a CMc project enters the construction phase, however, the project relationships mirror the relationships in a design-award-build project. As a result, the information presented in this topic generally applies to the construction phase of an owner-CMc contract. For example, the construction phase provisions in the AIA standard form CMc agreements (A121/CMc–2003 and A131/CMc– 2003) are based on the corresponding design-award-build contract documents.

In design-build projects, the relationship between a design-builder and a construction contractor bears many similarities to the owner-contractor relationship in a traditional design-award-build project. For possible ways to structure construction contracts in the design-build context, refer to AIA Document A142–2004, Agreement Between Design-Builder and Contractor, in the AIA Design-Build family of documents. When an architect contracts with a design-builder to provide architecture services in a design-build project, the architect should keep in mind that the scope of architecture services during construction will depend on how construction contract administration will be handled and may differ markedly from an architect's conventional role.

THE PARTS OF A CONSTRUCTION CONTRACT

In the traditional language of the construction industry, the owner-contractor *agreement* is the document that the owner and contractor sign and that sets out the most fundamental or essential terms of their understanding, such as payment terms. The construction *contract*, by contrast, consists of the owner-contractor agreement and everything that is incorporated into that agreement, whether those additional documents are physically attached as exhibits to the agreement or are simply incorporated into the agreement by reference.

> A contract is an agreed-upon set of mutual promises that gives each party a legal duty to the other and the right to seek a remedy for the other party's breach of its duties. A "letter of intent" or "memorandum of understanding" may not contain actual mutual promises. In that case, it may not be legally enforceable and therefore not a contract.

A construction contract normally includes the following essential documents: owner-contractor agreement, general conditions, supplementary or other conditions, drawings, and specifications. A construction contract also includes any authorized changes to the provisions in these documents. Changes made before the agreement is signed are typically made by addendum. Modifications made after the agreement is signed can be made in whatever way the construction contract itself provides or permits; alternatives include change orders, construction change directives, and minor changes in the work typically issued as architects' supplemental instructions.

Not all documents that are prepared and distributed by the architect are part of the construction contract. Documents prepared solely to describe bidding procedures or bidding requirements do not need to be incorporated into the contract, and confusion can be avoided by omitting them from the list of documents incorporated into the contract. When construction work is procured by negotiation instead of bidding, the request for proposals does not need to be part of the contract if the contractor's proposal or other contract documents set out all of the duties of the contracting parties. Similarly, shop drawings and other contractor submittals, even when approved by the architect, typically should not be incorporated into the construction contract. Incorporating approved submittals would alter the contractor's work requirements when a submittal varies from the original contract documents.

The fact that a construction contract may contain at least four initial written documents (agreement, general conditions, supplementary conditions, and specifications) naturally leads to the question: What subject matter goes where? The answer lies partly in practicality and partly in industry practice and tradition. One factor to consider is who is responsible for the content of the document. The agreement and conditions (general, supplementary, and any other) are ultimately the responsibility of the owner as they contain those matters that should be decided by the owner, such as insurance coverage or the amount of any liquidated damages. The specifications (Division 01 and higher), on the other hand, are the architect's responsibility and generally contain information that is within an architect's expertise. More detailed answers to "what goes where" are available in AIA Document A521–1993, Uniform Location of Subject

Matter. Additional guidance may be found in MasterFormat™ section numbers and titles published by the Construction Specifications Institute.

Owner-Contractor Agreement

As a general rule, the meaning or enforceability of a contract is not affected when a document is incorporated by reference rather than physically attaching it to the agreement. However, attaching a copy of the incorporated document has the practical benefit of better communication between the parties and decreases the chance of disputes resulting from misunderstanding.

The construction agreement typically identifies the parties and the architect, defines the contractor's scope of work by incorporating the construction drawings and specifications, states when the work will begin and when it is to be completed, states the amount the contractor will be paid or describes how that amount will be determined, and describes payment procedures. The agreement incorporates into the contract the conditions (general, supplementary, etc.) and any addenda or other documents. This may be done either by reference or by attaching the documents to the agreement.

General Conditions

This document, which may also be called "terms and conditions" or "general provisions," describes in detail the relationship between owner and contractor. A set of general conditions is designed to apply generically to a project delivery method or other project type. Although the architect is not a party to the construction contract, the general conditions describe responsibilities the architect has during construction; these provisions may be incorporated by reference into the owner-architect agreement as well. Structuring a construction contract with a separate general conditions document instead of including those provisions within the construction agreement itself normally has no effect on the meaning or enforceability of the provisions. An exception occurs when a precedence clause is included that states which document will override in the event of a conflict among the documents.

Supplementary Conditions

General conditions typically must be adapted to suit the particular requirements of a specific project. Supplementary conditions list such additions, deletions, or other changes to the general conditions. AIA Document A503–2007, Guide for Supplementary Conditions, is a resource for drafting them. The practice of making changes to general conditions in a separate set of supplementary conditions originated in the pre–computer age and is likely to decline as computers are increasingly used to generate contract documents. When general conditions are adapted by making changes directly in the general conditions document itself, a separate supplementary conditions document is unnecessary.

Special Conditions or Other Conditions

Other documents that modify the general conditions may be used. For example, some owners have standard modifications, or special conditions, to be used for their projects. In such instances, project contract documents may include both special conditions (describing the owner's typical requirements) and supplementary conditions (describing project-specific requirements).

Drawings

These are the graphic and pictorial portions of the contract documents that show the design, location, configuration, and dimensions of the work. Drawings typically include plans, elevations, sections, details, schedules, and diagrams.

Specifications

These are the written requirements for materials, equipment, systems, standards, and workmanship for the work. Specifications include both technical requirements and administrative or procedural requirements.

Addenda

An addendum is issued before the construction agreement is signed to change or interpret provisions of the proposed contract. An addendum may include graphic as well as written material and can change or interpret the conditions of the contract as well as the drawings and specifications.

Change Orders

A change order is a document signed by the owner and contractor (and by the architect when required by the general conditions) after the contract is signed to modify the work requirements. A change order may also change the amount the contractor is to be paid and the time allowed to complete the work.

Construction Change Directives

When provided for by the construction contract, a construction change directive permits the owner to direct a change in the work when the owner and contractor are initially unable to agree on the cost or time required for a change in the work. Typically, the architect prepares and signs a construction change directive, which the owner also signs.

Minor Change in the Work

The construction contract may authorize the architect to order a minor change in the work that does not involve a change either in the amount the contractor is to be paid or in the time to complete the work. Such orders are to be issued in writing and are binding on the owner and contractor.

Other Contract Modifications

The owner and contractor can also agree to modify their contract by signing a written amendment.

BASIS OF PAYMENT

The method used to determine how much the contractor will be paid has a significant effect on the construction contract. Relatively brief contract provisions are required to describe the contract sum when the contractor is to be paid a predetermined fixed amount or "stipulated sum." When the contractor is instead to be paid the actual amounts the contractor expends to do the work ("cost plus fee" or "time and materials"), defining exactly what categories of costs the contractor is allowed to charge to the owner requires considerable detail. Even further provisions are required when the contractor guarantees a maximum price for a project done on a cost-plus basis.

Stipulated Sum

In this type of contract, the contractor agrees to do the entire scope of work for a stated or fixed amount. Under this arrangement, the owner has the advantage of knowing the cost of the work at the time the contract is signed. A stipulated sum contract is almost always used when the work is competitively bid and may also be used in negotiated contracts. The contractor's profit (or loss) is determined by how the contractor's actual costs incurred compare to the amounts assumed in the bid or proposal.

Cost Plus Fee

Under this arrangement, the owner reimburses the contractor for the cost of all labor, materials, subcontracts, and other items required to complete the work (referred to as the "cost of the work" in AIA contract documents). The owner also pays the contractor a fee to allow for overhead and profit. The fee may be a fixed sum or may be a

AIA contract documents intentionally do not establish an order of precedence among contract documents that would apply in the event of an inconsistency. They require the contractor to consult the architect or owner when a discrepancy is encountered, allowing them to decide on the best course of action rather than leaving the resolution to the contractor.

percentage of the cost of the work. Establishing the fee as a fixed sum enables the contractor to reduce the cost of the work without reducing its profit. But even in a cost-plus contract with a fixed fee, the owner does not know what the cost of the work will be when the contract is signed. This disadvantage may be outweighed by other considerations, as in the following situations:

- To meet the owner's desired completion schedule, construction must be started before the design is completed, and the design-award-build project delivery method cannot be used.
- Other factors prevent the owner from knowing at the outset of construction what the exact scope of work will be, for example, when the owner will provide the interior finish work for office space to be leased to tenants.
- Construction quality or special construction requirements are more important than cost, such as in defense projects or research facilities.

Particularly in larger cost-plus contracts, a control estimate or target price may be established based on a preliminary cost estimate. This control estimate can be used to monitor costs as they are incurred and billed to the owner.

Guaranteed Maximum Price

This is a variation of the cost-plus-fee arrangement, in which the contractor assumes the risk that the construction cost will not exceed a stated amount. Unlike other cost-plus contracts, a contract with a guaranteed maximum price (GMP) must include a defined scope of work; without a measurable scope of work, the GMP serves no purpose. Contractors commonly commit to a GMP when construction documents are only 60 to 70 percent complete; larger contingencies can be expected when the construction documents are less complete. In a GMP contract, the contractor is entitled to an increase in the GMP for changes in the scope of work.

A construction manager doing construction work under a cost-plus contract with a GMP is sometimes referred to as a CM "at risk." Correspondingly, if no GMP is established in the cost-plus contract, the CM may be described as "not at risk." However, the terms "at risk" and "not at risk" are ambiguous and should be used with caution. Even if there is no GMP, a construction manager-constructor performs the construction work (directly or through subcontracts) and may incur a loss if the fee does not cover expenses.

When a GMP contract contains a percentage (not fixed) fee, the contractor has a financial incentive to incur the maximum allowable cost and thereby receive the maximum fee. One way to counter this tendency is for the owner and contractor to share the savings, that is, to split the difference between the allowed GMP and the actual cost-plus-fee amount. The proportion of the split can be in whatever percentages the parties agree.

A GMP contract can be adapted in other ways to adjust the cost risks carried by the owner and contractor. For example, the contractor may be able to obtain fixed prices from some subcontractors for their scopes of work; these fixed prices, along with the contractor's associated fee, can be included in the general construction contract, thereby reducing the scope of work that is subject to cost variation.

Unit Price

A unit price is a fixed amount the contractor will be paid for a specified unit of a material or service. Unit prices are used when the quantity of work the contractor will perform cannot be known at the outset, for example, to set the cost for rock excavation or other types of earthwork. Unit prices are used more extensively in construction of civil engineering work than in construction of buildings, although they are often used in building renovation projects and to obtain prices for tenant construction. The unit price method requires a specific description of the work (for example, types of rock excavation may need to be defined) and, during construction, a measurement of the amount of work actually performed (for example, volume of rock excavated). The contractor's cost in performing some kinds of work is dependent on the volume, so care should be taken in estimating how much work will be required on a unit price basis. If the actual amount of work varies significantly from the estimated amount, an adjustment in the unit price may be required to be fair to one party or the other.

OTHER SPECIFIC PROVISIONS

Following is a brief discussion of selected provisions commonly found in construction contracts.

> Construction contracts typically contain definitions of key terms. When the definition of a term is not provided in the contract itself, the term should be given its ordinary and customary meaning in the construction industry.

Project and Work

As used in standard form AIA Contract Documents, the term "work" refers to what the contractor provides under a particular contract. The term "project" refers to the owner's entire undertaking and, along with the contractor's work, generally includes such things as professional services; land acquisition; and furniture, furnishings, and equipment (FF&E). The project can be identified in the construction contract by name or other brief description. A description of the work is generally unnecessary because its scope is defined by the entire set of contract documents, including the construction drawings and specifications, which are incorporated by reference into the agreement. A short description of the work may be useful, however, when the project includes work to be performed by more than one prime contractor.

> *Contract parties:* Each party to a contract should be identified by its full legal name. This is particularly important when the party is an incorporated entity. Failure to accurately state a party's name in the agreement may complicate the resolution of any disputes.

Date of Commencement and Notice to Proceed

The owner may not be ready for construction to begin on the date the contract is signed. The contract can provide that work is to begin on another specified date or on a date to be established later in a notice to proceed that the owner will issue. A notice to proceed may be a letter or other document that states the date when the contractor may begin work and is signed by the owner (or by the architect, if authorized by the owner). A significant delay in issuing a notice to proceed may have an adverse effect on the contractor and give rise to a claim for increased costs or for additional time.

Contract Sum

Sometimes referred to as the contract price, this is the total amount that the owner will be required to pay the contractor. If the contract is for a stipulated sum, that fixed amount will be stated in the contract. At completion, the contract sum may be different because of change orders or other contract modifications. In a cost-plus-fee contract, however, the contract sum cannot be stated in the contract as a dollar amount; instead, the contract defines how the cost of the work will be determined and states the contractor's fee amount or percentage.

Progress Payments

Because of the length of time required to perform construction work, the contract typically requires the owner to make partial or progress payments as the work proceeds. Most standard-form construction contracts contain at least basic provisions for how and when such progress payments are to be made. Commonly, applications for payment are submitted monthly. The agreement may list the calendar date deadline for the contractor to make its applications. That date may be based on practical considerations, such as coordination with regularly scheduled project meetings where issues involving progress payments can be discussed and resolved. Other progress payment procedural requirements are typically described in the agreement and in the general conditions. They can be further detailed in the supplementary conditions and in Division 1 of the specifications. Cost-plus-fee contracts generally require more detailed payment provisions than stipulated sum contracts because the contractor is required to justify each of the costs charged to the owner.

Schedule of Values

To certify to the owner the amount to be paid, the architect must evaluate the contractor's application in light of both the scope of work described in the contract and the work completed. A schedule of values breaks down the entire scope of work into categories (such as by subcontract or specification division), which are each assigned a dollar value prior to work beginning. A schedule of values is indispensable for contracts that contain either a stipulated sum or a GMP. (A schedule of values is not required for cost-plus-fee contracts without a GMP, but its use may be considered as a tool for monitoring costs.) The schedule of values enables the architect to certify progress payments with some assurance that the total amount paid corresponds to the completion percentage of the work. To this end, the amount requested in each application for payment must reflect the quantity of work completed by category. In addition, the initial schedule of values must reflect the contractor's anticipated costs with reasonable accuracy. If work to be performed early in the construction process, such as site or foundation work, were assigned excessively high values, the contractor could be overpaid during the early phases of the work.

When the federal government is the owner, the government will determine the form of contract to be used. When the federal government is providing funding for construction work but is not the owner, applicable federal regulations need to be incorporated into whatever contract forms are used. AIA Document A201/SC–1999, Federal Supplementary Conditions of the Contract for Construction, may be used to adapt the A201 general conditions in this situation.

Retainage

Under traditional industry practice, some percentage of the value of the work completed may be deducted from the amount of each progress payment. This amount or retainage provides some additional assurance that the work can be completed for the unpaid contract amount, thus protecting the owner. The amount of retainage may vary by locale and custom, by project type, and by stage of completion of the work, but the details for any retainage and for any reduction or release of retainage funds must be spelled out in the contract. The amount of retainage on materials stored off-site may be set at a separate percentage. Some states have enacted statutes that affect when retainage must be paid or deposited for subsequent release, so any retainage provisions should be drafted with appropriate legal advice.

Substantial Completion

Requiring the contractor to complete the work by a stated date enables the owner to plan for occupancy and use of the project. The contractor's failure to meet that deadline generally constitutes a breach of contract. The standard for judging the contactor's performance for this purpose is "substantial completion" (that is, the project can be used for its intended purpose) instead of full or final completion (every contract requirement has been met). The concept of substantial completion is consistent with the way the common law resolves breach of contract claims. Even when the contract does not fix a required completion date, substantial completion still triggers other contract events. When substantial completion is reached, for example, the architect may be required to perform an inspection, or the method of calculating payments owed to the contractor may change.

Governing law: Construction contracts are typically interpreted under the law of a particular state, except in the case of federal government projects where federal contract law applies. Contracts designate the governing state law in order to avoid disputes over that issue and to increase the predictability of how contract provisions will be applied.

Final Completion and Final Payment

The requirements and procedures for final completion and final payment are distributed among the agreement, general and supplemental conditions, and Division 1 of the specifications. Unlike substantial completion, however, a required date for final completion is frequently not stated in the construction contract.

Three separate mechanisms may be found in construction contracts to ensure the contractor's responsibility for the quality of completed work. First, the contractor has a continuing contractual obligation to have performed the work in accordance with the contract documents. This obligation includes a general warranty against defective work (see, e.g., Section 3.5 of AIA Document A201–2007, General Conditions of the Contract for Construction). This warranty lasts until the expiration of the statute of limitations or statute of repose. Second, the contractor must comply with the specific terms of any product warranty that has been provided, for example, a 15-year warranty on a roofing system. These product-specific warranties are in addition to the general warranty and may be enforced for a longer time. Third, some construction contracts, such as those based on the A201, require the contractor to return to the site to correct defective work discovered within a year after substantial completion. This one-year period may sometimes be referred to, informally, as a "one-year warranty period," but that term is misleading because the contractor's warranty and other contractual responsibilities for defective work do not end one year after substantial completion.

Alternative Dispute Resolution

Unless a construction contract provides otherwise, the owner and contractor generally have a right to resolve contract disputes by litigating them in court with a trial by jury. With limited exceptions, this right can be waived by agreeing in the contract that disputes will be decided in another manner, such as mediation and arbitration. Most such arbitration agreements in construction contracts can be enforced under current law including the Federal Arbitration Act. Arbitration agreements may also contain procedural details regarding how arbitration is to be conducted. When the contract does not contain those details, they will be determined by the laws governing the arbitration procedure, which differ substantially among the states.

Consequential Damages

A party who breaches a contract is ordinarily liable to the other party for all damages that are the result of the breach, including both "direct" damages and "indirect" or "consequential" damages. In construction, an example of direct damages is the cost to repair defective work or to complete work left unfinished by the contractor. Consequential damages are losses that are not the immediate result of the breach, but are losses that the breaching party has reason to know the other party will likely incur when the contract is breached. In the construction of a hotel, for example, lost room rentals are consequential damages incurred by the owner when the contractor fails to complete the work by the date stated in the contract, provided that the contractor knew when the agreement was signed that the owner would suffer lost rent if the work was not completed on time. Contracts such as those based on the A201 may contain a waiver of consequential damages. When consequential damages are waived, only direct damages can be recovered when the contract is breached.

Liquidated Damages

Because it may be burdensome to determine the precise amount of damages that a party incurs when a contract is breached, the amount of damages may be predetermined or fixed as "liquidated damages" in the contract. The governing law restricts the ways that liquidated damages provisions can be applied, however, so legal advice is always recommended when including a liquidated damages provision. In construction, liquidated damages are most frequently used to set the amount of damages owed to the

The information in this chapter applies to general construction contracts, including those limited to interior construction work. Contracts for furniture, furnishings, and equipment fall into a separate category, however. Generally speaking, the purchase of FF&E is governed by Article 2 of the Uniform Commercial Code. This law differs markedly from general construction law, and only contract documents specifically intended for the purchase of FF&E, such as the AIA Interiors family of contract documents, should be used for that purpose.

owner for delay in completion of the work, generally on a per-day basis. Because such delay damages are typically consequential damages, any provision that waives consequential damages should specifically state that liquidated damages are not precluded. Care must be taken to ensure that a liquidated damages provision does not conflict with any waiver of consequential damages.

Statute of Limitations and Statute of Repose

The governing law restricts the length of time that lawsuits (or arbitrations) may be filed after damages are incurred or after a defect occurs or is discovered. This time period is established by a statute of limitations. Most states have also adopted another type of time restriction on claims against construction contractors (and architects), established by a statute of repose. Unlike a statute of limitations, a statute of repose begins to run at the end of construction or whenever services were last provided. Construction contracts may contain provisions that modify or further define these statutory time restrictions.

SUBCONTRACTS

An architect may have little or no direct communication with subcontractors when administering a construction contract. As a result, architects have less need to be familiar with construction subcontracts than with prime or general construction contracts. Subcontractors nevertheless perform a substantial percentage of construction work, and project success commonly depends on their performance.

The prime construction contract should provide the owner and architect the opportunity to review the qualifications of the subcontractors proposed for the principal portions of the work and, if necessary, the right to request that other subcontractors be used. In competitive bid situations, the contractor has likely relied on the bids submitted by the contractor's initially proposed subcontractors. As a result, substituting alternative subcontractors will frequently increase the contractor's costs. If an objection is made to a proposed subcontractor and another subcontractor is substituted, the owner should expect to pay the contractor for the increased cost unless the subcontractor initially proposed is demonstrably not capable of performing. When the prime contract is awarded by negotiation or when the prime contractor is a construction manager–constructor, the owner has additional opportunity to control the selection of subcontractors, and the contract should describe that process.

The prime construction contract should also require that subcontracts be governed by the same terms as the owner-contractor relationship. This flow-down serves to ensure that the responsibilities of subcontractors for their particular portions of the work match the responsibilities that the contractor has toward the owner. In addition, the prime contract should provide a means for the owner to require subcontractors to continue work in the event the contractor defaults on the prime contract. For example, the A201–2007, General Conditions requires that each subcontract be assigned to the owner, contingent on the contractor's default and on the owner's decision to accept the assignment.

In general, the law does not require a contractor to enter into a subcontract with any particular sub-bidder—even if its sub-bid is the lowest submitted and even if the contractor relied on that sub-bid to make its own bid. At the same time, the contractor can generally require a sub-bidder to honor its bid and enter into a subcontract based on that bid. This lack of symmetry is emblematic of the subcontractor's difficult position within the construction process. The subcontractor is affected by actions of the owner and other subcontractors but has no contract with those parties. Moreover, the subcontractor has no formal direct line of communication with the architect or engineering consultants. Depending on the terms of the subcontract, the subcontractor may have limited control over progress payments to be received from the contractor.

State laws provide some help to subcontractors to ensure they get paid for their work. Some states have enacted prompt payment statutes that may affect when progress payments and retainage must be paid. In addition, mechanic's lien statutes provide a way for subcontractors (as well as contractors) to enforce their rights to payment directly against owners that are not government entities. Under such statutes, a subcontractor providing labor or materials for construction work may assert the right to payment by filing a notice within a certain time. This filing begins a process that can result in a lien similar to a mortgage being placed on the construction site property. If the payment dispute is not resolved, the mechanic's lien can be foreclosed through litigation and the property sold to satisfy the payment. Using the mechanic's lien process, a subcontractor may be able to obtain payment from an owner even though the owner also paid the prime contractor in full. Faced with this risk, many owners seek to ensure subcontractors get paid by requiring that each application for payment be accompanied by subcontractors' lien waivers covering work paid for under prior applications for payment. Mechanic's lien statutes may, however, limit the enforceability of such lien waivers. Statutes governing mechanic's liens and prompt payment vary widely among the states, so legal counsel should be relied on for these matters.

For More Information

Smith, Currie & Hancock LLP's Common Sense Construction Law, edited by Thomas J. Kelleher Jr. (Wiley, 2005), provides further explanation of construction contracts as well as other areas of construction law.

CHAPTER 12

AIA Documents

12.1 The AIA Documents Program

Joseph L. Fleischer, FAIA

This chapter is based, in part, on Susan Van Bell, Esq.'s chapter in the 15th edition of The Handbook of Professional Practice *and Suzanne H. Harness, Esq. AIA's chapter in the 14th edition of* The Architecture Student's Handbook of Professional Practice.

AIA documents capture and convey the expectations, relationships, responsibilities, and rules that bring parties together for the design and construction of buildings.

The AIA was founded in 1857 by 29 architects who shared the goal of creating an organization that would recognize architects as professionals, as distinguished from the trade contractors who constructed buildings at that time, and that would "promote the scientific and practical perfection of its members."

Although the AIA mission statement has changed over the years, and its opinion of design-build has come full circle, the AIA remains committed to serving as (1) the voice of the architecture profession, and (2) the resource of choice for its members as they develop the knowledge needed to provide unsurpassed professional services. One important way the AIA speaks for its members, and provides a valuable resource to them, is through AIA Contract Documents®. The AIA publishes more than 100 standard form documents for use in the design and construction industry. These documents include agreements for design services, construction, construction management, and design-build. They also include general conditions documents to establish the terms and conditions of the contract for construction; instructions to bidders; qualification statements for architects and contractors; bonding forms; payment and change

Joseph Fleischer is a Partner Emeritus in Ennead Architects. Mr. Fleischer is a recognized expert in project budgeting and construction cost control, construction technology, and construction administration. He has served as Chair of the AIA's Risk Management Committee. He currently serves on the Institute's Contract Documents Committee, as Co-Chair of the AIA New York State Firm Management Committee, and is former Co-Chair of the Architects Leadership Council of the New York Building Congress.

order forms; and a request for information form. These standard forms may be modified to insert project-specific information, or may be edited further to change the standard text.

AIA CONTRACT DOCUMENTS DEVELOPMENT

The AIA has published standard form construction agreements for more than 125 years. Early in its history, the Institute recognized the need for a standard system of construction contracting. Working with the Western Association of Architects (which later merged into the AIA) and the National Association of Builders (which later became the Associated General Contractors of America), the AIA published its first standard form document in 1888. Entitled the Uniform Contract, this three-page agreement between owner and contractor contained many concepts that were carried forward into the first General Conditions of the Contract, published in 1911. The successor to that 1911 document is published today as A201™–2007, General Conditions of the Contract for Construction, and will be updated again in 2017.

In publishing the Uniform Contract, the AIA accomplished more than merely filling the need for a standardized construction contracting process. The document clarified, for the first time in American society, the AIA view of the appropriate roles of the owner, architect, and contractor during the construction process. It also firmly established, for nearly 100 years, the bright line separating the responsibilities of the architect and those of the construction contractor.

Benefits of Standard Forms

The industry's acceptance of the Uniform Contract marked the beginning of regulation of the construction process. The Uniform Contract established the steps the owner and contractor would take when entering an agreement to construct a building. The contract also established the most important benefit of standard forms: to ensure nationwide consistency and predictability in contracting and in the construction process. Predictability in the process controls the expectations of the parties and reduces their risks. Reducing the contractor's risk substantially benefits the owner because it results in lower bids that are not padded with contingencies to cover unknowns.

Another significant benefit of standard forms is the savings they achieve in transactional costs, as compared with custom-made contracts. One hour of an attorney's time is easily 10 or 20 times the cost of a standard form digital or paper document and is equivalent to the price of a license to use AIA Contract Documents software for an entire year. Standard forms also provide assurances that nothing important is left out of the contract and that the text is internally consistent. Attorneys appreciate these benefits and see the advantage in using a standard form and modifying it liberally to suit a particular project and their clients' needs, instead of incurring the legal malpractice risks inherent in creating a custom contract.

AIA standard forms are also more flexible than they once were. Available in both paper and digitally, with both "Documents and Demand" and licensing agreements, the documents are also now available under Web-based licensing agreements, which allow for editing and reviewing by multiple parties to the agreement, together with tracking systems that let each party know what modifications or choices have been made. The 2007 owner-contractor agreements and some owner-architect agreements provide check boxes for choosing a binding dispute resolution method. AIA Document A101™–2007, Agreement Between Owner and Contractor, additionally allows the parties to choose whether the architect will be the initial decision maker on claims between the owner and contractor, or whether a third-party, independent Initial Decision Maker (IDM) will be used.

The AIA also publishes some model, or alternative, language that can be added to standard forms to modify them to suit particular circumstances. Such model language is available in AIA Document A503™–2007, Guide for Supplementary Conditions; AIA Document B503™–2007, Guide for Amendments to AIA Owner-Architect Agreements; and AIA Document D503™–2011, Guide for Sustainable Projects. These "Guides" and others are available through AIA Contract Documents software and as free downloads from the AIA website. These Guides are very important to users of the AIA Document Program, in that they can be updated on a more regular basis than the normal updating cycle (see below), as new initiatives or issues impact the profession and its practitioners.

The Documents Committee

Since its early days, the AIA has maintained a committee of its members dedicated to the creation and revision of AIA Contract Documents. The AIA Documents Committee is drawn from practicing architects representing diverse geographic locations, size and type of practice, and specialized expertise. Committee appointments are made annually, although members are frequently reappointed for 10 years or more, based on their ongoing contributions, to provide continuity in document drafting. The Documents Committee meets at least three or four times annually and works with AIA staff attorneys and writers, as well as legal and insurance counsel, to draft and revise AIA documents. The committee generally revises documents on no more than a 10-year cycle to accommodate changes in practice and to respond to any relevant judicial decisions affecting interpretation of a document. As noted above, the Guides (their very existence unknown to many practitioners) are updated more regularly than the standard form documents, in order to assist the various parties in the industry with changes in the profession that impact the agreements or the way responsibilities are carried out.

Guiding Principles

Over a number of years, the AIA has developed what are called the Documents Drafting Principles, which guide the Documents Committee and AIA staff in preparing and revising AIA documents. These principles are as follows:

1. Establish and maintain, for nationwide application, standardized legal forms to enhance the stability of legal transactions in the design and construction industry.
2. Provide assistance to users who otherwise could not obtain knowledgeable legal counsel in a timely or economical fashion, by:
   - Providing standard documents as an alternative to costly custom-drafted documents
   - Promoting flexible use through the publication of supplemental guides that demonstrate, with model language and instructions, the adaptability of the standard documents to particular circumstances
   - Providing continuing education on the proper use of the documents
3. Strive for balanced and fair documents by:
   - Conforming to common law and statutory precepts adopted in the majority of jurisdictions
   - Allocating risks and responsibilities to the party best able to control them; to the party best able to protect against unexpected cost; or to the owner, when no other party can control the risk or prevent the loss
   - Seeking industry consensus among all parties whose interests may be significantly affected by individual documents
4. Publish documents that are subject to uniform legal interpretations so as to be predictably enforceable and, thus, reliable.
5. Use language that is unambiguous and comprehensible to users and interpreters (courts and lawyers) of the documents.
6. Where practices are consistent among regions, reflect industry customs and practices, rather than impose new ones; where practices are inconsistent or no guidelines for practice exist, provide a consensus-based model for practitioners to follow.

Allocation of Risk

The AIA intends that its agreements avoid unreasonable bias by first allocating risks and responsibilities to the party with the most knowledge of the risk and in the best position to control it. The agreements then allocate risk to the party best able to protect against unexpected cost by, for example, purchasing insurance. Risk is assigned to the owner, as the ultimate beneficiary of the project, only when no other party can control the risk or prevent the loss. The design and construction of buildings is a risky undertaking, so—to prevent an undue burden for any party, and to prevent any one interest (including that of architects) from being overrepresented—the Documents Committee strives to equitably balance risks.

Building Consensus

Starting with the Uniform Contract, the AIA has strived to produce documents that represent the consensus of the design and construction community. For that reason, the AIA seeks comment from industry liaison organizations representing contractors, subcontractors, owners, lenders, engineers, insurance and surety interests, and other interested stakeholders when drafting any new document or revising an existing one. So that no industry comment is overlooked, the AIA records all the comments it receives, and the Documents Committee reviews and discusses them thoroughly before agreeing to any changes in the existing text. The committee frequently meets in person with those who submit comments so committee members can gain a full understanding of the issue being presented. Through this process, the AIA works to provide documents that fully and fairly represent the interests of those stakeholders significantly affected by a particular document.

For example, in preparing documents for the 2007 release of the A201 family, which comprised over 40 new and revised documents, the Documents Committee sought comment from more than a dozen industry groups, including the Associated General Contractors of America, American Subcontractors Association, National Association of State Facilities Administrators, Commercial Owners Association of America, Associated Specialty Contractors, Council of American Structural Engineers, American Council of Construction Lawyers, the American Bar Association's Forum on the Construction Industry, and the American Arbitration Association. Similar outreach is done for the other document families as well.

The committee also sought input from outside experts in property, general liability, and errors and omissions insurance. Several AIA knowledge communities, including Technology in Practice, the Committee on the Environment, Small Project Practitioners, and Practice Management, as well as the Integrated Practice Board Discussion Group and the Large Firm Round Table, also provided guidance.

KEEPING PACE WITH THE INDUSTRY

In creating and revising documents, the AIA strives both to reflect and to anticipate the needs of the design and construction industry and to provide agreements that will serve the major delivery methods being used to construct building projects. Design and construction practices are always changing and the documents are also changed to remain relevant to industry needs.

Construction Contracts

Throughout the nineteenth and most of the twentieth centuries, design-bid/negotiate-build was the most common way to design and construct a project. In 2016 it is still the dominant project delivery method in the United States. The *2012 AIA Firm Survey: The Business of Architecture* reported that 55 percent of firm billings are derived from projects using the design-bid/negotiate-build delivery method.

▶ See "Demographics of Practice: 2012 AIA Firm Survey."

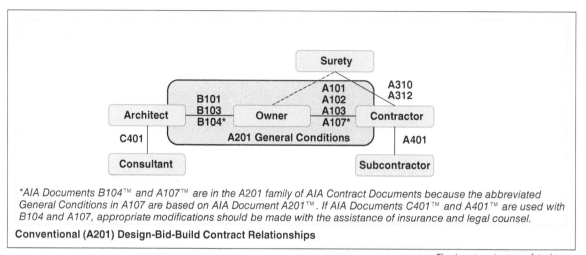

*AIA Documents B104™ and A107™ are in the A201 family of AIA Contract Documents because the abbreviated General Conditions in A107 are based on AIA Document A201™. If AIA Documents C401™ and A401™ are used with B104 and A107, appropriate modifications should be made with the assistance of insurance and legal counsel.

Conventional (A201) Design-Bid-Build Contract Relationships

The American Institute of Architects

FIGURE 12.1 **Conventional (A201) Design-Bid-Build Contract Relationships**

This method involves a sequential process whereby the architect completes the construction drawings and specifications and delivers them to the owner for approval. The owner then uses the architect's construction documents to obtain bids or proposals from construction contractors. AIA Contract Documents in the A201 (conventional) family serve the design-bid/negotiate-build delivery method (see Figure 12.1). Since 1967, the AIA has revised the A201 document and associated agreements and forms that rely on it every 10 years to keep it current with industry trends.

Construction Management

Construction management project delivery emerged in the 1970s, and the AIA responded with its Construction Manager as Adviser (CMa) family of documents in 1974, which were most recently updated in 2009. (See Figure 12.2.) The construction manager is an advisor to the owner and does not hold or assume any risk for the construction contracts. The owner holds construction contracts for each trade (multiple prime contracting) or may retain one general contractor. This model works well in some cases, but most owners look for a contractor to assume construction risk. To respond to that concern, Construction Manager as Constructor (CMc) agreements were developed in 1992 and also updated in 2009. (See Figure 12.3.) CMc can be thought of as a hybrid of CMa and design-bid-build because the construction manager serves as an advisor to the owner during the design phase (providing cost estimates and constructability reviews) and as a construction contractor during the construction phase. The construction manager may build the project at risk, by guaranteeing a maximum price,

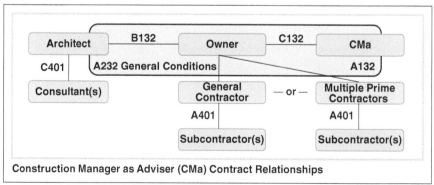

Construction Manager as Adviser (CMa) Contract Relationships

The American Institute of Architects

FIGURE 12.2 **Construction Manager as Adviser (CMa) Contract Relationships**

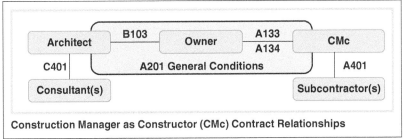

Construction Manager as Constructor (CMc) Contract Relationships

The American Institute of Architects

FIGURE 12.3 **Construction Manager as Constructor (CMc) Contract Relationships**

or on a cost-plus-fee basis. The CMc approach in which the construction manager guarantees a maximum price to the owner (using AIA Document A133™–2009, Standard Form of Agreement Between Owner and Construction Manager as Constructor where the basis of payment is the Cost of the Work Plus a Fee with a Guaranteed Maximum Price) is a popular delivery method that now rivals design-build delivery.

Both of the construction management families of documents were revised and updated in 2009. A discussion of those updates is included in the next section.

Design-Build

In 1985 the AIA was the first organization to publish standard form design-build documents. The AIA revised and restructured these documents in 1996 and made major revisions again in 2004 to keep pace with industry changes. The modified and renumbered 2004 documents, which presented an entirely new approach to design-build delivery were revised again in 2014. (See Figure 12.4.) The documents are A141™–2014, A142™–2014, and B143™-2014, respectively.

The 2004 revisions also included two new design-build documents. These were AIA Document B142™–2004, recently replaced by AIA Document C141™–2014, an agreement between the owner and a design-build consultant; and AIA Document G704/DB™–2004, replaced by AIA Document G744™–2014, a new form for acknowledging substantial completion of the design-build project. Other key documents in the design-build family include AIA Document C441™–2014, Standard Form of Agreement Between Architect and Consultant for a Design-Build Project, and AIA Document A441™–2014, Standard Form of Agreement Between Contractor and Subcontractor for a Design-Build Project. Recent releases in this family include AIA Document A145™–2015, Agreement Between Owner and Design-Builder for a One or Two Family Residential Project, AIA Document G742™–2015, Application and Certificate for Payment for a Design-Build Project, and AIA Document G743™–2015, Continuation Sheet for a Design-Build Project.

Design-Build Contract Relationships

The American Institute of Architects

FIGURE 12.4 **Design-Build Contract Relationships**

PART 4: CONTRACTS AND AGREEMENTS

Design Contracts

The design process is also continually changing. When comments were solicited for the 2007 revisions to the 1997 owner-architect agreements, the industry and AIA internal groups shared these concerns: the two-part format of AIA Document B141™–1997, phases vs. services, basic services and additional services, errors and omissions insurance, standard of care, green design, the architect as initial decision maker, ownership of instruments of service, and designing to the owner's budget.

Standard form of architect's services documents are versatile and may be used to provide the scope of services in any owner-architect agreement at the time of contracting, or combined with AIA Document G802™–2007, Amendment to the Professional Services Agreement, to create a modification to any existing owner-architect agreement. Appropriately modified, standard form services documents may be used to provide the consultant's scope of services in an architect-consultant agreement such as AIA Document C401™–2007, Agreement Between Architect and Consultant.

The resulting document, B101™–2007, Standard Form of Agreement Between Owner and Architect, is a one-part agreement that consolidates and replaces B141™–1997 and B151™–1997. AIA Document B101™–2007 sets forth the architect's services during five phases: schematic design, design development, construction documents, bidding/negotiation, and construction contract administration. It also contains a number of novel additions, including a specifically defined professional standard of care, an explicit requirement that the architect carry insurance, and a recognition that environmentally responsible design must be a part of every design project. (Subsequent to the 2007 release, and in support of the AIA Board's support for further efforts in the area of sustainable design, a number of documents were developed to support projects designated as a Sustainable Project. These "SP" versions of key documents are addressed later in this chapter and further described in the AIA Document Synopses by Family included in this *Handbook*. AIA Document B101™–2007 returns to the concept of "basic" and "additional" services and explicitly sets forth basic services in Article 3. Additional services, listed in Article 4, may be simply thought of as any service that is not a basic service. Additional services may be included in the agreement when it is executed, or added as the project proceeds. Also, AIA Document B101™–2007 substantially revises the instruments of service provisions. The new provisions clarify the architect's ownership rights, while more liberally granting licenses to the owner for use of the instruments of service upon project completion or the agreement's termination. AIA Document B101™–2007 retains the requirement that the architect design the project to the owner's budget, but strengthens the owner's obligation to identify the budget in the agreement and to modify it appropriately as the project proceeds.

To provide an agreement for the specialist architect, or the architect who may initially provide services for a special scope of work (e.g., a security evaluation) and then provide traditional design and contract administration services, the AIA divided the text of AIA Document B101™–2007 into two parts: the agreement portion and the services portion. These two documents are, respectively, B102™–2007, Standard Form of Agreement Between Owner and Architect Without a Predefined Scope of Architect's Services, and B201™–2007, Standard Form of Architect's Services: Design and Construction Contract Administration. AIA Document B102™–2007 may also be combined with other scope of service descriptions, such as AIA Document B203™–2007, Site Evaluation and Planning, to create an agreement. The AIA currently publishes 14 scope of services documents, all numbered in the B200 series. It is anticipated that these scope of services documents will be expanded in number and revised as appropriate between now and the 2017 release of the Conventional (A201) family of documents.

Another significant revision to the 2007 A201 family design agreements was the introduction of three new documents geared to the size and complexity of the project.

AIA Document B103™–2007, Standard Form of Agreement Between Owner and Architect for a Large or Complex Project, is based on B101 but contains revisions and incorporates assumptions that are specifically geared toward large or complex projects, such as that the owner will retain third parties to provide cost estimates and project

The American Institute of Architects

FIGURE 12.5 **Small Projects Contract Relationships**

schedules, and may implement fast-track, phased, or accelerated scheduling. For example, in B103 the architect does not prepare cost estimates, but agrees to design the project to meet the owner's budget for the Cost of the Work at the conclusion of the Design Development Phase Services.

AIA Document B104™–2007 is for use in "midsize" projects or projects of limited scope. B104 is an abbreviated version of B101. However, a significant difference is that B104 is not used with A201 General Conditions but, instead, B104 is used in conjunction with AIA Document A107™–2007, Standard Form of Agreement Between Owner and Contractor for a Project of Limited Scope, which it incorporates by reference. The general conditions are set forth in A107.

Finally, the 2007 revisions included two documents specifically developed for use in small projects. (See Figure 12.5.) AIA Document B105™–2007, Standard Form of Agreement Between Owner and Architect for a Residential or Small Commercial Project, and AIA Document A105™–2007, Standard Form of Agreement Between Owner and Contractor for a Residential or Small Commercial Project, make up the Small Projects family of documents. The goal in developing B105 was to provide a document that would be understandable and accessible, particularly to the homeowner client. The format was simplified to be less formal and more user friendly. Paragraph numbering was removed, and the document is two pages plus the cover. B105 contains seven abbreviated articles. There are only two phases of Basic Services, Design and Construction, that are each described under the Architect's Responsibilities in Article 1. B105 adopts A105 by reference as it sets forth the architect's responsibilities during the construction phase. General conditions are contained within A105.

AIA CONTRACT DOCUMENTS 2015

After updating the A201 family in 2007, the AIA revised the Construction Management family and the two bond forms. It also published new scope of services documents and new agreements for use in digital practice, integrated project delivery, housing, and sustainable design, and construction. Recently published scopes and agreements include a series of Master Agreement Documents in 2014 for use by owners, architects, contractors, and consultants in support of ongoing relationships where specific tasks are carried out under Service Orders or Work Orders. These agreements can be found in the Conventional family of documents. Lastly, a teaming agreement for the pursuit of projects, AIA Document C102™–2015, Agreement Between Team Manager and Team Member for the Purpose of Responding to a Solicitation and Pursuing a Project, has just been released for the purpose of confirming the relationship between parties if the pursuit of a project is successful. The organization of the documents, by series and family, and the document releases made through 2015 are discussed below.

Document Series

Documents are organized by series using a letter prefix to represent the type of agreement or document. For example, owner-contractor agreements are found in the A series and contract administration forms are found in the G series.

- A-series: Owner-contractor documents
- B-series: Owner-architect documents

▶ "Construction Phase Services" addresses the architect's observation and reporting of the progress and quality of the work and its conformance to the design intent expressed in the contract documents.

- C-series: Architect or Owner-consultant documents
- D-series: Miscellaneous documents
- E-series: Exhibits
- F-series: (Reserved for future content)
- G-series: Contract administration and project management forms

Document Families

A family of documents is a type of classification that refers to the type of project or project delivery method addressed by the documents. The documents within each family provide a consistent structure and text base to support the major relationships on a design and construction project. Understanding these family groupings helps architects select the most appropriate agreements and forms for a project. These classifications include:

- Conventional (A201), including Master Agreements
- Construction Manager as Adviser (CMa)
- Construction Manager as Constructor (CMc)
- Design-Build
- Integrated Project Delivery (IPD)
- Interiors
- International
- Program Management
- Small Project
- Digital Practice
- Contract Administration and Project Management Forms

Digital Practice

In April 2007, the AIA published two new standard form documents that address a growing concern in the design and construction industry: transmitting data in a digital working environment and maintaining control over its future use. Some of these initial documents have been updated as noted herein. AIA Documents C106™–2013, Digital Data Licensing Agreement, and E201™–2007, Digital Data Protocol Exhibit, allow contracting parties to share digital data in accordance with agreed-upon protocols for transmission, format, and use of the data.

Rather than deal with data transmission issues on an agreement-by-agreement basis, the AIA decided to create one standard form, AIA Document E201™–2007, Digital Data Protocol Exhibit. The parties may incorporate E201™–2007 into their agreements and modify it to suit the specialized transmission needs of each project. AIA Document E201™–2007 allows parties to determine the transmission method, data format, and permitted uses for a customizable list of the data that will be transmitted throughout the life of the project. The E201™–2007 exhibit may be used to standardize transmission methods and data formats across an entire project because it requires that each party incorporate the exhibit into all other agreements for design or construction for the project.

AIA Document C106™–2013 provides a licensing agreement for two parties who otherwise have no existing licensing agreement relating to the use and transmission of digital data. Some or all of the digital data may be subject to copyright protection, such as the architect's or a consultant's instruments of service. AIA Document C106™–2013 allows a Transmitting Party (1) to grant a Receiving Party a limited non-exclusive license for the Receiving Party's use of Digital Data on a specific project, (2) to set forth procedures for transmitting the data, and (3) to place restrictions on the license granted. Parties that have previously executed AIA agreements for design services or construction, or an agreement that incorporates AIA Document A201™–2007, General Conditions of the Contract for Construction, have already entered into licensing agreements pursuant to the provisions in those agreements.

In late 2008, the AIA introduced Document E202™–2008, Building Information Modeling Protocol Exhibit, to provide the contractual structure needed to manage the use of building information modeling (BIM). Like E201™–2007, AIA Document E202™–2008 is not a stand-alone agreement, but is an exhibit to attach to any agreement for design services or construction on a project where the project team will use BIM. Parties executing AIA Document E202™–2008 agree to incorporate it into any other agreement for services or construction on the project, thus ensuring consistency in BIM protocols and procedures across the project. This document establishes the procedures and protocols the parties agree to follow with respect to the development and management of the model throughout the course of the project.

In addition to AIA Document C106™–2013, the AIA released a number of other documents in support of the Digital Practice family. AIA Document E203™–2013, Building Information Modeling and Digital Data Exhibit, AIA Document G201™–2013, Project Digital Data Protocol Form, and AIA Document G202™–2013, Project Building Information Protocol Form. As of today, the development and use of digital formats for the design and construction of projects, including the production and use of the architect's instruments of service, continues to evolve.

Integrated Project Delivery

Beginning in 2007, the AIA turned its attention toward a newly emerging delivery model, integrated project delivery (IPD), beginning with publication of a guide document and then developing three different sets of documents for use in projects using IPD at varying levels of integration (see Figure 12.6).

Integrated project delivery is a model for delivering a construction project that integrates people, systems, and practices from the beginning of the design phase. This model, which is intended to increase efficiency and reduce waste, was initially described in "Integrated Project Delivery: A Guide" (IPD Guide), a manual that is free for download at www.aia.org/ipdg. Written by a collaboration of the AIA's Documents Committee and AIA California Council, the IPD Guide sets forth several IPD principles and provides a roadmap, by project phase, for achieving those principles.

The AIA took additional steps to lead the design and construction industry toward this more efficient and collaborative working environment through the 2008 release of two new types of IPD standard form contract documents, the A295 documents (also referred to as the Transitional documents), and the Single Purpose Entity (SPE) documents.

The A295 documents consist of AIA Document B195™–2008, an owner-architect agreement, and AIA Document A195™–2008, a guaranteed maximum price (GMP) owner-contractor agreement, both of which incorporate AIA Document A295™–2008, General Conditions of the Agreement for Integrated Project Delivery. The A295 documents provide a smooth transition from traditional delivery methods because they are based on a commonly used delivery model whereby the general contractor provides

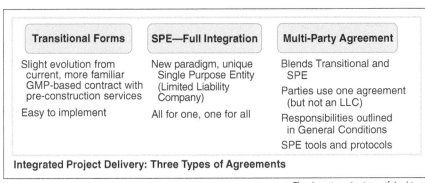

Transitional Forms	SPE—Full Integration	Multi-Party Agreement
Slight evolution from current, more familiar GMP-based contract with pre-construction services	New paradigm, unique Single Purpose Entity (Limited Liability Company)	Blends Transitional and SPE
Easy to implement	All for one, one for all	Parties use one agreement (but not an LLC)
		Responsibilities outlined in General Conditions
		SPE tools and protocols

Integrated Project Delivery: Three Types of Agreements

The American Institute of Architects

FIGURE 12.6 **Integrated Project Delivery: Three Types of Agreements**

preconstruction services, such as cost estimating and constructability reviews, working in tandem with the architect during the design phase. The A295™–2008 General Conditions document departs from tradition, however, because instead of setting forth the duties of the owner, architect, and contractor in separate silos, it creates a collaborative working environment by integrating the duties of each participant with the activities of the other two, and describes them sequentially for each of the IPD phases, from conceptualization through construction.

The Single Purpose Entity documents, by contrast, are not based on a traditional delivery model, but represent an entirely new way to deliver a project. To achieve a closer alignment of interests, the AIA developed AIA Document C195™–2008, Standard Form Single Purpose Entity Agreement for Integrated Project Delivery. Using C195™–2008, the owner, architect, construction manager, and perhaps other key project participants each become members of a single purpose entity, the SPE, whose purpose is to provide the skilled services necessary to design and construct the project. The SPE is a limited liability company, a business entity readily recognizable and available in all jurisdictions, that provides the benefit of limited liability to its members. The owner-member provides funding for the project under AIA Document C196™–2008, the agreement between the SPE and the project owner. The architect, construction manager, and other non-owner members provide services to the SPE using AIA Document C197™–2008, an agreement between the SPE and any non-owner SPE member. The SPE itself does not perform professional services, but provides those services through contracts with its own members or with other licensed professionals. Under AIA Document C197™–2008, the non-owner members are reimbursed for the costs they incur in providing services. They may earn profit through the achievement of project goals (goal achievement compensation), and a shared savings provision (incentive compensation). If one member earns profit, all members earn profit. For that reason, members are motivated to help each other achieve goals and monitor costs. This highly collaborative process has the potential to result in a high-quality project for the owner, and substantial monetary and intangible rewards for the other members.

In 2009, the IPD family was completed with publication of AIA Document C191™–2009, Standard Form Multi-Party Agreement for Integrated Project Delivery. C191™–2009 provides a third type of agreement model on the IPD spectrum. C191™–2009 establishes the basic legal framework for a multi-party agreement for integrated project delivery. C191™–2009 integrates the owner, architect, contractor, and perhaps other key project participants, under one agreement from the outset of the project. The parties are required to communicate, share information, and make decisions in a collective manner; establish project goals and compensation criteria based on the success of the project; collectively manage and allocate risk; and use BIM and other technologies to effectively manage the project.

AIA Document C191™–2009 reflects a significant departure from traditional delivery models in that it aligns the success of the individual parties with project success. At the same time, C191™–2009 maintains the familiar roles and responsibilities of each of the parties. Accordingly, C191™–2009 takes the IPD collaborative process further than the Transitional documents but not as far as the SPE documents.

Construction Management

In 2009, the AIA updated and revised the documents in the Construction Manager as Adviser family and the Construction Manager as Constructor family.

The documents were revised to conform to the updates made in the 2007 A201 family of documents, including the dispute resolution check box; selection of an Initial Decision Maker in AIA Documents A132™–2009, A133™–2009, and A134™–2009; and establishment of digital data protocols, with AIA Documents E201™–2007 and E202™–2008 referenced in the agreements. Each of the "A" series documents noted above also have their "SP" counterparts.

Other substantive changes unique to construction management were also made.

For example, in the Construction Manager as Adviser family, the payment application process and payment application forms were revised to better accommodate the difference between projects where the owner contracts with one general contractor and projects where the owner contracts with multiple prime contractors for construction of the work. In the case where the owner contracts with one general contractor, the construction manager reviews the contractor's periodic payment applications (AIA Document G732™–2009) and supporting materials and, upon certification, forwards each payment application and the supporting materials to the architect for review and certification. In the case of multiple prime contractors, the construction manager reviews the individual periodic payment applications (AIA Document G732™–2009) and supporting materials from each of the trade contractors. The construction manager uses data from the individual periodic payment applications to prepare a project application and certificate for payment (AIA Document G736™–2009) and a summary of the contractors' applications (AIA Document G737™–2009), and forwards those summary documents to the architect for review and certification for payment. The architect is then required to review and certify only the project application and certificate for payment, not each individual contractor application for payment.

In recognition of the special interparty relationships that exist between the owner, architect, and construction manager as constructor, the AIA recently released AIA Document B133™–2014, Agreement Between Owner and Architect, Construction Manager as Constructor Edition, to reflect the unique aspects that accompany the construction manager's transition from advisor to constructor as the project develops, and the impact this relationship shift has on the architect's services.

Program Management

Just as the methods and approaches to project design and project delivery have changed substantially over the last 50 years, so too has the owner's approach to managing and overseeing their projects. Throughout much of the twentieth century, large corporate entities, and both public and private developers of multiple projects, have created large, in-house "facilities" groups to oversee the planning and design of the capital improvements required to meet their business needs or fulfill their missions. More recently, many of these entities have determined that it is the business interest to outsource these services. Beginning in 2012, the AIA began to address this emerging approach to project development and oversight. The result was the 2013 release of the Program Management family of documents, the newest of the AIA Document Families.

The Program Management series was initially envisioned as a relationship between owner and a program manager for a Multiple Project Program. This vision has since been expanded to cover the management and oversight of a single, often complex, project. The essence of the program manager's role is to assist an owner from the outset of the owner's vision for a multi-building project program, through to the completion of the entire building program. That role includes advice on the selection of a design manager for the entire multi-building project program, selection of individual building design teams, or if the design manager carries out the preliminary designs for the buildings, architect of record for each building, and the contractors or construction managers, as appropriate, for individual building projects. The program manager then has the responsibility for the implementation and oversight of the entire program.

In 2013, the AIA published three new standard form documents to address the growing need for these services. AIA Document C171™–2013, Standard Form of Agreement Between Owner and Program Manager, for use in a Multiple Project Program, AIA Document B171™–2013, Standard Form of Agreement Between Owner and Design Manager for use in a Multiple Project Program, and AIA Document B172™–2013, Standard Form of Agreement Between Owner and Architect for Architect of Record Services. The AIA subsequently released AIA Document C172™–2014,

Standard Form of Agreement Between Owner and Program Manager for use on a Single Project. Each of these documents is described in greater detail in the AIA Document Synopses by Family section of this *Handbook*.

Bond Forms

In 2010, with the support and feedback of industry stakeholders, the AIA revised the Bid Bond, and Performance Bond and Payment Bond forms.

AIA Document A310™–2010, Bid Bond, is a simple, one-page form that establishes the maximum penal amount that may be due to the owner if the selected bidder fails to execute the contract or fails to provide any required performance and payment bonds. In addition to generally updated language, A310™–2010 adds language allowing the owner and contractor to extend the period of acceptance of the contractor's bid for up to 60 days without obtaining the surety's consent. A310™–2010 also can be used by subcontractors when a contractor requires a bid bond.

AIA Document A312™–2010, Performance Bond and Payment Bond, is one form that incorporates two bonds: one covering the contractor's performance, and the other covering the contractor's obligations to pay subcontractors and others for materials and labor. In addition, A312™–2010 obligates the surety to act responsively to the owner's requests for discussions aimed at anticipating or preventing a contractor's default.

As with Document A310™–2010, the language of Document A312™–2010 has been updated. Some other changes made to the A312™–2010 Performance Bond include the addition of language clarifying that the owner's failure to comply with the notice requirements of Section 3.1 does not release the surety from its obligations under the bond except to the extent the surety demonstrates actual prejudice. The A312™–2010 Performance Bond also shortens the notice period for surety default under the bond from 15 days to 7 days. Further, the limit of the surety's obligation to the amount of the bond does not apply if the surety elects to undertake and complete the contract itself.

Changes made to the A312™–2010, Payment Bond include an increase in the period of time in which the surety must answer a claimant's claim from 45 days to 60 days, and added language stating that a failure of the surety to answer or make payment in the time period specified is not a waiver of the surety's and contractor's defenses to the claim, but may entitle the claimant to attorneys' fees.

Housing and Other Owner-Architect Agreements

Since 2007, the AIA has introduced two additional A201 family owner-architect agreements that are based on AIA Document B101™–2007. They are AIA Document B108™–2009, Standard Form of Agreement Between Owner and Architect for a Federally Funded or Federally Insured Project, and AIA Document B106™–2010, Standard Form of Agreement Between Owner and Architect for Pro Bono Services.

AIA Document B108™–2009 is a standard form of agreement between owner and architect for building design and construction contract administration that is intended for use on federally funded or federally insured projects. B108™–2009 was developed with the assistance of several federal agencies and contains terms and conditions that are unique to federally funded or federally insured projects. It is an update of AIA Document B181™–1994 but is based on AIA Document B101™–2007 and incorporates the 2007 revisions.

AIA Document B106™–2010 is a new standard form of agreement between owner and architect for building design, construction contract administration, or other professional services provided on a pro bono basis. The architect's pro bono services are professional services for which the architect receives no financial compensation other than compensation for reimbursable expenses. A table format is provided which the parties use to designate the scope of the architect's pro bono services and the maximum number of hours to be provided by the architect for each designated pro bono service.

In 2010, the AIA introduced three documents for use in residential construction projects:

- AIA Document B107™–2010, Standard Form of Agreement Between Developer-Builder and Architect for Prototype(s) for Single Family Residential Project
- AIA Document B109™–2010, Standard Form of Agreement Between Owner and Architect for a Multi-Family Residential or Mixed Use Residential Project
- AIA Document B509™–2010, Guide for Supplementary Conditions to AIA Document B109™–2010 for use on Condominium Projects

AIA Document B109™–2010 is based on B103™–2007. B109™–2010 Standard Form of Agreement Between Owner and Architect for a Multi-Family Residential or Mixed Use Residential Project is a standard form of agreement between owner and architect for building design and construction contract administration for a multifamily residential or mixed-use residential project. B109™–2010 contains terms and conditions that are unique to these types of projects and also incorporates the basic assumptions contained in B103™–2007, such as owner-provided cost estimating and scheduling, as well as fast-track, phased, or accelerated scheduling. B109™–2010 contains the same division of Basic and Additional Services as in B101™–2007 and B103™–2007, but adds a new Pre-Design Services article that includes items such as assessment of project feasibility, layout, and regulatory requirements. B109™–2010 is not intended for use on condominium projects.

To assist users who wish to modify AIA Document B109™–2010 for use in condominium projects, the AIA published AIA Document B509™–2010, Guide for Supplementary Conditions to AIA Document B109™–2010 for use on condominium projects. B509™–2010 is not an agreement but a guide that provides model language with explanatory notes to assist users in adapting B109™–2010 for use on condominium projects.

The final owner-architect agreement published in 2010 tailored for residential construction, AIA Document B107™–2010 (formerly B188™–1996), Standard Form of Agreement Between Developer-Builder and Architect for Prototype(s) for Single Family Residential Project, is intended for use in situations where the architect will provide limited architectural services in connection with a single-family residential project. B107™–2010 is not based on B101™–2007 or B103™–2007 and it does not have a related general conditions document, but is instead a stand-alone agreement between the architect and developer-builder. B107™–2010 anticipates that the developer-builder will perform the construction.

Sustainable Design and Construction

Most recently, the documents library has been enhanced with the addition of documents developed to address issues associated with sustainable design and construction.

The AIA first published AIA Document D503™–2011, Guide for Sustainable Projects, including Agreement Amendments and Supplementary Conditions. D503™–2011 is not an agreement, but is a guide that discusses the roles and responsibilities faced by owners, architects, and contractors on sustainable design and construction projects. D503™–2011 also discusses certification systems, codes, and legislation affecting sustainable design and construction projects. D503™–2011 contains model provisions for modifying or supplementing the A201™–2007 general conditions, the A101™–2007 owner-contractor agreement, and the B101™–2007 owner-architect agreement. D503™–2011 also discusses the applicability of key concepts to other delivery models such as design-build, construction management, and integrated project delivery.

In May 2012, as the next step after publication of D503™–2011, the AIA published five documents for use on sustainable projects. These documents are based on underlying documents in the conventional (A201) family of AIA Contract Documents, with modifications that address the risks, responsibilities, and opportunities unique to

PART 4: CONTRACTS AND AGREEMENTS

projects involving substantial elements of sustainable design and construction. Similar sustainable project documents have now also been developed for both the CMa and CMc families. The Sustainable Projects documents are as follows:

- AIA Document A101™–2007 SP, Standard Form of Agreement Between Owner and Contractor, for use on a Sustainable Project where the basis of payment is a Stipulated Sum
- AIA Document A201™–2007 SP, General Conditions of the Contract for Construction, for use on a Sustainable Project
- AIA Document A401™–2007 SP, Standard Form of Agreement Between Contractor and Subcontractor, for use on a Sustainable Project
- AIA Document B101™–2007 SP, Standard Form of Agreement Between Owner and Architect, for use on a Sustainable Project
- AIA Document B103™–2007 SP, Standard Form of Agreement Between Owner and Architect for a Large or Complex Sustainable Project
- AIA Document C401™–2007 SP, Standard Form of Agreement Between Architect and Consultant, for use on a Sustainable Project
- AIA Document A132™–2007 SP, Standard Form of Agreement Between Owner and Contractor, for use on a Sustainable Project, Construction Manager Adviser Edition
- AIA Document A232™–2007 SP, General Conditions of the Contract for Construction, for use on a Sustainable Project, Construction Manager as Adviser Agreement
- AIA Document B132™–2007 SP, Standard Form of Agreement Between Owner and Architect, for use on a Sustainable Project, Construction Manager as Adviser Edition
- AIA Document C132™–2009 SP, Standard Form of Agreement Between Owner and Construction Manager as Adviser, for use on a Sustainable Project
- AIA Document A133™–2009 SP, Standard Form of Agreement Between Owner and Construction Manager as Constructor, for use on a Sustainable Project where the basis for payment is the Cost of the Work Plus a Fee with a Guaranteed Maximum Price
- AIA Document A134™–2009 SP, Standard Form of Agreement Between Owner and Construction Manager as Constructor, for use on a Sustainable Project where the basis for payment is the Cost of the Work Plus a Fee without a Guaranteed Maximum Price

The Sustainable Projects documents provide a process to develop and implement a program for sustainable design and construction projects. AIA Document A201™–2007 SP introduces a number of new definitions and terms that are unique to the Sustainable Projects documents. In addition, AIA Document B101™–2007 SP sets forth a newly defined scope of "Architect's Services for Sustainable Projects," that requires the architect to conduct a sustainability workshop and develop a sustainability plan that identifies the owner's sustainable objectives for the project, outlines sustainable measures necessary to achieve the sustainable objective, and allocates responsibility for each of the sustainable measures to the project team member in the best position to perform the sustainable measure. The requirements of the sustainability plan, with the owner's approval, will be further developed as the design for the project progresses and, as appropriate, will ultimately be incorporated into the drawings and specifications. The sustainability plan itself is also incorporated as a contract document.

In addition to setting forth this process, the sustainable projects documents contain other provisions related to issues specific to these kinds of projects, such as use of untested materials, the effect of substitutions on achievement of the sustainable objective, and waiver of consequential damages.

The sustainable projects documents were developed for use on a wide variety of sustainable projects, including those in which the owner's sustainable objectives include obtaining a sustainability certification, such as LEED (Leadership in Energy and Environmental Design), or those in which the sustainable objective is based on incorporation of performance-based sustainable design or construction elements. In addition, as new "green" codes are developed, the process outlined in the sustainable projects documents will help project participants navigate the requirements of code compliance. Currently structured and numbered as an overlay to various documents in the Conventional and Construction Manager families of documents, the structure of future documents may change, but the commitment to sustainable design is here to stay.

Using AIA Contract Documents

AIA Contract Documents are available in paper, in AIA Contract Documents® software, and on AIA Documents on Demand®. A Web-based AIA Contract Documents license is now available, and will be enhanced in the coming years. AIA Contract Documents software uses Microsoft Word to allow users to easily modify AIA documents using the "track changes" feature, and to e-mail them in Word or PDF formats. AIA software is currently available with an annual subscription that provides access to all AIA Contract Documents through a number of different license models. AIA Documents on Demand allows users to purchase most of the documents and forms in the AIA Contract Documents library online, fill in the open fill points, and print the completed document.

The AIA registers copyrights in nearly all of its standard form contract documents, claims trademark protection in its document numbers, and has registered the trademark AIA Contract Documents®. The AIA provides notice to document users that documents may not be reproduced or excerpted without express written permission from the AIA. For documents purchased in paper format, the AIA grants written permission in the footers of most documents to reproduce a maximum number of 10 copies of the completed document for use in connection with a particular project. Some documents purchased in paper format, such as General Conditions documents, may not be reproduced.

AIA software users may reproduce an unlimited number of copies of the documents they generate, but only for use on their own projects, and only for use on the project for which the document was created. Software users must comply with the End User License Agreement (EULA) provided for review and acceptance prior to purchasing the software.

The AIA registers copyrights and enforces copyright violations in order to protect the integrity of its valuable intellectual property, but copyright registration protects document users as well. Because AIA documents have a reputation for fairness, some parties attempt to take advantage of that reputation by scanning or copying an AIA document, deleting some or all of the AIA standard text, changing the content to suit their own interests, and then passing on the completed work as an AIA document with the AIA trademarked logo and copyright notice still intact. While these abuses do occur, copyright and trademark protection minimize their frequency and give the AIA the legal right to take action against the infringing parties. To report copyright or trademark violations of AIA Contract Documents, e-mail AIA legal counsel at copyright@aia.org.

LOOKING AHEAD

Over the next few years, the AIA will continue to revise existing documents and publish new agreements and forms. Major efforts will include revisions to the Design-Build family and preparation for the 2017 revisions to the A201 family, as well as application of sustainable design and construction concepts to additional delivery methods. New documents and revisions to existing ones will reflect input from industry stakeholders, changes in design and construction industry practices, and judicial decisions affecting owners, architects, consultants, and contractors. The Documents Committee will sift through the data and use its best efforts to develop the consensus required to produce documents that will admirably serve their intended purposes. The committee will continually seek new members who are willing to commit significant hours of volunteer time to ensure that AIA documents retain their stature as the industry standard. If you would like more information about serving as a member of the AIA Documents Committee, please send a message to docinfo@aia.org.

For More Information

AIA Contract Documents Reference Materials: www.aia.org/contractdocs/reference. AIA Contract Documents: www.aiacontracts.org/

12.2 AIA Contract Documents

CONVENTIONAL (A201) DESIGN-BID-BUILD

Key Attributes

- For use when the owner's project is divided into separate contracts for design (architect) and construction (contractor).
- Suitable for conventional project delivery (design-bid-build).
- Owner retains architect.
- Architect and his/her consultants prepare drawings and specifications.
- Architect assists owner in obtaining bids/proposals, and then owner awards contract(s) for construction.
- Contractor(s) and surety(ies) obligate to owner for bid, performance, and payment bonds.
- Contractor and subcontractors build the work.
- Versions of AIA Documents A101™, A201™, A401™, B101™, B103™, and C401™ developed specifically for use on sustainable projects are also available (e.g., designated as AIA Document A101™–2007 SP).

Conventional (A201) Design-Bid-Build Contract Relationships

AIA Documents B104™ and A107 ™ are in the A201 family of AIA Contract Documents because the abbreviated General Conditions in A107 are based on AIA Document A201™. If AIA Documents C401™ and A401™ are used with B104 and A107, appropriate modifications should be made with the assistance of insurance and legal counsel.

DOCUMENTS: AIA Documents **A101**™, Owner/Contractor Agreement—Stipulated Sum; **A102**™, O/C Agreement—Cost of the Work Plus a Fee, with GMP; **A103**™, O/C Agreement—Cost of the Work Plus a Fee, No GMP; **A107**™, O/C Agreement—Project of Limited Scope; **A201**™, General Conditions of the Contract for Construction; **A310**™, Bid Bond; **A312**™, Performance Bond/Payment Bond; **A401**™, Contractor/Subcontractor Agreement; **B101**™, Owner/Architect Agreement; **B103**™, O/A Agreement—Large or Complex Project; **B104**™, O/A Agreement—Project of Limited Scope; and **C401**™, Architect/Consultant Agreement.

SMALL PROJECTS

Key Attributes

- Suitable for residential or small commercial projects and other projects of relatively low cost and brief duration.
- These documents—AIA Documents B105™ and A105™—are, in effect, conventional design-bid-build documents (i.e., AIA Documents B101™ and A101™/A201™) "stripped down" to the essentials.
- These documents feature the use of Stipulated Sum and Integrated General Conditions.

Small Projects Contract Relationships

DOCUMENTS: AIA Documents **A105**™, Owner/Contractor Agreement, for a Residential or Small Commercial Project; and **B105**™, Owner/Architect Agreement, for a Residential or Small Commercial Project.

CONSTRUCTION MANAGER AS ADVISER (CMA)

Key Attributes

- Owner retains an architect and a construction manager, who acts as an additional advisor to the owner.
- Prime contractor(s) and subcontractor(s) are responsible for construction.
- Construction manager gives owner construction management advice through design and construction phases—increased expertise in managing a project from start to finish.
- Versions of AIA Documents A132™, A232™, B132™, and C132™ developed specifically for use on sustainable projects are also available (e.g., designated as AIA Document A132™–2009 SP).

CMa (2009) Contract Relationships

DOCUMENTS: AIA Documents **A132**™, Owner/Contractor Agreement, CMa Edition; **A232**™, General Conditions of the Contract for Construction, CMa Edition; **A401**™, Contractor/Subcontractor Agreement; **B132**™, Owner/Architect Agreement, CMa Edition; **C132**™, Owner/Construction Manager as Adviser Agreement; and **C401**™, Architect/Consultant Agreement.

CONSTRUCTION MANAGER AS CONSTRUCTOR (CMC)

Key Attributes

- Single party (construction manager) provides construction management services in preconstruction phase *and* then completes construction (constructor).
- Gives construction manager (constructor) responsibility and control over construction work via direct contract(s) with subcontractor(s).
- Construction phase services are paid on the basis of cost of work plus a fee either with (AIA Document A133™) or without (AIA Document A134™) a guaranteed maximum price.
- Versions of AIA Documents A133™ and A134™ developed specifically for use on sustainable projects are also available (e.g., designated as AIA Document A133™–2009 SP).

CMc (2009) Contract Relationships

DOCUMENTS: AIA Documents **A133**™, Owner/Construction Manager as Constructor Agreement, where the basis of payment is the cost of the work plus a fee with a guaranteed maximum price; **A134**™, Owner/Construction Manager as Constructor Agreement, where the basis of payment is the cost of the work plus a fee without a guaranteed maximum price; **A201**™, General Conditions of the Contract for Construction; **A401**™, Contractor/Subcontractor Agreement; **B133**™, Owner/Architect Agreement, Construction Manager as Constructor Edition; and **C401**™, Architect/Consultant Agreement.

DESIGN-BUILD

Key Attributes

- Owner enters into a contract with a single entity design-builder.
- Design-builder is then obligated to both design and construct the project.

- Owner may also hire a consultant to assist owner in working with design-builder.
- Design-builder then enters into contracts with architect and/or construction contractor(s), if necessary.
- Design-builder may be
  - a developer or single purpose entity (design and construction in one shop).
  - an architect-led organization.
  - a contractor-led organization (most often the case).
- For a one- or two-family residential project, see AIA Document A145™–2015, Owner Design/Builder Agreement for a One or Two Family Residential Project

Design-Build Contract Relationships

DOCUMENTS: AIA Documents **A141**™, Owner/Design-Builder Agreement; **A145**™, Owner/Design-Builder Agreement for a One or Two Family Residential Project; **A142**™, Design-Builder/Contractor Agreement; **A441**™, Contractor/Subcontractor Agreement for a Design-Build Project; **B143**™, Design-Builder/Architect Agreement; **C141**™, Owner/Consultant Agreement for a Design-Build Project; and **C441**™, Architect/Consultant Agreement for a Design-Build Project.

PROGRAM MANAGEMENT—MULTIPLE PROJECTS

Key Attributes

- For use in a program with more than one project. Suitable for conventional project delivery (design-bid-build).
- Owner retains a program manager to assist the owner in an advisory capacity, on matters that impact the entire program, during design and construction.
- Owner retains a design manager to assist the owner and the program manager in developing and establishing program. Design manager develops the program's design standards and performs schematic design and design development services for each project to develop a transfer package for the architect of record for each project in the program.
- Owner retains architect(s) of record to complete the design and perform construction administration services for each project.
- Contractor(s) and subcontractors build the work.

Program Management Contract Relationships

*AIA Documents B171™, B172™, and C171™ can be modified and utilized in non-design-bid-build project delivery methods as well. If AIA Documents B171, B172, and C171 are used in other delivery methods, appropriate modifications should be made with the assistance of insurance and legal counsel.

DOCUMENTS: AIA Documents **B171**™, Owner/Design Manager Agreement, for use in a multiple project program; **B172**™, Owner/Architect Agreement, for architect of record services; and **C171**™, Owner/Program Manager Agreement, for use in a multiple project program.

PROGRAM MANAGEMENT—SINGLE PROJECT

Key Attributes

- For use on a single project. Suitable for conventional project delivery (design-bid-build).
- Owner retains a program manager to assist the owner in an advisory capacity on matters that impact the project during design and construction.
- Owner retains an architect to design the project and perform construction administration services.
- Contractor(s) and subcontractors build the work.

The C172 ™–2014 contains optional cost estimating and construction administration services for the program manager to perform. If the program manager is to perform cost-estimating services, the owner can identify the program manager as the cost consultant in B103 ™–2014.

DOCUMENTS: AIA Documents **C172**™, Owner/Program Manager Agreement, for use on a single project.

INTEGRATED PROJECT DELIVERY (IPD): TRANSITIONAL DOCUMENTS

Key Attributes

- Integrated project delivery is an emerging process, and these Transitional Agreements are a comfortable first step to IPD.
- A collaborative project delivery approach that utilizes the talents and insights of all project participants through all phases of design and construction.
- Structured similar to existing construction manager as constructor agreements.

IPD Transitional Documents Contract Relationships

If AIA Document A401™ or C401™ is to be used on a project with the Transitional Forms, appropriate modifications should be made with the assistance of insurance and legal counsel.

DOCUMENTS: AIA Documents **A401**™, Contractor/Subcontractor Agreement; **A295**™, General Conditions of the Contract for Integrated Project Delivery; and **C401**™, Architect/Consultant Agreement.

INTEGRATED PROJECT DELIVERY (IPD): MULTI-PARTY AGREEMENT

Key Attributes

- These agreements more fully integrate the project parties into IPD.
- Owner, architect and contractor, at a minimum, enter into one contract (Multi-Party Agreement).
- The Multi-Party Agreement allows for sharing of risk and reward in a fully integrated collaborative process.

IPD Multi-Party Agreement Contract Relationships

If AIA Document A401™ or C401™ is to be used on a project with the Multi-Party Agreement, appropriate modifications should be made with the assistance of insurance and legal counsel.

DOCUMENTS: AIA Documents **A401**™, Contractor/Subcontractor Agreement; **C191**™, Multi-Party Agreement for Integrated Project Delivery; and **C401**™, Architect/Consultant Agreement.

INTEGRATED PROJECT DELIVERY (IPD): SINGLE PURPOSE ENTITY (SPE)

Key Attributes

- These agreements more fully integrate the project parties into IPD.
- Creates a limited liability company (single purpose entity) for the purpose of furnishing the planning, design, and construction of the project through separate contracts with appropriate entities.
- The SPE allows for complete sharing of risk and reward in a fully integrated collaborative process.

DOCUMENTS: AIA Documents **C195**™, SPE Agreement for Integrated Project Delivery; **C196**™, SPE/Owner Agreement for IPD; **C197**™, SPE/Non-Owner Member Agreement for IPD; **C198**™, SPE/Consultant Agreement for IPD; and **C199**™, SPE/Contractor Agreement for IPD.

Source: Original Text and Source: *TAHPP*, 15ᵗʰ Edition

12.3 AIA Contract Documents Synopses by Family

Joseph L. Fleischer, FAIA

AIA Contract Documents® are divided into nine "families" by project type or delivery method. The Documents by Family category includes two groups of documents not branded as families: Digital Practice Documents and Construction Administration and Project Management Forms.

- Conventional (A201)
- Construction Manager as Adviser (CMa)
- Construction Manager as Constructor (CMc)
- Design-Build
- Integrated Project Delivery (IPD)
- Interiors
- International
- Program Management
- Small Projects
- Digital Practice Documents
- Construction Administration and Project Management Forms

The document families reflect the various legal and working relationships in similar project types. Documents for the same families are linked by common terminology and procedures and may adopt one another by reference. By way of example, the relevant terms of A201–2007 are adopted by reference in several agreements, including A101–2007, A102–2007, A103–2007, A401–2007, B101–2007, and B103–2007.

More than 150 AIA contract and administrative forms are available in digital form today. Some documents are also available in paper, though the future is primarily in the world of the flexible digital documents and Web-based licenses. The precursor of these documents was the Uniform Contract, an owner-contractor agreement first published in 1888. This was followed, in 1911, by the AIA's first standardized general conditions for construction. The 2007 edition of the AIA Document A201 is the 16th edition of those general conditions. The primary, or flagship documents of the AIA are now revised and updated in a 10-year cycle. The newest version of A201 is scheduled for release in the Spring of 2017.

Many practices common to the construction industry today became established through their inclusion in the AIA's general conditions for construction and its other standardized documents. While the AIA documents have had a profound influence on the industry, the influence also runs the other way. The AIA regularly revises its documents to take into account developments in the construction industry and the law. Standardized documents for design-build, different types of construction management, international practice, integrated project delivery, program management and sustainable design have been published in recent years. Likewise, all of the documents have been updated to address new methods of communication and the dissemination of information in terms of digital data and building information modeling. Because AIA documents are frequently updated, users should consult an AIA component or www.aia.org to confirm current editions. This Synopsis is accurate through June 30, 2015.

The AIA documents are intended for nationwide use and thus are not drafted to conform to the law of any one state. With that caveat, however, AIA contract documents provide a solid basis for contract provisions that are enforceable under existing law at the time of publication. Case law on contracts for design and construction has, for the past century, been based largely on the language in AIA standardized documents. The documents are generally recognized to be fair and balanced for all participants in the design and construction process.

CONVENTIONAL (A201) FAMILY

Use of the Conventional (A201) family of AIA Contract Documents may be appropriate when the owner's project is divided into separate contracts for design (with the architect) and construction (with one or more contractors). This is the most commonly used family of AIA documents because the documents are suitable for the conventional delivery approach of design-bid-build. These documents can be used on small to large projects.

A101–2007, Standard Form of Agreement Between Owner and Contractor where the basis of payment is a Stipulated Sum

AIA Document A101™–2007 is a standard form of agreement between owner and contractor for use where the basis of payment is a stipulated sum (fixed price). A101 adopts by reference, and is designed for use with, AIA Document A201™–2007, General Conditions of the Contract for Construction. A101 is suitable for large or complex projects. For projects of a more limited scope, use of AIA Document A107™–2007, Agreement Between Owner and Contractor for a Project of Limited Scope, should be considered. For even smaller projects, consider AIA Document A105™–2007, Agreement Between Owner and Contractor for a Residential or Small Commercial Project.

A101–2007 SP, Standard Form of Agreement Between Owner and Contractor, for use on a Sustainable Project where the basis of payment is a Stipulated Sum

AIA Document A101™–2007 SP is a standard form of agreement between owner and contractor for use on sustainable projects where the basis of payment is a stipulated sum (fixed price). A101–2007 SP is based on AIA Document A101™–2007, Standard Form of Agreement Between Owner and Contractor, where the basis of payment is a Stipulated Sum, with modifications that address the risks, responsibilities, and opportunities unique to projects involving substantial elements of sustainable design and construction (sustainable projects). A101–2007 SP adopts by reference, and is designed for use with, AIA Document A201™–2007 SP, General Conditions of the Contract for Construction for use on a Sustainable Project.

A102–2007 (formerly A111–1997), Standard Form of Agreement Between Owner and Contractor where the basis of payment is the Cost of the Work Plus a Fee with a Guaranteed Maximum Price

This standard form of agreement between owner and contractor is appropriate for use on large projects requiring a guaranteed maximum price, when the basis of payment to the contractor is the cost of the work plus a fee. AIA Document A102™–2007 is not intended for use in competitive bidding. AIA Document A102–2007 adopts by reference and is intended for use with AIA Document A201™–2007, General Conditions of the Contract for Construction. NOTE: A111–1997 expired in 2009.

A103–2007 (formerly A114–2001), Standard Form of Agreement Between Owner and Contractor where the basis of payment is the Cost of the Work Plus a Fee without a Guaranteed Maximum Price

AIA Document A103™–2007 is appropriate for use on large projects when the basis of payment to the contractor is the cost of the work plus a fee, and the cost is not fully known at the commencement of construction. AIA Document A103–2007 is not intended for use in competitive bidding. A103–2007 adopts by reference, and is intended for use with, AIA Document A201™–2007, General Conditions of the Contract for Construction. NOTE: A114–2001 expired in 2009.

A107–2007, Standard Form of Agreement Between Owner and Contractor for a Project of Limited Scope

AIA Document A107™–2007 is a stand-alone agreement with its own internal general conditions and is intended for use on construction projects of limited scope. It is intended for use on medium- to large-sized projects where payment is based on either a stipulated sum or the cost of the work plus a fee, with or without a guaranteed maximum price. Parties using AIA Document A107–2007 will also use A107 Exhibit A, if using a cost-plus payment method. AIA Document B104™–2007, Standard Form of Agreement Between Owner and Architect for a Project of Limited Scope, coordinates with A107–2007 and incorporates it by reference.

For more complex projects, parties should consider using one of the following other owner-contractor agreements: AIA Document A101™–2007, A102™–2007, or A103™–2007. These agreements are written for a stipulated sum, cost of the work with a guaranteed maximum price, and cost of the work without a guaranteed maximum price, respectively. Each of them incorporates by reference AIA Document A201™–2007, General Conditions of the Contract for Construction. For single-family residential projects, or smaller and less complex commercial projects, parties may wish to consider AIA Document A105™–2007, Agreement Between Owner and Contractor for a Residential or Small Commercial Project.

A121–2014, Standard Form of Master Agreement Between Owner and Contractor where Work is provided under Multiple Work Orders

AIA Document A121™–2014 is a Master Agreement between the owner and contractor. It is intended for use when the contractor's scope of work will subsequently be specified through the use of one or more Work Orders. A121–2014 provides only the common terms and conditions that will be applicable to each Work Order. Use of A121 plus a Work Order creates a contract that includes both the terms and the scope of work. A121–2014 is coordinated for use with AIA Document A221™–2014, Work Order for use with Master Agreement Between Owner and Contractor. The Master Agreement plus Work Order contracting method allows multiple scopes of work to be issued quickly without the necessity to renegotiate the terms and conditions of the contract. It may be used on projects with a stipulated sum; cost of the work plus a fee, with or without a guaranteed maximum price; or other payment method determined by the parties. If using a cost-plus payment method, the parties will also use A121 Exhibit A, Determination of the Cost of the Work.

A201–2007, General Conditions of the Contract for Construction

The general conditions are an integral part of the contract for construction for a large project and they are incorporated by reference into the owner-contractor agreement. They set forth the rights, responsibilities, and relationships of the owner, contractor, and architect. Though not a party to the contract for construction between owner and contractor, the architect participates in the preparation of the contract documents and performs construction phase duties and responsibilities described in detail in the general conditions. AIA Document A201™–2007 is adopted by reference in owner-architect, owner-contractor, and contractor-subcontractor agreements in the Conventional (A201) family of documents; thus, it is often called the "keystone" document.

A201–2007 SP, General Conditions of the Contract for Construction, for use on a Sustainable Project

AIA Document A201™–2007 SP, General Conditions of the Contract for Construction, for use on a Sustainable Project, sets forth the rights, responsibilities, and relationships of the owner, contractor, and architect. The general conditions are an integral part of the contract for construction for a sustainable project, and A201–2007 SP is incorporated by reference into AIA Document A101™–2007 SP, Standard Form of Agreement Between Owner and Contractor, for use on a Sustainable Project where the basis of payment is a Stipulated Sum. A201–2007 SP is based on AIA Document A201™–2007, General Conditions of the Contract for Construction, with modifications that address the risks, responsibilities, and opportunities unique to projects involving substantial elements of sustainable design and construction (sustainable projects). Though not a party to the contract for construction between owner and contractor, the architect participates in the preparation of the Contract Documents and performs construction phase duties and responsibilities described in detail in the General Conditions.

A221–2014, Work Order for use with Master Agreement Between Owner and Contractor

AIA Document A221™–2014 is a Work Order that provides the contractor's scope of work, contract time, contract sum, and other terms pertinent to the specific Work Order. It is intended for use when the owner and contractor have entered into a Master Agreement setting forth the common terms and conditions applicable to all Work Orders. A221–2014 is not a stand-alone agreement and must be used in conjunction with a Master Agreement. A221–2014 is coordinated for use with AIA Document A121™–2014, between Owner and Contractor. The Master Agreement plus Work Order contracting method allows multiple scopes of work to be issued quickly without the necessity to renegotiate the terms and conditions of the contract. It may be used on projects with a stipulated sum; cost of the work plus a fee, with or without a guaranteed maximum price; or other payment method determined by the parties. If using a cost-plus payment method, the parties will also use A121 Exhibit A, Determination of the Cost of the Work.

A401–2007, Standard Form of Agreement Between Contractor and Subcontractor

AIA Document A401™–2007 establishes the contractual relationship between the contractor and subcontractor. It sets forth the responsibilities of both parties and lists their respective obligations, which are written to parallel AIA Document A201™–2007, General Conditions of the Contract for Construction, which A401–2007 incorporates by reference. AIA Document A401–2007 may be modified for use as an agreement between the subcontractor and a sub-subcontractor, and must be modified if used where AIA Document A107™–2007 or A105™–2007 serves as the owner-contractor agreement.

A401–2007 SP, Standard Form of Agreement Between Contractor and Subcontractor, for use on a Sustainable Project

AIA Document A401™–2007 SP, Standard Form of Agreement Between Contractor and Subcontractor, for use on a Sustainable Project, establishes the contractual relationship between the contractor and subcontractor on a sustainable project. A401–2007 SP is based on AIA Document A401™–2007, Standard Form of Agreement Between Contractor and Subcontractor, with modifications to coordinate its use with the other Sustainable Projects documents in the Conventional (A201) family of AIA Contract Documents. It sets forth the responsibilities of both parties and lists their respective obligations, which are written to parallel AIA Document A201™–2007 SP, General Conditions of the Contract for Construction, for use on a Sustainable Project. A401–2007 SP incorporates A201–2007 SP by reference. A401–2007 SP may be modified for use as an agreement between the subcontractor and a sub-subcontractor on a sustainable project.

A503–2007 (formerly A511–1999), Guide for Supplementary Conditions

AIA Document A503™–2007 is not an agreement, but is a guide containing model provisions for modifying and supplementing AIA Document A201™–2007, General Conditions of the Contract for Construction. It provides model language with explanatory notes to assist users in adapting AIA Document A201–2007 to specific circumstances. A201–2007, as a standard form document, cannot cover all the particulars of a project. Thus, AIA Document A503–2007 is provided to assist A201–2007 users either in modifying it, or developing a separate supplementary conditions document to attach to it. NOTE: A511–1999 expired in 2009.

A521–2012, Uniform Location of Subject Matter

AIA Document A521™–2012 provides general guidance to users preparing bidding and construction contract documents for determining the proper location of information to be included in bidding documents, the contract for construction, general conditions, supplementary conditions, and Division 01 General Requirements and Divisions 02–49 Specifications.

A701–1997, Instructions to Bidders

AIA Document A701™–1997 is used when competitive bids are to be solicited for construction of the project. Coordinated with AIA Document A201™, General Conditions of the Contract for Construction, and its related documents, AIA Document A701–1997 provides instructions on procedures, including bonding requirements, for bidders to follow in preparing and submitting their bids. Specific instructions or special requirements, such as the amount and type of bonding, are to be attached to, or inserted into, A701.

B101–2007 (formerly B151–1997), Standard Form of Agreement Between Owner and Architect

AIA Document B101™–2007 is a one-part standard form of agreement between owner and architect for building design and construction contract administration. AIA Document B101–2007 was developed to replace AIA Documents B141™–1997 Parts 1 and 2, and B151–1997 (expired 2009), but it more closely follows the format of B151–1997. Services are divided traditionally into basic and additional services. Basic services are performed in five phases: schematic design, design development, construction documents, bidding or negotiation, and construction. This agreement may be used with a variety of compensation methods, including percentage of construction cost and stipulated sum. B101–2007 is intended to be used in conjunction with AIA Document A201™–2007, General Conditions of the Contract for Construction, which it incorporates by reference.

B101–2007 SP, Standard Form of Agreement Between Owner and Architect, for use on a Sustainable Project

AIA Document B101™–2007 SP is a one-part standard form of agreement between owner and architect for sustainable building design and construction contract administration. B101–2007 SP is based on AIA Document B101™–2007, Standard Form of Agreement Between Owner and Architect, with modifications that address the risks, responsibilities, and opportunities unique to projects involving substantial elements of sustainable design and construction (sustainable projects). B101–2007 SP follows B101–2007 in the division of services into Basic and Additional Services. B101–2007 SP also includes a new scope of services section that sets forth services unique to sustainable projects.

B102–2007 (formerly B141–1997 Part 1), Standard Form of Agreement Between Owner and Architect without a Predefined Scope of Architect's Services

AIA Document B102™–2007 replaces and serves the same purpose as B141–1997 Part 1 (expired 2009). AIA Document B102–2007 is a standard form of agreement between owner and architect that contains terms and conditions and compensation details. B102–2007 does not include a scope of architect's services, which must be inserted in Article 1 or attached as an exhibit. Separation of the scope of services from the owner-architect agreement allows users the freedom to append alternative scopes of services. AIA standard form scopes of services documents that may be paired with B102–2007 include AIA Documents B203™–2007, Site Evaluation and Planning; B204™–2007, Value Analysis; B205™–2007, Historic Preservation; B206™–2007, Security Evaluation and Planning; B209™–2007, Construction Contract Administration; B210™–2007, Facility Support; B211™–2007, Commissioning; B214™–2007, LEED® Certification; B252™–2007, Architectural Interior Design; and B253™–2007, Furniture, Furnishings and Equipment Design.

B103–2007, Standard Form of Agreement Between Owner and Architect for a Large or Complex Project

AIA Document B103™–2007 is a standard form of agreement between owner and architect intended for use on large or complex projects. AIA Document B103–2007 was developed to replace AIA Documents B141™–1997 Parts 1 and 2, and B151™–1997 (expired 2009) specifically with respect to large or complex projects. B103–2007 assumes that the owner will retain third parties to provide cost estimates and project schedules, and may implement fast-track, phased, or accelerated scheduling. Services are divided along the traditional lines of basic and additional services. Basic services are based on five phases: schematic design, design development, construction documents, bidding or negotiation, and construction. The architect does not prepare cost estimates, but designs the project to meet the owner's budget for the cost of the work at the conclusion of the design development phase services. This document may be used with a variety of compensation methods. B103–2007 is intended to be used in conjunction with AIA Document A201™–2007, General Conditions of the Contract for Construction, which it incorporates by reference.

AIA Document B103™–2007 SP, Standard Form of Agreement Between Owner and Architect for a Large or Complex Sustainable Project

AIA Document B103™–2007 SP is a standard form of agreement between owner and architect intended for use on large or complex sustainable projects. B103–2007 SP is based on AIA Document B103™–2007, Standard Form of Agreement Between Owner and Architect for a Large or Complex Project, with modifications that address the risks, responsibilities, and opportunities unique to projects involving substantial elements of sustainable design and construction (sustainable projects). B103–2007 SP assumes that the owner will retain third parties to provide cost estimates and project schedules, and may implement fast-track, phased, or accelerated scheduling. Services are divided along the traditional lines of basic and additional services. B103–2007 SP also includes a new scope of services section that sets forth services unique to sustainable projects. This document may be used with a variety of compensation methods. B103–2007 SP is intended to be used in conjunction with AIA Document A201™–2007 SP, General Conditions of the Contract for Construction, for use on a Sustainable Project, which it incorporates by reference.

B104–2007, Standard Form of Agreement Between Owner and Architect for a Project of Limited Scope

AIA Document B104™–2007 is a standard form of agreement between owner and architect intended for use on medium-sized projects. AIA Document B104–2007 is an abbreviated version of B101™–2007. AIA Document B104–2007 contains a compressed form of basic services with three phases: design development, construction documents, and construction. This document may be used with a variety of compensation methods. B104–2007 is intended to be used in conjunction with AIA Document A107™–2007, Standard Form of Agreement Between Owner and Contractor for a Project of Limited Scope, which it incorporates by reference.

B106–2010, Standard Form of Agreement Between Owner and Architect for Pro Bono Services

AIA Document B106™–2010 is a standard form of agreement between owner and architect for building design, construction contract administration, or other professional services provided on a pro bono basis. The architect's pro bono services are professional services for which the architect receives no financial compensation other than compensation for reimbursable expenses. A table format is provided which the parties use to designate the scope of the architect's pro bono services and the maximum number of hours to be provided by the architect for each designated pro bono service. If the architect is providing construction phase services, B106–2010 is intended to be used in conjunction with AIA Document A201™–2007, General Conditions of the Contract for Construction, which it incorporates by reference. NOTE: B106–2010 is available in AIA Contract Documents® software, but not in paper. An interactive B106 form is available free of charge from AIA Documents on Demand®.

B107–2010 (formerly B188–1996), Standard Form of Agreement Between Developer-Builder and Architect for Prototype(s) for Single Family Residential Project.

AIA Document B107™–2010 is a standard form of agreement between developer-builder and architect for design of one or more prototype(s) for a single-family residential project. AIA Document B107–2010 is intended for use in situations where the architect will provide limited architectural services in connection with a single-family residential project. Under B107–2010, the architect's services consist of development of Permit Set Documents and limited construction phase services for the first residence of each prototype design constructed by the developer-builder in the development. This document anticipates that the developer-builder will have extensive control over the management of the project, acting in a capacity similar to that of a developer or speculative builder of a housing project, and that the developer-builder is an entity that has experience with applicable residential building codes, selection of materials and systems, and methods of installation and construction. NOTE: B188–1996 expired in 2012.

B108–2009 (formerly B181–1994), Standard Form of Agreement Between Owner and Architect for a Federally Funded or Federally Insured Project

AIA Document B108™–2009 is a standard form of agreement between owner and architect for building design and construction contract administration that is intended for use on federally funded or federally insured projects. AIA Document B108–2009 was developed with the assistance of several federal agencies and contains terms and conditions that are unique to federally funded or federally insured projects. B108 sets forth five traditional phases of basic services: schematic design, design development, construction documents, bidding or negotiation, and construction. Two other types of services are delineated in the document: optional services and additional services. B108 is structured so that either the owner or the architect may be the entity providing cost estimates. NOTE: B181–1994 expired in May 2011.

B109–2010, Standard Form of Agreement Between Owner and Architect for a Multi-Family Residential or Mixed Use Residential Project

AIA Document B109™–2010 is a standard form of agreement between owner and architect for building design and construction contract administration for a multifamily residential or mixed-use residential project. B109–2010 contains terms and conditions that are unique to these types of projects. B109–2010 is based on AIA Document B103™–2007, Standard Form of Agreement Between Owner and Architect for a Large or Complex Project. AIA Document B109–2010 uses the traditional division of services into Basic and Additional Services but adds a new Pre-Design Services article that includes items such as assessment of project feasibility, layout, and regulatory requirements.

B121–2014, Standard Form of Master Agreement Between Owner and Architect for Services provided under Multiple Service Orders

AIA Document B121™–2014 is a Master Agreement Between the Owner and Architect. It is intended for use when the architect's scope of services will subsequently be specified through the use of one or more Service Orders. B121–2014 provides only the common terms and conditions that will be applicable to each Service Order. Use of B121 plus a Service Order creates a contract, referred to as the Service Agreement, that includes both the terms and the scope of services. B121–2014 is coordinated for use with AIA Document B221™–2014, Service Order for use with Master Agreement Between Owner and Architect. The Master Agreement plus Service Order contracting method allows multiple scopes of services to be issued quickly without the necessity to renegotiate the terms and conditions of the Service Agreements.

B144™ARCH-CM–1993, Standard Form of Amendment to the Agreement Between Owner and Architect where the Architect provides Construction Management Services as an adviser to the Owner

AIA Document B144™ARCH-CM–1993 is an amendment to AIA Document B141™–1997 for use in circumstances where the architect, already under contract to perform architectural services for the owner, agrees to provide the owner with a package of construction management services to expand upon, blend with, and supplement the architect's design and construction contract administration services described in AIA Document B141–1997.

B201–2007 (formerly B141–1997 Part 2), Standard Form of Architect's Services: Design and Construction Contract Administration

AIA Document B201™–2007 replaces B141–1997 Part 2 (expired 2009). AIA Document B201–2007 defines the architect's traditional scope of services for design and construction contract administration in a standard form that the owner and architect can modify to suit the needs of the project. The services set forth in B201–2007 parallel those set forth in AIA Document B101™–2007: the traditional division of services into basic and additional services, with five phases of basic services. B201–2007 may be used in two ways: (1) incorporated into the owner-architect agreement as the architect's sole scope of services or in conjunction with other scope of services documents, or (2) attached to AIA Document G802™–2007, Amendment to the Professional Services Agreement, to create a modification to an existing owner-architect agreement. B201–2007 is a scope of services document only and may not be used as a stand-alone owner-architect agreement.

B202–2009, Standard Form of Architect's Services: Programming

AIA Document B202™–2009 establishes duties and responsibilities where the architect provides the owner with programming services. The architect's programming services are set forth in a series of iterative steps, from a broad identification of priorities, values, and goals of the programming participants to working with the owner to confirm the owner's objectives for the project. The programming services also include information gathering to develop performance and design criteria, and developing a final program of project requirements. AIA Document B202–2009 may be used in two ways: (1) incorporated into the owner-architect agreement as the architect's sole scope of services or in conjunction with other scope of services documents, or (2) attached to AIA Document G802™–2007, Amendment to the Professional Services Agreement, to create a modification to an existing owner-architect agreement. B202–2009 is a scope of services document only and may not be used as a stand-alone owner-architect agreement.

B203–2007, Standard Form of Architect's Services: Site Evaluation and Planning

AIA Document B203™–2007 is intended for use where the architect provides the owner with services to assist in site selection for a project. Under this scope, the architect's services may include analysis of the owner's program and alternative sites, site utilization studies, and other analysis, such as planning and zoning requirements, site context, historic resources, utilities, environmental impact, and parking and circulation. AIA Document B203 may be used in two ways: (1) incorporated into the owner-architect agreement as the architect's sole scope of services or in conjunction with other scope of services documents, or (2) attached to AIA Document G802™–2007, Amendment to the Professional Services Agreement, to create a modification to an existing owner-architect agreement. B203–2007 is a scope of services document only and may not be used as a stand-alone owner-architect agreement. B203 was revised in 2007 to align, as applicable, with AIA Document B101™–2007.

B204–2007, Standard Form of Architect's Services: Value Analysis, for use where the Owner employs a Value Analysis Consultant

AIA Document B204™–2007 establishes duties and responsibilities when the owner has employed a value analysis consultant. This document provides the architect's services in three categories: pre-workshop, workshop, and post-workshop. The services include presenting the project's goals and design rationale at the value analysis workshop, reviewing and evaluating each value analysis proposal, and preparing a value analysis report for the owner that, among other things, advises the owner of the estimate of the cost of the work resulting from the implementation of the accepted value analysis proposals. AIA Document B204–2007 may be used in two ways: (1) incorporated into the owner-architect agreement as the architect's sole scope of services or in conjunction with other scope of services documents, or (2) attached to AIA Document G802™–2007, Amendment to the Professional Services Agreement, to create a modification to an existing owner-architect agreement. B204–2007 is a scope of services document only and may not be used as a stand-alone owner-architect agreement. B204 was revised in 2007 to align, as applicable, with AIA Document B101™–2007.

B205–2007, Standard Form of Architect's Services: Historic Preservation

AIA Document B205™–2007 establishes duties and responsibilities where the architect provides services for projects that are historically sensitive. The range of services the architect provides under this scope spans the life of the project and may require the architect to be responsible for preliminary surveys, applications for tax incentives, nominations for landmark status, analysis of historic finishes, and other services specific to historic preservation projects. AIA Document B205–2007 may be used in two ways: (1) incorporated into the owner-architect agreement as the architect's sole scope of services or in conjunction with other scope of services documents, or (2) attached to AIA Document G802™–2007, Amendment to the Professional Services Agreement, to create a modification to an existing owner-architect agreement. B205–2007 is a scope of services document only and may not be used as a stand-alone owner-architect agreement. B205 was revised in 2007 to align, as applicable, with AIA Document B101™–2007.

B206–2007, Standard Form of Architect's Services: Security Evaluation and Planning

AIA Document B206™–2007 establishes duties and responsibilities where the architect provides services for projects that require greater security features and protection than would normally be incorporated into a building design. This scope requires the architect to identify and analyze the threats to a facility, survey the facility with respect to those threats, and prepare a risk assessment report. Following the owner's approval of the report, the architect prepares design documents and a security report. AIA Document B206–2007 may be used in two ways: (1) incorporated into the owner-architect agreement as the architect's sole scope of services or in conjunction with other scope of services documents, or (2) attached to AIA Document G802™–2007, Amendment to the Professional Services Agreement, to create a modification to an existing owner-architect agreement. B206–2007 is a scope of services document and may not be used as a stand-alone owner-architect agreement. B206 was revised in 2007 to align with AIA Document B101™–2007.

B207–2008 (formerly B352–2000), Standard Form of Architect's Services: On-Site Project Representation

AIA Document B207™–2008 establishes the architect's scope of services when the architect provides an on-site project representative during the construction phase. B207–2008 provides for agreement on the number of architect's representatives to be stationed at the project site, a schedule for the on-site representation, and the services that the on-site representative will perform. The on-site representative's services include attending job-site meetings, monitoring the contractor's construction schedule, observing systems and equipment testing, preparing a log of activities at the site, and maintaining on-site records. The owner will provide an on-site office for the architect's on-site representative. AIA Document B207–2008 is a scope of services document only and may not be used as a stand-alone owner-architect agreement. NOTE: B352–2000 expired in 2010.

B209–2007, Standard Form of Architect's Services: Construction Contract Administration, for use where the Owner has retained another Architect for Design Services

AIA Document B209™–2007 establishes duties and responsibilities when an architect provides only construction phase services and the owner has retained another architect for design services. This scope requires the architect to perform the traditional contract administration services while design services are provided by another architect. B209–2007 may be used in two ways: (1) incorporated into the owner-architect agreement as the architect's sole scope of services or in conjunction with other scope of services documents, or (2) attached to AIA Document G802™–2007, Amendment to the Professional Services Agreement, to create a modification to an existing owner-architect agreement. AIA Document B209–2007 is a scope of services document only and may not be used as a stand-alone owner-architect agreement. B209 was revised in 2007 to align, as applicable, with AIA Document B101™–2007.

B210–2007, Standard Form of Architect's Services: Facility Support

AIA Document B210™–2007 focuses attention on providing the owner with means and measures to ensure the proper function and maintenance of the building and site after final completion. This scope provides a menu of choices of services, including initial existing condition surveys of the building and its systems, evaluation of operating costs, and code compliance reviews. AIA Document B210–2007 may be used in two ways: (1) incorporated into the owner-architect agreement as the architect's sole scope of services or in conjunction with other scopes of services documents, or (2) attached to AIA Document G802™–2007, Amendment to the Professional Services Agreement, to create a modification to an existing owner-architect agreement. B210–2007 is a scope of services document only and may not be used as a stand-alone owner-architect agreement. B210 was revised in 2007 to align, as applicable, with AIA Document B101™–2007.

B211–2007, Standard Form of Architect's Services: Commissioning

AIA Document B211™–2007 requires that the architect, based on the owner's identification of systems to be commissioned, develop a commissioning plan, a design intent document, and commissioning specifications. It also requires that the architect review the contractor's submittals and other documentation related to the systems to be commissioned, observe and document performance tests, train operators, and prepare a final commissioning report. AIA Document B211–2007 may be used in two ways: (1) incorporated into the owner-architect agreement as the architect's sole scope of services or in conjunction with other scope of services documents, or (2) attached to AIA Document G802™–2007, Amendment to the Professional Services Agreement, to create a modification to an existing owner-architect agreement. B211–2007 is a scope of services document only and may not be used as a stand-alone owner-architect agreement. B211 was revised in 2007 to align, as applicable, with AIA Document B101™–2007.

B212–2010, Standard Form of Architect's Services: Regional or Urban Planning

AIA Document B212™–2010 establishes duties and responsibilities where the architect provides the owner with regional or urban planning services. This scope provides a menu of choices of regional or urban planning services, grouped under four phases: Inventory and Data Gathering; Analysis and Judgment; Preparation of Design Alternatives; and Finalization of Preferred Plan.

AIA Document B212–2010 may be used in two ways: (1) incorporated into the owner-architect agreement as the architect's sole scope of services or in conjunction with other scope of services documents, or (2) attached to AIA Document G802™–2007, Amendment to the Professional Services Agreement, to create a modification to an existing owner-architect agreement. B212–2010 is a scope of services document only and may not be used as a stand-alone owner-architect agreement.

B214–2012, Standard Form of Architect' Services: LEED® Certification

AIA Document B214™–2012, Scope of Architect's Services: LEED® Certification, establishes duties and responsibilities when the owner seeks certification from the U.S. Green Building Council's Leadership in Energy and Environmental Design (LEED) program. B214–2012 may be used to provide the scope of services for a prime architect who is providing LEED Certification services as an Additional Service, or, in the alternative, for an architect who is providing only LEED Certification services as a consultant to the owner. Although some of the architect's services vary based on whether the architect is performing its services as the prime architect or as a LEED consultant, in either case the architect's services include conducting a LEED Workshop, preparing a LEED Certification Plan, and Project registration and submission of LEED Documentation. B214–2012 may be (1) incorporated into the owner-architect agreement as the architect's sole scope of services or in conjunction with other scopes of services documents, or (2) attached to AIA Document G802™–2007, Amendment to the Professional Services Agreement, to create a modification to an existing owner-architect agreement. B214–2012 is a scope of services document only and may not be used as a stand-alone owner-architect agreement.

B221–2014, Service Order for use with Master Agreement Between Owner and Architect

AIA Document B221™–2014 is a Service Order that provides the architect's scope of services, and other terms pertinent to the specific Service Order. It is intended for use when the owner and architect have entered into a Master Agreement setting forth the common terms and conditions applicable to all Service Orders. B221–2014 is not a stand-alone agreement and must be used in conjunction with a Master Agreement. B221–2014 is coordinated for use with AIA Document B121™–2014, Master Agreement Between Owner and Architect for Services provided under Multiple Service Orders. Use of B221 plus a Master Agreement creates a contract, referred to as the Service Agreement, that includes both the terms and the scope of services. The Master Agreement plus Service Order contracting method allows multiple scopes of services to be issued quickly without the necessity to renegotiate the terms and conditions of the Service Agreements.

B252–2007, Standard Form of Architect's Services: Architectural Interior Design

AIA Document B252™–2007 establishes duties and responsibilities where the architect provides both architectural interior design services and design services for furniture, furnishings, and equipment (FF&E). The scope of services in AIA Document B252–2007 is substantially similar to the services described in AIA Document B152™–2007. Unlike AIA Document B152™–2007, AIA Document B252–2007 is a scope of services document only and may not be used as a stand-alone owner-architect agreement. B252–2007 may be used in two ways: (1) incorporated into the owner-architect agreement as the architect's sole scope of services or in conjunction with other scope of services documents, or (2) attached to AIA Document G802™–2007, Amendment to the Professional Services Agreement, to create a modification to an existing owner-architect agreement. B252 was revised in 2007 to align, as applicable, with AIA Document B101™–2007.

B253–2007, Standard Form of Architect's Services: Furniture, Furnishings and Equipment Design

AIA Document B253™–2007 establishes duties and responsibilities where the architect provides design services for furniture, furnishings, and equipment (FF&E). The scope of services in AIA Document B253–2007 is substantially similar to the services described in AIA Document B153™–2007. Unlike AIA Document B153™–2007, AIA Document B253–2007 is a scope of services document only and may not be used as a stand-alone owner-architect agreement. B253–2007 may be used in two ways: (1)

incorporated into the owner-architect agreement as the architect's sole scope of services or in conjunction with other scope of services documents, or (2) attached to AIA Document G802™–2007, Amendment to the Professional Services Agreement, to create a modification to an existing owner-architect agreement. B253 was revised in 2007 to align, as applicable, with AIA Document B101™–2007.

B503–2007 (formerly B511–2001), Guide for Amendments to AIA Owner-Architect Agreements

AIA Document B503™–2007 is not an agreement, but is a guide containing model provisions for amending owner-architect agreements. Some provisions, such as a limitation of liability clause, further define or limit the scope of services and responsibilities. Other provisions introduce different approaches, such as fast-track construction. In all cases, these provisions are provided because they deal with circumstances that are not typically included in other AIA standard form owner-architect agreements. NOTE: B511–2001 expired in 2009.

B509–2010, Guide for Supplementary Conditions to AIA Document B109–2010 for use on Condominium Projects

AIA Document B509™–2010 is not an agreement, but a guide containing model provisions for modifying and supplementing AIA Document B109™–2010, Standard Form of Agreement Between Owner and Architect for a Multi-Family Residential or Mixed Use Residential Project. It provides model language with explanatory notes to assist users in adapting AIA Document B109–2010 for use on condominium projects. B109–2010, as a standard form document, cannot address all of the unique risks of condominium construction. AIA Document B509–2010 is provided to assist B109–2010 users either in modifying it, or developing a separate supplementary conditions document to attach to it.

B727–1988 (EXPIRED), Standard Form of Agreement Between Owner and Architect for Special Services

AIA Document B727™–1988 expired on April 30, 2012. AIA Document B727 provided only the terms and conditions of the agreement between the owner and architect, with the description of services inserted in the agreement by the parties or attached in an exhibit. Users of B727 who wish to use an agreement that only contains terms and conditions may use AIA Document B102™–2007, Standard Form of Agreement Between Owner and Architect without a Predefined Scope of Architect's Services. Like B727, AIA Document B102 is a standard form of agreement between owner and architect that provides agreement terms only. B102–2007 does not include a scope of architect's services, which must be inserted in Article 1 or attached as an exhibit to B102–2007. Users of B727 may also wish to consider using AIA Document B105™–2007, Standard Form of Agreement Between Owner and Architect for a Residential or Small Commercial Project. AIA Document B105 contains fewer terms and conditions than B102 and it contains an abbreviated scope of services for use in design and construction administration in small projects.

C101–1993 (formerly C801–1993), Joint Venture Agreement for Professional Services

AIA Document C101™–1993 is intended for use by two or more parties to provide for their mutual rights and obligations in forming a joint venture. It is intended that the joint venture, once established, will enter into an agreement with the owner to provide professional services. The parties may be all architects, all engineers, a combination of architects and engineers, or another combination of professionals. The document provides a choice between two methods of joint venture operation. The "division of compensation" method assumes that services provided and the compensation received will be divided among the parties in the proportions agreed to at the outset of the project. Each party's profitability is then dependent on individual performance of pre-assigned tasks and is not directly tied to that of the other parties. The "division of profit and loss" method is based on each party performing work and billing the joint venture at cost plus a nominal amount for overhead. The ultimate profit or loss of the joint venture is divided between or among the parties at completion of the project, based on their respective interests. NOTE: C801–1993 expired in 2009.

C102™–2015, Standard Form of Teaming Agreement Between Team Manager and Team Member for the Purpose of Responding to a Solicitation and Pursuing a Project

AIA Document C102™–2015 is intended to allow multiple or cross-disciplinary parties to form a team to provide services necessary to submit a proposal, in response to a solicitation, for a shared opportunity project. C102™–2015 is not limited to use within a single project delivery method and can be used for responses to requests for proposals, design competitions, design-build competitions or public/private partnerships. C102 provides that one party will serve as the team manager, and that the team manager will enter into separate teaming agreements with each of the team members. There could be one, or multiple, team members. Each would enter into a separate C102 agreement with the team manager. If the team is awarded the project, the team manager will contract directly with the owner for the project. Each team member has a separate agreement with the team manager for services or work to be performed on the project, the terms of which will have been negotiated in advance with an agreement for such services or work, and made a part of C102 as Exhibit A. When the team manager enters into an agreement with the owner for the project, C102 terminates and the agreement between the team manager and team member, attached as Exhibit A, becomes effective.

C401–2007 (formerly C141–1997), Standard Form of Agreement Between Architect and Consultant

AIA Document C401™–2007 is a standard form of agreement between the architect and the consultant providing services to the architect. AIA Document C401–2007 is suitable for use with all types of consultants, including consulting architects. This document may be used with a variety of compensation methods. C401–2007 assumes and incorporates by reference a preexisting owner-architect agreement known as the "prime agreement." AIA Documents B101™–2007, B103™–2007, B104™–2007, B105™–2007, and B152™–2007 are the documents most frequently used to establish the prime agreement. C401–2007 was modified in 2007 to be shorter and more flexible by "flowing down" the provisions of the prime agreement, except as specifically stated in C401. NOTE: C141–1997 expired in 2009.

C401–2007 SP, Standard Form of Agreement Between Architect and Consultant, for use on a Sustainable Project

AIA Document C401™–2007 SP, Standard Form of Agreement Between Architect and Consultant, for use on a Sustainable Project, is a standard form of agreement between the architect and the consultant providing services to the architect on a sustainable project. C401–2007 SP is based on AIA Document C401™–2007, Standard Form of Agreement Between Architect and Consultant, with modifications to coordinate its use with the other Sustainable Projects documents in the Conventional (A201) family of AIA Contract Documents. C401–2007 SP is suitable for use with all types of consultants, including consulting architects. This document may be used with a variety of compensation methods. C401–2007 SP assumes and incorporates by reference a preexisting owner-architect agreement known as the "prime agreement."

C421–2014, Standard Form of Master Agreement Between Architect and Consultant for Services provided under Multiple Service Orders

AIA Document C421™–2014 is a Master Agreement Between the Architect and Consultant. It is intended for use when the consultant's scope of services will subsequently be specified through the use of one or more Service Orders. C421 is suitable for use with all types of consultants, including consulting architects. C421–2014 provides only the common terms and conditions that will be applicable to each Service Order and may incorporate by reference a preexisting owner-architect agreement known as the Prime Agreement. Use of C421 plus a Service Order creates a contract, referred to as the Service Agreement, that includes both the terms and the scope of services. C421–2014 is coordinated for use with AIA Document C422™–2014, Service Order for use with Master Agreement Between Architect and Consultant. The Master Agreement plus Service Order contracting method allows multiple scopes of services to be issued quickly without the necessity to renegotiate the terms and conditions of the Service Agreements.

C422–2014, Service Order for use with Master Agreement Between Architect and Consultant

AIA Document C422™–2014 is a Service Order that provides the consultant's scope of services, and other terms pertinent to the specific Service Order. It is intended for use when the architect and consultant have entered into a Master Agreement setting forth the common terms and conditions applicable to all Service Orders. C422–2014 is not a stand-alone agreement and must be used in conjunction with a Master Agreement. Additionally, C422–2014 incorporates by reference a preexisting owner-architect agreement known as the Prime Agreement. C422–2014 is coordinated for use with AIA Document C421™–2014, Master Agreement Between Architect and Consultant for Services provided under Multiple Service Orders. This document may be used with a variety of compensation methods. Use of C422 plus a Master Agreement creates a contract, referred to as the Service Agreement, that includes both the terms and the scope of services. The Master Agreement plus Service Order contracting method allows multiple scopes of services to be issued quickly without the necessity to renegotiate the terms and conditions of the Service Agreements.

C727–1992, Standard Form of Agreement Between Architect and Consultant for Special Services

AIA Document C727™–1992 provides only the terms and conditions of the agreement between the architect and the consultant—the description of services is left entirely to the parties, and must be inserted in the agreement or attached in an exhibit. It is often used for planning, feasibility studies, postoccupancy studies, and other services that require specialized descriptions.

D503–2013, Guide for Sustainable Projects, including Commentary on the AIA Sustainable Projects Documents

AIA Document D503™–2013 is a guide that discusses the roles and responsibilities faced by owners, architects and contractors on sustainable design and construction projects. D503–2013 includes a discussion of environmental product ratings, certification systems and jurisdictional requirements that may be applicable to sustainable projects. D503 also contains an in depth, section-by-section commentary on AIA Sustainable Project documents A101™–2007 SP, A201™–2007 SP, A401™–2007 SP, B101™–2007 SP, and C401™–2007 SP and AIA Document B214™–2012, Architect's Services: LEED® Certification. D503–2013 includes a sample Sustainability Plan that readers can use for assistance when preparing a Sustainability Plan unique to their project.

CONSTRUCTION MANAGER AS ADVISER (CMA) FAMILY

Use of the Construction Manager as Adviser (CMa) family of AIA Contract Documents may be appropriate when the owner's project incorporates a fourth prime player—the construction manager—on the construction team (owner, architect, and contractor) to act as an independent advisor on construction management matters through the course of both design and construction. The Construction Manager as Adviser (CMa) approach enhances the level of expertise applied to managing a project from start to finish. In its purest form, this approach preserves the CMa's independent judgment, keeping that individual from being influenced by any monetary interest in the actual labor and materials incorporated in the construction work. Documents in the CMa family can be used on small to large public and private sector projects.

A132–2009 (formerly A101CMa–1992), Standard Form of Agreement Between Owner and Contractor, Construction Manager as Adviser Edition

AIA Document A132™–2009 is a standard form of agreement between owner and contractor for use on projects where the basis of payment is either a stipulated sum (fixed price) or cost of the work plus a fee, with or without a guaranteed maximum price. In addition to the contractor and the architect, a construction manager assists the owner in an advisory capacity during design and construction.

The document has been prepared for use with AIA Documents A232™–2009, General Conditions of the Contract for Construction, Construction Manager as Adviser Edition; B132™–2009, Standard Form of Agreement Between Owner and Architect, Construction Manager as Adviser Edition; and C132™–2009, Standard Form of Agreement Between Owner and Construction Manager as Adviser. This integrated set of documents is appropriate for use on projects where the construction manager only serves in the capacity of an advisor to the owner, rather than as constructor (the latter relationship being represented in AIA Documents A133™–2009 and A134™–2009). NOTE: A101CMa–1992 expired in 2010.

A132–2009 SP, Standard Form of Agreement Between Owner and Contractor, for use on a Sustainable Project, Construction Manager as Adviser Edition

AIA Document A132™–2009 SP is a standard form of agreement between owner and contractor for use on sustainable projects, where the basis of payment is either a stipulated sum (fixed price) or cost of the work plus a fee, with or without a guaranteed maximum price. In addition to the contractor and the architect, a construction manager assists the owner in an advisory capacity during design and construction. A132–2009 SP is based on AIA Document A132™–2009, Standard Form of Agreement Between Owner and Contractor, Construction Manager as Adviser Edition, with modifications that address the risks, responsibilities, and opportunities unique to projects involving substantial elements of sustainable design and construction (sustainable projects).

The document has been prepared for use with AIA Documents A232™–2009 SP, General Conditions of the Contract for Construction, for use on a Sustainable Project, Construction Manager as Adviser Edition; B132™–2009 SP, Standard Form of Agreement Between Owner and Architect, for use on a Sustainable Project, Construction Manager as Adviser Edition; and C132™–2009 SP, Standard Form of Agreement Between Owner and Construction Manager as Adviser, for use on a Sustainable Project. This integrated set of documents is appropriate for use on sustainable projects where the construction manager only serves in the capacity of an advisor to the owner, rather than as constructor (the latter relationship being represented in AIA Documents A133™–2009 SP and A134™–2009 SP).

A232–2009 (formerly A201CMa–1992), General Conditions of the Contract for Construction, Construction Manager as Adviser Edition

AIA Document A232™–2009 sets forth the rights, responsibilities, and relationships of the owner, contractor, construction manager, and architect. A232–2009 is adopted by reference in owner-architect, owner-contractor, and owner-construction manager agreements in the CMa family of documents. Under A232–2009, the construction manager serves as an independent advisor to the owner, who enters into a contract with a general contractor or multiple contracts with prime trade contractors. NOTE: A201CMa–1992 expired in 2010.

CAUTION: Do not use A232–2009 in combination with agreements where the construction manager takes on the role of constructor, such as in AIA Document A133™–2009 or A134™–2009.

A232–2009 SP, General Conditions of the Contract for Construction, for use on a Sustainable Project, Construction Manager as Adviser Edition

AIA Document A232™–2009 SP sets forth the rights, responsibilities, and relationships of the owner, contractor, construction manager, and architect on a sustainable project where the construction manager is an advisor. A232–2009 SP is adopted by reference in owner-architect, owner-contractor, and owner-construction manager agreements in the CMa family Sustainable Projects documents. Under A232–2009 SP, the construction manager serves as an independent advisor to the owner, who enters into a contract with a general contractor or multiple contracts with prime trade contractors. A232–2009 SP is based on AIA Document A232™–2009, General Conditions of the Contract for Construction, with modifications that address the risks, responsibilities, and opportunities unique to projects involving substantial elements of sustainable design and construction (sustainable projects).

CAUTION: Do not use A232–2009 SP in combination with Sustainable Project documents where the construction manager takes on the role of constructor, such as in AIA Document A133™–2009 SP or A134™–2009 SP.

A533–2009 (formerly A511CMa–1993), Guide for Supplementary Conditions, Construction Manager as Adviser Edition

Similar to AIA Document A503™–2007, AIA Document A533™–2009 is a guide for amending or supplementing the General Conditions document, AIA Document A232™–2009. AIA Documents A533–2009 and A232–2009 should only be employed on projects where the construction manager is serving in the capacity of advisor to the owner and not in situations where the construction manager is also the constructor (CMc document–based relationships). Like A503–2007, this document contains suggested language for supplementary conditions, along with notes on appropriate usage. NOTE: A511CMa–1993 expired in 2010.

B132–2009 (formerly B141CMa–1992), Standard Form of Agreement Between Owner and Architect, Construction Manager as Adviser Edition

AIA Document B132™–2009 is a standard form of agreement between owner and architect for use on building projects where construction management services are to be provided under a separate contract with the owner. It is coordinated with AIA Document C132™–2009, an owner-construction manager as advisor agreement, where the construction manager is an independent advisor to the owner throughout the course of the project. Both AIA Documents B132–2009 and C132–2009 are based on the premise that one or more separate construction contractors will also contract with the owner. The owner-contractor agreement is jointly administered by the architect and the construction manager under AIA Document A232™–2009, General Conditions of the Contract for Construction, Construction Manager as Adviser Edition. NOTE: B141CMa–1992 expired in 2010.

B132–2009 SP, Standard Form of Agreement Between Owner and Architect, for use on a Sustainable Project, Construction Manager as Adviser Edition

AIA Document B132™–2009 SP is a standard form of agreement between owner and architect for use on sustainable projects where construction management services are to be provided under a separate contract with the owner. B132–2009 SP is based on AIA Document B132™–2009, Standard Form of Agreement Between Owner and Architect, Construction Manager as Adviser Edition, with modifications that address the risks, responsibilities, and opportunities unique to projects involving substantial elements of sustainable design and construction (sustainable projects). It is coordinated with AIA Document C132™–2009 SP, an owner-construction manager as advisor agreement for use on sustainable projects, where the construction manager is an independent advisor to the owner throughout the course of the project. Both AIA Documents B132–2009 SP and C132–2009 SP are based on the premise that one or more separate construction contractors will also contract with the owner. The owner-contractor agreement is jointly administered by the architect and the construction manager under AIA Document A232™–2009 SP, General Conditions of the Contract for Construction, for use on a Sustainable Project, Construction Manager as Adviser Edition.

C132–2009 (formerly B801CMa–1992), Standard Form of Agreement Between Owner and Construction Manager as Adviser

AIA Document C132™–2009 provides the agreement between the owner and the construction manager, a single entity who is separate and independent from the architect and the contractor, and who acts solely as an advisor (CMa) to the owner throughout the course of the project. AIA Document C132–2009 is coordinated for use with AIA Document B132™–2009, Standard Form of Agreement Between Owner and Architect, Construction Manager as Adviser Edition.

Both C132–2009 and B132–2009 are based on the premise that there will be a separate construction contractor or multiple prime contractors whose contract(s) with the owner will be jointly administered by the architect and the construction manager under AIA Document A232™–2009. AIA Document C132–2009 is not coordinated with, and should not be used with, documents where the construction manager acts as the constructor for the project, such as in AIA Document A133™–2009 or A134™–2009. NOTE: B801CMa–1992 expired in 2010.

C132–2009 SP, Standard Form of Agreement Between Owner and Construction Manager as Adviser, for use on a Sustainable Project

AIA Document C132™–2009 SP provides the agreement between the owner and the construction manager, a single entity who is separate and independent from the architect and the contractor, and who acts solely as an advisor (CMa) to the owner throughout the course of a sustainable project. C132–2009 SP is coordinated for use with AIA Document B132™–2009 SP, Standard Form of Agreement Between Owner and Architect, for use on a Sustainable Project, Construction Manager as Adviser Edition.

C132–2009 SP is based on AIA Document C132™–2009, Standard Form of Agreement Between Owner and Construction Manager as Adviser, with modifications that address the risks, responsibilities, and opportunities unique to projects involving substantial elements of sustainable design and construction (sustainable projects). The Construction Manager as Adviser plays a critical role in assisting the owner and architect in establishing the Sustainable Objective and Sustainable Measures for the project.

Both C132–2009 SP and B132–2009 SP are based on the premise that there will be a separate construction contractor or multiple prime contractors whose contract(s) with the owner will be jointly administered by the architect and the construction manager under AIA Document A232™–2009 SP. C132–2009 SP is not coordinated with, and should not be used with, documents where the construction manager acts as the constructor for the project, such as AIA Documents A133™–2009 SP or A134™–2009 SP.

G701CMa–1992, Change Order, Construction Manager-Adviser Edition

AIA Document G701™CMa–1992 is for implementing changes in the work agreed to by the owner, contractor, construction manager advisor, and architect. Execution of a completed AIA Document G701™–2001 indicates agreement upon all the terms of the change, including any changes in the Contract Sum (or Guaranteed Maximum Price) and Contract Time. It provides space for the signatures of the owner, contractor, construction manager advisor, and architect, and for a complete description of the change. The major difference between AIA Documents G701CMa–1992 and G701–2001 is that the signature of the construction manager advisor, along with those of the owner, architect, and contractor, is required to validate the change order.

G704CMa–1992, Certificate of Substantial Completion, Construction Manager-Adviser Edition

AIA Document G704™CMa–1992 serves the same purpose as AIA Document G704™–2000, except that this document expands responsibility for certification of substantial completion to include both the architect and the construction manager.

G714CMa–1992, Construction Change Directive, Construction Manager-Adviser Edition

AIA Document G714™CMa–1992 serves the same purpose as AIA Document G714™–2007, except that this document expands responsibility for signing construction change directives to include both the architect and the construction manager.

G732–2009 (formerly G702CMa–1992), Application and Certificate for Payment, Construction Manager as Adviser Edition

AIA Document G732™–2009 serves the same purposes as AIA Document G702™–1992. The standard form AIA Document G703™–1992, Continuation Sheet, is appropriate for use with G732–2009. NOTE: G702CMa–1992 expired in 2010.

G736–2009 (formerly G722CMa–1992), Project Application and Project Certificate for Payment, Construction Manager as Adviser Edition

Use AIA Document G736™–2009 with AIA Document G737™–2009, Summary of Contractors' Applications for Payment. These forms are designed for a project where a construction manager is employed as an advisor to the owner, but not as a constructor, and where multiple contractors have separate, direct agreements with the owner.

Each contractor submits separate AIA Documents G732™–2009 and G703™–1992, payment application forms, to the construction manager-advisor, who collects and compiles them to complete G736–2009. AIA Document G737–2009 serves as a summary of the contractors' applications with totals being transferred to AIA Document G736–2009. The construction manager-advisor can then sign G736, have it notarized, and submit it along with the G737 to the architect. Both the architect and the construction manager must certify the payment amount. NOTE: G722CMa–1992 expired in 2010.

G737–2009 (formerly G723CMa–1992), Summary of Contractors' Applications for Payment, Construction Manager as Adviser Edition

Use AIA Document G736™–2009 with AIA Document G737™–2009, Summary of Contractors' Applications for Payment. These forms are designed for a project where a construction manager is employed as an advisor to the owner, but not as a constructor, and where multiple contractors have separate, direct agreements with the owner.

Each contractor submits separate AIA Documents G703™–1992 and G732™–2009, payment application forms, to the construction manager-advisor, who collects and compiles them to complete AIA Document G736–2009. AIA Document G737–2009 serves as a summary of the contractors' applications with totals being transferred to G736. The construction manager-advisor can then sign G736, have it notarized, and submit it along with the G737 to the architect. Both the architect and the construction manager must certify the payment amount. NOTE: G723CMa–1992 expired in 2010.

CONSTRUCTION MANAGER AS CONSTRUCTOR (CMC) FAMILY

Use of the Construction Manager as Constructor (CMc) family of AIA Contract Documents may be appropriate when the owner's project employs a construction manager who will complete the construction and also provide construction management services. Under the Construction Manager as Constructor (CMc) approach, the functions of contractor and construction manager are merged and assigned to one entity that may or may not give a guaranteed maximum price (GMP), but which typically assumes control over the construction work by direct contracts with the subcontractors. Documents in the CMc family can be used on small to large private sector projects.

A133–2009 (formerly A121CMc–2003), Standard Form of Agreement Between Owner and Construction Manager as Constructor where the basis of payment is the Cost of the Work Plus a Fee with a Guaranteed Maximum Price

AIA Document A133™–2009 is intended for use on projects where a construction manager, in addition to serving as advisor to the owner, assumes financial responsibility for construction of the project. The construction manager provides the owner with a guaranteed maximum price proposal, which the owner may accept, reject, or negotiate.

Upon the owner's acceptance of the proposal by execution of an amendment, the construction manager becomes contractually bound to provide labor and materials for the project and to complete construction at or below the guaranteed maximum price. The document divides the construction manager's services into two phases: the preconstruction phase and the construction phase, portions of which may proceed concurrently in order to fast-track the process. AIA Document A133–2009 is coordinated for use with AIA Documents A201™–2007, General Conditions of the Contract for Construction, and B103™–2007, Standard Form of Agreement Between Owner and Architect for a Large or Complex Project. NOTE: A121CMc–2003 expired in 2010.

CAUTION: To avoid confusion and ambiguity, do not use this construction management document with any other AIA construction management document.

A133–2009 SP, Standard Form of Agreement Between Owner and Construction Manager as Constructor where the basis of payment is the Cost of the Work Plus a Fee with a Guaranteed Maximum Price, for use on a Sustainable Project

AIA Document A133™–2009 SP is based on AIA Document A133™–2009, Standard Form of Agreement Between Owner and Construction Manager as Constructor where the basis of payment is the cost of the work plus a fee with a guaranteed maximum price, with modifications that address the risks, responsibilities, and opportunities unique to projects involving substantial elements of sustainable design and construction (sustainable projects).

A133–2009 SP is intended for use on sustainable projects where a construction manager, in addition to serving as advisor to the owner, assumes financial responsibility for construction of the project. The construction manager provides the owner with a guaranteed maximum price proposal, which the owner may accept, reject, or negotiate. Upon the owner's acceptance of the proposal by execution of an amendment, the construction manager becomes contractually bound to provide labor and materials for the project and to complete construction at or below the guaranteed maximum price. The document divides the construction manager's services into two phases: the preconstruction phase and the construction phase, portions of which may proceed concurrently in order to fast track the process. AIA Document A133–2009 SP is coordinated for use with AIA Documents A201™–2007 SP, General Conditions of the Contract for Construction, for use on a Sustainable Project, and B103™–2007 SP, Standard Form of Agreement Between Owner and Architect for a Large or Complex Sustainable Project.

CAUTION: To avoid confusion and ambiguity, do not use this construction management document with any other AIA construction management document.

A134–2009 (formerly A131CMc–2003), Standard Form of Agreement Between Owner and Construction Manager as Constructor where the basis of payment is the Cost of the Work Plus a Fee without a Guaranteed Maximum Price

Similar to AIA Document A133™–2009, AIA Document A134™–2009 is intended for use when the owner seeks a construction manager who will take on responsibility for providing the means and methods of construction. However, in AIA Document A134–2009 the construction manager does not provide a guaranteed maximum price (GMP). A134–2009 employs the cost-plus-a-fee method, wherein the owner can monitor cost through periodic review of a control estimate that is revised as the project proceeds.

The agreement divides the construction manager's services into two phases: the preconstruction phase and the construction phase, portions of which may proceed concurrently in order to fast-track the process. A134–2009 is coordinated for use with AIA Documents A201™–2007, General Conditions of the Contract for Construction, and B103™–2007, Standard Form of Agreement Between Owner and Architect for a Large or Complex Project. NOTE: A131CMc–2003 expired in 2010.

CAUTION: To avoid confusion and ambiguity, do not use this construction management document with any other AIA construction management document.

A134–2009 SP, Standard Form of Agreement Between Owner and Construction Manager as Constructor where the basis of payment is the Cost of the Work Plus a Fee without a Guaranteed Maximum Price, for use on a Sustainable Project

AIA Document A134™–2009 SP is based on AIA Document A134™–2009, Standard Form of Agreement Between Owner and Construction Manager as Constructor where the basis of payment is the cost of the work plus a fee without a guaranteed maximum price, with modifications that address the risks, responsibilities, and opportunities unique to projects involving substantial elements of sustainable design and construction (sustainable projects).

Similar to AIA Document A133™–2009 SP, A134–2009 SP is intended for use when the owner seeks a construction manager who will take on responsibility for providing the means and methods of construction of a sustainable project. However, in AIA Document A134–2009 SP the construction manager does not provide a guaranteed maximum price (GMP). A134–2009 SP employs the cost-plus-a-fee method, wherein the owner can monitor cost through periodic review of a control estimate that is revised as the project proceeds.

A134–2009 SP is based on AIA Document A134™–2009, Standard Form of Agreement Between Owner and Construction Manager as Constructor where the basis of payment is the cost of the work plus a fee without a guaranteed maximum price, with modifications that address the risks, responsibilities, and opportunities unique to projects involving substantial elements of sustainable design and construction (sustainable projects).

The agreement divides the construction manager's services into two phases: the preconstruction phase and the construction phase, portions of which may proceed concurrently in order to fast-track the process. A134–2009 SP is coordinated for use with AIA Documents A201™–2007 SP, General Conditions of the Contract for Construction, for use on a Sustainable Project, and B103™–2007 SP, Standard Form of Agreement Between Owner and Architect for a Large or Complex Sustainable Project.

CAUTION: To avoid confusion and ambiguity, do not use this construction management document with any other AIA construction management document.

B133–2014, Standard Form of Agreement Between Owner and Architect, Construction Manager as Constructor Edition

AIA Document B133™–2014 is a standard form of agreement between owner and architect intended for use on projects where an owner employs a construction manager to act as an advisor during the preconstruction phase. At a time to be mutually agreed upon by the owner and the construction manager, and in consultation with the architect, the construction manager prepares a guaranteed maximum price proposal or control estimate, as applicable, for the owner's review and acceptance. Thereafter, the construction manager constructs the project on a cost of the work plus a fee basis, either with or without a guaranteed maximum price, and the architect provides contract administration services during the construction phase. B133–2014 assumes that the construction manager will provide cost estimates and schedules for the project. B133–2014 is intended to be used with AIA Document A201™–2007, General Conditions of the Contract for Construction, which it incorporates by reference and either A133–2009, Standard Form of Agreement Between Owner and Construction Manager as Constructor where the basis of payment is the Cost of the Work Plus a Fee with a Guaranteed Maximum Price or A134–2009, Standard Form of Agreement Between Owner and Construction Manager as Constructor where the basis of payment is the Cost of the Work Plus a Fee without a Guaranteed Maximum Price.

DESIGN-BUILD FAMILY

Use of the Design-Build family of AIA Contract Documents is appropriate when the project delivery method is design-build. In design-build project delivery, the owner enters into a contract with a design-builder who is obligated to design and construct the project. The design-builder then enters into contracts with architects and construction contractors, as needed. Design-build documents can be used on small to large projects.

A141–2004, Agreement Between Owner and Design-Builder

AIA Document A141™–2004 replaces AIA Document A191™–1996 and consists of the agreement and three exhibits: Exhibit A, Terms and Conditions; Exhibit B, Determination of the Cost of the Work; and Exhibit C, Insurance and Bonds. Exhibit B is not applicable if the parties select to use a stipulated sum. AIA Document A141–2004 obligates the design-builder to execute fully the work required by the design-build documents, which include A141 with its attached exhibits, the project criteria and the design-builder's proposal, including any revisions to those documents accepted by the owner, supplementary and other conditions, addenda and modifications. The Agreement requires the parties to select the payment type from three choices: (1) stipulated sum, (2) cost of the work plus design-builder's fee, and (3) cost of the work plus design-builder's fee with a guaranteed maximum price. A141–2004 with its attached exhibits forms the nucleus of the design-build contract. Because A141 includes its own terms and conditions, it does not use AIA Document A201™.

A141–2014, Agreement Between Owner and Design-Builder

AIA Document A141™–2014 replaces AIA Document A141–2004, Standard Form of Agreement Between Owner and Design-Builder, and consists of the Agreement portion and Exhibit A, a Design-Build Amendment that is executed when the owner and design-builder have agreed on the contract sum. Additionally, A141–2014 includes two exhibits, Exhibit B, Insurance and Bonds, and Exhibit C, Sustainable Projects. AIA Document A141–2014 forms the nucleus of the contract for design-build between the owner and design-builder.

Design-build is a process in which the owner contracts directly with one entity to provide both the design and construction of the project. The design-builder may be a design-build entity, an architect, construction contractor, real estate developer, or any person or entity legally permitted to do business as a design-builder in the jurisdiction where the project is located. The design-builder's organization may take a variety of legal forms, such as a sole proprietorship, a partnership, a joint venture, or a corporation. An architect or architectural firm choosing to function as a design-builder may directly contract to perform design-build services or, alternatively, may form a separate corporate entity or joint venture for design-build.

In A141–2014, the owner provides a set of owner's criteria establishing the owner's requirements for the project. Thereafter, the design-builder will review the owner's criteria, develop a preliminary design, and then provide a proposal to the owner regarding the contract sum. Upon mutual agreement, the owner and design-builder will execute the Design-Build Amendment to establish the contract sum and document the information upon which the contract sum is based. The Design-Build Amendment also includes the determination for the cost of the work, if the contract sum is based on a cost of the work with or without a guaranteed maximum price.

A142–2004, Agreement Between Design-Builder and Contractor

AIA Document A142™–2004 replaces AIA Document A491™–1996 and consists of the agreement and five exhibits: Exhibit A, Terms and Conditions; Exhibit B, Preconstruction Services; Exhibit C, Contractor's Scope of Work; Exhibit D, Determination of the Cost of the Work; and Exhibit E, Insurance and Bonds. Unlike AIA Document B491–1996, AIA Document A142–2004 does not rely on AIA Document A201™ for its general conditions of the contract. A142–2004 contains its own terms and conditions.

A142–2004 obligates the contractor to perform the work in accordance with the contract documents, which include A142 with its attached exhibits, supplementary and other conditions, drawings, specifications, addenda, and modifications. Like AIA Document A141™–2004, AIA Document A142–2004 requires the parties to select the payment type from three choices: (1) Stipulated Sum, (2) Cost of the Work Plus Design-Builder's Fee, and (3) Cost of the Work Plus Design-Builder's Fee with a Guaranteed Maximum Price.

A142–2014, Agreement Between Design-Builder and Contractor

AIA Document A142™–2014 replaces AIA Document A141™–2004, Standard Form of Agreement Between Design-Builder and Contractor, and consists of the Agreement portion and four exhibits: Exhibit A, Terms and Conditions; Exhibit B, Insurance and Bonds; Exhibit C, Preconstruction Services; and Exhibit D, Determination of the Cost of the Work.

A142–2014 obligates the contractor to perform the work in accordance with the contract documents, which include A142 with its attached exhibits, supplementary and other conditions, drawings, specifications, addenda, and modifications. Like AIA Document A141™–2014, AIA Document A142–2014 requires the parties to select the payment type from three choices: (1) stipulated sum, (2) cost of the work plus design-builder's fee, and (3) cost of the work plus design-builder's fee with a guaranteed maximum price.

A145–2015, Standard Form of Agreement Between Owner and Design-Builder for a One or Two Family Residential Project

AIA Document A145™–2015 is intended to be used for a one- or two-family residential project and consists of the Agreement portion and Exhibit A, a Design-Build Amendment that is executed when the owner and design-builder have agreed on the contract sum. A145–2015 is a streamlined document developed to meet the needs of residential owners and design-builders. For commercial or multifamily design-build projects, AIA Document A141™–2014, Agreement Between Owner and Design-Builder, is more appropriate.

Design-build is a project delivery method in which the owner contracts directly with one entity to provide both the design and construction of the project. It is important to recognize that a design-builder assumes responsibility and liability for both the design services and construction work. Prior to entering into this agreement, any person or entity that wishes to act as the design-builder should consult with its legal counsel and insurance advisors. Some states may restrict or prohibit design-build practices under statutes that regulate architectural registration, contractor licensing, or incorporation of professionals. Additionally, federal, state, or local law may impose specific requirements on contracts for residential construction. The requirements for single-family and two-family projects may be different. The owner should consult local authorities or an attorney to verify requirements applicable to this agreement.

Although A145 shares some similarities with other documents in the AIA's Design-Build family, A145 is not coordinated for use with those documents, and should *not* be used in tandem with agreements in the Design-Build family without careful side-by-side comparison of contents.

A441–2008, Standard Form of Agreement Between Contractor and Subcontractor for a Design-Build Project

AIA Document A441™–2008 is a fixed-price agreement that establishes the contractual relationship between the contractor and subcontractor in a design-build project. AIA Document A441–2008 incorporates by reference the terms and conditions of AIA Document A142™–2004, Standard Form of Agreement Between Design-Builder and Contractor, and was written to ensure consistency with the AIA 2004 Design-Build family of documents. Because subcontractors are often required to provide professional services on a design-build project, A441 provides for that possibility.

A441–2014, Standard Form of Agreement Between Contractor and Subcontractor for a Design-Build Project

AIA Document A441™–2014 establishes the contractual relationship between the contractor and subcontractor in a design-build project. AIA Document A441–2014 incorporates by reference the terms and conditions of AIA Document A142™–2014,

Standard Form of Agreement Between Design-Builder and Contractor, and was written to ensure consistency with the AIA 2014 Design-Build family of documents. Because subcontractors are often required to provide professional services on a design-build project, A441–2014 provides for that possibility.

B142–2004, Agreement Between Owner and Consultant where the Owner contemplates using the design-build method of project delivery

AIA Document B142™–2004 provides a standard form for the up-front services an owner may require when considering design-build delivery. The consultant, who may or may not be an architect or other design professional, may perform a wide ranging array of services for the owner, including programming and planning, budgeting and cost estimating, project criteria development services, and many others, commencing with initial data gathering and continuing through to postoccupancy. AIA Document B142–2004 consists of the agreement portion and two exhibits, Exhibit A, Initial Information, and Exhibit B, Standard Form of Consultant's Services. Exhibit B provides a menu of briefly described services that the parties can select and augment to suit the needs of the project.

B143–2004, Standard Form of Agreement Between Design-Builder and Architect

AIA Document B143™–2004 replaces AIA Document B901™–1996 and establishes the contractual relationship between the design-builder and its architect. AIA Document B143–2004 consists of the Agreement, Exhibit A, Initial Information, and Exhibit B, Standard Form of Architect's Services. Exhibit B provides a menu of briefly described services that the parties can select and augment to suit the needs of the project.

B143–2014, Standard Form of Agreement Between Design-Builder and Architect

AIA Document B143™–2014 replaces B143–2004, Standard Form of Agreement Between Design-Builder and Architect. B143–2014 establishes the contractual arrangement between the design-builder and the architect. B143 does not provide a fixed scope of architect's services, but instead includes an extensive menu of services from which the owner and architect may select.

AIA Document B143 can be used for a number of different contractual scenarios that may arise on a design-build project. If the design-build entity lacks the internal capacity to provide architectural services, or is required to separately contract for architectural services by virtue of local license regulations or other legal requirements, the design-build entity can use B143 to enter into an agreement with an architect to perform all of the architectural services on the project. B143 can also be used, however, where the design-builder directly performs some of the architectural services under its agreement with the owner. In this instance, B143 can be used to contract with additional architects that will provide portions of the architectural services. For example, the design-build entity may retain an architect to only provide a preliminary design, while the design-builder will use either a separate architect or its own forces to develop the construction documents and perform contract administration services.

C141–2014 (formerly B142–2004), Agreement Between Owner and Consultant for a Design-Build Project

AIA Document C141™–2014, provides a standard form for the up-front services an owner may require when considering design-build delivery. The consultant, who may or may not be an architect or other design professional, may perform a wide ranging array of services for the owner, including programming and planning, budgeting and cost estimating, project criteria development services, development of bridging documents, and services in connection with construction of the project. AIA Document C141–2014 consists of the Agreement and Exhibit A, Consultant's Services. Exhibit A provides a menu of briefly described services that the parties can select and augment to suit the needs of the project. NOTE: AIA Document B142–2004 expired on December 31, 2015.

C441–2008, Standard Form of Agreement Between Architect and Consultant for a Design-Build Project

AIA Document C441™–2008 establishes the contractual relationship between the architect and a consultant providing services to the architect on a design-build project. AIA Document C441–2008 is suitable for use with all types of consultants, including consulting architects and may be used with a variety of compensation methods. C441 assumes and incorporates by reference a preexisting prime agreement between design-builder and architect. C441–2008 was written to ensure consistency with AIA Document B143™–2004, Standard Form of Agreement Between Design-Builder and Architect, and with other documents in the AIA 2004 Design-Build family of documents.

C441–2014, Standard Form of Agreement Between Architect and Consultant for a Design-Build Project

AIA Document C441™–2014 establishes the contractual relationship between the architect and a consultant providing services to the architect on a design-build project. AIA Document C441–2014 is suitable for use with all types of consultants, including consulting architects and may be used with a variety of compensation methods. C441 assumes and incorporates by reference a preexisting prime agreement between the design-builder and architect. C441–2014 was written to ensure consistency with AIA Document B143™–2014, Standard Form of Agreement Between Design-Builder and Architect, and with other documents in the AIA 2014 Design-Build family of documents.

G704DB–2004, Acknowledgement of Substantial Completion of a Design-Build Project

Because of the nature of design-build contracting, the project owner assumes many of the construction contract administration duties performed by the architect in a traditional project. Because there is not an architect to certify substantial completion, AIA Document G704™DB–2004 requires the owner to inspect the project to determine whether the work is substantially complete in accordance with the design-build documents and to acknowledge the date when it occurs. AIA Document G704DB–2004 is a variation of AIA Document G704™–2000 and provides a standard form for the owner to acknowledge the date of substantial completion.

G742–2015, Application and Certificate for Payment for a Design-Build Project

AIA Documents G742™–2015, Application and Certificate for Payment for a Design-Build Project, and G743™–2015, Continuation Sheet for a Design-Build Project, provide convenient and complete forms on which the design-builder can apply for payment and the owner can certify the amount due. The forms require the design-builder to show the status of the contract sum to date, including the total dollar amount of the work completed and stored to date, the amount of retainage (if any), the total of previous payments, a summary of change orders, and the amount of current payment requested. AIA Document G743–2015 breaks the contract sum into portions of the work in accordance with a schedule of values prepared by the design-builder as required by Section 9.2 of AIA Document A141–2014. NOTE: The AIA does not publish a standard schedule of values form.

AIA Document G742–2015 serves as both the design-builder's application and the owner's certification of the amount due. Its use can expedite payment and reduce the possibility of error. The form also allows the owner to certify an amount different than the amount applied for, with explanation provided by the owner.

G743–2015, Continuation Sheet for a Design-Build Project

AIA Documents G742™–2015, Application and Certificate for Payment for a Design-Build Project, and G743™–2015, Continuation Sheet for a Design-Build Project, provide convenient and complete forms on which the design-builder can apply for payment and the owner can certify the amount due. The forms require the design-builder to show the status of the contract sum to date, including the total dollar amount of the work completed and stored to date, the amount of retainage (if any), the total of previous payments, a summary of change orders, and the amount of current payment requested. AIA Document G743–2015 breaks the contract sum into portions of the work in accordance with a schedule of values prepared by the design-builder as required by Section 9.2 of AIA Document A141–2014. NOTE: The AIA does not publish a standard schedule of values form.

G744–2014, Certificate of Substantial Completion for a Design-Build Project

Because of the nature of design-build contracting, the project owner assumes many of the construction contract administration duties performed by the architect in a traditional project. Because there is not an architect to certify substantial completion, AIA Document G744–2014 requires the owner to inspect the project to determine whether the work is substantially complete in accordance with the design-build documents and to identify the date when it occurs. AIA Document G744–2014 is a variation of AIA Document G704™–2000 and provides a standard form for the owner to certify the date of substantial completion.

INTEGRATED PROJECT DELIVERY FAMILY

Integrated project delivery (IPD) is a collaborative project delivery approach that utilizes the talents and insights of all project participants through all phases of design and construction. The AIA provides agreements for three levels of integrated project delivery. *Transitional Forms* are modeled after existing construction manager agreements and offer a comfortable first step into integrated project delivery. The *Multi-Party Agreement* is a single agreement that the parties can use to design and construct a project using integrated project delivery. The *Single Purpose Entity (SPE)* creates a limited liability company for the purpose of planning, designing, and constructing the project. The SPE allows for complete sharing of risk and reward in a fully integrated collaborative process. AIA documents for IPD can be used on large private sector commercial projects.

A195–2008, Standard Form of Agreement Between Owner and Contractor for Integrated Project Delivery

AIA Document A195™–2008 is a standard form of agreement between owner and contractor for a project that utilizes integrated project delivery. AIA Document A195–2008 primarily provides only the business terms and conditions unique to the agreement between the owner and contractor, such as compensation details and licensing of instruments of service. A195 does not include the specific scope of the contractor's work; rather, it incorporates by reference AIA Document A295™–2008, General Conditions of the Contract for Integrated Project Delivery, which sets forth the contractor's duties and obligations for each of the six phases of the project, along with the duties and obligations of the owner and architect. Under A195–2008, the contractor provides a guaranteed maximum price. For that purpose, the agreement includes a guaranteed maximum price amendment as Exhibit A.

A295–2008, General Conditions of the Contract for Integrated Project Delivery

AIA Document A295™–2008, provides the terms and conditions for AIA Documents A195™–2008 Standard Form of Agreement Between Owner and Contractor for Integrated Project Delivery, and B195™–2008, Standard Form of Agreement Between Owner and Architect for Integrated Project Delivery, both of which incorporate AIA Document A295–2008 by reference. Those agreements provide primarily only business terms and rely upon A295–2008 for the architect's services, the contractor's preconstruction services, and the conditions of construction. A295 not only establishes the duties of the owner, architect, and contractor, but also sets forth in detail how they will work together through each phase of the project: conceptualization, criteria design, detailed design, implementation documents, construction, and closeout. A295 requires that the parties use building information modeling.

B195–2008, Standard Form of Agreement Between Owner and Architect for Integrated Project Delivery

AIA Document B195™–2008 is a standard form of agreement between owner and architect for a project that uses integrated project delivery. AIA Document B195–2008 primarily provides only the business terms unique to the agreement between the owner and architect, such as compensation details and licensing of instruments of service. B195 does not include the specific scope of the architect's services; rather, it incorporates by reference AIA Document A295™–2008, General Conditions of the Contract for Integrated Project Delivery, which sets forth the architect's duties and scope of services for each of the six phases of the project, along with the duties and obligations of the owner and contractor.

C191–2009, Standard Form Multi-Party Agreement for Integrated Project Delivery

AIA Document C191™–2009 is a standard form multiparty agreement through which the owner, architect, contractor, and perhaps other key project participants execute a single agreement for the design, construction, and commissioning of a project. AIA Document C191–2009 provides the framework for a collaborative environment in which the parties operate in furtherance of cost and performance goals that the parties jointly establish. The non-owner parties are compensated on a cost-of-the-work basis. The compensation model is also goal-oriented, and provides incentives for collaboration in design and construction of the project. Primary management of the project is the responsibility of the project management team, comprised of one representative from each of the parties. the project executive team, also comprised of one representative from each of the parties, provides a second level of project oversight and issue resolution. The conflict resolution process is intended to foster quick and effective resolution of problems as they arise. This collaborative process has the potential to result in a high-quality project for the owner, and substantial monetary and intangible rewards for the other parties.

C195–2008, Standard Form Single Purpose Entity Agreement for Integrated Project Delivery

AIA Document C195™–2008 is a standard form single purpose entity (SPE) agreement through which the owner, architect, construction manager, and perhaps other key project participants, each become members of a limited liability company. The sole purpose of the company is to design and construct a project using the principles of integrated project delivery established in Integrated Project Delivery: A Guide. AIA Document C195–2008 provides the framework for a collaborative environment in which the company operates in furtherance of cost and performance goals that the members jointly establish. To obtain project funding, the company enters into a separate agreement with the owner. To design and construct the project, the company enters into separate agreements with the architect, construction manager, other non-owner members, and with non-member consultants and contractors. The compensation model in the non-owner member agreements is goal-oriented and provides incentives for collaboration in design and construction of the project, and for the quick and effective resolution of problems as they arise. This highly collaborative process has the potential to result in a high-quality project for the owner, and substantial monetary and intangible rewards for the other members.

C196–2008, Standard Form of Agreement Between Single Purpose Entity and Owner for Integrated Project Delivery

AIA Document C196™–2008 is a standard form of agreement between a single purpose entity ("the SPE") and a project owner, called the owner member. AIA Document C196–2008 is intended for use on a project where the project participants have formed the SPE using AIA Document C195™–2008, Standard Form Single Purpose Entity Agreement for Integrated Project Delivery. AIA Document is coordinated with AIA Document C195–2008 in order to implement the principles of integrated project delivery, including the accomplishment of mutually agreed goals.

C196 provides the terms under which the owner member will fund the SPE in exchange for the design and construction of the project. The SPE provides for the design and construction of the project through separate agreements with other members, including an architect and construction manager, using AIA Document C197™–2008, Standard Form of Agreement Between Single Purpose Entity and Non-Owner Member for Integrated Project Delivery. The SPE may also enter into agreements with non-member design consultants, specialty trade contractors, vendors, and suppliers.

C197–2008, Standard Form of Agreement Between Single Purpose Entity and Non-Owner Member for Integrated Project Delivery

AIA Document C197™–2008 is a standard form of agreement between a single purpose entity ("the SPE") and members of the SPE that do not own the project, called non-owner members. AIA Document C197–2008 is intended for use on a project where the parties have formed the SPE using AIA Document C195™–2008, Standard Form Single Purpose Entity Agreement for Integrated Project Delivery. C197–2008 is coordinated with C195–2008 in order to implement the principles of integrated project delivery, including the accomplishment of mutually agreed goals. All members of the SPE, other than the project owner, will execute C197–2008.

AIA Document C197–2008 provides the terms under which the non-owner members provide services to the SPE to complete the design and construction of the project. The specific services the non-owner members are required to perform are set forth in the Integrated Scope of Services Matrix, which is part of the C195–2008 Target Cost Amendment and is incorporated into the executed C197–2008. In exchange for the non-owner members' services, the non-owner members are paid the direct and indirect costs they incur in providing services. Additionally, C197 allows for the non-owner members to receive profit through incentive compensation and goal achievement compensation.

C198–2010, Standard Form of Agreement Between Single Purpose Entity and Consultant for Integrated Project Delivery

AIA Document C198™–2010 is a standard form of agreement between a single purpose entity ("the SPE") and a consultant. AIA Document C198–2010 is intended for use on a project where the parties have formed the SPE using AIA Document C195™–2008, Standard Form Single Purpose Entity Agreement for Integrated Project Delivery. C198–2010 is coordinated with C195–2008 in order to implement the principles of integrated project delivery. The specific services the consultant is required to perform are set forth within the document as well as the Integrated Scope of Services Matrix, which is part of the C195–2008 Target Cost Amendment. In addition to traditional compensation for services, C198–2010 allows for the consultant to receive additional profit through incentive compensation and goal achievement compensation.

C199–2010, Standard Form of Agreement Between Single Purpose Entity and Contractor for Integrated Project Delivery

AIA Document C199™–2010 is a standard form of agreement between a single purpose entity ("the SPE") and a contractor. AIA Document C199–2010 is intended for use on a project where the parties have formed the SPE using AIA Document C195™–2008, Standard Form Single Purpose Entity Agreement for Integrated Project Delivery. C199–2010 is intended to be a flexible document. C199 can be used for a contractor that only provides construction services, or it can also be used for a contractor that will provide both pre-construction and construction services. C199 is not intended for use in competitive bidding and relies upon an agreed to contract sum, which can be either a stipulated sum (fixed price) or cost of the work plus a fee, with a guaranteed maximum price. In addition to compensation for the contract sum, C199 allows for the contractor to receive additional profit through incentive compensation and goal achievement compensation.

Use of the Interiors family of AIA Contract Documents is appropriate for furniture, furnishings and equipment (FF&E) procurement services and for FF&E procurement combined with architectural interior design and construction services. The Interiors documents procure FF&E under a contract separate from design services, preserving the architect's independence from any monetary interest in the sale of those goods. AIA Document B152™ may be used as the owner-architect agreement for the design of both FF&E and architectural interiors. AIA Document B153™ is not suitable for construction work, such as major tenant improvements, and is used for design services related solely to FF&E. AIA documents in the Interiors family can be used on small to large tenant projects.

A151–2007 (formerly A175ID–2003), Standard Form of Agreement Between Owner and Vendor for Furniture, Furnishings and Equipment where the basis of payment is a Stipulated Sum

AIA Document A151™–2007 is intended for use as the contract between owner and vendor for furniture, furnishings and equipment (FF&E) where the basis of payment is a stipulated sum (fixed price) agreed to at the time of contracting. AIA Document A151–2007 adopts by reference and is intended for use with AIA Document A251™–2007, General Conditions of the Contract for Furniture, Furnishings and Equipment. It may be used in any arrangement between the owner and the contractor where the cost of FF&E has been determined in advance, either through bidding or negotiation. NOTE: A175ID–2003 expired in 2009.

A251–2007 (formerly A275ID–2003), General Conditions of the Contract for Furniture, Furnishings and Equipment

AIA Document A251™–2007 provides general conditions for the AIA Document A151™–2007, Standard Form Agreement between Owner and Vendor for Furniture, Furnishings and Equipment where the basis of payment is a Stipulated Sum. AIA Document A251–2007 sets forth the duties of the owner, architect and vendor, just as AIA Document A201™–2007, General Conditions of the Contract for Construction, does for building construction projects. Because the Uniform Commercial Code (UCC) governs the sale of goods and has been adopted in nearly every jurisdiction, A251–2007 recognizes the commercial standards set forth in Article 2 of the UCC, and uses certain standard UCC terms and definitions. A251 was renumbered in 2007 and was modified, as applicable, to coordinate with AIA Document A201–2007. NOTE: A275ID–2003 expired in 2009.

A751–2007 (formerly A775ID–2003), Invitation and Instructions for Quotation for Furniture, Furnishings and Equipment

AIA Document A751™–2007 provides (1) the Invitation for Quotation for Furniture, Furnishings and Equipment (FF&E) and (2) Instructions for Quotation for Furniture, Furnishings and Equipment. These two documents define the owner's requirements for a vendor to provide a complete quotation for the work. The purchase of FF&E is governed by the Uniform Commercial Code (UCC), and AIA Document A751–2007 was developed to coordinate with the provisions of the UCC. NOTE: A775ID–2003 expired in 2009.

B152–2007 (formerly B171ID–2003), Standard Form of Agreement Between Owner and Architect for Architectural Interior Design Services

AIA Document B152™–2007 is a standard form of agreement between the owner and architect for design services related to furniture, furnishings, and equipment (FF&E) as well as to architectural interior design. AIA Document B152–2007 divides the architect's services into eight phases: programming, pre-lease analysis and feasibility, schematic design, design development, contract documents, bidding and quotation, construction contract administration, and FF&E contract administration. B152 was renumbered in 2007 and modified to align, as applicable, with AIA Documents

B101™–2007 and A201™–2007. AIA Document B152–2007 is intended for use with AIA Documents A251™–2007, General Conditions of the Contract for Furniture, Furnishings and Equipment, and A201™–2007, General Conditions of the Contract for Construction, both of which it incorporates by reference. NOTE: B171ID–2003 expired in 2009.

B153–2007 (formerly B175ID–2003), Standard Form of Agreement Between Owner and Architect for Furniture, Furnishings and Equipment Design Services

AIA Document B153™–2007 is a standard form of agreement between the owner and architect for design services related solely to furniture, furnishings and equipment (FF&E). AIA Document B153–2007 divides the architect's services into six phases: programming, schematic design, design development, contract documents, quotation, and FF&E contract administration. B153 was renumbered in 2007 and modified to align, as applicable, with AIA Documents B101™–2007. AIA Document B153–2007 is intended for use with AIA Document A251™–2007, General Conditions of the Contract for Furniture, Furnishings and Equipment, which it incorporates by reference. NOTE: B175ID–2003 expired in 2009.

INTERNATIONAL FAMILY

The International family of AIA Contract Documents is for U.S. architects working on projects located in foreign countries. Because U.S. architects usually are not licensed in the foreign country where a project is located, these agreements identify the U.S. architect as a consultant, rather than an architect. AIA documents in the International family can be used on small to large projects.

B161–2002 (formerly B611INT–2002), Standard Form of Agreement Between Client and Consultant for use where the Project is located outside the United States

AIA Document B161™–2002 is designed to assist U.S. architects involved in projects based in foreign countries, where the U.S. architect is hired on a consulting basis for design services and the owner will retain a local architect in the foreign country. The document is intended to clarify the assumptions, roles, responsibilities, and obligations of the parties; to provide a clear, narrative description of services; and to facilitate, strengthen, and maintain the working and contractual relationship between the parties. Because of foreign practices, the term "owner" has been replaced with "client" throughout the document. Also, since it is assumed that the U.S. architect is not licensed to practice architecture in the foreign country where the project is located, the term "consultant" is used throughout the document to refer to the U.S. architect. NOTE: B611INT–2002 expired in 2009.

B162–2002 (formerly B621INT–2002), Abbreviated Standard Form of Agreement Between Client and Consultant for use where the Project is located outside the United States

AIA Document B162™–2002 is an abbreviated version of AIA Document B161™–2002, Standard Form of Agreement between Client and Consultant. The document is designed to assist U.S. architects involved in projects based in foreign countries where the U.S. architect is hired on a consulting basis for design services and a local architect will be retained. The document is intended to clarify the assumptions, roles, responsibilities, and obligations of the parties; to provide a clear, narrative description of services; and to facilitate, strengthen, and maintain the working and contractual relationship between the parties. Because of foreign practices, the term "owner" has been replaced with "client" throughout the document. Also, since it is assumed that the U.S. architect is not licensed to practice architecture in the foreign country where the project is located, the term "consultant" is used throughout the document to refer to the U.S. architect. NOTE: B621INT–2002 expired in 2009.

Use of the Program Manager family of AIA Contract Documents may be appropriate when the owner involves one or more additional consultants (program manager and/or design manager) to assist with program wide design and construction issues. The Program Manager approach enhances the level of expertise applied to managing a program from start to finish.

B171–2013, Standard Form of Agreement Between Owner and Design Manager for use in a Multiple Project Program

AIA Document B171™–2013 is a standard form of agreement between owner and design manager for use in a program with more than one project and where design management services are to be provided under a separate contract with the owner. It is coordinated with AIA Document C171™–2013, an owner-program manager agreement, where the program manager is an independent advisor to the owner throughout the course of the program. The design manager is required to assist the owner and the program manager in developing and establishing the owner's program. Additionally, the design manager provides limited architectural services for each project in the program. Upon the development of the program, the design manager is required to develop the design standards, which will provide a functional, aesthetic, and quality framework for the projects in the program. After establishment of the design standards, the design manager performs schematic design and design development architectural services for each project in the program in order to develop a transfer package that the owner can provide to the architect(s) of record for each project in the program. Both AIA Documents B171–2013 and C171–2013 are based on the premise that one or more separate architects of record and construction contractors will also contract with the owner for final design and construction of each project. AIA Document B172™–2013, Standard Form of Agreement Between Owner and Architect for Architect of Record Services, is intended to be used as the agreement between the owner and each architect of record. The architect of record is responsible for preparation of the construction documents, and related design and bidding phase services, and administration of the owner-contractor agreement on a project-by-project basis.

B172–2013, Standard Form of Agreement Between Owner and Architect for Architect of Record Services

AIA Document B172™–2013 provides the agreement between the owner and the architect of record, an entity who is separate and independent from the program manager and design manager, and who acts as a project specific architect. AIA Document B172–2013 is coordinated for use with AIA documents C171–2013, Standard Form of Agreement Between Owner and Program Manager for use in a Multiple Project Program, and B171™–2013, Standard Form of Agreement Between Owner and Design Manager for use in a Multiple Project Program. The architect of record is responsible for preparation of the construction documents, based on criteria received from the owner in a "transfer package," and related design and bidding phase services, and administration of the owner-contractor agreement on a project-by-project basis. AIA Document B172–2013 may also, with some modifications, be appropriate for use in other circumstances where an architect is asked to prepare construction documents based on the preliminary design work of another, and to provide related bidding and contract administration services for a project.

C171–2013, Standard Form of Agreement Between Owner and Program Manager, for use in a Multiple Project Program

AIA Document C171™–2013 is a standard form of agreement between owner and program manager for use in a program with more than one project. The program manager assists the owner in an advisory capacity, on matters that impact the program, during design and construction. The program manager's basic services primarily relate to overseeing the development and implementation of the owner's program and include creating a program management plan to describe the scope of the program and related requirements; managing program related information across the multiple projects in the program; developing a program-wide budget and schedule; and establishing quality control guidelines. The document has been prepared for use with AIA Documents B171™–2013, Standard Form of Agreement Between Owner and Design Manager for use in a Multiple Project Program, and B172™–2013, Standard Form of Agreement Between Owner and Architect for Architect of Record Services. This integrated set of documents is appropriate for use on projects where the program manager only serves in the capacity of an advisor to the owner.

Although titled "for use in a Multiple Project Program," AIA Document C171, with appropriate modifications, is also suitable for use in a program that consists of only a single project.

C172–2014, Standard Form of Agreement Between Owner and Program Manager for use on a Single Project

AIA Document C172™–2014 is a standard form agreement between owner and program manager for use on a single project. The program manager assists the owner in an advisory capacity on matters that impact the project during design and construction. The program manager's basic services include creating a program management plan to describe the scope of the project and related requirements, managing project-related information, developing a budget and schedule, and establishing quality control guidelines. C172–2014 also contains cost estimating and construction administration services that the parties may select as additional services. Unlike in the Construction Manager as Adviser family of documents, where the construction manager has some shared responsibilities with the architect, in C172 the program manager does not have shared responsibilities with other project participants or authority to act directly on behalf of the owner with respect to the responsibilities of the architect or contractor. C172–2014 is primarily intended to be used with the A201™–2007 family of documents.

SMALL PROJECTS FAMILY

Use of the Small Projects family of AIA Contract Documents may be appropriate when a project is straightforward in design; of short duration (less than one year from start of design to completion of construction); without delivery complications, such as competitive bidding; and when project team members already have working relationships. AIA documents in the Small Projects family are suitable for residential projects, small commercial projects, or other projects of relatively low cost and brief duration.

A105–2007 (formerly A105–1993 and A205–1993), Standard Form of Agreement Between Owner and Contractor for a Residential or Small Commercial Project

AIA Document A105™–2007 is a stand-alone agreement with its own general conditions; it replaces AIA Documents A105™–1993 and A205™–1993. AIA Document A105–2007 is for use on a project that is modest in size and brief in duration, and where payment to the contractor is based on a stipulated sum (fixed price). For larger and more complex projects, other AIA agreements are more suitable, such as AIA Document A107™–2007, Standard Form of Agreement Between Owner and Contractor for a Project of Limited Scope. AIA Documents A105–2007 and B105™–2007, Standard Form of Agreement Between Owner and Architect for a Residential or Small Commercial Project, comprise the Small Projects family of documents. Although A105 and B105 share some similarities with other agreements, the Small Projects family should *not* be used in tandem with agreements in other document families without careful side-by-side comparison of contents. NOTE: A105–1993 and A205–1993 expired in 2009.

B105–2007 (formerly B155–1993), Standard Form of Agreement Between Owner and Architect for a Residential or Small Commercial Project

AIA Document B105™–2007 is a standard form of agreement between owner and architect intended for use on a residential or small commercial project that is modest in size and brief in duration. AIA Documents B105–2007 and A105™–2007, Standard Form of Agreement Between Owner and Contractor for a Residential or Small Commercial Project, comprise the Small Projects family of documents. B105–2007 is intended for use with A105–2007, which it incorporates by reference. B105 is extremely abbreviated and is formatted more informally than other AIA agreements. Although AIA Documents A105 and B105 share some similarities with other AIA agreements, the Small Projects family should NOT be used with other AIA document families without careful side-by-side comparison of contents. NOTE: B155–1993 expired in 2009.

DIGITAL PRACTICE DOCUMENTS

AIA Digital Practice documents may be used for any projects involving digital data or Building Information Modeling. AIA Document C106™ provides a licensing agreement for transmission of digital data when not included in the prime agreement. AIA Documents E201™ and E202™ are exhibits that establish protocols for managing digital data and Building Information Modeling. These documents can be used on small to large projects.

C106–2013, Digital Data Licensing Agreement

AIA Document C106™–2013 serves as a licensing agreement between two parties who otherwise have no existing licensing agreement for the use and transmission of digital data, including instruments of service. AIA Document C106–2013 defines digital data as information, communications, drawings, or designs created or stored for a specific project in digital form. C106 allows one party to (1) grant another party a limited nonexclusive license to use digital data on a specific project, (2) set forth procedures for transmitting the digital data, and (3) place restrictions on the license granted. In addition, C106 allows the party transmitting digital data to collect a licensing fee for the recipient's use of the digital data.

NOTE: AIA Document C106–2013 replaced C106–2007, which expired on December 31, 2014.

E201–2007, Digital Data Protocol Exhibit

AIA Document E201™–2007 is not a stand-alone document, but must be attached as an exhibit to an existing agreement, such as the AIA Document B101™–2007, Standard Form of Agreement Between Owner and Architect, or A101™–2007, Agreement Between Owner and Contractor. Its purpose is to establish the procedures the parties agree to follow with respect to the transmission or exchange of digital data, including instruments of service. AIA Document E201–2007 defines digital data as information, communications, drawings, or designs created or stored for a specific project in digital form. E201 does not create a separate license to use digital data, because AIA documents for design or construction, to which E201 would be attached, already include those provisions. Parties not covered under such agreements should consider executing AIA Document C106™–2007, Digital Data Licensing Agreement.

E202–2008, Building Information Modeling Protocol Exhibit

AIA Document E202™–2008 is a practical tool for managing the use of building information modeling (BIM) across a project. It establishes the requirements for model content at five progressive levels of development, and the authorized uses of the model content at each level of development. Through a table the parties complete for each project, AIA Document E202–2008 assigns authorship of each model element by project phase. E202 defines the extent to which model users may rely on model content, clarifies model ownership, sets forth BIM standards and file formats, and provides the scope of responsibility for model management from the beginning to the end of the project. Though written primarily to support a project using integrated project delivery (IPD), E202–2008 may also be used on projects delivered by more traditional methods. E202 is not a stand-alone document, but must be attached as an exhibit to an existing agreement for design services, construction or material. NOTE: E202 is available in AIA Contract Documents software, but is not available in print.

E203–2013, Building Information Modeling and Digital Data Exhibit

AIA Document E203™–2013 is not a stand-alone document, but must be attached as an exhibit to an existing agreement, such as the AIA Document B101™–2007, Standard Form of Agreement Between Owner and Architect, or A101™–2007, Agreement Between Owner and Contractor. Its purpose is to establish the parties' expectations for the use of digital data and building information modeling (BIM) on the project and provide a process for developing the detailed protocols and procedures that will govern the development, use, transmission and exchange of digital data and BIM on the project. Once agreed to, E203–2013 states that the relevant protocols and procedures will be set forth in AIA Documents G201™–2013, Project Digital Data Protocol Form and G202™–2013, Project Building Information Modeling Protocol Form. E203 does not create a separate license to use digital data because AIA documents for design or construction, to which E203 would be attached, already include those provisions. Parties not covered under such agreements should consider executing AIA Document C106™–2013, Digital Data Licensing Agreement.

G201–2013, Project Digital Data Protocol Form

AIA Document G201™–2013 is a form that is coordinated for use with AIA Document E203™–2013, Building Information Modeling and Digital Data Protocol Exhibit. Its purpose is to document the agreed upon protocols and procedures that will govern the transmission, use and exchange of digital data on a project, such as electronic project communications, submittals, contract documents and payment documents. G201–2013 is not designed to address building information modeling protocols and procedures, which is the purpose of AIA Document G202™–2013, Project Building Information Modeling Protocol Form.

G202–2013, Project Building Information Modeling Protocol Form

AIA Document G202™–2013 is a form that is coordinated for use with AIA Document E203™–2013, Building Information Modeling and Digital Data Protocol Exhibit. Its purpose is to document the agreed upon protocols and procedures that will govern the development, transmission, use and exchange of building information models on a project. It establishes the requirements for model content at five levels of development, and the authorized uses of the model content at each level of development. Through a table completed for each project, AIA Document G202–2013 assigns authorship of each model element by project milestone. G202 defines the extent to which model users may rely on model content, clarifies model ownership, and sets forth building information modeling standards and file formats.

CONTRACT ADMINISTRATION AND PROJECT MANAGEMENT FORMS

AIA Construction Administration and Project Management forms are generally useful for all project delivery methods. The variety of forms in this group includes qualification statements, bonds, requests for information, change orders, construction change directives, and payment applications and certificates. These forms can be used on small to large projects.

A305–1986, Contractor's Qualification Statement

An owner preparing to request bids or to award a contract for a construction project often requires a means of verifying the background, references, and financial stability of any contractor being considered. These factors, along with the time frame for construction, are important for an owner to investigate. Using AIA Document A305™–1986, the contractor may provide a sworn, notarized statement and appropriate attachments to elaborate on important aspects of the contractor's qualifications.

A310–2010, Bid Bond

AIA Document A310™–2010, a simple, one-page form, establishes the maximum penal amount that may be due to the owner if the selected bidder fails to execute the contract or fails to provide any required performance and payment bonds.

A312–2010, Performance Bond and Payment Bond

AIA Document A312™–2010 incorporates two bonds—one covering the contractor's performance, and the other covering the contractor's obligations to pay subcontractors and others for material and labor. In addition, AIA Document A312–2010 obligates the surety to act responsively to the owner's requests for discussions aimed at anticipating or preventing a contractor's default.

B305–1993 (formerly B431–1993), Architect's Qualification Statement

AIA Document B305™–1993 is a standardized outline form on which the architect may enter information that a client may wish to review before selecting the architect. The owner may use AIA Document B305–1993 as part of a request for proposal or as a final check on the architect's credentials. Under some circumstances, B305–1993 may be attached to the owner-architect agreement to show—for example, the team of professionals and consultants expected to be employed on the project. NOTE: B305–1993 was renumbered in 2007, but its content remains the same as in AIA Document B431™–1993 (expired 2009).

D101–1995, The Architectural Area and Volume of Buildings, 1995 Edition

This document establishes definitions for methods of calculating the architectural area and volume of buildings. AIA Document D101™–1995 also covers interstitial space and office, retail, and residential areas.

D200–1995, Project Checklist

The project checklist is a convenient listing of tasks a practitioner may perform on a given project. This checklist will assist the architect in recognizing required tasks and in locating the data necessary to fulfill assigned responsibilities. By providing space for notes on actions taken, assignment of tasks, and time frames for completion, AIA Document D200™–1995 may also serve as a permanent record of the owner's, contractor's, and architect's actions and decisions.

G601–1994, Request for Proposal—Land Survey

AIA Document G601™–1994 allows owners to request proposals from a number of surveyors based on information deemed necessary by the owner and architect. G601–1994 allows owners to create a request for proposal through checking appropriate boxes and filling in project specifics, thus avoiding the costs associated with requesting unnecessary information. G601–1994 may be executed to form the agreement between the owner and the land surveyor once an understanding is reached.

G602–1993, Request for Proposal—Geotechnical Services

Similar in structure and format to AIA Document G601™–1994, AIA Document G602™–1993 can form the agreement between the owner and the geotechnical engineer. It allows the owner to tailor the proposal request to address the specific needs of the project. In consultation with the architect, the owner establishes the parameters of service required and evaluates submissions based on criteria such as time, cost, and overall responsiveness to the terms set forth in the request for proposal. When an acceptable submission is selected, the owner signs the document in triplicate, returning one copy to the engineer and one to the architect, thus forming the agreement between owner and geotechnical engineer.

G612–2001, Owner's Instructions to the Architect

AIA Document G612™–2001 is a questionnaire, drafted to elicit information from the owner regarding the nature of the construction contract. AIA Document G612–2001 is divided into three parts: Part A relates to contracts, Part B relates to insurance and bonds, and Part C deals with bidding procedures. The order of the parts follows the project's chronological sequence to match the points in time when the information will be needed. Because many of the items relating to the contract will have some bearing on the development of construction documents, it is important to place Part A in the owner's hands at the earliest possible phase of the project. The owner's responses to Part A will lead to a selection of the appropriate delivery method and contract forms, including the general conditions. Part B naturally follows after selection of the general conditions because insurance and bonding information is dependent upon the type of general conditions chosen. Answers to Part C will follow as the contract documents are further developed.

G701–2001, Change Order

AIA Document G701™–2001 is for implementing changes in the work agreed to by the owner, contractor, and architect. Execution of a completed AIA Document G701–2001 indicates agreement upon all the terms of the change, including any changes in the contract sum (or guaranteed maximum price) and contract time. The form provides space for the signatures of the owner, architect, and contractor, and for a complete description of the change.

G701S–2001, Change Order, Subcontractor Variation

AIA Document G701S™–2001 modifies AIA Document G701™–2001 for use by subcontractors. Modifications to G701–2001 are shown as tracked changes revisions—that is, additional material is underlined; deleted material is crossed out. NOTE: G701S–2001 is not available in print, but is available in AIA Contract Documents® software and from the AIA Documents on Demand® service.

G702–1992, Application and Certificate for Payment

AIA Documents G702™–1992, Application and Certificate for Payment, and G703™–1992, Continuation Sheet, provide convenient and complete forms on which the contractor can apply for payment and the architect can certify that payment is due. The forms require the contractor to show the status of the contract sum to date, including the total dollar amount of the work completed and stored to date, the amount of retainage (if any), the total of previous payments, a summary of change orders, and the amount of current payment requested. AIA Document G703–1992 breaks the contract sum into portions of the work in accordance with a schedule of values prepared by the contractor as required by the general conditions. NOTE: The AIA does not publish a standard schedule of values form.

AIA Document G702–1992 serves as both the contractor's application and the architect's certification. Its use can expedite payment and reduce the possibility of error. If the application is properly completed and acceptable to the architect, the architect's signature certifies to the owner that a payment in the amount indicated is due to the contractor. The form also allows the architect to certify an amount different than the amount applied for, with explanation provided by the architect.

G702S–1992, Application and Certificate for Payment, Subcontractor Variation

AIA Document G702S™–1992 modifies AIA Document G702™–1992 for use by subcontractors. Modifications to G702–1992 are shown as tracked changes revisions—that is, additional material is underlined; deleted material is crossed out. NOTE: G702S–1992 is not available in print, but is available in AIA Contract Documents® software and from the AIA Documents on Demand® service.

G703–1992, Continuation Sheet

AIA Documents G702™–1992, Application and Certificate for Payment, and G703™–1992, Continuation Sheet, provide convenient and complete forms on which the contractor can apply for payment and the architect can certify that payment is due. The forms require the contractor to show the status of the contract sum to date, including the total dollar amount of the work completed and stored to date, the amount of retainage (if any), the total of previous payments, a summary of change orders, and the amount of current payment requested. AIA Document G703–1992 breaks the contract sum into portions of the work in accordance with a schedule of values prepared by the contractor as required by the general conditions. NOTE: The AIA does not publish a standard schedule of values form.

G703S–1992, Continuation Sheet, Subcontractor Variation

AIA Document G703S™–1992 modifies AIA Document G703™–1992 for use by subcontractors. Modifications to G703–1992 are shown as tracked changes revisions—that is, additional material is underlined; deleted material is crossed out. NOTE: G701S–1992 is not available in print, but is available in AIA Contract Documents® software and from the AIA Documents on Demand® service.

G704–2000, Certificate of Substantial Completion

AIA Document G704™–2000 is a standard form for recording the date of substantial completion of the work or a designated portion thereof. The contractor prepares a list of items to be completed or corrected, and the architect verifies and amends this list. If the architect finds that the work is substantially complete, the form is prepared for acceptance by the contractor and the owner, and the list of items to be completed or corrected is attached. In AIA Document G704–2000, the parties agree on the time allowed for completion or correction of the items, the date when the owner will occupy the work or designated portion thereof, and a description of responsibilities for maintenance, heat, utilities, and insurance.

G705–2001 (formerly G805–2001), List of Subcontractors

AIA Document G705™–2001 is a form for listing subcontractors and others proposed to be employed on a project as required by the bidding documents. It is to be filled out by the contractor and returned to the architect for submission to the owner. NOTE: AIA Document G705–2001 was renumbered in 2007, but its content remains the same as in AIA Document G805™–2001 (expired 2009).

G706–1994, Contractor's Affidavit of Payment of Debts and Claims

The contractor submits this affidavit with the final request for payment, stating that all payrolls, bills for materials and equipment, and other indebtedness connected with the work for which the owner might be responsible has been paid or otherwise satisfied. AIA Document G706™–1994 requires the contractor to list any indebtedness or known claims in connection with the construction contract that have not been paid or otherwise satisfied. The contractor may also be required to furnish a lien bond or indemnity bond to protect the owner with respect to each exception.

G706A–1994, Contractor's Affidavit of Release of Liens

AIA Document G706A™–1994 supports AIA Document G706™–1994 in the event that the owner requires a sworn statement of the contractor stating that all releases or waivers of liens have been received. In such event, it is normal for the contractor to submit AIA Documents G706–1994 and G706A–1994 along with attached releases or waivers of liens for the contractor, all subcontractors, and others who may have lien rights against the owner's property. The contractor is required to list any exceptions to the sworn statement provided in G706A–1994, and may be required to furnish to the owner a lien bond or indemnity bond to protect the owner with respect to such exceptions.

G707–1994, Consent of Surety to Final Payment

AIA Document G707™–1994 is intended for use as a companion to AIA Document G706™–1994, Contractor's Affidavit of Payment of Debts and Claims, on construction projects where the contractor is required to furnish a bond. By obtaining the surety's approval of final payment to the contractor and its agreement that final payment will not relieve the surety of any of its obligations, the owner may preserve its rights under the bond.

G707A–1994, Consent of Surety to Final Reduction in or Partial Release of Retainage

This is a standard form for use when a surety company is involved and the owner-contractor agreement contains a clause whereby retainage is reduced during the course of the construction project. When duly executed, AIA Document G707A™–1994 assures the owner that such reduction or partial release of retainage does not relieve the surety of its obligations.

G709–2001, Work Changes Proposal Request

This form is used to obtain price quotations required in the negotiation of change orders. AIA Document G709™–2001 is not a change order or a direction to proceed with the work. It is simply a request to the contractor for information related to a proposed change in the construction contract. AIA Document G709–2001 provides a clear and concise means of initiating the process for changes in the work.

G710–1992, Architect's Supplemental Instructions

AIA Document G710™–1992 is used by the architect to issue additional instructions or interpretations or to order minor changes in the work. It is intended to assist the architect in performing its obligations as interpreter of the contract documents in accordance with the owner-architect agreement and the general conditions of the contract for construction. AIA Document G710–1992 should not be used to change the contract sum or contract time. It is intended to help the architect perform its services with respect to minor changes not involving adjustment in the contract sum or contract time. Such minor changes are authorized under Section 7.4 of AIA Document A201™–2007.

G711–1972, Architect's Field Report

The architect's project representative can use this standard form to maintain a concise record of site visits or, in the case of a full-time project representative, a daily log of construction activities.

G712–1972, Shop Drawing and Sample Record

AIA Document G712™–1972 is a standard form by which the architect can log and monitor shop drawings and samples. The form allows the architect to document receipt of the contractor's submittals, subsequent referrals of the submittals to the architect's consultants, action taken, and the date returned to the contractor. AIA Document G712–1972 can also serve as a permanent record of the chronology of the submittal process.

G714–2007 (formerly G714–2001), Construction Change Directive

AIA Document G714™–2007 is a directive for changes in the work for use where the owner and contractor have not reached an agreement on proposed changes in the contract sum or contract time. AIA Document G714–2007 was developed as a directive for changes in the work which, if not expeditiously implemented, might delay the project. Upon receipt of a completed G714–2007, the contractor must promptly proceed with the change in the work described therein. NOTE: G714–2001 expired in 2009.

G715–1991, Supplemental Attachment for ACORD Certificate of Insurance 25-S

AIA Document G715™–1997 is intended for use in adopting ACORD Form 25-S to certify the coverage required of contractors under AIA Document A201™–2007, General Conditions of the Contract for Construction. Since the ACORD certificate does not have space to show all the coverages required in AIA Document A201–2007, the Supplemental Attachment form should be completed, signed by the contractor's insurance representative, and attached to the ACORD certificate.

G716–2004, Request for Information (RFI)

AIA Document G716™–2004 provides a standard form for an owner, architect, and contractor to request further information from each other during construction. The form asks the requesting party to list the relevant drawing, specification, or submittal reviewed in attempting to find the information. Neither the request nor the response received provides authorization for work that increases the cost or time of the project.

G801–2007 (formerly G605–2000), Notification of Amendment to the Professional Services Agreement

AIA Document G801™–2007 is intended to be used by an architect when notifying an owner of a proposed amendment to the AIA's owner-architect agreements, such as AIA Document B101™–2007. NOTE: G605–2000 expired in 2009.

G802–2007 (formerly G606–2000), Amendment to the Professional Services Agreement

AIA Document G802™–2007 is intended to be used by an architect when amending the professional services provisions in the AIA's owner-architect agreements, such as AIA Document B101™–2007. NOTE: G606–2000 expired in 2009.

G803–2007 (formerly G607–2000), Amendment to the Consultant Services Agreement

AIA Document G803™–2007 is intended for use by an architect or consultant when amending the professional services provisions in the AIA's architect-consultant agreement, AIA Document C401™–2007. NOTE: G607–2000 expired in 2009.

G804–2001, Register of Bid Documents

AIA Document G804™–2001 serves as a log for bid documents while they are in the possession of contractors, subcontractors, and suppliers during the bidding process. The form allows tracking by bidder of documents issued, deposits received, and documents and deposits returned. AIA Document G804–2001 is particularly useful as a single point of reference when parties interested in the project call for information during the bidding process.

G806–2001, Project Parameters Worksheet

AIA Document G806™–2001 is an administrative form intended to help maintain a single standard list of project parameters including project objectives, owner's program, project delivery method, legal parameters, and financial parameters.

G807–2001, Project Team Directory

AIA Document G807™–2001 is used as a single point of reference for basic information about project team members including the owner, architect's consultants, contractor, and other entities. AIA Document G807–2001 differs from AIA Document G808™–2001, Project Data, which contains only data about the project and project site. G807–2001 should be carefully checked against the owner-architect agreement so that specific requirements as to personnel representing the owner and those involved with the architect in providing services are in conformance with the agreement.

G808–2001, Project Data

AIA Document G808™–2001 is used for recording information about approvals and zoning and building code issues gathered in the course of providing professional services. AIA Document G808–2001 should be completed piece by piece as a project progresses and periodically reviewed to ensure information relevance. The attached worksheet, AIA Document G808A™–2001, Construction Classification Worksheet, can be used to supplement the G808–2001.

G808A–2001, Construction Classification Worksheet

AIA Document G808A™–2001, Construction Classification Worksheet, can be used to supplement AIA Document G808™–2001, which is used for recording information about approvals and zoning and building code issues gathered in the course of providing professional services. AIA Document G808–2001 should be completed piece by piece as a project progresses and periodically reviewed to ensure information relevance. AIA Document G808A–2001 can help a design team work through the range of code compliance combinations available before choosing a final compliance strategy.

G809–2001, Project Abstract

AIA Document G809™–2001 establishes a brief, uniform description of project data to be used in the tabulation of architect marketing information and firm statistics.

The intent is to provide a single sheet summary where information can be sorted, compiled, and summarized to present a firm's experience. Information compiled in AIA Document G809–2001 can support planning for similar projects and answer questions pertaining to past work.

G810–2001, Transmittal Letter

AIA Document G810™–2001 allows for the orderly flow of information between parties involved in the design and construction phase of a project. It serves as a written record of the exchange of project information and acts as a checklist reminding the sender to tell the recipient what exactly is being sent, how the material is being sent, and why it is being sent.

Index

Page numbers followed by *f* and *t* refer to figures and tables, respectively.